the
AMERICANA ANNUAL

1974

AN ENCYCLOPEDIA OF THE EVENTS OF 1973
YEARBOOK OF THE ENCYCLOPEDIA AMERICANA

EDITORIAL STAFF

contents

FEATURE ARTICLES OF THE YEAR

Contributors—**Robert Shogan** and **C. Herman Pritchett.** The complex story of the Watergate affair is reported in lucid detail by a Washington correspondent. The constitutional aspects of the scandals are examined by a professor of political science, with special attention to the office of the presidency.

Contributors—**Frederic Golden, Robert E. Chrien, Peter E. Glaser,** and **Thomas L. Kimball.** In late 1973 the United States and other major industrial nations suddenly found themselves in the midst of a fuel crisis. This series of reports explains what happened and why, and it also explores some of the other sources of energy that must be tapped to supply future generations.

Contributors—**Robert M. Levine, Neill Macaulay,** and **Richard N. Cooper.** With little fanfare, Brazil has produced an "economic miracle" of its own and now bids to become one of the world's economic superpowers. This feature tells how the Latin American giant has achieved such remarkable growth and also highlights some of the problems it still faces.

Contributor—**Nora Kelly.** One of the most colorful law-enforcement forces in the world, the Royal Canadian Mounted Police observed its 100th anniversary in 1973. Today's Mounties have come a long way from their beginnings, and to their old traditions has been added the latest in modern technology.

Contributors—**Wilcomb E. Washburn, Andrew H. Malcolm,** and **Rudy Platiel.** The protracted siege of Wounded Knee, S. Dak., by a band of armed militants served to dramatize the demands of American Indians for a better life. The history of relations between the Indians and the federal government provides a background to today's headlines.

SPECIAL REPORTS

Pages 70-665 Alphabetical Section
(partial listing)

preface

It was the Year of Watergate. Not within memory has any single story so dominated the flow of news during an entire year as did the tortuous unwinding of the series of scandals that came to be known collectively as Watergate.

"And the pall of the Watergate . . . is upon us," Associate Justice Harry A. Blackmun told the American Bar Association in August. And that is as good a description as any of the miasma that blanketed official Washington in 1973 and seeped into virtually every segment of American life.

After all the disclosures, allegations, and suspicions surrounding Watergate and its attendant evils, the year ended with one burning question confronting Congress and the people: Should the President of the United States be impeached? The answer to that question would probably chart the course of American history for years to come.

Altogether it was a bad year for President Nixon, a sad year for America, and a troublesome year around the world. The start of the year found the President, flushed with his resounding reelection triumph, moving ahead confidently to reshape the executive branch and continue his mastery over Congress with new programs in the domestic and foreign fields. The long-awaited disengagement of U. S. forces in Vietnam further enhanced his prestige. But within months the revelations of Watergate, notably through Senator Ervin's committee hearings, had left the White House staff in a shambles, impaired the confidence of the people in their leaders, and seriously called in question the President's very ability to govern.

For the American people, just emerging from the ordeal of the Sixties, the burdens of Watergate weighed heavily upon the national conscience. In addition, the public had to cope with soaring prices, scarcity of meat and other essentials, and, late in the year, shortages of gasoline and heating fuels.

For much of the world the year brought recurring currency crises, energy shortages in some nations even worse than that in the United States, and dangerous rates of inflation. In the Middle East, smoldering passions exploded into the most violent of the four wars between Israel and its Arab neighbors.

The Watergate affair—subject of this volume's opening feature, "The Year That Shook America"—had many strange aspects, not the least of which was that the major headline of 1973 actually concerned a story that broke in June 1972 when the Democratic headquarters were burglarized. But the event had passed largely unremarked by an electorate then intent on returning President Nixon to office with one of the greatest election landslides in history.

As painful and traumatic as the experience may have been, however, Watergate may yet be seen as a turning point that set the United States on a new and healthy course, one of greater devotion to the democratic principles that established the nation. In this respect, the bungled burglary at Watergate, by shedding light on some of the murky doings in high places, may actually have helped to save the country.

S. J. FODERARO, *Senior Executive Editor*

Representatives of the four participants in the Paris peace talks sign the cease-fire agreement ending the hostilities in Vietnam, at the International Conference Center, Paris, January 27.

CHRONOLOGY 1973

NIXON INAUGURATED TO 2D TERM

LYNDON JOHNSON DIES AT 64

VIETNAM CEASE-FIRE SIGNED

JANUARY

S	M	T	W	T	F	S
		1	2	3	4	5	6
7	8	9	10	11	12	13
14	15	16	17	18	19	20
21	22	23	24	25	26	27
28	29	30	31			

JANUARY

1 Britain, Denmark, and the Republic of Ireland officially join the European Economic Community (Common Market).

3 The first session of the 93d U. S. Congress convenes.

11 U. S. President Richard M. Nixon announces Phase 3 of the economic stabilization program, ending all mandatory wage and price controls except in the food, health care, and construction industries.

14 The Miami Dolphins defeat the Washington Redskins, 14–7, in professional football's 7th Super Bowl game.

15 The United States suspends all offensive military action in North Vietnam.

17 Proclaiming the ratification of a new constitution, Philippine President Ferdinand E. Marcos announces the indefinite continuation of martial law.

20 President Nixon and Vice President Spiro T. Agnew are inaugurated for second terms. ● Amilcar Cabral, a leader of the black African independence movement, is assassinated in Conakry, Guinea.

22 Former U. S. President Lyndon Baines Johnson, 64, dies following a heart attack at his Texas ranch. ● The U. S. Supreme Court declares unconstitutional all state laws prohibiting or restricting a woman's right to obtain an abortion during her first three months of pregnancy. ● George Foreman defeats Joe Frazier to become the world's heavyweight boxing champion.

23 In Paris, Henry Kissinger and Le Duc Tho initial agreement "to end the war and bring peace with honor in Vietnam and Southeast Asia." ● A volcanic erruption occurs on the island of Heimaey, off Iceland.

26 Belgium's King Baudouin administers oath of office to coalition government headed by Edmond Leburton.

27 In Paris, representatives of the United States, South Vietnam, North Vietnam, and the Vietcong sign the Vietnam cease-fire agreement. ● Outgoing U. S. Secretary of Defense Melvin Laird announces that the military draft has ended.

29 President Nixon presents to Congress the budget for fiscal year 1974.

30 U. S. Sen. John C. Stennis (D-Miss.) is shot and seriously wounded by apparent robbers in front of his Washington, D. C., home. ● South Vietnam and the Communists accuse each other of cease-fire violations.

President Nixon is sworn in for second term, January 20. Chief Justice Burger officiates as Mrs. Nixon holds Bible.

UPI

FEBRUARY

S	M	T	W	T	F	S
				1	2	3
4	5	6	7	8	9	10
11	12	13	14	15	16	17
18	19	20	21	22	23	24
25	26	27	28			

U.S. DEVALUES DOLLAR BY 10%

FIRST U.S. WAR PRISONERS RETURN

ISRAELIS DOWN LIBYAN JETLINER

FEBRUARY

2 Pope Paul VI nominates 30 new cardinals.

10 U. S. Vice President Agnew reports to President Nixon on his tour of eight Southeast Asian nations.

11 Gen. Alfredo Stroessner is reelected to a fifth term as president of Paraguay.

12 U. S. Secretary of the Treasury George P. Shultz announced a 10% devaluation of the U. S. dollar against nearly all of the world's major currencies.
● The first group of released U. S. prisoners of the Vietnam War arrives at Clark Air Force Base, the Philippines.

14 The United States and North Vietnam announce that they have agreed to establish a Joint Economic Commission to administer reconstruction aid to North-Vietnam.

15 The United States and Cuba sign a five-year agreement to curb hijacking. A similar pact is signed by Canada and Cuba. ● The U. S. Department of Defense announces that the number of daily U. S. air strikes against North Vietnamese and Pathet Lao troops and munition movements in Laos has increased by about 100 within the last week.

17 The White House announces the nominations of L. Patrick Gray and G. Bradford Cook as director of the Federal Bureau of Investigation and chairman of the Securities and Exchange Commission, respectively.

21 Representatives of the Laotian government and the Communist Pathet Lao sign an agreement to end the war in Laos. ● Israeli fighter planes down a civilian Libyan jetliner in the Israeli-occupied Sinai Peninsula; 106 persons are killed.

22 The United States and China announce that they have agreed to establish a liaison office in their respective capitals. ● "At the request of the Royal Laotian government," U. S. B-52 bombers strike Communist troop positions in Laos less than 24 hours after the cease-fire went into effect.

26 Australia, a military ally of South Vietnam during the Vietnam War, establishes diplomatic relations with North Vietnam.

28 Militant American Indians, holding 11 persons hostage at Wounded Knee, S. Dak., exchange gunfire with federal officers. ● In general elections in the Republic of Ireland, a coalition of the Fine Gael party and the Labour party defeats the Fianna Fail party, which has governed the nation since 1957.

Libyan Airlines plane was shot down over Sinai by Israeli jets, killing 106, February 21.

UPI

Vietnam War POW, Navy Comdr. Raymond A. Vohden, arrives at Travis AFB on February 14.

UPI

U.S. ENVOY SLAIN IN SUDAN
BIG POWERS BACK VIETNAM TRUCE
DOWNEY RELEASED BY CHINESE

S	M	T	W	T	F	S
				1	2	3
4	5	6	7	8	9	10
11	12	13	14	15	16	17
18	19	20	21	22	23	24
25	26	27	28	29	30	31

UPI

Funeral of U. S. diplomats slain by terrorists in Sudan, Washington, D. C., March 7.

UPI

MARCH

2 In Khartoum, the Sudan, Cleo A. Noel, Jr., newly appointed U. S. ambassador, George C. Moore, outgoing U. S. chargé d'affaires, and Guy Eid, Belgium's chargé d'affaires, are shot and killed by Palestinian guerrillas. ● In Paris, the foreign ministers of 12 governments, including the United States, China, and the Soviet Union, sign formal declaration supporting Vietnam cease-fire agreement.

4 In legislative elections in Chile, the opposition Democratic Confederation (CODE) retains its majority with 54.7% of the vote.

5 During a strike by French air controllers, two London-bound Spanish jets collide over Nantes, western France, killing 68 persons.

7 In the first general election in Bangladesh, the Awami League of Sheikh Mujibur Rahman retains a large parliamentary majority.

11 France's Gaullist-led government wins an absolute majority in elections for the National Assembly. ● A state of emergency is declared in Bermuda following the assassination of Sir Richard Sharples, governor of the British colony, and his aide.

12 Argentina's military government declares Peronist candidate Héctor J. Cámpora the winner of the March 11 presidential elections. ● Authorities in China release John T. Downey, a U. S. intelligence agent shot down over China in 1952.

14 Liam Cosgrave is sworn in as prime minister of the Republic of Ireland.

15 David K. E. Bruce is named to head the U. S. liaison office in Peking.

17 In Phnom Penh, Cambodia, President Lon Nol declares a state of emergency and imposes a 9 P. M. curfew after a bomb destroys the barracks of the presidential guard. Forty-three persons are killed in the attack.

21 The United States vetoes a resolution of the UN Security Council urging construction of a new Panama Canal. ● The U. S. Department of Labor reports the highest monthly increase in the Consumer Price Index in 22 years.

29 President Nixon announces an immediate price ceiling on beef, pork, and lamb. ● All remaining U. S. troops in South Vietnam are withdrawn and the last 67 U. S. prisoners of war are released in Hanoi.

John Thomas Downey (center), CIA agent held in Red China 21 years, is freed on March 12.

4

APRIL

S	M	T	W	T	F	S
1	2	3	4	5	6	7
8	9	10	11	12	13	14
15	16	17	18	19	20	21
22	23	24	25	26	27	28
29	30					

U.S. CONSUMERS BOYCOTT MEAT
PICASSO IS DEAD AT 91
TOP WHITE HOUSE AIDES QUIT

APRIL

2 President Nixon and South Vietnamese President Nguyen Van Thieu open a two-day conference at the San Clemente (Calif.) White House. ● U. S. consumers begin a week-long meat boycott.

5 The nomination of L. Patrick Gray as director of the FBI is withdrawn.

8 Pablo Picasso, 91, dies at his home near Mougins, France. ● Following two weeks of unrest and violence in Sikkim, the Indian government takes over administrative control of the protectorate.

10 Three Palestinian Al Fatah guerrilla leaders are killed during an Israeli commando raid in southern Lebanon. Saeb Salam, premier of Lebanon, resigns following the raid. ● Pakistan's National Assembly adopts a new national constitution.

15 In Turkey, Naim Talu forms a new government.

16 Pentagon officials report that U. S. planes have bombed North Vietnamese positions in Laos following a major North Vietnamese ground attack. It was the second such raid since the Laotian cease-fire went into effect.

17 President Nixon announces that as a result of "intensive new inquiries" begun on March 21 "major developments" occurred in the Watergate case.

21 The UN Security Council condemns Israel for military attacks in Lebanon and "all acts of violence which endanger or take innocent human lives."

23 Presidential adviser Henry Kissinger announces that the United States seeks a "new Atlantic Charter" with its European allies.

24 A High Political Council, consisting of Lon Nol and three of his political opponents, begins governing Cambodia.

25 A new 17-man cabinet, headed by Amin Hafez, is formed in Lebanon.

27 William D. Ruckelshaus, administrator of the Environmental Protection Agency, is named acting director of the FBI. ● The Central Committee of the Soviet Communist party approves a series of personnel changes in the ruling Politburo.

30 On nationwide television, President Nixon accepts personal responsibility for the Watergate case. White House assistants H. R. Haldeman and John D. Ehrlichman, and Attorney General Richard G. Kleindienst resign; the President requests and accepts the resignation of Presidential Counsel John Dean; and Secretary of Defense Elliot L. Richardson is named to succeed Kleindienst.

U. S. housewives, protesting high prices, staged a meat boycott in early April.

UPI

5

SIEGE OF WOUNDED KNEE ENDS
MONTREAL CAPTURES HOCKEY TITLE
U.S. LAUNCHES SKYLAB MISSION

MAY

S	M	T	W	T	F	S
		1	2	3	4	5
6	7	8	9	10	11	12
13	14	15	16	17	18	19
20	21	22	23	24	25	26
27	28	29	30	31		

UPI

The Montreal Canadiens won the Stanley Cup by beating the Chicago Black Hawks in the sixth game, May 10.

NASA

MAY

4 Gen. Alexander M. Haig, Jr., is named an assistant to President Nixon.

7 Israel marks the 25th anniversary of its independence.

8 The 70-day confrontation between Indians and federal agents at Wounded Knee, S. Dak., ends.

10 A special federal grand jury indicts John N. Mitchell and Maurice H. Stans on charges of perjury and conspiring to defraud the United States and to obstruct justice. ● James R. Schlesinger is named secretary of defense; William E. Colby is designated to succeed Schlesinger as director of the Central Intelligence Agency. ● The New York Knickerbockers defeat the Los Angeles Lakers to win the National Basketball Association title. ● The Montreal Canadiens win the National Hockey League championship, defeating the Chicago Black Hawks.

11 U. S. District Court Judge William Matthew Byrne, Jr., dismisses all charges against the defendants in the Pentagon Papers case, Dr. Daniel Ellsberg and Anthony J. Russo, Jr. ● Ending a 163-day political crisis in the Netherlands, a 16-member cabinet, headed by Premier Joop den Uyl, is sworn in.

15 The price of gold reaches $128.50 an ounce on the Paris bullion market—a new high.

17 The Senate Select Committee on Presidential Campaign Activities, headed by Sen. Sam J. Ervin (D-N. C.), opens hearings on the Watergate case.

18 Archibald Cox, former U. S. solicitor general, is appointed special prosecutor in the Watergate investigation.

19 In Bonn, West German Chancellor Brandt and Soviet Communist Party Chairman Brezhnev sign a 10-year agreement calling for economic, industrial, and technical cooperation.

23 The U. S. Senate confirms the nomination of Elliot L. Richardson as attorney general.

25 Héctor J. Cámpora is inaugurated as president of Argentina. ● Skylab 1 astronauts Capt. Charles Conrad, Jr., Comdr. Joseph Kerwin, and Comdr. Paul J. Weitz are launched from Cape Kennedy.

29 The Canadian government announces that it will withdraw its cease-fire observers from Vietnam within 60 days. ● Thomas Bradley, 55-year-old black city councilman, is elected mayor of Los Angeles.

Skylab 1 astronauts Conrad, Kerwin, and Weitz blast off from Cape Kennedy, May 25.

JUNE

S	M	T	W	T	F	S
					1	2
3	4	5	6	7	8	9
10	11	12	13	14	15	16
17	18	19	20	21	22	23
24	25	26	27	28	29	30

SOVIET SST CRASHES IN PARIS
SECRETARIAT WINS TRIPLE CROWN
BREZHNEV BEGINS U.S. VISIT

JUNE

1 In Greece, the Council of Ministers issues a decree abolishing the monarchy and proclaiming the nation a "presidential parliamentary republic."

3 A Soviet supersonic TU-144 crashes at the Paris air show, killing the six crew members aboard and seven residents of a nearby village.

6 President Nixon names former Secretary of Defense Melvin R. Laird to the White House staff.

7 President Nixon nominates Clarence M. Kelley, police chief of Kansas City, Mo., as FBI director. ● West German Chancellor Brandt begins four-day state visit to Israel.

8 Generalissimo Francisco Franco, leader of Spain since 1939, appoints Adm. Luis Carrero Blanco as premier.

9 Secretariat wins the Belmont Stakes to become the first horse to win racing's Triple Crown since Citation in 1948.

13 Representatives of the United States, South Vietnam, North Vietnam, and the Vietcong sign communiqué calling for an end of all cease-fire violations. ● President Nixon orders a freeze on all consumer prices for up to 60 days.

15 Meeting in Copenhagen, Denmark, the 15-member North Atlantic Treaty Organization (NATO) agrees to restudy its political, economic, and military set-up in view of "profound changes" in the international situation.

16 Soviet Party Chairman Brezhnev begins nine-day visit to the United States.

17 Johnny Miller, a 26-year-old Californian, wins the U. S. Open golf championship.

18 Military leaders in Brazil select Gen. Ernesto Geisel for a five-year presidential term, beginning March 15, 1974.

21 The U. S. Supreme Court issues a series of decisions giving the states and local communities new authority to tighten rules governing obscenity.

22 President Nixon and Soviet Chairman Brezhnev sign an agreement pledging that their countries will not worsen relations with any other nation so as to provoke a nuclear war. ● The Skylab 1 astronauts return to earth following 28 days in space.

29 President Nixon assures Congress that U. S. military activity in Cambodia will end by August 15. ● In Chile, armed forces loyal to President Salvador Allende crush an anti-government revolt. ● President Nixon names Gov. John A. Love (R-Colo.) director of the new Energy Policy Office.

UPI

Curiosity-seekers surround the nose section of a Soviet supersonic transport plane that crashed during the Paris air show, June 3.

USSR Party Chairman Brezhnev whispers to President Nixon at welcoming ceremonies for Brezhnev at the White House on June 18.

UPI

7

QUEEN ELIZABETH VISITS CANADA

NIXON HOLDS WATERGATE TAPES

SKYLAB 2 ASTRONAUTS IN SPACE

JULY

S	M	T	W	T	F	S
1	2	3	4	5	6	7
8	9	10	11	12	13	14
15	16	17	18	19	20	21
22	23	24	25	26	27	28
29	30	31				

NASA

The crew of Skylab 2—Garriott, Bean, and Lousma—pose in front of the space vehicle that took them into orbit on July 28.

JULY

3 The 35-nation Conference on Security and Cooperation in Europe opens in Helsinki, Finland.

5 Britain's Queen Elizabeth II and Prince Philip end a 10-day tour of Canada.

8 In Italy, Mariano Rumor is sworn in as premier of a new center-left coalition government. (The government of Premier Giulio Andreotti had fallen on June 12.) ● Premier Takieddin Solh heads a new 22-member cabinet in Lebanon.

10 Britain grants complete independence to the Bahamas, a chain of 700 islands in the Atlantic Ocean.

13 Argentina's Congress accepts the resignation of President Héctor J. Cámpora.

16 U. S. Secretary of Defense Schlesinger admits that U. S. B-52 bombers secretly attacked Cambodia in 1969 and 1970. ● The White House confirms that all presidential meetings and telephone conversations have been recorded secretly since the spring of 1971. ● In parliamentary elections in Guyana, the People's National Congress of Prime Minister Forbes Burnham wins a two-thirds majority.

17 In Afghanistan, Lt. Gen. Mohammad Daud Khan overthrows King Mohammad Zahir Shah.

18 The White House outlines Phase 4 of President Nixon's economic program; the freeze on food (except beef) and health-care prices ends.

20 President Nixon returns to the White House following a one-week stay in Bethesda (Md.) Naval Hospital for treatment of viral pneumonia.

21 France explodes the first nuclear device of its current series over Mururoa Atoll in the Pacific.

23 President Nixon refuses to release presidential tapes concerning the Watergate case.

28 Skylab 2 astronauts Capt. Alan L. Bean, Maj. Jack R. Lousma, and Dr. Owen K. Garriott begin a 59-day mission in space. ● About 600,000 rock music fans attend a one-day festival in Watkins Glen, N. Y.

31 President Nixon and Japan's Premier Tanaka meet at the White House. ● Canada officially withdraws from the four-nation International Commission of Control and Supervision (ICCS) as its 249-member observer force leaves Vietnam for home. In Washington, U. S. officials announce that Iran is to succeed Canada on the ICCS.

BAHAMAS NEWS BUREAU

Prince Charles of Britain salutes the new nation of the Bahamas as British rule of nearly 300 years ended in Nassau on July 10.

AUGUST

S	M	T	W	T	F	S
			1	2	3	4
5	6	7	8	9	10	11
12	13	14	15	16	17	18
19	20	21	22	23	24	25
26	27	28	29	30	31	

AGNEW UNDER CRIMINAL PROBE

700 KILLED IN MEXICO QUAKE

JUDGE DEMANDS WATERGATE TAPES

AUGUST

2 In Ottawa, Canada, representatives of the 32 members of the Commonwealth nations attend opening session of nine-day conference. ● A devastating fire destroys an amusement center in Douglas, Isle of Man, and takes the lives of 51 persons.

5 Two Arab terrorists hurl grenades and fire machine guns into a crowded lounge at the Athens, Greece, airport; 3 persons are killed and 55 are injured.

6 U. S. Vice President Spiro T. Agnew announces that he is "under investigation for possible violations of the criminal statutes."

10 President Nixon signs a bill establishing a four-year farm program with a new method of subsidizing wheat, feed grains, and cotton.

12 Jack Nicklaus wins the Professional Golfers' Association (PGA) tournament by four strokes—his 14th major golf title, a record.

15 U. S. bombing in Cambodia officially ends. ● In a televised speech, President Nixon asserts that it is "time to turn Watergate over to the courts," and "for the rest of us to get on with the urgent business of our nation."

19 After being sworn in as the first president of Greece, George Papadopoulos promises amnesty for some 300 political prisoners.

20 In Laos, rebels stage an unsuccessful coup against the government of Prince Souvanna Phouma.

22 During President Nixon's first news conference since March 15, the President announces the resignation of William P. Rogers as secretary of state; presidential aide Henry A. Kissinger is named to the post.

24 The United States and Thailand announce that the United States will begin a phased withdrawal of U. S. troops and aircraft from Thailand.

28 In New Delhi, representatives of India and Pakistan sign an agreement calling for the release of 90,000 Pakistani prisoners held in India and for the settlement of other issues related to the 1971 India-Pakistan war. ● A predawn earthquake rips through the central part of Mexico, destroying villages and towns and leaving approximately 700 persons dead.

29 Federal Judge John J. Sirica orders President Nixon to release to him tape recordings of White House conversations involving the Watergate case. The White House announces that the President "will not comply" with the order. ● China announces that the 10th Congress of its Communist party was held on August 24–28.

Stunned victims of a massive earthquake that struck Orizaba, Mexico, on August 28 sit in the ruins of their home.

UPI

ALLENDE DIES IN CHILE COUP
UN ADMITS 3 NEW MEMBERS
PERÓN ELECTED IN ARGENTINA

SEPTEMBER

S	M	T	W	T	F	S
						1
2	3	4	5	6	7	8
9	10	11	12	13	14	15
16	17	18	19	20	21	22
23	24	25	26	27	28	29
30						

SEPTEMBER

1 The government of Libya announces the nationalization of 51% of the assets of all oil companies operating in the country.

2 Railroad workers in Canada return to work following a 9-day nationwide strike.

5 Officials of 76 nations gather in Algiers for the fourth conference of nonaligned nations.

10 Norway's Socialist bloc of parties wins a one-seat majority in two-day general elections.

11 Chile's President Salvador Allende is overthrown and dies during a violent military coup.

14 In Vientiane, Laos, representatives of the government and the Pathet Lao sign an agreement creating a coalition government.

15 Following the death of King Gustaf VI Adolf of Sweden, Crown Prince Carl Gustaf becomes King Carl XVI Gustaf.

16 Sweden's Social Democratic party of Prime Minister Olof Palme polls 43.6% of the vote and loses seven seats in elections, but remains in power.

18 At the opening of the 28th annual UN General Assembly, the Bahamas, East Germany, and West Germany are admitted as members.

20 Billie Jean King defeats Bobby Riggs in a $100,000 winner-take-all tennis match in Houston.

21 The U. S. Bureau of Labor Statistics reports that U. S. food prices climbed by 6.1% in August—the highest monthly increase since 1946.

23 Juan Perón is elected president of Argentina. ● Meeting in Nairobi, Kenya, finance ministers of 20 nations agree to postpone reforming the world's monetary system until a July 31, 1974, deadline.

26 Rep. Carl Albert, speaker of the U. S. House of Representatives, refuses to act "at this time" on Spiro T. Agnew's request for a House inquiry into allegations that the vice president received kickbacks from contractors in Maryland.

29 In exchange for the release of one Austrian and two Soviet Jews held by Arab guerrillas, the Austrian government announces that group transit of Soviet Jewish emigrants through Austria would no longer be permitted. ● Two Soviet cosmonauts complete a two-day orbital flight aboard Soyuz 12 —the USSR's first successful manned space flight since April 1971. ● Poet W. H. Auden dies at the age of 66.

In Chile, after Allende's overthrow, troops search a section of Santiago in which the U. S. consulate is located, September 27.

OCTOBER

S	M	T	W	T	F	S
	1	2	3	4	5	6
7	8	9	10	11	12	13
14	15	16	17	18	19	20
21	22	23	24	25	26	27
28	29	30	31			

WAR ERUPTS IN THE MIDDLE EAST
AGNEW QUITS AS VICE PRESIDENT
COX FIRED AS WATERGATE PROBER

OCTOBER

5 Canada's Prime Minister Trudeau announces that diplomat Jules Léger has been named as Canada's 21st governor-general.

6 A major war breaks out in the Middle East as Israeli forces fight Syrian troops along the Golan Heights and Egyptian forces along the Suez Canal.

10 Spiro T. Agnew resigns as vice president of the United States and pleads no contest to one count of income tax evasion.

12 President Nixon nominates Gerald Ford, the Republican leader of the House of Representatives, as the nation's 40th vice president.

14 Amid student demonstrations for a return of constitutional government, Thailand's King Phumiphol Aduldet appoints Sanya Dharmasakti as premier, succeeding Thanom Kittikachorn, who resigned.

17 In Kuwait, the minister of the 11 nations of the Organization of Arab Petroleum Exporting Countries agree on a plan of reduced oil production and oil exporting.

18 In Norway, a new minority Labor government, with Trygve M. Bratteli as premier, is sworn in.

20 Following a disagreement with the White House over the Watergate tapes, Archibald Cox is dismissed as special prosecutor, Elliot Richardson resigns as attorney general, and William Ruckelshaus leaves as deputy attorney general. ● In Moscow, U. S. Secretary of State Kissinger and Soviet Communist party chairman Brezhnev discuss the Middle East situation.

21 The Oakland Athletics defeat the New York Mets, four games to three, to win baseball's World Series.

23 President Nixon agrees to submit the Watergate tapes to Federal District Court Judge John J. Sirica.

24 A cease-fire agreement, the second in two days, goes into effect in the Middle East.

27 The UN Security Council approves the establishment of a UN peacekeeping force in the Middle East.

29 In provincial elections in Quebec, the Liberal party of Premier Robert Bourassa captures 102 of 110 legislative seats with 54% of the vote.

31 A worldwide alert of U.S. military forces, instituted on October 25, ends. ● The White House announces that two Watergate tapes sought by the prosecution do not exist.

Israeli artillerymen fire 155-mm guns at Syrian positions along the Golan Heights, October 12.

UPI

NIXON PROPOSES ENERGY ACT

CEASE-FIRE IN MIDDLE EAST

GREEK COUP OUSTS PRESIDENT

S	M	T	W	T	F	S
				1	2	3
4	5	6	7	8	9	10
11	12	13	14	15	16	17
18	19	20	21	22	23	24
25	26	27	28	29	30	

NOVEMBER

1 President Nixon announces the nomination of Sen. William B. Saxbe (R-Ohio) as attorney general. Leon Jaworski, a conservative Texas Democrat, is named to succeed Archibald Cox as special Watergate prosecutor.

2 The U. S. Department of Labor reports an October unemployment rate of 4.5%—the lowest level since June 1970.

6 In off-year elections, Brendan T. Byrne (D) and Mills E. Godwin, Jr. (R) are elected governor of New Jersey and Virginia, respectively; Abraham D. Beame (D) wins New York City's mayoralty race; and black mayoralty candidates are victorious in Detroit and Raleigh, N. C.

7 The United States and Egypt announce that they have agreed to reestablish diplomatic relations, which were suspended in June 1967. ● The U. S. Congress overrides the presidential veto of a bill limiting presidential power to wage war without congressional approval. ● President Nixon asks Congress to pass an emergency energy act, relaxing environmental requirements, reducing auto speeds, and imposing daylight saving time on a year-round basis.

11 Egypt and Israel sign a cease-fire agreement.

13 After reporting the worst monthly trade deficit in British history, the British government adopts a series of measures to improve its balance of payments, cut the money supply, and deal with labor problems threatening widespread power blackouts.

14 Britain's Princess Anne and Capt. Mark Phillips are married in Westminster Abbey, London.

16 The Skylab 3 astronauts—Lt. Col. Gerald P. Carr, Lt. Col. William R. Pogue, and Dr. Edward G. Gibson—are launched from Cape Canaveral beginning a scheduled 84-day mission aboard the earth-orbiting Skylab space station. ● President Nixon signs into law a bill authorizing the Alaskan pipeline.

25 In a bloodless military coup in Greece, Lt. Gen. Phaidon Gizikis, commander of the First Army, replaces George Papadopoulos as president. The civilian cabinet of Premier Spyros Markezinis is dismissed. ● President Nixon announces a series of steps to cut energy consumption, including a reduction in home heating oil deliveries and a cut in gasoline production.

26 An Arab heads of state conference opens in Staouéli, Algeria.

29 Egyptian-Israeli military talks collapse; the two sides exchange machine gun and mortar fire. ● More than 100 persons are killed and 100 are injured in a department store fire in Kumamoto, Japan.

UPI

Egyptian and Israeli Army officers shake hands after discussing supplies for Egyptian units inside Suez City, as UN officer (right) observes, November 2.

OCTOBER

S	M	T	W	T	F	S
	1	2	3	4	5	6
7	8	9	10	11	12	13
14	15	16	17	18	19	20
21	22	23	24	25	26	27
28	29	30	31			

WAR ERUPTS IN THE MIDDLE EAST
AGNEW QUITS AS VICE PRESIDENT
COX FIRED AS WATERGATE PROBER

OCTOBER

5 Canada's Prime Minister Trudeau announces that diplomat Jules Léger has been named as Canada's 21st governor-general.

6 A major war breaks out in the Middle East as Israeli forces fight Syrian troops along the Golan Heights and Egyptian forces along the Suez Canal.

10 Spiro T. Agnew resigns as vice president of the United States and pleads no contest to one count of income tax evasion.

12 President Nixon nominates Gerald Ford, the Republican leader of the House of Representatives, as the nation's 40th vice president.

14 Amid student demonstrations for a return of constitutional government, Thailand's King Phumiphol Aduldet appoints Sanya Dharmasakti as premier, succeeding Thanom Kittikachorn, who resigned.

17 In Kuwait, the minister of the 11 nations of the Organization of Arab Petroleum Exporting Countries agree on a plan of reduced oil production and oil exporting.

18 In Norway, a new minority Labor government, with Trygve M. Bratteli as premier, is sworn in.

20 Following a disagreement with the White House over the Watergate tapes, Archibald Cox is dismissed as special prosecutor, Elliot Richardson resigns as attorney general, and William Ruckelshaus leaves as deputy attorney general. ● In Moscow, U. S. Secretary of State Kissinger and Soviet Communist party chairman Brezhnev discuss the Middle East situation.

21 The Oakland Athletics defeat the New York Mets, four games to three, to win baseball's World Series.

23 President Nixon agrees to submit the Watergate tapes to Federal District Court Judge John J. Sirica.

24 A cease-fire agreement, the second in two days, goes into effect in the Middle East.

27 The UN Security Council approves the establishment of a UN peacekeeping force in the Middle East.

29 In provincial elections in Quebec, the Liberal party of Premier Robert Bourassa captures 102 of 110 legislative seats with 54% of the vote.

31 A worldwide alert of U. S. military forces, instituted on October 25, ends. ● The White House announces that two Watergate tapes sought by the prosecution do not exist.

Israeli artillerymen fire 155-mm guns at Syrian positions along the Golan Heights, October 12.

UPI

NIXON PROPOSES ENERGY ACT
CEASE-FIRE IN MIDDLE EAST
GREEK COUP OUSTS PRESIDENT

NOVEMBER

S	M	T	W	T	F	S
				1	2	3
4	5	6	7	8	9	10
11	12	13	14	15	16	17
18	19	20	21	22	23	24
25	26	27	28	29	30	

NOVEMBER

1 President Nixon announces the nomination of Sen. William B. Saxbe (R-Ohio) as attorney general. Leon Jaworski, a conservative Texas Democrat, is named to succeed Archibald Cox as special Watergate prosecutor.

2 The U. S. Department of Labor reports an October unemployment rate of 4.5%—the lowest level since June 1970.

6 In off-year elections, Brendan T. Byrne (D) and Mills E. Godwin, Jr. (R) are elected governor of New Jersey and Virginia, respectively; Abraham D. Beame (D) wins New York City's mayoralty race; and black mayoralty candidates are victorious in Detroit and Raleigh, N. C.

7 The United States and Egypt announce that they have agreed to reestablish diplomatic relations, which were suspended in June 1967. ● The U. S. Congress overrides the presidential veto of a bill limiting presidential power to wage war without congressional approval. ● President Nixon asks Congress to pass an emergency energy act, relaxing environmental requirements, reducing auto speeds, and imposing daylight saving time on a year-round basis.

11 Egypt and Israel sign a cease-fire agreement.

13 After reporting the worst monthly trade deficit in British history, the British government adopts a series of measures to improve its balance of payments, cut the money supply, and deal with labor problems threatening widespread power blackouts.

14 Britain's Princess Anne and Capt. Mark Phillips are married in Westminster Abbey, London.

16 The Skylab 3 astronauts—Lt. Col. Gerald P. Carr, Lt. Col. William R. Pogue, and Dr. Edward G. Gibson—are launched from Cape Canaveral beginning a scheduled 84-day mission aboard the earth-orbiting Skylab space station. ● President Nixon signs into law a bill authorizing the Alaskan pipeline.

25 In a bloodless military coup in Greece, Lt. Gen. Phaidon Gizikis, commander of the First Army, replaces George Papadopoulos as president. The civilian cabinet of Premier Spyros Markezinis is dismissed. ● President Nixon announces a series of steps to cut energy consumption, including a reduction in home heating oil deliveries and a cut in gasoline production.

26 An Arab heads of state conference opens in Staouéli, Algeria.

29 Egyptian-Israeli military talks collapse; the two sides exchange machine gun and mortar fire. ● More than 100 persons are killed and 100 are injured in a department store fire in Kumamoto, Japan.

UPI

Egyptian and Israeli Army officers shake hands after discussing supplies for Egyptian units inside Suez City, as UN officer (right) observes, November 2.

DECEMBER

S	M	T	W	T	F	S
						1
2	3	4	5	6	7	8
9	10	11	12	13	14	15
16	17	18	19	20	21	22
23	24	25	26	27	28	29
30	31					

FORD BECOMES VICE PRESIDENT
BRITAIN SETS 3-DAY WORK WEEK
SPANISH PREMIER ASSASSINATED

DECEMBER

1 David Ben-Gurion, the founding father of Israel, dies at the age of 87.

3 The small U. S. spacecraft Pioneer 10 sails through the radiation belts of Jupiter and transmits color photographs of the planet.

4 William E. Simon is named by President Nixon to head the new Federal Energy Office. John A. Love had resigned earlier as the President's energy adviser. ● Denmark's ruling Social Democrats suffer heavy losses in parliamentary elections.

5 Truck drivers in several states stage wildcat highway blockades to protest higher fuel prices and lower speed limits.

6 Gerald R. Ford is sworn in as the 40th vice president of the United States.

9 Britain, the Republic of Ireland, and the Protestant and Roman Catholic leadership of Northern Ireland agree to establish a Council of Ireland, which will act as liaison between Dublin and Belfast.

10 The U. S. government ends wage and price controls in the auto industry; in exchange, three manufacturers agree to limit price increases on 1974 models.

11 Nelson A. Rockefeller (R) announces his resignation as governor of New York.

13 To counter disruptions in Britain's energy supply, Prime Minister Heath announces that a three-day work week would be imposed on most British industries beginning Jan. 1, 1974.

16 O. J. Simpson of the Buffalo Bills establishes a season's rushing record for professional football (2,003 yards).

17 Arab guerrillas attack a U. S. jetliner in Rome, Italy, killing 31 persons.

18 The USSR launches Soyuz 13, a two-man space mission.

20 Luis Carrero Blanco, premier of Spain since June 1973, is assassinated in Madrid.

21 The first Arab-Israeli peace conference opens in Geneva. ● To deal with Japan's current oil shortage and inflation, Premier Tanaka declares a state of emergency.

22 The first session of the 93d Congress adjourns without enacting emergency energy legislation.

29 Generalissimo Franco names Minister of the Interior Carlos Arias Navarro premier of Spain.

31 In parliamentary elections in Israel, the Labor alignment of Premier Golda Meir loses some strength but remains in power.

WIDE WORLD

Spanish Premier Luis Carrero Blanco was killed when an explosive device was set off beneath a Madrid street, blowing his auto to pieces, December 20.

THE YEAR THAT SHOOK AMERICA

Sen. Sam J. Ervin, Jr.

"And the pall of the Watergate, with all its revelations of misplaced loyalties, of strange measures of the ethical, of unusual doings in high places ... is upon us. It is something that necessarily touches us all, irrespective of political inclination. The very glue of our ship of state seems about to become unstuck. There is a resultant fear of consequent grave damage to the democratic processes of which we have been so proud, and in which we firmly have believed, and which we have proclaimed to the world. Seemingly, there is an environment of diffuse but broad taint and corruption in our public life."

—Associate Justice Harry A. Blackmun, Aug. 5, 1973

The Watergate, where Democratic committee offices were burglarized.

BY ROBERT SHOGAN
Washington Bureau, "Los Angeles Times"

On Jan. 8, 1973, seven men went on trial in the U. S. district court in Washington, D. C., charged with conspiracy, burglary, and violation of federal wiretapping laws in connection with the break-in at the National Democratic Committee headquarters in the Watergate office building in Washington on June 17, 1972. The defendants were only supporting players in a legal and political drama that had already stirred intense controversy. The controversy would soon swell into a momentous government scandal, the worst in modern U. S. history.

The clouds of suspicion would reach the highest levels of President Richard M. Nixon's administration, casting a shadow over the President himself. Two former members of his cabinet and one key member of

his White House staff would come under indictment. Others of his trusted advisers would resign. The Congress and the courts would be brought into confrontation with the Chief Executive. And the crisis of disbelief would bring the nation closer to impeachment of a President than at any time in more than a century.

Amid these events came the news on October 10 that Vice President Spiro T. Agnew had resigned (see the article on page 20). This episode, although not related to Watergate, further shook the confidence of many Americans in their elected leaders.

BREAK-IN TRIAL AND COVER-UP REVELATIONS

During the 1972 election campaign, Democrats had charged that the Watergate break-in was part of a far-flung effort to undermine political opposition to Nixon. Several publications, notably the Washington *Post,*

President Nixon, in a television address to the nation from the Oval Office of the White House on August 15, proclaims his innocence of any complicity in the Watergate affair.

had published reports of political espionage, alleging involvement of high-level members of the Nixon campaign organization and the administration. The Office of Federal Elections in the General Accounting Office had turned up evidence of irregularities in the handling of Nixon campaign funds.

But the President had denied these charges. At a news conference on August 29, 1972, he said that as a result of a report by his counsel, John W. Dean III, he could state "categorically . . . that no one in the White House staff, no one in this administration, presently employed, was involved in this very bizarre incident."

Trial. As the trial opened before Chief Judge John J. Sirica, there was still no proof to the contrary. The grand jury probe of the break-in—which resulted in indictment of the seven men on Sept. 15, 1972—had been promised by Atty. Gen. Richard G. Kleindienst to be "the most extensive . . . since the assassination of President Kennedy."

Five of the men on trial had been arrested in the Democratic party headquarters. One was James W. McCord, Jr., security coordinator (at the time of his arrest) for the Committee for the Re-election of the President and a former Federal Bureau of Investigation (FBI) agent and Central Intelligence Agency (CIA) employee. The others were Bernard L. Barker, Frank A. Sturgis, Virgilio R. Gonzalez, and Eugenio R. Martinez—all residents of Miami, Fla., and foes of the Cuban leader Fidel Castro. Their mission at the time of their arrest included adjustment of electronic equipment that had been installed previously. The two arrested after June 17 were G. Gordon Liddy, counsel (at the time of his arrest) to the Finance Committee to Re-elect the President and a former White House aide and former FBI agent, and E. Howard Hunt, Jr., a former White House aide and retired CIA employee.

A few days after the trial opened, Hunt and the four Miamians

pleaded guilty. Liddy and McCord stood trial and were convicted on all charges on January 30. Sentencing was set for March 23.

First Evidence of Cover-Up. Judge Sirica said publicly that he was "not satisfied" that all the facts had been brought out and urged a congressional inquiry. On February 7 the Senate responded by creating a seven-member committee—the Senate Select Committee on Presidential Campaign Activities, headed by Sam J. Ervin, Jr. (D-N. C.)—to investigate all irregularities in the 1972 presidential campaign.

But it was Sirica's own persistence that produced the first major evidence of a cover-up. On March 20, with the threat of a heavy sentence hanging over his head, McCord wrote Sirica a letter in which he asserted that the defendants had been under "political pressure" to remain silent and charged that perjury had been committed. Sirica disclosed McCord's letter on March 23, when he postponed sentencing of McCord, sentenced Liddy to a prison term of from 6 years, 8 months to 20 years, and imposed "provisional" maximum sentences on the other five. Later—at the final sentencing on November 9—Liddy's sentence was unchanged; Hunt received a prison term of 2½ to 8 years; McCord, a term of 1 to 5 years; and the others, lesser sentences.

The disclosure of McCord's letter heightened the pressure on President Nixon, who had already been embarrassed by Watergate disclosures during the Senate Judiciary Committee hearings on his nomination on February 17 of L. Patrick Gray III to be permanent director of the FBI. Gray, who had been acting director since the death of J. Edgar Hoover

CONGRESSIONAL QUARTERLY, INC., 1973

The Senate Select Committee on Watergate meets in the Senate Caucus Room. Seated at center is committee chairman Sen. Sam Ervin of North Carolina, with committee vice chairman Sen. Howard Baker of Tennessee seated on his right and chief counsel Samuel Dash on his left.

UPI

Archibald Cox (above), whom President Nixon appointed Watergate special prosecutor, was dismissed by Nixon over White House tapes issue. *John Dean III* (right) former presidential counsel, testifies at Senate hearings.

CONSOLIDATED NEWS PICTURES, INC.

on May 2, 1972, had admitted to the committee on March 22 that John Dean had "probably" lied to the FBI during its Watergate investigation.

Events then moved swiftly. On April 5 the President announced withdrawal of the Gray nomination. On April 15 the President met with Attorney General Kleindienst and Asst. Atty. Gen. Henry E. Petersen, who told him that high officials at the White House and the reelection committee had been involved in trying to cover up the Watergate affair.

White House Reversal. On April 17, Nixon publicly announced that "major developments" in the case had led him to start his own investigation. White House Press Secretary Ronald L. Ziegler told newsmen that all previous White House statements on Watergate were to be considered "inoperative."

Amid a flood of published leaks about the revived investigation, John Dean issued an extraordinary statement on April 19, declaring that he would not "become a scapegoat in the Watergate case." The President's two top aides, H. R. Haldeman and John D. Ehrlichman, hired a private attorney to represent them in the investigation.

Top-Level Resignations. On April 26 came the first in a series of top-level resignations brought on by Watergate. Jeb Stuart Magruder, who had been deputy director of the reelection committee, quit as policy development director in the Department of Commerce. The next day, Acting FBI Director Gray also quit after it was disclosed that—at the suggestion, according to Gray, of Dean and Ehrlichman—he had burned "highly sensitive" papers taken from the safe in Howard Hunt's White House office.

On April 30 the White House announced the dismissal of Dean and the resignations of Haldeman, Ehrlichman, and Kleindienst. In a televised address, the President praised Haldeman and Ehrlichman and asked that they not be prejudged. He explained that Kleindienst had quit only because of his closeness to persons involved in the investigation and announced that he had named the secretary of defense, Elliot L. Richardson, as the new attorney general. Richardson, the President said, would have the authority to name a special prosecutor to take over the investigation. Nixon accepted responsibility for Watergate, although he denied prior knowledge of it, and vowed to turn his full attention to other vital national problems.

Pentagon Papers Involvement. But even then, shocking new disclosures were being made at the trial in Los Angeles, Calif., of Daniel Ellsberg and Anthony J. Russo, Jr., on charges of espionage, theft, and conspiracy in connection with the "Pentagon Papers" (a top-secret account of U. S. involvement in Indochina, given to newspapers in 1971). Newsmen dubbed the trial "Watergate West" when W. Matthew Byrne, Jr., the presiding judge, disclosed on April 27 that two of the convicted Watergate conspirators, Hunt and Liddy, had been involved in a burglary of the files of Ellsberg's former psychiatrist in September 1971. Later it was disclosed that the burglary had been part of an independent probe of the Pentagon Papers leak carried out by a special unit known as the "plumbers," under the supervision of Ehrlichman and a White House aide, Egil Krogh, Jr.

JUDGE JOHN J. SIRICA presided over Watergate case.

A few days after the burglary disclosure, the Department of Justice belatedly informed Judge Byrne that telephone conversations of Ellsberg had been overheard through an FBI wiretap. The tap was one of 17 placed on the telephones of government officials and newsmen supposedly to prevent leaks of national security information. The burglary and tapping prompted Judge Byrne to dismiss on May 11 the charges against Ellsberg and Russo on grounds of "improper government conduct." Later—on September 4—Ehrlichman, Krogh, Liddy, and David R. Young, a former White House staffer, were indicted by a Los Angeles grand jury for their connection with the burglary. Krogh pleaded guilty to a federal civil rights violation in the case on November 30.

The Vesco Case. Meanwhile, on May 10, a federal grand jury in New York City had indicted two former cabinet members. They were John N. Mitchell, who had resigned as attorney general on March 1, 1972, to head the reelection committee, and Maurice H. Stans, who had resigned as secretary of commerce on Feb. 15, 1972, to become chairman of the reelection finance committee. The charges stemmed from a $200,000 Nixon campaign contribution by New Jersey financier Robert L. Vesco, who was trying to block a federal inquiry into his handling of mutual funds.

Further White House Explanation. In the wake of these new blows to his administration, President Nixon on May 22 again spoke out publicly on Watergate. He reiterated his own innocence in the break-in and cover-up but conceded that there had been "wide-ranging" efforts by some members of his administration to conceal aspects of the case.

The President confirmed that he had ordered the creation of the "plumbers" unit, although he denied authorizing the burglary of the psychiatrist's office. The special investigative unit had been set up in 1971, he said, after a proposed intelligence operation—which would have sanctioned surreptitious entry, wiretapping, and other measures "in specified situations related to the national security"—was scrapped in 1970, mainly because of J. Edgar Hoover's objections. Because some of the persons involved in the Watergate break-in had past CIA affiliations, the President said he had been concerned that an intensive Watergate probe might turn up some connection with the CIA, which he said he mistakenly believed might have been involved. Accordingly, he had ordered Ehrlichman and Haldeman to prevent such disclosures. But he concluded that his instructions unintentionally seemed to have fostered efforts to impede the probe. *(Continued on page 22)*

THE AGNEW CASE

Sudden Resignation Ends Vice President's Career

BY MARQUIS CHILDS
Contributing Editor, St. Louis "Post-Dispatch"

UPI

Former Vice President Agnew just prior to his October 15 address to the nation explaining his resignation.

The ordeal of Spiro Theodore Agnew, which ended with his resignation of the vice presidency of the United States on October 10, began long before the charges against him surfaced in public. By early June the U. S. attorney in Baltimore, George Beall, had progressed sufficiently in the case so that on July 3 he could present his evidence to U. S. Attorney General Elliot L. Richardson. Two months before, Beall had informed Agnew's lawyers of the seriousness of the charges of bribery, conspiracy, and tax evasion that were being documented.

First Public Response. The first news accounts of the action to be taken against the vice president appeared on August 7, and the next day Agnew called a nationally televised press conference to denounce the charges as "damned lies." It was an impressive performance, with the vice president standing before the crowded conference and pledging full cooperation with the prosecutors, since he had "nothing to hide." Here was the No. 2 man in the U. S. government—a man who stood clear of the Watergate wreckage. He declared, as he was to declare repeatedly in the days ahead, that he would never resign.

After the conference Agnew flew to Palm Springs, Calif., to stay at Frank Sinatra's estate. As vice president, he had come to enjoy the friendship of Sinatra and other celebrities. Before being tapped by Richard Nixon as his running mate in 1968, Agnew had never been in the big time. As the charges were developed by Beall, the picture that emerged was of a relatively obscure politician in Baltimore county, with two years as governor of Maryland, trying to keep up with the social and political demands of increasingly higher office.

In the overheated atmosphere of Washington, D. C., the report spread that President Nixon wanted his vice president to resign. This would be the simplest way out. Whether Nixon ever brought himself to ask Agnew, face to face, to step down has been a matter of dispute. The relationship between them had been cordial enough, but never frank. At any rate, in early September, the President sent one of his aides, Bryce N. Harlow, to suggest resignation. Harlow outlined the seriousness of the charges, which on conviction could bring a prison term. As far as was publicly known at the time, Agnew gave little indication that he would do anything but fight.

Defense and Defiance. Agnew defended himself privately and later in a more or less public form against charges that, while holding public office in Maryland in the 1960's, he had accepted campaign contributions from individuals who later received government contracts. Such a practice, he argued, was part of a well-established pattern of political fund-raising in Maryland as well as elsewhere in the nation. What he was saying in private conversation was that the line between a campaign contribution and a gift of money intended as a bribe was thin. As he well knew, this defense would touch a sensitive nerve among many members of Congress.

But even while he was breathing defiance and accusing the Department of Justice of news leaks intended deliberately to destroy him, he was engaged, as was later shown, in plea bargaining to mitigate his sentence and escape a jail term. As Attorney General Richardson surveyed the case made by the U. S. attorney in Baltimore, he was increasingly concerned during this period that Agnew, while under the cloud of charges being brought against him, might inherit the presidency. Richardson kept urging action that would resolve the impasse.

Agnew meanwhile was fighting to keep before the public the image of a stern law-and-order official being persecuted by his enemies. On September 14 the vice president requested a meeting with the Republicans' best-known conservative, U. S. Sen. Barry Goldwater of Arizona, to discuss the suggestion that he resign. Goldwater agreed that, in case of guilt, resignation was in order. On receiving the vice president's assurance of innocence, Goldwater telephoned the White House, rebuked Harlow for the suggestion and the pressure it represented, and then flew home to Phoenix.

Disturbed by what seemed a rift in the party's ranks, Harlow and a White House lawyer, J. Fred Buzhardt, Jr., promptly took a plane to Phoenix to present the evidence to Goldwater. The senator is reported to have indicated, with his usual candor, that even if Agnew were "as guilty as John Dillinger," the thing that mattered was fair treatment by the Department of Justice. On September 29, in an address before the National Federation of Republican Women, Agnew denounced the

news leaks about his case and once again affirmed his innocence of all charges. The conservative audience cheered him and gave him several standing ovations.

Appeal to the House. One of the most dramatic developments came when, without any prior announcement, Agnew moved to get the case out of the courts and into the political arena of the House of Representatives. On September 25 he wrote a letter and also went to Capitol Hill to ask Speaker Carl Albert (D-Okla.) to have the House conduct an investigation into the charges against him. In the letter Agnew expressed his belief that "the Constitution bars a criminal proceeding of any kind" against a vice president while in office. This issue of whether the Constitution forbids the indictment of an incumbent vice president was to be raised repeatedly.

For Speaker Albert, the Agnew request posed an embarrassing issue. It seemed to be an invitation to begin impeachment proceedings. If such proceedings led to removal of the vice president—and if the presidency should become vacant before the vice presidency was filled—Albert would be next in the line of succession. The presidency under such circumstances was the last thing he wanted. In any event, Albert probably would have denied Agnew's request, which briefly made big headlines. But on September 25, Albert had received a telephone call from Attorney General Richardson, saying that grand jury proceedings were about to begin, with a number of witnesses and a store of accumulated evidence. Richardson expressed the opinion that an indictment would be returned. That was enough to tip the scales if the speaker had been in any doubt. The next day he announced that the House would take no action.

Pressures and Counterpressures. Agnew's move was widely interpreted to be another and highly significant thrust in the war of nerves with the White House and the Department of Justice. If a vice president could be impeached, so also could a president who found himself in a sea of troubles; this was the fear of men around the President. The example would be highly unwelcome. In the interval, the Department of Justice held that a vice president could be indicted while in office.

On September 27 the prosecutors in Baltimore began to present their evidence to the federal grand jury, with a parade of Agnew's friends and associates—contractors, architects, and others out of his days as Baltimore county executive and as governor—giving secret evidence. On September 28, Agnew's lawyers filed a suit to stop the grand jury probe, and in another dramatic countermove on October 3, they won the right to investigate Department of Justice news leaks, including the power of subpoena.

Even as the skirmishing grew fiercer, the end was in sight. The plea bargaining had been going on all this time. On September 13 it had reached a climax when—to the astonishment of Assistant Attorney General Henry E. Petersen—Judah Best, one of the vice president's lawyers, proposed a package deal. The vice president would plead nolo contendere (no contest—the equivalent of a guilty plea without the actual admission) on a one-count charge. In return, he would resign and would be assured of no jail sentence. It was this proposal that Best took to Florida on October 5 for a long bargaining session with Buzhardt, who was with the President's party at Key Biscayne. They settled on the wording of a statement in which Agnew would acknowledge evading income taxes in 1967. This bargain was ratified tentatively on October 8 in a meeting with Walter E. Hoffman, the federal district judge assigned to handle procedural matters in the case. But Judge Hoffman refused to make a commitment on the sentence that Agnew could expect without word from the Department of Justice. That question was resolved the next day by Attorney General Richardson, who recommended against a prison sentence.

Resignation. In a surprise appearance before Judge Hoffman in Baltimore on October 10, the vice president read from a statement in which he announced his decision to resign and to plead nolo contendere to the charge of failing to report $29,500 of income received in 1967.

"I admit that I did receive payments during the year 1967 which were not expended for political purposes and that, therefore, these payments were income taxable to me in that year and that I so knew," the 39th vice president of the United States said in the hushed courtroom.

At the same time the Department of Justice released a 40-page memorandum citing the detailed charges against the vice president. According to legal specialists, they would have added up to a 50-count indictment. Judge Hoffman sentenced Agnew to a fine of $10,000 and three years' unsupervised probation. From the bench, the judge said he would have sent the vice president to prison if it had not been for Richardson's plea for leniency. The memorandum showed sworn testimony to the effect that up to December 1972, Agnew had received envelopes containing money paid him by Baltimore associates in search of favors.

Yet even as he bowed out, Agnew reasserted his innocence in a televised address on October 15 and denounced "scurrilous and inaccurate" reports as the reason for the charges against him and for his resignation. He said that his plea was not an admission of any guilt but a "no contest" pleading to "still the raging storm."

"Let me reiterate here," he said, "that I have never as county executive of Baltimore county, as governor of Maryland, or as vice president of the United States, enriched myself in betrayal of my public trust. My current net worth, less than $200,000, is modest for a person of my age and position. Every penny of it can be accounted for from lawful sources."

Praising both President Nixon and U. S. Rep. Gerald R. Ford (R-Mich.), who had been named as his successor, Agnew told his television audience that this was his farewell and final address. Thus ended the career of the man who a year before had been considered the leading contender for his party's presidential nomination in 1976.

Background. Agnew was born in Baltimore on Nov. 9, 1918, the son of a Greek immigrant. After serving as an Army officer in World War II, he received a law degree from the University of Baltimore in 1947, entered law practice, and changed his political affiliation from Democrat to Republican. Agnew served as county executive of Baltimore county (1962–67) and governor of Maryland (1967–69). He became vice president in 1969.

(For subsequent developments on the vice presidency, see UNITED STATES.)

SENATE Watergate Committee Chairman Sam Ervin, Jr. (standing, left), swears in witness James McCord (standing, far right) in the Senate Caucus Room.

HOWARD BAKER (R-Tenn.), vice chairman of the Senate Watergate Committee.

Cox as Special Prosecutor. At the same time, the President cited Richardson's choice of Archibald Cox as special Watergate prosecutor as reason for confidence that the truth would be "brought out in an orderly way." Cox, a Harvard law professor and former solicitor general under Presidents Kennedy and Johnson, was sworn into office on May 25, with a broad mandate to investigate not only the Watergate case but also the 1972 controversy over the settlement of antitrust litigation against the International Telephone and Telegraph Corporation (ITT).

SENATE WATERGATE HEARINGS

While Cox recruited his staff and reviewed the evidence, public attention focused on the televised hearings of the Senate Watergate committee, which began on May 17. Besides Chairman Ervin, the committee consisted of three Democrats—Herman E. Talmadge of Georgia, Daniel K. Inouye of Hawaii, and Joseph M. Montoya of New Mexico—and three Republicans—Vice Chairman Howard H. Baker, Jr., of Tennessee, Edward J. Gurney of Florida, and Lowell P. Weicker, Jr., of Connecticut. Samuel Dash, a Georgetown University law professor, was selected by Ervin as chief counsel. The hearings were criticized by some on the grounds that the publicity they generated might make it impossible to conduct future criminal trials in the case.

McCord Testimony on Cover-Up. The first witnesses were middle-level officials of the reelection committee, who told how the committee was organized and described initial attempts to cover up evidence. James McCord testified that John J. Caulfield, a former White House and reelection committee aide, had secretly promised him executive

EDWARD GURNEY (R-Fla.), a member of the committee.

clemency, money, and eventually a job if he would keep silent at the trial. According to McCord, Caulfield indicated that the President knew of the offer. Later, the committee heard testimony that a total of $400,000 in Nixon campaign funds was funneled to the defendants and their lawyers for legal fees and support of the defendants' families.

Magruder's Admission of Perjury. The testimony of Jeb Stuart Magruder on June 14 provided the committee and the public with the first direct account by an admitted high-level participant in the break-in and cover-up. Magruder said that at a campaign strategy meeting in Key Biscayne, Fla., on March 30, John Mitchell had given tacit approval to plans for bugging the Democratic headquarters. The project was part of an intelligence-espionage program proposed by G. Gordon Liddy after two of Liddy's earlier and more grandiose plans had been rejected, Magruder continued. Magruder also testified that Gordon C. Strachan—an aide to Haldeman, Nixon's chief of staff—knew of the Watergate plans. But to his knowledge, Magruder said, Nixon was not aware of the plot. Magruder admitted lying under oath before the federal grand jury and said he had told Haldeman of his perjury.

Dean's Controversial Allegations. Magruder was followed on the witness stand by John Dean, who provided the most damaging testimony against Nixon. Dean implicated the President, as well as Haldeman, Ehrlichman, and himself in the cover-up. On Sept. 15, 1972—the day the seven conspirators were indicted—Nixon congratulated him on his work on the case, Dean said. Since Dean believed the President knew of his efforts to conceal the involvement of high-level officials, he took the statement as a sign of the President's approval of the cover-up.

JOHN EHRLICHMAN, a former White House adviser.

LEON JAWORSKI replaced Cox as special prosecutor.

Further, according to Dean, on March 13, 1973, the President not only told him that payment of $1 million to Watergate defendants "was no problem" but also referred to his discussion of possible executive clemency for Howard Hunt. When he warned the President on March 21 that a continued cover-up would require "more perjury and more money," Nixon did not seem "particularly concerned," Dean said. In five days of testimony, Dean stuck to his story, although most of it was unsupported by other evidence.

Dean also gave the committee documents pertaining to the so-called White House "political enemies" project. Included were lists of politicians, businessmen, labor leaders, journalists, and others who were considered political foes of the administration, as well as memorandums—one from Dean to Ehrlichman, dated Aug. 16, 1971—outlining a strategy of retribution against such "enemies."

In the face of Dean's charges, the White House stood firm on Nixon's denial of involvement in his May 22 statement. And several later witnesses sharply disagreed with Dean's version of events.

Mitchell's Explanation. John Mitchell denied that he had given approval to the Watergate bugging, as charged by Magruder. But he admitted withholding information from the President during the investigation of the crime because he feared that Nixon would "lower the boom" on those responsible and thus damage his reelection chances. For the same reason, Mitchell said, he shielded the President from any knowledge of the break-in at the office of Ellsberg's psychiatrist and a number of other incidents that he referred to as White House "horrors."

Ehrlichman's and Haldeman's Rebuttals. On July 24, Ehrlichman began five days of testimony in which he denied all charges of illegal conduct on his part and also denied that the President had approved the offering of executive clemency to Watergate defendants. Ehrlichman said that the President had not received a full report on the case until April 14, 1973, when Ehrlichman reported on the results of his own inquiry. He said Nixon had told him on March 30 to take over the Watergate investigation from Dean because the President was "satisfied that John Dean is in this so deeply that he simply cannot any longer have anything to do with it."

In his appearance before the committee, beginning on July 30, Haldeman, like Ehrlichman, denied any illegal acts on his part and said that he and Nixon were "badly misled" by Dean's denials of high-level involvement in the bugging or cover-up. He said that the President did not intend to compliment Dean for "containing" the Watergate scandal, as Dean inferred, but merely meant to give him "a pat on the back" for three months of hard work.

THE WHITE HOUSE TAPES

Meanwhile, in an appearance before the Senate committee on July 16, Alexander P. Butterfield—the head of the Federal Aviation Administration and a former White House aide—had revealed that "for historical purposes" Nixon had taped most conversations in his White House and Executive Office Building offices since early 1971. Both the Senate committee and Special Prosecutor Cox immediately sought access to the tapes, which they regarded as essential evidence in the case. Their efforts had been spurred when Haldeman testified before the committee that

the President had permitted him to listen to the tapes of two White House meetings, which Haldeman said demonstrated the President's innocence in the cover-up.

Presidential Refusal. But in a letter to Ervin of July 23, Nixon refused the request for the tapes, arguing that to release them to the Senate committee would violate the doctrine of separation of powers and the principle of executive privilege.

On July 26, the President formally defied subpoenas obtained by the Senate committee and by Cox on July 23, demanding certain of the tapes, along with the documents bearing on the case. Both Cox and the committee appealed to Judge Sirica, with Cox moving first.

On August 29, Sirica ordered the President to make the tapes available to him so that he could screen out material covered by executive privilege and turn over information bearing on the case to the grand jury. This decision was appealed to the Court of Appeals for the District of Columbia, which on October 12 upheld the substance of Sirica's ruling.

UPI

L. PATRICK GRAY, former acting director of the FBI.

Offer of Summary. The President, who had indicated that he would take the case to the Supreme Court, suddenly switched strategies. On October 19 he proposed to turn over a summary of the tapes to Sirica and the Senate committee. Sen. John C. Stennis (D-Miss.) would be entrusted with all the tapes so that he could verify the summary. Cox was ordered to abandon efforts to get the tapes and other documents from the White House.

When Cox announced on October 20 that he would not accept the order, Nixon instructed Attorney General Richardson to dismiss Cox. Richardson resigned, declaring that he felt bound to protect Cox's freedom of action. Richardson's deputy, William D. Ruckelshaus, also refused to fire Cox, and he resigned too. It was left to Solicitor General Robert H. Bork, who was next in line of succession as attorney general, to dismiss Cox.

Promise of Tapes and Aftermath. These actions provoked an outburst of protest from the public and Congress, and Nixon retreated. On October 23 the White House discarded the Stennis plan and promised to turn the tapes over to Sirica. The President then appointed a new special prosecutor, Leon Jaworski, a Texas lawyer and former president of the American Bar Association.

But then, on October 31, came another shock. The White House announced that two of the nine taped conversations subpoenaed on July 23 were missing—and maintained that they never existed. Later it was disclosed that an 18-minute segment of one of the seven remaining tapes was blank.

These disclosures heightened criticism of the administration. New suspicions were voiced on a number of issues, including the settlement of anti-trust litigation against ITT, the operations of the "plumbers" unit, political contributions from dairy producers, and the President's personal finances. A number of prominent publications, senators, and organizations demanded the President's resignation, and the House of Representatives authorized a formal inquiry into impeachment.

The President fought back. He proclaimed his innocence, vowed never to resign, and promised to make full disclosures, which he said would vindicate him. At year's end it was clear that the task of regaining public confidence and preserving his presidency confronted Nixon with the gravest challenge of his career.

FOUR LEADING FIGURES IN THE WATERGATE AFFAIR

CONSOLIDATED NEWS PICTURES

JOHN WESLEY DEAN III, a former counsel to President Nixon, was a key witness in the early stages of the Senate Committee's hearings on the Watergate affair. He implicated former members of the administration in the planning of the Watergate break-in and in the cover-up that followed. In his most sensational testimony, Dean charged that the President was partly responsible for the cover-up. Although Dean acknowledged that he himself had participated in some aspects of the cover-up, he said that he had finally reported the matter to federal prosecutors. In October 1973, Dean pleaded guilty to one count of conspiring to obstruct justice and defraud the United States.

Dean was born in Akron, Ohio, on Oct. 14, 1938. After attending Colgate University and American University, he graduated from Wooster College and Georgetown University Law School. He was briefly employed by a Washington law firm before becoming chief minority counsel to the judiciary committee of the House of Representatives. Later he served with the National Commission on the Reform of Criminal Laws and as a deputy associate U. S. attorney general, acting as a liaison with Congress. President Nixon appointed him one of his counsel in 1970. In August 1972, Nixon said Dean had conducted an investigation of the Watergate affair that had cleared members of the White House staff. Dean later denied investigating Watergate. He resigned from the White House staff on April 30, 1973, at the President's request.

JOHN DANIEL EHRLICHMAN, former assistant to President Nixon for domestic affairs, was implicated by witnesses before the Senate Watergate Committee in some aspects of the Watergate case. Ehrlichman himself was the committee's most belligerent witness. In his testimony, he denied all the charges and named John Wesley Dean III as a focus of Watergate illegalities. Ehrlichman was also associated with the activities of the "White House Plumbers," a group that searched a psychiatrist's office for records pertaining to Daniel Ellsberg, who had admitted giving copies of the Pentagon Papers to several newspapers. Ehrlichman denied that the plumbers' activities had been illegal, but he was indicted for burglary, conspiracy, and perjury in connection with the case.

Ehrlichman was born in Tacoma, Wash., on March 30, 1925. He graduated from the University of California at Los Angeles and Stanford Law School and practiced law in Seattle. At UCLA he was a classmate of H. R. Haldeman. He was a key aide in Richard M. Nixon's campaigns for the presidency in 1960 and 1968. He was appointed counsel to the President in 1969 and later assistant for domestic affairs.

J. P. LAFFONT/SYGMA

Ehrlichman, a Christian Scientist, was renowned in the White House for his spartan habits, his efficiency, and his loyalty to the President. He resigned on April 30, 1973, saying that his usefulness had been impaired by rumor although he was innocent of wrongdoing.

J. P. LAFFONT/SYGMA

HARRY ROBBINS (BOB) HALDEMAN, former chief of the White House staff under President Nixon, was accused in testimony by John Wesley Dean III before the Senate Watergate Committee of having had some knowledge of the cover-up of the Watergate affair. In his own testimony before the committee, Haldeman denied the accusations and maintained that Dean had misled the White House in his reports of the Watergate case. He was confident that President Nixon would be cleared of any knowledge of or complicity in the affair. His testimony included the dramatic admission that he had kept in his home for a time several key tape recordings of conversations between Nixon and persons implicated in the investigation.

Haldeman was born in Los Angeles on Oct. 27, 1926. He graduated from the University of California at Los Angeles and for 20 years was an executive with the J. Walter Thompson Company, an advertising agency, in New York City and Los Angeles. He was associated with all of Nixon's campaigns for office beginning in 1952. He was named White House chief of staff in 1969 and was regarded as one of the President's closest advisers. His influence derived from the fact that almost every document and visitor that reached the President came to Haldeman first. Haldeman resigned on April 30, 1973, affirming his noninvolvement in Watergate but declaring that the pressures of the inquiry would impede the performance of his White House duties.

JOHN NEWTON MITCHELL, former U. S. attorney general, accused by some witnesses before the Senate committee of complicity in the Watergate affair, testified to the committee that he had no prior knowledge of the break-in and denied taking part in the cover-up. In a separate proceeding, he was indicted on charges of perjury, conspiring to obstruct justice, and conspiring to defraud the United States by a New York grand jury investigating the financial dealings of Robert L. Vesco.

Mitchell was born in Detroit on Sept. 5, 1913. After graduating from Fordham University and the Fordham Law School, he practiced law in New York City for 32 years. He met Richard M. Nixon in 1963, and in 1966 his law firm merged with Nixon's. After managing Nixon's presidential campaign in 1968, he remained a close adviser to the President. He was appointed attorney general and acted sternly to enforce the laws. In notable rebuffs, the Senate rejected two Supreme Court nominees that Mitchell had recommended to the President. Mitchell's second wife, Martha, attracted wide publicity for her uninhibited public statements that alternately amused and angered official Washington. Mitchell resigned as attorney general in March 1972 to become director of the Committee for the Re-election of the President. He resigned this post on July 1, 1972, two weeks after the Watergate break-in.

J. P. LAFFONT/SYGMA

RICHARD G. WEST

THE WATERGATE STORY—A CHRONOLOGY

June 17, 1972—Bernard L. Barker, James McCord, Eugenio Martinez, Frank Sturgis, and Virgilio Gonzalez are arrested at the Democratic National Headquarters in the Watergate complex, Washington, D. C.

June 22—President Nixon states that the "White House has had no involvement whatever" in the incident.

July 1—John Mitchell resigns as Nixon's campaign chairman. Clark MacGregor is named to the post.

Sept. 15—Seven men (the five arrested June 17 and former administration aides G. Gordon Liddy and Howard Hunt) are indicted on charges of conspiring to break into the Democratic National Headquarters.

Oct. 26—Campaign manager MacGregor acknowledges the existence of a special Republican campaign fund controlled by top administration officials, but denies that the fund had been used for espionage.

Nov. 7—President Nixon is reelected.

Jan. 11, 1973—Hunt pleads guilty to all six charges against him.

Jan. 15—Four other defendants—Barker, Gonzalez, Martinez, and Sturgis—plead guilty.

Jan. 30—A U. S. district court jury finds Liddy and McCord guilty of conspiracy, second-degree burglary, attempted wiretapping and bugging.

Feb. 8—Sen. Sam J. Ervin, Jr. (D-N. C.) is named chairman of a select committee to investigate the case.

March 2—President Nixon states that the investigation of the case conducted by John Dean III, the White House counsel, "indicated that no one on the White House staff" in July–August 1972 was "involved in or had knowledge of the Watergate matter."

April 17—President Nixon reports that as a result of his own special investigation "major developments" have occurred in the case. • All previous White House statements on Watergate are declared "inoperative."

April 27—Patrick Gray 3rd resigns as acting director of the FBI. • William Matthew Byrne, Jr., the judge in the Pentagon Papers trial, releases Justice Department memorandum stating that Hunt and Liddy burglarized the office of Daniel Ellsberg's psychiatrist so as to steal Ellsberg's medical records.

April 30—Attorney General Kleindienst and presidential advisers H. R. Haldeman and John D. Ehrlichman resign; Dean is dismissed. Secretary of Defense Elliot Richardson is named attorney general.

May 2—Justice Department charges that the Finance Committee to Re-elect the President failed to report and monitor records on a $200,000 contribution by Robert L. Vesco, a New Jersey financier.

May 7—The Washington *Post* wins a Pulitzer Prize for its investigation of the Watergate case.

May 10—A special federal grand jury indicts Mitchell, Maurice W. Stans, Harry L. Sears, former majority leader of the New Jersey Senate, and Robert L. Vesco on charges of conspiring to defraud the United States and obstruct justice.

May 11—Judge Byrne dismisses all charges against the defendants in the Pentagon Papers case.

May 17—Ervin committee begins public hearings.

May 18—Elliot L. Richardson names Archibald Cox as special prosecutor in the Watergate case.

May 22—Nixon acknowledges that although in the interest of national security there were "wide-ranging efforts" to conceal aspects of the case, the President was "not aware" of the cover-up.

May 24—U. S. Attorney Harold H. Titus, Jr., announces that Jeb Stuart Magruder, Nixon's deputy campaign manager, has agreed to plead guilty and serve as a witness for the prosecution.

June 12—Forced to testify before Ervin committee, Stans denies any involvement in the Watergate affair.

June 25—Dean tells the Ervin committee that he had participated in the cover-up and that Nixon had some knowledge of the cover-up after June 1972.

June 27—The White House calls Dean the "mastermind" of the cover-up.

July 10—Mitchell tells Ervin committee that he concealed information from the President about Watergate so as not to hurt his reelection bid.

July 16—The White House confirms that since early 1971 virtually all presidential meetings and telephone conversations have been recorded secretly.

July 24—Before the Ervin committee, Ehrlichman seeks "to refute every charge of illegal conduct" on his part.

July 26—President Nixon refuses to comply with subpoenas ordering him to release the Watergate tapes.

July 30—Before the Ervin committee, Haldeman asserts that the President and himself had no "knowledge of or involvement in" the Watergate affair. Haldeman also states that he had recently listened to the tapes of a presidential meeting with Dean.

July 31—Rep. Robert F. Drinan (D-Mass.) introduces a resolution calling for the President's impeachment.

Aug. 2—Richard Helms, former CIA director, testifies that he had to resist White House pressures to involve the CIA in the Watergate cover-up.

Aug. 16—Magruder pleads guilty to one count of plotting to bug the Democratic headquarters and to the cover-up.

Aug. 30—The White House announces that it will seek a review of Sirica's order of Aug. 29 requiring the President to turn over to him for private review the presidential tapes involving Watergate.

Sept. 4—Ehrlichman, White House "plumbers unit" supervisor Egil Krogh, Jr., Liddy, and Donald R. Young are indicted by a grand jury in connection with the break-in at the office of Ellsberg's psychiatrist.

Oct. 3—Donald H. Segretti testifies about the dirty tricks he played on 1972 Democratic presidential candidates.

Oct. 12—The U. S. District Court of Appeals for D. C. holds, 5–2, that President Nixon must turn over his Watergate tapes to the U. S. District Court.

Oct. 19—Prosecutor Cox rejects a compromise presidential plan on releasing the tapes. • Dean pleads guilty to a single count of conspiring to cover-up the truth of Watergate.

Oct. 20—Attorney General Richardson refuses to dismiss Cox and resigns; Deputy Attorney General Ruckelshaus follows suit; Solicitor General Robert H. Bork fires the special prosecutor.

Oct. 23—The President agrees to submit the tapes to Sirica.

Oct. 31—White House lawyer J. Fred Buzhardt asserts that two key tapes sought by the prosecution do not exist.

Nov. 1—Sen. William B. Saxbe (R-Ohio) is named attorney general; Houston lawyer Leon Jaworski (D) is appointed special prosecutor succeeding Cox.

Nov. 9—Original Watergate defendants are sentenced to prison by Judge Sirica.

Nov. 21—White House counsel Buzhardt tells Sirica that an 18-minute segment of a subpoenaed tape is blank. • Sirica names a panel of experts to "study the authenticity and integrity of the tapes."

Nov. 26—White House turns over to the court the subpoenaed tapes. • Rose Mary Woods, Nixon's personal secretary, tells Sirica that she made a "terrible mistake" of accidentally erasing a portion of the 18 minutes of the subpoenaed tapes.

Nov. 27—Ervin committee suspends hearings.

Nov. 28—Buzhardt testifies in court that there were a "number" of blank sections on subpoenaed tapes.

Nov. 30—President Nixon signs legislation extending Watergate grand jury six months to June 4, 1974.

Dec. 19—Sirica upholds the President's claim of executive privilege on portions of the subpoenaed tapes.

—Compiled by James E. Churchill, Jr.

WIDE WORLD

SPECIAL prosecutor Archibald Cox (center) is sworn in as Attorney General Richardson looks on. Later Cox was fired and Richardson resigned.

Watergate v. the Constitution

The Scandal Posed Serious Questions About the Power of the Presidency

By C. HERMAN PRITCHETT
University of California, Santa Barbara

Watergate and its aftermath engulfed the Nixon administration and the nation in a series of constitutional crises unparalleled in U. S. history and raised grave doubts about the viability of fundamental constitutional arrangements. The basic issue that emerged was whether the power of the modern U. S. President, which has steadily increased since the 1930's, had become so great as to destroy the balance of powers provided for in the Constitution, rendering the chief executive unaccountable to Congress, the courts, and the people.

EXECUTIVE PRIVILEGE

The initial constitutional issue raised by Watergate was "executive privilege," which President Nixon asserted to justify his refusal to make executive documents or records available to Congress. Although presidents on numerous occasions have refused congressional demands for information, the claim of "executive privilege" is relatively recent. It had never before been asserted in an effort to immunize a President's aides from possible prosecution for criminal acts.

WIDE WORLD

LOWELL WEICKER (R-Conn.) of the Watergate Committee.

As Applied to Members of Executive Branch. As the Watergate and other hearings began to develop in 1973, the President issued a policy statement on March 12, saying: "Under the doctrine of separation

of powers, the manner in which the President personally exercises his assigned executive powers is not subject to questioning by another branch of government." The same principle, he held, prevented members of his staff from being questioned because "their roles are in effect an extension of the Presidency." He specifically refused to permit Presidential Counsel John W. Dean III to testify at the Senate confirmation hearings on L. Patrick Gray III as permanent director of the Federal Bureau of Investigation.

In testifying on April 10 before Senate committees meeting to consider the question of executive privilege, Atty. Gen. Richard G. Kleindienst contended that Congress had no power to order any of the 2.5 million employees of the executive branch to testify before its committees if the President barred their appearance. But within a week the administration had abandoned this extreme position.

On April 17, Nixon announced that his staff had worked out "ground rules" with the Senate Select Committee on Presidential Campaign Activities, headed by Sam J. Ervin, Jr. (D-N. C.)—a bipartisan committee established on February 7 to investigate the Watergate affair. Under these rules, all members of the White House staff would appear voluntarily when requested by the committee, but executive privilege could be asserted on particular questions. The Senate committee began its hearings on May 17, receiving testimony from a number of White House aides, including John Dean.

E. HOWARD HUNT pleaded guilty in the Watergate trial.

As Applied to White House Documents. On May 18, Elliot L. Richardson—whose confirmation to succeed Kleindienst as attorney general had been held up in the Senate pending his appointment of a special Watergate prosecutor—named Archibald Cox to that position. Since Cox was in the Department of Justice (an executive branch), no claim of executive privilege could be made to justify refusal of White House documents to him, but he soon encountered other resistance.

On July 16 came the startling disclosure that the President's conversations in his White House and Executive Office Building offices had been tape-recorded since 1971. Both Cox and the Senate Watergate committee immediately asked the President for tapes and records concerning Watergate. Nixon refused these requests on July 23, and subpoenas were filed the same day. Nixon also refused to honor these.

Court Response to Senate Subpoenas. On August 9 the committee filed suit in the U. S. district court to secure enforcement of its subpoenas. This was the first suit by a congressional committee against a President in U. S. history, although not the first time a President had been subpoenaed (see "Compulsory Appearance" below). Chief Judge John J. Sirica dismissed the suit on October 17, holding that no statute authorized a federal court to take jurisdiction of a civil complaint of this kind. Legislation was immediately introduced in Congress to give the courts jurisdiction over any civil action brought by the Senate committee.

Court Response to Cox Subpoena. There was no jurisdictional problem so far as the Cox subpoena was concerned, since Cox was seeking the tapes for the clearly appropriate purpose of preparing possible criminal prosecutions and presentation of evidence to the grand jury. But in a letter on July 23 from Charles Alan Wright, the President's legal consultant, Cox was told that as a member of the executive branch he was subject to the instructions of his superiors and could "have access to presidential papers only as and if the President sees fit

to make them available." White House counsel did not question the power of the court to issue a subpoena to the President but said he had no obligation to obey it.

On July 26, Judge Sirica ordered Nixon to explain by August 7 why he should not be compelled to release the tapes to Cox. In a notable courtroom confrontation between Cox and Wright on August 22, Cox contended that Nixon could not be a "proper judge" of whether the public interest required release of the tapes to the grand jury because, Cox noted, his closest aides were involved and the evidence might be material to accusations against the President himself. Wright emphasized the argument in his letter of July 23 to Cox that "questions of separation-of-powers are in the forefront when the most confidential documents of the Presidency are sought in the Judicial Branch."

Seeking a middle ground, Judge Sirica on August 29 ordered Nixon to submit the tapes to him for his private inspection so that he could decide whether they should be released to the grand jury. He would permit such use, he said, only if the material could be screened to protect national security interests and important presidential conversations unrelated to Watergate. Judge Sirica then stayed his order to permit appeal.

After making an unprecedented effort to effect a compromise, the Court of Appeals for the District of Columbia ruled on October 12, by a vote of 5 to 2, that Nixon must turn the tapes over to Sirica, thus substantially upholding Sirica's own ruling. The President, said the court, "is not above the law's commands," and in this case the court felt that the prosecutor had made a powerful showing that the tapes were directly relevant to the grand jury investigation. The court concluded that the grand jury has a right to every man's evidence, even that of the President, unless protected by constitutional, common law, or statutory privilege and that "the Constitution mentions no executive privilege, much less any absolute executive privilege."

Presidential Responses. The court gave the President five days to appeal the ruling to the Supreme Court, and it was assumed that he would do so, since he had indicated earlier that he "would abide by a definitive decision of the highest court." Instead, on October 19, Nixon announced a compromise whereby he would release to the federal court and to the Senate committee a personally prepared summary of the conversations on the tapes, to be authenticated by Sen. John C. Stennis (D-Miss.). He asserted that this arrangement had been approved by the chairman and vice chairman of the Senate committee. In addition, he directed Cox, "as an employee of the executive branch, to make no further attempts by judicial process to obtain tapes, notes or other memoranda of presidential conversations."

Cox immediately pointed out that this action was not in compliance with the court order and made it clear that he would defy Nixon's instructions to him. Cox was dismissed by a presidential order on October 20, but not before Attorney General Richardson and his deputy, William D. Ruckelshaus, had relinquished their offices rather than carry out orders to dismiss Cox in violation of the agreement with the Senate that Cox would have completely independent investigatory powers. On November 14, Judge Gerhard A. Gesell of the U. S. district court ruled that the firing of Cox had been illegal, since it violated the departmental regulation specifying that he could be removed only

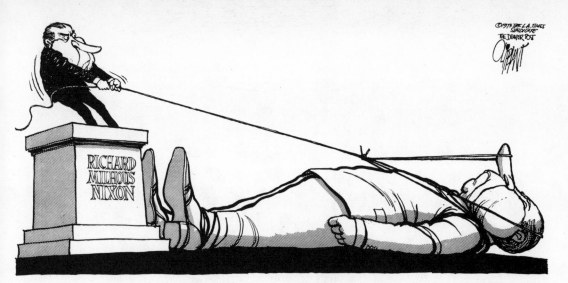

President Nixon And Watergate-- Favorite Target Of Cartoonists

(Right) *"Remember, not a word to him about sordid political activities."*

WASHINGTON'S NEW TOURIST ATTRACTION: Crowds line up outside the Senate Caucus Room for admission to the Watergate hearings.

for "extraordinary improprieties," which had not been alleged. But this was a declaratory judgment, which neither the court nor Cox sought to enforce. Meanwhile, the President had authorized Wright to inform Sirica on October 23 that he would relinquish the subpoenaed tapes to the court. (For the aftermath in regard to missing or defective tapes, see the article beginning on page 14.)

On November 5, Cox was replaced as special prosecutor by Leon Jaworski, who was assured by the White House of complete freedom of action. But because of doubts about the degree of independence that Jaworski could exercise, 55 senators sponsored a bill on November 21 providing for an independent prosecutor to be appointed by a three-judge panel of the U. S. district court. Judges Sirica and Gesell, taking the unusual step of commenting publicly on pending legislation, expressed the view that appointment of a prosecutor by the judicial branch would violate the separation of powers. But several constitutional experts testified before the Senate Judiciary Committee that the Constitution explicitly authorizes Congress to vest appointment of "inferior officers . . . in the courts of law."

Summary. It is now established, by the judicial decisions in the "tapes case," as well as by President Nixon's abandonment of his original extreme claims, that executive privilege does not give the President an absolute right to decide what evidence he will supply to Congress and that a subpoena will lie against the President to compel the production of executive records demonstrably relevant to a criminal investigation or prosecution. Admittedly, there are areas of confidentiality or national security where resistance is justified, but the courts will review any presidential claims of secrecy and will make the final decision.

CRIMINAL LIABILITY AND OTHER ISSUES

Other constitutional aspects of Watergate included questions of the criminal liability of an incumbent President, the ability of other branches to compel a President to appear before them, impeachment, and presidential accountability.

Criminal Liability. The possibility, especially as suggested by John Dean's testimony before the Senate committee, that the President might have engaged in a cover-up of Watergate amounting to criminal conspiracy to obstruct justice stirred speculation about the liability of an incumbent President to criminal prosecution. The brief submitted by Nixon's lawyers to Judge Sirica on August 7 argued for complete presidential immunity. Because of his office the President is "above the process of any court or the jurisdiction of any court to bring him to account as President." Only after the President has been convicted on impeachment and stripped of his office can he be tried, they argued.

As yet there has been no test of this theory. The experience of Vice President Agnew (see the article on Agnew, page 20), as well as of Aaron Burr, who was indicted for treason in 1807, established that the vice president can be indicted without first having been convicted on impeachment.

MAURICE STANS, former secretary of commerce.

Compulsory Appearance. On several occasions the Senate Watergate committee suggested that Nixon meet with the committee, but no effort was made to compel his appearance. The issue of compulsory appearance was raised—although no subpoena was issued for the President—by attorneys for Egil Krogh, Jr., a White House aide indicted in California in connection with the "Pentagon Papers" case.

The principal precedent was the subpoena issued by Chief Justice John Marshall for President Thomas Jefferson to appear as a witness and produce relevant papers at the Burr trial in Alexandria, Va., in 1807. It is generally thought that Jefferson defied the subpoena. Actually, he refused to leave the seat of government to attend the trial because it would "leave the nation without an executive branch," but he expressed willingness to give a deposition under oath in Washington.

Impeachment or Resignation. Although there was some talk of impeachment of President Nixon earlier in the year, it was not until the dismissal of Cox that this step was seriously supported. The House Judiciary Committee began its investigation of the case for impeachment in October. The President has no defenses against an impeachment investigation; he is obliged to supply all information requested. If impeachment (equivalent to indictment) were ultimately voted by a majority of the House, the trial in the Senate would be a long and disruptive experience, during which the ability of the President to govern would be in grave jeopardy. For this reason there was pressure for the President to resign, an action he repeatedly refused to consider.

Presidential Accountability. Finally, the prospect that Nixon—with his credibility destroyed or impaired by Watergate—might nevertheless serve out his term led many to consider the advantages of a parliamentary system, under which an executive whose standing has been impaired can be promptly removed by a legislative vote of no confidence. But this is hardly a feasible alternative. The strong presidency has generally worked well, and a guaranteed four-year term has helped to ensure stability and responsibility in governmental policy and administration.

BRUCE ROBERTS/RAPHO GUILLUMETTE

The Energy Squeeze

Americans Now Face a Future of Power Restrictions As Supplies Fail to Keep Pace with Soaring Demand

By FREDERIC GOLDEN
Science Editor, "Time" Magazine

It was a year when the term "energy crisis" impressed itself dramatically on the national consciousness. Early in 1973, shortages of heating oil in scattered parts of the United States forced the midwinter shutdown of many schools and factories. By the stifling summer months, utilities were again reducing voltages in major urban areas—cutting the efficiency of air conditioners, shrinking the size of pictures on TV screens, and dimming overhead lights. But brownouts were not the only indignity. For the first time since World War II, many service stations shut off their pumps and hung out signs reading "No gas today."

In October, while the administration was still arguing that the energy squeeze was only a "problem," not a "crisis," the situation became critical indeed. War broke out in the Middle East, and several Arab states declared an embargo on sales of crude oil to the United States. Although the embargo on Mideastern crude (about 6% of U. S. consumption) was not very effective, it forced America to recognize that shortages might not be easily overcome through increased imports. The nation could no longer count on limitless supplies of cheap energy.

The Problems. Simple statistics told the story. Although Americans account for only 6% of the world's population, they are consuming a third of the world's energy. Nor is their voracious appetite abating. The demand for electricity alone is doubling every decade. To fill this gap, the United States must depend increasingly on oil, which supplies 46% of U. S. energy needs, and on natural gas, which supplies 32%.

"...the average American will consume as much energy in the next seven days as most other people in the world will consume in an entire year. We have only 6 percent of the world's people in America, but we consume over 30 percent of all the energy in the world."
—President Richard M. Nixon, in a broadcast on the energy crisis, Nov. 7, 1973.

A partial solution to the energy crisis may result if geothermal steam from deep in the earth can be used to produce electricity.

JACK FIELDS/PHOTO RESEARCHERS, INC.

Drilling for offshore oil—a vital energy need but a potential threat to the environment.

Arabs' Embargo Struck Hard at Western Nations

Americans had been listening for some years to the "Jeremiahs" of ecology and had noted their warnings that the undisciplined exploitation of nature's riches today would lead to a debased, impoverished life tomorrow. In late 1973, the United States got its first taste of such a tomorrow.

In 1972, most Americans regarded the energy squeeze as a small cloud on a very distant horizon. But by Dec. 31, 1973, the nation had gone to a fuel allocation program, Sunday closings of filling stations, lowered home thermostats, and reduced commercial air service. It had experienced energy-related industrial layoffs, a browned-out Christmas, and, in some cities, a gasoline-less New Year. In other countries, conditions were much worse.

The event that brought the energy crisis to full international flower was the agreement between 11 Arab states, on Oct. 17, 1973, to reduce their production and export of crude oil and to embargo its sale to some nations deemed friendly to Israel. The Netherlands, one of the countries under embargo, banned Sunday driving in late October. Germany and Japan, foreseeing a drastically reduced flow of the inexpensive oil that had fueled their "economic miracles," imposed strict conservation measures. Britain, already struggling with labor slowdowns in coal mining and transportation,

imposed an especially harsh austerity plan, with a three-day work week (for three days' pay) in most factories, offices, and stores, effective Jan. 2, 1974.

Partial restoration of Arab oil production was announced on Christmas Day, but by this time there were fresh worries. Major petroleum-exporting nations—from Indonesia in the East to Venezuela and Bolivia in the West—had begun to raise prices exponentially. The crude oil that was being sold at between $2 and $3 per barrel (42 gallons) in late 1972 was priced at between $14 and $19 per barrel on Dec. 31, 1973. The economic effects of the anticipated massive flow of capital from consuming to producing states was impossible to calculate. At the very least, industrialized nations which were heavy importers could expect balance-of-payments problems and inflation due to increased manufacturing costs. Third World nations without oil deposits might face the serious threat of setbacks in their fragile programs of development.

In these troubled waters, where nations were using petroleum as an instrument of national policy, the U. S. ship of state seemed to be sailing without a rudder. Though the United States was the largest producer of crude oil (as well as its largest consumer), its government had long operated without a clearly defined energy program or the mechanism to create and enforce one. Incredibly, it had to go to the large private oil companies for information about domestic production and reserves, data that the corporations were often reluctant to disclose.

In the year of Watergate, with its revelations of massive secret contributions by corporate managers to the 1972 Nixon campaign, it was not surprising that many Americans greeted the President's November 7 declaration of a full-fledged energy crisis with skepticism and a suspicion that the shortages were either illusory or artificially induced. For their part, the petroleum executives bemoaned the public's ignorance of basic facts. Were Americans unaware that the costs of exploration and drilling had skyrocketed? How could they be persuaded that all mining involved some environmental risk? Could they be convinced that easily accessible deposits were being exhausted, that deposits 20,000 feet underground were many times more expensive to tap than those only 10,000 feet down, and that prices must reflect such additional costs?

The enlargement of the new Federal Energy Office and the appointment, on Dec. 4, 1973, of William Simon as its director were generally welcomed as evidence of the administration's wish to abandon piecemeal responses to the crisis.

Meanwhile, conservationists could take comfort in the developments of late 1973 in the United States. Some environmental safeguards were weakened in the rush to promote fuel production, but ecological sanity was entering through the back door. It could be detected in the greater funding of research on such nonpolluting energy sources as the geothermal and solar, in the greater attention to mass transit problems and recycling technologies, and in the declining demand for large cars and electric tie racks. It seemed that Americans were beginning to face up to the imminent demise of the "cowboy economy" of unlimited consumption and waste, and were looking for ways to make the best of the bountiful—but finite—system sometimes described as "Spaceship Earth."

WILLIAM CUMMINGS
The Encyclopedia Americana

Yet stores of these vital fuels are fast running short. Even with expanded drilling in the Gulf of Mexico and other offshore areas and the use of Alaska's North Slope fields, experts estimate that U. S. oil reserves could be depleted in another 20 years. The situation in natural gas is even worse; supplies of this exceptional "clean" fuel may well be exhausted by the mid-1980's.

Once self-sufficient in energy, the United States is now supplementing its oil and gas supplies with overseas purchases, mostly from sources in the Western Hemisphere. But in the future, the nation will have to rely more and more on oil from the Middle East—which is thought to be the repository of as much as 75% of the world's reserves—and perhaps on natural gas from the Soviet Union.

The Consequences. Such imports could have important repercussions for Americans. For one thing, the price of fuel is almost certain to go up. As former Secretary of Commerce Peter G. Peterson puts it: "The era of cheap energy is over. Popeye has run out of cheap spinach." The price of Arabian crude oil doubled between the mid-1960's and early 1973. During the last three months of 1973 it quadrupled, with no guarantee that additional price rises would not follow. Other producing countries—including Venezuela, a major supplier of crude for the U. S. market—posted comparable price rises.

But higher prices may not be the only consequence. By 1980, the United States may be paying $30 billion or more per year for imported oil. If that is the case, not only may the U. S. balance of payments be dangerously strained, but the nation may be vulnerable to what some foreign-policy specialists are calling "energy blackmail." A demonstration of Arab pressure on the United States and other nations friendly to Israel came after the outbreak of war in the Middle East in October 1973. Eleven Arab oil-producing nations announced a monthly reduction in exports of oil. The cutback was set at 5% off each previous month's sale, starting at the September level. Soon after, four Persian Gulf States—Kuwait, Qatar, Bahrain, and Dubai—announced a total

"We could offer to rent him a camel."

THE LEADING OIL PRODUCERS

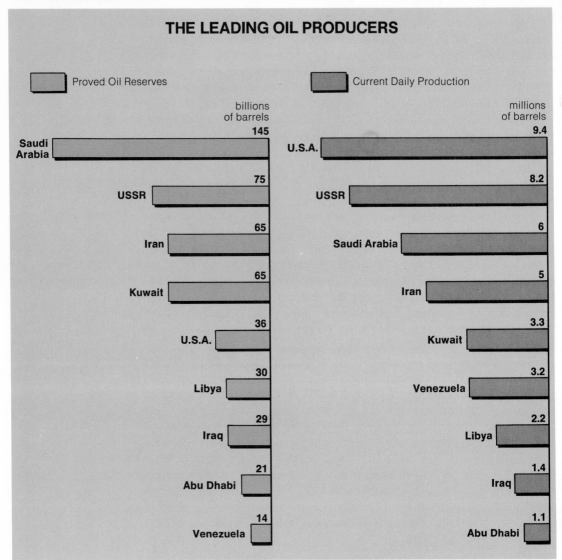

Proved Oil Reserves

Current Daily Production

billions
of barrels

millions
of barrels

	Proved Oil Reserves (billions of barrels)
Saudi Arabia	145
USSR	75
Iran	65
Kuwait	65
U.S.A.	36
Libya	30
Iraq	29
Abu Dhabi	21
Venezuela	14

	Current Daily Production (millions of barrels)
U.S.A.	9.4
USSR	8.2
Saudi Arabia	6
Iran	5
Kuwait	3.3
Venezuela	3.2
Libya	2.2
Iraq	1.4
Abu Dhabi	1.1

EDITOR'S NOTE: CURRENT DAILY PRODUCTION DATA PREDATES THE ARAB CUTBACK OF LATE 1973.

embargo of oil shipments to the United States. Saudia Arabia, Iraq, Libya, and Algeria joined in the boycott, one of whose chief targets was the Netherlands, which ships petroleum products to several other western European nations. (See also MIDDLE EAST.) On December 25, the Arab states eased the production cutback. But to several European nations and Japan, which had long imported most of their petroleum from the Middle East, the effect had already been devastating. Japan had declared a state of emergency on December 21. Britain was forced to extraordinary austerity measures, including a three-day work week.

The total embargo against the United States, the Netherlands, and some other countries remained in force into 1974. Its major effect in the United States might be considered to have been psychological, since more oil was being imported during early December of 1973 than during the comparable period in 1972, due to leaks in the Arab dike and the availability of additional oil elsewhere. Nevertheless, U. S. vulnerability to future energy blackmail was well established, because, in the short run, the gap between domestic demand and domestic supply seemed certain to increase.

Dire predictions of future woes were heard in 1973, some of them consciously exaggerated in order to spur action (see accompanying box). Yet some skeptics in Congress and elsewhere were convinced that the 1973 shortages of fuel were deliberately engineered by major suppliers to force prices up, to reduce import controls, to drive small independent fuel dealers out of business, and to break down the resistance of environmental groups to such controversial activities as the extension of offshore drilling. Yet, even if there was what Sen. Henry Jackson (D-Wash.) called a "premeditated plan" to control supplies in 1973, the threat of a future crunch is quite real. As conservative a journal as William Buckley's *National Review* stated: "We never have had much truck with Rachel Carson and her proliferating descendants. But the energy crisis, we conclude, is no bit of do-it-yourself apocalyptic; and, having looked at the figures, we are hereby worried."

Factors in the Crisis. If the situation is indeed so perilous, how did the world's leading industrial power ever get itself into such a mess? In part, the answer is complacency. With the exception of a few solitary voices, Americans believed that they had access to an inexhaustible well of cheap energy. The fact that, in real terms, the cost of energy did not rise from the late 1940's to the early 1970's, may have had a lulling effect on the public.

A share of responsibility for the crisis also lies with the growing environmental movement. However well-meaning, these interests have succeeded in blocking sorely needed new power plants, especially nuclear reactors—which still produce no more than 5% of America's electrical energy.

Lastly, much of the blame must rest with the government, whose energy policies have been confusing, to say the least. No fewer than 69 government agencies and a dozen congressional committees exercise authority on energy questions. While some have encouraged conserva-

AMERICAN GAS ASSOCIATION

Natural gas in liquid form is transported in "LNG" carriers—among the most expensive afloat because they must keep the "gas" at −260°F (−162°C).

A DIRE PICTURE OF THE FUTURE

A book entitled The Energy Crisis, *by Lawrence Rocks and Richard P. Runyon of Long Island University's C. W. Post College, received much attention in 1973. In what is otherwise a scholarly examination of the energy problem and its ramifications, the authors have included a fable about possible things to come that rivals Orwell's* Nineteen Eighty-Four *in pessimism, showing how higher fuel prices, brownouts, and other inconveniences could conceivably be the first stage of a vast calamity in the United States.*

This horror story begins when worsening fuel shortages compel the government to impose rationing. Subsequently, the number of cars on the highways dwindles and auto manufacturers are forced to lay off many thousands of workers. These shutdowns have a "domino effect," spreading first to such industries as steel and aluminum, which depend heavily on Detroit *for orders, and later hitting many other manufacturers. As the economic paralysis worsens, the stock market sinks to an all-time low. Freight carriers are so severely crippled by lack of fuel that farmers are unable to ship produce to the cities.*

As the country totters on the brink of economic disaster, the President wins authority from Congress to impose controls, not only on the use of energy, but also on prices, wages, profits, and many other aspects of American economic life. To protect this program and ensure universal compliance with its provisions, increasingly harsh laws are passed depriving dissidents of traditional legal safeguards under the Bill of Rights. As one set of controls and restrictions follows another set of controls and restrictions in this scenario, the United States of America falls completely into a dictatorship.

FREDERIC GOLDEN

tion, others—the Tennessee Valley Authority, for example—are still basically committed to promoting energy consumption.

Countermeasures. In response to growing criticism, President Nixon took a number of steps in 1973 to develop a single national energy policy, including a temporary relaxation of quotas on imported oil and the creation of new incentives to encourage exploitation of domestic fuel reserves. In June he announced the formation of a federal Energy Policy Office to be headed by Gov. John A. Love of Colorado. In September the President presented to Congress seven legislative proposals, including authorization for the Alaskan oil pipeline, for deepwater offshore ports for large oil tankers, and for establishing new strip mining standards which would result in additional surface coal production. On November 7, after the Arab states had announced their crude oil embargo, he asked Congress to enact an emergency energy bill giving him broad powers to relax environmental standards and regulate transportation schedules. Admitting that the shortage was now a crisis, he asked the states to reduce highway speed limits to 50 miles an hour, and urged Americans to lower home temperatures by 6 degrees. Later in the month, the legislators passed measures authorizing construction of the Alaska pipeline and requiring the President to establish allocation programs for crude oil and all refinery products.

Early in December, Governor Love resigned and Deputy Treasury Secretary William E. Simon was named director of a reorganized Federal Energy Office. Although Congress adjourned before Christmas without giving final approval to the emergency energy bill, the new energy "czar" was already in full swing. Refineries had been ordered to produce more heating oil and less gasoline from available crude oil. Filling stations had been asked to limit each sale and to close on Sundays. A gasoline rationing system was being readied for introduction at a future date, if necessary, and year-around daylight saving time was to begin on Jan. 6, 1974. As 1973 ended, industry was being given high priority in the allocation of fuel supplies in order to minimize the threat of recession and unemployment. Private car owners, on the other hand, were being warned by Simon to expect substantially diminished supplies of gasoline, and substantially higher prices.

Perhaps most significant in the long run was the President's introduction of the plan he called "Project Independence," designed to make the United States self-sufficient in energy by 1980. Though the target date was widely described as unrealistic, the proposal itself and its support by Congress encouraged everyone. Heavy emphasis was to be placed on development of the fast breeder nuclear reactor—not the favorite device of the environmentalists. But also to be explored were such alternatives as solar energy, geothermal power, harnessing of the winds and tides, magnetohydrodynamics (or MHD), fuel cells, liquefaction of coal, extraction of oil from shale, and the most promising energy source of the distant future—nuclear fusion.

Crash Program Required for Alternative Fuel Sources

But if any or all of these efforts are to be successful, they must be attacked with all the enthusiasm—and funding—that was put into the effort to land men on the moon. Certainly, the payoff from such a crash program could be even more important to America's well-being. For, as the nuclear-submarine pioneer Adm. Hyman G. Rickover has said: "The energy crunch is the most serious problem that has ever faced the United States, including the Civil War."

Nuclear power plant in San Clemente, Calif., with rated capacity of 430 megawatts of electricity.

The Energy Squeeze / NUCLEAR ENERGY

By Robert E. Chrien
Physicist, Brookhaven National Laboratory

The potential of nuclear technology as a supplier of the world's energy needs in the future rests on three power-producing concepts, represented by three reactor types: the U-235-fueled thermal fission reactor, the fast breeder reactor, and the fusion reactor. Of these, only the first has demonstrated both technical and commercial feasibility. The second—the fast breeder—has been technically, but not commercially, demonstrated; while the third—the fusion reactor—has not yet been proved successful in either category. In order to appreciate the utility of these devices, one must consider carefully the time scale in which they can be developed in relation to world supplies of nuclear fuel.

At the present time, fission reactors—principally of the light-water moderated thermal type—are supplying a small but continuously increasing fraction of the electrical power needs of the United States and some other nations. The number of nuclear plants ordered by U. S. utilities increased sharply in the late 1960's and early 1970's, as concern mounted over supplies of available fossil fuels, especially the low-sulfur-content types that have minimal polluting properties. At the beginning of 1973, 27 licensed nuclear plants existed in the United States, accounting for only 5% of U. S. generating capacity. Some 55 plants were under construction, 34 were being reviewed prior to the issuance of construction permits, and an additional 43 had been ordered by utilities but were not yet reviewed by the Atomic Energy Commission (AEC), which has regulatory responsibility.

Based on conservative forecasts of population growth and energy needs, nuclear generation in the United States is expected to reach 132,000 megawatts by 1980 and 1.2 million megawatts by the end of the 20th century. Total U. S. electricity production in 1972 was about 400,000 megawatts. According to these projections, U. S. consumption by the year 2000 would be five times the 1972 amount, with nuclear installations supplying about 60% of the total. Similar trends are expected in Europe. It must be noted, however, that the above projections take for granted the successful introduction of breeder reactors which will effectively use the world's uranium supply.

The Importance of the Breeder. The thermal fission reactors now in operation use the relatively rare uranium isotope U-235, which makes up 0.7% of the content of natural uranium and which fissions under bombardment by slow neutrons. At projected rates of consumption, presently known uranium ore reserves, if used only in this type of reactor, would not last beyond the end of this century, since over 99% of the content of the ore would be wasted.

On the other hand, virtually all of the ore that is mined would be utilized for energy production by breeder reactors, should they be successfully introduced. In the breeder, the nonthermally fissile U-238 isotope—99.3% of natural uranium—is converted, by a series of nuclear reactions, into the nuclide Pu-239, which, like U-235, fissions under thermal neutron bombardments. In a properly designed reactor, the amount of Pu-239 produced can exceed the amount of nuclear fuel consumed. Hence the name "breeder reactor"—a device which converts the nonproductive U-238 to useful fuel.

41

The breeder reactor cycle is thus the only way to unlock the very large energy content in the earth's available uranium ores. This energy supply is much larger than is available from the fossil fuels —oil, gas, and coal. If we represent the energy content of fuel by the symbol Q, which stands for one billion billion (10^{18}) thermal units, then the fuel resources available in the United States can be represented as follows: gas, 0.7Q; oil, 1.5Q; coal, 30Q; and uranium, 619Q, of which only 4.3Q is available as U-235 and the rest as U-238. Present U. S. consumption of total energy is between 0.1 and 0.2Q per year. The attractiveness of the breeder concept is evident from these figures.

The importance of the time scale in breeder development lies simply in the fact that if present use of uranium in thermal non-breeder reactors continues, the available uranium reserves will be sufficient, at best, for short-term relief of the energy crisis. Economic use of these reserves depends on the introduction of breeders before the end of this century or before uranium resources are virtually used up. An alternate breeder concept utilizes thorium to produce the fissile nuclide U-233. Such a thorium–U-233 cycle would permit use of the world's large thorium reserves.

The Promise and Problems of Fusion. A quite different approach to energy production is presented by the process of nuclear fusion. In this process, nuclei of deuterium and tritium contained in a hot plasma (a gas of electrically charged atoms) combine to produce helium in a thermonuclear reaction that generates an enormous amount of energy.

At present the AEC fusion program is investigating four parallel technical approaches to fusion power; (1) the steady-state toroidal systems, the best example of which is the tokamak, invented in the USSR; (2) the steady-state open systems, or magnetic mirrors; (3) the pulsed high density, "theta pinch" device; and (4) pulsed laser fusion, the newest and perhaps the most promising approach. In all of these techniques, the primary fuels are deuterium and tritium. The so-called DT cycle requires the presence of a lithium blanket to breed tritium to fuel the reaction. Since tritium is bred during the process, the principal fueling materials that must be provided are deuterium and lithium.

The critical problem in controlling fusion has been that of confining a superhot plasma in a small volume for a time long enough to produce sustained thermonuclear reactions. Scientists feel that they are close to a solution. However, between the elimination of this obstacle in the laboratory and the development of a true fusion reactor capable of power production, several awesome engineering problems must be overcome. Among these are the following: (1) the development of radiation resistant materials to enclose the reactor; (2) the problem of extracting heat energy from the reactor; (3) the assurance of safety in reactor design, including the handling of tritium; and (4) the challenge of producing power at competitive cost.

Fusion power plant capacities of 5,000 megawatts are envisioned, the inner structures of which will become highly radioactive. The replacement of components which will undergo the severe radiation damage caused by neutrons from the reactor core will necessitate designing equipment capable of handling tons of materials having exceedingly high radioactivity levels.

Finally, the fusion problem involves formidable costs in money and time. It is estimated, for example, that the development of a test plant that produces only a few megawatts of power will require several hundreds of millions of dollars and that even this small-scale test may not be feasible before the year 2000.

Clearly, fusion power is not the answer to our short-term energy needs. If successful, however, it could solve the energy question for mankind for a virtually unlimited span of time.

The greatest attraction of the fusion approach to power generation lies in the vast store of energy that is available in the cheap fuels deuterium and lithium. There is sufficient deuterium in the world's oceans to supply world energy needs—at 15 times the projected rate of consumption in the year 2000 —over the expected lifetime of the sun! Lithium is present on earth in large enough quantities to produce energy, at the same projected level, for several million years. A single hot spring in Nevada is now yielding dissolved lithium at a rate sufficient to supply all present U. S. energy needs, if it could be used in fusion reactors.

Fusion has other advantages as well. The high temperatures in a fusion reactor result in high thermal efficiency (55%), reducing the effect of thermal pollution. Waste heat could, in fact, be directed to seawater desalting or other uses. Furthermore, the only radioactive fuel by-product, tritium, has a relatively short half-life of 12.3 years, constituting much less of an environmental hazard than the long-lived decay products from fission reactors and posing less of a problem in disposal. In the long run, the hardest problems to be overcome by fusion developments may well be the engineering difficulties associated with moving fusion out of the laboratory and into a practical power plant.

In May 1973, nuclear explosives were detonated underground in Rio Blanco county, Colo., to release natural gas.

USAEC PHOTO

Solar furnace at Odeillo in the French Pyrenees Mountains has 63 movable flat mirrors that reflect the sun's rays. It can deliver 1,000 kilowatts to the material it heats.

The Energy Squeeze / SOLAR ENERGY

Scientists Seek to Tap Limitless Power of Sun

BY PETER E. GLASER
Vice President, Arthur D. Little, Inc.

The adequacy of our energy sources and the plans to meet our increasing demands have become a priority item on the U. S. agenda. This "energy crisis," as it has come to be called, is complicated by the fact that it is accompanied by a loss of faith in technology. We are nowhere near as eager today to adopt new technology—nuclear fission, for example—as we were even 10 years ago. In light of our chronic inability to foresee the consequences of energy consumption, this prudence is justified. Up to the present, however, generation of energy has always involved the transformation of some earthly material (the fuel) into another material (the waste). We are now rediscovering an energy source that does not require an earthly fuel and does not generate wastes: the sun.

The energy supplied by the sun to the earth is the equivalent of about 232 trillion horsepower per minute. By way of comparison, U. S. energy consumption during all of 1973 was some 30 trillion horsepower.

In his energy message of April 1973, President Nixon stated: "My new budget triples our solar energy research and development efforts to a level of $12 million. A major portion of these funds would be devoted to accelerating the development of commercial systems for heating and cooling buildings."

Solar Heating and Cooling. By 1985, energy consumed in heating and cooling buildings will amount to 21% of the total energy used in the United States. The amount of solar energy received by an average building is 6 to 10 times the amount required to heat the building. Experts report that by 1985, 10% of all buildings could use solar energy for heating and cooling.

There is already a substantial technical base for the development of solar energy heating and cooling. For example, solar hot-water heaters are used in Japan, Australia, Israel, and the Soviet Union. These heaters can be equipped with auxiliary electric heaters to provide hot water on cloudy days. In the last 25 years, about 20 houses and laboratory installations in the United States have been at least partially heated with solar energy on an experimental basis. Economic studies have shown that solar heating when used in combination with an auxiliary heat source fueled by oil, gas, or electricity, can approach and, in some cases, surpass in economy the performance of conventional fuel heating systems. In almost all cases the cost of solar heating is less than that of electric heating. More recently, solar air conditioning has been shown to be technically feasible.

A typical solar heating and cooling system is shown in the diagram. Its three basic components —the solar collector, the circulating fluid, and the heat storage medium—can be combined with temperature and humidity controls, pumps, fans and motors, and a heat-activated refrigeration unit to make a system which will provide either heating or cooling with negligible operating and maintenance costs. The combination of solar heating and cooling is attractive because solar collectors can be utilized both in winter and summer. Cooling with solar energy has an added advantage in that it is generally most effective in the warmest climates, since the hotter the sunshine, the more efficient the cooling system.

In the not-so-distant future, solar heating and cooling systems can also include solar cells for producing electricity. The electricity can be stored in batteries and used to supplement power from utility companies. A house incorporating such solar cells in the solar collector has already been constructed at the University of Delaware, but the widespread application of this technique will have to await the cost reduction expected to result from the mass production of solar cells.

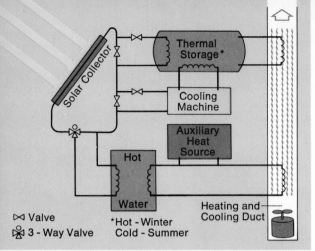

⋈ Valve
⋈ 3 - Way Valve
Hot - Winter
Cold - Summer

Heating and Cooling Duct

ARTHUR D. LITTLE, INC.

A typical solar heating and cooling system. A solar collector mounted on the roof absorbs solar energy and transfers the heat to a circulating fluid, which carries the heat to storage. Heat may cool the building.

A number of buildings now being planned will include solar heating and cooling. Recently, the Massachusetts Audubon Society in Lincoln, Mass., announced that it plans to build the world's first office building designed to rely on solar energy to provide 60% of its heating and cooling needs.

Solar energy cannot be used for heating and cooling of buildings without the cooperative efforts of the architect, the builder, the developer, and the equipment supplier. The design of buildings which will incorporate solar heating and cooling systems should take into account all of the building components which can play a role in the conversion and conservation of energy. These include windows, roof shape and material, floors, exterior color, and building orientation.

Conversion of Solar Energy into Electricity. A number of techniques for converting solar energy into electricity are being investigated for implementation over the next few decades, and if they are successful they will offer important alternatives for meeting energy demands in the 21st century.

The oldest idea is that of a power plant based on the use of solar energy to generate steam. A solar-powered steam engine was a central attraction at the 1878 Paris World Exposition. Recently, large-scale terrestrial solar power plants have been proposed for construction in the Arizona

desert. Arrays of reflecting mirrors would focus the sun's rays on collectors to produce steam to drive a turbine generator set.

Solar cells have been used successfully in spacecraft (most recently Skylab) to convert solar energy directly into electricity. On the ground, one square mile of solar cells, even with an efficiency as low as 10%, could generate 180,000 kilowatts when the sun shines. Solar cells could be mounted on the rooftops of buildings to produce electricity for household, office, or small industrial applications. Here, too, the obstacle to development is the high cost of these cells pending the introduction of mass production techniques.

There are two drawbacks common to all forms of terrestrial solar energy conversion. First, the amount of solar energy available is not constant. Second, a good deal of solar energy is absorbed in the atmosphere and thus never reaches the solar collector.

These drawbacks can be eliminated if the solar energy collection occurs in a satellite placed in an orbit around the earth, 22,300 miles (35,900 km) away, where the sun shines nearly 24 hours a day. This concept has recently been shown to be technically feasible and to have a potentially attractive economic cost competitive with those of other advanced energy production methods.

The orbiting solar cells would be arranged in large solar collectors to produce electricity, which would then be converted to microwave energy and transmitted to a receiving antenna on earth, where it would be converted back into electricity. The satellite could transmit to earth power equivalent to as many as 20 nuclear power plants.

Another possibility for generating electricity with solar energy is the concept of a heat engine based on the difference in temperatures of sea water at the surface and at great depths. Such ocean thermal power plants, which could be located in the Gulf Stream, for example, could provide a very large amount of power.

Conclusions. The above are examples of some of the long-range solar energy applications under consideration. Many are still in an early stage of development, and it is too soon to tell which would be the most useful over the long term. Solar heating and cooling of buildings represent a promising near-term potential which industry appears willing to explore. With active government support, solar energy has the potential to meet many of the anticipated energy needs of the 21st century.

The Energy Squeeze / # ENERGY AND THE ENVIRONMENT

BY THOMAS L. KIMBALL
Executive Vice-President,
National Wildlife Federation

As the most affluent nation in the world, the United States has developed an appetite for energy which threatens to exhaust domestic oil and natural gas reserves by 1990. But that isn't all. If Americans continue to consume energy at the present annual growth rate of more than 4%, it is unlikely that the country will achieve a high-quality natural environment. Despite new federal antipollution laws, the nation is on a treadmill where every move to improve air and water quality is offset by the

hunger for more of everything—from larger automobiles to electric combs.

We desecrate our land by stripping it of minerals, making scant provisions for reclamation. Coal mining is now shifting from scarred, eroded Appalachia to the Northern Great Plains, an area rich in mineral deposits. Thus, unbelievably, the majestic West—with its invigorating air and sparkling streams—has become the next intended victim of national energy demands.

In short, unless we can diminish the national exponential energy growth and improve pollution abatement technology, the United States is well along a course leading to environmental disaster. Have we reached the "point of no return"? Not yet—but we will soon, unless we modify some national practices and revamp life styles.

The answer? Conserve energy—make better use of what we have. This will alleviate the growing shortage of fossil fuels *and* help reduce environmental pollution.

We must focus not on how much energy we *can* supply in the next 15 years, but how much we *must* supply if we reduce waste and adopt sound conservation practices designed to give consideration to the aesthetic and natural values that contribute so much to the quality of life.

Conservation by Sectors. Reliable studies indicate that through reasonable conservation measures we can continue to provide 1973 levels of consumer service while we also decrease total projected energy consumption in 1990 by one fourth. We can slash predicted fossil fuel usage in half. How? Consider energy use in the following sectors:

Transportation. About 25% of all U. S. energy is used for transportation. Currently we rely on low-efficiency methods. Automobiles account for 55.3% of this energy consumption, trucks for 21.1%, and aircraft for 7.5%. The most efficient systems—bus, railway, waterway—account for only 16.1%. *Conservation potential:* If one half of the freight traffic and one third of the passenger traffic are shifted to the more efficient carrier systems, the change would save 20% in transportation energy, or 5% of total energy consumption in the United States.

Residential and Commercial. The residential and commercial sectors account for slightly more than one fifth of total energy consumed. Space heating alone requires 18% of the total energy. Potential savings are truly significant. It has been estimated that if FHA minimum insulation standards were met, energy required for heating could be reduced by 42% and energy for cooling by 25%. Requirements for interior lighting energy can be reduced 25% by lowering lighting levels and using fluorescent lamps, according to a 1972 report of the White House Office of Emergency Preparedness (OEP). Another 10% to 30% energy saving can be realized in water heating, refrigeration, and appliances. *Conservation potential:* About a 35% saving, or 7.5% of total national energy consumption.

Industry. About 25% of all energy produced is put to use in the industrial sector. Major industrial users—primary metals, chemicals, petroleum—account for more than one half. The steel industry, which by itself uses 6% of all U. S. energy, can reduce its energy consumption by one half, according to the OEP report, by converting to basic oxygen burners. (This conversion was about half complete in 1973.)

Production of new aluminum consumes almost 3% of the total electric energy supply. Although aluminum recycling requires only one fifth as much energy as does refining, less than 5% of the nation's aluminum was being produced by the recycling method in 1972.

"With the possible exception of the primary metals sector," stated the OEP report, "all ... (industries) could easily cut energy demand by 10–15% over a period of time by accelerated retirement of old equipment, more energy-conscious process design, and upgrading and increased maintenance of existing equipment." *Conservation potential* (without recycling): 6–10% of national energy consumption.

Utilities. The utilities use almost one third of all energy. *Conservation potential:* Considerable— through more efficient heat use and by smoothing out power peaking cycles.

Overall Savings by 1990. Energy consumption could be reduced by as much as 34 million billion BTU per year, or about one fourth of predicted total need.

Steps to Eliminate Energy Waste. Immediate action should be taken along the following lines:

• *Institute a "truth in energy" program.* It should be made mandatory that manufacturers indicate, by label, the energy required to produce a finished product. As an extension of this principle, full public exposure of all facts relating to issues of controversy in the energy field should be required, and full legislative and administrative access to such facts should be guaranteed.

• *Require full and early public disclosure of all energy plans and assure public participation in decision-making.*

• *Revise price structures.* Rates should increase as the volume of consumption increases. Also, pricing should include full costs of restoring land damaged by minerals extraction.

• *Revise tax structures.* Recycling should be promoted by altering tax schedules to reduce freight rates for transportation of scrap iron and to increase the use of re-refined oil. The highest degree of use of all manufactured products must be encouraged. (Do we really need to throw away containers and aluminum beer cans?) Tax incentives might also be used to encourage private research and development on improved energy technology, improved transmission, more efficient heat transfer, emission controls, and the production of energy as a by-product of solid waste disposal.

• *Revise administrative structures.* Government research and development activities should be consolidated. Regulation should be separated from promotion and development functions in government agencies.

• *Prevent monopoly over energy sources.* Oil companies own approximately 45% of known U. S. uranium reserves and 30% of coal reserves.

• *Revise building codes* to require greater insulation, improved space heating, reduced water use.

• *Increase government and industry research on cleaner and more efficient energy technologies.* Solar, geothermal, and magnetohydrodynamics research received federal funding of $3 million annually before 1973. Nuclear fusion, the ultimate energy source, should get top-priority attention.

• *Require government agencies to set the example* in establishing high-quality energy conservation and pollution abatement practices.

• *Require that highway trust funds be made available to meet urban mass transit objectives.*

• *Strive for simpler life styles.* The private citizen should rediscover the healthy pleasures of walking and bicycling. He should conserve gasoline by car-pooling, driving slower, and consolidating errands. Mass transit and recycling centers must be supported, and returnable bottles used. Less energy should be expended to heat and cool homes.

The time for further debate is past. *We must act now!*

BOOMING
BRAZIL

By Robert M. Levine
Associate Professor of History
State University of New York at Stony Brook

Brazil's economic upsurge in the last 10 years has been hailed as an "economic miracle." Under the military regime that took office in 1964, Brazil has moved from the status of a semideveloped country—with a stagnant industrial output, rampant inflation, and recurrent balance-of-payments crises—to a position of rapid industrialization and decreasing dependency on international economic conditions.

Through an imaginative exchange rate system adopted in 1968, under which the value of its currency is changed as often as necessary to keep its products competitive in the international market, Brazil attained a strong balance of payments position. Inflation, which stood at about 90% in 1964, had been reduced to 15.7% in 1972. Its gross national product (GNP), estimated variously at between $35.5 billion and $53 billion in 1972, placed Brazil among the world's 12 leading nations. This figure represented an extraordinary growth rate of 10.4%, compared with a GNP growth rate of 9% for Japan, 6.4% for the United States, and 3% for West Germany.

Although called a "miracle," Brazil's economic growth has resulted from skillful management within an authoritarian framework. Without this framework—in which the military regime and its civilian administrators have had complete freedom to manipulate a massive array of incentives, constraints, and national controls—it is unlikely that the "miracle" would have occurred, at least in the form that it has taken since 1964.

The results of the government's economic planning are clearly impressive. Yet some Brazilians, noting that the military government has consciously selected economic goals over social priorities, have criticized the regime's indifference to the problem of income distribution. They point also to regional inequities within Brazil's vast territory. The boom has centered in the Rio de Janeiro–Minas Gerais–São Paulo triangle in the southeast, while the impoverished northern and northeastern regions have fallen further behind. Some observers express concern over Brazil's growing military power, noting that billions of dollars are spent on ultramodern weapons systems and that Brazil, which may become a nuclear power by 1980 or 1985, has refused to sign the Nuclear Limitations Treaty. Some of Brazil's Spanish-speaking neighbors, including Paraguay and Bolivia, have fallen into Brazil's politico-economic orbit, and others actively fear Brazilian encroachment.

São Paulo, with some 6,000,000 people, is South America's largest and fastest-growing city.

MANCHETE/PICTORIAL PARADE

ECONOMIC PLANNING AND GROWTH

In September 1971, Brazil's president, Gen. Emilio Garrastazú Médici, revealed the First National Plan of Economic and Social Development, projecting economic goals for 1974 and beyond. Designed to build on the dynamic momentum achieved since the military government's departure in 1967 from traditional methods of economic planning, the new program outlined a list of far-flung objectives calculated to remove Brazil from the constraints of past dependence. Among the goals were (1) to vault from the status of semidevelopment to full development within a generation, (2) to double per capita income by 1980, and (3) to sustain indefinitely the annual 8–10% growth rate of the GNP, first achieved in 1968 under Finance Minister Antônio Delfim Netto.

Background. At the time of the military coup of March 31–April 1, 1964, Brazil was in a state of near economic chaos. In the first three months of 1964, prices rose by 25%. Overvalued exchange rates discouraged exports, leading to systematic deficits in the balance of payments. Rigid rate ceilings on public utilities prevented the purchase of new equipment despite growing needs. As a result, such public services as railroad transportation, telephones, and coastal shipping neared paralysis. Affluent Brazilians invested in real estate or converted their cash into foreign currencies on the black market and sent their savings abroad.

Between 1964 and 1967, economic improvement came slowly, stimulated by massive foreign aid proffered by the United States, which looked favorably on the military regime and its anti-Communist posture. Brazilian officials, led by Finance Minister Roberto Campos, attempted to neutralize inflation, restore foreign confidence, and use the tax structure as an "instrument of orientation" in the allocation of resources and investments. The annual inflation rate of 90% in 1964 had been cut in half by 1966. But it was apparent that only bold and imaginative planning would enable Brazil to achieve its economic objectives. That kind of planning came under the regime's second finance minister, Antônio Delfim Netto, who took office in 1967.

Industrial Upsurge. Led by Delfim Netto, Brazil's economic planners have spurred growth in a variety of new areas. Electric energy production will be increased by 30 million kilowatts by 1988 through the construction of some 75 new hydroelectric stations. The largest, at Sete Quedas Falls, will alone produce 10 million kilowatts, equal to the entire Brazilian demand in 1970. By absorbing idle industrial capacity, steel and cement production has been boosted to the point where steel output is expected to double by 1976 to 12 million tons. Under government impetus, new shipbuilding will triple Brazil's domestic fleet in that year. Automobile production has soared. From virtually nothing 15 years ago, Brazil now manufactures 600,000 cars annually and will produce a million by 1980.

The automotive industry's growth typifies the unique and rather bold approach to economic development under Delfim Netto. All automobile manufacturing firms in Brazil are foreign, including Volkswagen, Ford, General Motors, Chrysler, Toyota, and Fiat. To Brazilians, the existence of complete foreign control of their most dynamic industry has been rationalized by the fact that the vast capitalization required to establish the industry came entirely from abroad, thereby costing the country nothing. By 1973, automobile, bus, and truck manufacturers

Oil refinery at Duque de Caxias. Brazil's oil production is only about a third of its consumption.

Industry and Agriculture

Brazil leads the world in coffee production and exporting. New trees, like these growing in a nursery, replace older ones.

Brazil manufactures 600,000 automobiles annually. This is the assembly line of the Volkswagen plant in São Paulo.

employed 64,000 workers—lowly paid by foreign standards (a major factor in the foreign companies' decision to invest heavily in Brazil) but among the best paid of the domestic work force.

Delfim Netto's unique step combining savings and consumption as a formula for development, initiated in 1967, set the stage for the automobile boom and the general economic surge between 1968 and 1973. Basically, he chose the affluent sector of the urban population to be the catalyst of his consumer development program. Marshaling private investment through generous tax incentives, he created a bloc of nearly a million shareholders in a carefully controlled investment scheme designed to increase savings and stimulate industrial output. Allowing Brazilians to divert up to 25% from their income taxes into special investment funds, Delfim not only increased the number of individual taxpayers but accumulated substantial investment capital through the new accounts.

In turn, the funds—a form of forced savings—directly stimulated the automobile and other consumer industries. An astounding percentage—77%—of all redeemed tax accounts were used to finance new cars. Once a luxury for the very rich, automobiles—particularly the ubiquitous Volkswagen Beetle—flooded the highways and streets of the country, instantly becoming the most obvious sign of prosperity for the middle-upper bracket of the taxpaying population.

Effects on International Relations. The euphoria of economic success has led Brazil's leaders to take surprisingly independent stances on economic issues affecting its international relations. The cruzeiro was revalued by 3% in relation to the newly devalued U. S. dollar in February 1973, thus making Brazilian exports less costly to European and Japanese buyers. Brazil has extended friendly overtures to new trading partners, notably West Germany and Japan. And, wholly uncharacteristically in view of its strident domestic anti-Communism, it has negotiated agricultural sales to the Soviet Union and China.

ECONOMIC VERSUS SOCIAL PRIORITIES

Since the mid-1960's the population of Brazil—the largest nation of Latin America—has reached 100 million, and the country has become predominantly urban (58% in September 1972). Although industry has led the way in the economic upsurge—increasing its output by 14% in 1972—agriculture, the mainstay of nearly half the population, expanded by only 4%, barely keeping pace with the population growth. While coffee prices rose significantly toward the end of 1972, overall coffee production fell by 5%. Black beans, which with manioc flour comprise the principal staple of the Brazilian diet, doubled in price in early 1973 and disappeared from some markets. Despite the success of new initiatives in bringing domestic economic stability, the fact remains that nearly half the population continues to subsist outside the market economy.

Problems of Income Distribution. In consciously selecting economic over social goals, the government allowed prices to rise as rents, utility rates, and other formerly controlled items were freed from constraints. While the government kept wage increases low, profits were left largely unrestricted. Tax exemptions up to 50% were granted for investment in priority industries, mostly located in the northern part of the country. As a result, exports increased, manufactures boomed, and profits rose—and the gap between the rich and the poor widened. The

This hydroelectric plant on São Francisco River at Paulo Afonso Falls supplies power to the entire northeastern area of Brazil.

cost of living outstripped real wages, rendering the economically active work force—estimated at 31.2 million in September 1972—the victim of the very miracle heralded by Brazilian officials.

Brazilians have rarely offered public criticism of the regime's indifference to the problem of income distribution. But in May 1973, Agriculture Minister Cirne Lima, a spokesman for ranching interests in the state of Rio Grande do Sul, resigned over uncontrolled increases in food prices. Writing in *Ceres,* the magazine of the United Nation's Food and Agriculture Organization, he suggested that Brazil's growth rate be slowed to 7–8% a year to allow for more equitable distribution of income. In his letter of resignation, published in one Brazilian newspaper but censored from others, he questioned the philosophical basis of the regime's development formula, stating that in his view "the quest for efficiency and productivity [had] crushed the interests of Brazilian producers . . . to the benefit of multinational corporations."

Regional Inequities. The decline in real wages—by as much as 69% between 1960 and 1970—was accompanied by an increase in regional inequities, especially in the north and northeast. New jobs in Recife, the major city of the northeast, have grown at an annual rate since 1964 of 3.2%. But its labor force, swelled by interregional migrations and the highest regional birthrate in Brazil, has increased by the alarming rate of 3.7% a year over the same period. Many workers in the northeast earn less than $20 monthly, while unemployment exceeds 17%, according to official figures, and is probably much higher. Seasonal unemployment and chronic underemployment add to the suffering of the region's poor. In this context the government's model industrial projects are dwarfed by economic reality. Outmigration from northern Brazil crowds southern cities, principally São Paulo, and exacerbates social tensions.

THE "MIRACLE" AND THE FUTURE

The debate over the impact and meaning of the Brazilian "miracle" can be summarized, in part, under the following points:

(1) The per capita yearly income—only $430 in 1972 and projected at $520 for 1975—still lags behind many Latin American nations, including Argentina ($880) and Venezuela ($950). Confronted with similar statistics, Delfim Netto, speaking for the government, blandly remarks that "distribution of income is a problem that affects the whole world."

(2) It is possible that the domestic market, restricted essentially to only half the population, is already on the way to saturation. Nearly 600,000 television sets and one million refrigerators are produced annually, but most Brazilians who can afford them already have them. Although it is hoped that exports will take up most of the slack, 40% of manufactured exports are from foreign-owned firms, and luxury consumer goods, in any case, do not contribute significantly to the overall standard of living.

(3) To maintain its current growth rate, Brazil must take serious economic risks. Planning Minister João Paulo Reis Velloso has stated that foreign investment must grow at a level of 6% annually merely to sustain present conditions. Any change in the international marketplace threatens to upset the status quo, as does the possibility of a

BRAZIL · Information Highlights

Official Name: Federative Republic of Brazil.
Area: 3,286,478 square miles (8,511,965 sq km).
Population (1972 est. census): 98,850,000. Density, 28 per square mile (11 per sq km).
Chief Cities (1970 census): Brasília, the capital, 272,002; São Paulo, 5,921,796; Rio de Janeiro, 4,252,009; Belo Horizonte, 1,235,001.
Government: *Head of state,* Emilio Garrastazú Médici, president (took office Oct. 1969). *Head of government,* Emilio Garrastazú Médici. *Legislature*—National Congress: Federal Senate and Chamber of Deputies. *Major political parties*—Aliança Renovadoro Nacional (ARENA); Movimento Democratico Brasileiro (MDB).
Major Religious Group—Roman Catholics.
Language: Portuguese (official).
Education: *Expenditure* (1969), 17.5% of total public expenditure. *School enrollment* (1969)—primary, 12,294,343; secondary, 3,629,375; technical/vocational, 602,016; university/higher, 346,824.

Monetary Unit: Cruzeiro (6.13 cruzeiros equal U. S.$1, July 1973).
Gross National Product (1972 est.): $45,500,-000,000.
Economic Indexes: *Industrial production* (1970), 167 (1963 = 100); *agricultural production* (1971), 136 (1963 = 100); *consumer price index* (1972), 110 (1971 = 100).
Manufacturing (major products): Processed foods, chemicals, textiles, metals, machinery, motor vehicles, transportation equipment, petroleum products, paper, fertilizers.
Major Agricultural Products: Coffee (ranks 1st among world producers, 1971), corn (world rank 3d, 1972), cassava (world rank 1st, 1971), soybeans, rice, sugarcane, beans, bananas, oranges, cacao, tobacco, livestock, forest products.
Major Minerals: Manganese (ranks 3d among world producers, 1971), iron ore, bauxite, gold, petroleum, natural gas.
Foreign Trade (1972): *Exports,* $3,990,000,000; *Imports,* $4,723,000,000. *Chief trading partners* (1970)—United States (took 25% of exports, supplied 32% of imports); West Germany (9%—13%); Argentina (7%—6%); Japan; Netherlands.
Tourism: Receipts (1971), $36,000,000.
Transportation: *Motor Vehicles* (1970), 3,020,-500 (automobiles, 2,324,300); *railroads* (1971), 19,894 miles (32,015 km); *merchant fleet* (1972), 1,185,000 gross registered tons; *major national airlines,* VARIG, VASP.
Communications: *Telephones* (1972), 2,064,950; *newspapers* (1969), 257 (daily circulation, 3,393,000).

recession abroad or the election of a less favorable administration in the United States in 1976 or later. Brazil's debt service comprises nearly 10% of its currency holdings. Simply to maintain its present rate of growth, it must achieve the highest rate of savings (around 25%) in its history. The very elements that constitute the strengths of the economic upsurge may become potential liabilities overnight.

(4) The regime's much publicized programs for social development to date have not produced significant results. The attempt to industrialize the northeast represents, for the most part, restatements of earlier plans by previous governments to resolve socioeconomic problems without altering the social structure. The figures of economic inequity remain unchallenged. The richest 5% of the population received 28% of the nation's income in 1960 and 34% in 1970. The share of the poorest 40% shrank from 10% in 1960 to a pitiful 8% ten years later.

Brazil's extraordinary growth has taken place under tightly controlled conditions impossible in democratic nations and at the expense of the lower classes. Its economic progress in coming years must be measured not only in terms of its aggregate economic indicators but with respect to the quality of life yielded by that progress.

BOOMING BRAZIL / The Hinterland

By NEILL MACAULAY, *Associate Professor of History, University of Florida*

Brazil's great underpopulated and underdeveloped hinterland contains about two thirds of the nation's land area and 8% of its people. This region lies north of the 15th parallel (15° south latitude)—which passes just north of the new capital of Brasília—and inland from the states occupying the northeastern "bulge." It includes the state of Bahia west of the São Francisco River, the southern halves of Piaui and Maranhão, most of the state of Goiás, half of Mato Grosso, all of the states of Pará, Amazonas, and Acre, and the territories of Rondônia, Roraima, and Amapá. All of the region is tropical, where freezes are unknown, but little of it is torrid. Temperatures are moderated by elevation in the plateau areas and by the large volume of flowing water in the Amazon lowlands.

Former Boom-and-Bust Cycles. The Portuguese who colonized Brazil in the 16th century settled along the coast and for nearly 100 years had little interest in the vast interior of the South American continent. Later, as sugar plantations flourished on Brazil's northeastern coast, cattlemen in search of new pastures pushed inland along the São Francisco River. The economic decline of the sugar plantations in the late 17th century dealt the complementary cattle industry a severe blow, leaving the São Francisco Valley in the underpopulated and depressed state in which it remains today.

North and west of the São Francisco Valley lies the much larger basin of the Amazon River. The discovery of gold and diamonds near the headwaters of the São Francisco and upriver along a number of the Amazon's southern tributaries resulted in the great rush of the early 18th century and the scattering of a few permanent settlements

The Trans-Amazon Highway is being cut through the Amazon forest from near Belém to the Peruvian border.
MANCHETE/PICTORIAL PARADE

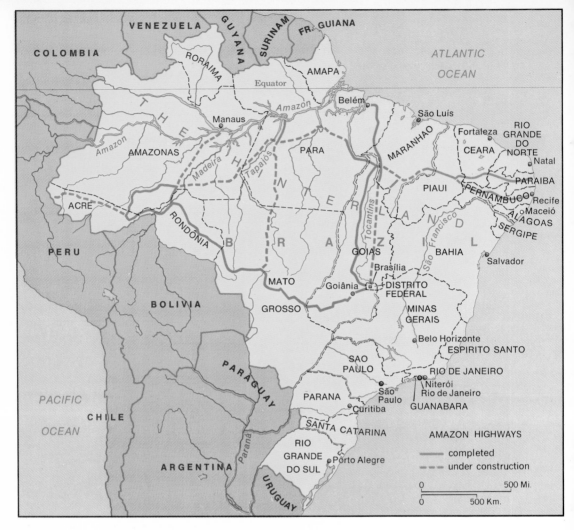

The map shows Brazil with states labeled, including AMAZONAS, PARÁ, MARANHÃO, CEARÁ, PIAUÍ, BAHIA, GOIÁS, MATO GROSSO, MINAS GERAIS, SÃO PAULO, PARANÁ, SANTA CATARINA, RIO GRANDE DO SUL, and neighboring countries. Cities include Manaus, Belém, São Luís, Fortaleza, Natal, Recife, Maceió, Salvador, Brasília, Goiânia, Belo Horizonte, Rio de Janeiro, Niterói, São Paulo, Curitiba, Pôrto Alegre. Rivers include the Amazon, Madeira, Tapajós, Tocantins, São Francisco, Paraná. "THE HINTERLAND" and "BRAZIL" are spread across the map.

AMAZON HIGHWAYS
— completed
--- under construction

0 ———— 500 Mi.
0 ———— 500 Km.

through the hinterland, from what is now the state of Minas Gerais through the states of Goiás and Mato Grosso to the Bolivian border. When most of the mines were depleted late in the 18th century, Goiás and Mato Grosso were plunged into a depression from which they are just now emerging.

The Amazon heartland also has had its cycle of boom-and-bust. Little attention was paid to the great river until the middle of the 19th century, when a large world demand arose for rubber, the principal source of which was the *Hevea brasiliensis,* a tree that grew only in the lowland Amazon forest. Migrants poured into the rubber country from impoverished northeastern Brazil, forest Indians were killed or enslaved by rubber hunters, and Manaus was transformed from jungle outpost to pretentious metropolis. The Amazon rubber boom collapsed in the second decade of the 20th century as plantation rubber from Southeast Asia, produced from Brazilian seeds, flooded the market and drove prices down to levels that made the gathering of forest rubber uneconomical. Thereafter, exploitation of this vast region was left largely to hunters, fishermen, lumbermen, and Brazil nut gatherers.

The São Francisco Valley Today. The São Francisco River, navigable for more than 1,000 miles (1,600 km), has long served as the "highway" of the *sertão*—the semiarid northeastern interior, a harsh land characterized by cacti, thorny thickets,

and blazing sun—which, except during years of severe drought, affords pasture for limited numbers of livestock. Since 1960 the Brazilian government has been studying the feasibility of irrigated agriculture along the São Francisco, but large-scale colonization is not planned for the valley. The most important use now being made of the São Francisco's water is in generating electric power at the huge Paulo Afonso Falls dam for cities of the northeast.

Savanna Country, Status and Prospects. Most of the Brazilian hinterland is *campo cerrado,* seasonally well-watered grasslands strewn with stunted trees. This savanna country stretches from the lowlands of Piauí and Maranhão across the plateaus of Goiás and central Mato Grosso (650–4,000 feet, or 200–1,200 meters, in elevation) to the Bolivian border. It is predominantly cattle country, although scattered mining operations produce modest quantities of iron ore, manganese, nickel, crystal, semiprecious stones, gold, and diamonds. Boosters of this area maintain that it has great agricultural potential, but experts doubt that even modern fertilizers can render economically productive the thin and porous topsoils that cover most of the region.

Focus on the Amazon Forest. In the late 1950's the Brazilian government promoted settlement in the upland *campo cerrado* by the construction of Brasília. The new national capital was then linked to the Amazon lowlands by the completion of the

Brasília-Belém Highway. In the 1960's, hundreds of new settlements sprang up along the highway, which descends into the forest zone about 250 miles (400 km) south of Belém. In the 1970's the occupation of the Amazon forest became almost an obsession with the Brazilian government. The Trans-Amazon Highway is being cut through the forest south of the great river from near Belém to the Peruvian border.

Agriculture. At the agricultural colonies spaced at 6-mile (10-km) intervals along completed stretches of the highway, men and boys sport T-shirts emblazoned with the motto *Integrar para não entregar*—"Integrate [the Amazon into the nation] so as not to give [it] up." Unless Brazil occupies the area, Brazilian alarmists warn, the United Nations, or a similar body, will one day resolve that this last livable and uninhabited region on earth must be forcibly opened to the world's excess population.

Thousands of settlers from all parts of Brazil, but especially from the depressed northeast, have accepted the government's offer of 249-acre (100-hectare) homesteads along the Trans-Amazon Highway. The colonists, with generous credit and technical assistance from the government, are now growing food crops in jungle clearings. Although the government has decreed that half the area of each homestead must remain in forest, environmentalists fear that the fragile Amazon ecology cannot withstand even the limited clearing operations officially approved. The *várzea* area, closest to the river but mostly beyond the reach of the highway, is the part of the lowlands most suitable for sustained agriculture because of the floods that annually renew the fertility of the soil. Commercial plantings of jute have been successful there.

While ecologists warn of the possible destruction of the forest, ethnologists deplore the inevitable disappearance of many of Brazil's remaining tribal Indians. Imported diseases, alcoholism, and clashes with other Brazilians will surely take a large toll of the tribes, despite the government's best efforts to protect them.

Other Activities. The participation of private capital in the development of the hinterland has been encouraged by laws allowing Brazilian companies and individuals to invest up to half of their income-tax liabilities in enterprises north of the 15th parallel. Despite the emphasis on maintaining the Amazon as Brazilian, important concessions have been made there to private U. S. capital, which is responsible for large-scale plantings of rice and pulpwood and the exploitation of important manganese deposits in Amapá. The few oil wells that have been brought into production in the Brazilian Amazon have raised expectations of Brazil's eventually sharing in the petroleum boom now under way in neighboring Peru. But between the Peruvian border area and Amapá, there is little indication of mineral wealth beneath the Amazon forest.

BOOMING BRAZIL / NOVEL EXCHANGE RATE SYSTEM SUPPORTS THE ECONOMIC SURGE

BY RICHARD N. COOPER
Professor of Economics, Yale University

Brazil's economic boom has been due in part to a novel exchange rate system adopted in 1968. The system involves changes in the value of Brazil's currency, the cruzeiro, by 1–2% as often as necessary to keep Brazil's products competitive with those in other countries, as measured by differential movements in domestic prices. This has meant eight to ten devaluations a year, varying in frequency from two weeks to ten weeks. The exact amount and timing of the devaluations —but not the principles underlying the strategy— are kept secret until the time of announcement, to frustrate potential speculators against the cruzeiro. Speculation is also inhibited by the high interest rates in Brazil, which make it attractive to hold Brazilian assets despite the periodic devaluations.

Inflation and the New System. During the 1950's and early 1960's, Brazil experienced an inflation rate of over 20% yearly, rising sharply until 1964. Yet the government attempted to maintain a fixed exchange rate between its currency and other leading currencies. This policy necessitated an extensive system of exchange controls and other devices to limit payments abroad. Despite these devices, rapid price increases compelled frequent devaluation. The military regime that took office in 1964 attempted to bring the rampant inflation under control by a strong contraction of the domestic economy. It succeeded in reducing the inflation from 84% in 1964 to about 24% in 1968. But inflation could not be eliminated in a short period without a severe and prolonged depression—and perhaps not even then, given the deep inflationary expectations that had been built up for nearly two decades.

The government therefore took two important steps to mitigate the damaging effects of rapid inflation. First, it raised the interest rates (or allowed them to rise) above the rate of inflation so that fixed-interest loans would not subsidize borrowers at the expense of lenders. Second, it introduced frequent, small (but cumulatively significant) devaluations of the cruzeiro, keyed to the difference between Brazil's inflation and inflation among its major trading partners.

Advantages for Brazil. The new system has had three important advantages for Brazil. First, speculation against the cruzeiro has sharply diminished from earlier years, thereby adding to the available investment funds in Brazil. Second, Brazil has been able to lift the tight exchange controls and other devices for coping with periodic balance-of-payments crises—devices that distorted the economy, fostered corruption, and impeded the growth of exports. Third, Brazil has avoided the disturbing jolts to the domestic economy that formerly attended currency devaluation, for those devaluations were much larger and hence often had a decisive effect on calculations of profitability. At the same time, Brazil's exchange rate has been stabilized in the short run and thus has not been subject to extreme disturbance from

PORTRAIT OF BRAZIL'S ECONOMIC RISE

Annual Rate of Economic Growth

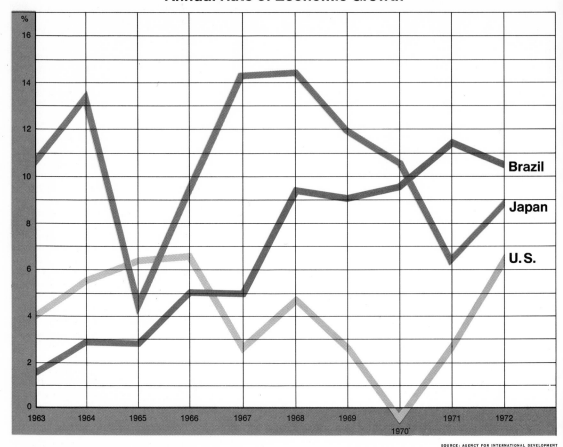

Brazil

Japan

U.S.

SOURCE: AGENCY FOR INTERNATIONAL DEVELOPMENT

Exports

Billions of U.S. Dollars

SOURCE: UNITED NATIONS

Annual Rate of Inflation

Percent

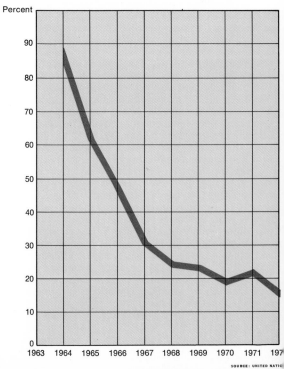

SOURCE: UNITED NATIO

ECONOMIC 'MAGICIAN'

MANCHETE/PICTORIAL PARADE

Antônio Delfim Netto, who took office as Brazil's minister of finance in 1967, not only won the support of the military high command for his daring but competent efforts to curb inflation and boost productivity but also gained the respect of foreign observers.

Delfim Netto was born in the city of São Paulo on May 1, 1928. After earning a doctorate in economics from the University of São Paulo, he immediately joined the university faculty. He began his public career as an employee of the São Paulo state highway department, then rose to the board of directors of São Paulo's powerful chamber of commerce, and finally, at the state level, was appointed to the post of secretary of finance.

A bachelor with a legendary reputation for hard work, Delfim Netto has been called an "economic Henry Kissinger" and the "Brazilian magician." A minor aide to Roberto Campos, the military regime's first finance minister, he catapulted from relative obscurity in 1967, when at the age of 38 he was chosen by Brazil's military leadership to replace Campos. Although he won the leadership's firm support for his economic "magic," he was rumored occasionally to have gone too far and to be on the verge of ouster, moving either to the post of governor of the state of São Paulo or to an international monetary agency. These rumors increased when Gen. Ernesto Geisel won the power struggle within the military high command to follow Gen. Emilio Garrastazú Médici—Delfim Netto's principal backer—as Brazilian president in 1974. But as of 1973 he had shown remarkable longevity in view of his outspokenness in a government noted for preferring blandness and teamwork in its higher echelons.

The respect that he earned abroad has been reflected in many observers' reference to him as Brazil's de facto prime minister. His energies have been spent chiefly in fostering international confidence in Brazil's economic future, securing loans and trade arrangements, and heading a professional team of skilled and pragmatic economists—many from Brazilian universities—who control and manipulate Brazil's massively planned economy.

Some foreign observers find him distressingly apolitical and cold to the problems of the Brazilian poor, 80% of whom earn less than the national per capita income. Delfim has shrugged off such criticism, perceiving his job in long-run terms and denying any future political ambitions. With a change in presidential administration approaching—as of March 1974—his plans remained indefinite.

ROBERT M. LEVINE

the international monetary system—originally laid down at the Bretton Woods Conference in 1944 and embodied in the Articles of Agreement of the International Monetary Fund—have been challenged with such severity in the early 1970's that they have largely broken down, and discussions have been attempting to repair or replace them.

One of the contenders is a system of "crawling pegs"—or "gliding parities," as it has also been called. Since most countries have a rate of inflation much lower than Brazil's, balance-of-payments equilibrium could be maintained by having the official exchange-rate parity crawl at a maximum rate of 2–3% a year instead of trotting at 10–15%. Because of these broader global considerations, interest in Brazil's exchange-rate system is high, for it represents an inadvertent experiment with the proposed gliding parity system.

But every country has unique features that call for caution in drawing lessons for other countries. Brazil's international reserves have risen very sharply since 1968, suggesting that its devaluations, based on relative price movements, have been excessive. Nonetheless, the experiment is sufficiently interesting—and the results are so satisfactory—that monetary officials around the world will watch carefully its continuing evolution. One frequently expressed fear—that steady devaluation will worsen inflation—has not been borne out in Brazil's case. Inflationary pressures, while still high, are substantially less than when Brazil operated under supposedly fixed exchange rates.

For a profile of Ernesto Geisel, Brazil's newly named president, see BIOGRAPHY; for a discussion of 1973 political events in Brazil, see page 146.

market forces, as was true of the flexible exchange rates prevailing among major currencies in the period following devaluation of the U. S. dollar in 1973. Brazil's economy and, in particular, its exports have done well under the new system.

Global Considerations. Brazil's new system has been called a "trotting peg" system because at each moment the exchange rate is "pegged" to the official rate, but the official rate is frequently changed. This system commands considerable attention abroad because the rules of

A SELECTION OF BOOKS ON BRAZIL

Azevedo, Fernando de, *Brazilian Culture: An Introduction to the Study of Culture in Brazil,* tr. by W. R. Crawford (1950; reprint, Hafner Pub. Co. 1971).

Bergsman, Joel, *Brazil: Industrialization and Trade Policies* (Oxford 1970).

Burns, E. Bradford, *A History of Brazil* (Columbia Univ. Press 1971).

Castro, Josué de, *Death in the Northeast* (Random House 1966).

Conrad, Robert, *The Destruction of Brazilian Slavery, 1850–1888* (Univ. of Calif. Press 1972).

Cunha, Euclides da, *Rebellion in the Backlands,* tr. by Samuel Putnam (Univ. of Chicago Press 1944).

Freyre, Gilberto, *The Masters and the Slaves: A Study in the Development of Brazilian Civilization,* tr. by Samuel Putnam, 2d English ed. (Knopf 1956).

Graham, Richard, *A Century of Brazilian History Since 1865: Issues and Problems* (Knopf 1969).

Havighurst, Robert J., and Moreira, J. Roberto, *Society and Education in Brazil* (Univ. of Pittsburgh Press 1969).

Levine, Robert M., *The Vargas Regime: The Critical Years, 1934–1938* (Columbia Univ. Press 1970).

Prado, Cáio, Jr., *The Colonial Background of Modern Brazil,* tr. by Suzette Macedo (Univ. of Calif. Press 1967).

Roett, Riordan, ed., *Brazil in the Sixties* (Vanderbilt Univ. Press 1972).

Rosenbaum, H. Jon, and Tyler, William G., eds., *Contemporary Brazil: Issues in Economic and Political Development* (Praeger 1972).

Stein, Stanley J., *Vassouras: A Brazilian Coffee County, 1850–1900* (Harvard Univ. Press 1957).

Stepan, Alfred, *The Military in Politics: Changing Patterns in Brazil* (Princeton Univ. Press 1971).

Wagley, Charles, *An Introduction to Brazil,* rev. ed. (Columbia Univ. Press 1971).

Wagley, Charles, ed., *Race and Class in Rural Brazil,* 2d ed. (Columbia Univ. Press 1963).

Wirth, John D., *The Politics of Brazilian Development, 1930–1954* (Stanford Univ. Press 1970).

COURTESY THE ROYAL CANADIAN MOUNTED POLICE

The Royal Canadian Mounted Police execute the "dome" formation, one of the 12 maneuvers they perform at their world-famous Musical Ride.

THE MOUNTIES

BY NORA KELLY
*Coauthor, "The Royal Canadian
Mounted Police: A Century of History"*

Royal Canadian Mounted Police: 100 Years of Proud Tradition

In 1973, as the Royal Canadian Mounted Police celebrated its 100th anniversary, the variety of its responsibilities and the vast area of its jurisdiction made it unique among the police forces of the world. Its members handle all of the federal policing in Canada, all provincial policing in eight of the ten provinces (excepting only Ontario and Quebec), and the municipal policing of more than 150 small municipalities. They constitute the only police at work in those areas not incorporated as provinces —the Yukon Territory and the Northwest Territories. The organization also operates the Canadian Security Service, which investigates espionage and subversion.

The force has increased greatly since its inception, when it had only 150 men. Regular uniformed RCMP members numbered 10,481 in 1973, with special constables and civilian members bringing total personnel to more than 14,000. The organization consists of 12 operational divisions, most of which have jurisdiction over specific provinces or geographical areas. There are 41 subdivisions and almost 700 detachments.

To perform all of its functions, the RCMP must be active in the air and on the water as well as on land. Its Marine Services operate a fleet of more than 30 vessels on both coasts and the Great Lakes, while land detachments operate hundreds of small boats on smaller inland waters. These are engaged variously in the inspection of vessels, customs and excise work, and patrol duty connected with provisions of the Migratory Birds Convention Act. The RCMP Air Division has more than 20 aircraft of various types, including helicopters, at 16 locations across Canada. It transports laboratory experts, prisoners, witnesses, and members of the force carrying on investigations in remote areas. It also performs important duties in times of civil emergency and in searches for lost persons, escaped prisoners, and wanted criminals.

Other increasingly important branches are the Telecommunications Branch and the National Police Services. The former maintains the Telex system and both stationary and mobile radio networks that link all RCMP divisions throughout Canada. National Police Services, through their Headquarters Identification Branch, divisional offices, and regional crime detection laboratories, provide expert services to all Canadian police forces and to foreign police forces when appropriate.

The RCMP also has offices in other countries for visa control and liaison duty. The first foreign liaison office was established in Washington, D. C., during World War II. (At the same time, the U. S. Federal Bureau of Investigation set up an office in the Canadian capital, Ottawa, site of RCMP head-

quarters.) Today, 20 RCMP liaison and visa control offices are scattered throughout the world to facilitate cooperation with other police forces and to ensure immigration security.

Beginnings. On May 23, 1893, an enabling bill was passed for the creation of a body of mounted police to enforce federal laws on the vast western Canadian plains known then as the North-West Territories. The plan called for the enlistment of able-bodied men of good character who were between the ages of 18 and 40 and could ride a horse. They were organized to clear the plains area of unscrupulous whisky traders who were demoralizing the Indians, to collect customs dues, and generally to establish law and order in anticipation of settlement.

The original 150 recruits spent the winter of 1873–74 at Lower Fort Garry, or "Stone Fort," 20 miles (32 km) north of the present city of Winnipeg, Manitoba. By spring another 150 men, recruited in eastern Canada, had joined this group.

On July 8, 1874, 275 scarlet-tunicked horsemen began their first operation, a now famous march west toward the foothills of the Rocky Mountains. The objective was to set up police posts at three main points on the Great Plains, and to establish law and order within that enormous triangle by patrolling out of these and subsidiary police posts. Through patient negotiations, the force established friendly relations with the Indian tribes, who were induced to sign treaties with the government of Canada. The whisky trade was suppressed and the lawlessness that had flourished in the region soon came to an end. The force had begun to make itself known, and by 1877 posts had been established at Fort MacLeod, Swan River (Livingstone), Fort Walsh, Fort Saskatchewan, Battleford, and Fort Calgary.

In the early summer of 1884, the North-West Mounted Police detachment at Battleford warned that the Métis—persons of mixed Indian and European (usually French) blood—were demanding redress of alleged grievances. There soon were reports that Louis Riel, a leader in earlier disturbances in the Red River area, had reappeared. Finally, on March 26, 1885, at Duck Lake in what is now Saskatchewan, there occurred the armed clash that marked the beginning of the Northwest Rebellion of 1885.

All of Canada was aroused by this threat, and militia units were quickly organized in other parts of Canada and sent to the area. The NWMP and the militia joined forces. The rebels were defeated, and the rebellion was virtually over by mid-May 1885. The North-West Mounted Police had assisted in meeting a major challenge.

Growth of the Force. As peace was restored and more settlers went west, the strength of the organization was increased. Several years before the Klondike Gold Rush in the late 1890's, the need for law enforcement in the north became evident, and NWMP jurisdiction was extended, first into the Yukon and later to other northern areas.

In 1905 the provinces of Alberta and Saskatchewan were formed from the original North-West Territories. Satisfaction with the work of the "Old Originals" led the new provinces to contract with the federal government for the continued services of the Royal North-West Mounted Police (the "Royal" had been bestowed to their name by King Edward VII in 1904), with the provincial governments sharing in the cost.

By 1919 the force was doing the federal policing of all four western provinces and northern Canada, while another police force, the Dominion Police, had similar responsibilities in eastern Canada. In 1920 the RNWMP was authorized to enforce federal laws in all of Canada, and its name was changed to the Royal Canadian Mounted Police. At that time, it absorbed the Dominion Police and moved its headquarters from Regina, Saskatchewan, to Ottawa. In 1928 the force again became responsible for provincial police duties in Saskatchewan, and later it made similar agreements with all of the other provinces except Ontario and Quebec, which had their own provincial police.

The Force Today. The modern RCMP has re-

The "Mounties" use power toboggans on Baffin Island, north of the Arctic Circle.

"Mounties" in patrol cars cover thousands of miles of road and highways throughout Canada.

Today's Mounties Make the Most of Modern Technology

RCMP technicians use a computerized videotape system to store fingerprints of all Canadians convicted of serious crimes.

The forensic laboratories of the RCMP are among the most modern in the world.

sponsibilities in municipal, provincial, federal, and international policing. Subjects of investigation vary from illicit stills to drug trafficking, from safe cracking to smuggling, from counterfeiting to the finding of lost persons, from traffic accidents to espionage.

Men on northern duty—traveling by power toboggan since the last dog team was inactivated in March 1969—check the welfare of Eskimos. Dogmasters supervise specially trained police service dogs that sniff out illicit drugs hidden in travelers' suitcases or in goods lying in customs sheds. When an American jetliner, skyjacked over Alaska and bound for Cuba, landed in Vancouver, an unarmed subinspector talked the armed skyjacker into giving himself up. These are but a few examples of the varied roles and activities of the RCMP today.

The Canadian Police Information Centre (CPIC), at the Ottawa headquarters, forms part of the National Police Services, through which the RCMP serves all Canadian police. Data stored in its $40 million computer system includes information about known criminals, stolen property, and all registered firearms. Through typewriter-like terminals in their own offices, all major police agencies can obtain Canadian information within seconds, and American information within minutes—since the CPIC also houses a terminal linked to an FBI police-information computer in Washington.

The Identification Branch in Ottawa has a videofile system for storage and retrieval of fingerprints. All prints are recorded on magnetic tape and can be retrieved within seconds by a computer and projected on a television screen for comparison.

Five main crime detection laboratories operate across Canada. In one recent year, 17,521 examinations were made in 73 categories, including human blood identification and grouping, X-ray inspection of parcels, identification of explosive materials, serial number restoration, urine analysis for drugs, deciphering of charred documents, and semen and spermatozoa examination.

To combat organized crime, the RCMP has set up 17 national crime intelligence units across Canada. These units gather specific intelligence about organized crime and criminals, supplementing the material in the CPIC. This intelligence is then stored at the RCMP National Central Repository in Ottawa for future use.

An RCMP radio network of nearly 1,200 fixed stations, more than 3,500 mobile radios, and about 1,000 portable radios covers populated mainland areas and many parts of the far north. Police cars, boats, and planes all have two-way radios. The force has a Telex system at all main points from coast to coast. A color-sensitive Wire Photo Service transmits photographs of documents and fingerprints with true fidelity over a distance of 4,000 miles.

Training and Education. The needs of the force have changed greatly since it was established, and with the new demands has come a change in the training and education of its members. The formal basic training period of recruits is six months. This is followed by another six months of on-the-job training under specially qualified supervisors. In accord with government policy, more bilingual (French- and English-speaking) recruits are being engaged. Although the ability to ride a horse was one of the criteria in 1873, horsemanship is no longer a requirement and is now taught only to members of the famous Musical Ride. Besides the period of initial training, regular members receive additional in-service training, advanced training, and refresher courses and attend the Canadian Police College. Many mounted policemen study university subjects on their own time through part-time attendance at classes or through correspondence courses. Others, sponsored by the force in a program begun in 1935, attend universities or technical colleges on a full-time basis.

The requirements for joining the force as a regular member have also changed since the force was first organized. The applicant must be a Canadian citizen or British subject 19 to 30 years of age, single, have a valid Canadian driver's license, have at least an 11th grade education, be between 5'8" and 6'5" tall, have no criminal record, be of good character, and be able to speak, read, and write English or French. Some departments requiring special skills employ applicants with specialized degrees. For example, the Commercial Frauds Sections based in various Canadian cities are partly staffed by RCMP members with degrees in commerce and law.

International Cooperation. Interpol, an international clearinghouse for the exchange of information and mutual assistance between member police agencies, is represented by a National Central Bureau at RCMP headquarters in Ottawa. This bureau acts on behalf of all accredited police forces in Canada. In 1972 the RCMP commissioner, W. L. Higgitt, became the president of Interpol.

In addition to its work with foreign law-enforcement agencies through Interpol, the RCMP deals directly with some of these through its liaison offices abroad. In 1968 the FBI asked the RCMP for assistance in locating James Earl Ray, the suspected murderer of Martin Luther King, Jr. A five-man team of the RCMP spent almost five weeks checking 250,000 applications for Canadian passports. Ray had used an assumed name, but a constable recognized the accompanying photograph and this led to Ray's capture in Europe. FBI director J. Edgar Hoover wrote a personal letter thanking the constable for his assistance.

Evaluation. The force has not altogether escaped criticism. There have been occasional complaints by its own members and some outside criticism of its performance of certain tasks, such as its enforcement of the law on Indian reserves, where poverty has embittered the Indians' relations with the police.

The most severe criticism in the force's history has arisen from its strict enforcement of laws governing the use of marihuana and other "soft" drugs. The widespread use of such drugs by young people, especially in the late 1960's, resulted in many convictions and consequent criminal records. In this instance, the force, as a visible target, was unfairly drawing fire from those whose proper quarrel was with the statute itself. As the use of drugs by young people began to diminish after 1970, so too did criticism of the RCMP.

The force is also condemned by some political dissidents, who tend to view it as an arm of the establishment that they oppose, especially when it is used as an internal security service. Such feelings are far from widespread, however. When the initials "RCMP" were removed from patrol cars and the word "Police" was substituted, the public protested so vehemently that the initials were replaced. It seems clear that most Canadians admire the Mounted Police and take pride in the fame that it has achieved beyond the borders of Canada.

THE AMERICAN INDIAN

Uprising at Wounded Knee Publicized Plight Of Native Americans and Their New Militancy

BY WILCOMB E. WASHBURN
Director, Office of American Studies,
Smithsonian Institution

The American Indian, once the fastest disappearing segment of the population of the United States, is now the most rapidly growing group. Estimates of Indian population differ, but the official census of 1970 records 792,730 Indians—up 51.4% from the 1960 census. More than half of all American Indians—an estimated 542,897 in 1973—live on or near reservations and are served to some degree by the Bureau of Indian Affairs under the Department of the Interior. The remainder are scattered throughout the country, with an increasing number in large Midwestern and Western cities. Indeed, 340,367 Indians (including some of those on or near reservations), live in urban areas—that is, metropolitan areas of 50,000 or more inhabitants and places of 2,500 or more inhabitants outside metropolitan areas.

Legal Status. American Indians occupy a special legal status within the United States. Although all Indians are citizens—as provided by the Indian citizenship act of 1924—they retain, in their tribal capacity, rights derived from treaties signed by the United States with their tribes prior to 1871, when Congress ordered a cessation of treaty-making with Indian tribes.

The Indians are the only ethnic group that is separately represented by a special government agency—the Bureau of Indian Affairs (BIA). Although subject to continuing and bitter criticism by Indians, the BIA functions as a guardian of the land base and the rights reserved to Indians by the treaties. The trusteeship role assumed by the United States in behalf of federally recognized Indian tribes has been necessary to prevent exploitation of Indians by individual non-Indians and by state and local governments. Nevertheless, the ponderous restrictions imposed on actions by Indians have continued to be an irritant.

Economic Status. The percentage gains in employment and income made by Indians since 1960 have been greater than those made by other groups, but the Indians still lag behind because of the low economic base from which they started. An economist, Alan L. Sorkin, noted in the study *American Indians and Federal Aid* (1971) that "an Indian reservation can be characterized as an open-air slum." Although varying in different locations, unemployment rates on reservations averaged between 37% and 51% during the period 1958–67, and there has been very little improvement since that time. The 1973 rate was 37%. If temporary employment is joined with unemployment, the rate of unemployment and underemployment is 55%. Nevertheless, the

(Continued on page 66)

(Opposite) Sacred Heart Church, site of 1890 massacre,
became the symbol of the 1973 siege at Wounded Knee.
WIDE WORLD

The Second Battle of

WOUNDED KNEE

BY ANDREW H. MALCOLM
"The New York Times"

American Indian Movement leader Dennis Banks.

"Gentlemen," the voice crackled over the radio, "the village of Wounded Knee is clear." Those words, spoken on May 8, 1973, by a U. S. marshall, marked the end of the occupation of Wounded Knee, S. Dak., one of the more dramatic, bitter, and bizarre episodes in recent U. S. history.

Seizure and Demands. Ten weeks earlier, members of the American Indian Movement (AIM) and its supporters had seized the historic village on the Pine Ridge Indian Reservation in South Dakota to dramatize their demands for reform in Indian tribal government in general and the overthrow of the local elected Oglala Sioux government in particular. Armed with rifles, shotguns, and bottles filled with gasoline, about 300 militants seized the town on the night of February 27. While guns fired and drums beat, some residents sneaked to safety. But the occupiers, many of them Indians from Midwestern cities, captured 11 hostages in the hamlet—a dusty collection of old, small homes and trailers in a scrubby prairie valley where in 1890 the U. S. Army massacred almost 300 members of Sioux bands as they turned in their arms. That battle was the last of the Indian wars. The Indian occupiers in 1973 hoped to strike a responsive chord of guilt among many non-Indian Americans aware of past injustices to the Indians.

The sight of Indians with braided hair riding horses bareback attracted hundreds of newsmen from as far away as West Germany. The newsmen's television cameras and other equipment and their questions and the Indians' theatrics created what could be described as almost a bizarre circus atmosphere, were it not for the seriousness of the confrontation. In a reversal of the traditional movie roles, federal lawmen encircled the Indians and watched the scene from hills overlooking Wounded Knee—which was named for an injury once inflicted on a Sioux by a Crow Indian. But soon tempers flared. Exchanges of high-powered gunfire became almost nightly occurrences. Parachute flares drifted across the winter sky, many starting grass fires on landing. Tracer bullets zipped overhead, while Indian and federal negotiators met almost daily, sometimes beside an old tepee. They made little progress, although the arrival of South Dakota's U. S. senators, George McGovern and James G. Abourezk, did secure the hostages' release on March 1.

The Indians wanted major revisions in the tribal constitution, adopted under the Indian Reorganization Act of 1934, that established an elected tribal government to replace the traditional chiefs and their factions. Government negotiators dispatched from Washington, D. C., under mounting pressure to return law and order to the village, refused constitutional concessions, fearing the precedent-setting impact on the elected tribal organizations that govern reservation Indians.

Premature Agreement. On April 5 an agreement to end the occupation was announced. The occupiers would give up when further talks began in Washington between their leaders and government officials on April 7. The leaders went to Washington. But the agreement contained no specific provisions for the actual surrender, and the occupation continued into the spring. Fatigue, bitterness, and deadly gunfire began to take their toll. Lloyd Grimm, a U. S. marshall, had been shot and paralyzed on March 26. Others on both sides were wounded. Frank Clearwater—one of the militants, who was wounded on April 17—died on April 25. Two days later, Lawrence Lamont, a 31-year-old Oglala Sioux, was killed. A tenuous cease-fire was promptly arranged and negotiations continued. On May 5, Indian elders supporting the occupiers received a letter from acting White House counsel Leonard Garment. It reiterated an earlier promise to dispatch federal representatives to the embattled 2,500-square-mile (6,500-sq-km) Pine Ridge reservation to discuss Indian grievances, specifically violations of an 1868 treaty promising the Sioux, among other things, half of what is now South Dakota.

End of Confrontation. On May 6 both sides announced an agreement to end the confrontation, and two days later they did. But the cost had been high—two dead, $5 million in police costs, and untotaled damage to the bullet-pocked town where homes were vandalized, burned down, or fouled by wastes. Many returning residents stayed only long enough to survey their losses. The promised talks were held 10 days later, and they continued sporadically. But no concrete results were announced or anticipated. In June, AIM leader Russell Means repeated demands that Indians be allowed to negotiate with the government as a sovereign nation, as they did before 1868. And other Indians promised "more Wounded Knees." On July 3 the Sacred Heart Roman Catholic Church, with its white steeple that had become a symbol of the 70-day occupation, mysteriously burned to the ground. And in the oppressive prairie summer heat, diseased and starving dogs picked over the ruins of what was the Second Battle of Wounded Knee.

A member of the American Indian Movement (AIM) stands guard at a roadblock thrown up around Wounded Knee.

Attempting to end the confrontation at Wounded Knee, U. S. government negotiators and AIM leaders meet on April 5. Left to right are Kent Frizzell, a federal negotiator; Ramon Robideaux, AIM chief counsel; and AIM members Wallace Black Elk and Russell Means.

Armed Indians at Wounded Knee. Behind them is Sacred Heart Church, which the Indians used as a residence during the 70-day occupation.

Alcatraz Island, in San Francisco Bay, was held by Indians in 1970 as a symbol of the pan-Indian spirit.

census of 1970 revealed a median income among Indian families of $5,832, compared with $6,864 for blacks and $11,549 for whites. Thus the gap between Indians and blacks has narrowed strikingly since 1960, when the income of nonreservation Indians was nearly that of nonwhites but the income of reservation Indians was only half as much. The number of Indian families with incomes below the officially defined poverty threshold ($3,743 for a nonfarm family of four in 1970) was down dramatically from earlier years, but one third of all Indian families are still below the line.

Changes in U. S. Government Policy. Government policy toward the Indian has become increasingly concerned with, and solicitous of, Indian needs and aspirations. The "termination" era of the immediate post–World War II period, during which Democrats and Republicans alike sought to terminate the federal trusteeship status and to force Indians into the mainstream of American life, has been repudiated. Although efforts during the Kennedy and Johnson administrations sought to raise the standard of living and increase the educational opportunities of Indians, the specter of termination continued to hang over Indians until expressly rejected by the Nixon administration in a statement issued by the President on July 8, 1970. The statement not only repudiated "termination" as a policy of the executive branch but enunciated a policy of "self-determination without termination." That is, the Indians would be allowed to determine their own future without, however, losing the protection of the federal trust relationship.

Indian tribal identity in the following years was strengthened. Indian voices were increasingly heard, Indian leadership in the BIA was expanded, and Indian land wrongfully taken by the government—as in the case of Blue Lake in New Mexico, a religious shrine of the Taos Pueblo Indians—was returned to the Indians. Congress, as well as the White House, became more accommodating toward Indian viewpoints, and Indians found places on the staffs of both the House and the Senate committees dealing with Indian affairs.

From the time of John Marshall, chief justice of the United States from 1801 to 1835, the judicial branch of government has been sympathetic to Indian rights. In the 1960's and early 1970's the courts handed down an unusual number of decisions—often in cases brought

INDIANS IN CANADA: *ACTION IN THE COURTS*

BY RUDY PLATIEL
"The Globe and Mail," Toronto

Decisions by the Supreme Court of Canada on aboriginal land rights not covered by treaty and on the rights of Indian women reverberated throughout Canada during 1973.

Supreme Court Decisions. In a 4-to-3 decision on January 31, the federal Supreme Court rejected the aboriginal land claims of the Nishga Indians to a large area of northern British Columbia. The majority opinion reflected the federal government's policy, never before tested in the highest court, of refusing to recognize the aboriginal rights of Indians not covered by treaty. Although a legal defeat, the decision contained elements of political victory. On February 7, Prime Minister Pierre Trudeau told a group of British Columbia chiefs, "Perhaps you have more legal rights than we thought." On February 14, the Yukon Native Brotherhood presented to the Trudeau government a proposal—with terms similar to those of the Alaska Native Claims Settlement Act of 1971 —for settling the claims of the Yukon's 5,000 Indians and *métis* (persons of mixed blood). The government agreed immediately to negotiate the claims, signaling a major policy change, and on August 8, Indian Affairs Minister Jean Chrétien announced that the federal government would consider compensating natives for the loss of lands never ceded by treaty.

In a 5-to-4 decision on August 27, the Supreme Court rejected arguments by two Indian women that the loss of their legal Indian status through marriage to non-Indians is a violation of the federal Bill of Rights. The majority held that although the Indian Act of 1952 discriminates against Indian women in stripping them (but not men) of Indian status and reserve rights, it does not involve guaranteed rights and freedoms and thus does not violate the Bill of Rights. Indian organizations had warned that a favorable decision could destroy the Indian act and lead to a "white takeover" of Indian reserves by non-Indian husbands.

Other Events. On September 6, the Supreme Court of the Northwest Territories granted the territories' Native Brotherhood the right to file a caveat (legal warning of interest) on land covering about one third of the territories. Indian leaders felt that the decision strengthened their stand in opposing federal plans for a highway and oil and gas pipelines, pending settlement of land claims under existing treaties. In Quebec, leaders of 6,000 Cree Indians and Inuits (Eskimos) used both the courts and public forums in their battle against the planned flooding of their wilderness area by the provincial James Bay hydroelectric project. Echoes of U. S. Indian militancy resounded in Ottawa on August 30, when 200 youths seized and held the federal Indian Affairs building for 24 hours.

by newly formed Indian legal aid groups—confirming or upholding a liberal interpretation of Indian land, water, hunting, and fishing rights. Among these was a series of suits brought on behalf of the Paiute Indians of the Pyramid Lake reservation in Nevada against the U. S. Department of the Interior and the states of California and Nevada. The result was a ruling, in November 1972, that the Interior Department had violated its trust and treaty obligations by allowing excessive amounts of water to be diverted from Pyramid Lake for use in irrigating non-Indian lands, thereby imperiling the lake and with it the Indians' livelihood.

Rise of Indian Militancy. The rapid rise of radical Indian organizations in the late 1960's and early 1970's did not coincide with a period of repression or unusual economic distress. On the contrary, it coincided with a period of increasing recognition, by both government and the public at large, of Indian aspirations and the need to achieve those aspirations with Indian advice and leadership. The "Red Power" movement, like the "Black Power" movement from which it drew ideas and help, paradoxically exploded in the face of the generation that lifted the lid off the disabilities experienced by Indians at the hands of previous generations of whites.

Radical Indian organizations, such as the American Indian Movement (AIM), had begun as attempts to deal with the frustrations felt by urban Indians trapped in the poverty and despair of cities. AIM, for

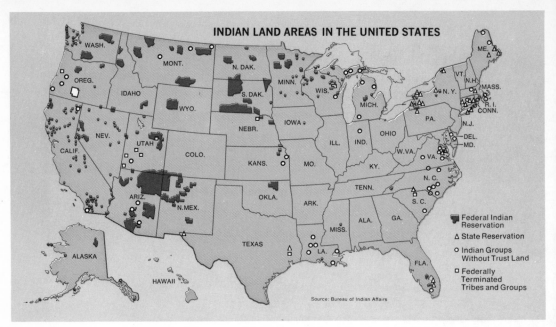

INDIAN LAND AREAS IN THE UNITED STATES

Federal Indian Reservation
△ State Reservation
○ Indian Groups Without Trust Land
□ Federally Terminated Tribes and Groups

Source: Bureau of Indian Affairs

example, was at first a local Minneapolis organization, which engaged in such activities as sending observers to follow police officers and monitor charges of brutality in the handling of intoxicated Indians. AIM soon emerged as the spokesman for grandiose policies of reform of federal-Indian relations, as in the 20 demands of the AIM leaders during the occupation of the BIA building in Washington, D. C., in early November 1972. In the main, those demands called for reinstating a treaty-making relation between the "Indian tribes and nations" and the federal government.

The change of focus was encouraged by the attention given the movement by the media, particularly the electronic media with their need for news conveyed in terms of movement and activity. With each accession of publicity, the importance of the radical leaders was magnified and that of the traditional leaders—especially the elected tribal leaders on reservations who sought to work within the system—was diminished. The culmination of the radical movement and the confrontation to which it led between the militant urban Indian leaders and the tribal leaders operating in the context of the federally protected—or "controlled," as the radicals would assert—reservation system was dramatized in the events at Wounded Knee, S. Dak., discussed in the accompanying article.

Militants Versus the "Establishment." Do the militants express the will of the Indian people? The self-respect of many Indians, both young and old, was bolstered by the radicals' forceful and even contemptuous rejection of white authority. But the wisdom of throwing a wrench into machinery that was steadily being converted to the support of Indian aspirations was questioned by many others. Most worrisome of all was the direct assault by the radicals on the system of electing tribal leaders. In their assault on Richard Wilson, the elected tribal leader of the Oglala Sioux, the AIM radicals strengthened the Oglala faction that wished to abolish the system of elections authorized, and officially accepted, by the Sioux in the Indian Reorganization Act of 1934. Instead, the militants sought a reversion to the more decentralized, nonelective, but consensus-implying "traditional chiefs" system of leadership.

Radicals Challenge the System

The radicals received unexpected support early in July from a ruling of the Supreme Court of Ontario, Canada, which declared that the council of hereditary chiefs of the Six Nations Indian Reserve near Brantford, Ontario, should be managing the reserve, rather than an elected Indian council imposed by the Canadian government in 1924. So inadequate was press coverage of the Wounded Knee episode that many observers, including Indians from other tribes, were for a long time unaware that the concept of an elected tribal leadership was under assault there.

A cynical observer might see the conflict between the new militants and the existing Indian establishment as a mere struggle for power. Certainly the struggle for power explains more about the conflict than do the expressions of ideals to be sought and evils to be fought that were recorded in the manifestos of both groups. Both sides want more autonomy and greater prosperity for Indian people. Existing tribal leaders believe that these objectives can be obtained by utilizing the system, of which they are now a part, to obtain those ends. The radicals, utilizing techniques that bring maximum publicity, state similar objectives in extreme terms and with rhetorical excesses. The central problem is how to determine Indian sentiment and how to continue the gains that Indians have achieved in the past. Every proposed change in Indian policy, even the Indian Reorganization Act of 1934, has created violent factions among Indian people who have divided for or against the proposed changes. The same split is evident in the current situation.

Proposed BIA Reorganization. The aftermath of the turmoil in Indian affairs in 1972 and 1973 has been a proposed reorganization of the BIA, which in mid-1973 was both literally and figuratively shattered. Hearings on a structure of reorganization were instituted in the summer of 1973 by the Senate's Indian affairs subcommittee, headed by Sen. James G. Abourezk (D-S. Dak.). Abourezk refused to allow Marvin Franklin, the acting commissioner of Indian affairs, to testify before the subcommittee on the ground that Franklin was serving illegally, since he had not been nominated to the position or confirmed by the Senate following the dismissal of top bureau officials in the aftermath of the sacking of the BIA building by AIM members. In October, President Nixon nominated Morris Thompson, Alaska area director of the BIA, as commissioner. He is an Athabaskan Indian.

A SELECTION OF BOOKS ON AMERICAN INDIANS

Cardinal, Harold, *The Unjust Society: The Tragedy of Canada's Indians* (Hurtig, M. G. 1969).

Deloria, Vine, Jr., *Custer Died for Your Sins: An Indian Manifesto* (Macmillan 1969).

Dockstader, Frederick J., *Indian Art in America*, 3d ed. (N. Y. Graphic 1968).

Dockstader, Frederick J., *Indian Art in Middle America* (N. Y. Graphic 1964).

Driver, Harold E., *The Americas on the Eve of Discovery* (Prentice-Hall 1964).

Driver, Harold E., *Indians of North America*, 2d ed., rev. (Univ. of Chicago Press 1969).

Drucker, Philip, *Cultures of the North Pacific Coast* (Chandler Pub. 1965).

Fey, Harold E., and McNickle, D'Arcy, *Indians and Other Americans: Two Ways of Life Meet*, rev. ed. (Harper 1970).

Fiedler, Leslie A., *The Return of the Vanishing American* (Stein & Day 1968).

Hagan, William T., *American Indians* (Univ. of Chicago Press 1962).

Hertzberg, Hazel W., *The Search for an American Indian Identity: Modern Pan-Indian Movements* (Syracuse Univ. Press 1971).

Jennings, Jesse D., *Prehistory of North America* (McGraw 1968).

Josephy, Alvin M., Jr., *The Indian Heritage of America* (Knopf 1968).

Levine, Stuart, and Lurie, Nancy O., eds., *The American Indian Today* (Edwards, Everett 1968).

Lurie, Nancy O., and Leacock, Eleanor B., eds., *North American Indians in Historical Perspective* (Random House 1971).

Oswalt, Wendell H., *This Land Was Theirs: A Study of the North American Indian* (Wiley 1966).

Owen, Roger C., and others, eds., *The North American Indians: A Sourcebook* (Macmillan 1967).

Spencer, Robert F., and others, *The Native Americans: Prehistory and Ethnology of the North American Indians* (Harper 1965).

Steiner, Stanley, *The New Indians* (Harper 1968).

Underhill, Ruth M., *Red Man's Religion: Beliefs and Practices of the Indians North of Mexico* (Univ. of Chicago Press 1965).

Washburn, Wilcomb E., ed., *The Indian and the White Man* (reissue; Anchor Bks. 1970).

Washburn, Wilcomb E., *Red Man's Land/White Man's Law: A Study of the Past and Present Status of the American Indian* (Scribner 1971).

Willey, Gordon R., *An Introduction to American Archaeology; vol. 1, North and Middle America* (Prentice-Hall 1966).

UN peacekeeping forces move from Cairo into Sinai
desert to supervise Arab-Israeli truce in October.

1973

REVIEW
OF THE YEAR

Victims of a gas-storage tank explosion on Staten Island, N. Y., are placed in coffins and lifted out by crane.

ACCIDENTS AND DISASTERS

Accidents continued in 1973 to be the leading cause of death among Americans through the age of 38. For U. S. residents of all ages, accidents constituted the fourth-leading cause of death, trailing only heart disease, cancer, and stroke. Motor-vehicle deaths in 1973, at first expected to exceed the 1972 U. S. total of 56,600, were later estimated to have totaled 1,000 below that record-breaking high. This was due to the decline in the death toll in November and December after the reduction of highway speed limits to conserve fuel.

Motor Vehicle Safety. The failure of the driving public in the United States to fully utilize safety belts and harnesses—now provided on nearly all passenger cars—has been estimated to cost about 14,000 lives each year. The introduction of seat belt interlock systems, which prevent drivers from starting their motors when the belts are not in place, was expected to add only slightly to the use of these restraints by the public. Studies indicated that only 25% to 35% of motorists were using seat belts in 1972.

Controversy over installation of air-bag systems in U. S. cars was expected to continue into 1974.

Bicycle Safety. On Sept. 29, 1973, the U. S. Consumer Product Safety Commission, in its initial ranking of the products over which it has jurisdiction, cited the bicycle as the most hazardous. The new agency, created by Congress in 1972, announced that bicycles are responsible each year for over 350,000 injuries requiring emergency-room treat-

ment. According to the National Safety Council, bicycle fatalities rose to more than 1,000 in 1972.

Legislation varies as to safety precautionary measures required for bicycles, but basic requirements for reflectorization on front and rear, pedals, and sides are gradually being standardized.

Drownings. An examination of the circumstances surrounding the 930 deaths by drowning that occurred as a result of boating accidents in 1971 revealed that only 20% of the victims used life-saving devices, although 65% had such devices available in the boat, as required under the federal Boat Safety Act.

VINCENT L. TOFANY
President, National Safety Council

—— MAJOR ACCIDENTS AND DISASTERS OF 1973 ——

AVIATION

Jan. 22—A chartered jetliner carrying Nigerian Muslims home from a pilgrimage to Mecca crashes and burns while landing in a fog in northern Nigeria, killing 176 persons; this crash and one near Moscow in 1972, in which the same number of people were killed, are the two worst crashes in civil aviation history.

Jan. 29—Egyptian jet crashes in Kyrenia Mountains of northern Cyprus, killing all 38 persons aboard.

Feb. 19—Soviet jetliner bursts into flames and breaks apart while landing at Prague, killing 66 persons.

Feb. 28—Polish Air Force plane crashes outside of Szczecin, near the Baltic Sea, killing 15 persons, including the interior ministers of Poland and Czechoslovakia and eight military leaders.

March 5—Two London-bound Spanish jetliners collide during a strike by air controllers; one of the planes explodes and crashes, killing all 68 aboard, but the other plane safely crash-lands with a damaged wing.

March 19—South Vietnamese passenger plane crashes near Ban Me Thout, killing all aboard (46–52 persons).

April 10—British charter plane crashes during a heavy snowfall near Basel, Switzerland, killing 104.

April 30—The foreign minister and 24 diplomats from Southern Yemen are killed in an air crash in Southern Yemen.

May 25—Soviet airliner crashes in southern Siberia, during a gunfight between a would-be hijacker and an armed guard; all 40 persons aboard are killed.

May 31—Indian jetliner crashes in New Delhi, killing 48 of the 65 persons aboard.

June 1—Brazilian plane explodes and crashes while attempting to land at São Luís, killing all 23 persons aboard.

June 30—Mexican DC-9 hits a mountain peak near Mexico's Pacific coast and explodes; all 27 persons aboard die.

U. S. ACCIDENT FATALITY TOLL			
	1970	1971	1972
All accidents	115,000	115,000	117,000
Leading causes			
Motor vehicles	54,800	54,700	56,600
Falls	17,800	17,900	17,400
Drownings	7,300	7,300	7,600
Burns	6,800	6,700	6,800
Poisons (other than gases)	3,000	3,500	3,700
Firearms	2,300	2,400	2,400
Poison gases	1,600	1,600	1,600
Source: U. S. National Safety Council estimates.			

--------- **MAJOR ACCIDENTS AND DISASTERS OF 1973 (continued)** ---------

AVIATION (continued)

July 11—Brazilian jetliner crashes in flames near Paris, killing 122 of the 134 persons aboard.

July 23—U. S. jetliner crashes shortly after taking off from Tahiti, killing 78 of the 79 persons aboard.

July 23—U. S. turbojet crashes during a storm near St. Louis, Mo., killing 36 of the 44 persons aboard.

July 31—U. S. jetliner crashes and burns while landing in a fog at Boston, killing 88 of the 89 persons aboard.

Aug. 13—Spanish jetliner explodes and crashes after hitting treetops while attempting to land in a thick fog near La Coruña, Spain, killing all 85 persons aboard.

Sept. 11—Yugoslav airliner crashes into a mountain peak near Titograd, Yugoslavia, killing all 42 persons aboard.

Dec. 23—Chartered jetliner bound for Morocco crashes near the Mediterranean coast, killing all 106 persons aboard.

LAND AND SEA TRANSPORTATION

Feb. 22—Crowded ferry collides with a Japanese freighter on the Rangoon River in Rangoon, Burma, killing more than 200 persons.

March 13—Bus smashes headlong into another bus in Antofagasta, Chile, killing 45 persons.

March 18—Massive traffic accident, in which 32 vehicles pile up on a highway near Barrie, Ontario, results in the deaths of 43 persons.

March 22—Two Norwegian freighters are lost in a storm off the coast of New Jersey; only one survivor is found of the 62 men in the crews of the two ships.

May 2—Bus accident near Salvador, Brazil, kills 39 persons, including 13 children.

May 5—Two river passenger boats collide near Dacca, Bangladesh, killing at least 250 persons.

July 7—Bus plunges into water near Alwar, India; 78 persons are killed and eight survive; more could have been saved but they belonged to two different high-caste communities and refused to share a single safety rope.

July 21—Bus plunges into a river in northeastern Iran, killing 48 persons, including 22 children.

Dec. 24—Ferry sinks in the Gulf of Guayaquil of southwestern Ecuador, near the Peruvian border, killing at least 109 persons; most of the more than 250 passengers were going home for Christmas.

STORMS, FLOODS, LANDSLIDES, AND COLD SPELLS

Jan. 10—Tornado cuts through farming town of San Justo, Argentina, 60 miles (97 km) south of Santa Fe; 46 persons are killed and some 300 are injured.

March 10–May 25—Mississippi River floods along 1,400 miles (2,255 km) of its course; it reaches its highest stage since 1785 at St. Louis, at 43.3 feet (13.2 meters), and remains above flood stage for a record 76 days; 26 persons are left dead, 39,000 are left homeless, and damage is estimated at $100 million.

March 24–31—Heavy rains in Tunisia cause floods that leave some 150 persons dead and 26,000 homeless.

April 12–26—Two weeks of storms in Bangladesh kill hundreds of persons and injure thousands; unofficial estimates of the death toll are nearly 1,000.

April 26—Torrential rain causes mudslide in Quito, Ecuador, killing at least 25 persons, crushing seven houses, and damaging others; some 2,000 persons flee their homes.

April–June—Severe storms sweep Indonesian islands of Palue and Flores, killing some 1,650 persons.

May 26–28—Tornadoes, heavy rains, and flash floods hit 10 states in the South and Middle West of the United States; 47 persons are killed, and crops and property are destroyed.

July–August—Storms and floods hit northern and central Mexico; hundreds are killed and thousands are left homeless; crop damage is estimated at $50 million.

August—Flooding of the Indus River system in Pakistan results in the deaths of more than 300 persons and the destruction of millions of acres of crops, thousands of cattle, and hundreds of thousands of homes.

November—Typhoon winds and torrential rains sweep the central and northern coastal provinces of South Vietnam, killing at least 60 persons and destroying thousands of acres of rice crops and tons of harvested rice supplies; 150,000 persons are forced out of their homes.

Dec. 10–25—Nearly 200 persons die during a severe cold wave that blankets northern India; most of the victims are poor people who lack proper clothing and shelter.

FIRES AND EXPLOSIONS

Feb. 10—Explosion in gas storage tank on Staten Island in New York City kills 40 workmen.

March 19—Series of underground gas explosions in Bihar state, in eastern India, kills at least 47 coal miners.

June 24—Fire sweeps through a New Orleans bar, killing 32 persons; late in the year a young man in Los Angeles confesses to setting the fire.

Aug. 4—Fire ravages a large amusement center at Douglas, on the Isle of Man; 51 persons are killed, making the fire the worst in Britain since World War II.

Sept. 1—Upper stories of a hotel in downtown Copenhagen burn, killing 35 foreign tourists, including 19 Americans.

Oct. 15—Fire fanned by high winds destroys an 18-block area of Chelsea, Mass., an industrial suburb of Boston; some 280 houses and 520 industrial or commercial buildings are destroyed and 1,000 are left homeless.

Nov. 16—Flames sweep up a staircase in a Los Angeles apartment house, killing 24 persons and injuring 52; it is the worst residential fire in the city's history.

Nov. 29—Department store in Kumamoto, Japan, is destroyed by fire during a big sale; at least 100 of the approximately 2,500 people in the store are killed.

EARTHQUAKES

Jan. 30—Earthquakes in western Mexico kill 52 persons.

Aug. 28—Earthquake rips through central Mexico; some 700 persons are killed and countless injured.

Blanket-wrapped body of a victim of the crash of a Brazilian jetliner near Paris is carried from the wreckage.

UPI

ADVERTISING

Expenditures for advertising in the United States rose 11% in 1973, resulting in a two-year growth rate of 20%. Canadian advertising grew 8% during the year despite severe government regulation.

UNITED STATES

The energy crisis was reflected in U. S. advertising in 1973. Government intervention continued, and the industry stepped up self-policing and consumer information and protection programs.

Government Relations. Consumer protection was broadened at the local level, as more states, cities, and towns began regulating advertising and manufacturing. Local, as well as national, advertisers were threatened by retroactive advertising and were required to run ads correcting false or misleading claims. The industry responded with intensified self-regulatory programs. Individual companies concentrated on providing consumers with more product information in ads, and instituted procedures to handle complaints about product quality and service and to correct abuses.

Advertising Copy. Two dominant ad themes reflected the economic pressures felt in 1973. The energy crisis emerged as a dominant subject, with ads urging (and explaining) fuel conservation techniques. Consumer worries over purchasing power, induced by the inflation, got attention in numerous campaigns stressing value, economy, and ways to extend dollars.

The naming of competitors in advertising grew rapidly. From deodorants and shavers to insurance

MASON REESE, a seven-year-old New York boy, ate his way to national fame by starring in TV commercials.

and Wall Street, copy featured direct comparisons between specific brands. Comparisons between name-brand shavers became so intense during 1973 that advertising in this category ended in the courts, after mediation efforts of the Federal Trade Commission (FTC) and media failed. The industry was worried that if seemingly conflicting comparisons of products proliferated, advertising credibility could suffer. One hope was that self-imposed guidelines on competitive claims might be developed.

Mass Media. Regulatory and consumerist bodies bore down on the quality of children's television programming and the quantity and selling techniques of commercials on these shows. The television industry responded by upgrading TV fare for youngsters, scrutinizing programs for excessive violence, and tightening guidelines for ads. The FTC formed four committees of consumer groups to draft a voluntary code for advertising to children.

Paper costs and postal rate increases prompted many magazines to change to smaller page sizes, with the consequent result of smaller ads. Newspapers, feeling the pinch of the newsprint shortage, limited ads and circulation. Meanwhile, despite labor opposition, automated composing and editing increased for both advertising and editorial copy. The attrition in the number of newspapers slowed down.

Advertising Spending. The 11% rise in expenditures to $25.5 billion in 1973 was caused in part by the growth in network spot TV advertising, which rose 14.7% to $3.6 billion. Gains in advertising in publications were modest—3.1% for magazines, to $1.48 billion; 5.2% for newspapers, to $1.16 billion; and 3.5% for business publications, to $803 million. All other media, from matchbook covers to billboards, posted a 9.6% increase, to $6.4 billion. Once again local advertising grew faster than national. Local advertising rose 11.5%, to $11.4 billion and national went up 9.1%, to $14.1 billion.

IN NEW TWIST, major oil companies encourage customers to use less of their product instead of more.

CANADA

Television advertising was the main concern of the Canadian advertising industry in 1973, but spending increased in all fields of advertising.

Television Advertising. Quebec enacted stringent legislation in 1973 regulating television ads directed at viewers 13 years old or younger. The Canadian Radio and Television Commission issued tough rules on TV clutter—limiting the number of commercials to run in a given period of time. The industry responded with vigorous self-policing, ranging from a voluntary reduction of commercial time on children's programs to the enforcement of the industry's code of ad standards. Efforts were made to ban the importation of television commercials produced outside of Canada.

Advertising Spending. Ad volume was up 8% in Canada in 1973, reaching $1.42 billion in spending. The growth resulted in the following totals: newspapers, $480 million; periodicals, $144.8 million; other publications, $267.8 million; and outdoor advertising, $121 million. Local advertising rose faster than national advertising during the year.

EDWARD H. MEYER
President and Chairman of the Board
Grey Advertising Inc.

AFGHANISTAN

A classic, almost bloodless, coup ended the Afghan monarchy on July 17, 1973. King Mohammed Zahir abdicated on August 12 after a 40-year reign. The intelligentsia cheered, the countryside little noticed, but the new republic, whatever form it takes, will ultimately affect the destinies of all Afghans—and possibly their neighbors.

Political Developments. Prime Minister Abdul Zahir resigned in December 1972 and Mohammed Musa Shafiq took over his office. Shafiq's seven-month government achieved genuine movement, but 10 years of relative legislative and administrative lassitude, combined with a postponement of the elections, caused a crisis in Afghanistan's political and economic direction. Lt. Gen. Mohammed Daud

Mohammed Zahir Shah, deposed ruler of Afghanistan.

KEYSTONE

——— AFGHANISTAN • Information Highlights ———

Official Name: Republic of Afghanistan.
Location: Central Asia.
Area: 250,000 square miles (647,497 sq km).
Population (1973 est.): 18,300,000. Density, 70 per square mile (27 per sq km).
Chief City (1971 est.): Kabul, the capital, 318,100.
Government: *Head of state,* Lt. Gen. Mohammed Daud Khan, president (took office July 1973). *Head of government,* Lt. Gen. Mohammed Daud Khan, prime minister (took office July 1973). Legislature—Shura (dissolved July 1973).
Languages: Pushtu and Dari (Persian)—both official.
Education: *School enrollment* (1970)—primary, 540,687; secondary, 121,699; technical/vocational, 7,646; university/higher, 7,397.
Monetary Unit: Afghani (45 afghanis equal U. S.$1, Aug. 1973).
Gross National Product (1971 est.): $1,575,000,000.
Economic Indexes: *Agricultural production Index* (1971), 109 (1963=100); *consumer price index* (1972), 110 (1970=100).
Manufacturing (major products): Textiles, cement, processed fruit, sugar, carpets.
Major Agricultural Products: Wheat, corn, rice, sugar beets, barley, cotton, fruits and nuts, sheep, karakul skins.
Major Minerals: Natural gas, coal, salt, lapis lazuli.
Foreign Trade (1970): Exports, $86,000,000; imports, $75,-000,000. *Chief trading partners* (1970)—USSR (took 38% of exports, supplied 34% of imports); India (19%—9%); United Kingdom (16%—4%).
Tourism: Receipts (1971), $10,800,000.
Transportation: *Motor vehicles* (1969), 49,000 (automobiles, 30,800); *major national airline,* Ariana Afghan Airlines.
Communications: *Telephones* (1972), 20,960; *newspapers* (1970), 18 (daily circulation, 101,000).

Khan (prime minister in 1953–63 and brother-in-law of the king) seized power with the assistance of the nation's largely Soviet-trained military forces. On July 18 his Central Committee named him founder and president of the Republic of Afghanistan.

Daud appointed a civilian cabinet with himself as prime minister, but governed mainly through the Central Committee. A new constitution, consistent with both Islamic and socialist ideals, was being written. The free press newspapers ceased publication, at least temporarily.

The new government thwarted a purported countercoup by arresting former Prime Minister Mohammed Hashim Maiwandwal and his followers. Maiwandwal reportedly committed suicide after admitting that he had a part in the attempted coup. The regime accused a "foreign power" (presumably Pakistan or a country operating through Pakistan) of complicity. Other countercoup rumors delayed reform, and policy and ideological disagreements among the power elite added to the suspense.

Economy. Bumper crops in 1973 helped Afghanistan recover from the famine threats of the preceding three years. Impetus from the Shafiq cabinet boosted internal development and increased exports. After the coup, a slowdown occurred as the republic sought to map its economic policies.

Foreign Affairs. Before the coup, Afghanistan moved toward closer relations with Iran and Pakistan, and a treaty governing the distribution of the Hilmand River waters was signed with Iran in March. The new republic declared its intention to remain nonaligned, but some observers noted an initial tilt toward the USSR—probably a natural reaction to the pro-Western sympathies of the monarchy. Although Iran immediately recognized the republic, the new regime was reexamining the Hilmand treaty. The Afghans expressed concern over arrests of opposition leaders in the North-West Frontier and Baluchistan Provinces of Pakistan, but hoped the problems of regional autonomy could be settled by peaceful means. Pakistan accused Afghanistan of meddling in its internal affairs. Relations among the three countries gradually were improving as the year ended.

LOUIS AND NANCY HATCH DUPREE
American Universities Field Staff

AFRICA

Drought victims on the Mali–Upper Volta border scramble for sacks of bran dropped by French army planes and intended for animals.

The year 1973 saw grave drought in the sub-Sahara region and in Ethiopia and continued ethnic conflict in central Africa. There seemed to be advances in coordination of guerrilla actions against Rhodesia and Portuguese Mozambique during the year, and France received several rebuffs from her former colonies.

INTRA-AFRICAN RELATIONS

Organization of African Unity (OAU). The 41-nation Organization of African Unity held its 10th heads-of-state meeting, a stormy one, in Addis Ababa, Ethiopia, May 26–29.

The dispute between Ethiopia and Somalia over the Ogaden Desert in southern Ethiopia, where most residents are nomadic Somalis, was submitted to arbitration at the meeting. Backed by the Arab nations, Somalia claims on ethnic grounds an area which Ethiopia says forms one third of its territory. The disputed area, over which fighting occurred in 1964, took on new importance recently when oil and natural gas were reportedly discovered there. The issue was turned over to an eight-member OAU mediation committee.

Libya, suspected of having encouraged Somalia's claim on Ethiopia, failed in an attempt to get the OAU headquarters moved from Addis Ababa to Cairo, Egypt. Libya's attempt was a protest against Ethiopia's diplomatic ties with Israel—ties that were broken by Ethiopia later in the year. Passing a milder resolution than Libya demanded, the OAU warned Israel that continued aggression against Arab nations might lead the OAU to take collective economic reprisals.

Most unexpected was the reconciliation between Uganda's president, Gen. Idi Amin, and Tanzania's president, Julius K. Nyerere, whose countries have had serious border clashes in the past two years. At the height of a speech in which Amin regaled OAU members with laughter, he suddenly advanced with outstretched hand to President Nyerere, who was obliged to return the proffered friendship. Ethiopia's emperor, Haile Selassie, headed a mediation committee that worked out agreements between these formerly hostile neighbors, opening the way for renewal of the East African Community composed of Kenya, Tanzania, and Uganda.

OCAM. Delegates to the Afro-Malagasy-Mauritius Common Organization, better known by its French acronym OCAM, met in Dakar, Senegal, in early August. Present members of the 12-year-old French-speaking economic unit include Senegal, the Ivory Coast, Gabon, Togo, Dahomey, Niger, Upper Volta, the Central African Republic, Rwanda, and Mauritius. Besides favorable economic arrangements with each other and with France, OCAM nations share an airline, Air Afrique; a postal and telecommunications system; a small merchant fleet; and cooperating schools that train personnel in road maintenance, animal husbandry, and cultural and language programs. The meeting reflected concern over the defection of six former members. Zaire and the Malagasy Republic (formerly Madagascar) withdrew in order to sell their sugar at higher prices in foreign markets. Mauritius is believed to have objected because some of its revenue from copper and iron-ore exports went to support poorer neighbors.

(*Continued on page 78*)

INFORMATION HIGHLIGHTS ON THE COUNTRIES OF AFRICA

Nation	Population (in millions) 1973 est.	Capital	Area (in sq. miles)	Head of State and/or Government (as of Jan. 1, 1974)
Sovereign Nations				
Algeria	15.5	Algiers	919,593	Houari Boumédienne, president
Botswana	.7	Gaborone	231,804	Sir Seretse Khama, president
Burundi	3.9	Bujumbura	10,747	Michel Micombero, president
Cameroon	6.2	Yaoundé	183,569	Ahmadou Ahidjo, president
Central African Republic	1.6	Bangui	240,535	Jean Bedel Bokassa, president
Chad	4.0	Fort-Lamy	495,754	Ngarta Tombalbaye, president
Congo	1.0	Brazzaville	132,047	Marien Ngouabi, president
				Henri Lopès, prime minister
Dahomey	2.9	Porto-Novo	43,483	Mathieu Kerekou, president
Egypt	36.9	Cairo	386,660	Anwar el-Sadat, president and premier
Equatorial Guinea	.3	Malabo (Santa Isabel)	10,831	Francisco Macias Nguema, president
Ethiopia	26.8	Addis Ababa	471,777	Haile Selassie I, emperor
				Aklilou Habte-Wold, prime minister
Gabon	.5	Libreville	103,346	Albert B. Bongo, president
Gambia, The	.4	Banjul	4,361	Sir Dauda K. Jawara, president
Ghana	9.9	Accra	92,099	I. K. Acheampong, chairman National Redemption Council
Guinea	4.2	Conakry	94,926	Sékou Touré, president
				Lansana Beavogui, premier
Ivory Coast	4.6	Abidjan	124,503	Félix Houphouët-Boigny, president
Kenya	12.0	Nairobi	224,959	Jomo Kenyatta, president
Lesotho	1.1	Maseru	11,720	Moshoeshoe II, king
				Leabua Jonathan, prime minister
Liberia	1.2	Monrovia	43,000	William R. Tolbert, president
Libya	2.1	Tripoli and Benghazi	679,360	Muammar el-Qaddafi, president Revolutionary Command Council
				Abdul Salam Jallud, prime minister
Malagasy Republic	7.5	Tananarive	226,657	Gabriel Ramanantsoa, head of governme
Malawi	4.8	Zomba	45,747	H. Kamuzu Banda, president
Mali	5.5	Bamako	478,765	Moussa Traoré, president
Mauritania	1.3	Nouakchott	397,954	Mokhtar O. Daddah, president
Mauritius	.9	Port Louis	720	Sir Raman Osman, governor-general
				Sir Seewoosagur Ramgoolam, prime minister
Morocco	17.4	Rabat	172,413	Hassan II, king
				Ahmed Osman, premier
Niger	4.2	Niamey	489,190	Hamani Diori, president
Nigeria	59.6	Lagos	356,668	Yakubu Gowon, president Federal Military Government
Rhodesia	5.6	Salisbury	150,803	Clifford W. Dupont, president
				Ian D. Smith, prime minister
Rwanda	3.9	Kigali	10,169	Juvenal Habyalimina, president
Senegal	4.2	Dakar	75,750	Léopold S. Senghor, president
				Abdou Diouf, premier
Sierra Leone	2.8	Freetown	27,700	Siaka P. Stevens, president
				Sorie I. Koroma, prime minister
Somalia	3.0	Mogadishu	246,200	Mohammed Siad Barre, president Supreme Revolutionary Council
South Africa, Rep. of	21.7	Pretoria and Cape Town	471,444	J. J. Fouché, president
				Balthazar J. Vorster, prime minister
Sudan	17.4	Khartoum	967,497	Jaafar al-Numeiry, president
Swaziland	.5	Mbabane	6,704	Sobhuza II, king
				Makhosini Dlamini, prime minister
Tanzania	14.3	Dar es Salaam	364,899	Julius K. Nyerere, president
Togo	2.0	Lomé	21,622	Étienne Eyadema, president
Tunisia	5.6	Tunis	63,170	Habib Bourguiba, president
				Hedi Nouira, premier
Uganda	9.3	Kampala	91,134	Idi Amin, president
Upper Volta	5.7	Ouagadougou	105,869	Sangoulé Lamizana, president
				Gérard Kango Ouedraogo, premier
Zaire	18.7	Kinshasa	905,565	Mobutu Sese Seko, president
Zambia	4.7	Lusaka	290,585	Kenneth D. Kaunda, president
				Mainza Chona, prime minister
Nonsovereign Nations				
Angola	6.1	Luanda	481,351	Overseas state of Portugal; administered by a governor-general
French Territory of the Afars and the Issas	.1	Djibouti	8,494	Overseas territory of France; administere by a council of government
Mozambique	8.2	Lorenço Marques	302,329	Overseas state of Portugal; administered by a governor-general
Portuguese Guinea (Guinea-Bissau)	.6	Bissau	13,948	Overseas province of Portugal; administered by a governor
South West Africa (Namibia)	.7	Windhoek	318,260	Status in dispute; claimed by South Africa and the United Nations; administered by South Africa
Spanish Sahara	.091	Aiún	102,700	Overseas province of Spain; administere by a governor-general

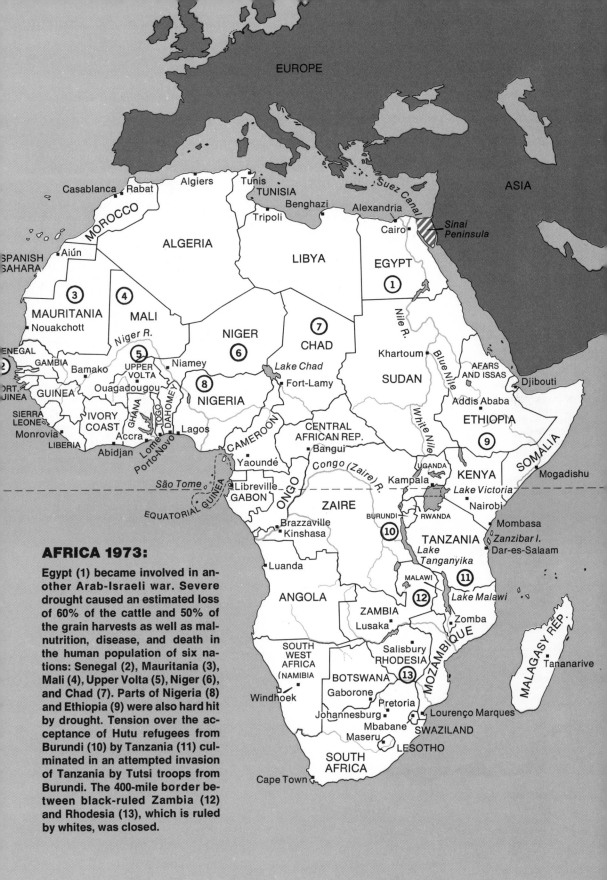

EUROPE

ASIA

Casablanca • Rabat
Algiers
Tunis
TUNISIA
Benghazi
• Tripoli
Alexandria
Cairo
Suez Canal
Sinai Peninsula

MOROCCO

ALGERIA

LIBYA

EGYPT ①

SPANISH SAHARA

• Aiún

MAURITANIA ③
• Nouakchott

MALI ④

NIGER

⑦
CHAD

Nile R.

Khartoum •

AFARS AND ISSAS
• Djibouti

Niger R.

⑥

Lake Chad
Fort-Lamy

SUDAN

Blue Nile

SENEGAL ②
GAMBIA
• Bamako
UPPER VOLTA ⑤
• Niamey
Addis Ababa •

ETHIOPIA

PORT. GUINEA
GUINEA
• Ouagadougou
⑧
NIGERIA

White Nile

⑨

SOMALIA

SIERRA LEONE
IVORY COAST
GHANA
TOGO
DAHOMEY
• Lagos
CENTRAL AFRICAN REP.

KENYA

Mogadishu •

Monrovia •
LIBERIA
• Accra
Lomé
Porto-Novo
• Abidjan
CAMEROON
• Bangui
UGANDA
• Kampala
Lake Victoria
Mombasa •

São Tome
• Yaoundé
Congo (Zaire) R.
Nairobi •

ONGO
• Libreville
GABON
ZAIRE
BURUNDI
RWANDA
Zanzibar I.

EQUATORIAL GUINEA

TANZANIA

Dar-es-Salaam

⑩
Lake Tanganyika
⑪

• Brazzaville
Kinshasa

• Luanda

MALAWI

ANGOLA
⑫
Lake Malawi
• Zomba

ZAMBIA
• Lusaka

MOZAMBIQUE

MALAGASY REP.

SOUTH WEST AFRICA (NAMIBIA)
Salisbury
RHODESIA
⑬
• Tananarive

• Windhoek
BOTSWANA
• Gaborone
Pretoria •
Lourenço Marques •

Johannesburg •
Mbabane •
SWAZILAND

Maseru •
LESOTHO

SOUTH AFRICA

Cape Town •

AFRICA 1973:

Egypt (1) became involved in another Arab-Israeli war. Severe drought caused an estimated loss of 60% of the cattle and 50% of the grain harvests as well as malnutrition, disease, and death in the human population of six nations: Senegal (2), Mauritania (3), Mali (4), Upper Volta (5), Niger (6), and Chad (7). Parts of Nigeria (8) and Ethiopia (9) were also hard hit by drought. Tension over the acceptance of Hutu refugees from Burundi (10) by Tanzania (11) culminated in an attempted invasion of Tanzania by Tutsi troops from Burundi. The 400-mile border between black-ruled Zambia (12) and Rhodesia (13), which is ruled by whites, was closed.

(*Continued from page 75*)
Others who have withdrawn are the Cameroon, Chad, and the Congo Republic. OCAM members were also concerned about criticism that they were being controlled economically by France and that they ignored the large English-speaking African bloc, including Nigeria. Senegal's president, Léopold S. Senghor, a principal backer, said, "If OCAM did not exist, we would have to invent it." A final communiqué reasserted that the union was vital to their interests and that they had "renewed dimensions of international cooperation."

Ethnic War in Burundi. Massacre flared again in tiny Burundi in central Africa, as it did in 1972 when over 50,000 of the majority but vassal Hutu people (making up 85% of the total population of 3.6 million) were killed by the ruling minority of Tutsi people. Many Hutus fled to their northern neighbor, Hutu-ruled Rwanda, and to camps in Tanzania. On May 12, vengeful Hutu students led ill-equipped Hutu refugees back into Burundi in an attempt to topple the hated Tutsi government of Col. Michel Micombero, but the Hutus were decimated. The UN and the OAU seemed powerless to halt the alleged genocide.

Tanzania's acceptance of Hutu refugees brought an invasion of Tutsi troops from Burundi on June 30, and eight Tanzanians were killed. Tanzanian dockworkers reacted by stopping the shipment of goods to and from landlocked Burundi. On July 12, Tanzanian troops repelled a new invasion of Burundi forces. The tension was relieved by a conciliating meeting of the presidents of the two countries on July 21, but Hutu deaths still occur and Hutus still stream into Tanzania for safety.

Guerrilla Warfare in Rhodesia. Guerrilla warfare escalated, particularly in northeast Rhodesia. In January 1973, after guerrillas attacked a bridge and police station at Mount Darwin, and several Rhodesian troops were killed by exploding land mines, Prime Minister Ian Smith closed Rhodesia's borders with Zambia, where guerrillas allegedly are based. On July 5, terrorists abducted nearly 300 black students and staff from a Catholic school near Centenary, most of whom were soon rescued by Rhodesian forces. Observers reported that Rhodesian and South African troops retaliated by helping Portuguese troops force guerrillas into ambushes near Tete, Mozambique.

AFRICA IN WORLD AFFAIRS

United Nations. UN delegates from 50 nations met on April 14 in Oslo, Norway, to discuss racism and colonialism in Africa. They urged the UN to adopt economic and cultural sanctions against South Africa. Leaders of nine nationalist groups from southern Africa came together for the first time in Oslo and called for UN support of armed struggle against white minority governments.

Britain and the United States vetoed a UN Security Council resolution on May 22 to extend UN sanctions against Rhodesia to South Africa and Portuguese Africa. Britain said that the resolution declared economic war against all of southern Africa. The United States argued that the resolution was unenforceable.

British Commonwealth. At the 32-nation Commonwealth conference in Ottawa, Canada, in early August, a variety of issues affecting Africa were raised, including opposition to the racial policies of white minority governments in South Africa,

Rhodesia, and the Portuguese areas, and a pledge to help independence movements there.

Arab-Israeli War. Before the fourth Arab-Israeli war began on October 6, Israel had diplomatic relations with 29 African countries. A month later these had shrunk to six: the Ivory Coast, Malawi, the Republic of South Africa, Botswana, Lesotho, and Swaziland. The reasons given for breaking ties include Israel's refusal to return occupied Arab territory and the threat of Arab economic retaliation. Since 1970, OAU leaders have taken even stronger pro-Arab, anti-Israeli stands. At a conference of nonaligned nations in Algeria in September, Col. Muammar el-Qaddafi of Libya offered compensation for any financial loss incurred by participating nations in a break with Israel. Saudi Arabia and Libya have already given such aid to some African countries that have broken with Israel. The swing away from Israel was encouraged by Arab financial aid to drought-stricken African states.

Anti-French Action. The year saw significant breaks away from France's economic and military influence. Demonstrations against French involvement in Chad affairs were led by President François Tombalbaye. Mauritania abandoned the franc zone, introduced its own new currency unit, and pulled its reserves out of Paris. In the Malagasy Republic, the forced removal of French military units, French withdrawal from the governor's mansion, and imposition of restrictions on French investors marked a revolution in relations. Observers wondered if the economies of these countries could survive this loosening of French ties.

Portugal: Alleged Mozambique Massacre. A London *Times* article of July 10 charged that Portuguese soldiers massacred over 400 men, women, and children on Dec. 16, 1972, in the village of Wiriyamu on the Nyantawatawa River for helping guerrillas fighting for Mozambique national liberation. The two Catholic priests cited as source of the massacre story were reported to be in prison in the Mozambique capital of Lourenço Marques. Priests who were expelled from the area later supported the massacre story, saying that it was the fourth and the worst mass killing in the area near the Rhodesia border in the past two years. Portuguese officials denied the story and said that neither the village nor the river appeared on their maps, but they promised to conduct an inquiry.

Portugal: Disputed Independence of Guinea (Bissau). National liberation guerrilla forces in Portuguese Guinea, or Guinea (Bissau), unilaterally declared independence from Portugal on September 24. The guerrillas, who have been fighting Portuguese rule in the West African country since 1959, claim control of two thirds of the rural area.

Over 70 states have accorded diplomatic recognition to Guinea-Bissau. A UN General Assembly vote in November favoring admission was not expected to be ratified in the Security Council, since Britain and the United States, which abstained from the General Assembly vote, would probably veto it. Portugal, which still holds the towns, claims the independence declaration is "just a propaganda stunt."

United States. The United States continued to support Africa's development plans and political independence aims but did not interfere in South African and Portuguese African affairs. The United States was the largest contributor to the drought-stricken areas of West Africa. After President Idi Amin threatened to jail Americans, the United States

closed its embassy in Uganda. At the White House in October, President Richard M. Nixon met with President Félix Houphouët-Boigny of the Ivory Coast, President Mobuto Sese Seko of Zaire, and President Sangoulé Lamizana of Upper Volta.

DROUGHT

West Africa. Africa's worst drought of this century threatened some 25 million people living in the area of about 965,000 square miles known as the Sahel (Arabic for border) on the southern edge of the Sahara Desert in six formerly French-ruled countries: Mauritania, Senegal, Mali, Upper Volta, Niger, and Chad. The UN, especially its affiliated Food and Agriculture Organization, and the following nations, have cooperated in giving relief: the United States, Soviet Union, China, West Germany, France, Canada, Belgium, Italy, Spain, and the Netherlands. As of October, the United States had given most—$47 million out of a total international contribution of $154 million.

By November, after rain brought relief, UN officials said that the worst of the famine was past. Estimates hold that as a whole the six stricken nations have lost 60% of their cattle and 50% of their grain harvests. In order to survive, farmers ate the seeds for next year's harvest. With temperatures reaching 120°, livestock (particularly cattle) died in the millions from lack of water. Many cattle tenders, who were forced to migrate to towns in search of food, no longer have herds and will be unable to return to their former nomadic life. The drought's effects on the region's human population are incalculable. Malnutrition, disease, and deaths, especially of the very young and the aged, were widespread throughout the Sahel.

The drought, which came after six years of poor rains, has set back the pace of development in the six countries, four of which are included in the UN's list of the world's poorest countries. Ironically, improved Western-aided health standards have upset the precarious balance of soil, plant cover, animals, and man. The number of people and animals in the area has doubled in the last 30 years. The resulting overpopulation and overgrazing have reduced the limited supply of land capable of sustaining life, and an estimated 250,000 square miles (647,500 sq km) of the Sahel have become desert in the last half century.

Ethiopia. As of early November, deaths from a drought in central and northern Ethiopia numbered at least 50,000. A UN report held that the total could reach 100,000. Minor rains, which usually fall in February, did not materialize, and the crisis was felt by April and May. The sun burned much of the grain in the fields, causing cattle to die in large numbers from lack of fodder and water. In May, starving people from the provinces of Shoa, Wallo, and Tigre, all north of Addis Ababa, the capital, streamed into towns for food. The government established 13 refugee camps, and food and other relief supplies have been sent from abroad, with Britain alone contributing $300,000 plus food from government and private sources.

STOLEN ART WORKS

Wide publicity accompanied arrangements in November to return a stolen 100-year-old statue held in reverence by a West African tribal kingdom. To the 40,000 people of Kom, one of 17 independent kingdoms in the United Republic of Cameroon, the 64-inch wooden statue of a man embedded with slave beads and wearing a copper headpiece has great significance. On rare ceremonial occasions the statue, which symbolizes peace and the unity of the people, was brought out of its sanctuary. On Aug. 20, 1966, it was reported missing from the royal palace, and an anguished search for it proved fruitless. A substitute figure carved in 1968 was not accepted, and the people claimed that there would be no peace until Afo-A-Kom was found.

A more intensive search for the statue was undertaken by an American Peace Corps worker, Craig Kinzelman, then serving in the Cameroon. Kinzelman discovered a picture of the statue in a museum catalog, and it was verified to be the stolen Afo-A-Kom by a fellow Peace Corps worker, Evan Schneider. Among those whom Kinzelman alerted were Cameroon officials, the American ambassador to the Cameroon, the U. S. Department of State, and a New York *Times* reporter residing in the Cameroon. A New York *Times* article about the stolen statue induced Warren Robbins, director of the Museum of African Art in Washington, D. C., to raise $25,000 for the statue's purchase from Aaron Furman, the New York City art dealer who owned the statue and had offered it for sale for $60,000. In December, the statue was returned to the village from which it had been stolen, bringing jubilation to the king and people of Kom.

At the annual meeting of the African Studies Association in Syracuse, N. Y., in November, the Kom statue incident evoked discussion about suspected widespread thievery of African art. Art historians believe that much African art in museums was originally stolen and that the illicit traffic may be controlled by Muslim Africans, who lack reverence for the human image.

Stolen African art was also discussed at the UN on November 7. Zaire's representative proposed a resolution deploring the removal of art objects from poor countries. The Assembly was asked to initiate international action to insure prompt restitution of expropriated monuments, museum pieces, and other works of art.

ECLIPSE

On June 30 a rare eclipse of the sun caused darkness across 4,600 miles of Africa from Mauritania on the Atlantic to the Somalia Republic on the Indian Ocean. Near the juncture of Algeria, Mali, and Niger, the eclipse lasted 7 minutes and 3.9 seconds. Only two longer eclipses have occurred in the last 1,433 years. The next eclipse of this length will not occur until the year 2150.

Astronomers and other scientists from France, the Soviet Union, and the United States, along with amateur observers and the curious, monitored the eclipse, some from ships off Mauritania. Others, including scientists supported by the U. S. National Science Foundation, watched in Akjouti and Chinguetti, Mauritania, and at Loiyengalani on the southeastern shore of Kenya's Lake Rudolph. Two specially equipped planes followed the path of the eclipse: a U. S. Air Force jet and an Anglo-French Concorde. Anthropologists also observed the effects on primitive people of this most scientifically monitored eclipse of all time.

FRANKLIN PARKER
West Virginia University

AGNEW, Spiro T. See pages 20–21.

FOREIGN AGRICULTURE USDA

Harvesting wheat in Japan. Increasing amounts of wheat are imported to meet burgeoning consumer demand.

agriculture

In the United States, 1973 was the year for record farm production and major federal farm legislation. Preliminary estimates indicated that world agriculture production had rebounded from the weather-induced decline of 1972. This article is a general roundup of how agriculture fared in 1973 —production, trends, scientific developments, and other news. It consists of three sections: (1) World Agriculture; (2) U.S. Agriculture; and (3) U.S. Agricultural Research.

World Agriculture

World agricultural production became a critical concern in nearly every nation in 1973 because food and fiber stocks were at the lowest levels in at least 20 years. Preliminary reports indicated that world output recovered from the weather-induced production dip in 1972, which had caused scores of countries to scramble hard to find reserves to maintain their agricultural economies and to provide food for their people.

"The world food situation in 1973 is more difficult than at any time since the years immediately

following the devastation of the second World War," declared Addeke H. Boerma, director general of the United Nations Food and Agriculture Organization (FAO). "There is . . . little if any margin against the possibility of another widespread harvest failure in 1973," he added, "and the world has become dangerously dependent on current production and hence on weather conditions."

If early indications hold, world output of agricultural, fishery, and forest products in 1973 will rise substantially above the 1972 index number of 123 (1961–65 average = 100).

Because most agricultural products are consumed in the year following production, shortages pinched hard in some areas in 1973, particularly in the developing lands. "Per capita food production in the developing countries . . . has now fallen back to the level of 1961–65," Boerma said.

It was some relief, then, to note that production prospects in 1973 were brighter than the results in 1972. The stakes were so huge that the U.S. Department of Agriculture (USDA) took an unusually hard look at the situation late in 1973.

USDA Grain Report. The USDA findings were presented in a paper by USDA economist William R. Gasser at conference in Atlanta on October 1–3. He focused on grain production, the key indicator of worldwide farm output. Total grain production was up in the United States, Canada, Australia, the USSR, and China. European and Indian grain outputs were almost equal to their 1972 levels, and Indian coarse-grain production was up substantially. Rice production also was up in major producing regions. Total world grain production for 1973 was estimated at almost 900 million metric tons. The USDA called it "an unprecedented leap" of 50 million tons above the production in 1972, and the 1973 total was 30 million tons more than the previous record in 1971.

This sharp increase mainly was due to high prices and strong demand for nearly all grains, which encouraged farmers to increase plantings and use better seeds and fertilizers. Also, more favorable weather and crop conditions in key areas, including South Asia and the USSR, boosted prospects. Gasser cautioned, however, that late-year crop failures were possible in China and the USSR. He also noted that the disastrous drought in West Africa continued, and that Turkey, Syria, Cyprus, Jordan, and North Africa also suffered drought.

Despite the setbacks of 1972, mainly from unfavorable weather in the Soviet Union and other key production areas, the "green revolution" continued to have an impact during 1973. "The misfortunes experienced in Asia," Gasser reported, "highlight the problems of applying the improved technology rapidly enough to increase output sufficiently to keep up with population growth." Without the higher-yielding grain varieties, India's drought-reduced output, for example, would have been as much as 20% lower, he said.

In 1973, floods in Pakistan were the most severe in history. The August floods damaged or destroyed about one million tons of stored wheat and about 600,000 tons of the rice crop. However, Bangladesh recorded a 20% gain in food-grain production.

In Africa and the Middle East, 1973 was not a good farm year. Droughts in northern, eastern, and southern Africa were overshadowed by an extreme drought in Mauritania, Mali, Chad, Senegal, Upper Volta, and Niger, where decimation of livestock by

the drought will have long-term effects. Herd losses were as high as 80%.

FAO Proposals. In a series of international meetings in late 1973, the Food and Agricultural Organization submitted proposals aimed at easing the precarious food and fiber situation. Director General Boerma called on governments "to take cooperative action ... by increasing export availabilities and economizing on nonhuman uses of wheat and at the same time to share available supplies according to some internationally acceptable criteria so as to ensure distribution on an orderly and fair basis to all countries." He also called for talks on ways to achieve international agricultural adjustments to "reduce the wide and dangerous fluctuations in world food supplies and prices."

WORLD FARM OUTPUT

In late 1973, the FAO issued preliminary data on world farm output in 1972. Total and per capita food production declined in developed and less-developed regions. The decline was severe in South Asia, East Asia, Latin America, and Africa.

Major factors were winterkill and a dry summer that cut Soviet grain output. Drought cut grain crops in Argentina and Australia. A below-normal monsoon reduced India's grain production. Drought and typhoons damaged Philippine rice and corn crops. A wet fall hampered the U. S. corn and soybean harvest. Peru's anchovy catch failed, cutting high-protein fishmeal output for livestock feeding. Mauritania, Mali, Chad, Senegal, Upper Volta, and Niger had a fifth consecutive year of severe drought.

North America. In 1972, total farm output in North America approximately equaled the record level of 1971, which was about 10% above the 1968–70 average. A decrease of about 6% in Canada's total production was offset by a slight increase in the U. S. output, according to the FAO.

In Canada, grain harvests in 1972 were down 10% from 1971. The wheat crop was about the same as in 1971 but it was still 25% below the 1965–69 average. A 10% increase in plantings was offset by lower yields. Canadian feed-grain output in 1972 was off 15% from the 1971 output. Oilseed production was lower by nearly a third, with most of the decline being in rapeseed. The 1972 sugar-beet output in Canada was lower, too. Canada's beef production rose by more than 2% in 1972, and its herd of beef animals has been increasing. Its milk output was up slightly, while its pork output was down 5%, and its egg production was lower.

Latin America. In 1972, farm production in Latin America rose by 1% over 1971, but per capita output declined by 1%. The FAO data showed that Argentina, Colombia, and Peru had relatively good years, but that Brazil and Chile fell behind, especially in wheat production. Latin America's totals for leguminous seeds, oil seeds, tobacco, cotton, citrus fruit, and other fruit were all higher than in 1971. Sugar output was up in Argentina, Bolivia, Brazil, Columbia, and Peru, but down in Cuba and several other countries. The better wheat crops in Argentina, Colombia, and Peru were counterbalanced by an extremely poor crop in Brazil and a reduced crop in Chile. Latin America's total wheat output of some 12.4 million tons was better than in 1971.

Nicaragua suffered setbacks from severe drought. Paraguay's crops of soybeans and cotton were much better in 1972 but below 1970 records. Belize (British Honduras) suffered from too much rain,

and Mexico lost yields to dry weather. Barbados, Costa Rica, the Dominican Republic, El Salvador, Guatemala, Guyana, and Haiti had spells of drought that hurt crops and grazing.

Western Europe. Outstanding farm output in 1972 in Western Europe matched the bumper harvests of 1971, according to the FAO. France had the highest gain, 10% over the previous year. Wheat harvested in the 20 countries in Western Europe was down about 1%. Barley output rose 4% to record highs. Oats were down, but corn production continued its upward trend. Sugar-beet output was down 9%, and potato plantings continued to decline in several countries. Milk and cheese production rose. France became the world's leading butter producer, as its 1972 output of 515,000 tons exceeded that of the United States. Beef output declined 6% in Western Europe in 1972; mutton and lamb production were off slightly, too, but pork production rose slightly.

Eastern Europe. Despite the severe crop failures in the USSR, farm results in eastern Europe were generally good in 1972. FAO data showed that expansion in total output was fastest in Rumania. Poland's growth rate greatly exceeded expectations; moreover, its livestock sector expanded more rapidly than total output and recorded the highest rate of increase in eastern Europe. Crop production rose rapidly in Hungary and Bulgaria, but livestock in both countries contributed little to the overall expansion. Results in Czechoslovakia and East Germany were good, based on a fairly balanced performance of the livestock and grain sectors.

In contrast, the Soviet output was disappointing. Production in 1972 was down 4.6%, reflecting an 8% decline in crop production and only small gains in livestock production. A harsh and dry winter damaged at least one third of the plantings, and then a prolonged drought hit some of the most fertile areas in the west. However, crops were good in Kazakhstan, the Urals, and Siberia. Tractors, combines, trucks, and other materials were rushed to these remote regions to make the most of the harvest.

Middle East. Farm output in the Middle East in 1972 was consistent with recent trends, being up 5% over the previous year. According to the FAO, cereal production was 10% more than that of the good results of 1971. Record grain crops were produced in Iraq and Syria, and output also was good in Egypt, Iran, Jordan, Lebanon, Libya, and Saudi Arabia. Turkey's grain output was down 12% but other Turkish crops, such as vegetables, legumes, and cotton, were above levels of a year earlier. Iran's output of most crops was better than in 1971, but droughts cut output in Cyprus and Yemen.

Africa. FAO data showed that a 2% growth in agricultural production in Africa in 1972 was not shared by all countries. Favorable weather allowed considerable expansion in production in northwest Africa, while the output in East and Central Africa recovered from the drought-affected levels of 1971. West Africa's plight from prolonged drought bordered on famine, and the FAO pressed international emergency relief because of drastic food shortages in large areas of Chad, Gambia, Mali, Mauritania, Niger, Senegal, and Upper Volta. Drought also affected southern Africa, where production fell sharply.

Far East. In the developing lands of the Far East, failure of the monsoon in 1972 resulted in poor farm performance in most regions. Output fell by about 3%, according to the FAO. The decline in

agricultural production was particularly sharp in India, which accounts for nearly half of the regional output. Bangladesh, Nepal, and Indonesia also suffered. The Philippines sustained losses from floods, but output was higher in Pakistan.

In China, grain production fell 4% in 1972, 240 million tons below the record level in 1971. The year was the driest in north China since 1921, and natural disasters were prevalent countrywide.

Japan's downtrend in farm production was halted in 1972. The rice crop was larger than in 1971 by 9%, but harvests of wheat, barley, oats, and maize were reduced because plantings were smaller.

Oceania. Serious drought hurt Australia, where the wheat harvest dropped 25% and was less than half the record crop of 1968. Outputs of barley and oats were reduced by about 50%. In New Zealand, however, wheat and other grains were produced in quantities only slightly below the record 1971 levels.

JOE WESTERN, *Kominus Agri-Info Associates*

U. S. Agriculture

U. S. agriculture prospered in 1973. Farm production in the United States broke all records, exceeding by far even the record levels of 1972. The incredible outpouring of U. S. food and fiber came after a year of worldwide agricultural shortages—especially in the USSR—that made world trade expand greatly and pushed prices far above the previous levels for most commodities.

Nevertheless, the increased U. S. production and a larger worldwide agricultural output barely met the rising demand and fell short of providing stocks for rebuilding depleted food reserves. Consequently, the U. S. Congress enacted drastic new farm legislation aimed at encouraging production. The new law departed sharply from the practices and policies that had prevailed during the past four decades, in which the planting of crops was restricted by the U. S. government and payments and subsidies were given to farmers to compensate for any loss of income resulting from the restrictions. The new legislation moved U. S. farmers closer to full competitiveness in the world market.

New Legislation. The new farm bill was signed into law by President Richard M. Nixon on August 10 and was to be effective for four years, beginning in 1974. Restrictions were ended on the planting of almost all crops except peanuts, rice, tobacco, and sugar. The old system of payments and price supports being used to persuade farmers to reduce plantings was suspended and replaced with a new system of "target prices." Target prices were established for the key crops of corn, wheat, and cotton. If market prices fell below these, the government would pay farmers the difference, based on normal yields on allotment acreages. Farmers would also then be eligible for price-support loans from the government at lower levels. If market prices remained above the target prices, no payments were to be made and loans would be available only at the lower levels.

Target prices were to be as follows: for wheat, $2.05 a bushel, well below the July 1974 futures price (as of Sept. 13, 1973) of $4.08; for corn, $1.38 a bushel, below the December 1974 futures contract price of $2.13 a bushel; and for cotton, 38 cents a pound, below the December 1974 futures price of 54 cents a pound. The target prices were to be adjusted later to take into account changes in costs and per-acre yields. The price-support loan level for wheat was $1.37 a bushel; for corn, $1.10 a bushel; and for cotton, 25 cents a pound.

At the option of the secretary of agriculture, farmers may be required to set aside certain acreages from production. For 1974 crops, however, Secretary of Agriculture Earl L. Butz announced there would be no limits on the planting of wheat, feed grains, and cotton.

Government payments of any kind were limited to $20,000 per person. This is a major development, as the limit since 1970 had been $55,000 per *crop*, and before 1970 there had been no limitation on government payments.

Another major change imposed by the new law was that the price targets were in specific dollar figures. Previous U. S. agricultural price policies had aimed at achieving a certain percentage of "parity."

Hatchery workers in Georgia kill baby chicks to protest the freeze on meat prices while the cost of feed rises.

Parity was the yardstick used for four decades to measure the purchasing power of farmers in terms of production, based on the period of 1910–14, when farmers were supposedly receiving "fair" prices for their products.

Production. In 1973, U. S. farm output of crops and livestock reached an index number of 115 (1967 = 100), up from the previous record of 111 in 1972, and far above the index of 95 a decade earlier.

Plantings for harvest totaled about 317 million acres in 1973, up 26 million acres from 1972. Yields per acre were high for many crops, but not record breaking. One reason was that the increase in planting brought into use some less productive land. The larger crop production offset smaller livestock, dairy and poultry output, resulting in an increase in total farm output in 1973.

Production of corn was at a record high in 1973, with nearly 5.7 billion bushels, up 2% from 1972, Sorghum grain totaled a record 971 million bushels, up 18% from the previous year's yield. Corn, sorghum, oats and barley are the major livestock feed grains. The total tonnage of all four feed grains was a record 208 million tons, 4% more than in 1972.

Total production of grains raised for foods was 57.3 million tons in 1973, up 11% from the previous year. The wheat crop was a record 1.7 billion bushels, up 12% from 1972, but the output for rye and rice were down from the previous year.

The output of oilseeds—soybeans, peanuts, cottonseed, and flaxseed—totaled a record 54.7 million tons, up 19% from 1972. The most important of the oilseed crops in 1973 was the soybean crop, with a record volume of nearly 1.6 million bushels, up 23% from 1972.

Production of livestock was down in 1973, sinking below even the low output of the previous year. Rising feed costs, severe weather and its effects on the weight of the animals, a consumer boycott occasioned by record-breaking meat prices, and a price freeze on red meats all contributed to holding down production.

The spring pig crop failed to meet expectations, and spring replacements of feeder cattle were off sharply. The restricted supplies of cattle and hogs for slaughter in the spring pushed prices substantially above 1972 levels.

Milk production was down 3% in 1973, from the 120.3 billion pounds of 1972. The reason was that the sharp rise in feed costs had led farmers to feed less grain to their cows, causing production to decline despite high consumer demand. The high beef prices encouraged many dairy farmers to cull and liquidate marginal dairy cows, accelerating the long-term drop in the number of U. S. cows.

Income. Rocketing prices and a growing worldwide demand for food enriched U. S. farmers in 1973 as never before. The increased demand stemmed from production failures in many parts of the world and rising personal incomes. In addition, devaluations of the U. S. dollar in 1973 made U. S. goods substantially cheaper in export markets.

Gross sales of farm products in 1973 were estimated at $82.5 billion, up from $69 billion a year earlier. At times in 1973, realized net farm income was running at a projected annual rate of nearly $25 billion, some $5 billion more than the record 1972 rate. The jump in net income was achieved despite an unusually high rise in expenses for feed, fertilizer, seed, and other needed products.

Retail food prices rose sharply in 1973 despite indications of larger crops. Smaller reserve stocks, supply disruptions, continued uncertainty over supplies of livestock-related products, and a sustained demand in domestic and foreign markets kept an upward pressure on prices.

For all of 1973, retail food prices averaged 20% above those in 1972. In an effort to slow the rise in prices of domestic food and feed, President Nixon in midyear ordered export controls on some strategic products, mainly soybeans and related products.

Consumption. The per capita food consumption for the United States in 1973 declined for the first time since 1965, falling an estimated 1% below that of 1972. A 2% dip in livestock-related foods outweighed a 1% increase in crop foods. The index of per capita consumption for 1973 was placed at 102.7 (1967 = 100), down from 103.7 in 1972.

Meat and egg consumption was off the most, followed by poultry. Fish and dairy consumption stayed about the same. There were sharp increases in the consumption of fruit, processed vegetables, processed potatoes, and vegetable oils. There were declines in consumption of fresh vegetables and potatoes, coffee, and cocoa.

Consumer resistance to higher prices and limited supplies caused the drastic decline in the consumption of most livestock-related foods. The per capita consumption of red meat dropped 5% below that of 1972, and the consumption of chicken fell 2%.

Exports. The poor 1972 crop year in many parts of the world, a sharp increase in demand, and the two devaluations of the U. S. dollar—making American goods cheaper abroad—combined to push farm exports to a record high of $12.9 billion in the 1973 fiscal year. The total was 60% higher than that of the previous fiscal year.

The realignment of foreign currencies in relation to the U. S. dollar resulted in a 20% to 35% increase in purchasing power in many European countries and an increase of about 27% in Japan. Foreign buyers swarmed after U. S. cotton, tobacco, feed grains, fruits, vegetables, nuts, and meat products. As developing countries advanced economically the amount of U. S. farm exports to them steadily increased. Farm exports to developing Asian countries totaled $2.2 billion in the fiscal year, up $600 million from the preceding fiscal year.

Assets and Land Values. The value of U. S. farm real estate on Jan. 1, 1973, was $258.7 billion, up from $230.5 billion a year earlier. With other assets added in, the total assets of U. S. farmers on Jan. 1, 1973, were valued at $383.5 billion, up from $341.1 billion a year earlier. Farmers' debts totaled $73.6 billion, up from $66.9 billion. So the net worth of U. S. farmers on Jan. 1, 1973, was $309.9 billion, up from $274.2 billion a year earlier. The farmers' debt-asset ratio thus declined from 19.6% to 19.2% in one year.

JOE WESTERN, *Kominus Agri-Info Associates*

U. S. Agricultural Research

Agricultural research in the United States has been a function of the federal government since 1839, when the U. S. Congress appropriated $1,000 for "the collection of agricultural statistics, and for other agricultural purposes." Today, the Agricultural Research Service (ARS) of the Department of Agriculture is the principal agricultural research agency of the federal government.

The chief objective of ARS is to carry on a balanced program of agricultural research and development that gives consideration to improving the well-being and living conditions of the people and to increasing the efficiency of production of crops and livestock. During fiscal year 1973, Congress appropriated $203 million for ARS research in areas ranging from the improvement of farm practices to human nutrition.

Beef Production Research. Intensive research efforts are currently underway at ARS to help farmers produce more meat—especially beef. They involve breeding, feeding, and management research, more attention to improving pasture, range, and forage production, and research on ways of increasing the protein content and quality of feed grains.

One ARS study, for example, showed that, generally, young bulls will produce 25% to 40% more lean meat than steers on the same diet. A related study showed that Holstein-Friesian dairy steers may become an even more important source of beef. Tests showed that such steers produced acceptable carcasses and gained as well, if not better, in the feedlot than steers of the Hereford breed.

Another ARS study found that heat stress can affect the estrous cycle of heifers. The scientists found that feeding the heifers a high-energy, low-fiber diet and providing plenty of water will help the cattle adjust when moved from cold to hot climates just prior to the breeding season.

The percentage of unsaturated fats in beef can be increased through selective feeding. ARS research shows that the greatest changes to beef carcass fat composition are likely to come from feeding "protected" polyunsaturated oils to cattle. The "protection" involves treating polyunsaturated vegetable oil—a mixture of safflower oil and casein—with formaldehyde. This prevents the oil from becoming saturated as it passes through the cow's digestive system.

Several million acres of once-productive rangeland in arid and semiarid areas that were lost to noxious shrubs can now be regained for grazing. ARS scientists at Las Cruces, N. Mex., developed and tested equipment that will uproot shrubs, make a good seedbed, plant seed, and distribute brush over the seeded strip to shade the ground—all in a single pass over the land. On planting trials in New Mexico, about 50% of the seedings using the experimental machine were considered successful.

Plant Protein Research. Current research efforts aimed at producing more protein from plants center on genetic improvement, better control of weeds, insects, and diseases, improved harvest equipment, and better understanding of the plants' total nutritional needs. For example, scientists have found that one bacterium inhibits the activity of other bacteria in soybeans. This may provide an approach to the biological control of the most costly and widespread of soybean diseases—bacterial blight—which is responsible for an average annual loss of 2.2% of the soybean crop.

Protein from cottonseed may soon reach the dinner table because of a newly developed milling process now ready for commercial use. When run through the ARS-developed "Liquid Cyclone Process" (LCP), each 100 tons of cottonseed should yield about 25,000 pounds of high-quality edible flour that contains about 65% protein. Thus, cottonseed flour could make a major contribution toward easing the global problem of protein malnutrition.

Pest Control. Insects that eat and otherwise destroy crops receive priority attention from ARS scientists, who estimate that we are in a continuing fight against 10,000 kinds of insects, 1,500 plant diseases, and 256 animal diseases that are already established in the United States.

One answer is the use of integrated pest management programs against insect enemies. This approach maximizes the use of naturally beneficial insects, but also relies on other techniques—chemical, cultural, biologic, and genetic. Crops now included under integrated programs are cotton, apples, alfalfa, sweet corn, and tobacco.

Initial field tests of muscalure, a newly identified sex attractant for houseflies, show that the attractant more than triples the flies' response to the traps and baits currently in use. Muscalure's potential value in reducing the need for insecticides is greatly enhanced by its ability to attract both males and females.

In a related study, ARS scientists found that resmethrin, a synthetic insecticide related to pyrethrum, is exceptionally effective against both flies and cockroaches when it is applied as a superfine dust. Applied in a confined area, it knocks down stable flies within 10 minutes and houseflies within 30 minutes. Within a few hours of knockdown, the flies are dead. Roaches exposed to resmethrin die within 24 hours. Resmethrin is virtually harmless to warm-blooded animals.

Environmental Research. Conservation and proper management of the soil, water, and air are, in essence, the preservation of life itself. The Agricultural Research Service is rising to the challenge of ensuring clean air and water with studies on sediment, erosion, drainage, and irrigation. These studies range from water harvesting—collecting water from areas that have been treated to increase rain and snow runoff—to studies of the usefulness of current weather modification programs, such as the seeding of clouds to produce rain. Other studies include responses of various plants to air pollution, effects of heavy metals upon soils, and the impact of air pollutants upon plant food chains and agricultural productivity.

Composting Sewage. New ways of coping with municipal sewage sludge are being investigated. As with the problem of disposing of livestock and poultry manure, it may prove practical to distribute the municipal sludge on cropland to improve soil nutrients. A team of scientists incorporated a variety of industrial and domestic sludge into a 75-acre test site at Beltsville, Md. In one field trial, the sludge was buried in trenches 2 feet wide and 2 to 4 feet deep, then covered with a 1-foot layer of soil. Other incorporation methods, such as deep disking or rotary tilling, are also being tested. Drain lines have been installed that empty into a man-made pond so that groundwater and surface runoff can be captured, controlled, and studied.

These experiments will enable the scientists to determine the amount of sludge that can be applied to land for maximum benefit and minimum hazard. The study has led to large-scale testing of composting sewage sludge by environmental agencies in the Washington, D. C., area.

MARCELLA M. MEMOLO
U. S. Agricultural Research Service

AIR FORCE, U. S. See DEFENSE FORCES.
AIR TRANSPORTATION. See TRANSPORTATION.

ALABAMA

The year 1973 was a legislative year in Alabama, and although there were other important developments in the state, most of the more noteworthy events involved the state legislature.

Reapportionment. Alabama's legislature convened in regular biennial session on May 1, but immediately recessed to meet in special session to deal with the reapportionment question. The purpose of the session was to develop a reapportionment plan that the federal courts might accept in lieu of the plan they had ordered into effect in January 1972.

The legislature enacted a reapportionment plan that, like the court plan, provided for single-member legislative districts. One of the major objections voiced against the court plan had been that it failed to give sufficient consideration to existing precinct and county lines. Consequently, the legislature's plan followed established county and precinct boundaries more closely.

The legislative plan was criticized as racially and politically gerrymandered to the disadvantage of the black population and to the advantage of incumbent legislators. In August, the court rejected the legislature's plan and ordered full compliance with its original plan so that it might be effectively implemented at the 1974 elections.

Regular Legislative Session. In contrast to previous sessions, the legislature passed appropriations measures well before the end of the regular session in September. The appropriations for the current biennium included $262 million for the general operations of the state government, $1.17 billion for education, and $81 million for mental health. The legislature also approved a bond issue totaling approximately $180 million to finance capital improvements in the state educational system. These appropriations amounted to a major breakthrough in fiscal support, but in other areas the regular session of the legislature was characterized by factionalism and controversy. As a result, few measures of importance were enacted.

The major bill enacted was a controversial ethics law that requires legislators and state officials to make public disclosure of their personal finances. It also prohibits them from receiving any other governmental income or from having any financial interest in any firm that does business with the state. The measure was also applicable to newsmen who cover the state legislature or the state government. This provision was challenged in court immediately after its enactment into law.

The legislature also proposed a constitutional amendment designed to revise the existing provisions of the constitution relating to the state judiciary. In May, a constitutional study commission recommended a proposed new constitution for the state, and the amendment substantially paralleled the judicial article proposed by the constitutional commission. The amendment provided for the establishment of a unified structure of courts operating under the general supervision of the chief justice of the state supreme court. The original proposal would have replaced the present heterogeneous set of local inferior courts with a uniform system of district courts. However, the measure was amended in the legislature to permit municipalities to retain their present municipal courts if they so desired. Voters approved the amendment in a special referendum held on December 18.

──────── ALABAMA • Information Highlights ────────

Area: 51,609 square miles (133,667 sq km).
Population (1972 est.): 3,510,000. *Density:* 69 per sq mi.
Chief Cities (1970 census): Montgomery, the capital, 133,386; Birmingham, 300,910; Mobile, 190,026; Huntsville, 137,802.
Government (1973): *Chief Officers*—governor, George C. Wallace (D); lt. gov., Jere Beasley (D); secy. of state, Mabel Amos (D); atty. gen., William Baxley (D); treas., Agnes Baggett (D); supt. of education, LeRoy Brown; chief justice, Howell T. Heflin. *Legislature*—Senate, 35 members (33 Democrats, 2 vacancies); House of Representatives, 106 members (99 D, 2 R, 1 National Democratic party of Alabama, 4 vacancies).
Education (1972–73): *School enrollment*—public elementary, 407,737 pupils, 16,523 teachers; secondary, 375,646 pupils, 17,207 teachers; nonpublic, 54,300 pupils, 2,370 teachers; colleges and universities, 110,514 students. *Public school expenditures*, $432,282,000 ($590 per pupil). *Average teacher's salary*, $8,262.
State Finances (fiscal year 1971): *Revenues*, $1,519,367,000 (4% general sales tax and gross receipts taxes, $230,852,000; motor fuel tax, $123,603,000; federal funds, $483,801,000). *Expenditures*, $1,405,080,000 (education, $636,476,000; health, welfare, and safety, $277,442,000; highways, $266,787,000). State debt, $769,941,000 (Sept. 30, 1971).
Personal Income (1972): $11,699,000,000; per capita, $3,333.
Public Assistance (1972): $230,839,000. *Average monthly payments* (Dec. 1972)—old-age assistance, $71.61; aid to families with dependent children, $75.03.
Labor Force: *Nonagricultural wage and salary earners* (July 1973), 1,103,100. *Average annual employment* (1972)—manufacturing, 327,800; trade, 205,660; government, 219,600; services, 143,400. *Insured unemployed* (Sept. 1973)—13,300 (1.6%).
Manufacturing (1971): *Value added by manufacture*, $4,530,900,000. Primary metal industries, $731,400,000; chemicals and allied products, $532,900,000; textile mill products, $404,100,000; paper and allied products, $394,000,000; apparel and othe, textile products, $343,400,000; food and kindred products, $340,200,000.
Agriculture (1972): *Cash farm income*, $987,854,000 (livestock, $616,394,000; crops, $303,369,000; government payments, $68,091,000). *Chief crops* (in order of value, 1971)—Cotton lint; peanuts (ranks 3d among the states, 1972); soybeans; corn.
Mining (1972): Production value, $333,440,000 (ranks 21st among the states). *Chief minerals*—Coal, $173,225,000; cement, $56,200,000; stone, $37,594,000; petroleum, $30,000,000.
Fisheries (1972): *Commercial catch*, 39,564,000 pounds ($18,326,000). *Leading species by value*, shrimp, $14,661,000; croaker, $1,174,000; oysters, $701,000.
Transportation: Roads (1972), 79,036 miles (127,193 km); motor vehicles (1972), 2,092,971; railroads (1972), 4,567 miles (7,350 km); public airports (1972), 90.
Communications: *Telephones* (1973), 1,762,900; *television stations* (1971), 16; *radio stations* (1971), 189; *newspapers* (1973), 24 (daily circulation, 743,000).

Other Events. In June, national attention was focused on the case of two black Montgomery girls who allegedly were sterilized—without their parents' informed consent—as a result of surgery arranged by the Montgomery community-action agency's family-planning clinic. The incident precipitated a review of the guidelines regulating the operations of federally financed family-planning agencies, but administrative changes at the state level were expected to result in closer state supervision of family-planning programs and more uniform requirements for the provision of sterilization surgery.

On the Fourth of July, Sen. Edward M. Kennedy of Massachusetts spoke at the "Spirit of America" celebration in Decatur, where Gov. George C. Wallace was presented with a patriotism award. Democratic National Chairman Robert Strauss also spoke at the meeting. The presence of these national political figures was widely interpreted as an effort toward unification of the Democratic party in anticipation of the 1976 presidential election.

Spring Storms. On the night of May 27, a series of tornadoes caused extensive damage to various localities in central and northeastern Alabama. The storms, which were among the most destructive in the state's history, caused many injuries and widespread destruction of homes and other property. Eight deaths were attributed to the severe weather.

JAMES D. THOMAS, *The University of Alabama*

ACRES OF PIPE to be used in the trans-Alaska oil pipeline, which was approved by the U. S. Congress in 1973, are stored in this yard in Valdez, Alaska.

ALASKA

The legal and political struggle to get on with the building of a pipeline from the Prudhoe Bay oil fields to the port of Valdez dominated the public activity of Alaskans in 1973.

Trans-Alaska Pipeline. The U. S. Circuit Court of Appeals on February 9 ruled the proposed trans-Alaska oil pipeline to be in conflict with provisions of the Mineral Leasing Act of 1920 and barred Secretary of the Interior Rogers C. B. Morton from granting Alyeska, a consortium of oil companies, a permit to construct the line. On April 2 the U. S. Supreme Court refused to hear an appeal.

Pipeline proponents, backed by the Nixon administration, then turned to Congress, where the Senate and House each passed divergent bills to amend the 1920 act and to authorize pipeline construction.

The conference committee compromise was passed by the House and the Senate on November 12 and November 13, respectively, and was signed by the President on November 16. The act granted a trans-Alaska oil pipeline right-of-way without further proceedings under the National Environmental Policy Act and limited the right of judicial review to constitutional grounds only. The Alyeska consortium must pay the full cost of control and removal of pollution directly created by its operations.

Native Claims. By the end of 1973, more than 77,000 Alaskan Eskimos, Aleuts, and Indians had been declared eligible for benefits under the Alaska

Native Claims Settlement Act of 1971. At least 5,000 other claims were rejected. Twelve native regional corporations and 170 native villages had been organized and were in the process of selecting lands made available to them under the act. These corporations will also share the $962.5 million monetary settlement. The largest corporation, Doyon Ltd., announced plans to build a two-story office building covering a half-block of downtown Fairbanks.

Legislation. In contrast to the long sessions of recent years, the 1973 legislative session ended on its 90th day. The state House of Representatives organized under a biparty coalition with Rep. Tom Fink, an Anchorage Republican, as speaker. The state Senate elected Terry Miller, Republican of Fairbanks, as its president.

The session was a quiet one. The lawmakers turned down Gov. William Egan's proposed tax increases and squelched a pay raise for state employees, but gave them improved health insurance coverage. They also passed a program that limited entry to the state's fisheries, adopted an occupational safety and health act, established a new employment security funding system, and authorized appointment of a student member to the Board of Regents of the University of Alaska. Finally, they adopted a budget of $352.9 million, about $4 million less than Governor Egan had requested.

Special Legislative Session. Governor Egan called the Legislature into special session on October

---

———— ALASKA · Information Highlights ————

Area: 586,412 square miles (1,518,807 sq km).
Population (1972 est.): 325,000. Density: 0.6 per sq mi.
Chief Cities (1970 census): Juneau, the capital, 6,050; Anchorage, 48,081; Fairbanks, 14,771; Ketchikan, 6,994; Kodiak, 3,798.
Government (1973): *Chief Officers*—governor, William A. Egan (D); lt. gov., H. A. Boucher (D); atty. gen., John E. Havelock (D); treas., Robert D. Stevenson; commissioner of education, Marshall L. Lind; chief justice, Jay A. Rabinowitz. *Legislature*—Senate, 20 members (11 Republicans, 9 Democrats); House of Representatives, 40 members (20 D, 19 R, 1 Independent).
Education (1972–73): *Enrollment*—public elementary schools, 58,155 pupils, 2,338 teachers; public secondary schools, 27,200 pupils, 1,804 teachers; nonpublic schools, 600 pupils, 60 teachers; colleges and universities, 11,698 students. *Public school expenditures*, $118,563,000 ($1,473 per pupil). *Average teacher's salary*, $15,176.
State Finances (fiscal year 1971): *Revenues*, $430,922,000 (total sales tax and gross receipts taxes, $22,238,000; motor fuel tax, $10,936,000; federal funds, $150,058,000). *Expenditures*, $475,714,000 (education, $187,593,000; health, welfare, and safety, $40,608,000; highways, $90,983,000). *State debt*, $300,533,000 (June 30, 1971).
Personal Income (1972): $1,678,000,000; per capita, $5,162.
Public Assistance (1972): $20,324,000. *Average monthly payments* (Dec. 1972)—old-age assistance, $125.46; aid to families with dependent children, $211.65.
Labor Force: *Nonagricultural wage and salary earners* (July 1973), 116,400. *Average annual employment* (1972)—manufacturing, 8,100; trade, 16,700; government, 40,700; services, 13,800. *Insured unemployed* (Sept. 1973)—3,400 (5.1%).
Manufacturing (1971): *Value added by manufacture*, $197,700,000; food and kindred products, $70,200,000; lumber and wood products, $26,200,000; printing and publishing, $14,200,000.
Agriculture (1972): *Cash farm income*, $4,767,000 (livestock, $2,841,000; crops, $1,729,000; government payments, $197,000). *Chief crops* (in order of value, 1971)—Hay, silage, potatoes, barley.
Mining (1972): *Production value*, $321,915,000 (ranks 23d among the states). *Chief minerals*—Petroleum, $237,340,000; sand and gravel, $35,102,000; natural gas, $31,080,000; coal, $6,000,000.
Fisheries (1972): *Commercial catch*, 390,137,000 pounds (80,733,000). *Leading species by value*, salmon, $32,700,000; crabs, $31,806,000; halibut, $10,517,000; shrimp, 3,242,000.
Transportation: *Roads* (1972), 7,817 miles (12,580 km); *motor vehicles* (1972), 150,655; *railroads* (1972), 544 miles (875 km); *public airports* (1972), 537.
Communications: *Telephones* (1970), 85,000; *television stations* (1971), 7; *radio stations* (1971), 19; *newspapers* (1973), 7 (daily circulation, 76,000).

17 to consider a revision of the oil legislation passed during the 1972 session. He told the lawmakers that he had worked out an agreement with the oil companies which, if approved by the Legislature, would avert a court suit contesting the constitutionality of parts of the 1972 oil package. In response, the Legislature adopted a 20-mill tax on property used in the exploration, production, and transportation of oil and natural gas and set limits on local taxation of such property. It also deleted two portions of the right-of-way leasing act that had been strongly opposed by the oil companies, but created a five-man regulatory pipeline commission.

Special Congressional Election. In a special election on March 6, voters elected state Sen. Don Young (R), to fill the unexpired term of U. S. Rep. Nick Begich (D), who had been missing since October 1972 and presumed dead in a plane crash. Young defeated state Democratic Chairman Emil Notti in a close race.

Education. Dr. Robert W. Hiatt was appointed president of the University of Alaska to replace the retiring president, William R. Wood.

The federal government transferred the Arctic Health Research Center and the Arctic Environmental Research Laboratory to the ownership and operation of the University of Alaska, on whose Fairbanks campus the facilities are located.

Economy. The 1973 salmon catch totaled only 1,134,353 cases, a record low for this century. However, prices were the highest in years.

Imports to the state jumped 8% in 1972 to $49 million, much of the increase consisting of jet fuels. Canadian imports increased, while those from Japan fell off considerably.

Alaska ranked 35th among the states receiving military contracts in 1972, with $107 million or 0.33% of the total.

RONALD E. CHINN
University of Alaska

ALBANIA

The Ideological and Cultural Revolution continued to dominate the domestic scene in the People's Republic of Albania (PRA) during 1973. Although the PRA persisted in its efforts to expand its ties with other nations, it also appeared to have strengthened its relations with China.

The Ideological and Cultural Revolution. Decrying the growth of "harmful foreign bourgeois influences," especially among the nation's youth, the regime ordered the removal of television antennas capable of receiving foreign transmissions. The Albanian leaders also launched campaigns to eliminate worker absenteeism and "vagabondism" and "hooliganism" among the young.

The Albanian Party of Labor (APL) initiated a new program of "mass ideological reeducation" to ensure the ultimate success of the Ideological and Cultural Revolution.

Enver Hoxha, first secretary of the APL, severely criticized the nation's intellectuals for their "liberal" and "anti-Marxist attitudes" in two major speeches, delivered on March 15 and June 26, respectively. APL Central Committee members Fadil Paçrami and Todi Lubonja, who maintained close ties with the intelligentsia, were dropped from that body and expelled from the party for "manifestations of liberalism" in the performance of their duties and in their private lives.

ALBANIA • Information Highlights

Official Name: People's Republic of Albania.
Location: Southern Europe, western coast of the Balkan peninsula.
Area: 11,100 square miles (28,748 sq km).
Population (1973) est.): 2,300,000. *Density,* 199 per square mile (77 per sq km).
Chief Cities (1970 est.): Tiranë, the capital, 171,300; Shkodër, 55,300; Durrës, 53,800.
Government: *Head of state,* Haxhi Lleshi, president of the presidium (took office 1953). *Head of government,* Maj. Gen. Mehmet Shehu, premier (took office 1954). First secretary of the Albanian Party of Labor, Gen. Enver Hoxha (took office 1941). *Legislature* (unicameral)—People's Assembly (all members of the Albanian Democratic Front).
Language: Albanian (official).
Education: *School enrollment* (1970)—primary, 555,300; secondary, 80,400; university/higher, 25,500.
Monetary Unit: lek (4.15 leks equal U. S.$1, June 1973).
Gross National Product (1971 est.): $1,040,000,000.
Industrial Production Index (1969), 195 (1963=100).
Manufacturing (major products): Processed foods, textiles, cement, tobacco products.
Major Agricultural Products: Corn, sugar beets, wheat, cotton, potatoes, tobacco.
Major Minerals: Chromium ore (ranks 4th among world producers, 1971), petroleum, lignite, copper, iron-nickel ore.
Foreign Trade (1964): *Exports,* $60,000,000. *Imports,* $98,-000,000. *Chief trading partners* (1964)—China (took 40% of exports, supplied 63% of imports); Czechoslovakia (19%—10%).
Transportation: *Railroads* (1971), 126 miles (203 km).
Communications: *Daily newspapers* (1972), 2 (daily circulation, 146,000).

Before this latest cultural crackdown had run its course, a number of officials had been removed from office, including the first secretary of the Union of Albanian Labor Youth, the chairman of the Albanian Writers and Artists Union, and the secretary of the presidium of the People's Assembly. By late 1973, the APL seemed to have tightened its grip over all aspects of Albanian culture.

Political and Economic Developments. Petro Dode was elected to the secretariat of the APL Central Committee in February. The Seventh Congress of the Union of Albanian Women, which met on June 11–14, reelected Vito Kapo as president. In December 1972, Myqerem Fuga had been appointed to head the newly created ministry of light and food industry.

According to the 1973 economic plan, industrial output was expected to be 10.4% greater and agricultural production was expected to be 6.6% higher than in 1972. During 1972 industrial production had risen by 10.5% and agricultural output had increased by 12.4%.

Foreign Relations. Sino-Albanian cultural exchanges increased during the year, and China continued to be Albania's chief trading partner. The Albanians also seem to have been pleased by the leadership and policy decisions of the 10th Congress of the Chinese Communist party.

Albania's relations with the USSR remained tense. The Albanians denounced Soviet Communist party leader Leonid Brezhnev's June visit to Washington and refused to participate in the 35-nation European Security Conference on the grounds that it was merely a "device to ensure Soviet hegemony in Europe."

During 1973, Albania established diplomatic relations with Malta, Nigeria, Senegal, Cameroon, Argentina, and Tunisia. The Albanians, however, ignored a U. S. overture to normalize relations and subsequently accused the United States of "plotting to overthrow the Allende government in Chile" and "encouraging and supporting Israeli aggression" against the Arabs.

NICHOLAS C. PANO
Western Illinois University

——————— ALBERTA · Information Highlights ———————

Area: 255,285 square miles (661,189 sq km).
Population (1972 est.): 1,666,000.
Chief Cities (1971 census): Edmonton, the capital (438,152); Calgary (403,319); Lethbridge (41,217); Red Deer (27,674); Medicine Hat (26,518).
Government: *Chief Officers* (1973)—lt. gov., J. W. Grant MacEwan; premier, Peter Lougheed (Progressive Conservative); atty. gen. and prov. secy., C. Mervin Leitch (P. C.); prov. treas., Gordon T. W. Miniely (P. C.); min. of educ., Louis D. Hyndeman (P. C.); chief justice, Sidney Bruce Smith. *Legislature*—Legislative Assembly: 75 members (49 Progressive Conservative; 24 Social Credit; 1 New Democratic party; 1 Independent).
Education: School enrollment (1969–70)—public elementary and secondary, 413,576 pupils (19,821 teachers); private schools, 5,342 pupils (317 teachers); Indian (federal) schools, 3,553 pupils (174 teachers); college and university, 28,551 students. *Public school expenditures* (1970)—$381,436,000; average teacher's salary (1970 est.), $8,489.
Public Finance (fiscal year 1973 est.): *Revenues,* $1,310,-900,000 (sales tax, $106,000,000; income tax, $299,600,000; federal funds, $273,400,000). *Expenditures,* $1,479,200,-000 (education, $455,500,000; health and social welfare, $525,000,000; transport and communications, $113,600,000).
Personal Income (1971): $5,544,000,000; average annual income per person, $3,405.
Social Welfare (fiscal year 1973 est.): $118,300,000 (aged and blind, $2,000,000; dependent and unemployed, $86,-900,000).
Manufacturing (1969): Value added by manufacture, $702,-810,000 (food and beverages, $172,374,000; nonmetallic mineral products, $68,378,000; fabricated metals, $67,-917,000; chemical and chemical products industries, $66,-221,000; primary metals, $52,346,000; wood industries, $50,501,000).
Agriculture (1972 est.): *Cash farm income* (exclusive of government payments), $901,581,000 (livestock and products, $517,882,000; crops, $371,392,000). *Chief crops* (cash receipts)—wheat, $164,921,000 (ranks 2d among the provinces); barley $68,918,000 (ranks 2d); rapeseed, $60,965,000 (ranks 2d); sugar beets, $12,162,000 (ranks 1st); potatoes, $11,796,000 (ranks 5th).
Mining (1972 est.): *Production value,* $1,926,571,000. *Chief minerals* (cash value)—crude petroleum, $1,247,064,000 (ranks 1st among the provinces); natural gas, $322,225,-000 (ranks 1st); natural gas by-products, $238,801,000 (ranks 1st); coal, $52,773,000 (ranks 2d); sulfur, $17,072,-000 (ranks 1st).
Forest Products (1969): Lumber, 429,133,000 board feet (ranks 4th among the provinces).
Transportation: *Roads* (1970), 97,425 miles (156,786 km); *motor vehicles* (1970), 768,759; *railroads* (1971), 6,245 track miles (10,050 km); *licensed airports* (1971 est.), 56.
Communications: *Telephones* (1970), 742,231; *television stations* (1972), 47; *radio stations* (1972), 22; *daily newspapers* (1972), 7.
(All monetary figures given in Canadian dollars.)

ALBERTA

Natural gas, oil, coal, wheat, and beef cattle claimed the attention of Albertans in 1973, as did labor unrest in transportation and other services. But bountiful crops and rising demand for agricultural products and fuel brought continued prosperity.

Legislation and Politics. The Legislative Assembly, which met from February 15 to May 10, approved a $1.5 billion budget, with no tax increases, and passed some 50 other bills. Chief among them was a property-tax reduction plan.

The government's candidate, Progressive Conservative Stewart McCrae, won the June 25 by-election to fill the assembly seat vacated by the death on February 25 of Leonard Werry, who was also a cabinet member. McCrae won easily over a field that included leaders of the Social Credit and Liberal parties. Premier Peter Lougheed announced the appointment of Helen Hunley as solicitor-general. She was the first woman to be named to a cabinet post in Alberta.

The most serious political controversy arose from actions of the federal government, first in imposing a temporary ban on beef exports and then in levying an export tax on crude oil. Albertans regarded both measures as attempts to control consumer prices in eastern Canada at the expense of western producers. Most of Canada's oil comes from Alberta, where 80% of oil and gas rights are provincially owned. With external trade under federal jurisdic-

tion and natural resources under provincial control, the confrontation promises to be prolonged.

Coal and Oil Sand. A coal-mining operation, developed for the Japanese market, encountered serious problems when a deep-pit mine was abruptly closed for cost reasons. A $1 billion oil-sand development, announced by Premier Lougheed in September, was jeopardized by the federal oil export tax.

J. W. CHALMERS, *University of Alberta*

ALGERIA

In 1973, Algeria was concerned with the Arab-Israeli conflict and the establishment of economic self-sufficiency. The nation was host to two important international conferences during the year.

Nonaligned Nations Conference. President Houari Boumédienne emerged as the acknowledged leader of the nonaligned nations at their fourth summit conference held in Algiers on September 5–9. Delegates, including 55 heads of state and government, ratified 90% of the resolutions offered by the Algerians and established a coordinating committee headed by Boumédienne, who also became their spokesman before the United Nations.

Stressing the Algerian theme of economic self-sufficiency, resolutions emphasized the necessity and right of participants to control foreign investments; restrict operations by multinational corporations; nationalize foreign companies while determining the amount and nature of compensation; and participate in worldwide trade and monetary negotiations. Boumédienne also announced the formation of a new development fund. Finally, the general Arab plan for the "Yom Kippur War" against Israel seems to have been worked out in private meetings among the heads of Middle Eastern states attending the conference.

Arab-Israeli War. On October 14–15, a week after the outbreak of the Arab-Israeli war, President Boumédienne went to Moscow as spokesman for the nonaligned nations and negotiator for the Arab nations involved in the war. He apparently helped solidify Soviet commitments to continue the flow of

——————— ALGERIA · Information Highlights ———————

Official Name: Democratic and Popular Republic of Algeria.
Location: North Africa.
Area: 919,593 square miles (2,381,741 sq km).
Population (1973 est.): 15,500,000. Density, 16 per square mile (6 per sq km).
Chief Cities (1966 census): Algiers, the capital, 943,142; Oran, 328,257; Constantine, 253,649; Annaba, 168,790.
Government: *Head of state,* Houari Boumédienne, president (took office June 1965). *Head of government,* Houari Boumédienne.
Languages: Arabic (official), French.
Education: *Expenditure* (1968), 17.6% of total public expenditure. *School enrollment* (1968)—primary, 1,585,682; secondary, 177,382; technical/vocational, 40,684; university/higher, 10,681.
Monetary Unit: Dinar (4.093 dinars equal U. S.$1, Aug. 1973).
Gross National Product (1971 est.): $5,300,000,000.
Economic Indexes: *Industrial production* (mining) (1970), 125 (1963=100); *agricultural production* (1971), 107 (1963=100); *consumer price index* (1967), 104 (1963= 100).
Manufacturing (major products): Processed foods, wine, liquefied natural gas, cement, petroleum products.
Major Agricultural Products: Wheat, citrus fruits, wine grapes, olives, dates, figs, tobacco, fish, livestock.
Major Minerals: Petroleum, natural gas, iron ore.
Foreign Trade (1971): *Exports,* $730,000,000; *Imports,* $1,162,-000,000. *Chief trading partners* (1970)—France (took 24% of exports, supplied 38% of imports); West Germany (24% —9%); Italy (7.5%—8.5%); USSR (6.6%—4%).
Transportation: *Motor Vehicles* (1971), 243,200 (automobiles, 137,200); *railroads* (1971), 2,417 miles (3,889 km); *major national airline,* Air Algérie.
Communications: *Telephones* (1972), 199,000; *newspapers* (1970), 4 (daily circulation, 275,000).

ALGERIAN Foreign Minister Abdel Aziz Bouteflika was chairman of the meeting of the foreign ministers of the nonaligned nations in Algiers in September.

Emigration to France. On September 19 the Algerian government suspended the emigration of Algerian workers to France until the Paris government could guarantee "the safety and dignity" of the 750,000 Algerians already there. The move followed the murder of 11 Algerians in France after a berserk Algerian killed a French bus driver in Marseilles in August. Some 25,000 Algerians a year sought jobs (mainly semiskilled) in France because of the lack of work at home. Nearly half of the able-bodied men in Algeria were unemployed or worked part-time, while Algerians in France sent about 10% of their salaries back to their families.

Oil and Agrarian Reform. Algerians raised crude oil prices from about $3.60 to $5 a barrel in November and cut production by 25% in solidarity with Arab policies, but also to conserve resources. Exploration for new oil sources intensified, with contracts being granted to several foreign companies. U. S. oil firms continued to operate in Algeria after November despite a boycott on shipments of natural gas and oil to the United States. Capital needs for developmental projects precluded total nationalization of foreign oil concerns in 1973.

There were intensified efforts during the year to mobilize popular support for the regime's programs of agrarian reform and socialist administration of industry, but the development of an enthusiastic mass response was hampered by the weakness of the labor unions and the National Liberation Front (FLN), Algeria's only political party, together with the domination of most institutions by the military. The regime's concentration on developing heavy industry with $1 billion of annual oil and gas revenues continued unabated in 1973.

STUART SCHAAR
Brooklyn College, City University of New York

arms to the Arabs at the moment that the United States announced its intention to rearm Israel.

Algeria sent Egypt two airborne fighter squadrons, one bomber squadron, and an armored brigade. Syria received Algerian medical supplies and personnel. In early November, Boumédienne met individually with Arab leaders who were confronted with problems over the cease-fire and U. S. Secretary of State Henry Kissinger's peace proposals.

The Algerians claimed that they neither accepted nor rejected the UN cease-fire, but would do what was best to enhance Arab unity. However, they had earlier argued that the war had to go on until the rights of the Palestinians had been guaranteed. Boumédienne foresaw a protracted guerrilla struggle within Israel, fought by Palestinians to a "final victory," as the only long-term solution. Egypt, faced with extraordinary Israeli and Great Power pressure, accepted Kissinger's cease-fire plan without sending Algiers progress reports on negotiations. By late November, Boumédienne's efforts at organizing a special meeting of African foreign ministers to deal with the Middle East crisis had floundered. But he did succeed in convoking a summit meeting of Arab heads of state, despite Cairo's lukewarm enthusiasm for the meeting.

The Arab heads of state met in Algiers on November 26–28, and drew up a declaration of their stand on the Arab-Israeli conflict. They also agreed to exert economic pressure on other countries to persuade them to influence Israel to sign a peace settlement in accordance with Arab demands. The Arabs, therefore, would continue to manipulate oil exports according to the "attitude of every country toward the Arab cause." (See also MIDDLE EAST.)

ANTHROPOLOGY

The year 1973 was a quiet one in anthropology. The 71st annual meeting of the American Anthropological Association (AAA) was held in Toronto, Canada, late in 1972, and the ninth International Congress of Anthropological and Ethnological Sciences (ICAES) met in Chicago in September 1973. The year was marked by the death of Sir Edward Evan Evans-Pritchard, a British social anthropologist.

AAA Meeting. At the AAA meeting in Toronto, Edward H. Spicer, president-elect for 1973–74, delineated three trends and related problems confronting the association and the profession. They were: the integration of the aims and efforts of the various branches and organizations in anthropology; the problem of how anthropologists view themselves in relation to the society in which they operate; and the widening of the field of anthropology, with new interests and new concepts brought into focus by recent international meetings.

Of greatest interest were sessions on the problems of ethnohistory; discussions of what constitutes ethical behavior of social scientists; the development of films as both recording and teaching devices; the films of the teaching of sign language to the chimpanzee Washoe; and the ad hoc committees formed to deal with problems of American Indian legislation and education. Considerable numbers of Canadian and U. S. American Indians were present at the meeting. They expressed resentment at being studied by anthropologists and at the same time asked for help in maintaining their cultural institutions.

JIM PURKS, FLORIAD DEPARTMENT OF STATE

UNDERWATER ARCHAEOLOGIST W. A. Cockrell holds human skull uncovered in Florida. About 10,200 years old, it is oldest yet found in eastern United States.

ICAES Meeting. The theme of the ninth International Congress of Anthropological and Ethnological Sciences was "One Species, Many Cultures." The meeting was organized by Dr. Sol Tax of the University of Chicago, the elder statesman of anthropology and the organizer of international congresses. Anthropologists from many nations attended, and the meeting sessions were translated into French, German, English, Russian, and Spanish.

New Books. During 1973 continuing and developing interests of anthropologists were reflected in the publication of a number of significant books and articles. In *The Mountain People*, Colin Turnbull describes the Ik, once a hunting and gathering people whose hunting territory was turned into a national game preserve by the Ugandan government. The Ik were given land and told to become farmers, but the land is arid and incapable of supporting farming. The Ik are slowly starving to death, and all the social bonds necessary in a hunting culture have collapsed. According to Turnbull, when survival is sufficiently threatened, everything else is sacrificed. Turnbull concludes that human values are only a characteristic of a particular form of survival, and that man "is perfectly capable of associating for purposes of survival without being social." Turnbull gloomily wonders if this sounds too much like our own society. Others have pointed out, however, that the Ik represent an isolated case of a specialized people abruptly uprooted from their way of life.

Other significant new books were published, including Turnbull's *Africa and Change* and Elvin

Hatch's *Theories of Man and Culture.* Several new textbooks with new approaches to the study of the discipline also were published in 1973. They included *Evolving Life Styles* by Elbert W. Stewart, *Man's Place in Nature* by Charles F. Hockett, and *Human Nature* by James F. Downs.

New Papers. Scholarly and research papers pointed to interests in Europe, primate behavior, symbol and myth in belief systems, and reevaluations of basic concepts of culture, society, and anthropology. Europe as a field of study has in the past been neglected by many anthropologists. In 1973, however, the *American Anthropologist* published nine articles on rural European social organization (Vol. 75, No. 3, June 1973). In an article "Rethinking Culture," Paul Bohannan of Northwestern University extended a plea for a reexamination of the concept of culture (*Current Anthropology,* Vol. 14, No. 4, October 1973). Roger M. Keesing enunciated a need for "a new cognitive model of culture which can be systematically related to sociological, biological, ecological, and other realms, not merely abstracted from them" (*Southwestern Journal of Anthropology,* Vol. 28, No. 4, Winter 1972). Lastly, Raoul Naroll and Richard G. Sipes proposed a new standard ethnographic sample, which is intended as a sampling universe for cross-cultural surveys and as a data quality control measure for such surveys (*Current Anthropology,* Vol. 14, No. 1–2, February–April 1973).

There also has been an increasing number of articles on cognitive anthropology (the study of the empirical belief systems of peoples), and they frequently make use of symbolic algebra or mathematics. A number of papers on the anthropology of art and aesthetics also appeared.

Peking Man Fossils. A Chicago investment broker, Christopher G. Janus, has been searching for the fossils of Peking Man, missing since 1941 when they were being transported out of China for safekeeping by a detachment of U. S. Marines. The fossils disappeared when the Japanese army captured the Marines. Janus has been on the Chinese mainland and on Taiwan, but he has had no luck in locating the fossils so far. Janus has said that he intends to continue the search. A reward has been offered for information leading to their recovery.

The fossils originally were found by J. G. Anderson, W. C. Pei, and others from 1921 to 1937. Fortunately, most of the bones had been cast and studied intensively by the German anthropologist Franz Weidenreich before they were lost. The casts were sent to laboratories in many parts of the world.

Evans-Pritchard. Sir Edward Evan Evans-Pritchard, a professor of social anthropology at the University of Oxford from 1946 to 1970, died on Sept. 11, 1973. He was a major figure in British social anthropology and, indeed, in the world. Evans-Pritchard's fieldwork was done mainly among the Azande and Nuer of southern Sudan. His best-known books, *Witchcraft, Oracles and Magic among the Azande* (1937) and *The Nuer* (1940), have been universally recognized as brilliant contributions to anthropological theory. He was a prolific writer on kinship and religion, a president of the Royal Anthropological Institute and first chairman of the Association of Social Anthropologists of the British Commonwealth. He was an honorary member of the American Academy of Arts and Sciences, and he was knighted by Queen Elizabeth in 1971.

HERMAN J. JAFFE, *Brooklyn College*

PREHISTORIC MEN lived along the lower Illinois River valley. Archaeologists at the Koster site found these remains of a village dating from the 6th century B. C.

ARCHAEOLOGY

Further discoveries of Australopithecine remains in Africa, the exploration of neolithic and mesolithic villages in Europe and the Near East, studies of pre-Columbian communities in the Americas, an autopsy on a well-preserved 2,000-year-old corpse in China, and the discovery of a pair of glass slippers from the 4th century A. D. made news in archaeology in 1973. The trend toward an interdisciplinary approach to archaeological research was illustrated by the use of a computer for data analysis at the famous Koster site in Illinois.

WESTERN HEMISPHERE

Research on the Incas of Peru, finds relating to the early inhabitants of Panama and Trinidad, and the discovery of a potentially important new site in New Jersey were among the important events of 1973 in Western Hemisphere archaeology. In Illinois, computer technology was assisting in the work of teams of researchers at the Koster site.

Peru. Archaeologists from Brandeis University have completed the major phase of their research at Huanuco Pampa, a former provincial capital of the Incas. A map of the city ruin is nearly com-

pleted, and some 104 structures have been investigated. Initial studies confirm that one area of the city was concerned with communal feedings. This and other recovered data suggests that the strictly structured Inca society regulated even individual living arrangements.

Ecuador. The Smithsonian Institution completed a successful archaeological project near Guayaquil which resulted in the recovery of some 250 skeletons associated with ceramic urns. The burials date from the Milagro period (about 1400–1500 A. D.) and are characteristic of that culture. An earlier burial complex was also noted at this site, possibly dating from 200–500 A. D.

Venezuela. Recent excavations in western Venezuela have produced a series of carbon-14 dates ranging from 900 B. C. to 500 A. D., during which time corn (maize) and, later, manioc were cultivated. The origins for this formative phase of agriculture in Venezuela are thought to be traceable to the Amazon basin.

Panama. Archaeologists working in stratified rock shelters along the upper Río Chiriquí have reported collecting sufficient data to identify a Río Chiriquí prehistoric cultural sequence. Earliest occupations are attributed to the Talamancan phase, beginning about 4600 B. C., and feature edge-ground cobbles, bifacially flaked celt-like wedges, and a variety of scraper types. The succeeding Boquete phase (about 2100 B. C.) is characterized by smaller, frequently polished stone tools. Pottery occurs sometime after 1000 B. C. and is associated with a flaked-tool industry. Several stages of ceramic development are noted, culminating in the classic Chiriquí ceramic phase of 1000–1500 A. D.

Trinidad. Various investigations on the island of Trinidad are revealing a prehistory of greater complexity than had been realized. The oldest culture on Trinidad, a hunting and gathering phase termed Banwari I, dates from about 5200 B. C. All later periods are grouped into Banwari II, beginning about 4200 B. C. Current work is being directed at a hilltop site, Poonah Road, where milling stones and celts are being recovered from up to 32 inches (80 cm) of refuse. Other sites being excavated are classified as neo-Indian and were occupied variously from 20 to 940 A. D.

Alabama. During the summer of 1973, archaeologists surveyed some 12 sites in Clarke county in southwestern Alabama and 7 sites in neighboring Monroe county near Claibourne. One of these sites was identified as a large prehistoric quarry for the manufacture of stone tools.

Some 3 miles north of Daphne, Ala., University of Alabama personnel investigated a Mobile Bay shell midden some 500 feet (150 meters) long and 80 to 130 feet (25–40 meters) wide. Preliminary excavations in one area have revealed two cultural zones separated by about 3 feet (nearly a meter) of sand. Artifacts from the upper zone include three partially restorable vessels, a large-mouthed pot, and two shallow bowls with incised designs. These items appear to date from the Historic Period—about 1700–1800 A. D. The lower cultural zone resembles the Fort Walton Period (about 1400–1700 A. D.) and features grit-tempered ceramics.

Arkansas. A second season of excavations was undertaken at the Ferguson site by the Arkansas Archaeological Survey. Despite inclement weather several stages of mound construction were identified and excavated.

Three occupation periods have been recognized at the site. The earliest occupation dates from about 7000 B. C. and is attributed to various Archaic hunters. Around 300 A. D., a village grew up at this location and was occupied by a population oriented to agriculture. About 1350 A. D. the Ferguson site became a ceremonial center for pre-Caddoan people, and at that time the prominent mound features were constructed, lasting until 1500 A. D.

Illinois. Excavations continued at the important Koster site in the lower Illinois River valley. There excavators have identified 15 distinct cultural horizons dating back to 6000 B. C. In its fifth season, the Koster site attracted some 120 scientists and students, who worked under the direction of Northwestern University personnel.

A computer is being used at the Koster site to absorb and sort out the vast stratigraphic and artifactual data as it is exposed. Archaeologists feel that the computer can assist them in identifying recovery patterns and possibly even suggest productive areas to excavate.

New Jersey and Pennsylvania. Archaeologists from Seton Hall University continued their project at the prehistoric village site near Tocks Island on the Delaware River in northwestern New Jersey, uncovering an area of about 300 feet (90 meters) by 70 feet (20 meters). The excavators noted that this particular site does not possess the regular posthole features commonly identified with other Late Woodland palisaded villages. Accordingly, it would seem that warfare was not common in the Tocks Island area prior to the advent of European contact.

Farther south along the Delaware River, personnel from the University of Pennsylvania have reported what they believe to be one of the most important archaeological sites in the eastern United States. Located northwest of Stockton, N. J., this deeply stratified site may eventually reveal a record of man's past back to the Paleo-Indian Period, or about 10,000 B. C.

Oregon. Excavations sponsored by the Smithsonian Institution are continuing near Seaside, Oreg., with attention being focused on the Par-tee site. A new series of carbon-14 dates confirms the occupation of this large maritime-oriented village from 245 to 915 A. D. Excavations have produced artifact types from the earliest occupation levels.

Washington. The discovery of iron tools at the Lake Ozette village site has prompted archaeologists in the state of Washington to speculate that extensive trade routes may have existed along the Pacific Coast 500 years ago. The tools, fashioned to be used like adzes, may have been traded down (or south) along the Pacific Coast after originating among the Siberian Eskimo, who are known to have had metal tools in the 15th century.

GEORGE E. PHEBUS
Smithsonian Institution

EASTERN HEMISPHERE

Excavation in the Eastern Hemisphere produced surprising discoveries even in such well-explored archaeological areas as the Roman and Egyptian.

Steps Toward Man. At Lake Rudolph in northern Kenya, the same stratum which yielded a 2.8 million-year-old cranium in 1972 yielded fragments of a 6-year-old child and the femur of an adult female in 1973. This leg bone looks much more like a modern human femur than does the leg bone found with the Australopithecines of South Africa.

Another Australopithecine skull was found in South Africa in the Sterkfontein Caves, which earlier produced fossil men. This 2-million-year-old cranium is also thought to be that of a female.

Neanderthal Ingenuity. Studies in which thermoluminescence is used to measure radiation damage in crystalline objects have demonstrated conclusively that Neanderthal flint users of the Mousterian Culture sometimes heated their raw material before chipping tools from it. Such sophisticated thermal modification seems surprising for an industry over 50,000 years old. Mousterian flint mines were also found in Switzerland.

Paleolithic Puzzle. An Australian discovery difficult to evaluate consists of *Homo erectus* skulls, like that of Java Man, with radiocarbon dates from the end of the Pleistocene—rather than the middle of it, as expected. The simple pebble tools prove little, as they were used in Southeast Asia by Stone Age man until the present day.

Stone Age Villages. In the well-watered valleys of the Zagros Mountains of what is now Luristan, in western Iran, the Ice Age hunters had plenty of game available, so they ranged only short distances from their cave habitations. They made their tools at flint outcroppings. A study of the Neolithic farmers shows that they brought the flint to their riverside villages to flake. The agriculturists did little hunting, but relied upon fish to supplement their crops. At this time, the numerous caves in this district were used only by goat-herders, as temporary shelters.

In eastern Jutland (Denmark), both the winter and summer villages have been located for a band of Mesolithic hunters who made a distinctive local form of pottery. The seacoast summer encampment had very flimsy shelters for the exploitation of marine resources such as clams, seals, and gull eggs. The newly discovered winter settlement, some 10 miles (16 km) inland, shows semi-subterranean houses with turf walls and branch-covered roofs. Elk and aurochs (giant wild oxen) provided food in winter, and fur-bearing animals were taken with transverse arrowheads for their pelts.

Bronze and Iron Ages. In a desert in eastern Iran, near Shahdad, the oldest-known city in Iran is being explored by Iranian archaeologists. The urbanites who built the city on the Xabis Plain before 4000 B. C. were devoted to a series of goddesses, including a horned deity of animals. Among the numerous bronze objects are seals and a flag depicting lions, bulls, and another goddess with her retinue. The pictographic writing in the city appears to be older than that of Mesopotamia.

Omanari tumulus graves, first excavated scientifically in Kuwait, were being investigated by professional archaeologists in Oman itself. The skeleton graves contain black and red pottery, steatite vessels, and some bronze implements. These cemeteries of the early 3d millennium B. C. occur near copper workings, but no cities or habitations have yet been located.

A remarkable factory site for such steatite vessels has been discovered on Saudi Arabia's Tarut Island, in the Persian Gulf. The vessels seem to have been carved there from Halafian to Omanari times (about 5000 to 3000 B. C.). The incised decorations consist of mat-and-weave and stepped patterns and depictions of plants and animals.

A Danish engineering firm has verified that the ancient Egyptians used real chalk mortar for the construction of the pyramid of Khufu in the 2d millennium B. C. Previously the Greeks had been credited with the invention of mortar.

Votive deposits in the southern Belgian subterranean course of the Lesse River, which enters a mountain to reemerge further downstream near Han-sur-Lesse, have greatly illuminated the insufficiently known Bronze Age of Belgium. Offerings of knives were made at one place, axes and spearheads at others. These weird underground precincts, picketed by stalactitic formations, were used as places of execution by La Tene III Celts. These finds were made in a project combining the problems of both cave and underwater archaeology.

The burial of a noble warrior uncovered in a tumulus at Altrier, Luxembourg, contained wood datable (by tree-ring chronology) to 461 B. C. and earlier, thus ending conclusively the long debate as to whether or not the La Tene Iron Age started before 450 B. C. The cremated body, deposited in an imported bronze Etruscan stamnos, was equipped with a sword, a gold armlet, and a bronze and coral fibula, or clasp, with four faces in relief.

Archaeological "Autopsy" in China. The early Western Han royal grave found in Hunan Province in 1972, containing the body of a noblewoman dead about 2,000 years, also had hundreds of normally perishable artifacts preserved by a kaolin clay and charcoal cover. The body, the best-preserved human corpse ever recovered archaeologically, has now been intensively scrutinized. The 50-year-old woman must have died of heart disease, but she also suffered from a pea-sized tubercular tumor in each lung.

Roman Discoveries. At Vindolanda, a Roman fort in Northumberland, England, a clay and heather deposit over the archaeological debris saved perishable materials such as tools of wood and clothing. Documents have been recovered, providing new materials for historians and archaeologists.

Oplonti, a third town destroyed by the eruption of Vesuvius that buried Pompeii and Herculanum, has apparently been located. The first discoveries center on a villa with a huge atrium (central hall), a mosaic floor, and complete bathing facilities. Painted stucco works on the walls resemble three-dimensional lace.

Urban decay and the socioeconomic processes which affect the prestige of various parts of cities were being investigated by the late Swedish king, Gustaf VI (who was also an archaeologist), and Dr. C. E. Ostenberg at Acquarosa, Italy. They were excavating an Etruscan city to reveal its ground plan and clues to its inhabitants' everyday life, rather than to find artistic objects.

Amateur archaeologists in Cologne, Germany, brought forth from an otherwise simple burial site the remains of a youngish woman with a pair of glass slippers. Dating from the 4th century A. D., these are the first such slippers found intact, although fragments had been known from other sites in the Roman Empire. No Cinderella, the woman is thought to have been a prostitute.

Ancient Churches. Under the present-day Church of St. Thomas in Tyre (Sur), Lebanon, an international team revealed successively superposed Crusader and Byzantine churches and a Roman building that may also have been a church. Under the Crusader's church were buried six archbishops, one of them sitting upright on a throne.

RALPH M. ROWLETT
University of Missouri, Columbia

ESTO

The new headquarters of the American Institute of Architects in Washington, D. C., was designed, appropriately enough, by The Architects' Collaborative, Inc.

architecture

The year 1973 was marked by evolving standards and conflicting directions in architecture. On the one hand, a humanizing trend in housing and urban renewal was evident. On the other hand, there was a continuing increase in the magnitude of significant building projects. Among architects themselves there was official uncertainty over the determination of universally acceptable standards of architectural merit.

Professional Values. In 1973, The American Institute of Architects (AIA) failed to award its annual gold medal, the profession's highest honor. This lapse stemmed from a recognition that design skill alone could no longer be the prime standard of achievement when architecture is increasingly linked with the issues of urban change, ecology, energy use, and social policy. Future awards await the development of a fuller definition of architectural merit.

Urban Renewal and Housing. Conventional tactics of sweeping demolition and grim replacement structures were giving way to a more humane approach in redevelopment circles. In the Twin Parks area of the Bronx, N. Y., public agencies are building 4,000 new housing units on several scattered sites, and are rehabilitating 1,000 older units. By assigning this work to a variety of well regarded firms—including John Johansen, James Polshek, Mitchell-Guirgola, Richard Meier, Giovanni Pasanella, and Prentice & Chan, Ohlhausen—the Urban Development Corporation and the N. Y. City Housing Authority brought unusual quality and diversity to pub-

lic housing, and softened its potentially disruptive effects on a changing older neighborhood.

In St. Louis, Mo., a similarly humane proposal for selective rebuilding of the socially troubled Pruitt-Igoe housing project was rejected by governmental agencies. Instead, the project's 31 slab-shaped buildings will be demolished. This paradoxical act symbolizes the futility of 1950's urban renewal policies, and may lead to more imaginative planning in the future.

Immensity. At the same time, other architects were still being swept up in a societal trend toward hugeness and inhuman scale. In New York, Minoru Yamasaki's World Trade Center, dedicated in 1973, includes twin 110-story towers 1,350 feet (405 meters) tall and comprises 10 million square feet of space for 130,000 workers and visitors. This world record for height was soon broken by Chicago's 1,450-foot-high (435-meter) Sears Tower. Designed by Skidmore, Owings & Merrill, the Sears building consists of nine "megamodules" 75 feet square that range in height from 50 to 110 stories and produce a stepped profile and a variety of floor sizes. Embracing 4.5 million square feet, this is the world's largest private office building to date.

Plans were published for a still taller structure, the CN Tower in Toronto. This concrete and steel shaft will rise 1,805 feet (542 meters) and serve tourist and broadcasting functions. Consulting architects are John Andrews/Webb Zerafa Menkes Housden.

Skidmore, Owings & Merrill finished the design of another enormous building, the 2.3 million-square-foot New York Convention Center, whose main exhibit level alone will cover 13 acres.

The Dallas–Fort Worth airport, projected to be the world's largest, opened its first section in 1973.

This complex will eventually have 14 horseshoe-shaped terminals, each over a mile in circumference, and will cover an area of 27 square miles, more than the three major airports of New York, Chicago, and Los Angeles combined.

Commercial Buildings. Structures of less overwhelming scope provided better opportunities for architectural skill and subtlety. I. M. Pei's 88 Pine Street, a 32-story office tower in Manhattan, displays a highly refined curtain wall of white-painted aluminum and broad undivided windows. Raymond & Rado's 2 Dag Hammarskjöld Plaza, also in New York, is a self-effacing glass office structure of 16 stories with a connecting sculpture garden privately built for public use on plaza space leased from the city.

San Francisco's building boom produced two outstanding hotels in 1973. The 7-sided Hyatt Regency is a busy sightseeing stop due to its "futuristic" 17-story lobby. Architect-developer John Portman, here and in earlier projects, has shown the economic value of generous architectural spaces. The Hyatt on Union Square by Skidmore, Owings & Merrill is a more restrained and sensitively detailed building. Its genius lies in a deferential yet imaginative relationship to its old urban setting.

In Kansas City, Harry Weese's Crown Center Hotel is distinguished by a lobby carved into a rocky bluff and landscaped to make a skylit indoor park.

Columbus, Ind., a showplace of modern architecture under the patronage of civic leader J. Irwin Miller, gained its first major work of urban design, the Gruen Associates' Courthouse Center. The center is a shopping and entertainment mall tautly faced in glass. Intended to revive the old retail area, it is notable for its provision of a large interior civic space, the Commons.

Transit. In 1973 the first new U. S. rapid transit system in two generations was completed in the San Francisco Bay area. Its designers gave major architectural expression to the 37 stations and the elevated structures. Perhaps the most prominent and ingenious station is Hallidie Plaza in San Francisco's core, designed by Skidmore, Owings & Merrill as a mini-park stepping down from the street to the subway level.

Cultural Buildings. The Sydney (Australia) Opera House was completed 16 years after its design was chosen in an international competition. Danish architect Jørn Utzon's winning entry was a romantic vision of billowing concrete shells. However, engineering and construction problems, design changes, rising costs, and political intrigue slowed the project, forcing Utzon's resignation before its completion. Final costs were estimated at an exorbitant U. S. $150 million. Yet, the Opera House, dramatically situated in Sydney Harbor, may well become Australia's most memorable landmark.

HYATT REGENCY, SAN FRANCISCO

THE HYATT REGENCY, a new hotel in Embarcadero area of San Francisco, Calif., has an exciting atrium-lobby that features immense live trees and a brook that runs over a rock-lined bed. The anodyzed aluminum sphere at center is the height of a four-story building. The hotel was designed by John Portman & Associates.

THE STUDENT UNION at California Polytechnic State University, San Luis Obispo, was designed by Esherick Homsey Dodge and Davis.

WAYNE THOM FOR ESHERICK HOMSEY DODGE AND DAVIS

The American Institute of Architects' national headquarters design was also selected by competition, in 1962. The plans of Mitchell and Guirgola satisfied a knowledgeable client, but not Washington's dogmatic Fine Arts Commission. After two more of their designs were vetoed, they quit and were succeeded by The Architects Collaborative (TAC). TAC's effort is a clearly contemporary design carefully related to the 175-year-old Octagon House which shares its site.

Plans for the John F. Kennedy Library were unveiled in 1973. I. M. Pei's controversial design calls for a 7-story truncated glass pyramid set into an open circular courtyard near the Harvard campus.

Educational Buildings. In the United States, Victor Lundy's Intermediate School 53 in New York City and Earl Flansburgh's Kent Elementary School in Charlestown, Mass., proved that low budgets do not preclude quality. Both schools use staggered and stepped brick walls to achieve a distinctive, accommodating scale compatible with their neighborhoods.

Canadian design in university structures continued to show unusual sophistication. Alberta's University of Lethbridge is a concrete megastructure boldly sited in an otherwise untouched landscape. Erickson/Massey's design integrates teaching space, labs, offices, and dormitories in a single linear building. The University of Winnipeg's Centennial Hall occupies space above and between existing campus buildings. Architects Moody Moore Rattray Peters Searle Christie gave this pragmatic multipurpose structure a bright industrial expression. In Vancouver, Rhone & Iredale, faced with limited land for the University of British Columbia's Sedgewick Library, built below a pedestrian mall, capitalizing on a gentle slope and preserving several large trees.

Preservation and Recycling. The year 1973 saw the continuing erosion of the characteristic Parisian skyline by skyscrapers. In Barcelona, Spain, there was destructive renovation of Gaudí's famous Casa Milá. In New York, plans were announced to alter Frank Lloyd Wright's Guggenheim Museum.

On the positive side, a $2.2 million restoration of Boston's Faneuil Market district was begun. In New York, nine federal row houses, including one by John McComb, were relocated within lower Manhattan and restored. Restoration of Dankmar Adler & Louis Sullivan's Auditorium Building, in Chicago, was sponsored by Roosevelt University.

At Princeton University, Gwathmey & Siegel ingeniously salvaged a fire-ruined campus landmark, Whig Hall, by building modern spaces within the still usable outside shell. In Tacoma, Wash., Allan Liddle converted a 1920 bank into the Tacoma Art Museum, leaving the neoclassic exterior intact and radically altering the interior.

Awards. In 1973, AIA honor awards were given to John Andrews for Gund Hall, Harvard, Cambridge, Mass.; Joseph Esherick for the Cal Poly Student Union, San Luis Obispo, Calif.; Gourley/ Richmond for Radcliffe faculty housing, Cambridge, Mass.; Harry Weese for the Chicago Time-Life Building; William Kessler for public housing, Wayne, Mich.; Skidmore, Owings & Merrill for the American Can Company Building; Marcel Breuer and Herbert Beckhard for St. Francis de Sales Church, Muskegon, Mich.; RTKL Associates for Fountain Square Plaza, Cincinnati, Ohio; Loebl, Schlossman, Bennett & Dart for St. Procopius Abbey; and to Edward Cuetara and McCue Boone, Tomsick, Moore-Turnbull for private residences.

TAC won an invited competition for the Johns-Manville headquarters near Denver, Colo. Bard Awards of the City Club of New York for excellence in architecture and urban design went to: Davis-Brody's East Midtown Plaza; Bronx State Rehabilitation Center, Bronx, N. Y., by Gruzen & Partners; Morris Lapidus' Bedford-Stuyvesant Community Pool, Brooklyn, N. Y.; and Twin Parks housing, Bronx, N. Y., for separate projects by Richard Meier and Prentice & Chan, Ohlhausen.

JOHN PASTIER
Architecture Critic, Los Angeles "Times"

ARCTIC REGIONS. See POLAR RESEARCH.

ARGENTINA

The return to power of the exiled, 78-year-old former dictator Juan Perón overshadowed all other events in Argentina in 1973. During the course of the year, four chief executives occupied the Casa Rosada, the presidential residence, in Buenos Aires. Gen. Alejandro Lanusse vacated the premises after Dr. Héctor Cámpora, victor in the March elections, was inaugurated in May. Cámpora resigned in July to make way for the return of Perón, whereupon the president of the House of Deputies, Raúl Lastiri, temporarily assumed the Argentine presidency. Perón himself moved into the executive mansion in October.

March Elections. Despite misgivings in the armed forces, General Lanusse made good his promise to return the country to civilian rule. Elections were held on March 11, 1973, for the first time since 1964. Perón, who had been exiled from his homeland in 1955, was barred from running for the presidency and remained abroad, but his hand-picked surrogate, Cámpora, representing the Peronist coalition called the Justicialista Liberation Front, was the overwhelming winner in the election. Cámpora gathered about 50% of the total vote, as against 21% for his closest opponent, Ricardo Balbín of the Radical Civic Union (UCRP). The military government subsequently ruled that another election to achieve a simple majority was unnecessary. Thus, on May 25, the Peronists returned to power after 18 years of proscription and ostracism, and the military returned to its barracks for the first time since 1966.

The Cámpora Administration. As the victors faced the difficult task of national reconstruction, they were deeply divided between leftist and rightist factions which disagreed over how far the "revolution" should go. In May, Rodolfo Galimberti, leader of the leftist Peronist Youth, was forced to resign, and on May 25, during Cámpora's inauguration ceremonies, major street confrontations occurred between leftist and rightist Peronist demonstrators.

The inaugural speech itself called for a political and social truce based on such old ideas as economic independence, redistribution of income, and solidarity with the "anti-imperialist struggles" of the "Third World." The new regime immediately released most political prisoners and granted a general amnesty. Cámpora's cabinet appointments were designed, through balance, to satisfy the rival factions, but divisions remained deep.

On June 20, as several million people gathered near Ezeiza Airport outside Buenos Aires to welcome Perón on his return from exile, a shoot-out near the speaker's platform claimed at least 30 lives and left hundreds wounded. Perón's plane was diverted to a local air base, and the next day he addressed a shocked nation to appeal for unity. Apparent responsibility rested with a rightist goon squad organized to discredit the left.

September Elections. On July 13, after seven weeks in office, President Cámpora and his vice president, Vicente Solano Lima, resigned. Raúl Lastiri, president of the Chamber of Deputies, became the new executive as indicated by the laws of succession, and new elections, in which Perón himself would be eligible to run, were called for September 23. Perón then called for the institutionalization of the Justicialista movement, whose progressive secretary general, Juan Abal Medina, was replaced by

———— ARGENTINA • Information Highlights ————

Official Name: Argentine Republic.
Location: Southern South America.
Area: 1,072,158 square miles (2,776,889 sq km).
Population (1973 est.): 25,300,000. *Density,* 23 per square mile (9 per sq km).
Chief Cities (1970 census): Buenos Aires, the capital, 2,972,453; Rosario (met. area), 810,840; Córdoba (met. area), 798,663.
Government: *Head of state,* Juan Perón, president (took office Oct. 1973). *Head of government,* Juan Perón. *Legislature*—National Congress. *Major political parties*—Justicialista Liberation Front; Radical Civic Union.
Language: Spanish (official).
Education: *Expenditure* (1969), 2% of gross national product. *School enrollment* (1972)—primary, 3,699,007; secondary, 1,058,945; technical/vocational (1969), 519,079; university/higher, 351,287.
Monetary Unit: Peso (5.00 pesos equal U.S.$1, Aug. 1973).
Gross National Product (1972 est.): $28,210,000,000.
Economic Indexes: *Industrial production* (1972), 198 (1963=100); *agricultural production* (1971), 97 (1963=100); *consumer price index* (1972), 811 (1963=100).
Manufacturing (major products): Iron and steel, automobiles, machinery, processed foods, cement, chemicals.
Major Agricultural Products: Wheat, corn, grapes, oats, sugarcane, sorghum, barley, sunflower seeds (ranks 1st among world producers, 1972), cattle, sheep.
Major Minerals: Petroleum, natural gas, zinc, manganese, tungsten, beryllium, coal.
Foreign Trade (1971): Exports, $1,740,000,000. Imports, $1,868,000,000. *Chief trading partners* (1971)—Italy (took 15% of exports, supplied 6% of imports); United States (9%—22%); Netherlands (9%—2%); Brazil (6%—11%).
Tourism: Receipts (1971), $52,980,000.
Transportation: *Motor vehicles* (1970), 2,194,400 (automobiles, 1,439,600); *railroads* (1971), 24,548 miles (39,905 km); *merchant fleet* (1972), 1,401,000 gross registered tons; *major national airline,* Aerolineas Argentinas.
Communications: *Telephones* (1972), 1,825,532; *newspapers* (1971), 176.

a conservative four-man executive committee. This reduced the influence of the Peronist Youth, the movement's most progressive organization. Clearly, Perón had swerved to the right.

The aging and ailing Perón briefly entertained the idea of running for president on a unity slate, with his old adversary, Ricardo Balbín, leader of the UCRP, as his vice presidential candidate. But Balbín's party refused to accept that liaison and, instead, Perón settled for the nomination of his 42-year-old wife, the politically conservative Isabel. After a brief campaign they won nearly 62% of the votes, while Balbín tallied 24.5%. On October 12, Perón received the presidential sash that he had been forced to remove more than 18 years earlier.

Economic Developments. In June 1973, Cámpora outlined the Peronist economic program. In a message to Congress he proposed a redistribution of income to be accomplished by a reduction of some prices, a general freeze on others, and a wage increase of at least 25% (with no increases in costs to be passed on to the consumer). Wages would then be frozen for two years while the government achieved full employment, low-income housing construction, the reorganization and reform of the tax structure, the reduction of bank interest rates, and the "rationalization" of the marketing system. Cámpora indicated that legislation would soon be forthcoming on such matters as the nationalization of bank deposits, the regulation of meat and grain exports, the control of foreign investment, and the utilization of idle land.

At midyear, the economic outlook was mixed. During the first half of 1973, as compared with the first six months of 1972, exports of meat and meat products declined in quantity, but, due to high international prices, they increased in total value. Wheat and grain sorghum exports were up sharply during this period. However, Lanusse had drastically overcommitted the wheat crop and, early in August, Argentina suspended shipments and bought wheat

from the United States at very high prices to meet internal demands and foreign commitments.

Although the trade balance was favorable and exchange reserves were high, Argentina's foreign indebtedness totaled some $7.3 billion. The president of the Central Bank claimed that Argentina did not need to renegotiate the debt "at present." In September, the Congress passed legislation to nationalize bank deposits and levied a tax on the productive potential of land.

Political Violence. The Peronist political triumph did not put an end to guerrilla activities. In addition to a series of kidnappings (and the recovery of huge ransoms), the guerrillas assassinated several military officers and, on September 25, shot and killed José Rucci, a top labor leader. At first, the leftist People's Revolutionary Army (ERP) was accused of Rucci's murder, but later there was speculation that extreme right-wing elements might have been responsible.

The military leaders, obviously frightened for their own safety, pressured the Peronists to condemn "subversion" and to prevent the possession of arms and explosives by private citizens. Perón himself vehemently condemned guerrilla activities in several speeches. In September, the ERP was outlawed by presidential decree.

International Developments. In foreign affairs Argentina attempted to achieve an independent position between the capitalist and Communist blocs and to regain ground lost to Brazil in their competition for influence in South America. Early in the year, Chile received a credit of $100 million to purchase Argentine products, and Cuba, recognized by the new government on May 28, was granted a credit of $200 million, later increased by a billion dollars. Relations with both Paraguay and Uruguay were cool. Paraguay allied itself with Brazil in a dispute over regional river development, and Uruguay moved toward a Brazilian-style political regime.

United States relations were strained by Argentina's renewed ambitions for hemispheric leadership, by its call for reform of the Organization of American States, and by its increased hostility toward, and attempt to control, foreign capital.

Perón in Office. Within a few weeks of Perón's inauguration on October 12, it became evident that he intended to consolidate his power by dealing vigorously with leftist critics both within and outside of the Justicialista movement. This was seen in the suppression or disavowal of left-leaning publications, a police raid on the headquarters of the Peronist Workers Youth organization, and pressure on state governors to purge their administrations of leftist officials.

Urgent problems confronted the president as the year drew to a close. To achieve his basic goals he had to effectively redistribute income, eliminate the guerrilla movement, generate constant economic growth, and redirect wealth and political power to the interior provinces, particularly to explosive Córdoba, where loyalty to Peronism was not strong.

In the face of his people's great—perhaps unrealistic—expectations, Perón was not ignoring the lesson of Chile and its September military coup. He was attempting to create a dependable officer corps by retiring the old-guard soldiers who had exercised power since 1966, and restoring rank to officers who had been loyal to him in 1955.

JAMES R. LEVY
University of New South Wales, Australia

ARIZONA

The major political events in Arizona in 1973 were an unsuccessful attempt to remove the governor from office, the rewriting of school financing laws in conjunction with tax reform, and a conflict-of-interest scandal in the legislature.

Campaign Against the Governor. An all-out drive to remove Gov. Jack Williams (R) from office by using the recall device of the Arizona constitution failed in 1973. The drive had been led by the United Farm Workers, under the leadership of Cesar Chavez, who were opposed to Williams because he had signed a controversial farm labor bill. The recall drive gained the formal support of the state Democratic party, although some top Democrats refused to participate in the campaign on the grounds that it was doomed to failure. Far more than the required number of signatures were obtained on recall petitions, but when they were submitted many names were thrown out as not being those of qualified electors and others for having been obtained by deputy voter registrars, a practice declared illegal by Attorney General Gary K. Nelson (R). A final determination by Secretary of State Wesley Bolin (D) held that the number of valid signatures filed was constitutionally insufficient, and Governor Williams remained in office.

The Legislature. During its regular 1973 session the Arizona legislature abolished the current laws for financing education. A special session beginning in October attempted to agree on a new school revenue package. Despite general agreement that the

———— **ARIZONA • Information Highlights** ————

Area: 113,909 square miles (295,024 sq km).
Population (1972 est.): 1,945,000. *Density:* 16 per sq mi.
Chief Cities (1970 census): Phoenix, the capital, 581,562; Tucson, 262,933; Scottsdale, 67,823; Tempe, 63,550; Mesa, 62,853; Glendale, 36,228; Yuma, 29,007.
Government (1973): *Chief Officers*—governor, Jack Williams (R); secy. of state, Wesley Bolin (D); atty. gen., Gary K. Nelson (R); treas., Ernest Garfield (R); supt. of public instruction, Weldon F. Shofstall (R); chief justice, Jack D. H. Hays. *Legislature*—Senate, 30 members (18 Republicans, 12 Democrats); House of Representatives, 60 members (38 R, 22 D).
Education (1972–73): *Enrollment*—public elementary schools, 385,278 pupils, 16,248 teachers; public secondary schools, 156,506 pupils, 7,005 teachers; nonpublic schools, 29,700 pupils, 1,270 teachers; colleges and universities, 110,468 students. *Public school expenditures,* $518,612,000 ($1,110 per pupil). *Average teacher's salary,* $10,863.
State Finances (fiscal year 1971): *Revenues:* $951,180,000 (3% general sales tax and gross receipts taxes, $193,983,000; motor fuel tax, $70,518,000; federal funds, $196,576,000). *Expenditures,* $831,263,000 (education, $399,332,000; health, welfare, and safety, $81,944,000; highways, $159,958,000). *State debt,* $88,969,000 (June 30, 1971).
Personal Income (1972): $8,364,000,000; per capita, $4,300.
Public Assistance (1972): $53,840,000. *Average monthly payments* (Dec. 1972)—old-age assistance, $79.97; aid to families with dependent children, $126.59.
Labor Force: *Nonagricultural wage and salary earners* (July 1973), 696,000. *Average annual employment* (1972)—manufacturing, 97,200; trade, 151,000; government, 139,500; services, 111,900. *Insured unemployed* (Sept. 1973)—8,700 (1.6%).
Manufacturing (1971): *Value added by manufacture,* $1,384,600,000. Electrical equipment and supplies, $291,600,000; nonelectrical machinery, $230,400,000; primary metal industries, $182,700,000; food and kindred products, $113,100,000; printing and publishing, $85,600,000; fabricated metal products, $72,000,000.
Agriculture (1972): *Cash farm income,* $871,252,000 (livestock, $479,986,000; crops, $342,253,000; government payments, $49,013,000). *Chief crops* (in order of value, 1971)—Cotton lint, lettuce, hay, wheat.
Mining (1972): *Production value,* $1,050,881,000 (ranks 9th among the states). *Chief minerals*—Copper, $913,869,000; molybdenum, $35,886,000; sand and gravel, $25,174,000.
Transportation: *Roads* (1972), 47,085 miles (75,774 km); *motor vehicles* (1972), 1,184,972; *railroads* (1972), 2,052 miles (3,302 km); *public airports* (1972), 104.
Communications: *Telephones* (1973), 1,166,400; *television stations* (1971), 12; *radio stations* (1971), 76; *newspapers* (1973), 12 (daily circulation, 481,000).

state should assume a larger share of educational costs and must therefore levy increased taxes, the special session was deadlocked when the Senate and House passed widely differing bills, and a conference committee was unable to effect a compromise. Just before Christmas the Legislature recessed for the holidays without taking any final action.

Arizona Republicans, who have controlled both houses of the legislature since 1966, were faced with a scandal in 1973 when it was alleged that two Republican committee chairmen had an interest in the sale of retirement annuities to state employees. The Republican leadership of the House of Representatives stripped both men of their chairmanships and announced a broad investigation of conflict-of-interest problems in the legislature.

Local Elections. Phoenix voters administered a decisive setback to federal and state highway planners in May when they voted heavily against the construction of the Papago Freeway, a major east–west superhighway that would have cut through downtown Phoenix. Millions of dollars had already been spent on land acquisition and clearing, and at the end of 1973 it was still uncertain what would be done with the abandoned freeway land.

In November the Charter Committee, the political organization that has dominated the Phoenix government since 1949, suffered a setback when an Independent candidate won one of the six seats on the City Council, all of which had previously been held by Charterites. However, Timothy Barrow was unopposed as Charter candidate to succeed Mayor John Driggs. In Tucson, Democrats won the three council seats at stake and converted a 4–2 Republican majority to a 5–1 Democratic margin.

JOHN P. WHITE, *Arizona State University*

ARKANSAS

Reform, innovation, and fiscal irregularities highlighted the activities of state and local governments in Arkansas during 1973.

Legislature. During its regular session, a modernized General Assembly, with the number of standing committees reduced to 10 in each chamber and with a streamlined system for scheduling and locating bills, passed a record 893 acts. A number of these bills involved educational programs. Communities were authorized to establish state-supported junior colleges (an act that was generating increasing controversy); free textbooks for high school students were approved; and a kindergarten program was inaugurated. Capital punishment was reinstated for certain crimes, but was not made mandatory. Under the new law, the jury decides in a separate hearing whether a convicted person will be sentenced to death or life imprisonment without parole. The federal Equal Rights Amendment, prohibiting discrimination as to sex, was not ratified by the Arkansas legislature. By not adjourning sine die, the legislature, although limited by the constitution to a 60-day biennial session, provided for an unprecedented annual session by agreeing to reconvene in January 1974.

While most of Gov. Dale Bumpers' bills were passed, executive-legislative relations lacked the harmony of his first term. Some significant bills were vetoed, such as one that would have allocated 7% of the general revenue fund to cities and counties and another that would have begun a highway between Pine Bluff and Little Rock.

Fiscal Irregularities. While the practices of national public figures were being investigated in the Watergate hearings, a number of local irregularities were being uncovered in Arkansas. The Legislative Joint Auditing Committee exposed local officials who were embezzling public funds. A state department admitted to overcharging for travel expenses in order to create a public relations slush fund. The Community Investment and Development, Inc., was charged with gross mismanagement. The Arkansas Electric Cooperatives and the Milk Producers Institute were accused of making illegal campaign contributions. And two state senators were convicted for failing to pay federal income taxes.

Education. The Little Rock school board and the plaintiffs in the desegregation controversy that began in 1956 agreed to a two-year moratorium on litigation. A federal judge dissolved segregated black school districts in Conway county and integrated the students into adjoining white districts.

Prisons. A federal judge relinquished his jurisdiction over the state prisons in 1973 after the state correctional system had been restructured. Other federal court orders directed Pulaski and other counties to bring their jails and prison farms up to constitutional standards.

Obituary. The state was saddened by the death on February 22 of Winthrop Rockefeller, governor of Arkansas for two terms beginning in January 1967. Rockefeller had been the first Republican governor of Arkansas since 1874. During his tenure far-reaching reforms were initiated.

WILLIAM C. NOLAN, *Southern State College*

───────── ARKANSAS · Information Highlights ─────────

Area: 53,104 square miles (137,539 sq km).
Population (1972 est.): 1,978,000. *Density:* 37 per sq mi.
Chief Cities (1970 census): Little Rock, the capital, 132,483; Fort Smith, 62,802; North Little Rock, 60,040; Pine Bluff, 57,389; Hot Springs, 35,631; Fayetteville, 30,729.
Government (1973): *Chief Officers*—governor, Dale Bumpers (D); lt. gov., Robert C. Riley (D); secy. of state, Kelly Bryant (D); atty. gen., Jim Guy Tucker (D); treas., Nancy J. Hall (D); commissioner of education, A. W. Ford; chief justice, Carleton Harris. *General Assembly*—Senate, 35 members (34 Democrats, 1 Republican); House of Representatives, 100 members (99 D, 1 R).
Education (1972–73): *Enrollment*—public elementary schools, 245,457 pupils; 10,008 teachers; public secondary schools, 213,600 pupils; 10,603 teachers; nonpublic schools, 12,100 pupils; 530 teachers; colleges and universities, 52,198 students. *Public school expenditures,* $269,549,000 ($652 per pupil). *Average teacher's salary,* $7,613.
State Finances (fiscal year 1971): *Revenues,* $720,235,000 (3% general sales tax and gross receipts taxes, $120,-162,000; motor fuel tax, $79,720,000; federal funds, $228,-798,000). *Expenditures,* $651,864,000 (education, $272,225,-000; health, welfare, and safety, $133,972,000; highways, $137,941,000). *State debt,* $110,969,000 (June 30, 1971).
Personal Income (1972): $6,640,000,000; per capita, $3,357.
Public Assistance (1972): $130,071,000. *Average monthly payments* (Dec. 1972)—old-age assistance, $69.42; aid to families with dependent children, $112.49.
Labor Force: *Nonagricultural wage and salary earners* (July 1973), 628,400. *Average annual employment* (1972)—manufacturing, 184,000; trade, 117,600; government, 109,000; services, 78,900. *Insured unemployed* (Sept. 1973)—8,500 (1.8%).
Manufacturing (1971): *Value added by manufacture,* $2,420,-000,000. Food and kindred products, $335,400,000; electrical equipment and supplies, $269,700,000; paper and allied products, $222,200,000; lumber and wood products, $201,800,000; chemicals and allied products, $127,900,000.
Agriculture (1972): *Cash farm income,* $1,485,359,000 (livestock, $673,596,000; crops, $730,139,000; government payments, $81,624,000). *Chief crops* (in order of value, 1972) —Soybeans, cotton lint (ranks 4th among the states), rice (ranks 1st), hay.
Mining (1972): *Production value,* $258,121,000 (ranks 27th among the states). *Chief minerals*—Petroleum, $57,-535,000; bromine and bromine compounds, value not available.
Transportation: *Roads* (1972), 78,680 miles (126,620 km); *motor vehicles* (1972), 1,075,373; *railroads* (1972), 3,582 miles (5,765 km); *public airports* (1972), 73.
Communications: *Telephones* (1973), 993,500; *television stations* (1971), 7; *radio stations* (1971), 119; *newspapers* (1973), 35 (daily circulation, 438,000).

Metropolitan Museum of Art visitors view $1 million Greek vase. Museum officials claim it was bought; Italian government says it was smuggled from Italy.

art

In 1973, emphasis in the art world continued on periods and groups that were previously relatively ignored. The avant-garde also aroused interest.

REDISCOVERIES AND NEW EMPHASES

19th Century Academic Art Reexamined. Italian Ottocento (19th century) painting from American collections was shown at the New York Cultural Center, Columbia (S. C.) Museum of Art and Science, Cummer Gallery of Art (Jacksonville, Fla.), and M. I. T. (Cambridge, Mass.). It featured such painters as Giovanni Boldini, Gaetano Chierici, Silvestro Lega, and Giovanni Segantini.

Important exhibitions were also devoted to little-known 19th century artists of northern Europe. They included Jean-Leon Gérome (Dayton Art Institute, Minneapolis Institute of Arts, and the Walters Art Gallery, Baltimore), Sir Lawrence Alma-Tadema (Metropolitan Museum, New York), and professors of the Düsseldorf Academy and their U. S. pupils (National Collection of Fine Arts, Washington).

Women in Art. Among rediscovered 19th century artists was Lilly Martin Spencer, mother of 13, who was an accomplished realist painter of sentimental subjects (National Collection). More important was the impressive showing made by contemporary women artists. Major group shows—Women Choose Women (New York Cultural Center), Open

A. I. R. (A. I. R. Gallery, New York), and Unmanly Art (Suffolk Museum, Stony Brook, N. Y.)—sought "to redress the balance of the male-dominated art establishment." Works ranged from photo-realism to conceptualism. Womanspace, the first all-woman gallery on the West Coast, opened in Los Angeles to provide "a sympathetic environment in which women's art can be seen apart from male preoccupations."

Numerous distinguished exhibitions by women succeeded in New York without benefit of a "sympathetic environment"—Women Printmakers (New York Public Library), Lee Krasner's abstract paintings (Whitney Museum and Marlborough Gallery), Chryssa's neon-tube constructions (Denise Rene), Mary Frank's stoneware sculpture (Zabriskie), and Margaret Israel's reliefs and assemblages (Cordier & Ekstrom). Other noteworthy exhibitions included those of Miriam Schapiro (Emmerich), Alice Wilson (Whitney), Alice Trumbull Mason (Whitney), and the 19th century impressionist Mary Cassatt (Metropolitan).

American Indian Art and Graffiti. An important consideration in the publicizing of neglected or ignored art is the fostering of group pride. Thus, in addition to exhibits of internationally recognized traditional Indian arts (Metropolitan and the National Gallery of Art, Washington), work by contemporary Indians was shown (M. I. T. and the Peabody Museum, Cambridge).

In New York, graffiti were recognized as a largely Puerto Rican, apparently all-male, art form. Hugo Martinez, a City College student, formed United Graffiti Artists to foster self-expression in a studio rather than on the subways and walls, which cost the city more than $2 million a year to clean. Connoisseurs of graffiti by such "masters" as MICO, Spin-a-Roo, and Kool Breeze have already defined the distinct Manhattan, Bronx, and Brooklyn styles.

Traditional and Early Modern American Art.
Exhibitions highlighted varieties of 19th century realism. Works of John Singer Sargent, Theodore Robinson, Childe Hassam, and William Chase, from the Horowitz collection, were shown at the Metropolitan. Images of the American frontier appeared at the Whitney and paintings of the Great American West at the Kennedy Gallery (New York). A large exhibition of oils, watercolors, and drawings of Winslow Homer traveled from the Whitney to the Los Angeles County Museum of Art and the Chicago Art Institute. American impressionists were seen at the National Gallery, Whitney, Cincinnati Museum of Art, and North Carolina Museum of Art, Raleigh.

Early American modernists on view included Oscar Bluemner, Stuart Davis, Charles Demuth, Arthur Dove, John Marin, Georgia O'Keeffe, Charles Sheeler, Joseph Stella, and Max Webber in Pioneers of American Abstraction (Crispo, New York). A retrospective of Alfred Maurer was at the National Collection and several New York City galleries.

Photography. Appreciation of photography as a fine art continued to expand. In New York the Scott Elliot Gallery opened with calotypes (first photographs on paper) by William Talbot and Octavius Hill. Other "old masters" of photography shown included Eadweard Muybridge (Stanford University in 1972, New York Cultural Center in 1973); Edward Weston, Ansel Adams, and Wynn Bullock (Pasadena Art Museum); and Diane Arbus (Museum of Modern Art, New York). Thematic exhibits included 225 Press Photos from 50 years of newspapers (Museum of Modern Art) and The Painterly Photograph, 1890–1914, from the Stieglitz collection (Metropolitan).

THE AVANT-GARDE

Within the avant-garde, various forms of abstraction, new realism, and conceptualism continued to flourish. At the Whitney Biennial, 229 works represented most of the current trends. But more and more critics questioned the wisdom of vast surveys that often submerge individual achievement.

Abstract Art. Color-field abstraction was fashionable, as evidenced by an exhibit of Jules Olitski at the Rubin Gallery (New York) and most notably in his retrospective at the Boston Museum of Fine

Arts and the Whitney. Other color-field painters shown in New York included Morris Louis (Emmerich), Larry Poons (Knoedler), and Ellsworth Kelly (Museum of Modern Art). Other approaches to color, such as the lyrical abstractions of Philip Woffard, were revealed in Way of Color, the 33d Corcoran Biennial in Washington. Other avant-garde painters shown in New York were Sam Francis (Whitney), Roy Lichtenstein (Castelli), Frank Stella (Castelli), and Gene Davis (Fischbach). Also seen were Jim Dine (Sonnabend), Larry Rivers (Marlborough), and Kenneth Noland (Emmerich).

New Realism. Current interest in photography and 19th century realism, willingness to challenge "establishment" assumptions, and, more significantly, the need for perceptual, emotional, and intellectual expansion contributed to the recent revival of representational art. "New realism," therefore, variously manifested itself in photo-, magic, close-up, mini-, maxi-, hard-edge, and soft-focus realisms. The multiplicity of approaches was reflected in two differently organized group shows held simultaneously at the New York Cultural Center—Realist Revival and Realism Now. Also in New York were one-man shows of realists John Salt (O. K. Harris), Horacio Torres (Goldowsky), Joseph Raffael (Hoffman), and Malcolm Morley (Stefanotty). The work of photo-realists Chuck Close, Richard Estes, Don Eddy, and Robert Bechtle toured German museums in Stuttgart, Frankfurt, and Wuppertal.

Thanks to new realism, two popular realists enjoyed a revival. Norman Rockwell had a retrospective at the Danenberg Gallery, and Andrew Wyeth had one at the De Young Museum (San Francisco).

Sculpture. Big outdoor, environmental sculpture threatened to make most gallery sculpture look trivial. David von Schlegell's project at Storm King, N. Y., and Richard Serra's *Shift* on an estate in Canada were particularly impressive. In New York, gallery sculpture, however, was most effective. It included works by the Englishmen Reg Butler (Matisse), Isaac Witkin (Elkon), Tim Scott (Rubin), and Anthony Caro (Emmerich) and interesting new objects and constructions by Americans Donald Judd and painter Robert Rauschenberg (both Castelli). Outstanding was the retrospective of the late Eva Hesse (Guggenheim Museum, New York).

Jackson Pollock's Blue Poles *was sold for $2 million, the highest price ever paid for an American painting.*

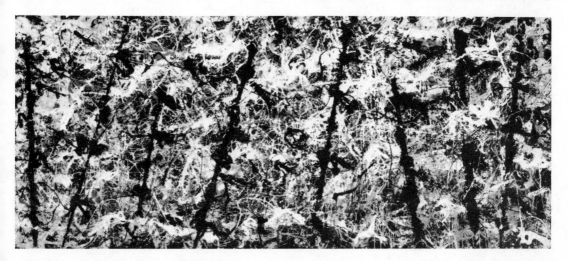

NEW VAN GOGH MUSEUM in Amsterdam is the permanent home of the van Gogh family collection. Dr. Vincent van Gogh (left), nephew of the painter, supervised the architects and designers and the final arrangement of the paintings.

Conceptual Art. As an international phenomenon often supported by political and idealistic action programs, conceptual art continued to win converts. One of its strongest exponents, the influential German artist Joseph Beuys, received two exhibits in New York (Gibson and Feldman Fine Arts). Other impressive presentations included Mel Bochner's Non-verbal Structures (Sonnabend) and Bruce Nauman's retrospective (Whitney).

RETROSPECTIVES AND OTHER EXHIBITIONS

Old Masters. The Hermitage State Museum in Leningrad and the Pushkin Museum in Moscow sent the first exhibit of Western art from the USSR to the United States. Masterpieces covering 50 years of French art from Monet to Leger were displayed at the National Gallery, Knoedler Gallery, and in Detroit. The Chicago Art Institute mounted a major old-master restrospective—88 paintings by Renoir.

There were many old-master exhibitions of the graphic arts. A most interesting collection of Roman drawings and prints of the First Maniera (Mannerist) was shown at the Rhode Island School of Design, Providence. Other exhibitions included 200 early Italian engravings (National Gallery); Italian master drawings from Christ Church, Oxford (Morgan Library, New York; Cleveland; St. Louis; Washington; and Philadelphia); and French master drawings (New York Cultural Center). Prints and drawings by Abraham Bloemaert were at the Metropolitan, and drawings by Inigo Jones were shown in the Banqueting House, which he designed, in London. Modern European drawings from the Kröller-Müller National Museum (Otterlo, Netherlands), including 35 superlative works by van Gogh, traveled to the Museum of Modern Art, Chicago, Ottawa, and San Antonio.

Modern Masters. A retrospective of the distinguished Swiss modernist Ferdinand Hodler was seen for the first time in the United States (University Art Museum, Berkeley; Guggenheim; Busch-Reisinger Museum, Cambridge). Another "first" at the Guggenheim was the Malevich collection from Amsterdam's Stedelijk Museum. A "first" at the National Gallery was modern painting and sculpture—large-scale works by 23 Americans.

Other modern masters exhibited were Hans Hofmann (Corcoran Gallery, Washington), Marcel Duchamp (Philadelphia Museum of Art, Museum of Modern Art, and Art Institute of Chicago), Amédée Ozenfant (Knoedler), Kurt Schwitters (Marlborough), and Arshile Gorky (Feigen). Also shown were Wassily Kandinsky (Pace and Lefebre), Soutine (Marlborough), and Miro (Matisse and Museum of Modern Art).

Canadian Art World. At the National Gallery of Canada (Ottawa), Canadians saw French drawings, paintings, sculpture, and tapestry; Quebec painters from the André and Maurice Corbeil collection; and a retrospective for Claude Tousignant. Americans saw Canadian landscapes in The Artist and the Land, 1670–1930, at the Elvehjem Art Center (Madison, Wis.).

Unusual Exhibitions. Several exhibitions dealt with unusual material—paintings by maximum-security prisoners (National Collection), 44 kinds of highly expressive modern musical notation (Baltimore Museum of Art), and the multitudinous uses of gold (Metropolitan). A presentation of fakes and forgeries, with originals for comparison, could be studied at the Minneapolis Institute of Arts.

Non-Western Art. African art was seen in a splendid array of textiles (Los Angeles County Museum of Art) and Dogon carvings (Brooklyn Mu-

seum, then on tour). Eskimo art was at the De Young Museum. Asia House (New York) displayed Indian miniatures and the arts of Isfahan.

Ancient Chinese art recovered from tombs in the last 20 years was sent by China to the Petit Palais in Paris and the Royal Academy in London, indicating the interest of the Communist government in China's imperial past. Chinese bronzes and classical landscapes were shown at the Metropolitan. Exhibitions of Japanese art focused on Japanese representation of Europeans and assimilation of their techniques— 19th century prints (Philadelphia Museum of Art) and 16th and 17th century Namban painting and ceramics (Japan House, New York).

MUSEUMS AND COLLECTIONS

Looting and Theft. A spectacular controversy surrounded the calyx krater painted by Euphronios, which the Metropolitan bought in 1972 for $1 million. The Italian government charged that the vase was illegally smuggled out of Italy, while the museum maintained it was a lawful acquisition. The dispute dramatized the scandal of the worldwide looting and theft of art. Theft of art objects increased 14% in 1973. Authorities estimate that in the last 15 years 25,000 works of ancient and other art have been stolen from Italian museums, churches, and archaeological sites, and that $7 million worth of antiquities are stolen annually from sites in the Mediterranean area. Many objects go to museums. The problem is so serious that Interpol published its first list of "most wanted" paintings. UNESCO sponsored the first conference on the problem.

Art, Ethics, and the Law. The Metropolitan was also the focal point of argument concerning the reattribution, sale, or trade of 300 paintings. After censure from the College Art Association, it became clear that new procedures were needed both to guide and protect museums. The Metropolitan agreed to consider more carefully the interest of the public in future "de-acquisitioning."

The Practicing Law Institute (New York) began holding workshops on the legal and business problems of museums and artists. The Association of International Museum Directors sponsored a special conference in Berlin to discuss an unprecedented move by German authorities who sought to hold a guest curator responsible for a $250,000 deficit at the 1972 Kassel Documenta. The U.S. House of Representatives began hearings on a bill to aid the general improvement of museums.

New Museums. In Amsterdam a new home was built for the van Gogh family collection, formerly at the Stedelijk. In Florence the 16th century Vasari corridor, damaged in World War II, was reopened, linking the Uffizi Gallery with the Pitti Palace. In Rome, Pope Paul VI opened a Vatican gallery of modern art. The 600 works are by such masters as Picasso, Braque, Klee, Kandinsky, and Kokoschka.

Appointments. Four museums gained new directors. Merrill Rueppel was named for the Boston Museum of Fine Arts; Thomas Armstrong for the Whitney; E. Laurence Chalmers, Jr., for the Chicago Art Institute; and Everett Fahy for the Frick Collection.

Auctions and Sales. So many price records were set that one auctioneer admitted that money no longer seemed to mean anything. At Christie's (London) a landscape by Aelbert Cuyp, whose most expensive work previously brought $130,600, was sold for $1,522,500. At Kornfeld and Klipstein (Zürich)

Toulouse-Lautrec's *Grande Loge* became, at $160,-000, the most expensive print ever sold at auction. Georgia O'Keeffe's *Poppies,* sold for $120,000 at Sotheby Parke Bernet (New York), set a new record for a work by a living American. The National Gallery paid $1.1 million for *Femme nue* (1910), an analytic cubist Picasso that was the highest price ever paid for his work. Jackson Pollock's *Blue Poles,* sold to the National Museum of Australia for $2 million, was the costliest American painting.

AWARDS, HONORS, AND GRANTS

The National Endowment for the Arts awarded a grand total of $38.2 million to museums, other institutions, and individuals in the arts. More than 100 fellowships were granted to artists and photographers. Art historian Meyer Schapiro received an award from the Art Dealers' Association of America. On his 86th birthday Chagall was given his own museum by the French government, the first it had ever dedicated to a living artist.

OBITUARIES

Pablo Picasso (91), one of history's greatest artists, died in southern France. About 40 masterworks from his collection of works by other painters were given to the Louvre. The disposition of more than 10,000 of his own works remained in doubt, since he left no will. (See also OBITUARIES.)

Other notables in the art world who died in 1973 were the Americans Edward Steichen (93), photographer (see also PHOTOGRAPHY); Robert Goldwater (66), director, Museum of Primitive Art, New York; Philip Evergood (72), painter; and Robert Smithson (35), earth sculptor.

VICTOR H. MIESEL, *University of Michigan*

ANCIENT CHINESE bronze cooking vase is part of the exhibition China sent to London and Paris in 1973.

UPI

ASIA

In Bangkok, Thailand, antigovernment riots by students resulted in the overthrow of the 10-year-old military regime of Thanom Kittikachorn.

For Asia, 1973 was the year of a food scare, an energy crisis, U. S. disengagement from the war in Southeast Asia, and several changes of government. There was economic progress in East Asia but a general condition more closely approximating stagnation in South Asia.

FOOD SCARCITY

Millions of tons of grain had to be shipped to Asia since poor planning and adverse weather conditions had sharply cut agricultural output in South Korea, the Philippines, Indonesia, Malaysia, Cambodia, Thailand, Burma, Bangladesh, and India. Scarcity became more widespread than ever in India (one million children annually die of diseases related to malnutrition there), although India imported about 2 million tons of food grain. More favorable rains later in the year prevented even worse consequences. Bangladesh had to import 2.5 million tons. Deaths from starvation were reported in Indonesia, which imported 1.5 million tons of rice. In Burma, black market food prices were four times the controlled price.

By the end of the year the population of Asia had surpassed the 2.2 billion mark—constituting almost 60% of the world's total—and it was still growing at a rate of about 2.3% per year. This meant that by the end of the year there were 50,-600,000 additional new mouths to feed. But even though it had been shown that the "green revolution" of superior seeds, more fertilizer, and increased irrigation had not provided the decade or two of food security that generally had been hoped for, no government seemed inclined to rely less on agricultural investment and institute an all-out population curtailment program.

In China, where the population growth rate has been about 1.7%, positive economic incentives to check population growth were limited to free birth-control devices, and attempts to use negative sanctions, such as the withholding of food from already large expanding families, seemed too unpopular to sustain. Although India planned to triple its outlay for family planning in its next plan, it cut its planned expenditure in 1973.

Bangladesh planned to spend at least 15% of its plan budget for such measures when it begins, but in the meantime it allocated very little. Pakistan, the Philippines, and Thailand, all of whom have annual population increase rates surpassing 3%, have no programs worth mentioning. Only Japan appeared to keep its population growth rate near the 1% level. The experience of 1973 suggested the necessity of a population decline on the continent of Asia, but few world leaders seemed to perceive it.

The Oil Crisis and Economic Development. The traditional goal of providing a better life for an ever-growing population received a new shock during 1973. Like the West, much of Asia was shocked by the Arab cutoff of oil. Japan, which had enjoyed an economic growth rate of 11.5% in 1972, still expected its Gross National Product (GNP) to rise by 9% in 1973. But the Arab energy squeeze created near panic in its sorely dependent economy, which had just begun to experience an inflation rate of over 20% and an adverse balance of trade as a consequence of the 40% upward revaluation of the yen over the past few years. In India automobile fuel prices doubled. Its Arab allies had been less concerned with the eventual destination of its exports than punishing the Western companies that delivered India's petroleum. India's GNP had not increased more than 2% in 1972–73, and various other shortages had already curtailed its industrial output.

Moderately high energy-based economies in other countries were also adversely affected by the end of the year: Hong Kong, whose economy has been jumping at a rate of around 17% the last few

years; Pakistan, which after a couple of disastrous years finally managed a 6.5% increase in GNP in 1972–73; and Taiwan and South Korea, which managed large increases in output but where increased fuel costs threatened such growth rates. The effect seemed to be less dramatic but no less serious on such relatively stagnant economies (in 1973) as those of Afghanistan, Sri Lanka (Ceylon), Burma, Bangladesh, Thailand, South Vietnam, and the Philippines.

China seemed little affected because it has adequate oil supplies and because it relies heavily on human labor. As has been the pattern since 1968, at least 2 million middle school graduates were sent to the countryside in October to provide rural labor, many of them permanently. (In 1972, China's growth in GNP seems to have slowed from its normal 9%–10% to around 6%–7%.) Indonesia, because of its oil reserves, appeared to be little affected, and Iran, because it increased its substantial oil exports, would probably have a GNP increase above the 13% it had forecast for itself earlier in the year.

Vietnam and U. S. Disengagement. In January, a Vietnam cease-fire, withdrawal, peace, and reunification agreement was initiated by U. S. presidential adviser Henry Kissinger and the North Vietnamese negotiator Le Duc Tho. It was a complex 18-page agreement that resulted in the exchange of thousands of prisoners and provided a presumably graceful withdrawal of U. S. troops from the combat area. The United States had spent nearly $150 billion on the war and lost about 46,000 soldiers in combat. It is estimated that there had been more than 1.1 million combat deaths among the North and South Vietnamese and over 1 million civilian deaths. But the agreement, while stopping the loss of life in North Vietnam and Laos, did not end the war in either South Vietnam or Cambodia. Both the North Vietnamese and the United States continued to resupply their allies. An average of about 5,000 Vietnamese were killed each month for the remainder of the year. The United States sent at least 500 more planes, 200 gunships, 600 tanks, 150,000 tons of bombs, and 200,000 tons of artillery shells after the truce. The North Vietnamese sent tanks, SAM II missiles, and at least 40,000 new troops to the South, while building roads and fuel pipelines. Le Duc Tho and Kissinger met in Paris on December 20 to exchange complaints about breakdowns in the cease-fire.

U. S. bombing had probably prevented the takeover of the official Cambodian government by the North Vietnamese-backed insurgents at midyear. However, by year's end the Cambodian army again appeared to be weakening under the siege and attacks by the smaller, Khmer Rouge rebel forces. The number of civilians killed and orphans created in the embattled towns in the 50-mile (80-km) perimeter surrounding the capital, Phnom Penh, numbered in the tens of thousands. During much of the year President Lon Nol had difficulty in preserving a united government. His palace was attacked from the air in March. To shore up his prestige, a four-man government with In Tam as premier was instituted in May. In Tam resigned in October, complaining of powerlessness under the president, but Lon Nol rejected the resignation. However, In Tam offered his resignation again on December 7. On December 26, Lon Nol appointed Foreign Minister Long Boret premier.

After 20 years of intermittent war, peace finally came to Laos. The United States appeared to be willing to allow the newly worked out compromise to stand. Prince Souvanna Phouma again became premier in the provisional government. The non-Communists got the ministries of finance, interior, and defense, but the Pathet Lao got the ministry of foreign affairs, an organizational advantage in the Consultative Council, and an equal number of seats in the provisional coalition government instead of the 25% it was given in 1962. It was believed that Hanoi would withdraw a major portion of its 60,000 troops from Laos, although perhaps not all of them as had been stipulated in the agreement.

The declining presence of U. S. forces in the region made it easier to overthrow a U. S.-backed military dictatorship in Thailand. The United States had already withdrawn several thousand troops and over 100 planes when in October students took to the streets to protest the corrupt and arbitrary rule of the regime of Marshal Thanam Kittikachorn. After unprecedented street fighting involving over one million citizens against one of Asia's more formidable armies, Premier Thanam left for the United States, and in his place the king appointed a university dean, Dr. Sanya Dharmasakt. The result seems to have been a liberal revolution, a rarity in Asia today. A committee has been established to investigate reports of massive corruption on the part of the past rulers, corruption involving perhaps $20 million of public funds. At the same time a constitution was being written that would redistribute land and provide for the subsidization of education as well as create a democratic government. Although student leaders said they would campaign for the elimination of American bases and the creation of a more independent Thailand, the revolution had created little overall anti-Americanism in the country.

The Asian Structure of Power. With the pullout of U. S. troops from Vietnam, Thailand, and Taiwan the power structure in Asia became more diffuse. As the United States reduced its presence in the area, the Soviet Union announced its desire to

MEMBERS of international commission supervising the Vietnam cease-fire confer with American officer (right).

UPI

establish an Asian collective-security system. Iran, perhaps the most pro-Western of all the Asian nations, somewhat surprisingly endorsed the idea. But other Asian nations have been considerably less than enthusiastic.

China regards the Soviet proposal coolly as a device for its own encirclement. Premier Kakuei Tanaka of Japan balked at the idea during his visit to Moscow in October. The Soviet political leader Leonid Brazhnev attempted to get India to accept it during his trip there in November, but the resulting agreement, which had much to say about trade and development assistance, had nothing to say about collective security.

Smaller Asian nations have been silent about the Soviet idea, which suggests that Asia does not seem to be eager to have another Western power fill any supposed power vacuum. Iraq and Syria in West Asia may welcome Russian military influence, but such pro-Soviet South Asian nations as Afghanistan, India, and Bangladesh continued to prefer to keep their relations as purely economic as possible.

China and Japan, the more natural leaders of Asia (so long as India languishes in near economic stagnation), did not greatly increase their hegemony during 1973. Japan continued to scatter substantial sums of aid about, but the new precariousness of its own economy undercut its position. China seemed more concerned with establishing trade relations with Japan and the West than in trying to influence the affairs of other Asians. Its support for the rebels in Cambodia and Vietnam has been indirect and from all appearance rather modest.

One of the most dramatic shifts in power came as a consequence of quite sizable purchases of military equipment from the United States by Iran. Over $3 billion was allocated for the purchase of hundreds of the most advanced U. S. aircraft, laser-guided bombs, and other complex equipment. A

U. S. DIPLOMAT Henry Kissinger confers informally with Communist China's Chairman Mao Tse-tung (right) and Prime Minister Chou En-lai in Peking in February.

UPI

force of 1,700 tanks was projected. Such a force was expected to give Iran superiority over Soviet-aided Iraq in the Persian Gulf region. Pakistan in turn purchased some of Iran's old F5's, and also some old Starfighters from Saudi Arabia. But its forces would still be no match for those of India, which has a standing army of more than 900,000. The largest air force in Asia is probably South Vietnam's, which suggests that power in Asia has become fairly widely dispersed.

Transition. Some of the 1972 trends continued into 1973. The spirit of South Asian détente was strengthened when Pakistan, India, and Bangladesh agreed to exchange prisoners. And Pakistani Prime Minister Ali Bhutto got permission from his new Assembly to recognize Bangladesh when he deemed it appropriate.

China continued its trade expansion. Its world trade grew from $5.8 billion in 1972 to around $7 billion in 1973. Trade with the United States jumped ten-fold to around $900 million. Most of it was in the form of grain purchases, but it made the United States China's second-largest trading partner. Japan stayed on top by exchanging about $1.1 billion in goods. Trade with the Soviet Union fell to about $200 million from around $250 million the year before.

The press was again on the defensive in Asia. In the Philippines, the press was permitted to report news of crimes only after the courts had given their verdict. Sri Lanka's government broke up the largest newspaper chain in the country, a chain that happened to have opposed it in the last general election. Premier Nguyen Van Thieu in Vietnam, Bhutto in Pakistan, and Mujibur Rahman in Bangladesh were among those rulers who took further action to curtail the press in 1973.

The Chinese government did not relax its hold over the populace. Some moderate leaders who had fallen into disfavor were rehabilitated, and a few new faces appeared at the top of an enlarged politburo at the 10th Party Congress in 1973.

A few trends were reversed during the year. Burma seemed to be ending its 10-year policy of isolation. Gen. Ne Win initiated contact with the World Bank and the Asian Development Bank. He also sought bids from nearly 50 foreign companies to search for off-shore oil. Although his government controlled most of the economy down to the local retailers, economic progress has been slow and the black market vigorous. Ne Win also paid visits to Japan, Thailand, Indonesia, and Malaysia.

Some new governments were formed. Afghanistan's king, Mohammed Zahir Shah, was overthrown by the army. Lt. Gen. Mohammed Daud Khan, who had followed a pro-Soviet and anti-Pakistan foreign policy during an earlier term as Afghanistan's premier, became head of the newly proclaimed republic. A civilian revolt of 15,000 brought down the government of the autocratic *chogyal* in tiny Sikkim. At this ruler's request, India's troops marched in to save him, but they set up a more liberal and democratic government.

A major shift of government came for the 1,000 tribes of 2.6 million people in Papua New Guinea. Australia granted them self-government on December 1. Many citizens wondered if a stable country could be shaped by a people divided into 500 diverse language groups.

RALPH C. MEYER
Fordham University at Lincoln Center

astronomy

Although important astronomical progress was made in 1973 in studies of the moon, the sun, and other objects of the solar system, some of the most exciting developments of the year pertained to identifications of "black holes," to events in the nuclei of galaxies, and to cosmology.

Instrumentation. The surface of the large dish at the Arecibo Ionospheric Observatory in Puerto Rico is being refigured to make it spherical to within a tolerance of 0.12 inches (3 mm). The sensitivity will be increased 100-fold for radio work and 1,000-fold for radar work. It will then be possible to construct a radar map of Venus as accurate as our present lunar radar maps.

Curtailment of funds for a high-energy astrophysical orbiting observatory dealt a severe blow to progress in this very exciting field of physical science. Meanwhile, valuable astronomical observations (of solar activity, especially) were undertaken during the year from the orbiting Skylab. (See SPACE EXPLORATION.)

Solar Eclipse. On June 30, 1973, an eclipse of the sun crossed much of the Atlantic Ocean and Africa. Some 3,500 people gathered in 7 cruise ships to view the event, and it was also observed from numerous ground stations. Although the eclipse lasted only 10 minutes at any point on the ground, one group of scientists, by following the path of the eclipse in a supersonic Concorde airliner, was able to extend its observation to 74 minutes to secure infra-red data and study coronal motions.

Moon. Analyses of lunar data were beginning to give a broad general picture of the probable history and internal structure of the moon. Measurements of subsurface temperatures and rock conductivities showed that the rate of heat loss from the interior is about one third that of the earth. Seismic wave data show that to a depth of more than 600 miles (about 1,000 km) the material is rigid. Moonquakes and meteorite impacts on the far side show seismic P waves but no S waves, suggesting a semi-melted core with a radius of about 450 miles (700 km) and a temperature of $1,500°K$ ($2,700°F$).

The surface of the moon seems to be covered everywhere with rubble. The low density crust may be 45 miles (70 km) thick on the far side, but the maria on the near side may be primarily basalt. In a few locations, solid rock may lie just a few miles below the surface.

The fossil magnetism of lunar rocks indicates crystallization in a magnetic field about 100 times the strength of the present lunar field. H. C. Urey and S. K. Runcorn have suggested that the rocks may have been magnetized at a time when the interior of the moon was cold and the moon itself was magnetized like a permanent magnet. Later heating of the moon's interior would have destroyed this strong magnetic field.

In spite of differences from one surface point to another, the most common chemical elements show a remarkable uniformity in abundance. Compared to the solar system "average," as defined by carbonaceous chondrites, the lunar surface is about 6 times richer in aluminum, calcium, and titanium, and about 4 times poorer in sodium, magnesium, and iron. The interior almost certainly has a different

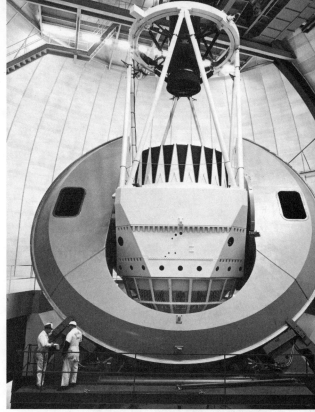

MAYALL TELESCOPE at Kitt Peak, Arizona, began operations in 1973. Its 158-inch primary mirror will allow astronomers to see objects at the fringe of the universe.

composition. Existing crustal differences in chemical composition are probably produced by the effects of bombardment and destruction of the original crust, followed by lava flows and other events.

Age determinations show that lunar rocks seem to fall into two groups. The very ancient ones are about 4.47 billion years old, while the old highland rocks and basalts appear to be about 3.95 billion years old. A battering by planetesimals occurred about 4 billion years ago. Over a period of about 600 million years, the surface was churned up, rocks were melted, and mare basalts were produced. The existence on the moon of xenon isotopes—which can be produced by the fission of plutonium, whose half life is 82 million years—gives evidence that there was plutonium in the original lunar rocks, indicating that the moon contained at least some material processed in a supernova explosion.

Sun. Observations from the orbiting solar observatory OSO-7 and from Skylab gave important data on solar flares. Analyzing OSO-7 data, D. J. Forrest observed gamma rays whose explanation required a stream of fast protons impinging upon gases in the solar atmosphere to produce positron-electron annihilation radiation and decay of excited deuterons. Other observers reported hard X rays in the range of 30 to 40 keV (thousand electron volts), lasting one minute, and connected with a longer burst of lower energy X rays.

The corona is a very inhomogeneous structure, characterized by "holes" where temperatures are some $600,000°K$ ($1,100,000°F$) below that of the surrounding gas and which are deficient in the emission of X rays and ultraviolet radiation.

(Continued on page 109)

107

Lubos Kohoutek, Czech astronomer, stands before a photograph of comet bearing his name.

KOHOUTEK

A Flop to Earthlings, Ballyhooed Comet Pleased Scientists

Comet Kohoutek was discovered by the Czech astronomer Lubos Kohoutek on March 7, 1973, while he was using a 32-inch (81-cm) Schmidt telescope at the Hamburg Observatory. The comet was first detected beyond the orbit of Mars. Since Kohoutek seemed to be a large comet—its solid nucleus was estimated to have a diameter of 25 miles (40 km)—and since comets brighten as they approach the sun, many astronomers expected that it would become a spectacular object as it approached perihelion on December 28, assuming it would brighten in the same ratio as do most comets. But as it neared the sun it did not become a conspicuous object like comet Bennett in 1970, although it was visible with field glasses if the observer knew where to look. However, the public's disappointment over the comet's display was balanced by the comet's value to astronomers.

Path of the Comet. Comets are believed to exist in great numbers at the outer fringes of the solar system, and they are presumed to represent debris left over when the solar system was formed 4.6 billion years ago. Comet Kohoutek made a long, long journey from the outer solar system to the sun, which it swung around at a distance of about 13.2 million miles (21.2 million km) on December 28. The comet hurtled through the inner solar system at a speed of about 70,000 miles (115,000 km) per hour and made its closest approach to earth—75 million miles (120 million km) —early in January when it was outward bound from the inner solar system. Its discoverer said that it "very probably" was a new comet that had never been around the sun before.

The orbit of Kohoutek showed it to be a new comet, moving in a path indistinguishable from a parabola. Hence, its period of revolution around the sun is extremely long. It may take about 75,000 years before the comet returns to the inner solar system. Alternatively, perturbations caused by the planets may eject Kohoutek from the solar system, never to return.

Structure and Composition. A generally accepted theory holds that comets are "icebergs" consisting of frozen water (H_2O), methane (CH_4), and ammonia (NH_3), and other substances containing much refractory material, possibly in the form of silicate dust. As a comet approaches the sun, its temperature rises and the frozen gases begin to volatilize and escape from its surface. At this stage the cloud of material surrounding the original solid nucleus forms a fuzzy envelope, or coma. Also, the solar wind—the fast-moving charged-particle stream from the sun—strips material away from the comet, thereby producing its tail. A bright comet will show a small nucleus (the original "iceberg"), an immediately surrounding cloud of newly evaporated gases (the extended coma), and a tail that can be a few million miles to 100 million miles (160 million km) long. Since comet Kohoutek was making its first visit near the sun, its solid nucleus had never been volatilized before. Presumably, observation and subsequent analysis of its coma and tail could provide information on the primordial matter of the solar system.

Observational Program. Comet Kohoutek was discovered months before its closest approach to the sun, so there was plenty of time to plan cooperative observations from numerous observatories, the manned Skylab space station, the Venus-bound Mariner 10, two earth-orbiting unmanned satellites, rockets, balloons, and aircraft. Furthermore, the comet passed so close to the sun that it was possible to determine some of the effects of solar radiation on the cometary constituents.

The Skylab 3 crew—astronauts Gerald Carr, Edward Gibson, and William Pogue—obtained a wealth of data by using various telescopes and cameras, including a special far-ultraviolet camera for high-resolution photographs of radiations from hydrogen. Much of the gas ejected from a comet scatters or reemits far-ultraviolet light that cannot penetrate through the earth's atmosphere; thus, the camera aboard the spacecraft gave a new view. Two of the astronauts went outside their space station to photograph the comet on December 25 and 29. On the earlier date its tail was 15 million miles (24 million km) long and showed such colors as blue-silver, reds, and yellows.

Valuable observations also were made from the unmanned Mariner 10, the orbiting astronomical observatory Copernicus, and the orbiting solar observatory OSO 7. These observations included direct photographs that record rapid changes in the comet's tail as well as scans of spectral regions, particularly those unobservable from the ground. Rockets fired from the earth's surface were used for many experiments, such as searching for radiation from helium. Ground-based observations were made at observatories in West Virginia, Arizona, California, Hawaii, and Chile, and the Jet Propulsion Laboratory tried to obtain radar reflections from the nucleus of the comet.

In spite of the fact that comet Kohoutek was less than spectacular, the intensive observational program is sure to yield valuable insights into the primordial material of the solar system.

LAWRENCE H. ALLER

Mercury and Venus. From its reflection spectrum, T. McCord and J. B. Adams have inferred that the planet Mercury is covered by a lunar-like soil rich in dark material of high iron and titanium content. Radar studies of Venus have shown its equatorial regions to contain shallow craters ranging in diameter from 20 miles (32 km) to 100 miles (160 km).

Jupiter and Its Moons. The space probe Pioneer 10, which passed near Jupiter on Dec. 4, 1973, sent back data relating to the magnetic field of the planet. (See SPACE EXPLORATION.) At year's end, scientists were examining the data to ascertain whether, as J. Warwick had suggested, the center of Jupiter's magnetic field is located some 30,000 miles (50,000 km) from the center of the planet. The axis of the field is tilted about 8°–10° with respect to the axis of Jupiter's rotation.

From infra-red reflectivities, McCord and S. T. Ridgway have identified water ice on three of Jupiter's satellites—Europa, Ganymede, and Callisto.

Comets. The first comet of the year was discovered on January 11, after it had passed perihelion and was already receding from the sun. Comet Kohoutek (discovered March 7) reached maximum brightness near Christmas (see opposite page).

Stellar Satellite. A planet-like companion with a mass less than 1% that of the sun has been found for the dwarf star Epsilon Eridani. It revolves at a distance of 750 million miles (1,200 million km) in a period of 25 years.

X-Ray Sources, "Black Holes," and Pulsars. X-ray sources now identified include strong sources for hard (2–10 keV) X rays near the center of our galaxy, with luminosities 25,000 times that of the sun. Other sources include Cygnus X3, a number of X-ray "stars" and pulsars, and "soft" X-ray-emitting supernova remnants such as Vela X.

Cygnus X3 (distance, 25,000–30,000 light years) was detected as a source of X-ray, infra-red, and radio emissions. Its X-ray emission shows a periodicity of 4.8 hours, suggestive of a binary (double star) that may involve a pulsar or "black hole." Its radio flux has shown rapid fluctuations, including a 200-fold increase in one day.

Attention is increasingly directed to a small class of X-ray pulsars which show rapid pulses in addition to long period variations suggestive of eclipses. Herculis X1 (HZ Herculis) shows identical optical and X-ray periods. It is suggested that the X-ray source is on the surface of a neutron star which revolves around a more "normal" star.

Conventional radio frequency pulsars can be detected only if they are comparatively nearby. An object such as the Crab pulsar could be seen only as an X-ray or optical pulsar if placed behind a thick cloud of ionized hydrogen. Recently, the Crab pulsar was found to emit gamma rays in synchronism with its optical pulses. The Vela pulsar is observed to emit X rays, but is not seen optically.

Pulsar sizes are deduced to range from about 30 to 105 miles (50 to 170 km). Individual splotches on their surfaces, believed to produce beams of high-energy particles, radiation, and other emissions, are about 1.5 miles (2.5 km) across.

Cosmology. The ratio of the brightness of a galactic nucleus to that of the rest of the galaxy varies from one object to another. The ratio is relatively low in the Seyfert galaxies and similar types with active nuclei, and is relatively high in the so-called N galaxies. It has been suggested that quasars may represent simply the very bright nuclei of galaxies whose outer portions are dim.

Quasar red shifts are usually interpreted in terms of recession velocities. R. Carswell and P. A.

AMERICAN SCIENCE AND ENGINEERING, INC.; ASTROPHYSICAL JOURNAL; NASA

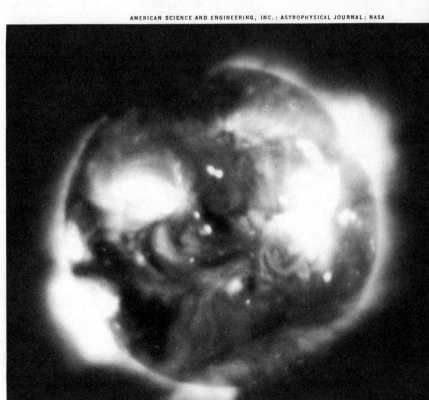

THE SOLAR CORONA, the hot outer layer of the sun, was captured in this X-ray photograph by the crew of Skylab 1 on May 28, 1973.

Strittmatter at the University of Arizona found that the quasar OH 471, discovered at Ohio State, has a red shift corresponding to a recession velocity 0.9c, or nine tenths of the speed of light, and a distance of 1.2 billion light years.

The existence of background gamma radiation that is probably isotropic has raised some questions in the minds of cosmologists. Its apparent extragalactic origin has led to the suggestion that it may originate from matter annihilation occurring at boundaries where clusters of galaxies composed respectively of matter and anti-matter impinge on each other. This interpretation is strongly challenged, however. No anti-particles occur in cosmic rays, and G. Steigman argues that there is no requirement that the universe contain large quantities of anti-matter anywhere.

Anniversary. Commemorative ceremonies were held in many places throughout the world in 1973 to mark the 500th anniversary of the birth of the Polish astronomer Copernicus. Prominent among the celebrations were those at the National Academy of Sciences in Washington, D. C., in April, and at the Extraordinary General Assembly of the International Astronomical Union in Warsaw, in September.

LAWRENCE H. ALLER
University of California, Los Angeles

ATLANTA

In Atlanta, the highlights of 1973 included the adoption of the first new city charter in 100 years and the election of the city's first black mayor.

City Charter. The 1973 Georgia General Assembly adopted a new Atlanta city charter to replace the one in effect since 1874. The new charter strengthens the administrative position of the mayor, but separates executive and legislative functions. The former Board of Alderman, consisting of 18 members elected at large, was replaced by an 18-member City Council, six members of which are chosen at large and 12 by districts. The Atlanta school board was reduced from 10 at-large members to nine members—three chosen at large and six by districts.

Elections. Elections to fill the new posts in the charter, which took effect in January 1974, were held in October 1973. Vice Mayor Maynard Jackson became Atlanta's first black mayor by defeating incumbent Sam Massell, the city's first Jewish mayor, in a runoff election. Nine black and nine white members were elected to the City Council, and white alderman Wyche Fowler defeated black civil rights activist Hosea Williams in the race for the presidency of that body. Five black and four white members were elected to the school board. A little more than half the population of Atlanta is black.

Crime. Crime continued to be a serious problem. In 1973, Atlanta was tagged as the "Murder Capital of the United States." Statistics of the Federal Bureau of Investigation showed that the homicide rate in Atlanta was twice the national average. Other crime also continued to rise, but by the end of the year the city had well underway a $20 million "Impact" program designed to reduce street crime and burglary. The city also added four new helicopters to its aerial patrol and launched an $8 million Target Hardening and Opportunity Reduction (THOR) program, which provides security inspectors to assist Atlantans in securing their homes and businesses against intruders.

Construction. Plans for more skyscrapers in downtown Atlanta were announced in 1973, even as work was begun on a 70-story hotel, which was expected to be one of the two tallest inns in the world. (The other is a hotel being built in Chicago by the same firm.) Plans were also announced for a high-rise convention-shopping-participant sports complex on a 21-acre site near Georgia Tech. The complex, which was expected to cost more than $150 million, was to include four 45-story and two 40-story buildings and a 1,000-room hotel.

In residential construction, the age of the condominium dawned in Atlanta, with the building of some 4,000 units during 1973. By early August, however, the effective interest rate on home loans had reached 8.3% for new homes and 8.5% for resales—the highest in the nation. Whereas the first six months of 1973 set a new record for housing and condominium construction, the final figures for the year were expected to reflect a decline in total residential construction due to an end of a decade of great activity in apartment building.

MARTA. The Metropolitan Atlanta Rapid Transit Authority (MARTA) began to acquire land for its planned 50-mile (80-km) rapid rail transit system and announced that inflation and new plans had boosted the anticipated cost of the system by $450 million to $1.79 billion. Still, MARTA officials said that because of a larger federal share than first expected the project could still be financed out of revenues from the special Atlanta sales tax of 1%. MARTA also repeated its promise to keep city bus fares at 15 cents for a seven-year period, begun in 1972, and to complete the rail system by 1980, with initial lines opening in 1978.

GENE STEPHENS, *Georgia State University*

ATOMIC ENERGY. See special feature beginning on page 41; see also NUCLEAR ENERGY.

NEW MAYOR of Atlanta, Ga., Maynard Jackson, is the first black mayor of a major city in the South.

UPI

Queen Elizabeth officially opened Sydney's new Opera House (above), as Navy helicopters flew over and boats converged in Sydney Harbour.

AUSTRALIA

A mixture of nationalism and Socialist doctrine took Australia along new paths in 1973. The Australian Labor party (ALP) government released a flood of legislation described by one critic as "the result of 23 years of dreaming" while the party was out of power. It also announced plans for a comprehensive federally financed health scheme, expanded the public service, and voted a substantial increase in funds for education. But polls showed that the tide of support for the ALP had ebbed by mid-year, and a national referendum in December on wage and price controls showed a further erosion in public support for the Labor government.

Economic prosperity was sustained in 1973 by high export prices for wool, meat, grain, and minerals, but a 13% inflation threatened real gains in the economy. The government moved to curb foreign investment.

In the international sphere, initiatives were directed toward closer association with the Third World nations. Whitlam made his first visit as prime minister to the People's Republic of China.

Politics. In a year of political shock tactics, the Labor government created more than 50 commissions, boards of inquiry, and committees of experts. Dozens of legislative measures were introduced in Parliament. But the Senate, where the Australian Labor party lacked a majority, managed to delay or substantially to amend some of the government bills, including those on the composition of electorates, on monopolies and restrictive trade practices, on conciliation and arbitration of industrial disputes, on a nationally funded health scheme, and on the form of the oath of allegiance for naturalization.

In the first half of the year the parliamentary and trade union wings of the ALP appeared to work in harmony. However, well before the end of the government's first year in office, strains and open differences came to the fore in sharply differing views expressed by Prime Minister Gough Whitlam and the newly elected federal president of the party, Robert Hawke. Hawke opposed the government when it sought in December to gain federal control over incomes by referendum; Hawke and Whitlam also disagreed on the desirability of increasing taxation to curb inflation. The personalities of these two ambitious leaders clashed as each claimed to speak for the Labor movement.

Successive polls showed that the public continued to support the prime minister. But support for his party declined, particularly after the middle of the year. Elections in Victoria and New

─────────── AUSTRALIA • Information Highlights ───────────

Official Name: Commonwealth of Australia.
Location: Southern Hemisphere between the Pacific and Indian oceans.
Area: 2,967,900 square miles (7,686,848 sq km).
Population (1973 est.): 13,300,000. *Density,* 5 per square mile (2 per sq km).
Chief Cities (1971 census, metropolitan areas): Canberra, the capital (city district), 141,795; Sydney, 2,717,069; Melbourne, 2,388,941; Brisbane, 816,987; Adelaide, 809,466.
Government: *Head of state,* Elizabeth II, queen; represented by Sir Paul Hasluck, governor-general (took office April 1969). *Head of government,* Gough Whitlam, prime minister (took office Dec. 1972). *Legislature—*Parliament: Senate and House of Representatives. *Major political parties—*Labor party; Liberal party; Country party.
Language: English (official).
Education: *Expenditure* (1967), 11.9% of total public expenditure. *School enrollment* (1968)—primary, 1,768,000; secondary, 1,080,524; technical/vocational, 189,985; university/higher, 164,528.
Monetary Unit: Australian dollar (.6723 A. dollar equals U. S. $1, Sept. 1973).
Gross National Product (1972 est.): $40,500,000,000.
Economic Indexes: *Industrial production* (1971), 145 (1963 = 100); *agricultural production* (1971), 121 (1963 = 100); *consumer price index* (1972), 139 (1963 = 100).
Manufacturing (major products): Petroleum products, steel, meat, heavy machinery, chemicals, processed foods, automobiles.
Major Agricultural Products: Wool (ranks 1st among world producers, 1971), wheat, sugarcane, barley, fruit, tobacco, raisins (world rank 2d, 1972), dairy products, sheep.
Major Minerals: Bauxite (ranks 2d among world producers, 1971), iron ore (world rank 3d, 1971), lead (world rank 3d, 1971), coal, nickel, copper, petroleum, natural gas, uranium, tin, gold, silver.
Foreign Trade (1972): Exports, $6,304,000,000; Imports, $4,555,000,000. *Chief trading partners* (1970)—Japan (took 27% of exports, supplied 14% of imports); United States (12%—22%); United Kingdom (11%—21%).
Tourism: Receipts (1972), $155,000,000.
Transportation: *Motor vehicles* (1971), 4,958,000 (automobiles, 3,993,900); *railroads* (1971), 25,495 miles (41,028 km); *merchant fleet* (1972), 1,184,000 gross registered tons; *major national airline,* Qantas Airways.
Communications: *Telephones* (1972), 4,151,622; *newspapers* (1970), 58 (daily circulation, 4,028,000).

South Wales confirmed the Liberals in office, with a marked swing away from the ALP. In Western Australia a by-election crucial to the Labor government was won by only 30 votes, allowing Premier John Tonkin to remain in office. In a referendum held on December 8, 65% of the voters turned down the government's bid to control income; 55% rejected its bid to control prices.

The visit of Yugoslavia's prime minister, Džemal Bijedić, in March coincided with the biggest political storm of the year. Before the visit, the attorney general, Sen. Lionel Murphy, accused the previous attorney general, the Liberal Sen. Ivor Greenwood, of having been too tolerant toward Croatian terrorists in Australia. (These Croatians, according to Yugoslavia, are trained in terrorist tactics in Australia, then return to Yugoslavia to work for Croatian secession through terrorism.) On March 16, Murphy, in company with federal police, raided the Melbourne headquarters of the Security Intelligence Organization, apparently to take files relating to the Croatian liberation movement. The raid created a major political stir. On April 5 the Liberal-dominated Senate passed a vote of no-confidence in Senator Murphy as attorney general, the first such motion to carry. Countering this censure, the Labor-dominated House of Representatives passed a motion of confidence in him after Whitlam had declared that no vote other than that of the House had any effect on the fate of ministers.

Shortly after praising Prime Minister Bijedić on his arrival in Australia, Whitlam was embarrassed by the disclosure that three Australians who were members of a Croatian organization captured by Yugoslav security forces in 1972 had been summarily executed in Yugoslavia a week before the Yugoslav prime minister's visit.

Domestic Policy. The government's position on public ownership of the energy resources of uranium, oil, natural gas, and coal changed in the course of the year. After a forthright declaration that full Australian ownership of these resources would be required and the requirement would be enforced, Whitlam softened "Australian ownership" to "Australian control." However, forces within the cabinet held the view that foreign investors should be given no equity in new energy projects but should only be guaranteed supplies of the minerals in return for investment funds. (See also MINING.)

The Economy. Overheating in the economy was characterized by full employment (less than 1.5% registered for unemployment assistance), a surfeit of unfilled jobs, sharp rises in wages, a rash of strikes, and serious inflation, with food prices and housing costs showing the sharpest increases. Though business prospered, the business community was sharply critical of the government, accusing it of excessive spending that put damaging strains on the private sector.

A 26% increase in the money supply and heavy deficit spending by the government fueled the inflation. Export income from rural products, minerals, and manufacturing was at a record high, and although capital inflow was cut, overseas balances remained high in spite of successive revaluations and a mid-year 25% cut in tariff duties.

The budget presented in August increased federal revenues to A.$11.481 billion (up 17%) and raised outlays to A.$12.168 billion (up 16%). It provided A.$843 million for assistance to education and increased social services payments. The budget increased taxes on gasoline, cigarettes, and wine and spirits, and taxation was increased for farmers, manufacturing companies, and mining enterprises.

In an effort to dampen demand for housing and ease private spending, interest rates rose in October to their highest level within memory—8½% for short-term federal bonds. Meanwhile strikes resulted in cutbacks in power and materials, which in turn slowed production, leading to shortages. Plentiful rain in most farm and pastoral areas, combined with a strong advance in prices for primary products, sustained prosperity in the rural sector. The stock market drifted almost 30% from its peak in January, and after a mild rally showed continued weakness.

Foreign Affairs. In November, Prime Minister Whitlam, winding up his 11-month role as minister for foreign affairs, called attention to moves undertaken "to stabilize" Australia's relationships with the United States, Japan, China, and Indonesia. (Indonesia was referred to as "our great next-door neighbor.") Support of these relationships was intended to give Australia "a clear," constructive, and forward-looking role" in the western Pacific. Whitlam said he believed Australia could now help materially in improving those relations. It had been his design to reassure Japan about access to raw materials. In regard to China, Whitlam visited Peking and assured China on his departure that Australia's friendship was "unshakable and unswerving." However, Whitlam's proposal for a new regional grouping of the nations of Asia and the Pacific was coolly received in the area. Indonesia was particularly aloof in commenting on the proposal.

Other initiatives in foreign policy included an exchange of diplomatic representatives with North Vietnam, North Korea, and East Germany.

Defense forces were trimmed. Early in the year the government announced that all Australian combat troops would be withdrawn from Malaya-Singapore by the end of 1973, thus effectively ending support for the ANZUK pact.

The Sydney Opera House. The Sydney Opera House, which took about 15 years to build and cost about A.$100 million, was opened on October 20 by Queen Elizabeth II. As a background for the opening there were harbor festivities in which 1,000 pigeons and 60,000 balloons were released; fireboats put on a water display. At night a crescendo of fireworks preceded the concert attended by the queen.

R. M. YOUNGER
Author, "Australia and the Australians"

AUSTRIA

Three important events occurred on Jan. 1, 1973: Austria took its seat for a two-year term on the UN Security Council; the trade agreement between Austria and the European Economic Community (EEC) went into effect; and the value-added tax was introduced in Austria. Later in the year Austria caused something of an international furor, when in order to effect the release of hostages taken in Austria by Arab guerrillas, the government agreed to close a Jewish transit facility near Vienna.

International Incident. On September 28, two armed Arab guerrillas raided a Moscow–Vienna train just after it left Czechoslovakia, and seized an Austrian customs official and three Soviet Jews bound for Israel. To free the hostages, Austrian Chancellor Bruno Kreisky agreed to provide a plane for the guerrillas to fly to Tunisia and to close the Jewish transit facility at Schönau Castle, near Vienna. The castle had been leased by the Jewish Agency and to a degree was beyond Austrian control and sovereignty. The Austrian government feared that the continued operation of the transfer center would lead to further guerrilla activity and make Austria a battleground of Israeli-Arab antagonism.

In spite of a personal appeal by Israeli Premier Golda Meir and an appeal by U. S. President Richard M. Nixon, Chancellor Kreisky refused to reverse the government's decision. Jews from the Soviet Union were still permitted to use Austria as a transfer point, but were required to proceed at once to Israel, without lengthy stopovers in Austria. Schönau Castle was not closed finally until December 10, when a new "Provincial Red Cross Aid Station for Refugees and other Transients" was opened at Wöllersdorf, 25 miles (40 km) south of Vienna.

Politics. In January the ruling Socialist party lost its absolute majority in the municipal elections in Graz. The party also lost ground in the Carinthia municipal elections on March 25.

At the end of May a referendum was held in Vienna on the city government's plan to erect a university institute in a local park. This would have necessitated the felling of some 70 trees. Conservationists and the press were successful in defeating the move. As a result, on June 2, Felix Slavik resigned as mayor of Vienna on the grounds that he lacked the confidence of the Socialist party organization. He was replaced by Leopold Gratz, the Socialist parliamentary floor leader. On July 13 the municipal council announced its early dissolution.

Economic Developments. The Austrian economy continued to expand with a growth rate of more than 6% in 1972 and, according to estimates, again

in 1973. Inflation continued. The overall increase in retail and consumer prices amounted to 7.4% in 1972. Unemployment was practically nonexistent in 1973, and Austria continued to recruit foreign workers, mostly from Yugoslavia and Turkey. Foreign workers numbered well over 200,000 and accounted for about 8% of the labor force.

The value-added tax was levied at the rate of 16%. A reduced rate of 8% was levied on such items as basic foodstuffs, books and newspapers, tourism, the rental of immovable property, and certain professional services.

Under the trade agreement of July 22, 1972, and the interim agreement of Oct. 1, 1972, between Austria and the EEC, tariffs were being gradually eliminated on industrial goods at the rate of 20% a year until ending on July 1, 1977. For certain "sensitive items"—such as special steels, aluminum, and paper—the period for the reduction of the tariffs was extended. Most of these tariffs were to end on Jan. 1, 1980, but the tariffs on paper were to extend to Jan. 1, 1984. A solution for the marketing of agricultural products remained to be worked out.

Premier Aleksei Kosygin of the USSR visited Austria on July 2–5 and signed an economic cooperation accord. The Soviet Union agreed to open a bank in Vienna in order to facilitate trade between the two countries.

In the international dollar crisis of the first half of 1973, Austria followed the lead of West Germany, revaluing the schilling upward by 2.25% on March 13, and by 4.8% on July 3. The midpoint rate (the average of the buying and selling rates) of the schilling stood at 28.82 per U. S. dollar in January 1973 and at 17.35 in July 1973.

Winter Olympics. On Feb. 4, 1973, the International Olympic Committee awarded the 1976 Winter Olympic games to Innsbruck, Austria.

E. C. HELMREICH
Bowdoin College

AUSTRIA • Information Highlights

Official Name: Republic of Austria.
Location: Central Europe.
Area: 32,374 square miles (83,849 sq km).
Population (1973 est.): 7,500,000. *Density,* 230 per square mile (89 per sq km).
Chief Cities (1971 census): Vienna, the capital, 1,603,408; Graz, 249,211; Linz, 204,627; Salzburg, 127,455.
Government: *Head of state,* Franz Jonas, president (took office for 2d 6-year term June 1971). *Head of government,* Bruno Kreisky, chancellor (took office April 1970). *Legislature*—Federal Assembly: Federal Council and National Council. *Major political parties*—Socialist party; Austrian People's party; Freedom party.
Language: German (official).
Education: *Expenditure* (1969), 7.9% of total public expenditure. *School enrollment* (1969)—primary, 886,990; secondary, 377,990; technical/vocational, 216,109; university/higher, 56,290.
Monetary Unit: Schilling (17.35 schillings equal U. S.$1, July 1973).
Gross National Product (1972 est.): $18,800,000,000.
Economic Indexes: *Industrial production* (1972), 175 (1963=100); *agricultural production* (1971), 107 (1963=100); *consumer price index* (1972), 143 (1963=100).
Manufacturing (major products): Processed foods, chemicals, textiles, iron and steel, electrical goods, paper, machinery and tools, wood products.
Major Agricultural Products: Rye, wheat, barley, potatoes, sugar beets, oats, forest products.
Major Minerals: Magnesite, iron ore, lignite, petroleum, natural gas, antimony.
Foreign Trade (1972): Exports, $3,883,000,000; Imports, $5,216,000,000. *Chief trading partners* (1970)—West Germany (took 23% of exports, supplied 41% of imports); Switzerland (11%—7%); Italy (9%—7%).
Tourism: Receipts (1972), $1,679,300,000.
Transportation: *Motor vehicles* (1971), 1,751,300 (automobiles, 1,325,200); *railroads* (1971), 4,062 miles (6,537 km); *major national airline,* Austrian Airlines.
Communications: *Telephones* (1972), 1,546,719; *newspapers* (1971), 32 (daily circulation, 2,187,000).

1974 STYLING

American Motors added this sporty Matador five-passenger coupe to its 1974 line. Free-standing, energy-absorbing front and rear bumpers are standard.

AMERICAN MOTORS CORPORATION

The 1974 Ford Mustang II is planned as the forerunner of a new class. It is 19 inches shorter than the 1973 model and 7 inches shorter than 1964 original.

THE FORD MOTOR COMPANY

The Chevrolet Laguna for 1974 has the popular rear "opera-window" roofline treatment. This Laguna S-3 is a sporty hardtop coupe.

THE GENERAL MOTORS CORPORATION

automobiles

Nearly all automobile manufactures in the United States and Canada established new production records during the 1973 model run. Production of 9,915,803 1973-model cars in the United States brought the industry within 1% of realizing the "10-million-car-year." The U. S. industry had never before exceeded even 9 million cars in any model run. It had built 8,631,886 1972 models and 8,842,000 1965 cars—the previous all-time peak.

Truck production in the United States also was proceeding at a record pace of close to 3 million units a year—after 1972 output of 2,482,503 trucks.

The Canadian industry produced 1,002,546 cars and trucks in the first seven months of 1973, compared with 876,841 for the same 1972 period. This total for 1973 included 783,084 cars, up from 679,-025, and 219,462 trucks, up from 197,816.

1973 MODEL PRODUCTION

General Motors (GM), Ford Motor Company, and Chrysler Corporation all set records through the 1973 run. GM for the first time surpassed 5 million cars, reaching 5,403,023. This exceeded GM's former high of 4,630,357, attained in 1972, by 16%.

Ford Motor's total of 2,562,625 cars edged out the 2,472,317 high reached in 1966. Chrysler's 1,623,469 total exceeded the 1,588,571 total of 1968 for its new record. American Motors Corporation (AMC) built 320,786 1973-model cars, more than 60,000 above its 1972 output but short of its 1965-model record of 391,366.

GM accounted for 54.49% of all 1973 cars built, up from 53.64% the previous year; Ford Motor, 25.84%, down from 27.47%; Chrysler Corpora-

tion, 16.37%, up from 15.82%, and American Motors, 3.24%, up from 3.00%. Ford's share of the U. S. output was affected by the fact it is the largest builder of cars in Canada for sale in the United States.

Trends. The 1973-model year was highlighted by sharp rises in production of intermediate, compact, and subcompact body styles—accompanied by a pronounced falloff in demand for standard-size cars. This trend was particularly evident in the last months of the 1973-model season, when gasoline shortages in many parts of the United States accelerated sales of smaller-size cars and hampered regular-size model retail deliveries. The "Big Three" automakers announced many plant closings and worker layoffs. Only AMC, primarily a maker of small cars, reported higher sales.

Intermediate models that showed the greatest gains in 1973 included the restyled Chevrolet Monte Carlo, with its "fixed" rear windows; Oldsmobile Cutlass; Buick Century; Pontiac LeMans; Mercury Montego; and Dodge Coronet. Chevrolet's compact Nova and subcompact Vega, Ford's compact Maverick, Plymouth's compact Valiant, and AMC's compact Hornet and subcompact Gremlin also had substantially higher 1973 output totals.

For four makes, compact or intermediate series proved "best sellers" in 1973. These included AMC (Hornet), Plymouth (Valiant), Dodge (Coronet), and Mercury (Montego). At the other end of the price spectrum, however, top-of-the-line models enjoyed record sales, as well.

Sports Cars. The long-slumping sports-car segment of the market apparently "bottomed out" and made a slight recovery, helped by restyled Pontiac Grand Prix and Firebird models and Chevrolet's Camaro. The Ford Mustang, longtime sales leader in the "pony car" category, held its lead over Camaro prior to a major revamping of the Mustang for 1974. The Mustang II was diminished in size and power for 1974 in keeping with the trend toward smaller cars.

THE 1974 MODELS

Of the four safety-equipment devices required by the Department of Transportation for 1974 models, the one most affecting consumers was the interlock ignition system connected to new inertia-reel seat-and-shoulder belts for the driver's seat and the right front passenger seat. In order to start any 1974 car, it is necessary for both the driver and the right front passenger to connect the seat-and-shoulder belts to their appropriate buckles. Unbuckling after starting actuates a buzzer-warning light signal similar to that used on 1973 models to call attention to unfastened belts. An actuating "bypass" button within the engine compartment is installed for use should correct connection of the seat belts still fail to permit the driver to start the ignition.

The three other government-directed changes in safety equipment affecting 1974 cars include: strengthening of front and rear bumpers so that both withstand impacts of up to 5 miles (8 km) per hour without damage to safety-related components such as lights and latches; addition of a second accelerator pedal return spring to safeguard against malfunctioning of the primary spring, and added protection in roofs against rollover "crushing."

Permissible exhaust-emission levels were unchanged for 1974 cars except for a slight reduction in the ceiling on nitrous oxide limits allowable on cars sold in California. However, the Environmental Protection Agency (EPA) declared interim 1975-model standards final.

U. S. PASSENGER CAR PRODUCTION

Company and make	1972 models	1973 models	Company and make	1972 models	1973 models
AMERICAN MOTORS CORPORATION			Cougar	53,702	60,628
Ambassador	44,364	49,114	Comet	82,359	94,691
Hornet	71,055	102,569	Subtotal Mercury Division	421,626	462,674
Gremlin	61,717	85,181	Total Ford Motor Company	2,371,387	2,562,625
Matador–Rebel	54,813	52,700	**GENERAL MOTORS CORPORATION**		
Javelin–AMX	27,176	31,222	Buick	420,847	455,824
Total AMC	259,125	320,786	Riviera	33,728	34,080
			Century	225,346	298,467
CHRYSLER CORPORATION			Apollo		32,793
Valiant	256,431	316,837	Subtotal Buick Division	679,921	821,164
Barracuda	18,450	22,213	Cadillac	227,713	253,388
Satellite–Belvedere	81,272	127,440	Eldorado	40,074	51,451
Fury	280,362	280,330	Subtotal Cadillac Division	267,787	304,839
Subtotal Plymouth Division	636,515	746,820	Chevelle	357,820	328,538
Chrysler	204,764	234,229	Nova	367,999	391,158
Imperial	15,794	16,729	Chevrolet	906,541	941,114
Coronet–Charger	159,758	212,816	Corvette	27,004	30,465
Dart	172,109	176,069	Camaro	68,651	96,756
Sportsman		51,153	Monte Carlo	163,085	233,691
Challenger	26,663	32,596	Vega	394,592	395,795
Polara–Monaco	149,914	153,057	Subtotal Chevrolet Division	2,285,692	2,417,517
Subtotal Dodge Division	508,444	625,691	Cutlass	334,582	405,519
Total Chrysler Corporation	1,365,517	1,623,469	Oldsmobile	374,702	417,522
FORD MOTOR COMPANY			Toronado	48,900	56,226
Club Wagon	32,884	17,396	Omega		60,363
Torino–Fairlane	360,222	331,798	Subtotal Oldsmobile Division	758,184	939,630
Ford	794,438	857,685	Pontiac	274,081	374,375
Mustang	125,093	134,867	LeMans–Tempest	169,993	248,785
Thunderbird	57,814	87,269	Firebird	29,951	46,313
Maverick	136,925	201,393	Grand Prix	91,961	153,899
Pinto	347,825	341,470	Ventura II	72,787	96,500
Subtotal Ford Division	1,855,261	1,971,878	Subtotal Pontiac Division	638,773	919,872
Lincoln	45,969	58,636	Total General Motors Corporation	4,630,357	5,403,023
Mark IV	48,591	69,437	**CHECKER MOTORS**	5,500	5,900
Montego	135,092	156,805	Total U. S. production	8,631,886	9,915,803
Mercury	150,473	150,550			

Source: Automotive News

Canada did not require ignition interlocks on its 1974 cars, nor did it appear likely to order exhaust limits making necessary catalytic converters on 1975 models. Leadless gasoline will be needed to use with converter-equipped cars to prevent catalyst fouling, but service stations in both the United States and Canada planned to add leadless gasoline pumps in the summer of 1974. Catalyst material will be of platinum-palladium metal, imported from South Africa.

Models and Innovations. Four fewer models were offered by U. S. auto producers in 1974 than in 1973. The industry's total dropped to 300 1974 models as Ford joined Chrysler and AMC in dispensing with convertibles. The last remaining North American convertible manufacturer was GM, with a total of six models. Styling innovations that spread in 1974 included the coupe with unopenable rear windows, which had contributed to the popularity of GM's 1973 model intermediates, "opera" (side) rear windows, and hatchback two-door models.

Labor. After a national strike in September, lasting less than two weeks, Chrysler Corporation and the United Automobile Workers reached a contract renewal agreement that featured a voluntary overtime provision and acceptance of the union's demand for pensioned retirements after 30 years of service without regard to age. This agreement covered three years and affected both U. S. and Canadian workers. Prices of 1974 models were increased to compensate for government-directed safety and emissions equipment, but the new labor accord was interpreted as a cost-rise factor likely to occasion further price increases.

Imports. Approximately 1,275,000 imported new cars were sold in the United States in the first 8 months of 1973, compared with 1,071,000 in the same period in 1972. Steep foreign currency revaluations that boosted prices of German and Japanese

cars in the United States failed to slow the sales pace. About 9,500,000 imported cars were in operation in the United States.

MAYNARD M. GORDON
Editor, "Motor News Analysis"

BAHAMAS, The

On July 10, 1973, the Bahamas became independent, ending more than 250 years (1719–1973) of almost continual British rule. The new nation, composed of approximately 700 islands and keys of which only 29 are permanently inhabited, became a member of the Commonwealth of Nations and continued to recognize the queen of England as the symbolic head of state. At the independence ceremonies in Nassau, capital of the Bahamas, the queen was represented by Prince Charles, heir to the throne. On Aug. 1, 1973, Sir Milo Boughton Butler, a native Bahamian, was appointed by the queen as governor-general, a post that is primarily ceremonial.

On independence day, Lynden O. Pindling became the first prime minister of the Bahamas. Pindling, a 44-year-old Bahamian trained in law at the University of London, had been the prime mover behind the drive for independence, which was supported by most of the Bahamian population.

He had served in the legislative branch of government from 1956 until 1967, when the Progressive Liberal party (PLP), of which he is the leader, became the majority party and named him premier. In the election of September 1972, Pindling and his PLP following captured an impressive 59% of the popular vote and, as promised in the campaign, moved directly forward toward independence.

Tourism is the main industry of the islands, pumping an estimated $270 million into the economy in 1973. Other industries include the production of over a billion tons of salt, one million cases of rum, and five million barrels of cement. There is an oil refinery, which eventually expects to increase its daily production to 450,000 barrels, making it one of the largest in the world. A second refinery is expected to begin operations in 1974, in conjunction with a deepwater port for supertankers on Grand Bahama. The new nation is also something of a financial center, with branches of about 300 banking institutions located there.

THOMAS G. MATHEWS
University of Puerto Rico

WORLD MOTOR VEHICLE DATA

Country	1972 cars produced	1972 trucks produced	1972 vehicle registrations
Argentina	207,623	70,599	2,539,000
Australia	389,424	77,493	5,049,800
Austria	381	5,874	1,414,206
Belgium	252,832	18,621	2,399,584
Brazil	408,712	200,273	4,015,000
Canada	1,147,280	317,220	8,306,418
Czechoslovakia	154,454	28,483	1,351,650
Finland	...	1,250	880,056
France	2,992,959	335,361	15,975,000
Germany, East	143,000	28,000	1,727,906
Germany, West	3,521,540	294,442	16,758,529
Hungary	...	10,890	471,548
India	38,828	51,220	1,181,000
Italy	1,732,379	107,414	12,291,700
Japan	4,022,289	2,272,149	19,857,877
Mexico	163,005	66,761	1,937,446
Netherlands	87,396	12,270	3,156,000
Poland	91,000	65,100	866,400
Portugal	...	326	628,478
Rumania	29,000	42,000	125,000
Spain	600,559	94,658	3,584,715
Sweden	317,962	33,027	2,513,089
Switzerland	...	1,179	1,620,838
United Kingdom	1,921,311	408,119	14,276,682
United States	8,828,205	2,482,503	112,999,125[1]
USSR	728,000	648,000	5,400,000
Yugoslavia	108,029	18,383	1,021,960
World total	27,886,168	7,691,615	262,174,539[2]

[1] Excludes Puerto Rico, 664,895; Virgin Islands, 29,669, and Canal Zone, 20,546. [2] Includes all countries, of which others with registrations in excess of or approaching 1,000,000 were: Denmark, 1,367,742; South Africa, 2,200,693; New Zealand, 1,128,901; Venezuela, 982,914, and Norway, 969,244. Nineteen countries assembled 1,272,056 cars and 300,766 trucks during 1972. Of these, Belgium led in 1972 car assemblies with 669,121, while South Africa led in trucks with 109,316. Source: Motor Vehicle Manufacturers Association of the United States, Inc.

--- BAHAMAS · Information Highlights ---

Official Name: Commonwealth of the Bahamas.
Location: Atlantic Ocean, southeast of Florida.
Area: 5,380 square miles (13,935 sq km).
Population (1973 est.): 200,000. Density, 34 per square mile (13 per sq km).
Chief Cities (1970 census): Nassau, the capital, 101,503.
Government: *Head of state,* Elizabeth II, queen, represented by Sir Milo Butler, governor-general (took office Aug. 1973). *Head of government,* Lynden O. Pindling, prime minister (took office July 1973). *Legislature*—Parliament: Senate and House of Assembly. *Major political party*—Progressive Liberal party (PLP).
Language: English (official).
Education: *School enrollment* (1969)—primary, 35,169; secondary, 16,748; technical/vocational, 399.
Monetary Unit: Bahamian dollar (1 B. dollar equals U. S. $1, July 1973).
Gross National Product (1970 est.): $390,000,000.
Manufacturing (major products): Cement, automotive parts, petroleum products, rum.
Major Agricultural Products: Cucumbers, sweet peppers, tomatoes, okra, fish, forest products.
Foreign Trade (1971): Exports, $265,000,000; Imports, $508,000,000. *Chief trading partners*—United States; United Kingdom; Canada.
Tourism: Receipts (1973 est.), $270,000,000.

BALTIMORE

Among the major occurrences on the Baltimore scene in 1973 were wide-ranging debates over a proposed new stadium; the approval of the building of Coldspring, an elaborate new housing concept; a prison flare-up; and adoption of a city budget that exceeded $1 billion. Also occurring in the city was the investigation by a special grand jury of Vice President Spiro T. Agnew and others.

New Stadium. The Baltimore City Council, by an 11–6 vote, passed a resolution endorsing the construction of a new stadium in downtown Baltimore. The new domed sports complex, was recommended by the Maryland Sports Complex Authority. The council's action paved the way for the Maryland General Assembly to use the state's credit to back the sale of revenue bonds to finance the construction of the complex. A dissident group planned a petition drive for a referendum to block the complex, but its early efforts seemed ineffectual.

Housing. An altogether new and architecturally exciting urban community known as Coldspring received approval by the City Council and the federal Department of Housing and Urban Development. The $200 million project consists of 3,800 middle- and upper-income housing units covering 370 acres of largely vacant land overlooking the Jones Falls Expressway. The project, which would house more than 12,000 residents, was designed by Moshe Safdie, the Israeli architect, and will require eight to 10 years to complete. The residents of Coldspring will be racially and economically mixed, and it will offer a new style of urban living for moderate to upper-income families.

Violence and Crime. In March, 75 prisoners took over the west wing of the Maryland Penitentiary and threatened to kill the seven guards taken as hostages until a force of about 140 guards and policemen stormed the prison, firing plastic bullets from shotguns, and ended the two-hour riot. The rioting prisoners, none of whom was injured, demanded to talk to a state legislator about "racist" and "rotten" conditions in the prison.

Police statistics on major crimes in Baltimore for the first three months of 1973 showed an overall decline of 14%, including a 5.5% drop in violent crimes such as murder, rape, and robbery. Property crimes dropped 16.5%, according to Baltimore police statistics. These statistics followed comparable data issued by the Federal Bureau of Investigation for 1972, which ranked Baltimore second only to New York in per capita murders, rapes, robberies, and assaults.

Agnew Probe. In midsummer it was announced that a federal grand jury in Baltimore was investigating allegations of contract kickbacks against Vice President Agnew, who was Baltimore county executive (1962–66) and governor of Maryland (1967–69), and others. The investigation was extended to income tax evasion. N. Dale Anderson, Agnew's successor as county executive, was indicted in August and again in October. Vice President Agnew pleaded no contest to one count of income tax evasion and resigned his post on October 10.

Finances. The City Council adopted a record fiscal 1974 city budget of $1,158,553,654. It fixed the property tax rate at $5.83 per $100 assessed valuation.

WILLIAM F. AMELIA
The Equitable Trust Co., Baltimore

KEYSTONE

PRE-ELECTION scene in Bangladesh. Awami League candidates used symbol of country-boat and picture of Prime Minister Mujib.

BANGLADESH

Bangladesh, until late 1971 the eastern province of Pakistan, held its first national elections as an independent state in 1973 and made significant concessions to Pakistan in an effort to secure recognition of its independence and the regularization of its international status. The country is subject to natural disasters such as flooding. Since independence it has also had to cope with dislocations caused by its brief war for independence. Bangladesh continued in 1973 to be a land divided, crippled by sporadic violence and a shaky economy.

Internal Politics. The government of Sheikh Mujibur Rahman (Sheikh Mujib) is the only one independent Bangladesh has possessed. The hero of East Pakistan before independence, Sheikh Mujib had been briefly jailed and then dramatically released by Pakistan's President Ali Bhutto. Mujib is called the "father of Bangladesh." Widely known and loved, Mujib is largely unassailable as the head of the well-entrenched Awami League.

Parliamentary elections were held on March 7. Mujib campaigned throughout the country, using a Soviet helicopter. His opposition—scattered among 14 parties—was disorganized and weak. With about a 50% turnout of those eligible to vote, Mujib's party captured almost all of the 300 seats at stake. Described as a mandate by enthusiastic supporters,

——— **BANGLADESH** • Information Highlights ———

Official Name: People's Republic of Bangladesh.
Location: South Asia.
Area: 55,126 square miles (142,776 sq km).
Population (1973 est.): 83,400,000. *Density*, 1,500 per square mile (580 per sq km).
Chief Cities (1971 est.): Dacca, the capital, 915,000; Chittagong, 458,000; Khulna, 403,000; Narayanganj, 389,000.
Government: *Head of state*, Abu Sayeed Choudhury, president (took office Jan. 1972). *Head of government*, Mujibur Rahman, prime minister (took office Jan. 1972). *Legislature* (unicameral)—Jatiyo Sangsad. *Major political parties*—Awami League; National Awami party (Bhashani); National Awami party (Muzaffar).
Languages: Bengali (official), English.
Monetary Unit: Taka (7.346 takas equal U. S.$1, June 1973).
Gross National Product (1971 est.): $4,300,000,000.
Consumer Price Index (1972), 205 (1963=100).
Manufacturing (major products): Jute products, cotton textiles, processed foods, wood products.
Major Agricultural Products: Jute (ranks 1st among world producers, 1972), rice, sugarcane, tea, oilseeds, pulses.
Major Minerals: Natural gas, coal, limestone, clay, glass.
Foreign Trade (1971): Exports, $263,000,000; Imports, $331,000,000. *Chief trading partners* (1971)—United States (took 20% of exports, supplied 32% of imports); United Kingdom (10%—9%); West Germany (3.6%—7.4%).
Transportation: *Motor vehicles* (1969), 36,800 (automobiles, 22,400); *major national airline*, Bangladesh Biman.

this unbalanced victory suggested that, lacking a viable opposition, Bangladesh's democracy would be rudimentary at best.

It was estimated in June that about 2,000 political murders had occurred in Bangladesh in the first 16 months of the country's independence. Most of these murders reflected inter-party struggles and retaliations. Militant government supporters used violence in rooting out the opposition; and the opposition, itself divided, retaliated in kind. Armed terrorism revived at the close of 1973. Even in student elections at Dacca University in September, a number of students were machine-gunned to death by terrorists.

Within weeks of the election, the domestic political climate had deteriorated very seriously. There were public demonstrations against food shortages, high costs, and corruption in the government. Some of the demonstrations were organized by the leadership of opposition groups. But the opposition groups were concerned with more than shortages and prices. Some, like that led by 91-year-old Maulana Bhashani, articulated strong anti-Indian, anti-Hindu sentiments. They argued that they had not sought independence from Pakistan in order to become a colony of India. Some even expressed doubts about the wisdom of independence from Pakistan.

Mujib continued to wrestle with the bureaucracy of his government and to shake up his cabinet. In December, President Choudhury resigned, and it is apparent from the unrest and violence in the country that Mujib does not control the domestic situation. Yet his opponents are not strong enough to offer a viable political alternative.

Foreign Affairs. The allies of Bangladesh are chiefly the Soviet Union and India. In regard to the latter, Mujib's goal has been friendship coupled with independence; but there is every reason to believe that in the months to come Bangladesh will remain the client state of India that it has been from the beginning. The Soviet Union has given Bangladesh international support and some economic aid, though not as much as the United States. Until late in 1973 relations with the United States had been decidedly cool. But perhaps in response to generous U. S. economic aid, government efforts to control criticism of the United States have begun to have an effect.

Bangladesh's main opponent has been Pakistan. Bangladesh has insisted that Pakistan recognize its independence, that the Bengalis held in Pakistan be released when Bangladesh releases Pakistani prisoners of war, that a small number of Pakistani soldiers be tried for war crimes, and that Pakistan accept perhaps 250,000 Biharis (a non-Bengali, Muslim minority in Bangladesh, loyal to Pakistan in the 1971 war) as immigrants.

Much of 1973 was spent in bargaining over these issues. In an agreement made in New Delhi, India, in August, Bangladesh made considerable concessions. Despite its insistence that no prisoners of war be released (and especially those accused of war crimes) until Pakistan granted recognition, Bangladesh agreed to the repatriation of the bulk of the prisoners of war and abandoned its insistence that the 195 soldiers accused of war crimes be tried in Bangladesh. (Prime Minister Bhutto of Pakistan has blocked, with China's support, the entry of Bangladesh into the United Nations until the 195 are released.) In its turn, Pakistan agreed to accept about 50,000 Biharis. But Pakistan is not anxious to accept large numbers of unskilled laborers like the Biharis, regardless of the "moral" obligation it might have toward them as a result of Bihari support for Pakistan in 1971.

Economy. At the end of 1972 there had been guarded optimism that Bangladesh would somehow be able to shake off the effects of the war and put its economy together. But such optimism turned out to be premature, to judge by the events of 1973.

Bangladesh's economy is almost entirely agricultural, producing jute, tea, food grains, and spices. It continues to sell its jute on the world markets. But its attempts to reach self-sufficiency in foodstuffs have failed, and the foreign exchange earned from jute has been frittered away in the purchase of food rather than of machinery, spare parts, and other modern economic essentials.

A severe food shortage was evident by spring. It was estimated that a shortage of about 2.5 million tons of foodstuffs would have to be made up by gifts and purchases from abroad. But there is considerable dispute about how much food is needed or how many people are actually consuming the food that is raised domestically or imported from or given by other countries.

Bangladesh does receive important infusions of foreign aid, through the United Nations and from individual countries. By March 1973 the United States had extended $300 million of aid since the end of the war, with another $100 million probably to be granted by year's end. India contributed more than $300 million in the same period.

To compound the economic plight of Bangladesh, there are recurring natural disasters. Heavy rains in the spring resulted in widespread flooding, although the damage done was subject to considerable dispute. A further strain is placed on the economy by the relentless increase of population. There is an annual increase of about 3% for a population approaching 85 million, which has made real economic growth for the population impossible.

It is apparent that the economic difficulties of the country are only partly the result of the war. It is also clear that the government of Mujib has not been able to secure control of the economic forces in the country, nor has it been able to effect a rational distribution of what is available in the way of the necessities of life.

CARL LEIDEN
University of Texas at Austin

BANKING

The rapid expansion that characterized the U. S. economy in 1972 moderated somewhat in 1973. Growth in real output declined from an annual rate of 8% in the first quarter to 3.4% in the third. Nevertheless, this diminished increase in economic activity was sufficient to reduce the national unemployment rate from 5.1% in December 1972 to 4.8% in November 1973.

Despite Phase 4 controls, price inflation (which was spurred by sharp increases in food costs) continued to be a serious problem throughout the year.

International Aspects. Because of a worsening U. S. trade balance, the dollar came under heavy pressure in the international money markets early in the year. As a result of the deteriorating balance-of-payments position, the government announced on February 12 that the dollar would be devalued by 10%. This move, coupled with the decision of the major Western trading nations to allow their currencies to "float" in relation to the dollar, paved the way for substantial improvements in the U. S. trade position. September 1973, for example, saw a trade surplus of $873 million, the largest single-month surplus in over eight years.

Nonetheless, rising interest rates in Europe and uneasiness over exchange rates resulted in significant outflows of funds from the United States. The balance of payments (on an official settlements basis) did not show significant improvement. (See also INTERNATIONAL FINANCE.)

Monetary Policy. U. S. monetary policy in 1973 was directed primarily toward reducing the rates of price and cost inflation without jeopardizing economic growth. To this end, the discount rate was raised from 4.5% to a record 7.5% by the end of the third quarter. The Federal Reserve System's open-market operations, while attempting to maintain some parity with rates available in Europe, were simultaneously directed toward accommodating the banking system's need for reserves.

In a further action designed to restrain the rising demand for credit, the Federal Reserve on May 16 imposed marginal reserve requirements on large denomination certificates of deposits issued by member banks that had $10 million or more as of that date. The net effect of these actions was to maintain funds availability at a very high price.

Bank Reserves and Money Supply. Relative to the sharp increases in the fourth quarter of 1972, bank deposits and reserves and the money supply grew less rapidly during the first half of 1973. Average money supply increased at a rate of 4.6% in the first quarter and 6.7% in the second.

The lower rate of expansion in the first quarter reflected the reduction in dollar cash balances resulting from speculative outflows into foreign currencies. In the second quarter, the continuing impact of enlarged demand for funds by consumers and businesses, coupled with special features such as unusually large personal income tax refunds in May and June, contributed to the higher rate of monetary expansion.

Despite the Federal Reserve's continued net purchases of Treasury securities, bank borrowing of reserves (which were high at the end of 1972) increased steadily as the year progressed.

Interest Rates, Loans, and Investments. Short-term interest rates, responding to the actions of the monetary authorities, rose in the first quarter. Loan demand (particularly the business loan component) was extremely strong, growing 18% annually.

Short-term rates continued to surge upward during the second quarter, under the combined pressure of strong demand for short-term credit and a policy of monetary restraint. As a result, total loan demand expanded at the rate of 9.8% in the second quarter. This slackened pace reflected a significant decline in business loan growth, accompanied by a slower expansion in both consumer loans and loans to nonbank financial institutions.

The rate of growth in loan demand declined considerably in the second half of the year. Interest rates, which had risen steadily throughout much of the third quarter, leveled off and then declined as the year came to a close.

Changes in Prime Rate. The high levels of loan demand that prevailed through much of the year led to increases in the prime rate (the lowest rate charged by large banks to their biggest and best short-term business borrowing customers) from 6% on January 4 to a record high of 10% by the end of the third quarter. As loan demand slackened, however, the prime rate declined somewhat in the fourth quarter. But by the end of the year, some banks were again charging 10% to their best customers.

In response to the sharply rising cost of short-term business credit, the Federal Reserve on May 16 required its member banks to adopt a two-tier, or "dual prime role," structure. While the prime interest rate for loans to large businesses would fluctuate with money-market rates generally, the small-business prime rate was to be much steadier. This change was designed to offer a more favorable short-term borrowing rate to small customers.

Bank Regulation. The Board of Governors of the Federal Reserve System approved changes in Federal Reserve Regulation Q effective July 1. The amendments to Regulation Q increased the ceiling rates on interest for member banks on passbook savings deposits by 0.5%, and on small denomination time deposits from 0.25% to 0.75% on various maturities. Ceilings were suspended on minimum deposits of $1,000 with maturities of four years or more. These amendments became necessary in order to allow banks to compete for time deposits in the face of the rapidly rising short-term rates on market securities.

Proposed Legislation. In August, President Nixon proposed legislation to Congress that would bring major changes to banks and savings institutions and could result in higher interest rates on consumer savings. Reaction to the proposals was varied, and congressional deliberation was expected to be lengthy.

The Canadian Economy. The Canadian economy grew at a relatively slow rate through the first part of the year, the rate of growth being slightly above 3.5%. Unemployment declined from about 5.8% to 5.3% by the end of June. Price inflation was a problem throughout the first half of the year, with consumer prices increasing at an 8.1% annual rate.

In order to combat these inflationary pressures, the central bank adopted a more restrictive monetary policy. The discount rate was increased in three steps, from a 5¼% rate in April to 6¾% by the end of August. Short-term interest rates responded to these moves by rising steadily from about 3.8% in January to 6.5% by the end of August.

CLIFTON H. KREPS, JR.
University of North Carolina at Chapel Hill

BELGIUM

Belgium in 1973 enjoyed much improved economic conditions, and there was relatively little civil violence, but the nation's linguistic-political problem, involving Flemish-speaking and French-speaking (Walloon) Belgians, continued to be troublesome throughout the year.

Economic Affairs. The economy, which had been sluggish in 1972, improved at an increasing tempo in 1973. Exports rose steadily, with the balance of trade turning favorable in the first quarter of the year. The index of industrial production, including building construction, was 7% higher in May 1973 than it was in the same month of 1972, and unemployment declined.

However, inflation was a cause of continuing concern, and the government introduced a number of measures to combat it. Among these were a tightening of terms and conditions for installment credit purchases, a lengthening of the two-month notification period required of major businesses that planned to increase prices, and a restriction of credit facilities.

A comprehensive labor agreement between employers and the major trade unions was signed on February 17, calling for an increase in annual vacation time from three to four weeks by 1975.

Political Developments. The ministry of Gaston Eyskens, formed in January 1972, resigned on Nov. 22, 1972. After 66 days of negotiations, Socialist party cochairman Edmund Leburton, a Walloon, succeeded in forming a new cabinet. It took office Jan. 26, 1973.

The Eyskens ministry had fallen on issues arising from the Flemish-Walloon language dispute which has plagued Belgium for several decades. The chief problem in forming the new cabinet was that of obtaining the support of a two-thirds majority in

---

────── BELGIUM • Information Highlights ──────

Official Name: Kingdom of Belgium.
Location: Northwestern Europe.
Area: 11,781 square miles (30,513 sq km).
Population (1973 est.): 9,800,000. *Density,* 821 per square mile (317 per sq km).
Chief Cities (1971 census): Brussels, the capital, 1,074,726 (metropolitan area); Antwerp, 222,775; Ghent, 148,166; Liège, 144,875.
Government: *Head of state,* Baudouin I, king (acceded July 1951). *Head of government,* Edmund Leburton, prime minister (took office Jan. 1973). *Legislature*—Parliament: Senate and Chamber of Representatives. *Major political parties*—Christian Social party; Socialist party; Liberty and Progress party (Liberals); People's Union; French Speaking Front; Walloon Union.
Languages: French, Flemish (both official).
Education: *Expenditure* (1968), 5% of gross national product. *School enrollment* (1968)—primary, 1,018,334; secondary, 847,605; technical/vocational, 518,709; university/higher, 69,634.
Monetary Unit: Franc (35.86 francs equal U. S.$1, July 1973).
Gross National Product (1972 est.): $33,000,000,000.
Economic Indexes: *Industrial production* (1972), 148 (1963=100); *agricultural production* (Belgium-Luxembourg, 1971), 130 (1963=100); *consumer price index* (1972), 142 (1963=100).
Manufacturing (major products): Steel, metals, textiles, cut diamonds, chemicals, glass, electronics, machinery.
Major Agricultural Products: Sugar beets, potatoes, wheat, oats, barley, flax, hay.
Major Minerals: Coal, iron ore.
Foreign Trade (Belgium-Luxembourg, 1972): *Exports,* $16,081,-000,000. *Imports,* $15,605,000,000. *Chief trading partners* (1970)—West Germany (took 25% of exports, supplied 25% of imports); France (20%—18%); Netherlands (19%—16%).
Tourism: Receipts (with Luxembourg, 1971) $370,000,000.
Transportation: *Motor vehicles* (1971) 2,439,000 (automobiles, 2,054,100); *railroads* (1971), 2,575 miles (4,144 km); *merchant fleet* (1972), 1,192,000 gross registered tons; *major national airline,* SABENA.
Communications: *Telephones* (1972), 2,161,744; *newspapers* (1970), 55.

Parliament. Under the terms of the constitutional reforms of 1971, a two-thirds vote is required for the implementation of basic solutions of the linguistic controversy.

Leburton achieved the necessary strength by enlarging the Socialist and Social Christian coalition to include the Liberals. The broadened coalition controled 76% of the seats in Parliament, but there was some discontent on the fringes of the component parties.

Leburton was the first Walloon Socialist to hold the office of prime minister since World War II. The cabinet was large. It included 22 ministers and 14 secretaries of state (adjunct ministers), compared with 19 ministers and 10 secretaries of state in the previous cabinet. Excluding the prime minister, 10 ministers and 5 secretaries of state were French-speaking, 11 ministers and 8 secretaries of state were Flemish-speaking, and one secretary of state was German-speaking. The Leburton cabinet was also the first ever to have two women members.

An obstacle in obtaining Flemish support for the cabinet was Leburton's lack of facility in Flemish. Since the Socialists would not join the coalition unless Leburton became prime minister, concessions had to be made in the distribution of portfolios and on specific issues. The result of such concessions was the mammoth cabinet, two Flemish deputy premiers, and the making of promises that might prove difficult to fulfill. For example, the "free" (church) schools were promised more generous state subsidies, and assurances were given that the city of Brussels, a bilingual enclave in Flemish-speaking territory, would be restricted in size for some period of time, despite pressure for expansion.

Military Draft Policy. Public discontent with conscription induced the government to announce major changes in policy. First, a proposal to end student deferments was withdrawn in the face of strong protests. Later, it was announced that combat units pledged to NATO were to be all-volunteer by 1976, while draftees were to have only homeguard duties, with the period of service reduced from 12 months to six.

New University. Even the centuries-old University of Leuven did not escape involvement in the bitter language dispute between Flemings and Walloons. In 1968 the French-language faculties were ordered to move to another city. It was decided that a separate university, called Louvain-la-Neuve, would be constructed in a town about 20 miles (32 km) southeast of Brussels. The first 800 students attended classes there in 1972–73. Enrollment in the new university was expected eventually to approach 25,000.

Labor Trouble. A difficult local employment situation was highlighted by the desparate measures resorted to by a group of workers in the Liège region. When the government failed to grant a subsidy to a bankrupt pressing machine plant to save it from liquidation, some 50 employees took over the factory. After operating it for several months, the workers announced that they wished to return the plant to capitalist management and threatened to blow it up unless the government reversed its decision on the subsidy. On September 10, the prime minister agreed to review the case, and the workers' ultimatum was withdrawn.

AMRY VANDENBOSCH
University of Kentucky

BIOCHEMISTRY

The year 1973 was an exciting one in biochemistry as scientists continued to probe for greater understanding of key processes in body chemistry.

Cell Protection Against Foreign DNA. An example of a palindrome is the phrase attributed to Adam in the Garden of Eden, "Madam I'm Adam," in which the words (or letters) can be read from left to right or right to left. This sort of formation has become the focus of one of the more interesting speculations as to how cells protect themselves against foreign DNA (deoxyribonucleic acid). One system found in the bacterium *Escherichia coli* has been studied. In this case it seems that the host DNA is modified by the addition of some specific methyl groups in a characteristic way, whereas foreign DNA that does not contain the appropriate methyl groups is attacked and degraded. The ability to degrade the foreign DNA appears to reside in an endonuclease called R1, which makes a break in each of the two strands of the DNA double helix.

One way to explain how the enzyme cleaves both strands of the DNA is to assume that the recognition sites for a cleavage are palindromic and that the enzyme recognizes the same base sequence in opposite directions on the two DNA strands. Interesting new work by J. E. Mertz and R. W. Davis and by Joe Hedgpeth, H. M. Goodman, and H. W. Boyer appeared to show that this is indeed the case.

Synthesis of DNA. One intriguing problem in the synthesis of DNA stems from the fact that DNA is synthesized by an enzyme moving in a single direction, whereas the two chains of the DNA molecule are encoded in opposite directions. One explanation, proposed by R. Okazaki in 1968, is that the DNA chains are synthesized in short pieces that are later joined together. Newer work by S. Hirose, R. Okazaki, and S. Tamanoi has shed some light on how these short fragments are synthesized.

Apparently each Okazaki fragment of DNA has a short piece of RNA that is removed before the total synthesis of the fragment is finished. Different methods of estimating the amount of RNA contained in the DNA segment reveal that a segment of DNA about 2,000 nucleotides long contains an RNA segment of between 50 and 100 nucleotides. The first base of the DNA chain is always cytidine and the last base of the RNA is always a pyrimidine, so it seems plausible that a specific sequence determines the point of switch from RNA to DNA.

Reverse Transcriptase. Reverse transcriptase, discovered in 1971, is an enzyme that can synthesize DNA by using an RNA template. Until 1973 it was thought that reverse transcriptase activity was unique to RNA tumor viruses or virus-infected tumor cells. However, Chil-Yong Kang and H. M. Temin apparently detected a reverse transcriptase in chicken embryo cells, and it apparently is biochemically distinct from the enzymes found in tumor viruses. What function this enzyme might have in the chick cell is not yet known.

Muscle Growth. Weightlifting enthusiasts and other athletes are quite familiar with the enlargement of muscles with exercise. The biochemical mechanism by which this occurs has been under study, and some new work by C. K. Jablecki, J. E. Heuser, and Seymour Kaufman sheds some interesting light on this mechanism.

It has been known for some time that RNA synthesis is an important prerequisite to muscle en-

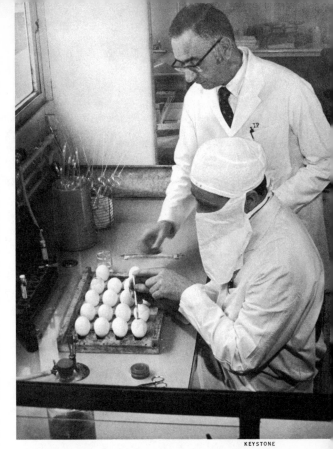

FLU VACCINE believed effective against present and future strains was developed at the Pasteur Institute.

largement. However, the new work seems to suggest that the important site for this RNA synthesis is the connective tissue rather than the muscle fibers themselves. When muscles are injected with radioactive precursors of RNA, the radioactivity is found to be located almost exclusively in the connective tissue. Very little of the radioactivity is found in the muscle fibers themselves. No radioactivity is found associated with the connective tissue when RNA synthesis inhibitors are administered. This work may also prove to be important in understanding the enlargement of heart muscle.

Life on the Moon? Rock samples brought back from the moon have been tested to detect any amino acids, which are key building blocks of life. R. Modzeleski and his co-workers used an ion-exchange column to analyze extracts of the lunar samples. Although the amounts detected were extremely small, such amino acids as glycine, aspartic acid, glutamic acid, and serine were found in samples of lunar materials. No amino acids were found from tests of the surface of one of the astronauts' gloves, suggesting that the origin of the amino acids was indeed the samples brought from the moon.

Polyunsaturated Fats. J. F. Connolly, M. Noonan, and M. G. Harrington used a technique to bypass the rumen of suckling lambs and fed these lambs substitute diets rich in polyunsaturated fatty acids. Analysis of the body fat of the diet-fed lambs showed that these lambs contained 10 times as much polyunsaturated fatty acid as a control group did, and there was no perceptible difference in the taste of the meat.

STEPHEN N. KREITZMAN, *Emory University*

Biography

A selection of biographical sketches of persons prominent in the news during 1973 appears on this and the following pages. The subjects include men and women from many parts of the world, and representing a wide variety of pursuits. The list is confined to living persons; for biographical data on prominent people who died during the year, see OBITUARIES (beginning on page 432). Unless otherwise indicated, all articles in this section are by Henry S. Sloan, Associate Editor, Current Biography.

AARON, Henry

The winter of 1973–74 could, to some extent, have been the one of Henry Aaron's discontent. As he drew near Babe Ruth's career home-run record of 714 in September, Henry said he was hopeful of breaking the mark before the season's end. He did not want to sit around all winter and fret about it. Aaron came within one homer of tying the mark when time ran out for 1973. He and all baseball had to await the start of the 1974 season when it was expected that the Atlanta star would better the mark that had been expected to stand forever.

Aaron, an outfielder and later a first baseman, had been a fine all-around hitter for the Milwaukee Braves before he became classed as a slugger. In 1956, his second full season with Milwaukee (he was injured part of the 1954 season), he led the National League in batting with 200 hits, only 26 of them homers, and an average of .328. The next year, though, he set the pace in home runs with 44 and runs batted in with 132, and was voted the league's most valuable player.

It was then that he began to realize his potential as a home-run hitter. He clouted 30 or more each season after that, except for 1964 when he dropped to 24 and 1968 when he hit 29. His high was 47 in 1971. He belted 45 in 1962 and 44 in 1963 and 1966, the first year that the Braves played in Atlanta, and in 1969. In most of these seasons he batted over .300.

One by one, Hammerin' Hank overtook noted home-run hitters in career totals. In 1968 he passed Lou Gehrig (492) and the 500 mark. The following year he

HENRY AARON (right), *Atlanta Braves slugger, closed to within one of Babe Ruth's all-time home run record in 1973. With him is Willie Mays, third on homer list.*

WIDE WORLD

moved ahead of Mel Ott (511), Ed Mathews, the former Braves' leader (512), Ted Williams (521), Jimmy Foxx (534), and Mickey Mantle (536) to a 554 total. Only Willie Mays at 600 and Ruth were ahead. It took Aaron two more seasons to catch the aging Mays. He passed the 600 level in 1971 and moved into second place in 1972, becoming the leading right-handed homer hitter (Ruth batted left-handed) and finished the season at 673 with Willie at 654. (Mays retired with a 660 total). Aaron passed the 700 mark on July 21 and hit No. 713 on September 29, the day before the season finale. He batted .301 for the year, his 20th in the major leagues, and kept his career average near .311.

Aaron's winter could not have been one of complete discontent. He had a new bride, the former Mrs. Billye Williams, whom he married in October to help him celebrate his 40th birthday on February 5. He could look over the long list of records he had compiled. They show he is fourth overall in runs scored with 2,060 and fourth in hits with 3,509. His 11,288 times at bat are the most in the National League and close to Ty Cobb's major-league record of 11,429. In addition, Aaron could read some of the more than 30,000 letters he had received from fans.

BILL BRADDOCK

AGNEW, Spiro T. See special report beginning on page 20.

ALBERT, Carl

In his third year as speaker of the U. S. House of Representatives, Oklahoma Democrat Carl Albert was "a heartbeat away" from the presidency from Oct. 10, 1973, when Spiro Agnew resigned as vice president, until December 6, when House Republican Minority Leader Gerald Ford was sworn in as Agnew's successor. Albert did not relish the prospect of succeeding to the presidency, and he may have influenced President Nixon in his choice of Ford as a surefooted vice-presidential replacement.

During the year, Albert voiced sharp criticism of the administration on the handling of the economy and the energy crisis and the impoundment of funds allocated by Congress, and he voted to curb the President's war-making powers. In October he endorsed a preliminary House Judiciary Committee inquiry into the possible impeachment of President Nixon in connection with the Watergate affair. Albert is credited with having brought about a number of recent reforms in the House, such as opening committee meetings to the public and facilitating the flow of legislation to the House floor.

Background. Carl Bert Albert was born on May 10, 1908, in McAlester, Okla., where his father was a farmer and coal miner. After graduating from the University of Oklahoma with a degree in political science in 1931, he became a Rhodes scholar at Oxford University, where he obtained a law degree in 1934. During World War II he served with the U. S. Army Air Force in the Pacific and rose to the rank of lieutenant colonel. Elected to the House of Representatives from Oklahoma's 3d congressional district

in 1946, he generally supported the policies of the Truman, Kennedy, and Johnson administrations, championed the interests of the farmers, and earned a reputation as a consensus-seeker and conciliator. A protégé of the late Speaker Sam Rayburn of Texas, Albert became Democratic whip in 1955 and was elected House majority leader in 1962. He succeeded John McCormack as speaker of the House on Jan. 21, 1971.

BAKER, Howard Henry, Jr.

A Republican U. S. senator from Tennessee, Howard Henry Baker, Jr., was vice chairman and ranking minority member of the Senate Select Committee on Presidential Campaign Activities. When the committee began its televised hearings on the Watergate case, Baker declared that he favored "a full, thorough, and fair investigation." The part he played in the hearings impressed most television viewers and moved him into a position of influence in national politics.

Baker worked in harmony with the chairman, Sen. Sam J. Ervin, Jr. (D-N. C.). His attitude contributed to the absence of partisanship shown by the committee. He refused to express an opinion on the revelations in testimony, remarking that he would save his judgments for his final report.

Baker was considerate but adroit in dealing with witnesses. His questions often dealt with the motives that impelled people to act as they admitted they had. He asked witnesses what they thought might be done to prevent such abuses as were revealed in the Watergate affair. His manner was usually relaxed, and he engaged with Ervin in an exchange of biblical quotations and anecdotes.

Background. Baker was born at Huntsville, Tenn., on Nov. 15, 1925. His father was elected to the U. S. House of Representatives for seven consecutive terms. Baker attended the University of the South and Tulane University and graduated from the University of Tennessee Law College. He practiced law in Knoxville, Tenn.

In 1964 he lost an election for U. S. senator from Tennessee, but he was elected to the Senate in 1966 and 1972. Regarded as a leading conservative, he was unsuccessful in 1969 and 1971 in attempts to win the senate minority leadership.

Baker is married to the daughter of the late Senate Minority Leader Everett McKinley Dirkson (R-III.).

RICHARD G. WEST

BEAME, Abraham David

On Nov. 6, 1973, Democrat Abe Beame was elected mayor of New York City, winning decisively with about 60% of the vote, even though he had three major opponents (representing the Republican, Liberal, and Conservative parties). Thus Beame, the incumbent city comptroller, was rewarded for months of effort that included winning in the Democratic four-way primary and primary runoff elections and campaigning vigorously before November—despite being the odds-on favorite. He had trudged, he said in his victory speech, "20,000 miles of city streets."

Mayor Beame, inaugurated on Jan. 1, 1974, was expected to emphasize efficiency and cost-cutting. Campaigning, he also stressed crime control and the need for cooperation, rather than confrontation, between elements of the community.

Background. Beame was born on March 20, 1906, in London, the son of Polish-Jewish parents who took him to New York three months later. The family's name was originally Birnbaum, which was legally changed to Beame in about 1912. The young Beame grew up in cold-water flats on Manhattan's Lower East Side. An eager student, he graduated from City College in 1928 with an accounting degree. He worked in an accounting firm and taught high-school accounting, at the same time becoming increasingly involved in Democratic

politics in Brooklyn. In 1946 he was appointed assistant city budget director and in 1952, budget director. Beame successfully ran for city comptroller in 1961. He lost the mayoral election of 1965 to John V. Lindsay, but in 1969 he was overwhelmingly elected comptroller. Beame and his wife, Mary, have two sons.

WESLEY F. STROMBECK

BRADLEY, Thomas

Thomas Bradley—lawyer, former policeman, and city councilman since 1963—took office on July 1, 1973, as the mayor of Los Angeles, Calif. He became the first black mayor of that city, which with a population of some 3 million (less than 18% of it black) is the third-largest U. S. city, after New York and Chicago.

Bradley, a Democrat, was making his second bid for the office, both times against Sam Yorty, incumbent mayor since 1961 and a maverick Democrat. Bradley defeated Yorty with a landslide victory in the nonpartisan election on May 29, winning 56% of the vote. Although race was not the predominant issue of the campaign, Yorty tried to depict his opponent as a "dangerous radical" and a captive of the militants. Bradley stressed his own record as a political moderate and crime fighter, who represented all the people, and made integrity of government a major issue.

Following his victory, Bradley promised to "save Los Angeles from the kind of decay that has overtaken so many cities in our country." Since taking office, he has initiated measures to reduce street crime, combat pollution, establish a city ombudsman, limit the ultimate growth of the city's population to 4 million, and facilitate construction of a $4 billion rapid transit rail system for the greater Los Angeles area.

Background. One of the seven children of a sharecropper, Bradley was born in Calvert, Texas, on Dec. 29, 1917, and went with his family to Los Angeles at the age of 7. He attended the University of California, Los Angeles, on an athletic scholarship and became a track star but left the university in 1940 and joined the Los Angeles police department. Studying law at night, he obtained a law degree from Southwestern University School of Law, Los Angeles, in 1956. After retiring from the police force in 1961, he entered law practice and became active in Democratic politics. In 1963 he was elected to the Los Angeles city council, becoming the first black member of that body.

BRANDT, Willy

In May 1973, Willy Brandt, West German chancellor and chairman of the Social Democratic party of Germany (SPD), achieved one of the major objectives of his *Ostpolitik* (Eastern policy), when the West German parliament ratified the Basic Treaty, which he had concluded with the East German government in 1972. By the treaty the two Germanys recognized each other as separate, sovereign states and pledged themselves to good-neighborly, peaceful coexistence. The chancellor also negotiated a series of economic, cultural, and air traffic accords with Soviet Communist party chief Leonid I. Brezhnev when the latter paid a visit to Bonn in the spring.

Brandt's rapprochement with East Germany bore fruit in increased East-West German contacts. Millions of West Germans and West Berliners visited the German Democratic Republic (DDR), and at least those East Germans who had to attend to "pressing family matters" were allowed to go to the West. Travel between West Berlin and West Germany also moved smoothly in sharp contrast to the delays of previous years.

On the other hand, Brandt was unsuccessful in efforts to dissuade the United States from pursuing its plan of reducing the American military presence in West Germany. Disclosures of U. S. wiretapping activities in the Federal Republic added to the existing tension between West Germany and the United States, as did Brandt's neutral stance during the Arab-Israeli

war. Previously, however, on a visit to Israel in June, the first ever paid by a West German chancellor to that country, Brandt had made it clear that conflicting interests and Bonn's international obligations (to the European Economic Community, for example) might no longer permit it to back Israel as unreservedly as it had done in the past.

Domestically the chancellor began losing ground, as public opinion polls indicated. Unchecked inflation, increased taxes, and failure to carry out long-promised reforms antagonized a growing number even of his own party friends. A more radical wing of the SPD, representing mainly younger members, called for socialization of banks and other major concerns. At the annual party congress in Hanover, Brandt clearly faced serious challenges in his own camp.

Background. Willy Brandt was born in Lübeck on Dec. 18, 1913. He joined the SPD in 1930 at the age of 16, but soon switched to the more militant Socialist Workers party. After spending the Nazi era in exile in Norway and Sweden, he resumed his German citizenship in 1948 and rejoined the SPD.

Brandt was elected a member and later president of West Berlin's parliament, and in 1957 he became mayor of West Berlin. After unsuccessful bids for the chancellorship in 1961 and 1965, he became foreign minister in a coalition government formed by the Christian Democratic Union and the SPD in 1966. When the coalition broke up in 1969, Brandt became chancellor of a coalition government of the SPD and the small Free Democratic party. This coalition won a substantial majority in the elections of 1972. In 1971, Brandt was awarded the Nobel Peace Prize in recognition of his efforts to bring about a détente between East and West.

ANDREAS DORPALEN

BREZHNEV, Leonid Ilich

Leonid Brezhnev, secretary general of the Soviet Communist party, chairman of the party Politburo, and member of the Supreme Soviet Presidium, received more publicity in 1973 than any other Soviet leader. A fourth volume of his collected works was issued and worshipfully reviewed, while his record in World War II was praised in new memoirs by a Soviet general. Brezhnev also received two high awards—the Lenin Peace Prize from his own government, and the title of Hero of the People's Republic of Bulgaria. When the Soviet Communist party began issuing new identification cards to its members, card number 1 was assigned to the deceased Lenin and number 2 to Brezhnev. Yet he was still "first among equals" in the Soviet leadership rather than a supreme dictator like Stalin.

During 1973, Brezhnev made official visits to eight foreign countries, including Bulgaria, Czechoslovakia, East Germany, Poland, and France. His May journey to Bonn resulted in new Soviet–West German treaties of economic cooperation and cultural exchange, while a November trip to New Delhi was the occasion for signature of a pact promising Soviet technical aid to India for 15 more years. His most important visit, however, was in June to the United States, where he and his delegation concluded 11 agreements concerning commerce, scientific exchange, arms limitation, and nuclear nonaggression. Besides lengthly conversations with President Nixon, Brezhnev made speeches to U. S. congressmen and business leaders, trying to convince them of the possible benefits from future large expansion of U. S.-USSR trade.

As a result of negotiations in Moscow during October between U. S. Secretary of State Henry Kissinger and Brezhnev, the United States and the USSR acted jointly to obtain a cease-fire in the 1973 Arab-Israeli war.

At year-end it appeared that Brezhnev was at a high point in his strength in the USSR and that he had suffered no significant repercussions from his close personal dealings with President Nixon. This seemed to confirm that Brezhnev's policy of détente with the Western powers was still operative.

Background. Brezhnev, who looks like a successful capitalist businessman rather than a Communist politician, was born in Dneprodzerzhinsk, the Ukraine, on Dec. 19, 1906. He has had a versatile career, working as a surveyor, agricultural administrator, metallurgical engineer, regional Communist party chief, high-ranking army political officer, and secretary of the party's central apparatus. From 1960 to 1964 he served as president of the USSR. After helping to oust Nikita Khrushchev from power in October 1964, he replaced Khrushchev as head of the Soviet Communist party.

ELLSWORTH RAYMOND

BRUCE, David Kirkpatrick Este

To David K. E. Bruce, a distinguished U. S. diplomat who has served under five presidents, the year 1973 meant emerging from retirement once more to accept a challenging assignment. In March, President Nixon appointed him chief of the new liaison office in Peking—the nation's first representative in China since the Communists took power in 1949.

President Nixon said that it was "very important to appoint a man of great stature to this position." At the age of 75, Bruce was regarded as well fitted to work with the Chinese leaders Mao Tse-tung and Chou En-lai, his contemporaries in age.

Background. Bruce was born in Baltimore, Md., on Feb. 12, 1898. He studied at Princeton and the University of Maryland and was an artilleryman in France during World War I. Bruce practiced law in Baltimore, served a year as U. S. vice consul in Rome, and engaged in business and farming until 1940, when he began a broader career.

He was chief representative of the American Red Cross in Britain for a year, and in 1941 joined the wartime U. S. Office of Strategic Services, whose European operations he headed from 1943 to 1945. After a year each as assistant secretary of commerce and chief of the Economic Cooperation Administration's mission to France, he was named by President Truman in 1949 as ambassador to France. He persuaded France to accept West German rearmament.

His service in this post was followed by a year as undersecretary of state and a year as special representative to the European Coal and Steel Community. President Eisenhower named him ambassador to West Germany in 1957, and President Kennedy appointed him in 1961 to the Court of St. James's in Britain, where he continued under President Johnson until he retired in 1969. Bruce returned to public life in 1970, when President Nixon named him head of the U. S. delegation to the Vietnam peace talks in Paris. A year later, he retired again.

RICHARD G. WEST

BURGER, Warren E.

In 1973, its fifth year under Chief Justice Warren E. Burger, the U. S. Supreme Court continued on its moderately conservative course, strengthening governmental authority in some areas, extending liberal principles in others. Although Burger generally voted along "strict constructionist" lines, he sometimes followed an independent course, as in the court's decision to legalize abortion, in which he voted with the majority.

In its first school desegregation case involving a major Northern city, the court, with Burger concurring, ordered the city of Denver to effect full-scale integration of its school districts. He dissented from the court's decision to strike down state laws aimed at giving government assistance to private parochial schools. Burger supported opinions strengthening law enforcement, including one that permitted police to search motorists arrested on minor charges for evidence of more serious crimes.

Another landmark decision was the court's ruling (5–4) that permitted state and local authorities to define obscenity in judging books, plays, and films. In writing the majority opinion, Burger asserted that "to equate the free and robust exchange of ideas . . . with commercial exploitation of obscene material demeans . . . the First Amendment. . . ."

Burger in 1973 again proposed reforms for the judicial system. In November he urged that all trial lawyers receive special training and certification, as is done in England. He also proposed that basic legal education be reduced from three to two years, followed by specialized courtroom training and internship. Earlier, to reduce pressure on the courts, he had advocated a screening process to limit the number of appeals that losing parties might take above the district court level.

Background. Born in St. Paul, Minn., on Sept. 17, 1907, Warren Earl Burger attended the University of Minnesota, and graduated with honors from the St. Paul (now Mitchell) College of Law in 1931. Combining law practice with teaching, he became active in Republican politics. In 1953, President Eisenhower appointed him assistant attorney general in charge of the Justice Department's civil division. In 1956 he became judge of the District of Columbia U. S. Court of Appeals. Following appointment by President Nixon, Burger became the 15th U. S. chief justice on June 23, 1969, succeeding Earl Warren.

CHOU EN-LAI

At 75, Premier Chou En-lai remained a top leader of the Chinese Communist party, second only to Chairman Mao Tse-tung. His major task in 1973 was to restore the party framework that had been wrecked by the purge of Defense Minister Lin Piao in 1971. Through complicated maneuvering, Chou formed an alignment of ideological divisions within the party that promised to sustain him in power.

Chou emerged triumphant from the 10th Congress of the party, held in August 1973. He was named first among the five vice chairmen of the Central Committee and was elected to the Politburo and its Standing Committee, the highest ruling body of China. The party congress confirmed the rehabilitation of a number of his old colleagues, purged during the 1966–69 Cultural Revolution. Also elected to the Central Committee were diplomats who had worked closely with Chou in improving relations with the United States.

But Chou was not unopposed. His pragmatic approach was criticized because he departed from the basic teachings of Chairman Mao. The dramatic rise of Wang Hung-wen, a militant leader of the Cultural Revolution, to third place in the party hierarchy showed that the strength of the radical forces, Chou's major rival, was far from waning.

In foreign policy, Chou's object was to contain the Soviet Union. His détente with the United States, his cultivation of friendly relations with Western Europe, and his support of the Third World were all directed at curbing Soviet influence. He also played an important part in bringing about the peace settlement in Vietnam in 1973. Chou's interest in improving relations with the United States was borne out by his agreements with Henry A. Kissinger, President Nixon's emissary, to establish liaison offices in Peking and Washington and to increase Chinese-U. S. trade and cultural exchanges.

Background. Chou En-lai was born in Shaohing (Shaohsing), Chekiang, in 1898. He graduated from high school in 1917 and then studied in Japan and in France, where he joined the Chinese Communist party in 1922. Returning to China in 1924, he quickly became a leader of the party.

Named premier of the Communist government upon its establishment in 1949, Chou has since held that post, displaying extraordinary administrative and diplomatic talents. He represented China at such important international conferences as the Geneva Conference (1954) and the Bandung Conference (1955).

Chou supported the Maoists during the Cultural Revolution, while attempting to curb the militancy of the Red Guards. Toward the end of the Cultural Revolution he emerged as a national leader, when China's return to political stability needed his moderation and flexibility.

CHESTER C. TAN

COLBY, William E.

On May 10, 1973, William E. Colby, a career clandestine operative for the U. S. government, was named by President Nixon as director of the Central Intelligence Agency, succeeding James R. Schlesinger. Colby had been serving for two months as deputy director of operations, heading the CIA's clandestine overseas services. At confirmation hearings of the Senate Armed Services Committee, he was closely questioned about his past activities, including his role as director of the controversial Phoenix "pacification" program in Vietnam. He asserted that under his direction, the CIA would downgrade its secret political operations overseas and that its "primary focus" would be on foreign intelligence gathering. With reference to the illegal involvement of CIA agents in the Watergate burglaries, he declared that he would "reinforce very vigorously" the principle that the CIA was not to be involved in domestic intelligence activities.

Background. William Egan Colby was born in St. Paul, Minn., on Jan. 4, 1920, the son of an Army officer. A graduate of Princeton University and Columbia Law School, he began intelligence work in 1943 with the Office of Strategic Services, serving behind enemy lines in occupied Europe. In 1950 he joined the CIA, and during the next few years he worked in its clandestine operations while officially listed as a foreign service officer on the staffs of the U. S. embassies in Stockholm and Rome. He went to Vietnam in 1959 as first secretary of the U. S. embassy in Saigon. In 1962 he became chief of the Far East Division at CIA headquarters in Virginia, taking charge of the agency's Vietnam operations. From 1968 to 1971, Colby directed the U. S. "pacification" program in South Vietnam. He returned to the CIA in early 1972 as executive director-controller. His appointment as director was confirmed by the Senate on Aug. 1, 1973.

COX, Archibald

Appointed by Attorney General Elliot L. Richardson on May 18, 1973, as special prosecutor in the Watergate case, Archibald Cox was dismissed on October 20 on the order of President Nixon.

When he assumed his office with a large staff, Cox, a Democrat, bore the responsibility of investigating

ARCHIBALD COX was dismissed as special prosecutor of Watergate affair in October. His firing was protested around the nation.

UPI

WIDE WORLD
WILLIAM O. DOUGLAS receives pat from Chief Justice Burger after he set record for longevity on high court.

activities of a Republican administration in several areas. He demanded and was promised complete independence of action and pledged to follow the trail of evidence wherever it might lead.

Indictments were expected from the grand juries working with Cox on Watergate and in the areas of "dirty political tricks" and illegal campaign contributions from corporations, into which his Watergate inquiries had led him. Several key figures in the case pleaded guilty and agreed to cooperate with the prosecution.

But Cox had difficulty obtaining potential evidence from the White House. In July, when he requested for the grand jury nine specific tapes of White House conversations, the President refused to yield them, claiming executive privilege. Cox obtained a subpoena, and his move was partially upheld by Judge John J. Sirica in U. S. District Court and by the Circuit Court of Appeals.

When the President offered a compromise involving summaries of the tapes, Cox would not accept it. The President ordered Cox not to move further in court to obtain the tapes. When Cox would not obey, he was discharged. Attorney General Richardson and Deputy Attorney General William Ruckelshaus also lost their jobs in this "Saturday Night Massacre."

Background. Cox was born in Plainfield, N. J., on May 17, 1912. After graduating from Harvard College and the Harvard Law School, he practiced law in Boston from 1938 to 1941. He served in the office of the U. S. solicitor general and in the Labor Department until 1945, when he was named lecturer in law at Harvard. Appointed professor in 1946, he taught until 1961, when President Kennedy named him solicitor general. He continued in this post under President Johnson until 1965, when he was named Williston professor of law at Harvard.

RICHARD G. WEST

DEAN, John W., III. See page 26.

DOUGLAS, William O.

Associate Justice William O. Douglas of the U. S. Supreme Court reached a milestone on Oct. 29, 1973, when on completion of 34 years and 196 days on the high court he became the longest-serving justice in its 184-year history. The most persistent champion of human liberties among U. S. jurists and the mainstay of the dwindling liberal minority on the "Nixon Court," Douglas had often fought lonely battles to safeguard individual rights and to protect the natural environment.

During 1973 he attracted public attention by such actions as the freeing of the "Fort Worth Five" on bail, and his unsuccessful effort to block U. S. bombing of Cambodia. In his dissent from the court's landmark decision on obscenity he asserted that "the idea that the First Amendment permits government to ban publications that are 'offensive' to some people puts an ominous gloss on freedom of the press." But although he was concerned about erosion of First Amendment rights and about government encroachment on citizens' privacy in this "Orwellian era," he was optimistic in the long run, maintaining that "the people of this country are still the sovereigns."

Douglas continues to engage in such activities as hiking, mountain climbing, and world travel with his fourth wife, the former Cathleen Hefferman. At 75, he has no plans to retire.

Background. The son of a circuit-riding Presbyterian missionary, William Orville Douglas was born on Oct. 16, 1898, in Maine, Minn., and grew up in the state of Washington, where he worked his way through Whitman College. After graduating in 1925 from Columbia University Law School, he joined a Wall Street law firm for two years. He taught at Columbia, and then at Yale University, which made him Sterling professor of law in 1932. He became chairman of the Securities and Exchange Commission in 1937. Appointed by President Franklin D. Roosevelt, he took his seat on the Supreme Court in 1939 and soon became a leading member of the court's liberal faction. Throughout the post-World War II McCarthy era, he remained a consistent defender of individual rights, and during the court's liberal period under Chief Justice Earl Warren, in the 1950's and 1960's, he was responsible for a number of landmark decisions. Douglas is the author of a number of works on the law and conservation.

ECHEVERRÍA ALVAREZ, Luis

Mexican President Luis Echeverría Alvarez continued, in 1973, to implement his economic reform program, designed to modernize Mexican industry, promote employment, establish greater government control over foreign investment, and provide fairer distribution of wealth. In March and April he undertook a four-week "mission of peace," visiting Canada, Great Britain, France, Belgium, the USSR, and China. The tour, intended to promote Mexican political and economic interests, was also seen as a means of demonstrating Mexico's independence of the United States. During this trip Echeverría succeeded in persuading France and China to adhere to a protocol committing nuclear powers to refrain from using nuclear arms in Latin America.

After a military coup overthrew Chile's Marxist government in September, Echeverría declared three days of mourning for its late president, Salvador Allende, and offered asylum to opponents of the new regime.

Background. The son of a civil servant, Luis Echeverría Alvarez was born in Mexico City on Jan. 17, 1922. He graduated from the law school of the National University of Mexico in 1945 and joined its faculty in 1947. A member of Mexico's ruling Institutional Revolutionary party from 1946, he served in various party and government posts before his appointment, in 1964, to the key cabinet position of minister of the interior.

Echeverría was elected president of Mexico in July 1970 and inaugurated in December of that year. Although he had employed harsh measures against student rioters when he was interior minister, he acquired a liberal reputation as president. He drew criticism from old-guard and right-wing elements for taking a conciliatory approach toward leftist dissenters and for introducing far-reaching economic and social reforms.

EHRLICHMAN, John D.   See page 26.

ERVIN, Sam J., Jr.

As chairman of the U. S. Senate Select Committee on Presidential Campaign Activities, Sam J. Ervin, Jr., a Democratic senator from North Carolina, became a national figure through the committee's televised hearings, beginning in May 1973, which first aired the story of the Watergate affair.

While witness after witness testified on aspects of the Watergate break-in and the subsequent cover-up, Ervin emphasized that the committee's duty was to establish the facts and report to the Senate. He had to bear in mind the criminal inquiry into the case then being conducted by the special prosecutor, Archibald Cox, and a grand jury.

An authority on the U. S. Constitution, Ervin maintained the right of Congress to examine activities of the executive branch of government. He challenged the concept of executive privilege advanced by President Nixon to bar access to tapes of White House conversations and caused a subpoena to be issued for some that were believed to contain valuable evidence. The subpoena was dismissed in court. At Ervin's behest, Congress later approved legislation permitting the committee to subpoena documents from the President. Late in 1973 the committee subpoenaed hundreds of such documents, but the subpoena was not honored.

The committee comprised three Democrats besides Ervin and three Republicans, but Ervin succeeded generally in excluding any show of partisan friction in the hearings. After finishing its Watergate phase, the committee held televised hearings on political espionage and trickery (popularly called the "dirty tricks") and on campaign financing.

Presiding in an atmosphere of drama, Ervin created a notable image by his bearing and by his apt and aphoristic quotations from the Bible. He also enjoyed relating anecdotes of his legal career, which often made a telling point.

Background. Samuel James Ervin, Jr., was born at Morganton, N. C., on Sept. 27, 1896. He graduated from the University of North Carolina and Harvard Law School. In World War I, he served with the U. S. 1st Division in France, where he was twice wounded and received several decorations.

He began to practice law in Morganton in 1922. He was a state legislator and a judge of the Burke county criminal court and of the state superior court before serving one term in the U. S. House of Representatives (1947–48). Ervin was an associate justice of the North Carolina supreme court from 1948 to 1954. Appointed to fill a U. S. Senate vacancy in 1954, he was elected to the Senate that year and was reelected in 1956, 1962, and 1968. Citing his advancing age, Ervin announced late in 1973 that he would not seek reelection in 1974.

In 1954, Ervin sat on the committee that recommended the censure of Sen. Joseph R. McCarthy (R-Wis.). A civil libertarian, Ervin opposed surveillance of civilians by the Army, computerized data banks, and a "no-knock" crime bill.

RICHARD G. WEST

FORD, Gerald Rudolph

On Oct. 12, 1973, Gerald R. Ford, 60-year-old minority leader of the U. S. House of Representatives, was nominated by President Nixon to become the 40th

WIDE WORLD

(Above) *Gerald Ford, who became vice president in December, appears at a reception with his wife, Betty, and daughter, Susan.* (Right) *Sen. Sam J. Ervin, Jr., gained prominence as chairman of the Senate Watergate committee.*

UPI

vice president of the United States. The office became vacant two days earlier when Spiro T. Agnew resigned after having pleaded *nolo contendere* to a charge of federal income tax evasion. Ford was named while President Nixon was facing threats of impeachment and calls for his resignation.

After an intensive investigation by the House and Senate, Ford was confirmed. On December 6 he was installed in the nation's second-highest administrative office and in direct line of succession to the presidency. Ford thus became the first person nominated and approved under the provisions of the 25th Amendment, which was ratified in 1967.

Ford's long record in the House had been marked by strong party loyalty, dogged hard work, and a complete absence of any hint of scandal. These qualities, and his ability to get along with members of both political parties, were pertinent to his selection. In a national atmosphere of scandal, charges, disbelief, vituperation, and disdain of politicians, a man of solid honor and purest reputation was needed. After being nominated as vice president, Ford disclaimed any intention to run for "president, vice president, or anything else in 1976."

During his 25 years of service in the House, Ford emphasized the need for fiscal responsibility and a strong defense. In 1948–49, Ford served in the House with Nixon and the two became good friends. In 1965, Ford became minority leader of the House, replacing Charles A. Halleck. During the years of the two Nixon administrations, Ford has been a consistent supporter of the President's policies. In 1970, Ford worked for the impeachment of Supreme Court Justice William O. Douglas. In 1972, Ford made a 10-day visit to China, and on his return he stated that high Chinese officials exhibited a "great deal of interest in

... the sufficiency of our military capability." Ford has the reputation of being a boring public speaker but a most effective political vote trader and an effective representative of his constituents. He has been dubbed "Mr. Clean" by journalists.

Background. Gerald Ford was born in Omaha, Neb., on July 14, 1913, and grew up in Grand Rapids, Mich. In 1935, he graduated from the University of Michigan, where he played center on two undefeated national championship football teams. He earned a law degree from Yale University in 1941 and then served in the Navy for 47 months as an aviation operations officer, rising to the rank of lieutenant commander. After a period of private law practice, Ford first won election to the House from the Fifth District of Michigan in a tough 1948 campaign in which he had the support of Sen. Arthur H. Vandenberg. Ford was reelected for 12 consecutive terms, the last starting in 1973. The new vice president is married to the former Elizabeth Bloomer. The Fords, who live in Alexandria, Va., have three sons and a daughter.

WALTER DARNELL JACOBS

FOSSE, Bob

Bob Fosse, director and choreographer, became in 1973 the first person ever to win the "triple crown" of show business, achieving top honors of the Broadway theater, motion pictures, and television within a single year. In March he received two "Tony" awards for his work as director and choreographer of the Broadway musical *Pippin,* as well as an "Oscar" for his direction of the film *Cabaret.* In May he received three "Emmy" awards for producing, directing, and choreographing Liza Minnelli's television special *Liza with a "Z."* His current directorial projects include the film *Lenny,* starring Dustin Hoffman as the late comedian Lenny Bruce, and a forthcoming Broadway musical based on the play *Chicago,* starring his third wife and long-time collaborator, Gwen Verdon, from whom he is now separated.

Background. Robert Louis Fosse was born in Chicago, Ill., on June 23, 1927, the son of a vaudevillian. He received dance training at an early age, appeared in variety shows in his teens, and performed with U. S. Navy entertainment units in the Pacific during World War II. After a year of studying acting with the American Theatre Wing and several years of singing and dancing in stage, motion picture, and television musicals, Fosse was hired in 1954 as choreographer for the Broadway musical *The Pajama Game,* for which he won his first "Tony." Other Broadway hits for which he did the choreography include *Damn Yankees* (1955), *Bells Are Ringing* (1956), and *New Girl in Town* (1957). He made his debut as a theatrical director with *Redhead* (1959), staged *How to Succeed in Business Without Really Trying* (1961), and was co-director of *Little Me* (1962). In Hollywood, Fosse choreographed the films *My Sister Eileen* (1955), *The Pajama Game* (1957), and *Damn Yankees* (1958). He scored a major triumph on Broadway as director-choreographer and co-star with Gwen Verdon in *Sweet Charity* (1966). He also directed and choreographed its less successful 1969 film version, starring Shirley MacLaine.

GANDHI, Indira

Prime Minister Indira Gandhi, who had gained a commanding position on the Indian political scene in 1971 and 1972, was confronted by a series of economic and political troubles during 1973, and there was a considerable erosion of her popularity and power.

Although she had promised in election campaigns to abolish poverty, she was unable to stem the tide of economic reverses. In part these were due to natural disasters, including the worst droughts in a decade, and in part to governmental policies or lack of policies. Measures that her government took to deal with the serious food shortage and rising prices, such

as nationalization of the wholesale trade in wheat and substantial imports of food grains, were costly and only partially effective. The country was plagued with food riots, communal riots, a revolt of the provincial armed constabulary in Mrs. Gandhi's own state of Uttar Pradesh, and other forms of violence.

Amid mounting charges of corruption in her party and government mismanagement, Mrs. Gandhi was faced with serious problems in several states, six of which had to be placed under President's Rule.

In foreign affairs, Mrs. Gandhi had greater success. She visited Nepal in February and Sri Lanka in April, and took an active part in the Commonwealth heads of state conference in Canada and the nonaligned nations' meeting in Algeria.

Background. The only daughter of Jawaharlal Nehru, Indira Gandhi was born in Allahabad on Nov. 19, 1917. She was educated in India and at Oxford. On her return to India she took an active part in the independence movement, and she was imprisoned in 1942–43 by the British. In 1942 she married a Parsi lawyer, Feroze Gandhi, by whom she had two sons. Gradually she and her husband became estranged, especially after 1947 when she became virtually a full-time hostess for her father. She was president of the Congress party in 1959–60, and minister of information and broadcasting in 1964–66. In January 1966 she became prime minister of India. In the fall of 1969 the Congress party split, and her wing of the party gained increasing support. In the fifth general elections, in 1971, she was given a decisive majority in the Lok Sabha (lower house).

NORMAN D. PALMER

GEISEL, Ernesto

In June 1973, Brazilian President Emilio Garrastazú de Médici and the chiefs of the nation's armed services announced that former Gen. Ernesto Geisel was their choice to lead the nation during the 1974–79 presidential term. For four years, the president-designate had been the manager of Petrobrás, the government oil monopoly, where he had proved himself an efficient and foresighted administrator, forceful but prudent. Médici assured the nation that Geisel "will not permit any deviation from the economic, social, and political philosophy of the revolutionary order." Geisel was formally elected president by the military regime's rubber-stamp electoral college on Jan. 15, 1974.

Background. Ernesto Geisel was born on Aug. 3, 1908, in the mountain town of Bento Gonçalves, Rio Grande do Sul, the youngest of five children of a German-born schoolteacher. There was little money in the family until Geisel's sister won a state lottery, which enabled Ernesto and his brother Orlando to attend the Brazilian Military Academy. Both were eventually to become four-star generals. Orlando was minister of the army in 1973.

As a lieutenant, Ernesto Geisel took part in the suppression of the Communist-led revolt of 1935. He rose steadily in the army hierarchy during the dictatorship of Getúlio Vargas (1937–45) and the democratic period that followed it. A protégé of Marshal Humberto de Alencar Castelo Branco, Geisel helped to plan and execute the 1964 coup that ousted the government of João Goulart.

With Castelo Branco installed as president, Geisel became secretary general of the National Security Council, which was responsible for purging the country of subversives. Geisel later headed the Supreme Military Tribunal. He retired from the army in 1969 to take up his post at Petrobrás.

NEILL MACAULAY

HAIG, Alexander Meigs, Jr.

One of President Nixon's most trusted diplomatic advisers and emissaries, Alexander Meigs Haig, Jr., a full general in the U. S. Army, was appointed by Nixon

in May 1973 as White House chief of staff to succeed H. R. (Bob) Haldeman, who had resigned in the wake of the Watergate affair. Haig resigned from the Army after objections that an Army officer should not serve in the White House.

Haig's new duties involved ensuring that decisions were made and implemented, overseeing staff operations, and dealing with delicate problems. By training and experience, he was considered by many to be well qualified for the task. By year's end he was embroiled in the controversy over a key "gap" in a tape recording subpoenaed in the Watergate investigation.

Background. Haig was born in Philadelphia on Dec. 2, 1924. Orphaned at age 10, he worked to save money for a college education. He attended the University of Notre Dame and then entered the U.S. Military Academy at West Point, where he graduated in 1947 and was commissioned a 2d lieutenant.

After years of varied assignments, Haig filled staff posts in Washington early in the 1960's and was a deputy special assistant to the secretary of defense. In this decade he graduated from the Naval and Army war colleges and received a master's degree.

During the Vietnam War he was a battalion and brigade commander with the 1st Infantry Division in 1966–67. From 1967 to 1969 he was regimental commander and deputy commandant at West Point.

Haig's knowledge of foreign affairs and his talent for diplomacy were recognized in 1969, when he was named senior military adviser to Henry Kissinger, then the President's chief adviser on national security. A year later, Haig became a deputy assistant to the President for national security. His several missions to Southeast Asia prepared the groundwork for a cease-fire agreement in Vietnam. Within two years he won promotions to brigadier general and major general. Early in 1973, he was named Army vice chief of staff with the rank of full general, being advanced over 240 generals and skipping the rank of lieutenant general.

RICHARD G. WEST

HALDEMAN, H. R. See page 26.

HEATH, Edward

British Prime Minister Edward Heath's Conservative government faced critical economic problems in 1973 while also dealing with continuing troubles in Ireland. In December, the prime minister displayed his legendary stubbornness by announcing a three-day work week rather than meeting coal miners' wage demands that he deemed economically unjustifiable.

In September, in an attempt to clarify the Irish situation, Heath visited Dublin—the first such official visit by a British prime minister since 1922. A new Northern Irish executive was formed in December, consisting of Catholic and Protestant groups, drawn from the Assembly elected in June by proportional representation. But extremist opposition persisted, IRA violence continued, and future relations between the north and south of Ireland remained unsettled.

Britain's formal entry into the European Economic Community (EEC, or Common Market) on Jan. 1, 1973, was the culmination of a policy with which Heath had been identified for more than 10 years. The prime minister spent much time in 1973 denying that EEC membership was in any way responsible for rises in food prices in Britain, and stressing that the benefits of membership would take time to materialize. After the October Arab oil boycott, Heath joined with French President Georges Pompidou in a controversial policy seen by their opponents as pro-Arab and disruptive of EEC harmony.

Until October, Heath continued to identify himself with the economic strategy of "going all out for growth," hoping that the inflationary consequences of such a course would be limited by an improvement in Britain's terms of trade, a leveling off of world commodity prices, an increase in exports, and the success

CENTRAL PRESS FROM PICTORIAL PARADE

EDWARD HEATH, British prime minister, ordered three-day work week in face of critical energy shortage.

of the Prices and Incomes policy. Phase II of that policy was introduced in April, and Phase III in November.

In October and November the Heath strategy appeared to have been undermined. First, the Arab oil embargo was expected to enlarge an already huge British balance of payments deficit, and in November the miners and the power engineers took industrial action against Phase III, causing an immediate fuel crisis. Heath subsequently declared a state of emergency and announced the energy-saving short work week.

The Heath government's reputation did not seem to suffer very greatly as the result of a scandal that saw the resignation in May of two ministers who had associated with call girls. Nor did the Labour opposition capitalize fully on the government's failure to contain inflation at an acceptable level. On the other hand, the Liberals made inroads into Conservative strength in two November by-elections. Polls showed that many voters were disillusioned with both major parties, as well as with both major-party leaders.

Background. Edward Richard George Heath was born in Broadstairs, Kent, on July 9, 1916, and was educated at Balliol College, Oxford. After military service during World War II, he entered the civil service as an administrator of civil aviation. From 1950 he represented Bexley, a London suburb, as a Conservative in Parliament. Successively party whip, minister of labour, and lord privy seal, he was elected Conservative party leader in 1965 and became prime minister after the Conservative victory in 1970.

A. J. BEATTIE

HUROK, S.

S. Hurok, master showman and world citizen, continued at the age of 85 to carry on his life's work—presenting top artistic talent at moderate prices to the widest possible audiences. On May 21, he was honored at a gala concert at New York's Metropolitan Opera House in recognition of his 85th birthday and his 60 years as an impresario in the service of the performing arts. The program, a benefit for the Performing Arts Research Center of the New York Public Library at Lincoln Center, included such luminaries as Van Cliburn, Isaac Stern, and Margot Fonteyn and was attended by artists, diplomats, and leaders of society.

In recognition of Hurok's pioneering contributions to U. S.-Soviet cultural exchange, the USSR sent members of the Bolshoi Ballet to take part in the event. Price Alfonso de Borbón of Spain presented Hurok with his country's highest honor, the Medal of Isabel la Católica. New York's Mayor John V. Lindsay gave Hurok the city's Diamond Jubilee Medal and its highest cultural award, the Handel Medallion, with an inscription honoring him as a "daring innovator, international pioneer and leader in the living arts."

Background. Solomon Hurok was born in the Ukrainian village of Pogar on April 9, 1888, the son of a hardware dealer. In 1905 he was sent by his father to Kharkov to study business, but he decided instead to go to the United States and arrived there the next year. After supporting himself at various jobs, he began in 1911 to arrange concerts for workers' organizations—featuring, among others, the violinist Efrem Zimbalist. His "Music for the Masses" concerts in New York City soon were attracting overflow audiences. Since 1913, Hurok has presented to U. S. audiences hundreds of distinguished international artists—including Anna Pavlova, Feodor Chaliapin, Artur Rubinstein, Isadora Duncan, and Marian Anderson—and such ensembles as the Ballets Russes, the Moscow Art Players, and the Vienna Boys' Choir. He has exercised a major influence on the dance through his presentation of the world's leading ballet companies and dance groups. "I feel younger than I did 25 years ago," Hurok said at age 85. "That's because I'm in love—with this business."

JAWORSKI, Leon

Leon Jaworski, a Democrat and a Texas lawyer with a long record of public service, took office on Nov. 5, 1973, as special prosecutor in the Watergate case. He succeeded Archibald Cox, who was dismissed on October 20 when he refused to comply with a presidential order not to seek White House tapes and records. In announcing Jaworski's appointment on November 1, Acting Attorney General Robert H. Bork said that Jaworski would have the same job charter and guidelines as his predecessor but that he had been promised full freedom of action in seeking release of presidential documents. It also was stipulated that he could not be dismissed without the consensus of eight congressional leaders—the majority and minority leaders of the House and Senate and the chairmen and ranking minority members of the judicial committees of both houses.

By mid-December, Jaworski had expressed satisfaction with White House cooperation in making relevant documents available, and Congress deferred action on bills calling for court appointment or congressional approval of the special prosecutor.

Background. Jaworski was born in Waco, Texas, on Sept. 19, 1905. He received a law degree from Baylor University in 1925 and was admitted to the Texas bar in that year. His record of public service includes his roles as a prosecutor in the first major war crimes trials in the European theater during World War II, as assistant to the attorney general in the Kennedy and Johnson administrations, and as an adviser to President Johnson. A past president of the American Bar Association, Jaworski at the time of his appointment was a senior partner in a Houston law firm.

SUE R. BRANDT

KELLEY, Clarence M.

Clarence M. Kelley, chief of police of Kansas City, Mo., was named director of the Federal Bureau of Investigation (FBI) on June 7, 1973, by President Nixon, who called him "the best man in the country for the position." A veteran of 33 years in law enforcement, including 21 years with the FBI, Kelley was confirmed by a unanimous Senate vote on June 27 and was sworn into office on July 9. He is the first permanent director

CLARENCE KELLEY became director of the FBI in July. He had been serving as chief of police of Kansas City, Mo.

UPI

since J. Edgar Hoover, who headed the FBI for nearly 50 years until his death in May 1972. Hoover's successor, L. Patrick Gray 3d, who resigned as acting director in April 1973 after admitting involvement in the Watergate affair, was temporarily replaced by William D. Ruckelshaus.

At the Senate confirmation hearings, Kelley asserted that he would enhance the bureau's professionalism and restore its self-confidence, while doing everything in his power to keep it free of partisan politics. He promised a more relaxed atmosphere and a more open policy toward the public and the news media, and also invited congressional review of FBI activities, as well as "participatory management" by its employees. Although committed to "law and order," Kelley believes that crime can be controlled without violating "human rights and dignities."

Background. Born in Kansas City, Mo., on Oct. 24, 1911, Clarence Marion Kelley was educated at the University of Kansas and the law school of the University of Kansas City. After Navy duty in World War II, he was employed by the FBI from 1940 to 1961, when, as head of the bureau's office in Memphis, Tenn., he was offered the post of police chief of Kansas City. An advocate of modern technology in police work, Kelley introduced round-the-clock helicopter patrols and computerized data systems in his department. He is credited with reducing crime by 25% in Kansas City.

KING, Billie Jean

When she was 11 years old, Billie Jean Moffitt was excluded from an official tennis tourney picture because she was wearing shorts instead of a tennis skirt. This was soon after she had taken up the game and determined to be a world champion. She dedicated the next 18 years to achieving her goals on the courts and fighting the staid establishment. Her battles with tennis officialdom were chiefly over the size of the prizes awarded to women compared with those for men.

To get the money conditions changed, she became, with Mrs. Gladys Heldman, one of the prime movers of "Women's Lob." Billie Jean, who does not smoke, welcomed the sponsorship of Virginia Slims cigarettes because it gave the females some independence from federation-operated activities. She was suspended many times until the pros and the establishment could get together on sanctioning. By 1971, when she was rated the top woman player, Mrs. King not only was the first woman athlete to win over $100,000 in a year but she also won more than any of the American men players.

Billie Jean was born in Long Beach, Calif., on Nov. 22, 1943. About 10 years later her parents told her she could no longer play football with the boys and to find some other sport to replace softball. She discovered tennis at a public park, saved her money to buy a racquet, and went on to become one of the game's

finest competitors and greatest champions as well as one of its most controversial stars.

When she was 17, Miss Moffitt gained her first major title. She and Karen Hantze won the doubles at Wimbledon in 1961. Billie Jean married Larry King, a fellow student at Long Beach State College in 1965. The following year she began strings of three straight victories in the U. S. indoor and at Wimbledon. In 1967 she took the Australian title and, after Wimbledon, won the U. S. singles, the doubles with Rosemary Casals, and the mixed doubles with Owen Davidson. This was the first triple victory since Sarah Palfrey Cooke's in 1941.

Billie Jean began winning again in 1971 when she took the three U. S. titles—indoor, clay court, and open. In 1972 she won the French, Wimbledon, and U. S. opens, losing only one set in 22 matches. In 1973 she triumphed again at Wimbledon, increasing her victories there to 17—five singles, nine doubles, and three mixed doubles. She wound up the year by humbling Bobby Riggs on a television spectacular billed as the "Battle of the Sexes." (See also Sports, page 535.)

BILL BRADDOCK

KING, Carole

Singer, songwriter, and pianist Carole King, one of the brightest stars in the recent history of show business, strikes a responsive chord among today's young popular music fans with her "soft rock" songs. They are characterized by a flowing, rhythmic sound based on jazz but emphasizing the lyrics rather than the beat, expressing "the way kids feel today," as one fan commented. Her album *Tapestry*, released in 1971, became the best-selling rock album of all time, topping the 10-million mark in sales by mid-1973. In the LP album *Fantasy*, released in 1973, Miss King moved beyond the romantic themes of her earlier works to comment on such topics as drug addiction and racial discrimination. The highlight of her personal appearances in 1973 was her free concert in May in New York's Central Park, where she sang to an enthusiastic crowd of 70,000.

Carole King was born in New York City on Feb. 9, 1941, the daughter of a salesman and a schoolteacher. She attended Queens College for a year before dropping out to marry Gerry Goffin, an aspiring chemist who shared her enthusiasm for popular music. For several years, the couple worked as songwriters for New York music publisher Don Kirschner, turning out such hits as "Will You Love Me Tomorrow?," "Up on the Roof," and "A Natural Woman."

Having decided to end her marriage and songwriting partnership with Goffin in 1968, Carole moved

WIDE WORLD

BILLIE JEAN KING is shown in action at Wimbledon, where in 1973 she won her fifth singles championship.

to the West Coast where she soon became a successful solo vocalist and recording star. In 1972 the National Academy of Recording Arts and Sciences presented Carole with four Grammy awards for the 1971 season. *Tapestry* was voted the best album of the year, and her rendition of its title song was cited as the best female vocal performance in the pop music field. She also received awards for "You've Got a Friend," the best song, and "It's Too Late," the best single record of 1971. Her other LP albums include *Writer: Carole King* (1970), *Music* (1971), and *Rhymes & Reasons* (1972). Carole makes her home in the Los Angeles area with her second husband, bassist Charles Larkey.

KISSINGER, Henry Alfred

The mercurial career of Henry A. Kissinger continued its upward spiral throughout 1973. A year of intense worldwide activity was capped by two achievements—becoming secretary of state and winning the Nobel Prize for peace.

Kissinger retained his position as assistant to the President for national security affairs while assuming

UPI

HENRY KISSINGER climaxed an eventful year in 1973 by becoming U. S. secretary of state and winning the Nobel Peace Prize. Here he speaks to UN General Assembly.

the new job of secretary of state on September 22. This indication of President Nixon's high regard for Kissinger also was reflected in the many diplomatic missions that Kissinger undertook.

A cease-fire agreement in Vietnam was obtained in January through Kissinger's negotiations with Le Duc Tho, the North Vietnamese representative. Although it was followed by many violations and reports of build-ups for offensive action, the agreement permitted the United States to disengage from the war and to gain the release of its prisoners of war. Kissinger and Le Duc Tho were named co-winners of the Nobel Prize for peace for their efforts in the negotiations, but Tho refused to accept the award.

The détente with the Soviet Union, which formed the basis for Kissinger's policy of balance-of-forces diplomacy, seemed to come apart in October when the Arab-Israeli war broke out. Kissinger was faced with threats of unilateral Soviet intervention in the conflict, but he responded by recommending an alert of U. S. forces and supporting a UN resolution to end the fighting. The conflict was halted, and Kissinger contended that the détente and Nixon's close acquaintance with Leonid Brezhnev had made that possible while avoiding a major confrontation with the Soviet Union. Kissinger later suggested that the United States might make a formal guarantee of the borders of Israel.

Throughout the year Kissinger made repeated trips to world capitals, visiting leaders in the USSR, Japan, China, the Middle East, and other places. Everywhere, Kissinger's seemingly limitless energy and his intelligence characterized his activity.

Background. Henry Alfred Kissinger was born in Fürth, Germany, on May 27, 1923. His family went to New York City in 1938. During World War II he served in the U. S. Army where he came to the attention of Fritz Kraemer, who sponsored his education at Harvard University. He graduated *summa cum laude* in 1950 and earned a Ph. D. in 1954. He served with the Council on Foreign Relations, and in 1957 published *Nuclear Weapons and Foreign Policy*. Kissinger advised various governmental agencies and headed a special studies project for the Rockefeller Brothers Fund. He directed Harvard's Defense Studies Program from 1959 to 1969, when he went to Washington with a leave of absence from Harvard.

WALTER DARNELL JACOBS

KOSYGIN, Aleksei Nikolayevich

Soviet Premier Aleksei Kosygin in 1973 continued to rank second among Soviet leaders only to Leonid Brezhnev, the secretary general of the Communist party. On Jan. 1, 1973, Kosygin was given the honor of presenting to the Soviet people on radio and TV the New Year's greetings from the USSR government and the Communist party Politburo.

During 1973, Kosygin made six official visits to foreign countries, including a goodwill trip to Yugoslavia and attending a meeting of the Soviet–East European Mongolian "Council of Mutual Economic Assistance" in Czechoslovakia. In Iran he was the guest of honor at the opening of a steel mill built with Soviet assistance. His April visit to Stockholm resulted in Soviet-Swedish treaties concerning cultural exchange and maritime shipping. In Vienna during July he concluded Soviet-Austrian pacts for cultural exchange, economic cooperation, and motor vehicle traffic control.

Kosygin's most important journey, however, was in mid-October to Cairo, where he discovered that the Egyptian military situation was deteriorating in the 1973 Arab-Israeli war. His talks with Egyptian President Anwar el-Sadat apparently focused on ways to settle the Middle East crisis. After he returned to Moscow, the USSR began to cooperate with the United States in obtaining a cease-fire in the Middle East.

Although the 69-year-old Kosygin is one of the oldest members of the Politburo, there was no sign in 1973 that this tall dour man desired to retire.

Background. Kosygin was born of a worker's family in St. Petersburg (now Leningrad) on Feb. 20, 1904. He is a skilled economist and since 1939 has held such high posts as chairman of the State Planning Committee, vice premier of the USSR, premier of the Russian Soviet Republic, and head of the ministries for the textile industry, light industry, the consumer goods industry, and finance. He was a Politburo member from 1945 to 1952, and he has been a member since 1957. Following the ouster of Nikita Khrushchev as premier in 1964, Kosygin succeeded him. In the post-Khrushchev period he has never had as much official publicity as Brezhnev, but the two men work together as co-leaders, dividing important assignments between them.

ELLSWORTH RAYMOND

LE DUC THO

The chief North Vietnamese negotiator during the Paris peace talks that lasted three years and resulted in a cease-fire agreement in January 1973, Le Duc Tho was awarded the Nobel Peace Prize jointly with Henry A. Kissinger on October 16. But a week later, Le Duc Tho rejected the prize, saying that "peace has not yet really been established in South Vietnam." And, in fact, the level of fighting there increased steadily through the year after the two negotiators met in June to sign an accord strengthening the cease-fire. They met again in Paris in December to discuss "matters of mutual interest." But by year's end most of the terms of the January truce had yet to be carried out.

Background. The career of Le Duc Tho, like the careers of many other life-long revolutionaries, is not well documented—and very little is publicly known about his personal life. He was born in 1911 or 1912 in what is now North Vietnam and received training in radiotelegraphy. In 1929 he joined the Indochina Communist party. The French colonial masters of Indochina held Le Duc Tho in jail at various times; during World War II he may have been in China with Ho Chi Minh or in jail in Indochina. With the start of the war against the French in Indochina, Le Duc Tho began to rise in the party hierarchy, gaining a leadership position in the south. With the ouster of the French, he returned north. He is a member of the Politburo and secretary of the central committee of the Vietnam Workers (Communist) party. Le Duc Tho is graceful in manner but unbending in putting forth his country's position. He writes poetry that is frequently militant.

WESLEY F. STROMBECK

LÉGER, Jules

The distinguished diplomat Jules Léger was designated on Oct. 5, 1973, as Canada's 21st governor-general, effective in mid-January 1974. At the time of his appointment he was serving as Canada's ambassador to Belgium and Luxembourg. Léger, who succeeds the retiring governor-general, Roland Michener, is the fourth native Canadian and the second French-Canadian to be named to that office. The other native governors-general were Vincent Massey (1952–59), Georges P. Vanier (1959–67), and Michener; Vanier was a French-Canadian. As the personal representative of the British sovereign, the governor-general fulfills the role of Canadian head of state on behalf of the crown and represents Canada on ceremonial and symbolic occasions.

Léger was born in St.-Anicet, Quebec, on April 4, 1913. He studied at the College of Valleyfield and the University of Montreal law school and received a doctor of letters degree in 1938 from the University of Paris. In 1938–39 he was associate editor of the Ottawa daily newspaper *Le Droit*. Léger joined the Canadian department of external affairs as third secretary in 1940 and in 1940–42 also taught diplomatic history and current affairs at the University of Ottawa. He went abroad in 1943 and served successively as a member of the Canadian mission in Santiago, Chile, as first

secretary in London, and on conference duty with the United Nations General Assembly in Paris.

After returning to Canada in 1949, Léger was executive assistant to Prime Minister Louis St. Laurent before being appointed assistant undersecretary of state for external affairs in 1951 and ambassador to Mexico in 1953. Thereafter, in 1954, he became undersecretary of state for external affairs. In 1958–62 he represented Canada on the North Atlantic Council and the Organization for Economic Cooperation and Development. Thereafter he was ambassador to Italy (1962–64) and ambassador to France (1964–68). From 1968 until his appointment as ambassador to Belgium and Luxembourg on Feb. 16, 1973, Léger served as undersecretary of state with responsibility for arts, bilingualism, and education. He is a brother of Paul-Émile Cardinal Léger, retired archbishop of Montreal.

MEANY, George

George Meany, president of the nearly 14 million-member AFL-CIO, brought his labor federation back into alignment with the Democratic party and into determined opposition to the Nixon administration in 1973, ending his "political neutrality" during the 1972 presidential campaign. Although he continued to serve on the Cost of Living Council's labor-management advisory committee, Meany became increasingly critical of the President's economic policies, as living costs, especially food prices, outdistanced wage gains. He assailed the administration's proposals for minimum wages, pensions, and unemployment compensation as falling far short of labor's needs and denounced the President's veto, in September, of labor's proposed minimum-wage bill as "a callous, cruel blow" to the nation's working poor. He demanded a vigorous investigation of the Watergate affair, which he saw as a "large-scale subversion of the democratic political process." Meany broke with tradition by refusing to invite President Nixon to the October biennial AFL-CIO convention at Miami Beach.

In the 1973 struggle to control California's grape workers between Cesar Chavez' United Farm Workers and the International Brotherhood of Teamsters, Meany gave solid support to the AFL-CIO-affiliated Farm Workers. He warned in December against succumbing to "Arab blackmail" in the fuel crisis, and declared that labor would go along with "fair and equitable" energy conservation programs.

Background. Born in New York City on Aug. 16, 1894, William George Meany left school at 16 to enter the plumbing trade. In 1922 he became business agent of his union local. He was elected president of the New York State Federation of Labor in 1934 and secretary-treasurer of the American Federation of Labor in 1939. After serving on the War Labor Board in World War II, he played a leading role in the postwar expansion of the union movement. He was elected president of the AFL in 1952 and of the merged AFL-CIO in 1955.

MEIR, Golda

Premier Meir of Israel, who was named the "most admired" woman of the year in a Gallup Poll released in December 1973, faced the 25th anniversary year of her country's independence with determination "to convince the Arabs that Israel is here to stay and cannot be defeated." The continued Arab hostility toward Israel culminated in the Yom Kippur war, when Egypt and Syria launched an attack on the Jewish state on October 6.

Although Israel scored some gains in the 17-day struggle, it paid a high price in casualties. At the urging of U. S. Secretary of State Henry Kissinger, Mrs. Meir agreed in December to take part in Mideast peace talks at Geneva and did not rule out the possibility of relinquishing some of the Arab territory occupied by Israel since 1967 in return for secure borders.

Despite assurances of continued U. S. support, Israel found itself increasingly isolated on the diplomatic front at the end of 1973, partly as a result of the oil crisis, which made many nations increasingly dependent on the good graces of the Arab states. On the home front, Mrs. Meir's critics charged that Israel was inadequately prepared at the time of the October war. In the elections of December 31, Mrs. Meir's Labor group suffered a setback but managed to retain control of the government.

Background. A native of Kiev, Russia, Golda Meir (Mrs. Morris Myerson) was born Golda Mabovitch on May 3, 1898. Brought to the United States at the age of eight, she spent her formative years in Milwaukee, Wis. She studied at a teachers college and became interested in socialism and Zionism. In 1921 she emigrated to Palestine, where she worked on a kibbutz and later helped organize the labor confederation Histadruth. From 1946 to 1948 she served in its executive branch and headed the political department of the Jewish Agency. She was a signer of Israel's declaration of independence in 1948. She served as minister to the Soviet Union (1948–49), as minister of labor (1949–56), as foreign minister (1956–66), and as secretary general of the Mapai (Labor) party (1966–68). On March 17, 1969, she became Israel's fourth premier, succeeding Levi Eshkol.

GOLDA MEIR, premier of Israel, led her country in the fighting against Egypt and Syria in 1973. Her party remained in power despite losses in the December elections.

WIDE WORLD

MITCHELL, John N.   See page 26.

NIXON, Richard M.

For President Richard Nixon, 1973 was a year of increasing travail. In January he was inaugurated for a second term and in the same month he announced the end of U. S. involvement in the Vietnam War. Within months, however, his aspirations for his second term were a shambles as the Watergate scandals decimated his staff, eroded his popular support, and brought into question his capacity to govern. The year ended amid real gloom, as the President announced that the country faced a shortage of energy in the wake of a war in the Middle East and an Arab oil embargo.

Foreign Affairs. On January 23 the President announced that agreement had been reached on a peace accord to end the longest war in U. S. history. The agreement resulted in an exchange of war prisoners for which he and Dr. Henry Kissinger received much acclaim.

In October, Israelis and Arabs fought another brief but bloody war. Israeli losses of men and materials were high and the United States agreed to furnish Israel with replacement weapons while appealing to the Soviet Union and the Arab coalition to begin

negotiations. On October 25, Nixon placed U. S. forces on alert in response to a reported Soviet threat of unilateral action. The next day, however, the Soviets agreed to support a U. S. plan for an international peace-keeping force without big-power participation. The President and Secretary of State Kissinger undertook negotiations to bring the two sides together to search for a permanent settlement of the dispute.

Domestic Affairs. President Nixon interpreted his landslide victory in 1972 as a mandate to decentralize the federal bureaucracy, reduce or eliminate federal programs, and share federal revenues with state and local governments. He impounded money appropriated for programs with which he disagreed, vetoed legislation that he did not want, and dismantled agencies whose missions he questioned. Although all but one of his vetoes were sustained, his impoundments were overturned in lower federal courts in most instances. Major changes were made in the President's cabinet and his White House staff during the year, primarily as a result of the Watergate affair. Clearly the most historic departure was that of Vice President Spiro Agnew, who pleaded no contest on October 10 to a charge of income tax evasion, and resigned the same day. Using the provisions of the 25th Amendment to the Constitution for the first time, President Nixon nominated House Minority Leader Gerald R. Ford (R-Mich.) to the vice presidency. Congress confirmed his nomination on December 6.

Political Troubles. The series of events known collectively as the Watergate affair dominated the news throughout 1973 and led to widespread speculation that Nixon would be impeached or forced to resign. By November his popularity, according to the Gallup Poll, had leveled off at an all-time low of 27% approval. (See Watergate feature beginning on page 14.) The President was also criticized for a variety of actions with which he or his aides were charged, including alleged favoritism in handling an antitrust case involving the International Telephone and Telegraph Corporation, the President's payment of a nominal income tax for several years, and the substantial and questionable expenditure of public funds for Nixon's homes in Florida and California. It was further alleged that he reversed a milk price support decision in return for a large campaign contribution from the dairy industry. The President promised full disclosure of evidence to answer the various charges.

The Economy. Inflation dominated economic considerations during 1973. Nixon imposed a price freeze on June 13 to cover everything except wages, rents, and agricultural products at the farm level. In July he announced his Phase 4 economic program, which removed most controls in order to allow prices to seek their "natural" level. In the face of a growing fuel shortage caused by increased demand, decreased domestic sources, and an Arab embargo on oil shipments to the United States, the President on November 7 outlined a far-reaching program to curb the consumption of fuel. He asked for authority to take steps to alleviate the shortage.

Background. Richard M. Nixon was born in Yorba Linda, Calif., on Jan. 9, 1913. After serving in the Navy during World War II he was elected to the U. S. House from California in 1946 and to the Senate in 1950. He served as vice president with President Eisenhower and received the Republican nomination for President in 1960. After being narrowly defeated by John F. Kennedy he ran for governor of California and lost in 1962. He joined a law firm in New York City but maintained his interest in Republican party affairs. He was nominated and elected President in 1968 and was reelected in 1972.

ROBERT J. HUCKSHORN

PAPP, Joseph

The dynamic producer and director of the New York Shakespeare Festival, Joseph Papp became perhaps the most influential figure in the U. S. theater when in March 1973 he was given control over all dramatic production at Lincoln Center for the Performing Arts in New York City. To offset expected deficits, Papp has been engaged in a massive fund-raising effort for his projects. Convinced that "the living playwright...is a resource we must treasure, nourish, and produce," he designated the center's 1,140-seat Vivian Beaumont Theater for new plays "reflecting the great issues of our times." Shakespeare productions will be staged in the smaller Mitzi E. Newhouse Theater (formerly the Forum Theater).

In November, Papp's production of David Rabe's new play *Boom Boom Room* opened at the Beaumont to largely unfavorable reviews. Earlier, on August 17, a televised version of Papp's Broadway production of Rabe's controversial *Sticks and Bones*—a mordant satire about a Vietnam veteran's return to his family—was finally seen on television after CBS had tried to postpone it indefinitely. The production was the second of a series that Papp is scheduled to produce for CBS television.

Background. Papp was born Joseph Papirofsky in Brooklyn, N. Y., on June 22, 1921. After serving in the U. S. Navy, he studied acting and directing at the Actors Laboratory Theatre in Hollywood, Calif., and began to meet some success in the early 1950's as a director in New York's off-Broadway theater and as a stage manager for CBS-TV. Determined to bring free theater to the public, Papp founded in 1954 the New York Shakespeare Festival, which took a fresh approach to Shakespearean drama. Operating on a shoestring budget, he presented its productions at various locations before moving into the new Delacorte Theater in New York's Central Park in 1962. In the mid-1960's, Papp acquired the Public Theater complex in lower Manhattan as headquarters for his Shakespeare Festival. While continuing to present free productions of Shakespeare in the park during the summer, he has greatly expanded his operations, bringing to Broadway such hits as the rock musical *Hair* (1968) and Jason Miller's Pulitzer Prize-winning play *That Championship Season* (1972).

PAUL VI, Pope

The wide-ranging concerns of Pope Paul VI during 1973, the 10th year of his pontificate, were expressed in a series of meetings at the Vatican with representatives of other churches, secular states, and secular movements. In declaring 1975 a Holy Year, the Pope emphasized the importance of the interior renewal of the church. His public statements during the year called attention to the needs of those suffering from war and famine.

In January the prime minister of Israel, Golda Meir, met with the Pope at the Vatican. It was the first time that a head of the Israeli government had met with a pope. A Vatican spokesman, however, pointed out that the visit did not necessarily indicate papal support of the Israeli position in the political struggles in the Middle East.

Another historic meeting took place in May when Paul VI exchanged the kiss of peace with the Coptic Orthodox Patriarch Amba Shenouda III in a ceremony marking the 16th centenary of the death of St. Athanasius. An ecumenical commission was established to study relationships between the two churches, which have been separated for 1,500 years.

In May, Paul VI announced that 1975 would be a Holy Year. He had considered, the pontiff said, whether such a tradition should continue and had concluded that it could help promote "the interior renewal of man." On June 10, Pentecost Sunday, he declared the Holy Year to be dedicated to the theme of reconciliation. Protestants were invited to participate, in particular the World Council of Churches (WCC). Reaction from the WCC was favorable, although a spokesman expressed the hope that the Holy Year would not be an

WIDE WORLD

NEW YORK STATE THEATER

UPI

(Above, left) *President Nixon joins composer Irving Berlin in singing* God Bless America *at reception for former POWs.* (Above) *Pope Paul VI greets a young girl during Lenten visit to a church in Rome.* (Left) *Joseph Papp, stage producer, took major post at Lincoln Center, New York.*

occasion for new dogmatic pronouncements nor be characterized by a great emphasis on indulgences.

In March the pope created 30 new cardinals, including three Americans. As a result the College of Cardinals reached an all-time high of 145 members, but the pope announced that only 120 of these would be eligible to take part in the election of a new pope. He also indicated that some bishops probably would participate in the next papal election.

On June 21, Paul VI celebrated the 10th anniversary of his election. Dutch bishops took the occasion to publish a pastoral letter on "the ministry of Peter," in which they observed that although the local churches want respect for their own contributions, "it is the duty of the Holy See to defend the treasure of the faith." In reply Pope Paul thanked the bishops for their "public and moving testimony of hierarchical communion with the See of Peter." The exchange of letters was an attempt to ease the tensions that had developed in recent years between the Dutch Bishops' Conference, headed by Cardinal Bernard Alfrink, and the pope.

In his Easter address Paul VI called for continued efforts to build a genuine peace in the Middle East, Northern Ireland, and Indochina. On Pentecost Sunday he appealed for a spirit of reconciliation, particularly in Northern Ireland where Protestant and Catholic extremists continued their programs of terror. The hundreds of thousands of Africans threatened with starvation as a result of a drought in the sub-Sahara region were the subject of another papal appeal in May.

JOSEPH A. O'HARE, S. J.

PERÓN, Juan D.

The 78-year-old former dictator Juan D. Perón completed a notable political comeback on Oct. 12, 1973, when he was inaugurated president of Argentina, a post from which he had been ousted 18 years earlier.

On March 11, the Peronist movement had shown its strength in Argentina's first free elections since 1966, as Perón's hand-picked candidate, Hector Cámpora, won the presidency. But Cámpora, who was inaugurated on May 25, was unable to forge unity among the leftist and rightist elements of the amorphous Peronist movement, and resigned after 50 days in office. Perón, who had returned to Argentina from his exile in Spain on June 20, then announced his own candidacy, pledging a policy of peace and conciliation. With his third wife, Isabel, as his vice-presidential running mate, he was elected on September 23, winning 62% of the vote.

Amid continued urban guerrilla violence, Perón began to crack down on leftist elements within his divided movement. He managed to bring some degree of economic stability to the country and to stem the tide of inflation, and in December announced a three-year economic program aimed at freeing Argentina from "foreign financial, technological, and commercial control." There were doubts, however, that Perón's state of health would permit him to continue for very many years as Argentina's president.

Background. The son of a middle-class landowner, Juan Domingo Perón Sosa was born on Oct. 8, 1895, in Lobos, Buenos Aires Province. He graduated from Argentina's national military college at 18, with a com-

mission as a sublieutenant, and in the years that followed he rose through the ranks of the army. Following a mission to Italy, where he became an admirer of the fascist dictator Benito Mussolini, he helped organize a right-wing clique of officers that overthrew Argentina's civilian government in 1943. By 1944 he was vice president and minister of war, in addition to serving as head of the labor secretariat, a position empowering him to institute major reforms that won him the support of Argentina's working masses.

Elected president in 1946, Perón (with the moral support of his second wife, Eva, who shared his popularity) developed the industrial sector of the Argentine economy and created a strong welfare state, combining nationalism, populism, and state socialism. By the early 1950's, political persecution, corruption, and economic mismanagement had created growing discontent, and in 1955 Perón was overthrown in a military coup. While in exile, however, Perón maintained his influence over his many followers in Argentina. In November 1972 he returned to Argentina and organized a political coalition, the Justicialist Liberation Front, but made no move to attain power and left the country after four weeks.

POMPIDOU, Georges

Perhaps the biggest story concerning President Pompidou of France in 1973 was the matter of his health. Sketchily reported, it was a mystery that remained unresolved. In late spring, rumors that he was seriously ill seeped into print. Photographs showed his face unnaturally swollen; presidential appointments were canceled. But inquiries brought only bland official reassurances. The public was left with tales of cortisone treatment for rheumatism or some other disorder—and speculation about an early presidential election.

Nevertheless, Pompidou performed animatedly during his January and June press conferences. He carried out a round of visits in Europe, Africa, and Asia—from Iceland to Ethiopia to China—and received various foreign statesmen at home. His position remained unshaken despite some loss of support in the March legislative elections. Appealing to fears of communism, he escaped dependency on the centrists but gave ground to his ambitious allies, the Independent Republicans. Retaining the loyal Pierre Messmer as premier, he continued to absorb snubs and criticism from intransigent old Gaullists to whom he was both a latecomer and the man who had publicly posed his presidential candidacy in January 1969—a virtual act of treachery while President de Gaulle (who had fired Pompidou as premier) still intended remaining in office. He reconstructed his cabinet in April, parting company with Defense Minister Michel Debré, an old rival and a "hard" Gaullist who had in any event become something of a liability because of legislation he sponsored eliminating most student draft deferments.

Expressing irritation with press criticism, authoritarian and secretive in style, Pompidou was remote from the public and hardly in touch with Parliament. He was preoccupied with assuring the primacy of France in Western Europe, the independence of both against the superpowers, and the continuing supply of petroleum to a booming economy.

Background. Pompidou was born in Montboudif in central France on July 5, 1911. Graduated at the top of his class from the prestigious École Normale Supérieure in 1934, he taught school for ten years. He was appointed to General de Gaulle's staff after the Liberation in 1944 and remained after de Gaulle resigned in 1946. In 1951, Pompidou joined the Rothschild bank; he returned briefly to de Gaulle's staff in 1958, and then rejoined the bank in 1959. In April 1962 he replaced Debré as premier. A faithful executant and confidant of the general, he distinguished himself by his resolute handling of the 1968 nationwide strikes and disorders. Too successful, he was sacked almost at once. But following de Gaulle's political miscalculation and resignation in 1969, Pompidou readily won election to the presidency with 58% of the vote.

JOHN C. CAIRNS

QADDAFI, Muammar el-

Colonel Qaddafi, the 31-year-old president, or chairman, of the Revolutionary Command Council of the Libyan Arab Republic, emerged in 1973 as a pivotal influence in world affairs because of the vast wealth in petroleum resources under his control. The most militant of the heads of Arab states aligned against Israel, he supplied much of the financial and logistical support for the Egyptian and Syrian military forces in their conflict with Israel in October. He then opposed all compromise with the Jewish state following the Middle East war. Qaddafi has been a leading sponsor of the Palestinian guerrilla movement. Through economic and diplomatic pressure he persuaded a number of countries of black Africa to sever ties with Israel.

Earlier in the year Qaddafi took steps to gain total control of foreign-held oil resources in Libya and tried unsuccessfully to effect a political merger between his country and Egypt. In April he launched a massive "cultural revolution" to rid Libya of foreign influences and impose his unique brand of "Islamic socialism."

Background. The son of a Bedouin farmer of Berber stock, Muammar el-Qaddafi was born somewhere in the Libyan desert in 1942. Among the chief influences of his early life were his family's long resistance to Italian colonial rule, and the rise of Gamal Abdel Nasser in Egypt, whom he came to idolize. He graduated from the University of Libya in 1963 and entered the national military academy at Benghazi. There he found a group devoted, like himself, to the overthrow of King Idris of Libya. In September 1969 a Revolutionary Command Council of young officers under Qaddifi's leadership staged a bloodless coup against the monarchy and established the Libyan Arab Republic. Qaddafi promoted public works projects, evacuated British and U. S. military bases from Libyan soil, confiscated the property of the Italian and Jewish communities, and imposed strict adherence to Koranic doctrine. After serving as premier from 1970 to 1972, he continued, as head of the Revolutionary Command Council, to hold the dominant position in the Libyan Arab Republic.

RAY, Dixy Lee

In February 1973, Dixy Lee Ray was named by President Nixon to be chairman of the Atomic Energy Commission (AEC), the first woman to occupy this position. A marine biologist and holder of a doctor's degree, she had been a member of the commission, director of the Pacific Science Center, and associate professor of zoology at the University of Washington in Seattle.

Public understanding of science has been promoted by Dr. Ray for many years, and she has been aware of the widespread apprehension of danger in nuclear power plants. Her predecessor as head of the AEC, James R. Schlesinger, observed that she would contribute to solving the commission's problem of "balancing the demands of energy and environment."

In May, Dr. Ray moved to assert the AEC's independence from the Congressional Joint Committee on Atomic Energy by reorganizing the AEC staff despite some opposition by the committee. She also separated the responsibility for the development of nuclear power reactors from the responsibility for their safety by creating an independent Division of Reactor Safety Research. Critics of the AEC, especially environmentalists, previously had protested that the centralization of these responsibilities in one division amounted to a conflict of interest.

Background. Dixy Lee Ray was born in Tacoma, Wash., on Sept. 3, 1914. She received B. A. and M. A.

U. S. ATOMIC ENERGY COMMISSION

DIXY LEE RAY became the first woman to head the Atomic Energy Commission. She is a marine biologist.

degrees from Mills College, Oakland, Calif., and taught in public schools from 1938 to 1942. She earned a Ph. D. in biological science from Stanford University in 1945 and joined the teaching staff at the University of Washington in 1945.

Her scientific specialty has been the study of marine invertebrates. She received the William Clapp award in marine biology in 1959 and was a member of the President's Task Force on Oceanography in 1969. In that year she was chosen Seattle's "Maritime Man of the Year." She has been associated with the American Association for the Advancement of Science's committee on public understanding of the sciences.

RICHARD G. WEST

RICHARDSON, Elliot Lee

After many years of governmental service at high levels, Elliot L. Richardson resigned as attorney general of the United States in October 1973.

Richardson's resignation was prompted by an order from President Nixon that he fire special Watergate prosecutor Archibald Cox. Richardson maintained that Nixon had assured him that Cox would be able to operate without interference from the White House. When Nixon decided to fire Cox for seeking tapes of presidential conversations through the courts, Richardson considered the agreement broken, refused to fire Cox, and resigned.

This end to Richardson's period of service came less than six months after he first headed the Department of Justice. Richardson had been sworn in as attorney general in May 1973. His administrative skills and reputation for probity preceded him to the Department of Justice. At the time of his appointment, Nixon described him as "one of the ablest men ever to hold the office of attorney general." Immediately prior to that, he had served as secretary of defense, beginning in January 1973. Richardson had little time to prove himself as secretary of defense, serving only from January to May 1973. In that period, he continued the policies of Melvin R. Laird, consolidated several commands, and closed some bases. When Richard G. Kleindienst resigned as attorney general on April 30, Nixon tapped Richardson to replace him. He was also placed in charge of the Watergate investigation.

Richardson, classified as a moderate Republican, had long been considered a future possibility for national elective office. His departure from the Nixon administration removed him from active public life for the first time since 1963. After the elections in November 1973, Richardson was reportedly offered the job of attorney general of New Jersey, but the 53-year-old

Republican declined the offer. It was expected that Richardson would return to his native Massachusetts and reenter politics actively.

Background. A member of a socially prominent family, Elliot Lee Richardson was born in Boston on July 20, 1920. After military service in the Army in World War II he received an LL. B. degree *cum laude* in 1947 from Harvard Law School, where he was editor of the *Harvard Law Review*. He served as law clerk to Judge Learned Hand and to Supreme Court Justice Felix Frankfurter before entering private practice in 1949. He worked as an aid to Sen. Leverett Saltonstall of Massachusetts in 1953 and 1954. In 1958 he served briefly as acting head of the Department of Health, Education, and Welfare (HEW), and from 1959 to 1961 as U. S. attorney for Massachusetts. He served as lieutenant governor of Massachusetts (1965–67), as that state's attorney general (1967–69), and as undersecretary of state from 1969 until June 1970. He was secretary of HEW until January 1973 when he became secretary of defense.

WALTER DARNELL JACOBS

RUMOR, Mariano

On July 8, 1973, the veteran Christian Democratic leader Mariano Rumor became premier of Italy for the fourth time in his career. He brought back into power a Center-Left coalition that includes Christian Democrats, Socialists, Social Democrats, and Republicans. His government—Italy's 35th since the fall of Mussolini 30 years earlier—replaced the Center-Right coalition of Premier Giulio Andreotti, who had tried to govern the country without the Socialists for 15 months but was forced to resign on June 12 because he was unable to command an effective majority. Rumor, who heads the powerful middle-of-the-road Dorotheans within the faction-ridden Christian Democrats, returned to the premiership under an arrangement among party leaders that placed his chief rival, Amintore Fanfani, in the highest post—as party secretary.

Rumor had been serving for 15 months as minister of the interior, and in that capacity he had proceeded vigorously against organized crime and politically inspired violence. On becoming premier, he promised "shock therapy" to combat inflation, stimulate the economy, and reform health, educational, and other services. During his first few months in office, he met some success in instituting an austerity program designed to revive Italy's industrial capacity and in combatting inflation with such measures as a price freeze on consumer goods and limitations on bank credit.

Background. Rumor was born in Vicenza, Italy, on June 16, 1915, the son of a printer and newspaper publisher. He received a doctorate in literature from the University of Padua in 1939 and then taught in a secondary school and took part in the moderately liberal Catholic Action movement. After serving in World War II, he joined the new Christian Democratic party and soon demonstrated skill as a specialist in labor problems and as an organizer and conciliator.

Rumor was elected to the constitutional assembly in 1947 and to the national Chamber of Deputies in 1948 and held various subcabinet posts before being appointed in 1959 as minister of agriculture, a position he held until 1963. He was minister of the interior in 1963–64 and secretary of the Christian Democratic party from 1964 to 1969. His negotiating skill resulted in the reconstitution of the collapsed Center-Left coalition in December 1968, and he became premier. Thereafter he headed two other successive governments until his abrupt resignation in the wake of a general strike in July 1970.

SADAT, Anwar el-

Since 1970, President Sadat of Egypt has promised his people a "year of decision," a year of "total confrontation" with Israel. That year was 1973.

UPI

(Above) *Anwar el-Sadat* (left), *with Saudi Arabia's King Faisal. The Egyptian president enhanced himself among Arabs with 1973 war.* (Right) *William Saxbe, U.S. attorney general.*

UPI

Dealing with student disturbances in January, Sadat showed considerable leniency. But a few weeks later he began a purge of the Arab Socialist Union, removing a number of journalists and intellectuals. Subsequently, however, he pardoned most of the purged party members and the students.

Sadat was shrewd in his relations with the disparate elements of the Arab world, garnering support from Libya, Saudi Arabia, Syria, and Jordan. After assuming personal direction and employing emergency powers he was able to organize the Egyptian armed forces for a coordinated strike against Israel on October 6, the Jewish holy day of Yom Kippur. He led his nation into a war in which the Egyptians did remarkably well and through which they gained distinct political and psychological advantages against the Israelis. Sadat thus forced the Israelis to begin negotiating on somewhat more flexible terms than they had always insisted upon. And by mobilizing the oil money of conservative Saudi Arabia, he made the war possible and its aftermath promising.

During 1973, President Sadat became his own premier as well as the military governor-general of Egypt. Personally, Sadat is less flamboyant, less dominating than his predecessor, Gamal Abdel Nasser. But Sadat has achieved a level of leadership in the Arab world in three years that eluded Nasser in nearly 20 years.

Background. Sadat was born on Dec. 25, 1918, in a village in the Nile Delta. In 1938 he and Gamal Abdel Nasser formed a secret group with other army officers to work for the liberation of Egypt from its feudal monarchy and British influence. This group was the nucleus of the officers' committee that overthrew King Faruk in 1952.

Speaker of the National Assembly (1961–68), Sadat was appointed vice president in December 1969. He was elected to the presidency on Oct. 15, 1970, after the death of President Nasser.

CARL LEIDEN

SAXBE, William B.

Sen. William B. Saxbe (R-Ohio) was named by President Nixon on Nov. 1, 1973, as attorney general to succeed Elliot L. Richardson, who had resigned following the dismissal of Archibald Cox as special Watergate prosecutor. The outspoken Saxbe, in his own words a "hard-liner on law enforcement," has generally supported Nixon administration policies, although on occasion he directed verbal darts at the President. For example, in December 1972 he suggested after the administration's resumption of bombing raids in North Vietnam that Nixon seemed to have "left his senses."

Although Saxbe was originally skeptical of the President's protestations of innocence in the Watergate cover-up, he later became convinced that Nixon "acted honorably" in the affair. During judiciary committee hearings, he pledged to "restore morale to the Justice Department, and he promised to support the new special Watergate prosecutor Leon Jaworski against White House pressure. He was confirmed by the Senate (75–10) on December 17.

A retired colonel of the Ohio National Guard, Saxbe declared his intention to remove himself from the Justice Department's reopened investigation of the shooting of four Kent State University students by Ohio guardsmen in 1970. Saxbe postponed being sworn in as attorney general until Jan. 4, 1974, in order to complete five years of Senate service and so qualify for a congressional pension.

Background. William Bart Saxbe was born in Mechanicsburg, Ohio, on June 24, 1916. He graduated from Ohio State University in 1940, and after obtaining his LL. B. degree there in 1948 he joined a Columbus law firm. From 1947 to 1954 he was a member of the Ohio state legislature, serving as majority leader (1951–52) and as speaker (1953–54). He was attorney general of Ohio, 1957–58 and 1963–68. In 1968 he was elected to the U. S. Senate.

SCHLESINGER, James R.

In one of the top-level reorganizations of the U. S. government resulting from the Watergate affair, James R. Schlesinger, director of the Central Intelligence Agency (CIA), became secretary of defense on July 2, 1973, replacing Elliot Richardson. In his five months as CIA director, Schlesinger streamlined the agency and downgraded its cloak-and-dagger activities, taking steps to prevent future CIA involvement in covert domestic operations.

In public statements during his early weeks as defense secretary, Schlesinger defended the secret U. S. bombing raids in Cambodia in 1969–70, opposed amnesty for draft evaders, pledged renewed U. S. air support for South Vietnam in the event of attacks from

North Vietnam, and warned that the USSR was closing a technological gap by successful development of multiple-warhead missiles. Schlesinger took part in efforts to bring about a settlement of the Arab-Israeli war, and on October 25 he issued a precautionary military alert in response to apparent Soviet preparations to send troops to the Middle East.

Background. James Rodney Schlesinger was born in New York City on Feb. 15, 1929. He graduated *summa cum laude* from Harvard University in 1950 and obtained his Ph. D. in economics from Harvard in 1956. After teaching economics at the University of Virginia from 1955 to 1963, he joined the Rand Corporation in 1963 and became its director of strategic studies in 1967. He was appointed assistant director of the Bureau of the Budget in 1969, and he served as assistant director of the Office of Management and Budget in 1970–71. After becoming director of the Atomic Energy Commission (AEC) in August 1971, he demonstrated his conviction that a nuclear test at Amchitka Island in Alaska posed no hazard by taking his family to the test site. He also reorganized the AEC to emphasize civilian programs, created an office on environmental and safety affairs, and promoted research on nonnuclear sources of energy. Schlesinger is the author of *The Political Economy of National Security* (1960) and coauthor of *Issues in Defense Economics* (1967).

SIMON, William E.

On Dec. 4, 1973, Deputy Secretary of the Treasury William E. Simon was named by President Nixon as director of the newly created Federal Energy Office, succeeding John A. Love, who resigned after five months as "energy czar." Simon's powers in the cabinet-rank post exceeded those of his predecessor, in that he had full operating responsibility for energy programs, rather than a mere coordinating role. In the weeks that followed his nomination, Simon issued guidelines and regulations for the conservation of energy, calling for reductions in nonessential use of fuel by business and government, while giving priority in fuel allocation to emergency services and vital industries. He encouraged the use of car pools and public transportation and called on motorists to limit themselves voluntarily to 10 gallons of gasoline a week. On December 27 he announced the establishment of a standby gasoline rationing program, but expressed optimism that its actual use might be avoided.

Born in Paterson, N. J., on Nov. 27, 1927, William Edward Simon was educated in private schools and graduated from Lafayette College with a B. A. degree in 1951. He began his career in 1952 with Union Securities in New York, was named a vice president of Weeden & Co. in 1957, and, in 1964, joined the Wall Street investment banking firm of Salomon Brothers. He was a senior partner of that firm and head of its government and municipal securities department when he was appointed deputy treasury secretary. In the federal post, Simon acted as chairman of the President's oil policy committee. He was largely responsible for revisions in the mandatory oil import program in the spring of 1973.

SIMPSON, O. J.

Early in the first quarter at Shea Stadium on Dec. 15, 1973, the game was stopped and the ball was given to O. J. Simpson as the crowd of 47,740, mostly New York Jets fans, cheered. The 26-year-old running back of the Buffalo Bills had just broken the season record for yards gained by rushing that had been put in the books in 1963, presumably forever, by Jim Brown, the great Cleveland back.

O. J. went into this final game of the season needing 61 yards to better the record. His teammates had promised to clear the way for him, but he didn't need their word. "We have the cockiest offensive line in football. They think they can do anything for me," he said.

The line and "The Juice," as they call him, went to work quickly, and he spun away for 57 yards on the Bills' 71-yard drive for a touchdown. The next time Buffalo got the ball, Simpson whirled off tackle for 6 yards, and history was made. Actually, he gained 200 yards in that game, running his season total to 2,003. Brown's old mark was 1,863. Simpson had broken the record for yards gained in a game at the start of the season. He rushed for 250 yards against the New England Patriots, bettering Willie Ellison's mark by 3 yards. In the final game O. J. carried the ball 34 times for a season total of 332, breaking Brown's mark of 305.

Simpson followed with another performance that was typical of the man who had been acclaimed the greatest college back five years before. In appearing before the massed press and TV cameras after the game, O. J. brought along his 10 teammates on the offensive team—the fellows "who had made the record possible."

Orenthal James Simpson was born in San Francisco on July 9, 1947. As a follower of the 49ers, he once ran into Jim Brown near the stadium and puckishly told him that he was going to be a better back. O. J. does not run over his opponents as Brown did. He slithers past them. He is rated faster than Brown, is a capable receiver, and, on occasion, has passed on the option play.

Simpson was a star at San Francisco City College and at the University of Southern California where he gained nationwide acclaim. He led the Trojans to the top in 1967 and 1968 and was awarded the Heisman Trophy as the best college player in 1968.

Simpson was grabbed as the top choice in the 1969 draft by Buffalo. He did his best, but the Bills' style was not designed for him. After Lou Saban became coach and with better blockers, the Bills' and Simpson's performances improved. In 1972, O. J. led the league in yards gained with 1,251 and was named to the All-Pro team. He ended 1973 with the three all-time rushing records, some minor ones, and wild public acclaim. *Sporting News* named Simpson "Sports Man of the Year," and Associated Press voted him the NFL's most valuable player in 1973.

BILL BRADDOCK

O. J. SIMPSON, Buffalo Bills superstar, romped for 2,003 yards in 1973 to establish new season record.

THE BUFFALO BILLS

UPI

JOHN J. SIRICA, presiding judge in the Watergate case. In 1973 he engaged in a legal struggle with President Nixon for custody of White House tape recordings.

SIRICA, John J.

The key figure in the search during 1973 for the facts in the Watergate affair was the tenacious chief judge of the U. S. District Court for the District of Columbia, John J. Sirica. His elicited information may implicate the White House in the 1972 burglary of Democratic headquarters and related events. In January 1973, as the presiding judge in the trial of the Watergate burglars, Sirica drew testimony from defendants by provisional sentences, later modified, that ranged up to 40 years. The action brought him criticism from some civil libertarians, but gained very high praise elsewhere for "stubbornly and doggedly pursuing the truth."

On August 29 the judge, in a historic ruling, ordered President Nixon to turn over to him certain tape recordings of White House conversations to aid a grand jury investigation. When the President refused to comply on the ground of executive privilege, the U. S. Circuit Court of Appeals for the District of Columbia basically upheld Sirica's ruling. Judge Sirica was faced with having to cite the President for contempt, but on October 23, President Nixon decided to turn over the tapes to him. The revelation that 18 minutes of a key conversation were obliterated, allegedly by the error of the President's personal secretary, prompted Sirica to have the tapes examined by technical experts for possible evidence of tampering. The experts found that at least five erasures had been made on the tape.

Background. The son of an Italian immigrant barber, John Joseph Sirica was born in Waterbury, Conn., on March 19, 1904, and grew up in poverty, mainly in Florida and Louisiana. He took his law degree at Georgetown University in 1926. From 1930 to 1934 he served as an assistant U. S. attorney for the District of Columbia, then went into private law practice. He was hired in 1944 as counsel for a congressional committee investigating the Federal Communications Commission. In 1949 he joined the Washington law firm of Hogan & Hartson, and won a reputation as a skillful trial lawyer. Named by President Eisenhower to the federal bench in 1957, Sirica became known as tough but scrupulously honest. He became chief judge of the U. S. District Court in Washington in 1971.

SUHARTO

General Suharto was elected to a second five-year term as president of Indonesia by the People's Consultative Assembly on March 22, 1973. Unopposed, he was elected by acclamation. In his New Year television address to the nation he expressed gratification that security and national stability had made progress possible in various sectors.

On March 27, President Suharto announced the formation of a new cabinet, which he called the Second Development Cabinet. The 22-man cabinet contains seven professors and only three military men. Not members of the cabinet but entrusted with important duties were Brigadier General Ali Said, who was to serve as attorney general, and General Sumitro, who was to serve as commander of the Command to Restore Law and Order. President Suharto placed Sultan Hamengku Buwono, the newly elected vice president, in charge of People's Welfare and the supervision of the administration of the national development program. Gen. Maraden Panggabean was named minister for defense.

President Suharto had been very critical of the operation of political parties under the Sukarno regime, charging that they were too numerous and fought for their own interest rather than the public interest. A simplification of the political party system in accordance with his views was accomplished in January. Four Islamic parties were merged into the Partai Persatuan Pembanguan. Five non-Islamic parties—the Indonesian Nationalist party, the Movement for the Defense of Indonesian Independence, the Catholic party, the Protestant Christian party, and the Party of the Masses—were merged into the Partai Demokrasi Indonesia.

Background. General Suharto was born on June 8, 1921, in Central Java. He enlisted in the Netherlands Indies army but joined the revolutionary forces at the end of World War II and became an officer in the Indonesian army. A relatively obscure major general when the Communists attempted to take over the government on Sept. 30, 1965, he became the leader in crushing the coup and reshaping his country. In March 1966, President Sukarno relinquished all executive powers to Suharto. In 1967 the People's Consultative Assembly named him acting president and the following year elected him president for a five-year term.

AMRY VANDENBOSCH

TANAKA, Kakuei

On Dec. 22, 1972, after the general election held December 10, Japan's Diet reelected Kakuei Tanaka as premier. At the same time, he formed his second cabinet, actually a coalition of powerful faction leaders within the majority, business-backed Liberal-Democratic party (LDP).

Nicknamed "Kaku-san" by the press, Tanaka at age 55 is the youngest premier since the end of World War II. Often called the "computerized bulldozer," he is identified as a conservative, who supports Japan's mixed capitalistic system and at the same time points up problems inherent in rapid growth: inflation, urbanization, and environmental disruption.

In a new world of multipolar international politics, Premier Tanaka has become a familiar figure in jet-powered summit diplomacy. During 1973 he conferred with President Nixon in Washington, visited Western Europe, engaged in tough bargaining with Soviet leaders Leonid Brezhnev and Aleksei Kosygin in Moscow, and planned a visit to Southeast Asia early in 1974.

Early Career. Tanaka was born on May 4, 1918, in Nishiyama, Niigata prefecture. He was the only son among seven children in a poor family. At age 15, after completing primary school, he entered the construction business and, while attending night school in Tokyo, established his first business firm. Drafted into the army at age 20, he served for two years in Manchuria. Immediately after the war, in 1945, he reentered the construction business. With no university connections and only brief experience in the bureaucracy, Tanaka emerged as a unique member of Japan's elite, which had traditionally been dominated by university-trained ex-bureaucrats.

Politics. He was first elected to the House of Representatives in 1947, held various portfolios in five

(Above) *Kakuei Tanaka, premier of Japan, met with world leaders in 1973.* (Right) *Canadian Prime Minister Trudeau, dancing with wife, Margaret. Their second son was born on Christmas.*

different cabinets, and served the LDP as secretary-general. As premier he reestablished diplomatic relations with the People's Republic of China, in 1972. He reaffirmed the close relationship with the United States under the Mutual Security Treaty in 1973. At home, he has supported a National Development bill, which incorporates his famous plan to "remodel the Japanese archipelago." At first very popular among Japanese for his vigor, Tanaka saw his support eroded during 1973 by the problems of inflation, trade balances, and pollution. On December 22 he was obliged to declare a state of emergency to deal with the Arab embargo on oil shipments and with inflation. Politically he was threatened by his old rival and member of the cabinet, Finance Minister Takeo Fukuda.

Private Life. Premier Tanaka and his wife, Hana, have one daughter and one grandson. Since childhood he has been fond of writing and he also likes to sing folk songs. Like millions of his fellow-Japanese, he is an avid golfer (handicap: 18).

ARDATH W. BURKS

TRAIN, Russell Errol

In September 1973, Russell E. Train was confirmed by the U. S. Senate as the new head of the Environmental Protection Agency (EPA). With 8,000 employees and a budget of billions of dollars, the EPA administers the laws that are designed to purify and preserve the environment in which Americans live. As he took office, Train observed that the nation was entering a time of "testing the public commitment to environmental progress." He was confident that the commitment would be honored.

Noting that advances had been made in controlling pollution in several fields, Train declared that the EPA must adjust to realities and fit its programs into the economic and social fabric of the nation. However, Train and his agency faced enormous difficulties. Problems that existed when he took office became massive before year-end. The gravest was the energy crisis arising from crude-oil shortages. As a result the nation may have to use fuels with greater pollution potential, thereby lowering standards for cleaner air.

Background. Russell E. Train was born at Jamestown, R. I., on June 4, 1920. He graduated from Princeton and Columbia University law school and was admitted to the District of Columbia bar in 1949. For eight years his legal work with committees of Congress and the Treasury Department mainly dealt with internal

revenue and taxation. From 1957 to 1965 he was a U. S. Tax Court judge.

Train enlisted early in the cause of conservation. He was a vice president of the World Wildlife Fund (1959–69), president of the African Wildlife Leadership Foundation (1959–69), and president of the Conservation Foundation (1965–69). In 1969–70 he was undersecretary of the interior, and in 1970 he was appointed chairman of the Council on Environmental Quality.

RICHARD G. WEST

TRUDEAU, Pierre Elliott

As the leader of Canada's minority Liberal party government in 1973, Pierre Elliott Trudeau had to lay aside his philosopher-king image and become a practical politician. The results of the 1972 election made it evident that his academic approach to political and social issues and his self-isolation during his first four years as prime minister had alienated many Canadians. But despite repeated challenges from the Progressive Conservative party, Prime Minister Trudeau refused to be toppled. He clung to power with the support of the New Democratic party and occasionally, the Social Credit party.

Activities in 1973. For Trudeau, the year included a great deal of fence-mending, with trips to various parts of Canada and conferences with disaffected areas, particularly western Canada. He also visited China.

A developing area of federal-provincial conflict came into focus in 1973 in connection with the energy crisis, since natural resources are under the control of individual provinces. By introducing national energy policies, Trudeau annoyed the western provinces, which have all the oil, whereas most of the consumers are in eastern Canada.

Taking note of the election platforms of the other major parties, Trudeau introduced far-reaching legislation on social welfare, regional development, and oil and other energy policies. As a result, he seemed more firmly established politically than he was at the beginning of the year. The sweeping electoral victory of the Quebec Liberal party, which was returned to power on October 29, contributed to a rise in the popularity of Trudeau and the Liberals nationally.

Background. Trudeau was born in Montreal on Oct. 18, 1919. He received a law degree from the University of Montreal in 1943. After studying economics, political science, and law abroad, he became active in Quebec as a lawyer specializing in labor law and civil-liberties

cases and as a teacher and writer. His recent books include *Federalism and the French Canadians* (1968) and *Approaches to Politics* (1970).

Trudeau first gained experience in federal politics in 1949–51, when he served as economic adviser to the St. Laurent government. In 1965, Trudeau was elected to Parliament as the Liberal candidate for Montreal–Mount Royal. He became parliamentary secretary to Prime Minister Lester B. Pearson in 1966, minister of justice and attorney general in 1967, and leader of the Liberal party, succeeding Pearson, in 1968. He took office as prime minister on April 20, 1968, following a victory marked by a frenzied enthusiasm known as "Trudeaumania." On March 4, 1971, he was married to Margaret Sinclair. The son born to them on Dec. 25, 1971, was the first child born to an incumbent prime minister since 1869. On Christmas Day 1973, another son was born to the Trudeaus.

W. A. McKAY

WALDHEIM, Kurt

During 1973, his second year as secretary general of the United Nations, Kurt Waldheim's conception of his role in world affairs became increasingly clear. A diplomatist in the European tradition and a staunch believer in the UN, he felt that the need for international cooperation "has never been so great or so urgent." He asked the member states whether they wanted an effective organization or merely a forum for the pursuit of national policies.

Waldheim felt that both he and the UN had a coordinating role to play, not only in the solution of political problems but also in such measures as relief for the victims of the Managua earthquake and alleviation of starvation in Bangladesh. He considered his part in the international conference on Vietnam in Paris from February 26 to March 3 a "breakthrough" and a "positive development," though he could not sign the final conference document as he was not the representative of any one country.

His visit to the Paris conference was one of a number of trips made in 1973 to survey the problems and to meet world leaders, including one to the Indian subcontinent and the Far East. He conferred on February 5 with Prime Minister Indira Gandhi, and also visited Pakistan and Bangladesh; in March he addressed the 15th session of the Economic Committee for Latin America; and he visited Africa for the 10th anniversary of the Organization of African Unity (OAU) on May 25.

Waldheim's interest in a solution to the problems in the Middle East was apparent both in his review of peace efforts prepared for the Security Council in May, and in his tour of five Middle Eastern countries from August 27 to September 4. His conception of his role in the peace-keeping function of the UN was shown by his efforts toward achieving the Middle Eastern cease-fire and the speed with which he organized the UN emergency force there; by his welcome for the New Delhi agreement reached by India, Pakistan, and Bangladesh on August 28; and by his attendance at the opening in Helsinki, Finland, on July 3 of the conference on Security and Cooperation in Europe.

Background. Waldheim was born near Vienna on Dec. 12, 1918. Educated at the Consular Academy at Vienna and the University of Vienna, where he took a law degree, he joined the foreign service in 1945. He led the Austrian observer mission to the UN in 1955–56, headed his country's first delegation to the UN in 1958, and was Austria's permanent representative there from 1964 to 1968. He returned to the UN as permanent representative in 1970, and ran unsuccessfully for the Austrian presidency in 1971. He was elected to a five-year term as UN secretary general by the General Assembly on Dec. 22, 1971, and took office on Jan. 1, 1972.

RICHARD E. WEBB

WHITE, Patrick

Australian author Patrick White, who won international acclaim for his novels reflecting the loneliness, isolation, and emptiness of modern man, was awarded the 1973 Nobel Prize for literature, becoming the first Australian to be accorded that honor. In announcing the award, the Swedish Academy cited his "epic and psychological narrative art, which has introduced a new continent into literature" and noted that he had given Australia "an authentic voice that carries across the world at the same time as his achievement contributes to the development . . . of contemporary literature." Indicating that White was chosen for the entire range of his work, including his latest novel, *The Eye of the Storm* (1973), the academy also cited his "unbroken creative power," his "onslaught against vital problems," and his capacity for extracting from language "all its power and all its nuances, to the verge of the unattainable."

Background. Patrick Victor Martindale White was born on May 28, 1912, in London, England, where his parents were vacationing. He spent his early years in Sydney, returning to England at 13 for schooling at Cheltenham College. After studying modern languages at King's College, Cambridge, and graduating in 1935, he spent several years traveling in Europe and America. His first novel, *Happy Valley*, was published in London in 1939. After World War II service in the Royal Air Force, White returned to Australia, determined to come to terms with his Australian heritage. His reputation as an international literary figure was established with his novel *The Tree of Man* (1955). His other novels include *The Living and the Dead* (1941), *The Aunt's Story* (1948), *Voss* (1957), *Riders in the Chariot* (1961), *The Solid Mandala* (1966), and *The Vivisector* (1970). He also has written four plays.

WHITLAM, Gough

Prime Minister Gough Whitlam of Australia pursued in 1973 his program of domestic reforms and a more independent foreign policy that had brought his Labor party into power the previous year. He took steps to end military conscription, to bar discrimination on the basis of race or sex, to return tribal lands to aborigines, to relax censorship of the arts, to allow 18-year-olds to vote, and to make divorce easier to obtain. Having ended Australia's involvement in Vietnam, he established closer ties with Communist China, Indonesia, and Japan, while diminishing Australia's dependence on the United States and Britain. He protested French nuclear tests in the Pacific and proposed a regional grouping of Asian and Pacific nations, with Australia acting as an "honest broker."

During the year, Whitlam faced serious problems at home: inflation, strikes, disputes between states and the federal government, and large losses for the Labor party in state and local elections. A general decline in his popularity in public opinion polls suggested that he had moved too fast. In November, Whitlam relinquished his secondary post of minister of foreign affairs.

Background. (Edward) Gough Whitlam was born in the Melbourne suburb of Kew, Victoria, on July 11, 1916, and attended private schools and Sydney University. After World War II service in the Royal Australian Air Force, he entered law practice and became active in the Labor party. Elected to the national House of Representatives in 1952, he served on the joint parliamentary committee on constitutional review (1956–59). Succeeding Arthur Calwell as parliamentary leader of the Labor party in 1967, he revitalized it, purging doctrinaire elements and broadening popular appeal. In the 1972 national elections, Labor defeated the Liberal-Country party coalition, ending its 23-year rule and gaining a nine-vote margin in the 125-member House of Representatives. Whitlam succeeded William McMahon as prime minister on Dec. 5, 1972.

The first American-made rotary combustion (Wankel) outboard engine began experimental runs in 1973.

BOATING

Plans for elimination of the famed U. S. Coast Guard "weather cutters," anticipation of a revolutionary rotary combustion outboard motor, and continued enthusiasm for boating, as reflected by the record number of boats on the nation's waters, were boating highlights of 1973.

Elimination of "Weather Cutters." Although the U. S. Coast Guard is beset by rising costs and an ever-increasing demand for services, the Office of Management and Budget slashed deeply into Coast Guard appropriations for fiscal 1974. The first victims are expected to be five so-called "weather cutters," which have been operating in the Atlantic and Pacific oceans since 1942. These ships, stars of countless dramas both fictional and real, stay on station for weeks at a time in midocean, relaying meteorological information, providing navigational aids and oceanographic data, and standing ready to speed to vessels in distress.

It is expected that by June 1974, only one cutter will be on station—some 200 miles (322 km) off the Delaware coast. The budget reductions also reflect a trend toward decreasing the number of relatively low work load operational facilities in the Coast Guard. Twelve rescue stations, mostly in the Great Lakes, were decommissioned.

Rotary Combustion Outboards. In 1966, the Outboard Marine Corporation, manufacturer of both Johnson and Evinrude outboards, signed license agreements with the Curtiss-Wright Corp. to build and sell rotary combustion engines. The engines, popularly called "Wankels" after their inventor Felix Wankel, employ a triangular rotor that revolves instead of pistons that move up and down, as in conventional engines. Because complicated valves are eliminated, the engines are about two thirds the size and weight of conventional engines of equivalent horsepower. After several years of secrecy, general announcements of the project were made in 1972. Details have not been released, but size and weight appear to be consistent with the present conventional outboards, the largest of which is 150 horsepower. The exact horsepower of the new Wankel is still secret, but it has been estimated at 250. At present the Wankels are used only ex-perimentally in racing. They probably will not be offered for sale until at least 1975.

Racing. Spectators at the Hennessy Grand Prix offshore powerboat race on July 18 were treated to a thrilling neck-and-neck battle won by Robert ("Doc") Magoon, a Miami eye surgeon, who roared across the finish line only 50 feet (15.2 meters) ahead of the boat driven by Giorgio Mondadori of Italy. Magoon, a three-time winner, covered the 181.3 mile (291.8 km) course off the New York–New Jersey shore at an average speed of 73.28 mph (117.9 km/hr).

The Annapolis-to-Newport race, held in mid-June, was won by the 68-foot (20.7 meter) ketch, *Equation,* owned by John T. Potter of Oyster Bay, N. Y., sailing the course in 57 hours and 19 minutes and breaking the record time set in 1965 by 4 hours and 18 minutes. (See also Sports—*Yachting.*)

Statistics. Although the number of registered boats increased by some 400,000, fatalities as a result of boating accidents during 1972 stood at 1,437, compared with 1,582 in 1971. Total boating accidents showed little change, with 3,942 recorded in 1972 and 3,909 the previous year. Capsizing and falling overboard remained the major causes of loss of life. Authorities believe that as the stringent regulations prescribed by the Federal Boat Safety Act of 1971 come into effect, the trend toward fewer accidents will continue.

Boating continued to be a major form of recreation. The Boating Industry Association estimated that retail spending on the sport would reach $4 billion for 1973, an increase of $400 million over the previous year. A record fleet of 10 million boats —including some 5 million outboard, 643,000 sailboats without power, and 2.4 million rowboats, canoes, and miscellaneous craft—were estimated to be sailing the nation's waters.

ZACK TAYLOR, *Boating Editor, "Sports Afield"*

BOLIVIA

The military became increasingly involved in the running of the Bolivian government during 1973, indicating the failure of President Hugo Banzer Suárez to establish a non-military political base since the ouster in August 1971 of the leftist government of

Juan Torres. Nevertheless, the Banzer regime reaped some economic benefit from an unpopular currency devaluation instituted late in 1972, and apparently retained substantial support among Bolivians of the professional and middle classes.

Political Affairs. In 1971, Banzer had established an uneasy ruling coalition based on the military and on two political parties with a tradition of mutual antagonism—the Socialist Bolivian Falange (FSB) and the National Revolutionary Movement (MNR). By 1973, the strains of coalition had caused partisan bickering and had weakened both parties. After an abortive coup attempt in April, Banzer reshuffled his cabinet, giving the military two more posts.

In May, Andrés Selich, a popular officer who led the coup that brought Banzer to power, was arrested for plotting against the President and was killed during an interrogation by security agents. This caused a showdown between the military and President Banzer, who removed the commander in chief of the armed forces and made several changes in the military hierarchy.

In August, the government announced the suppression of an attempted coup by right-wing extremists in the Falange, and on September 23 it arrested 86 labor leaders on charges of implication in a Marxist plot to overthrow the regime. A few days later, the President named a new cabinet composed exclusively of military officers and civilians pledged not to run in the elections that were planned for 1974. In November, Banzer reshuffled his cabinet again and, in a surprise move, announced that he would not be a candidate for reelection in 1974.

The leftist guerrilla movement remained fragmented and demoralized in 1973, but the growing strength of the radical clergy posed a new dilemma for the government of staunchly Roman Catholic Bolivia. In January, a declaration signed by more than 100 priests criticized the regime for its continuing repression of the universities and the judiciary and for its violation of basic civil rights.

Economic Affairs. Faced with continuing large deficits in government budgets and with a weakening

──────── BOLIVIA • Information Highlights ────────

Official Name: Republic of Bolivia.
Location: West central South America.
Area: 424,163 square miles (1,098,581 sq km).
Population (1973 est.): 5,000,000. *Density,* 12 per square mile (5 per sq km).
Chief Cities (1969 est.): Sucre, the legal capital, 58,000; La Paz, the actual capital, 525,000; Cochabamba, 157,000.
Government: *Head of state,* Hugo Banzer Suárez, president (took office Aug. 1971). *Head of government,* Hugo Banzer Suárez. *Legislature*—Congress (suspended Sept. 1969): Senate and Chamber of Deputies.
Languages: Spanish (official), Quechua, Aymara.
Education: *Expenditure* (1969), 26.2% of total public expenditure. *School enrollment* (1969—primary, 663,829; secondary, 76,244; technical/vocational, 9,692; university/higher, 27,352.
Monetary Unit: Peso (20 pesos equal U. S.$1, July 1973).
Gross National Product (1972 est.): $1,140,000,000.
Economic Indexes: *Agricultural production* (1971), 135 (1963 = 100); *consumer price index* (1971), 156 (1963 = 100).
Manufacturing (major products): Processed foods, textiles, leather goods, cement, glass ceramics.
Major Agricultural Products: Sugarcane, corn, potatoes, wheat, rice, coffee, bananas.
Major Minerals: Tin (ranks 3d among world producers, 1971), antimony (world rank 3d, 1971), silver, petroleum, lead, zinc, tungsten, gold, copper.
Foreign Trade (1971): *Exports,* $212,000,000; *Imports,* $171,-000,000. *Chief trading partners* (1970)—United Kingdom (took 38% of exports, supplied 5% of imports); United States (33%—31%); Japan (9.5%—16.4%); Argentina (4.7%—10.3%).
Transportation: *Motor vehicles* (1970), 48,000 (automobiles, 19,200); *railroads* (1971), 2,236 miles (3,599 km); *major national airline,* Lloyd Aereo Boliviano.
Communications: *Telephones* (1972), 44,200; *newspapers* (1970), 21.

foreign exchange position, the Banzer government had adopted the Stabilization and Development Act in October 1972. The principal stabilization measure was a major currency devaluation. The plan committed Bolivia to a strategy of export-led growth. In 1973, some $500 million in external financing for a three-year investment program was being allocated principally to the directly productive sectors, especially agriculture, mineral ores, and the oil industry. Previous governments had channeled the bulk of foreign funds into public works and infrastructure. Banzer was clearly stressing output.

The devaluation of the peso was unpopular but it produced a marked improvement in the investment climate of the country and a resultant large inflow of capital. Furthermore, by increasing the competitiveness of the export sector, the devaluation relieved pressure on the budget resulting from the large deficits of the State Mining Corporation (COMIBOL) and spared the government the necessity of reducing miners' salaries or fringe benefits.

International Affairs. In 1973, Bolivia became involved in a growing rivalry between Brazil and Argentina, partly because it offered these nations a "back door" to the Andean Group common market, of which it is a member. In addition, Brazil's reported investment in the development of Bolivian iron ore deposits at Mutun alarmed Argentina, which was counting on the ore for its steel industry.

THOMAS M. MILLINGTON
Hobart and William Smith Colleges

BONDS. See STOCKS AND BONDS.
BOOK PUBLISHING. See PUBLISHING.

BOSTON

An airplane crash and a freak accident highlighted the news in Boston during 1973. The local elections brought about little change in government.

Disasters. On July 31, a Delta Airlines jet crashed at Boston's Logan Airport while attempting to land in poor weather. A total of 88 persons were killed. An investigation into the cause of the crash was still underway at the end of the year.

On September 10, in a freak accident, a heavily loaded truck struck a supporting pillar of the Tobin Bridge, a two-level structure over the Mystic River that is one of the main arteries for auto traveling to and from the northern suburbs of the city. Almost 200 feet of the upper roadway collapsed, forcing a complete closing of the bridge. The lower level was reopened on a limited basis on November 20, but officials estimated that final repairs would not be completed until mid-1974 at the earliest.

Part of the Tobin Bridge passes over the city of Chelsea, directly north of Boston. On October 14, a fire ravaged a 20-block area of Chelsea. See MASSACHUSETTS.

Elections and City Government. Elections for the City Council and School Committee were held on September 25, with only some 30% of the eligible voters participating. All of the incumbents who sought reelection won. Former Congresswoman Louise Day Hicks received the most votes of all candidates for the Council. Mrs. Hicks, who has long been noted in the city as a foe of busing and other measures to reduce racial imbalance in the schools, thus returned to city politics.

The Boston School Committee and the State Education Commission were at odds throughout the

CHRISTIAN SCIENCE center in Boston, designed by I. M. Pei & Partners and Araldo Cossutta. The Church Administration Building is at left.

year on plans to bring the city's schools into compliance with the state's racial imbalance law, which prohibits a nonwhite enrollment of more than 50% in any school. Racial tensions in some of the city's high schools were evident during the year. Dorchester High was closed for several days in May after a series of disturbances with racial overtones.

In governmental affairs, Mayor Kevin H. White announced that Boston's tax rate for 1974 would be the same as 1973 and that the city would continue on a strict austerity budget. The mayor's announcement caused some disappointment, as many homeowners had expected a tax decrease.

Urban Renewal. Two urban renewal projects—both privately financed in part—were in the news during the year. In the spring the Christian Science Church, which has its world headquarters in Boston, completed work on a 10-acre center surrounding the original Mother Church (built in 1894). The complex includes a 26-story administration building, a 500-car garage and a public park built around a reflecting pool 670 feet (210 meters) long. The project adds to a number of renewal projects taking place in Boston's "Back Bay" section.

Another urban renewal plan fared less well in 1973. The proposed Park Plaza development—a retail-residential complex at the edge of the historic Boston Common—was kept in limbo by a state ruling that the environmental impact of the structures was unacceptable. At the end of the year the fate of the $266 million plan was very much in doubt.

HARVEY BOULAY
Boston University

BOTANY

Interactions between plants and the environment, plants and plants, plants and animals, and plants and man were stressed by various researchers in 1973. The year produced findings of interest relating to the process of double fertilization, to somatic cell genetics, and to the use of fossils to compare embryo development.

Plant Ecology. The reason for the existence of bare areas (halo areas) associated with shrub stands within grasslands in California has been subject to debate and study for 10 years. Some attributed the bare areas to allelopathy (volatile toxins from shrubs which poisoned herb seedlings), others to animal activity or to competition for moisture.

In 1973, J. P. Halligan announced that he had investigated the herb pattern associated with the shrub called coastal sage (*Artemisia californica*) to determine which of the three explanations correctly described the cause of bare areas. His research demonstrated that vegetation patterns and bare areas did not result from a single causative agent, but from the interaction of factors which produced a series of changed conditions: (1) through volatilization, the shrubs added chemicals that were toxic to certain herbs (allelopathy); (2) the size of small mammal populations greatly increases in the shrubs, and they partially or entirely eliminate certain plant species of the grassland; and (3) a checkerboard pattern of moist and dry conditions developed under each shrub which greatly affected the herb growth.

Double Fertilization. Recent data on the process of fertilization in flowering plants, obtained from ultrastructure studies, was summarized in 1973 by W. A. Jensen and related to traditional information. The recent data indicated that the pollen tube from the germinated pollen grain grows into the embryo sac by first entering one of the two synergid cells which compose the egg apparatus. The two sperm nuclei located in the pollen tube are discharged into one synergid cell. One sperm migrates and makes contact with the plasma membrane of the egg cell, and the other with the plasma membrane of the large central cell. The fusion with the plasma membranes prevents any additional entrance of sperm nuclei. After passing through the membranes one sperm nucleus fuses with the polar nuclei located in the center cell.

Thus, "double fertilization" results from fusion by the two sperm nuclei, one within the egg and the other within the central cell. It is now known that the synergid cells, formerly considered insignificant, are critical cells which are important in the process of double fertilization, a process essential for embryo development in flowering plants.

Plant Pathology. Recent knowledge obtained about somatic cell genetics of flowering plants has made it possible to develop mutants of single haploid cells, a technique that suggests the possibility of a major advance in selective breeding. The new knowledge has been used to develop variants of tobacco that are resistant to methionine sulfoximine, which is a structural chemical analog of the natural toxin methionine. Methionine is a toxin produced by a bacterial pathogen causing wildfire disease, which attacks the leaves of tobacco.

Peter A. Carlson announced in 1973 that it was possible to obtain mutants which have an altered response to this bacterial pathogen, by recovering somatic cells which were resistant to the toxin. These resistant cells can be used for performing cell transplants to produce experimentally strains of tobacco resistant to wildfire disease.

Fossil Plant Study. Two botanists, C. N. Miller and J. Brown, reported the discovery of the oldest known plant embryos. At least 260 million years old, they were found in seeds of a fossilized conifer cone from the Glass Mountains of Texas.

Miller and Brown also reported that embryo growth had been completed within the seeds before they were dispersed—a process similar to that found in modern living plants. Previous evidence has suggested that plants which lived during the Paleozoic Era—230–600 million years ago—possessed embryos which did not form until the seed had been dispersed from the plant and landed in a suitable growing site. The development of an embryo before seed dispersal may provide for a better chance of seedling survival, and this suggests that the modern sequence of embryo growth may have evolved as an adaptation to a less hospitable environment. The newly discovered seeds containing developed embryos support such a hypothesis, since they were from a geologic period when the earth's environment was becoming cooler and drier.

DAVID E. FAIRBROTHERS
Rutgers University

BRANDT, Willy. See BIOGRAPHY.

BRAZIL

Brazil's military bosses named a new president in June 1973, as the country entered its 10th year of authoritarian rule. Ernesto Geisel, an army general, like his three predecessors, was chosen by "The System"—the incumbent president and about a dozen high-ranking chiefs—and his nomination was ratified by the National Renewal Alliance (ARENA), the government political party (see also BIOGRAPHY).

After an unexciting six-month campaign, during which press censorship remained in effect, a vote was taken on Jan. 15, 1974, in the ARENA-dominated Electoral College, an assembly of national congressmen and state legislators, and Geisel was proclaimed president-elect over token opposition from the Brazilian Democratic Movement (MDB), Brazil's only other legal political party.

"The System." The events of 1973 clearly demonstrated that the legal political parties, Congress, the judiciary, and the state legislatures were no more than window dressing for a dictatorship of n.ilitary men and civilian technocrats. While President Emilio Garrastazú Médici and the armed forces were busy fighting corruption and subversion,

suppressing the political opposition, and delivering nationalistic rhetoric, the technocrats, headed by Finance Minister Antônio Delfim Netto, ran the government and created most of its policy. With Brazil's economy continuing to boom, the soldiers seemed inclined to give their civilian partners free rein. There certainly has been less military interference in day-to-day governing in recent years than there was during pre-1964 civilian administrations. On major issues, Delfim Netto occasionally has said "no" to the military and had his way. One general described the regime as "an economic dictatorship with the support of the military."

While supreme authority rested with the handful of generals and admirals comprising "The System," lesser officers were likely to be punished for playing politics. Brazilian officers have been taught respect for the civilian technicians in government and contempt for the old political class. For real or imagined enemies of the new order there was no tolerance. Early in the year Luís Carlos Prestes, Brazil's widely admired Communist party chief, was forced to leave his Brazilian hiding place for exile in the USSR. In April, soldiers and police rounded up and jailed hundreds of educators, journalists, student leaders, and other dissidents.

Criticism of the Regime. With the press heavily censored and most political meetings banned, the Roman Catholic Church remained the principal forum for criticisms of the government. From the pulpits came denunciations of the arbitrary arrests and the mistreatment, including torture, of prisoners. In May a conference of bishops issued a 30-page document protesting the political repression and the manipulation of economic policy to "make the rich richer and the poor poorer." The bishops' manifesto, the most outspoken in years, was immediately suppressed by the regime.

The government countered church criticism with claims of significant social progress. According to the government, the settlement of the Amazon was providing good homes and decent employment for thousands of migrants from the poverty-stricken Northeast, an area of prime concern to the bishops. Continuing gains were posted by MOBRAL, the agency in charge of the government's literacy drive. The adult illiteracy rate, according to MOBRAL, had been reduced to less than 27% in every state and territory in Brazil.

Nevertheless, some government officials agreed with the bishops that there had been little, if any, improvement in the standard of living in the poorest areas of the country. Luís Cirne Lima resigned as agriculture minister in May, charging that the regime's policies favored urban interests at the expense of rural Brazil. Earlier the government had acknowledged that rapid industrialization threatened to lower the quality of life in the cities and had enacted anti-pollution controls.

Inter-American Affairs. Brazil in 1973 continued to expand its influence in Latin America while retaining good relations with the United States. Brazilian military and financial aid poured into Bolivia, Paraguay, and Uruguay to prop up friendly right-wing governments on Brazil's vulnerable southern borders. At the same time, Brazil undertook some long-range economic development projects in these countries, which seemed destined to become virtual satellites of their giant neighbor. Among the projects launched in 1973 were the laying of a 1,600-mile (2,600-km) natural gas pipeline from Bolivia

to Brazil and the construction on the Paraná River of the Itaipu dam complex, expected to be the world's largest hydroelectric facility, which will inundate a large stretch of Paraguayan territory.

In a border-town meeting with Venezuelan President Rafael Caldera in February, President Médici sought to allay the fears of Brazil's neighbors by denying that his country was striving for political or economic hegemony in Latin America.

While the United States insisted that it was not sponsoring Brazil for the leadership of Latin America, relations between the governments of the two countries were especially cordial in 1973. William Crimmins, one of the State Department's ablest Latin American specialists, was named U. S. ambassador to Brazil in June.

In June the U. S. government lifted its ban on the sale of supersonic military aircraft to Latin America, and Brazil immediately placed an order with the Northrop Corporation for 48 new F-5E jet fighters. These warplanes, together with a squadron of Mirage fighters that Brazil is buying from France, should make the Brazilian air force by far the most formidable in South America.

New Bridge. A centuries-old Brazilian dream came close to realization in 1973. Work neared completion on a 9-mile-long (14-km) bridge across the neck of Guanabara Bay between the cities of Rio de Janeiro and Niterói.

(*For additional articles about Brazil's economic boom and an "Information Highlights" table, see special report on pages 46–57.*)

NEILL MACAULAY, *University of Florida*

BREZHNEV, Leonid I. See BIOGRAPHY.
BRIDGES. See ENGINEERING, CIVIL.

BRITISH COLUMBIA

The New Democratic party government of Premier David Barrett, which marked its first full year in office in September 1973, spent much of the year in implementing programs and policies outlined in its first legislative session in late 1972. Walter Stewart Owen took office as lieutenant governor of British Columbia on March 19. He succeeded John R. Nicholson, who retired.

Legislation and Government Activity. The 1973 legislative session passed a wide range of measures. Social services legislation included provisions for a guaranteed minimum income of $200 monthly for all senior citizens and free medical drugs for all persons above the age of 60. The hours and wages act was amended to raise the minimum wage to $2.25 an hour by Dec. 15, 1973, and to $2.50 an hour by June 4, 1974. Government employees received substantial pay increases in line with an announced policy of closing the gap between private industry and civil service wage levels.

Amendments to the park act created 10 new provincial parks and expanded several existing parks. Other new legislation provided for increasingly strict control over private developments in parks and recreation areas. The people of British Columbia became active owners in the forest industry when the government established the Ocean Falls Corporation to manage the pulp mill at Ocean Falls, bought Plateau Mills Ltd. at Vanderhoof, and acquired a 79% interest in the Canadian Cellulose Company Ltd., with pulp mills at Prince Rupert and Castlegar. Commissions were formally established to review

—— BRITISH COLUMBIA • Information Highlights ——

Area: 366,255 square miles (948,597 sq km).
Population (1973 est.): 2,315,000.
Chief Cities (1972 est.): Metro Victoria, the capital (199,-000); Metro Vancouver (1,098,000).
Government: *Chief Officers*—Lt. gov., Walter S. Owen; premier and min. of finance, David Barrett (New Democratic party); atty. gen., Alexander B. Macdonald (NDP); prov. secy., Ernest Hall (NDP); min. of educ., Eileen Dailly (NDP); min. of labor, William King; chief justice, John L. Farris. *Legislature*—Legislative Assembly, 55 members (38 New Democrat, 10 Social Credit, 5 Liberal, 2 Progressive Conservative).
Education: *School enrollment* (June 1973)—public elementary and secondary, 537,106 pupils; private schools (Sept. 71), 21,777 pupils; Indian (federal) schools (1972–73), 2,947 pupils; college and university, 37,500 full-time students. *Public school expenditures* (1973 est.), $435,786,195; median teacher's salary (Sept. 1972), $11,479.
Public Finance (fiscal year 1972–73): *Revenues*, $1,667,217,819 (sales and fuel taxes, $418,397,000; income and inheritance taxes, $430,986,000; natural resources taxes, $220,048,294). *Expenditures*, $1,621,421,248 (education, $435,786,195; health and social services, $580,634,161).
Personal Income (1972): $9,164,000,000; average annual income per person, $4,078.
Human Resources (fiscal year 1973–74 est.): $229,070,705 (aged, disabled and blind, $67,503,000; social allowance recipients and dependents, $120,495,000).
Manufacturing (1972 est.): $4,722,100,000 (wood industries, $1,582,100,000; paper and allied industries, $789,800,000; food and beverages, $758,700,000).
Agriculture and Products (1972): *Cash farm receipts*, $243,-447,000 (livestock, $168,657,000; crops, $71,677,000). *Chief products* (cash receipts): Dairy products, $57,907,000; cattle and calves, $49,280,000; fruit, $28,959,000; eggs, $24,-155,000.
Mining (1972): *Production value*, $637,200,000. *Chief minerals:* Copper, 467,012,000 lbs; crude oil, 24,954,000 bbl; zinc, 268,348,000 lbs; coal, 6,026,000 tons; lead, 194,250,000 lbs; molybdenum, 28,042,000 lbs.
Forest Products (1972): Lumber, 9,466,000,000 board feet; pulp, 4,909,000 tons; paper and paper board, 1,853,000 tons.
Fisheries (1972): Wholesale marketed value: $154,821,000. Leading species: Salmon, 164,386,000 pounds ($114,349,-000).
Transportation: *Roads* (1972), 28,498 miles (45,952 km); *motor vehicles* (1972), 1,162,581; *railroads* (1972 est.), 4,826 main track miles (7,766 km).
Communications (1972): *Telephones*, 1,160,333; *television stations*, 122; *radio stations*, 54; *daily newspapers*, 18.
All monetary figures given in Canadian dollars.

energy policies and land use, and plans were announced for major changes in provincial labor laws at the fall session of the legislature.

Economic Developments. Generally, the economy showed marked advances over 1972. Although sparked by the forest industry, the gains were noticeable in every sector. A survey of private and public investments for 1973 showed an estimated expenditure of $4.1 billion, compared with $3.7 billion in 1972. Sectors expecting gains included public utilities, trade, housing, and government. Improvement in the employment situation was perhaps the most significant development. The seasonally adjusted unemployment rate in August 1973 was 5.6%, compared with 7.7% in August 1972. Inflationary pressures increased substantially, with sharp gains in food prices highlighting this trend.

Canada's largest single railway expansion program in more than 50 years was announced in July. At a cost of $325 million, the British Columbia Railway and the Canadian National Railway will jointly develop northern British Columbia and provide a rail route bypassing the Fraser Canyon. An economic study of the northern rail development suggests that the program will generate 18,000 jobs in the resources industries and 17,000 more jobs in the service sector.

J. R. MEREDITH, *Director*
B. C. Bureau of Economics and Statistics

BUCK, Pearl. See OBITUARIES.
BUDDHISM. See RELIGION—*Oriental Religions.*
BUILDING AND CONSTRUCTION. See HOUSING.

BULGARIA

Bulgaria continued under the stern rule of the aging Todor Zhivkov, who has been first secretary of the Communist party since 1954. His long illness in February–April only temporarily slowed down his activities. In Bulgaria's foreign policy, Soviet leadership continued to be recognized, and in domestic politics the Soviet Union was still considered a model.

Ideological Uniformity. Reports of the June meeting of the Warsaw Pact Communist leaders in the Crimea emphasized friendship, mutual respect, and identity of views between Secretary Zhivkov and Leonid Brezhnev of the USSR. On September 9, the 29th anniversary of the Communist takeover in Bulgaria, Brezhnev received Bulgaria's highest decoration, that of "Hero of the People's Republic of Bulgaria." Various agreements providing for "ideological cooperation" were concluded with the Warsaw Pact countries.

In numerous instances during the year, government and party leaders warned the population against détente in the field of ideology as well as against "misinformation, violence, racism, and fascism coming from the West." For example, almost all Bulgarian reports from Helsinki on the Conference on Security and Cooperation in Europe contained comments that "free flow of information and people" might mean a revival of "cold war" for the Western "imperialists."

Domestic Politics. The Communist party membership increased to more than 700,000, some 9% of the population. In May a conference of heads of political departments and secretaries of party committees in the armed forces recommended reorganization of the committees and took steps to attract worthy officers.

Control over intellectual life has been entrusted to Liudmila Zhivkov, the 30-year-old daughter of Bulgaria's ruler, who was appointed head of the state committee on art and culture. Notwithstanding her ideological orthodoxy, Miss Zhivkov permitted the previously ostracized poet Blaga Dimitrova to be given the Writers' Union award for her latest book, *Underground Sky,* and she allowed Vera Mutafchieva to publish her ideologically unorthodox novel, *A Card Game for Two.*

Bulgaria's growing alcoholism and crime were extensively discussed in the National Assembly, and amendment of the penal code was recommended by several deputies.

Economy. On March 13 the government issued a decree providing for a 42.5-hour five-day week for over 300 selected enterprises. A 46-hour six-day week remains the norm for the rest of the country.

Throughout the year officials appealed to the nation for "socialist competition," for fulfillment of the sixth five-year plan (1971–1975), as well as for "higher social productivity of labor." They also indicated that a reform of wage scales, a new labor code, and a new law on social insurance will be completed and implemented by 1975. By that time the five-day working week is to be introduced nationwide.

According to government forecasts the overall goal of a 9.9% increase in industrial growth in 1973 will be met. Instead of 35%, as planned, only 20% of capital investment could be used for modernization. Milk production continued to decrease. Retail goods turnover, however, increased faster than planned, and housing construction exceeded the planned 7.4% increase.

New regulations were issued against "nonlabor income" in such fields as profits from rents, sales of property, private sheep breeding, and private housing construction. No family is allowed to own more than one place for permanent residence, and living quarters cannot have a floor area larger than 120 square meters (1,292 sq ft). A one-family country house cannot be larger than 60 square meters (646 sq ft).

Foreign Affairs. In July the chairman of the USSR's Supreme Soviet, Nicolai Podgorny, visited Sofia, Bulgaria's capital, and the following month Premier Stanko Todorov went to Moscow. The main features of both countries' five year plans for 1976–1980 were defined and synchronized at these meetings. In March and April, Bulgaria and Yugoslavia negotiated an agreement establishing joint Bulgarian-Yugoslav manufacture of washing machines and electirc irons.

The main directions of foreign trade did not change. Over 50% of it was with the Soviet Union and some 27% with the rest of the COMECON countries. Great efforts were made to intensify trade with the non-Communist countries, however.

In May, Bulgarian Foreign Minister Petar Mladenov visited Athens. Several agreements concerning trade, consular service, and cultural exchange were signed. In June, Minister of Machine Building Ivan Popov visited Austria to sign a ten-year agreement on economic cooperation based on the most-favored national principle. In the same month the Shah of Iran visited Sofia, and agreements were reached providing for a balanced trade amounting to $200 million during the period 1973–77. Similar agreements were signed with Iraq. In July, French Premier Pierre Messmer visited Sofia, and plans for increased trade were agreed upon.

JAN KARSKI
Georgetown University

BULGARIA • Information Highlights

Official Name: People's Republic of Bulgaria.
Location: Southeastern Europe.
Area: 42,823 square miles (110,912 sq km).
Population (1973 est.): 8,700,000. Density, 199 per square mile (77 per sq km).
Chief Cities (1970 est.): Sofia, the capital, 876,900; Plovdiv, 250,000; Varna, 224,700.
Government: *Head of state,* Todor Zhivkov, chairman of the Council of State and first secretary of the Communist party (took office July 1971). *Head of government,* Stanko Todorov, premier (took office July 1971). *Legislature* (unicameral)—National Assembly (all members of the Fatherland Front).
Language: Bulgarian (official).
Education: *Expenditure* (1969), 4.7% of net material product. *School enrollment* (1969)—primary, 1,064,200; secondary, 377,788; technical/vocational, 274,836; university/higher, 95,706.
Monetary Unit: Lev (0.94 lev equals U. S.$1, July 1973).
Gross National Product (1972 est.): $11,100,000,000.
Economic Indexes: *Industrial production* (1971), 237 (1963 = 100); *agricultural production* (1970), 158 (1957–59 = 100); *consumer price index* (1971), 103 (1963 = 100).
Manufacturing (major products): Processed foods, machinery and equipment, chemicals, steel, tobacco products clothing, petroleum products.
Major Agricultural Products: Corn, wheat, barley, fruits, sugar beets, tobacco.
Major Minerals: Lignite, iron ore, coal, zinc, copper, lead.
Foreign Trade (1972): *Exports,* $2,603,000,000; *Imports,* $2,-548,000,000. *Chief trading partners* (1970)—USSR (took 54% of exports, supplied 52% of imports); East Germany (9%–9%); Czechoslovakia (4%–5%); Poland.
Tourism: Receipts (1971), $113,000,000.
Transportation: *Railroads* (1971), 2,476 miles (3,985 km); *merchant fleet* (1972), 742,000 gross registered tons; *major national airline,* Bulgarian Airlines "BALKAN."
Communications: *Telephones* (1972), 534,257; *newspapers* (1971), 12 (daily circulation, 1,632,000).

BURMA

Burma's dictator Ne Win, who gave up his military rank of general a year earlier, took the first tentative steps in 1973 toward abandonment of the extreme isolationist foreign policy pursued by his military government since 1962. The actions appeared to be part of a general loosening of the political and economic policies of one of the most rigidly controlled non-Communist countries, and reflected a relaxation in Southeast Asian affairs stemming from the end of the Vietnam War and from improved relations between the United States and China, Burma's powerful neighbor.

Ne Win paid visits to Thailand, Malaysia, and Indonesia during the year in a significant break from his previous policy of almost complete noninvolvement in regional affairs. Former Premier U Nu's departure from his exile base in neighboring Thailand was exacted as the price for greater Burmese participation in area political affairs.

Partly in response to mounting economic difficulties, Ne Win also opened the door to new foreign economic activity. He actively sought aid from the World Bank and from the Asian Development Bank, and he invited foreign firms to bid for offshore oil exploration contracts.

Economy. Bad weather and population growth combined to terminate Burma's rice exports—an extraordinary circumstance in a land that was once the world's ranking exporter of the grain. For the first time since it regained its independence from British colonial rule in 1948, Burma made no advance commitments for the export of its rice in 1973. So extreme was the shortage of the grain within the country that the government lifted various controls on the sale of rice, which farmers had been holding back or not growing at all because of insufficient profit incentives. The result was a doubling of the price of the grain.

The previously rigidly applied "Burmese Way to Socialism" was further relaxed by the denationalization of part of the industrial sector. Several small industries using local raw materials were permitted to return to personal ownership and engage in private trade.

─────────── **BURMA • Information Highlights** ───────────

Official Name: Union of Burma.
Location: Southeast Asia.
Area: 261,789 square miles (678,033 sq km).
Population (1973 est.): 29,800,000. Density, 113 per square mile (44 per sq km).
Chief Cities (1969 est.): Rangoon, the capital, 1,717,600 (1968 est.); Mandalay, 393,000; Moulmein, 169,000.
Government: Head of state, Ne Win, Chairman of the Revolutionary Council (took office March 1962). Head of government, Ne Win, premier. Legislature—Parliament (dissolved March 1962).
Languages: Burmese, English (both official).
Education: Expenditure (1967), 16.8% of total public expenditure. School enrollment (1969)—primary, 3,328,000; secondary, 699,615; technical/vocational, 4,080; university/higher, 45,891.
Monetary Unit: Kyat (4.862 kyats equal U. S.$1, July 1973).
Gross National Product (1971 est.): $1,959,000,000.
Agricultural Production Index (1971), 111 (1963=100).
Manufacturing (major products): Processed foods, textiles, tobacco products, wood products.
Major Agricultural Products: Rice, groundnuts, sesame, tobacco, sugarcane, millet, cotton, forest products.
Major Minerals: Petroleum, lead, zinc, salt.
Foreign Trade (1972): Exports, $118,000,000; Imports, $98,-000,000. Chief trading partners (1970)—Japan (took 9% of exports, supplied 23% of imports); United Kingdom (9%—9%); India (7%—15%).
Transportation: Motor vehicles (1970), 60,800 (automobiles. 29,800); railroads (1971), 1,925 miles (3,098 km); major national airline, Burma Airways.
Communications: Telephones (1971), 27,000; newspapers (1971), 44.

Politics. Political controls were also lessened during the year as Burma prepared for two ballots: a December 1973 referendum on a constitution to replace the one overthrown by Ne Win in 1962, and January 1974 one-party elections to the new legislature. The constitution, modeled after the constitutions of the Eastern European countries, received 90% endorsement in the December vote. Largely Ne Win's own creation, it was not intended to reintroduce democratic government in the country, but the Burma Socialist Program party, the only political organization allowed by the new constitution, presumably would play a more important role in the government of the country, while the army would play a less obvious role.

Insurgencies. The liberalization of Burma's government was partly designed to conciliate opposition to the Ne Win dictatorship, but it seemed to have no impact on the continuing insurgencies. The most important of these were the Chinese-aided Communist insurgents in the northeast. Perhaps 5,000 in number, the Communists pushed steadily southward. Shan and Kachin ethnic minority rebellions (in the northeastern and northern regions, respectively) boasted approximately 4,000 partisans each. In the eastern part of the country, insurgents who were once followers of ousted Premier U Nu totaled about 1,000, but Nu himself had abandoned leadership of this group (many of whom are Karens).

RICHARD BUTWELL
State University of New York at Brockport

CALIFORNIA

Tax, budgetary, and public policy issues were highly controversial in California during 1973. The political highlights included a court-adopted redistricting plan, a jockeying for position by those who sought to succeed Ronald Reagan as governor in 1974, and the election of a black mayor of Los Angeles (see LOS ANGELES).

Tax Issues. As a result of miscalculations and a one-cent increase in the sales tax in December 1972, the state finished fiscal year 1973 with an embarrassing $826 million surplus. The governor and state legislative leaders became embroiled in a controversy over what to do with the surplus. Some legislators wished to spend it on projects that had been delayed. Others wanted to return the money to the taxpayers, but not necessarily in relation to the amount paid. Still other legislators and the governor wanted it returned to taxpayers in proportion to their individual burdens.

After more than three months of political maneuvering, Governor Reagan and his supporters emerged victorious in legislative action. About $721 million was to be returned; one half of it through a six-month cut of one cent in the sales tax, and the remainder by a rebate on 1973 income taxes that would average 30%. The sales tax was scheduled to increase again on April 1, 1974, in time for high taxes to become an issue once again during the gubernatorial campaign.

While the issue of the disposal of the surplus was being debated, supporters of the governor circulated petitions for an initiative petition that would place on the ballot an extremely complex plan to amend the state constitution so as to mandate a 15-year-long gradual reduction in state taxes. This proposed constitutional amendment, strongly

─────── CALIFORNIA • Information Highlights ───────

Area: 158,693 square miles (411,015 sq km).
Population (1972 est.): 20,468,000. *Density*, 130 per sq mi.
Chief Cities (1970 census): Sacramento, the capital, 257,105; Los Angeles, 2,809,596; San Francisco, 715,674; San Diego, 697,027; San Jose, 445,779; Oakland, 361,561.
Government (1973): *Chief Officers*—governor, Ronald Reagan (R); lt. gov., Ed Reinecke (R); secy. of state, Edmund G. Brown, Jr. (D); atty. gen., Evelle J. Younger (R); treas., Ivy Baker Priest (R); supt. of public instruction, Wilson C. Riles; chief justice, Donald R. Wright. *Legislature*—Senate, 40 members (19 Democrats, 19 Republicans, 2 vacancies); Assembly, 80 members (50 D, 29 R, 1 vacancy).
Education (1972–73): Enrollment—public elementary schools, 2,750,000 pupils, 112,000 teachers; public secondary schools, 1,820,000 pupils, 77,500 teachers; nonpublic schools, 336,200 pupils, 14,060 teachers; colleges and universities, 1,063,043 students. *Public school expenditures*, $4,408,596,000 ($1,000 per pupil). *Average teacher's salary*, $12,700.
State Finances (fiscal year 1971): *Revenues*, $12,007,955,000 (5% general sales tax and gross receipts taxes, $1,798,-409,000; motor fuel tax, $669,847,000; federal funds, $3,-248,241,000). *Expenditures*, $10,637,439,000 (education, $3,270,770,000; health, welfare, and safety, $3,356,727,000; highways, $1,331,126,000). *State debt*, $5,727,925,000 (June 30, 1971).
Personal Income (1972): $102,374,000,000; per capita, $5,002.
Public Assistance (1972): $2,989,993,000. *Average monthly payments* (Dec. 1972)—old age assistance, $111.94; aid to families with dependent children, $210.54.
Labor Force: *Nonagricultural wage and salary earners* (July 1973), 7,512,200. *Average annual employment* (1972)—manufacturing, 1,530,900; trade, 1,627,700; government, 1,495,100; services, 1,358,500. *Insured unemployed* (Sept. 1973)—184,700 (3.1%).
Manufacturing (1971): Value added by manufacture, $27,568,-200,000. Transportation equipment, $4,708,300,000; food and kindred products, $3,769,300,000; electrical equipment and supplies, $3,249,000,000; nonelectrical machinery, $2,-156,700,000; fabricated metal products, $1,755,600,000; printing and publishing, $1,448,500,000.
Agriculture (1972): *Cash farm income*, $5,596,499,000 (livestock, $2,205,784,000; crops, $3,268,272,000; government payments, $122,443,000). *Chief crops* (in order of value, 1972)—Grapes (ranks 1st among the states); hay (ranks 1st); tomatoes (ranks 1st); lettuce.
Mining (1972): Production value, $1,891,953,000 (ranks 3d among the states). *Chief minerals*—Petroleum, $945,472,-000; natural gas, $194,334,000; cement, $187,006,000; sand and gravel, $163,789,000.
Fisheries (1972): *Commercial catch*, 639,764,000 pounds ($91,-898,000). Tuna, $71,096,000; salmon, $4,304,000; flounder, $3,348,000; jack mackerel, $2,216,000.
Transportation: *Roads* (1972), 165,990 miles (267,128 km); *motor vehicles* (1972), 12,367,181; *railroads* (1972), 7,385 miles (11,885 km); public airports (1972), 277.
Communications: *Telephones* (1973), 14,381,400; *television stations* (1971), 49; *radio stations* (1971), 384; *newspapers* (1973), 127 (daily circulation, 5,836,000).

supported by Reagan, became the only measure on the ballot at a special election on November 6. Voters recognized that the issue before them was important, but a poll just before election showed many of them to be confused and uncertain. Doubtful voters said no, and the proposal gained the support of only 45.5% of the voters.

State Budget. The state budget for the 1974 fiscal year set an all-time record for California and for all state governments. It totaled $9.339 billion, a 28% increase over the previous year. The largest increase—more than $1 billion—came in intergovernmental transfers of shared taxes and grants to school districts and other local governments. Other increases came in funds to purchase parklands and provide salary increases for state employees.

Reductions in the budget from the previous year were primarily in the fields of education, public health, prisons, and welfare. In these areas Governor Reagan projected declining clientele levels. The governor also acted to overrule a proposed increase in the appropriation for the Coastal Zone Conservation Commission. In all, he vetoed budget items amounting to $80 million.

Death Penalty. Perhaps the most dramatic new legislation in 1973 was the reenactment of the death penalty. This represented a response to a referendum in 1972 in which two out of three voters favored restoration. It was also a response to a

number of spectacular murders and trials during the year. The law imposes a mandatory death sentence for 11 categories of murder. It was designed to avoid the legal objections the U. S. Supreme Court had made to state laws in which the death sentence was to some degree optional. The law went into effect on Jan. 1, 1974.

Higher Education. The Legislature established the California Postsecondary Education Commission (CPEC) to replace the Coordinating Council for Higher Education, which had lost credibility with the Legislature. The CPEC has responsibility for planning and coordinating all education beyond high school. Although the 23-member commission is restricted to an advisory role, it is responsible for developing a new master plan for higher education to replace that of 1960 and for keeping the plan updated.

Other New Legislation. Other measures passed included a Forest Practices Act that imposes new rules on the timber industry for greater erosion control, stream protection, and replanting regulations. Another law provided for new programs for child day-care, preschools, and immigrant children's care.

New regulations were imposed upon mortgage brokers, some of whom have allegedly engaged in unethical practices, such as making misleading claims and issuing false advertising, charging excessive fees, and requiring "balloon" payments of large size as a last payment, forcing many debtors to borrow more to pay them and thus remain indefinitely in debt. Laws affecting women in relation to taxes and credit were liberalized. And the sabertooth cat was made the official state fossil.

Once again the Legislature refused to pass no-fault automobile insurance laws. It also rejected proposals to legalize bingo and to create a state lottery.

Vetoes. During the legislative session Governor Reagan vetoed 171 bills, an all-time state record. All of his vetoes were sustained, and indeed no gubernatorial veto has been overriden in California since 1946.

Redistricting. The state supreme court appointed a committee of three court "masters"—retired judges—to draw up a redistricting plan if the Legislature and the governor could not agree on one acceptable to the court. The masters announced their plan in August, after which it was considered by the court and finally adopted in November. The plan provides new districts that were drawn with the aid of a computer, which processed data on population shifts reflected in the 1970 census.

California sends 43 representatives to the U. S. Congress, has a 40-member state Senate, and an 80-member state Assembly. Some of the incumbents face an uncertain future in the 1974 elections as a result of the redistricting.

1974 Gubernatorial Race. Governor Reagan has long insisted that he will not run for reelection in 1974. As a result, both parties had a number of men volunteering early for candidacy. It would be only the second race in over 50 years in which there will be no incumbent.

At least a dozen candidates had announced their intentions or were making obvious moves toward running. At year-end the prospects were for vigorous, expensive primary elections in both major parties.

CHARLES R. ADRIAN
University of California, Riverside

CAMBODIA

American combat participation in the Cambodian theater of the Indochina war, and in Indochina as a whole, ended on August 15, when a U. S. Congress-ordered bombing halt took effect. The subsequent military collapse of the anti-Communist Lon Nol government was widely expected but did not occur. A peaceful settlement of the Cambodian war also did not take place, however, making the Khmer republic the only Indochinese country without an active political dialogue between Communist and anti-Communist rivals.

The War. Both the Lon Nol government and the insurgent Communist "Khmer Rouge" seemed exhausted as a result of the often fiercely waged war. In August, when the bombing stopped, the defenses of the capital of Phnom Penh seemed in peril. But the Communists did not move to take the city. In subsequent weeks, government forces—fighting far better than had been expected—successfully defended Kompong Cham (Cambodia's third-largest city) and opened Route 4 linking Phnom Penh to Kompong Som. But 3½ years of fighting had left the Khmer army badly battered.

The Khmer Rouge had been seriously weakened by the American bombing and were hampered by the monsoon rains, which ended in November. At the time of the bombing halt, three fourths of the country was in the rebels' hands; but the government controlled most of the cities. Khmer Rouge forces totalled an estimated 50,000, about one fourth the size of the government's army.

U. S. Military Role. President Richard M. Nixon had declared in May that U. S. bombing of Communist forces in Cambodia, particularly of the North Vietnamese, would continue until the Communists accepted the cease-fire offered them by President Lon Nol. But the American leader failed to appreciate mounting antiwar sentiment in Congress, which resulted in an act requiring the cessation of U. S. bombing in Cambodia by August 15. President Nixon accused Congress of "abandonment of a friend" and promised the Lon Nol regime all the aid allowed by law.

Termination of the U. S. air war against the Communists in Cambodia ended 160 consecutive days of extremely heavy American bombing, involving 430 bombers and fighter-bombers. The American air role in Cambodia had begun secretly 4½ years earlier when Prince Sihanouk was still in power. U. S. bombing in 1971–72 may have accounted for the survival of the Lon Nol regime.

Arms and other supplies continued to flow into Cambodia from the United States after August. The U. S. General Accounting Office charged that the Nixon administration was illegally advising the Khmer army on the use of such equipment in violation of a congressional ban on such advice.

Diplomacy. President Nixon's surprise midyear statement that "extremely delicate" negotiations were in progress—involving Lon Nol, Prince Sihanouk, and the Khmer Rouge—was not followed by a political settlement. The Phnom Penh government even denied knowledge of such activity. But the United States had talks with both China and North Vietnam on ending the fighting in Cambodia.

There were no signs of any negotiations between the different Cambodian sides as the year's end approached. But there were signs of growing diplomatic backing for Prince Sihanouk. The USSR, which previously played a very delicate political game, called Sihanouk the "sole legal representative" of the Cambodian people and cut the size of its Phnom Penh embassy to three aides.

Politics. The United States, pressing Lon Nol for a negotiated settlement with his foes in the field, also pushed the Khmer president to broaden participation in his hitherto quite unrepresentative and autocratic government. In April a four-man "High Political Council" was formed (comprising Lon Nol as chairman, together with key anti-Communist leaders Prince Sirik Matak, Cheng Heng, and In Tam), and in May, In Tam, rival of Lon Nol, became premier. This compromise failed to bring political peace to the different anti-Communist factions, however, and the 59-year-old, crippled President Lon Nol remained the dominant, if not decisive, leader of the government. Premier In Tam resigned in December.

Sihanouk's Strategy. Ousted leader Prince Sihanouk, who is living in Peking, said in October that he might resign from the government-in-exile because of differences with the Khmer Rouge, who had been his foes when he headed the Cambodian regime before 1970. He expressed his pleasure with Chinese and North Vietnamese aid. He made it clear that he was unwilling to negotiate with the United States, thus reversing an earlier position. Sihanouk's cause gained international support during the year, mainly from "nonaligned" countries. But the likelihood that the prince himself would again head a Cambodian government seemed remote, because of his differences with both friends and foes.

Economy. Inflation was severe during the year; the cost of living increased about 60%. But there were no acute food or other shortages at the year's end, although rice had earlier been in short supply. The government met the demands of its own payroll obligations by increasing the money supply. Speculators and hoarders bought up many vital items, also adding to inflationary pressures. The government's budget deficit for the year appeared to be approximately U. S.$40 million.

RICHARD BUTWELL
State University of New York at Brockport

——————— CAMBODIA • Information Highlights ———————

Official Name: Khmer Republic.
Location: Southeast Asia.
Area: 69,898 square miles (181,035 sq km).
Population (1973 est.): 7,800,000. Density, 112 per square mile (43 per sq km).
Chief Cities (1962 census): Phnom Penh, the capital, 393,995; Battambang, 38,780; Kompong Cham, 28,532.
Government: Head of state, Gen. Lon Nol, president (took office March 1972). Head of government, In Tam, premier (took office May 1973). Legislature—Parliament: Senate and National Assembly.
Languages: Khmer, also called Cambodian (official), French.
Education: Expenditure (1967), 21.6% of total public expenditure. School enrollment (1969)—primary, 989,464; secondary, 126,791; technical/vocational, 5,798; university/higher (1968), 11,094.
Monetary Unit: Riel (275 riels equal U. S.$1, Oct. 1973).
Gross National Product (1971 est.): $655,000,000.
Consumer Price Index (1972), 284 (1963=100).
Manufacturing (major products): Paper, textiles, tobacco products, sawnwood.
Major Agricultural Products: Rice, corn, rubber, beans, sweet potatoes and yams, forest products, fish.
Major Minerals: Coal, phosphate, iron ore.
Foreign Trade (1971): Exports, $15,000,000; Imports, $78,-000,000. Chief export customers: South Vietnam; Hong Kong; Singapore; France. Chief import suppliers: United States; Japan; Singapore; Hong Kong.
Tourism: Receipts (1971), $300,000.
Transportation: Motor vehicles (1971), 37,500 (automobiles, 26,400); railroads (1971), 403 miles (649 km); major national airline, Air Cambodge.
Communications: Telephones (1971), 8,000; newspapers (1968), 26 (daily circulation, 145,000).

CANADA

During farewell ceremonies at a South Vietnamese airport in July, a South Vietnamese general shakes hands with the 249 members of the Canadian truce team.

At the opening of Parliament on Jan. 4, 1973—the first session after the general election of October 1972—the Liberal party government of Pierre Elliott Trudeau seemed to hold a very precarious lease on life. That election reestablished a minority government, with 109 Liberals, 107 Progressive Conservatives, 31 New Democrats, 15 Social Credit members, and 2 Independents in the 264-seat House of Commons. Most Canadians predicted an early collapse of Trudeau's Liberal government and the accession of Robert Stanfield's Progressive Conservative party. But the Liberals clung to power in 1973 with the help of the New Democratic party and, occasionally, the Social Credit party.

On October 5, Prime Minister Trudeau announced that Jules Léger had been appointed as the 21st governor-general of Canada, to succeed Roland Michener, who retired officially on November 30. At the same time the prime minister announced that Léger would not assume office until mid-January 1974 and that Michener would continue to serve until then. On December 28, Trudeau named Bora Laskin as the new chief justice of Canada, succeeding Gérald Fauteux, who retired.

For the first time, Canada was host for the meeting of the heads of government of the Commonwealth, which was held in Ottawa on August 2–10. Internationally, Canada found itself involved in peacekeeping missions in both the Far East and the Middle East. Prime Minister and Mrs. Trudeau made an official visit to China in October. Relations with the United States were marked by growing demands for limits on U. S. ownership of Canadian industries and curbs on U. S. investment in Canada.

DOMESTIC AFFAIRS

By custom, a government that is defeated on the basis of its initial program of legislation is obliged to resign, and the governor-general then calls on the leader of the opposition to form the government. But when a government survives the early attacks on its programs, it is entitled—if defeated after a number of months—to ask the governor-general to dissolve Parliament and call a general election.

By surviving throughout the year, the Trudeau government outran the threat of having to hand over the reins to Robert Stanfield or face an election. At the same time, the New Democratic party —which succeeded in influencing most legislation in the direction of greater nationalism and more social concern—lost some of the sting that it had appeared to have during the 1972 election campaign. During that campaign the party leader, David Lewis, had attacked multinational corporations and called for more Canadian control of industry, trade, and commerce, particularly in relation to subsidiaries of U. S. companies operating in Canada.

Major Challenges to Trudeau Government. A series of moves by the Liberals—chiefly in enlarging policies announced on January 4—brought sufficient support from the New Democrats that the government survived three no-confidence motions of the Progressive Conservatives during the first half of January. These moves included the promise to

hold a western Canadian economic conference, together with a promise to review the railway freight rate structure, and the announcement of a variety of regional economic development and social welfare policies.

The federal budget, introduced by Finance Minister John Turner on February 19, incorporated a number of ideas culled from the election platforms of opposition parties, including cuts in personal income and corporation taxes, increased aid to regions with economic problems, and boosts in welfare and pension payments. When the budget passed by a 143–102 vote on February 28, the government negotiated another major hurdle in its plan for survival.

A rapid and unprecedented rise in the cost of living—equal in April to a 6.6% increase in one year—and prospects of an even higher rate of increase for foodstuffs forced the government in May to establish a food prices review board under the guidance of Beryl Plumptre, a former chairman of the Canadian Consumer Council. After hearing evidence and conducting an investigation of food production and marketing, Mrs. Plumptre reported that "food prices were not rocketing out of control." But many Canadians were so angered at spectacular rises in the prices of some foods, especially beef and other meat products, that they were unwilling to agree. Robert Stanfield seized the occasion to introduce on June 14 a motion of no-confidence in the government because of its mishandling of the economy and the lack of action to check rising prices. Like the others, this attempt by the Progressive Conservatives to bring down the government was unsuccessful.

Sharp focus on the national energy situation, brought about by the Arab oil embargo following the Arab-Israeli conflict in October, provided additional ammunition for the opposition. At that time, the part of Canada east of the Ottawa River, which had always relied on imported oil, prepared for a cold, oil-short winter, and the government was vilified for its lack of preparation for this national emergency. On December 3, Robert Stanfield announced his intention of bringing an end to the Trudeau administration within one week.

But in a major speech to Commons on December 6, Trudeau announced his government's fuel policy. It included a continuation of the price freeze on heating oil and other petroleum products, the establishment of a national petroleum corporation to buy oil and to enter the field of exploration and development, and extension to Montreal, Quebec, of the pipeline (from Edmonton, Alberta) that now terminates at the Ottawa River, on the Ontario-Quebec border. This announcement had the effect of rallying the New Democratic party behind the government and defusing Stanfield's no-confidence motion, introduced on December 10.

The Energy Situation. At least until the Arab oil embargo, there was little evidence of crisis in the Canadian energy situation. Ontario, Quebec, and Manitoba announced at an early date that their electrical output would not be seriously affected. Exports of petroleum to the United States continued at a record level—about 1 million barrels a day— and there was no immediate reason to curtail exports. To do so would not have benefited Canadians, since there were no adequate means of transporting oil from western Canada—where all the oil is produced, chiefly in Alberta—to the oil-short areas of eastern Canada. Those areas relied almost entirely on imported oil, chiefly from Venezuela. And because imported oil had always been cheaper than Alberta oil, there had been great resistance to an extension of the oil pipeline. When the prime minister called for the pipeline extension, he was greeted with some hostility by the Quebec government and spokesmen for the Maritime provinces. But his announcement of a price freeze on heating oil and other petroleum products, extending to Jan. 31, 1974, was accepted by consumers.

Federal Action Before Embargo. After permitting an increase in oil shipments to the United States in January, Energy Minister Donald Macdonald announced on February 15 a licensing system for export of all grades of crude oil. The announcement was in response to a report of the National Energy Board, saying in part that "production from all sources in Canada will not be able to supply the potential export and domestic market demand after 1973." This decree was followed in June by a government prohibition on the export of gasoline and heating oil except when approved by the board.

In September the federal government moved to impose what was in effect an export tax on crude oil of 40 cents a barrel. This tax was raised to $1.90 a barrel, effective December 1, and was scheduled to rise to $2.20 on Jan. 1, 1974. Premier Peter Lougheed of Alberta, the oil companies, and the U. S. Department of State all predicted serious consequences for western Canada's oil industry as a result of the tax.

APLOMB: *Justin, son of Prime Minister and Mrs. Trudeau* (right), *greets a visiting dignitary in August.*

Other Post-Embargo Action. The Arab oil embargo, which dislocated shipments not only from the Middle East but from Venezuela and other suppliers, gave a new impetus to the concept of oil self-sufficiency for Canada and revived interest in pipeline extension. Meanwhile, Energy Minister Macdonald recommended the use of trucks and trains to carry Alberta crude oil overland to the eastern provinces, as well as tankers to carry the oil on the St. Lawrence Seaway and from British Columbia ports by way of the Panama Canal.

On December 27, Macdonald announced that Canada would increase its export tax on crude oil to about $6.50 a barrel on Feb. 1, 1974, unless some other arrangement was made at a federal-provincial conference scheduled for late January 1974. The $6.50 rate, he said, would cover the widening differential between Canada's frozen domestic price on crude oil—about $4.00 a barrel—and the going rate on world markets. About the same time the Arab countries and Venezuela announced prices on their crude oil, effective Jan. 1, 1974, representing a 470% and 400% increase, respectively, in one year.

Alberta's Responses. Following the increase in the federal export tax on crude oil to $1.90, the Alberta government broke off talks with the federal government on the issue of energy. Under the Canadian constitution, the provinces have control over the natural resources within their borders, but the federal government has jurisdiction over international and interprovincial trade. Premier Lougheed not only called the federal export tax the most restrictive ever taken against a province but also objected to a lack of consultation with Alberta on the part of the federal government. But the breakdown was resolved in November, following federal-provincial talks, and Lougheed expressed willingness

---

THE CANADIAN MINISTRY
(According to precedence, December 1973)

Pierre Elliott Trudeau, Prime Minister
Paul Martin, Leader of the Government in the Senate
Mitchell Sharp, Secretary of State for External Affairs
Allan J. MacEachen, President, Queen's Privy Council
Charles M. Drury, President of the Treasury Board
Jean Marchand, Minister of Transport
John N. Turner, Minister of Finance
Jean Chrétien, Minister of Indian Affairs and Northern Development
Donald S. Macdonald, Minister of Energy, Mines and Resources
John C. Munro, Minister of Labour
Gérard Pelletier, Minister of Communications
Jack Davis, Minister of the Environment and of Fisheries
Jean-Eudes Dubé, Minister of Public Works
S. Ronald Basford, Minister of State for Urban Affairs
Donald C. Jamieson, Minister of Regional Economic Expansion
Robert K. Andras, Minister of Manpower and Immigration
James A. Richardson, Minister of National Defence
Otto E. Lang, Minister of Justice and Attorney General
Herb Gray, Minister of Consumer and Corporate Affairs
Robert D. G. Stanbury, Minister of National Revenue
Jean-Pierre Goyer, Minister of Supply and Services
Alastair W. Gillespie, Minister of Industry, Trade and Commerce
Stanley Haidasz, Minister of State
Eugene F. Whelan, Minister of Agriculture
Warren Allmand, Solicitor General of Canada
J. Hugh Faulkner, Secretary of State of Canada
André Ouellet, Postmaster General
Daniel J. MacDonald, Minister of Veterans Affairs
Marc Lalonde, Minister of National Health and Welfare
Jeanne Sauvé, Minister of State for Science and Technology

LOUIS ST. LAURENT (1882–1973)

UPI

Louis Stephen St. Laurent, Canada's 12th prime minister and the second French-Canadian to serve in that office, died on July 25, 1973, at his home in the city of Quebec. Known familiarly as "Uncle Louis" or "Monsieur Canada," he led his country to maturity as a sovereign state within the British Commonwealth and greatly enhanced its status as an international power. A prominent lawyer, St. Laurent entered national politics at the age of 59 to accept what was intended as a World War II assignment in the cabinet of W. L. Mackenzie King. He served as the nation's first secretary of state for external affairs (1946–48) and succeeded King as Liberal party leader and prime minister (1948–57).

St. Laurent was born of French-Irish parentage in Compton, Quebec, on Feb. 1, 1882, the son of a country storekeeper. He received a law degree from Laval University in 1905 and became a professor of law there in 1914. Later he distinguished himself both in representing the federal and provincial governments in constitutional cases and as a corporation lawyer. He was president of the Canadian Bar Association from 1930 to 1932.

After accepting appointment to Mackenzie King's cabinet in 1941, St. Laurent won election to Parliament the next year. His early efforts as minister of justice were directed toward backing the war effort with a policy of total conscription. He took part in the founding conference of the United Nations in 1945, headed Canada's delegation to the first sessions of the United Nations General Assembly (1946, 1947), and successfully negotiated Canada's bid for a Security Council seat and a voice in the peace treaty negotiations. He was among the first to enunciate the concept of the North Atlantic Treaty Organization (NATO).

As prime minister, St. Laurent promoted construction of the St. Lawrence Seaway, completed negotiations for Newfoundland to join the Canadian Confederation in 1949, made the Supreme Court of Canada the final court of appeal, and led Canada into participation in NATO. His party was defeated in 1957, and the next year he retired from politics.

HENRY S. SLOAN

---

to see crude oil price increases "phased in" over a period of time.

The suggestion by Lougheed in late 1972 that he would propose a substantial increase in the price of natural gas brought an immediate objection from Ontario, a major consumer of Alberta gas. It soon became obvious that Lougheed was attempting to use the near-monopoly position of his province in the energy field to wrest concessions in other areas from the consuming provinces, particularly in freight rate differentials on east- and west-bound trains, in the tax-sharing field, and in a share of the multimillion-dollar petrochemical industry. In June, Premier William Davis of Ontario announced his intention of testing the constitutionality of Alberta's gas-pricing policy in the courts.

Increasing pressure on Canada's limited oil and gas reserves brought the Athabasca oil sands in northern Alberta back into the picture as an economical source of oil. Disappointed by the meager results of drilling along the Atlantic coast and in

Striking rail workers storm their way into Parliament buildings to protest attempts to force their return to work.

the Canadian far north and encouraged by rising world prices for oil, Premier Lougheed announced on September 18 that Syncrude Canada Ltd., a firm owned by oil companies, would proceed with its development of the sands under a new agreement with the province. Under the agreement, royalties would be 50% of profits, and the newly formed government agency, Alberta Energy Co., would have an option to purchase 20% of the operating plant. Great Canadian Oil Sands Ltd., which opened the first plant in the sands in 1968, currently produces 66,000 barrels of synthetic crude oil a day.

Major Legislation. By the time of the summer adjournment of Parliament on July 27, a number of important measures had been passed. Among these were a cut in personal income taxes of 5% (including a previously scheduled 3% reduction), a reduction from 49% to 40% in the corporate tax rate for manufacturing and processing industries, and removal of federal sales and excise taxes on a wide range of goods. Also approved was support for the 1976 Olympic Games at Montreal through the sale of commemorative stamps and coins, as well as a national lottery. The first coins and lottery tickets went on the market in December. But there was a great deal of uneasiness not only about the high cost of being the host country but also about the possibility of providing security arrangements sufficient to prevent another tragedy like that as Munich in 1972. The federal treasury board forecast a $217 million deficit in the Olympic Games budget.

An emergency session of Parliament was called on August 27 to legislate an end to the national rail strike (*see below*). It remained in session until September 21 to deal with problems posed by the rising cost of living. Major changes in national oil policies formulated at this time have been noted. In addition, bills were passed to increase family allowance payments and boost pensions of retired public servants to take into account the full effect of inflation. During the fall session, which opened on October 15, Parliament passed the long-awaited foreign investment review bill, which would establish an agency to screen some foreign investments and would restrict expansion of foreign-controlled firms.

As a result of increased expenditures for measures needed to offset the effects of inflation and to reduce unemployment, supplementary appropriations for the 1973–74 fiscal year were introduced on November 7. These appropriations, totaling about $1 billion, brought the forecast government spending in fiscal 1973–74 to a record $20.3 billion.

The Economy, Labor, and Strikes. Despite ever-increasing inflation, the economy remained generally strong. The gross national product—which stood at $102.9 billion at the end of 1972—had increased to an annual level of $112.6 billion in the first quarter of 1973. Thereafter the rate of increase dropped as a result of the government's efforts to slow the economy with cuts in federal spending and higher interest rates to discourage private borrowing and spending. Strikes and shortages of materials were other factors, especially in the last half of the year. By October, the cost of living had risen 8.7% above the previous October, and food prices had soared by almost 17% in the same period. These increases meant the worst inflationary year for Canada since 1951. Nationwide, the seasonally adjusted rate of unemployment remained below the 6.5% level in December 1972. (See also LABOR—*World Labor*.)

Canada's housing shortage was aggravated by a nationwide seven-month elevator constructors' strike, which was ended in late March. But other strikes, including a 68-day garbagemen's strike in Hamilton, Ontario, and a two-month machinists' strike against Air Canada, were a source of public annoyance. The seven-month mining strike at Buchans, Newfoundland, was settled in October.

THE CANADIAN ECONOMY

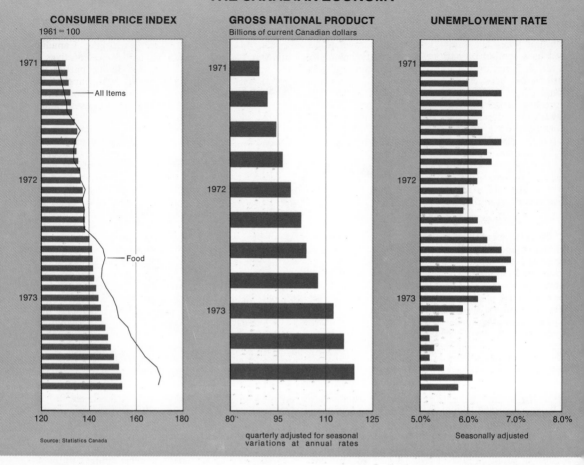

CONSUMER PRICE INDEX
1961 = 100

All Items

Food

120 140 160 180

Source: Statistics Canada

GROSS NATIONAL PRODUCT
Billions of current Canadian dollars

1971

1972

1973

80 95 110 125

quarterly adjusted for seasonal
variations at annual rates

UNEMPLOYMENT RATE

1971

1972

1973

5.0% 6.0% 7.0% 8.0%

Seasonally adjusted

The strike of nonoperating railway workers, which began as a series of rotating regional strikes in July, became a complete shutdown by August 27, when Parliament legislated a return to work on the basis of a 34-cent-an-hour increase for 1973 and a 7.5% increase in 1974. The average 1973 wage for nonoperating workers was $3.53 an hour before the settlement.

As Parliament met, about 150 militant workers stormed the Centre Block on Parliament Hill and left only after some damage had been done and a number of persons injured. The violence grew out of a demonstration by some 1,800 workers who had gathered to protest being legislated back to work. The terms imposed by Parliament were those that the workers had rejected some weeks earlier. As a result, there were a number of holdout locals, and full rail service was not restored for almost two weeks after the settlement. The railway strike left thousands of holiday visitors stranded in Newfoundland and Prince Edward Island when ferries operated by the Canadian National Railways ceased to operate.

Federal-Provincial Conferences. In 1879, John A. Macdonald, Canada's first prime minister after Confederation, introduced his "National Policy," which was based on the assumption that as the railways were pushed into western Canada settlers would follow, creating a market for eastern Canada's manufactured goods and providing a source of raw materials. Meetings of the premiers of the western provinces—British Columbia, Alberta, Saskatch-

ewan, and Manitoba—were called in March and June 1973 to plan a strategy that would put an end to this policy, which they maintain has been pursued tacitly until the present day, and to give westerners a better deal on freight rates, agricultural policies, and regional industrialization.

Thus, when the four premiers met Prime Minister Trudeau at the western economic opportunities conference at Calgary, Alberta, on July 24–26, the prime minister was faced with demands to assist westerners to process their raw materials at home— a plan that would become possible only if transportation disparities were removed and the port of Churchill, Manitoba, were made more useful for trans-Atlantic shipping. Trudeau was also asked to pass legislation permitting the provinces to invest in chartered banks—all of which are privately owned in eastern Canada—so that capital might be more readily available for western development.

Participants in the historic western conference agreed that it might be years before its success or failure could be determined. Other federal-provincial conferences throughout the year were devoted to such subjects as finance, housing, and tax-sharing.

Other Events. In late June and early July, Queen Elizabeth II visited Prince Edward Island, which was celebrating 100 years of participation in Canadian confederation, and took part in the Royal Canadian Mounted Police centennial celebrations in Saskatchewan and Alberta. (See feature article on page 58.) In August, she welcomed the delegates to the Commonwealth conference in Ottawa.

At a provincial dinner in her honor at Toronto on June 25, the queen sounded a new note in relationships when she said, "I want the Crown to be seen as a symbol of national sovereignty belonging to all. It is not only a link between Commonwealth nations, but between Canadian citizens of every national origin and ancestry. The Crown is an idea more than a person and I would like the Crown in Canada to represent everything that is best and more admired in the Canadian ideal." Although the queen did not visit Quebec, her tour of other parts of Canada was considered a success.

For the native Indian and Eskimo peoples of Canada, the year brought some progress, especially in their struggle to establish aboriginal land rights. (See report on Indians of Canada, page 67.)

INTERNATIONAL AFFAIRS

Canada's peacekeeping efforts in 1973 reflected the active and constructive role in world affairs first developed for Canada by former Prime Minister Louis St. Laurent in the late 1940's. The visits of Canadian leaders to China and the USSR in 1973 were seen as efforts to establish cordial relations with the national superpowers.

Peacekeeping. After the signing of the Vietnam peace treaty in Paris on January 27, the first contingent of Canadian soldiers and civilians left Montreal to join similar forces from Hungary, Poland, and Indonesia—the other members of the four-country International Commission of Control and Supervision (ICCS). They arrived in Saigon on January 29. Canada had established relations with the South Vietnamese government at Saigon, and, in

February, Canada formally recognized the government of North Vietnam.

On March 15, Mitchell Sharp, the Canadian minister for external affairs, and representatives of the Social Credit and New Democratic parties visited Saigon, where they heard that peacekeeping efforts were being blocked by noncooperation among the former combatants, as well as dissension and a lack of cooperation within the ICCS.

On April 7, four ICCS members, including one Canadian, were killed when their helicopter was shot down while on duty with the peacekeeping force. By late May the ineffectiveness of the effort had become so evident that Canada announced the withdrawal of its troops within 60 days. "We have come to the conclusion . . .," Sharp said, "that the Canadian concept of the functioning of the international commission has not been accepted and that it would be in the interest of all concerned if we were now to withdraw." The external affairs minister also expressed the belief that Canadian withdrawal would not have "any significant effect upon prospects for peace in Vietnam."

By October 30, Canada found itself once again involved in a peacekeeping exercise. On that date External Affairs Minister Sharp announced that the Canadian government had agreed to provide support for the United Nations Emergency Force (UNEF) in the Middle East. The purpose of the UNEF was to supervise implementation of the United Nations Security Council resolutions calling on Israeli and Egyptian combatants to move back to cease-fire lines established on October 22, after fighting had broken out between Israel and Arab nations on October 6. By year-end, Canada had sent more than 1,000 men, together with equipment, to the Middle East. On this peacekeeping mission the Canadian government had greater support from the various political parties and the public than had been evidenced in the Vietnam mission, but some doubt was cast on the effectiveness of the UNEF efforts in the face of big-power aid to the combatants.

Foreign Visits. In October, Prime Minister and Mrs. Trudeau made a 10-day visit to China. The meeting between Trudeau and Chairman Mao Tse-tung in Peking on October 13 occurred on the third anniversary of the recognition agreement between the two countries. At a banquet on October 11, Premier Chou En-lai referred to Trudeau—who had visited China as a private citizen in 1960—as "our old friend." During the visit, it was agreed that consulates would be opened in the cities of Vancouver and Canton.

In November, External Affairs Minister Sharp spent some time in the USSR, talking with Soviet leaders. During discussions with Soviet Foreign Minister Andrei A. Gromyko, the Middle East situation was given particular attention.

Neither of these visits produced spectacular results. They were used instead as occasions for commercial and cultural agreements, including a three-year trade agreement with China, that probably would have been reached in the normal course of international relations. But the feeling was widespread in Canada that the establishment of cordial relations with the national superpowers might make it easier to discuss divergent views and misunderstandings and thus make spectacular agreements unnecessary.

W. A. McKAY
University of Toronto

CANADA • Information Highlights

Official Name: Canada.

Location: Northern North America.

Area: 3,851,809 square miles (9,976,185 sq km).

Population (June 1973 est.): 22,095,000. *Density,* 5 per square mile (2 per sq km).

Chief Cities (1971 census): Ottawa, the capital, 302,341; Montreal, 1,214,352; Toronto, 712,786; Edmonton, 438,-152; Vancouver, 426,256.

Government: *Head of state,* Elizabeth II, queen (represented by Jules Léger, governor-general; took office Jan. 1974). *Head of government,* Pierre Elliott Trudeau, prime minister (took office April 1968). *Legislature—* Parliament: Senate and House of Commons. *Major political parties*—Liberal; Progressive Conservative; New Democratic; Social Credit.

Languages: English, French (both official).

Education: *Expenditure* (1969), 8.9% of gross national product. *Public school enrollment* (1972)—primary (grades 1–6), 2,746,722; secondary (grades 7–12), 2,-511,667; university/higher, 478,413.

Monetary Unit: Canadian dollar (0.9990 C. dollar equals U. S.$1, Sept. 1973).

Gross National Product (3d quarter 1973 est.): $119,008,-000,000.

Economic Indexes: *Industrial production* (Oct. 1973), 211.6 (1961=100); *agricultural production* (1972), 150.5 (1961=100); *consumer price index* (Oct. 1973), 154.3 (1961=100).

Manufacturing (major products): Pulp and paper, petroleum products, iron and steel, motor vehicles, aircraft, machinery and equipment, aluminum, chemicals.

Major Agricultural Products: Barley (ranks 2d among world producers, 1972), oats (world rank 3d, 1972), wheat.

Major Minerals: Nickel (ranks 1st among world producers, 1971), asbestos (world rank 1st, 1971), silver (world rank 1st, 1971), gold (world rank 3d, 1971), iron ore.

Foreign Trade (1972): *Exports,* $19,977,000,000. *Imports,* $18,654,000,000. *Chief trading partners* (1972)—United States (took 70% of exports, supplied 69% of imports); United Kingdom (6.6%—5.1%).

Tourism: Receipts (1972), $1,226,000,000.

Transportation: *Motor vehicles* (1971), 8,823,200 (automobiles, 6,967,200); *railroads* (1971), 43,983 miles (70,-782 km); *merchant fleet* (1972), 2,381,000 gross registered tons; *major national airlines,* Air Canada; CP Air.

Communications: *Telephones* (1972), 10,290,305; *newspapers* (1971), 115 (daily circulation, 4,605,000).

(All monetary figures given in Canadian dollars.)

LES GRANDS BALLETS CANADIENS

LES GRANDS BALLETS CANADIENS, of Montreal, in a scene from Tchaikovsky's The Nutcracker, *choreographed by Canadian Fernand Nault.*

CANADA: CULTURAL AFFAIRS

The 1973 cultural scene in Canada is reviewed in this article. It consists of the following sections: (1) general survey, including the theater, film, music, dance, and the visual arts; (2) Canadian literature; and (3) French Canadian literature.

General Survey

In 1973, Canadian cultural activity reflected an all-round steady growth in the nation. There was some concern over the inflation spiral, which increased expenses more rapidly than the box-offices could increase revenues. However, the pumping of public funds into the deficit areas provided timely aid in most instances. The federal government's cultural spending was close to $400 million. In addition, all of the Canadian provinces boosted their contributions to the cultural pot, with the apparent approval of the taxpayers. In a speech in September, André Fortier, director of the Canada Council, which oversees the country's cultural affairs, said, "Three quarters of Canada's population are now within reach of professional theatres and concert halls, making the performing arts as democratic in terms of audience as professional sport."

Parochialism Versus Internationalism. The usually placid Canadian cultural scene was disturbed in mid-October when 14 eminent French Canadian producers boycotted the celebration of the 25th anniversary of Canadian Film Awards. The action was in keeping with the incipient, possibly malignant, cultural nationalism that is spreading throughout the country. Throughout 1973, in various parts of Canada, there was a notable increase of bitter talk about the alleged baleful influence of "foreigners." In Quebec, for example, a minority separatist feeling is

directed against anything not specifically French-Canadian oriented. However, while the views of the cultural parochialists are important and often get the headlines, the internationalists are predominant and evidently content with what "foreigners" are doing in the Canadian cultural milieu. In 1973, Canadian audiences in sell-out numbers welcomed such non-Canadian attractions as the Leningrad Philharmonic Orchestra, the Melos Quartett from Stuttgart, Spanish guitarist Mario Escudero, the Zen Buddhist Orchestra from Japan, the Bolshoi Ballet, the Katakali Theatre from India, the Ivory Coast Dancers, and Marcel Marceau from France.

Theater. Canadian theater in 1973 rode the crest of moderate inflation. Expenses were very high, the box-office was very good, and government grants were very generous. In February, the Stratford Festival Company achieved notable success with its first European tour, playing in Poland, the Soviet Union, Denmark, the Netherlands, and Britain. The company's home season was successful both artistically and financially, with advance ticket sales surpassing the million-dollar mark for the first time. The Festival Theatre featured Shakespeare's *The Taming of the Shrew, Othello,* and *Pericles,* and Goldsmith's *She Stoops to Conquer.* The smaller Avon Theatre performed Turgenev's *A Month in the Country* and Gogol's *The Marriage Brokers.*

Nearby in Niagara-on-the-Lake, Canada's Shaw Festival Theatre enjoyed a rousing first season in its new $3 million building, opened in June by Queen Elizabeth. The house was filled to 97% of capacity for 118 performances of three productions.

The National Art Centre Theatre in Ottawa was also well attended, as was the Citadel Theatre in Edmonton. In Quebec City, Le Grand Théâtre played to 395,000 patrons, a 36% increase over the 1972 opening year. Toronto's two well-established the-

158

aters, the free-enterprise Royal Alex and the subsidized St. Lawrence Centre, enjoyed a good season. A great deal of local attention was directed to the Toronto Free Theatre's offerings of Canadian plays. Also successful was the popular Neptune Theatre in Halifax, which offered a mature and varied bill ranging from *Hedda Gabler* to *Charlie Brown.*

On the negative side, many people were disappointed by the closing, in May, of the Canadian Theatre Centre, a helping agency for the whole theater business in Canada. Founded in 1956, it had been effective in setting up the successful National Theatre School in Montreal and Toronto and in developing many other advantages for Canada's burgeoning theater. Policy differences between Anglophones and Francophones were largely responsible for the phasing-out of the operation.

Film. There were several notable film events. The First International Festival of Films on the Human Environment was held for four days in Montreal, with 400 films entered from 25 countries. After 10 years of inactivity, the Stratford Film Festival was revived successfully. The 25th anniversary celebration of Canadian Film Awards in October was marred by Canadian internal squabbles. In the same month, the private Canadian Film Institute sponsored FILMEXPO, a fortnight of film shows of the past. One week of FILMEXPO was devoted to Canadian entries, the other to international offerings.

Music. In 1973 music enjoyed a customary good year from Newfoundland to the Northwest Territories. The most newsworthy event was the 25th anniversary of the Canadian Opera Company. Wagner's *Die Götterdämmerung,* Verdi's *Rigoletto,* Beethoven's *Fidelio,* Lehár's *The Merry Widow,* and Rossini's *The Barber of Seville* were produced with great artistic and financial success. The company also won high praise for its world premiere performance on September 8, in Toronto, of *Heloise and Abelard* by Charles Wilson of London, Ontario. In Hamilton, Ontario, the opening of an $11 million art center in September was highlighted by a stunning premiere of *A Contemporary Mass* by the popular composer Galt MacDermot. Toronto's Louis Applebaum was commissioned to compose a major orchestral fanfare for the opening of the center.

In early summer, the new Ottawa-based National Arts Centre Orchestra made a five-week tour of the Soviet Union, Poland, Italy, the Netherlands, and Britain. The tour was very successful, reinforcing a growing Canadian national pride in the group. In June, the annual Mariposa Folk Festival drew big crowds to Toronto's Centre Island. The audiences seemed pleased with the offering of 150 concerts and workshops.

Dance. Canada's three major ballet companies were all handsomely subsidized in 1973. Nonetheless, Montreal's accomplished Les Grands Ballets Canadiens had problems during the year as a result of the familiar performing arts syndrome—expanding costs and stable box-office. The group received $330,000 from the federal coffers and $75,000 from the city. It requested $800,000 from the Quebec provincial treasury and received $200,000. Despite a rewarding artistic season it finished the season with some financial difficulty.

The immensely successful Royal Winnipeg Ballet, a group of classical dancers who thrive on fun and spoofs and who have toured in many parts of the world, entertained a quarter of a million people in the home season. They made a smash hit of their new rock-ballet, *What to Do Till the Messiah Comes.* The Toronto-based National Ballet Company did well at home and abroad with its traditional, basically conservative repertoire.

Modern dance is developing a large and loyal audience in Canada, and modern dance groups had a successful year in all the provinces. La Groupe de la Place Royale, of Montreal; the Contemporary Dancers, of Winnipeg; and the Toronto Dance Theatre are among the best-known and most admired modern dance ensembles. The popular variety and folk dance group, the Feux Follets company of Quebec province, pulled up stakes and settled down at a new permanent base at the Confederation Centre in Charlottetown, P. E. I.

Visual Arts. In 1973 one of the most interesting events in the field of visual arts was a non-happening—the temporary shutdown of the Montreal Museum of Fine Arts. Because the many activities of the MMFA, one of Canada's great galleries, could no longer be encompassed by its stodgy 1860 building, a $6 million, two-year face-lifting job was approved and begun in May 1973. The museum's directors launched a unique public relations program, designed to keep the institution's public image bright. Instead of storing MMFA treasures in warehouses during the shutdown, the directors decided to lend art works periodically to other galleries throughout Canada. The MMFA achieved excellent publicity, and a safe, productive sharing of important art works was ensured.

Early in 1973 the Canada Council Art Bank announced its first purchases—1,100 works by 194 Canadian artists at a total cost of $670,000. These works, including paintings, graphics, sculptures, and ceramics, are rented by the Art Bank to federal gov-

THE CANADIAN OPERA COMPANY staged world premiere of new opera, Heloise and Abelard, *in September. Allan Monk and Heather Thomson sang the title roles.*

ROYAL WINNIPEG BALLET dancers appear in What to Do Till the Messiah Comes, a new ballet choreographed by Norbert Vesak that was given its world premiere in January.

ROYAL WINNIPEG BALLET

ernment departments for display in public buildings. The idea is to provide financial and psychological help to artists and to encourage the purchasing of Canadian art by the private sector. The initial grant of $5 million, given the Art Bank by its parent, Canada Council, is to be used over a period of five years.

Miscellaneous. A great many miscellaneous happenings filled out the cultural mosaic in Canada in 1973. A long-overdue act by the federal government set up Heritage Canada, a multimillion-dollar national trust devoted to the preservation of major historic structures and natural beauty sites. At Saint-Tite, in Quebec, the world's only French-language rodeo and stampede was attended by 300,000 fans. The First Canadian Olympic Bash, celebrated in Toronto in May, was a joyful get-together of Canadian artists to promote interest in the 1976 Olympics to be held in Montreal. The Molson Prizes, worth $15,000 each and awarded annually by the Canada Council, were presented to Dr. John Deutsch, economist and principal of Queen's University; Alfred Pellan, a distinguished painter from Quebec; and George Woodcock, author and Vancouver University professor.

Personalities. Ottawa-born Bruce Swerdfager was named general manager of the Stratford Festival operations, succeeding William Wylie of Winnipeg, who died suddenly. Robin Phillips, an Englishman whose background includes experience with both the Royal Shakespeare Festival and the Chichester Festival, was appointed Stratford's artistic director. In an interesting juggling of posts, Hugh Davidson, chief musician of the National Arts Centre, switched jobs with Guy Huot, who had headed the music department of the Canada Council. Professor Richard Courtney of the University of Calgary was elected president of the prestigious Canadian Conference of the Arts. The Montreal Symphony Orchestra announced that its new director, beginning in 1975, would be Rafael de Burgos, currently director of the Madrid National Orchestra.

Obituaries. Several Canadians prominent in cultural affairs died in 1973. Among them were Peter Dwyer, former director of the Canada Council; Sir Ernest MacMillan, the "statesman of Canadian music"; Dr. Arnold Walter, long associated with the music faculty of the University of Toronto; and Kathleen Fenwick, curator of prints at the National Gallery of Canada.

WALTER B. HERBERT
Consultant on Canadian Cultural Matters

Canadian Literature

In 1973 a continuing concern for Canada, notably for the country's natural resources, was evident in many of the books that were published. It was hearteningly apparent also that Canadian books are steadily improving both in content and in appearance.

Public Affairs. In a year when Canada's politicians were deeply concerned with the international problems of oil shortages, energy crises, and pollution, Wade Rowland's *The Plot to Save the World* came as a timely reminder of what is at stake. The work, his third on environmental matters, describes the 1972 Stockholm Conference on the Human Environment, at which 114 nations met. *One Cosmic Instant,* subtitled *Men's Fleeting Supremacy,* by John A. Livingston tells how man has brought about the extinction of various animal and plant species. In *The Arctic Imperative,* Richard Rohmer looks at Canada's vast Arctic and sub-Arctic regions and pleads for planned development that does not upset the ecology. Farley Mowat's *Tundra* chronicles man's Arctic explorations and adventures. It is the third volume in his *Top of the World* trilogy.

French Canada and its problems inspired several books. In *Wanted: A Single Canada,* Joseph T. Thorson, head of the Single Canada League, speaks out for a single-language Canada, claiming that the concept of a dual French-English Canada disagrees with the original terms of the country's constitution. *Bilingualism and Biculturalism,* by Hugh R. Innis, is a clarified version of the report of the Canadian government's Royal Commission on these subjects. *Parti Québecois Manifesto* is an English translation by Pierre Bourgault of the radical Parti Québecois manifesto, which calls for virtual separation of Quebec from the rest of Canada. Historian Dale Thomson's *Quebec Society and Politics: Views from the Inside* is a collection of essays about Quebec by prominent thinkers from that province.

Biography and Autobiography. *Stanfield,* by Geoffrey Stevens, is a thorough study of Robert Stanfield, the leader of the Progressive Conservative party in Canada. Stevens, Ottawa correspondent of *Time,* is particularly interesting in his report of the leadership convention that ended John Diefenbaker's reign as party leader and launched Stanfield's. *Half-breed,* the autobiography of Maria Campbell, tells how a northern Saskatchewan half-breed Indian girl fought her way through poverty, prostitution, dope addiction, and alcoholism to survival and self-respect.

History. *Policy By Other Means: Essays in Honour of C. P. Stacey,* edited by Michael Cross, is a collection of historical essays honoring Canada's leading military historian. Betty Lee's two-volume *Love and Whisky* is a fine, highly readable history of the Dominion Drama Festival, and of Canadian drama generally. In *Voyage to the Edge of the World,* Alan Edmonds tells how, in 1970, the Canadian research ship *Hudson* became the first vessel to circumnavigate North and South America, Bernard Epps' *The Outlaw of Megantic* is the biography of Donald Morrison, who was a 19th century Canadian outlaw.

Poetry. F. R. Scott, still a master craftsman, produced his eighth volume of poetry, *The Dance Is One.* It contains new poems reflecting his celebrated wit and precision, and also includes some engaging translations of poetry from Quebec and France.

Lovers and Lesser Men further enhances the reputation of Irving Layton. Many of the poems are set in Greece, and their spirited, singing lines demonstrate that Layton, like Yeats, feels and expresses himself more passionately as he grows older.

George Bowering's *The Sensible* is a single romantic poem. Alfred G. Bailey selected his best poems, spanning a long career, in *Thanks for a Drowned Island.* Paul J. Marcotte's *Quebec Revisited and Other Poems* tells how an individual's old-fashioned search for salvation conflicts with the complexities of the modern world. *Waiting for Wayman* is the first volume of verse by Tom Wayman, a young poet, much of whose writing shows promise. Some of his poems are realistic and some are humorous. Louis Dudek edited *All Kinds of Everything,* a book of poetry for young people that is filled with happy choices.

Fiction. In her excellent fifth novel, *The Book of Eve,* Constance Beresford-Howe writes with skill, restraint, and rare authority about her heroine, Eva, who has just received her first old-age pension check and walks out on her sick but aggravating husband of 40 years. She leaves her home in Montreal's Notre Dame de Grâce section and starts a new and different life, one that contains love, in Montreal's east end.

Admirers of Alden Nowlan's volumes of fine poetry can now enjoy his first novel, *Various Persons Named Kevin O'Brien.* Nowlan has a poet's eye for detail, and his descriptions of the existence in a Nova Scotia village are true to life.

Jim Willer's *Paramind* is a chilling futuristic story about "Paramind," an incredibly complex electronic device that gives the world "electric government." Quebec writer Yves Theriault's two short novels, *Kesten* and *Cul De Sac,* translated by Gwendolyn Moore, were published in one volume. Christie Harris' 10th book, *Once More Upon a Totem Pole,* is another fine work of children's fiction.

Miscellaneous. *The Case Against the Drugged Mind,* by Andrew I. Malcolm, is a disturbing book. In it he speaks out strongly against the worsening of what was once called "the problem of drug abuse" but is now more often referred to as "the understandable fact of drug use."

Donald Waterfield's *Land Grab* tells how Oliver Buerge fought the British Columbia Hydro and Power Authority in a six-year court battle to get adequate compensation for his farm, which was flooded by the construction of the High Arrow water storage dam on the Columbia River.

A Vision of Canada, with text by art critic Paul Duval and designed by painter A. J. Casson, is a splendidly illustrated study of the McMichael Canadian Collection of art at Kleinburg, Ontario. Colin McCullough's *Stranger in China* is a journalist's first-hand view of China's Cultural Revolution.

Peter Such, in *Soundprints,* deals in lively fashion with six contemporary Canadian composers. Journalist Adrian Waller's *Guide to Music* has wit and charm. Adrian Waller also wrote *Theatre on a Shoestring,* a guide for amateur theater groups. *Window on the Sea,* with text by novelist Ernest Buckler and photographs by Hans Weber, is a sensitive portrayal of Nova Scotia's landscape and people.

DAVID SAVAGE, *Simon Fraser University*

FRENCH CANADIAN LITERATURE

Theater remained in the forefront of French-Canadian literature in 1973. Remarkably, the year's greatest literary success was *La Sagouine,* a monologue by Antoine Maillet; it owes as much to the novel as to the drama. Of the other playwrights who published during the year, one must acknowledge André Ricard (*Alcide 1ᵉʳ*) and Dominique de Pasquale (*Oui, Chef* and *Larme à l'oeil ou l'arme au poing*). At present, the theater seems to be the place where the Quebecois rediscover themselves— or their image.

Poetry. The poets are muted, but they have not disappeared. Proof of this is *La Main au feu,* the recent collection of Roland Giguère, one of the best of the living French-language poets. The heir of surrealism and automatism, he traces his own path by way of a completely personal symbolism. The young Michel Beaulieu, with *Variables,* seems to be reinvigorating lyricism, while re-creating rhythms.

Fiction. The year's literary high point was undoubtedly the return of André Langevin to the novel, with *L'Élan d'Amérique.* The novel's complex psychological universe links it, in a way, with Faulkner's works, whereas Langevin's previous novels related more to surrealism. The playwright Michel Tremblay published a novel, *C'ta Ton Tour, Laura Cadieux,* but it was more or less a dramatic theme transposed into novelistic form. Tremblay's style, which is too deliberately popular, is disappointing.

Marie-Claire Blais' novel, *Un Joualonais, sa joualonie,* was scarcely a success. Roch Carrier, in *Le 2 Millième Étage,* describes a group of tenants resisting demolitionists. Although amusing, it lacks the tragic dimension that strengthened his previous works. *Les Princes,* by Jacques Benoit, offered a theme new to French Canadian literature: a story of dogs in a realistic and fantastic setting.

Nonfiction. Jean-Marie Poupart wrote a tonic essay, *Les Récréants.* Unacademic, it discusses various literary problems, particularly the technique of the detective story.

Three other essays were remarkable. In *Indépendances,* Pierre Vadeboncoeur questions the spirit of the system and deciphers the language of the counterculture. Jean Éthier-Blais, in *Signets III,* examines, through literary works, the situation of French Canadians. But his rather haughty (and conservative) approach is very different from that of Jean Bouthillette, who, in *Le Canadien français et son double,* illuminates without condescension the nature of Quebec's relations with English-speaking Canada.

ANDRÉ MAJOR, *Literary Critic, Montreal*

CARIBBEAN

Agricultural production in the Caribbean Islands, notably that of sugar, continued to decline in 1973. With the unstable situation in the Middle East, oil extracted from and refined in the Caribbean area took on increased industrial and economic importance. Important steps were taken during the year toward the integration of regional economies with the formation of the Caribbean Common Market, effective in August 1973.

On the political side of the spectrum, several of the smaller polities of the region took initial steps on the road to full independence. In an unprecedented move, the prime ministers of Trinidad and Tobago, Guyana, Jamaica, and Barbados met with Cuban Premier Fidel Castro as a first step in establishing diplomatic relations as well as pooling some of their common interests.

Agriculture. The spring months in the Caribbean are usually dry. In 1973, however, the drought extended well into the middle of summer. For the second year in a row, summer tropical storms were very infrequent. The Lesser Antilles, from Trinidad north, felt the worst effects of the drought. The Greater Antilles, from Puerto Rico westward, received some relief from occasional heavy rains related to storm patterns moving northward across and out of the Caribbean.

Sugar output dropped in Trinidad, Barbados, St. Kitts, and Antigua, but the Dominican Republic registered a slight increase. Cuba's output also increased. Its estimated production for 1973 was put at slightly more than 5 million tons. In Puerto Rico, the drought forced the closing of the last privately owned and operated sugar *central* as production on that island dropped to 3.6 million tons.

Industry. As a result of the current scarcity of oil and the constantly growing demand for it, petroleum and its by-products are playing an increasingly important role in the industrial sector of the economies of the Caribbean communities. Refineries are scattered throughout the Caribbean from Trinidad north to Antigua and eastward from St. Croix to Cuba. There are also refineries on Curaçao and Aruba, two offshore islands near South America.

Petroleum products are being shipped more and more frequently in enormous supertankers. Consequently, the islands have been pressed into providing enlarged port facilities which can accommodate ships hauling 500,000 tons of crude oil. Designs for the construction of such superports were being planned by Puerto Rico on the small offshore island of Mona and by the Bahamas on Grand Bahama Island. Tentative plans for such ports were also discussed in the Dominican Republic, Haiti, and Jamaica. These schemes were being undertaken over the vehement protests of ecologists and conservationists, who fear the impact of such industrial development on the islands' beaches and coral reefs.

Politics. The Bahamas became independent of Britain in July (see BAHAMAS). A number of other small Caribbean islands explored the possibilities of achieving full independence. Eric Gairy, premier of Grenada, was in London in July to secure a firm date for the granting of independence to his people. February 1974 was the date agreed upon. However, there was opposition to this step. In Antigua, Premier George Walter announced its intention of bringing independence to that island, although no target date had been set by year's end. Walter also faces growing opposition to this plan.

The six islands of the Netherlands Antilles, which with Surinam and the Netherlands form the tripartite Kingdom of the Netherlands, are being moved reluctantly toward independence by the Netherlands. The announced projected date for independence is 1975. The three principal islands, Aruba, Bonaire, and Curaçao, lie just off the coast of Venezuela. Most of the population of the island of Aruba, as well as some inhabitants of Bonaire and Curaçao, came at one time or another from Venezuela. Perhaps as a result, the inhabitants of the Netherlands Antilles speak not only Dutch and English, but also Papiamento, a creole dialect, which is closely related to Spanish. The economy of these islands is closely related to the refining of Venezuelan crude oil. In 1973, a four-hour ferry service joined the islands with the Venezuelan coast, assuring even closer social and economic ties.

Relations with Cuba and the African States. Political history was made in the Caribbean when, at the end of August, the prime ministers of the English-speaking Commonwealth nations of Barbados, Trinidad and Tobago, Jamaica, and Guyana met with Prime Minister Fidel Castro of Cuba. They had taken the initiative in opening up formal diplomatic relations with Cuba. The occasion for this minisummit was provided by the intention of some of these prime ministers to attend the conference of nonaligned nations in Algiers in September.

One concrete result of the meeting was the agreement to allow Cuba to use the commercial airports of Trinidad, Barbados, and Guyana in working out a route that would link Cuba and these nations with the nations of Africa. A closer relationship with the nations of Africa seemed to be a major common interest of the minisummit participants. Closer ties between the black states of the Caribbean and the African nations came closer to fruition with the offer made at Algiers by Prime Minister Michael Manley of Jamaica to send volunteer fighters from Jamaica and Guyana to the Organization of African Unity, which is spearheading the struggle to free the remaining colonial territories in Africa.

Cuba's ties with the rest of the Caribbean were further strengthened by the visit of a group of sugar technicians to the island. They went to Cuba to explain a new process whereby animal feed can be produced from sugar cane stalk refuse.

Violence and Political Unrest. Many of the small islands of the Caribbean were the scene of violence and political unrest. St. Croix in the Virgin Islands witnessed the murders of numerous victims of racial tension from 1972 through late 1973. In Trinidad, a small guerrilla force has operated in the northern mountain range for almost a year. Guerrilla invasions of the Dominican Republic and Haiti kept the military forces in both countries occupied for several weeks. In Haiti, President Jean-Claude Duvalier, installed for life, took advantage of the opportunity provided by the defeat of the guerrilla forces to carry out a major reshuffling of some 49 top government officials.

Only one election was held in the Caribbean in 1973 and that was on the tiny island of Montserrat. Chief Minister Austin Bramble called for the election even though he and his party, which controlled all seven seats of the legislature, still had two more years to govern. Bramble and his party were kept in power.

Regional Cooperation. In 1973, after five years of successful operation, the Caribbean Free Trade Association (CARIFTA) took an important forward step. At a preliminary meeting held in April in Georgetown, Guyana, 10 heads of member governments, all of English-speaking nations, tentatively agreed to the creation of a Caribbean Economic Community or Caribbean Common Market (CARICOM). On July 4, the heads of the four largest English-speaking states, Trinidad and Tobago, Barbados, Jamaica, and Guyana, meeting at Chaguaramas Bay in Trinidad, signed a 52-page document marking the creation of a common market composed of their nations. Representatives of six smaller states in the Caribbean requested a year's delay before entering into the agreement, which went into effect in August 1973. Antigua refused to consider joining the Caribbean Common Market because it feared an adverse effect on its economy through the subsequent loss of revenues from tariffs.

The agreement provided for a common tariff policy and a uniform policy of industrial incentives among participating members. Among the other subjects of agreement that were outlined were shipping, air transportation, health, travel, and labor relations. It is quite possible that the Bahamas, Belize, and even Antigua may also be incorporated into the Caribbean Economic Community by May 1974 when the six smaller states join the organization. The new organization is a tribute to the successful management of CARIFTA, which can now be seen as having been a preliminary stage in the formation of the Caribbean Common Market.

Dr. William Demas, the secretary general of CARIFTA and the guiding spirit behind the formation of the Caribbean Common Market, apparently feeling that his mission had been accomplished, announced his intention to resign his post. His announcement aroused opposition among the heads of member governments who felt that Demas was needed to guide the new Common Market.

Another important announcement of a resignation from a major regional organization was made by Dr. W. Arthur Lewis, president of the Caribbean Development Bank. Dr. Lewis, who was the bank's first president, plans to return to Princeton University. After only four years of operation, the Caribbean Development Bank has capital amounting to over $65 million. Almost half of this capital comes from the United States, slightly more than one third comes from Canada and Britain, and the remainder comes from Colombia, Venezuela, and West Germany. The impact that the workings of the bank have on the Caribbean region is still to be measured.

THOMAS G. MATHEWS, *University of Puerto Rico*

CASALS, Pablo. See OBITUARIES.
CATHOLIC CHURCH. See RELIGION.

CENSORSHIP

The greatest exercise of censorship by government in the United States continued to be censorship at the source, the withholding of information from the public by officials largely working in the federal executive branch. The Nixon administration is counted the most closed administration—and covertly punitive—in recent decades by organizations and students of press-government relations.

The absolute right of a President to withhold information from Congress, the courts, and the people on plea of executive privilege, as variously guaranteed by some readings of the Constitution, was uniquely tested in 1973 when a federal district court ordered President Nixon to deliver materials thought to contain evidence bearing on investigation of possible criminal acts by administration officials and supporters. An appellate court rejected an administration effort to have the order dismissed. After insisting that he would not do so, President Nixon acceded to the court's order. (See special report on Watergate, page 14.)

The new Reporters Committee for Freedom of the Press detailed in its second "press censorship newsletter" 14 major instances of federal efforts to restrict news coverage.

Congress unearthed a noteworthy instance of secrecy in the deliberate falsification of records of bombing missions in Southeast Asia where, despite government assurances to the contrary, the government had mounted a 14-month secret bombing campaign against Communist targets in Cambodia.

Scholars, consumers, and conservationists increasingly turned to the courts as provided in the Freedom of Information Act to gain the right to see materials they thought improperly kept secret by governmental agencies. The results were mixed.

Noting that the act exempted disclosures that might affect national security, the Supreme Court ruled that "Congress, not the court . . . has ordained unquestionable deference to the Executive's use of the 'secret' stamp." In issue was the attempt of 33 members of Congress to see certain documents about an underground nuclear test on Amchitka Island. An appeals court had earlier ordered a lower court to review the materials to determine if any nonsecret sections could be separated. The Supreme Court held there could be no such inspection.

When a scholar tried to force open Federal Bureau of Investigation files compiled for law enforcement purposes, a Supreme Court ruling effectively placed the files beyond public inspection.

Victories in removal of the secrecy stamp were not of the dimensions of the defeats. A public interest law firm did force public release of private rulings, records occurring when a taxpayer challenges decisions of the Internal Revenue Service. Pleas that items sought were properly withheld under terms of the act relating to internal office memoranda did not avail agencies trying to keep secret manuals to employees carrying information concerning policies affecting the puplic.

The Interagency Classification Review Committee announced in March that over a 9-month period the number of persons authorized to classify documents was reduced by 64% and that 28 million documents had either lost their secrecy stamp or been scheduled for release sooner than intended at time of classification. Legislation has been proposed to guarantee nondisclosure of materials surviving review by the committee. Congress has received a bill that would revise the Federal Criminal Code. Jail sentences of from three to five years and fines of from $25,000 to $50,000 would face officials leaking information, coworkers who knew of but did not report the act, reporters who did not report the act and turn over the material to the government, and newspaper or broadcast officials who participated in making the unauthorized information public. Passage of the bill remains highly uncertain.

Administration vs. the Media. Antagonism of the Nixon administration toward the press has been much noted. Leakage of high-level inter-office memoranda has revealed administration plans and proposals to harass and intimidate the media. These papers as well as announcements by the President and his assistants indicate the administration's concern with the networks' handling of news and documentaries. Clay Whitehead, director of the White House's Office of Telecommunications Policy, seemed to be suggesting bargaining when he held out the tempting offer of longer, even permanent, broadcast franchises to stations if the networks could be brought to a level of greater responsibility and accuracy in news coverage.

To several public interest groups, White House pressure on government-funded television reached a point by mid-1973 that justified a charge of censorship of programing of the Corporation of Public Broadcasting. The groups filed a lawsuit in May asking that public television programing for the fiscal year 1974 be rescinded on grounds that it was tainted by the White House and that funds be distributed to production centers and local stations to avoid government interference or intimidation.

In a rare case in which the government sought to impose prior restriction on publication, the authors and the intended publisher of a book on the Central Intelligence Agency fought to keep intact a substantial section that the agency sought to expunge. The Supreme Court declined to review an appellate court ruling that the CIA is privileged to delete classified materials from the book because the co-author, a former employee, had taken an oath of secrecy as a condition of employment.

Pornography. In a series of 5–4 decisions, the Supreme Court agreed in 1973 on "concrete guidelines to isolate 'hard core' pornography from expression protected by the First Amendment." Dissenting justices viewed the decision as an invitation to "state-ordered regimentation of our minds." The court left the determination of obscenity to the "average" person and what he understands of the standards of morality of his community. As a result, many state legislatures and municipal councils moved back into an area of control they had all but given up and began writing new obscenity statutes and ordinances.

Publishers and film-makers were perplexed by the decisions, which were appealed. They argued that what one community will accept as legitimate candor in expression will be rejected by another, and that books and movies made safe from challenge by any community will often lack substance.

Censorship in Court. Trial courts are continuing the practice of limiting information by direct order of silence to defense lawyers, prosecutors, and police officials and by limiting access of reporters to the proceedings. The practice has culminated in orders, contested by two networks, forbidding artists to sketch courtroom scenes either in the courtroom or from memory outside it.

Generally, such orders will be held unconstitutional on appeal. A federal appellate court ruled that the trial judge exceeded constitutional bounds in ordering two Baton Rouge, La., newsmen not to report an injunction hearing. However, the appellate court also ruled that reporters should obey court orders of silence even where there is a strong presumption of unconstitutionality and should seek redress through the appeals procedure.

The Media and Society. While civil liberties groups continued to assail the media for self-censorship, special interest groups continued to fault them for not properly policing themselves. Despite the threat of boycott by lay religious groups, the Columbia Broadcasting System (CBS) reran an episode of a comedy (*Maude*) using abortion as a theme. However, many of the network's affiliates yielded to outside pressure and dropped the rerun. Civil liberties groups called that action an "insidious" abridgement of press freedom.

CBS decided not to show as scheduled the critically acclaimed anti-Vietnam War play, *Sticks and Bones,* while U. S. prisoners of the war were being repatriated. When the network later made the play available, a majority of its affiliates refused to pick it up and no advertiser supported it.

Censorship: World View. By all yardsticks, censorship exists in most countries. A Freedom House study of 151 countries, updated in mid-1973, found less than a third to be free of governmental controls; only Gambia in Africa and only Israel and Lebanon in the Middle East enjoyed freedom.

In its annual summary (January 1973) the International Press Institute (IPI) looked back on "a year of lost battles." By IPI's assessment barely one out of five countries could claim freedom of information. The most serious infringement by government on press freedom, the institute reported, had occurred in the Philippines where "the most courageous and frank press in Asia" has been silenced. In midyear the IPI adopted five resolutions deploring the status of press freedom, singling out for special notice conditions in the Philippines, Singapore, Sri Lanka, Chile, and Greece.

The Inter-American Press Association's annual review of conditions in the Western Hemisphere found total press censorship in Cuba and Haiti. Extensive controls were exerted by Panama, Paraguay, Brazil, Chile, Peru, Ecuador, and Uruguay.

PAUL FISHER
Director, Freedom of Information Center
University of Missouri

CENTRAL AMERICA

Still reeling from the devastation wrought by the earthquake that leveled the capital of Nicaragua on Dec. 23, 1972, Central America suffered additional natural calamities in 1973, including a severe drought. Political maneuvering looking to elections in 1974 attracted some attention in Guatemala and Costa Rica, while the shaky condition of the once-promising Central American Common Market was of concern not only in those two republics but also in the three other nations—Honduras, Nicaragua, and El Salvador—that had banded together in 1961 to create this regional economic community.

(For developments in the Republic of Panama, see PANAMA.)

Regional Economic Problems. The 1973 drought, the most prolonged in 30 years, affected all of Central America and caused the worst agricultural crisis there in half a century. Resulting losses, estimated at more than $100 million, forced the five republics to import basic foodstuffs and reduced the production of sugar, a major source of export earnings in the area, by about 60%.

The future of the Central American Common Market (CACM), which had been disrupted by the brief war between Honduras and El Salvador in

CENTRAL AMERICA—Information Highlights

Nation	Population (in millions)	Area (in sq mi)	Capital	Head of State and/or Government
Costa Rica	2.0	19,575	San José	José Figueres Ferrer, president
El Salvador	3.8	8,260	San Salvador	Arturo Armando Molina, president
Guatemala	5.6	42,042	Guatemala City	Carlos Arana Osorio, president
Honduras	3.0	43,277	Tegucigalpa	Gen. Oswaldo López Arellano, president
Nicaragua	2.2	50,193	Managua	Roberto Martínez Lacayo, Alfonso Lovo Cordero, Edmondo Paguaga Irias, governing council

1969, remained in doubt in 1973. Honduras, which had withdrawn from the market in 1970, did not participate in an August 1973 meeting at which market problems were discussed, and one of the four remaining members, Costa Rica, appeared to be contemplating withdrawal due to unfavorable balances in its Central American trade. Meanwhile, the increase in bilateral trade agreements between Central American republics in 1973 indicated the evolution of a possible substitute arrangement for the CACM.

Nicaragua. The destruction of the Nicaraguan capital, Managua, on Dec. 23, 1972, affected life in that country throughout 1973. Some 6,000 persons had been killed during the earthquake, and 20,000 injured. More than half the city's population of 300,000 was made homeless, and about 90% of Managua's business capacity was obliterated, a loss that was reflected in a 1973 decline of 40% in government income. This decline added to the burden of the huge reconstruction costs facing the republic.

After declaring martial law and partially evacuating the city, the government began the task of rebuilding Managua. Special agencies were established to coordinate the work and to function under the guidance of the country's most prestigious political figure, Gen. Anastasio Somoza Debayle. (Somoza, a former president, was expected to resume that office after the ratification of a new constitution in 1974.) After some argument, it was decided that Managua was to be rebuilt at its present site. Somoza estimated that the massive effort would require 10 years, and that it might take two years to complete the necessary demolition work.

Some evidence of progress was to be seen in 1973. Managua's schools, for example, were reopened in June, and most basic services were restored before the end of the year. On the other hand, some phases of the program were obviously lagging, and this provided fuel for political debate over the pace of reconstruction.

The rebuilding effort received considerable assistance from outside sources, both governmental and private. The government of the United States and other nations, the Inter-American Development Bank, the Organization of American States, and many private groups, such as the Wisconsin Partners of the Americas, provided food and supplies, technical assistance, and financial aid. Industrial corporations also made substantial contributions.

Costa Rica. On April 14, 1973, Costa Rica experienced its own earthquake. Though less devastating than the Managua quake, it registered 6.7 on the Richter scale, killed at least a score of people, and virtually destroyed several small towns northeast of the capital city of San José. Losses were estimated at more than $15 million.

Costa Rica was also hard hit by the drought, which further reduced its rice and corn crops, and, paradoxically, by floods in the banana-growing regions, which severely damaged that export crop. The Costa Rican economy in 1973 faced a serious imbalance of trade and an escalating inflation. The cost of living was estimated to have risen by about 20% during the year, with the cost of basic food items rising at an especially rapid pace.

Despite such economic problems and a minor scandal arising from President José Figueres Ferrer's personal and financial connection with Robert Vesco, the international financier implicated in the U. S. Watergate affair, the Figueres-backed candidate in the upcoming Costa Rican elections appeared to face little serious opposition.

Guatemala. In Guatemala too, opposition parties seemed to be entering the 1974 electoral campaign with little chance of success. Brig. Gen. Kjell Laugerud García not only had the endorsement of incumbent President Carlos Arana Osorio but was running as the coalition candidate of two major parties, the Institutional Democratic party (PID) and the National Liberation Movement (MLN).

Economically, Guatemala seemed the most fortunate Central American republic in 1973, with a booming economy, due mainly to record export prices for bananas, coffee, meat, and sugar. The Central Bank of Guatemala recorded the highest monetary reserve level in the nation's history, and outside investors were finding the country attractive.

El Salvador. Economic advances in El Salvador were less dramatic, but some significant gains were registered, particularly in the mounting of long-range projects. In January 1973 a $38 million loan was obtained from the Inter-American Development Bank. This was augmented in May with a $27 million loan from the World Bank to assist construction of a geothermal power plant and expand electrical facilities in El Salvador. Economic growth was also promoted by a number of other grants, including one to develop irrigation facilities and agricultural opportunities in the north.

Honduras. The government of Honduras operated through 1973 under the leadership of Gen. Oswaldo López Arellano, who had overthrown the constitutionally elected regime of Ramón Ernesto Cruz in a bloodless coup on Dec. 4, 1972. Long a dominant figure in Honduras, López had seized power once before in 1963. He had named himself president in 1965, and had served until 1971. The lack of real resistance to his new assumption of presidential power was due in great measure to exasperation with the Cruz government, a two-party coalition regime too divided to act decisively.

Economic planning in Honduras continued to lay stress on the expansion of the nation's road network. An $18 million loan, the sixth of a series of such loans, was granted by the World Bank to help finance a four-year highway construction and improvement project, the ultimate aim of which was to open new lands to agriculture and forestry.

ROBERT L. PETERSON
University of Texas at El Paso

CEYLON. See SRI LANKA.

CHEMISTRY

In 1973, the American Chemical Society published a 600-page report entitled "Chemistry in the Economy." The publication, resulting from a 3-year study and announced in Congress, helped to bring into focus the far-reaching social and economic changes brought about by chemical science and technology. One notable change was toward a life-style of convenience encouraged by petrochemicals, made into convenience items such as plastics, wash-and-wear textiles, and detergents.

Fuel. With shortages of natural gas and petroleum developing in 1973, the $20 billion petrochemical industry faced shortages of raw materials, which were either used for motor fuels or shipped abroad where prices were higher. One manufacturer of disposable laboratory ware said his supplies of styrene were cut nearly in half. Some firms reground polystyrene; but prices of this scrap rose more than 600%. Automobile makers, too, felt a shortage of materials for making plastic parts and items such as vinyl seat covers.

Some countries faced with fuel shortages, notably India, built bio-gas plants to convert sewage and animal wastes to fertilizer and methane, a fuel gas. In the United States the process aroused little interest, but in 1973, *The Mother Earth News* announced the successful operation of a bio-gas plant on an Indiana farm. The methane produced was burned in a gas stove and gas lights and was also used as fuel for a stationary automobile engine. Another plant in progress is intended to supply a gas range, gas lights, refrigerator, space and water heaters, and an automobile engine. The gas is said to be usable directly from the plant or could be compressed and stored for later use.

Pollution. A study by the U. S. Geological Survey indicated that each year some 2.5 million tons of chemicals are washed down by rain and snow over New England alone. For example, it was estimated that 11 pounds of calcium fall on each square mile of the region each day. Other estimates on a pounds-per-square-mile-per-day basis are magnesium, 2; potassium, 3; sodium, 5; chlorides, 9; and sulfates, 76, about half of which is sulfuric acid.

Atmospheric sulfates in concentrations of 8 to 12 micrograms per cubic meter have been found to aggravate certain respiratory disorders, such as bronchitis and croup. Sulfates in the atmosphere exceed this range in the eastern United States, are about equal in the Midwest, and are lower in the West. Sulfates are formed from sulfur dioxide, which is formed during the burning of fossil fuels. Power plants are major offenders in sulfate pollution.

The environmental consequences of the dioxin TCDD, a very toxic compound known to cause birth defects in animals, was cause for concern. TCDD was found as a contaminant in the pesticides PCP and 2,4,5-T. PCP, or pentachlorophenol, was widely used as a replacement for mercury to control slime molds in paper-pulp manufacture, but when PCP is discharged to the environment it is as hazardous to aquatic life as mercury. PCP was also used as a fungicide and even in shampoos. Dioxins might be formed after these pesticides are discharged into the environment, and indications are that they can accumulate. In one test, 1 part per million was added to soil, and 350 days later 54% was still present.

Evidence continued to accumulate showing that man has added substantial quantities of mercury to the environment. Analysis of core samples containing dated layers of sediments taken from the Santa Barbara basin off the coast of California showed that mercury levels about 1,500 years ago were about 0.04 mg per kilogram of dry sediment. During the 19th century mercury levels increased to 0.06 mg, and since 1950 they have increased to about 0.12 mg. This finding supported previously reported data. For example, since 1950 the average annual deposition of mercury in the Greenland ice sheet is about double that deposited beginning about 800 B. C.

At least one scientist, Henry A. Schroeder of Dartmouth Medical School, who has spent 30 years analyzing trace metals, is concerned more about cadmium, lead, and nickel carbonyl in the environment than about mercury. He found that lead shortened the life span of animals, caused heart disease, and inhibited important enzyme activity. He also found that cadmium impaired enzyme function and caused high blood pressure. Significantly, in Japan, where there is more cadmium in the environment than in the United States, the leading cause of death is cerebral hemorrhage.

Ions. A scientist at the University of California at Berkeley suggested that air pollution causes malaise, tension, and irritability, as well as increased susceptibility to respiratory diseases. He proposed that atmospheric small ions—charged particles produced by cosmic rays from space or radioactivity in the earth's crust—react with pollutants in the air to form larger ions that are physiologically inert.

Small negative ions are thought to lower blood levels of the chemical serotonin and thus to produce a tranquilizing effect. In contrast, positive ions raise the serotonin level and increase reactivity. In fact, positive ions might be responsible for the notorious ill winds such as the foehn in Germany and the sharav in the Mideast that cause several disorders including tension, irritability, and quarrelsomeness. Israeli scientists compared meteorological conditions before, during, and after a sharav and found that although ion concentration increased from 1500 to 2600 per cubic centimeter, the positive to negative ratio, normally 1.2 to one, increased to 1.33 to one. Victims were relieved when allowed to breathe air charged with negative ions or given drugs that depressed serotonin production.

Helium. Helium, a scarce element, was the center of a court battle. The U. S. Department of the Interior wished to terminate contracts to buy and store helium in accordance with a conservation program initiated in 1960 when basic research programs were strong, the space age was in its infancy, and a scarcity of helium was feared. Helium is used for various specialized purging, pressurizing, and leak-detection applications; for underwater breathing atmospheres; and for very low temperature research. By 1973 the curtailment of research and space activities resulted in a surplus of helium and, with 35 billion cubic feet in storage, Interior said it had enough. However, some authorities said that termination of the conservation program would be short-sighted because new technology under development would require large quantities of helium. Some predicted uses included low-temperature power transmission and low-temperature magnetic levitation of transportation systems.

Polywater. The controversy that arose in 1969 when the Russian physicist B. V. Deryagin and associates claimed to have prepared a strange new com-

pound, called polywater or anomalous water, by condensing ordinary water into quartz or glass capillary tubes was resolved. After exhaustive testing, Deryagin himself admitted that the material was only water contaminated with impurities, such as silicates and sodium, dissolved out from the tubes. Thus polywater is probably silic acid or silica gel, and Deryagin suggested that the clouds of Venus are probably of the same material—water vapor condensed on silica nuclei.

Polywater, said to be heavier and more stable than water, had been studied by eminent bodies such as the National Bureau of Standards, and its military potential was investigated by the British Navy and the Pentagon. One scientist had even speculated that if polywater escaped into waterways, it might change oceans into a form of water unable to support life.

Cardiac Pacemakers. General Electric announced development of a new sodium-bromine battery for cardiac pacemakers. It was said to last about 10 years, compared with 24 to 28 months for conventional batteries, thus reducing costs of surgical replacement. The new battery is safer, less expensive, and just as long-lasting as nuclear-powered batteries. It is about the size of five stacked 50-cent pieces and consists of a bromine cathode, a sodium amalgam anode, and an aluminum oxide ceramic electrolyte which, being solid, prevents contact between the reactive materials and self-discharge that reduces life of other chemical batteries. Its shelf life is almost unlimited. Human implantation is expected in about two years.

Forensic Science. Forensic science, which until recently was mostly a collection of disconnected laboratory techniques that might or might not be admissible as court evidence, showed signs of being jelled into a scientific discipline. The Law Enforcement Assistance Agency made grants of $600,000 each to six universities to acquire equipment and personnel for carrying on graduate studies in crime detection. Although many disciplines are involved, analytical chemistry with emphasis on modern methods of instrumental analysis is central to any crime laboratory.

A nuclear chemist at the Pennsylvania State University developed a kit for obtaining scene-of-the-crime evidence regarding persons who fired a gun. Instead of the customary wax, a thin film of very pure liquid cellulose is applied to a suspect's hands, peeled off, and placed in a reactor where it is bombarded with neutrons that render metals associated with gunpowder, such as barium, antimony, and copper, radioactive. The inventor of the kit claimed that a hand that pulled a trigger could be distinguished from a hand that merely held a gun.

Another method identifies a hand merely in contact with metal. The skin is sprayed with a solution of 8-hydroxyquinoline and examined under ultraviolet light. If the hand was in contact with steel, a dark purple is produced; with copper, a light purple; with galvanized iron, bright yellow; and with aluminum, mottled yellow.

Origin of Life. In 1969, the Creation Research Society persuaded the California State Board of Education to rule that science textbooks describe the biblical account of Creation as well as evolution and the chemical theory of the origin of life. This drew fire from scientists and science organizations. In 1973 the California board revised its ruling and said that the Creation theory was to be described in social science texts and the discussion of evolution and the origin of life was to appear in a more speculative form in science texts.

Art Forgeries. Art forgers found that copying 19th and early 20th century works was profitable because the styles are easy to mimic and many of the materials used then are still available. Carbon-14 analysis was found useful for detecting such forgeries. The technique is based on the fact that since 1945 nuclear explosions have increased the content of carbon-14 in the environment and therefore its content in organisms alive after 1945 should be greater than in those that died before 1945. For example, linseed oil, commonly used in artist's paint, is prepared from flax seed, and its carbon-14 content should reflect the environment existing when the seed was harvested. Scientists at the Carnegie-Mellon University in Pittsburgh found that linseed oil prepared in 1968 contained nearly twice as much carbon-14 as that prepared in 1945. Similar results were obtained for paint samples.

EUGENIA KELLER
Managing Editor, "Chemistry" Magazine

CHICAGO

Chicago, now the second-largest metropolitan area in the United States, saw several politicians convicted in 1973 and its police department torn by scandal. A cloud of suspicion even hung over Chicago's powerful Mayor Richard J. Daley for one of the few times in his long public career. There was also a stalemate over a regional transit authority and a new expressway, and the city's public school teachers went on strike.

Crime Among Officeholders and Police. Otto Kerner, a judge on the bench of the U. S. Appeals Court for the 7th District and former Democratic governor of Illinois, was sentenced to three years in prison and fined $50,000 for accepting racetrack stock at bargain prices in return for influencing legislation and racing board appointments on behalf of special racing interests. Kerner was the first judge of the nation's second-highest court to be convicted while still a member of the court.

Edward J. Barrett, Cook county clerk, a state and county Democratic officeholder for more than 40 years and a close political ally of Mayor Daley, was sentenced to three years and fined $15,000 for accepting $180,000 in kickbacks in exchange for purchasing voting machines.

Two Chicago aldermen were convicted of accepting bribes in rigging zoning board cases, and several others were indicted or under grand jury investigation for abuse of their public office.

A widespread scandal hit the Chicago police department, with 35 policemen convicted, primarily for shakedowns of taverns and clubs. High-ranking police officers were involved, and public pressure forced Police Superintendent James Conlisk to resign.

Politics and a Challenge to Daley. James R. Thompson (R), U. S. attorney in Chicago who organized and directed the staff that obtained the conviction of Kerner and other politicians, emerged as a powerful figure. Federal grand juries were also investigating various activities of state and suburban officeholders in a sweeping crackdown on public malfeasance. Political insiders expected Thompson to turn his string of courtroom victories into a platform for a bid for the mayor's office in 1975, but so far he has turned down offers to run.

WORLD'S TALLEST BUILDING, the 110-story Sears Tower in Chicago is scheduled for completion in 1974.

For the first time in five mayoral elections, Mayor Daley was expected to face an opponent in the Democratic primary in 1975. Alderman William Singer, an independent Democrat who led a delegation of 59 regulars that managed to unseat Daley and his party regulars in the 1972 Democratic National Convention, announced that he would seek the mayoral nomination. Daley still maintained control of the city council, with 42 of the 50 aldermen backing him. However, disclosures that Daley personally ordered $2.9 million in municipal insurance business given to a firm associated with one of his sons brought the mayor's practices under close scrutiny. The mayor subsequently ordered all city insurance to be put up for competitive bid and promised a public explanation of the incident.

Civil Rights. The Chicago Plan, a voluntary program to get minority workers into the construction industry, was a failure. It will be replaced by the Philadelphia Plan, under which contractors in federally financed jobs will be forced to hire specific numbers of minority members.

Congressman Ralph Metcalfe, representing a predominantly black district on Chicago's South Side, conducted four days of public hearings and compiled an 80-page report accusing the police of brutality against blacks and other minorities.

Transportation. The Chicago Transit Authority (CTA), the public transportation system for the city and some suburbs, began the year in a severe financial crisis. The CTA announced cutbacks in bus and rapid transit service and an increase in the basic 45-cent fare. The state, Cook county, and the city provided emergency funds to avert the fare hike and most of the cutbacks. However, the aid only deferred the financial problems of the CTA. After long controversy, the Illinois General Assembly passed legislation authorizing a regional transportation authority, but the plan still requires voter approval.

Another controversial transportation issue was the Crosstown Expressway, a north-south superhighway proposed along Chicago's West Side. Mayor Daley supported it, but Gov. Daniel Walker (D) and the Citizens Action Program opposed it. A maneuver to get congressional legislation to permit the city to build the expressway without state approval failed.

Education. After a two-week strike in January that closed public schools, Chicago teachers accepted an agreement that shortened the school year and increased salaries. It was the third time in four years that the city's teachers had struck.

DAVID E. HALVORSEN, *"Chicago Tribune"*

CHILD WELFARE. See SOCIAL WELFARE.
CHILDREN'S LITERATURE. See LITERATURE.

CHILE

After three turbulent years in power, Chile's Marxist government, led by Salvador Allende Gossens, was violently overthrown on Sept. 11, 1973. The coup, mounted by the armed services, followed a series of increasingly disruptive mass protests that occurred against a background of rampant inflation, strikes, food shortages, and terrorist acts by both rightist and leftist groups. During the military's attack on the Presidential Palace, President Allende and his press secretary, Aristides Olivares, reportedly committed suicide.

The Military Regime. After the coup, a four-man military junta headed by Gen. Augusto Pino-

Riot police stand guard outside gutted Presidential Palace in Santiago, Chile, after overthrow of government.

chet Ugarte, commander in chief of the army, took over the government. Other junta members included the commander of the air force, Gen. Gustavo Leigh Guzmán; the commander of the navy, Adm. José Toribio Merino Castro; and the chief of *carabineros* (national police), Gen. César Mendoza Dorán.

The Congress was dissolved and a state of siege declared. All the Marxist parties in the Popular Unity (UP) coalition—Socialists, Communists, and MAPU—were declared illegal and the Christian Democratic (PDC) and other opposition parties ordered into indefinite recess. The nation's largest labor group, the Central Unica de Trabajadores (CUT), was also outlawed. The government returned the vast majority of state-run factories and businesses to the executives who had managed them before President Allende was elected. It also announced that the "door is open" for negotiations on compensation for nationalized U. S. copper properties.

Pay raises scheduled by the ousted government for October 1 to offset the effects of a cost of living that had soared by 323% since August 1972 were canceled. The national currency, the escudo, was devalued drastically on October 1.

Allende's death did not end the fighting. Throughout September and October, the military and national police encountered snipers and resistance as they arrested more than 8,000 suspected Chilean and foreign supporters of Allende. Several hundred Bolivians, Cubans, and other foreigners, including a few Americans, were ousted from the country. On October 6, the government reported that 513 persons had been killed since September 11, including 37 policemen and soldiers. This report was disputed by outside sources, which claimed that many thousands had died and that the incoming regime had engaged in summary executions and torture.

In a 14-point communiqué which followed announcement of a new cabinet, the junta charged Allende with "artificially encouraging a sterile—and often bloody—class struggle," with nullifying de-

cisions of the Congress and the judiciary, and with doing little about the nation's economic paralysis.

Immediately after the coup, the junta broke off diplomatic relations with Cuba and North Korea. In turn, the Soviet Union, its East European allies, and Yugoslavia suspended diplomatic relations with Chile. By late September, the new regime had been recognized by 28 governments, among them the United States, Britain, France, Argentina, and Peru.

CHILE • Information Highlights

Official Name: Republic of Chile.
Location: Southwestern coast of South America.
Area: 292,257 square miles (756,945 sq km).
Population (1973 est.): 10,400,000. *Density,* 34 per square mile (13 per sq km).
Chief Cities: Santiago, the capital, 2,900,000 (1970 census, metropolitan area); Valparaíso (1969 est.), 289,500.
Government: *Head of state,* Gen. Augusto Pinochet Ugarte, president (took power Sept. 1973). *Head of government,* Gen. Augusto Pinochet Ugarte. *Legislature—* Congress (dissolved Sept. 1973). *Major political parties*—Marxist parties banned; other parties "recessed" Sept. 1973.
Language: Spanish (official).
Education: *Expenditure* (1969), 10.6% of total public expenditure. *School enrollment* (1969)—primary, 1,980,-815; secondary, 267,769; technical/vocational, 85,987.
Monetary Unit: Escudo (270 escudos equal U. S.$1, Nov. 1973).
Gross National Product (1972 est.): $7,690,000,000.
Economic Indexes: *Industrial production* (manufacturing) (1972), 143 (1962=100); *agricultural production* (1971), 115 (1963=100); *consumer price index* (1972), 1,278 (1963=100).
Manufacturing (major products): Iron and steel, petroleum products, pulp and paper, chemicals, metal products.
Major Agricultural Products: Wheat, sugar beets, potatoes, corn, grapes, citrus fruits, rapeseed, fish.
Major Minerals: Copper (ranks 2d among world producers, 1971), nitrates and iodine, iron ore, coal, gold, potash.
Foreign Trade (1972): Exports, $811,000,000; Imports, $1,-300,000,000. *Chief trading partners* (1970)—United States (took 14% of exports, supplied 37% of imports); Latin American Free Trade Association (12%—20%); United Kingdom (12%—6%).
Transportation: *Motor vehicles* (1970), 325,800 (automobiles, 176,100); *railroads* (1971), 6,041 miles (9,721 km); *merchant fleet* (1972), 382,000 gross registered tons; *major national airline,* LAN-CHILE (Línea Aérea Nacional de Chile).
Communications: *Telephones* (1972), 389,609; *newspapers* (1971), 122 (daily circulation, 803,000).

SALVADOR ALLENDE (1908–1973)

WIDE WORLD

President Salvador Allende Gossens of Chile, Latin America's first freely elected Marxist chief of state, died on Sept. 11, 1973, at La Moneda, the presidential palace in Santiago, during a military coup that overthrew his government. He reportedly took his own life to avoid surrender.

As the candidate of Unidad Popular, a five-party leftist coalition, Allende had been elected to succeed Christian Democrat Eduardo Frei as president on Sept. 4, 1970, receiving a narrow plurality of 36.3% in a three-way race. His election was confirmed by Congress on October 24. Sworn into office on Nov. 3, 1970, Allende soon began to implement his "anti-oligarchic" and "anti-imperialist" program designed to establish socialism within a democratic framework. He nationalized natural resources, basic industries, public utilities, and banks, raised the wages of industrial workers, undertook an ambitious land redistribution program, and established diplomatic ties with Cuba and the Chinese People's Republic.

Almost from the beginning, however, Allende's government faced massive problems. Food shortages, price increases, and his failure to restrain extremist elements incurred the hostility of Chile's powerful middle class. He saw many of his programs blocked in Congress by the Christian Democrats and Nationalists.' The U.S. government, angered by the expropriation of the largely American-owned copper industry, imposed an "invisible blockade" that effectively isolated Chile from the world money market. By the late summer of 1973, as rampant inflation, crippling strikes, and political violence brought Chile to the brink of civil war, the military abandoned its traditional political neutrality and moved against the Allende government.

The son of a lawyer and the grandson of a physician, Salvador Allende Gossens was born in Valparaíso on July 26, 1908. He earned a medical degree (1932) at the University of Chile, where he was active in socialist politics and was twice jailed. A founder of Chile's Socialist party in 1933, he was elected to the Chamber of Deputies (1937) and served as minister of health in the popular-front government of Pedro Aguirre Cerda (1939–42). In 1945 he entered the Chilean Senate, and from 1965 to 1969 served as its president. He made unsuccessful bids for the national presidency in 1952, 1958, and 1964. The Soviet Union awarded him a Lenin Peace Prize in April 1973.

HENRY S. SLOAN

The March Elections. Late in 1972, a nation-wide trucking strike had been resolved only when Allende named the Army chief of staff, Gen. Carlos Prats González, as minister of the interior. The presence of Prats and two other military officers in the cabinet helped restore public calm preceding the parliamentary and municipal elections held on March 11, 1973.

The results of the election surprised most observers, as Allende's UP coalition increased its share of the popular vote to 43.4% (from 36.3% in 1970). The opposition Christian Democratic and National parties, organized into the Democratic Confederation (CODE), gained 54.7% of the vote.

Copper Strikes and Abortive Coup. On April 19, a strike broke out involving 13,000 copper miners at Chile's largest mine, El Teniente in Roncágua. President Allende refused to negotiate with the workers, who were demanding a 41% wage boost. After May 30, when a miner was killed by army troops, violent outbreaks involving the strikers, their sympathizers, the *carabineros,* and military personnel increased sharply. Subsequently, white-collar workers went on a sympathy strike at the Chuquicamata mine. Since the two mines normally produce two thirds of all Chilean copper, an important economic consequence of the strikes was a sharp reduction in copper exports.

Symptomatic of the worsening crisis was a coup attempt by an army contingent in Santiago on June 29, which was quickly put down by troops under General Prats. The copper workers at El Teniente voted to end their 10-week-old strike on July 2.

Murder of Arraya. On July 27, the country was shocked by the assassination of Cmdr. Arturo Arraya, the president's naval aide. Some groups tried to link the killing to the militant leftist Movimiento de la Izquierda Revolucionário (MIR). The government attributed both the murder and the June coup attempt to an extremist right-wing group calling itself *Patria y Libertad* (Fatherland and Liberty). Its leader, Roberto Thieme, was arrested.

Truck Strike. Meanwhile, on July 26, the country's most crippling strike had begun. On that day the 40,000 members of the truck owners federation went on strike over their inability to obtain the spare parts and new vehicles promised by the government in resolving their previous strike of October-November 1972. The truck owners were joined during the next 46 days by bus owners, professional people, and other groups. By mid-August the strike had cost the economy an estimated $100 million.

President Allende sought to resolve the crisis on August 9 by nominating General Prats as minister of defense and the Air Force commander, Gen. César Ruíz Danyan, as minister of public works and transport. On August 19, however, General Ruíz resigned, claiming that Allende refused him sufficient powers to settle the strike, including the freedom to name other military officers as his subordinates in the transport ministry. The situation worsened when Ruíz was told that his resignation from the cabinet also implied his resignation as commander of the Air Force. Senior officers put the Air Force on alert and demanded that Allende reinstate Ruíz in his former command. They relented on August 28, when Allende announced a new cabinet with another general named to the transport post.

Congressional Censure and Prats Resignation. On August 22, the CODE majority in the Congress passed a resolution censuring the government for not observing the constitution and calling on the four military ministers in the cabinet to insist on a fundamental change of policy. On the following day, General Prats resigned his positions after meetings with the general staff and demonstrations outside of his home by groups that included the wives of prominent officers. He was replaced by his close friend General Pinochet.

Concerned that the armed forces might not continue to support his government, Allende sought to make new military command appointments, some of which were circumvented by the military who—along with the police—were trying to control the wave of violence by right- and left-wing extremists.

BEFORE the revolution, groups of Santiago housewives protest against the Allende government's economic policies.

UPI

The September Coup. The insurrection of September 11 began with the seizure of the port city of Valparaíso by the Chilean Navy. Allende then received the junta's ultimatum calling for his resignation. He refused, saying in a radio broadcast that he was "ready to resist with whatever means, even at the cost of my life, as a lesson in the ignominious history of those who have strength but not reason." When he did not resign, army troops attacked the palace, quickly overcoming the handful of police and Allende supporters defending it.

Before the day had ended, the new junta government was established and Allende's suicide announced. No independent autopsy preceded the late president's burial on September 12.

Economic Affairs. In 1972, Chile's export earnings had dropped by over $100 million, due principally to declining world copper prices. Meanwhile, imports had risen by more than $300 million, leaving a huge trade deficit. August production estimates for the year 1973 showed a decline in copper tonnage, attributed mainly to strikes. However, with copper prices bouncing back on world markets, export earnings were showing no further drop in 1973.

Agricultural production remained low. Food imports, which had risen from $149 million in 1969 to $444 million in 1972, continued to increase, with a total of nearly $550 million forecast for 1973. On October 15, the Pinochet government sought to reduce food imports and spur agricultural productivity by raising the prices of essential food items.

Death of Neruda. Pablo Neruda, who won the 1971 Nobel Prize for Literature, died on Sept. 23, 1973, at the age of 69, a victim of cancer. The state of siege prevailing in late September precluded a state funeral, but several thousand mourners, singing the *Internationale,* were permitted to attend the funeral of the much admired poet, a long-time Communist party member.

NEALE J. PEARSON, *Texas Tech University*

AFTER the military coup, Chileans seek news of relatives or friends who may be inside the National Stadium in Santiago, a makeshift detention center.

UPI

CHINA

Visiting Canadian Prime Minister Trudeau imitates one of the statues behind him in Loyang cave. Looking on are Premier Chou En-lai, Mrs. Trudeau, and a provincial official.

Control of China, the world's most populous nation, is claimed by two opposing regimes—the People's Republic of China (Communist China), on the mainland, and the Republic of China (Nationalist China), on the offshore island of Taiwan.

THE PEOPLE'S REPUBLIC OF CHINA

The 10th Congress of the Chinese Communist party was held in August 1973 to reconstruct the party framework, badly damaged after the purge of former Defense Minister Lin Piao in 1971. Premier Chou En-lai (see BIOGRAPHY), leader of the moderates, remained second in command after Chairman Mao Tse-tung. But the dramatic rise of Wang Hung-wen, a young radical leader from Shanghai, indicated the increasing power of the leftists, led by Chiang Ch'ing, Mao's wife. The new party constitution designated no political successor to Chairman Mao.

Peking's relations with Moscow remained tense. The Chinese opposed the East-West détente in Europe, which would allow the Soviet Union to concentrate more forces on its Chinese border. China's encouragement of Western European unity and its support of the Third World's struggle against "superpower hegemony" were chiefly directed toward containing Soviet influence.

Party Congress. The 10th Congress of the Chinese Communist party was held on August 24–28. It was attended by 1,249 delegates, representing a party membership of 28 million. The congress received no advance publicity, and it lasted for an unusually short period. These curious circumstances may be attributed to the desire of the leadership to avoid open wrangling and rifts that might arise from factional rivalries.

The primary object of the congress was to reconstruct the party framework that had been shattererd first by the Cultural Revolution of 1966–69 and then, in 1971, by the purge of Lin Piao, Chairman Mao's designated successor. The task was a formidable one, for the rivalries among the moderates, the radicals, the senior leaders, and the military were severe and extensive.

After much jockeying and manipulation, the congress finally elected 195 full members and 124 alternates to the Central Committee. The new committee was said to combine the old, the middle-aged, and the young, so there would be no paucity of successors to Chairman Mao. Elected to the Central Committee were many high-ranking leaders purged during the Cultural Revolution. Notable among them were Teng Hsiao-p'ing, former general secretary of the party, and T'an Chen-lin, a former vice premier. The Central Committee also included as full members Ch'iao Kuan-hua, deputy foreign minister; Huang Chen, head of the liaison office in Washington; and Huang Hua, Chinese representative to the United Nations. These three had worked closely with Chou in improving U. S. relations.

New Alignments. At its first plenary session on August 30, the party's Central Committee elected five vice chairmen, the principal deputies to Chairman Mao. Premier Chou was named first among the five, and Wang Hung-wen second. Others named were K'ang Sheng, an elder of the party, who was believed to have been in charge of security affairs; Yeh Chien-ying, executive vice chairman of the party's Military Affairs Commission; and Li Teh-sheng, chief political commissar of the army.

The Central Committee also elected 21 full members and four alternates to the Politburo, the highest ruling body in China. The Politburo, in turn, appointed a Standing Committee of nine to rule when the Politburo was not in session. Included in this smaller committee were Chairman Mao, the five vice chairmen of the Central Committee, and three

others: Tung Pi-wu, acting president of China; Chang Ch'un-ch'iao, chairman of the Shanghai Revolutionary Committee; and Chu Teh, the old marshal who had led the Red Army to victory in 1949.

The various elections and appointments confirmed Chou En-lai as second in command after Mao Tse-tung, and the moderates who follow Chou gained ground in the new power alignment. But the radical group that formerly led the Cultural Revolution was not ignored. Though Chiang Ch'ing, Mao's leftist wife, and Yao Wen-yuan, her protégé, were not elected to the Standing Committee, they remained members of the Politburo. Chang Ch'un-ch'iao, another close associate of Chiang Ch'ing, was not only appointed to the Standing Committee but also served as secretary general of the party congress.

Of greatest significance is the spectacular rise of Wang Hung-wen, who apparently is in third position in the party hierarchy after Mao and Chou. Wang, a 38-year-old former textile mill worker, had been a militant leader during the Cultural Revolution. He later became a vice chairman of the Shanghai Revolutionary Committee and was generally regarded as a protégé of Chang Ch'un-ch'iao.

Denunciation of Lin Piao. In his report to the congress, Premier Chou denounced the late Defense Minister Lin Piao and recounted the events leading up to his death. Chou told the congress that Lin Piao plotted two coups d'etat—the first at a plenary session of the ninth Central Committee in August 1970 and the second on Sept. 8, 1971, when an attempt was made to assassinate Mao and set up a rival Central Committee. On September 13, after his conspiracy had collapsed, Lin "surreptitiously boarded a plane, fled as a defector to the Soviet revisionists in betrayal of the party and country, and died in a crash at Undur Khan in Mongolia." Chou castigated Lin Piao as a "bourgeois careerist, conspirator, double-dealer, renegade, and traitor."

New Party Constitution. The congress adopted a new party constitution that deleted all reference to Lin Piao, designated in the previous constitution as Chairman Mao's successor. The new constitution named no successor, and the omission prompted speculation that after Mao's death China would be ruled by a collective leadership, including the five vice chairmen of the Central Committee.

Wang Hung-wen, in his report on the new constitution, told the congress that China would undergo revolutions like the 1966–69 Cultural Revolution many times in the future. Though the new constitution calls on all organizations to accept the centralized leadership of the party, it maintains that the masses must have the freedom to speak out against erroneous political views without fear of retaliation.

Labor, Women, and Youth. In line with its policy of political normalization, China took steps to restore the labor unions that had been dissolved during the Cultural Revolution. In those days, the labor unions were regarded as political strongholds of Liu Shao-ch'i, chairman of the People's Government. In April 1973, the labor unions in Peking and Shanghai were reestablished, setting examples for other cities to follow in reorganizing labor.

The Federation of Women, which ceased functioning during the Cultural Revolution, was also restored. At a women's congress held in Wuhan, delegates were urged to oppose the old idea of male superiority and to promote equality of the sexes.

The Communist Youth League, also shattered during the Cultural Revolution, was reestablished in the various provinces and regions. The reconstruction of the youth apparatus was to give the party leadership more effective control over young people and to encourage them to take part in supervised political activities at an early age. Those admitted to the league would have some special status, but none would be exempt from a period of compulsory labor in rural areas.

In 1973, some 2 million graduates from colleges and middle schools were sent to the countryside to work with the farmers. Many were dispatched to remote border regions to settle there. Compulsory rural assignments have caused widespread discontent among the youth. Not only do they find rural life uncongenial, but they often are unable to support themselves. They earn less work points than the farmers, and they receive no extra income from such sideline activities as raising chickens and growing vegetables.

Nuclear Test and Missiles. On June 27, China conducted its 15th nuclear test. The hydrogen bomb, set off in the atmosphere at the Lop Nor test site in the remote Sinkiang region, was estimated by the U. S. Atomic Energy Commission to be in the 2- to 3-megaton range.

While China continued to make advances in the development of nuclear warheads, the development of delivery missiles was slower than expected. In 1972, China deployed some 1,000-mile (1,600-km) medium-range missiles and probably had begun deploying a 1,500-mile (2,400-km) intermediate-range missile, capable of striking Soviet targets in Siberia and American targets in the Western Pacific. But her multistage missile, with a capability range of more than 3,000 miles (4,800 km), reaching almost all targets in the Soviet Union, was not expected to be ready for deployment until 1974. Further, it was uncertain when an intercontinental ballistic missile, capable of striking all targets in the United States, could be produced.

Economic Development. Industrial production for the first half of 1973 surpassed the planned targets in 80 major industries, including steel, machine tools, and textiles. In some cases the targets were exceeded by as much as 50%. A remarkable advance was made in the electronics industry. In the first five months of 1973, production of radios and TV sets increased, respectively, by 89% and 93% over the same period in 1972.

China's major industrial concern is the renovation and modernization of her production facilities. Many factories are old, and their equipment is antiquated. To remedy this situation, China began to purchase high-technology manufactured products from the West and to send technical missions abroad to acquire advanced industrial knowledge.

Agriculture suffered reverses in the first half of 1973. Drought hit 12 provinces and regions in northern China, and heavy rains did extensive damage to crops in the south. To offset the effects of these natural disasters, rural authorities were permitted to shift manpower and capital from industry to agriculture. In the north, extensive well-drilling programs were undertaken to irrigate arid land.

Foreign Trade. Parallel with its efforts to normalize foreign relations, Peking began expanding its trade with the West. To finance imports of Western capital goods, China is now beginning to purchase on credit. Peking also agreed to pay foreign royalties and grant licenses to foreign patent-holders. To earn more foreign exchange for imports, China raised the price of its exports—sharply in regard to many items.

Chinese export expansion, however, is likely to remain minimal for some time, since there are several obstacles to be overcome. Not only does China have limited agricultural production, but its manufactured goods have yet to develop markets abroad, and product adjustments must be made to meet standards acceptable in the West.

U. S. Relations. Peking continued its rapprochement with Washington in 1973. On February 22, after extensive talks in Peking between Chinese leaders and Henry A. Kissinger, then President Nixon's foreign affairs adviser before he became secretary of state, a joint communiqué announced that China and the United States would establish respective liaison offices in Washington and Peking. The move was hailed as a significant diplomatic breakthrough after more than two decades of mutual isolation.

In November, Secretary of State Kissinger visited Peking again for four days of talks with Chairman Mao and Premier Chou. In the joint communiqué issued on November 14, the United States reaffirmed the "one-China" principle, which is regarded by Peking as essential to normalizing relations. The two sides agreed to expand their liaison offices and to increase trade and cultural exchanges.

U. S. Trade and Cultural Exchanges. The value of Sino-American trade exceeded $500 million by August 1973, and it was expected that the total for the year would approach $1 billion. China's largest commodity purchase, by far, from the United States was grain, but China also bought cotton, fertilizer, and tobacco.

However, rapid expansion of Sino-American trade is impeded by two factors: blocked accounts and the failure so far of the United States to grant most-favored-nation status to China. In 1950 the American government froze Chinese assets in the United States amounting to about $78 million, and the Chinese Communists expropriated American properties in China valued at about $250 million. Claims regarding these monies must be settled before China will receive U. S. government-backed credits and most-favored-nation tariff treatment. Peking and Washington have initiated talks on these claims and are expected to reach an early settlement.

Cultural exchanges between China and the United States increased notably after the Chou-Kissinger meeting in February. Chinese visitors to the United States in 1973 included groups of journalists, water-conservation experts, high-energy physicists, librarians, and a gymnast team. Among Americans invited to visit China were a medical group, a scientific group, a group of elementary and high school teachers, amateur basketball and swimming teams, and the Philadelphia Orchestra.

Canadian Relations. On October 10, Prime Minister Pierre Elliott Trudeau of Canada arrived in China for a six-day visit. Upon becoming prime minister in 1968, Trudeau had set about to normalize relations with China, and Canada had recognized Peking in 1970.

Prime Minister and Mrs. Trudeau were warmly welcomed by Premier Chou and several thousand cheering children at the Peking airport. Trudeau had a series of long talks with Chou and conferred for two hours with Chairman Mao, who was reported to be alert and keen, asking many questions about the economy and social problems of Canada.

On October 13, Chou and Trudeau signed a trade agreement that stressed long-term commercial contracts, especially in regard to aluminum, wood pulp, nickel, sulfur, and potash. Agreements were also reached on the establishment of consular relations and on the exchange of cultural, medical, and scientific missions.

In an earlier accord, signed on October 5, China agreed to purchase up to 224 million bushels of wheat from Canada at an estimated cost of $1 billion. The wheat is to be shipped over a three-year period, beginning in January 1974. Canada's trade with China, totaling about $300 million in 1973, is expected to grow rapidly.

Western European Relations. In 1973, China made diligent efforts to cultivate relations with countries in Western Europe. In May, Peking sent a valuable collection of archeological objects for exhibit in Paris and London.

In June, Foreign Minister Ch'i P'eng-fei went to Britain and France and invited British Prime Minister Edward Heath and French President Georges Pompidou to visit China. The French president arrived in Peking on September 11 to confer with Chairman Mao and Premier Chou. While they did not agree on all world problems, their views converged on many points. China supported France's efforts to affirm a European identity and develop European unity, but it objected to the establishment of an East-West détente in Europe. In a joint communiqué issued on September 17, the two sides declared that they were against "all hegemony," but they named no nation striving for such a position.

China's active diplomacy in Europe was motivated largely by the desire to curb Soviet influence in the West. In China's view, a détente in Europe would allow the Soviet Union to concentrate more troops on the Chinese-Soviet border. Consequently, Peking's support of the European Common Market (EEC) and its attack, as a "plot," on the Soviet-in-

spired European security conference were directed toward encouraging Western European unity against the Soviet Union.

Sino-Soviet Antagonism. China's relations with the Soviet Union remained strained in 1973. No progress was reported regarding the Sino-Soviet border negotiations, for Moscow has no intention of giving up territory that Peking claims was seized by czarist Russia.

The Soviet Union concentrated from 45 to 48 divisions along the Chinese border during the year and accelerated the settlement of Russian farmers in the disputed area. To strengthen its claim to former Chinese territories, the Soviet government changed the names of towns in eastern Siberia from Chinese to Russian.

Both China and the Soviet Union launched violent verbal attacks against each other. One of the most severe against the Soviet Union was delivered by Premier Chou in his report to the 10th Congress. "The Soviet revisionist ruling clique, from Khrushchev to Brezhnev," Chou said, "has made a socialist country degenerate into a social-imperialist country." He denounced the Soviet leadership as "the new czar" and likened Soviet criticism of China to "an old trick of Hitler's." Chou also called on the Chinese people to prepare for a surprise attack on China by Soviet forces. In spite of such vilification, however, there was no evidence of serious military threats along the border by either country.

New Relations with Japan. In March, pursuant to an agreement reached in 1972, China and Japan exchanged envoys for the first time. In establishing diplomatic relations with Tokyo, Peking hoped that Japan would cooperate in curbing Soviet influence in the Far East. The Chinese government publicly supported Japan's claim to four islands north of Hokkaido that have been occupied by the Soviet Union since the end of World War II. On the other hand, China opposed Japan's participation in the proposed joint Soviet-Japanese development of oil and gas resources in eastern Siberia.

In April, to influence Japanese public opinion, Peking sent a Chinese mission to Japan, headed by Liao Ch'eng-chih, president of the China-Japan Friendship Association. The 50-member group visited various places in Japan, including Hokkaido, where there is strong feeling for return of the four Soviet-held islands.

In April, China and Japan agreed in principle to laying an underseas cable between the two countries by 1975. But Sino-Japanese negotiations for establishing intercountry air service met with difficulties as Tokyo stood firm against Chinese demands that flights between Japan and Taiwan be discontinued.

Southeast Asia. China played an important role in bringing about the Vietnam cease-fire accord in January. It pushed for a settlement, not only to avoid straining relations with the United States, but also to check Soviet influence in Indochina. In an agreement reached in Hanoi in June, Peking promised substantial economic aid for the reconstruction of North Vietnam.

In other developments, China strongly criticized the United States for bombing raids against Cambodian Communist positions in the summer of 1973. Also, China was building two roads from Yunnan province to northeastern Laos, in a determined effort to increase its influence in Indochina.

The Third World. China has adopted a pose as the champion of the interests of the Third World in

UPI

CELEBRATING opening of U. S. liaison office in Peking are (l. to r.) Sen. Warren Magnuson, Chiao Kuanhua of the foreign ministry, liaison chief David Bruce.

its struggle against the domination of the "superpowers." Speaking before the UN Security Council on June 14, Huang Hua, the Chinese representative, blamed the Soviet Union and the United States for tensions in the Middle East, calling them "the two superpowers which have today taken the place of former imperialist powers as the principal rivals for hegemony."

When the Arab-Israeli war broke out in October, Peking accused Israel of aggression and declared support for the Arabs. The Chinese delegates at the United Nations declined to support the American-Soviet resolution calling for a cease-fire in the Middle East. Peking assailed the Soviet Union for "betraying" the Arabs by not giving them sufficient support to attain their objectives.

To maintain buffer zones between both the Soviet Union and India, China cultivated the friendship of Iran and strengthened its relations with Pakistan. The Chinese government reiterated its support for the "common struggle of the African peoples against imperialism and neocolonialism," and, in regard to Latin America, it made efforts to strengthen its ties with Argentina after the leftist regime of President Juan D. Perón was returned to power.

REPUBLIC OF CHINA

Taiwan suffered diplomatic reverses in 1973, but its economy continued to grow. Foreign trade increased, even with countries that recognized Communist China. Under the leadership of Premier Chiang Ching-kuo, the morale and efficiency of the government improved. Also, Taiwan resolutely refused to negotiate with Peking toward peaceful reunification.

Government. President Chiang Kai-shek had not appeared in public for more than a year, but a photograph of him and his family, released in July 1973, indicated that he had recovered from a long illness. Control of the government, however, rested with his eldest son, Chiang Ching-kuo, appointed premier in May 1972.

Apparently a courageous and efficient leader, Premier Chiang initiated reforms and vigorously attacked problems of government corruption and laxity. His stringent regulations were firmly enforced, resulting in improved morale and efficiency. Also, Premier Chiang eased tensions between native Taiwanese and Chinese of mainland origin by appointing a number of Taiwanese to his cabinet. His frequent informal visits to rural areas gained him a favorable public image.

Rejection of Peking Overtures. Early in 1973, Peking launched a vigorous campaign to persuade Taiwan to reunite with mainland China. Calling the Chinese on Taiwan "our flesh and blood," the Communists broadcast assurances of fair treatment for the Taiwanese upon reunification. Peking remarked on Taiwan's growing isolation within the international community and glowingly reported the achievements, economic and diplomatic, of Communist China. On March 1, the Chinese Communists announced that they were ready to hold direct reunification negotiations with the Nationalist government.

The Communist offer, however, was resolutely rejected by the Nationalists. Taipei broadcast that Nationalist China "will always oppose the Communists and never compromise with them." In a resolution on June 28, the Standing Committee of the ruling Kuomintang party declared full support for Chiang's refusal to have any contact with Peking.

U. S. Relations. Taiwan was gravely concerned over the agreement between the United States and Communist China to establish liaison offices in Peking and Washington. The Nationalists, viewing the move as a step toward full United States recognition of Peking, were apprehensive that the American agreement with the Communists would reduce their own influence in Washington.

The Nationalist government repeatedly inquired about the American position, receiving assurances that the United States would honor the mutual defense treaty and continue to maintain diplomatic relations with Nationalist China. Nevertheless, it was apparent that Washington intended, in the long run, to normalize relations with Peking.

Japanese Ties. Nationalist China's economic relations with Japan continued in 1973, although the two countries severed diplomatic relations in 1972. Trade reached new highs, and Japanese investments flowed unabated into Taiwan. In Tokyo, the Nationalists established the Association for Far Eastern Relations to assume trade and consular services, while overall supervision of Japanese business in Taiwan was borne by the Interchange Association in Taipei. Trade between Taiwan and Japan was expected to reach $2 billion in 1973, with Taiwan's exports increasing sharply, thereby narrowing its adverse trade balance with Japan.

Diplomatic Reverses. Taipei broke off diplomatic relations with Spain in April, when Madrid recognized Peking. It was reported that Thailand, an old friend of Nationalist China, was discreetly reducing its relations with Taiwan in an attempt to appease Communist China.

Amid these developments, Taiwan looked to Africa and Latin America to strengthen its diplomatic posture. In Africa, vigorous programs were launched to promote Chinese investment there and establish agricultural cooperative enterprises. Regarding Latin America, in August, Vice President C. K. Yen visited Paraguay, Brazil, Costa Rica, and Guatemala to cultivate friendly relations.

Economy. Taiwan's economy continued to advance in 1973, with an annual estimated growth rate of 11%. Expansion was particularly strong in the industrial sector, where the growth rate was expected to reach 24.5%. A $30 million program related to agriculture was launched in July to improve marketing systems for farm produce, to establish factories in the rural areas, and to promote research for modernizing agricultural methods.

Foreign Trade. Despite international political problems, Taiwan's total trade for the first 10 months of 1973 reached $6 billion, up 46% over the same period in 1972. Taiwan's largest trade partner is the United States, and in 1972, Taiwanese exports to the United States exceeded imports by $686 million. Recognizing the inflationary danger from such a surplus, the Nationalist government began to take steps to narrow the favorable trade balance by increasing the purchase of American products, especially grain and soybeans.

Taiwan's flourishing trade is attributed partly to the bargain prices of its goods, but another factor is the effort by both government and private enterprise to promote commerce with all non-hostile nations, including those having no diplomatic relations with Taipei. In 1973, Taiwan maintained trade relations with over 130 countries.

Inflation. While the trade surplus brought in large foreign reserves, it also gave rise to domestic inflation. The wholesale price index rose by 11.68% in the first two months of 1973. To cope with the situation, the government adopted a number of measures, including tighter credit, a ban on certain nonessential construction, and price controls on some basic commodities, such as fertilizer, flour, soybean meal, and cotton goods.

CHESTER C. TAN, *New York University*

CHOU EN-LAI. See BIOGRAPHY.

NATIONAL CHINA • Information Highlights

Official Name: Republic of China.
Location: Islands about 100 miles off the southeastern coast of the Chinese mainland.
Area: 13,885 square miles (35,961 sq km).
Population (1973 est.): 15,000,000. *Density,* 1,080 per square mile (415 per sq km).
Chief Cities (1970 est.): Taipei, the capital, 1,740,800; Kaohsiung, 806,300; Tainan, 468,300.
Government: *Head of state,* Chiang Kai-shek, president (reelected for 5th 6-year term March 1972). *Head of government,* Chiang Ching-kuo, premier (took office May 1972). *Legislature* (unicameral)—Legislative Yuan.
Language: Mandarin Chinese (official).
Education: *Expenditure* (1969), 16.5% of total public expenditure. *School enrollment* (1969)—primary, 2,428,-041; secondary, 1,028,752; technical/vocational, 155,-947; university/higher, 184,215.
Monetary Unit: New Taiwan dollar (38.10 NT dollars equal U. S.$1, Sept. 1973).
Gross National Product (1972 est.): $6,915,000,000.
Economic Indexes: *Industrial production* (1972), 495 (1963=100); *agricultural production* (1971), 193 (1952–56=100); *consumer price index* (1972), 131 (1963=100).
Manufacturing (major products): Petroleum products, processed foods, textiles, electrical machinery, electronics, chemicals, apparel.
Major Agricultural Products: Sugarcane, bananas, mushrooms, pineapples, rice, tea, vegetables, sweet potatoes, fish.
Major Minerals: Coal, natural gas.
Foreign Trade (1971): *Exports,* $2,135,000,000. *Imports,* $1,990,000,000. *Chief trading partners* (1971)—United States (took 41% of exports, supplied 30% of imports); Japan (12%–39%); Hong Kong (7%–2%); West Germany (4%–4%).
Tourism: Receipts (1970) $89,700,000.
Transportation: *Motor Vehicles* (1970), 98,500 (automobiles, 49,500); *railroads* (1971), 621 miles (999 km); *merchant fleet* (1971), 1,322,000 gross registered tons; *major national airline,* China Airlines Limited.
Communications: *Telephones* (1972), 492,307.

SITTING AREA provided by the builders of a New York City skyscraper. Several such areas, with radiant heating units in canopy roofs and undulating sidewalks of earth-colored brick, attempt to lend a "country lane" atmosphere to a city street.

CITIES AND URBAN AFFAIRS

American cities were confronted with energy shortages, transportation problems, an increasing number of violent crimes, and growing congestion during 1973. However, the cities did develop some new responses in meeting these challenges, particularly in looking toward limited, ordered expansion as a desirable goal.

Energy Shortage. The first and most immediate concern for the cities was the shortage of energy, which became acutely apparent late in the year. Because of the interdependence of urban areas and their reliance on power for homes, businesses, communications, and transit, the energy shortage threatened to alter drastically the nature of urban life. Automobiles and trucks, on which cities have depended for their livelihood, were threatened not only with shortages of fuel but also with the possibility that their use within urban centers would be severely curtailed. Some cities facing energy shortages and environmental problems adopted innovative plans and solutions to meet the crises, but it was generally feared that environmental standards for air and water pollution would be among the first casualties of the energy crisis.

Transportation. Cities such as Seattle and San Diego implemented free or very low-cost mass transit systems within their central areas, thereby encouraging shifts from automobile to bus transportation. In other cities, such as Boston and Washington, D. C., parking surcharges were proposed to discourage the use of private automobiles. Although support for such proposals was only scattered, these alternatives seemed sensible and perhaps inevitable given the strains that existing transportation systems place on energy supplies and environmental quality. Moreover, the willingness of the federal government to utilize the multibillion-dollar Highway Trust Fund for the construction and operation of mass transit systems emphasized the urgency of the transportation problems.

Housing. The demand for more urban housing units mounted, but the existing economic situation—especially high interest rates for mortgages and home improvement loans—prohibited extensive construction and renovation. A few cities encouraged programs of "urban homesteading." In such a program an abandoned inner-city dwelling is sold to a citizen for a minimal price, usually one dollar, on the condition that he promised to rehabilitate the house by his own efforts or through contracts with competent workmen. The first urban homesteading program began in Wilmington, Del., in August. Although not ambitious in size it received considerable publicity, and other cities began to follow suit.

Crime. Cities were still plagued by violent crime, a nagging problem that arose in the late 1960's and has shown little sign of dissipating. Although claims of reduced crime were advanced by officials in some cities and at the federal level, crimes against persons, notably murder and rape, were on the rise. Many cities shifted to individual emergency telephone numbers to make reporting of crimes easier, only to find that citizens kept the lines jammed with nonemergency calls.

Limits on Growth. In a sharp break with tradition, the country's long-accepted goals of growth, expansion, and progress were questioned in a significant number of cities during 1973. Historically, the United States has congratulated itself on every record set—fastest-growing urban area, biggest shopping center, largest population, most new homes, and so on. But in 1973 its citizens registered their shock and dismay at the ever-increasing congestion, blight, smog, and loss of open space. The protest of persons of every social, economic, and political description was expressed in the approval of laws limiting growth and the election of candidates who called for limited, ordered expansion.

Throughout the country issues of land use and open space dominated state and local legislative bodies, which had been accustomed to thinking that schools, taxes, and law and order were of the highest priority. During 1973, the environmental movement went beyond rhetorical concern and took practical forms. There were population ceilings and building moratoria, and jurisdictions were created solely for governing growth in geographically defined areas.

In densely populated Dade county (Miami), Fla., for example, one building moratorium after another was approved. This resulted in a near-ban on construction in the county until land-use plans are written and implemented. Officials and citizens hoped that a limited-growth policy, probably including a population ceiling, would be included in the county's revised master plan.

Fairfax county, Va., a Washington suburb, was once labeled the "fastest growing large county in the nation." However, in 1973 its board of supervisors, at the urging of alarmed citizens, suspended

sewer construction (and thus residential construction) in the entire county. The county government also began turning down many requests for rezoning that called for higher building densities.

Perhaps the most dramatic and prophetic opposition to expansion occurred in California in 1973. Residents of Los Angeles revolted against their own bigness and transcended political and racial boundaries to elect a mayor who advocated limiting the city's population to 4 million while characterizing the previously planned-for 10 million as "insane." The new mayor, Thomas Bradley, strongly favored curbs on housing developments that have consumed open space. He also favored mass transit in this car capital, which once boasted about having the "most miles of freeway." Many of those who voted for Bradley in 1973 on the basis of his stand on environment-limited growth were opposed to him in the previous mayoralty election on grounds of political ideology and race. (Bradley is the city's first black mayor.)

Bradley's election illustrates a trend now pervading California and emerging in other states. In a late-1972 referendum, the California electorate imposed a ban on all building construction along the Pacific coast from the Oregon border to Mexico. During 1973, very few new structures were permitted along the shoreline, and these were built only by specific state permit.

Environment-Oriented Officials. In California, as in other states, a new kind of local official has emerged. He is sensitive to the environment and the quality of life and is resistant to conventional pressures for "progress." Of California's 296 county supervisors, 140 have been elected in the last two years. Never before in California's history has there been such a large-scale dismissal of experienced, well-known incumbents in exchange for relative amateurs. Many of these elections turned on issues of growth control and stricter zoning. City councils also experienced revolutionary changes. At the 1973 spring convention of the California League of Cities, the 500 mayors and councilmen present were asked if they attributed their election primarily to their position on environmental issues. More than 70% raised their hands.

Blacks in Urban Leadership. Urban leadership in the United States has been shifting more and more into the hands of blacks. In three major cities, blacks won the mayoralty election and joined the growing ranks of black elected officials. In Los Angeles, black Councilman Thomas Bradley defeated incumbent Sam Yorty; in Atlanta, Maynard Jackson was elected over Mayor Sam Massell; and Detroit's new black mayor, Coleman Young, beat former police commissioner John Nichols. These examples indicated the ability of blacks to attract votes, regardless of race. Another measure of the growing strength of minority candidates was the respectable showing of Black Panther Bobby Seale in both the primary and run-off mayoral elections in Oakland, Calif.

The spirit among these black political leaders was practical and conciliatory. Detroit's Young told reporters after his victory that his first task was to show the whites of his city that he did not have "horns."

Black mayors from the South showed their willingness to forge valuable political alliances when they met with Gov. George Wallace at the mayors' annual meeting in Tuskegee, Ala. Such conciliation was prompted by the realization that it would be difficult to achieve progress for urbanites of any race by using an extremist strategy.

Federal Aid to Cities. Strong leadership at the national level was diminished by two developments. The first was the introduction of the Nixon administration's fiscal year 1974 budget, which proposed cuts in a number of domestic programs on which urban areas had come to depend. Justification for the cuts was largely rhetorical, and the cities' leaders reacted negatively. They criticized the administration for misleading them with the claim that the newly enacted general revenue-sharing program was intended to supplement, not replace, existing urban programs. Changes in federal programs had little effect on the burden of local taxpayers, and national surveys of citizen attitudes toward government, especially a year-end Harris poll conducted for a congressional subcommittee, yielded negative results.

By midyear the public debate over the budget was pushed to the back pages by the revelations of government scandals known as the Watergate affair. This was the second development that weakened strong national leadership. As attention in the United States continued to be focused on the Watergate aspect of national affairs, the plight of the cities was largely neglected. Through this neglect, however, cities may have begun to look to themselves for the means to solve some of their most pressing problems. While continued federal participation in the affairs of state and local governments was thought necessary, the federal government remained largely inactive. National executive leadership was severely impaired, and the congressional session failed to pass key administration proposals, such as special

revenue-sharing funds for locally controlled community development. A coalition of state, city, and county officials was formed in Washington to press for jointly agreeable federal programs, but the prospect of their having much effect seemed dim because the national administration was preoccupied.

RICHARD E. THOMPSON
President, Revenue Sharing Advisory Service, Inc.

CIVIL LIBERTIES AND CIVIL RIGHTS

Investigations during 1973 of the Watergate affair revealed a number of threats to American civil liberties. A pattern of insensitivity to individual rights by the executive branch of the federal government became evident. It was discovered that President Nixon had approved of a plan for domestic surveillance that included burglary, opening of mail, and wiretapping. Critics of the administration, particularly members of the press, were harassed by FBI investigations and threats of prosecution. And members of a White House group called the "plumbers" were indicted in September for burglary.

The investigations by a Senate committee and by the special Watergate prosecutor's office also raised important constitutional questions, including the scope of a President's authority in the name of executive privilege to withhold information from congressional committees and grand juries, and the possible prejudice to criminal prosecutions arising out of the extraordinary publicity generated by the congressional inquiry into Watergate. (See a special report on Watergate on pages 14–33.)

During the year the U. S. Supreme Court took a more conservative turn, reflecting the majority views of the four justices appointed by President Nixon, usually joined by Justice Byron White. Although many important decisions favored civil liberties, the proportion of rulings favorable to individual rights was the lowest in 16 years.

Free Speech. The Supreme Court substantially reduced the restraints forged by the Warren Court on censorship of literature and stage performances alleged to be obscene. Material that has *any* redeeming social importance will no longer be constitutionally protected unless it also has "serious" literary, artistic, political, or scientific value. Perhaps more important was the holding that courts will henceforth apply state or local standards rather than a single federal standard in evaluating material challenged as obscene.

The Supreme Court also dealt a blow to the right of citizens to know about government action. In its first ruling under the Freedom of Information Act of 1966, it rejected a claim by Rep. Patsy Mink (D-Hawaii) and 36 other members of Congress and accorded the executive branch broad discretion to withhold information "in the interest of the national defense or foreign policy." Lower courts have generally been more generous in allowing access to government documents, and as the year ended several cases were on the way to the Supreme Court attempting to limit the Mink case.

In other free-expression cases, the court sustained a student's claim that she had been wrongfully expelled from a university for publication of "indecent speech"; refused to hear a case in which a man was convicted of shouting obscene words in a public street; and declined to disturb lower-court rulings that struck down a California statute too broadly prohibiting defacement of the American flag and that permitted a New York teacher to wear a black armband on Vietnam moratorium day.

Freedom of the Press. The Department of Justice, modifying administration policy, announced in October that it would henceforth subpoena the notes of news reporters only in exceptional cases and then only on the personal authority of the attorney general.

A clarifying decision on the extent to which reporters can be coerced through court order to reveal notes of confidential interviews seemed likely

in the proceedings involving Vice President Spiro Agnew, but when Agnew resigned the case was mooted. (See special report on Spiro Agnew, pages 20–21.) During the year, the Supreme Court refused to review two contempt convictions against newspersons and scholars for refusing to disclose such information, and congressional attempts to frame new legislation bogged down in committees.

A sharply divided Supreme Court handed down rulings in two important cases involving news media where constitutional rights conflicted. In one case the court upheld the refusal of the Federal Communications Commission to require broadcasters to sell time to advertisers for comment on controversial issues. And in the other the court sustained a ruling of the Pittsburgh Commission on Human Rights that prohibited the Pittsburgh *Press* from running help-wanted columns by sex, as "Help Wanted— Male" and "Help Wanted—Female."

Rights of Women. Feminists prevailed in several Supreme Court actions in addition to the Pittsburgh *Press* case. In its most important decision, the court invalidated Texas and Georgia statutes placing restrictions on abortions. In a broad opinion the court prohibited any state interference with a decision of a woman relying on her physician's judgment to have an abortion during the first three months of pregnancy, and imposed severe limitations on laws restricting abortions during the second three months. Several members of Congress proposed constitutional amendments to reverse the decision.

Meanwhile, the Equal Rights Amendment became stalled in the ratification process after 30 of a required 38 state legislatures passed it. (See also WOMEN'S LIBERATION MOVEMENT.)

Religion. In a series of cases challenging public aid to church-related schools, the court reaffirmed a strict view of the "establishment" clause of the First Amendment. It struck down various forms of tax credits, tuition reimbursement, and other forms of aid on the ground that they embodied impermissible religious motives and would entangle the state with church schools. But the court sustained a South Carolina statute establishing an Educational Facilities Authority to help institutions of higher learning construct and finance buildings not used for worship or for a divinity school.

Civil Rights and the Rights of the Poor. The Supreme Court broadly condemned racial segregation in Northern public schools by holding that a finding of intentional segregation in any part of a school system would support a finding of such segregation in the entire system. The court also barred state support to so-called private academies that had been set up in certain Southern states to evade desegregation rulings. Other decisions gave broad interpretations to federal civil rights statutes in housing, employment, and voting.

The most important decision, however, rejected a broadly conceived challenge to school financing in Texas. A closely divided court refused to follow certain state rulings and found that the Texas system did not violate the equal-protection clause of the Fourteenth Amendment even though it resulted in substantially unequal expenditures for the state's pupils solely because they lived in school districts with different financial capacities to support education. A contrary ruling would have forced a historic reexamination of the nation's system of school financing.

Rights of Criminal Suspects. No consistent pattern developed in cases challenging the fairness of criminal convictions. For example, the Supreme Court struck down warrantless police searches of automobiles 25 miles from Mexico despite a statute authorizing searches close to a border. But it relaxed the restrictions on warrantless searches of motor vehicles lawfully in the custody of police and affirmed convictions for transporting stolen goods despite claims that confessions had been improperly obtained.

The court also issued inconsistent rulings in a series of cases involving the application of the double-jeopardy clause. And it narrowed the protection of the privilege against self-incrimination in two cases while holding unconstitutional a state law requiring defendants to give advance notice of an alibi defense in the absence of a reciprocal requirement on the prosecution.

The death penalty was reinstated in several states for specific crimes, such as murder of a police officer. This was done despite the 1972 Supreme Court ruling holding that capital punishment was cruel and unusual punishment, at least if imposed "wantonly and freakishly." Court tests are expected.

Terror raids by narcotics agents shocked civil libertarians in 1973. Operating under state or federal "no knock" statutes, agents often disguised in shabby attire and refusing to identify themselves broke into homes where they expected to find drugs. In some instances innocent persons had their homes raided and ransacked, and they were threatened with death if they resisted.

Voting Rights. In the area of legislative apportionment, the Supreme Court reaffirmed the principle of strict equality in the drawing of district lines for the U. S. House of Representatives. However, with respect to state legislatures it upheld larger variations in population among legislative districts and refused to apply the usual apportionment rules to special units of government—watershed and flood-control districts—on the ground that the constituents most affected by these suits could be given greater voting power than other citizens.

The court also rejected challenges to several state laws. These included a 50-day residence law and a New York statute that required a voter to enroll in the party of his choice before the general (November) election in order to be permitted to vote in the next primary.

Rights of Other Groups. The Supreme Court again afforded aliens broad protection when it held that state restrictions on them were "inherently suspect"; in two cases the court ruled that aliens could not constitutionally be denied admission to the bar or excluded from employment in a state's civil service.

Persons of illegitimate birth were helped when the court invalidated a New Jersey statute limiting certain welfare payments to families with legitimate or adopted children and in another case ruled that a state could not deny illegitimate children the right to sue their fathers for support.

But government employees were unable to persuade the Supreme Court to overthrow rulings upholding statutes forbidding political action by civil servants. (See also CRIME; LAW.)

NORMAN DORSEN
New York University School of Law

CLEVELAND

A mayoral election was the highlight of 1973 in Cleveland. The year was also marked by much renewal of the city's downtown section.

Mayoral Election. In a mayoral campaign bristling with reluctance, Cleveland voters on November 6 retained Mayor Ralph J. Perk for a second two-year term. The Republican defeated an unexpected opponent, Mercedes Cotner, a Democrat and clerk of the City Council, by a vote of 90,839 to 57,488.

Twelve days before the election Mrs. Cotner moved into a vacuum created as the Democratic nominee, James M. Carney, withdrew for unexplained personal reasons. He jerked his hat from the ring 10 days after the city's October 2 primary in which Perk received about 55% of the total vote. Cleveland customarily is heavily Democratic. Carney, a businessman and real estate investor, and Arnold Pinkney, Cleveland board of education president and a Democrat, had lost to Perk in 1971.

The first announced mayoral candidate, the Rev. Alfred M. Waller, a Baptist minister backed by Congressman Louis Stokes, withdrew on July 29 when his appeal failed to attract expected support. Stokes' "21st District Caucus," which had sought to unify black political strength locally and nationally, began to run into defections in 1972. One who broke away was Pinkney; declining to run himself, he supported Carney.

Attempted murder and a reported connected murder preceded the election campaigning. The director of Cleveland's federally funded model cities program, Robert E. Doggett, was shot in the back on August 6 near his office. Nine days later the body of Jerald A. Johnson, suspected of having wounded Doggett, was found in the Ohio River near Petersburg, Ky. Model cities contracts were believed at the heart of the crimes. A special Cuyahoga county grand jury investigated the case.

Downtown Revival. Signs of the viability of the city's core were plentiful in 1973. Two motion picture theaters that had been dark reopened with entertainment and dining facilities. The State Theater's lobby became the Playhouse Square Cabaret on April 18, and the nearby Palace Theater opened for similar use in November. The first featured the songs of Jacques Brel for more than 30 weeks, in November breaking Cleveland's record for continuous theatrical performances, set 45 years before by *Abie's Irish Rose.*

A block from these theaters, the intersection of Euclid Avenue and Huron Road was changed late in the year to a garden mall. Two blocks to the north the 22-story, 265-suite Ernest J. Bohn Tower opened on January 9 as the latest Cleveland Metropolitan Housing Authority (CMHA) apartment house. This building, for senior citizens, was named for a former CMHA director.

Near the Tower a large apartment-and-shopping complex, Park Centre, admitted its first tenants in 1973. Construction of the $35 million building was continuing at year's end.

An agency of the Higbee Company, a department store, bought 4 acres at the westerly edge of the downtown section. Plans were drawn to renovate this section as a living-shopping-dining center. Cleveland State University began clearance of land in the Euclid–East 19th Street region for its $6 million law school.

Sports. First steel was raised for Nickolas Mileti's basketball and hockey arena south of Cleveland. Mileti is a principal owner of Cleveland professional basketball, hockey, and baseball franchises. Negotiations neared completion under which the 80,000-seat, 42-year-old Municipal Stadium would be leased to the Cleveland Browns' football team management and others for 10 years. Improvements costing $10 million were planned.

Business. Cleveland, a major steel-making center and producer of durable goods, maintained a record level of business activity throughout 1973.

JOHN F. HUTH, JR.
"The Plain Dealer," Cleveland

COIN COLLECTING. See HOBBIES.
COLLEGES. See EDUCATION; UNIVERSITIES.

COLOMBIA

Despite substantial political alienation, constitutional government appeared more firmly established than ever in Colombia at the end of 1973. The Liberal and Conservative parties spent most of the year jockeying for a dominant position inasmuch as the National Front government, a 15-year-old experiment in coalition politics, is scheduled to end in 1974. In spite of another resurgence of guerrilla activity, the economy performed admirably.

Political Affairs. The scheduled end of the National Front arrangement with presidential elections in March 1974 meant that both the Liberals and Conservatives were free in 1973 to nominate candidates for president. Since 1958 the presidency had been alternated between Liberals and Conservatives every four years.

The Liberal convention in June revealed serious divisions in the party. Former President Carlos Lleras Restrepo, the leading contender for the

---

——— COLOMBIA · Information Highlights ———

Official Name: Republic of Colombia.
Location: Northwest South America.
Area: 439,736 square miles (1,138,914 sq km).
Population (1973 est.): 23,700,000. *Density,* 49 per square mile (19 per sq km).
Chief Cities (1972 est.): Bogotá, the capital, 2,500,000; Medellín, 1,090,000; Cali, 920,000; Barranquilla, 700,000.
Government: *Head of state,* Misael Pastrana Borrero, president (took office Aug. 1970). *Head of government,* Misael Pastrana Borrero. *Legislature*—Congress: Senate and House of Representatives. *Major political parties*—Liberal party; Conservative party; National Popular Alliance (ANAPO).
Language: Spanish (official).
Education: *Expenditure* (1969), 12.7% of total public expenditure. *School enrollment* (1968)—primary, 2,733,432; secondary, 654,066; technical/vocational, 191,573; university/higher (1969), 85,339.
Monetary Unit: Peso (23.75 pesos equal U. S.$1, July 1973).
Gross National Product (1972 est.): $7,360,000,000.
Economic Indexes: *Industrial production* (1970), 148 (1963=100); *agricultural production* (1971), 140 (1963=100); *consumer price index* (1972), 245 (1963=100).
Manufacturing (major products): Textiles, beverages, iron and steel, petroleum products, cement, footwear, apparel, machinery.
Major Agricultural Products: Coffee (ranks 2d among world producers, 1972), bananas, cotton, sugarcane, tobacco, potatoes, corn, rice, cattle.
Major Minerals: Petroleum, iron ore, gold, coal, platinum.
Foreign Trade (1972): *Exports,* $743,000,000; *Imports,* $836,000,000. *Chief trading partners* (1970)—United States (took 37% of exports, supplied 48% of imports); West Germany (14%—8.5%); Latin American Free Trade Association (11%—9%).
Tourism: *Receipts* (1971), $41,470,000.
Transportation: *Motor vehicles* (1969), 285,500 (automobiles, 150,500); *railroads* (1971), 2,092 miles (3,366 km); *merchant fleet* (1972), 232,000 gross registered tons; *major national airline,* AVIANCA (Aerovias Nacionales de Colombia).
Communications: *Telephones* (1972), 1,005,771; *newspapers* (1971), 36 (daily circulation, 2,369,000).

presidential nomination, called for a new alignment of Liberals with the moderate wing of the Conservative party. Following his defeat for the nomination, he walked out of the convention and the Liberals nominated Alfonso Lopez Michelsen, leader of the party's left wing. The Conservatives nominated Alvaro Gomez Hurtado.

In spite of the campaign rhetoric, much of the National Front arrangement seemed likely to endure past 1974. An agreement appeared to have been reached on a sharing of cabinet posts and other political spoils no matter who is elected president. The only major opposition to the two old-line parties will come again from former dictator Gustavo Rojas Pinilla's populist National Popular Alliance (ANAPO), which nearly won the 1970 elections. This time, ANAPO's candidate was to be Rojas' daughter, Maria Eugenia Rojas de Moreno Diaz.

At the end of the year both Liberals and Conservatives seemed to discount the threat of ANAPO. The only unknown in the campaign was whether Carlos Lleras Restrepo would try to form a last-minute coalition of Liberals and moderate Conservatives in an attempt to regain the presidency.

Guerrilla Activity. The three major guerrilla groups operating in Colombia—the Maoist Popular Liberation Army (EPL), the Castroite Army of National Liberation (ELN), and the Moscow-oriented Colombian Revolutionary Armed Forces (FARC)—were all active during 1973. Several leading political and social figures were kidnapped early in the year, but were subsequently released. In May, the leader of the Liberal party in the department of Córdoba, German Gomez Pelaez, was kidnapped and subsequently killed by members of the EPL.

Government response to the kidnappings and to several attacks on isolated army posts was the roundup and trial in Bucaramanga of 120 guerrilla suspects. Those convicted were sentenced to imprisonment on the Pacific island of Gorgona.

Economy. Colombian austerity in the preceding decade began to pay off in a period of sustained economic growth. The 1973 growth rate was slightly better than the 1972 increase of 7.4%. Continued high world prices for a number of agricultural products, including coffee, plus several other favorable factors, combined to produce increased export revenues. Imports did not increase as rapidly as exports, and substantial capital inflows allowed prepayment of some international loans.

Much of the capital inflow was in the form of economic assistance, of which $310 million came from the ten member nations of the Colombian Consultative Group. In a June meeting, the group expressed its satisfaction with Colombia's development program and promised further aid through 1974 at or above 1973 levels. The only problem area was the rate of inflation, which rose to 14% during the first five months of 1973.

Foreign Affairs. During July and August, Colombia took steps to normalize its participation in the Andean Group—a common market arrangement among Colombia, Venezuela, Ecuador, Peru, Bolivia, and Chile. The government asked for congressional approval of the 1969 Treaty of Cartagena that established the group. It also issued two measures designed to bring treatment of foreign capital into line with Andean Foreign Investment Code provisions, until approval of the treaty has been obtained.

ERNEST A. DUFF
Randolph-Macon Woman's College

COLORADO

Colorado continued as a battleground for environmental issues in 1973. The state also gained a new governor and passed some significant legislation in the longest legislative session in its history.

Politics. John A. Love, who was first elected governor of Colorado in 1962, resigned in July 1973, with 17 months left in his third term, to accept a presidential appointment as director of the new White House Office of Energy Policy. (In December, Love quit the post and returned to Denver to practice law.) His 1970 Republican running mate, Lt. Gov. John D. Vanderhoof, stepped up to the governorship amid predictions that his tenure would be more lively than the serene course steered by Love.

A minor scandal at the State Penitentiary came to light shortly after the change in command, and Vanderhoof acted promptly to suspend the acting warden. A state grand jury investigation was begun into a variety of charges, including complaints that prison officials had misappropriated food and other supplies for personal use. Vanderhoof made some changes in state department heads and pledged to pursue his predecessor's priority program of attempting to control Colorado's booming growth in land development.

Legislature. Despite the efforts of Love and Vanderhoof, attempts by the Colorado legislature to enact a land-use bill collapsed toward the end

--------- COLORADO • Information Highlights ---------

Area: 104,247 square miles (270,000 sq km).
Population (1972 est.): 2,357,000. *Density:* 23 per sq mi.
Chief Cities (1970 census): Denver, the capital, 514,678; Colorado Springs, 135,060; Pueblo, 97,453; Lakewood, 92,787; Aurora, 74,974; Boulder, 66,870; Arvada, 46,814.
Government (1973): *Chief Officers*—governor, John D. Vanderhoof (R); acting lt. gov., Ted L. Strickland (R); secy. of state, Byron A. Anderson (R); atty. gen., John P. Moore (R); treas., Palmer Burch (R); commissioner of education, Calvin M. Frazier; chief justice, Edward E. Pringle. *General Assembly*—Senate, 35 members (22 Republicans, 13 Democrats); House of Representatives, 65 members (37 R, 28 D).
Education (1972–73): *Enrollment*—public elementary schools, 312,960 pupils, 12,264 teachers; public secondary schools, 265,040 pupils, 12,280 teachers; nonpublic schools, 35,-200 pupils, 1,700 teachers; colleges and universities, 115,657 students. *Public school expenditures,* $513,045,000 ($955 per pupil). *Average teacher's salary,* $10,280.
State Finances (fiscal year 1971): *Revenues,* $1,104,058,000 (3% general sales tax and gross receipts taxes, $156,873,-000; motor fuel tax, $78,309,000; federal funds, $297,423,-000). *Expenditures,* $1,003,385,000 (education, $449,505,-000; health, welfare, and safety, $194,708,000; highways, $183,852,000). *State debt,* $120,119,000 (June 30, 1971).
Personal Income (1972): $10,485,000,000; per capita, $4,449.
Public Assistance (1972): $184,155,000. *Average monthly payments* (Dec. 1972)—old-age assistance, $76.10; aid to families with dependent children, $178.98.
Labor Force: *Nonagricultural wage and salary earners* (July 1973), 834,700. *Average annual employment* (1971)—manufacturing, 117,700; trade, 180,800; government, 187,-000; services, 134,700. *Insured unemployed* (Sept. 1973)—6,200 (1.0%).
Manufacturing (1971): *Value added by manufacture,* $2,088,-500,000. Food and kindred products, $501,000,000; non-electrical machinery, $190,500,000; fabricated metal products, $149,400,000; printing and publishing, $144,100,000; stone, clay, and glass products, $133,500,000; electrical equipment and supplies, $129,200,000.
Agriculture (1972): *Cash farm income,* $1,770,676,000 (livestock, $1,396,479,000; crops, $303,291,000; government payments, $70,906,000). *Chief crops* (in order of value, 1972)—Hay, wheat, corn, sugar beets (ranks 3d among the states).
Mining (1972): *Production value,* $421,698,000 (ranks 19th among the states). *Chief minerals*—Molybdenum, value not available; petroleum, $109,836,000; coal, $36,500,000; sand and gravel, $31,951,000.
Transportation: *Roads* (1972), 81,870 miles (131,753 km); *motor vehicles* (1972), 1,547,598; *railroads* (1972), 3,572 miles (5,748 km); *public airports* (1972), 74.
Communications: *Telephones* (1973), 1,592,500; *television stations* (1971), 11; *radio stations* (1971), 94; *newspapers* (1973), 26 (daily circulation, 756,000).

of the six-month session. The legislature passed a $221 million plan increasing state support for public schools, an action that together with a healthy surplus in the state treasury promised property tax reductions for most Colorado landowners.

The legislature also imposed a uniform statewide cigarette tax of 10 cents a pack, doubling the old level but also ending local cigarette taxes. After three years of trying, it approved a no-fault automobile insurance law and also passed a record $1.4 billion state budget. A tough capital punishment bill, which would have made death the only penalty for a number of major crimes, was rejected.

Denver. Colorado's capital city lost in an important U. S. Supreme Court decision in August. The court, in the first such ruling affecting a northern school district, declared that the Denver public schools had allowed a pattern of racial discrimination to continue by not taking affirmative action to correct it in one area of the city.

Voters in the Denver area approved a $1.56 billion regional transportation district, but a few weeks later a very small turnout of metropolitan area voters rejected a proposal for a regional services program. Late in 1973, Denver and its suburbs engaged in a bitter battle over the city's annexation policies.

Ecology. Colorado, a battleground for environmental issues, became involved in several disputes with the federal government. Perhaps the most serious dispute was that between Denver and the U. S. Army when it was revealed that the military was not destroying stockpiles of nerve gases as scheduled. The gas and other toxic chemicals are stored at the Rocky Mountain Arsenal, north of Denver, in an area where the city proposes to extend a new runway for Stapleton International Airport.

There was also an environmental battle between the state and the Atomic Energy Commission (AEC) over traces of radioactive hydrogen found in the water supply of Broomfield, a suburban city north of Denver. The AEC's Rocky Flats plant, operated by the Dow Chemical Company, was suspected by state officials as the source of the pollution.

FREDERICK W. BROWN, JR., *The Denver Post*

COMMONWEALTH OF NATIONS

During 1973 the Commonwealth gained a new member, the Bahamas, and was concerned with Anglo-Maltese relations and with economic matters.

New Member. A new member, the 33d, was added to the Commonwealth of Nations when the Bahamas became independent on July 10, 1973. Prince Charles, the Prince of Wales, represented Queen Elizabeth II at the independence celebrations from July 6 to 11. Sir Milo Butler, the first Bahamian governor-general, took office on August 1. (See also BAHAMAS.) Independence for Grenada as of Feb. 7, 1974, was approved in London on June 6, 1973.

Meetings. The 19th Commonwealth Conference met in Ottawa, Canada, on August 1–10. The meeting reviewed world political and economic problems. According to the final communiqué, "mutual understanding of conflicting viewpoints was achieved." The 8th conference of heads of government of Commonwealth Caribbean countries, held in Georgetown, Guyana, from April 24 to 27, decided to establish a Caribbean Community, including a common market, to come into effect on May 1, 1974.

COMMONWEALTH OF NATIONS

Component	Area (sq mi)	Pop. (mid-1972 estimate)	Status
EUROPE			
Great Britain & islands of British seas[1]	94,528	55,967,000	Sovereign state
Gibraltar	2	30,000	Dependent territory
Malta	122	325,000	Sovereign state
Total in Europe	94,652	56,322,000	
AFRICA			
Botswana	231,804	690,000	Sovereign state
British Indian Ocean Territory	30	2,000	Dependent territory
Gambia	4,361	380,000	Sovereign state
Ghana	92,099	9,090,000	Sovereign state
Kenya	224,959	12,070,000	Sovereign state
Lesotho	11,720	970,000	Sovereign state
Malawi	45,747	4,670,000	Sovereign state
Mauritius (and dependencies)	809	830,000	Sovereign state
Nigeria	356,668	58,020,000	Sovereign state
Rhodesia	150,803	5,690,000	Internally self-governing colony[2]
St. Helena	47	5,000	Dependent territory
Ascension	34	1,000	
Tristan da Cunha	40	300	
Other islands	41	......	
Seychelles	145	60,000	Dependent territory
Sierra Leone	27,700	2,630,000	Sovereign state
Swaziland	6,704	430,000	Sovereign state
Tanzania	364,899	14,000,000	Sovereign state
Uganda	91,134	10,460,000	Sovereign state
Zambia	290,585	4,420,000	Sovereign state
Total in Africa	1,900,329	124,418,300	
AMERICA			
Antigua	171	70,000	West Indies Associated state
Bahamas	5,380	190,000	Sovereign state
Barbados	166	240,000	Sovereign state
Belize (British Honduras)	8,867	130,000	Dependent territory
Bermuda	20	60,000	Dependent territory
British Virgin Islands	59	11,000	Dependent territory
Canada	3,851,809	21,850,000	Sovereign state
Cayman Islands	100	10,000	Dependent territory
Dominica	290	72,000	West Indies Associated state
Falkland Islands (and dependencies)	6,198	3,000	Dependent territory
Grenada	133	100,000	West Indies Associated state
Guyana	83,000	750,000	Sovereign state
Jamaica	4,232	1,920,000	Sovereign state
Montserrat	38	12,000	Dependent territory
St. Kitts-Nevis-Anguilla	138	70,000	West Indies Associated state
St. Lucia	238	120,000	West Indies Associated state
St. Vincent	150	90,000	West Indies Associated state
Trinidad and Tobago	1,980	1,040,000	Sovereign state
Turks and Caicos	166	6,000	Dependent territory
Total in America	3,963,135	26,744,000	
ASIA			
Bangladesh	55,126	76,600,000	Sovereign state
Brunei	2,226	140,000	Internally self-governing sultanate
Cyprus	3,572	650,000	Sovereign state
Hong Kong	399	4,080,000	Dependent territory
India	1,266,598	563,490,000	Sovereign state
Malaysia	127,316	11,000,000	Sovereign state
Singapore	224	2,150,000	Sovereign state
Sri Lanka (Ceylon)	25,332	13,030,000	Sovereign state
Total in Asia	1,480,793	671,140,000	
OCEANIA			
Australia	2,967,900	12,960,000	Sovereign state
Christmas Island	52	3,000	External territory
Cocos Islands	5	1,000	External territory
Norfolk Island	14	2,000	External territory
Papua New Guinea	178,260	2,580,000	External territory
British Solomon Islands Protectorate	10,983	170,000	Dependent territory
Fiji	7,055	540,000	Sovereign state
Gilbert and Ellice Islands	342	60,000	Dependent territory
Nauru[3]	8	7,000	Sovereign state
New Hebrides	5,700	90,000	Anglo-French condominium
New Zealand	103,736	2,900,000	Sovereign state
Niue Island	100	5,000	Dependency
Tokelau Islands	4	2,000	Dependency
Pitcairn Island	2	100	Dependent territory
Tonga	270	90,000	Sovereign state
Western Samoa	1,097	150,000	Sovereign state
Total in Oceania	3,275,528	19,560,100	
Grand Total[4]	10,714,437	898,184,400	

[1] Includes Northern Ireland, Channel Islands, and Isle of Man. [2] Rhodesia declared its independence Nov. 11, 1965, but technically retains Commonwealth status. [3] Nauru is a special member. [4] Does not include British Antarctic Territory, Australian Antarctic Territory, or Ross Dependency (New Zealand).

COMMONWEALTH OF NATIONS' representatives met in Ottawa, Canada, in August, with Canadian Prime Minister Pierre Trudeau acting as host.

British Military Bases on Malta. On Dec. 27, 1972, Malta's Prime Minister Dom Mintoff asked that Britain pay an additional 10% on the agreed rent for Maltese military bases or give up the bases by March 31, 1973, but the deadline passed without any action being taken. Malta was, however, admitted to full membership in the conference of nonaligned nations in Algeria in September, after giving a pledge that British troops would be out of Malta by the end of 1979, the date at which the current Anglo-Maltese defense agreement expires.

Aid to Commonwealth Territories. On Jan. 1, 1973, the Commonwealth Development Corporation, a British government agency, was operating 216 projects in 39 countries and had a total investment commitment of £202.4 million (the pound equals about $2.40). By July 1, 1973, the Commonwealth Development Finance Company, a private corporation owned by businesses based in the Commonwealth, had investments totaling £32.3 million and was operating 145 projects in various parts of the world.

Britain provided other assistance, including a number of loans, among them £3.1 million to Guyana toward the cost of a £9.5 million electricity pro-

gram; a capital grant of £7 million to Lesotho; and two economic aid loans to Sri Lanka (formerly Ceylon) totaling £1.86 million. Three loans, of £5 million, £3.3 million, and £3.5 million, were made to India. The Seychelles received a grant of £2.3 million toward improving the water supply for its capital, Mahe. A loan agreement with Bangladesh providing for £2 million assistance was signed in Dacca on May 18.

Bermuda. The governor of Bermuda, Sir Richard Sharples, and his aide-de-camp, Captain Hugh Sayers, were shot and killed while walking on the grounds of Government House on March 10. The crime was not solved by year's end. Sir Edwin H. C. Leather was sworn in as Sir Richard's successor.

Visits. Queen Elizabeth II and the Duke of Edinburgh visited Ontario, Prince Edward Island, Regina, and Calgary, Canada (June 25–July 5).

RICHARD E. WEBB
Former Director, Reference and Library Division
British Information Services, New York

COMMUNICATIONS. See POSTAL SERVICE; TELE-
COMMUNICATIONS; TELEVISION AND RADIO.

COMPUTERS

In the computer field the most important events of 1973 were the resolutions of two lawsuits brought by competitors against International Business Machines Corporation (IBM), the world's largest supplier of electronic data processing (EDP) products.

IBM and the Courts. The first of the two antitrust suits against IBM to be concluded in 1973 was settled out of court in January by consent of the litigants. In return for withdrawing its five-year-old charge that IBM had exercised monopoly powers in marketing large-scale computers, Control Data Corporation received IBM's Service Bureau Corporation (SBC) subsidiary and a package of other concessions valued in excess of $146 million. Since Control Data paid IBM $16 million for SBC, the total benefits to Control Data were about $130 million. The most notable aspect of the case involved Control Data's agreement to destroy a computerized index ("data base") it had developed from the millions of documents IBM had been ordered to submit as evidence in this and related antitrust cases.

Two of those other cases—one brought by the Justice Department and the other by Telex Computer Products, Inc.—were still pending. Both complained that the destruction of the index violated a pretrial order against destroying any records. The end result was that Control Data and IBM were chastised by the court for the *fait accompli,* but the settlement was allowed to stand. It is a tribute to the computer's power to retrieve information from masses of raw data that this "data-base incident" became paramount even though copies of all the original documents always were available to all parties.

The Telex case, resolved in September, was noteworthy for many reasons. It was the first of 11 antitrust suits against IBM to end in a court judgment, and it resulted in the largest total damage award in antitrust history—$352.5 million, or three times actual found damages as stipulated by the Sherman Antitrust Act. Also, the decision established a precedent whereby products designed for attachment to another manufacturer's products may constitute a separate and legitimate market.

Briefly, Telex Computer Products manufactures peripheral equipment (such as memory devices) designed to be compatible with IBM central processing units (CPU's). Telex charged that IBM selectively reduced prices on its own peripherals when it found them vulnerable to Telex competition, and that IBM deliberately designed its CPUs to hinder the development of compatible peripherals. IBM claimed that a manufacturer has a natural monopoly power over all devices designed exclusively for attachment to its own products. Therefore, argued IBM, a market for "plug-compatible" equipment cannot exist, and IBM could not be guilty of restraining it. IBM also countersued Telex for theft of trade secrets.

Judge A. Sherman Christensen accepted Telex's contention that IBM had priced its products in a "predatory" manner, rejecting IBM's argument on the grounds that IBM recognized the existence of a plug-compatible market by reacting to it. The judge also ordered Telex to pay IBM $21.9 million for misappropriating IBM trade secrets. He later announced that his calculation of revenues lost by Telex due to IBM's predatory pricing actions did not take into account that some of the products from which Telex would have derived those revenues were developed from the information it had misappropriated. Accordingly, he reduced the award to Telex by $93 million, dropping the total to $259.5 million.

Point-of-Sale Terminals. Advances in microminiaturization, coupled with the development of standard product identification codes, brought about a wave of new specialized computer terminals for retail applications. Sears Roebuck, J. C. Penney, and Montgomery Ward were replacing conventional cash registers with sophisticated data-capture devices, and pilot installations were under way in several large supermarket chains.

Pocket-Sized Calculators. About 6 million pocket-sized digital calculators were produced in 1973. These tiny electronic devices first became popular less than two years earlier when simple four-function $(+, -, \times, \div)$, six-digit models were priced at about $100. By the end of 1973 more sophisticated eight-digit models were priced under $40.

New Technologies. The most dramatic technological advances in 1973 were associated with computer memories. In February, RCA demonstrated what it described as the "first holographic optical computer memory able to perform the full-cycle data processing operations of write, store, read, and erase." Cambridge Memories, a Massachusetts firm, reported deliveries of a solid-state storage device ("Dotram") that could replace the popular spinning-disk type of computer memory. IBM announced a complete random-access memory with a capacity of more than 8,000 bits (binary digits) of information on a semiconductor chip smaller than three-tenths of a square inch.

ALAN R. KAPLAN
Editor, "Modern Data" Magazine

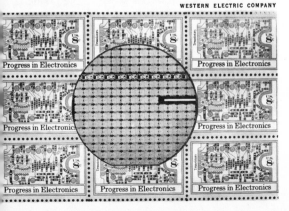

546,000 (COUNT 'EM) TRANSISTORS: Two-inch wafer contains 130 silicon gate memory integrated circuit chips, each chip containing 4,200 transistors. Stamps in background were issued in honor of transistors.

WESTERN ELECTRIC COMPANY

CONNECTICUT

Taxes, food prices, the oil supply, and legislative reapportionment were among Connecticut's major concerns in 1973. Most of these issues were the subjects of legislative or court action.

In May, Gov. Thomas J. Meskill appointed Lt. Gov. T. Clark Hull, Jr., and state treasurer Robert I. Berdon to the state superior court. Peter L. Cashman, a Republican leader of the state Senate, was sworn in as the new lieutenant governor in June and was also appointed chairman of the state's newly created Council on Human Services.

CONNECTICUT · Information Highlights

Area: 5,009 square miles (12,973 sq km).
Population (1972 est.): 3,082,000. *Density:* 633 per sq mi.
Chief Cities (1970 census): Hartford, the capital, 158,017; Bridgeport, 156,542; New Haven, 137,707; Stamford, 108,798; Waterbury, 108,033; New Britain, 83,441.
Government (1973): *Chief Officers*—governor, Thomas J. Meskill (R); lt. gov., Peter L. Cashman (R); secy. of state, Gloria Schaffer (D); atty. gen., Robert K. Killian (D); treas., Alden A. Ives (R); commissioner of education, William J. Sanders; chief justice, Charles S. House. *General Assembly*—Senate, 36 members (23 Republicans, 13 Democrats); House of Representatives, 151 members (93 R, 58 D).
Education (1972–73): *Enrollment*—public elementary schools, 478,528 pupils, 19,343 teachers; public secondary schools, 195,001 pupils, 14,825 teachers; nonpublic schools, 107,900 pupils, 5,200 teachers; colleges and universities, 129,911 students. *Public school expenditures*, $770,000,000 ($1,241 per pupil). *Average teacher's salary*, $11,200.
State Finances (fiscal year 1971): *Revenues*, $1,364,625,000 (6.5% general sales tax and gross receipts taxes, $265,217,000; motor fuel tax, $103,215,000; federal funds, $270,088,000). *Expenditures*, $1,463,181,000 (education, $498,033,000; health, welfare, and safety, $270,651,000; highways, $224,476,000). *State debt*, $2,171,123,000 (June 30, 1971).
Personal Income (1972): $16,466,000,000; per capita, $5,342.
Public Assistance (1972): $249,186,000. *Average monthly payments* (Dec. 1972)—old-age assistance, $107.22; aid to families with dependent children, $247.91.
Labor Force: *Nonagricultural wage and salary earners* (July 1973), 1,221,100. *Average annual employment* (1972)—manufacturing, 402,000; trade, 233,500; government, 164,400; services, 198,500. *Insured unemployed* (Sept. 1973)—30,100 (2.6%).
Manufacturing (1971): Value added by manufacture, $6,049,300,000. Transportation equipment, $1,012,100,000; nonelectrical machinery, $815,300,000; electrical equipment and supplies, $675,900,000; fabricated metal products, $643,300,000; primary metal industries, $404,300,000.
Agriculture (1972): *Cash farm income*, $164,364,000 (livestock, $101,255,000; crops, $62,600,000; government payments, $509,000). *Chief crops* (in order of value, 1971)—Tobacco, hay, apples, potatoes.
Mining (1972): Production value, $28,451,000 (ranks 46th among the states). *Chief minerals*—Stone, $15,370,000; sand and gravel, $10,739,000; feldspar, value not available; lime, value not available.
Fisheries (1972): *Commercial catch*, 4,911,000 pounds ($1,498,000). *Leading species by value*—Lobster, $657,000; oysters, $231,000; clams, $207,000.
Transportation: *Roads* (1972), 18,531 miles (29,822 km); *motor vehicles* (1972), 1,791,011; *railroads* (1972), 664 miles (1,069 km); *public airports* (1972), 14.
Communications: *Telephones* (1973), 2,185,000; *television stations* (1971), 5; *radio stations* (1971), 58; *newspapers* (1973), 28 (daily circulation, 967,000).

New $40 million Gold Star Memorial Bridge (right) spans Thames River between Groton and New London.

Legislation. The General Assembly adopted a $1.2 billion budget for fiscal 1973–74. Republicans, in control of the executive and legislative branches, lowered the state's sales tax from 7% to 6½%, abolished the dividends tax, provided property tax relief for the elderly, and revised various business taxes. Regulatory commissions were created to control hospital costs and prices of petroleum products.

A bill to restore the death penalty for certain crimes passed by a narrow margin. An address before the Assembly by Chief Justice Charles S. House —the first such address in state history—was responsible in part for judicial reforms that included creation of an organized crime task force and a division of criminal justice in the judicial department.

In a reversal of a 1972 action, the Assembly adopted the proposed 27th (Equal Rights) Amendment to the U. S. Constitution. A permanent commission on the status of women was also created. The Council on Human Services was charged with coordinating and improving the work of the state's health, welfare, correction, and other social service agencies. Two mental retardation facilities received an emergency appropriation of $4.3 million, and $5 million was allocated to upgrade the standards of the state's mental health institutions. No abortion legislation was passed, but the public health council issued guideline regulations.

A solid waste agency, known as the Resources Recovery Authority, was created with bonding power of $250 million to establish statewide refuse disposal and recycling facilities. The Assembly also established a state department of commerce and restored observance of Veterans Day to November 11.

Court Actions. The two-year struggle for legislative reapportionment ended on June 18, when the U. S. Supreme Court ruled that the General Assembly's reapportionment (Saden) plan does not violate the one-man, one-vote principle. On July 26, Connecticut's attorney general, Robert K. Killian, announced that the state had filed suit against 20 major oil companies, charging violation of state and federal antitrust laws. Connecticut became the second state (after Florida) to sue oil firms.

Transportation. A bus strike halted service in the major cities during the winter months. The settlement, which was agreed to in March, guaranteed payment by the state of losses and operating expenses for two years, after which local transit districts are to take over. A $4.4 million monorail system for Bradley International Airport (near Hartford), used by 2.3 million passengers annually, is to be built in 1974.

Higher Education. Legislation adopted by the General Assembly allows out-of-state college students to qualify for in-state tuition rates if they demonstrate financial independence and establish residence in Connecticut. Glenn W. Ferguson, formerly president of Clark University, took office as president of the University of Connecticut on August 15.

Economic and Other News. The employment situation improved, except in the construction industries. Agriculture continued to decline, but production of shade-grown tobacco increased from 3.62 million to 5.89 million pounds. By May 1973 the state's 50-cents-a-ticket lottery, which began operation in February 1972, had sales totaling $50.2 million. Payments in prizes amounted to $20.4 million, and net revenue, $22.6 million.

GEORGE ADAMS
Connecticut State Library

CONSUMERISM

Consumers and their advocates, as well as members of the business community, wondered if the consumer movement had peaked-out in 1973. After the publication of Ralph Nader's *Unsafe at Any Speed* in 1965, consumerism received major public attention. However, during 1973 public concern for consumers' interests appeared to have hit a plateau or, possibly, to have begun a decline.

Inflation. Major U. S. consumer concern in 1973 centered on the problem of inflation. Selected statistics indicate the seriousness of that problem. During 1972, when Phase II of President Nixon's price and wage control policies were in effect, there was a relatively mild rate of inflation of 3.4%. However, during the first five months of 1973, following the institution of Phase III, which removed mandatory price controls and decontrolled rents, prices rose at a seasonably adjusted annual rate of 8.3%. As a result, on June 13 the President imposed a freeze on nearly all prices, except of raw ·farm products and rents.

On July 19, Phase IV went into effect, with the freeze lifted for most foods, except beef. On August 12, the freeze was lifted on all other items, except gasoline and oil. On September 12 the price freeze on beef was lifted.

The major price increase was in August, when the Consumer Price Index rose by 1.9%, or 22.8% on a seasonally adjusted annual basis. Food accounted for 80% of the increase.

By October it was apparent that the worst of the inflation had not passed. That month prices increased by 9.6% on a seasonally adjusted annual basis, with fuel costs leading the price increases. Food prices probably will never return to their previous lower levels, but the magnitude of their inflation during 1973 was not anticipated for 1974. (See also ECONOMY OF THE U. S.)

Octane Ratings. From the consumer's point of view, when buying gasoline the most significant thing, other than price, is the octane rating. A fringe benefit for consumers from Phase IV was the requirement by the Cost of Living Council that octane ratings be posted on gasoline pumps. The knowledgeable consumer reduces the octane rating of the gasoline he uses for his car until the engine begins to "knock," then he uses a gasoline having an octane rating just above that level. This practice has two advantages: first, the consumer does not buy a higher priced gasoline than his car engine needs; second, using the proper octane gasoline lessens the pollution emission of the engine.

Federal Consumer Legislation. No major consumer bills were enacted in 1973, and those that were had relatively minor importance. Among them were laws prohibiting televising commercials for little cigars and tampering with automobile odometers.

The most significant consumer bill considered during 1973 was one that would establish a Consumer Protection Agency. There are two basic versions of the bill. One would establish the agency within the White House; the other would make it an independent agency. Almost unanimously, consumer advocates favor an independent agency that would have far-reaching powers and be relatively free from political pressure. The controversy about the bill has been going on for a number of years, and it seems unlikely that Congress will act on it in the near future.

DEL MONTE CORPORATION

NEW LABELING system, adopted voluntarily by some food processors, tells consumers the nutritional value.

Consumer Product Safety Commission. The most significant consumer law enacted in 1972 established the Consumer Product Safety Commission (CPSC). During 1973, under the chairmanship of Richard O. Simpson, CPSC operations began to take shape. Charged with protecting the public against "unreasonable risks of injury," CPSC, called the most powerful independent federal agency ever created by Congress, has the authority to regulate safety features on most consumer products, many of which had not been subject to federal controls. In 1973, CPSC required that mattresses be made of material that will not catch fire from dropped lighted cigarettes. It also banned outright the sale of aerosol spray adhesives, acting on a report that exposure to the spray may cause chromosome damage in adults and birth defects in children. Further, it removed the "Little Wonder TV Antenna" from the market because of the danger of electrical shock.

Important to the success of CPSC is the National Electronic Injury Surveillance System (NEISS). Through NEISS, product-related injuries are reported by teletype from emergency rooms of 119 selected hospitals across the United States. These hospitals are considered to be a representative sample for the continental United States. NEISS by no means supplies a complete accounting of product-related injuries, since injuries treated in doctors' offices, at home, or by direct hospital admission are not reported. However, it does provide a rapid method of alerting CPSC to products on the market that cause consumer injuries.

There is some concern among the business community that CPSC will be unreasonable and unreal-

istic. But Chairman Simpson denied this charge. For example, he stated that CPSC would not require safety features for an electric toaster that might push its price up to $150. However, if a safety feature costing $1.00 or $1.50 would make a toaster considerably safer, such a feature would be required.

Food and Drug Administration. The Food and Drug Administration (FDA) took two actions in 1973 of major significance to consumers. It issued a final order requiring manufacturers of cosmetics to list ingredients on product labels. The new labeling requirement will cover all cosmetic labels ordered from printers after March 31, 1974; and after March 31, 1975, all cosmetic products must be so labeled. These dates permit manufacturers to clear out current stocks and redesign and order new labels. The FDA order makes it mandatory for cosmetic ingredients to be listed in descending order of prevalence and by standardized names. Fragrances and colors may be labeled, simply, as "fragrances and colors."

Nutritional labeling, the FDA's other significant action, is considered by the agency to be one of the most ambitious programs it has ever undertaken. From labels, consumers will know exactly what nutrients are in the food they buy. Not only will the labels list the ingredients in the food package, but, in a standard format, they will also give what nutrients and in what quantities the food provides. Such labels will permit consumers to compare the nutritional value of different foods by a uniform standard.

The nutritional label on a food package will list the caloric content and how much protein, carbohydrates, and fat a serving of the food will provide. In addition, it will also show the percentage of the U.S. Recommended Daily Allowance (U.S. RDA) of protein and seven essential vitamins and minerals per serving. The label may also list how much unsaturated and saturated fat, cholesterol, and sodium the food contains, and it may give the percentage of the U.S. RDA for an additional dozen vitamins and minerals.

The FDA labeling program is voluntary on the part of food purveyors unless nutritional claims are made on labels or in advertising. In that case, FDA standards must be met. Already several major food processors and supermarket chains are using the FDA labeling standards, and most others are expected to follow, by choice or because of competitive pressures.

Federal Trade Commission. The Federal Trade Commission (FTC) was involved in three key consumer issues in 1973. Because of action initiated by the FTC in 1959 against deceptive and misleading advertising of Geritol, a U.S. district judge imposed fines of $456,000 against Geritol's manufacturer, the J. B. Williams Co., and of $356,000 against the Parkson Advertising Agency, a wholly owned subsidiary of J. B. Williams.

In June the U.S. Court of Appeals for the District of Columbia upheld the FTC's authority to make binding rules defining as illegal business practices it considered unfair or deceptive. The case was a crucial test of the FTC's regulatory powers.

For many years the S & H Green Stamp Company has been involved with the FTC regarding its stamp redemption procedures. In 1973 the company agreed to redeem its stamps at any of its redemption centers for cash at the rate of 50 cents per 300 stamps or $2.00 per book of 1,200 stamps, at the option of the customer.

State Consumer Legislation. Considerable state consumer legislation was introduced in 1973 in various legislatures, but the number of bills passed and their importance was minimal. Several states enacted no-fault automobile insurance laws, bringing to 19 the number of states having such laws. The quality of the no-fault insurance laws varies, and no doubt there will eventually be a national standardized law. (See also INSURANCE.)

Several significant state consumer bills were enacted in 1973. Connecticut provided its Consumer Protection Commission with powers similar to those held by the Federal Trade Commission. Massachusetts became the only state to enact mandatory nutrition, ingredient, and open-date labeling, to become fully effective by the end of 1974. In New Hampshire a law was passed mandating the public display of the prices of more than 200 of the best-known prescription drugs, listing both generic and brand names. The California Department of Consumer Affairs now requires that all persons who repair, service, or maintain major home appliances must register with its Bureau of Repair Service.

Better Business Bureaus. The Council of Better Business Bureaus (BBB) reported that in the first five months of 1973 its bureaus handled an average of 3,340 service contacts per month. (Service contacts are divided into inquiries and complaints.) During this period, 78% of the recorded service contacts were prepurchase inquiries. For the estimated 9.6 million BBB service contacts for 1973, 1.2 million were customer complaints.

Canadian Consumerism. Like the United States, Canada was plagued by inflation, particularly of food prices. The Canadian government appointed a Food Prices Review Board to investigate the nature and causes of food-price increases in Canada. It was hoped that the board would allay fears and restore Canadians' confidence in its food industry.

The major Canadian government agency for consumer protection is the Department of Consumer and Corporate Affairs. In 1973 the department became responsible for administering the new textile labeling act. The act requires that every textile manufacturer or seller must list the fibers contained in a fabric, using the generic name for each. From June 1, 1973, the labels must be permanently attached to the product.

Several provinces have enacted legislation outlawing or restricting the growing "pyramid selling" operations in Canada. Pyramid selling is undoubtedly the most successful get-rich-quick promotion ever operated on a large scale in Canada. In pyramid selling the seller hopes to make "big" money by persuading investors to buy distributorships that give investors the right to sell the company's products; but, more important, this gives them ths right to sell distributorships to other investors. An investor who buys a distributorship for, say, $5,000 then has the right to sell distributorships to others and keep perhaps 50% of the fee. Money is made not in selling the product but in selling distributorships. This pyramiding of the number of distributorships makes this scheme a fraud. Since all provincial governments maintain offices to handle consumer inquiries and complaints, Canadians can easily get help in regard to pyramid selling and other such schemes.

STEWART M. LEE
Geneva College

Texas police remove the body of the 25th murder victim of a Houston area homosexual ring that included Elmer Henley and David Brooks (left). The bodies of 27 boys were found in the worst mass slaying in U.S. history.

CRIME

What is crime? Who is a criminal? When should the penalty be made to fit the crime? When should the penalty be tailored to fit the criminal? Fundamental questions such as these came under intense inquiry during 1973.

The Meaning of "Crime." The concept of "crime," a concept traditionally applied to such behavior as murder, robbery, and rape, was extended deep into the political and commercial world during the year.

The Watergate scandal, the plea of *nolo contendere* by former Vice President Agnew to a charge of income tax evasion, and continuing attention to "white-collar" crimes, such as air and noise pollution, illegal campaign contributions, and consumer fraud, all called for reexamination of the meaning of "crime" and the proper response to "criminal" behavior.

In addition, some maintained that far more serious "crimes," such as racism, sexism, and international aggression, were being ignored in discussions of "crime," while trivial kinds of behavior, such as petty larceny, and so-called "victimless" offenses, such as drunkenness, prostitution, and narcotics possession, were monopolizing criminal justice resources.

Agnew Case. The Agnew case highlighted a number of these basic issues. In accepting the former vice president's plea, Judge Walter E. Hoffman noted that ordinarily he would sentence lawyers, bankers, and accountants who violated income tax laws to jail, but that he was willing to go along with the government's contention that Agnew had been punished adequately in terms of his loss of office and reputation. Also, by agreeing to plead *nolo contendere,* the former vice president had saved the nation the travail of an extended and divisive courtroom encounter. The light sentence—unsupervised probation for three years and a fine of $10,000 —was the government's concession to Agnew in return for his plea of no contest. The government also agreed not to prosecute Agnew for extortion or bribery, though it alleged that it had enough evidence to convict him on charges of these crimes.

Negotiated Justice. In negotiated justice, the defendant "cops a plea," that is, he pleads guilty to lesser offenses than those with which he was originally charged. This procedure pervades American criminal justice, involving more than 90% of the felony cases in many jurisdictions. Its advantages,

in addition to those specified in the Agnew case, include the saving of time and money by the government and the possibility of reaching a "fairer" outcome than that specified in the literal letter of the law. Its disadvantages include the possibility of undue coercion on those defendants who seek leniency rather than run the risk of being convicted of more serious crimes although they believe they are innocent.

Equal Justice Under Law? Perhaps the most serious issue raised by the Agnew case was the feeling that defendants with astute attorneys, high social status, or similar resources can work out bargains for themselves that are better than any bargains that can be obtained by persons in less favorable social positions. Susan A. Urban, a New York City resident, wrote to a newspaper after the Agnew case, "I have a friend who is serving a seven-year sentence in prison after being convicted of committing a robbery of $2. No force was used. My friend is poor. He is also black. He and thousands like him join me in a sense of outrage at this dual system of justice."

Victims of Crime. Events in 1973 not only raised fundamental questions about what properly can be labeled as "crime" and how crime should be dealt with. For the first time in recent history, events also concentrated attention on the victims of crime—persons long neglected and often harassed by the criminal justice system.

This development was highlighted by the convening of the first International Symposium on Victimology in Jerusalem, Israel, early in September. Delegates from more than 30 nations presented papers

BANDIT, wearing a Mardi Gras mask and waving a revolver, holds up a bank in a suburb of New Orleans, La.

UPI

that called for return of the victim to primary consideration in the criminal justice process. Among other things, it was noted that crime victims often are harshly dealt with when they present their complaints. During trial, the crime victim is often forced to miss work without reimbursement from the state, and he or she will sit neglected while rival attorneys maneuver trial delays. If a plea is negotiated, the victim is rarely consulted or informed about the outcome. If a fine is levied against the criminal, the collected money goes to the public treasury rather than to the victim who suffered injury or loss because of the criminal act.

The study of "victimology," a term coined in 1947 by the Rumanian jurist Binyamin Mendelsohn, took concrete form during 1973 not only in discussions during the Jerusalem conference but also in various pioneering studies. In a paper titled "On Being Mugged: The Event and Its Aftermath," published in *Urban Life and Culture* in October 1973, Robert Lejeune and Nicholas Alex of the Herbert H. Lehman College in New York examined the responses of 17 mugging victims to their experience. They concluded that the victim "emerges from his mugging as much bewildered as he is morally indignant." The bewilderment, the authors noted, is largely a function of the victims' loss of belief in their invulnerability and an undermining of their feeling of trust and their ability to judge accurately.

Tangible concern for crime victims has been manifested by the proliferation of programs to provide state funds to reimburse crime victims for loss of earnings and medical expenses. During 1973, Illinois became the ninth jurisdiction in the United States to establish a program to compensate crime victims. In addition, Sen. John McClellan and Sen. Mike Mansfield sponsored legislation that would provide federal funds to pay 90% of the costs of state crime-victim compensation programs. If enacted, this measure undoubtedly would lead to inaugurations of programs throughout the country.

In Canada, at the beginning of 1973, the government opened negotiations with provincial authorities regarding federal financial support for the provincial crime-victim compensation efforts. Unlike the U. S. states, Canadian provinces usually tie crime-victim compensation to workmen's compensation programs, and they allow awards for pain and suffering as well as for actual out-of-pocket expenses. Eight of the ten Canadian provinces have victim compensation programs. The programs have been described by Allen M. Linden, a law professor at Osgoode Hall in Toronto, as hybrid types of things. "We have a little bit of criminal justice, a little bit of tort law, and a little bit of welfare."

Crime Statistics. The *Uniform Crime Reports* (*UCR*) is an annual inventory of criminal statistics published by the Federal Bureau of Investigation. Undoubtedly, the most unusual development in many years in regard to the *UCR* was the concession by then Attorney General Elliot L. Richardson that the figures presented a skewed picture of the true crime conditions in the country. "It is universally recognized," he said, "that only a fraction of all crimes committed are reported to the police at all."

The *UCR,* concentrating on crimes known to the police, inevitably reflects biases in the reporting of offenses as well as idiosyncracies in the tabulations made by individual police departments. In regard to forcible rape, for instance, many women fail to report the offense to the police because they feel

SHOT by New York City police while trying to rob Harlem bank, wanted criminal Mace Brown lies dead on sidewalk.

there is nothing to be gained; in fact, a more trust-worthy police department may report more rape offenses because more victims will have the confidence to report offenses to it. Some auto thefts are not registered officially until 24 hours after the original report, and thus temporarily "borrowed" or perhaps "misplaced" vehicles are never reported on official files in some cities. In contrast, they are tabulated in other cities.

In 1973 the *UCR* showed that Phoenix, Ariz., had the highest larceny rate in the nation—well ahead of such cities as New York, Detroit, Los Angeles, and Washington, where crime is believed to flourish to a much greater extent. In an interview, Phoenix Police Sgt. Edna Hurt, head of the crime analysis section, said that her city's poor record was due to thoroughness in reporting. "We count everything here," Sergeant Hurt said, "even if it involves a garbage can or a garden hose." Cities often do not record such minor thefts.

What can be said for the *UCR* is that it generally reflects the same biases year after year, and therefore some real trends can be discerned. For 1972, the *UCR* crime index rate for the United States decreased by about 3%. For particular crimes, the following changes were recorded in 1972 as compared with 1971. Murder was up 5%, forcible rape was up 10%, robbery was down 4%, aggravated assault was up 5.5%, burglary was down 2%, larceny of over $50 was down 3%, and auto theft was down 7%. Steering-column locking devices probably were a major factor in the decline in auto theft. Activities of the women's lib movement are believed to have made more women willing to report rape.

Death Penalty. More than a third of the states had restored capital punishment to their statute books by the end of 1973. Legislators were interpreting the Supreme Court's 1972 five-to-four decision ruling capital punishment unconstitutional as applicable only to situations in which the death penalty is an optional sentence. The new statutes declare the death penalty is mandatory for various specified offenses, including aircraft hijacking and treason (Georgia), illegal sale of cocaine or heroin to someone who dies from using the purchased drug (Connecticut), and rape of a person under 11 years of age (Florida). In most states, the approach has been to mandate the death penalty for killings by

prison inmates and for murder when there are aggravating circumstances (such as murder by a hired killer or by a person with a previous conviction for homicide) and no mitigating facts (such as the youth of the offender). Meanwhile, it remains arguable whether the Supreme Court will find the new laws constitutionally sound; until and unless it does, the actual infliction of the death penalty will remain in abeyance.

Crime in the News. In August, police in Houston, Texas, discovered the graves of 27 teen-age boys who had been the victims of homosexual abuse and murder—the largest mass murder in the history of the United States. Elmer Wayne Henley, 17, and David Owen Brooks, 18, led the police to shallow graves they had helped to dig at several sites in the Houston area during the preceding three years. Brooks told police that after each slaying, the victim's body was immediately wrapped in plastic, placed in a wooden box built by Dean Allen Corll, and then taken to one of three burial sites. Crushed lime rock was liberally sprinkled over the corpses to reduce the odor.

The story first broke on August 8 when Henley summoned the police after killing Corll, a 33-year-old electric utility company worker. Henley told the police that Corll was solely responsible for the murders. Over the next five days, Henley and Brooks led the police to the graves of the victims. The police said the victims had been invited to attend parties given by Corll, sexually assaulted, and then killed. Henley and Brooks were indicted for murder on August 14.

On Jan. 18, 1973, Juan V. Corona, a 38-year-old farm labor contractor from Yuba City, Calif., was convicted for the murder of 25 itinerant farm workers in northern California in 1971. In February he was sentenced to 25 consecutive terms of life imprisonment for what was at that time the biggest mass murder in U. S. history.

On Sept. 6, 1973, W. A. (Tony) Boyle, former president of the United Mine Workers (UMW), was arrested and charged with murder in the 1969 killing of rival UMW leader Joseph A. Yablonski, his wife, and daughter. Boyle, 71, failed in a suicide attempt later in the month.

GILBERT GEIS
University of California, Irvine

PRESIDENTS Héctor J. Cámpora (left) of Argentina and Osvaldo Dorticós Torrado of Cuba embrace in Buenos Aires after reestablishment of diplomatic relations.

CUBA

The Cuban government in 1973 made headway in institutionalizing the socialist revolution and integrating Cuba into the Soviet-bloc economy. While an agreement was concluded with the United States to combat air and sea hijackings, there was little relaxation of tension between Havana and Washington. Cuba lost a friend with the fall of the socialist regime in Chile, but gained a diplomatic ally in newly Peronist Argentina. During the year Premier Fidel Castro left the governing of Cuba to the bureaucrats and assumed the role of spokesman for the USSR in the "Third World."

Sugar. For the second consecutive year, Cuban sugar production fell below 5 million tons in 1973. Since 1970 Cuba's share of world sugar production has declined from 12% to 6%. In 1973, Cuba lost its place as Latin America's leading sugar producer for the first time in more than a century, as Brazil took the lead, with over 6 million tons. Bad weather, shortages of fertilizers and insecticides, mechanical breakdowns, and problems of labor mobilization were factors in the disappointing performance of Cuba's sugar industry in 1973.

Aid and Trade. Other developments on the economic front were more encouraging to the regime. Early in the year it was disclosed that the USSR was writing off much of the huge debt owed to it by Cuba. All payment on the debt, said to amount to more than $4 billion, was to be suspended until 1986, and all interest charges were dropped. In addition, the USSR granted Cuba a $330 million loan for the development of Cuban agriculture, industry, and mining. In return the USSR received a lien on all minerals mined in Cuba. The Soviets were especially interested in the island's nickel deposits, comprising about 40% of the world's known reserves.

Other partners of Cuba in the Council for Mutual Economic Assistance (Comecon), the Soviet-led trading bloc, pledged aid in 1973. Poland advanced credits for the modernization of the Cuban sugar industry and the expansion of the Havana shipyards. The Cubans promised to repay the Poles with sugar, fruit, nickel, and tobacco. A similar arrangement was made with Czechoslovakia for the financing of a Cuban cement factory and a plant to manufacture refrigerators and other kitchen goods. Cuba's Comecon partners seemed satisfied that their aid would be utilized in accordance with the principles of "Socialist planning."

Court Reforms. In 1973, Communist legal experts were busy revamping Cuba's judiciary, a hodgepodge of revolutionary tribunals and regular courts from pre-Castro days. Under a new, integrated system, courts will be presided over by mixed panels of professional judges and "lay" judges —representatives of official organizations like the Committees for the Defense of the Revolution. "The administration of justice," President Osvaldo Dorticós declared in September, "must be at the service of revolutionary power, at the service of the historic objectives of the Revolution, and every interpretation of the law ... must be based on the cardinal principles of the Cuban Socialist Revolution." During the year the death penalty was decreed for "crimes against the national and popular economy," murder, and certain sexual offenses.

The Premier. On July 26, Premier Castro, who is famous for speaking extemporaneously for hours on end, for the first time read his annual speech commemorating the birth of the Cuban Revolution in 1953. In the relatively brief, 93-minute speech Castro condemned the "reactionary thesis" advanced by leaders of some developing countries that both the United States and the Soviet Union are basically imperialistic. The United States, he insisted, is the principal enemy of the "Third World," while the USSR is its best friend.

Castro repeated this argument in September at the fourth conference of nonaligned nations in Algeria. There he was challenged from the floor by Cambodian Prince Norodom Sihanouk, who reminded his colleagues of the USSR's diplomatic relations with the "reactionary" Lon Nol government.

--------- CUBA • Information Highlights ---------

Official Name: Republic of Cuba.
Location: Caribbean Sea.
Area: 44,218 square miles (114,524 sq km).
Population (1973 est.): 8,900,000. *Density,* 197 per square mile (76 per sq km).
Chief Cities (1970 census): Havana, the capital, 1,755,400; Santiago de Cuba, 276,000; Camagüey, 196,900.
Government: *Head of state,* Osvaldo Dorticós Torrado, president (took office July 1959). *Head of government,* Fidel Castro Ruz, premier (took office Feb. 1959).
Language: Spanish (official).
Education: *Expenditure* (1966), 16.1% of total public expenditure. *School enrollment* (1969)—primary, 1,427,607; secondary, 266,651; technical/vocational, 60,332; university/higher, 31,035.
Monetary Unit: Peso (0.80 peso equals U.S.$1, July 1973).
Gross National Product (1970 est.): $4,500,000,000.
Economic Indexes: *Industrial production* (1965), 116 (1963=100); *agricultural production* (1971), 133 (1963=100).
Manufacturing (major products): Sugar products, tobacco products.
Major Agricultural Products: Sugarcane, tobacco, rice, oranges and tangerines, sweet potatoes and yams.
Major Minerals: Nickel (ranks 4th among world producers, 1971), manganese, salt, chromium ore.
Foreign Trade (1970): *Exports,* $1,043,000,000; *Imports,* $1,-300,000,000. *Chief trading partners* (1968)—USSR (took 45% of exports, supplied 61% of imports); Czechoslovakia (6%—4%); East Germany (6%—4%); France (2%—5%).
Transportation: *Motor vehicles* (1969), 102,000 (automobiles, 71,000); *railroads* (1971), 3,281 miles (5,280 km); *merchant fleet* (1972), 398,000 gross registered tons; *major national airline,* Empresa Consolidada Cubana Aviación.
Communications: *Telephones* (1972), 274,949; *newspapers* (1971), 15.

Arab leaders, incensed by Cuba's recognition of Israel, joined Sihanouk in denouncing Castro. After the conference Cuba broke diplomatic relations with Israel and Castro left Algeria for a tour of Hanoi and the "liberated areas" of South Vietnam.

Inter-American Relations. Early in the year there was a slight thaw in relations between Cuba and the United States. On February 15 the two nations formally agreed to extradite or punish with "the most severe penalty" any person "who seizes, removes, appropriates or diverts . . . an aircraft or vessel" of one country and takes it to the other. Although U. S. spokesmen cautioned that the hijacking agreement did not foreshadow broader ties with Havana, Secretary of State-designate Henry Kissinger testified on September 10 that he hoped soon to begin consultation with Washington's "friends in Latin America" which might lead to a change in the Cuban policy of the United States.

By this time Havana's friends in the Organization of American States (OAS) had rounded up 11 of the 12 votes necessary to end the official embargo that the OAS had imposed on trade with Cuba in 1964. On September 11, however, the anti-embargo forces lost a vote with the fall of Salvador Allende's socialist government in Chile. With the tide apparently turned against Cuba in the OAS, the State Department instructed U.S. ambassadors in Latin America to ignore Kissinger's remarks about a possible reassessment of U. S. policy toward Cuba.

Generally, however, Cuba's position in Latin America was strengthened in 1973. The new Peronist government in Argentina established diplomatic relations with Havana in May and granted Cuba a credit of $200 million for the purchase of Argentine food and agricultural machinery. Mexico, which had never adhered to the OAS boycott, began discussions with Cuba on a proposal to exchange Mexican petroleum for Cuban nickel and chrome.

NEILL MACAULEY
University of Florida

CYPRUS

Cyprus was the scene of conflicts among the Greek Cypriots in 1973. Archbishop Makarios III confirmed his right to remain both archbishop and president of the island republic.

Conflicts. Archbishop Makarios faced political agitation in 1973 from Gen. George Grivas, with whom he had worked for independence from Britain and *enosis* (union) with Greece in the 1950's. Grivas again strongly supported *enosis* in 1973. Makarios, however, wished to maintain Cyprus as an independent, unitary state, although he did not hide his feelings that *enosis* might come later. The archbishop realized that the Turkish Cypriot minority, who constitute about 18% of the population, were so unalterably opposed to union that it was not at this time a realistic solution, particularly since the Turkish government was also vehemently opposed.

Grivas remained in hiding during 1973, but his supporters staged guerrilla raids and the Greek Cypriots were caught up in an increasingly violent atmosphere. Pro-Grivas islanders were themselves victims of terrorist attacks, apparently in retaliation. In late July, Christos Vakis, the minister of justice, was kidnapped by the Grivas side and not released until late August. In October an attempt to assassinate Makarios was thwarted.

──────── CYPRUS • Information Highlights ────────

Official Name: Republic of Cyprus.
Location: Island in the eastern Mediterranean Sea.
Area: 3,572 square miles (9,251 sq km).
Population (1973 est.): 600,000. *Density,* 179 per square mile (69 per sq km).
Chief Cities (1970 est.): Nicosia, the capital, 115,000 (metropolitan area); Limassol, 51,500; Famagusta, 42,500.
Government: Head of state, Archbishop Makarios III, president (reelected for a 3d term Feb. 1973). *Head of government,* Archbishop Makarios III. *Legislature* (unicameral)—House of Representatives. *Major political groups*—Greek Cypriots; Turkish Cypriots.
Languages: Greek, Turkish (both official), English.
Education: *Expenditure* (1969), 14.8% of total public expenditure. *School enrollment* (1969)—primary, 71,236; secondary, 39,221; technical/vocational, 4,218; university/higher, 580.
Monetary Unit: Pound (0.3454 pound equals U. S.$1, July 1973).
Gross National Product (1972 est.): $693,000,000.
Economic Indexes: *Industrial production* (mining, 1972), 79 (1963=100); *agricultural production* (1971), 169 (1963=100); *consumer price index* (1972), 119 (1967=100).
Manufacturing (major products): Cement, cigarettes, wines and spirits.
Major Agricultural Products: Citrus fruits, potatoes, grapes, olives, carrots, barley.
Major Minerals: Copper, iron pyrites, asbestos, chromium ore, sulfur.
Foreign Trade (1972): Exports, $134,000,000; Imports, $320,-000,000. *Chief trading partners* (1970)—United Kingdom (took 41% of exports, supplied 29% of imports); West Germany (12%—7%); France (4%—4%).
Tourism: Receipts (1971), $35,200,000.
Transportation: *Motor vehicles* (1971), 79,100 (automobiles, 63,000); *merchant fleet* (1972), 2,015,000 gross registered tons; *major national airline,* Cyprus Airways.
Communications: *Telephones* (1972), 47,589; *newspapers* (1971), 12 (daily circulation, 85,000).

In August, President George Papadopoulos of Greece reaffirmed his government's commitment to an independent Cyprus. He asked Grivas, who though born in Cyprus was also a Greek army officer, to cease his underground campaign and not to push for *enosis.* Grivas rejected the appeal, but Makarios praised Papadopoulos' initiative as a step toward restoring unity to the Cypriot Greeks.

Elections. Since no candidate opposed Makarios for the presidency of Cyprus, the elections of February 1973 were canceled and Makarios was by law automatically reelected. He later said that this, his third 5-year term, would be his last. Following the announcement that Vice President Fazil Küçük would not seek a third term, Rauf Denktaş was proclaimed the new vice president when a second candidate withdrew from the race.

Challenge of the Metropolitans. Makarios' right to be president was strongly challenged by the island's three pro-*enosis* metropolitans, who along with him made up the Holy Synod. They were Gennadios of Paphos, Anthimos of Kitium, and Kyprianos of Kyrenia. In 1972 the three had declared that it was against canon law for Makarios to serve as both president and archbishop. After the start of his third term in 1973 they ordered him defrocked. Makarios, who had the support of the Greek Cypriot population and of Archbishop Ieronymos, the primate of Greece, and other Orthodox prelates outside Cyprus, turned against Gennadios, whom the three had agreed should act as the island's archbishop. Makarios declared that Gennadios' see was vacant, and a new metropolitan was elected by the populace, according to custom.

Makarios brought together a major synod of the Greek Orthodox Church, including the patriarchs of Antioch and Alexandria. In August the synod upheld Makarios and defrocked the three metropolitans. Makarios later divided up the sees of Kitium and Kyrenia.

GEORGE J. MARCOPOULOS
Tufts University

CZECHOSLOVAKIA

The most significant events in Czechoslovakia in 1973 involved stepped-up endeavors to improve its relations with the West, especially West Germany and the United States. Czechoslovakia was aided by the Soviet Union's desire for a rapprochement with the United States and for some sort of European détente. The "pragmatists" within the leadership of the Czechoslovak Community party, led by Party Chief Gustav Husák, appeared to have gained greater leverage at the expense of inveterate hardliners and managed to contain somewhat the repression of the preceding years.

Pact with West Germany. After protracted negotiations, Czechoslovakia and West Germany reached agreement on May 30 on a treaty normalizing relations after 35 years of hostility. Under the terms of the agreement, the Munich Pact of 1938, which awarded the Sudetenland region of Czechoslovakia to Germany, was to be regarded by both countries as "void with regard to their mutual relations." The new agreement reaffirmed "the inviolability of their common frontier now and in the future" and called for "further steps for the comprehensive development of their mutual relations."

The accord was made possible by Czechoslovakia's tacit retreat from its previous insistence that West Germany recognize the Munich Pact to have been invalid from the outset. Instead, the new treaty confirmed the validity of laws promulgated during the German administration of the Sudetenland from Sept. 30, 1938, to May 9, 1945. It also stipulated that it would "not constitute any legal basis for material claims" by Czechoslovakia.

The treaty was scheduled to be signed when German Chancellor Willy Brandt paid an official visit to Prague in September. But Brandt's visit was postponed until December 11 (when the signing took place) because of the refusal of Czechoslovakia to recognize West Germany's right to represent West Berlin in Prague.

Relations with the United States. Czechoslovakia's relations with the United States improved in 1973. The treatment of U. S. correspondents was better and some were granted interviews with high-ranking Communist officials. The government was anxious to reopen dialogue with the United States on the previously deadlocked issue of compensation for U. S.-owned properties nationalized after World War II and thus to pave the way for increased trade and access to U. S. technology. U. S. Secretary of State William P. Rogers paid an official visit to Prague in July and signed a consular convention to regularize trade and travel between the countries.

Government. President Ludvík Svoboda, although 77 years old and rumored to be in poor health, was elected to a second five-year term by a unanimous vote of the Federal Assembly in March. In the same month, Jaromír Obžina was named minister of the interior to replace Radko Kaska, who died in a plane crash. Minister of Culture Miloslav Brůžek, who had led the regime's repressive policies in the realm of culture, was succeeded in May by Antonín Klusák, son-in-law of President Svoboda.

Economy. The basic economic tasks set by the Five-Year Plan continued to be fulfilled in 1973. By midyear, industrial production had risen 6.1% over the corresponding period in 1972, output of consumer goods had increased by 4.9%, construction by 5.8%, freight transportation by 4.1%, foreign trade by 10.9%, and domestic retail trade by 5.2%. Labor productivity in industry climbed by 5.4% and in construction by 3.7%.

The population's monetary income increased by 5.9%. The average monthly pay reached about $180 in industry and about $200 in construction, while living costs were said to have remained essentially unchanged.

On the other hand, absenteeism at work reached 4.28% in the first half of 1973, compared with 4.18% in the first six months of 1972. One out of eight enterprises failed to meet its planned goals, and the quality and assortment of some durable and textile consumer goods were found lacking. But the worst performance was registered again in residential housing construction. Only 40.7% of the apartment construction planned for 1973, and only 26.4% in the capital city of Prague, were completed by mid-1973.

Tightened Penal Code. Czechoslovakia paralleled the USSR's policy of stressing détente in foreign relations while at the same time tightening domestic controls. The Federal Assembly enacted several laws in April providing for stricter penalties for a number of offenses and to facilitate criminal prosecution. The maximum prison sentence for capital crimes was raised from 15 to 25 years (with the death penalty left intact), and the penalty for leaving or attempting to leave the country without official authorization was increased to 10 years for persons entrusted with state secrets.

Punishment by up to three years' imprisonment was provided for those who spread "untrue reports about the international position of Czechoslovakia or its foreign policy which could harm the interests of the republic." A new penalty of "protective surveillance" was instituted to follow imprisonment. Thus, a person who had already served a jail term could be placed under police controls for an additional one to three years.

------ CZECHOSLOVAKIA • Information Highlights ------

Official Name: Czechoslovak Socialist Republic.
Location: East central Europe.
Area: 49,370 square miles (127,869 sq km).
Population (1973 est.): 15,000,000. *Density,* 293 per square mile (113 per sq km).
Chief Cities (1970 census): Prague, the capital, 1,078,096; Brno, 335,918; Bratislava, 283,539; Ostrava, 278,737.
Government: *Head of state,* Ludvík Svoboda, president (took office for 2d 5-year term March 1973). *Head of government,* Lubomír Štrougal, premier (took office Jan. 1970). Communist party secretary general, Gustáv Husák (took office April 1969). *Legislature*—Federal Assembly: Chamber of Nations and Chamber of the People.
Languages: Czech, Slovak (both official), Hungarian, German, Russian.
Education: *Expenditure* (1969), 7.5% of total public expenditure. *School enrollment* (1969)—primary, 2,002,053; secondary, 390,057; technical/vocational, 274,178; university/higher, 133,524.
Monetary Unit: Koruna (5.20 koruny equal U. S.$1, July 1973).
Gross National Product (1972 est.): $32,900,000,000.
Economic Indexes: Industrial production (1972), 211 (1963=100); agricultural production (1970), 113 (1957–59=100); consumer price index (1972), 100 (1969=100).
Manufacturing (major products): Chemicals, machinery, petroleum products, glass and ceramics, textiles, footwear, processed foods, iron and steel, automobiles, beverages.
Major Agricultural Products: Rye, oats, sugar beets, potatoes, wheat, corn, grapes, vegetables.
Major Minerals: Lignite, coal, magnesite, iron ore, kaolin, antimony.
Foreign Trade (1972): *Exports,* $4,662,000,000. *Imports,* $5,124,000,000. *Chief trading partners* (1971)—USSR (took 32% of exports, supplied 34% of imports); East Germany (11%—6%); Hungary (6%—5%).
Tourism: *Receipts* (1971), $61,200,000.
Transportation: *Motor Vehicles* (1971), 1,125,300 (automobiles, 918,200); *railroads* (1971), 8,275 miles (13,317 km); *merchant fleet* (1972), 103,000 gross registered tons; *major national airline,* Ceskoslovenske Aerolinie.
Communications: *Telephones* (1972), 2,111,996; *newspapers* (1970), 28 (daily circulation, 3,641,000).

UPI

A march to protest the killing of a Mexican-American boy by a Dallas policeman erupts into violence, July 28.

Anniversary. Soviet Communist party leader Leonid Brezhnev visited Prague in February for the 25th anniversary of the establishment of Communist rule in Czechoslovakia. As part of the celebration, President Svoboda announced an amnesty for the estimated 50,000 Czechs who fled the country after the Soviet invasion in 1968.

EDWARD TABORSKY
University of Texas at Austin

DALLAS

Dallas continued to grow in 1973, when the city's population passed 900,000—an increase of 55,000 over 1970. The creation of the Dallas–Fort Worth Standard Metropolitan Statistical Area (SMSA) in April made Dallas part of the largest SMSA (estimated population: 2,500,000) in Texas and the twelfth-largest in the nation. This "Southwest Metroplex" was expected to have 3,600,000 residents by 1985.

The development of two "new towns" northwest of Dallas is further evidence of the region's dynamic population growth. Flower Mound New Town will open in mid-1974, with the expectation of 70,000 residents by 1985, while Las Colinas will open late in 1974 with plans for 50,000 residents by 1980.

Economy. Overall, the economy of Dallas was prosperous in 1973, and the future appeared bright. The unemployment rate was 3% in June, and it declined as the year progressed. Although the local consumer price index rose considerably during the year, it was at a rate lower than that of many other U.S. cities. Wages and productivity both improved as labor and industry averted crippling strikes.

Several major building projects contributed to the city's economic growth. The $35.5 million City Hall complex, designed by I. M. Pei and Partners, was under construction, with a completion date of April 1976. This complex, to be fronted by a 6.5-acre park, will have three levels of underground parking facilities. Tunnel walkways will connect the complex with the recently expanded Dallas Memorial Auditorium-Convention Center.

A consortium of business and civic leaders is developing a greenbelt-park in downtown Dallas that will be known as Thanks-Giving Square. Thanks-Giving Square celebrates America's ancient heritage at the center of commercial downtown with a garden and fountains and a small, white chapel.

The Union Terminal area of Dallas is the site of a proposed $200 million development (including a major hotel, restaurants, shops, and tourist facilities) to be sponsored jointly by the city of Dallas and a group of private investors.

Transportation. In September, the new Dallas–Fort Worth Regional Airport was officially dedicated. This 17,000-acre facility, hailed by aviation experts as the world's most advanced, began regular commercial service in January 1974. With the opening of the new regional airport, Love Field, formerly Dallas' commercial airport, was converted into the nation's largest general aviation airport. A system of ground transportation (SURTRAN) serves the new airport, Dallas, Fort Worth, and major suburbs.

Environment. In June, local environmentalist groups won a victory in a referendum that defeated a measure that included "canalization" of the Trinity River and construction of several dams. Also during the year the city council took two important steps to improve the environment: it passed an ordinance to control the proliferation of signs and billboards, and it approved the creation of a historical preservation district in the Swiss Avenue area, where many of the city's fine old homes were threatened by commercial developers.

Chief Resigns. Police Chief Frank Dyson, widely regarded as a liberal, resigned in October because of controversy over his handling of a July riot.

BEN J. WALLACE AND ROBERT V. KEMPER
Southern Methodist University

DAMS. See ENGINEERING, CIVIL.

American Ballet Theatre's lavish new full-length production of Tales of Hoffmann *featured Cynthia Gregory and Jonas Kage (right).*

dance

The state of the economy in 1973 afflicted dance with a number of problems, including a major strike, but the year, nevertheless, was esthetically a rich one. And in dance, as in most fields, names made news. Some names, such as Melissa Hayden, Agnes de Mille, Rudolf Nureyev, Martha Graham, and Fred Astaire, were familiar, and some, such as Nadezhda Pavlova and Igor Terentiev were new.

Ballet. The spring season of the New York City Ballet was marked by the celebrations attendant on the retirement of that company's senior ballerina Melissa Hayden. The various honors accorded Miss Hayden in her last season included a new ballet, *Cortège Hongrois,* choreographed for her by NYCB's ballet master George Balanchine, and a proclamation from Gov. Nelson Rockefeller in recognition of her "contribution to dance in New York State." Miss Hayden danced her last performance with the company at the Wolf Trap Farm Park in Vienna, Va.

The NYCB fall season celebrating the company's 25th anniversary and the 40th anniversary of George Balanchine's arrival in the United States was canceled on November 13 when the dancers walked out because of a failure of the musicians' union to reach an agreement with management. After a month the dispute was resolved and the holiday season of performances of *The Nutcracker* began.

The American Ballet Theater (ABT) had a successful winter season. But their summer stint at the New York State Theater looked bleak at first. Guest star Carla Fracci was available for few performances, and Natalia Makarova, who had decided to become a freelance guest with companies in Europe appeared with ABT in only one performance of *Swan Lake.* Their absence gave opportunities to younger soloists in the company, and

Karena Brock distinguished herself in a number of roles, as did Martine van Hamel in *Swan Lake* and Zhandra Rodriguez in *Giselle.*

New works in the ABT repertoire included a revival of Eugene Loring's *Billy the Kid* and a production of Peter Darrell's *Tales of Hoffmann,* based on the Offenbach opera. A full-evening ballet, it showed off the company well and was a good vehicle for ballerinas Cynthia Gregory, Carla Fracci, and Eleanor D'Antuono.

The City Center Joffrey Ballet suffered a major cutback in funds from its parent organization, the City Center of Music and Drama (a loss of nearly a quarter of a million dollars), which forced it to curtail its 1973–74 season. But the company offered Frederick Ashton's *The Dream* and Leonide Massine's *Parade,* both significant works.

Modern Dance. Probably the most important event in modern dance this year was the revival of Martha Graham's *Clytemnestra,* a full-evening work (1958) which had not been performed since Miss Graham last danced the title role in 1967. When it was presented by the Martha Graham Dance Theater at the Alvin Theater in New York in May, the role of Clytemnestra was danced at alter-

nate performances by Mary Hinkson and Pearl Lang. The significance of the revival went beyond merely giving dance fans another opportunity to see *Clytemnestra,* for in training other dancers to perform it, Miss Graham has made possible the preservation of this work, which is considered by many to be her masterpiece.

Other well-known works presented by the Graham Dance Theater included *Appalachian Spring, Cave of the Heart, Seraphic Dialogue,* and *Secular Games.* The company also offered the world premiere of Miss Graham's *Myth of a Voyage* (music by Alan Hovhaness, sets by Ming Cho Lee), another dance-drama based on Greek myth. Writing in the New York *Times,* Anna Kisselgoff stated that, although not as good as Miss Graham's earlier *Circe,* the new work was "witty and visually stunning."

The late José Limón (died 1972), who had taught at the Juilliard School for many years, was honored in May by a program of the Juilliard Dance Ensemble, including premieres of works by Anna Sokolow, Kazuko Hirabayashi, and Daniel Lewis. And in September, the Cubiculo presented the New York premiere of James Waring's *Feathers,* dedicated to the American trapeze artist Vander Barbette, who died in August.

At the Guggenheim Museum in September, Erick Hawkins reminded dance audiences that modern dance does not have to be grim or tragic by performing his comic solo *Squash,* the last part of his *8 Clear Places.* On the same program Hawkins' company returned to Greek myth, the more familiar territory of modern dance, in the performance of a work-in-progress, *Greek Dreams, With Flute.*

Merce Cunningham's revival of his full-evening work *Canfield* (1969) at the Brooklyn Academy of Music in July was a failure with both critics and audiences. But if Cunningham is exhausting the patience of his admirers in his own land, his prestige in Europe (like that of many American modern dancers and choreographers) remains undiminished. John Cage was commissioned to provide an original work for the Paris Opéra Ballet. The result, *A Day or Two,* with a score by Cage and decor by Jasper Johns, was presented during the Paris Festival d'Automne and had a considerable success.

The Paul Taylor Dance Company did well with its season in London, with ballet dancer Rudolf Nureyev appearing as a guest in two works, *Book of Beasts* and *Aureole.* The world's most famous male classical dancer, Nureyev has occasionally appeared with other modern groups, and he fitted easily into Taylor's, the most classically oriented of modern companies.

Visiting Companies. The National Ballet of Canada had its first season at the Metropolitan Opera House in April and May, with the ubiquitous Nureyev as guest star. Presenting a repertoire of such works as *Swan Lake, Sleeping Beauty, La Sylphide,* and *The Moor's Pavane,* the company made a very favorable impression. They were praised particularly for the high level of performance in mime roles and for the work of soloists Veronica Tennant, Vanessa Harwood, Karen Kain, and Frank Augustyn.

The Stuttgart Ballet from Germany followed the Canadians at the Metropolitan with a repertoire consisting mostly of full-length ballets (*Romeo and Juliet, Eugene Onegin,* and *Swan Lake*) choreographed by John Cranko and starring Marcia Haydee, Richard Cragun, and Egon Madsen. As in their previous American visits, the company was enthusiastically applauded. Special attention was focused on Cranko's *Swan Lake,* which had its American premiere in May. Cranko rejected most of the traditional choreography and in his reworking of the ballet placed greater emphasis on Prince Siegfried as a tragic hero.

In June and July a large group of dancers from the Bolshoi Ballet of Moscow performed at the Metropolitan. The full Bolshoi company had not appeared in the United States for seven years, and this group of dancers was limited in repertoire mostly to short exhibition pieces or excerpts from larger works, such as *Giselle, Swan Lake,* and *Spartacus.* The typical Bolshoi bravura style of Raissa Struchkova and other mature artists contrasted interestingly with the somewhat more restrained work of Ludmilla Semenyaka, Marina Leonova, and other younger dancers. The greatest attention was given to a brilliant 17-year-old ballerina, Nadezhda Pavlova, who had won the grand prize in the International Ballet Competition in Moscow less than 10 days before the Bolshoi troupe arrived in New York.

For the first time a group of young students from the Bolshoi Dance Academy accompanied regular members of the company on a foreign tour, and they were extremely impressive and appealing. One of the youngest of them, 13-year-old Igor Terentiev, was singled out as a potential great star.

The interest in folk, or ethnic, dance, increasing noticeably in recent years, continued in 1973 with a continual parade of companies from foreign countries. Prominent among them were the Mazowske company from Poland; the Krasnayarsk Dance Company from Siberia; the Bayanihan Philippine Dance Company, on its sixth U. S. tour; and the Ballet Folklorico of Mexico, which looked a bit slicker in 1973 because it omitted the Aztec ritual dances which were formerly an important part of its repertoire. Other folk dance companies that visited the United States included the Jamaica National Dance Theater, the National Folklore Ballet of Ecuador, the Inbal Dance Company from Israel, the George Zamfir Ensemble from Rumania, and the National Folk Ensemble of Pakistan.

Other Kinds of Dance. The World's Professional Ballroom Dancing Championship was held in the United States for the first time in October 1973. Sponsored by Arthur Murray, Inc., the competition took place at the Felt Forum in New York. The contestants were 51 couples from 27 countries. Hans Peter and Inge Fisher, of Australia, won first prize in Latin American dancing, and the first prize in the Modern Exhibition style was won by Richard and Janet Gleave from Britain.

Choreographer Agnes de Mille founded the Agnes de Mille Heritage Dance Theater "to do for America's native dances and songs what Moiseyev has done for Russia's: that is to revitalize our great traditions creatively and dynamically." With grants from private sponsors, the Rockefeller Foundation, and the National Endowment for the Arts, she founded the company under the aegis of the North Carolina School of the Arts in Winston-Salem. The new group gave its first performances in Winston-Salem in April and made its first tour in October and November, beginning in Richmond, Va., and ending in East Lansing, Mich.

Special Events. During the year homage was paid to three of the most influential living figures in

RETIRING ballerina Melissa Hayden (center) is honored by George Balanchine and colleagues of New York City Ballet.

GUEST STAR with the National Ballet of Canada, Rudolf Nureyev partners Veronica Tennant in La Sylphide.

the dance world. On April 30, the Film Society of Lincoln Center presented a gala tribute to the stage and screen star Fred Astaire, whom the choreographer George Balanchine has termed "the greatest dancer in the world." Astaire and his most famous partner, Ginger Rogers, were present at the program which consisted of excerpts from Astaire's films.

On May 21, similar tribute was paid to Sol Hurok, who was celebrating his 60th anniversary as an impresario and his 85th birthday. Hurok, who has been the American manager of such dancers as Isadora Duncan, Anna Pavlova, Margot Fonteyn, and Rudolf Nureyev and of such companies as the British Royal Ballet, the Canadian National Ballet, the Stuttgart Ballet, and the Bolshoi Ballet, was honored by a gala program at the Metropolitan Opera House featuring performances by many of his artists, including Miss Fonteyn, Andrés Segovia, and Van Cliburn.

In November, Martha Graham, who has received the highest awards New York City can offer, including the Handel Medallion (1970), was presented with a special scroll from the mayor honoring her long service to modern dance, which "has added new dimensions to the arts." The occasion was the publication of her book *The Notebooks of Martha Graham* (Harcourt Brace Jovanovich).

Dance and Other Media. Other distinguished dance books published during the year were *Martha Graham, A Biography* by Don McDonagh (Praeger); *Speak to Me, Dance with Me* by Agnes de Mille (Atlantic–Little, Brown); *Starring Fred Astaire* by Stanley Green and Burt Goldblatt (Dodd, Mead); *The Busby Berkeley Book* by Tony Thomas and Jim Terry with Busby Berkeley (New York Graphic Society); and *The New York City Ballet* by Lincoln Kirstein (Knopf).

Both of the most discussed dance films of the year starred Rudolf Nureyev. The first, *I Am a Dancer,* showed him performing in a variety of ballets with such partners as Margot Fonteyn and Carla Fracci. The second, and more successful, was a filmed performance of the Russian ballet *Don Quixote,* directed by Nureyev and Sir Robert Helpmann, both of whom danced leading roles along with Lucette Aldous and members of the Australian Ballet.

A large gap in the catalog of recordings of ballet scores was filled when two record companies issued performances of Sergei Prokofiev's full-length *Romeo and Juliet.* The version released by London Records, which was billed as the world premiere stereo recording, was played by the Cleveland Orchestra conducted by Lorin Maazel. It was followed within days by the release of Angel Records' version played by the London Symphony conducted by André Previn. Both were widely praised.

In dance criticism an important event was the appointment by the *New Yorker* magazine of its first dance critic. In the past, reviewing dance had been a secondary duty of the magazine's music critic. But in the spring, the editor of the *New Yorker* created a separate column for dance reviews and engaged the critic Arlene Croce, editor and publisher of *Ballet Review* and author of *The Fred Astaire and Ginger Rogers Book.*

Two major performer/choreographers died during the year, John Cranko and Mary Wigman.

WILLIAM LIVINGSTONE, *"Stereo Review"*

DEATHS. See OBITUARIES.

The Navy F-14 has been hailed as the most advanced all-weather, carrier-based aircraft ever to be developed for the U.S. Navy. The plane is armed with Phoenix missiles.

DEFENSE FORCES

The year 1973 began with considerable enthusiasm for the budding relaxation in tensions, or détente, between the United States and the Soviet Union, but paradoxes arose in regard to defense policy for the two superpowers, their allies, and others as the year unfolded.

There were many events that suggested that détente was becoming a reality, with the Cold War confrontation being replaced by a more peaceful era. For example, a negotiated cease-fire was obtained in Vietnam in January. In addition, the Russians and Americans said they desired to extend the limitations on strategic weapons established in the 1972 Strategic Arms Limitation Talks (SALT); discussions were held between the United States and the Soviet Union and their respective allies on the possibility that the two superpowers would withdraw some of their military forces from Europe; and Soviet Foreign Minister Andrei A. Gromyko suggested that the five permanent members of the UN Security Council cut their military budgets by 10%, with part of the funds thus saved to be used to assist developing nations.

The peaceful tenor suggested by these events was amplified by U. S. President Richard Nixon in his welcoming remarks to Soviet leader Leonid Brezhnev during the latter's June visit to Washington. The President spoke of "lifting the burden of armaments from the world and building a structure of peace."

In contrast, there was evidence that détente was not yet at hand. For example, the Soviets reportedly tested impressive new strategic systems, and the U. S. defense budget for fiscal 1974 rose to $79 billion, higher than the peak spending during the Vietnam War. In the late fall détente survived its sternest test to date when the United States and the USSR cooperated to secure a cease-fire between their respective client states after war had broken out in the Middle East. (See MIDDLE EAST.)

United States

According to Henry Kissinger, national security adviser to the President and secretary of state, détente with the Soviet Union came as a result of American strength, not in spite of it. President Nixon and Kissinger gave every indication they believed that détente would continue only if the United States retained sufficient military power to discourage the Soviet Union from seeking to take advantage of the new era of relaxation either at the bargaining table or elsewhere. Thus the stage was set in 1973 for careful negotiations with the Soviets concerning additional efforts to settle outstanding differences and to dampen the arms competition, with the backdrop being the tailoring of U. S. military and diplomatic moves to discourage possible Soviet threats to use force.

Strategic Offensive Forces. The long-range bombers and missiles of the Strategic Air Command (SAC) and the submarine-launched missiles of the Navy are the basic U. S. deterrents against possible attacks on the American homeland. In 1973 these forces included 1,000 Minuteman intercontinental ballistic missiles (ICBMs), 54 Titan ICBMs, 425 B-52 bombers, 73 FB-111 bombers, and 656 Polaris and Poseidon submarine-launched ballistic missiles (SLBMs). The numbers of ICBMs and SLBMs were the maximum permitted by the 1972 SALT agreement with the Soviet Union, which did not include any limitations on aircraft.

A major debate developed over whether and with what speed the Department of Defense should prepare for the possibility that the bombers and the SLBM force might need to be replaced late in the 1970's to counter improvements in Soviet forces. The most strenuous argument centered on the Nixon administration's request to speed up the development of a replacement for the sea-based deterrent force, which consisted of 41 nuclear-powered submarines

REENLISTMENT bonus checks are displayed by servicemen at Fort Jackson, S. C. Despite such incentives, the number of men attracted to the volunteer armed forces fell far short of hoped-for strength.

and the 656 missiles they carry. The Pentagon wanted to advance the deployment date of the first new submarine-and-missile combination from 1980 to 1978. In the Senate, efforts to block the Pentagon's desire for a speedup failed by a narrow margin—47 against to 49 in favor.

The subject of the controversy is called the Trident system (formerly the undersea long-range missile system), which consists of two components. One is an entirely new submarine, which would be larger and presumably less vulnerable to Soviet antisubmarine warfare (ASW) than current subs. The other is a new Trident SLBM, which will have a longer range than the current models. The price tag for 10 Trident submarines was estimated to be $13 billion. According to Pentagon planners the Trident system should provide an adequate sea-based deterrent for the remainder of the 20th century.

There was less argument over the Pentagon's request for nearly $500 million to continue development of a new bomber designated the B-1. This funding request was less controversial than that for Trident because Congress was asked only to approve the construction of three prototype aircraft for tests to determine the operating reliability of the plane. A more fundamental debate on the B-1 may come in 1974 or 1975 when the Pentagon may seek authorization for 241 B-1 bombers at a 1973 estimated price of $55 million each. Although smaller and lighter than the B-52, the B-1 is described by the Air Force as a replacement for that aging SAC veteran. Proponents of the new bomber claim that it will have a quick-reaction take-off capability to enable it to become airborne before a missile attack hits. The first B-1 is scheduled to fly by 1975.

Three relatively noncontroversial and much less expensive programs were designed to enhance the fighting capabilities of the existing fleet of bombers. One program involved structural modifications in 80 B-52s to preserve their operating life. Another concerned the procurement of additional short-range attack missiles (SRAM), which will be carried by B-52 and FB-111 aircraft. The third program called for the development of a subsonic-cruise armed-decoy (SCAD) missile. This missile is designed to imitate the flight characteristics of a B-52 and thus assist in confusing enemy antibomber radar defenses so that the B-52s can more readily reach their targets.

The U. S. ICBM force underwent upgrading in several areas during 1973. Some older Minuteman missiles were replaced by the newer Minuteman III. The silos housing ICBMs were improved in regard to protection against near misses by enemy warheads. Greater flexibility in setting the targets for some ICBMs was attained by providing a rapid retargeting capability. Upgrading the SLBM force included continuation of the program to replace 496 Polaris missiles with the newer Poseidon missiles. It was generally believed that both the Minuteman III and the Poseidon missiles carry a number of multiple independently targeted reentry vehicles (MIRVs).

A new missile system might be required to replace the ICBMs in the future. However, less than $100 million was invested in research on the advanced ballistic reentry system (ABRES) program.

Strategic Command and Control. The strategic nuclear forces would be unable to operate effectively in wartime if the command of their capabilities were destroyed or seriously degraded. Because of the increasing ability of the Soviet Union to strike at strategic command and control centers, additional efforts were made to ensure the continued operation of such centers in case of attack. One effort centered on a three-year program to equip seven Boeing 747 aircraft so that they could direct the use of the strategic forces while airborne. Another effort involved the further testing of the Sanguine extremely low-frequency communications system, which is designed to enhance communications with missile-launching submarines when they are submerged.

Strategic Defensive Forces. The strategic defensive forces are designed to provide warning against enemy bomber and missile attack and to defend against such attacks. The United States has been permitting its antibomber forces to decline because the Soviet long-range bomber force has remained at approximately 140 bombers and 50 tanker aircraft, and these planes were growing old. However, the United States continued to conduct research on possible antibomber defenses as a precaution against any future Soviet buildup of a new bomber force. These efforts included research on an over-the-horizon radar to detect approaching bombers farther away; an airborne radar warning and control system (AWACS) to be carried aboard Boeing 707 aircraft; an improved manned inceptor (IMI); and an improved surface-to-air missile, the SAM-D.

Early warning of an ICBM, SLBM, or FOBS (Fractional Orbital Bombardment System) attack on the United States is provided not only by a network of land-based radars but also by sensor equipment on satellites. In 1973 the installation of additional coastal radars made some improvement in the U. S. ability to detect SLBM warheads.

DIRECTORY OF MAJOR U. S. MISSILES

Missile	Status[1]	Service	Range (nautical miles)[2]	Propulsion
Surface-to-Surface				
Asroc[3]	O	Navy	. . .	Solid
Dragon[4]	O	Army	1,000 statute mi.	Solid
Lance	O	Army	. . .	Storable liquid
Honest John	O	Army	20	Solid
Minuteman I, II, III	O	AF	6,300+	Solid
Pershing 1A	O	Army	400 statute mi.	Solid
Polaris A-2, A-3[5]	O	Navy	1,500 and 2,500	Solid
Poseidon[5]	O	Navy	2,500	Solid
Sergeant	O	Army	25–75	Solid
Shillelagh	O	Army	short	Solid
Subroc[3]	O	Navy	long	Solid
Titan II	O	AF	6,000+	Storable liquid
Tow[4]	O	Army	3 km	Solid
Trident	D	Navy	4,000	Solid
Surface-to-Air				
Chaparral	O	Army	. . .	Solid
Hawk	O	Army	30 km	Solid
Improved Hawk	P	Army	. . .	Solid
Nike Hercules	O	Army	75+	Solid
Redeye	O	Army	. . .	Solid
Sam-D	D	Army	. . .	Solid
Sea Sparrow	O	Navy	. . .	Solid
Sea Sparrow, NATO	P	Navy, NATO	. . .	Solid
Spartan	P	Army	Few hundred statute mi.	Solid
Sprint	P	Army	25 statute mi.	Solid
Standard	O	Navy	. . .	Solid
Stinger	D	Army	. . .	Solid
Talos	O	Navy	65+	Solid or ramjet
Tartar	O	Navy	10+	Solid
Terrier	O	Navy	20+	Solid
Air-to-Air				
Agile	D	Navy	. . .	Solid
Falcon	O	AF	5+	Solid
Genie	O	AF	. . .	Solid
Phoenix	P	Navy	60	Solid
Sidewinder	O	AF–Navy	. . .	Solid
Sparrow	O	AF–Navy	. . .	Solid
Sparrow III (Advanced)	D	AF–Navy	. . .	Solid
Air-to-Surface				
Bullpup	O	AF	2+	Liquid
Condor	D	Navy	medium	Solid
Hound Dog	O	AF	500+	Turbojet
Maverick	P	AF	. . .	Solid
SCAD	S	AF	. . .	Turbojet
Shrike	O	AF–Navy	. . .	Solid
SRAM	D	AF	. . .	Solid
Standard ARM	O	AF–Navy	. . .	Solid
Walleye	O	AF–Navy	10	None
Zuni	O	Navy	5	Solid
Air-to-Surface/Surface-to-Surface				
Harpoon	D	Navy	60	Solid

[1] Status code: D, under development; O, operational; P, production; S, study. [2] One nautical mile equals 1.15 statute miles or 1.85 km. [3] Antisubmarine missile. [4] Anti-tank missile. [5] Submarine-launched ballistic missiles, approximate ranges.

The 1972 SALT agreement called for the superpowers to limit their antiballistic missiles (ABMs) to one site for defending an ICBM base and one site for defending the national capital. Accordingly, the U. S. terminated construction of an ABM site at Malstrom, Mont., leaving only the ABM site at Grand Forks, N. Dak., under construction. The Nixon administration did not seek funds to develop the second ABM site permitted for Washington, D. C., but held that option open.

The American civil defense effort, which is designed to lessen the effects of a nuclear attack on the United States, received a very low priority in fiscal 1974. Only $89 million was requested out of a total U. S. defense budget of nearly $75 billion. The reasons for such a meager amount were varied. There was a general presumption that war can be deterred due to the presence of the U. S.

strategic forces. There was a widespread belief that little could be done to save any Americans near points of thermonuclear detonations. Also, there was a belief that an attempt to develop an extensive civil defense system would appear provocative to the Soviet Union, perhaps creating an incentive for Moscow to undertake substantially increased arming efforts.

General-Purpose Forces. General-purpose forces consist of both conventional units and tactical nuclear units of the Army, Navy, Air Force, and Marine Corps. Their purpose is to deter, if possible, and fight, if necessary, wars below the level of nuclear exchanges involving the homelands of the two superpowers. The effects of détente and the conclusion of the Vietnam War could be seen in the 1973 reductions of U. S. general-purpose forces. For example, the United States maintained 16 active combat divisions in 1973, as compared with 22 such divisions in 1968 at the height of the Vietnam War. There were 163 tactical fighter squadrons as compared with 210 in 1968. Airlift squadrons were reduced from the 1968 high of 63 to 34 in 1973. Similarly, the number of major warships declined from 434 to 253.

Although the reductions in personnel and equipment were substantial, several developmental programs were kept in progress to ensure that the general-purpose forces would be equipped with advanced weapons in the future. Such development included the F-15 jet fighter for the Air Force, the F-14 jet for the Navy, and a nuclear-powered aircraft carrier. New types of short-range guided missiles, a new main battle tank, and new helicopters were also being developed and evaluated.

The U. S. Army, Navy, and Air Force have sponsored research on lasers that thus far has been "revolutionary," Defense Department sources said in 1973. The Army is investigating use of the laser against air attacks, the Navy is investigating laser defenses against guided missiles, and the Air Force is investigating laser defenses against antiaircraft fire. Prototype military laser experiments were expected by 1975, and it was forecast that some laser weapons probably would be operational by 1984.

ARTIST'S conception of the U. S. Navy's proposed Trident submarine launching a long-range guided missile.

OFFICIAL U.S. NAVY PHOTOGRAPH

Military and aerospace agencies were expected to spend more than $300 million annually for military laser research and development.

The All-Volunteer Army. The draft for the Army ended shortly after the beginning of 1973, and the all-volunteer Army concept was put into effect. The results for the first year of the program were disappointing, as the Army generally failed to obtain the number of new enlistments required to maintain the prescribed force levels. For example, in June, July, and August—months thought to be the best for recruiting—the Army failed to meet its enlistment goals by 9%, 24%, and 19%, respectively. The official response to the low enlistment rates was that the all-volunteer Army was a new program that in time would produce the desired results.

An interesting statistic regarding Army enlistments in 1973 was the unusually high percentage of black volunteers. In July blacks accounted for 34.6% of the enlistments, whereas blacks accounted for only 13% of the 18–35 age group.

Personnel Changes. During 1973 there were substantial changes in the leadership of the defense establishment. Henry Kissinger, national security adviser to the President, became secretary of state on September 22. He retained his post as national security adviser.

Melvin R. Laird was succeeded as secretary of defense by Elliot L. Richardson, the former secretary of health, education, and welfare, on January 29. After the resignation of Attorney General Richard G. Kleindienst on April 30, Richardson quit the Pentagon and served as attorney general until his resignation on October 20. James R. Schlesinger succeeded Richardson as secretary of defense on June 28. He had previously served as chairman of the Atomic Energy Commission and director of the Central Intelligence Agency. David Packard, who had served as the deputy secretary of defense under Laird, was succeeded on January 23 by William P. Clements, Jr., a businessman.

The three service secretaries were Howard H. Callaway, Army; John W. Warner, Navy; and John L. McLucas, Air Force. Adm. Thomas H. Moorer served as the chairman of the Joint Chiefs of Staff. Gen. Creighton W. Abrams was the Army chief of staff; Adm. Elmo R. Zumwalt was the chief of naval operations; Gen. George S. Brown became the chief of staff of the Air Force upon the retirement of Gen. John D. Ryan; and Gen. Robert E. Cushman was the commandant of the Marine Corps.

North Atlantic Treaty Organization (NATO)

In the fall the U. S. Senate came within several votes of accepting the "Mansfield resolution," which was offered by Sen. Mike Mansfield (D-Mont.), the majority leader of the Senate. This effort to reduce American troop strength in Europe called for the withdrawal of 200,000 troops over a 3-year period, or an overall cut of 40%. Originally it appeared that the resolution would pass the Senate. However, very heavy lobbying by the most prominent Pentagon spokesmen resulted in the defeat of the move by the narrow margin of 51 opposed to 44 in favor.

The Nixon administration based its opposition to the Mansfield resolution primarily on the argument that it was poor strategy for the United States to reduce its troop strength unilaterally at a time when Washington was attempting to bargain with the Soviet Union to achieve a mutual reduction of the military forces of both nations. The point made by the administration was that if the United States unilaterally reduced its troops in Europe before agreements for mutual reduction could be obtained from the Soviet Union, then Moscow would be under little pressure to reduce its forces. Furthermore, it was argued that the United States needed the troops in Europe to ensure that the Soviets understood that it would be foolhardy to engage in a conventional or tactical nuclear invasion of Western Europe because of the depth of the U. S. commitment as represented by substantial American forces in Europe.

Those supporting the Mansfield resolution cited several reasons for their point of view. One was that in an era of détente fewer U. S. troops would be required in Europe because the threat from the Soviet Union was decreasing. Another argument was that the Western European members of NATO had ample manpower and economic resources to take over more of the defense task, thereby freeing the United States from a burden it has carried for more than two decades. It was also pointed out that the United States faced economic difficulties that could be more easily overcome if the costs of maintaining U. S. troops in Europe could be substantially decreased.

One of the most important items on the 1973 agenda for NATO was the initial meetings with the Soviet Union and the other members of the Warsaw Pact to discuss what was originally termed Mutual

BRITISH FLEET heading for Gibraltar despite the protests of Spain is led by a missile destroyer.

Balanced Force Reductions. Later in the year the name of the discussions was changed to Mutual Force Reductions. Some feared that the dropping of the word "balanced" meant that the Americans had begun to give in to Soviet bargaining tactics, which would mean that the United States would not insist on Soviet troop withdrawals being equal to those made by the United States.

The entire matter of possible withdrawal of U. S. troops from Europe, whether as a unilateral American reduction or in association with some type of Soviet troop withdrawal, created one of the most difficult problems the NATO alliance has faced in a number of years. One of the problems associated with the possibility of mutual troop withdrawals was the fear that once some or all the American and Soviet troops had left Europe, Moscow could much more easily reintroduce military forces in Europe than could Washington.

A controversial suggestion was that a reduction of American forces could be compensated for by wider NATO reliance on new "clean" tactical nuclear weapons. Those making this suggestion held that small and clean nuclear weapons—weapons that create very little if any long-lasting radiation hazards—could be extensively used in the defense of Western Europe without excessive damage to that densely populated area.

There were a number of other suggestions. The most debatable of these was the suggestion that an enlarged British-French strategic nuclear force could compensate for a decline in American troop strength.

Other problems arose for NATO during 1973. In Iceland there was considerable public demand to revise an agreement with the United States that governs the operation of the U. S. naval station at Keflavík. The primary function of the base is to maintain aerial and electronic surveillance of Soviet ships and submarines entering the North Atlantic. The agitation to close or reduce the functions of the base was aggravated by a dispute between Iceland and Britain over the possession of fishing rights off the Icelandic coast.

Late in the year relations between Washington and the NATO states were strained because of the Arab-Israeli war. Washington accused its allies of failing to support its assistance to Israel, and in turn the NATO states accused the United States of overresponding in terms of assistance to Tel Aviv.

Soviet Union

On August 17 Secretary of Defense James R. Schlesinger announced that the Soviet Union had demonstrated a MIRV capability. The news of the MIRV tests was not unexpected in Washington, as it was generally believed to be only a matter of time until Soviet scientists and engineers perfected what their American counterparts had developed several years earlier. Nevertheless the news about the MIRV tests was viewed with alarm by some members of Congress, including Sen. Henry M. Jackson (D-Wash.), who had warned at the time of the SALT-1 accords in 1972 that the Soviets must not seek to move from rough parity in strategic weapons to superiority. What particularly bothered those worried about the Soviet MIRV program was the possibility that Moscow would add MIRVs to the already greater numbers of ICBMs and SLBMs that the Soviet Union was permitted under the SALT-1 agreements. Should this happen the Soviet Union could emerge by the end of the 1970's with considerably more warheads capable of striking the United States than the United States could threaten to fire against the Soviet Union.

In evaluating the significance of the Soviet MIRV tests, Schlesinger stated that it was reasonable to assume that the Soviets would require several years to complete their MIRV testing, which would mean that they could start to deploy MIRVs on ICBMs by 1975. He suggested that by 1979 the Soviet MIRV program could advance to the point where the USSR would have as many MIRV warheads as the United States, and that by the early to mid-1980's the Soviets could possess "a very formidable force structure." Whether the Soviet Union would seek to achieve substantial superiority in both the number and the size of its warheads remained an important but unanswerable question in 1973. Schlesinger issued this warning: "As the Soviets close the technological gap and acquire MIRV capabilities, improved warheads and guidance, the United States is not in a position to tolerate the numerical or quantitative advantages presently possessed by the Soviet Union."

Not all those concerned with national defense matters shared the pessimism of some regarding the possible Soviet intentions for MIRVs. The optimistic view was that the Soviets merely intended to attain a number of warheads similar to that possessed by the United States, perhaps somewhat fewer be-

SOVIET aircraft carrier being built in 1973 and guided missile destroyer (artist's conception).

cause the Russian warheads are larger than the American ones. It was contended that such behavior would be consistent with the proposition that the Soviets would be content to live with rough strategic parity, knowing if they sought superiority it would trigger an American response and the arms race would again be in full force.

Missile Site Inspections. The news of the Soviet MIRV tests brought to the fore a particularly difficult problem that had been shunted aside during the SALT-1 negotiations. This is the matter of how inspections may be performed to guarantee that a nation is living up to any agreement regarding the number of MIRVs it has deployed on missiles. The heart of the problem is that MIRVs inside the nose cone of a missile cannot be detected by satellite photographs, the means by which the number of deployed missiles is checked. The only known way of determining how many MIRVs are in a missile nose cone is to inspect the nose cone. Since 1946, when the United States first suggested on-site inspection of Soviet and American military forces, Moscow has steadfastly rejected the idea.

Without inspection, many Americans would not trust the Soviets to abide by any MIRV number-limitation agreement emerging from the SALT-2 negotiations, and the Soviets have not changed their view of on-site inspection. Thus the stage was set for difficult bargaining in regard to MIRVs at the SALT-2 sessions. Failure to reach agreement could result in American deployment of more MIRVs on more missiles to compensate for uncertainty as to how many the Soviets might be deploying.

Soviet ICBMs. In addition to their MIRV progress the Soviets tested four new ICBMs in 1973 and one new missile for use aboard the new Delta-class submarine. In Washington it was generally felt that the Soviet activity was a continuation of a long-standing effort to improve the quality of its missile forces by developing missiles with greater accuracy, range, and throw-weight capabilities. Furthermore, it was not certain whether the Soviets meant to deploy all four of the new ICBMs. Secretary Schlesinger suggested that two of the new missiles might be in competition to replace the standard SS-11; that the new missile designated SSX-18 was the replacement for the largest Soviet missile, the SS-9; and that the remaining new missile, the SSX-16, could be designed to be a mobile ICBM.

Naval Forces. For several years Western observers have noted substantial efforts by the Soviet Union to increase the firepower and range of its naval forces. This trend continued in 1973 as new vessels were added to an already impressive force of cruisers, submarines, and helicopter aircraft carriers. At the Black Sea naval shipyard at Nikolayev, a full-size aircraft carrier was taken from the construction drydock, and in its place a similar ship was being built. The new carriers are approximately 900 feet (275 meters) long and have an angled flight deck about 600 feet (185 meters) long. They probably displace about 40,000 tons, making them smaller than the largest U. S. carriers.

Backfire Bomber. A new Soviet bomber remained something of a question mark with regard to the extent to which Moscow may deploy it. The plane is a supersonic swing-wing craft called Backfire. Should the Soviets build substantial numbers of this plane, considerable pressure would be generated in Washington to provide new air defenses and possibly to buy the B-1 bomber.

Warsaw Pact Nations

During 1973 there were no dramatic changes in the conventional armed forces of the Soviet Union and the Warsaw Pact nations. These forces are arranged as a counterweight to NATO forces, and they have been undergoing a gradual modernization program. In this program older models of guns and tanks are gradually being replaced.

People's Republic of China

Despite continued progress in building a nuclear arsenal, the Chinese possessed no nuclear threat against the United States in 1973. Pentagon spokesmen thought that it was possible that the Chinese would deploy a 3,000- to 3,500-mile (4,800- to 5,600-km) missile by late 1974. Such a missile would be capable of hitting targets in all of the Soviet Union and portions of Alaska.

Officials in Washington did not think the Chinese would be able to perfect an ICBM that was capable of being fired against the rest of the United States until 1975 at the earliest. However, they said that the Chinese were developing a large three-stage liquid-fueled ICBM that was expected to have a range of 5,000 to 7,000 miles (8,000 to 11,250 km) —a range that would enable it to reach most major cities and military targets in the Soviet Union and the United States.

It appeared that the Chinese placed a high priority on nuclear weapons that could be used against the Soviets. They reportedly have built medium-range jet bombers that can carry nuclear bombs, and they have built some liquid-fueled medium-range ballistic missiles. It was expected that these missiles would be replaced by a solid-fuel type.

The 2.5 to 3 million-man Chinese army was still largely an infantry force in 1973. However Peking appeared to be increasing the amount of armor in its army and to be converting some infantry divisions to mechanized units.

The results of Chinese research efforts were becoming visible in the form of new aircraft and naval vessels. The F-9 is a Chinese-designed jet fighter bomber. The bulk of the Chinese navy still consisted of diesel-powered submarines, which were produced in increasing numbers in China. Additions to this force include a new diesel class of submarine and a new Chinese-built destroyer armed with surface-to-surface missiles. It was not clear when the Chinese would produce submarines capable of launching missiles, but it was generally believed in Washington that this development was only a matter of time.

France

U. S. sources reported in 1973 that France was building sites in the southeastern region of the country for a group of IRBMs with thermonuclear warheads, and that French nuclear weapons tests in the Pacific Ocean involved detonation devices for the new thermonuclear warheads. France already has two groups of nine IRBMs, which are deployed in central France and have atomic warheads.

The French fleet includes two missile-launching submarines. A third, *La Foudroyant,* was scheduled to join the fleet in late 1974, and two more were to be added by 1978.

(See also DISARMAMENT AND ARMS CONTROL.)

ROBERT M. LAWRENCE
Colorado State University

DELAWARE

Partisan politics at the state level in Delaware were relatively quiet following the elections of 1972, which gave both major parties a share in the control of state government. Sherman W. Tribbitt, a Democrat, was inaugurated as governor on January 19. Eugene D. Bookhammer, a Republican, continued as lieutenant governor, having been reelected as a result of intense ticket-splitting, which has become a trend in the state. Governor Tribbitt was successful in furthering the efforts of his conservationist predecessor, Republican Russell W. Peterson, to protect the coastal zone of Delaware from incursions by heavy industry and to regulate all uses of the state's extensive wetlands.

Legislation. The close balance between Democrats and Republicans in the General Assembly, where the Republicans have a majority of only one in each house, made for some interesting maneuvers between the governor and the legislators. The governor was able to effect a working relationship with the Senate after the defection of one Republican member of that party's caucus, but the Republicans in the House stood firm, maintaining party cohesion in spite of their marginal majority.

The coastal zoning act of 1971, which prohibited further construction of heavy industries along Delaware's coastline, won acclaim as a landmark for both the state and the nation. In June, Governor Tribbitt signed into law a new wetlands act, which aims at regulating all uses of the extensive wetland area of the state, including the construction of condominiums, trailer parks, and marinas. Passage of

--------- DELAWARE • Information Highlights ---------

Area: 2,057 square miles (5,328 sq km).
Population (1972 est.): 565,000. *Density:* 290 per sq mi.
Chief Cities (1970 census): Dover, the capital, 17,488; Wilmington, 80,386; Newark, 21,078; Elsmere, 8,415.
Government (1973): *Chief Officers*—governor, Sherman W. Tribbitt (D); lt. gov., Eugene Bookhammer (R); secy. of state, Robert H. Reed (D); atty. gen., W. Laird Stabler, Jr. (R); treas., Mary D. Jornlin (R); supt. of public instruction, Kenneth C. Madden; chief justice, Daniel L. Herrmann. *General Assembly*—Senate, 21 members (11 Republicans, 10 Democrats); House of Representatives, 41 members (21 R, 20 D).
Education (1972–73): *Enrollment*—public elementary schools, 71,950 pupils, 3,070 teachers; public secondary schools, 62,367 pupils, 3,295 teachers; nonpublic schools, 18,500 pupils, 870 teachers; colleges and universities, 24,263 students. *Public school expenditures,* $143,900,000 ($1,162 per pupil). *Average teacher's salary,* $11,100.
State Finances (fiscal year 1971): *Revenues,* $346,027,000 (total sales tax and gross receipts taxes, $45,395,000; motor fuel tax, $19,120,000; federal funds, $51,163,000). *Expenditures,* $370,152,000 (education, $171,402,000; health, welfare, and safety, $51,788,000; highways, $52,330,000). *State debt,* $433,372,000 (June 30, 1971).
Personal Income (1972): $2,815,000,000; per capita, $4,983.
Public Assistance (1972): $31,325,000. *Average monthly payments* (Dec. 1972)—old-age assistance, $91.13; aid to families with dependent children, $117.03.
Labor Force: *Nonagricultural wage and salary earners* (July 1973), 238,100. *Average annual employment* (1972)—manufacturing, 72,300; trade, 48,300; government, 34,400; services, 39,700. *Insured unemployed* (Sept. 1973)—3,000 (1.5%).
Manufacturing (1971): Value added by manufacture, $1,281,000,000; food and kindred products, $187,300,000.
Agriculture (1972): *Cash farm income,* $156,608,000 (livestock, $103,186,000; crops, $51,447,000; government payments, $1,975,000). Chief crops (in order of value, 1971) —Corn, soybeans, potatoes, hay.
Mining (1972): Production value, $2,388,000 (ranks 50th among the states). *Chief minerals*—Sand and gravel, $2,364,000; clay, $22,000; gem stones, $2,000.
Fisheries (1972): *Commercial catch,* 10,648,000 pounds ($1,869,000). *Leading species by value* (1971): Clams, $1,079,000; oysters, $191,000; crabs, $112,000.
Transportation: *Roads* (1972), 5,104 miles (8,214 km); *motor vehicles* (1972), 316,512; *railroads* (1972), 291 miles (468 km); *public airports* (1972), 2.
Communications: *Telephones* (1973), 410,300; *radio stations* (1971), 15; *newspapers* (1973), 5 (daily circulation, 180,000).

this legislation brought into sharp focus the controversy between the state planning office and Sussex county officials over who has control of zoning and land use in the state's southern wetlands. The widespread introduction of multiple-occupant housing and recreational facilities—with the dredging, filling, and dumping that accompany such development—has raised serious problems in maintaining the ecological balance needed to sustain fish, birds, and plant life in coastal areas.

Gubernatorial Appointments. Daniel F. Wolcott, chief justice of the state supreme court, died on July 10, and the governor appointed Associate Justice Daniel L. Herrmann to the chief justiceship. William Duffy, of the court of chancery, was named to Herrmann's place, and Judge William T. Quillen became the new chancellor.

Economic and Other News. Delaware's economy showed a slight improvement, with 6,000 more persons employed in 1973 than in 1972. Strikes in the automobile assembly plants were of short duration. Ambitious plans for the construction of a central-city shopping mall in Wilmington, connected with the new Federal Plaza, had to be abandoned because of a cutback in federal funds.

PAUL DOLAN, *University of Delaware*

DENMARK

Denmark's voters showed their opposition to growing taxes and government bureaucracy in 1973. The ruling Social Democratic government was defeated in parliamentary elections in December, and the principal opposition parties also suffered serious setbacks. A major victor was the newly formed Progress party, which had promised tax reductions and lessened government interference in private affairs. The elections were held at a time of serious economic problems including strikes, a huge deficit in the balance of payments, and runs on the krone.

Political Affairs. The government of Prime Minister Anker Jørgensen was on a precarious course, with only a two-vote majority in the Folketing (legislature). He had to call for new elections on November 8 after his government was defeated by a vote of 86–86 on an income tax measure.

In the elections held on December 4, voters elected representatives of 10 parties to the Folketing, twice as many parties as in the previous legislature. The Social Democrats remained the country's largest party, but fell from 70 seats to 46 in the 179-member Folketing. The new Progress party became the second-largest, with 28 seats, and the Moderate Liberal party, with 22 seats, became the third-largest party. The new premier was Poul Hartling of the Moderate Liberal party.

Economic Problems. At the start of the year Denmark's Nationalbank purchased bonds and kroner as part of its efforts to support the plunging currency. The U. S. dollar devaluation in February further unsettled the unstable krone, necessitating the bolstering of the currency even in the late fall. The bank raised interest rates in March to an unprecedented high of 11%.

The shaky economy was further imperiled when some 258,000 workers left their jobs on March 21, beginning a three-week strike that caused the nearly complete shutdown of Danish industries. The strikers won an approximate 7.5% wage increase including fringe and pension benefits, but the country's economy was seriously damaged.

——————— DENMARK • Information Highlights ———————

Official Name: Kingdom of Denmark.
Location: Northwest Europe.
Area: 16,629 square miles (43,069 sq km).
Population (1973 est.): 5,100,000. *Density,* 298 per square miles (115 per sq km).
Chief Cities (1971 est.): Copenhagen, the capital, 618,900; Aarhus, 241,300; Odense, 166,700; Aalborg, 155,400.
Government: *Head of state,* Margrethe II, queen (acceded Jan. 1972). *Head of government,* Poul Hartling, prime minister (took office Dec. 1973). *Legislature* (unicameral) —Folketing. *Major political parties*—Social Democratic party; Progress party; Conservative People's party; Liberal Democratic party; Radical Liberal party; Center Democratic party; Socialist People's party.
Language: Danish (official).
Education: *Expenditure* (1969), 17.7% of total public expenditure. *School enrollment* (1969)—primary, 534,000; general secondary, 215,890; technical/vocational (1968), 171,629; university/higher, 71,770.
Monetary Unit: Krone (5.799 kroner equal U. S.$1, Aug. 1973).
Gross National Product (1972 est.): $19,000,000,000.
Economic Indexes: *Industrial production* (manufacturing, 1971), 153 (1963=100); *agricultural production* (1971), 103 (1963=100); *consumer price index* (1972), 164 (1964=100).
Manufacturing (major products): Beverages, processed foods, machinery, ships, chemicals, furniture, textiles, ceramics.
Major Agricultural Products: Barley, sugar beets, oats, dairy products, cattle, hogs, fish.
Major Minerals: Peat, lignite, salt, kaolin.
Foreign Trade (1972): *Exports,* $4,417,000,000. *Imports,* $5,070,000,000. *Chief trading partners* (1970)—United Kingdom (took 19% of exports, supplied 13.5% of imports); Sweden (16%—16.5%); West Germany (12%—18.5%); United States (4%—8.4%).
Tourism: *Receipts* (1971), $386,900,000.
Transportation: *Motor vehicles* (1972), 1,374,000 (automobiles, 1,149,700); *railroads* (1971), 1,208 miles (1,944 km); *merchant fleet* (1972), 4,020,000 gross registered tons; *major national airline* (with Norway and Sweden), Scandinavian Airlines System (SAS).
Communications: *Telephones* (1972), 1,793,926; *newspapers* (1971), 56 (daily circulation, 1,829,000).

Denmark's balance-of-payments deficit for the first six months of 1973 was 4.8 billion kroner, compared with 1.9 billion for the same period in 1972. The rate of expansion in chemical, shipbuilding, and ceramic industries amounted to a low of 2%, compared with the normal 15% expansion rate characteristic of these concerns. Opposition parties stressed the country's economic troubles and charged the government with responsibility for a "total breakdown of fiscal policy."

Foreign Affairs. Folketing debate in April focused on U. S. proposals for expanded Atlantic cooperation. An early interest cooled later, and the Danes stated their opposition to changes in NATO and to aid to the United States either in solving the dollar crisis or in modifications of positions adopted by the European Economic Community. Meetings between Foreign Minister K. G. Andersen and U. S. Secretary of State William Rogers in June were cordial in tone, but the results as measured in signed agreements proved to be meager.

The royal family visited Finland and Sweden, participated in the funeral ceremonies for Sweden's King Gustaf VI Adolf in September, and spent some days in the Faeroe Islands and in Iceland. As part of a program of the restoration of Icelandic manuscripts to their homeland, Queen Margrethe delivered the two oldest Icelandic lawbooks, *Jónsbók* and *Grågåsen,* during her visit to Reykjavík.

New Abortion Legislation. The Folketing passed a law in May enabling women to obtain abortions as part of their normal health benefits. Special permission for an abortion would be necessary after the 12th week of pregnancy, with a requirement of social, medical, or other reasons for such medical treatment.

RAYMOND E. LINDGREN
California State University, Long Beach

DETROIT

The election of the city's first black mayor and a bitter strike by public school teachers were the major events of 1973 in Detroit.

Elections. Coleman A. Young, a veteran state senator, was elected mayor of Detroit in the nonpartisan November 6 city election. He defeated former police commissioner John F. Nichols, 231,786 to 217,479. Three newcomers were elected to the nine-member city council, which is now composed of a majority of persons considered to be "liberals" who would be cooperative with Young.

One of the major tasks of the new mayor was the reorganization of the city government as required by a new city charter, which was approved by voters, 186,041 to 141,095. The new charter, effective July 1, 1974, will establish a five-member police commission appointed by the mayor to replace the present single commissioner, create an ombudsman office to investigate citizen complaints against city agencies, and set up new agencies to protect consumers and the city's environment.

Schools. A strike by Detroit teachers delayed the opening of school for 43 days until October 18. To meet the state requirement of a school year of 180 days, the Christmas and Easter vacations were reduced, Saturday classes were scheduled, and the school year lengthened to June 29, 1974. The strike ended when the Detroit Board of Education and Detroit Federation of Teachers agreed to submit the dispute over salary and class size to compulsory arbitration. The more controversial issue of teacher "accountability" (teacher evaluation plan) was submitted to a panel appointed by Gov. William Milliken. The teachers' union and its top officers were fined a total of $228,000 for contempt for failure to obey a court order to return to work under a Michigan law prohibiting strikes by public employees. The union also was to pay the school district damages of $2.5 million. The union appealed both the fines and the damages.

The 13-member central school district was given a new look by the election on November 6 of six new members. Four incumbents were defeated, and two did not seek reelection. The shift was expected to give a more powerful voice in citywide school affairs to Detroit's eight regional school districts.

A 1% income tax, to benefit schools effective July 1, was replaced by a seven-mill ($7 per $1,000 assessed valuation) property tax approved by voters on September 11. The income tax was imposed by the school board under authority granted in February.

Renaissance Center. Ground was broken on May 22 for the Renaissance Center to be built on Detroit's waterfront. The center, a complex of a hotel, stores, and office buildings, is to be built over a 10-year period at a total cost of $500 million. The Ford Motor Company and General Motors Corporation, with $6 million each, headed a list of 48 investors who committed $37,150,000 to the $200 million first phase of the project.

Auto Talks. A nine-day strike by United Automobile Workers (UAW) employees at Chrysler Corporation began September 14 and was settled with agreement on a new three-year contract. Ford and the UAW agreed on a new contract on October 26, just 75 minutes before a strike deadline. The UAW and General Motors reached agreement on November 19.

CHARLES W. THEISEN, *The Detroit "News"*

UPI

In Washington, D.C., Soviet Communist party chairman Brezhnev and U.S. President Nixon sign agreement to negotiate treaty to reduce nuclear arms.

Disarmament and Arms Control

Nuclear arms control and disarmament efforts were characterized by stalemate and reappraisal in 1973. The ongoing U.S.-USSR Strategic Arms Limitation Talks (SALT) reached no new agreements nor saw prospective ones take shape during the year, and the same was true for the Conference of the Committee on Disarmament, the chief forum for negotiating nonstrategic arms control measures.

The first phase of the bilateral negotiations, SALT 1, was completed in 1972 with two pacts—(1) a treaty limiting Soviet and U.S. antiballistic missile (ABM) systems, and (2) an interim arrangement freezing offensive strategic missiles of both sides at approximately current levels for up to five years. The ABM treaty was approved by the U.S. Senate in August 1972. The interim agreement froze the number of American land-based intercontinental ballistic missiles (ICBMs) and submarine-launched ballistic missiles (SLBMs) at 1,710 and permitted the Soviet Union to have a total of 2,358 ICBMs and SLBMs. This interim agreement was approved by Congress in September 1972 after the adoption of a reservation proposed by Sen. Henry Jackson (D-Wash.). · It specified that in the future the president should not enter into any treaty that would "limit the United States to levels of intercontinental strategic forces inferior" to those permitted for the Soviet Union.

Goals and Problems of SALT 2. The second phase of SALT began in Geneva, Switzerland, in November 1972 and recessed a year later in what appeared to be a complete deadlock. The U.S. team was led by Ambassador U. Alexis Johnson, who succeeded Gerard C. Smith on February 1, and the Soviet team was again headed by Deputy Foreign Minister Vladimir S. Semyonov. According to the American-Soviet agreement signed by President Richard Nixon and Secretary General Leonid I. Brezhnev in Washington on June 21, 1973, the lofty objectives of SALT 2 are to complete by the end of 1974 a permanent treaty to limit the number and quality of offensive strategic weapons on both sides and, if possible, to reduce the offensive strategic weapons inventory of each side. According to a White House release, this "solemn commitment" is designed to "broaden the scope of an agreement to include limits on qualitative improvements as well as numbers of weapons," to "provide for subsequent reductions," and to "allow for immediate agreements in areas where limiting competition may be urgent."

Underlying these broad goals were the perplexing problems that have dogged strategic arms control efforts from the start. For instance, the problem of definition remained. The Soviet Union argues that a strategic weapon is one that can penetrate the homeland of an adversary, and therefore U.S. tactical aircraft based in Western Europe are strategic weapons. The United States insists they are not strategic weapons—that they are there for the defense of Europe only. Also, the problems af arms control are made difficult by the complexity of strategic land, sea, and air weapons systems; by technical developments; and by geographical differences between the Soviet Union and the United States.

Developments Since SALT 1. The 1972 interim agreement on offensive weapons limited the number of missile launchers on both sides, but it permitted each side to augment its strategic power through improvements in nuclear submarines, bombers, and warhead systems. Both sides have done this, and there has been debate as to which has gained more.

DISCUSSING SALT are (left to right) *Sen. Henry Jackson, Armed Forces subcommittee chairman; Fred Iklé, Arms Control and Disarmament Agency director; and U. S. Ambassador-at-Large U. Alexis Johnson.*

The United States, taking advantage of its lead in MIRV (Multiple Independently Targeted Reentry Vehicle) technology, has continued the process of fitting each of its land-based and submarine-launched missiles with several nuclear warheads, each capable of reaching a different target. In spite of Moscow's larger number of missile launchers, Washington had a lead of about 5,700 to 2,500 in the number of targeted warheads at the time of the SALT 1 agreement, and it has substantially increased this lead since then. In the category of strategic bombers, which are not covered by the interim agreement, the United States has approximately 500 planes to 140 for the USSR, and the United States has been improving the weapons carried by its planes. The United States also has been improving the range of its submarine-launched missiles.

Soviet strategic developments since SALT 1 have been more visible and dramatic than those of the United States, and some Western observers regard them with alarm. Within its numerically superior limit permitted by the interim agreement, Moscow has further strengthened the throw-weight capacity of its large ICBMs. It now has some 300 giant SS-9 missiles with a throw-weight of 13,000 pounds each, compared with an average throw-weight of approximately 2,000 pounds for the Minuteman missile, which makes up the bulk of the U. S. land-based strategic force. The Soviet navy is building 12 to 13 nuclear submarines a year, compared with 6 for the United States. The new U. S. submarines carry 16 missiles each, whereas the Soviet Delta-class subs carry 12. It is estimated that the Soviet Union has 3-to-1 missile throw-weight advantage.

On August 17 the U. S. defense department announced that Moscow had successfully flight-tested its own MIRV system. Depending on how rapidly this technology can be applied and in the absence of any agreed limitations, the Soviet Union could combine multiple warheads with its superior missile throw-weight and thus achieve significant missile superiority over the United States unless Washington were permitted approximate equality in missile launchers and undertook a major effort to increase the throw-weight of its own missile force.

Taking into account many complex factors, including the lead time required to apply weapons technology, Western experts disagree over which side now has or in 1980 will have the strategic advantage. Those who are concerned about Moscow's increasing strategic capability often point to other Soviet military developments. In 1973 the Soviet navy continued its modernization program, was more widely deployed in the world's oceans, and was rapidly approaching parity with the U. S. Navy. The Soviet army has more than 2 million men compared with 800,000 for the U. S. Army. The Soviet air force has about 8,250 combat aircraft, whereas the U. S. Air Force has about 5,750.

The International Institute for Strategic Studies in London estimated that both the United States and the USSR spent approximately $85 billion in 1973 for defense, but that the Soviet Union spent a significantly larger portion for military research and development.

Outlook for SALT 2. The year-end stalemate in the SALT negotiations is not likely to be easily broken, at least by a comprehensive agreement to limit further or cut back major offensive strategic systems. This forecast is based on the complex problems involved, the apprehension in some quarters about growing Soviet military capability and intentions, and the renewal of the U. S. debate on the doctrine of "flexible response," which has a direct bearing on arms control measures.

On June 30, Fred C. Iklé succeeded Gerard C. Smith as director of the U. S. Arms Control and Disarmament Agency, and on July 2, James R. Schlesinger became secretary of defense. Both men are advocates of developing a greater capacity for a more "flexible and controlled" U. S. response in the face of a nuclear attack by the Soviet Union. This view challenges the concept of "assured destruction," which holds that the United States can best deter a nuclear first strike by targeting U. S. missiles on Russian population centers and by having U. S. missiles sufficiently protected to have enough left over to deliver unacceptable damage to the Soviet Union after absorbing a first strike.

For the past decade the U. S. strategic posture has relied primarily on the targeting of Soviet cities and industrial complexes, although some missiles have been aimed at military installations, such as airfields and command centers. The current debate is a matter of emphasis. However, if those seeking a more diversified strategic arsenal prevail, it will mean that the United States will have to take further measures to ensure the survivability of its missiles.

In view of the growing Soviet missile technology and the U. S. objective of achieving a capability for a broader range of nuclear options, Washington will probably insist on approximate numerical equality in delivery vehicles in any permanent limitation on offensive systems. On December 4, Senator Jackson warned against the growing Soviet strategic power, noted the "impasse" in SALT negotiations, and recommended that the United States and the Soviet Union each reduce its total number of ICBMs, strategic bombers, and missile-launching submarines to 1,760 or fewer to help equalize the nuclear payload of both sides.

Geneva Disarmament Conference. The Conference of the Committee on Disarmament (CCD) opened its 1973 session at Geneva on February 20. When the session ended on August 30, the conference had no progress to report to the United Nations General Assembly. A deadlock between the

United States and the Soviet Union over proposals for a partial ban on underground nuclear tests and a ban on chemical arms has stymied the disarmament conference for two years. Despite the lack of progress, Soviet delegate Aleksei A. Roschin said that the conference still was a "necessary and useful international forum for the consideration of disarmament problems." This view was implicitly supported by the American delegate, Joseph Martin, Jr.

The United States and the Soviet Union share the chairmanship of the conference. The other members are Argentina, Brazil, Bulgaria, Burma, Canada, Czechoslovakia, Egypt, Ethiopia, France, Great Britain, Hungary, India, Italy, Japan, Mexico, Mongolia, Morocco, Netherlands, Nigeria, Pakistan, Poland, Rumania, Sweden, and Yugoslavia.

Other Developments. The People's Republic of China remains a nonparticipant in formal arms control negotiations despite the fact that it has made "tremendous progress" in its capacity to build and deliver nuclear weapons, according to a statement by Sen. Strom Thurmond (R-S. C.) after a briefing by CIA Director Richard Helms on Jan. 9, 1973.

On July 18, France signed Protocol II of the 1967 Treaty of Tlatlelolco, which bans nuclear weapons from Latin America. The United States and Britain had previously signed this treaty, and the People's Republic of China has indicated that it plans to do so. The Soviet Union has shown no indication that it will sign.

On December 11, Japanese Premier Kakuei Tanaka said he planned to seek Diet (parliament) approval to ratify the 1969 Nuclear Nonproliferation Treaty early in 1974.

ERNEST W. LEFEVER
The Brookings Institution

DISASTERS. See ACCIDENTS AND DISASTERS.
DISTRICT OF COLUMBIA. See WASHINGTON, D. C.

DOMINICAN REPUBLIC

The political violence which has characterized life in the Dominican Republic for many years continued during 1973, but the nation's president, Gen. Joaquín Balaguer, remained in firm control of the government and was reported to be contemplating a campaign for reelection in 1974. Economic conditions showed only slight improvement.

Violence and Repression. On Feb. 4, 1973, a small guerrilla band landed on the south coast, in Azua province. Some 2,500 government troops were sent in pursuit, and, on February 17, the regime announced that the leader of the invaders, Col. Francisco Caamaño, leader of the Constitutionalist forces in the 1965 civil war, had been killed, along with most of the other guerrillas.

During the crisis, the government organized a major show of military force in Santo Domingo. It also arrested a number of political opponents. Juan Bosch and other leaders of the largest opposition party, the Dominican Revolutionary party (PRD), went into hiding. Bosch did not resume public activity until May 5.

Another major incident of violence was the murder on March 28 of Gregorie Garcia Castro, one of the country's leading journalists. The national journalists' union denounced an aide of President Balaguer, Socrates Pichardo, as the "intellectual author" of the murder, although three police officers were arrested for actually executing it.

Political Maneuvers. In 1972, talks had begun among four major opposition parties looking to the formation of a common front against President Balaguer, should the rumor of his intention to seek reelection in 1974 prove true.

Although agreement appeared near in January 1973, the PRD suddenly broke off negotiations, a move attributed to a split between Juan Bosch and other party leaders over the advisability of collaboration with rival antigovernment groups. Several PRD officers were expelled or resigned from the party, and negotiations were resumed later in the year. Early in November, an agreement in principle was announced, but later Bosch broke with the PRD and formed his own party. In the meantime, President Balaguer was demonstrating his continuing control over the military by transferring army officers from one cabinet post to another.

Economic Affairs. Some economic progress was made in 1973. In January a new oil refinery was inaugurated near Santo Domingo. It was said to be capable of processing most of the petroleum products consumed in the country. Also in January, two sizable loans, one from the Inter-American Development Bank for $24.8 million and another for $13 million from the International Development Association of the World Bank, were received for agricultural development. Later in the year, however, it was announced that the country would have to import extraordinarily large quantities of foodstuffs because of insufficient domestic production.

In May a $2 million government program to develop the fishing industry was announced. A part of the Inter-American Bank loan was to be used for this purpose.

Dispute with Puerto Rico. Some tension developed with Puerto Rico during the year over the issue of a "superport" for oil tankers that the Puerto Rican government was planning to build on the island of Mona, between the two countries. There was some indication that the Dominican Republic might claim sovereignty over Mona.

ROBERT J. ALEXANDER
Rutgers University

— DOMINICAN REPUBLIC • Information Highlights —

Official Name: Dominican Republic.
Location: Eastern two thirds of the island of Hispaniola in the Caribbean Sea.
Area: 18,816 square miles (48,734 sq km).
Population (1973 est.): 4,800,000. *Density,* 250 per square mile (90 per sq km).
Chief Cities (1970 census): Santo Domingo, the capital, 671,-400; Santiago de los Caballeros, 155,200.
Government: *Head of state,* Joaquín Balaguer, president (took office for 2d 4-year term July 1970). *Head of government,* Joaquín Balaguer. *Legislature*—Congress: Senate and Chamber of Deputies. *Major political parties*—Reformist party; Dominican Revolutionary party.
Language: Spanish (official).
Education: *Expenditure* (1969), 16% of total public expenditure. *School enrollment* (1969)—primary, 726,398; secondary, 102,707; technical/vocational, 4,636; university/higher, 18,817.
Monetary Unit: Peso (1 peso equals U. S.$1, Aug. 1973).
Gross National Product (1972 est.): $1,745,000,000.
Economic Indexes: *Industrial production* (manufacturing, 1969), 124 (1963=100); *agricultural production* (1971), 120 (1963=100); *consumer price index* (1972), 117 (1963=100).
Manufacturing (major products): Sugar, processed foods, metallurgical products, petroleum products.
Major Agricultural Products: Sugarcane, rice, coffee, cacao, peanuts, bananas and plantains, tobacco, forest products.
Major Minerals: Bauxite, nickel, salt.
Foreign Trade (1972): *Exports,* $347,000,000. *Imports,* $321,-000,000. *Chief trading partner* (1970)—United States (took 75% of exports, supplied 53% of imports).
Transportation: *Motor vehicles* (1971), 68,600 (automobiles, 44,800); *major national airline,* Dominicana de Aviación.
Communications: *Telephones* (1972), 55,982; *newspapers* (1971), 7.

NEW YORK CITY'S Addiction Services Agency used mobile centers to offer treatment to drug addicts and to explain the state's new drug law.

DRUG ADDICTION AND ABUSE

In 1973 the rate of increase of narcotic addiction and other forms of drug abuse that marked former years appeared to have slowed. Governmental activities were highlighted by the issuance of a federal strategy paper on ways to control drug abuse. Also, the National Commission on Marihuana and Drug Abuse rendered its final report.

Incidence. Although accurate statistics are difficult to obtain, indirect measures show the first meaningful changes in the rate of appearance of new addicts. The number of new heroin addicts continued a decline that started in 1969. In New York City alone, heroin deaths fell below the 2,000 recorded in 1971. Property crimes have shown an absolute drop in those cities where aggressive narcotic treatment and control activities are under way. The waiting lists for treatment slots have all but disappeared in most communities. It has become possible to treat 175,000 addicts per year. Estimates of the number of narcotic addicts remain at between 500,000 and 600,000, including those in treatment.

With regard to nonnarcotic drugs the picture is mixed. The consumption of hallucinogens may also have leveled off. Sedatives—particularly methaqualone (Quaalude, Sopor), a nonbarbiturate sleeping pill—continue to be widely used. (In consequence, the federal government imposed new restrictions late in September 1973 on the sale of methaqualone.) Amphetamines have been brought under much stricter prescription control, and their misuse has decreased. Cocaine, a related stimulant, has increased in popularity. Marihuana and hashish remain widely used, especially by young adults.

Governmental Efforts. The first federal strategy paper for drug abuse and drug traffic prevention appeared in 1973. Issued by the Strategy Council which consists of involved government department heads and the directors of the drug abuse control and prevention agencies, the report emphasized that supply and demand must be simultaneously reduced if the current abuse situation is to be brought under control. Treatment must be available to those who want it, and at the same time, the quantity of abusable drugs must be reduced.

Federal—and other—authorities see heroin addiction as the most serious of the illicit drug problems. A multimodality treatment system is available in many communities so that the addict can enter the treatment mode best suited for him. In 1973, about 75,000 people were enrolled in methadone maintenance programs. This procedure is now viewed as an interim step toward a complete drug-free recovery, and it is no longer thought of as a lifelong maintenance program. About 100,000 addicts are in some form of nonmaintenance treatment facility—therapeutic communities, detoxification and aftercare, or civil-commitment programs.

In line with the federal strategy guidelines President Nixon recommended to Congress new legislation that would sharply reduce the availability of bail for major heroin traffickers and provide minimum mandatory sentences for them. Life imprisonment without possibility of parole is recommended for major repeat offenders.

The Special Action Office for Drug Abuse Prevention (SAODAP) has been attempting to coordinate and give direction to the federal effort in education, training, research, and treatment. The 14 governmental agencies, involved in these activities will be reduced to six by 1974. The SAODAP is a temporary agency that will be disbanded in 1975. At that time a new National Institute on Drug Abuse will be established within the Department of Health, Education, and Welfare.

The fragmented federal drug law enforcement effort will be unified by the creation of the Drug Enforcement Administration (DEA) in the Department of Justice, according to Reorganization

Plan Number Two of 1973. All enforcement and control agencies will come under a single administration.

During 1973 officials claimed considerable success for drug control measures. Drug seizures and arrests attained an all-time high. Sixty tons of opium, morphine base, and heroin were confiscated in the United States and abroad by governmental officials. The seizures affected the price of heroin, which doubled, and in the eastern United States a severe heroin shortage occurred. The heroin content of street heroin "bags" dropped from 12 to 3 or 4%.

Another major reorganization move is the decentralization of resources to the states. Single state agencies have been formed to set priorities and finance local treatment programs. Block grants are awarded to the state agencies for this purpose. The federal effort in research, training, and demonstration projects will continue.

New York Legislation. New York State in 1973 enacted very stringent legislation against dangerous drug possession and sale. Provisions include minimum mandatory sentences without possibility of parole, discontinuance of plea bargaining, and jail terms that may exceed those for murder. The lack of response to the treatment effort and the continuing high level of addict-related crimes were the reasons given for recourse to the more punitive legislation.

Other Approaches. Some new and innovative approaches to the management of drug abusers are being attempted. One of these is TASC (Treatment Alternatives to Street Crime). At the time of arrest the addict is offered treatment as a condition of release or parole. This relieves congestion in the judicial system, and the possibility of the addict entering into a productive existence through treatment is enhanced.

One approach not recommended in the federal strategy is heroin maintenance—the giving of heroin to the addict so that he will not have to resort to crime. It is believed that providing heroin would seriously increase the number of people becoming addicted because heroin must be given to take home for injection every 4 to 6 hours. Methadone requires only that the solution be swallowed once a day in a clinic. Longer-acting drugs are under study at Veterans Administration hospitals and other treatment centers.

An effort is being made to place the abused barbiturates into Schedule Two, the category that requires a narcotic-type, nonrefillable prescription and now includes the narcotics and amphetamines. In so doing, better control over supplies can be maintained.

Marihuana. Marihuana is not considered as hazardous as narcotics, and its penalty structure has been adjusted so that the federal statute and the statutes of 44 states make its possession a misdemeanor. In five other states the judge has the discretion of trying it as a felony or a misdemeanor. One state, Oregon, now makes simple possession a violation punishable by a fine. The National Commission on Marihuana and Drug Abuse, headed by Raymond P. Shafer, former governor of Pennsylvania, has recommended decriminalization for marihuana (making possession of small amounts and private use a noncriminal act).

The Strategy Council report makes the following points about marihuana: (1) Our understanding of marihuana's effects is still very incomplete. (2) A substantial increase in usage would accompany decriminalization or legalization. (3) More significantly, the drug would be incorporated into the customs and values of the society. In the case of alcohol and tobacco this incorporation has proved to be irreversible when it became clear that these would be dangerous drugs. Therefore, important areas of ignorance should be cleared up before a complete removal of criminal sanctions occurs.

Drugs and Violence. In its report, the Shafer Commission had some interesting comments about the effects of drugs upon violent criminal behavior. It found alcohol to be the drug most strongly associated with violent crimes and with reckless and negligent operation of motor vehicles. An increasing number of reports are linking barbiturate and amphetamine users with criminal behavior, especially assaultive offenses. Research data linking cocaine use and criminal behavior are generally lacking; however, the pharmacologic effects of the drug suggest a potential for violence similar to that shown for amphetamines. Marihuana use, in and of itself, is neither causative of nor directly associated with either violent or nonviolent crime.

The use of opiates, especially heroin, is associated with acquisitive crimes such as burglary and shoplifting, ordinarily committed for the purpose of securing money to support addiction. Opiate users are less likely to commit assaultive offenses. Except in relatively rare instances generally related to drug-induced panic and toxic reactions, users of hallucinogens, nonbarbiturate sedative-hypnotics, and glue and similar volatile inhalants are not inclined toward assaultive, criminal behavior. Some of these substances can induce violent behavior.

Personnel Changes. In 1973 the four heads of the major federal drug abuse programs resigned. Dr. Jerome H. Jaffe, director of the Special Action Office for Drug Abuse Prevention; Dr. William E. Bunney, Jr., director of the Division of Narcotic Addiction and Drug Abuse of the National Institute of Mental Health; Myles J. Ambrose, director of the Office of Drug Abuse Law Enforcement; and John E. Ingersoll, director of the Bureau of Narcotics and Dangerous Drugs relinquished their positions.

SIDNEY COHEN, M. D.
Executive Director, Council on Drug & Alcohol Abuse, University of California, Los Angeles

EARTHQUAKES

Earthquake activity in 1973 was much less than usual, and there were few casualties, except for two disastrous quakes in Mexico. Seismologists have been seeking a way to predict earthquakes so that people can flee an area before a quake strikes. During the year their hopes were raised by findings that confirmed an earthquake-prediction theory first developed by Soviet scientists in 1969.

Earthquake Activity. The intensity of an earthquake is measured on the basis of a scale devised by the American seismologist Charles F. Richter. Each number on the Richter scale represents a quake ten times as strong as the one of next lower magnitude. For example, an earthquake of magnitude 8 is ten times stronger than one of magnitude 7, which in turn is ten times stronger than one of magnitude 6, and so on.

The first damaging earthquake of the year 1973 occurred on January 30 in Mexico about 100 miles (160 km) southeast of Colima, killing 52 persons

and injuring 390. This quake had a magnitude of 7.8 on the Richter scale. On August 28 the most damaging quake of the year occurred in central Mexico near Tierra Blanca. Although only of magnitude 7, it caused approximately 700 deaths and was felt as far away as Mexico City, about 175 miles (280 km) northwest of Tierra Blanca.

On February 21 a quake of magnitude 5.75 was felt from Santa Barbara to San Diego along the coast of California. Only five persons were injured, but property damage in Oxnard and Camarillo was reported at $1 million.

East and south of Honshu, Japan, there were 26 minor shocks of magnitude 4 to 5 in January, 17 such shocks in February, and only 7 in March, clearly indicating a tapering off in activity. However, the shocks increased in number to 18 in April, indicating a rise in activity again. As a result the residents of Tokyo are becoming as jittery as those in San Francisco, fearful as to when they will have their next big quake. The fact that the Tokyo area had these minor shocks can be considered a good sign rather than a bad one because the energy released in minor shocks lessens the energy buildup. Although it is still debatable whether frequent minor shocks are a safety valve or a warning of something bigger to come, this writer inclines to the former view.

Earthquake Prediction. The front line of research in seismology still is the attempt to find a way of predicting earthquakes. As early as 1969 Soviet scientists announced that the ratio of the velocities of the two main earthquake waves, called P waves and S waves, changed before quakes struck in the Garm region of Tadzhik. The ratio of the velocity of the primary or compression wave (P wave) to that of the secondary or shear wave (S wave) normally is a constant, 1.75, and formerly was considered to be always a constant. However, the Soviet scientists found that as strain was de-

veloping some time before a quake, the velocity ratio became much smaller and then gradually increased to its normal value, whereupon the earthquake occurred. These findings have been confirmed in Japan and the United States, particularly in the case of the San Fernando earthquake of Feb. 9, 1971.

Soviet and American scientists now are working on the problem as a combined team. They have found that the variation in the velocity ratio is the same for large and small quakes, but that the time prior to the quake when the change becomes noticeable is a function of the size of the developing quake. In the case of the San Fernando quake (magnitude 6.4), a decrease in the velocity ratio occurred as much as three-and-one-half years before the quake struck. In the case of a larger quake, say of magnitude 8, the evidence would probably begin to show up about 30 years before the quake.

While there are some minor differences among the U.S.-USSR collaborators, it is generally agreed that the chief factor in the variation of the ratio of the velocities is the variation in the velocity of the P wave. When a rock is strained, as shown in laboratory experiments, the volume of the rock is increased, its shape is changed, cracks and interstices develop, and as a result the velocity of the P wave decreases. When these cracks are filled with underground water, the velocity of the P wave would be expected to increase back to normal, and laboratory tests have shown that P-wave velocities are higher in water-saturated rock than in unsaturated rock. Thus, it can be concluded that close watch of the velocity ratio in a region bids fair to give some warning of an impending quake.

J. JOSEPH LYNCH, S. J.
Director, Fordham University Seismic Observatory

EASTERN ORTHODOX CHURCH. See RELIGION.
ECOLOGY. See ENVIRONMENT.

Residents of Tecomán, Mexico, inspect the remains of a store that collapsed during a January earthquake.

WIDE WORLD

"We've come a long way since Phase One."

Economy of the U.S.

The year 1973 brought continued strong gains in production levels but was marred by accelerating inflation and developing anxiety associated with energy shortages. Uncertainties over fueling the U. S. economy at recent high levels, international monetary stabilization, and economic leadership brought the year to a close with instability the keynote and considerable fear of sharp economic recession. Further economic dislocations were thought by some to be foreshadowed by widely fluctuating stock prices, but certainly declines in two mainstays of recent prosperity, housing and automobile production, were cause for concern.

Since the mid-1960's when the United States tried combining high-level domestic production with war finance, the nation has been plagued by wage and price spirals. Withdrawal from direct participation in Indochina hostilities did not end the problem, however. Worldwide food and resource short-

ages, together with the declining value of the dollar, imposed a foreign demand on top of an already high level of domestic demand to push prices up at an even faster rate. By the fourth quarter of 1973, "real" output of the economy—after adjustment for price increases—was rising only a little over 1%, the slowest since the last quarter of 1970. And prices were rising in the last quarter at the fastest rate since 1951.

Gross National Product. The GNP, the broadest measure of the economy's performance, approached $1.3 trillion for all of 1973, a showing that was up 11.5% over 1972. This compared with a gain of about 9.4% in 1972 over 1971, but in 1973 more of the increase was in prices. The real output of the economy and price increases were more nearly evenly divided in 1973, but the swift rate of increase in prices toward the end of the year contributed further to the nation's pessimistic out-

THE U.S. ECONOMY IN 1973
Everything Is Go–Including Prices

GROSS NATIONAL PRODUCT

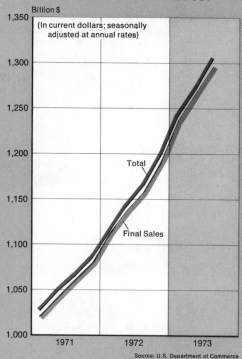

Billion $
(In current dollars; seasonally adjusted at annual rates)

Total
Final Sales

Source: U.S. Department of Commerce

UNEMPLOYMENT RATE

Percent
(Seasonally adjusted)

Total

Married Men

Source: U.S. Department of Labor

INDUSTRIAL PRODUCTION

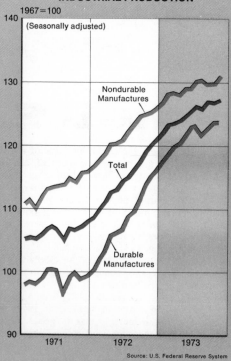

1967=100
(Seasonally adjusted)

Nondurable Manufactures

Total

Durable Manufactures

Source: U.S. Federal Reserve System

CONSUMER PRICE INDEX

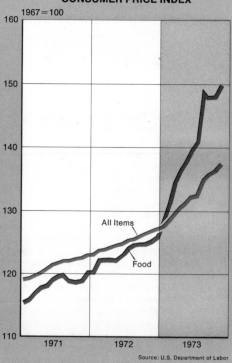

1967=100

All Items

Food

Source: U.S. Department of Labor

*SECRETARY OF THE TREASURY George Shultz intro-
duced the administration's Phases 3 and 4 in 1973.*

look for the immediate future. With fuel shortages
an obvious push to further price rises, the outlook
for at least the first six months of 1974 became
much less rosy than the total showing for 1973
would seem to have indicated.

Prices. Rises in prices traced a jagged pattern
upward in 1973 as the nation went through more
of the administration's economic phases. With the
end of Phase 2 in January, more permissive wage-
price controls brought widespread increases, and
Phase 3 was replaced by Phase 4 in two steps in
July and August. A two-month price freeze in mid-
June, which excluded agricultural produce, produced shortages that intensified pressure on food
prices when lifted because rising raw material prices
pressed against fixed final product price.

Consumer prices for the year rose nearly 9%,
heavily pushed by a 22% increase in food prices.
Wholesale prices rose 17% during the year, regis-
tering the sharpest advance since 1947. And while
prices of industrial commodities were going up
13%, prices of farm products and processed foods
were advancing 27%. The occasional dips in some
prices during the year proved to be illusory and
unsustained.

Production. Industrial production made solid
gains, particularly in the first three quarters of the
year. As measured by the Federal Reserve Board's
Index of Industrial Production (1967 = 100), output rose from 115.2 for all of 1972 to 125.2 for
the first 10 months of 1973. This gain compares
with a rise of 8.4 for 1972 and only 0.2 for 1971.
Contributing to the overall showing was the continued strong steel production pace, with 1973
heading for record levels. Production in the first
10 months of the year was running at a rate substantially ahead of the 1969 record of 140 million
tons. Automobile output, too, probed new record
levels as domestic production measured by cars and
trucks assembled passed the 9.7 million mark for the
year, up about 10% from 1972.

But the dampener came in the fourth quarter
when the Arab oil embargo dramatized fuel shortages, and auto makers were faced with product
redesign to accommodate a limited supply of more
expensive gasoline for years to come. The immediate question was what this would do to 1974 levels
of production, not only of cars but also of energy-
propelled business in general.

Sales and Profits. The outlook for business
generally was strong in the first three quarters of
the year as sales and profits bounded ahead. Total
sales for all business averaged $18 billion a month
higher in the first three quarters over the monthly
average for all of 1972, which in turn had shown
a monthly average increase of $12 billion over 1971.
Inventories were being drawn down compared with
preceding years until near the end of the year.
Profits, too, were heading for record high levels.
At a seasonally adjusted annual rate corporate
profits before taxes were averaging $129 billion
for the first three quarters of the year, up sharply
from $98 billion for 1972 and $85 billion for
1971.

Adding to and reflecting the highly favorable
business climate that prevailed during most of 1973
was spending for new plant and equipment. The
total for the year rose to about $100 billion, up
13% from 1972, which had gained 8.2% over 1971.
It was noted that not all such expenditures in 1973
added to productive capacity, since pollution-control
outlays increased in significance during the year.
But general business optimism continued on through
the end of the year, as it was announced that business expected to add another 12% to outlays for
new plant and equipment in 1974.

Farm income rose sharply during 1973, reflecting
in part worldwide shortages in food supply and in
part price adjustments within the American economy. Net farm income was running as high as a
quarter above the preceding year through the first
three quarters of the year. And one of the net beneficiaries in the total U.S. economic picture was the
nation's balance of payments. While the U.S.
showed a net import balance of $4.6 billion for
all of 1972, the 1973 results for the first three
quarters showed an average net export balance of
$3 billion on goods and services. Contributing to
this markedly better showing was dollar devaluation,
which had improved the position of U.S. goods in
foreign markets.

Spending. Government spending added margin-
ally to GNP during the year, chiefly through the
purchases of goods and services by state and local
governments. Federal spending was held nearer
1972 levels through the first half of the year. The
increased pace of business activity helped generate
additional tax receipts to keep down but not eliminate the federal deficit effect on price rises. While
federal defense spending levels have been relatively
stable over the last few years, indications near the
end of 1973 were that increases might be in the
offing for 1974. State and local spending continued
on an upward course, reflecting the continued rise
in demand for local services as well as general
price increases.

Consumer spending rose sharply in 1973, as consumers confronted with a host of stimuli spent
more, generally got less, and tried to keep up with
advancing prices. Shortages developed in the supply of some items, and there were instances of
buyer resistance to higher prices. Personal con-

sumption expenditures were advancing 11% over most of the year, as compared with an 8.5% increase a year earlier. And even accounting for a drop of 1.3% in retail sales in December, consumers at the retail level ran up a volume of $504 billion for the year, up 12% from 1972. Durable goods sales, particularly automobiles, accounted for the drop in consumer spending at the end of the year. Consumer's spirits were further dampened by layoffs in the automobile, airline, and other industries.

Personal Income and the Labor Force. Contributing to the generally optimistic outlook of consumers during most of the year was the rise in personal income. The gain in personal income was running ahead of 1972 by 10% over the first three quarters. At the same time the average work week was rising, and average hourly earnings for production workers in private nonagricultural employment was rising from $3.74 to $3.99. The labor force expanded by some 2.5 million workers, and the unemployment rate dropped from 5.0% at the beginning of the year to 4.5% by October, although it was returning to the 4.8% level by the end of the year.

Savings and Credit. In their efforts to expand purchasing power, however, consumers were not relying on increased earnings alone. Savings rates were declining from the highs of 8.1% of disposable personal income registered in 1970 and 1971 to 6.2% in 1972 to 5.7% by the third quarter of 1973. At the same time installment credit continued to expand, and by the end of the third quarter consumer credit outstanding was up 10% from the beginning of the year. This rise compared with a 14% rise for all of 1972 over 1971. Consumers were also stimulated by more generous tax refunds due to overwithholding in the preceding year, as well as increases in social security checks which had come toward the end of 1972.

Outlook. Aside from the persistent and rising rate of inflation, there were other danger signs. Stock prices, which have a certain forecasting value, began to weaken early and this trend continued through the year, after a pickup in the fall. At the same time bond yields were increasing, and interest rates climbed to records as demands for funds increased. The prime rate, that rate charged to the most credit worthy corporations, rose to 10% in September, was cutback to 9½% in October, and rose back to 10% in December. A major victim of

higher interest rates was housing, where a severe decline set in, partly due to higher financing costs, partly to overbuilding in some areas. From a record high of over 2.4 million private housing starts early in the year, the total had declined to 1.6 million by October, and the outlook was generally gloomy for the industry in the period just ahead.

As a whole the year 1973 showed signs of considerable vigor in the industrial sector and in the outlook for business generally. Rising levels of production, expanding outlays for new plant, increasing employment, and high levels of profit all pointed up the general level of prosperity. However, the continuation of inflation at an even higher rate during the year indicated that corrective measures being taken were not adequate and that additional steps would have to be taken. The decline in housing construction levels and, at year end, the impact of the energy crisis were indications that 1974 would not be as favorable economically as was 1973.

The slowdown in housing was expected to continue, and there was widespread speculation as to the effects of increased energy costs on the economy. Surveys taken on consumer groups late in 1973 indicated considerable pessimism, and one initial impact was a sharp cutback in consumer purchases of durable goods, particularly automobiles. Whether the effect would be one which would reverberate through the economy, extending from cuts in consumer purchases to layoffs to cutbacks in production to further unemployment, remained to be seen.

More technically, whether a recession was a proper forecast—that is, whether there would be two consecutive quarters of the year in which real gross national product showed a decline—was being debated among economists as 1973 ended. Certainly, the year closed on a lower note than had prevailed over most of it, as far as productive performance was concerned. But whether the impact of the energy crisis on the continuing and accelerating rate of inflation would be such as to push the economy into deeper trouble was still a matter of uncertainty.

(See also INTERNATIONAL FINANCE; INTERNATIONAL TRADE; LABOR; STOCKS AND BONDS; UNITED STATES. For economic developments in other nations, see articles on the individual countries.)

JACKSON PHILLIPS
Vice President, Moody's Investors Service

AUTO PRODUCTION, a key economic indicator, was being curtailed because of a gasoline shortage as 1973 ended. A New Jersey assembly plant (left) is closed temporarily.

ECUADOR

The military government of Gen. Guillermo Rodríguez Lara remained in power throughout 1973. This regime had supplanted Ecuador's last civilian government, headed by Dr. José María Velasco Ibarra, which was overthrown on Feb. 16, 1972. Official spokesmen rejected the possibility of elections or of yielding power to civilians until substantial progress had been achieved toward realizing the military's goals for the country. These goals called for major economic and social changes and administrative reform in Ecuador. Much of the program was incorporated in a comprehensive five-year plan launched in 1973.

Political Affairs. Civilian political parties were not suppressed after the 1972 coup but were sharply discouraged. A Democratic Restoration Front, composed of left to center parties, called for elections within a year, but the Communist party declared its support for the military government. A fairly severe military attitude, plus new affluence from oil revenues, cooled much partisan criticism. A rising number of strikes and student disorders occurred as the year progressed, however.

At the administrative and policy-making level, political division reflected the factionalism within the armed forces. A "Brazilian," or generally conservative and repressive faction, was opposed by a "Peruvian" or leftist-to-progressive faction. President Rodríguez sought to maintain a middle, or moderate, position. There were many changes in the military hierarchy and in cabinet posts during 1973, and civilian "specialists" appeared to be returning to power gradually during the year. As a rule, policy disputes appeared to be fueled less by clashes of personality than by ideological differences and specific economic problems, a distinct contrast to the civilian politics of the recent past.

Land Distribution Proposal. One of the major issues was an as yet undefined land distribution program that was to involve the allocation of about 240,000 acres (100,000 hectares) of land to some 20,000 families. Undecided was the question of whether this acreage would come from expropriated private land (much of it owned by Guayaquil's entrepreneurial and traditional landed group) or from virgin lands in undeveloped eastern Ecuador.

The question had wide-ranging social and economic implications. The country needs much capital to develop its economic plan, but a radical policy would preclude the development of mixed public and private Ecuadorian capital sources and would jeopardize chances of attracting foreign funds.

Petroleum and the Five-Year Plan. Ecuador's five-year blueprint, called the Integral Plan for Transformation and Development, is controlled by the National Planning Committee. The plan, which was outlined in 1972, contemplates the use of mixed capital sources, both national and foreign, and involves the development of both "socialist" and "capitalist" techniques for management of the capital market, foreign trade, and investment in selected industrial and social sectors. It calls for rigorous and "moralizing" (socially justifiable) use of petroleum revenues, which are beginning to add immeasurably to the country's economic potential. The Ecuadorian State Petroleum Corporation (CEPE) had renegotiated all contracts with foreign oil companies, altering the terms substantially in Ecuador's favor, and only a few companies chose to withdraw as a result.

In the past, Ecuador enjoyed modest rewards from exploitation of its coastal petroleum and gas deposits. On Aug. 15, 1972, the nation began to export oil from much more productive fields east of the Andes. By the end of 1973, a pipeline and other facilities built by a Texaco-Gulf consortium were operating nearly to their 250,000-barrel daily capacity. Expansion to a capacity of 400,000 barrels was being projected by the consortium.

The Integral Plan earmarks much oil revenue for specific uses. Nearly half is to go for electrification in a program designed to triple the nation's woefully inadequate installed generating capacity. Agricultural diversification was also to be subsidized, and nearly $40 million was to be spent annually on irrigation works, a 50-fold increase over the average of the 1950's and 1960's.

The plan is to be integrated with decisions by the Andean Group Commission (the planning body of the 6-member common market), which has assigned to Ecuador quasi-monopoly roles in petrochemicals and in several metal-working and toolmaking lines.

International Affairs. Ecuador's leftward movement under military control brought about the development of trade and investment relations with several Soviet bloc countries, and even mild approbation from Cuban dictator Fidel Castro.

In an ongoing dispute over the extent of territorial waters, the seizure of U.S.-owned tuna fishing boats continued at a reduced rate in 1973. The U.S. Congress urged that American naval vessels loaned to Ecuador's navy be taken back.

The Israeli-Arab war in October improved the already favorable Ecuadorian position as a new major oil producer. During 1973, the base price of Ecuadorian oil to all importing countries was raised from $2.50 to over $5.00 per barrel, and the nation's petroleum was being sought eagerly by many countries, including Brazil, Peru, Colombia, Mexico, and the United States.

PHILIP B. TAYLOR, JR.
University of Houston

ECUADOR • Information Highlights ————

Official Name: Republic of Ecuador.
Location: Northwest South America.
Area: 109,483 square miles (283,561 sq km).
Population (1973 est.): 6,700,000. Density, 57 per square mile (22 per sq km).
Chief Cities (1970 est.): Quito, the capital, 528,100; Guayaquil, 794,300.
Government: *Head of state*, Gen. Guillermo Rodríguez Lara, president (took office Feb. 1972). *Head of government*, Gen. Guillermo Rodríguez Lara. *Legislature*—Congress (suspended June 1970).
Language: Spanish (official).
Education: *Expenditure* (1969), 25% of total public expenditure. *School enrollment* (1969)—primary, 975,480; secondary, 194,682; technical/vocational, 55,659; university/higher, 31,921.
Monetary Unit: Sucre (25.25 sucres equal U.S.$1, Aug. 1973).
Gross National Product (1972 est.): $1,695,000,000.
Economic Indexes: *Industrial production* (manufacturing, 1971), 241 (1963=100); *agricultural production* (1971), 124 (1963=100); *consumer price index* (1972), 147 (1965=100).
Manufacturing (major products): Processed foods, textiles, petroleum products.
Major Agricultural Products: Bananas, coffee, cacao, potatoes, rice, sugarcane, cotton, fish, forest products.
Major Minerals: Petroleum, gold, silver.
Foreign Trade (1972): *Exports*, $322,000,000; *Imports*, $327,000,000. *Chief trading partners* (1970)—United States (took 39% of exports, supplied 33% of imports); Japan (17%—12.4%); West Germany (10%—12.6%).
Transportation: *Motor Vehicles* (1970), 63,400 (automobiles, 27,000); *railroads* (1971), 661 miles (1,064 km); *major national airline*, Compañia Ecuatoriana de Aviación.
Communications: *Telephones* (1971), 150,000; *newspapers* (1970), 25 (daily circulation, 250,000).

THE NEW YORK TIMES

Campus in a bubble: This plastic air dome in Columbia, Md., will house a branch of Ohio's Antioch College. It is an experiment in inexpensive and deliberately impermanent construction that may prove to be a highly flexible means of providing educational shelter.

THE NEW YORK TIMES

education

The U. S. Supreme Court rendered decisions in 1973 on several issues of paramount importance to both public and private education. In their impact on the operation and support of educational institutions, these rulings rival in significance the racial segregation decision of 1954.

The cost of education continued to rise (see the special report on college costs, page 221). Enrollments tended to taper off except at the preprimary level, where gains of almost one third were recorded. Issues in the news in 1973 included the status of women in higher education, the year-round school plan, and busing to achieve racial balance.

COURT DECISIONS

In one long-awaited ruling, the U. S. Supreme Court upheld the constitutionality of systems of school finance based partly on property taxes. In another, the court voided various forms of state aid to nonpublic schools. Other Supreme Court decisions dealt with specific instances of racial segregation or discrimination.

Property Tax Financing. In a landmark 5-to-4 decision involving a challenge to the constitutionality of the Texas school finance system, the Supreme Court ruled on March 21 that there is no constitutional right to education and thus no constitutional remedy for disparities between rich and poor school districts. The decision left intact the local property tax system on which most states depend heavily for financing their schools.

Previously, a lower court in Texas had ruled that the local property tax system used to finance schools in that state violated constitutional guarantees of equal protection because it made the quality of education dependent on the wealth of the local school district rather than of the state as a whole. For example, in the San Antonio system, where the suit arose, property values in the school districts ranged from $5,429 per student in a low-income district to $45,095 in a wealthy suburban district.

Educators expressed relief at the court's refusal to overturn the school finance laws of Texas. It had been predicted that the financing of public schools in every state except Hawaii would be thrown into chaos if use of local property taxes were declared unconstitutional. The attorneys general of 30 states had joined in telling the high court that "a genera-

tion of litigation" would be spawned if the lower court ruling were upheld, since financing not only of schools but of other vital government services, such as police protection, could be affected.

Justice Lewis F. Powell, Jr., who wrote the majority opinion, stated that the need for tax reform is apparent but that "the ultimate solution must come from lawmakers and from the democratic pressures of those who elect them." Justice Thurgood Marshall, in dissent, described the decision as "a retreat from our historic commitment to equality of educational opportunity."

School Consolidation Decision. In a 4-to-4 decision on May 21, the U. S. Supreme Court blocked consolidation of the 70% black city school system of Richmond, Va., with the 90% white school systems of adjacent Henrico and Chesterfield counties. The tie vote—with Justice Lewis F. Powell, Jr., formerly of Richmond, abstaining—had the effect of upholding the judgment of the Fourth U. S. Circuit Court of Appeals, which in June 1972 had ruled against the city-sought merger.

The appellate court had held that the constitutional rights of black residents of Richmond were not being violated by requiring them to attend an increasingly black school system. It also expressed the judicial view that the decision of the district court judge who had ordered the three-way consolidation was an attempt to restructure local government.

Leaders of the Legal and Educational Fund, Inc., of the National Association for the Advancement of Colored People, joined with their old foes on the Richmond school board in the effort to win high court approval of the consolidation plan. In turning down the merger—which was opposed by the two counties, the state of Virginia, and the Nixon administration—the high court gave no opinion on whether the Constitution requires black cities and white suburbs to trade pupils to desegregate the schools of both.

The decision attracted wide attention because similar consolidation plans have been sought in Detroit, Hartford, Boston, and other cities with predominantly white suburban school systems in adjacent counties. Opponents of massive busing to achieve racial balance were jubilant, as were advocates of the neighborhood school concept. City school officials saw the ruling as accelerating the white flight to the neighboring counties. But winners and losers alike agreed that the quality of education in predominantly black city school systems is of major importance. In November the U. S. Supreme Court agreed to hear the case involving Detroit.

Private School Aid. On June 25 the U. S. Supreme Court ruled that tuition reimbursement and tax deductions for parents of children attending parochial and other nonpublic schools are unconstitutional as violations of the ban on state aid to religious institutions. By a vote of 6 to 3, the court invalidated a Pennsylvania plan that would have reimbursed parents by as much as $75 for each child in a nonpublic elementary school and $150 in a nonpublic secondary school. By the same margin the court disapproved a New York plan for providing tax deductions for parents of children attending parochial or other nonpublic schools. As a result of these decisions the Nixon administration's support of legislation to provide federal income tax credit probably will be abandoned.

The Committee for Public Education and Religious Liberty, which had challenged the New York laws, hailed the decision as "a major victory for religious freedom and church-state separation . . . ." Spokesmen for Roman Catholic groups, which are hard-pressed to support parochial schools, condemned the decision and warned that public schools would face serious difficulties if forced to absorb private school pupils. In New York alone, about 750,000 students, or 20% of the state's elementary and secondary enrollment, attend nonpublic schools.

Segregation in the North. School systems in other parts of the nation must take the same sweeping steps to overcome racial segregation as the Southern states, according to a 7-to-1 ruling of the U. S. Supreme Court on June 21. Systemwide desegregation will be required in instances where "plaintiffs prove that school authorities have carried out a systematic program of segregation affecting a substantial portion of the students, schools, teachers, and facilities within the school system." The ruling, which grew out of a case involving the schools of Denver, Colo., was the first school segregation case of its kind from outside the South on which the high court has ruled.

Segregation in Private Schools. In a decision of far-reaching importance, U. S. District Judge Albert V. Bryan, Jr., ruled on July 29 that private schools cannot practice racial discrimination. In a suit involving the admission of black pupils to two Virginia private schools, Judge Bryan noted that neither of the schools had ever admitted a black pupil and that race seemed to be the basis for selection. Damages were awarded to the two protesting families. An attorney for the Southern Independent Schools Association, with a membership of 395 private schools enrolling 180,000 pupils in seven Southern states, declared that the ruling would be appealed to the U. S. Supreme Court if necessary. Most affected by the decision are the segregated white academies of the Deep South. Some 1,000 of these small private schools have sprung up in the last decade, supported largely by white parents who do not wish to send their children to integrated public schools.

BACK-TO-SCHOOL FIGURES

Estimates from the U. S. Office of Education indicate a total enrollment of 59.3 million students in U. S. schools and colleges in the fall of 1973. Education is the chief occupation of 30% of the population.

Educational costs have continued to rise. Expenditures for educational institutions of all levels are estimated at $96.7 billion in the school year 1973–74, compared with $89.4 billion the previous year. Again, the total expenditure approaches 8% of the gross national product, according to the U. S. Office of Education.

Elementary and Secondary Enrollments. Enrollment in elementary schools continued to decline, dropping from 35,744,000 in the fall of 1972 to 35,100,000 in 1973—a decrease of 1.7%, the same percentage drop as occurred the previous year. The declining birthrate is now affecting the number of children in the age group 5 to 13 years.

High school enrollment continued to rise slightly, from an estimated 15,319,000 in 1972 to 15,510,-000 in 1973. The number of graduates in 1974 is expected to exceed the 1973 figure of 3,100,000—the largest graduating class up to that time.

Preprimary Figures. During the period 1964–72, the number of children in the 3-to-5 age group decreased from 12,496,000 to 10,166,000. Yet the enrollment in preprimary education programs in the United States increased by almost one third—to a new high of 4,231,000 in 1972. The percentage of the age group enrolled in all such programs increased from 25.5% to 41.6%, according to the U. S. Office of Education. Particularly striking was the increase in prekindergarten enrollment, which rose from 471,000 in 1964 to 1,277,000 in 1972. Kindergarten enrollment increased during the same period from 2,716,000 to 2,954,000.

Costs. Expenditures for elementary and secondary schools in 1973–74 are expected to total $61.5 billion ($55.9 billion for public and $5.6 billion for nonpublic schools). For higher education, the estimate is $35.2 billion ($23.8 billion for public and $11.4 billion for private institutions).

State legislatures and the federal government are called on to play a larger role in financing education. Although local sources still account for more than 50% of school revenues, federal and state contributions have increased to more than 7% and 40%, respectively. In the past 10 years, federal revenues have risen by more than $2 billion, state revenues by $11 billion, and local revenues by $13 billion. More than two fifths of state and local government spending is for education.

Taxpayers have expressed their dissatisfaction with costs and other aspects of the education program by voting against school bond issues. During the fiscal year 1972, fewer than half of the school bond issues presented to the nation's voters were approved, according to the U. S. Office of Education. In San Diego, Calif., for example, every bond issue in the past six years has been turned down. Many other large cities—among them Los Angeles and Detroit—lack resources to meet changing demands on education because of taxpayers' refusal to vote bond issues.

President Nixon has proposed abolishing practically all present programs for federal aid to elementary and secondary education and replacing them with educational revenue-sharing. Federal funds for education would be channeled to state and local governments with only broad guidelines on how the money can be spent. Local school officials have opposed the plan because they fear a reduction in funds from the federal government.

HIGHER EDUCATION

College enrollments, which nearly tripled in the 20-year period 1952–72, are approaching a plateau, according to a survey of enrollment trends by *U. S. News and World Report*. The fall 1973 enrollment was up only about 2% from the preceding year. Some observers cite the fact that the annual growth in the number of 18-year-olds is beginning to slow down. Other factors influencing enrollment trends are the end of the military draft, which eliminated one reason for attending college, and changes in the attitudes of young people.

Changing Attitudes. Many young people are disenchanted with the values of a college education and are reluctant to incur large debts for their schooling. They have found that a degree is no guarantee of a job and that there are other ways of getting an education. Uncertainties about the cost and value of a college education are causing many young people to delay college entrance to work for

a while, travel, or just think things over. Many are seeking "a more vocationally meaningful college experience" and are shifting from liberal arts programs to vocational preparation.

Shifts in Enrollment. Changing attitudes have had a marked effect on enrollments in most of the liberal arts colleges, especially the small private institutions. The great shift has been to the public colleges and universities, which accounted for 74% of the total college enrollment in 1972, compared with only 52% in 1952. In this 20-year period the gain in student enrollment in public institutions was 5,019,000, or 456%; in private institutions the gain was 1,067,000, or 103%. Public two-year community colleges are continuing to attract thousands of new students with an expanding curriculum of career courses. These colleges, convenient and inexpensive, showed a 5.3% increase in enrollment in 1972–73 over the preceding year.

Young people entering college today have a wide range of choice among the small and medium-sized private colleges. But the prestigious private institutions—such as those in the Ivy League—are full to overflowing. The same situation exists at the popular and less expensive state universities, which have more applications than they can accommodate.

Law and medical schools also are overflowing. An estimated 40,000 young people are seeking admission to medical schools, with about 13,900 places available. Openings available in law schools total 37,000, and some 120,000 students have taken the law school admission test of the Educational Testing Service.

Colleges have resorted to active recruiting programs to attract more students. Admissions officers are visiting high schools over a wide area. For 25 years the students have been the active seekers of college admission. Now the institutions, especially the small private colleges, are seeking the students.

Effects of the New Age of Majority. The 26th Amendment to the U. S. Constitution, giving 18-year-olds the right to vote, has resulted in a lowering of the age of majority to 18 in most states. It has resulted in the virtual disappearance of the *in loco parentis* policy, under which colleges served as substitutes for parents.

Higher institutions already were treating students as adults before the amendment was passed. Some administrators predict that colleges eventually will deal almost exclusively with students. The tradition of mailing grades and disciplinary reports to parents appears doomed. Students can sue and be sued. Financial aid programs, usually based on a standardized form known as the Parents' Confidential Statement, may be challenged on the grounds that only the student's own financial status applies.

A ruling of the U. S. Supreme Court on June 11 upheld the right of state universities to charge higher fees for out-of-state students. The lowering of the age of majority may make it easier for students to establish legal residence and qualify as state students. If such a trend develops, it would affect the financial operation of public institutions accustomed to rely on added income from tuition charges for out-of-state students.

Colleges for Women. The trend toward coeducation, which only a few years ago seemed to presage the end of women's colleges as single-sex institutions, is being challenged. Barbara W. Newell,

(Continued on page 222)

COLLEGE COSTS:

UP, UP, UP

The cost of attending college has risen every year for the past decade. In the last four years alone, basic costs have risen 30% at private colleges and 25% at public colleges, according to the U. S. Office of Education. In 1973–74 the average charge for tuition alone was between $150 and $200 more than in the previous academic year.

Current Costs, Private and Public. The U. S. Office of Education estimated that at private institutions the average basic charge—for tuition, board, and room but nothing else—was $3,281 for the year 1973–74, an increase of 7% over the previous session. Books, clothing, transportation, and incidentals required at least $500 more. Since 1963–64, when the average basic cost was only $1,815, attendance costs have increased at least 80%. The largest increases have occurred in the well-known private colleges on the East Coast. Harvard told its students to expect a total cost of about $5,400 for attendance in 1973–74. Princeton and Yale suggested $5,380 and $5,050, respectively.

Costs at public institutions also have risen, but in a slightly less dramatic fashion. Basic charges averaged $926 in 1963–64, according to the U. S. Office of Education. In 1973–74 the average cost was $1,492—an increase of 60% during the decade and of 6% over the 1972–73 session. Additional fees—billed separately from charges for tuition, room, and board—tended to bring the total cost in public colleges to about $2,000. These figures are for state residents. Most state institutions charge higher tuition for out-of-state students.

Cost-Cutting. College administrators are concerned over the effect of increased costs on student enrollment, especially in the smaller liberal arts colleges, many of which are already facing deficits. Although economies in operation are difficult to achieve in an era of generally rising costs, institutions are seeking to cut expenses by various means. These include increases in class size, fewer replacements of faculty members who retire or resign, a growing reluctance to grant tenure, and curtailment of many nonacademic activities.

Plight of the Middle-Income Family. As costs increase, middle-income families are finding it increasingly difficult to finance college education for their children. A study by the New York *Times* indicated that four of the five major financial-aid programs administered by the U. S. Office of Education tend to exclude students from families with incomes above the $12,000–$15,000 range. Even the Guaranteed Student Loan Program, the chief source of federal assistance for middle-income students, concentrates increasingly on the neediest, although all income groups are eligible according to the law. Inadequate funding of authorized federal programs adds further to the problem.

Cost Gaps and National Controversy. Some educators maintain that increases in college costs are not out of line with the rise in average income of the U. S. family during the past decade. But there is a widening gap between costs at private and public institutions, and many of the private colleges are losing students to the less expensive state-supported community and four-year colleges.

In a study, *The Management and Financing of Colleges,* released in September, the nonprofit Committee for Economic Development recommended that public colleges increase their undergraduate tuition charges to 50% of the cost of instruction per student. Such charges now cover less than 25%, with the rest coming from state subsidies. Charges at private colleges cover more than 60%, according to the study. The committee also recommended that the doubling of tuition be accompanied by large increases in direct aid to students, based on need—with the recipients free to choose between public and private colleges. Earlier, the Carnegie Commission on Higher Education, the College Entrance Examination Board, and others had made similar proposals.

These recommendations added to the existing national controversy over social versus individual benefits of higher education and the question of who should bear the major share of the cost—the public or the individual. Also involved are the issue of public aid to private institutions, the competition between public and private colleges, and the probability of further pressure on middle-income students, who would pay a larger share of the costs but might be ineligible for aid based on need.

Aid to Planning. The prospect seems to be that college costs will continue to rise. The College Scholarship Service of the College Entrance Examination Board, which compiles and distributes to institutions detailed reports on the financial needs of students, has developed a formula to enable families to project the probable cost of four years at college. It suggests that the charges for 1973–74 be multiplied by 4.18 to reach a total four-year figure for resident students in private colleges, and 4.29 for commuter students. The factors for public four-year colleges are 4.25 for resident students and 4.30 for commuting students.

EDWARD ALVEY, JR.

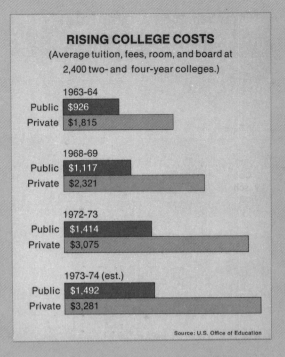

RISING COLLEGE COSTS
(Average tuition, fees, room, and board at 2,400 two- and four-year colleges.)

1963-64
Public $926
Private $1,815

1968-69
Public $1,117
Private $2,321

1972-73
Public $1,414
Private $3,075

1973-74 (est.)
Public $1,492
Private $3,281

Source: U.S. Office of Education

CLOSED-CIRCUIT TELEVISION is part of the security system of one New York City junior high school. Here, a faculty member talks to a tardy student.

president of Wellesley College, charged that coeducation has "increased, rather than lessened, male domination of American higher education." In 1973 she launched a $70 million centennial development program with a pledge to "affirm the need for equal education for women."

All the prestigious "Seven Sisters" women's colleges have flirted with coeducation to various degrees. Of these colleges, only Vassar is fully coeducational, although Radcliffe is a part of Harvard except in name. Barnard has cross-registration with Columbia University. Mount Holyoke and Smith have male exchange students living on campus for limited periods, and Wellesley and Bryn Mawr have male nonresident exchange students from nearby schools. But none of the last four grant degrees to men.

In the 12-year period 1960–72, the number of colleges exclusively for women declined from 298 to 146. Most of those remaining are small Catholic schools. Currently, fewer than 2% of women students attend women's colleges, although 40% of all college students are women. Despite charges that coeducation is male-dominated—even in the former women's colleges—the trend to coeducation continues. Arrangements for the temporary exchange of students between men's colleges and women's colleges have become popular. In time, it is possible that the legality of single-sex institutions will be challenged on an equal-rights basis.

Women in Higher Education. Men received preferential treatment at all levels of higher education, according to a Carnegie Commission on Higher Education report, *Opportunities for Women in Higher Education,* released in September 1973. Women faculty members earn approximately $2,000 less annually than their male counterparts. Although the majority of the country's high school graduates are women, the percentage of female participation in higher education declines steadily as the level of professional training increases. The report calls for the removal of "all improper barriers to the advancement of women in higher education." It recommends better counseling at the high school level, a more equitable admissions policy for women at coeducational institutions, and a larger percentage of female employees in administrative and instructional positions. Clark Kerr, chairman of the commission, estimated that it would take a quarter of a century—"a generation of effort"—to rectify the present inequalities.

According to a U.S. Office of Education survey, released in April, women comprised 22.5% of the nation's 254,930 full-time college and university faculty members in 1972–73. Male faculty members earned an average salary of $14,352 annually, while females received $11,865. The salary gap is widest at the university level, where men received an average annual salary of $15,829, compared with $12,325 for women. It is smallest at two-year colleges, where the figures are $12,889 for men and $11,862 for women.

This survey revealed that of the 57,297 female faculty members, only 9.7% have achieved the rank of full professor, compared with 25.5% of the males. Only 17.1% of the women are associate professors, 36.4% are assistant professors, and 36.8% are instructors. The proportion of women faculty members in universities has changed little in the last 10 years, rising from 19% to 20.6%.

OTHER DEVELOPMENTS

Busing to improve racial balance in schools—a hotly debated issue in U.S. education in 1972—remained controversial in 1973, although new provisions for busing were inaugurated without violence as schools opened in the fall. Teachers' strikes delayed the opening of schools in at least 10 states, with the most serious in Michigan. Among newer ideas in education, the year-round school plan found favor in a growing number of schools.

Busing. Although the majority of Americans favor integration, only a small proportion favor busing as a means of achieving this goal, according to a midyear Gallup Poll. Yet large-scale busing prevails in various areas. In Alexandria, Va., where some elementary schools had been 97% white and others 96% black, about 43% of the elementary pupils were being bused to achieve racial balance in 14 elementary schools. In Memphis, Tenn., some 27,000 children were being transported to achieve a better balance in 139 schools. But enrollment is down in the public school system, which is now 68% black. Many of the white pupils have shifted to the city's 85 private schools.

Teachers' Strikes. Officials of both the National Education Association (NEA) and the American Federation of Teachers, AFL-CIO, said that the strike situation nationally in 1973 was not alarming. An NEA spokesman declared that teachers were seeking smaller classes and more control of the teaching environment, as well as increased monetary return for their work.

On September 4, the 10,500 teachers in Detroit, with the nation's fifth-largest school system, struck over salary and class size. Detroit's 330 public schools remained closed for six weeks until a new one-year agreement was reached on October 15. The board of education and the Detroit Federation of Teachers also agreed to drop all claims for damages against each other. Schools opened on October 17.

One of the nation's longest school strikes occurred in Philadelphia early in 1973. The walkout actually began in September 1972, when teachers in the 280,000-pupil system struck for three weeks over pay, length of work day, and proposed assign-

ment changes. The strike was resumed on Jan. 8, 1973, and continued for more than seven weeks. Top leaders of the Philadelphia Federation of Teachers—which represents 11,000 of the 13,000 city teachers and 5,000 auxiliary personnel—were jailed, and 790 teachers were arrested for blocking entrances to schools. Finally, a tentative agreement on a new four-year contract was reached on February 27, forestalling a general strike set for midnight of that day by more than 40 local unions supporting the teachers. Total cost of the new contract was estimated at $68.6 million.

Year-Round School Plan. A growing number of schools are following a year-round schedule, according to a survey by the New Jersey Department of Education. More than 300,000 students in 31 states are studying in some form of extended school year. Most of the new programs operate on a staggered attendance plan, known as the "45-15" system, under which three fourths of the students are in school nearly all year, with 45 class days (9 weeks) in school, followed by 15 class days (3 weeks) of vacation. The new plan provides more efficient use of school buildings and equipment. Savings from capital school construction costs in fast-growing communities have been another factor.

In Prince William county, Va., where the plan has been used on the elementary- and middle-school levels since 1971, the 12-month operation has already resulted in substantial savings. School officials in that fast-growing county estimate that some $40 million in school construction costs might be saved in the next eight years if the plan were used on a large scale. The Virginia legislature has appropriated $1 million to support trial year-round programs in six selected school systems.

The plan is regarded as a means of improving the quality of education. The long summer vacation—a time of forgetting for many students—is eliminated, and the amount of reteaching is reduced. Both teachers and pupils find the shorter nine-week courses of study more conducive to learning. Although there has been some initial opposition from parents, most of them eventually become enthusiastic about the plan. The children seem to make more steady progress, and their attitudes toward school are improved.

Teachers have mixed feelings about the year-round plan. Where it is in effect, they usually have the option of a 9-month or 11½-month teaching contract. Most men teachers select the longer period and increase their salaries by one third.

EDWARD ALVEY, JR.
Mary Washington College

EGYPT

The year 1973 was the year of total confrontation that President Anwar el-Sadat had long promised the Egyptian people. Maintaining himself in power domestically, despite student demonstrations and political dissidence, Sadat mobilized the support of much of the Arab world to shore up his attack on Israel in October. The conflict ended with definite political gains for the Egyptians and, for the first time, the prospects of real concessions on the part of the Israelis. In November a visit to Cairo by U. S. Secretary of State Henry Kissinger produced the resumption of diplomatic relations with the United States. At the same time, union with Libya seemed a dead issue.

Domestic Affairs. The year opened in Cairo with major student demonstrations and riots. The government closed the universities (to be opened a month later) and blamed the disturbances on what it termed "leftists." Perhaps in a related move, the government began in early February to purge the Arab Socialist Union, the sole political party. The purge tended to center on the media; at least 64 journalists and intellectuals were removed from party and jobs.

In March, Aziz Sidky resigned as premier. Sadat named himself premier and military governor-general, while retaining the office of president. In effect he added to his emergency powers, which were already substantial. He continued to insist that Egypt should be on a war footing and that domestic affairs would have to take lower priority because of the necessity of war with Israel. In February, consistent with this ordering of priorities, Sadat announced the scrapping of a number of long-range developmental projects in favor of a "war budget" that would free funds for the struggle with Israel.

By April, President Sadat's program of "total confrontation" was in full swing, with "battle committees" and "control centers" a part of the new attempt to mobilize popular support. In September a confident Sadat pardoned about 200 students and journalists and also vacated the purge order of the media that had been announced in the spring.

During the year Egypt continued to explore the possibilities of a $400 million pipeline connecting the Mediterranean with the Gulf of Suez. In October an American firm, the Bechtel Corporation, agreed to build this pipeline. Earlier, in May, Exxon and Mobil signed agreements to explore for oil in Egypt.

President Sadat was firmly in control throughout the year, and Egypt's apparent gains in the fourth war with Israel seemed to assure his popularity.

War with Israel. The war with Israel—the fourth since 1948—broke out in October. It was merely

---
EGYPT • Information Highlights

Official Name: Arab Republic of Egypt.
Location: Northeastern Africa.
Area: 386,660 square miles (1,001,449 sq km).
Population (1973 est.): 36,900,000. *Density,* 88 per square mile (34 per sq km).
Chief Cities (1970 est.): Cairo, the capital, 4,961,000; Alexandria, 2,032,000; Giza, 712,000; Port Said, 313,000.
Government: *Head of state,* Anwar el-Sadat, president (took office Oct. 1970). *Head of government,* Anwar el-Sadat, premier (took office March 1973). *Legislature* (unicameral) —People's Assembly. *Political party*—Arab Socialist Union.
Languages: Arabic (official), English, French.
Education: *Expenditure* (1969), 21% of total public expenditure. *School enrollment* (1969)—primary, 3,618,750; secondary, 1,357,972; technical/vocational, 245,862; university/higher, 197,055.
Monetary Unit: Pound (0.3906 pound equals U. S.$1, Sept. 1973).
Gross National Product (1972 est.): $7,250,000,000.
Economic Indexes: *Industrial production* (1969), 136 (1963= 100); *agricultural production* (1971), 125 (1963=100); *consumer price index* (1972), 117 (1967=100).
Manufacturing (major products): Cotton textiles, processed foods, fertilizer, iron and steel, petroleum products, chemicals, clothing, cement.
Major Agricultural Products: Cotton, forage plants (berseem), rice, wheat, millet, corn, sugarcane, fish.
Major Minerals: Petroleum, phosphate, iron ore, natural gas, gypsum.
Foreign Trade (1972): *Exports,* $825,000,000; *Imports,* $899,-000,000. *Chief trading partner* (1971)—USSR (took 40% of exports, supplied 13.5% of imports).
Tourism: Receipts (1971), $85,000,000.
Transportation: *Motor vehicles* (1971), 176,200 (automobiles, 141,500); *railroads* (1971), 3,036 miles (4,885 km); *merchant fleet* (1972), 243,000 gross registered tons; *major national airline,* Egyptair.
Communications: *Telephones* (1968), 365,000; *newspapers* (1969), 14 (daily circulation, 712,000).

the culmination of months of complicated maneuvers on the part of Egyptians, Arabs in general, the Israelis, and the superpowers.

In January, Sadat refused the plea of Syria to reopen the war with Israel. In February he sent Hafez Ismail, his adviser on national security affairs, to Washington to explore once again the possibility of American support. In the same month Ismail journeyed to Moscow where his reception was described as "cool." In February also, the Israelis by error shot down a Libyan civilian jet liner over the Sinai, but the incident itself did not produce trouble. Some days earlier Israeli and Egyptian jet aircraft engaged in a short air battle over Suez.

In June the Egyptians fired surface-to-air missiles at Israeli jets over Sinai. In the same month the Egyptians, suggesting that the 1947 partition plan for Palestine be reexamined, spoke in favor of the creation of a Palestinian state on the west bank of the Jordan River. The proposal stirred considerable controversy in the Arab world. In late August, Sadat visited Saudi Arabia, Qatar, and Syria; then in early September Jordan's King Hussein and President Hafez al-Assad of Syria visited Cairo. Diplomatic relations with Jordan were resumed at that time. It is apparent that at these conferences the decisions for the renewal of the war were made and support was promised by the Saudis for the Arab combatants, Syria and Egypt.

The Egyptians on the Suez front and the Syrians on the Golan front achieved tactical surprise in the attack initiated by them on October 6. The Egyptians crossed the canal in force but failed to exploit their advantage by penetrating very deeply into the Sinai. The Israelis chose to fight on their northern front against Syria first; they then turned to deal with the Egyptians. They forced a small beachhead on the west side of the canal, dividing the Egyptian forces. They then expanded the beachhead, surrounded Suez city, encircled the Egyptian Third Corps, caught in a pocket on the eastern bank, and moved to within 50 miles (80 km) of Cairo.

A cease-fire was tentatively agreed to on October 22, but fighting did not stop until several days later. Although the Israelis demonstrated once again their military superiority, the Egyptians performed much better than they had on any previous occasion.

Egypt demanded that the Israelis withdraw to the positions held at the time of the October 22 cease-fire and refused to exchange prisoners until they did. Israel would not fall back but did agree to the provisioning by a 100-truck convoy of the trapped Egyptian Third Corps. On November 11, Egypt and Israel signed a six-point cease-fire that called for a continuous supplying of the trapped Egyptian forces and an exchange of war prisoners.

The exchange of prisoners began on November 14. At the same time a peace conference was proposed, to be held in Geneva on December 18, and attended by Syria, Israel, Egypt, Jordan, the United States, the USSR, and the United Nations, represented by Secretary General Kurt Waldheim.

After the November 11 agreement, Israeli-Egyptian military talks were held on the Cairo-Suez road. But the cease-fire was frequently violated by both sides, and when an impasse was reached on Israeli troop withdrawals the talks were suspended on November 29. Egypt did not agree to attend the peace conference until December 8, and both countries remained on a war footing. Nonetheless the conference began what no doubt will be extended negotiations. It is clear that the Israelis ultimately will make major concessions.

Relations with Libya. Egypt continued to resist complete union with Libya in 1973. On September 1, the day the union was to have been completed, Libya reluctantly agreed to a process of gradual union. The October war drove the two countries farther apart: Libya disapproved of the way the war was conducted and the terms of the cease-fire. On December 1, Libya announced that it had closed, at least temporary, its embassy in Cairo.

(See also MIDDLE EAST.)

CARL LEIDEN
University of Texas at Austin

UPI

JUBILANT Egyptian troops plant their flag in territory they captured from the Israelis in the early stages of the October Middle East war. The land, on the east bank of the Suez Canal, had been occupied by the Israelis since 1967.

ELECTIONS

Democratic and Republican leaders cautiously assessed the results of scattered off-year elections in the United States in 1973 in light of the Watergate affair. Politicians reported little clear evidence that scandals within the Nixon administration had affected the voting. Republicans in general did less well than the Democrats, although local issues were often greater factors in the results.

State Elections. New Jersey voters on November 6 elected Democrat Brendan T. Byrne to the governorship by more than 2 to 1 over conservative Republican U. S. Rep. Charles W. Sandman, Jr., who had defeated Gov. William T. Cahill in the Republican primary. In his first campaign for elective office, Byrne had the advantages of a moderate program and freedom from taints of corruption that had plagued the outgoing administration and some Democratic city leaders. The landslide also gave Democrats control of both houses of the Legislature by large majorities.

In Virginia, voters elected as governor Mills E. Godwin, Jr., a former Democratic governor turned Republican. He narrowly defeated Lt. Gov. Henry Howell, a liberal-populist Democrat who ran as an independent. The Democrats did not run a candidate. Howell carried liberal and black precincts and the economically disadvantaged areas in southwest Virginia. Godwin attacked Howell for past support of school busing for racial balance and of gun control and for opposition to the state's right-to-work law. Both Democrats and Republicans lost seats in the Virginia House of Delegates, as independents gained. In Kentucky, Democrats strengthened their control of both houses.

New York voters chose Charles D. Breitel, Republican-Liberal, chief judge of the Court of Appeals over Democrat Jacob Fuchsberg. Voters rejected a $3.5 billion transportation bond issue intended to hold down commuter and transit fares.

Californians defeated a constitutional amendment to limit state tax collections. Gov. Ronald Reagan strongly supported the amendment, but opponents contended that it would shift costs to local governments unequally able to bear them. Texas and Rhode Island refused to increase legislative salaries, and Washington voters forced legislators to reduce a 193% salary increase to 5.5%. Maine and Rhode Island voted to permit state lotteries. Washington disapproved both an income tax plan and a lower drinking age for alcoholic beverages. North Carolina rejected liquor by the drink.

City Elections. In a nonpartisan primary on April 3, Los Angeles Mayor Sam Yorty trailed Thomas Bradley for reelection. Bradley became the city's first black mayor after his May 29 runoff-election defeat of Yorty by 56% of the vote. In Madison, Wis., on April 3, Paul Soglin, 27, former activist in the peace movement, defeated two-term conservative Republican Mayor William D. Dyke. Soglin had strong support from university students, minorities, and liberal Democrats. On April 3, St. Louis voters elected John Poelker, who had defeated Mayor Alphonso Cervantes in the Democratic primary.

By electing Maynard Jackson on October 16, Atlanta became the first major Southern city to choose a black for mayor. In the nonpartisan election, supporters of incumbent Mayor Sam Massell's reelection made the racial issue acrimonious. Jackson pledged an administration of racial cooperation.

GOVERNOR-ELECT of Virginia, Mills Godwin, Jr. (right), who had won the governorship once before as a Democrat, defeated a Democrat running as an independent.

Democrat Abraham D. Beame, city controller, won the mayoralty of New York on November 6, the first candidate of Jewish faith to do so. With 58% of the total vote, he left three other candidates far behind. Republicans won only 5 of the 43 City Council seats.

Cleveland's Republican mayor, Ralph Perk, won reelection, also on November 6, with 61% of the vote. Detroit elected its first black mayor, Democrat Coleman A. Young, in a close race with an independent, former police commissioner John F. Nichols. In Minneapolis, Democrat-Farmer-Labor candidate Albert J. Hofstede defeated Mayor Charles S. Stenvig, a law-and-order independent, in the first election in which municipal ballots identified candidates by party.

In Connecticut, Republicans lost control of 32 town governments to Democrats on November 6 while gaining in only 10. Dayton, Ohio, elected James H. McGee, a black, in a nonpartisan race for mayor. Clarence E. Lightner, elected in Raleigh, N. C., became the first black mayor in a metropolitan Southern city with a white majority. Maurice Ferre, millionaire native of Puerto Rico, was elected mayor of Miami, Fla. In Philadelphia, Democrat F. Emmett Fitzgerald, Jr., defeated Republican district attorney Arlen Specter. Democratic Mayor Frank L. Rizzo, feuding with the Democratic city organization, had supported Specter.

U. S. House of Representatives. In elections held to fill vacancies in the U. S. House, Republicans won in Alaska and Maryland and Democrats won in Louisiana and Illinois.

FRANKLIN L. BURDETTE
University of Maryland

ELECTRONICS

The electronics industry in the United States recorded its second consecutive $30 billion year in 1973, despite the administration's restrictive economic price controls. Much of this strength was due to consumer spending, with large increases recorded in sales of color television receivers, calculators, electronic watches and clocks, and photographic and audio equipment. For example, color TV receiver sales in the United States were up more than 16% over the previous year.

The most dramatic performance of 1973 was that of minicalculators, whose sales to consumers jumped from about 1.6 million units (worldwide) in 1972 to an estimated 11 million units in 1973, with at least 8 million of these being sold in the United States. Advancements in technology and higher production rates helped U. S. manufacturers of small calculators to cut the prices of many of their products by more than 50% between mid-1972 and mid-1973. At least one 8-digit, four-function, hand-held calculator retailed for as little as $39.

Semiconductor Sales Gains. Minicalculators were major contributors to a huge boost in the market for semiconductor components throughout the world in 1973. Following a mid-year review of the 1973 market for semiconductor devices, Texas Instruments, the leading supplier, forecast $1,617 million in U. S. factory shipments for the year, and a worldwide consumption of $3,430 million.

According to projections in the Texas Instruments report, consumer calculators alone were providing the impetus for $235 million in semiconductor shipments in 1973, representing a large gain over 1972. In addition, the increasing use of solid-state components in color TV sets was spurring growth in shipments of small-signal devices to about $393 million, while both the automotive and TV markets were stimulating shipments of power devices to an estimated $350 million for 1973.

A breakdown of markets within the semiconductor industry shows the consumer market as the largest segment for the first time, at $340 million. The estimates for 1973 also include $238 million in sales to the government (including military sales), $249 million in industrial sales, $303 million in sales to the computer industry, and $192 million in exports. The significance in the shift in component sales is best reflected by relating the 1973 estimate with 1971 sales totals. In that year government-military sales were still the largest segment, at $217 million, and consumer product use of semiconductor devices was the smallest segment, at $121 million.

Land Mobile Radio. In August, the White House Office of Telecommunications Policy (OTP) urged the Federal Communications Commission (FCC) to allocate new frequencies for mobile radio use on the basis of maximum competition in the industry. In a policy statement, OTP said the new portion of the radio spectrum available for mobile services should be allocated in blocks of sufficient size to encourage industry investment in new technologies and services.

However, in order to preserve flexibility and to avoid over-commitment to any particular service or technology, OTP recommended that a substantial portion of the available spectrum be held in reserve. OTP said this could then be allocated at a later date, as warranted by consumer demand. The White House agency also suggested to the FCC that another portion of the spectrum (about 14 megahertz) be allocated to telephone common carriers to provide for rate-regulated mobile phone service and ancillary dispatch services, as an extension to their regular phone service. In a letter to the FCC, the OTP said that its recommended policy would provide "the widest possible flexibility for serving the mobile communications needs" of the public.

Electronics in Photography. The National Association of Photographic Manufacturers predicted that the photo industry would become much more electronically oriented in the next few years. The association said it could foresee mass production of self-focusing lenses, an increase in integrated circuits for shutters and cameras, and a greater combination of photography and other video forms. It added that the so-called "instant cameras" undoubtedly would receive the biggest commercial push from electronic advances anticipated in the next decade.

Domestic Satellites. Following several years of policy development proceedings, the Federal Communications Commission issued five authorizations to build ground stations and domestic communications satellites worth slightly more than $330 million.

The applications approved by the FCC were filed by American Satellite Corp., jointly owned by Western Union International and Fairchild Industries; RCA Global Communications and RCA Alaska Communications; GTE Satellite Corporation, and National Satellite Services, a subsidiary of Hughes Aircraft; American Telephone and Telegraph; and the Communications Satellite Corporation (Comsat). The estimated cost of the earth stations totaled $32 million. Comsat applied for permission to construct, own, and operate four communications satellites to be used as part of AT&T's domestic satellite system, along with two telemetry, tracking, and control stations.

Report on Communications Research. The National Academy of Engineering released a report in 1973 stating that while the United States leads the world in advanced communications research, it lags in some important respects in applying that technology for the nation's benefit. Two areas in which shortcomings in new uses of telecommunications technology are most apparent, the report said, are in the improvement of the quality of generally available medical care and the quality of life in American cities.

The report, commissioned by the National Science Foundation, also indicated that despite U. S. technological supremacy over other developed nations, the country has not made much of a dent in the foreign market for advanced communications equipment.

Electronics and Theft Prevention. Electronic and related devices helped reduce theft-related merchandise cargo losses in the United States in 1973. Such losses have been estimated to run to more than $1 billion a year. Secretary of Transportation Claude S. Brinegar cited more rigid government standards and theft-prevention pilot programs as among the factors leading to the improvement. He also called for "an active, permanent program of theft prevention." Several new companies were formed during the year specifically to develop theft-prevention equipment for the transportation segment of the securities market.

RONALD A. SCHNEIDERMAN
"Electronic News"

ENERGY. See special feature beginning on page 34.

The Tavera Dam, completed in 1973, will provide hydroelectric power and irrigation water for much of the northern part of the Dominican Republic.

engineering, civil

Civil engineering is concerned with the design and construction of public and private projects related to the needs of the community, including buildings, transportation systems, and dams. In 1973 two gigantic civil engineering projects neared completion—the 1,450-foot (443-meter) Sears Tower in Chicago, the tallest building in the world to date, and an 11.6-mile (18.6-km) railroad tunnel in Japan, the second-longest in the world. This article covers the planning and construction that were under way in 1973 of bridges, canals and other waterways, dams, and tunnels. For coverage of developments in the other branches of civil engineering, see ARCHITECTURE; TRANSPORTATION.

BRIDGES

New bridges were completed in all parts of the world in 1973, including a new London Bridge, a parallel span to the Chesapeake Bay Bridge, a cable suspension bridge linking two Japanese islands, and a major bridge and highway system in Turkey.

United States. In 1973, a parallel span to the 4-mile (6.4-km) Gov. William Preston Lane, Jr., Memorial Bridge, crossing Chesapeake Bay in Maryland, was opened. The 38-foot (11.6-meter) wide, three-lane steel roadway bridge is situated 450 feet (137 meters) north of a companion two-lane structure built 20 years earlier. The new bridge carries westbound traffic, and the original structure is now reserved for eastbound traffic. Both spans have a vertical clearance of 186 feet (56.7 meters). They connect Annapolis to the eastern part of the state.

The new bridge, which cost some $120 million, is made up of four different types of bridge. The deep-water channel of the bay is crossed by a 2,950-foot (899-meter) suspension structure consisting of a 1,600-foot (488-meter) main span and two 675-foot (206-meter) side spans. The bridge also has welded girder spans, deck cantilever truss spans, and through cantilever truss spans.

Turkey. British and German contractors have spanned the Bosporus Strait at Istanbul to provide the first road link between European and Asian Turkey since the Persian chief Darius completed a pontoon bridge there in 500 B. C. The new six-lane bridge, which was opened in 1973, has a main suspension span of 3,523 feet (1,074 meters) and a 210-foot (64-meter) vertical clearance. Two side spans give the bridge a total length of 5,118 feet (1,560 meters), making it the fourth-longest in the world.

The bridge, which cost some $35 million, forms part of a peripheral highway around Istanbul, and was expected to carry 7.5 million vehicles per year. It was to be carried over the historic Golden Horn, a western arm of the Bosporus Strait, on a 3,133-foot (955-meter) combination continuous steel-plate girder and prestressed concrete bridge, scheduled for completion in 1974.

England. A new London Bridge across the Thames River was opened in 1973. This is the third bridge at that historic site in over 700 years. The first known bridge was completed in 1209 and stood for nearly 600 years. The second was built in 1831. It was abandoned after little more than a century and a quarter because it was too narrow for modern traffic and because foundation problems were causing it to distintegrate. The present bridge, started in 1968, was built in sections so that traffic could be maintained on the old bridge during the work.

The new London Bridge is 860 feet (262 meters)

long, 107 feet (33 meters) wide, has three spans, six traffic lanes, and two pedestrian walks. It was built of prestressed concrete with granite facing at a cost of nearly $10 million. Fascia stone from the 1831 bridge was shipped to Lake Havasu City, Ariz., and used in an authentic reproduction of the London span across an arm of the Colorado River.

Japan. The longest cable suspension bridge in the Orient, and the 10th longest in the world, was opened in 1973 to link the Japanese islands of Honshu and Kyushu. The bridge is 3,504 feet (1,068 meters) long, with a 2,336-foot (712-meter) central span and two 584-foot (178-meter) side spans. It has a vertical clearance of 200 feet (61 meters) above the sea. Steel towers rise 462 feet (141 meters) above water level. The deck will carry four lanes of traffic, but provisions have been made to widen it to six lanes when traffic demands.

CANALS AND OTHER WATERWAYS

Major shipping canals were being dug in the United States and Rumania in 1973, and a large-scale canal irrigation project was planned for India.

United States. A $500 million project got under way in 1973 to connect the highly developed Tennessee River with the Tombigbee River in Alabama. The 253-mile (407-km) ship canal was to form a navigable waterway from the central United States to Mobile, Ala., on the Gulf Coast. The project, which was expected to take 10 years or longer, was to include a 170-mile (274-km) channelization of the Tombigbee and the construction of five dams and ten locks.

The U. S. Corps of Engineers planned to dredge a continuous channel stretching 145 miles (233 km) from Delaware Bay to Cape Charles, Virginia. The canal, which would be 100 feet (30.5 meters) wide and 6 feet (1.8 meters) deep, would wind between the outlying barrier islands and the coasts of Delaware, Maryland, and Virginia. The Corps planned to use existing canals and channels wherever possible, but it was expected that 5 million cubic yards (3.8 million cu meters) would be dredged from approximately 50 miles (80 km) of the waterway.

Rumania. After a delay of 20 years, work was resumed in 1973 on a half-completed canal connecting Cernavoda, on the Danube River, and a point near Constanta, on the Black Sea. The canal was intended as a shortcut for Danube shipping.

Rumania was also engaged in digging a 186-mile (300-km) network of canals for the Sadova-Corabia irrigation project. This system was designed to distribute water from the Danube through canals and pipelines to the poor sandy soil region along the Danube Valley. The main canal was to be 230 feet (70 meters) wide. Rumania was planning to irrigate some 5 million acres (2 million hectares) by 1975.

India. What could be the world's biggest water project was planned by the Indian government to bring surplus water and floodwater from the Ganges River to irrigate the drought-prone south, central, and western regions of the subcontinent. A vast national water grid would link all the major rivers. Water would be taken from the snow-fed Ganges in the Himalaya and channeled south through a 2,200-mile (3,540-km) Grand Feeder Canal to the tip of the peninsula. The project was expected to cost between $3 and $4 billion, and would take 25 years to finish. Construction should start in the late 1970's.

This Ganges-Cauvery river link canal would be 245 feet (75 meters) wide, with depths varying from 10 to 25 feet (3–7.5 meters). The canal, big enough to take cargo vessels into the heart of India, would open up trade for undeveloped parts of the country. Feeder canals would take water to the dry regions.

DAMS

During 1973, major dams were under construction in North America, Europe, Africa, and the Middle East. Some were completed during the year.

United States. In 1973 the U. S. Corps of Engineers completed the Dworshak Dam, the third-highest dam in the country (after Oroville and Hoover). Dworshak Dam is a concrete gravity structure 717 feet (219 meters) high and 3,300 feet (1,006 meters) long. It contains 6.7 million cubic yards (5.1 million cu meters) of concrete. Dworshak

DWORSHAK DAM, on the north fork of the Clearwater River in central Idaho, became the highest concrete gravity dam in the United States when it was topped out at 717 feet (219 meters) in 1973.

is one of the last big dams in a Columbia River System program for flood control, power, recreation, and irrigation. It is located on the North Fork of Clearwater River in central Idaho. The $131 million dam, which took seven years to construct, has a powerhouse containing three generators with a capacity of 400,000 kw. Ultimately, it was expected to house six units capable of generating 1,060,000 kw. The dam impounds a 3.5 million acre-foot reservoir.

At the end of 1973, the U. S. Bureau of Reclamation was completing an earthfill barrier on Strawberry River near Duchesne, Utah. The $10 million Soldier Creek Dam has a crest length of 1,320 feet (402 meters), a maximum height of 250 feet (76 meters), and a volume of about 3.3 million cubic yards (2.5 million cu meters). It is located 7 miles (11 km) downstream from Strawberry Dam, which forms the present reservoir. The new dam will raise the reservoir level 45 feet (13.7 meters), and increase its capacity from 283,000 to more than 1 million acre-feet.

In the arid desert south of Casa Grande, Ariz., the U. S. Corps of Engineers was building Tat Momolikot Dam across the channel of Santa Rosa wash. The earth embankment has a maximum height of 90 feet (27 meters) at its right abutment in a rocky knoll. From that point the dam stretches 2.5 miles (4 km) across the valley until it tapers off to nothing as the ground rises to crest level. The embankment will contain about 4 million cubic yards (3 million cu meters) of fill. The $7 million structure was scheduled for completion in 1974.

Britain. The highest earthfill dam in Britain neared completion in 1973 at Empingham, England. The 3,600-foot (1,100-meter) long, 115-foot (35-meter) high structure will form a lake with a 3,113-acre (1,260-hectare) surface and a capacity for 162 million cubic yards (124 million cu meters) of water. The $42 million project will draw water for the reservoir from the Welland and Nene rivers.

West Germany. In 1973, West Germany put into operation a 3-mile (4.8-km) concrete dam spanning the mouth of the Eider River on the west coast of Schleswig-Holstein. The $60 million Eider Dam was built to protect the surrounding region from North Sea tidal floods and to control silting of the sandy riverbed. It incorporates sluices that permit unhindered passage for flood, tidal, and river water.

Syria. In 1973, Syria completed construction of a $300 million earthfill dam, some 213 feet (65 meters) high and 2.8 miles (4.5 km) long, across the Euphrates River near the town of Thawra in the northern part of the country. It is part of a hydroelectric complex begun in 1969 with Soviet assistance. The complex will ultimately have eight turbines generating 800,000 kw. By the end of 1975, Euphrates Dam will form a 50-mile (80-km) long reservoir, Lake Assad, which will cover 247 square miles (640 sq km). It was expected that the stored water would eventually protect more than 166 million acres (640,000 hectares) of semiarid land.

Ivory Coast. In 1969 the Republic of the Ivory Coast began an earth and rockfill dam across the Bandama River at Kossou for the largest power development ever undertaken in the country. Kossou Dam was completed in 1973, and its powerhouse began operating with a capacity of 175,500 kw. The dam is 4,921 feet (1,500 meters) long, 187 feet (57 meters) high, and contains 6.9 million cubic yards (5.3 million cu meters) of material. The lake behind the dam stretches for 112 miles (180 km) and

BOSPORUS BRIDGE, Istanbul, in 1973 provided first road link between European and Asian parts of Turkey.

has a maximum surface area of 716 square miles (1,855 sq km).

TUNNELS

In 1973 one of a pair of tunnels was completed allowing traffic to pass under the Continental Divide of North America. A railway tunnel was under construction in Japan, linking two of its major islands, and plans for a railway tunnel under the English Channel were announced.

United States. In 1973 the first of twin tunnels was opened to carry Interstate Highway 70 under the Continental Divide 60 miles (97 km) west of Denver. At a level of 11,000 feet (3,353 meters), it is the highest highway tunnel in the world. It is also the longest in North America, at 1.7 miles (3 km). The tunnel took five years to complete and cost $110 million. It replaces a 10-mile (16-km) road full of hairpin turns and switchbacks. Originally known as Straight Creek Tunnel, it was renamed Eisenhower Tunnel by the Colorado state legislature.

English Channel Tunnel. Britain and France agreed in 1973 to build a railway tunnel under the English Channel. Private consortiums from each country were to raise $2 billion for construction, but the tunnel was to be operated by an authority appointed by both governments.

TOKTOGUL DAM across the turbulent Naryn River, high in the mountains of the Kirghiz republic, USSR, neared completion in 1973.

FRÉMONT BRIDGE, across the Willamette River, Portland, Oreg. To avoid tying up one of the nation's busiest ports, some sections of the bridge were built off-river and very quickly hoisted into place. The 6,000-ton central arch, heavier than any bridge section ever lifted before, was set in position in March 1973.

The 32-mile (51.5-km) tunnel was to have two parallel tubes, each carrying a single track. They were to be linked by crossovers with a service tunnel between them. The train tubes would have a diameter of 22 feet (6.8 meters) and the service tunnel, a diameter of 11.5 feet (3.5 meters). The crossovers would counter the piston-like effect of high-speed trains moving through the tunnel. Boring through the chalk bed was to be done by rotary tunneling machines working from both ends. Construction was expected to start in 1975 and end in 1980.

The tunnel would connect Folkstone, England, and Calais, France, thereby linking the railroads of the continent and Britain. A trip from London to Paris should take about 3½ hours, in contrast to the nearly seven hours now required for the trip by train and ferry. Double-decker electric trains will shuttle cars and trucks through the tunnel.

Japan. The longest railway tunnel in Japan, and the second-longest in the world (after the Alps Simplon) was being bored under Kanmon Strait between Honshu and Kyushu islands. The dual-track Kanmon Tunnel is 11.5 miles (18.6 km) long and 31.5 feet (9.6 meters) wide.

WILLIAM H. QUIRK
"Contractors and Engineers" Magazine

ENVIRONMENT

The environmental movement gained momentum worldwide in 1973. A start was made in creating a body of international environmental law, particularly to protect the oceans. Cooperative planning and action under the auspices of the United Nations gained a stronger foothold during the year. Several nations established bilateral agreements to deal with environmental problems that transcended border lines, and individual countries showed greater concern about the environment their peoples live in.

Nevertheless, two obstacles to future rapid progress loomed significantly larger during the year. One was energy shortages in the developed countries. In the United States, for instance, pressure developed for easing environmental standards to permit the use of coal or high-sulfur oil. As the oil shortage worsened late in the year, there were growing fears that a number of environmental controls imposed in recent years might have to be relaxed to meet the energy crisis. The other obstacle was the less developed countries. They strongly urged that their industrial growth and improvements in the quality of life of their peoples had a higher priority than environmental protection.

UN Environmental Program Headquarters. On October 2, in Nairobi, Kenya, the Secretariat of the United Nations Environmental Program (UNEP) began work in its permanent headquarters. In preliminary ceremonies, the vast plaza of the 29-story cylindrical tower of the Kenyatta Center was festooned with flags of the 135 member states of the United Nations as 83-year-old Jomo Kenyatta, standing before a color guard of game wardens and forest rangers, unfurled the UN flag.

There was a fanfare of trumpets. *"Harambee"* (Swahili for "Let's pull together"), shouted Kenyatta, president of Kenya. *"Harambee!"* responded Maurice Strong, 43-year-old Canadian executive director of the UNEP. "We accept your slogan and your spirit!" After the speeches, Strong and his small secretariat staff repaired to their offices in the 29-story tower to carry out the work approved by the 58-nation Governing Council in its first meeting at Geneva in June 1973 and to prepare for the council's crucial second meeting at Nairobi in March 1974.

UN Program. At the Geneva meeting, the Governing Council of the UNEP examined a 15-point provisional agenda and set up a list of priorities, guided by the 109 recommendations made at the first United Nations conference on the Human Environment, which was held in Stockholm in 1972. The discussions and the concluding actions at the Geneva meeting underscored the determination of the less developed countries to use environmental concern as a lever for improvements in the quality of life rather than for mere protective action against air and water pollution.

The council allocated $5.5 million for programs to deal with human habitats, health, and well-being; land, water, and deserts; education, training assistance, and information; trade economics and transfer of technology; oceans; conservation of nature, wildlife, and genetic resources; energy; "earthwatch" monitoring of possible danger; and other matters.

A dispute arose over apportioning responsibility between the council and Executive Director Strong. The council decided to defer adoption of its General Procedures until its next meeting in March 1974. In the interim, Strong was given authority to proceed toward essential objectives.

Marine Pollution Control. Representatives of 71 countries took a major step in world environmental quality protection when they approved a new international convention on the oceans in November. However, it will take years before their respective national legislatures ratify it, as required.

The participating countries held a month-long meeting in London under the auspices of the Intergovernmental Maritime Consultative Organization, a UN agency first formed in 1948. They agreed to significant changes in tanker construction, including fitting tankers with devices that would monitor oil discharges. They also placed prohibitions on discharges within 50 miles (80 km) of land. Russell E. Train, who headed the U. S. delegation, described the agreement as "a historic milestone in the control of marine pollution."

The new convention covered accidental as well as intentional discharges of oil, sewage, garbage, and other noxious substances carried in bulk. Together with a 1972 convention prohibiting the dumping of poisonous wastes, the new convention would cover about half the causes of ocean pollution. The other half is attributed to pollutants that pass from the atmosphere to the oceans.

Under the convention, any tanker that is over 70,000 tons deadweight and is built after 1975 must be fitted with segregated ballast tanks. This would end pollution due to the use of cargo tanks for sea-water ballast that then is discharged at sea. As a consequence of this part of the convention a 70,000-ton tanker would lose more than 35% of its cargo-carrying capacity. (A much less drastic alternative to reducing pollution from tanker ballast water is described in MICROBIOLOGY—*Microbial Ecology*.)

The Law of the Sea Conference. Participants in the Law of the Sea Conference held a preparatory meeting during the summer of 1973. This conference was initiated by the UN General Assembly in 1970 to stabilize international rules governing na-

tional rights on the oceans and to establish the rules for mineral exploration and exploitation of the seabeds.

The Seabeds Committee established a subcommittee on marine pollution. During the preliminary discussions the subcommittee discussed the basic obligations and powers of states, jurisdictional and enforcement issues, and liability for pollution damage. It made genuine progress in establishing the groundwork for the full-dress conference, which was scheduled for Caracas, Venezuela, in 1974.

The full-dress conference will have to deal with many intricate and interrelated issues. For instance, what should be the limits of territorial sovereignty? How do fishing rights relate to the new boundaries? Can (or should) historic rights of free passage through coastal zones, straits, and archipelagoes be preserved? What are the rights of landlocked states? If an international ruling body for the oceans is established, what should be its authority? What are the economic, technological, and environmental implications of deep-seabed mining? How should any profits be distributed?

Also, should environmental-impact statements be required before any new exploration of oceans is permitted? Which United Nations agency should have primary responsibility for implementing environmental provisions? What machinery should be established to settle disputes?

International Whaling Commission. At the meeting of the International Whaling Commission (IWC) in June, the United States again proposed a global 10-year moratorium on commercial whaling. Although seven other member nations of the IWC supported the moratorium, it once again failed to be approved. However, the commission agreed to a 25% reduction in the 1974 quota for the Antarctic fin whale, the most seriously depleted of the currently harvested whales, and a moratorium on all harvests of this whale in three years. However, the IWC has no enforcement powers, and Japan and the USSR may not comply with its decisions.

Convention on Endangered Species. At the invitation of the U. S. government, representatives of 80 nations met in Washington, D. C., early in 1973 to conclude a convention on endangered species. The group agreed on March 2 to a new Convention on International Trade in Endangered Species of Wild Fauna and Flora, designed to preserve wildlife. The convention protects more than 500 species of animals and over 20,000 species of plants, whether taken from land or from the sea. It would prohibit commercial trade in 178 species of mammals, 113 birds, 44 reptiles, 26 mollusks, 8 fishes, and 6 amphibians. Also, 239 kinds of animals could be traded only if permits were granted by the exporting and importing countries.

Economic Commission for Europe. The Economic Commission for Europe (ECE) is one of the few international organizations comprising both Communist and non-Communist industrialized nations of the Western world. As a result, the ECE has a unique potential for promoting environmental cooperation between the East and West European nations. At a meeting in April a somewhat imprecise long-range program was adopted, dealing with air pollution, energy, water pollution, toxic wastes, transportation, tourism, and transborder pollution of the Black Sea.

European Committee on Automobile Pollution. Seven of the largest automobile manufacturers in Europe agreed to formulate a common approach to automobile safety and pollution problems. They formed the Committee of Common Market Constructors to pool information and to press for uniform standards both inside and outside the European Economic Community.

Leontief Study. Late in 1973 the United Nations commissioned a two-year study headed by Wassily Leontief, a Harvard economist and 1973 Nobel Prize winner. The study is to determine whether concern for the environment and measures to protect it would inhibit economic development in the less developed nations. The study will project future demographic characteristics, structure of production and consumption, use of natural resources, and state of the environment in various parts of the world.

World Environment Day. World Environment Day was observed on June 5, 1973. Among many working observances the same day were an international symposium in Stockholm on energy, environment, and development; a pollution-control congress in London; and the first international film festival on the human environment in Canada.

The UNEP promoted the observance of World Environment Day by staging a worldwide photography contest for pictures illustrating environmental problems and remedial activities. The winners in the professional, adult amateur, and young amateur categories will be awarded trips to UNEP headquarters in Nairobi after publication of the pictures on June 5, 1974.

American-Soviet Cooperation. Acting on the 1972 American-Soviet agreements for joint action in environmental protection, a joint working group met in Moscow in January and agreed on 22 projects dealing with endangered plant and animal species and wildlife management.

Another joint group working on air pollution met in Moscow in March and agreed on the development and testing of methods to control sulfur oxides and particulates emitted by fossil-fuel power plants, particularly fuel cleaning and wet stack-gas scrubbing technologies.

Still another joint working group interested in water quality met in Moscow in March and agreed to study pollution-control strategies for selected river basins as well as ways to protect Lake Baikal in Siberia and Lake Superior and Lake Tahoe in the United States.

Various joint programs relating to urban environment were developed as a result of a Soviet tour of five American cities in April. Soviet legal experts visiting the United States in May expressed particular interest in the Environmental Protection Agency when they were briefed on its regulatory and enforcement programs. Other Soviet-American working groups met in the United States to discuss earthquake prediction, marine oil pollution, air-pollution modelling and instrumentation, and meteorological monitoring and instrumentation.

Japanese-American Cooperation. Japan and the United States, following up a joint conference on new sewage-treatment technologies in late 1972, held a conference in January on solid-waste management and resource recovery and a conference in June on photochemical smog. Discussions on mobile sources of pollution have been held periodically.

Canadian-American Cooperation. In 1973 the United States and Canada immediately began to fulfill the mutual obligations of the Great Lakes Water

Quality Agreement of 1972. On the U.S. side almost all significant municipal wastewater treatment facilities, at which phosphorus removal is required, were being built or would soon receive construction grants from the Environmental Protection Agency.

Cooperating in the International Joint Commission (IJC), the United States and Canada established the Great Lakes Water Quality Board and the Research Advisory Board, as called for in the 1972 agreement. The two boards set up working groups to consider such problems as phosphorus loading, land drainage, and dredge-spoils disposal.

Canada and the United States also worked together on other transborder problems. Oil-spill contingency plans were developed for boundary waters on the Atlantic and Pacific coasts and in the Great Lakes, and joint studies of ecological conditions in the Puget Sound area were being planned. The two countries were working to reduce pollution in the St. John River basin between Maine and New Brunswick, and both nations were jointly monitoring water quality in the Red, Rainy, and St. Croix rivers under the IJC. Air-pollution problems in the Detroit-Windsor and Port Huron-Sarnia areas were being addressed by U.S. and Canadian officials at federal, state, provincial, and city levels.

Mexican-American Cooperation. In June negotiations began between the U.S. and Mexican governments to recommend a definitive solution to the problem of controlling salinity in the Colorado River, whose waters are used to irrigate 75,000 acres (30,351 hectares) in northwestern Mexico. An agreement reached in August called for the United States to build a desalting plant since drainage from irrigated lands in its western states carried salt into the river.

Action in the United States. By the end of 1973 the Environmental Protection Administration (EPA), under its new administrator, Russell E. Train, had granted one-year extensions to automobile manufacturers to meet the statutory automobile emission limits set by Congress under the Clean Air Act of 1970. Those limits had been intended to reduce carbon monoxide, hydrocarbon, and nitrogen oxide emissions from 1975–76 cars by 90% from 1970–71 levels. Instead, they were made applicable to 1976–77 cars. Demands by the auto industry for further delays in fitting cars with emission-control devices were rejected by the EPA at congressional hearings in November.

Construction of the trans-Alaska oil pipeline was expected to begin early in the spring of 1974, more than five years after the discovery of a vast reservoir of oil on Alaska's North Slope had touched off a raging environmental controversy. Legislation to permit construction of the pipeline cleared Congress in November. While environmentalists were expected to continue their challenge, construction permits were being processed by the Interior Department at year-end.

In October, the Senate passed and sent to the House a tough bill establishing federal standards for strip mining of coal. It prohibited surface mining where land reclamation was not feasible. It also required the Interior Department to adopt final regulations for all state mining controls and for mining on federal land if a state failed to adopt an acceptable plan.

Legislation was introduced by Rep. Martha Griffiths of Michigan to give recycled materials the same tax treatment as now applies to newly mined minerals and timber. Also, Connecticut began a solid-waste management project under the leadership of the General Electric Company.

A study made by the Midwest Research Institute in 1973 showed that the amount of recycled waste paper could be more than doubled by 1985 if the federal government provided incentives to industry. According to the study, the 1973 recycling rate of about 20% could be raised to 26% by 1985, thereby providing more than 15 million tons of recycled paper. The National Academy of Sciences had set a recycling goal of 35% by 1985, but the study showed this goal probably would not be reached by that date.

Action in Canada. Canada proceeded energetically with plans for a world conference and exposition on human settlements, especially cities, to be held in Vancouver in 1976. Fifty experts from 20 countries met in June 1973 to discuss and improve on preliminary plans drawn by the Canadian government. The program adopted was then forwarded to the Governing Council of the UNEP in Geneva. To be called Confex '76, the conference will exhibit 100 experiments in improving the quality of cities around the world and the life of city dwellers.

Action in Western Europe. The Belgian government, after much delay and international pressure, banned the netting of wild birds. It was estimated that 20 to 30 million migratory birds were captured annually before the ban.

The British government extended the powers and duties of statutory authorities in the areas of waste disposal, the licensing of mine dumps, urban noise, and the discharge of effluents in tidal rivers, estuaries, and the sea.

West Germany planned a high-speed tracked train that would travel the 500 miles (804 km) between Munich and Hamburg in less than two hours. For environmental reasons the Germans decided to use a magnetic suspension system rather than an air cushion. The former is more expensive than the latter, but it does not stir up dust or make noise.

Action in the Soviet Union. The Soviet Union adopted a new method of reclaiming worked-out strip mines. The scarred surface of the land is renovated by replacing various strata of soil and adding a heavy layer of topsoil.

In January the Soviet Union announced that it would establish a national environmental protection service to monitor air and water pollution throughout the country. The announcement also called for an expansion of green areas in cities and suburbs and better management of solid-waste disposal.

Action in Japan. Japan shifted responsibility for pollution control from the Environmental Agency to the Ministry of International Trade and Industry. Also, the Transport Ministry's Civil Aviation Bureau sought to double its appropriation for reducing aircraft noise around major commercial airports.

Action in India. The Indian government began "Operation Tiger" with $1 million from the World Wildlife Fund and about $6 million from the government. Eight 500-square-mile (1,300-square-kilometer) sanctuaries were to be set up for 500 tigers.

Action in Sudan. South of Khartoum, a $100 million irrigation project at the juncture of the Rahad and Blue Nile rivers was begun to convert 300,000 acres (121,400 hectares) of semiarid desert into productive farmland.

JACK RAYMOND, *Past President*
International Institute for Environmental Affairs

ETHIOPIA

Ethiopia's relationship with the French Territory of the Afars and Issas was clarified in 1973, but its relations with Somalia continued to disintegrate. Large quantities of natural gas were discovered during the year in the Ogaden region of Ethiopia, and the United States opened a communications base in the Indian Ocean.

International Relations. French President Georges Pompidou visited Ethiopia on Jan. 17, 1973, after a week's stay in Afars and Issas, the small French territory wedged into the east coast of Ethiopia. He announced that France had no intention of abandoning the colony of the Afars and Issas and that France supported "peace, stability, and progress" in the area. Ethiopia's emperor, Haile Selassie, who fears a French withdrawal from the colony would result in a bitter conflict between Ethiopia and Somalia over control of Afars and Issas and its harbor, was pleased with President Pompidou's statement. It was announced that France and Ethiopia would proceed with their cultural exchange program.

The German Democratic Republic (East Germany) established diplomatic relations with Ethiopia on February 1. Princess Anne of Britain visited Ethiopia on February 11 and 12. In the summer, Emperor Haile Selassie paid a state visit to the United States and was feted by President Richard M. Nixon.

Because of continued unrest and insecurity in the Ethiopian province of Eritrea, where a major U. S. military base is located (Kagnew), the United States had long been seeking a strategic area in the region in which to situate a new, possibly alternative, military base. On March 23, the U. S. Navy opened a communications base on the British-held island of Diego Garcia in the Indian Ocean, south of India and east of Ethiopia. The base was initially to house a radio station manned by 274 Navy personnel, an 8,000-foot (2,438-meter) aircraft runway, and a small harbor. There was some displeasure toward this move by some Ethiopian leaders.

───── ETHIOPIA • Information Highlights ─────

Official Name: Empire of Ethiopia.
Location: Eastern Africa.
Area: 471,777 square miles (1,221,900 sq km).
Population (1973 est.): 26,800,000. Density, 54 per square mile (21 per sq km).
Chief Cities (1970 est.): Addis Ababa, the capital, 795,900; Asmara, 218,360.
Government: *Head of state,* Haile Selassie I, emperor (proclaimed emperor April 1930). *Head of government,* Aklilou Habte-Wold, prime minister (took office April 1961). *Legislature*—Parliament: Senate and Chamber of Deputies.
Languages: Amharic (official), English.
Education: *School enrollment* (1969)—primary, 590,445; secondary, 114,443; technical/vocational, 6,168; university/higher, 4,636.
Monetary Unit: Ethiopian dollar (2.07 E. dollars equal U. S. $1, July 1973).
Gross National Product (1972 est.): $2,113,000,000.
Economic Indexes: *Agricultural production* (1971), 127 (1963=100); *consumer price index* (1972), 135 (1963=100).
Manufacturing (major products): Processed foods, textiles, cement, leather and shoes.
Major Agricultural Products: Coffee, cotton, sugarcane, corn, millet and sorghum, oilseeds, pulses, cattle, sheep.
Major Minerals: Salt, gold, natural gas, platinum.
Foreign Trade (1972): Exports, $168,000,000. Imports, $189,-000,000. *Chief trading partners* (1969)—United States (took 42% of exports, supplied 10% of imports); West Germany (10%—14%); Italy (7%—15%).
Tourism: Receipts (1970), $6,340,000.
Transportation: *Motor vehicles* (1970), 59,500 (automobiles, 47,200); *railroads* (1971), 675 miles (1,087 km); *major national airline,* Ethiopian Airlines.
Communications: *Telephones* (1972), 50,518; *newspapers* (1971), 9 (daily circulation, 46,000).

Somalia accused Ethiopia in May of planning a military attack on its territory near the Ogaden desert region. The Ogaden, where the population is predominantly Somali, has been claimed by both countries for a number of years, although Ethiopia presently controls the area. Ethiopia's prime minister, Aklilou Habte-Wold, claimed that Ethiopia was contemplating no attack but that "it is Somalia, which has amassed weapons, and . . . accused Ethiopia of massing troops." Somalia called on the Organization of African Unity (OAU) to intervene and urge Ethiopia "to desist from her preparation for an aggressive war against Somalia and reduce tension in the area by withdrawing her troops to their original and normal positions immediately." In response, the OAU established a commission made up of members from Guinea, Mali, Liberia, Nigeria, and Senegal to mediate the border dispute. The commission was to report back to the OAU.

Drought and Foreign Assistance. The northern and central provinces of Ethiopia continued to suffer from severe drought. It was estimated that between April and October more than 50,000 persons lost their lives because of the drought. The UN Food and Agricultural Organization promised 10,000 tons of wheat, corn, and sorghum to drought victims. Other international organizations and foreign governments pledged additional aid.

The World Bank loaned Ethiopia $5 million to help finance a $7 million project designed to improve slaughter facilities for Ethiopia's livestock industry. The United Nations High Commission for Refugees granted Ethiopia $150,000 for aiding 20,000 refugees in Ethiopia. The International Development Agency agreed to loan Ethiopia $16 million for an irrigation scheme and an agricultural study of the Rift Valley.

Technical agreements signed by Canada and Ethiopia were instrumentalized in 1973. Under the agreements, Canada provided Ethiopia with technical advisers and granted scholarships to a number of Ethiopian workers. Canada and Ethiopia also began joint exploration for minerals around the Omo River. In addition to small quantities of gold already discovered, it was believed that nickel, lead, and platinum were also to be found. For this venture, Canada was to provide three geologists, two helicopters, and a small number of engineers.

Because of an increased interest in Ethiopia by tourists, hoteliers from Italy, Japan, and the United States were considering the construction of additional hotels in Addis Ababa. In April 1973, Ethiopian Airlines extended its European network to include London.

Natural Gas Discovery. Ethiopia discovered natural gas in large quantities less than 30 miles (48 km) from the disputed Somalia frontier in the Ogaden region. The U. S. company Tenneco had been drilling in the area since February 1972. It seemed more than likely that large quantities of oil would also be found. If this is so, it would be the first major find in the entire East Africa region.

Books. A number of important books on Ethiopia appeared in 1973. The most notable included *Priests and Politicians: Protestant and Catholic Missions in Orthodox Ethiopia, 1830–1868,* by Donald Crummey; *Land Tenure Among the Amhara of Ethiopia,* by Allan Hoben; and *Decision-Making in Ethiopia,* by Peter Schwab.

PETER SCHWAB
State University of New York at Purchase

*PUSH EXPO '73 at the Chicago International Amphitheatre had the theme
"Save the black colleges." PUSH stands for People United to Save Humanity.*

ETHNIC GROUPS

Ethnic groups around the world continued their struggles for greater freedom, higher status, or a more powerful voice during 1973. One notable trend in the United States was the increasing number of blacks who won elected offices.

ETHNIC GROUPS IN THE UNITED STATES

The Administration and Ethnic Problems. Early in 1973 the Nixon administration was accused of failing to respect the interests of minority groups. James Farmer, formerly assistant secretary of the Department of Health, Education, and Welfare (HEW), stated that the President was isolated from contact with blacks and relied entirely on white aides to represent minority group interests. A group of black Southern mayors, while acknowledging benefits from federal antipoverty funds, accused the administration of failing to disperse these funds to black communities led by unsympathetic whites or less well-known blacks.

In February, the U. S. Commission on Civil Rights reported that most federal agencies were not adequately enforcing civil rights legislation. Laying the blame largely to a lack of "presidential leadership," the commission charged that the administration had "no government-wide plan for civil rights enforcement." Specifically, it registered the following complaints: (1) HEW's attempts to curtail funds to induce voluntary compliance in uncooperative school districts had not been effective, and HEW had made "virtually no effort to prevent the flow of federal funds to nonpublic schools which are enjoying discriminatory practices" or to cut off their tax exemptions; (2) the Office of Federal Contract Compliance had not developed "adequate proce-

dures to resolve . . . problems" in constraining contractors to hire more minority employees; (3) the Equal Economic Opportunity Commission (EEOC) had a growing backlog of complaints and was assigning low priority to enforcing agreements; and (4) the Civil Service Commission had not changed the "pronounced disparate treatment" of minorities in federal jobs.

Equal Employment Action. The foregoing charges may have spurred more vigorous action in government agencies, but most of the measures taken against discrimination in employment practices had already been set in motion. The EEOC was especially active. With the help of the Labor Department the agency constrained the American Telephone and Telegraph Company to pay the largest job-bias compensation ever awarded—$15 million to 15,000 women and minority male employees for past discriminatory practices and $23 million per year in pay increases to 36,000 women and minority group males who had been promoted to higher positions but not allowed to retain seniority.

The EEOC filed more than 100 suits against major corporations and labor unions, charging them with discrimination on the basis of race, color, national origin, religion, and sex. EEOC also filed suit in California against the Xerox Corporation for engaging in "policies which exclude Spanish-surnamed persons from employment."

The Justice Department also took measures against employment discrimination. It filed similar suits against the cities of Boston, Chicago, and Buffalo for discriminating against blacks and Spanish Americans in hiring firemen and policemen. The department charged that among Boston's 2,100 firemen there were only 16 blacks and three Spanish Americans, though blacks comprised 16% of the

city population and Spanish Americans 4%. Out of Chicago's 5,000 firemen, only 4% were Negro and 0.5% were Puerto Rican or Mexican American, though 32% of the city population were black and 11% were Spanish American.

Equal-opportunity employment was pressed by court authorities. A U. S. district court judge ordered Bridgeport, Conn., to hire blacks and Puerto Ricans to fill half the vacancies in the police force until they comprise 15% of the force. A federal district court judge ordered the U. S. Steel Corporation and the United Steelworkers Union to change hiring and seniority programs that were discriminatory. A district court judge approved a Delta Air Lines plan to open higher-level jobs to women and minority employees and to make a correction in back pay for losses due to discrimination.

School Desegregation. Federal courts continued to take the initiative in efforts to desegregate public school. U. S. District Court Judge John H. Pratt ordered HEW to direct 25 school districts in 12 states to submit new plans that would "eliminate the vestiges" of their formerly segregated systems by the fall of 1973, warning that refusal could result in legal action and a loss of federal aid. A circuit court supported the principle that city and suburban school districts should be merged to achieve racial balance but ordered a lower court to work out a new plan for busing children in metropolitan Detroit. A lower court had ordered a massive busing plan for that area without allowing suburban school districts sufficient opportunity to object in court.

DENNIS BANKS, American Indian Movement (AIM) leader, at bier of slain colleague Pedro Bissonette.

WIDE WORLD

The U. S. Supreme Court issued its first ruling concerning *de facto* segregation in a case involving Denver schools. The Denver school board had been accused of fostering racially segregated schools through manipulating school zones and school site selection. The Supreme Court ruled that in such situations "school authorities have an affirmative duty to effectuate a transition to a racially nondiscriminatory school system."

U. S. District Court Judge Albert V. Bryan, Jr., ordered two private schools in Virginia not to refuse admission to blacks, an order that affected 395 other private schools that had intervened in the case. Meanwhile, court-ordered integration was being wrought peacefully, though with reluctance. About 27,000 students were being bused between districts in Memphis to reduce the number of all-black schools, but more than 13,000 students were missing, having enrolled in private schools. Alexandria, Va., schools were integrated, as were the elementary schools and kindergartens in Little Rock, Ark., where the higher grades had already been integrated. (See also EDUCATION.)

Minority Group Actions. In the year following a presidential election the activities of minority groups seemed relatively quiescent. About 140 delegates attended the meetings of the National Black Assembly to develop ways of exerting more black political power, but many authorized delegates stayed away. The assembly decided to establish a series of model workshops in 10 cities and to set up a team to investigate "specific incidents of abuses against the black community."

The National Association for the Advancement of Colored People, despite the opposition of some members, continued to press for school integration. In its 64th annual convention the association censured the officials of its Atlanta chapter, who had consented to a local school plan to deemphasize integration. The chapter president had argued that the association should understand the problems of school systems where "there are no white kids around . . . to integrate with."

Black action groups seemed to have lost some of their momentum. The Rev. Ralph Abernathy resigned from the presidency of the Southern Christian Leadership Conference, citing financial difficulties in the organization and a lack of support from well-to-do blacks. However, in its annual meeting the organization's board of directors prevailed upon Abernathy to remain in office and instituted a number of major administrative changes.

The major issue confronting Spanish-American groups seemed to be the struggle between the Teamsters Union and Cesar Chavez's AFL-CIO United Farm Workers Union for the loyalty of California's largely Spanish-American farm labor force.

Ethnic-Group Status Trends. Statistics released in 1973 revealed trends in the changing statuses of ethnic minorities. Intermarriage between whites and nonwhites, a useful index of the degree of ethnic integration, was 63% higher in the 1960's than in the 1950's. The percentage of interracial marriages in the country rose from 0.44% to 0.70%.

Black representation in elected offices reached a record high in 1973. After the elections of the previous fall, 1,144 blacks held elected offices in the 11 states of the Deep South, 241 more than ever before and more than 10 times the number of blacks elected in 1965. Of 1,276 black candidates in the South, about half had won offices. They included 2

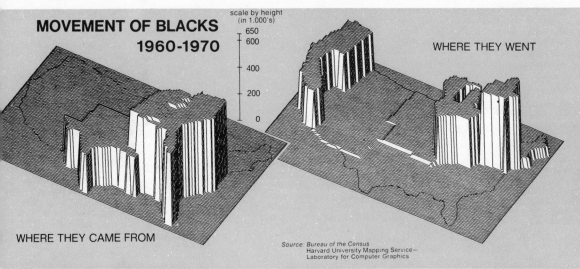

MOVEMENT OF BLACKS
1960-1970

WHERE THEY WENT

scale by height
(in 1.000's)

650
600

400

200

0

WHERE THEY CAME FROM

Source: Bureau of the Census
Harvard University Mapping Service—
Laboratory for Computer Graphics

congressmen, 6 state senators, 55 state representatives, and 38 mayors.

Municipal elections in 1973 brought blacks into prominent offices elsewhere. Most notable was Thomas Bradley's victory over incumbent Sam Yorty in a run-off election for mayor of Los Angeles. According to Bradley the election of a black mayor in a city having only a 15% to 18% black population showed that "people will listen to a candidate and make their judgment on merit instead of race or creed." Atlanta, Detroit, Dayton (Ohio), Grand Rapids (Mich.), and Raleigh (N. C.) also elected black mayors in 1973.

The inclusion of eight blacks and two Spanish Americans among the 25 new members of the Democratic National Committee augured for more minority-group influence in the Democratic party.

ETHNIC GROUPS IN OTHER COUNTRIES

Minorities in the Soviet Union. Indications of unrest among minorities in the Soviet Union continued to be in evidence, but they were not easy to distinguish from popular resistance against the government. The seriousness of these pressures was indicated by increased Soviet emphasis on nationwide policy and planning in an effort to minimize the economic and cultural differences between the national republics. Violence erupted in Georgia against new limitations on small private enterprises, including peasant farm products, and troops had to be sent in to restore order. Also, more Ukrainians were jailed for their part in the Ukrainian movement to achieve Ukrainian cultural and political autonomy.

Presumably as a control on Jewish emigration to Israel, the Soviet government instituted an exceedingly high tax on emigrants, amounting to several years of a professional person's salary. The action came as the U. S.-Soviet trade pact was being considered in Congress. Many congressmen sought to restrain the Soviet Union from imposing extortative exit fees on Jews by supporting an amendment denying most-favored-nation status to nations restricting emigration or imposing sizable exit fees. Soviet Jews indicated that despite assurance to the contrary Jewish emigration was still restricted. Moreover, some Jews attempting to emigrate were arrested and interrogated. Eight Jews demonstrating in support of their emigration requests were jailed for 16 days and severely beaten.

Ethnic Conflict in Southern Africa. The Portuguese military has been accused of many serious atrocities in the wars against black guerrillas in Angola and Mozambique. A group of diplomats from six nonaligned nations reporting for the United Nations Human Relations Commission charged Portugal with torturing black prisoners. The group reported that the Portuguese used napalm, defoliants, and herbicides against the black guerrillas.

Blacks in South Africa seemed more firmly under control than those in neighboring countries, but there was obvious evidence of unrest. Although illegal, there were 160 reported strikes by a total of 61,410 blacks in several industries in the first quarter of 1973. Black unions are not allowed, but a group of 200 metalworkers founded the first black union in the country. The South African government later introduced legislation that for the first time in 30 years would give black workers limited rights to strike.

Chief Gatsha Buthelezi, the black leader of Zululand, rejected offers by South African officials to discuss plans to consolidate his area with other areas. He declared he would "not allow ourselves to be used for a facade. While we accept that we are powerless, like all black people in this country, we cannot accept being used to create the impression that we have scope for negotiations when under these circumstances we have none at all." He agreed to "bow to the unilateral decrees of the white minority government."

Ethnic Conflict in the Philippines. Intermittent fighting between Muslims and the Philippine government continued on Mindanao. Early in 1973, President Ferdinand Marcos offered amnesty to Muslim rebels who would hand over their arms, but fewer than 300 accepted the offer. The Philippine government announced a desire to improve economic conditions of the Muslims. Nevertheless, fighting continued, forcing a reported 800,000 civilians on Mindanao to evacuate their homes. Fighting seemed to subside after a Philippine naval blockade cut the flow of military supplies to the insurgents.

ROBERT L. CANFIELD
Washington University, St. Louis

EUROPE

Sunday near Amsterdam, after a Netherlands government ban on Sunday automobile driving. Other countries took stringent measures in the fuel crisis.

For Europe the year 1973 opened in restrained optimism and closed in unrelieved gloom. The tasks for the first months seemed to be merely the completion of major undertakings already well advanced —continuance of the détente between Communist Eastern Europe and the West, revival of West European–American ties following the end of U. S. involvement in Indochina, reduction of inflation without restraint of economic growth, and strengthening of the economic reforms begun by new leaders in Eastern Europe. At the end of the year, however, the energy crisis precipitated by the cutback in oil supplies from the Arab countries threatened Western Europe with the gravest economic and political crisis since World War II.

East-West Détente. The relaxation of tension in the relations between the Communist and non-Communist states, begun in 1971–72, continued. Leaders of both Eastern and Western nations felt their national interest served by détente. The USSR, still embroiled in its rivalry with the People's Republic of China, sought not only to avoid military confrontation with the West but to profit from access to its technology, agricultural surpluses, and financial credits. West German Chancellor Willy Brandt completed the diplomatic agreements with East Germany, Poland, and Czechoslovakia that were the foundation of his new *Ostpolitik* (Eastern Policy), begun two years earlier.

The principal architect of the Soviet Union's new overtures to the West was Party Secretary Leonid Brezhnev. In April and May, Brezhnev reinforced his position in the Politburo by ousting two

of his critics—Vice Premier Pyotr Y. Shelest and Minister of People's Control Gennadi I. Voronov— and promoting two supporters of his Western policy —Foreign Minister Andrei Gromyko and Defense Minister Marshal Andrei Grechko. Later in May, Brezhnev became the first Soviet leader to pay an official visit to West Germany, where he concluded agreements on economic and cultural ties and opened negotiations with West German companies for the construction of several large projects in the Soviet Union. In June, Brezhnev visited U. S. President Richard Nixon in Washington, D. C., at which time both leaders declared their intention of proceeding rapidly with talks on strategic arms limitation. Europeans feared that in his talks with Brezhnev the President, under congressional pressure to withdraw part of the 300,000 U. S. troops stationed in Europe, had put too little emphasis on a reduction of the USSR's growing armaments in Eastern Europe.

East-West Talks. The Strategic Arms Limitation Talks (SALT) continued in Geneva. However, negotiators made little progress in discussions involving the technical problems of limiting such offensive weapons as nuclear bombers and medium-range rockets.

The talks arranged in 1972 on Mutual and Balanced Force Reductions between members of the North Atlantic Treaty Organization (NATO) and the Warsaw Pact finally opened in Vienna in 1973, after delays caused by quarrels over the number and status of the powers attending. The actual talks began officially on October 30 and were expected to

last more than a year. The first task was to reduce opposing forces in the crucial north-central region comprising West and East Germany, Poland, and Czechoslovakia. Whereas the tanks and tactical aircraft of the Warsaw Pact powers were almost three times superior, the NATO powers hoped to use their superiority in nuclear weapons for bargaining power.

Concrete decisions on troop reductions were tied to decisions on broader principles under discussion by the security conference in Helsinki. The Soviet and U. S. governments had agreed in May 1972 to call the conference. Six months of preparatory negotiations preceded the formal opening in July 1973. In September the 35 nations attending divided the work among three commissions. Subcommittees of the first commission were to draft a code of international good conduct and to recommend "confidence-building" measures. The second commission was to study plans for increasing trade, industrial and scientific cooperation, and collaboration on environmental problems. The third commission was to deal with "human questions"—including human rights, freer movements of persons, and wider cultural exchanges. (See also DISARMAMENT.)

Economic Progress in Eastern Europe. Governmental policy in Eastern Europe was a combination of firm political controls with increasing material rewards. Poland in particular, where riots of dissatisfied workers in the coastal towns had brought the Silesian miner Edward Gierek to power in 1970, enjoyed the benefits of a consumer-oriented policy. At the Polish Communist party conference in November, Gierek was able to announce that during the three years of his rule the national product had increased 27%, industrial production 33%, and farm production 19%—results that had been partly achieved with foreign aid from Russia and credits from the West.

East Germany remained the most spectacular example of economic success in Eastern Europe, even though First Party Secretary Erich Honecker continued the authoritarian controls of his predecessor Walter Ulbricht. Ulbricht himself, who had held the largely ceremonial role of president since 1971, died in August. The reinforcing of the Berlin wall and the barriers along the West German border and the use of currency requirements to discourage visits by West Germans emphasized the belief of the East German government that the isolation of its 17 million citizens from West Germany was an essential foundation for the "economic miracle" that had made the country the ninth industrial power in the world.

Like Russia, the East European countries cautiously sought greater technical and financial support from the West. East Germany profited from trade within the common external tariff of the European Economic Community (EEC, or Common Market) because of West Germany's insistence that the two states had remained legally one economic unit. Rumania was granted special access to EEC as a "developing" country, and the Council for Mutual Economic Assistance (COMECON) began informal contacts as preliminary to an increase of its trade with EEC. Since the exports to EEC of the European members of COMECON were primarily in foodstuffs, wood, tobacco, and other raw materials, COMECON members were concerned with removing the restrictions of EEC's common agricultural policy and protecting themselves against the regulations due to be imposed after January 1974 by the new common commercial policy. To make COMECON a genuine counterpart to EEC in the economic bargaining, the heads of government of the COMECON countries, meeting in Prague in June, decided to make a number of political and economic steps to strengthen the organization, including establishment of a multilateral payments scheme and agreement on more effective measures of harmonizing national economic plans. In March, the International Investment Bank of COMECON even floated a bond issue on the Eurodollar market.

The Enlarged Common Market. Before the energy crisis, EEC was primarily concerned with its own internal problems, including the integration of three new members (Ireland, Denmark, and Britain), the reworking of the exorbitantly expensive common agricultural policy, and the establishment of a number of new policies as laid down at the summit meeting of heads of state or government in Paris in October 1972.

Although membership in EEC remained unpopular with the majority of the British people, considerable stimulus to the work of the European Parliament was provided by the Conservative group of members of the British Parliament, who demanded greater legislative powers for the European Parliament and lessened dominance over that body by the Council of Ministers.

The West German government succeeded in forcing the French, who were the main beneficiaries of the common agricultural policy, to begin negotiations on a drastic reform of the policy that would reduce the subsidies to Europe's farmers. These subsidies were expected to reach almost 4 billion European units of account (predevaluation U. S. dollars) in 1973.

Bitter quarrels erupted during discussion of the financing of a regional fund to provide development aid to the poorer regions of the Community, especially in Italy, Ireland, and Britain. In December, the British threatened to paralyze energy policy if the Germans refused to agree to, and pay a large share of, a regional fund of more than $3 billion for the following three years.

EEC Without a Foreign Policy. Worsening relations with the United States failed to induce the EEC states to adopt a common foreign policy. President Nixon had called for a "year of Europe" to restore confidence in the U. S. government, which had been weakened during the Vietnam War, but his initiative failed. Distrust of the American economy was spurred by a second devaluation of the dollar in February, the grave harm to the political prestige of the presidency by the Watergate revelations, and worry over American military leadership magnified by failure to consult the European powers during the Arab-Israeli war, especially when Nixon placed American forces on a worldwide atomic alert.

Yet the will among EEC governments to find their own unified policy was entirely lacking. Many Europeans were apathetic about the "European idea" as World War II receded further in memory. Brandt, the only charismatic leader in Western Europe, was devoting his efforts to the success of his own *Ostpolitik*. French President Georges Pompidou continued to follow the Gaullist policy of French national independence, braving world outrage to carry out atomic tests in the Pacific and seeking a favored position for France with the oil-producing Arab states.

The Netherlands, placed under a total ban on oil supplies by the Arab states for its supposedly pro-Israeli attitude, failed to win support in EEC for its argument that the Treaty of Rome required its EEC partners to share with it their oil supplies. Instead, realizing their dependence upon oil supplies from the Arab countries, which constitute between 82% and 95% of their requirements, the EEC governments felt compelled to draw up a common declaration transparently sympathetic to the Arab cause in the Middle East.

The second summit conference in Copenhagen in December, the purpose of which was to review progress toward achieving the goals laid down at the previous summit, achieved little. The heads of state or government agreed to meet more frequently, to speed up planning for economic and monetary union, and to meet the energy crisis in a "concerted manner." In response to four Arab foreign ministers who paid an unexpected visit to the conference, it was agreed that Europe should seek to negotiate long-term agreements with the oil-producing countries, exchanging aid in industrial development for stable oil supplies at reasonable prices.

Political Unrest in Western Europe. The internal politics of the West European states were marked by increasingly bitter unrest. In Scandinavia, support for the long-entrenched Socialist parties was deeply eroded. In the September elections, the Swedish Social Democratic party led by Prime Minister Olof Palme, and its allies the Left Communists, saw their parliamentary majority reduced to two seats, while Norway's Labor party and its allies, vigorously opposed by an antitax protest movement, won a majority of only one seat. The biggest upset occurred in Denmark, where the protest vote against the vast cost of state services was thrown in support of a new Progress party led by Mogens Glistrup, a millionaire lawyer and self-proclaimed tax-dodger. As a result, the Social Democratic Prime Minister Anker Jørgensen was replaced in December by a minority government headed by the Liberal party leader Poul Hartling.

Similar parliamentary difficulties threatened to hinder governmental action in the Netherlands, where it required five months for Joop den Uyl to form a five-party coalition government. In Italy, Christian Democrat Mariano Rumor was able to renew a Center-Left coalition in July, but only after the Socialist party had split in two on the issue of joining the coalition. Even the strongly entrenched Gaullist party in France narrowly escaped electoral defeat in the parliamentary ballots of March 4 and 11, when pressed by a powerful Socialist-Communist coalition that emphasized financial scandals in the government, the personal rivalries within the Gaullist party, and especially the continuing inequitable distribution of income in France.

Political change in Greece was more violent. Following an unsuccessful attempt in June by the navy to overthrow the government of the military junta that had ruled since 1967, Premier George Papadopoulos deposed exiled King Constantine for alleged support of the coup and made himself president. Six months later, however, after he had used force to break up a student occupation of the central university buildings in Athens, the army overthrew Papadopoulos, making Lieut.-Gen. Phaedon Gizikis president and a civilian, Adamandios Androutsopoulos, premier. In December, extremists in Spain murdered Adm. Luis Carrero Blanco, a right-wing politician who had been appointed premier by Generalissimo Francisco Franco in June.

The British government of Conservative Prime Minister Edward Heath faced perhaps the most Herculean tasks of all. There was an increasingly violent dispute with fellow-NATO member Iceland over Britain's right to fish within 50 miles (80 km) of the Icelandic coast, which Iceland claimed unilaterally as its territorial waters. The dispute was finally settled in October with promises of severe restrictions on Britain's annual catch. Progress in the bloody conflict between Protestants and Catholics in Northern Ireland, in which almost a thousand people had been killed by the end of 1973, was painfully slow and uncertain. However, a milestone in negotiations was passed in December when the British and Irish governments and the Northern Ireland executive agreed to create a Council of Ireland which would have limited competence in both Eire and Northern Ireland.

Britain's internal economic problems were an aggravated form of those present in many West European countries. With inflation running at just under 10% and unemployment at the low figure of 2%, labor unrest in Britain expressed itself in bitter strikes that challenged the wage norms of the government's anti-inflation program. Sporadic strikes throughout the year cut automobile exports; and during the energy crisis the coal miners, electrical power engineers, and railroad workers simultaneously restricted their hours of work to compel the government to grant them higher wages. Harsh austerity measures to meet the crisis were announced in December, including a three-day work week and huge cuts in government spending.

The Energy Crisis. In December, the extent of the greatest crisis of the year—the energy crisis—was beginning to be glimpsed throughout Western Europe. Most European states had remained firmly neutral during the Arab-Israeli conflict, and Britain had even refused to supply spare parts for Israel's British-made tanks. Nevertheless, in November, the oil-producing Arab states imposed an overall cut in production of 25% as well as a total ban on supplies to the Netherlands and the United States. The initial cuts were to be followed by additional decreases of 5% each month if progress toward settlement of the Palestine question on Arab terms was not achieved. However, the December 1973 decrease was cancelled for most European countries, although an embargo continued for the Netherlands and the United States.

With Europe dependent on the Arab world for more than 70% of its oil supplies, much of which had been passing through the Dutch port of Rotterdam, the effects were quickly felt. A price rise of 70% in the remaining supplies threatened the balance of payments of most European countries and vastly increased inflation.

Expedients to deal with the fuel shortage included gasoline rationing, bans on Sunday driving, restrictions on airline flights, and reduction of hours for factories and shops. It seemed likely, moreover, that most European countries would experience a cessation of economic growth, large-scale unemployment, and a possible recession. Some Western politicians surmised that, as a result, the balance between East and West was in danger of being radically altered.

F. ROY WILLIS
University of California, Davis

*The strapless evening dress—a long, lean tube of
jersey, by Anne Klein—and the casual wrap coat
reflected the "not dressed to kill" mood of 1973.*

Fashion

241

Whether it was the influence of Women's Lib, a carry-over from the protest years, or just plain common sense being brought to bear on fashion, 1973's woman was not going to be pushed around. She was going to wear what she wanted to wear—which, in most cases, meant casual clothes touched up with her own personality.

"Not being dressed to the teeth," as the American designer Anne Klein put it, became the first rule of the new chic. The New York *Times* advised simply: "When in doubt, wear a sweater."

The '73 girl could take a bulky Irish sweater, for example, and tuck it into a knitted dirndl skirt with a sliver of a lizard belt, or she could go in for a simple pullover with a printed shirt. She could wear a sweater-dress to the office or out to dinner, a sweater-coat day or night.

The more sophisticated dresser could choose an import with a fox collar, wear a cashmere classic with a paillette skirt, or, if sufficiently extravagant, dress for evening with Yves Saint Laurent's $3,000 sweater beaded with golden pearls and paired with gray flannel slacks. The word casual and the mood casual took on a different meaning—not classic any longer and with a definite leaning toward opulence.

For the dress-as-you-please record, the cocktail-buffet-dinner scene, including both men and women, was conclusive. Women wore long skirts and pretty shirts (pantsuits becoming less and less visible) while men appeared in casual—rather flamboyantly casual—jackets and slacks with well-coordinated shirts. This way of dressing satisfied both men and women—women because they love long skirts without being "dressed to kill" and men because they dislike formal clothes but secretly enjoy being decked out in male plumage

Lengths and Silhouettes. Sights such as the following identified 1973 in terms of lengths and silhouettes:

Women streaked along city streets in dresses several inches above the knees, with miniskirts looking outdated. These lengths contrasted with a noticeable number of long skirts going shopping, to offices, and even to church. A few midcalf skirts were presented as trial balloons, but there were few takers.

The romantic look of big, flower-trimmed hats and long, full skirts appeared at fashionable resorts and racetracks.

Shirt dresses took on a new shape, with wrapped tops and flaring skirts Big smock tops continued to be popular for pants, and wide tent dresses and short caftans existed side by side with belted tents and chemises. For evening, long slip dresses with skinny cardigan jackets contrasted with blowy chiffons with big puffy sleeves.

Three coats dominated the entire coat story: (1) the easy cardigan style, self-belted or hanging loose and usually in pale shades of jersey or mohair, inspired by the casual syndrome and aptly called the "noncoat" by Bill Blass, one of its creators; (2) the coat-lover's coat in handsome wool or suede trimmed with flattering long-haired fur; (3) the big full-back steamer coat with raglan sleeves, revived from the 1940's.

(Continued on page 244)

THE SWEATER-DRESS—this one by Oscar de la Renta—hat with veil, and under-the-arm handbag made fashion news.

blue jeans

Once-Lowly 'Faded Blues' Scale Fashion Heights; 'A Sign of the Times'

LEVI STRAUSS & CO.

Blue jeans have taken a long walk on the fashion scene. After miles in the mass market they have arrived, front and center, in the realm of high fashion. This progression is contrary to the usual course of fashion, which customarily starts at the top and sifts down. But blue jeans are contrary. They are antifashion. They are nonfashion.

Genesis. Legend has it that the story started at Vassar College in the late 1930's, when the drama department was instituted and the girls working on sets were required to wear so-called "work clothes" made of fabrics known as denim or jean (jean fustian). The habit caught on, and in the spring there were the blue jeans on the grass outside the dormitories, washed and put out to fade in the sun. Thus "faded blues" began, a long process in those days compared to the instant doing with Clorox today. It is interesting to note that the fashion story originated with the Ivy League crowd, projecting the thinking that clothes do not matter.

At first, blue jeans were worn with cotton shirts, sweaters, or rain jackets. Then, in the 1940's, they were always rolled up and put with men's shirts worn outside, with a sweater tied around the waist. Not for years were they allowed in the classroom.

Then came the 1960's—the protest years, the hippies, the drifters. Long hair and jeans were the badges of antiestablishment, antistatus. They came to be adopted by all the teens, 20's, and 30's of both sexes who subscribed to the casual way of life and this "comfortable" way of dressing. Jeans became a more universal uniform than had ever before been seen in the United States, thereby attaining a status of their own. The more faded, the more tattered, and the more patched, the greater the symbolism. The preoccupation spread to Europe, and the international period began. The young traveled in jeans, whether thumbing a ride on the highways or jetting to Europe, whether drifters or youthful teachers, artists, or writers.

Phenomenon 1972–73. Beginning in 1972 and climaxing in 1973, jeans entered another bracket. Elaborately embroidered, jeweled, and patched— also deliberately frayed and faded—they were sold at unbelievable prices in the best-known boutiques in New York, California cities, London, Paris, and Rome. A rhinestone-studded suit at Giorgio's in Beverly Hills brought $100 for the jeans and $150 for the jacket; a T-shirt and jeans set at Proctor's in London, $112; a jeans jacket, $120 at the BBC in Paris; and—to top the list—jeans with "total encrustation," $500 at Serendipity in New York. A laundry in Brooklyn advertised that it "aged" jeans, and many old jeans were acquired by secondhand dealers and sold to boutiques.

The list of wearers read like a jet-set blue book: Lee Radziwill of London and New York, Italian designer Valentino, actor Steve McQueen, new star Lauren Hutton, and—making the best news story of all—Pilar Crespi, the daughter of titled parents in Rome, who was married in the ancestral castle and "went away" in jeans.

In the words of Peter E. Haas, president of Levi Strauss & Co., well-known maker of Levis, who received one of the Neiman-Marcus fashion awards of 1973, it felt "a little strange to rise from work clothes to high fashion, but we're not fighting it."

Children fell in line with gusto, refusing to wear anything else and insisting on the disreputable as the only "cool." With incorrigible ingenuity, they ripped out sleeves of jeans jackets and wore them tattered over old sweat shirts. Their college sisters made smart-ugly long skirts from two pairs of old jeans.

The demand was so great that scarcity became acute. Prices rose, and still the demand skyrocketed. Not only was denim in short supply, but indigo dye was running out. One reason for the increase in the wearing of "faded blues" was that the paler blue took less dye and thus became a commercial necessity. Fabrics other than denim copied the blues. Corduroy led the list. Even furs got on the bandwagon, with denim blue raccoon and opossum.

The jeans syndrome is a sign of the times, easily subject matter for the social studies or a doctoral thesis, instead of a fashion article. Yet blue jeans relate sturdily to fashion, inasmuch as they have become the key to the casual sports mood that dominates the clothes of this time.

RUTH MARY (PACKARD) DUBOIS

(Continued from page 242)

The Feminine Mood. Femininity was expressed in a variety of ways. There were hats with veils, not the delicate, old-time veiling but coarse, bold-pattered veils tied around berets, fur hats, or brimmed felts. "White shoulders" appeared in the strapless evening dresses of the 1940's and the one-shoulder style of the 1950's. A fresh camellia was worn on the shoulder or in the hair.

The Jeans Circuit. The two principal developments were the change from blue-jeans pants to blue-jeans skirts—long and sloppy, worn with fragile, lace-trimmed shirts—and the upswing to the jet set of the entire jeans fashion, with expensive jeans selling like wildfire all over the United States and Europe (see special report on the preceding page).

Accessory Bulletins. The spectator pump and oxford with stacked heels—white with black or navy for summer, in two shades of tan for fall—looked right with sweaters and sports clothes. The bronze kid sandal, bare and strappy, with a higher, thinner heel, came in for evening. It was distantly related to the bronze kid opera pump of the 1930's. Heels, in general, became higher and somewhat thinner but not shaped, while the big bulkies receded. Bracelets were big, bold bangles—masses of them, bright and noisy. The right necklace was "opera length" (21–30 inches), preferably in amber shades, amethyst, or rose quartz. Belts were popular again in all widths. Handbag news was the bag carried in the hand, not the bag swung from the shoulder, although the latter was still mass-produced.

Colors and Fabrics. Unlikely combinations such as calico and velvet in a dinner skirt were evidence of continuing antilogical moods. Gray flannel with spangles was another example. Sparkle invaded all fabrics. Metallics were blended with wool and mohair, and gold and silver Lurex stripes were characteristic of holiday sweaters. A new satin-chiffon was used in pink or blue dinner dresses and pajamas. Printed chiffon was loved in short and long dresses. Washable polyesters led the daytime parade. Qiana nylon matte jersey was great for traveling. Polka dots in all sizes, especially on green and red grounds, were found in long and short dresses.

THE CLOCHE, brimmed to the brow, was reminiscent of the 1920's and "very F. Scott Fitzgerald."

Cream, ivory, and vanilla shades were alternatives for white during the summer, and camel to deep-amber tones gave variety to fall beiges. Blue was the strongest color, from bright cornflower blue to faded blue. Reds were in the orange range. Pink was true flower pink. Nail polishes and lipsticks were red and strong pink—no more of the whitish look. Dark brown was a smart substitute for black. Gray and brown were often combined—gray velvet, for example, with dark-brown flannel.

International Aspects. For the first time, there was Franco-American collaboration in fashion when French and U. S. designers gave a fashion "spectacle" at Versailles in November to raise money to restore Versailles. The U. S. designers were Bill Blass, Anne Klein, Halston, Stephen Burrows, and Oscar de la Renta. French participants were Cardin, Givenchy, Dior, Ungaro, and Saint Laurent. Chairmen were U. S. socialites and titled Europeans.

The Japanese, with yen in plentiful supply, became the big spenders of 1973, buying art, antiques, racehorses, and fashion, among other things. They purchased fabrics and yarns to such an extent that many U. S. firms were short of both wool and cotton, and prices, especially in coats, soared. They bought ready-to-wear and couture models in Paris and the United States. Paris designer Ungaro set up boutiques in Japan with instant success, and the Japanese Suzuki-owned chain adapted French fashions and opened shops in Paris and Hong Kong. Kenzo, one of the foremost designers in Paris, is Japanese. Pure silks came from Japan as well as China and India.

China was being explored as a market. Catching on fast, the Chinese raised prices. A good example was cashmere, in demand in the United States. At the Canton Fair in April, most of the U. S. buying was in semiprecious jewelry. Chinese styles such as the pure silk pongee summer coat-jacket in U. S.

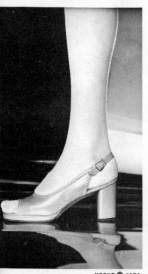

THE SLING-BACK SHOE, with small platform sole, and the oxford with fashion stockings looked right with 1973 clothes.

THE FASHION EDICT, "When in doubt, wear a sweater," covered a wide range—from a sleeveless pullover combined with a simple shirt and a cardigan to the opulent fur-trimmed or beaded sweater worn with a paillette skirt or with gray flannel slacks.

specialty shops tended to be high fashion, replacing the Mao suits of 1971–72. The "Shanghai shirt" was made by a Hong Kong designer of the resin-coated black silk worn by Chinese nannies.

Scottish and British imports in wool did well in the United States. Clan plaids made news in ankle-length kilts, which fit perfectly into the prevalent not-too-dressed-up thinking. They were liked for their quality and for the eternally young mood they represented.

Sportswear, the U. S. signature in fashion, was adopted all over the world. The fashion of sweaters, actually begun by the French designer Coco Chanel in the early 20th century but identified with the United States, became a trend in Paris and Rome, with Saint Laurent, Givenchy, and Valentino. Marc Bohan of Christian Dior announced that he would build his spring collection around the idea of the shirt. He did so with success, especially in his beautiful printed chiffons, given a new shapeliness with midriffs tucked from bustline to hipline. Saint Laurent's belief in the shirt was expressed in his belted shirt jacket worn with flannel pants. And as though by mutual consent, designers in both Europe and the United States put the timeless cardigan jacket and coat into the headlines.

Tennis spoke an international language, influencing fashion from beachwear to sports sweater. The derivation came partially from the motion picture (due in 1974) based on F. Scott Fitzgerald's novel *The Great Gatsby,* celebrating the 1920's.

Men's Fashions. The summary can be made in three words: vests, plaids, and bow ties. Vests returned for the first time in many years, in casuals rather than in conventional suits. They were made to match or contrast. The same plaid appeared in vest, jacket, and pants. A plaid or checked vest was worn with plain colors, or a plain jacket—a maroon blazer, for example—went well with plaid vest and slacks. Waist-length, sleeveless sweaters were made to take the place of vests. Bow ties were always wide, tied or tie-it-yourself, and came in plaids, dots, or plain shades. Four-in-hand ties were still wide, news being in splashy scenic patterns. A knee-length skirt for women, made of men's ties, originated in Deauville on the French Riviera. Named the Deauville Skirt, it was copied widely in the United States.

Pinstripes again became a predominant pattern in suit fabrics. All single-breasted jackets were two-buttoned. The white shirt was almost a rarity, colors and stripes being preferred with plain or patterned jackets. Drip-dry cord suits reappeared for summer. Knits and double-knits were basic for fall. Camel and green shades made the best-liked color combinations.

Children's Clothes. Children, too, were wearing what they wanted to wear—never mind what their parents might advise. This meant jeans for both girls and boys—which is no news. The news was in the style of the tops, an underwear type of T-shirt, inscribed souvenirlike with names of cities—New York, Miami, Houston, and so forth—or with crazy animals. Girls wore long dresses about as much as they did the previous year, but not more. Little boys often liked their fathers' bow ties. Subteen and early teen-age girls made their own denim jumpers from bib overalls.

Children's shop buyers say that fabric scarcities drove prices up 10% to 15%. How long the blue-jeans binge, the fabric shortage, and the no-news period would last was hard to predict. The only healthy aspect was that rich kids now looked like poor kids, by their own edict.

RUTH MARY (PACKARD) DuBois
Freelance Fashion Writer, Lecturer, and Columnist

FINLAND

Although facing an uncertain future, Finland made some important decisions in 1973. The president's term was extended. With Sweden's cooperation, steps were taken to stem migration of Finnish workers, and pacts were signed with the Soviet bloc's Council for Mutual Economic Assistance (COMECON) and the European Economic Community (EEC).

Political Affairs. The so-called UKK Law, enacted Jan. 18, 1973, by a 170–28 vote, continued Urho K. Kekkonen's presidential term to March 1, 1978. The outcome was interpreted as a tribute to the president's achievements during 17 years in office and as assurance that a steady hand would guide the nation in a difficult period.

On Sept. 4, 1973, a four-party coalition government led by Prime Minister Kalevi Sorsa, a Social Democrat, marked its first anniversary in power.

Migration. In the years since 1954, when a Nordic common labor market agreement was concluded, heavy emigration had occurred, particularly to neighboring Sweden. Alarmed by this "impoverishing export," Finland, on April 11, secured Sweden's agreement to require advance job assignments through the Finnish Employment Service. Other demographic concerns in Finland included a low and falling birthrate, mounting numbers of elderly people, and an accelerated exodus of the farm population into overcrowded cities.

The Economy. Factors inhibiting Finnish economic growth in 1973 included widespread strikes in the spring, intensified inflation, an unemployment rate of over 2%, unfavorable farming weather, foreign trade and payments imbalances, and doubts about the efficacy of proposed supplementary governmental policies. The gross national product

---

──────── FINLAND • Information Highlights ────────

Official Name: Republic of Finland.
Location: Northern Europe.
Area: 130,120 square miles (377,009 sq km).
Population (1973 est.): 4,800,000. Density, 36 per square mile (14 per sq km).
Chief Cities (1971 est.): Helsinki, the capital, 528,800; Tempere, 157,810; Turku, 156,900.
Government: *Head of state,* Urho Kaleva Kekkonen, president (took office March 1968 for 3d 6-year term, which was extended for an additional 4 years in Jan. 1973). *Head of government,* Kalevi Sorsa, prime minister (took office Sept. 1972). *Legislature* (unicameral)—Eduskunta. *Major political parties*—Social Democratic party (SDP); Finnish People's Democratic League (SKDL); Center party; Conservative party; Communist party; Finnish Rural party; Swedish People's party.
Languages: Finnish, Swedish (both official).
Education: *Expenditure* (1969), 23.9% of total public expenditure. *School enrollment* (1970)—primary, 416,966; secondary, 323,615; technical/vocational, 105,058; university/higher, 58,615.
Monetary Unit: Markka (3.69 markkaa equal U. S.$1, Aug. 1973).
Gross National Product (1972 est.): $12,000,000,000.
Economic Indexes: *Industrial production* (1972), 187 (1963 = 100); *agricultural production* (1971), 112 (1963 = 100); *consumer price index* (1972), 131 (1967 = 100).
Manufacturing (major products): Wood and paper products, ships, machinery, chemicals, metals, textiles, cement.
Major Agricultural Products: Oats, potatoes, sugar beets, rye, barley, wheat, forest products.
Major Minerals: Iron ore, copper, zinc, nickel, vanadium, chromium ore.
Foreign Trade (1972): Exports, $2,947,000,000. Imports, $3,-198,000,000. *Chief trading partners* (1970)—United Kingdom (took 19% of exports, supplied 13.5% of imports); Sweden (16%—16.5%); USSR (11%—14%); West Germany (10%—16%).
Tourism: Receipts (1971), $161,000,000.
Transportation: *Motor Vehicles* (1971), 874,800 (automobiles, 752,900); *railroads* (1971), 3,356 miles (5,400 km); *merchant fleet* (1972), 1,630,000 gross registered tons; *major national airline,* Finnair.
Communications: *Telephones* (1972), 1,289,592; *newspapers* (1971), 65.

(GNP) increased some 6%, and industrial production, 9%. In the first 8 months exports rose 16% and imports 25%, resulting in a large trade deficit and a sharp decline in foreign exchange holdings.

Bright spots in the economy included an impressive growth in shipbuilding facilities and orders, greater trade with Third World countries, and a continuing gain in income from tourism.

COMECON and the EEC. Progress was made in 1973 in institutionalizing Finland's trade relations with both the East and the West. On May 16, 1973, Finland became the first state with a free market economy to sign an accord with COMECON for economic, scientific, and cultural cooperation. Its immediate goals were exchange of information through a joint commission and the lowering of trade barriers by means of bilateral negotiations.

Implementation of a draft EEC free trade agreement, prepared in July 1972, was delayed by vigorous Communist opposition and by bitter contention over proposed short-term protective legislation. The EEC document was signed in Brussels on Oct. 5, 1973, but the parliament earlier had postponed action on a controversial package of trade protection laws. Despite an unexpected outburst of critical Soviet press comments, the Finnish parliament ratified the EEC accord in November.

International Affairs. Two long-pursued goals were attained in 1973. The European Security Conference was held in Helsinki in July, and, following a Finnish-sponsored gathering in the spring, seven Baltic states signed an anti-pollution and fishing grounds agreement in Poland in September.

Finns were becoming increasingly chagrined over the expression "Finlandization," used in a pejorative sense in Western countries to describe excessive pressure on a small nation's policies by a powerful neighbor. President Kekkonen sought to amplify the definition to convey a larger truth about Finland itself—a small country, defeated in war and left to its own resources, yet successful in preserving its independence and national dignity, in establishing friendly relations with the USSR, and in making contributions to world peace through policies of constructive neutralism.

Death of "The Flying Finn." The Finnish nation mourned the death on Oct. 2, 1973, of its celebrated distance runner Paavo Nurmi (76), many of whose track records remain unbroken.

JOHN I. KOLEHMAINEN
Heidelberg College, Ohio

FISHERIES

The U. S. fisherman saw prices for his products climb substantially in 1973, and the value of the total catch set a record even though production in many fisheries was lower than in preceding years.

Industry Trends. The trend in prices, value, and production became well established in 1972, the last year for which statistics were available. Total U. S. commercial fishery landings of 4.7 billion pounds were 5% less than in 1971; but the record $703.6 million value was 9% greater.

Seafood prices climbed still higher in 1973. At the peak of the high meat price crisis in midyear, they reached the point where some industry observers foresaw the possibility of price controls. Furthermore, the higher prices had the effect of weakening one of seafood's major selling points—that it is a cheap sources of high-grade protein. Seafood

LEADING FISHING COUNTRIES
(In millions of metric tons)

Country	1967	1968	1969	1970	1971
Peru	10.2	10.6	9.2	12.6	10.6
Japan	7.9	8.7	8.6	9.3	9.9
USSR	5.8	6.1	6.5	7.3	7.4
China (mainland)	5.2	5.4	5.5	6.3	6.9
Norway	3.3	2.9	2.5	3.0	3.0
United States	2.4	2.5	2.5	2.8	2.8
Six-nation total	34.8	36.2	34.8	41.3	40.6
Other countries	25.6	27.7	27.8	28.3	28.8
World catch	60.4	63.9	62.6	69.6	69.4

came close to being comparable to beef in price, a development that caused apprehension among seafood merchandisers. However, the U. S. fisherman did not profit in direct ratio to the higher market prices not only because imports supply well over 60% of the seafood consumed in the United States but also because the purchase of imported seafood made the devaluation of the dollar a major contributing factor to the higher prices.

Meanwhile, the increased demand for protein was causing some significant trends in respect to species caught and processed by the U. S. fisheries. Traditionally such bottom-fish species as hake and pollack have largely been ignored by American Pacific coast fishermen, although Japanese and Russian fleets are active in those fisheries there. However, major Alaskan producers are now studying these resources, and some already have geared their plants for processing or gone into production in anticipation of a booming bottom-fish industry.

Mullet. On the Gulf of Mexico even the lowly mullet, which for years has resisted all sorts of ambitious promotional programs, has been having its day. A brisk export market developed for mullet roe, Japan and France being the chief customers.

Shrimp. Japanese affluence continued to make Japan a major market for the world's choicest fishery products, with the result that it has been a formidable competitor of the United States and Europe as a market for the world's shrimp production. The U. S. demand for shrimp is apparently insatiable, and shrimping continued its lead as the country's most valuable fishery. The demand for shrimp trawlers continued to keep boatyards busy in 1973.

Tuna. The tuna fishery, like shrimp an exception to the generally static or deteriorating condition of the historical U. S. fisheries, continued to expand in 1973. More "superseiners" were brought to the fleet, including the largest to date, a 262-foot (80-meter) vessel capable of 2,000-ton catches.

International Negotiations. Fisheries negotiations with foreign nations in 1972 and 1973 brought both favorable and unfavorable results. Particularly disappointing was the failure of Mexico to renew its bilaterial fishing treaty with the United States; U. S. boats must now stay 12 miles (19.3 km) from the Mexican coast.

On the other hand, the 1970 reciprocal fishing agreement between the United States and Canada was extended for another year, and a two-year bilateral fishing agreement was signed between the United States and Poland. Among other things, it provided that Poland not fish for lobster in certain waters off the U. S. coast.

In a series of informal discussions the United States and the Soviet Union agreed on conservation needs off the American Pacific coast, but they remained at odds about the northwest Atlantic. U. S. proposals for a number of conservation measures were rejected at a meeting of the International Commission of Northwest Atlantic Fisheries at Copenhagen in June 1973.

World Catch. World fisheries production in 1971, the last year for which figures were available, reached 69.4 million metric tons, according to the UN Food and Agricultural Organization.

WILLIAM A. SARRATT
Editor, "The Fish Boat," New Orleans

FLORIDA

In 1973, major issues in the state of Florida were education reform, environmental protection, dishonesty in government, and majority rights for 18- to 20-year-olds.

Education. Concern about the quality of public education and the need for a more adequate school funding system culminated in the passage of an Omnibus Education Bill. The bill reflected the recommendations of Gov. Reubin O'D. Askew's Citizens' Committee on Education. Provisions included a new funding system to replace the old minimum foundations formula, a provision for the establishment of teacher education centers, a requirement for citizen advisory committees in school districts, a mandate for state colleges and universities to explore the development of accelerated degree programs, and several other changes.

--------- FLORIDA • Information Highlights ---------

Area: 58,560 square miles (151,670 sq km).
Population (1972 est.): 7,259,000. Density: 137 per sq mi.
Chief Cities (1970 census): Tallahassee, the capital, 72,586; Jacksonville, 528,865; Miami, 334,859; Tampa, 277,767; Saint Petersburg, 216,232; Fort Lauderdale, 139,590; Hollywood, 106,873.
Government (1973): *Chief Officers*—governor, Reubin O'D. Askew (D); lt. gov., Tom Adams (D); secy. of state, Richard B. Stone (D); atty. gen., Robert L. Shevin (D); treas., Thomas D. O'Malley (D); commissioner of education, Floyd T. Christian (D); chief justice, Vassar B. Carlton. *Legislature*—Senate, 40 members (25 Democrats, 14 Republicans, 1 Independent); House of Representatives, 120 members (77 D, 43 R).
Education (1972–73): *Enrollment*—public elementary schools, 769,700 pupils, 34,012 teachers; public secondary schools, 667,500 pupils, 33,239 teachers; nonpublic schools, 111,800 pupils, 5,010 teachers; colleges and universities, 225,232 students. *Public school expenditures*, $1,238,227,000 ($902 per pupil). *Average teacher's salary*, $9,740.
State Finances (fiscal year 1971): *Revenues*, $2,548,063,000 (4% general sales tax and gross receipts taxes, $715,227,000; motor fuel tax, $246,839,000; federal funds, $493,137,000). *Expenditures*, $2,410,817,000 (education, $1,185,232,000; health, welfare, and safety, $350,777,000; highways, $449,219,000). *State debt*, $1,021,038,000 (June 30, 1971).
Personal Income (1972): $30,397,000,000; per capita, $4,188.
Public Assistance (1972): $280,376,000. *Average monthly payments* (Dec. 1972)—old-age assistance, $79.58; aid to families with dependent children, $96.58.
Labor Force: *Nonagricultural wage and salary earners* (July 1973), 2,525,400. *Average annual employment* (1972)—manufacturing, 334,700; trade, 634,100; government, 440,500; services, 460,300. *Insured unemployed* (Sept. 1973)—32,200 (1.6%).
Manufacturing (1971): *Value added by manufacture*, $4,821,800,000; Food and kindred products, $979,100,000; chemicals and allied products, $434,600,000; electrical equipment and supplies, $408,200,000.
Agriculture (1972): *Cash farm income*, $1,680,740,000 (livestock, $464,033,000; crops, $1,198,524,000; government payments, $18,183,000). *Chief crops* (in order of value, 1972)—Oranges (ranks 1st among the states); grapefruit (ranks 1st); tomatoes (ranks 2d); sugarcane for sugar and seed (ranks 2d).
Mining (1972): *Production value*, $396,538,000 (ranks 20th among the states). *Chief minerals*—Phosphate rock, value not available; stone, $69,530,000; cement, $60,320,000.
Fisheries (1972): *Commercial catch*, 176,271,000 pounds ($55,711,000). *Leading species by value*, Shrimp, $21,067,000; lobster, $11,780,000; red snapper, $2,859,000; mullet, $2,613,000.
Transportation: *Roads* (1972), 93,310 miles (150,164 km); *motor vehicles* (1972), 4,534,300; *railroads* (1972), 4,157 miles (6,690 km); *public airports* (1972), 114.
Communications: *Telephones* (1973), 5,103,100; *television stations* (1971), 25; *radio stations* (1971), 289; *newspapers* (1973), 52 (daily circulation, 2,166,000).

"Gainesville 8's" Stanley Michelsen (with beard) *and Alton Foss* (far right) *after not guilty verdict was announced.*

Environment. Problems ranged from a temporary but critical water shortage in the St. Petersburg area to a severe flood along the Suwannee River. Crops were ravaged and over 1,000 people abandoned their homes, but property damage was less than expected because the north central Florida region affected is a thinly populated agricultural area.

The mushrooming population of central and southern Florida began to put a serious burden on the state's underground fresh water supply, and many government officials and citizen groups asked that the water recharge areas be protected from development. If these recharge areas stop feeding fresh water into the porous limestone aquifer, there will be an insufficient water supply. There would also be danger that the limestone will become contaminated by saltwater seeping up from below.

The state cabinet favors the appropriation of state funds to begin buying the 570,000-acre Big Cypress Swamp and 64,000 acres along the Kissimmee River. Attorney General Robert Shevin's suit to halt development of the 870-square-mile Green Swamp near Disney World was denied by a state court. U. S. Sen. Lawton Chiles introduced a bill calling on the federal government to buy Big Cypress Swamp. In spite of the majority support for protection or purchase of these areas through state or federal action, land development interests protested at public hearings on the Big Cypress Swamp in November.

Controversy surrounded Florida's oil spill law and the question of offshore oil drilling. Florida's beautiful beaches and the multimillion-dollar tourist industry which they support are such a major part of the state's economy that in 1970 the legislature passed a tough oil-spill law. This law, imposing full liability, was challenged unsuccessfully in Florida's supreme court by major oil companies. There is general concern that the energy crisis might be exploited to win government approval for offshore drilling before an adequate environmental impact study is completed. Governor Askew, Senator Chiles, and others are committed to resist such action.

Legislative Session. The legislature voted full majority rights to 18- to 20-year-olds despite public opposition to granting them gambling and drinking rights. Yet, it bowed to public sentiment by not ratifying the Equal Rights Amendment for women.

The legislature failed to deal forcefully with the issue of dishonesty in government. Legislative investigations substantiated allegations that Lt. Gov. Tom Adams had been using state employees and the power of his office for personal gain. A House committee recommended his impeachment, but on May 17 the House refused by 17 votes to impeach Adams.

Concerned over the Adams affair and press allegations of misconduct by two other cabinet members, reform-minded legislators introduced a bill requiring public disclosure of income by legislators and state officials. It was overwhelmingly defeated.

In other action, the legislature passed the Deceptive and Unfair Trade Practices Act to protect consumers; a bill defining landlord-tenant rights; a bill restricting interest rates; a bill prohibiting discrimination on the basis of sex; and several bills restricting land sales and development. Major land development projects now require environmental impact studies and governmental approval.

Economy. Unemployment remained below national levels in 1973. The closing of McCoy Air Force Base in Orlando was largely compensated for by growth induced by Walt Disney World. The outlook for the citrus industry was good. However, pollution reduced catches in the fishing industry.

"Gainesville 8" Trial. On August 31, in Gainesville, a federal jury acquitted seven members of the Vietnam War Veterans Against the War, and a supporter, of conspiring to disrupt the Republican National Convention in Miami Beach in 1972.

J. LARRY DURRENCE, *Florida Southern College*

During the height of the meat shortage in the United States in 1973, packing plants were virtually empty.

FOOD

Grain production in the United States, Canada, Australia, China, and the Soviet Union rose in 1973, while European and Indian production held steady and West Africa suffered from severe drought. Food prices were high throughout the world. Wheat, rice, and other grain stocks were at low levels in many countries, and the UN Food and Agricultural Organization called for international action to stockpile wheat, rice, and corn for domestic needs and for relief of emergency shortages. This article is divided into three sections: (1) World Food Supply; (2) U. S. Food Industry; and (3) Nutrition.

WORLD FOOD SUPPLY

When world food prices went up in 1973, many people blamed farmers or businessmen or the government. The truth is, weather was the main villain.

Reduced Food Production. The weather turned bad in many countries back in 1972, although the full effects on food supplies and prices were delayed. Then during 1973 the weather changed for the better, causing some forecasters to predict that the very tight supply-demand situation would ease in 1974.

Because most of the world had poor weather in 1972, a precarious food supply situation developed worldwide. About the only place with good weather was the United States, where the total agricultural output in 1972 rose 1% to a new high. In many countries, crop-growing conditions were miserable, dragging down total world agricultural production.

A hard winter and then a dry summer cut the Soviet grain crop in 1972. Drought reduced Argentina's and Australia's grain harvests. A below-normal rainy season limited India's grain crop, and droughts and typhoons damaged the Philippine rice and corn crops. Peru's anchovy catch failed, cutting high-protein fishmeal production, and the African sub-Saharan countries suffered their fifth straight year of drought.

As a result of these difficulties, total and per capita food production in 1972 declined in both the developed and less developed regions of the world. Each of the four major developing areas—South Asia, East Asia, Latin America, and Africa—had severe declines.

U. S. Role in Food Supply. The losses caused foreign buyers to beat a path to the United States. That country was the only major supplier with much grain for sale, and it was selling at attractive prices because of dollar devaluations and previous low crop prices. This led to a great increase in the value of U. S. agricultural exports—a rise from $8.1 billion in fiscal year 1972 to $12.9 billion in fiscal year 1973. Grains accounted for more than half the total value increase, and soybeans accounted for a fourth.

The Soviet Union bought about 28 million tons of grain in 1972–73 including 18 million tons from the United States. This buying reflected a major policy reversal by the USSR, which previously had resorted to belt tightening when its crops had been bad. But in 1972 the Soviet government decided to buy food abroad to maintain its citizens' diets and expand the livestock herds despite the grain shortages.

The much-discussed grain buying by the USSR accounted for about 16% of the $4.8 billion increase in U. S. agricultural exports in fiscal year 1973, while grain sales to Western Europe accounted for 30% of the increase and sales to Japan accounted for about 22%. Japan is the single largest importer of U. S. farm goods, taking over $2 billion worth in fiscal 1973.

Low Grain Stocks. Because of the small crops overseas, the dollar devaluations, and the expanded U. S. sales of farm goods abroad, the United States ended fiscal year 1973 with the lowest stocks of wheat since 1952. Stocks of the other three major wheat exporters—Canada, Australia, and Argentina—were also at the lowest levels in two decades. Grain stocks in many other countries also were down. Thus, wheat reserves to protect against major crop failures were very low. Moreover, world supplies of rice, another major food grain, were in even more precarious balance than wheat reserves.

249

These shortages prompted an emergency meeting of representatives of major grain-exporting countries in the fall of 1973. The meeting was called by Addeke Boerma, director general of the United Nations Food and Agriculture Organization, who warned that developing countries must obtain their minimum essential grain imports if they were to avoid possible starvation.

The worldwide concern over the tight food supply also found expression in Henry Kissinger's first speech as U. S. secretary of state. In his address to the United Nations General Assembly in September, Kissinger recommended "that a world food conference be organized under UN auspices in 1974 to discuss ways to maintain adequate food supplies and to harness the efforts of all nations to meet the hunger and malnutrition resulting from natural disaster."

The Role of the "Green Revolution." Students of agriculture may wonder what happened to the much-heralded "green revolution" that had been proclaimed the savior of agriculture in the developing areas in the 1960's. The drive to adopt improved technology in agriculture, symbolized by the "green revolution" slogan, did not end. When widespread bad weather occurs, it can temporarily overcome the technological advances toward increasing output, but it cannot keep these advances from having an effect. A crude estimate is that the low grain output in drought-stricken India in 1972 would have been 15% to 20% lower without the improved farm practices brought about by the "green revolution."

Food Supply Outlook. Just as bad weather in 1972 triggered the difficulties of short supplies in 1973, good weather in 1973 led to brighter production prospects for 1974. Total grain production in 1973 rose sharply in the United States, Canada,

PROTESTING the slaughter of horses for food, riders paraded in Washington, D. C., on May 13.

Australia, the USSR, and China. European grain production for 1973 was about equal to the level in 1972. The same was true for India's wheat crop, although its coarse grain production probably exceeded its 1972 output. Rice production was headed for an increase in the major producing regions. Also, world production prospects for protein meals pointed to record crops, led by larger production of soybeans in the United States and Brazil.

There were still major uncertainties, however. The exact size of the Soviet and Chinese grain crops in 1973 and the possible import purchases or export sales by the USSR and China remained subject to wide speculation. The disastrous drought in West Africa continued, and Pakistan reeled from the effects of summer floods. Turkey, Syria, Cyprus, Jordan, and much of North Africa had droughts in 1973, and their grain crops deteriorated. Jordan and Cyprus had almost complete wheat-crop failures.

Late in 1973, farmers in the United States, Canada, and Australia were encouraged to produce as much grain as possible in 1974. Larger grain production was stimulated by higher farm prices and special incentives. More irrigation facilities, better machinery, and improved seeds were bought up around the world, and farmers scrambled for limited fertilizer supplies.

These developments added up to possibly substantial production increases in 1974. Nevertheless, just as in 1972 and 1973, the weather in 1974 would play the dominant role in the food supply situation. Fortunately, in most years, the worldwide weather has been generally friendly.

In 1954–72, per capita food production in developed regions of the world increased about 1.5% annually. Increases in the poorer regions averaged about a third of that rate because their populations increased much faster.

BENJAMIN R. BLANKENSHIP, JR.
Economic Research Service
U. S. Department of Agriculture

U. S. FOOD INDUSTRY

For the food industry, 1973 was a year of turmoil marked by natural disasters, consumer boycotts, skyrocketing prices, food shortages, and price controls. For the consumer, it was a year of decision marked by substitutions in diets, going without high-priced foods, budget juggling, and frustration over food supplies.

Supply and Price Trends. The U. S. food supply was buffeted by many factors, yet it provided American consumers with perhaps the best food in the world. Prices of food rose at an unprecedented rate, and in August reached a high of 21.5% above those of a year earlier. Consumer reaction to prices, price controls, and shortages led to meat boycotts and increased interest in home freezing and canning. While prices dropped after August, most forecasts pointed to higher food prices in the future. Diets and buying habits changed due to higher prices and shortages of meat. Forecasts indicated that meat consumption would decrease to 180.3 pounds per capita in 1973, down from a previous high of 191.8 pounds, and that total meat production would be 2.5% less than that in 1972.

Although U. S. farm productivity has risen to the point where one worker now supplies food for 51 people, prices have increased because of many factors. The American consumer now spends over $600 a year on food, whereas 20 years ago he spent

"If you have to ask 'how much,' you can't afford one!"

$350. In the same period the percentage of income spent on food dropped from slightly under 20% to about 16%. However, in 1972 alone U. S. median family income rose 8.1% to $11,120.

Weather, lower yields, increased demands, and higher costs created problems in supply and increased prices. These and other factors, such as the price control program, led to reductions of food in the market system, which in turn caused price increases and emergency buying by consumers. With the lifting of the price freeze in mid-July, food supplies approached normal in the early fall, and the overall price index dropped in September and October. Although the cost of food in 1973 was much higher than the cost in 1972, the U. S. food industry was able to provide the country and the world with high-quality food without severe shortages.

Governmental Actions. Early in 1973, the U. S. Food and Drug Administration (FDA) published regulations on nutrition labeling of foods. The partly voluntary program is designed to inform the consumer of the nutrients in food. Basically the food industry supports this principle, but it has voiced disagreement with the use of the new U. S. Recommended Daily Allowance (USRDA) percentages of protein and seven essential vitamins and minerals in a serving. (See Nutrition, page 252.)

In other regulations, the FDA defined good manufacturing practices for thermally processed low-acid foods packaged in hermetically sealed containers. These regulations cover product preparation, establishment of thermal processes, operations in thermal-processing rooms, equipment and procedures, containers, processing and production records, deviations in processing, and personnel. As part of these regulations, each company must have an operating supervisor in the thermal-processing area who is certified by an FDA-approved school no later than September 1974.

Many other governmental actions affecting the food industry were taken in 1973. New or revised standards relating to product quality, composition, and packaging were published. Also, regulations controlling food fortification ingredients, food additives, and food colors were promulgated. Of major interest was the banning of diethylstilbestrol (DES) for use in pellets implanted in cattle and sheep to stimulate growth. DES had been shown to induce cancer in laboratory test animals, and under the Delaney amendment had to be discontinued. The ban in April affected the critical meat supply, and it was expected to add to the price of meat because a longer feeding period would be necessary for animals to reach market maturity.

Research. The food industry was involved in research on new foods, forms of food, processing techniques, packaging, and quality of food, fiber, and environment.

Armour and Company received an industrial achievement award from the Institute of Food Technologists in 1973 for developing a portable instrument that tests a raw carcass and accurately predicts its tenderness after cooking. This system, in combination with the U. S. Department of Agriculture quality grade system, should assist in improving meat quality in the future.

Intensive research has been carried out on new forms of food, food combinations and food supplements, and new protein sources. Textured vegetable protein (TVP), primarily from soybeans, has been widely investigated, and it has been used in a number of food products. TVP is high in nutritional value. When used in flour, concentrate, or isolate form, it can be combined with other foods as a supplement or extender or manufactured into specific products or analogues. In addition to providing another source of protein, TVP is used for diet purposes such as cholesterol-free or calorie-controlled foods. More than 700 million pounds of soybean products were consumed in the United States in 1972, and forecasts indicate 10 to 20 times this amount will be used by 1980.

Other new developments included: sorting of fruit automatically by using light transmittance to measure internal quality; the design and operation of a prototype production line for heat processing of military rations in flexible pouches; and the continued research and development of aquaculture (fish farming) utilizing catfish, trout, salmon, crayfish, and shellfish as the main crops.

KIRBY M. HAYES
University of Massachusetts

U. S. FOOD INDUSTRY

Group	Employees[1] (1,000) 1970	Employees[1] (1,000) 1971	Value added by manufacture (billions) 1970	Value added by manufacture (billions) 1971	Value of shipments (billions) 1970	Value of shipments (billions) 1971
Meat and poultry products	317.3	313.1	$4.4	$5.0	$25.0	$26.0
Dairy products	204.4	191.3	3.7	3.9	13.7	14.6
Canned, cured, frozen foods	267.8	265.4	4.3	4.7	11.0	12.1
Grain mill products	112.7	106.6	3.3	3.4	10.8	11.1
Bakery products	255.1	243.1	4.0	4.2	7.2	7.4
Sugar (raw and refined)	30.8	29.4	0.8	0.9	2.7	2.8
Confectionery and related products	84.7	79.7	1.6	1.6	3.3	3.4
Beverages, alcoholic and nonalcoholic	229.6	217.7	5.9	6.5	12.2	13.2
Miscellaneous food products[2]	136.8	136.2	3.9	4.0	11.9	12.6
Total[3]	1,639.2	1,582.4	$31.9	$34.2	$97.6	$103.3

[1] Excludes employees at central administrative offices, distribution warehouses, and other auxiliary establishments. [2] Includes animal and vegetable oils and fats, roasted coffee, macaroni, potato chips, etc. [3] Details may not add to totals because of rounding. Source: Annual Survey of Manufacturers, U. S. Bureau of the Census.

NUTRITION

The field of nutrition gained increased stature in 1973 as concern about the quality of food supply and diets grew. Nutrition became interwoven with consumerism, food regulations, and the food industry.

Food Prices and Supply. In the United States, 1973 proved that food and feed shortages and increased food prices can alter the nutritional situation. During 1973 the consumption of meat dropped to an estimated 180.3 pounds per capita from a 1971 level of 191.8 pounds per capita. On the nutritional level these figures mean that fish, poultry, and other protein sources became substitutes for meat, perhaps bringing an improvement in the general health of the public. Not only were family diets changed but away-from-home markets such as industrial feeding and school lunch programs were affected. Thus, price and supply caused alterations within the American diet and brought about an increased public interest in nutrition.

Nutrition Labeling. In late 1969 the White House Conference on Food, Nutrition, and Health recommended that the U. S. Food and Drug Administration (FDA) consider the development of a system for identifying the nutritional qualities of food. The first format for nutrition labeling was published in March 1972 with further regulations appearing throughout 1973. The well studied and tested program will have a profound effect on the entire food industry, on nutrition education, and on the consumer. Its aim is to have the label inform consumers what nutrients are in the food they buy.

The program, while voluntary, does require a manufacturer to use nutrition labeling when he adds any nutrient to the food or when he makes some nutritional claim on the label or in advertising. The package's nutrition panel will list how many calories and how much protein, carbohydrates, and fat a serving will supply. It will also show what percentage of the U. S. Recommended Daily Allowance (USRDA) of protein and seven essential vitamins and minerals a serving will provide. It may also show amounts of saturated and unsaturated fat, cholesterol, and sodium in the food as well as the percentages of USRDA for other vitamins and minerals.

The label format is designed to be easily understood and used by consumers, nutritionists, and other workers in the field. The basic design permits the user to determine quickly the size of a serving whether expressed in ounces, slices, units, or cupfuls. The quantities of nutrients are expressed in terms of a serving. Variations of the basic design are permitted to include food after cooking or showing nutrients in a finished product. Since the label shows percentage of USRDA, consumers need only add the percentages of all foods eaten in a day to determine their nutritional standing. Certain foods, such as infant and baby foods (smaller serving size and special RDA) and special dietary foods, are exempt from nutritional labeling requirements or are subject to special regulations.

While many segments of the food industry have spoken against the regulations on the basis of cost, inadequate information, dislike of format, and disagreement with the USRDA, all labels ordered after Dec. 31, 1973, must comply, as must food shipped interstate after Dec. 31, 1974. Although nutrition labeling regulations may not solve all nutrition problems, it is a giant step toward educating the consumer. (See also CONSUMERISM.)

Nutrition Education. Although nutrition labeling provides factual information, it does not substitute for consumer education. A unified approach to nutrition education for all levels of the population is needed, but there were few active and coordinated programs in 1973. A "Child Nutrition Education Act of 1973" that calls for the development of sound nutrition education programs for children, school food service personnel, and teachers, administered by the Department of Agriculture (USDA) was proposed, but not enacted.

Food Assistance Programs. Federally sponsored programs to provide food to the nation's children, elderly, and other needy groups are overseen by the USDA and the Department of Health, Education, and Welfare (HEW). The Child Food Service Programs ("School Lunch") of USDA represent a $2.6 billion a year industry and encompass three programs: School Lunch, School Breakfast, and Special Food Service. The programs have roughly 40 million daily participants (a child can participate in more than one program) with School Lunch having about 25 million. In November, President Nixon signed a law that provided additional federal assistance to the school lunch and school breakfast programs. The milk subsidy bill, which had been under fire, was funded at the same level as in 1972 and became effective November 1.

The Agriculture and Consumer Protection Act of 1973 amends the 1964 Food Stamp Act. Amendments include: implementation of a nationwide food stamp program by June 30, 1974; the redefinition of eligible foods to include imported items and seeds and plants for home gardens; semi-annual coupon allotment adjustment to reflect food price changes; and a provision to allow the elderly to use food coupons for meal purchases in communal dining situations, plus other broadening changes. Under HEW, which administers the Older Americans Act, nutrition programs for the elderly will receive USDA donated foods without regard to whether elderly people are needy. In May, President Nixon signed a bill extending aid to the elderly for three years but at reduced levels.

Food Quality. In August, the USDA's Consumer and Food Economics Institute began collecting nutrient data on composition of foods from food processors. The Nutrient Data Bank will computerize detailed data on nutrient composition for use by food scientists, consumers, and food manufacturers. The FDA is cooperating in the project.

Food additives and food ingredients generally recognized as safe (GRAS) were studied extensively. A select committee is reviewing the 533 GRAS substances and will advise the FDA on the safety of each ingredient. In July the FDA proposed establishing a classification of foods and of ingredients for direct addition to human food according to their purposes.

The Uniform Retail Meat Identity Standards Program, a voluntary program coordinated by the National Livestock and Meat Board and backed by government, industry, and consumer groups, is trying to reduce confusion and help the consumer by having each meat cut carry the same name wherever it is sold in the country. It is expected the program will be in wide use by the middle of 1974.

KIRBY M. HAYES
University of Massachusetts

FORD, Gerald R. See BIOGRAPHY; UNITED STATES.

FOREIGN AID

Economic assistance from industrialized nations to developing countries continued at levels well below official goals in 1972. Nonetheless the aid-receiving countries, except for the least developed, were achieving significant economic growth. Early data indicated that these trends continued in 1973.

Aid from Industrialized Nations. According to the Development Assistance Committee (DAC) of the Organization for Economic Cooperation and Development, the net flow of resources from DAC's 16 industrialized member nations—who account for about 95% of the economic aid to developing countries—totaled $19.4 billion in 1972, compared with $18.1 billion in 1971. In real terms, after accounting for price rises and exchange rate changes, the 1972 total declined an estimated 3% from the 1971 volume. Measured as a percentage of the gross national product (GNP) of the advanced nations, the 1972 flow of resources was 0.77%, down from 0.82% in 1971.

The most important component of this total resources flow is the concessional governmental aid known as official development assistance (ODA), which rose from $7.7 billion in 1971 to $8.6 billion in 1972. The ODA increase in real terms was calculated at around 1%. Expressed as percentage of donor GNP the ODA slipped from 0.35% to 0.34%, compared with a UN target of 0.7%.

Other components of the 1972 total included other official flows, $1.5 billion (1971, $1.3 billion); private investment and credits, $8.3 billion (1971, $8.2 billion); and grants by private voluntary agencies, $1 billion (1971, $900 billion).

The total aid amounted to about $10 per person in the developing countries, a decline of about 5% from 1971 in real terms and a reversal of the long-term average yearly increase of 3% from 1962 to 1972. Nonetheless the economies of the aid-receiving countries generally rebounded from slowdowns during 1970–71. The World Bank's 1973 annual report indicated a 6% GNP growth by developing countries in 1972, a 3% rise per capita after accounting for population increases. Raising the average were the nations exporting petroleum and manufactured goods in large volume. The 25 "least developed" countries showed only a 2.5% GNP growth in 1972 and no rise at all in GNP per capita.

Multilateral Assistance. Governmental contributions to international aid institutions continued to climb, reeaching a record $1.9 billion in 1972, up from $1.3 billion in 1971.

The World Bank group—the International Bank for Reconstruction and Development (IBRD), the International Development Agency (IDA), and the International Finance Corp.—approved a record $3.6 billion in development assistance in fiscal 1973, led by a 36% increase in IDA lending over 1972. For the first time, agriculture became the biggest single-sector recipient of IBRD and IDA funds, replacing transportation. World Bank President Robert S. McNamara, reporting a successful doubling of operations in 1969–73, proposed a further increase of 40% over the next five years involving $22 billion for nearly 1,000 aid projects.

The United Nations Development Program (UNDP) continued to expand with a $359 million program in fiscal 1973, up 10% from the previous year. The developing countries contributed about 60% of the funds for the UNDP projects.

CARL PURCELL—AGENCY FOR INTERNATIONAL DEVELOPMENT

DROUGHT-STRICKEN Africa receives U. S. food through Agency for International Development (AID). Here, workers in Dakar, Senegal, fill bags with sorghum.

U. S. Aid. The total U. S. economic aid flow in 1972 was $7.3 billion, up $0.5 billion over the year before in dollar terms but down from 0.64 to 0.63 in percentage of GNP. U. S. official development assistance, at $3.3 billion, dropped from 43% of the DAC total in 1971 to 40% in 1972 and from 0.32 to 0.29 in percentage of U. S. GNP.

In Congress, the House Foreign Affairs Committee initiated and the Senate Foreign Relations Committee approved a major overhaul of the foreign assistance law. U. S. bilateral economic assistance was focused on major problems common to developing countries, such as food, population, health, and education, with the aim of helping the poorest masses of people. An omnibus aid appropriation bill of $5.8 billion for fiscal 1974, passed in December 1973, included $1.3 billion for various economic assistance programs, mostly bilateral; $788 million for international development banks; $450 million for postwar economic help to the Indochina states, not including North Vietnam; and $925 million in military assistance and credit sales globally. Also in the bill was $2.2 billion in emergency arms aid to Israel.

Aid from Communist Nations. The USSR, the East European countries, and the People's Republic of China extended new economic credits and grants to noncommunist developing countries totaling $1.7 billion in 1972, fractionally below the 1971 level, according to the State Department. The main recipients were Near East and South Asian nations.

LEWIS GULICK
Staff Consultant, House Foreign Affairs Committee

253

FORESTRY AND LUMBERING

Conservation was the dominant issue in forestry during 1973. Proposals for a new federal department of natural resources, legislation to provide increased incentives to landowners to grow timber, and congressional authorization for a federal-state program of land-use planning were among the major developments in the United States. The year was also marked by litigation over timber-cutting programs on public lands.

Proposed New Department. At the request of the administration, Sen. Henry M. Jackson (D.-Wash.) introduced legislation to establish in the federal government a new Department of Energy and Natural Resources. To this new energy department would be transferred the Department of Agriculture's Forest Service and the Interior Department's Bureau of Land Management.

Federal Legislation. Legislation to continue the Agricultural Adjustment Program, authorized in 1970, was approved by both houses of Congress. The bills would give the secretary of agriculture authority to establish a "set-aside" program for wheat, feed grains, and cotton, and to provide for federal cost-sharing of vegetative cover on the set-aside acreage to prevent wind and water erosion. The bills also called for establishment of a $25 million Forestry Incentive Program to encourage owners of small nonindustrial woodlands to apply practices that would provide for reforestation of cutover, nonstocked, or understocked forest lands and for multiple-purpose management of the forest growth. Holdings under the plan may not exceed 500 acres.

The U. S. Congress also had under consideration a land-use bill which would authorize federal grants to states and encourage development of land-use planning programs.

Opposition to Increased Cutting. The Natural Resources Defense Council, joined by the Sierra Club and the Wilderness Society, brought suit in U. S. District Court for the District of Columbia for an injunction to halt the Forest Service from increasing timber sale offerings by 1.1 billion board feet, to a total of 11.8 billion feet, to help meet national needs for housing construction. The Forest Service maintained that the increased offering was still below the allowable cut which could be sustained annually by new growth.

Japanese Purchases. Increased Japanese purchases of U. S. softwood logs in the Pacific Northwest led to proposals for some restriction on U. S. exports. However, as a result of negotiations between Japanese officials and the U. S. ambassador in Tokyo, Japan agreed to reduce its purchases of U. S. softwood logs by 10.9% in the 1974 fiscal year. Japanese imports during the preceding year amounted to 2.52 billion board feet.

U. S. Forest Service. For the fiscal year 1974, President Nixon's budget requested a total of $456,-972,000 for the Forest Service of the U. S. Department of Agriculture. This was a cut of nearly $105 million from the amount appropriated for 1973. In Congress, however, the House increased the Forest Service appropriation by nearly $20 million over the budget request. Major items in the appropriation were $259,700,000 for protection and management of the national forests, $90,700,000 for forest roads and trails, $59,145,000 for forest research, and $27,760,000 for federal cooperation with states and private owners of forest lands.

The Forest Service in 1973 was administering 182,340,000 acres of national forests, 3,802,000 acres of national grasslands, 149,000 acres of land utilization projects, and 121,880 acres of research and experimental forests. Forest research was being carried on at eight regional forest experiment stations, at the Forest Products Laboratory in Madison, Wis., and at the Institute of Tropical Forestry in Puerto Rico.

Reforestation. The Forest Service reported that acreage planted to trees in 1972 totaled 1,680,175 acres. This was a decrease of 12,764 acres from the preceding year's figure. The total included plantings for wind barriers and for Christmas tree production. Of the total, nearly 1.3 million acres were planted by private landowners, 318,000 acres by federal agencies (chiefly the Forest Service), and 65,300 acres by states and local governments. The private planting included 920,540 acres planted by forest industries and other industries (mining, railroads, water, and power companies), the remainder being planted by farmers and other small owners.

Fire. Favorable weather helped to hold forest fire losses in the United States to moderate levels in the first half of 1973, but late summer brought some serious outbreaks in a number of localities in the Western states.

For the United States as a whole, the Forest Service reported a total of 124,554 fires in 1972, which burned a total of 2,641,166 acres. Of the more than 1.3 billion acres of forest and other wild lands classed as needing protection, about 7%, mostly in the Southern states, still lacked organized protection services. Some 29% of the burned area in 1972 was on these unprotected lands.

Lumber. Production of lumber in the United States in 1972 was estimated by the National Forest Products Association at 38,815,000,000 board feet, an increase of about 2.2 billion over 1971. Lumber output in the first four months of 1973 was running at a seasonally adjusted rate of about 1.7% above that recorded in 1972.

In Canada, lumber production in 1970 totaled 11,353,024,000 board feet, a decline of about 227 million feet from the preceding year. More than 95% of the total was softwood lumber.

The UN estimated world production of sawnwood in 1970 at 416,625,100 cubic meters, a 3 million increase over 1969. (One cubic meter equals 424 board feet.) About 75% of the total represented softwood (coniferous) sawnwood, but the bulk of the increase was in hardwood production.

The Soviet Union ranked first in lumber production, with 118,090,000 cubic meters, followed by the United States with 84,725,000 cubic meters, Japan with 42,989,000 cubic meters, and Canada with 26,776,000 cubic meters.

CHARLES E. RANDALL, *"Journal of Forestry"*

U. S. LUMBER PRODUCTION, 1971–72

(In million board feet)

Producing Regions	1971	1972
Southern pine region	7,734	8,337
Douglas fir region	8,283	8,892
Western pine region	10,019	10,436
California redwood region	2,312	2,423
Other softwoods	1,296	1,482
Total softwoods	29,744	31,570
Southern hardwoods	3,456	3,455
Appalachian hardwoods	1,259	1,460
Other hardwoods	2,234	2,329
Total hardwoods	6,949	7,244

GAMMA

In Paris, 100,000 French college students march on April 2 from the Gare de l'Est to the Place de la Nation to protest abolition of military deferments for students.

FRANCE

The French Republic moved through the year 1973 quietly and prosperously, without much visible change in internal or external policies. The serious domestic upheavals that some had predicted did not materialize. With minor political effervescence and social protest, this booming, introverted nation made its way through difficulties stemming from the international energy crisis that threatened its neighbors with restrictions and discomforts in the winter of 1973–74. By and large, the French under the regime of President Georges Pompidou were faring very well.

DOMESTIC AFFAIRS

Politics. The year began with predictions of trouble for the ruling Union of Democrats for the Republic (UDR) and its allies. Because of the tax-evasion and influence-peddling scandals of 1972, and the five-year united-action pact between the Communists and the Socialists, it was thought that the government might be toppled in the two-round March elections for the National Assembly. Other observers correctly predicted, however, that there would be no dramatic shifts. An important factor is that the constituencies are so drawn as to favor the rural conservative right.

The tough Minister of the Interior Raymond Marcellin opened the campaign on February 12 with tactics calculated to frighten the electorate about the consequences of a government defeat. The president himself brandished the possibility of defeat and subsequent institutional instability, but he intervened only from on high, using TV and radio to his advantage. Pompidou ordered the state radio and TV network to show Communist leader Georges Marchais extensively because "he frightens people" (though in fact Marchais was studiedly moderate),

FRANCE • Information Highlights

Official Name: French Republic.

Location: Western Europe.

Area: 211,207 square miles (547,026 sq km).

Population (1973 est.): 52,300,000. *Density,* 243 per square mile (94 per sq km).

Chief Cities (1968 census): Paris, the capital, 2,590,771; Marseille, 889,029; Lyon, 527,800; Toulouse, 370,796; Nice, 322,442.

Government: *Head of state,* Georges Pompidou, president (took office June 1969). *Chief minister,* Pierre Messmer, premier (took office July 1972). *Legislature*—Parliament: Senate and National Assembly. *Major political parties*—Union of Democrats for the Republic; Independent Republican; Socialist; Communist; Center for Democracy and Progress.

Education: *Expenditure* (1969), 22.3% of total public expenditure. *School enrollment* (1969)—primary, 5,019,837; secondary, 4,106,647; technical/vocational, 953,609; university/higher, 615,326.

Monetary Unit: Franc (4.250 francs equal U. S.$1, Sept. 1973).

Gross National Product (1972 est.): $186,000,000,000.

Economic Indexes: *Industrial production* (1972), 173 (1963 = 100); *agricultural production* (1971), 127 (1963 = 100); *consumer price index* (1972), 147 (1963 = 100).

Manufacturing (major products): Steel, machinery, metals, chemicals, automobiles, processed foods, textiles, aircraft, beverages, clothing.

Major Agricultural Products: Barley (ranks 3d among world producers, 1972), wheat (world rank 5th, 1972), oats, sugar beets, vegetables, apples, grapes, cattle, fish.

Major Minerals: Iron ore (ranks 4th among world producers, 1971), coal, bauxite, sulfur, potash, lead, zinc, natural gas.

Foreign Trade (1972): *Exports,* $25,848,000,000; *Imports,* $26,715,000,000. *Chief trading partners* (1970)—West Germany (took 24% of exports, supplied 25% of imports); Belgium-Luxembourg (13%—12%); Italy (12%—11%); United States (6%—9%).

Tourism: Receipts (1971), $1,451,300,000.

Transportation: *Motor vehicles* (1971), 16,321,000 (automobiles, 13,400,000); *railroads* (1971), 22,706 miles (36,540 km); *merchant fleet* (1972), 7,420,000 gross registered tons; *major national airline,* Air France.

Communications: *Telephones* (1972), 9,546,173; *newspapers* (1969), 106 (daily circulation, 11,957,000); *television stations* (1971), 106; *television sets,* 10,200,000.

255

PRESIDENT GEORGES POMPIDOU casts his ballot on March 4 as France elects a new National Assembly.

and he branded Socialist leader François Mitterrand an ambitious "left-wing fascist."

As March neared, the chances of an upset evaporated. Only the personal performances of Mitterrand and Finance Minister Valéry Giscard d'Estaing, probable candidates for the presidency in 1976, aroused public interest. Mitterrand called for social and electoral reform. Giscard predicted that socialism would wreck the economy, lower the living standard, and destroy the European Economic Community (Common Market). Premier Pierre Messmer, scarcely more than the president's spokesman, made no impression.

The first round took place on March 4. Nearly 25 million of the 30 million eligible voters went to the polls. More than 3,000 candidates ran for 490 seats. The initial outcome was a strong United Left showing. Some cabinet ministers were forced into the second round. Only 58 seats were won outright, through absolute majorities. The days preceding the March 11 runoff were filled with deals for withdrawals in favor of front-running candidates. The Gaullists arranged some reciprocal withdrawals with Jean Lecanuet's centralist Reformers. Knowing that even a trailing Socialist might draw more votes than a front-running Communist, Mitterrand vainly sought Marchais' approval of support for whatever candidate had the best chance. Marchais insisted on the pact. Allies, but hardly friends, Communists and Socialists retained their mutual suspicions. A splinter group of Radicals supported them. Those centrist Radicals behind Jean-Jacques Servan-Schreiber held aloof from them and the Lecanuet group. The always fragile center thus narrowed down.

The March 11 ballot gave the Gaullist coalition a working majority, with no need for the Reformers' support ("We ask nothing," Lecanuet remarked bitterly). But the UDR, with 185 seats, had an increased dependency on Giscard's Independent Republicans (54 seats) and Jacques Duhamel's Demo-

cratic center (21 seats). Evidently the electorate had responded as Pompidou had hoped to his dictum that it had a "simple choice of Marxist communism or freedom." Notwithstanding discontent with the governing coalition, the electorate's fear of Reds, riots, nationalizations, and tax reform carried the day. Down from 365 to 275 seats, the coalition might have to take account of demand for change.

All the same, the Communists (73 seats) had shown themselves weaker than the Socialists (89 seats), a result confirmed in the cantonal elections on September 30. The old hard-lining Gaullists who consider Pompidou less than de Gaulle's heir had been diminished by contrast with the loose hangers-on attracted by party success rather than doctrine. Whatever the ritual invocations of Gaullist ideology and vocabulary, "hard and pure" Gaullism was dying. Even if there was some truth in Giscard's observation that "France wants to be governed at the center," clearly neither his Independents nor the UDR represented anything of the kind. Pompidou received less than a mandate but more than a reprieve. Even the conservative Figaro admitted that the gerrymandered electoral districts did not reflect opinion accurately.

Contrary to expectation, Pompidou reappointed Messmer premier on April 2. Faithful to de Gaulle, and now to Pompidou, Messmer symbolized Gaullist orthodoxy though he did nothing to advance it. Truly representative of this orthodoxy was Michel Debré, who was replaced as defense minister by Robert Galley. Giscard's ambitions were strengthened by the appointment of the Independents' secretary general, Michel Poniatowski, as minister of health and social security. Foreign Minister Maurice Schumann, an old Gaullist who lost his Assembly seat in the elections, was replaced by Pompidou's chief of staff, Michel Jobert. In all, nine were dropped from the first Messmer cabinet.

Commentators were quick to say the elections and the new cabinet showed the desire for "social renewal." Messmer promised this as readily as his predecessor Jacques Chaban-Delmas once promised a "new society." Theoretically in line with the president's declared responsiveness to opinion was his April 3 proposal to reduce the presidential term from 7 to 5 years, effective in 1976. He gave no clear reason for urging this constitutional reform. Pompidou had his bill submitted to Parliament on a take-it-or-leave-it basis. Needing a three-fifths majority in the joint sitting, with the Gaullists deeply divided, the amendment had no chance. Debré and former Premier Maurice Couve de Murville rejected it as contrary to General de Gaulle's thought. Messmer scorned such idolatrous views of the 1958 constitution "as if it were an immutable monument, the least aspect of which must remain inviolate under pain of sacrilege." At his September 27 press conference, Pompidou snapped, "I don't have to take lessons in Gaullism from anybody—you heard me, anybody. . . . I don't say I'm doing what he would have done, but I defy anyone pretending to know what he would have done." The UDR rift went deep. On October 24, Pompidou broadcast his decision to let the matter drop until 1976.

A crisis of confidence loomed again for the regime. Giscard's Independents were increasingly ambitious rivals, biding their time. Hostility simmered between the old orthodoxy and Pompidou's "catchall Gaullism." Yet the insulation of executive power from parliamentary control was not reduced.

The Senate, though critical of the regime, remained harmless. The National Assembly, although it elected Edgar Faure, an active, moderate, and unorthodox Gaullist to its presidency on April 2, remained one of the most ineffectual elected bodies in the Western world. Deputies listened to ministerial reform proposals with complacency or cynicism, and applauded or booed Mitterrand's sneering attacks, but in 1973 the chamber showed little life. Arguing that only Parliament could handle the structural problems facing the nation, Faure infused no spirit into this pale assembly. Power in France remained at the president's Élysée Palace. Pompidou, a man with no parliamentary experience at all, continued de Gaulle's policy of ignoring the chambers between elections. "The result," noted a writer in *Le Monde,* "is a feeling of frustration. The state becomes a machine for alienating citizens, who no longer have a hand in shaping their destiny." The president's "principle of solitude" was said to threaten the regime.

But the administration's style remained tough. The new minister for cultural affairs, Maurice Druon, academician and novelist without party, came out swinging in May, denouncing the "intellectual terrorism" of "people who come to this ministry's door with a begging cup in one hand and a Molotov cocktail in the other." Thousands of actors, film stars, playwrights, poets, painters, sculptors, and singers marched against him in Paris on May 13, appalled by his negativism and cultural priorities (first, preservation of monuments; then, teaching; lastly, stimulation of the arts). Even the hard-lining director of the state radio and TV network, Arthur Conte, protested in October against government interference (on domestic and Middle East news). When the minister of information, Philippe Malaud (an Independent), denounced the radio service as "a den of Communists," Pompidou fired Conte and put Malaud in a minor cabinet post.

Wiretapping. Pompidou ignored parliamentary and press criticism of government wiretapping, an operation long practiced. Strangely, the storm over wiretapping in 1973 was broken by Michel Poniatowski's complaints to president, party, and press. The government offered no explanation or apology for this vast daily operation, covering from 1,000 to 5,000 phones of journalists, politicians, embassies, and various individuals, monitored by civil and military personnel under army direction. A Senate committee (Gaullists refusing participation) was informed by an official on June 19 that the operation was none of its business, that the purpose was control of political extremism, and that Senate supervision would harm state security. The committee's report in November denounced 99% of the taps as illegal, revealed obstruction of the inquiry by Pompidou and the cabinet, and declared the purpose to be not safeguarding of the state but political espionage and personal blackmail.

Wiretapping brought the government under heavy fire in December. Early in the month, the new offices of *Le Canard Enchaîné,* a famous satirical—and antigovernment—weekly, were discovered to have been "bugged." Premier Messmer quickly called the incident "a practical joke." But investigation proved that the installation was a sophisticated one, and members of Parliament, frustrated by past controversies, raised a clamor. The press, too, opened fire. Premier Messmer then called the incident "extremely bizarre," but the culprits remained at large.

Strikes and Violence. In March, thousands of students all over France struck against a new law eliminating draft deferments for most college students. Ritual stone-throwing by the demonstrators brought the usual tear-gassing and clubbing by riot police in the capital. Class boycotting, school closures, and street agitation, backed by trade unions,

"Me? I drank radioactive water," says the sign worn by one Parisian protesting current French nuclear tests.

followed for a month. The government finally promised restoration of some measure of deferment. One result of the agitation was increased public discussion of the purpose of military service.

The ghost of 1968's disorders appeared briefly again in Paris on June 21, when the government authorized the New Order, a racist, anti-Semitic party, to meet to protest the immigration of North African and black African workers into France. The predictable result was violent left-wing assault and serious personal and property damage. On June 28, both the New Order and the far-left, Trotskyite Communist League were outlawed. It was certain that the barely contained violence of French fringe groups would burst forth again.

Industrial strikes continued during 1973. Forbidden since 1964 to strike, air-traffic controllers went out from February 20 to March 20. When military controllers took over, pilots struck briefly against air hazards.

More significant socially was the immigrant workers' strike at the state-owned Renault automobile plant in Paris, which partially closed the factory in March and April. The Renault workers—representative of exploited, unskilled foreigners, many illegally in France and hence subject to employer blackmail—sparked stoppages at other plants. At issue generally was the government's declared program of raising minimum monthly wages to $200 and of making retirement available at age 50 on the existing terms covering age 65.

Concerning immigrants specifically, the government denied that racism and other hatred of foreigners was characteristic of French society, a disavowal that was too general to cover evidence across the past decades. A May Day workers' parade highlighted the plight of Spanish, Portuguese, and North African immigrants. Whether the United Left's election pledges to improve conditions for immigrant workers would have any results remained to be seen.

Other strike actions included a month-long protest, ending in mid-June, by social security employees against low wages, poor housing, and inefficient administration. Lip watch-factory workers in Besançon seized their plant on June 12, following warnings of imminent shutdown as a result of U. S. and Japanese competition. Continuing manufacture, they sold at wholesale prices, refused a government compromise plan preserving all but 400 jobs, and defied a court order to cease their action. Unions rallied in support, but eventually, during the August holiday season, busloads of police were sent in to evict them. A fruit and meat retailers' strike, protesting the government's November 2 measures to combat inflation by controlling already minimal profit margins, was another manifestation of economic and social discontent.

Scandals. At least two scandals (in addition to the wiretapping revelations) diverted the nation. The wider-reaching, perhaps, concerned the prestigious Bordeaux region wine industry. In June, tax inspectors impounded 2 million bottles bearing Cruse labels on suspicion of adulteration and fraudulent labeling. The affair, recalling struggles between Catholic growers and Protestant merchants, was envenomed by the political struggle between Finance Minister Giscard d'Estaing and Jacques Chaban-Delmas, the mayor of Bordeaux and a former premier, each of whom harbors presidential ambitions for 1976. Some observers suspected that the struggle stemmed from Giscard's effort to erode Chaban's reputation. But by October, 12 merchants were accused of violating the wine laws.

In a second scandal, the body of Marshal Philippe Pétain, the World War I hero who headed the collaborationist regime in World War II, was abducted from its tomb on the Île d'Yeu, off western France, on February 19, by a small group of right-wing supporters. The heavy casket was found two days later in a suburban Paris garage after the ring leader held a press conference, was arrested, and led the police to the hiding place. The intent to force an embarrassed government on the eve of elections to do what de Gaulle had always refused—to inter the disgraced marshal at the Douaumont war cemetery, near Verdun—failed. Pompidou had the body returned to the Île d'Yeu, but he also sent a wreath.

Economy. The French economy remained relatively healthy in 1973. Productivity was high. Fears of left-wing electoral success caused increased flow of liquid assets to Switzerland. Government victory reassured capital, and growth continued to be the administration's basic aim. Making gestures late in the year to curb food prices, Giscard had no overall program: "If we can avoid a policy of constraint, it would be much better for France."

Middle- and low-income housing remained desperately short, the gap between low and high wages enormous, and the inequities of taxation gross. The most dynamic presence may have been that of Jean Royer, minister of commerce and crafts (that is, small business and shopkeepers), with an unprogressive constituency like that to which Pierre Poujade appealed two decades ago.

Nuclear Testing. France continued atmospheric nuclear testing, despite its previous denials of intent to resume in 1973, at Mururoa atoll in the Pacific from July 21 to August 29. Australia and New Zealand obtained an injunction from the International Court of Justice on June 21, which France ignored. New Zealand sent frigates into the test zone. Various civilian boats defied the French ban, several being seized and the Canadian crew of one assaulted. A cascade of condemnations from Sweden to Peru and Japan had no effect.

Domestically, there was more protest over the testing from the press than from the street. Most shrill was the collision between the bishop of Orléans and the chief of staff of the navy in an escalating church–armed forces quarrel. Having spent some $15 billion, France was still decades behind the superpowers and falling further back.

FOREIGN AFFAIRS

The president and his foreign ministers maintained familiar positions on peace, security, and cooperation. They feared U. S. troop withdrawal from Europe but refused to widen the concerns of the North Atlantic Treaty Organization (NATO) in the economic sphere. Holding firmly to the Gaullist conception of a Europe of sovereign states, Pompidou at his September 27 press conference called for union by 1980. Disapproving the Mutual Balanced Force Reductions (MBFR) and Strategic Arms Limitation Talks (SALT) discussions, he supported the Soviet-initiated European security conference.

French relations with Britain were cordial. In Paris, on May 21–22, Pompidou and Prime Minister Edward Heath agreed that a proposed Atlantic summit was "premature" and that no special trade concessions should be made to the United States because

MEETING world leaders, President Pompidou shakes hands with U. S. President Nixon in Reykjavik, Iceland (left) and with USSR Chairman Brezhnev near Paris.

of the expanded Common Market, heavy U. S. defense commitments in Europe, and Europe's relatively strong recovery. In London in mid-November they toasted the signing of a treaty to construct and operate an English Channel tunnel costing $2 billion. The future of their vastly expensive Concorde supersonic transport remained dubious, sales being minimal and criticism in Britain severe.

Ten years after the signing of their historic treaty of cooperation, France and West Germany, though linked by economic and cultural exchanges, were divided on Europe's future. In Paris in January and in Bonn in June, Pompidou and Chancellor Willy Brandt agreed on asserting "a European identity," but their relations were cool. The French feared Brandt's acceptance of European neutralization in return for an active role in Eastern Europe. Some spoke of possible renewed German nationalism. For their part, the Germans reproached the French for so long opposing a united Europe and for still preventing reform of the Common Market agricultural policy that benefits France.

Pompidou's talks with Soviet Communist party General Secretary Leonid Brezhnev, in Russia in January and in France in June, did not quash French fears of a Soviet-American arrangement on Europe. France opposed a summit meeting of the European security conference powers, but concluded further scientific, technical, economic, and industrial accords with the Soviets. Foreign Minister Schumann visited Rumania in January. The Yugoslav foreign minister visited France in June. Premier Messmer and Foreign Minister Jobert visited Budapest and then Sofia in July to discuss possible industrial and cultural cooperation.

Though it banned a Paris conference on U. S. draft-dodger amnesty in January, the government continued to reproach the United States for insufficient dollar support, for requesting compensation of costs incurred in the 1966–67 eviction of American forces from France, and for possible collusion with the Soviet Union to neutralize Europe. The

Pompidou-Nixon meeting in Iceland on May 31 and June 1 solved no problems. The French discouraged a Nixon visit to Europe in the autumn and a summit meeting to sign a "new Atlantic Charter." They were skeptical about the November alert of U. S. forces during the Middle East war and unwilling to back U. S. reinforcement of Israel. To American reproaches, Le Monde retorted that Europeans were being treated like a schoolchild scoring zero for deportment.

Beneath a somewhat cool high-level standoff, Franco-Canadian exchanges were normal. De Gaulle's emphatic affirmation of French concern for Quebec had long since faded away. France's seizure of a Canadian boat defying the nuclear test-site ban, bringing charges that its crew was beaten and one man hospitalized, occasioned only futile protests and categoric French denials of assault.

In the Middle East, France remained friendly to the Arab states. It denied that Libya's Mirage jets were being used in the war and actively cultivated that oil-rich country, whose leader visited Paris in November. France urged the Common Market nations to coordinate their Middle East policies.

French relations with African and Asian states were good in 1973. Following a short stay in the Territory of the Afars and the Issas (the colony formerly known as French Somaliland) in mid-January, Pompidou visited Ethiopia. After an unprecedented visit to France in June by the Chinese foreign minister, Pompidou became the first West European head of state to visit Communist China, from September 11 to 17. In a delicate test, he met with Chairman Mao Tse-tung and Premier Chou En-lai to assure them that détente did not mean encouraging Russia to turn against the East. At the same time, he avoided expressing his own suspicion of Mutual Balanced Force Reductions. Thus disappointing his hosts, he was nonetheless criticized in the Soviet press. En route home, the president conferred briefly with the shah of Iran.

JOHN C. CAIRNS, *University of Toronto*

GARDENING AND HORTICULTURE

At no time since World War II has public enthusiasm for home gardening been so great as it was in 1973. Fruits, vegetables, ornamentals, and landscape plants all shared in the vast upsurge of interest. Three roses, two floribundas and one hybrid tea, took top honors in the All-America Rose Selections competition. A zinnia was the only gold medal winner among other All-America entries. Labor problems continued to plague commercial horticulturists during 1973.

Labor and Agricultural Mechanization. The report *Hard Tomatoes, Hard Times*—published by the Agribusiness Accountability Project, Washington, D. C., in late 1972 and written by James Hightower—indicted the land grant college system for failure to respond to the needs of rural America and for catering to the big farmer. The report charged that mechanization was causing "hard times" for the family farmer. The "hard tomatoes" in the title refers to a new variety of tomatoes, developed at the University of Florida, that is adapted to mechanical harvesting. The author apparently assumes that there is an ample supply of labor to perform the dirty, menial jobs now performed by machines that have been developed through long hours of research at various agricultural experiment stations. He further assumes that it is desirable to maintain these jobs and that bigness is necessarily counterproductive in dealing with sociological concerns such as unemployment. The fact is that domestic labor will not perform jobs such as hand-picking of strawberries, tomatoes, beans, and similar crops. Commercial horticulturists are currently faced with many problems other than labor shortages, and how quickly and how well these problems are solved will determine whether food shortages and high prices will continue to plague the American consumer.

All-America Selections. Once more the grueling two-year tests are completed, and three new All-America award-winning roses have been selected for 1974. These are the pink-orange Bahia, the fragrant pink Perfume Delight, and the pink and white bicolored Bon-Bon. Six other flowers and two vegetables won All-America medals.

Roses. Bahia is described as a very floriferous floribunda. The most important asset of a rose of the floribunda class is abundance of bloom, and certainly Bahia possesses that characteristic. The flowers of Bahia are 2½-inch blooms, of a vivid pink-orange color, borne in clusters of three to many. The double blossoms are made up of 20 to 30 petals, plus 10 to 18 petaloids. Their garden value is enhanced by the fact that they hold their bright color until the petals fall, all the while gently exuding a spicy fragrance. Bahia—a product of the well-known U. S. hybridizer, Walter E. Lammerts—resulted from a cross between Rumba and Tropicana.

Perfume Delight, a hybrid tea, is a richly fragrant clear pink rose. A creation of O. L. Weeks of California—who originated Gypsy, a 1972 winner—this magnificent rose sweetly contradicts the often-heard comment that modern roses do not have the fragrance of "those in my grandmother's garden." A single bloom of Perfume Delight will fill a room with fragrance. The coloring of Perfume Delight extends from the outermost to the innermost segments of the flower and lasts throughout its life. Thirty broad satiny petals make up the large, well-formed blooms, which often measure 5 inches in diameter. It is not surprising that this selection has beauty and a rich, spicy fragrance. Its ancestral background includes five All-America award winners, with three—Charlotte Armstrong, Mirandy, and Chrysler Imperial—noted for their fragrance.

Bon-Bon, an ideal landscaping floribunda, is densely covered with delightful pink and white bicolor blooms, beautifully displayed over masses of bright green leaflets. The flowers of this award-winner are borne in large clusters, opening continuously from spring until autumn frosts. Bon-Bon is as richly fragrant as it is colorful, and it has the additional asset of dropping its petals cleanly. The pink and cream buds in the clusters pop open to rounded, cupped 3½-inch blooms, each formed by as many as 25 petals of extraheavy substance. Bon-Bon comes from a famous line of ancestors, including such well-known names as Bridal Pink, Spartan, and Fashion. Its direct parents are Bridal Pink and Yellow Seedling 58-6792. It was hybridized in 1965 by William Warriner of California. Bon-Bon has a high degree of resistance to black spot and is exceptionally resistant to mildew.

Other Winners. The zinnia Scarlet Ruffles was the only gold medal winner from the All-America Selections of annuals for 1974. The bush acorn squash Table King won a silver medal. Bronze medals went to the zinnia Peter Pan, the marigold Showboat, the celosia Red Fox, the dianthus Magic Charms, the cosmos Diablo, and the waxbean Goldcrop.

New Books. An excellent reference, very moderately priced, for those interested in the growing of houseplants is *128 Houseplants You Can Grow*, by Rob Herwig. This book was first published in the Netherlands in 1971 and was translated and published in the United States in paperback in late 1972. All plants discussed are illustrated with good full-color photographs. The use of symbols to denote plant requirements enables the author to include a great deal of information in a small space. *Perennials*—by James Underwood Crockett and the editors of Time-Life Books, illustrated by Allianora Rosse —is an excellent source of information on the propagation, culture, and general care of perennials. It is well illustrated with full-color photographs and watercolors.

DONALD W. NEWSOM
Louisiana State University

GENETICS

During 1973 advances in genetics included the determination of the structure of an operator gene, the development of new techniques for detecting agents that produce mutations, and the analysis of the genes controlling conversion of atmospheric nitrogen to ammonia, a biologically useful compound.

Operator Gene Structure. In 1961, François Jacob and Jacques Monod of the Pasteur Institute in Paris formulated a theory for the regulation of gene function. It was based largely on their work with the genes of the bacterium *Escherichia coli* that control the metabolism of lactose, the lac operon. According to their operon theory, a special protein, called a repressor, present in the cells that do not need to digest lactose, binds to a specific region of deoxyribonucleic acid, or DNA. This DNA region, called the operator, is at or near the point at which transcription of the lac operon genes into their messenger ribonucleic acid (mRNA)

product starts. The binding of repressor to operator was postulated as the mechanism that prevents transcription and hence the expression of the lac operon genes. In 1973, Walter Gilbert, Nancy Maizels, and Allan Maxam, all of Harvard University, succeeded in isolating the operator and in determining its structure and mode of action.

Chemical analysis of the operator showed that it is a stretch of DNA containing 27 nucleotide base-pairs, 16 of which are arranged in a twofold symmetrical pattern. Repressor protein, isolated by Gilbert and B. Müller-Hill in 1966, consists of two identical halves. The symmetry of the operator allows each side of the repressor to bind simultaneously to an identical sequence of nucleotides. By comparing the sequence of bases in lac operon messenger RNA to the operator base sequence, the Harvard investigators showed that the initiation point for transcription lies in the operator. This finding provides chemical verification of the Jacob-Monod postulate. Detailed chemical analysis of the repressor-operator interaction is in progress.

Improved Detection of Mutagens. Mutagenic activity, or the ability to induce mutations, is a factor that must be tested in the safety evaluation of drugs, insecticides, and other chemicals to which we are exposed. It is convenient to test mutagenic effects on certain bacterial mutants in which mutations back to normal can be readily detected by simple growth tests. The mechanisms of mutation in bacteria and in man are thought to be similar. However, such tests on bacteria cannot be used reliably to evaluate mutagenic activity against man and other mammals because chemicals ingested by mammals are often modified by mammalian metabolism.

One procedure to overcome this problem is the "host-mediated assay" devised by Michael G. Gabridge and Marvin S. Legator of the U. S. Food and Drug Administration. In this assay, "tester" bacteria are placed in the abdomens of rats or mice that are being treated with a potential mutagen. In this way, mutations in the tester bacteria may be induced by the substance being tested and by its mammalian metabolic products. In 1973, Bruce Ames, Frank D. Lee, and William E. Durston of the University of California at Berkeley prepared an improved set of bacterial tester strains for mutagenic screening. The four strains contain mutations of different chemical types, and most mutagens will induce one or another of the strains to mutate back to normal. Ames, Lee, and Durston, with Edith Yamasaki, also showed that some of the chemical alterations induced by mammalian metabolism can be produced by treating the chemicals with an extract of mammalian liver. They then treated many carcinogens, compounds that produce cancer, with liver extract to effect in them the same changes that mammalian metabolic processes produce. Many of the carcinogens were found to be potent mutagens of the tester bacteria after treatment but not before. These results have led to the postulate that these carcinogens cause cancer by inducing mutations.

Transfer of Nitrogen-Reducing Genes. Only a relatively few species of microorganisms contain genes that can convert atmospheric nitrogen to ammonia. R. A. Dixon and John R. Postgate of the University of Sussex, England, and Raymond L. Streicher, Elizabeth G. Gurney, and Raymond C. Valentine of the University of California at Berkeley transferred these genes from one type of bacterium to another. This achievement is a significant step toward preparing hybrid organisms that can more effectively reduce atmospheric nitrogen to ammonia, a compound biologically useful in the synthesis of protein. This advance could eventually help alleviate the shortage of protein in some parts of the world.

FRANK G. ROTHMAN
Brown University

GEOGRAPHY

Geography in 1973 was characterized by an increasing trend toward the application of geographic knowledge, methodologies, and skills to the solution of real world problems. Also, more geographers were becoming involved in public policy studies at local, state, and federal levels of government.

Geography in Education. The significance of geographical research and training to the environmental movement and to such contemporary problems as urbanization, population growth, transportation, technological innovation, and housing has spurred college and university enrollments in geography courses. In the past decade the rate of growth of such enrollments has surpassed the rate of growth of overall college and university enrollment.

Geography as "effective environmental education" was the theme of the annual meeting of the National Council on Geographic Education, held in Washington, D. C., in 1973. Hundreds of geography teachers participated in workshops, paper sessions, training sessions, field trips, and demonstrations involving the use of geographical techniques and tools in environmental education programs.

AAG Meeting. A record number of geographers attended the annual meeting of the Association of American Geographers (AAG), held in Atlanta in 1973. AAG President Wilbur Zelinsky emphasized the issue of radical reform in geographers' approaches to contemporary social problems. Past President Edward Taaffe exhorted geographers to abandon arcane methodologies directed toward trivial issues and instead apply their sophisticated skills to man-environment relationships and regional geography. The paper and discussion sessions of the meetings covered a broad range of geographical subfields. In the papers, computer, mathematical, and statistical techniques characterized the research methodologies in such disparate fields as social geography and historical geography. The same techniques characterized the discussion sessions on economic, political, and urban geography; locational analysis; behavioral geography; biogeography; and cartography.

Research. Resource papers issued by the AAG during 1973 featured such varied topics as radar imagery in climatological research, man and the environment, the urban health care crisis, visual blight in America, and perspectives on environment. Geographers continued their seminal research on the assessment of natural hazards, urban goals and patterns of daily urban systems, and suburban black towns. The natural-hazards research is a two-year project at the Institute of Behavioral Science at the University of Colorado, and the other two assessments are projects of the AAG.

Exploration. The National Geographic Society (NGS) sent a team to investigate the eruption of Eldfell, Iceland's newest volcano, born on Jan. 23, 1973. The volcano's lava and cinders covered the island of Heimaey near Vestmannaeyjar, Iceland's

fifth-largest town and its most important fishing center. In addition, the NGS continued to sponsor research and publications covering broad areas in the natural and social sciences.

Land-Use Policy and Planning Program. Federal legislation on land-use policy and planning should provide ample opportunity for geographers to exercise their traditional but evolving skills in land-use mapping, classification, and interpretation. A federal classification system in which the individual states will develop land-use plans is envisioned. Supporting data from photographic surveys from Earth Resources Technology Satellite 1 (ERTS 1) and from the Skylab space station will be used to augment conventional aerial photographs and field reconnaissance surveys.

New Director of AGS. The American Geographical Society (AGS), the oldest geographical society in the United States, appointed a new director, Robert B. McNee. He looked forward to a resurgence in the research efforts of the AGS during his tenure.

J. WARREN NYSTROM
Association of American Geographers

GEOLOGY

Intensive exploration and data gathering on earth and nearby extraterrestrial bodies highlighted advances in geology during 1973. The acquisition of specimens, photographs, and tapes has been so extensive that detailed studies of the results of such major projects as the Apollo missions, the Deep-Sea Drilling Project, and the Earth Resources Technology Satellite program have lagged notably.

Lunar Geology. Under current plans manned exploration of the moon ended with the Apollo 17 mission in December 1972. The Apollo 17 findings supplemented but did not greatly alter previous results. Generally speaking there was disappointment in not finding rocks either as old or as young as hoped for. All the rock specimens were produced by melting and fractionation of previous rocks.

Only a few questionable moon rock samples older than 4 billion years are known. Cataclysmic events—probably gigantic collisions—were active in rock destruction and reconstitution 3.8 to 4.0 billion years ago, and most of the volcanic-flow rocks (basalts) date from 3.5 to 3.8 billion years ago, the time of the filling of the great circular "seas." Since then, little more than meteoric impacts has disturbed the lunar surface. At the time of discovery by the Apollo 17 crew, a deposit of "orange soil" was hailed as evidence of relatively recent volcanic activity. However, the age of this soil proved to be about 3.7 billion years.

Martian Geology. The Mariner 9 spacecraft returned 7,329 photographs of Mars taken during 698 orbits over a period of 349 days in 1971–72. Since then, a variety of photomosaic, topographic, and geologic maps have been prepared. The geologic features present some degree of geometric order, aside from ancient cratered regions that constitute about one half of the surface. A wide equatorial belt includes giant volcanic piles; deep chasms, rifts, or canyon systems; and large patches of chaotic terrain. Sinuous channels, some with branching tributaries, also occur in this zone and are generally considered to imply a history of running water. The polar regions display rudely concentric, layered, or stratified outcrops thought to relate to glacial action. Intermediate zones show wind-blown depositional

and erosional features. The wind-blown material, which appears to be very fine-grained, is derived mostly from the circumpolar regions.

Almost positive evidence of free-flowing water in the past and good possibilities of present subsurface frozen stores strengthen the probability that simple forms of life exist on Mars. Much thought is being given to the selection of a 1976 landing site for U. S. Viking landers, which will be equipped to search for organic material.

Surface of Venus. The first radar map of the topography of part of Venus revealed a cratered moonlike terrain. The craters are relatively flat, suggesting partial destruction by crustal adjustments.

Exploration of Ocean Bottoms. Deep-sea drilling from the research vessel *Glomar Challenger* went into its fifth year of operation in 1973. Since 1968 over 94,000 feet (28,570 meters) of core have been taken from over 450 holes at more than 300 localities. Four legs in its mission in the Indian Ocean revealed a very complex history of fragmentation, uplift, and subsidence. The oldest rocks, dated at 160 million years, are near the western coast of Australia. Beds of shallow-water shells and coal lying more than 3,280 feet (1 km) below sea level on a major ridge in the Indian Ocean indicate emergence and later subsidence. Other evidence gives an improved estimate that India ceased its northward movement 60 million years ago. The island of Madagascar has had a separate existence for 100 million years, much longer than supposed.

Two legs of the vessel's voyages explored Antarctic and sub-Antarctic ocean bottoms. Almost continuous glaciation of Antarctica for a period of 20 million years was established. The circum-Antarctic current became active in the middle Oligocene, and there was a change from dominantly calcareous to dominantly siliceous organic sediments in the Pliocene along the Antarctic convergence. (See also POLAR RESEARCH.)

Earthquake Prediction. Intensified studies of earthquakes in 1973 showed promise of leading to earthquake prediction and some degree of control. Past observations showed that destructive quakes are preceded by a variety of premonitory signs, including: (1) slight uplift or swelling of the surface, (2) changes in the electrical conductivity of the rocks, (3) increased emission of radioactive radon gas, (4) slight rise of water levels in nearby wells, (5) decrease and subsequent increase in small earth tremors, and (6) changes in the velocities of seismic waves passing through the fault area.

The ratio of the velocity of compressional waves to the velocity of shear waves shows a decrease from normal for some weeks or months and then a gradual increase to normal just before a quake. Also, the greater the quake, the earlier is the onset of a change in the ratio. Varied combinations of these two types of waves have been recorded in quakes in Japan, the USSR, and the United States.

Most of the premonitory phenomena are explained by ingenious theories advanced by scientists from Stanford, the California Institute of Technology, and the Lamont Geological Laboratory. In their scenario, intense compression along fault zones creates a network of small pervasive fractures. This breakage results in an increase of volume of the rock, forming microscopic spaces that provide passageways for the entry of groundwater. This is a slow process, but, depending on the volume of rock to be filled, penetration eventually nears saturation.

During the process small tremors increase, and a major slippage occurs because of weakening and the lubricating effects of saturation.

In experiments at the Rangely oil field in northwest Colorado the injection of water into an active fault zone increased the tremors to as many as 30 per month, whereas the withdrawal of water decreased the tremors to about 1 per month.

Earth-Orbiting Satellites. Earth Resources Technology Satellite 1 (ERTS 1), orbited in July 1972, provided significant results during 1973 as its instruments photographed about 188 scenes each day. These photographs are valuable to geologists in studying structural features, variations in rock composition, location of faults, lineaments, ancient volcanic features, regional relationships of mineral deposits, and landforms.

(See also ASTRONOMY; EARTHQUAKES; OCEANOGRAPHY; SPACE EXPLORATION.)

W. LEE STOKES, *University of Utah*

GEORGIA

The most interesting news in Georgia during 1973 centered on politics and scandals, both at home and in Washington.

U. S. Congress. The Rev. Andrew Young, an official of the Southern Christian Leadership Council and a former chairman of the Atlanta Community Relations Commission, took his seat in the U. S. House of Representatives in 1973. He was the first black congressman from Georgia, or any other part of the South, since Reconstruction. At about the same time, Sam Nunn, a 34-year-old attorney from Perry and former state representative, began his first full term in the U. S. Senate.

Georgia's other U. S. senator, Herman Talmadge, became something of a matinee idol in 1973. He received thousands of letters, many from admiring females, while he was appearing on daytime television as a member of the Senate committee investigating the Watergate affair and other alleged illegal activities during the 1972 election campaign.

Parole Controversy. Controversy, which has surrounded the operations of the Georgia Board of Pardons and Paroles for more than a decade, continued to haunt the panel in 1973. Board member Joseph G. Maddox was asked to resign by his fellow members when it was alleged that he had engineered the release from prison of a young heroin pusher after talking to the youth's father about the sale of real estate owned by Maddox. Maddox refused to resign and an investigation was continuing.

Meanwhile, it was charged that some state legislators had attempted to influence the board's parole decisions. State Sen. Maylon London reported that he had been offered a $35,000 "campaign contribution" in exchange for his influence in getting a parole for a drug pusher.

Legislature. The 1973 Georgia Assembly passed a $1.6 billion biennial budget, which included funds for huge pay raises for most state government officials, including the legislators. Lt. Gov. Lester Maddox was credited with (and blamed for) passage of the controversial pay hike, which was to go into effect while federal ceilings remained at 5.5% for most workers. After passing the Georgia House, the bill was voted down on a recorded vote in the Senate, but moments later Maddox, the presiding officer, let the bill pass on a new, unrecorded vote. Maddox, a former governor who plans to run for

─────── **GEORGIA** • Information Highlights ───────

Area: 58,876 square miles (152,489 sq km).
Population (1972 est.): 4,720,000. Density: 80 per sq mi.
Chief Cities (1970 census): Atlanta, the capital, 497,421; Columbus, 155,028; Macon, 122,423; Savannah, 118,349.
Government (1973): *Chief Officers*—governor, Jimmy Carter (D); lt. gov., Lester G. Maddox (D); secy. of state, Ben W. Fortson, Jr. (D); atty. gen., Arthur K. Bolton (D); treas., G. W. Hogan (D); supt. of schools, Jack P. Nix (D); chief justice, Carlton Mobley. *General Assembly*—Senate, 56 members (48 Democrats, 8 Republicans); House of Representatives, 180 members (151 D, 29 R).
Education (1972–73): *Enrollment*—public elementary schools, 686,601 pupils; 29,914 teachers; public secondary schools, 397,801 pupils; 20,023 teachers; nonpublic schools, 32,700 pupils; 1,740 teachers; colleges and universities, 135,710 students. *Public school expenditures*, $786,790,000 ($782 per pupil). *Average teacher's salary*, $8,644.
State Finances (fiscal year 1971): *Revenues*, $1,840,685,000 (3% general sales tax and gross receipts taxes, $361,222,-000; motor fuel tax, $165,714,000; federal funds, $536,-349,000). *Expenditures*, $1,786,007,000 (education, $818,-592,000; health, welfare, and safety, $379,652,000; highways, $244,099,000). *State debt*, $931,125,000 (June 30, 1971).
Personal Income (1972): $18,152,000,000; per capita, $3,846.
Public Assistance (1972): $374,684,000. *Average monthly payments* (Dec. 1972)—old-age assistance, $57.83; aid to families with dependent children, $100.23.
Labor Force: *Nonagricultural wage and salary earners* (July 1973), 1,697,000. *Average annual employment* (1972)—manufacturing, 473,200; trade, 362,900; government, 320,-900; services, 217,700. *Insured unemployed* (Sept. 1973)—13,300 (1.0%).
Manufacturing (1971): Value added by manufacture, $6,533,-200,000. Textile mill products, $1,210,600,000; transportation equipment, $1,188,700,000; food and kindred products, $776,600,000.
Agriculture (1972): *Cash farm income*, $1,502,230,000 (livestock, $786,774,000; crops, $634,392,000; government payments, $81,064,000). *Chief crops* (in order of value, 1971) —Peanuts (ranks 1st among the states); corn, tobacco (ranks 4th); cotton lint.
Mining (1972): Production value, $268,236,000 (ranks 26th among the states). *Chief minerals*—Clays, $143,760,000; stone, $81,141,000; cement, $27,200,000.
Fisheries (1972): *Commercial catch*, 17,544,000 pounds ($6,-802,000). *Leading species by value:* Shrimp, $5,611,000; crabs, $825,000; shad, $111,000.
Transportation: *Roads* (1972), 100,214 miles (161,274 km); *motor vehicles* (1972), 2,752,904; *railroads* (1972), 5,402 miles (8,693 km); *public airports* (1972), 107.
Communications: *Telephones* (1973), 2,820,800; *television stations* (1971), 16; *radio stations* (1971), 228; *newspapers* (1973), 34 (daily circulation, 1,037,000).

that office again in 1974, denied seeking passage of the pay raise and later led the Senate in a vote to repeal the measure. The repeal bill, as expected, failed to gain House approval.

The legislature also restored capital punishment for certain crimes. Airplane hijacking and treason are now punishable by death. Murder, rape, armed robbery, and kidnapping are punishable by death if the jury verdict includes a finding of at least one statutory aggravating circumstance.

One of the final acts of the 1973 General Assembly was to appropriate $3.2 million to begin a $35 million Georgia World Congress Center. The international showcase was held up by Gov. Jimmy Carter, who late in 1973 was still seeking private funding for the project. Meanwhile, some $80 million in conventions had been scheduled for the center, beginning in 1976.

Abortion Ruling. On January 22, the U. S. Supreme Court, in a 7–2 landmark decision, repealed Georgia's limited abortion law. The court held that Georgia had no right to interfere with abortions in the early stages of pregnancy when a doctor felt it was needed to safeguard the mother's health. The ruling, along with other related decisions, was interpreted to mean that abortion is legal in the first 13 weeks of pregnancy. By late 1973, abortion had become a big business in Atlanta, where an estimated 30,000 abortions a year were being performed for more than $5 million in fees.

GENE STEPHENS, *Georgia State University*

West German Chancellor Willy Brandt (second from left), during a five-day visit to Israel, passes a mural depicting World War II concentration-camp inmates in the Yad Vashem Museum in Jerusalem.

GERMANY

Germany is divided into two separate states. The Federal Republic of Germany (West Germany) is a democratic, parliamentary republic and a member of such Western organizations as the North Atlantic Treaty Organization (NATO), the European Coal and Steel Community, and the European Economic Community (Common Market). The German Democratic Republic (East Germany), also known as DDR from its German-language initials, is, in effect, a Communist one-party state. It is affiliated with the Warsaw Pact and the Council for Mutual Economic Assistance (COMECON), the Eastern counterparts of NATO and EEC.

Between these two states, West Berlin, a Western outpost within East Germany, maintains its precarious existence. Economically it is tied closely to the Federal Republic, but politically and militarily it has a separate status.

FEDERAL REPUBLIC OF GERMANY
(West Germany)

Following the electoral victory of the Social Democratic (SPD) and Free Democratic (FDP) parties in November 1972, a new SPD/FDP coalition government took over. It was headed again by Willy Brandt (SPD) as chancellor and Walter Scheel (FDP) as foreign minister. Since Brandt's *Ostpolitik* (Eastern policy) goals had been largely accomplished, the government's main tasks were domestic. Among these, the fight against inflation, tax reforms, workers' rights to profit-sharing and to participation in managerial decision-making, abuses in land development, and education were major issues.

These issues affected basic positions of both coalition partners. The SPD wished to finance reforms by tax increases while the FDP opposed new taxes as a deterrent to individual initiative. Other problems included the issue of private enterprise, or (as in the case of anti-inflationary measures) the problem of planned v. market economy. With negotiations dragging on, the government was subjected to growing charges of helplessness.

Political Parties. A major cause for these difficulties was the deepening ideological differences between the two coalition partners. In the SPD the younger members, but a good many older ones too, called for large-scale socialization of the nation, thus challenging the official party program which accepts West Germany's market economy. At the annual party congress in Hannover a considerable number of left-wingers were elected to the party directorate.

The FDP, a small party of old-line liberals and entrepreneurs, in turn had to reconcile its function as a brake on the reforming zeal of the SPD with the fact that many supported it only because of its coalition with the SPD. It thus steered a cautious course between its liberal credo and the need to accept such measures as curbs on real estate speculation and participation in management and institutionalized profit sharing for workers.

The Christian Democratic Union (CDU) and its Bavarian offshoot, the Christian Social Union (CSU), continued to oppose the Basic Treaty (negotiated with the DDR in 1972), which provided for the good-neighborly peaceful coexistence of the two German states. When CDU party chief Rainer Barzel proposed parliamentary rejection of the treaty, but support of a bill authorizing the entry of the Federal Republic into the United Nations along with

the DDR, he was disavowed by his party. He resigned and was succeeded by Helmut Kohl, minister-president of the Rhineland-Palatinate.

The Steiner Affair. West Germany, too, had its "Watergate," though on a far smaller scale. The key figure was one Julius Steiner, former CDU deputy, who claimed to have abstained from voting against Chancellor Brandt in a crucial no-confidence vote in April 1972. With the outcome depending on the slimmest of margins, he thus helped to assure Brandt's survival as chancellor. Steiner did so, he said, in return for a payment of 50,000 marks (about $16,000) which he received from a prominent SPD deputy, Karl Wienand. (Steiner also confessed to having served as an intelligence agent for both the Federal Republic and DDR, with the former's knowledge.) Wienand denied Steiner's assertions, which a Bundestag investigating committee found full of discrepancies. However, Wienand's testimony also left some matters unclear. By year's end the committee had not yet reached a decision regarding the Steiner affair.

Economic Conditions. Living costs increased at an annual rate of nearly 7% through most of the year. In order to check the inflation, the government imposed a 10% surcharge on high personal and business incomes and an 11% tax on new investments, besides disallowing previously granted tax write-offs in the case of the latter. At the same time public expenditures were sharply reduced. Interest rates also were raised, and the mark was revalued upward by 5.5%, in order to stem the influx of dollars. In September the rate of inflation did drop to 6.5% after having risen to almost 8% in midyear. Whether this was a permanent change for the better remained to be seen.

Despite the upward revaluation of the mark, exports kept expanding, except to the United States. There even such one-time money-makers as Volkswagen automobiles and Carribbean cruise ships no longer were profitable. As a result many West German entrepreneurs turned from exports to investments in the United States.

The Arabian oil boycott posed new problems for the economy. In mid-November the parliament enacted a law that was intended to conserve energy resources. Among the measures authorized by the law were tight speed limits and a ban on Sunday driving, both of which were imposed by the government to cope with the energy crisis.

Social Conditions. The presence of some 2.4 million "guest laborers" and their 1 million family members continued to be one of the country's most serious social problems. In 1973 foreign workers made up 10% of the West German labor force. Housing, schooling, and social services for these workers were generally inadequate, and hospital facilities were poor. Working conditions, too, were often unsatisfactory. In September, 2,000 of the 12,000 Turks employed by the Ford plant in Cologne struck in protest against various discriminatory practices to which they claimed they were being subjected. They won some concessions, including a pay raise.

The future of the foreign workers was uncertain. Most of them had one- or two-year renewable work permits, but at the end of November new hirings were barred because of the energy crisis. It was also announced that expiring work permits would be renewed only after careful examination of each individual case.

The improvement of the "quality of life," one of the SPD's election promises, was rendered more difficult by the financial retrenchment initiated by the government. This caused much discontent. A newly founded Committee for Workers' Concerns, sponsored by the lower echelons of the SPD and some labor unions, called for the nationalization of all health services, government guidance of investments, price controls, and tax exemptions for low-income groups. A nationwide meat boycott, launched during the summer, ended inconclusively. Pensioners, however, took comfort from a Federal Labor Court decision calling for revaluation of pensions in accordance with the declining purchasing power of the mark.

In 1972 deaths outnumbered births by about 30,000—the first such deficit in a peacetime year in many decades.

Cultural Life. West German universities continued to suffer from a shortage of facilities to accommodate all applicants for admission. The problem was somewhat eased by tightened admission standards. However, rejections could be challenged in court, and many were. Some U. S. universities offered to admit part of those who could not get into a West German university. Efforts also were made to persuade business concerns to hire high school graduates without university degrees for executive careers.

Several books on Hitler appeared in 1973, among them a 1,100-page biography by Joachim Fest. The tenor of these books and the ensuing discussion made it clear, however, that the new wave of Hitleriana had no political overtones.

——— WEST GERMANY • Information Highlights ———

Official Name: Federal Republic of Germany.
Location: North Central Europe.
Area: 95,743 square miles (247,973 sq km). West Berlin, 186 square miles (481 sq km).
Population (1973 est.): 59,400,000; West Berlin: 2,100,000. *Density*, 620 per square mile (240 per sq km).
Chief Cities (1970 est.): Bonn, the capital, 275,722; Hamburg, 1,793,600; Munich, 1,312,000; Cologne, 849,450.
Government: *Head of state*, Gustav Heinemann, president (took office July 1969). *Head of government*, Willy Brandt, federal chancellor (took office Oct. 1969). *Legislature*—Parliament: Bundesrat and Bundestag. *Major political parties*—Social Democratic party; Free Democratic party; Christian Democratic Union.
Language: German (official).
Education: *Expenditure* (1969), 11.2% of total public expenditure. *School enrollment* (1969)—primary, 6,098,-425; secondary, 4,280,996; technical/vocational, 2,086,-194; university/higher, 440,647.
Monetary Unit: Deutsche Mark (2.68 D. Marks equal U. S. $1, Dec. 1973).
Gross National Product (1972 est.): $242,500,000,000.
Economic Indexes: *Industrial production* (1972), 162 (1963=100); *agricultural production* (1971), 115 (1963=100); *consumer price index* (1972), 134 (1963=100).
Manufacturing (major products): Mechanical engineering products, automobiles, chemicals, iron and steel, ironware, tinware, hardware, textiles, processed foods, electrical machinery.
Major Agricultural Products: Rye (ranks 3d among world producers, 1972), oats (world rank 4th, 1972), barley, potatoes, sugar beets, hops, fish, forest products.
Major Minerals: Lignite (ranks 3d among world producers, 1971), coal, potash, iron ore, lead, petroleum, natural gas.
Foreign Trade (1972): *Exports*, $46,208,000,000. *Imports*, $39,763,000,000. *Chief trading partners* (1971)—France (took 12.5% of exports, supplied 13.3% of imports); Netherlands (10.7%—13.1%); United States (9.7%—10.3%).
Tourism: Receipts (1971), $1,577,000,000.
Transportation: *Motor vehicles* (1971), 15,738,100 (automobiles, 14,688,700); *railroads* (1971), 18,187 miles (29,267 km); *merchant fleet* (1972), 8,516,000 gross registered tons; *major national airline*, Deutsche Lufthansa.
Communications: *Telephones* (1972), 15,245,686; *newspapers* (1970), 1,093 (daily circulation, 19,701,000).

PRE-LENTEN CARNIVAL festivities in Bonn, West Germany, are highlighted by a mock invasion of the chancellery and a toast by Chancellor Brandt.

PICTORIAL PARADE

Foreign Affairs. In September the Federal Republic was admitted to the United Nations. Admission was by acclamation. Only Guinea objected, charging West Germany with supporting rebel activities in Guinea. In his inaugural speech Foreign Minister Scheel expressed West Germany's continuing hope for the eventual reunification of the two Germanys.

Relations with the United States were strained at times. Leftists objected to the bombing of North Vietnam in December 1972 and proposed withholding Bonn's contribution to the upkeep of American forces in West Germany. The disclosure that U. S. intelligence agents had been wiretapping German civilians and civilian organizations caused another furor.

Yet most Germans wished the U. S. military forces to stay on. Reports of the demand by the U. S. Congress for a reduction of the American military presence in Europe were received with dismay. Both Brandt and Scheel went to Washington to seek reassurance on this point, but they received no clear-cut commitment.

New difficulties arose over the neutral stance taken by Bonn in the Israeli-Egyptian war because of its dependence on Arab oil. The United States resented Bonn's ban on shipments of American supplies from West Germany to Israel. Bonn objected to United States criticisms on the grounds that its NATO obligations did not extend to matters involving Israel.

Brandt's *Ostpolitik* paid some new dividends. In May, Soviet Communist party chief Leonid I. Brezhnev visited Bonn. He signed a comprehensive 10-year agreement on economic, industrial, and technical cooperation; a cultural exchange pact; and an air traffic accord permitting West German flights to Japan via Siberia. Subsequently Moscow accepted a compromise with Bonn on the latter's right to be the diplomatic representative for West Berlin's

institutions and organizations—an issue, which had not been settled by the Four-Power Berlin Agreement of 1971.

After long negotiations the Federal Republic and Czechoslovakia initialed a friendship treaty in June. It proclaimed void the Munich Agreement of 1938, guaranteed the territorial integrity of both states, and pledged them to the peaceful settlement of disputes. After some delay caused by the (still unresolved) question of West Germany's right to represent West Berlin corporations and institutions in Czechoslovakia, the treaty was signed in December.

GERMAN DEMOCRATIC REPUBLIC
(East Germany)

The death of 80-year-old Walter Ulbricht on August 1 led to a reshuffling of top government posts in the DDR. Willi Stoph, the ailing long-time minister-president, became Ulbricht's successor as chairman of the State Council, a largely ceremonial position. Stoph was succeeded in the minister-presidency by Horst Sindermann, 58, who had been Stoph's deputy since 1971.

Politically active since his high school days, Sindermann had spent the entire Nazi era in penitentiaries and concentration camps. He belonged to the leadership of the (Communist) Socialist Unity party (SED) since its formation in 1946. As party head of the important industrial district of Halle, Sindermann made a name for himself as a capable organizer and administrator, but also as a rigorous ideologue. In 1967 he became a member of the Politburo of the SED.

The Economy. As always, East Germany's main economic problem was to reconcile industrial development with the demand for more consumer goods. In his first public speech as minister-president Sindermann promised to meet the "material and cultural needs" of the people. The drive to keep up

housing construction continued. Yet despite the full-scale application of mass-production techniques, including the widespread use of standardized prefabricated walls, doors, and windows, the housing shortage was not expected to be wholly relieved until 1990. Some of the consumer goods industries, such as clothing and furniture, were hampered by production difficulties.

Food supplies, on the other hand, grew more plentiful. Farming cooperatives expanded production. Their members earned good incomes, worked fewer hours than they had as private farmers, and enjoyed paid vacations and other social benefits. There were indications that they were abandoning the plots set aside for their private use since the additional income did not seem to them to be worth the additional work.

Social Conditions. While criminal statistics are not published regularly in the DDR, there were suggestions that criminal offenses were on the increase. Juvenile delinquency posed an especially serious problem: one out of two offenders was between 14 and 25 years old. Except in very grave cases, first offenders received suspended sentences. In the words of the solicitor general, they were considered victims of the "birthmarks of the old society" which the new social order had not yet completely erased. Part of the blame was also put on "imperialist propaganda" that kept alive "bourgeois ideology and lifestyles" through its mass media, but socialist society with its "contradictions and conflicts" could not be absolved of all responsibility.

Minor infractions of the law, such as petty thefts or traffic violations, were dealt with by some 23,000 special commissions. Such commissions are elected by every enterprise or institution that employs more than 50 people. The commissions could impose fines up to 150 marks. They also settled labor disputes over pay, vacations, dismissals, and similar questions.

In August, East Berlin hosted an "International Festival of Youth and Students" which was attended by 25,000 foreign delegates and guests. It presented some 1,500 political, cultural, and athletic events. Representatives of the independence movement in Portuguese Africa received special honors. A noteworthy feature was a series of free-wheeling discussions with spokesmen of the 800 West German delegates.

Foreign Affairs. Like the Federal Republic, the DDR was admitted to the UN in September. In the DDR's case, the Israeli delegate protested against its entry on the grounds that it had never accepted any coresponsibility for the Nazi crimes perpetrated on Jews and had refused to make any restitution. In his inaugural speech, Foreign Minister Otto Winzer stressed the permanence of the breakup of Germany into two separate states, sharply refuting his West German counterpart.

Earlier in the year, Britain and France established full diplomatic relations with East Berlin. The United States began talks on recognition, and a State Department delegation went to the East German capital to look for embassy quarters. However, formal ties had not yet been established by year's end.

Contrary to its long-standing hostility to Franco Spain, the DDR government recognized Spain in January. The move provoked protest rallies and sharply critical letters to East German newspapers. The objections were dismissed by *Neues Deutschland,* the chief SED daily, with the remark that "foreign policy cannot be based on emotions." The DDR was prepared, the paper noted, to establish diplomatic relations with any nation—"capitalist countries, monarchies and even dictatorships." Determined to play a role on the international stage, East Germany would not be held back by ideological reservations.

This was confirmed also by negotiations with the Vatican, conducted throughout the year, about the establishment of formal ties. In preparation for this move, several ecclesiastical districts which still formed part of West German dioceses were converted into separate units. Pope Paul VI thereupon appointed apostolic administrators in these areas. They were to become full-fledged bishoprics once relations between the Vatican and East Germany had been formalized.

PEACE AND TRADE TALKS were held in Bonn between USSR Communist party chief Leonid I. Brezhnev (left) and Chancellor Willy Brandt.

NEW UNITED NATIONS MEMBERS: East German Foreign Minister Otto Winzer (left) shakes hands with West German Foreign Minister Walter Scheel.

EAST-WEST GERMAN RELATIONS

In May the West German parliament ratified the Basic Treaty with East Germany. According to the treaty the two German states recognized each other as separate sovereign states. Bavaria challenged the treaty as unconstitutional, on the grounds that contrary to the intent of the West German constitution the treaty precluded an eventual reunification of the two Germanys. However, the West German constitutional court rejected this argument. The East German parliament ratified the pact a few days after the Bundestag approved it.

As a result of the 1972 traffic pact between East and West Germany, East-West contacts increased in 1973. Several million West Germans and West Berliners visited the DDR. East Germans still found it difficult to visit the West unless they were over 60, but by late April some 20,000 had been permitted to do so in cases involving "pressing family matters."

The DDR government was concerned about these contacts, since they led to invidious comparisons of East and West German living standards and might weaken the ideological ascendancy of the DDR regime. The government also feared clandestine intelligence operations, and ranking party members, officials, and others in sensitive jobs were forbidden to receive West German visitors in their homes. Concern over a black market in East German currency, which enabled West German visitors to buy up scarce East German goods cheaply, suggested one way to reduce the number of visitors: in October the amount of DDR currency that each visitor had to buy at the border was doubled.

The Escape Issue. The number of escapees from the DDR increased by several hundred in 1972 and was expected to reach the figure of 6,500 in 1973. The East German government blamed the relaxed controls on the transit routes between West Berlin and West Germany for the increase. Actually the number of people who fled via these roads seems

to have been rather small. The bulk of the refugees made their way to the West by way of the Eastern European countries. The Bonn government, fearful of the impact of these escapes on East-West German relations in general and on the smooth flow of traffic between West Berlin and West Germany in particular, threatened to prosecute or extradite to East Germany anyone who helped to arrange such escapes commercially.

Those who could afford to pay the going price of $10,000 to $15,000 for an arranged escape were chiefly highly trained professionals whose skills the DDR could ill afford to lose. One East Berlin hospital lost 59 doctors within a short time. DDR courts sought to stop these operations by imposing unusually stiff jail sentences on a group of escape arrangers who had been caught.

WEST BERLIN

While the 1971 Big-Four Berlin Agreement and the 1972 East-West German traffic pact increased the mobility of West Berliners, the city's legal ties to the Federal Republic remained a matter of dispute. The Big-Four accord authorized West German consulates to represent West Berlin residents in foreign countries. It made no such provision, however, for corporations and institutions. While the USSR agreed to extend West Germany's diplomatic authority to legal persons, Czechoslovakia, Hungary, and Bulgaria so far have not done so.

Considering West Berlin a separate political unit, the newly appointed Soviet consul general in West Berlin refused to call on its mayor as long as the city insisted on hoisting the West German flag along with West Berlin's flag at his formal reception. A compromise was finally reached on the occasion

─── **EAST GERMANY • Information Highlights** ───

Official Name: German Democratic Republic.
Location: North Central Europe.
Area: 41,766 square miles (108,174 sq km).
Population (1973 est.): 17,400,000. *Density*, 390 per square mile (150 per sq km).
Chief Cities (1971 census): East Berlin, the capital, 1,084,866; Leipzig, 583,311; Dresden, 500,051; Karl-Marx-Stadt, 298,335.
Government: *Head of state*, Willi Stoph, chairman of the Council of State (took office Oct. 1973). *Head of government*, Horst Sindermann, minister-president (took office Oct. 1973). First secretary of the Socialist Unity (Communist) party, Erich Honecker (took office May 1971). *Legislature* (unicameral)—Volkskammer (People's Chamber). *Major political party*—Socialist Unity party.
Language: German (official).
Education: *Expenditure* (1969), 8.3% of total public expenditure. *School enrollment* (1969)—primary, 2,485,367; secondary, 659,536; technical/vocational, 582,380; university/higher, 91,947.
Monetary Unit: Ostmark (1.78 Ostmarks equal U. S.$1, Aug. 1973).
Gross National Product (1972 est.): $35,300,000,000.
Economic Indexes: *Industrial production* (1972), 171 (1963=100); *agricultural production* (1970), 119 (1957-59=100); *consumer price index* (1971), 99 (1963=100).
Manufacturing (major products): Iron and steel, machinery, chemicals, transport equipment, electronic equipment, precision and optical instruments, fertilizers, synthetic rubber and fibers.
Major Agricultural Products: Rye (ranks 4th among world producers, 1972), potatoes, sugar beets, wheat, oats, barley.
Major Minerals: Lignite (ranks 1st among world producers, 1971), potash, salt, coal, copper.
Foreign Trade (1972): *Exports*, $6,184,000,000. *Imports*, $5,905,000,000. *Chief trading partners* (1971)—USSR (took 38% of exports, supplied 38% of imports); West Germany (10%—10%); Czechoslovakia (9%—9%); Poland (9%—6%).
Transportation: *Motor vehicles* (1971), 1,681,600 (automobiles, 1,267,800); *railroads* (1971), 9,108 miles (14,658 km); *merchant fleet* (1972), 1,198,000 gross registered tons; *major national airline*, Interflug.
Communications: *Telephones* (1972), 2,165,235; *newspapers* (1968), 40 (daily circulation, 7,608,000).

of the visit of the minister of agriculture of the African republic of Togo. During that visit both the Berlin and West German flags were raised, but with Togo's between them. Similarly the DDR would not allow West German sports organizations to act as spokesmen for West Berlin's athletes. Conversely, a West German sailing team withdrew from an East German meet on the Baltic Sea when the West Berlin flag was displayed there along with Bonn's black-red-and-gold flag.

Air Traffic. Hopes that West Berlin's airports might become transit stops rather than remain terminals for flights from the West also were disappointed. The USSR opposed the inclusion of West Berlin in international air traffic, while the Western powers on their part wished to avoid new controversies involving the city.

Economy. Possibly because of these difficulties, West Berlin's economy suffered setbacks. The number of visitors decreased in 1973 despite the city's improved accessibility. Similarly, instead of the originally expected influx of 30,000 West German workers, at most 23,000 actually arrived—notwithstanding special income subsidies of 8% and lower income taxes (30% less than in West Germany). The number of foreign workers remained correspondingly large; in one city district every third resident was a Turk. There was, however, a slight increase in the business the city did with the DDR and several other East European countries.

ANDREAS DORPALEN
The Ohio State University

GHANA

Ghana's economy was buoyed by soaring world prices for cocoa, and so the army-based government of Col. Ignatius K. Acheampong moved more confidently in 1973, its second year in power. (Acheampong, chairman of the so-called National Redemption Council, NRC, had seized power in a bloodless coup d'etat on Jan. 13, 1972.)

Domestic Affairs. One of the government's confidence came in its release of political prisoners. Immediately after the coup the NRC had imprisoned more than 1,300 memberes of the Progress party of former Prime Minister Kofi Busia, including cabinet members. By July 1973 all were released, although Gen. A. A. Afrifa (a leader of the 1966 coup) remained under "open arrest." Late in the year five prominent Ghanians were charged with treason and tried by a military tribunal. The accused included the former secretary general of the All-Africa Trades Union Federation and a former foreign minister.

Members of the NRC remained adamantly opposed to any resumption of political activity, however. In January, Acheampong issued a "Charter of Redemption," whose seven goals included "revolutionary discipline," "self-reliance," and "total manpower development and employment." Ghana would strive for a continental union government in Africa and would support national liberation movements in Southern Africa. But Acheampong indicated that leadership would remain in the hands of the military until the country's economy was sound. "We have put an end to politics," he proclaimed, stating that until economic stability is attained, "we do not think it is useful to discuss politics."

Some areas of domestic discontent did surface. In July the NRC issued a strong decree against

————— GHANA • Information Highlights —————

Official Name: Republic of Ghana.
Location: West Africa.
Area: 92,099 square miles (238,537 sq km).
Population (1973 est.): 9,900,000. *Density,* 104 per square mile (40 per sq km).
Chief Cities (1970 census): Accra, the capital, 633,880; Kumasi, 342,986; Sekondi-Takoradi, 161,071.
Government: *Head of state,* Col. Ignatius K. Acheampong, chairman of National Redemption Council (took office Jan. 1972). *Organ of government,* National Redemption Council. *Legislature*—National Assembly (dissolved Jan. 1972).
Languages: English (official), 50 tribal languages and dialects.
Education: *Expenditure* (1969), 20.3% of total public expenditure. *School enrollment* (1970)—primary, 1,389,804; secondary, 81,499; technical/vocational, 12,169; university/higher (1969), 4,759.
Monetary Unit: New cedi (1.15 new cedis equal U. S.$1, July 1973).
Gross National Product (1972 est.): $2,090,000,000.
Economic Indexes: *Industrial production* (1970), 154 (1963=100); *consumer price index* (1971), 177 (1963=100).
Manufacturing (major products): Processed agricultural products, wood products, cement.
Major Agricultural Products: Cacao (ranks 1st among world producers, 1972), corn, cassava, groundnuts, sweet potatoes and yams, forest products, livestock, fish.
Major Minerals: Diamonds (ranks 4th among world producers, 1971), gold, manganese, bauxite.
Foreign Trade (1972): *Exports,* $389,000,000. *Imports,* $290,-000,000. *Chief trading partners* (1970)—United Kingdom (took 23% of exports, supplied 24% of imports); United States (18%—18%); West Germany (10%—11%).
Tourism: Receipts (1972), $1,629,100.
Transportation: *Motor vehicles* (1970), 63,500 (automobiles, 36,500); *railroads* (1971), 592 miles (953 km); *merchant fleet* (1972), 166,000 gross registered tons; *major national airline,* Ghana Airways.
Communications: *Telephones* (1972), 49,123; *newspapers* (1970), 7.

rumor mongering. An individual spreading any statement "which was false and likely to cause fear or alarm or despondency to the public, or to disturb the public peace, or to cause disaffection against the National Redemption Council and the Executive Council, among the public or among members of the armed forces," would be liable to up to three years' imprisonment. In the same month, Acheampong condemned chiefs of the Volta Region, which had been governed until 1957 as the Trust Territory of British Togoland. He warned against any encouragement of secessionist feeling and disclosed that several chiefs had been arrested.

Economic Developments. The NRC stressed agricultural productivity, especially of food crops. Plans were announced for constructing a 50-mile irrigation canal from the Volta River to the Accra plains. Its excavation may be carried out by communal labor.

High cocoa prices, topping $1,500 per ton in July, enabled the NRC to transform its 1971 trade deficit of $95 million into a 1972 surplus of $100 million. Cocoa provided 54% of the exports. A dramatic increase in timber shipments (up more than 40%) and more effective import controls also helped.

Further steps were taken for government economic participation in privately owned businesses. In July negotiations were completed with timber and mining firms for 55% government holdings. Plans were announced for government shares of 40% in foreign-owned banking and insurance companies, and of 50% in brewing, broadcasting, and other endeavors.

International debt questions remained unsettled following the NRC's 1972 repudiation of nearly $100 million in medium-term debts. At the start of 1973, Ghana's external debt stood at $230 million long-term, $370 million medium-term, and $285 million short-term.

CLAUDE E. WELCH, JR.
State University of New York at Buffalo

Britain's royal newlyweds, Princess Anne and Capt. Mark Phillips, pass royal family as they leave Westminster Abbey (above) and wave from Buckingham Palace balcony.

GREAT BRITAIN

Britain officially became a member of the European Economic Community (EEC) on Jan. 1, 1973, but for reasons having little to do with British participation in the Common Market, 1973 proved to be a nightmarish year for the national economy.

Prime Minister Edward Heath's Conservative government began the year grappling with difficulties that included a high rate of inflation, an adverse balance of payments, the weakness of the British pound sterling, and a legacy of industrial troubles that had forced the declaration of four states of national emergency in the years 1970–72. The government sought to cope with these problems by "heating up" the economy under a lid of wage and price controls. By the end of 1973, a partial oil embargo by the Arab states and industrial action by coal miners and transportation workers had led the prime minister to declare yet another state of emergency, and Britons were facing a critical energy shortage, strict rationing, increased inflation and trade deficits, a three-day work week, and a huge rise in unemployment. There was no diminution in 1973 of violence by Catholic and Protestant groups

determined to block any moderate solution to the problem of Northern Ireland. But the year did provide the British people with one welcome distraction from their many problems—a royal wedding.

Royal Wedding. Princess Anne, 4th in the line of succession to the throne, was married on November 14 to Capt. Mark Phillips of the 1st Queen's Dragoon Guards. Some 2,000 guests in Westminster Abbey and many millions of television viewers around the world witnessed the colorful ceremony uniting the 23-year-old daughter of Queen Elizabeth II and the 25-year-old commoner, the son of a manufacturer.

ECONOMY

In late 1972, the British government had conceived the plan of containing inflation and promoting economic growth by combining stimulants to consumption and investment (through a generous use of the money supply) with a firm prices and incomes policy, one that was partly modeled on President Nixon's earlier experiments. On Nov. 6, 1972, Prime Minister Heath had introduced Phase I of that policy—a temporary freeze· on wages, prices, and dividends. In January 1973 the details of Phase II were revealed.

Phase II Economic Policies. Increases in incomes under Phase II were to be limited by a formula of "£1 plus 4%" in relation to increases in the previous year, with an absolute limit of £250 per year for any individual. Phase II went into effect in April, after a delay that necessitated the extension of Phase I (originally a 90-day freeze) through March.

A pay board was established. Dividend and price limits were imposed—administered by a prices board—and permissible price increases were governed by a formula that took account of productivity, increases in costs, and other factors. The government estimated that the provisions of Phase II should limit inflation to 7–8% per year. It was hoped that any adverse effects of inflation on the British balance of payments would be mitigated by the increased imports facilitated by the floating exchange rate, first introduced in 1971. It was recognized that a floating rate might also increase the import bill and thus add to demands for compensatory increases in incomes, but the government hoped that this effect would be limited both by an improvement in the terms of trade and by some moderation in the increase in international commodity prices.

The Trades Union Congress, the principal voice of labor, opposed Phase II, arguing that excessive wage increases were not responsible for inflation, and that if incomes were limited and inflation continued, a heavy and unjust burden would fall upon the old and the poorly paid.

The government pinned its major hopes on export-led and investment-backed growth, gambling that if its policy was pursued with sufficient firmness, the dividends of growth would offset the adversities of inflation. The leadership was also determined not to return to the uncertainties of the "stop-go" cycle of the 1950's and 1960's, with its attendant need for frequent deflationary measures and its consequent checks on growth.

The chancellor of the exchequer's March budget reflected his intention to stimulate growth by a light hand on public expenditure. Revenue was reduced by £120 million. Pensions were increased, and tax reliefs for the aged introduced. Sickness and unemployment benefits were raised. A value added tax (VAT) was to come into operation on April 1 (as announced in 1971). The rate was set at 10%, and the VAT was to replace the existing purchase tax and the selective employment tax.

Labor Difficulties. Phase II was scheduled to lapse at the end of October. During that month, slightly looser rules were published to govern Phase III, which was to take effect on November 1. Wage increases up to 7% or £2.25 were allowed. There was to be a "threshold guarantee," that is, the government would amend the Pay Code rules if

inflation exceeded expectations. Price and dividend controls continued.

The trade unions remained adamant in their opposition to the whole statutory policy, arguing that its rules were inadequate to deal with an inflation proceeding at an annual rate greater than 8%. In October, some workers in low-skilled trades were granted pay increases in excess of the Phase III formula, and, in November, the electrical power engineers, concerned about the narrowing differential between pay scales for skilled and unskilled labor, refused a Phase III offer and imposed a limitation on hours of work.

Finally, on November 12, the miners cancelled overtime work, despite the fact that the pay offer made to them was calculated under Phase III rules that had been largely couched with their special needs in mind. A slowdown by railway engineers followed, affecting deliveries of coal and making an energy crisis inevitable, since 70% of Britain's electrical power is produced by coal-fired generators.

State of Emergency. The final blow to the government's earlier expectations came when it appeared that the Arab oil embargo, first imposed in October, would hit Britain much harder than had originally been expected. On November 13 a state of emergency was declared in response to the fuel crisis, and later in the month the government ordered a 10% cut in fuel deliveries and urged drivers to observe a 50-mile-per-hour speed limit.

The government's economic calculations had clearly been upset. Assumptions about a favorable change in the terms of trade were wrecked by the oil embargo, which threatened to add enormously to the balance of payments deficit. That deficit had

---

GREAT BRITAIN · Information Highlights

Official Name: United Kingdom of Great Britain and Northern Ireland.
Location: Off the northwestern coast of Europe.
Area: 94,226 square miles (244,044 sq km).
Population (1973 est.): 57,000,000. *Density*, 590 per square mile (228 per sq km).
Chief Cities (1971 census): London, the capital, 7,379,-014; Birmingham, 1,013,366; Glasgow, 896,958; Liverpool, 606,834; Manchester, 541,468; Sheffield, 519,703.
Government: *Head of state*, Elizabeth II, queen (acceded Feb. 1952). *Head of government*, Edward Heath, prime minister (took office June 1970). *Legislature*—Parliament: House of Lords and House of Commons. *Major political parties*—Conservative party; Labour party; Liberal party.
Languages: English, Welsh (both official).
Education: *School enrollment* (1969)—primary, 5,835,093; secondary, 3,945,297; technical/vocational, 166,732; university/higher, 417,736.
Monetary Unit: Pound (0.4110 pound equals U. S.$1, Oct. 1973).
Gross National Product (1972 est.): $151,600,000,000.
Economic Indexes: *Industrial production* (1972), 130 (1963 = 100); *agricultural production* (1971), 122 (1963 = 100); *consumer price index* (1972), 159 (1963 = 100).
Manufacturing (major products): Iron and steel, motor vehicles, aircraft, textiles, chemicals, processed foods, petroleum products, electrical machinery.
Major Agricultural Products: Barley, oats, sugar beets, potatoes, wheat.
Major Minerals: Coal, iron ore, petroleum, natural gas, limestone, tin, gravel.
Foreign Trade (1972): *Exports*, $24,344,000,000. *Imports*, $27,860,000,000. *Chief trading partners* (1971)—Common Market (took 21% of exports, supplied 21.4% of imports); European Free Trade Association (15.2%—16%); United States (11.9%—11%).
Tourism: Receipts (1972), $1,369,000,000.
Transportation: *Motor vehicles* (1971), 14,273,900 (automobiles, 12,516,500); *railroads* (1971), 11,847 miles (19,064 km); *merchant fleet* (1972), 28,625,000 gross registered tons; *major national airlines*, BOAC (British Overseas Airways Corp.); BEA (British European Airways).
Communications: *Telephones* (1972), 16,143,102; *newspapers*, daily circulation (1968), 25,609,000.

already grown, revealing the extent to which, despite dramatic increases in exports, the stimulated boom and the depreciation of the pound had increased the import bill. Although in November the government could claim that British rates of inflation were considerably less than some others (those in France and Japan, for example), it was clear that Britain faced increased oil prices and the prospect of widespread strikes in a much less favorable balance-of-payments position than most other industrial countries.

Three-day Week. On December 13, the prime minister temporarily abandoned the policy of growth and announced new and extremely harsh austerity measures, claiming that a fuel shortage caused by continuing work slowdowns by coal miners, electrical engineers, and railway engineers made such a program necessary. The principal measure, designed to save fuel, was the limitation of most commercial and industrial establishments to a three-day work week and their employees to three days' pay, effective in the first full week of January 1974.

The government had been able to claim, even as late as December 1973, that its economic policies had produced a significant increase in employment and in industrial productivity per man. But by mid-January of 1974, while the nation's government and its 270,000 coal miners stubbornly held to their respective positions, more than 3 million people were estimated to have been laid off due to the shortened work week.

GOVERNMENT AND POLITICS

The nation's economic difficulties played a dominant role in domestic political affairs, as they did in most other aspects of British life in 1973.

Gains for Minor Parties. The alleged failure of the Conservative government to reduce the rate of inflation to an acceptable level was the main reason why the Tories lagged behind the Labour party opposition in the opinion polls through most of 1973. But the principal political effect of the government's troubles was not increased popularity for the opposition but greater support for minor parties, especially the Liberal party. Until the autumn, a number of polls showed the Liberals receiving support almost equal to that of each of the two major parties, and in July Liberal candidates won formerly safe Conservative seats in Ely and Ripon. Although Liberal advances had abated by fall, they were sufficient to show that the Labour party had failed to take advantage of the government's difficulties and that the public was disillusioned with the performance of both major parties.

Crisis Support. In November and December, and especially after the prime minister announced the imposition of the three-day maximum work week and blamed it on coal miners and other labor groups, public sentiment appeared to swing back toward support of the government. In mid-January of 1974, with industrial peace not yet reestablished, it appeared that the prime minister might call for new elections to take advantage of the trend.

Labour Party Developments. Although Labour candidates did well in the local elections held in April, internal developments in the party seemed to have an adverse effect on its fortunes. The left wing, represented especially by Wedgwood Benn, made a determined effort to swing the party away from its allegedly "centrist" tendencies, and was supported by the leaders of several major trade unions.

At the party's annual conference in October, the left tried to commit the party to nationalizing over 25 leading companies if returned to power. Former Prime Minister Harold Wilson, the party's leader, was able to defeat this move, but he emphasized that extensions of public ownership were still a main priority of the party, even if it remained inappropriate to specify the precise number of firms involved.

The party was united in its opposition to the government's prices and incomes policy and remained committed to repeal of the Industrial Relations Act. On the question of British participation in the Common Market, it was more divided, though officially opposed. In general, the complexion of the new "shadow cabinet," elected by Labour MP's, showed the degree to which the party's parliamentary contingent lagged behind in the leftward drift of the party as a whole.

Miniscandal. On May 22, Lord Lambton, undersecretary of state for defense, resigned from the government after revelations about his connections with call girls and his use of narcotics. Two days later Lord Jellicoe, leader of the House of Lords, admitted to having had "casual affairs" with prostitutes and gave up his senior cabinet post as lord privy seal. Despite a furor in the popular press, these incidents appeared to do little damage to the government's reputation. A Security Commission report in July concluded that state security had not been compromised.

The Tory Right. Within the Conservative party, the hostility between the government and Enoch Powell increased as a result of Powell's attacks on his colleagues. The former Conservative minister and spokesman for the right wing accused his party's leaders of bad faith, especially in their failure to moderate inflation by limiting the money supply. He also criticized British entry into the Common Market, but made no significant inroads into the support for Prime Minister Heath and his ministers among the Conservative rank and file.

Parliament and the EEC. The position of the British Parliament under the European Economic Community was a topic of concern throughout the year. British MP's at the European Parliament in Strasbourg were critical of the "formal set-piece" character of the debate there, and introduced a variant of the British Parliament's "question time" into the procedure. At home, a House of Commons select committee reported in November that legislation proceeding directly from the EEC Commission constituted a serious threat to British parliamentary control, and recommended the creation of a new permanent committees to review such legislation.

Agreement with Iceland. The Icelandic fisheries dispute, which arose in 1971 when Iceland unilaterally extended its offshore territorial waters from 12 miles to 50 miles, appeared to be settled by November 1973, when the Icelandic government agreed to allow trawling within the 50-mile limit and Britain agreed to reduce its annual catch. Live shots had been fired by an Icelandic vessel in March, and a British frigate was sent to protect British trawlers in May.

NORTHERN IRELAND

A fresh approach to settlement of the problem of Northern Ireland was being attempted in 1973, even as the killing of soldiers and private citizens by Protestant and Roman Catholic terrorists continued.

IN NORTHERN IRELAND, youngsters in Armagh (above) throw stones and bottles at the police who had stopped an unofficial march. Other children entered a poster contest open to both Protestants and Catholics. A typical entry (right) appeals to both sides in struggle to stop the fighting.

Power-Sharing Proposals. On March 8, a promised plebiscite was held in Ulster on the question of joining the Irish Republic. With the province's Catholics boycotting the referendum, only 58% of the qualified voters took part. Nearly all of them (57% of the total electorate) voted to remain part of the United Kingdom. On the assumption that this result would do something to reassure the Protestants that union with the Republic of Ireland would no longer be in question, the British government proceeded with plans for constitutional reform in Northern Ireland, the principal aim of which was to give the large Catholic minority greater representation in the Ulster government.

On March 20, an official white paper on Northern Irish reform was published. It contained the following principles:

• Ulster was to remain a part of the United Kingdom as long as a majority of its inhabitants so wished.

• Ulster would retain its 12-member representation in the British Parliament.

• A Northern Ireland Assembly of 80 members was to be created, to be elected by proportional representation.

• The committees of the Assembly were to be "balanced" in their representation of the Catholic and Protestant communities.

• Administration was to be vested in a new Northern Irish Executive, to consist of the Assembly committee chairmen.

• The military campaign against terrorism was to continue.

• Discrimination on religious grounds was to be illegal. (This was an attempt to deal with Catholic allegations that distribution of economic and social resources was biased in favor of Protestant groups.)

• There was to be consultation and cooperation with the government of Éire.

June Election. On June 28 the first elections to the New Assembly were held. More than 72% of the electorate voted, despite attempts to force a Catholic boycott. The election revolved around the acceptability of the white paper proposals. These

were supported by the "official" Unionist party of former Ulster Prime Minister Brian Faulkner, which won 22 seats, and by the major Catholic party, the Social Democratic and Labour party (SDLP), which won 19. The proposals were opposed by the Rev. Ian D. Paisley's Democratic Unionist party (8 seats) and William Craig's Vanguard group (7 seats). The bare majority won by the pro-white paper groups was made even more precarious by the ambivalent attitude of 13 dissident, or "non-official," Unionists elected to the Assembly, and by the weakness of Faulkner's hold on his own "official" Unionists. The moderate position was strengthened, on the other hand, by the non-sectarian Alliance party, which won 8 seats in the Assembly.

The British leadership, which had hoped to see a great victory for moderation, was somewhat disappointed. However, the success of the SDLP meant that, for the first time since 1922, Catholic-based politicians had achieved representation in the Ulster Assembly in something like just proportion to their electoral support in Ulster. The SDLP performance had also enhanced its claim to represent political Catholic forces against the revolutionary IRA.

Formation of the Executive. Great obstacles to peace remained. The first meeting of the new Assembly, on July 31, broke up in disorder because

CIVIL SERVANTS in Britain take part in work-hour walkouts to protest a government freeze on their wages.

of the determination of the Paisley and Craig parties to obstruct and destroy the idea of power-sharing between majority and minority groups. Moreover, the possibility of creating a bipartisan executive depended upon the negotiation of outstanding differences between Faulkner and the SDLP leaders. Faulkner stressed the need for the SDLP to renounce any intention to merge with the south, while the SDLP had serious reservations both about the British government's policy of internment of suspected terrorists and about the nature of the future links between Northern Ireland and Éire.

Agreement about the nature of the executive was reached, and all of its members were selected by the end of November. The 11-member body was to be headed by Faulkner and was to include five of his Unionist supporters, four SDLP representatives, and one member of the Alliance party.

Council of Ireland. The selection of the executive body cleared the way for a new top-level conference about the larger question of peace in Ireland. On December 9, after a four-day meeting in London, Faulkner, Heath, Prime Minister Liam Cosgrave of the Irish Republic, and various other delegates from Ulster, Éire, and Britain agreed to establish the Council of Ireland. It was to consist of seven members of the Ulster executive body and seven members of the Irish Republican government and was to serve as a permanent link between the province and the republic. The council was to have its own "secretariat" and was to be assisted by a 60-member consultative body made up equally of members of the Irish Republican Parliament and members of the Assembly of Northern Ireland.

The accord on December 9 included several major concessions on both sides, perhaps the most dramatic of which was Dublin's pledge to recognize that the present status of Ulster—that is, its link with Britain—could not be altered without a majority decision in the North to do so. Despite this concession, however, Protestant opinion in Northern Ireland became increasingly inflamed against both the new power-sharing executive and the Council of Ireland on the basis that both could represent steps toward the unification of Ulster and the Irish Republic.

By the end of December it was clear that weakening support for Faulkner within his own group of moderate Unionists was to pose one of the more serious threats to the success of the initiatives. On Jan. 7, 1974, four days after the first meeting of the new executive body, Faulkner lost control of his party and resigned as its leader, but he retained his post as Northern Ireland's chief executive and pledged to use his influence as head of the governing coalition to gain acceptance of the Council of Ireland agreement.

Violence. Terrorism waxed and waned through 1973. To the continuing killings in Northern Ireland were added numerous incidents in England—especially London—where bombings were apparently designed to pressure the British government in its Ulster policies. More than 200 persons were injured in two London explosions on March 8, several more by letter-bombs in London offices in August. Both the IRA and Protestant extremists were adamantly opposed to the Council of Ireland agreement, and there was a consequent escalation of bombings and shootings in December in Ulster and England.

A. J. BEATTIE, *The London School of Economics and Political Science*

SYGMA

PRESIDENT George Papadopoulos of the new Greek republic takes the oath of office (above). Exiled King Constantine and Queen Anne Marie are at right.

UPI

GREECE

Momentous political developments, including the abolition of the monarchic system and a bloodless military coup that toppled the government of George Papadopoulos, dominated events in Greece in 1973.

Challenges to Papadopoulos. George Papadopoulos began the year as Greece's regent, premier, minister of foreign affairs, and minister of planning and governmental policy. Early on, however, he met vocal opposition to his government, which had evolved from a military coup on April 21, 1967. Student boycotts, sit-ins, and demonstrations in the first four months of 1973 became the most marked antigovernmental agitations since 1967. The regime countered with police force, and it annulled the draft deferments of dissident students.

In April four retired generals, who had not participated in the 1967 coup, released the text of a letter in which they strongly called on Papadopoulos to restore democracy to Greece. That same month Constantine Caramanlis, the former conservative Greek premier (1955–63), issued a statement from Paris, his residence for the past 10 years. He boldly urged the Papadopoulos regime to resign and to give back actual rule to exiled King Constantine II. Though at that point Papadopoulos still recognized him as king of the Hellenes, Constantine had resided with his family in Rome since December 1967 when he had unsuccessfully tried to replace the leaders of the previous April's coup.

In May the government announced that it had forestalled a naval mutiny planned for the 23d of that month by several retired pro-royalist admirals and others whose intention it was to replace Papadopoulos. About this same time the captain of a Greek destroyer received asylum in Italy along with six junior officers and 24 sailors.

Abolition of the Monarchy. Unrest in the navy, long a royalist stronghold, gave the Papadopoulos regime an opportunity to turn publicly against King Constantine. Citing what he called the king's com-

plicity in the naval disturbances, Papadopoulos announced on June 1 that the monarchy was ended and that the king and his heirs were deposed. A republic was proclaimed with Papadopoulos as provisional president, and a referendum was set for July 29. Papadopoulos thus put himself in direct opposition to the 1968 constitution, which he had sponsored and which had retained the monarchy.

From Rome, King Constantine termed his deposition an illegal act and stated that he had no connection with the events in the navy. Announcing that he still considered himself to be lawful king of the Hellenes, he voiced his conviction that one day he would return to Greece to become the guardian of constitutional government.

The referendum of July 29 really did not give the electorate a chance to vote on the monarchy. It was designed to give a "yes" or "no" vote for the constitutional changes Papadopoulos desired in setting up a new regime with wide presidential powers that he would hold until 1981. Papadopoulos was the only candidate for president, and Gen. Odysseus Anghelis, the only candidate for the vice presidency, a position he had held since June 15. The final referendum results showed that 77.2% of the votes cast had been affirmative. Opponents of the regime, however, charged that there had been widespread occurrences of fraud and intimidation.

Papadopoulos was formally installed as president on August 19. That same day he abolished martial

AT A FOLK DANCE before his ouster, Papadopoulos (left) appears with Phaidon Gizikis (center), who replaced him, and military strong man Dimitrios Ioannidis (right).

law wherever it was in effect, and he announced an amnesty for about 350 political prisoners. Among these was Alexander Panagoulis, who had tried to assassinate Papadopoulos in 1968. The president also affirmed that suspended articles of the constitution dealing with civil liberties would be restored and that a freely elected parliament would meet in 1974. Papadopoulos named Spyros Markezinis

------------ **GREECE • Information Highlights** ------------

Official Name: Hellenic Republic.
Location: Southeastern Europe.
Area: 50,944 square miles (131,944 sq km).
Population (1973 est.): 9,100,000. *Density,* 173 per square mile (67 per sq km).
Chief Cities (1971 census): Athens, the capital, 862,133; Salonika, 339,496; Piraeus, 186,223; Patras, 110,632.
Government: *Head of state,* Phaidon Gizikis, president (took office Nov. 1973). *Head of government,* Adamantios Androutsopoulos, premier (took office Nov. 1973). *Legislature*—Parliament (dissolved 1967).
Language: Greek (official).
Education: *Expenditure* (1969), 10.7% of total public expenditure. *School enrollment* (1969)—primary, 948,097; secondary, 521,819; technical/vocational, 103,202; university/higher, 72,616.
Monetary Unit: Drachma (27 drachmas equal U. S.$1, Oct. 1973).
Gross National Product (1972 est.): $11,650,000,000.
Economic Indexes: *Industrial production* (1972), 245 (1963 = 100); *agricultural production* (1971), 130 (1963 = 100); *consumer price index* (1972), 126 (1963 = 100).
Manufacturing (major products): Construction materials, textiles, chemicals, petroleum products, processed foods, ships.
Major Agricultural Products: Olives (ranks 3d among world producers, 1972), tobacco, grapes, cotton, wheat, citrus fruits, tomatoes, raisins, sugar beets.
Major Minerals: Bauxite, lignite, magnesite, iron ore, chromium ore.
Foreign Trade (1972): Exports, $871,000,000; Imports, $2,346,-000,000. *Chief trading partners* (1971)—West Germany (took 20% of exports, supplied 19% of imports); France (9%—7%); United States (9%—6.6%); Italy (8.6%—9%).
Tourism: Receipts (1971), $305,300,000.
Transportation: *Motor vehicles* (1971), 391,700 (automobiles, 263,200); *railroads* (1971), 1,598 miles (2,571 km); *merchant fleet* (1972), 15,329,000 gross registered tons; *major national airline,* Olympic Airways.
Communications: *Telephones* (1972), 1,229,630; *newspapers* (1971), 107 (daily circulation, 682,000).

premier in October and installed a civilian cabinet.

Upheaval and Coup. On November 4 a memorial service for George Papandreou, a former Liberal premier who died in 1968, turned into an antigovernment demonstration. Numerous civilians and policemen were injured in street clashes. Demonstrations continued. By November 17 some 2,000 students were barricaded on the campus of Athens Polytechnic University, demanding the overthrow of the government. On that date troops crashed through the gates to quell the protest, and Papadopoulos reimposed martial law. The government succeeded in putting down the student rebellion with tanks, mass arrests, and courts martial. At least 13 persons were killed in the street.

The Papadopoulos regime had triumphed but it was not to endure long. On November 25, Papadopoulos was awakened at his seaside villa to discover that a coup was in progress. The strongman behind the coup was said to be Brig. Gen. Dimitrios Ioannidis, chief of the Greek military police. Papadopoulos was replaced as president by Lt. Gen. Phaidon Gizikis, who was promoted to full general. Adamantios Androutsopoulos, a civilian, became premier.

The new leaders overthrew Papadopoulos, they said, because he had betrayed the 1967 revolution. He had failed to reform Greek society and was leading the country toward a potentially chaotic "electoral adventure." The Gizikis government made it clear it would rule by decree indefinitely.

Resignation of Ieronymos. Archbishop Ieronymos, who had become primate of Greece in 1967 shortly after Papadopoulos' coup, faced mounting opposition during 1973 from within his own hierarchy over his conduct of church affairs. Unwanted by the Gizikis regime, Ieronymos resigned in December.

GEORGE J. MARCOPOULOS, *Tufts University*

GUINEA

There were few high-level changes in the government of Guinea in 1973 and none in the administrative structure created in 1972. The Parti Démocratique de Guinée (PDG) maintained control, and President Sékou Touré's popularity continued.

Political Developments. Throughout 1973, Radio Conakry broadcast news of various plots to overthrow the government. In April, the Central Committee ordered informational meetings held all over Guinea to alert everyone of such dangers.

The most traumatic event of 1973 was the January 20 assassination, in Conakry, of Amilcar Cabral, the leader of the liberation movement, the African Party for the Independence of Guinea and Cape Verde (PAIGC), based on neighboring Guinea-Bissau. Some of the direct participants in the assassination were arrested immediately. Hundreds of persons, many of them PAIGC members, were detained. Subsequently all but 50 were released and Touré pledged that the PAIGC would conduct the trials of the accused.

Foreign Affairs. In April, Liberian President William Tolbert and Sierra Leone's leader, Siaka Stevens, visited Conakry to confer on ways to strengthen ties between the three states. In June, Major Mathieu Kerekou, the leader of Dahomey, visited Conakry.

Guinea's relations with France did not improve measurably in 1973. Touré charged that Jacques Foccart, France's secretary-general for African affairs, is an active imperialist, who has been implicated in sending mercenaries against African nations.

In June, Touré denounced attempts to associate African states more closely with the European Economic Community (Common Market). He called on Africa to break away from neo-colonialism.

Economic Developments. Agricultural development fell short of government projections, partly due to the failure of the cooperatives to modernize. The output of many small factories also fell short of goals due to poor management and shortages of raw material.

Mining production exceeded expectations. Despite Touré's fear of foreign domination, he continued to seek investments to exploit Guinea's mineral wealth. The large bauxite complex at Boke was opened in May under the general control of the government's Compagnie des Bauxite de Guinée in cooperation with a consortium of foreign companies. A new 136-mile (218-km) railway connecting the complex to a new deepwater port at Kamsar was also put into operation. Full production of 6 million tons per year is expected in 1975. The smaller bauxite operation at Fria continued functioning under Guinean control in cooperation with several U. S. aluminum companies.

Guinea, Liberia, Algeria, Zaire, and Nigeria agreed to joint exploitation of the rich iron deposits in eastern Guinea. They contracted with a Japanese firm for plans to improve the port of Conakry and to build a $450 million trans-Guinea railroad, 500 miles (800 km) long, linking the mines to Conakry.

HARRY A. GAILEY
San Jose State University

GUYANA

The major event in Guyana in 1973 was the nation's second general election since independence.

Election. Contending for 53 seats in the National Assembly were 212 candidates, representing four parties. After the voting on July 16, Prime Minister Forbes Burnham's party, the People's National Congress (PNC), won 37 seats, the People's Progressive party of former Premier Cheddi Jagan, 14 seats, and the Guyana Liberator party, 2 seats.

Legislation. The election gave Prime Minister Burnham's government a two-thirds majority in the Assembly, which was its avowed objective. Burnham had declared that he wished this majority to make possible the creation of a strong government, and to enact measures abolishing the use of the British Privy Council as the highest court of appeal in Guyana, and to reduce the voting age from 21 to 18. The two measures, requiring two-thirds approval, were passed by the new Assembly.

――――――― **GUINEA • Information Highlights** ―――――――

Official Name: Republic of Guinea.
Location: West coast of Africa.
Area: 94,926 square miles (245,857 sq km).
Population (1973 est.): 4,200,000. *Density,* 43 per square mile (17 per sq km).
Chief Cities (1967 census): Conakry, the capital, 197,267; Kankan (1964 est.), 29,100.
Government: *Head of state,* Sékou Touré, president (took office for 2d 7-year term Jan. 1968). *Head of government,* Lansana Beavogui, premier (took office April 1972). *Legislature* (unicameral)—National Assembly. *Major political party*—Guinean Democratic party (PDG).
Languages: French (official), local languages, English.
Education: *Expenditure* (1965), 19.4% of total public expenditure. *School enrollment* (1968)—primary, 167,340; secondary, 41,736; technical/vocational, 5,334; university/higher, 942.
Monetary Unit: Sily (20.463 silys equal U.S.$1, July 1973).
Gross National Product (1971 est.): $325,000,000.
Manufacturing (major products): Alumina and aluminum products, processed foods, soap.
Major Agricultural Products: Coffee, palm oil and kernels, pineapples, rice, cassava, citrus fruits, groundnuts, sweet potatoes, bananas.
Major Minerals: Bauxite, diamonds, iron ore.
Foreign Trade (1971): Exports, $48,400,000; Imports, $68,500,000. *Chief trading partners* (1969)—Eastern Europe (took 26% of exports, supplied 31% of imports); France (11%—10%); United States (10%—28%).
Transportation: *Motor Vehicles* (1969), 20,000 (automobiles, 8,000); *railroads* (1971), 411 miles (661 km); *major national airline,* Air Guinée.
Communications: *Telephones* (1972), 7,488; *newspapers* (1971), 1 (daily circulation, 5,000).

――――――― **GUYANA • Information Highlights** ―――――――

Official Name: Republic of Guyana.
Location: Northeast coast of South America.
Area: 83,000 square miles (214,970 sq km).
Population (1973 est.): 800,000. *Density,* 10 per square mile (4 per sq km).
Chief City (1970 census): Georgetown, the capital, 167,068 (metropolitan area).
Government: *Head of state,* Arthur Chung, president (took office March 1970). *Head of government,* Forbes Burnham, prime minister (took office Dec. 1964). *Legislature* (unicameral)—National Assembly. *Major political parties*—People's National Congress; People's Progressive party; Guyana Liberator party.
Languages: English (official), various East Indian dialects.
Education: *Expenditure* (1969), 13.1% of total public expenditure. *School enrollment* (1969)—primary, 129,527; secondary, 55,911; technical/vocational, 2,639; university/higher, 1,085.
Monetary Unit: Guyana dollar (2.12 G. dollars equal U.S.$1, Aug. 1973).
Gross National Product (1971 est.): $270,000,000.
Consumer Price Index (1972), 124 (1964=100).
Manufacturing (major products): Processed foods, alumina.
Major Agricultural Products: Sugarcane, rice, corn, coconuts, livestock, fish.
Major Minerals: Bauxite, diamonds, gold.
Foreign Trade (1972): Exports, $143,000,000; Imports, $145,000,000. *Chief trading partners* (1971)—United Kingdom (took 27% of exports, supplied 31% of imports); Canada (25%—5.5%); Commonwealth Caribbean countries (17%—15%).
Transportation: *Motor Vehicles* (1971), 28,000 (automobiles, 19,600); *railroads* (1971), 40 miles (64 km).
Communications: *Telephones* (1972), 14,691; *newspapers* (1970), 3 (daily circulation, 44,000).

Election Protests. The results of the election were challenged. The People's Progressive party was especially vigorous in its claims that the government had used the army to coerce voters and steal votes. Cheddi Jagan declared that the result of the election was to establish a "fascist" regime in Guyana. The opposition objected particularly to changes in the electoral law which substituted the central counting of all votes in Georgetown for the traditional procedure of counting the votes locally and reporting the results to a central electoral headquarters. The PPP refused to take the legislative seats allotted to it.

Inter-American Affairs. On July 4, Guyana's representatives signed the Treaty of Chaguaramas, thus making Guyana a founding member of the Caribbean Community and Common Market. On September 2, Prime Minister Burnham played host to Cuban Premier Fidel Castro on the latter's first visit to an independent Commonwealth Caribbean country, and the two men subsequently traveled together to the conference of nonaligned nations in Algiers.

ROBERT J. ALEXANDER, *Rutgers University*

HAITI

Additional cracks appeared in the Haitian ruling group during 1973, but an inner core remained united behind the young president, Jean Claude Duvalier, who had succeeded his late father, the long-time dictator François ("Papa Doc") Duvalier, in April 1971. The economy continued to improve slowly for the small fraction of the population that benefits from tourism, light industry, and foreign investment, but remained stagnant for the great rural majority.

Political Affairs. The principal figures within the secretive Haitian ruling group in 1973 appeared to be Simone Duvalier (the mother of the president), Breton Claude (commander of the Dessalines Battalion), and Gracia Jacques (commander of the Presidential Guard). Throughout the year this triumvirate juggled various political factions while maintaining a rough balance of power.

In January 1973, the new minister of the interior, Roger Lafontant, was dismissed. This occurred barely two months after he himself had engineered the dismissal of his predecessor, the reputed strongman Luckner Cambronne. Lafontant, though no radical, had brought young men into the government at a rapid pace, threatening both the economic and political interests of the old guard, which was made up largely of faithful retainers of the former president.

At about the time of Lafontant's dismissal, the regime suffered two further embarrassments. On January 23, political opponents of the regime seized the U. S. ambassador, demanding ransom and a flight to safety for themselves and 12 young political prisoners. These terms were met and the victims were released unharmed. Also troublesome to Haiti's image was a series of violent clashes involving many of the several hundred candidates campaigning for 58 seats in the National Assembly. All proclaimed themselves Duvalierists, but the old guard battled youthful challengers up to election day (February 11).

Following these crises, calm returned to the country for a few months, although political intrigues continued. In June the government permitted Marie Denise, the ambitious sister of the president, to return home. On June 23, a mysterious

--------- HAITI • Information Highlights ---------

Official Name: Republic of Haiti.
Location: Western third of the island of Hispaniola in the Caribbean Sea.
Area: 10,714 square miles (27,750 sq km).
Population (1973 est.): 5,600,000. *Density,* 464 per square mile (179 per sq km).
Chief Cities (1971 census): Port-au-Prince, the capital, 419,-900; Cape Haïtien, 43,600.
Government: *Head of state,* Jean-Claude Duvalier, president for life (took office April 1971). *Head of government,* Jean-Claude Duvalier. *Legislature* (unicameral)—National Assembly. *Major political party*—Parti de l'Unité Nacionale.
Languages: French (official), Creole patois.
Education: *School enrollment* (1968)—primary, 291,000; secondary, 34,230; technical/vocational, 6,400; university/higher (1966), 1,527.
Monetary Unit: Gourde (5 gourdes equal U. S.$1, Aug. 1973).
Gross National Product (1971 est.): $462,000,000.
Consumer Price Index (1972), 138 (1963=100).
Manufacturing (major products): Processed foods, sugar.
Major Agricultural Products: Sugarcane, sisal, coffee, cacao, bananas, tobacco, corn, cassava.
Major Minerals: Bauxite, copper.
Foreign Trade (1971): Exports, $47,000,000; Imports, $60,000,-000. *Chief trading partners* (1970)—United States (took 60% of exports, supplied 46% of imports); Belgium-Luxembourg; France; Italy.
Transportation: *Motor vehicles* (1970), 13,100 (automobiles, 11,600).
Communications: *Telephones* (1972), 4,600; *newspapers* (1971), 7.

fire severely damaged the presidential palace, exploded the country's major munitions dump (which was located in the palace basement), and destroyed the security communications center.

Whatever the hidden reasons for or connections between these events, the regime in early August reshuffled political office holders in the most profound shakeup of Jean Claude's presidency. Some 50 military and civilian officials either lost their jobs or were assigned to lesser positions. Marie Denise again left the country, but several of her allies found themselves in important posts. When the dust had settled it appeared that only Cambronne's faction and a "Young Turk" movement in the armed forces had suffered severely. The triumvirate had survived, and a balance had been maintained among factions of the old guard, youthful aspirants to political positions, and moderate-nationalist reformers.

The Economy. Several new foreign owned firms launched operations in Haiti during 1973. Tourist activity was brisk, with over 100,000 visitors recorded for the second straight year as new hotels continued to be built and old ones refurbished. At the same time some capital was being repatriated, the banking business was expanding, and financial reserves were up.

Unfortunately for the majority of people, agriculture remained stagnant. Coffee production equaled that of 1972, but exports declined slightly. Sugar and molasses production was also lower, while sisal increased modestly and cocoa was unchanged.

International Relations and Foreign Aid. The year witnessed major improvements in Haiti's relation with Western nations. As its U. S. contacts continued to grow, Haiti rejoined the list of countries eligible to participate in U. S. military sales and credit programs.

Two substantial loans, for development of Haiti's port facilities and highways, had been announced by the Inter-American Development bank by October. Most strikingly, France initiated an ambitious 10-year program of scientific, technological, cultural, and economic aid.

KARL M. SCHMITT
The University of Texas at Austin

--------- **HAWAII** • Information Highlights ---------

Area: 6,450 square miles (16,706 sq km).
Population (1972 est.): 809,000. *Density:* 123 per sq mi.
Chief Cities (1970 census): Honolulu, the capital, 324,871; Kailua, 33,783; Kaneohe, 29,903; Hilo, 26,353; Waipahu, 24,150; Pearl City, 19,552; Wahiawa, 17,598.
Government (1973): *Chief Officers*—governor, John A. Burns (D); lt. gov., George R. Ariyoshi (D); atty. gen., George T. H. Pai (D); supt. of education, Shiro Amioka; chief justice, William S. Richardson. *Legislature*—Senate, 25 members (17 Democrats, 8 Republicans); House of Representatives, 51 members (35 D, 16 R).
Education (1972–73): *Enrollment*—public elementary schools, 98,700 pupils, 4,945 teachers; public secondary schools, 81,400 pupils, 3,455 teachers; nonpublic schools, 21,700 pupils, 910 teachers; colleges and universities, 35,155 students. *Public school expenditures,* $173,620,000 ($1,046 per pupil). *Average teacher's salary,* $10,900.
State Finances (fiscal year 1971): *Revenues,* $689,184,000 (4% general sales tax and receipts taxes, $177,859,000; motor fuel tax, $18,138,000; federal funds, $144,468,000). *Expenditures,* $720,094,000 (education, $290,256,000; health, welfare, and safety, $79,278,000; highways, $60,465,000). *State debt,* $679,043,000 (June 30, 1971).
Personal Income (1972): $3,991,000,000; *per capita,* $4,995.
Public Assistance (1972): $89,269,000. *Average monthly payments* (Dec. 1972)—old-age assistance, $105.95; aid to families with dependent children, $295.43.
Labor Force: *Nonagricultural wage and salary earners* (July 1973), 323,600. *Average annual employment* (1972)—manufacturing, 24,800; trade, 73,500; government, 79,400; services, 64,700. *Insured unemployed* (Sept. 1973)—10,300 (3.7%).
Manufacturing (1971): *Value added by manufacture,* $435,-000,000. Food and kindred products, $254,000,000; printing and publishing, $49,000,000; stone, clay, and glass products, $26,800,000; apparel and other textile products, $24,-300,000; fabricated metal products, $12,800,000; nonelectrical machinery, $4,700,000.
Agriculture (1972): *Cash farm income,* $234,544,000 (livestock, $46,238,000; crops, $177,198,000; government payments, $11,108,000). *Chief crops*—Sugarcane for sugar and seed; macadamia nuts; papayas; pineapples.
Mining (1972): *Production value,* $28,834,000 (ranks 45th among the states). *Chief minerals*—Stone, $14,506,000; cement, $11,233,000; sand and gravel, $1,972,000; pumice, $743,000.
Fisheries (1972): *Commercial catch,* 14,686,000 pounds ($5,-097,000). *Leading species by value*—Tuna, $3,559,000; red snapper, $234,000.
Transportation: *Roads* (1972), 3,591 miles (5,779 km); *motor vehicles* (1972), 426,219; *public airports* (1972), 23.
Communications: *Telephones* (1972), 447,263; *television stations* (1971), 10; *radio stations* (1971), 29; *newspapers* (1973), 5 (daily circulation, 238,000).

HAWAII

A booming economy, increasing activity by Japanese business interests, and, paradoxically, an unbalanced state budget were all part of the mosaic of life in Hawaii during 1973.

The Economy. During 1973, Hawaii's economy continued in a strong recovery from its 1970–71 slowdown. Unemployment dropped from 6.0 to 5.4% by midyear. Strongly contributing to the advance was an increase in national defense expenditures in the state, following the withdrawal of military units from Indochina to Hawaiian bases. A rise of about 20% in the number of tourists also stimulated business activity. By year's end, Hawaii welcomed approximately 2.6 million visitors—about three times the total resident population.

Increased Japanese Activity. Growing numbers of tourists were coming from Japan (some 300,000 in 1973), a circumstance that led hotels and shops in tourist areas to post bilingual signs and encourage their staffs to learn conversational Japanese. Indeed, several of the large hotels were owned by Japanese firms, as were a growing number of other enterprises in Hawaii.

The number of businesses owned by nonresident Japanese stood at 8 in 1959, just prior to statehood. By mid-1973, they totalled 84, with 50 of those having been established since 1970. During 1972 and 1973, the value of hotels and commercial firms acquired by Japanese enterprise in Hawaii considerably exceeded $100 million. This expansion followed sustained efforts by the state government

to attract capital from around the Pacific rim. It was undoubtedly furthered by the decline in the exchange value of the U. S. dollar.

Ecological Concerns. Questions as to the effects of continued economic growth and development on the environment and quality of life were repeatedly raised, sometimes in the courts. Legal suits in 1973 delayed construction of a new "interstate" highway across a valley in central Oahu and of a jet runway across a reef adjacent to the Honolulu International Airport. A state commission · was studying the feasibility of limiting the population growth of Hawaii as a means of checking environmental degradation.

A University of Hawaii research project began exploring means of using some of the natural heat being generated on the volcanically active Island of Hawaii as a source of electric power through a relatively non-polluting conversion process. Such heat conversion was already taking place elsewhere in the United States (in the Geysers area, north of San Francisco) and in six other nations.

Labor and Budget Problems. Public school teachers throughout the state went out on strike for two weeks in April over implementation of their first collective bargaining agreement. Their pay increase added to the state's deficit, since the 1973 legislature failed to enact a new tax bill. Facing higher salaries for other state employees, Gov. John A. Burns appointed a commission to study Hawaii's finances and report to the 1975 Legislature on how to balance the budget. No basic tax changes were expected in 1974—an election year for both the governor and the legislators.

ROBERT M. KAMINS, *University of Hawaii*

HEALTH CARE. See SOCIAL WELFARE.
HEART DISEASE. See MEDICINE.
HEATH, Edward. See BIOGRAPHY.
HIGHWAYS. See TRANSPORTATION.

HOBBIES

Developments in the various hobbies are discussed in this article. It consists of the following sections: (1) General Survey; (2) Coin Collecting; and (3) Stamp Collecting.

General Survey

In 1973, craft hobbies continued their spectacular growth. Needlecraft was the most widespread of the creative hand hobbies. In other craft areas, decoupage, stained glass, and leatherwork ranked high in popularity.

Needlecraft. Needlepoint, petit point, and rugmaking were engaged in with enthusiasm. String pictures and macrame also continued to attract numerous people. Kits, containing in one package all the materials and instructions needed to help in starting, were available in numerous designs and patterns.

Other Crafts. Among other crafts, the most popular were decoupage, a form of decorating which utilizes varnish or lacquer and printed paper cutouts; stained glass; flowers made from a wide variety of materials; bead work; and leathercraft. Egg decorating received a big boost with the introduction of plastic eggs in various sizes (the use of wild bird eggs is generally illegal).

Model Trains and Planes. Model railroading remained extremely popular. Enthusiasts delved into

narrow gauge, period railroading, and traction, and collected both scale models and toy trains. National Model Railroad Association membership reached an all-time high in 1973.

Model aviation also experienced growth despite anticipated shortages of balsa wood and fuel. Interest centered on radio-controlled airplanes; control-line models; free flight (gas powered); and R/C soaring models. Easily obtainable FCC licenses are required for all R/C model use.

Collecting Hobbies. Collecting hobbies thrived. Modelers had developed detailing and painting techniques that made low-cost plastic models, assembled with parts and decorated with paints available at hobby shops, look like custom-made museum pieces.

Scale-model soldiers of both past and present were available. More serious workers preferred cast-metal figures, but detailed plastic models were also popular. Meticulous painting, after careful research, is needed to ensure authenticity.

Hobby Organizations. There are hobby organizations for virtually all hobbies. Well-known organizations include the National Model Railroad Association, the Academy of Model Aeronautics, and the North American Model Boat Association.

HAROLD C. CARSTENS
Carstens Publications, Inc.

Stamp Collecting

The U. S. Postal Service left no doubt in 1973 that it was determined to promote its stamp business to help reduce deficits, even if this involved direct competition with private enterprise.

Postal Service Activities. At a symposium to which collectors and dealers were invited, officials of the new Stamps Department unveiled several programs that were ready for introduction or being developed. For example, a film that will urge youngsters to buy only domestic stamps as they are issued

U.S. COMMEMORATIVE STAMPS OF 1973		
Subject	Denomination	Date of issue
Love	8¢	Jan. 26
Ballooning aerogram	15¢	Feb. 10
Pamphleteer	8¢	Feb. 16
George Gershwin, composer	8¢	Feb. 26
Posting a Broadside	8¢	April 13
Copernicus	8¢	April 23
Postal people	10x8¢	April 30
Harry S. Truman	8¢	May 8
Post Rider	8¢	June 22
Boston Tea Party	4x8¢	July 4
Progress in Electronics	6¢, 8¢, 11¢, 15¢	July 10
Robinson Jeffers, poet	8¢	Aug. 13
Lyndon B. Johnson	8¢	Aug. 27
Henry O. Tanner, painter	8¢	Sept. 10
Postal Card centenary	6¢	Sept. 14
Willa Cather, novelist	8¢	Sept. 20
Drummer of Revolution	8¢	Sept. 28
Angus Cattle centenary	8¢	Oct. 5
Christmas	2x8¢	Nov. 7
Jefferson Memorial	10¢	Dec. 14

will be shown in elementary schools. Also, shops will be opened in 10,000 post-office lobbies to sell new issues plus such nonpostal items as albums, catalogues, posters, and nonmailable souvenir cards.

New Stamps. The U. S. government again violated its policy of releasing only 15 stamps a year for special occasions. In 1973 there were 35 commemoratives and a number of high-priced definitives with a total cost of $11.44. Two of these new issues —the postal workers stamps and the Amadeo P. Giannini commemorative—came in for criticism.

Avowedly to "pay tribute to postal workers," 10 different 8-cent stamps were authorized by Postmaster General E. T. Klassen. Their pictures and their text, which is printed on the gummed backside, laud the efficiency of mail-handling services. Since those services have deteriorated, the public regarded these commemoratives as ill-timed at best. The American Philatelic Society considered the issuance of 10 stamps, where one would have sufficed, as exploitative and assigned its "black blot" to them. It is given to all stamps intended more for revenue than for postal service.

After millions of new 21-cent stamps honoring the banker Giannini were printed, a collector who saw an advance photograph noted that the first name was erroneously spelled "Amedeo." Stocks had to be destroyed and costly new plates engraved.

Prices. The philatelic market reflected both increasing demands for rare classic stamps and the declining value of the U. S. dollar on the international market. Prices continued to soar, with most valuable specimens going to European and Japanese buyers at American auctions.

Stamp Shows. The Aero-Philatelic Club of Britain and the American Air Mail Society marked their 50th anniversaries with stamp shows and celebrations in Manchester, England, and Washington, D. C. International stamp shows were held in West Germany, Iceland, Poland, India, and Israel.

ERNEST A. KEHR, *Stamp News Bureau*

Coin Collecting

Early in 1973 the General Services Administration (GSA), an agency of the U. S. government, offered for sale coins from its hoard of nearly 3 million silver dollars minted during the late 19th century. Most attractive to collectors were uncirculated specimens from the Carson City mint that had been stored from the time of mintage. These coins were offered on a bid basis, with a minimum of $30 set for each Carson City coin.

NEEDLEWORK of all types reached unprecedented heights of popularity in the United States. Shown here is Erica Wilson, a leading authority and designer.

ERICA WILSON

Commemorative U. S. stamps issued during 1973 included two honoring recently deceased presidents—Harry S. Truman and Lyndon B. Johnson. The bicentennial of the Boston Tea Party was commemorated with a series of four stamps that together make one picture, and Paul Revere's ride was the subject of a stamp entitled Rise of the Spirit of Independence.

The Hobby Protection Act, signed by President Nixon on November 30, requires that copies of coins, paper money, tokens, and medals be "clearly and permanently marked" with the word "copy."

Increases in Prices. Political and financial uncertainties, precipitated in part by two devaluations of the U. S. dollar, forced the price of gold metal to more than $120 per ounce on the European exchanges. In the United States the price of common gold coins rose sharply. A common-date $20 gold piece, worth about $60 in 1972, climbed to more than $190 in mid-1973. By the end of the year the price had subsided somewhat.

A number of U. S. coins were offered or sold for more than $100,000. A 1794 silver dollar, uncirculated, was sold at auction for $110,000 by Superior Galleries of Los Angeles, Calif. Bowers and Ruddy Galleries, Inc., of Hollywood, Calif., offered for sale the Idler specimen of the 1804 dollar for $165,000, a new record price. A sale at $125,000 was reported for an "extremely high relief" variety MCMVII $20 gold piece.

Museum Sale. As part of its campaign to raise funds for other purposes, the Metropolitan Museum of Art in New York City sold to the American Numismatic Society of the same city a group of more than 6,000 ancient coins. The price of $150,000 was raised by donations from ANS members.

Eisenhower Dollar. First issued in 1971, the dollar has now met with apathy on the part of the American public. In 1971 and 1972 more than 275 million Eisenhower dollars were produced for circulation. By 1973 the novelty of the new "silver dollar"—actually made of copper and nickel—had faded, and no specimens were minted for circulation. The 1973 coinage was limited to pieces ordered by coin collectors.

Bicentennial. A number of proposals were considered for the bicentennial of American independence in 1976. In September the U. S. Congress approved a bill providing for the coinage of up to 60 million pieces containing 40% silver metal. Silver has not been regularly used in coinage—except for special coins for collectors—since 1970. In October the director of the mint announced a competition among American artists to design the bicentennial coinage.

Special Sets. During 1973 the United States continued production of proof coins for collectors. Such coins, sold in sets, have achieved sales of slightly more than 3 million proof sets per year; the 1972 figure was 3,267,667. For the first time, the 1973 sets included an Eisenhower dollar in proof condition. Previously, Eisenhower dollars had to be ordered separately.

Q. DAVID BOWERS
Author of "Coins and Collectors"

HONG KONG

The unprecedented rise in Hong Kong's stock market, which had begun in 1972, reached its peak in March 1973 and then fell sharply. The government was reorganized in 1973, the flow of immigrants from China was regulated, and measures were taken to conserve energy.

Stock Market. The stock market had risen rapidly in 1972, attracting wild speculation and heavy inflows of funds from overseas. The rise continued in the first part of 1973. The Hang Seng Index of the Hong Kong Stock Exchange—the local equivalent of the Dow Jones Average—soared from 869.14 on January 2 to 1,770.85 on March 5 in one of the maddest speculative bursts seen on any stock exchange outside of Tokyo. Thousands of people gave up their jobs and gambled on shares. They sold or mortgaged their property and used all their savings to buy stocks and shares. In early 1973 at least $620 million had been drained out of the banking system and thus out of the community's savings.

The government was aware of the dangers of the overheated stock market, and before it could introduce any controls, it was too late. In mid-March the market began to fall rapidly and by June the

—————— HONG KONG • Information Highlights ——————

Official Name: Hong Kong.
Location: Southeastern coast of China.
Area: 398 square miles (1,034 sq km).
Population (1973 est.): 4,500,000. *Density,* 10,360 per square mile (4,000 per sq km).
Chief City (1971 census): Victoria, the capital, 521,612.
Government: *Head of state,* Elizabeth II, queen (acceded Feb. 1952). *Head of government,* Sir Murray MacLehose, governor (took office 1971). *Major political parties*—Democratic Self-Government party; Labour party of Hong Kong; Socialist Democratic party.
Languages: English, Cantonese Chinese (both official).
Education: *Expenditure* (1969), 22.1% of total public expenditure. *School enrollment* (1969)—primary, 746,429; secondary, 254,617; technical/vocational, 13,383; university/higher, 19,874.
Monetary Unit: Hong Kong dollar (5.085 H. K. dollars equal U. S.$1, Feb. 1973).
Gross National Product (1971 est.): $4,080,000,000.
Consumer Price Index (1972), 139 (1963=100).
Manufacturing (major products): Textiles, clothing, furniture, jewelry, plastic articles, electronic components, household utensils, toys and games, ships.
Major Agricultural Products: Rice, vegetables.
Foreign Trade (1972): *Exports,* $3,477,000,000. *Imports,* $3,902,000,000. *Chief trading partners* (1970)—United States (took 42% of exports, supplied 13% of imports); United Kingdom (14%—8%); Japan (4%—24%); China.
Tourism: *Receipts* (1972), $377,000,000.
Transportation: *Motor vehicles* (1971), 144,200 (automobiles, 110,200); *railroads* (1971), 22 miles (35 km); *merchant fleet* (1972), 458,000 gross registered tons; *major national airline,* Cathay Pacific Airways.
Communications: *Telephones* (1972), 691,616; *newspapers* (1971), 69.

Hang Seng Index had plunged to 600, and on July 11 it reached 494. The average daily turnover on the four exchanges fell from about $90 million in January to less than $15 million in June. The Index fluctuated mainly between 500 and 750 throughout the summer and autumn, but sagged to 450 in December.

The collapse was mainly due to overseas speculators who withdrew their funds after making a quick profit and to the uncertainty about the government's policy on the control of speculation and monetary flows. The situation was further deteriorated by the government's domestic rent freeze, the recall by banks of loans on share collateral, and a 2.25% hike in interest rates.

Many people lost their life savings and went broke because of the collapse of the stock market. The wild speculation also led to inflation and a slowdown of investment in manufacturing, which is the main source of Hong Kong's income. Housing costs and the cost of living rose sharply.

Immigration. Chinese immigrants flooded into Hong Kong in 1973. In September they were entering at the rate of 240 per day. In September and November, 21,203 immigrants entered Hong Kong legally. In November an agreement was reached between China and Britain that no more than 75 persons per day could leave China for Hong Kong.

Government. The Hong Kong government underwent a drastic reorganization in 1973, when it adopted the recommendations of the McKinsey Report that was published in May 1973. Six powerful cabinet-level secretaries are now in charge of the six branches of government: economy, environment, housing, security, home affairs, and social services.

An exposure of police bribery led to a thorough investigation of police corruption. The investigation resulted in the flight of a police superintendent and the prosecution and "voluntary" resignation of a few other senior officers.

Fuel Conservation. In spite of the worldwide alarm over the oil crisis in 1973, Hong Kong did not face an immediate shortage. The Chinese government also assured that shipments of kerosene and diesel fuel to Hong Kong would be increased if necessary. However, in face of a possible shortage in the future, the government announced in December that neon lights for advertising could be used only between 6:00 P. M. and 10:30 P. M., gas stations could not supply motorists with fuel or oil in containers, and winter daylight saving time was introduced. No bans on Sunday motoring or cuts in speed limits were imposed.

Rain. A total of 121.55 inches (3,087.37 mm) of rain fell in the first nine months of 1973, making it the wettest year on record. The previous record of 119.75 inches (3,041.65 mm) was set in 1889.

DAVID CHUEN-YAN LAI, *University of Victoria*

HORTICULTURE. See GARDENING AND HORTICULTURE.
HOSPITALS. See MEDICINE.
HOTELS AND MOTELS. See TOURISM.

WIDE WORLD

HONG KONG SKYLINE: Office buildings and high-rise apartment houses replace older, smaller structures on the island. The old Cat Street market area (center, background) is being razed to make way for construction of more offices and shops.

MODULAR HOUSING in Jersey City, N. J. In modular construction, entire apartments are built in a factory and hauled to the building site, where they are fastened together.

HOUSING

In 1973 the U. S. housing field underwent dramatic changes stemming from a variety of forces. Early optimism with respect to continued high levels of housing production faded when mortgage funds all but disappeared at midyear, and there was a pronounced downturn in housing starts during the remainder of the year.

Subsidized housing suffered particularly because the Nixon administration had halted new commitments to subsidize low- and middle-income housing construction on Jan. 8, 1973. On the bright side, mobile home production continued to grow despite the general downturn in conventional housing, and demand for condominiums helped boost multifamily construction. In September, President Nixon outlined several legislative proposals and administrative actions that were designed to ease the mortgage credit situation and improve housing for the poor.

Early 1973 Optimism for Housing. Housing market analysts forecast that there would be a continued strong demand for housing throughout 1973, accompanied by a plentiful if somewhat more costly supply of mortgage funds. Although the 1972 production record of 2.4 million conventional-type housing starts was not expected to be matched in 1973, there was general agreement that housing demand would soften only slightly and that the level of housing starts would modestly decrease to 2.1 million, exclusive of mobile homes.

In contrast to the private sector's optimism about housing production in 1973, the federal government opened the year on a rather gloomy note by announcing an 18-month moratorium on all new commitments for subsidy housing under the Housing and Urban Development Act of 1968.

This act provides for two subsidy programs that are administered by the Federal Housing Administration (FHA). These programs are homeownership assistance under Section 235 of the act, and assistance to builders of rental units under Section 236. Each program provides for a federal subsidy that cuts the mortgage loan interest for eligible borrowers. Outstanding subsidy commitments were not affected by the moratorium, but without new commitments the number of subsidized housing starts in 1973 could not match the 1972 level.

One reason for the moratorium was that a number of serious problems had arisen in these subsidy programs in late 1972. The programs had experienced exceptionally high default and foreclosure rates, and there was evidence of mismanagement involving both the public and private sectors.

First-Half Boom, Second-Half Bust. All in all, the widely held forecasts for 1973 seemed well founded during the first six months of 1973 (see accompanying chart). However, a credit crunch, which most experts omitted from their forecasts, was apparent by June, when the rates for short-term Treasury bills exceeded the peak of 1969—the last credit crunch on record. The short-term rate increases resulted in pressures on long-term mortgage rates so that by September 1973 home mortgage interest rates on new and existing homes had climbed to the highest level in more than 2½ years.

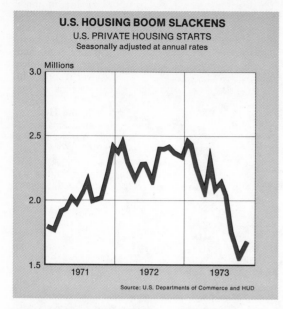

U.S. HOUSING BOOM SLACKENS
U.S. PRIVATE HOUSING STARTS
Seasonally adjusted at annual rates

Source: U.S. Departments of Commerce and HUD

Thus, at midyear 1973, the credit crunch caused a pronounced downturn in the home-building boom that had begun late in 1970. The midyear rate of just over 2 million units dropped substantially during the rest of 1973, so that housing starts fell well short of the forecast of 2.1 million units.

Housing costs continued to soar during 1973 despite the fall in starts, although the rate of increase slowed during the latter months of the year. The consumer price index (1967 = 100) listed home-ownership costs in April 1973 at 143.6, food prices at 136.4, and services at 137.0. These figures indicated that housing costs rose faster than the other inflation-sensitive items during the 1968–73 period.

Neighboring Canada provides an even more extreme example of rising housing costs. In Vancouver, for example, the average cost of a home increased from $23,970 in 1970 to $41,264 in 1973 —an increase that far surpassed the inflation rate in the United States.

Mobile Homes. Mobile homes are a large and growing segment of the U. S. housing stock. Throughout the 1970–73 housing boom, annual shipments of mobile homes increased dramatically. About 400,-000 units were shipped in 1970, 500,000 units in 1971, and 570,000 units in 1972. In 1973, the total was well over 600,000 units. Many experts foresee an annual production level of over 700,000 mobile homes by 1975 and nearly 1,000,000 units by 1980.

There are several reasons why the demand for mobile homes maintained the strength of prior years and why it is likely to do so in the foreseeable future despite the general decline in residential construction during 1973. First of all, mobile homes are an important source of low-cost housing, averaging an estimated $7,000 to $8,000 per unit in 1973. In the face of the federal government's moratorium on new commitments to subsidize housing construction, mobile home manufacturers provide an alternative source of low-cost housing.

Also, mobile homes are competing more favorably with conventionally constructed single-family homes with respect to size and style. There has been a distinct trend recently toward larger units that approach or even exceed "small home" size.

In 1960, 10-foot-wide (3-meter-wide) mobile homes were the standard of the industry, accounting for more than 90% of the total mobile-home production. During the next 13 years, changing tastes and improved technology resulted in a radical change in the size and shape of mobile homes. By 1973, 10-foot-wide mobile homes represented less than 5% of the total production, and manufacturers were producing mobile homes with widths in the range from 12 to 18 feet (3.7 to 5.5 meters). Changed also are the neighborhoods into which mobile homes may be placed. The larger, less mobile units may now be placed in planned unit developments with large recreation areas and increasingly larger lots.

Lenders have played an important role in the growth of mobile-home sales. Because of the relatively higher interest rates and shorter terms associated with mobile-home loans, mobile-home financing has long held promise for mortgage lenders. However, prior to 1969 most mobile home financing was done through finance companies and commercial banks, where the unit was treated as a chattel (personal property) and the typical terms were from five to seven years. In 1969, the Federal Home Loan Bank board authorized federal savings and loan associations to lend up to 10% of their assets in mobile-home loans. FHA and Veterans Administration programs were introduced for mobile-home financing, and credit unions moved in to compete for loans to finance the purchase of mobile homes.

In 1973, there was ample evidence of even greater movement by traditional mortgage lenders into the mobile-home field, pushing loan terms out farther into the future and making mobile homes an even more attractive alternative to conventionally constructed housing.

Multifamily Construction. The production of multifamily units provided strength to the residential construction market during most of 1973, just as in 1972. The rate of multifamily starts held closely to the one million mark in the first half of 1973 but declined during the second half.

Condominiums continued to enjoy widespread popularity during 1973. They offered the advantages of home equity during a period of record-breaking inflation, as well as property-tax and mortgage-interest deductions from taxable income.

Condominium ownership of housing was almost nonexistent in 1960 except in certain resort areas, whereas by 1970 more than 11% of all starts of ownership housing were under multifamily condominiums. It is likely that one out of every three ownership starts during 1973 was a condominium unit. This ratio becomes even higher in the larger urban areas, and many cities reported that condominiums accounted for over 40% of the new for-sale housing starts.

Mortgage Financing. In some respects, mortgage lending made the biggest housing news in the United States during 1973. One of the most critical indicators of the relative health of the nation's housing markets is the availability of mortgage funds. Short-term mortgage funds are needed to finance the construction phase of single-family and multifamily developments, and long-term mortgage funds are needed by investors in major multifamily projects and by prospective home buyers. A shortage of mortgage funds can burst the housing production bubble, as the year 1973 showed once again.

Thrift institutions—savings and loan associations and mutual savings banks—are the major source of

mortgage funds for the purchase of owner-occupied housing, and they were hit severely by the 1973 credit crunch. The mortgage-lending thrift institutions depend on savings inflows as their prime source of funds to lend for home purchases. When the U. S. Treasury and other federal agencies offer to pay savers at rates substantially higher than those they can receive on their thrift-institution passbook accounts, "disintermediation" takes place. Disintermediation is simply the diversion of funds away from a financial intermediary and directly into securities.

For the first nine months of 1973, monetary authorities followed a policy of tightening credit in order to lessen inflation. The treasury rate on three-month bills rose from 5% in January 1973 to a historic high of over 9% in early September. Thrift institutions are regulated with respect to how much they may pay on passbook and certain other accounts, and thus they found themselves at a competitive disadvantage. The impact of the high Treasury rates was seen in the record-setting net outflows of funds from the thrift institutions in the third quarter of 1973. The resultant famine in mortgage funds was a primary reason for the downturn in housing starts during the last half of 1973.

President Nixon's Housing Message. On Sept. 19, 1973, President Nixon announced his new housing plan. Specific administrative actions and legislative proposals in the President's message were aimed at easing the tight mortgage-credit situation and improving the supply of mortgage funds and access to them. In addition, President Nixon presented a new approach to the problem of housing the poor by proposing a program of direct cash assistance to those families who lack sufficient income for decent housing. Programs for subsidized housing were also included in the program of assistance, but on a very limited basis. There was no congressional plan to implement the President's proposals, at least until July 1, 1974.

STEPHEN D. MESSNER
The University of Connecticut

HOUSTON

Houston is the nation's sixth-largest city, and major events there in 1973—frequent floods, teacher discontent, a spectacular crime episode, and the still unsolved transit problem—reflected aspects of the urban situation in general.

Floods. The year 1973 was one of the wettest ever for the city of Houston, and the rains resulted several times in flooded homes and streets. The increasing floods were blamed on the spreading pavement accompanying urban development and on land subsidence caused by the pumping of underground water for industrial purposes. Geologists reported that some land in the Houston area had sunk nine feet during the last 30 years.

Teachers' Strike. An urban problem that Houston had in common with several other U. S. cities in 1973 was dissatisfaction among public school teachers over their pay increase and conditions in inner-city schools. The discontent culminated in late August with a teachers' strike on the opening day of the school year. The strike was spotty in effect, however, and lasted only one day.

Crime. Murder has become an everyday matter in large American cities, but on Aug. 8, 1973, a multiple murder case began to unravel in Houston that stunned the nation. Within a week, law-en-forcement officers had dug up 27 bodies in three different locations across the eastern part of Texas—in a common grave in Houston, in the Piney Woods area of East Texas, and on a Gulf of Mexico beach. The victims, all teenaged boys or young men, had been slain by a homosexual murder ring, police said. The 27 bodies were the most ever recorded in the United States considered to be victims of the same killer or killers. (See also CRIME.)

Transportation. In February 1973, the Houston City Council adopted the recommendations of a $774,000 transit study done by a Virginia consulting firm. The transit plan called for a $350 million expenditure in the next five years to improve the city's bus system and to lay the initial groundwork for an 80-mile system of busways and fixed guideway routes.

But after the council adopted the plan, the Texas legislature passed a bill that, with a majority vote of the residents, would have established a county-wide mass transit authority. Saddled with a vehicle emissions tax as its financing method and opposed by suburban city leaders who felt the authority would favor Houston, the issue went down to defeat at the polls in early October by a 3-to-1 margin.

Traffic was heavy not only on Houston's roadways but also on the city's international waterway, the Houston Ship Channel. With the third-busiest port in the nation, and located nearest the agricultural belt, Houston in 1973 was the exit point of about three fourths of the wheat sold to the Soviet Union in the Russian-American grain deal of late 1972. The first Russian grain ship docked at the Port of Houston in February 1973.

Politics. The year 1973 marked the end of the administration of Mayor Louie Welch. After 10 years as mayor, he stepped down to become chief executive of the Houston Chamber of Commerce. He was succeeded by Fred Hofheinz, who won a runoff election on December 4.

ADREN ETHERIDGE
The Houston "Post"

HUNGARY

Hungary continued, in 1973, to oscillate between a general trend toward increasing liberalization and, on the other hand, party-government efforts to preserve the essentials of the "socialist structure."

Domestic Politics. A prominent sociologist and former premier, Andras Hegedues, and philosophers Mihaly Vajda and János Kis were expelled from the Hungarian Socialist Workers' (Communist) party for "ideological and political views ... opposed to Marxism-Leninism." Four prominent nonparty scholars were severely criticized. Although foreign tourists annually spend over $160 million in Hungary, the party press frequently warned the population against "ideological contamination and infiltration."

The council of ministers issued a decree reducing the work week of civil servants to 44 hours. Some 155,000 persons benefited. The decree did not cover over 1,465,000 employees in socialized agriculture, industry, transportation, and trade.

The growing divorce rate aroused concern in official quarters. With over 25,000 divorces estimated for 1973, Hungary became the fourth-highest-ranking country in the world in terms of divorce rate. Similar concern was expressed over the increasing consumption of alcoholic beverages in Hungary. As of Oct. 1, 1973, physicians were permitted

------- HUNGARY • Information Highlights -------

Official Name: Hungarian People's Republic.
Location: Southeast central Europe.
Area: 35,919 square miles (93,030 sq km).
Population (1973 est.): 10,400,000. Density, 287 per square mile (111 per sq km).
Chief Cities (1970 census): Budapest, the capital, 1,940,212; Miskolc, 172,952; Debrecen, 155,122; Pécs, 145,307; Szeged, 118,490.
Government: *Head of state,* Pál Losonczi, chairman of the presidential council (took office April 1967). *Head of government,* Jenö Fock, premier (took office April 1967). *First secretary of the Hungarian Socialist Workers' (Communist) party,* János Kádár (took office Oct. 1956). *Legislature* (unicameral)—Parliament.
Language: Hungarian (official).
Education: *Expenditure* (1969), 7.3% of total public expenditure. *School enrollment* (1969)—primary, 1,177,887; secondary, 454,552; technical/vocational, 330,332; university/higher, 53,237.
Monetary Unit: Forint (9.39 forints equal U. S.$1, July 1973).
Gross National Product (1972 est.): $15,300,000,000.
Economic Indexes: *Industrial production* (1972), 164 (1963=100); *agricultural production* (1970), 118 (1957–59=100); *consumer price index* (1972), 108 (1967=100).
Manufacturing (major products): Machinery, machine tools, commercial vehicles, chemicals, pharmaceuticals, aluminum, steel, processed foods, cement, leather footwear, textiles.
Major Agricultural Products: Corn, wheat, potatoes, sugar beets, barley, grapes, wine grapes, rye, oats, pigs, sheep, fish.
Major Minerals: Bauxite, coal, petroleum, natural gas, lignite, manganese.
Foreign Trade (1972): *Exports,* $3,292,000,000; *Imports,* $3,-154,000,000. *Chief trading partners* (1970)—USSR (took 35% of exports, supplied 31% of imports); East Germany (9%—10%); Czechoslovakia (8%—8%); Poland, Italy, West Germany.
Tourism: *Receipts* (1971), $97,100,000.
Transportation: *Automobiles* (1971), 295,200; *railroads* (1971), 5,022 miles (8,082 km); *major national airline,* Malév-Hungarian Airlines.
Communications: *Telephones* (1972), 873,194; *newspapers* (1971), 27 (daily circulation, 2,251,000).

to prescribe contraceptive pills on demand to all women over 18 years of age.

Economy. The June session of Parliament devoted its deliberations almost exclusively to a final accounting with regard to the 1972 budget. The revenues amounted to $19.4 billion and expenditures to $19.6 billion, leaving a deficit of $200 million. Eighty-three percent of the revenues came from turnover and profit taxes, customs duties, and various payments by state and cooperative enterprises. Some 22% of the expenditures went for investment, 25% for "budgetary support" (subsidies, price supports, import-export price supplements, and so on), 8% for culture and education, and 16% for social purposes and public health.

As a result of the reforms of the New Economic Mechanism introduced in 1968, the national income was increasing annually at a rate of 6.2%, compared with 5.3% during the years 1961–67. A flexible economic policy, decentralization, and competition, as well as greater independence accorded nonstate enterprises, served the national economy well, according to the government press.

On May 16, Premier Jenö Fock inaugurated the Kiskore River dam and a series of irrigation systems in the Tisza Valley, which produces more than half of Hungary's agricultural yield. The new dam provides irrigation for 76,600 acres (31,000 hectares). The irrigated area will increase to 741,300 acres (300,000 hectares) by 1985. The Kiskore hydroelectric plant produces 120 million kilowatts of electric power annually.

Industrialization of corn and sugar beet production based on American experience proved successful. Instead of the planned 311,000-acre (126,000-hectare) units, over 544,000 acres (220,000 hectares) were used for that purpose. The main supplier of the machinery and technology for the project was John Deere, a U. S. firm.

Foreign Policy. In July, Hungarian Communist party chief János Kádár took part in the Crimean conference of Communist party leaders from Eastern Europe. Upon his return he initiated a press campaign for solidarity of the Communist countries and their support of a détente with the West that would advance the cause of socialism.

In December 1972, on the 25th anniversary of the first trade agreements between the USSR and Hungary, Soviet party leader Leonid Brezhnev visited Budapest. In July 1973 a North Vietnamese delegation headed by Premier Pham Van Dong arrived. Soon after, Kádár visited Yugoslavia. Also in July, Premier Pierre Messmer of France paid a visit. Negotiations aimed at establishing diplomatic relations with West Germany entered the final stage.

Foreign Trade. According to official data released in 1973, the balance of payments for 1972 was favorable—for the first time. The surplus amounted to $140 million, compared with a $500 million deficit in 1971. Trade with the Council for Mutual Economic Assistance (COMECON) countries resulted in a $220 million surplus, while that with other countries showed an $80 million deficit. In the first part of 1973, trade with the COMECON countries brought in a $240 million surplus; trade with others resulted in a $110 million deficit.

After long negotiations Hungary was admitted as the 82d member of the Council of the General Agreement on Tariffs and Trade (GATT).

On May 18 the traditional Budapest International Fair opened. Over 1,750 foreign and 1,223 Hungarian firms exhibited. Thirty-two countries participated. In September, Budapest was host to the International Exhibit of Agricultural and Feed Industry Machinery.

JAN KARSKI
Georgetown University

ICELAND

Icelandic foreign relations and economic stability were shaken in 1973 by the "codfish war" with Britain, an eruption of the volcano Helgafell, and devaluation and other economic problems.

The Fishing Conflict. Troubles with Britain and West Germany over the 50-mile (80-km) fishing limit led to many incidents and affected Icelandic relations with other countries. British trawlers fishing close to Iceland were constantly harassed. The Icelandic coast guard cut the British trawling lines, and ships were rammed. When Britain in May sent three frigates to protect the trawlers, a public demonstration in Reykjavík seriously damaged the British embassy, and Iceland appealed to the United Nations and to the NATO Council. The conflict even precipitated discussions on the 1951 defense treaty between Iceland and the United States. During these discussions Iceland sought to close the U. S. base at Keflavík. The British frigates withdrew on October 3, following Iceland's threat to sever diplomatic relations. Later in October, Premier Ólafur Jóhannesson and Britain's Prime Minister Edward Heath arrived at an agreement sharply reducing British fishing in Icelandic waters. Prime Minister Heath said that the "agreement will end an unhappy and dangerous situation which was damaging our relationship with a NATO ally."

Eruption of Helgafell. The sudden activity of this long-dormant volcano, beginning on January 23, nearly closed the harbor at Vestmannaeyjar and

ICELAND • Information Highlights

Official Name: Republic of Iceland.
Location: North Atlantic Ocean.
Area: 39,768 square miles (103,000 sq km).
Population (1973 est.): 210,000. Density, 5 per square mile (2 per sq km).
Chief City (1971 est.): Reykjavík, the capital, 82,900.
Government: *Head of state*, Kristján Eldjárn, president (took office for 2d 4-year term Aug. 1972). *Head of government*, Ólafur Jóhannesson, prime minister (took office July 1971). *Legislature*—Althing: Upper House and Lower House. *Major political parties*—Independence party; Progressive party; People's Alliance; Social Democratic party; Liberal Left party.
Language: Icelandic (official).
Education: *Expenditure* (1968), 12.7% of total public expenditure. *School enrollment* (1968)—primary, 27,356; secondary, 21,584; technical/vocational, 5,000; university/higher, 1,302.
Monetary Unit: Króna (87 krónur equal U.S.$1, July 1973).
Gross National Product (1972 est.): $600,000,000.
Consumer Price Index (1972), 275 (1963=100).
Manufacturing (major products): Fish products, clothing, shoes, chemicals, fertilizer.
Major Agricultural Products: Potatoes, hay, dairy products, fish, sheep.
Major Minerals: Shell sand, perlite, pumice, peat.
Foreign Trade (1972): *Exports*, $191,000,000; *Imports*, $234,000,000. *Chief trading partners* (1970)—United States (took 37% of exports, supplied 14.7% of imports); United Kingdom (13%—13.5%); USSR (8.2%—6.8%); Denmark (6.4%—9.7%).
Transportation: *Motor vehicles* (1971), 52,500 (automobiles, 46,100); *merchant fleet* (1972), 131,000 gross registered tons; *major national airlines,* Loftleider Icelandic Airlines; Icelandair.
Communications: *Telephones* (1972), 75,168; *newspapers* (1971), 5 (daily circulation, 96,000).

buried the island town under a layer of ashes. In the summer some hardy citizens dug their houses out and began to return despite rumbles from Helgafell and dangers from volcanic gases.

Devaluation and the Economy. A monetary devaluation in December 1972, followed by another in February, came as a surprise to the public, which also faced the imposition of price controls on January 1 as a replacement of the price freeze. The government met heated opposition but won a vote of confidence on March 5–6 by the narrow margin of three votes (31–28).

Inflation continued its ravages, possibly matching the cost rise of 20% in 1972. Yet the economy and foreign trade continued to expand, and fish exports reached a greater total value than they had during 1972. After the Icelandic government revalued the króna by 6% on April 30, a provisional law reduced prices by 2% on all goods and services.

RAYMOND E. LINDGREN
California State University, Long Beach

UPI

KEYSTONE

VOLCANIC ERUPTIONS in Icelandic islands southeast of Reykjavik in January forced many of the inhabitants to flee to the mainland. Three who returned (left) stroll past mounds of lava.

IDAHO

Legislative activities and a summer drought made news in Idaho in 1973.

Legislature. The legislature met for 65 days. The highlight was the unsuccessful attempt to repeal its 1972 ratification of the federal Equal Rights Amendment banning discrimination on the basis of sex. The hearings produced highly emotional testimony. This was followed by an attempt to re-call state Rep. Patricia McDermott of Pocatello because she voted against rescinding. The recall movement went to the courts for resolution.

The legislature also attempted to weaken present stream channel protection laws to allow developers more freedom, but Gov. Cecil D. Andrus vetoed that bill. It created interim committees to study land use, the Occupational Safety and Health Act and special education amendments, and reorganization of the executive department. The voters in 1972 mandated that there be no more than 20 executive agencies.

Environment and Natural Resources. Scant winter snowfall and an extremely dry summer left drought in the land and reservoirs dangerously low for irrigation and power production. The state, which relies largely on water for electric power, faces cutbacks to industry, business, and homes.

Dworshak Dam on the Clearwater River was completed, and power generation is under way. The pool behind the dam is now northern Idaho's best fishery.

IDAHO • Information Highlights

Area: 83,557 square miles (216,413 sq km).
Population (1972 est.): 756,000. *Density:* 9 per sq mi.
Chief Cities (1970 census): Boise, the capital, 74,990; Pocatello, 40,036; Idaho Falls, 35,776; Lewiston, 26,068; Twin Falls, 21,914; Nampa, 20,768.
Government (1973): *Chief Officers*—governor, Cecil D. Andrus (D); lt. gov., Jack M. Murphy (R); secy. of state, Pete T. Cenarrusa (R); atty. gen., W. Anthony Park (D); treas., Marjorie Ruth Moon (D); supt. of public instruction, Donald F. Engelking (D); chief justice, Charles R. Donaldson. *Legislature*—Senate, 35 members (23 Republicans, 12 Democrats); House of Representatives, 70 members (51 R, 19 D).
Education (1972–73): *Enrollment*—public elementary schools, 91,847 pupils, 3,793 teachers; public secondary schools, 92,816 pupils, 5,677 teachers; nonpublic schools, 6,100 pupils, 250 teachers; colleges and universities, 31,534 students. *Public school expenditures,* $136,290,000 ($772 per pupil). *Average teacher's salary,* $8,058.
State Finances (fiscal year 1971): *Revenues,* $370,723,000 (3% general sales tax and gross receipts taxes, $45,367,000; motor fuel tax, $28,802,000; federal funds, $93,932,000). *Expenditures,* $322,395,000 (education, $119,588,000; health, welfare, and safety, $40,433,000; highways, $80,668,000). *State debt,* $37,737,000 (June 30, 1971).
Personal Income (1972): $2,748,000,000; per capita, $3,635.
Public Assistance (1972): $38,371,000. *Average monthly payments* (Dec. 1972)—old-age assistance, $70.78; aid to families with dependent children, $179.15.
Labor Force: *Nonagricultural wage and salary earners* (July 1973), 242,200. *Average annual employment* (1972)—manufacturing, 43,200; trade, 56,700; government, 53,700; services, 36,500. *Insured unemployed* (Sept. 1973)—4,800 (2.5%).
Manufacturing (1971): Value added by manufacture, $669,000,000. Food and kindred products, $227,900,000; lumber and wood products, $165,600,000; chemicals and allied products, $118,600,000; printing and publishing, $23,100,000; fabricated metal products, $16,900,000; nonelectrical machinery, $15,700,000.
Agriculture (1972): *Cash farm income,* $859,090,000 (livestock, $397,734,000; crops, $410,289,000; government payments, $51,067,000). *Chief crops* (in order of value, 1972)—Potatoes (ranks 1st among the states); hay (ranks 4th); wheat, sugar beets (ranks 2d).
Mining (1972): Production value, $112,629,000 (ranks 33d among the states). Chief minerals—Silver, $23,609,000; phosphate rock, value not available; lead, $18,271,000; zinc, $13,784,000.
Transportation: *Roads* (1972), 57,144 miles (91,962 km); *motor vehicles* (1972), 509,203; *railroads* (1972), 2,668 miles (4,294 km); *public airports* (1972), 122.
Communications: *Telephones* (1973), 414,600; *television stations* (1971), 7; *radio stations* (1971), 50; *newspapers* (1973), 15 (daily circulation, 194,000).

Plans to place more land into Wilderness and National Recreational Areas and to designate more rivers as Wild and Scenic are progressing. Condemnation of private lands in Hells Canyon of the Middle Snake River has started.

Industries are being forced to improve both air and water quality, and old autos are being removed and reclaimed.

A tussock moth infestation in the Idaho forests is very serious. Since DDT is the only agent at present that offers adequate control, the difficult decision whether to lose thousands of acres of trees or risk further DDT pollution must be made.

Human Rights. The state Human Rights Commission has succeeded in improving the lot of the poor, minorities, school children, and working women. But its success displeased the conservative legislature, which cut its funds severely. The courts forced school districts to allow boys to wear long hair and girls to wear pants suits to school.

Finance. Legislative appropriations increased the general fund expenditures from $137.3 million to $153.6 million. The public schools' portion went from $47.8 million to $57.8 million and higher education's from $29.5 million to $31.8 million. Real property owners were given some tax relief when the public school levy was reduced from 30 mills to 27 mills.

CLIFFORD DOBLER, *University of Idaho*

ILLINOIS

In business, agriculture, and labor, 1973 was a very good year in Illinois. But in politics, the state that is proud of its heritage of distinguished public office-holders had reason to be dismayed.

The economy of Illinois was healthy. Most of the heavy steel industry and other manufacturing in the Chicago area prospered. Farmers, set back by severe Mississippi River floods in the spring, were reaping near-record harvests of soybeans and corn after a good summer growing season and were experiencing personal prosperity. Unemployment in the state was below the national average, and in metropolitan Chicago it was lower yet.

Politics. The turmoil in politics centered on Gov. Daniel Walker, an independent Democrat, who took office in January. Walker had bucked the regular Democratic organization of Chicago's Mayor Richard J. Daley for the party nomination and defeated incumbent Republican Richard B. Ogilvie in the fall of 1972.

Walker continued his successful populist campaign after he took the oath of office. He feuded with Daley's Democratic leaders in the legislature. The Democratic politicians and the Republican leadership on occasion found themselves aligned against Walker's policies.

Walker frequently went on television in "fly-arounds" to various major cities in the state. He took his case to the people and with a charismatic presentation earned the grudging admission of some veteran political observers that his tactics were effective.

In the General Assembly, it was a different matter. The Republicans held slight majorities in both houses. Walker brought in several out-of-staters for his cabinet. He also made some controversial appointments in the state.

The Republican-controlled Senate refused to confirm many of his choices, including seven women.

ILLINOIS • Information Highlights

Area: 56,400 square miles (146,076 sq km).
Population (1972 est.): 11,251,000. *Density:* 200 per sq mi.
Chief Cities (1970 census): Springfield, the capital, 91,753; Chicago, 3,369,359; Rockford, 147,370; Peoria, 126,963; Decatur, 90,397; Joliet, 80,378; Evanston, 79,808.
Government (1973): *Chief Officers*—governor, Daniel Walker (D); lt. gov., Neil F. Hartigan (D); secy. of state, Michael J. Howlett (D); atty. gen., William J. Scott (R); treas., Alan J. Dixon (D); supt. of public instruction, Michael J. Bakalis (D); chief justice, Robert C. Underwood. *General Assembly*—Senate, 59 members (30 Republicans, 29 Democrats); House of Representatives, 177 Members (89 R, 88 D).
Education (1972–73): *Enrollment*—public elementary schools, 1,480,475 pupils, 60,824 teachers; public secondary schools, 907,524 pupils, 45,676 teachers; nonpublic schools, 441,600 pupils, 16,520 teachers; colleges and universities, 414,208 students. *Public school expenditures,* $2,415,130,000 ($1,144 per pupil). *Average teacher's salary,* $11,564.
State Finances (fiscal year 1971): .*Revenues,* $5,000,989,000 (3.5% general tax and gross receipts taxes, $1,023,800,-000; motor fuel tax, $331,754,000; federal funds, $1,114,-760,000). *Expenditures,* $4,518,824,000 (education, $1,793,-585,000; health, welfare, and safety, $1,066,518,000; highways, $852,748,000). *State debt,* $1,621,647,000 (June 30, 1971).
Personal Income (1972): $57,675,000,000; per capita, $5,126.
Public Assistance (1972): $1,213,921,000. *Average monthly payments* (Dec. 1972)—old-age assistance, $66.69; aid to families with dependent children, $242.40.
Labor Force: *Nonagricultural wage and salary earners* (July 1973), 4,362,800. *Average annual employment* (1972)—manufacturing, 1,269,500; trade, 940,400; government, 654,800; services, 695,000. *Insured unemployed* (Sept. 1973)—49,300 (1.4%).
Manufacturing (1971): Value added by manufacture, $22,789,-800,000. Nonelectrical machinery, $3,502,000,000; food and kindred products, $3,097,400,000; electrical equipment and supplies, $2,809,000,000; fabricated metal products, $2,283,500,000; chemicals and allied products, $1,969,800,-000; printing and publishing, $1,993,200,000.
Agriculture (1972): *Cash farm income,* $3,640,621,000 (livestock, $1,463,589,000; crops, $1,933,153,000; government payments, $243,879,000). *Chief crops* (in order of value, 1972)—Corn (ranks 1st among the states); soybeans (ranks 1st); hay, wheat.
Mining (1972): Production value, $758,533,000 (ranks 10th among the states). *Chief minerals*—Coal, $389,300,000; petroleum, $122,283,000; stone, $97,121,000; sand and gravel, $62,960,000.
Transportation: *Roads* (1972), 130,187 miles (209,510 km); *motor vehicles* (1972), 5,417,021; *railroads* (1972), 10,822 miles (17,416 km); *public airports* (1972), 82.
Communications: *Telephones* (1973), 7,640,900; *television stations* (1971), 21; *radio stations* (1971), 222; *newspapers* (1973), 93 (daily circulation, 4,035,000).

The most controversial figure was Anthony Angelos a successful Chicago businessman, picked to be di rector of insurance. Various charges were made that Angelos bought the post with a $50,000 campaign contribution to Walker. Others charged that Angelos had liquor interests and therefore violated an Illinois law that prohibited the liquor industry from contributing to political campaigns. Angelos stepped down, but the controversy simmered on.

Walker and Daley finally reached a tentative political accord late in the year. One of the most critical issues in the state was establishment of a regional transportation authority for six counties of metropolitan Chicago. The public transportation system for Chicago is a good one, but the Chicago Transit Authority (CTA), five of six commuter railroads, and most suburban bus lines were losing money. The CTA situation was so critical that special appropriations were needed to keep it operating.

House Speaker Robert Blair, a Republican, and Walker both introduced transit bills. With political prestige at stake, Daley met with Walker and promised support for the governor's bill. The strategy was to get some Republican defections during a fall special session of the General Assembly. While the two parties were locked in a political stalemate the CTA warned that its financial situation was getting worse.

The Equal Rights Amendment to the U. S. Constitution banning discrimination on the basis of sex failed to pass in the legislature for the second time. There were no tax increases; two tax reduction bills, caught in partisan politics, failed. There was considerable rhetoric over a tough ethics bill for financial disclosures, but little action.

Cardiss Collins, a Democrat, became the first black woman from Illinois to win a seat in Congress. She won a special election to succeed her husband, who was killed in a plane crash.

New Laws. Nineteen-year-olds were permitted to buy wine and beer, as the drinking age was lowered. Leaf burning came back when the legislature took away the right of the state pollution control board to restrict it. A 17-member appointive state board of education was set up to supervise primary and secondary education in Illinois. Abortion laws were liberalized to permit abortions on demand in the first trimester of pregnancy.

Governor Walker's fiscal program was conservative. He introduced stringent reforms to curb the costs of the state's welfare program. The governor signed a new death penalty bill and another bill outlawing the so-called "Saturday night special," a cheap handgun used in many robberies.

Crime. In downstate Collinsville, a raid by federal narcotics agents on the home of a construction worker and his wife stirred national interest. Herbert Giglotto and his wife, Louise, were allegedly brutalized by agents of the federal Drug Abuse Law Enforcement Agency when the agents mistakenly entered their home on April 23. The incident spurred a U. S. Senate investigation, and a federal grand jury indicted 12 narcotics agents for illegal raids.

DAVID E. HALVORSEN, *"Chicago Tribune"*

GOVERNOR Daniel Walker of Illinois, at August press conference, denies campaign-fund irregularities.

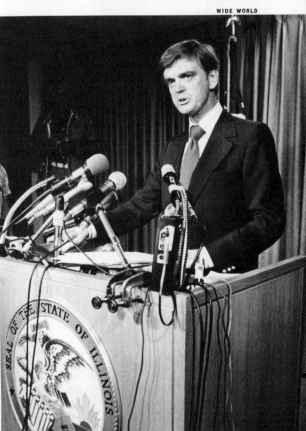

WIDE WORLD

New Delhi housewives carry signs and banners and beat empty tin cans as they march on the home of the food minister to protest high prices.

INDIA

For India, 1973 was one of the most troubled years since it gained its independence in 1947. The year was characterized by a rapid decline in national morale and performance, by violence and political instability in several states, by a weakening of the strong position that the ruling Congress party and its leader, Mrs. Indira Gandhi, had gained in 1971–72, by the worst drought in a decade, by serious food shortages and heavy food imports, and by the continuance of economic problems.

DOMESTIC AFFAIRS

President's Rule and Political Changes in the States. Political agitation, often accompanied by violence, led to the fall of Congress party governments in several states and the imposition there of president's rule, that is, temporary direct rule by the central government. The states included Andhra Pradesh in January, Orissa, Assam, Mysore, and Manipur in March, and Uttar Pradesh in June. In Andhra Pradesh the situation was particularly critical because of the agitation for the separation of the Andhra region from the more backward Telengana area and acute factional rivalry within the state Congress party. Not until December 10 was a new Congress ministry installed. This was headed by J. Vengal Rao from Telengana, with a leader of the Andhra region as deputy chief minister.

In Uttar Pradesh, units of the Indian army had to be called in in June to put down a revolt by large numbers of the Provincial Armed Constabulary (PAC)—the first large-scale rebellion of the PAC in any state—and by students, especially at Lucknow University. There were many casualties and resulting discontent with the government and the Congress party in this most populous state in India. In November, Mrs. Gandhi was responsible for installing a ministry in Uttar Pradesh and selecting the chief minister, H. N. Bahuguna. The ministry began

to attempt to repair the damage to the party and to restore law and order in preparation for state elections in early 1974.

In March the chief minister of Gujarat, chosen by Mrs. Gandhi in 1972, was forced to resign, to be succeeded by a stronger political leader. In Bihar the Congress party's chief minister resigned in June, to be replaced in early July by the first Muslim chief minister in that state.

In February the Union Council of Ministers was augmented by the appointment of three new cabinet members, two ministers of state, and eight deputy ministers. Mrs. Gandhi gave up the home ministry, appointing Umashankar Dikshit to that important post. On April 31 the minister of steel and mines, Mohan Kumaramangalam, a leftist legislator who had been one of Mrs. Gandhi's chief advisers, was killed in an airplane crash; another former deputy adviser, Dinesh Singh, who has been foreign minister, was expelled from the Congress party. In October, Barkatullah Khan, chief minister of Rajasthan and a Muslim, died suddenly of a heart attack, and was succeeded by Harideo Joshi, minister for power in the previous ministry.

In June, Guruji M. S. Golwalkar, the head (Sarsangchalak) of the Rashtriya Swayamsevak Sangh (RSS) since 1940, died. The RSS is closely associated with the Jana Sangh, a political party that faced a leadership crisis in 1973 when Balraj Madhok was expelled. Madhok, a founder-member and former party president, formed a new party—the National Democratic Jana Sangh.

In May the Lok Sabha (the lower house of parliament) passed the Constitution (Thirty-first Amendment) Bill to increase the elected membership in the Lok Sabha from 522 to 545.

Violent outbreaks and riots of major proportions, with heavy loss of life and property damage, occurred in several states during the year, notably

in Andhra Pradesh, Bihar, Madhya Pradesh, Maharashtra, Mysore, Uttar Pradesh, and West Bengal. In Andhra Pradesh the main cause was the separatist agitation. Communal riots were the principal source of disturbance in Bihar and Uttar Pradesh (leading to the clcsing of Aligarh Muslim University in Uttar Pradesh); but in the latter state the revolt of the PAC and university students in June attracted the most attention. Riots protesting against food shortages and high prices were particularly common in those states that were hardest hit by the serious drought.

Judicial Affairs. On April 24 the supreme court of India, after 69 days of hearings by 13 judges, handed down a historic judgment in the so-called fundamental rights cases. The majority of the judges upheld the power of Parliament to amend any part of the constitution, provided the amendment did not alter the basic structure or framework of the constitution. The majority decision ran to 217 pages.

On the following day Mrs. Gandhi departed from precedent by passing over three more senior judges and appointing Justice Ajit Nath Ray as the new chief justice of the supreme court. The three more senior judges promptly resigned. Mrs. Gandhi's decision was strongly criticized by leading lawyers and jurists, bar associations, most opposition political parties, and many Indian newspapers and publicists.

Sikkim. Following elections in Sikkim (a protectorate of India strategically located between Nepal, Bhutan, and Tibet) to the Sikkim State Council in January and a boycott of the council when it opened on March 28, an uprising in Sikkim was staged to demand the abdication of the ruler, Chogyal (King) Palden Thondup Namgyal, in favor of a popularly elected government. When his promises to make concessions did not still the demonstrations, the Chogyal called upon India for help.

Indian troops were sent into Sikkim on April 8, and the protectorate was placed under direct Indian administration. On May 8 an important agreement was signed in Gangtok, the capital of Sikkim, by the chogyal, by leaders of Sikkim's three political parties, and by the foreign secretary of India. The agreement provided for a legislative assembly for Sikkim elected on the basis of adult suffrage, an executive council responsible to the assembly, safeguards for minorities, and various administrative reforms.

THE ECONOMY

Economically, 1973 was one of the worst years since independence. The economic setbacks of 1972 continued into 1973, and in most cases were aggravated. This was particularly true of shortages of food and power, of unemployment, and of rising prices. The rate of growth of the national output, which had been 5.3% in 1969, fell even below the 1972 figure of between 1% and 2%. Food-grain production, which had risen to well above 100 million tons a year, hardly reached the 100 million figure in 1973. Because of this, the food shortage became particularly serious, and India, which two years previously had seemed to be on the verge of self-sufficiency in food production, was forced to reduce its reserves of food grains to a very low level and to import 9 to 10 million tons of grains.

Because the Indian government had decided against accepting any more food aid from the United States under the "food for peace" program, it was obliged to buy several million tons in the world markets; and since food prices had skyrocketed as a result of the worldwide food shortage and heavy purchases by the Soviet Union and China, it had to pay far higher prices for its food imports than it had contemplated. A Soviet offer of 2 million tons of wheat, made in late September, a rea-

─────── **INDIA · Information Highlights** ───────

Official Name: Republic of India.
Location: South Asia.
Area: 1,266,598 square miles (3,280,483 sq km).
Population (1973 est.): 600,400,000. Density, 470 per square mile (180 per sq km).
Chief Cities (1971 census): New Delhi, the capital, 292,857; Bombay, 5,968,546; Delhi, 3,694,451; Calcutta, 3,141,180; Madras, 2,470,288.
Government: *Head of state,* V. V. Giri, president (took office Aug. 1969). *Head of government,* Mrs. Indira Gandhi, prime minister (took office Jan. 1966). *Legislature—* Parliament: Rajya Sabha (Council of States) and Lok Sabha (House of the People). *Major political parties—* Congress (Ruling) party; Communist party; Jana Sangh; Congress (Opposition) party; Swatantra.
Languages: Hindi (official), English, 14 national languages.
Education: *Expenditure* (1966), 17.8% of total public expenditure. *School enrollment* (1965)—primary, 49,499,000; secondary, 7,650,102; technical/vocational, 450,101; university/higher, 1,054,273.
Monetary Unit: Rupee (7.843 rupees equal U. S.$1, Sept. 1973).
Gross National Product (1972 est.): $59,010,000,000.
Economic Indexes: *Industrial production* (1972), 153 (1963= 100); *agricultural production* (1971), 119 (1963=100); *consumer price index* (1972), 202 (1960=100).
Manufacturing (major products): Iron and steel, industrial machinery and equipment, chemicals, fertilizers, cotton and jute textiles, cement.
Major Agricultural Products: Rice (ranks 2d among world producers, 1972), wheat (world rank 3d, 1972), groundnuts (world rank 1st, 1971), barley, sesame, sugarcane, corn, rubber, cotton, tea (world rank 1st, 1972), rapeseed, jute.
Major Minerals: Coal, iron ore, manganese, mica, bauxite, chromium ore, salt.
Foreign Trade (1972): *Exports,* $2,415,000,000; *Imports,* $2,-230,000,000. *Chief trading partners* (1971)—United States (took 15% of exports, supplied 26% of imports); USSR (13%—6%); Japan (12%—6%); United Kingdom (11%—9%).
Tourism: Receipts (1971), $53,800,000.
Transportation: *Motor vehicles* (1970), 1,143,300 (automobiles, 619,000); *railroads* (1971), 37,006 miles (59,553 km); *merchant fleet* (1972), 2,650,000 gross registered tons; *major national airlines,* Indian Airlines; Air India.
Communications: *Telephones* (1972), 1,351,200; *newspapers* (1971), 821.

CUBAN PREMIER Fidel Castro is greeted by Indian Prime Minister Indira Gandhi at the New Delhi airport.

UPI

DISASTROUS floods and drought struck Rajasthan state. September floods (above) forced the inhabitants of this town in the western part of the state to live on rooftops. Drought in May (left) in the southeast dried up Lake Pichola in Udaypur, a man-made 15th century lake with a former maharajah's palace, now a hotel, in the background.

sonably favorable monsoon in most of the country, and a good *kharif* crop in the fall helped to alleviate the food crisis, and renewed hope that food-grain production for 1973–74 might reach the hoped-for target of 115 millions tons.

In March the government took over the wholesale trade in wheat in an attempt to bring down prices and assure adequate and equitable distribution. This measure was highly controversial, and did not achieve its objectives. In September the government admitted that its previously announced plan to nationalize the wholesale trade in rice was being shelved.

In 1973 large parts of India were hit by the worst drought in a decade. It was particularly serious in Maharashtra, Gujarat, Rajasthan, Andhra Pradesh, Mysore, and Orissa, but nearly two thirds of the country was affected.

On January 20 the National Development Council approved the planning commission's *Approach to the Fifth Five-Year Plan* (1974–79). This document envisioned a total outlay of slightly over $70 billion in both the public and private sectors during the fifth plan period, and a 5.5% annual growth rate (a level that India had not attained in any previous five-year period). It also assumed that gross foreign economic aid to be available during the plan period would be over $4 billion (a bold assumption in

view of the "aid weariness" of donor nations). Over three fifths of this would be needed for debt servicing. The draft five-year plan, made public in November, retained the basic outline of the "Approach" document, but slightly increased the estimates of total expenditures, in order to take account of rising prices.

The budget for the fiscal year 1973–74, presented to the Parliament by the finance minister, Y. B. Chavan, on February 28, provided for receipts of $6.98 billion and expenditures of $6.53 billion in the revenue account, and for receipts of $3.38 billion and expenditures of $3.95 billion in the capital account.

FOREIGN AFFAIRS

Foreign Visits and International Conferences.
Top Indian leaders made an unusually large number of trips abroad during the year, and an unusually large number of foreign dignitaries visited India. Mrs. Gandhi made official visits to Nepal in February and to Sri Lanka in April, thus symbolizing India's desire to maintain good relations with smaller neighbors. In June she made official visits successively to Yugoslavia, Canada, Fiji, and Tonga. In August she participated in the Conference of Commonwealth Heads of Government in Ottawa and in September in the fourth conference of non-

aligned nations in Algiers. The Indian foreign minister, Swaran Singh, accompanied her to both conferences, and he also made official visits to Japan in January, to Syria, Kuwait, Iraq, Czechoslovakia, and the German Democratic Republic in May and early June, to Finland, Sweden, Norway, and Denmark in June, and to Iran in July. President Giri made official visits to Malaysia in March and to Czechoslovakia in October.

Visits by Foreign Leaders to India. Among the top leaders of other countries who visited India during the year were the prime minister of Poland in January, the president of the Yugoslav Federal Executive and the prime minister of the German Democratic Republic in March, the prime minister of Australia in June, King Birendra of Nepal in October, and General Secretary Leonid Brezhnev of the Soviet Union in November. Brezhnev's was the first visit by a member of the top leadership of the Soviet Union since Premier Aleksei Kosygin's visit in 1968. It resulted in the signing of a 15-year economic agreement, covering an expansion of trade and Soviet aid to India to finance the development of Indian industrial plants.

One Asia Assembly. In February an important One Asia Assembly, sponsored by the Asia Press Foundation, was held in New Delhi. It was inaugurated by the secretary-general of the United Nations, Kurt Waldheim. Both President Giri and Mrs. Gandhi addressed the assembly.

Relations with Bangladesh and Pakistan. Relations with Bangladesh continued to be officially close and good, in spite of criticism by opposition groups in Bangladesh of the excessive dependence of their country on India. On April 17, after four days of talks in New Delhi, the foreign ministers of the two countries issued a joint declaration, proposing simultaneous exchange of Pakistani prisoners of war and civilian internees (except those who were to be held for trial on criminal charges), Bengalis detained in Pakistan, and Pakistanis in Bangladesh. This formula, with some modifications and elaboration, became the basis for a historic agreement signed in New Delhi on August 28 between high-level representatives of India and Pakistan. There was hope the agreement would usher in a new era in Indo-Pakistan relations and would pave the way for a peaceful resolution of the differences among the major states of the subcontinent. Such vexing issues as the Kashmir question and the recognition of Bangladesh by Pakistan were, however, not referred to in the agreement.

Relations with the United States. Relations between the United States and India, which had been strained for the previous two years, showed some signs of improvement in 1973. The desire for better relations, often expressed by top leaders of both countries, was symbolized by the appointment of Professor Daniel Patrick Moynihan, a former adviser to President Nixon, as U. S. ambassador to India, and of T. N. Kaul, India's most senior diplomat, a former foreign secretary of India, and a close adviser to Mrs. Gandhi, as Indian ambassador to the United States.

Two decisions of the Nixon administration that led to official and unofficial protests in India were the decision in March to lift the embargo on the supply of arms to Pakistan (and to India), and the decision in October, during the war in the Middle East, to send a naval task force into the Indian Ocean. India and the United States took very different positions during the Middle East crisis. Although India strongly supported the Arab side, it was adversely affected by the oil shortages and increased prices for crude oil, which India badly needed for its development program.

Ambassador Moynihan was able to persuade the Nixon administration to enter into an understanding with the government of India to liquidate a substantial part of the nearly $3.5 billion worth of rupees owed by India to the United States for U. S. food aid from 1956 to 1971. On December 13, Ambassador Moynihan and an official of the Indian government signed an agreement for the disposal by the United States of the equivalent of $2.2 billion of the "blocked rupee" holdings, which will be used over the next five years for development programs. The equivalent of another $1 billion will be retained by the United States for embassy expenses over a period of at least 15 years.

NORMAN D. PALMER, *University of Pennsylvania*

INDIANA

Republicans largely controlled Indiana politics in 1973. They had majorities in both houses of the legislature, which ended its annual session in April. Moreover, in January a Republican, Otis R. Bowen, became governor after having won the largest majority ever accorded an Indiana chief executive. This victory, along with the fact that he was the first governor elected since adoption of a constitutional amendment allowing an incumbent to seek a second consecutive term, enhanced his influence.

Legislation. New legislation covered a variety of topics. Eighteen-year-olds were given most of the legal rights and privileges of 21-year-olds, but 21 remained the legal age for purchase of alcoholic beverages. Sunday sales of such beverages were authorized for retailers grossing $100,000 annually, if half the total was for food. The right of public school teachers to engage in collective bargaining was recognized, but not their right to strike. Other laws restored capital punishment for designated crimes, legalized abortions, provided bonus payments for Vietnam veterans, and authorized the preservation of scenic rivers.

Items failing to win approval were: no-fault insurance, elimination of price-fixing for alcoholic beverages, collective bargaining for public employees generally, and ratification of the Equal Rights Amendment to the federal Constitution banning discrimination on the basis of sex.

Biennial Budget. The legislature adopted a budget authorizing $4.04 billion in state expenditures for the 1973–75 biennium. This budget, the largest ever, was accompanied by a tax revision to augment state support for elementary and secondary schools and to lessen the tax load on owners of property (the latter tax used almost entirely for support of local governments).

The Economy. Diversified manufacturing continued to dominate Indiana's economy, with unemployment declining slightly from 1972. Increased prices for farm products and generally favorable weather made 1973 a good year for farmers. Commencement of a new port facility on the Ohio River near Evansville offered early promise of a port that, in contrast to the one on Lake Michigan, can probably be used throughout the year. Further deterioration and decline of railroad freight service adversely affected scattered Indiana cities and towns.

──────── INDIANA • Information Highlights ────────

Area: 36,291 square miles (93,994 sq km).
Population (1972 est.): 5,291,000. *Density:* 146 per sq mi.
Chief Cities (1970 census): Indianapolis, the capital, 744,743; Fort Wayne, 178,021; Gary, 175,415; Evansville, 138,764; South Bend, 125,580; Hammond, 107,888; Anderson, 70,787.
Government (1973): *Chief Officers*—governor, Otis R. Bowen (R); lt. gov., Robert D. Orr (R); secy. of state, Larry Conrad (D); atty. gen., Theodore L. Sendak (R); treas., Jack L. New (D); supt. of public instruction, Harold Negley (R); chief justice, Norman F. Arterburn. *General Assembly*—Senate, 50 members (29 Republicans, 21 Democrats); House of Representatives, 100 members (73 R, 27 D).
Education (1972–73): *Enrollment*—public elementary schools, 656,578 pupils, 26,600 teachers; public secondary schools, 563,370 pupils, 25,900 teachers; nonpublic schools, 106,700 pupils, 4,320 teachers; colleges and universities, 194,132 students. *Public school expenditures,* $967,740,000 ($878 per pupil). *Average teacher's salary,* $10,300.
State Finances (fiscal year 1971): *Revenues,* $1,866,350,000 (4% general sales tax and gross receipts taxes, $404,083,000; motor fuel tax, $208,806,000; federal funds, $381,709,000). *Expenditures,* $1,748,782,000 (education, $857,018,000; health, welfare, and safety, $244,467,000; highways, $349,313,000). *State debt,* $570,159,000 (June 30, 1971).
Personal Income (1972): $23,235,000,000; per capita, $4,391.
Public Assistance (1972): $223,767,000. *Average monthly payments* (Dec. 1972)—old-age assistance, $54.81; aid to families with dependent children, $141.29.
Labor Force: *Nonagricultural wage and salary earners* (July 1973), 1,981,000. *Average annual employment* (1971)—manufacturing, 708,300; trade, 386,500; government, 301,200; services, 241,800; *Insured unemployed* (Sept. 1973)—15,400 (1.0%).
Manufacturing (1971): *Value added by manufacture,* $12,073,900,000. Electrical equipment and supplies, $1,935,200,000; primary metal industries, $1,836,700,000; transportation equipment, $1,607,200,000; nonelectrical machinery, $1,195,500,000; chemicals and allied products, $1,102,800,000; food and kindred products, $979,100,000.
Agriculture (1972): *Cash farm income,* $1,960,666,000 (livestock, $967,171,000; crops, $860,394,000; government payments, $133,101,000). *Chief crops* (in order of value, 1972)—Corn (ranks 3d among the states); soybeans (ranks 4th); hay; wheat.
Mining (1972): *Production value,* $305,816,000 (ranks 24th among the states). *Chief minerals*—Coal, $134,000,000; cement, value not available; stone, $47,165,000.
Transportation: *Roads* (1972), 90,908 miles (146,298 km); *motor vehicles* (1972), 2,902,522; *railroads* (1972), 6,405 miles (10,308 km); *public airports* (1972), 65.
Communications: *Telephones* (1973), 3,201,700; *television stations* (1971), 17; *radio stations* (1971), 159; *newspapers* (1973), 79 (daily circulation, 1,691,000).

Prison Revolt. A short but very threatening revolt of inmates at the state prison in Michigan City in September was quickly ended without loss of life. Governor Bowen was both commended and condemned for promising amnesty to end the uprising.

Desegregation. After continued failure of the Indianapolis school board to develop what was considered to be an adequate desegregation plan in accordance with court orders, federal circuit court Judge S. High Dillon in August appointed two commissioners to achieve this. The commissioners were mandated to develop a temporary plan covering Indianapolis schools for 1973–74 and a city-suburban designation plan for 1974–75. The plan for Indianapolis was implemented during the fall of 1973 through substantial busing of black pupils.

Indiana War Memorial. Beginning in 1953 the American Civil Liberties Union (ACLU) sought intermittently to obtain permission from the Indiana Department of the American Legion to hold a public meeting in the Legion-controlled Indiana War Memorial. The Legion contended that such use by the ACLU was inappropriate. The ACLU, however, won a 5-to-0 decision against the Legion in the state supreme court in January. Unable to obtain reversal of this decision, the Legion relented, and the ACLU held a meeting in the War Memorial in October.

DONALD F. CARMONY, *Indiana University*

INDIANS, American. See special feature beginning on page 62.

INDONESIA

The outstanding event in Indonesia in 1973 was the election of General Suharto to a second five-year term as president. The year was also marked by increased diplomatic activity. The Indonesian government fought effectively against inflation, and the production of oil within the republic was steadily increasing.

Politics. President Suharto's reelection was by acclamation; he had no opposition. Five days after his reelection on March 22 by the People's Consultative Assembly, Suharto announced the formation of a new cabinet. Its composition indicated a shift toward more civilians in the administration. Suharto relinquished the post of minister of defense and security and appointed Gen. Maraden Panggabean to this position. Including General Panggabean, who serves as commander of the armed forces, there are only three military men in the 22-member cabinet.

The governmental reorganization reflects President Suharto's emphasis on economic development as his major concern. The ministry is called the Second Development Cabinet.

President Suharto is planning to move his country toward a modified democratic political system—one that will be free of the excesses of the Sukarno years. The cabinet is instructed to prepare to hold general elections by 1977.

The budget for the fiscal year 1973–74 represented an increase of 14% over the previous year's budget.

In his report on March 12 to the People's Consultative Assembly, President Suharto stated that public order and security had been restored and the Communist movement in the country had been largely suppressed, but he warned that all danger had not been removed. Small-scale guerrilla activity was continuing in West Kalimantan, presumably in coordination with Communists operating in the neighboring Malaysian state of Sarawak. He called for the improvement of social conditions to combat communism.

Economy. When Suharto took over from Sukarno, the nation's most urgent problem was inflation. As a result of the stringent measures instituted by the Suharto government, the rate of inflation fell from 650% in 1966 to 2.5% in 1971. A rapid rise in the price of rice in the closing months of 1972 caused the rate of inflation to increase to 25%. This inflationary pressure was brought under control in 1973, however, by measures to stabilize the price of rice.

Production in nearly all sectors is increasing, but the low price of rubber on the world market imposes a severe handicap on Indonesia's rubber producers and tends to depress export earnings. The government is promoting the rapid development of the country's vast agricultural potential.

Oil production is steadily increasing and has become a very important factor in Indonesia's economy. Oil output has reached 1.4 million barrels a day, putting Indonesia in 10th place among the world's oil producers. About half of the government's budget and 45% of Indonesia's export earnings come from the oil industry.

Indonesia has developed a unique system of oil production control and management. Concessions have been abolished and oil production made a state monopoly, operated by a public corporation called

Pertamina (an acronym for Pertambangan Minjak dan Gas Bumi Nasional—State Gas and Oil Enterprise). From 15% to 20% of Indonesia's oil output is produced by Pertamina itself; the remainder is produced by foreign companies on the basis of production-sharing contracts. Pertamina receives a 65% (or more) share of the production by the foreign oil concerns. The State Gas and Oil Enterprise has developed into the largest single business organization in Indonesia, with a number of diversified interests.

Education. The Suharto regime is revamping Indonesia's educational system. After the nation achieved independence, education expanded tremendously at all levels; it was predominantly literary and aimed at training for university entrance. After completing a three-year study of the system, the Office of Educational Development drafted a program that is now being put into effect. The office found that about three fourths of the 22 million school-age children were enrolled in primary schools, but many dropped out after a few years. Sixty percent of the primary school teachers had no formal training. In spite of the heroic postindependence educational program, one half of the population was still illiterate. Some 360,000 students entered the institutions of higher learning, but their education had been so academic that many were unable to obtain positions after graduation.

The new program emphasizes practical subjects related to the students' world. Vocational training is stressed at the secondary level. Qualifications for admission to the universities and professional schools have been raised drastically, and enrollment in these institutions is to be restricted to a 4% increase per year. The new educational system accords with Suharto's policy of stressing economic development.

Foreign Relations. Indonesia in 1973 began to play a larger role in world affairs, in keeping with its position as the fifth-most-populous state in the world and by far the largest in Southeast Asia. In his address to the People's Consultative Assembly on March 12, Suharto described Indonesia's foreign policy as active but independent, opposed to all manifestations of imperialism and colonialism but ready to assist in promoting world peace. His government was particularly desirous of creating regional stability in Southeast Asia and would participate in all efforts to that end short of jeopardizing Indonesia's development program.

In pursuance of these principles Indonesia served as a member of the UN Security Council (1973–74) and was also a member of the International Commission for Control and Supervision of the Cease-Fire in Vietnam.

Indonesia sent a delegation headed by Foreign Minister Adam Malik to the summit conference of nonaligned nations in Algeria in September. Malik stated that Indonesia wanted to see the smaller states free to determine their own fate and stressed economic development as the role of the nonaligned countries in promoting peace.

An important diplomatic visitor to Indonesia was Prime Minister Gough Whitlam of Australia. During his stay in Jakarta (February 20 to 25), the prime minister and President Suharto discussed a wide range of common interests. Whitlam declared that his government's policy was to take a more independent position in international affairs and

———— INDONESIA • Information Highlights ————

Official Name: Republic of Indonesia.
Location: Southeast Asia.
Area: 735,269 square miles (1,904,345 sq km).
Population (1973 est.): 132,500,000. Density, 218 per square mile (84 per sq km).
Chief Cities (1971 census): Jakarta, the capital, 4,576,009; Surabaja, 1,556,255; Bandung, 1,201,730.
Government: *Head of state,* Suharto, president (took office for 2d 5-year term March 1973). *Head of government,* Suharto. *Legislature* (unicameral)—Dewan Perwakilan Rakyat (House of Representatives). *Major political parties* —Partai Persatuan Pembanguan; Partai Demokrasi Indonesia.
Languages: Bahasa Indonesia (official), Javanese, Sundanese, Madurese, other Malayo-Polynesian languages, English.
Education: *School enrollment* (1969)—primary, 12,802,415; secondary, 1,637,375; technical/vocational, 385,833; university/higher, 192,416.
Monetary Unit: Rupiah (374 rupiahs equal U. S.$1, July 1973).
Gross National Product (1972 est.): $8,940,000,000.
Economic Indexes: *Agricultural production* (1971), 129 (1963=100); consumer price index (1972), 76,463 (1963=100).
Manufacturing (major products): Processed foods, petroleum products, mineral products.
Major Agricultural Products: Rice (ranks 3d among world producers, 1972), rubber (world rank 2d, 1972), sweet potatoes and yams, copra, sugarcane, cassava, coffee, tea, palm oil, spices.
Major Minerals: Petroleum, tin, bauxite, nickel, coal.
Foreign Trade (1972): *Exports,* $1,854,000,000. *Imports,* $1,- 726,000,000. *Chief trading partners* (1971)—Japan; United States; Singapore; West Germany; Netherlands.
Tourism: Receipts (1971), $22,000,000.
Transportation: *Motor vehicles* (1971), 364,200 (automobiles, 238,600); *railroads* (1971), 4,926 miles (7,928 km); *merchant fleet* (1972), 619,000 gross registered tons; *major national airline,* Garuda Indonesian Airways.
Communications: *Telephones* (1972), 229,636; *newspapers* (1965), 85 (daily circulation, 709,000).

a more comprehensive and positive attitude with respect to regional cooperation. He looked forward to the emergence of a comprehensive regional organization to help free the Asia-Pacific area from great-power rivalries and intervention. The organization he suggested would not supplant the Association of Southeast Asian Nations but rather complement it.

The Australian prime minister declared that his government was committed to cooperation with the countries of the region for defense and development and that it would extend Indonesia an expanded assistance directed to its development priorities. The two political leaders agreed to broaden and intensify bilateral exchanges and cooperation in cultural affairs.

On his return to Canberra, Prime Minister Whitlam expressed his gratification at President Suharto's interest in the evolution of a more broadly based and representative regional forum. That there was not complete agreement by the two political leaders on the subject of an enlarged Asian regional organization was apparent from the statement by Foreign Minister Malik that Indonesia had no objection to Prime Minister Whitlam's proposed new organization if it were not political in nature. Indonesia wished to know what form the proposed organization would take and to what extent it would be enlarged.

What apparently troubled the Indonesian president and his foreign minister was China's relation to the proposed regional organization. Suharto's government had earlier broken off diplomatic relations with Peking, which under Sukarno had become close. Malik declared in January that the resumption of diplomatic relations between Indonesia and Communist China would be determined by Indonesia's judgment of its internal security situation. The Suharto government was understandably loath to afford Peking any opportunity to engage in subversive activities in Indonesia.

AMRY VANDENBOSCH
University of Kentucky

INSURANCE

The U. S. insurance business continued in 1973 to adjust to a changing social and economic environment. Consumerism, government, and competition all were catalysts in the process.

PROPERTY AND LIABILITY INSURANCE

For the second successive year there was a significant improvement in underwriting results producing a net gain of some $1.1 billion for the property-liability insurance business in 1972, according to the Insurance Information Institute. These results contrast with the substantial underwriting losses, after policyholder dividends, over the 15-year period ending with 1970. Improved underwriting results were attributed in part to relatively modest losses from catastrophes, a slight reduction in fire losses, a decline in crime losses, and a small improvement in auto insurance claim frequency. Increased operating efficiency and the benefits of the widespread introduction in recent years of mandatory deductibles on homeowners and other personal lines insurance policies also contributed to the favorable results.

Automobile Insurance. State legislatures showed growing interest in proposals to change from the traditional third-party liability system of automobile insurance to a system in which the person who suffers the loss is compensated by his own insurance company. In 1971 and 1972, a few states had enacted laws to reform their auto insurance systems, placing greater emphasis on so-called first-party, or no-fault, coverage. In 1973, several states—including Arkansas, Colorado, Connecticut, Hawaii, Kansas, Nevada, New York, and Utah—followed suit.

Economic losses from auto accidents increased in 1972 to an all-time high of $19 billion. In an effort to cut the costs of highway accidents, insurers accelerated their studies of the damageability and reparability of automobiles. and they began offering reductions of up to 20% on collision insurance premiums on 1973 private passenger cars in recognition of the improved standards on bumpers mandated by the federal government.

Other Developments. Insurers began comprehensive programs to upgrade state workmen's compensation laws following the report in July 1973 by the National Commission on Workmen's Compensation Laws. The report recommended 19 essential changes in programs, most of which involved expansion of the workmen's compensation coverage.

In view of the increasing demands and expectations of the consumer and the Consumer Product Safety Act of 1972, product liability continued to be an area of prime concern. Insurers acted vigorously to provide necessary inspection and loss-control services as businesses began to feel the full impact of the 1970 Occupational Safety and Health Act.

A new Property Insurance Plans Service Office was opened in 1973 to improve the services of the FAIR Plans (Fair Access to Insurance Requirements Plans) operating in 26 states, the District of Columbia, and Puerto Rico to make property insurance readily available to property owners having difficulty in obtaining coverage. The plans issued more than 840,000 new and renewal policies during 1972, and at the end of that year they were providing more than $21.3 billion in coverage.

Rate reductions of from 30% to 40% and an increase in the kinds of property eligible for coverage gave a boost to the flood insurance program run by the Federal Insurance Administration and the National Flood Insurers Association. In the fiscal year 1973, the number of policies in force throughout the nation increased 158%, and the amount of insurance in force jumped from $1.48 billion in 1972 to more than $4 billion.

Fire losses in the United States in 1972 exceeded $2 billion for the third time in history, but nevertheless were slightly lower for the second consecutive year. The most costly catastrophe of 1972 was Hurricane Agnes, which swept the eastern seacoast in June, causing an estimated insured loss of nearly $100 million.

LIFE INSURANCE

The average insured U. S. family had $26,900 worth of life insurance at the start of 1973. This was equivalent to slightly more than two years of that family's disposable personal income.

Purchases and Payments. New life insurance purchases amounted to $212 billion in 1972. Of this sum, $156 billion represented individually purchased ordinary and industrial life insurance. New purchases of group life insurance totalled $56 billion. During 1972 life insurance companies paid more than $18 billion in benefits to policyholders, annuitants, and other beneficiaries.

Investments. The assets of the 1,810 legal reserve life insurance companies totalled nearly $240 billion on Jan. 1, 1973. Corporate securities accounted for 47.1% and mortgages for 32.1% of these investment holdings. Loans to policyholders reached 7.5% of the total assets of the insurance companies. The net pretax earning rate of life insurance company investments in 1972 was 5.56%, the highest in 52 years.

Urban Program. The special Life Insurance Urban Investment Program, established by the industry to aid in the improvement of living conditions for people residing in blighted city neighborhoods, achieved its goal of $2 billion in 1972. This was the amount the participating companies had pledged to divert from their usual investments into special higher risk investments designed to benefit residents of urban core areas. Among projects financed through the program were housing, job-creating enterprises, and medical and community service facilities.

Equity Products. In addition to the mutual funds and variable annuities, which a number of companies are offering as equity-based products to supplement life insurance coverage, progress was made in 1972 in developing variable life insurance. This is a new kind of policy with an equity base. With a variable life policy, the reserves would be invested in securities, primarily common stocks. In early 1973, the Securities and Exchange Commission decided that the basic supervision of this type of policy would be maintained by state insurance departments.

HEALTH INSURANCE

A record 185 million persons had private health insurance in the United States at the start of 1973. Private health insurance policyholders received $21.4 billion in benefit payments in 1972. The coverage was provided by insurance companies, Blue Cross-Blue Shield organizations, other plans approved by medical societies, and independent plans. See SOCIAL WELFARE—*Health Care*.

KENNETH BLACK, JR., *Georgia State University*

SPACE IS AT A PREMIUM in the two-room New York City apartment of architect Douglas Kahn and his wife, interior designer Stephanie Mallis Kahn. The living room, decorated in a gray motif, includes an abundance of built-in space-saving devices.

INTERIOR DESIGN

Flexible and mobile are two words that best describe the current interior—in particular, that of the home. The open-space plan, created by removing the solid barriers that traditionally enclosed each room, has become increasingly popular during the 1970's. Within these reshaped spaces for living, furniture arrangements have become flexible. The room no longer requires a rigid, balanced grid placement. On the contrary, space is organized into active and quiet areas, shared or private areas, within one big environment.

Interior design has always been responsive to social change. People of the mid-1970's sense a restlessness in the air—a need for mobility or change. Noting that change is fundamental to our lives, a feature, "The Urge to Change," in the June 1973 issue of *House and Garden* quotes Emilie O'Mara, an expert in environmental psychology: "We're constantly changing and if we try to deny the fact, we are just deluding ourselves." Specifically, the article notes, we develop new tastes, our interests change,

our relationships alter, and we change physically and emotionally. As a result, many of us pull up roots, move on, and start over. Others, responding to the sense of security to be found in continuity and familiar places, find an alternative to moving. We change what we already have—revise it—for our altered personalities or way of life.

This personal urge for change is also evident in the new flexible furniture designs, particularly in seating pieces. They are modular, with an extraordinary versatility. The pieces are not necessarily chairs. Instead, they may be ottomans, with attached back bolsters and sometimes arms that can be removed so that the designer can assemble anything from a single chair to a room-long banquette, a conversation cluster, or an "island" of seating arrangements. These furniture designs, which are being produced by many European and U. S. manufacturers, are the new tools for creating a flexible or mobile scheme for living.

Residences. Not all individualists are purchasing the modular furnishings. Some are building islands for relaxing and active living. Such is the

THE NORTH SALEM, N. Y., country home of architectural designers Tony and Anne Kassel Woolner is a Plexiglas cylinder. The two-story, white-walled living room offers an excellent view of the surrounding woods and fields.

case of architect Douglas Kahn and his wife, the interior designer Stephanie Mallis Kahn, who live in a two-room New York City flat. Here the demands on the space were considerable. The main space (the original living room) was completely reshaped with built-in arrangements to accommodate sleeping, reading, listening to music, entertaining, and eating. Various levels were created with plywood seating-storage platforms, which were completely wrapped in gray carpeting. Walls and ceiling were painted gray to effect a total environment. The platforms to be used as seating were padded with a layer of waffle foam under the carpeting. The result is a lively series of levels set about in an asymmetric manner—the antithesis of the well-ordered, well-balanced room. It is perhaps the most extreme of the mobile and flexible approaches to interior design.

Whereas the Kahn apartment is an enclosed gray environment, the North Salem, N. Y., country home of architectural designers Tony and Anne Kassel Woolner is a Plexiglas cylinder—designed by the Woolners—open to the fields, the woods, and the sky. The living room, "protected" only by curving ribs of painted white wood that frame large panes of clear Plexiglas, soars two stories high. A feeling of joyous liberation emanates from within the nondelineated area.

The main furniture—a seating cluster, or island, seemingly in space—is composed of modular seating and storage units. Some seating units within a U-shaped formation have backs but no arms. Others are large ottomans intermittently fitted into the arrangement. Adjoining this formation of units, but facing in different directions, are platforms upholstered to form chaise longues. These platforms are higher than the other seating units and are attached to tables and cabinets of painted white wood. The various units are movable, and they can be used to form other more or less intimate conversational or relaxing arrangements, according to the occasion or the changing daylight or season outside.

Offices. The flexible and mobile approach to office design has been evident for several years. The open-space plan has been recognized since 1969, as has the formalized concept developed in Germany and known as *Bürolandschaft* ("office landscape"), where permanent walls are replaced by functional dividers such as screens, free-standing storage units, plants, or simply a cluster arrangement of work units to allow for expansion or contraction of office personnel. As a logical solution both economically and functionally, this flexible use of space is an accepted fact. Approximately 30% of all offices built or refurbished in 1973 have been planned on some formula of the *Bürolandschaft* system or the somewhat more flexible and personal open-space plan.

Schools. The justification of the flexible open plan for schools is more profound than mere economics. There has been a rethinking of the function and meaning of schools and teaching. The rigid, boxlike classroom has gone the way of rote education. Group activities within large airy spaces are more the rule. Space is flexible to allow change at will, to conform to groupings and regroupings of student activities. These activities may encompass electronic tutoring, television sessions, reading, studying, or group discussion—any or all happening simultaneously: furniture has become rudimentary: a few desks and seats ((sitting on the floor is common), some tables, carrels, and shelves or stacks for books and graphic materials—all are movable.

The St. Paul Open School—a public school for kindergarten through 12th grade, housed in a former industrial plant in St. Paul, Minn.—is an example of the use of "found space" as an alternative to new construction, as well as of flexible, open design. Few of the original walls were kept. The basic plan used by the designer, architect John Baymiller, was open, with space divided in interesting ways.

One area, in particular, was devoted to "environments"—detachable units made up of a series of enclosed platforms. The platforms, each large enough to accommodate from one to four occupants, were carpeted for warmth and comfort, as well as for the carpet's acoustical properties. They are set at varying levels on a demountable unistrut system and face different directions. Each serves as a step up to the next platform in the unit. The platforms function as cozy nooks for reading, studying, research, resting, "rapping," or getting away from it all.

JEANNE G. WEEKS
Harvey Probber Inc.

DESIGNED BY JOHN BAYMILLER, the St. Paul Open School, St. Paul, Minn., was built from a former industrial plant. Part of the school consists of "environments" (shown in photo) which serve as research, studying, and resting areas for the students.

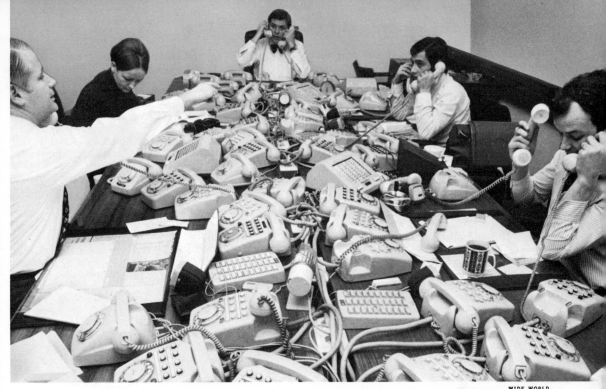

international finance

The devaluation of the American dollar in February caused a crisis on the international money market. In the office of a private currency broker in Frankfurt, West Germany (above), and on the Paris stock exchange (below), activity was frantic.

Although official negotiations toward reform of the international monetary system made little progress during 1973, the system began to reform itself. Early in the year large flows of capital swept away the patchwork, fixed-rate system devised at the Smithsonian Accord on Dec. 18, 1971, and left in their wake a new system with greater exchange-rate flexibility.

Throughout the year the international economy was subjected to substantial disturbances: rapid worldwide inflation, widespread shortages of agricultural commodities and petroleum, abrupt shifts of monetary policy in several major nations, wide swings in exchange rates, an unprecedented political crisis in the United States, and the outbreak of war in the Middle East. Yet despite all of these shocks the world economy continued to grow at or near record rates, and the volume of trade and investment both appear to have flourished.

SPONTANEOUS REFORM OF THE MONETARY SYSTEM

Barely six months after the Smithsonian Accord, the interim international monetary system showed signs of strain. Britain had allowed the pound to float in June 1972 after having lost $2.5 billion in defense of the Smithsonian central rate. And by end of 1972, despite the realignment of exchange rates, the U. S. trade deficit and the West German and Japanese trade surpluses were larger than ever.

During the first week of February speculators moved heavily into continental European currencies and the Japanese yen and out of dollars. Foreign central banks purchased roughly $8 billion in an effort to maintain the dollar values of their currencies within the Smithsonian bands of ± 2¼% from the negotiated central rates. The German central bank

alone purchased $6 billion and the Bank of Japan purchased $1.5 billion before the official foreign exchange markets were closed.

The Dollar Devaluation. After hasty international consultations, U. S. Secretary of the Treasury George Schultz announced that the dollar would be devalued by 10% (thus raising the official price of gold to $42.22 per ounce) and that the Japanese yen would be allowed to float. This attempt to patch up the Smithsonian Accord and thereby preserve the fixed rate system proved totally inadequate. Less than a month later, on March 1, most European central banks again stopped intervening in support of the dollar after having purchased roughly $3.6 billion in defense of the new central rates. The following day the Bank of France was almost alone in its effort to defend the February 12th central rates; however, after purchasing $500 million early in the day it also withdrew from support operations.

These large flows of capital led to a striking change in the international monetary system: the determination of exchange rates between major currencies largely by the interaction of private supply and demand rather than by official intervention in support of negotiated parities.

EXCHANGE RATE MOVEMENTS

As a first step toward monetary integration in the spring of 1972 the members of the European Economic Community (EEC) decided to limit fluctuations against each other's currencies within a 2¼% band inside the 4½% band permissible under the Smithsonian Accord—an arrangement that became known as the "snake in the tunnel." With the collapse of the Smithsonian Accord, the future of the snake was also in question. Six members of the EEC agreed to maintain the integrity of the snake even though the tunnel had dissolved in the general float. These six—Belgium, Denmark, France, Luxembourg, the Netherlands, and West Germany— were joined for purposes of the joint float by Norway and Sweden. Italy decided to drop out of the snake and float alone and Britain continued its independent float, although both countries are members of the EEC. In addition, the Canadian dollar, the Japanese yen, the Swiss franc, and the U. S. dollar floated separately.

From the reopening of the exchange markets on March 19 until the middle of May, exchange rates were remarkably stable; the snake stayed well within the limits of the old tunnel. However, from the second week in May until the first week of July the snake currencies and the Swiss franc began to rise against the dollar and most other floating currencies. The dollar depreciated most dramatically vis-à-vis the German mark, losing more than 20% of its value in marks from early spring to midsummer. During the first week of July there were large and erratic movements in exchange rates so that by the end of the week some New York banks had stopped trading in certain European currencies. From mid-March through the first week of July there had been no official intervention in support of the dollar price of the snake currencies; however, that weekend at a meeting of the Bank for International Settlements in Basel, Switzerland, an agreement was made to resume central bank intervention in support of orderly market conditions. Also an additional $6.25 billion in swap lines—short-term, reciprocal credit arrangements among central banks—was made available to the Federal Reserve, increasing the sum of swap facilities that the Fed could draw upon to $17.98 billion.

The official intervention that actually took place at that time was comparatively slight; by the end of July, Federal Reserve intervention in marks amounted to only $200.5 million equivalent while the German central bank purchased roughly $300 million in support of the dollar. Nonetheless, whether because of the psychological impact of the Basel agreement or because of shifts in interest rates and natural corrective factors set off by the preceding exchange rate changes, orderly market conditions were restored and the dollar price of the snake currencies began to fall. It continued to fall, somewhat irregularly, through much of the rest of the year. The outbreak of fighting in the Middle East and the rationing of petroleum exports by the Arabs led to a strengthening of the dollar relative to European currencies and the yen because the United States was relatively less dependent on external supplies of petroleum. By year-end, the dollar had regained on the average most of its value it had lost since the February devaluation.

Although the dollar fluctuated significantly in terms of the snake currencies and the Swiss franc, it remained remarkably stable in terms of the British pound, the Canadian dollar, the Italian lira, and the Japanese yen. Inasmuch as roughly three fourths of U. S. trade is with Canada, Italy, and Japan, the effective depreciation of the dollar was relatively modest.

BALANCE OF PAYMENTS

United States. During 1973 some of the most extreme payments imbalances began to ease. The U. S. balance of payments showed dramatic improvement. During the third quarter the U. S. trade balance was in surplus by more than $3 billion at an annual rate—the first trade surplus since the first quarter of 1971. However, optimism about the trend of the trade balance was tempered by the fact that most of the improvement was attributable to a rise in agricultural exports that is not likely to recur. There was also a marked improvement in net long-term capital flows as foreign direct investment in the U. S. accelerated and U. S. direct investment abroad slowed. At the close of 1973 the restrictions on U. S. capital outflows, first imposed a decade ago, were significantly eased. The interest equalization tax was slashed by two thirds, and the ceilings on direct investment outflows and bank lending abroad were substantially increased.

Japan. Japan's trade surplus through November 1973 was slashed to $3.75 billion from $7.75 billion in the same period of 1972, due largely to an upsurge in imports. The roughly 70% growth in imports during 1973 was attributable to the revaluation of the yen, the domestic economic boom, the sharp rise in world commodity prices, and the effects of liberalization of import controls and agreements with the United States to offset the bilateral surplus. Japan, which imports virtually all of its petroleum needs, was particularly hard hit by the energy crisis.

Germany. The German trade surplus showed few signs of diminishing. Despite the fact that at the end of 1973 the dollar price of the mark was roughly 50% higher than it had been in the spring of 1970, the German surplus continued to mount, surpassing the DM 20 billion attained in 1972.

INTERNATIONAL FINANCIAL CONDITIONS

Gold. Because the price of gold is widely regarded as a barometer of confidence in the international monetary system itself, it is not surprising that it fluctuated widely during 1973. Rising from a price of $65 an ounce in January 1968, the price of gold on the London market reached a record high of $127 early in the summer before falling to a price of roughly $112 at year-end. Official pronouncements and rising interest rates accounted for much of the downward trend in the gold price during the latter half of the year.

In late summer Valery Giscard d'Estaing, French minister of finance, announced that France would no longer insist that gold have a central position in the new monetary system. In November, Arthur Burns, chairman of the Federal Reserve Board, announced that the United States and six European nations had agreed to end the 1968 Washington Agreement that had created the two-tier gold market by prohibiting government purchases or sales on the private gold market. Because official holdings of gold are nearly 30 times larger than the annual volume of production in recent years, the possibility of official sales tended to depress the gold price. However, some European governments interpreted the end of the two-tier system as permitting official purchases as well.

Interest Rates. Central bank discount rates were at or near record levels in most major industrial nations as most governments attempted to tighten monetary policy to combat inflation. Interest rates in the Eurodollar market, the offshore market in dollar bank deposits, approached the extraordinarily high levels attained in 1969.

TOWARD A NEW INTERNATIONAL MONETARY SYSTEM

Contrary to some optimistic prognostications emanating from the Committee of Twenty (C-20), the International Monetary Fund (IMF) committee charged with designing the new international monetary system, the annual meeting of the IMF produced no tangible progress toward a negotiated reform. The principal accomplishment of the annual meeting, held in Nairobi, Kenya, was an agreement that the C-20 should complete a basic outline of international monetary reform by July 31, 1974. The Chairman of the C-20, Jeremy Morse of Britain, released a "First Outline of Reform" noting areas of agreement and issues yet to be resolved.

Signals for Adjustment. Although delegates agreed on the need to establish adjustment rules and sanctions falling symmetrically on surplus and deficit countries, they disagreed on how best to attain such an objective. The United States placed considerable importance on the movements of reserves as an objective indicator of imbalances, while other governments preferred to rely more heavily on subjective evaluation in consultation with an international group of experts.

Means of Adjustment. While there was a consensus that countries should initiate adjustment to external imbalances by use of domestic monetary or fiscal policy or by exchange rate changes rather than by means of controls on flows of goods and services, some nations favored substantial reliance on controls on capital flows—an option that the United States strongly opposed. The agreement with respect to the new exchange rate regime was described in the expression "stable but adjustable par values, with provision for floating in particular situations"—a phrase that is less a prescription for reform than a reflection of the divergence of opinion within the C-20.

Reserve Assets. It is generally agreed that Special Drawing Rights—perhaps modified and renamed—should take on the role of unit of account and principal reserve asset in the new system and, correspondingly, that the official reserve role of gold and holdings of national currencies should decline. Unfortunately, the technical details of how best to accomplish such a change were not yet clear in 1973.

As the year drew to an end, several observers asked why it was necessary to continue efforts to change the international monetary system in view of the success with which flexible exchange rates had insulated individual currencies and economies from a succession of serious foreign disturbances without significantly impeding trade and investment. Most officials felt that it was essential to continue the effort to develop a system of rules to govern conduct when national policies conflict. Since the exchange rate is an important political issue in most countries, governments will inevitably seek to influence its level. The fundamental task of reform is thus to devise a set of rules to guide official intervention. Without effective guidelines there is a danger that future economic conditions may lead governments to engage in competitive exchange-rate manipulation that could ultimately result in the unraveling of the fabric of world trade and investment.

RICHARD J. HERRING
University of Pennsylvania

INTERNATIONAL LAW. See LAW.

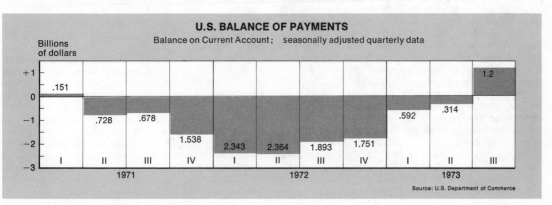

U.S. BALANCE OF PAYMENTS

Balance on Current Account; seasonally adjusted quarterly data

Billions of dollars

Source: U.S. Department of Commerce

international trade

The Russian bulk carrier Zakarpatye, said to be the first Soviet vessel ever to enter Lake Superior, is ready to take on wheat at Superior, Wis.

UPI

World trade showed exceptional growth in 1973 despite currency unrest, war in the Mideast, and shortages of commodities in many countries. In U. S. dollars, the value of world trade for the year was expected to reach nearly $500 billion, some 30% greater than in 1972. Trade of the world's two largest exporters, the United States and Japan, shifted abruptly. The U. S. trade balance, in large deficit during 1972, moved to a surplus of $1.7 billion. In contrast Japan, which had registered an exceptionally large 1972 surplus, reduced the excess of exports over imports by at least half. A Trade Reform Act of 1973 was passed by the U. S. House of Representatives at the end of the year and sent to the Senate for action.

Developments for the year are discussed in the following sections: (1) Trade Trends; and (2) Tariffs and Trade Restrictions.

TRADE TRENDS

The strong growth in world trade occurred in large part as a result of the unusual coincidence that all major developed nations were undergoing a boom at the same time. This situation stimulated competition for international industrial supplies and capital equipment. In addition, crop failures and poor harvests in large consuming and producing countries caused a sharp upturn in trade in agricultural products. The extensive rise in demand put great pressure on world prices, especially of primary commodities, which rose strongly.

Currency unrest, reflected in a second devaluation of the U. S. dollar in February and many subsequent movements, up and down, of other currencies, surprisingly had no discernible negative effect on the growth of world trade. Traditionally, traders have felt that stable currencies were an essential stimulus to trade expansion. Nor did the growing use of export restrictions appear to have noticeably slowed the increase. The United States, Canada, and various European Economic Community (EEC) or Common Market countries at one time or the other during the year limited the amount of exports in order to husband supplies for domestic use or to help control inflation.

After the outbreak of war between the Arabs and the Israelis in October, Arab crude oil was embargoed to the United States and the Netherlands in retaliation for their assistance to Israel, and produc-

tion was reduced in most Arab countries. It was not possible to estimate immediately the effect of those actions on world trade. However, because petroleum prices continued to rise sharply, the volume of world trade was more likely to change than the value.

On September 12–14, delegates from about 100 nations met in Tokyo, Japan, to initiate the seventh round of negotiations to cut tariffs, reduce other barriers, and generally liberalize world trade. These negotiations, considered the most important since the establishment of the General Agreement on Tariffs and Trade (GATT) in 1948, were expected to be given the broadest possible scope. Unlike previous sessions, they were to (1) include agricultural as well as industrial goods, (2) focus on reducing nontariff barriers, and (3) pay special attention to developing country problems. It was anticipated that detailed negotiating would begin in September 1974, following agreement on specific guidelines by the participating nations and passage of the new trade bill in Washington.

United States. The foreign trade of the United States improved in 1973 as abruptly as it had deteriorated in 1972. Exports totaled $70.8 billion for the entire year while imports were $69.1 billion. The surplus of $1.7 billion contrasted sharply with the 1972 deficit of $6.4 billion. The 24% rate of gain for imports was about the same as in the previous year, but exports jumped by 44%, more than three times as fast as in 1972. The expansion in these trade values was considerably strengthened by price increases which were generated by intense inflationary pressures around the world. In fact, after adjustment for price changes imports were only 5% greater in volume than in 1972. About half the rise in exports was accounted for by increased quantities of goods.

This turnaround in U. S. trade stemmed primarily from the booming business conditions abroad which strained indigenous capacity and brought heightened demand for American goods. The change in the competitiveness of U. S. products brought about by the devaluations of the dollar in December 1971 and February 1973 also aided foreign sales. Finally, the urgent need for imported grain in the largest countries, together with short supplies in two principal exporting nations, Australia and Argentina, brought about an unprecedented jump in sales of food and feed grains.

U. S. Exports. In January–December exports of agricultural products surged by 88% over the year 1972. Wheat shipments nearly tripled in value and those of soybeans and corn soared. The tremendous advance in wheat exports was due in part to huge requirements from the USSR placed, after a disastrous harvest, at advantageous prices in the summer of 1972. Both the People's Republic of China and India were short of grain and made large purchases in the U. S. market.

Nonagricultural exports of goods were also unusually strong in 1973. Shipments climbed to more than $50 billion, 33% above January–December 1972. The widespread rise included industrial supplies, machinery, and transport equipment.

U. S. Imports. Imports of foreign goods into the United States in 1973 were 24% higher than in the preceding year. All but a small part of the rise in the import value stemmed from higher prices, which occurred as a result of the second dollar devaluation and because of exceptionally strong inflation in other countries. With the worsening of the fuel situation, rising imports of petroleum and products added over $3 billion to the import bill for the entire year. Consumer goods purchased abroad rose by 16%, with most of the increase due to foreign cars and all of it resulting from higher prices. Food and beverage entries climbed by one fourth in value for the year, in large part because of higher prices for coffee and meat.

U. S. Balance of Payments. The U. S. payments balance in the first three quarters of 1973 showed a surplus of $1 billion measured by the balance on current account and long-term capital. This was a sizable improvement when compared with 1972. The significant reduction in the trade deficit in that period accounted for much of the shift for the better. There was also an improvement in the services account stemming from reduced deficits in tourism and military transactions and from greater investment income. Government and long-term private capital outflows, which had added to the 1972 trade deficit, shifted to a net inflow through September 1973.

The official reserve transactions balance, designed to measure current exchange market pressures on the dollar was deeply in deficit in the first quarter of 1973, but shifted to a surplus during the second and third quarters of the year as liquid private capital began to return to the United States.

Export-Import Bank. In fiscal year 1973 the Eximbank handled more business relating to U. S. exports than in any preceding year. It supported $10.5 billion of export sales, authorized $8.5 billion of loans, guarantees, and insurance, and more than $1.6 billion of discount loan commitments to U. S. commercial banks, and paid its 23d consecutive dividend to the U. S. Treasury.

Most of the $2.3 billion long-term loans authorized during the year covered the purchase of nonmilitary capital equipment and services. Principal items financed were jet aircraft for 37 countries, nuclear power and research projects for four countries, and petroleum extraction and refining equipment, primarily for Taiwan and Indonesia.

In fiscal 1973 President Nixon determined that it was in the national interest for the Eximbank to support exports to the USSR and Poland. Credits and guarantees were authorized to support $482 million of U. S. exports to four communist countries. An additional $51 million of exports was supported

by short- and medium-term programs. Among the larger credits were $86 million to the USSR for a truck plant, $22 million to Poland for two meat-processing plants, and $20 million to Rumania for jet aircraft.

Canada. Both exports and imports of Canada advanced by 23% in the first nine months of 1973. With exports valued at Canadian $17.8 billion and imports at C$16.7 billion through September, Canada's trade was in surplus by C$1.1 billion.

As usual, exchanges with the United States accounted for the major share of Canadian trade—in the nine-month period, 69% of shipments and 71% of imports. Responsible for more than half of the sales to the United States were automotive products, petroleum, lumber, and newsprint. Strikes on the Canadian railroads and in the pulp and paper in-

PRINCIPAL U.S. TRADING PARTNERS
(First eight months of 1973, in millions of dollars)

U. S. TRADING PARTNERS, 1972–73
(Millions of dollars)

Country	Exports & reexports		General imports	
	1972	Jan.–August 1973	1972	Jan.–August 1973
Total................	49,768	44,420	55,555	44,892
Australia.................	843	820	807	620
Belgium-Luxembourg.......	1,138	1,033	968	790
Brazil..................	1,243	1,057	942	745
Canada.................	12,415	9,653	14,909	11,715
Colombia...............	317	268	284	252
France.................	1,610	1,479	1,369	1,160
Germany, Fed. Rep........	2,811	2,332	4,249	3,549
Hong Kong..............	489	458	1,249	923
India[1]...................	350	281	427	281
Israel..................	558	598	222	189
Italy...................	1,430	1,392	1,756	1,337
Japan..................	4,965	5,316	9,064	6,470
Korea, South............	735	814	708	645
Mexico.................	1,982	1,788	1,632	1,487
Netherlands.............	1,851	1,800	639	523
Netherlands Antilles........	122	102	400	424
Philippines..............	366	299	484	429
South Africa, Rep. of........	602	464	325	250
Spain..................	930	864	600	501
Sweden.................	472	327	601	510
Switzerland..............	672	611	619	514
Taiwan.................	631	642	1,294	1,142
United Kingdom...........	2,658	2,210	2,986	2,403
USSR..................	547	894	95	118
Venezuela...............	924	659	1,298	1,026
Other countries and undisclosed shipments.....	9,107	8,259	7,628	6,889

[1] Exports exclude "special category" shipments for which information is withheld for security reasons. Source: U. S. Department of Commerce.

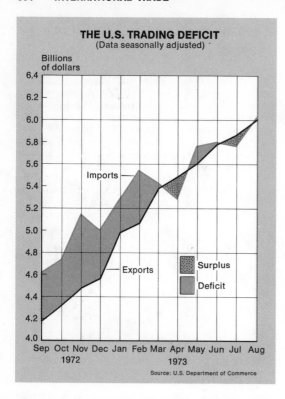

THE U.S. TRADING DEFICIT
(Data seasonally adjusted)

Billions of dollars

Imports

Exports

Surplus

Deficit

Sep Oct Nov Dec Jan Feb Mar Apr May Jun Jul Aug
1972   1973

Source: U.S. Department of Commerce

dustry during the summer tended to reduce third-quarter shipments somewhat. Gains in imports from the United States were concentrated in automotive products, industrial machinery, aircraft, and food.

In 1973, Japan replaced Britain as Canada's second most important trading partner. Imports from that nation remained near their record 1972 level through September, but sales of Canadian products to Japan soared by 75% as additional quantities of metals, lumber, and other resources moved at increased prices. The nine-month 1972 deficit of C$125 million shifted to a surplus of C$450 million in 1973. Canada's trade was also strong with the Common Market and Commonwealth nations.

Exports from Canada benefited greatly from booming world economic conditions. Notable increases were registered in sales of wheat, petroleum, iron ore, paper, and lumber. Controls temporarily imposed on selected commodities kept exports from rising even higher.

The current account of the Canadian balance of payments improved in the first half of 1973. The substantially greater trade surplus more than offset an increase in the deficit in the services account. Net capital movements dropped from inflows of C$1 billion in January–June 1972 to only C$400 million a year later. The major shift in these movements resulted from a decline of more than half a billion Canadian dollars in the net inflow of long-term funds.

Latin America. Benefiting from sharply rising world demand, production shortages, and general inflation, sales of basic Latin American products advanced strongly in value in the first six months of 1973. Prices for coffee, meat, sugar, cotton, wool, petroleum, and copper—all important export commodities from this area—jumped in the first quarter and continued upward as the year progressed. Exports from the 19 republics in the first half were

at least 15% above the level of the first half of 1972. Import growth lagged somewhat behind that of exports, as is usual, though the pattern varied widely from country to country.

The Brazilian trade and payments situation improved substantially in the first six months. Exports surged by 47% as a result of higher prices, especially for coffee and cacao, and a greater diversification of commodities. Increases in coffee prices more than compensated for low quantities available because of unfavorable climatic conditions. As imports advanced by only 30%, Brazil's trade balance moved to a slight surplus.

With inflation growing, inflow of capital limited by uncompetitive interest rates, and agricultural and mineral production reduced, the usual foreign trade deficit of Mexico expanded in 1973. Through July, a deficit of more than $800 million was recorded, about 30% more than in the preceding year. The 1972 rate of export growth was maintained, but imports, especially of capital goods and certain agricultural products, rose faster than in 1972. The rate of import growth was enhanced, as in Brazil, by the government's relaxation of import restrictions in order to combat domestic inflation.

Along with other oil-producing countries, Venezuela benefited in 1973 from higher prices for its main export product, even though the volume of shipments continued to drop, at least in the early months. Iron ore, also in great demand throughout the world, was sold in substantially greater quantities and at rising prices. Imports grew more slowly than exports so that Venezuela's favorable trade balance was likely to be higher for the year as a whole than 1972's $500 million. In signing the "Consensus of Lima," Venezuela agreed to enter the Andean Common Market, a group of Latin American countries bound to eventual establishment of a common external tariff and elimination of internal duties.

Western Europe. In the first half of 1973 the expansion in Western Europe's imports, measured in dollars, was 29%. At least half of this appeared to represent price increases. Exports advanced nearly as strongly in value, with prices also a significant factor.

Economic activity grew rapidly in the first half in the Common Market, which was enlarged to nine countries on January 1 with the formal accession of Britain, Denmark, and Ireland. Internal demand expanded, plant capacity was at high levels, labor shortages grew, and low stocks were replenished. These conditions brought a sizable rise in imports, while tending to limit exports. Thus, the Community's trade balance deteriorated. Notable exceptions to this deterioration, however, were Germany and the Netherlands.

West Germany's trade soared in both directions and the already large surplus expanded further. In the first six months of 1973, the excess of exports over imports totaled $5.5 billion, not far from the surplus of $6.8 billion in the full year 1972. The exceptional demand for German goods—up 33% in the first six months—occurred despite higher prices for its products in foreign currencies as a result of the revaluations of the Deutsche mark, including a fresh one at the end of June, and internal inflation caused by excessive demand. Imports were 27% greater in value through June partly as a result of rising commodity prices and partly because of an acceleration of domestic investment activity and higher consumer demand.

Dutch trade, as that of other European countries, expanded in the January–June period. Because exports rose 37%, several percentage points faster than imports, trade moved into balance, an exception to the usual Dutch deficit position. In an effort to combat inflation, however, the Dutch again revalued their guilder upward by 5% on September 17. This action was expected to retard exports and induce more goods to be imported as guilder prices dropped.

Italian exports proved an exception to the general expansionary trends in Western Europe as they were hard hit because of strikes, particularly in the first quarter of the year. After the signing of new labor agreements in April, there was some pickup, but through the first half sales to foreigners were little higher than in the two preceding half years. Agricultural exports were also limited because of the poor 1972 harvest. The trend of imports in contrast was sharply up, in part as a result of increased costs, which were boosted by the de facto devaluation of the lira. However, a prolonged strike by customs officials impeded import growth.

The British reported a mounting deficit during 1973. The deficit, which was £57 mililon a month in 1972, had grown to an average of £139 million per month through August. British exports moved with particular strength to the rest of the Common Market following its accession to that group at the beginning of the year. In total, exports advanced by 23% in value, with a sizable portion accounted for by volume increases. Of the 34% rise in import values, however, only about half represented a gain in quantity. Real growth was mainly in raw materials and machinery to aid the vigorously growing British investment in plant and equipment.

TARIFFS AND TRADE RESTRICTIONS

In the 9 months after the 93d U. S. Congress convened in January, 375 trade and related bills were introduced. A number of these, especially as inflation continued strong in the United States, related to the establishment of restrictions on U. S. exports in periods of short supply.

The most significant legislation being considered which related to U. S. trade and tariffs was the Trade Reform Act of 1973, submitted to the Congress in April by President Nixon. After 24 days of public hearings with testimony from 369 witnesses, and many subsequent months of work, the House Ways and Means Committee rewrote the trade bill. The House acted favorably in December and sent the bill to the Senate for final action during 1974.

There was considerable controversy surrounding the provision in the trade bill relating to the Soviet Union and other nonmarket countries. By this provision, the same duties could be charged on imports from them that are charged other nations if the president is satisfied the country does not place undue restrictions on emigration. Such restrictions allegedly practiced against Soviet Jews and other minorities were a major issue in the House debate on the bill, especially in light of the October war in the Middle East and Soviet involvement therein. It was also considered possible that further restrictions on credit to the nonmarket countries might be added to the bill.

The principal purposes of HR 10710, however, go far beyond this controversial issue. These are: (1) to renew and extend the authority of the president to enter into trade agreements with foreign countries for a period of five years; (2) to authorize the president to enter agreements providing for the reduction or elimination of nontariff barriers and other distortions of international trade; (3) to improve procedures for dealing with problems of unfair trade practices in the United States and abroad; (4) to improve adjustment assistance programs for workers and firms adversely affected by increased imports; and (5) to authorize the president to grant preferential tariff treatment to the exports of developing countries.

Late in October the nine Common Market countries opened negotiations in Brussels, Belgium, with 43 developing countries from Africa, the South Pacific, and the Caribbean aimed at consolidating the largest free-trade arrangements in the world. Many of these countries now have, and the others have been offered, the privilege of exporting goods duty-free to the Market. In return, some of these associated nations have eliminated duties on products coming from the EEC. The latter arrangement, the so-called "reverse preference," which has been opposed by the United States, will be under serious discussion in the negotiations, along with plans for the creation of special funds to guarantee developing countries' earnings from raw material exports and to use for development purposes. Negotiations are expected to continue into mid-1974.

With the accession of the United Kingdom to the Common Market in January 1973, all British extra-Community preferential trade agreements were terminated. The plans under discussion in Brussels would reinstitute arrangements with most developing Commonwealth countries and broaden their scope to all of the nine members.

FRANCES L. HALL
Director, International Trade Analysis Division
U. S. Department of Commerce

NON-COMMUNIST WORLD TRADE BY REGIONS, 1972–73

Quarterly figures expressed as annual rates
(Billions of dollars)

Area	1972				1973	
	1st Quarter	2d Quarter	3d Quarter	4th Quarter	1st Quarter	2d Quarter[1]
Total exports, f.o.b....	346.8	370.9	354.6	411.8	430.8	482.5
Developed areas						
United States and Canada..	66.4	71.3	65.9	79.5	85.9	96.8
Western Europe...........	179.2	191.9	174.8	212.9	220.6	252.5
Japan...................	24.6	26.3	30.1	33.5	30.3	34.6
Australia, New Zealand, South Africa...........	9.8	11.1	10.7	12.0	14.7	15.8
Developing areas						
Latin American republics...	14.7	16.3	16.9	16.8	17.6	18.0
Other Western Hemisphere	3.1	3.4	3.1	3.0	3.5	3.5
Middle East.............	17.3	17.6	17.0	16.5	19.7	21.0
Other Asia..............	17.6	19.2	21.2	22.1	23.0	24.4
Africa..................	13.4	13.2	14.2	14.8	14.9	15.2
Other countries..........	0.7	0.6	0.7	0.7	0.6	0.7
Total imports, c.i.f....	366.4	386.0	368.4	418.2	450.3	501.6
Developed areas						
United States and Canada..	74.8	80.4	77.2	85.9	90.7	99.7
Western Europe...........	191.6	201.6	186.1	219.5	240.2	267.6
Japan...................	21.7	22.1	23.5	26.7	29.3	37.6
Australia, New Zealand, South Africa...........	10.8	10.4	10.1	11.5	12.5	13.9
Developing areas						
Latin American republics...	15.7	17.5	18.2	18.5	18.6	20.4
Other Western Hemisphere...........	4.8	5.2	4.7	4.8	5.2	5.4
Middle East.............	11.0	11.2	10.2	11.5	12.9	13.5
Other Asia..............	21.8	23.7	24.4	25.0	25.4	27.5
Africa..................	13.0	12.6	12.9	13.6	14.0	14.5
Other countries..........	1.2	1.3	1.1	1.2	1.5	1.5

[1] Partly estimated.   Source: U. S. Department of Commerce.

IOWA

In 1973 a newly elected state legislature passed a record high budget for Iowa in the second-longest session in the body's history. Iowa farmers enjoyed an increase in crop production.

Legislature. The 65th General Assembly of Iowa met in its first session on Jan. 11, 1973. All 150 members had been elected in the November 1972 election because of reapportionment of both the House and the Senate.

Republicans controlled both houses, with 28 of the 50 seats in the Senate and 56 of the 100 House seats. The average age of the legislators was 45.2 years, the youngest in many years. The legislature was also the most inexperienced in history, with 59 of the 150 members serving their first legislative term.

Early in the year, Gov. Robert D. Ray (R) presented a record-setting budget of $1,579,103,139 for the 1973–75 biennium that called for no general tax increase even though it was 22.7% higher than the budget for the previous biennium. In April, Governor Ray submitted an amended budget, which increased the recommended appropriations to more than $1.6 billion. Final appropriations were nearly identical with those proposed by the governor. The state treasury had a surplus of more than $119 million at the end of the 1972–73 biennium, but this figure included more than $30 million received in federal revenue sharing.

The legislative regular session ran 168 days, making it the second longest in history. Several tax relief programs were passed. The first $4,000 of annual income was exempted from state income taxes. Property tax relief was granted to those over 65 years of age who have incomes of less than $6,000. The legislators agreed to phase out personal property taxes over a 10-year period, and the personal property tax on livestock was repealed outright.

The salaries of all top state officials—both administrative and judicial—and of county elected officials were raised. The annual salaries of the state legislators themselves were increased from $5,500 to $8,000 (beginning in 1975), and their weekly expense allowances were increased to $140. A new statute required candidates for public office and committees working in their behalf to disclose campaign contributions and expenses.

The legislators also authorized the establishment of health maintenance organizations in the field of preventive health care and of facilities for family medical practice. Appropriations for tuition grants to students at private colleges were increased to $12 million.

The sale of liquor and beer on Sunday under certain conditions was authorized and bingo and other games of chance were legalized. Finally, statewide voter registration was set for 1975.

Agriculture. Iowa farmers did well in 1973. Crop production was large, and the average prices for both corn and soybeans were twice what they had been in 1972.

More than 1.2 billion bushels of corn were harvested in Iowa in 1973, an increase of more than 1% over the record 1972 crop. Iowa farmers also harvested 282.6 million bushels of soybeans, an increase of more than 30% over the record 1972 crop.

Other News. Iowa's U. S. Sen. Harold Hughes (D) surprised his constituents by announcing that he would not be a candidate for reelection in 1974, but would instead be working with religious groups.

In August 1973, Iowa's unemployment rate dropped to 2.7%, with total employment of 1,302,900. This was down from 3.2% unemployed in August 1972.

RUSSELL M. ROSS, *University of Iowa*

IOWA • Information Highlights

Area: 56,290 square miles (145,791 sq km).
Population (1972 est.): 2,883,000. *Density:* 51 per sq mi.
Chief Cities (1970 census): Des Moines, the capital, 201,404; Cedar Rapids, 110,642; Davenport, 98,469; Sioux City, 85,925; Waterloo, 75,533; Dubuque, 62,309; Council Bluffs, 60,348.
Government (1973): *Chief Officers*—governor, Robert D. Ray (R); lt. gov., Arthur A. Neu (R); secy. of state, Melvin D. Synhorst (R); atty. gen., Richard C. Turner (R); treas., Maurice E. Baringer (R); supt. of public instruction, Robert Benton; chief justice, C. Edwin Moore. *General Assembly*—Senate, 50 members (28 Republicans, 22 Democrats); House of Representatives, 100 members (56 R, 44 D).
Education (1972–73): *Enrollment*—public elementary schools, 449,615 pupils, 16,565 teachers; public secondary schools, 199,259 pupils, 15,776 teachers; nonpublic schools, 70,900 pupils, 3,110 teachers; colleges and universities, 98,036 students. *Public school expenditures*, $652,731,000 ($1,058 per pupil). *Average teacher's salary*, $10,564.
State Finances (fiscal year 1971): *Revenues*, $1,233,936,000 (3% general sales tax and gross receipts taxes, $212,257,000; motor fuel tax, $107,062,000; federal funds, $251,550,000). *Expenditures*, $1,144,386,000 (education, $476,652,000; health, welfare, and safety, $153,113,000; highways, $286,507,000). State debt, $107,833,000 (June 30, 1971).
Personal Income (1972): $12,447,000,000; per capita, $4,318.
Public Assistance (1972): $125,407,000. *Average monthly payments* (Dec. 1972)—old-age assistance, $131.82; aid to families with dependent children, $187.76.
Labor Force: *Nonagricultural wage and salary earners* (July 1973), 963,300. *Average annual employment* (1972)—manufacturing, 223,300; trade, 225,000; government, 179,200; services, 161,200. *Insured unemployed* (Sept. 1973)—6,600 (0.9%).
Manufacturing (1971): Value added by manufacture, $3,941,100,000. Food and kindred products, $1,082,700,000; nonelectrical machinery, $788,200,000; chemicals and allied products, $341,700,000; electrical equipment and supplies, $340,900,000; printing and publishing, $225,500,000; fabricated metal products, $225,400,000.
Agriculture (1972): *Cash farm income*, $5,015,343,000 (livestock, $3,260,692,000; crops, $1,436,140,000; government payments, $318,511,000). *Chief crops* (in order of value, 1972)—Corn (ranks 2d among the states), soybeans (ranks 2d), hay, oats.
Mining (1972): Production value, $136,012,000 (ranks 31st among the states). *Chief minerals*—Cement, $53,650,000; stone, $44,281,000; sand and gravel, $21,556,000; coal, $7,300,000.
Transportation: *Roads* (1972), 112,831 miles (181,579 km); *motor vehicles* (1972), 1,841,680; *railroads* (1972), 7,903 miles (12,718 km); *public airports* (1972), 109.
Communications: *Telephones* (1973), 1,751,100; *television stations* (1971), 13; *radio stations* (1971), 110; *newspapers* (1973), 42 (daily circulation, 949,000).

IRAN

There were no major changes in Iran in 1973 in either domestic affairs or foreign relations. Rather there was an intensification and continuation of trends and policies visible for several years past. The two main themes, pursued by the shah's government under the premiership of Amir Abbas Hoveida, concerned economic development and the military strengthening of Iran.

Economic Development. In the last few years, Iran has been classed with Japan and Brazil as one of the world's fastest-growing economies, the current growth rate being about 14%. At the same time, the tendency to concentrate on sophisticated industries and on mechanizing agriculture could lead to unemployment and social problems, as the government now recognizes. There is also an emerging concern with the need for limiting population.

In announcing the new five-year plan in the Majlis on January 7, Premier Hoveida said that the

plan gave a higher priority than previous plans to agriculture and to social-welfare legislation aimed at reducing the gap between rich and poor. It is understood that the plan was modified to include projects involving income redistribution at the insistence of the shah, who is sensitive to the threat of social discontent.

Oil. In 1973, Iran, like other oil-producing states, made moves to increase national control over the industry and increase the revenues gained from it. On January 23 the shah warned the consortium of British, U. S., French, and Dutch oil companies operating in Iran that he would refuse to renew their contract after 1979 unless they agreed to increase the current production of almost 4.5 million barrels a day to 8.3 million by 1977.

This threat was succeeded very soon (March 20) by the shah's announcement of nationalization of the industry. (The oil companies had been originally nationalized in 1951, but this was reversed in 1954 by a 25-year agreement with the newly formed consortium.) Negotiations followed, resulting in the signing on May 24 of an agreement by Iran and the consortium that gave Iran "full and real control" of the oil industry within its borders. Under this pact oil production is to be increased to 8 million barrels a day by 1976. The National Iranian Oil Company took control of all facilities and operations, with the consortium remaining as technical adviser. The 30,000 square miles (77,700 sq km) in which the consortium had rights were to be reduced by 30%, but the areas remaining to it contain all current producing fields.

Iran, along with seven other members of OPEC (Organization of Petroleum Exporting Countries), signed an agreement in Geneva on June 2 under which a group of Western oil companies agreed to pay increases totaling 11.9% for crude oil. The demand for higher prices had been made to compensate for the devaluation of the U. S. dollar in February. In September and October the 11-member OPEC was again demanding yet higher prices.

On July 25 the shah revealed on a visit to Washington that Iran had signed a novel contract with an American firm, Ashland Oil Inc., to share 50–50 in producing, refining, and marketing oil.

Iran, which has a greater need for a steady cash flow of oil revenues than the Arab oil producers, did not join the latter in the oil embargo, which began in October, imposed on the United States and other countries classed as friendly to Israel.

Terrorist Activity. Iran, a monarchical state endeavoring to follow an internal policy of evolutionary reforms, continued to be a magnet for the activities of terrorists; and the government continued to deal firmly with them. Five Iraqi-trained Iranians convicted of sabotage and terror were executed on January 5, as were two men on January 11, convicted of the murder (August 1972) of Gen. Saied Taheri. On June 2 in Teheran a terrorist shot and killed Lt. Col. Lewis Hawkins, a U. S. military adviser; on June 15, Iranian security forces shot dead Reza Rezai, a guerrilla leader who they said had killed Hawkins and others.

Foreign Relations. Since the British withdrawal from the Persian Gulf area in 1971, Iran has been consciously playing the role of the stabilizing strong power of the area. This role is questioned and threatened by radical Iraq. It may at some point also be menaced by Iraq's patron and Iran's northern neighbor, the Soviet Union. In response to this,

───────── **IRAN • Information Highlights** ─────────

Official Name: Empire of Iran.
Location: Southwest Asia.
Area: 636,294 square miles (1,648,000 sq km).
Population (1973 est.): 31,100,000. Density, 47 per square mile (18 per sq km).
Chief Cities (1966 census): Teheran, the capital, 2,719,730; Isfahan, 424,045; Meshed, 409,616; Tabriz, 403,413.
Government: *Head of state,* Mohammed Reza Pahlavi, shah (acceded Sept. 1941; crowned Oct. 1967). *Chief minister,* Amir Abbas Hoveida, premier (took office Jan. 1965). *Legislature*—Parliament: Senate and Majlis (Lower House). *Major political parties*—Iran Novin party; Mardom party.
Languages: Persian (official), Turki.
Education: *Expenditure* (1969), 6.8% of total public expenditure. *School enrollment* (1969)—primary, 2,916,266; secondary, 930,053; technical/vocational, 23,335; university/ higher, 67,268.
Monetary Unit: Rial (68.17 rials equal U. S.$1, Sept. 1973).
Gross National Product (1972 est): $14,400,000,000.
Economic Indexes: *Industrial production* (1972), 356 (1963 = 100); *agricultural production* (1971), 126 (1963 = 100); *consumer price index* (1972), 126 (1963 = 100).
Manufacturing (major products): Petroleum products, iron and steel, textiles, processed foods, assembled automobiles, carpets.
Major Agricultural Products: Wheat, rice, barley, cotton, tobacco, fruits, fish (caviar).
Major Minerals: Petroleum (ranks 4th among world producers, 1972), natural gas, coal, iron, copper, lead, chromium ore.
Foreign Trade (1972): *Exports,* $2,964,000,000; *Imports,* $2,410,000,000. *Major export markets* (1970)—Japan, United Kingdom, India, United States. *Major import suppliers* (1970)—West Germany, Japan, United States, United Kingdom.
Tourism: Receipts (1970), $42,200,000.
Transportation: *Motor vehicles* (1971), 410,800 (automobiles, 331,200); *railroads* (1971), 2,742 miles (4,412 km); *merchant fleet* (1972), 181,000 gross registered tons; *major national airline,* Iran National Airlines.
Communications: *Telephones* (1971), 307,500; *newspapers* (1971), 29.

a vast and expensive program of modernizing Iran's armed forces is under way.

A massive increase of over 45% in military expenditure was the most striking feature of the budget that Premier Hoveida presented to the Majlis on March 4. Hoveida described defense as Iran's "top priority" and said that the government was resolved to turn Iran into a much more powerful nation since it was situated in "a very sensitive part of the world." On February 22 it had become known that Iran had contracted with the United States in recent months to buy more than $2 billion worth of sophisticated military equipment. This was described as the biggest single arms deal ever arranged by the Pentagon. It was also revealed that the U. S. military mission in Iran was to be augmented by several hundred men.

Diplomatic Meetings. Iran's excellent relations with the United States were symbolized by the state visit of the shah to Washington, July 24–27, during which he conferred at length with President Nixon. This was only one of a large number of visits testifying to Iran's growing importance. The shah visited Rumania (June 1–5) and signed an accord on long-term cooperation. Premier Hoveida conferred in London, April 12, and in Moscow, August 6–12. President Pompidou of France visited Teheran on September 18. President Bhutto of Pakistan was in Teheran from May 9 to 14. Iran is friendly toward Pakistan, and is cooperating in the suppression of the rebellion among the Baluchi tribesmen.

The foreign ministers of CENTO (the Central Treaty Organization) met in Teheran, June 10–11. However, in an interview with C. L. Sulzberger of the New York *Times* in April, the shah said his country had very little faith in CENTO, and intended to rely on its own strength as a matter of "crude reality."

ARTHUR CAMPBELL TURNER
University of California, Riverside

Official Name: Republic of Iraq.
Location: Southwest Asia.
Area: 167,925 square miles (434,924 sq km).
Population (1973 est.): 10,800,000. *Density,* 57 per square mile (22 per sq km).
Chief Cities (1970 est.): Baghdad, the capital, 2,183,800 (metropolitan area); Basra, 370,900; Mosul, 293,100; Kirkuk, 207,900.
Government: *Head of state,* Ahmed Hassan al-Bakr, president (took office July 1968). *Head of government,* Ahmed Hassan al-Bakr. *Major political parties*—Baath party; Kurdish Democratic party; Communist party.
Language: Arabic (official).
Education: *Expenditure* (1968), 5.5% of gross domestic product. *School enrollment* (1969)—primary, 1,040,968; secondary, 316,230; technical/vocational, 9,994; university/higher, 36,736.
Monetary Unit: Dinar (0.2961 dinar equals U. S.$1, Sept. 1973).
Gross National Product (1971 est.): $3,800,000,000.
Economic Indexes: *Agricultural production* (1971), 128 (1963 = 100); *consumer price index* (1972), 127 (1963 = 100).
Manufacturing (major products): Petroleum products, processed foods, textiles, cigarettes, cement.
Major Agricultural Products: Barley, wheat, rice, cotton, tobacco.
Major Minerals: Petroleum, sulfur.
Foreign Trade (1972): *Exports,* $1,184,000,000; *Imports,* $711,-000,000. *Chief trading partners* (1969)—Italy (took 24% of exports, supplied 8% of imports); France (20%—5%); Netherlands (9%—2%); United Kingdom (5%—12%).
Transportation: *Motor vehicles* (1971), 116,400 (automobiles, 71,800); *railroads* (1971), 1,395 miles (2,245 km); *merchant fleet* (1972), 121,000 gross registered tons; *major national airline,* Iraqi Airways.
Communications: *Telephones* (1970), 120,000; *newspapers* (1970), 4.

IRAQ

Iraq continued to be ruled throughout 1973 by the radical Baath party regime of President Ahmed Hassan al-Bakr and the Revolutionary Command Council. The Baath party completed five years of power in Iraq. An apparently serious threat to its position in July 1973 resulted in a strengthening of the authoritarian nature of the regime. Iraq continued to be at odds with several other states of the region, and it participated in the October war against Israel.

Oil: Agreement with IPC. Several months of negotiation were successfully concluded with the signing, announced on February 28 in Baghdad, of an agreement between the Iraqi government and the Western-owned Iraq Petroleum Company, whose oil fields and assets had been nationalized on June 1, 1972. The main terms of the complicated deal called for the company to pay Iraq about $350 million in arrears on account of royalties, expenses, and taxes. As compensation for nationalized assets, Iraq would deliver to IPC 15 million tons of crude oil (7 million in 1973 and 8 million in 1974) at Mediterranean terminals. IPC's biggest concession was to waive all claims to the North Rumaila field, which was nationalized without compensation in 1961. IPC agreed to increase production at the Basra field to 80 million tons by 1976.

Anti-Government Plot Crushed. The most important domestic event of the year was an abortive coup at the end of June, which led to the murder of one cabinet minister and two police officers and also resulted in the execution of 36 persons and the reorganization of the government. Most observers believe that the conspiracy reflected very deep rifts over policy within the ranks of the governing cabal itself.

It appears that Defense Minister Lt. Gen. Hammad Shihab and Interior Minister Lt. Gen. Sadoun Ghaidan, along with several army and security officers, were taken prisoner on June 30 at a banquet in Baghdad to which they had been invited by the ringleader, Col. Nazem Kazzar, chief of internal security. The captives were then taken to Zarbatiya, on the Iraq-Iranian border, where their captors were seized the next day by security forces. Kazzar was said to have shot Shihab dead and wounded Ghaidan when he found himself surrounded. He was alleged to have plotted to assassinate President Bakr and Vice President Sadam Hussein as a first step toward seizing power. Kazzar and 22 others were executed on July 7 after a trial before a special tribunal, and 13 more were executed on July 8. This brought to about 150 the number of those executed for conspiring against the regime since Bakr conspired successfully against the previous regime in July 1968; most of them had been exposed by Kazzar.

The constitution was amended by the Revolutionary Command Council on July 13 to give virtually unlimited authority to President Bakr. The changes made him "head of state, prime minister, and commander-in-chief." On July 17 plans were announced for the reestablishment of a parliament, which Iraq has been without for 15 years.

Relations with Pakistan. Normal diplomatic relations between Pakistan and Iraq were breached for two months after Pakistani police, disregarding diplomatic immunity, raided the Iraqi embassy in Islamabad on February 10, seizing large quantities of arms that had been smuggled into Pakistan and hidden in the embassy. Pakistan expelled the Iraqi ambassador and an attaché and recalled its ambassador from Baghdad. The arms scandal, in which some Pakistani politicians were implicated, is thought to have arisen from an Iraqi desire to bolster the separatist movement among the Baluchi tribesmen who straddle the Pakistani-Iranian border. Normal relations between Iraq and Pakistan were restored by an agreement made on April 25.

Border Dispute with Kuwait. Long-standing disputes with Iraq's tiny but wealthy neighbor Kuwait erupted on March 30 when troops clashed at the ill-defined frontier. It appears that Iraqi troops did cross several miles into Kuwaiti territory. The Arab League was active in mediating between the parties, and by March 26, Iraq had undertaken to pull its troops back. To reinforce these good intentions Saudi Arabia sent 15,000–20,000 soldiers into Kuwait on March 29 to bolster the sheikhdom's defenses. Motives for the Iraqi incursion were obscure but were thought to be connected with Iraq's desire to play a larger role in the politics of the Persian Gulf.

Position in Arab-Israeli Confrontation. Iraq joined in the war against Israel on October 10, sending about 18,000 troops to operate on Syrian soil. On October 7, in what was stated as reprisal for U. S. support of Israel, Iraq nationalized two American oil firms, Mobil and Exxon. But Iraq did not join the other Arab countries in cutting back oil production to penalize countries supporting Israel. Nor did it join the Arab leaders' meeting held in Algiers on November 26–28, objecting, as did Libya, to the Arab agreement to a cease-fire with Israel.

Earlier on August 10, an Iraqi Airways passenger jet en route from Beirut to Baghdad was intercepted by Israeli fighters and forced to land in northern Israel. The Israelis had thought that several Palestinian terrorist leaders were aboard the plane. When this was found not to be the case, the plane was allowed to proceed with all passengers.

ARTHUR CAMPBELL TURNER
University of California, Riverside

IRELAND

As the death toll from the sectarian strife in Northern Ireland continued to climb, politics in the Irish republic in 1973 reflected the strains of this ordeal.

New Government. Only a month after his return from a visit to the United States to discuss economic matters and the northern problem, Prime Minister Jack Lynch surprised many by dissolving Parliament (the Dáil) and announcing a general election to be held on February 28. Hoping to increase the number of his Fianna Fáil party's seats (69 out of 144), Lynch asked the electorate for a "clear and unmistakable mandate."

In one of the country's biggest electoral upsets, Fianna Fáil was defeated by a moderate coalition of Fine Gael and Labour, which won 54 and 19 seats, respectively. Fianna Fáil retained 69 seats, and 2 independents were returned. After 16 years in office (and after having governed the country for 35 of the last 41 years), the Fianna Fáil ministry resigned in favor of the coalition, headed by Liam Cosgrave. Son of William T. Cosgrave, head of government of the Irish Free State in 1922–32, the new prime minister had led the Fine Gael party since 1965. The coalition campaign had concentrated on social and economic issues, promising anti-inflation measures, tax reform, and more housing.

Cosgrave's new cabinet, named on March 14, included ten Fine Gael and five Labour ministers. Among them was Brendan Corish, leader of the Labour party, who became deputy premier and minister for health.

The I. R. A. The new government had pledged itself to take stern measures against the Irish Republican Army (I. R. A.) and other "illegal" organizations but soon found that the targets were as elusive as they had been during Lynch's administration. Political extremists continued to operate in the republic, and several persons suspected of being informers or spies working for the British army in the north were shot during the year.

--------- IRELAND • Information Highlights ---------

Official Name: Republic of Ireland (Éire).
Location: Island in the eastern North Atlantic Ocean.
Area: 27,136 square miles (70,283 sq km).
Population (1973 est.): 3,000,000. *Density,* 109 per square mile (42 per sq km).
Chief Cities (1971 census): Dublin, the capital, 566,034; Cork, 128,235.
Government: *Head of state,* Erskine H. Childers, president (took office June 1973). *Head of government,* Liam Cosgrave, prime minister (taoiseach) (took office March 1973). *Legislature*—Parliament: Senate (Seanad Éireann) and House of Representatives (Dáil Éireann). *Major political parties*—Fianna Fáil; Fine Gael; Labour party.
Languages: Irish (official), English (major).
Education: *Expenditure* (1968), 11.2% of total public expenditure. *School enrollment* (1968)—primary, 513,805; general secondary, 148,197; technical/vocational (1968), 46,-513; university/higher (1968), 25,660.
Monetary Unit: Pound (0.4071 pound equals U. S.$1, Aug. 1973).
Gross National Product (1972 est.): $5,100,000,000.
Economic Indexes: *Industrial production* (1972), 164 (1963=100); *agricultural production* (1971), 118 (1963=100); *consumer price index* (1972), 172 (1963=100).
Manufacturing (major products): Processed foods, clothing.
Major Agricultural Products: Potatoes, wheat, sugar beets.
Major Minerals: Gypsum, limestone, slate, clay, peat, lead.
Foreign Trade (1972): Exports, $1,611,000,000. Imports, $2,102,000,000. *Chief trading partners* (1971)—United Kingdom (took 66% of exports, supplied 50% of imports); United States (11%—9%); West Germany (3%—7.3%).
Transportation: *Motor vehicles* (1971), 466,800 (automobiles, 418,000); *railroads* (1971), 1,931 miles (3,108 km); *merchant fleet* (1972), 182,000 gross registered tons; *major national airlines,* Aer Lingus Teoranta; Airlinte Éireann.
Communications: *Telephones* (1972), 323,826; *newspapers* (1971), 7 (daily circulation, 694,000).

Other Developments. On August 30, Minister for Health Corish redeemed one of the coalition's campaign pledges by announcing the terms of a new comprehensive health insurance scheme that would guarantee every citizen almost free hospital care for a nominal sum. Another popular reform enacted was the abolition of the proficiency requirement in the Irish language for high school graduates. The language remained a mandatory subject in the school curriculum.

In the hope of easing strained relations with the United Kingdom, Cosgrave conferred twice with British Prime Minister Edward Heath (March 8 and July 2) in England. The two leaders discussed plans for reforming representative government and improving security measures in Northern Ireland. The I. R. A. letter bombing campaign, launched in England during August, underlined the need for closer cooperation between the Irish and British governments. The two prime ministers met again in Ireland on September 17.

On December 9, Cosgrave, Heath, and Brian Faulkner, chief of the Ulster executive body, agreed to establish a Council of Ireland in 1974. The Council was to serve as a link between the Dublin and Belfast governments, each of which will have seven members on the Council. Britain and the Irish republic pledged to guarantee that the status of Northern Ireland would not be changed except with the consent of a majority in the North.

Ireland gained a new president on May 30 to replace the venerable Éamon de Valéra (age 91) who had decided to retire from that post. The special election was won by Erskine Childers, English-born son of a prominent Protestant Republican and friend of De Valéra who had been executed in 1922 during the Irish civil war. Childers, of the Fianna Fáil, defeated the coalition candidate, Thomas O'Higgins, by a margin of 636,162 to 587,577.

L. PERRY CURTIS, JR.
Brown University

ISLAM. See RELIGION.

ISRAEL

It was a disquieting and ominous year for Israel. Although the Jewish state had now been in existence for a quarter century, its territorial extent and even its continued existence were still very uncertain. The perilousness of Israel's position was underscored. After the October war with the Arabs, it no longer could be assumed that Israel had an enormous margin of military superiority over its Arab neighbors, or that the extended frontiers achieved in 1967 provided the country with much greater security, or that friendship with the United States could be relied on with complete confidence. And the results of the parliamentary elections held on December 31 demonstrated that Prime Minister Golda Meir's hold over the electorate had weakened as a result of Israel's unpreparedness in the face of the Arab attack.

Domestic Events. In parliamentary balloting on April 10, Ephraim Katchalski, a 56-year-old biophysicist, was elected Israel's fourth president. He was sworn in on May 24. The candidate of the ruling Labor party, he received 66 votes to 41 for Ephraim Uhrbach, candidate of the National Religious party. Katchalski had served as head of the biophysics department of the Weitzmann Institute of

UPI

ISRAELI TROOPS dance a joyous hora after smashing across the Syrian border on October 11, five days after a new Arab-Israeli war began.

Science and as chief scientific adviser to the Ministry of Defense. On his election Katchalski changed his name to Katzir in compliance with the policy requiring state officials to have Hebrew names. Katzir succeeded Zalman Shazar, who had been president since 1963 and was retiring at the end of his second five-year term.

The 25th anniversary of the creation of the Israeli state was celebrated with considerable pomp in a military parade in Jerusalem on May 7. Jordan formally protested in the United Nations the holding of the parade in Jerusalem. There was also some domestic criticism.

A number of conciliatory moves were made toward Arabs in Israel and their families, in a policy described as "creeping normalization." The cabinet decided on May 13 to allow Arabs from outside Israel to visit Israeli-occupied areas throughout the year instead of only in summer as previously. It was also decided to permit Arabs in East Jerusalem who retained Jordanian citizenship to vote in municipal elections without having to register. On May 24 the executive committee of the Labor party agreed to open party membership to all Israeli Arabs who supported its program. The party already had several hundred Arab members admitted on an individual basis.

The lineup for the forthcoming general election became clear in summer and early fall. Premier Meir, who had considered retirement, announced on June 17 that she would run for re-election. A merger of four opposition parties (Herut, Liberal, Free Center, and State List) under the name of Likud was formed on September 5 in a bid to unseat the ruling Labor Alignment. In the elections on Sept. 11 for Histradut, the important general federation of labor, the Labor party and its Mapam ally lost some ground to Likud.

Israel continued to suffer both a serious inflation and consequent labor troubles. A three-month price freeze was announced on June 24 on imported and manufactured goods. The government also pledged not to introduce new taxes during the same period, and agreed to a 5% cost-of-living increase in July.

The first generation of Israeli leaders is now dying. The beloved patriarch David Ben-Gurion, a founding father and Israel's first premier, died on December 1, at the age of 87 (see OBITUARIES). Lt. Gen. Yakov Dori, first chief of staff of the Israeli forces, died at 73 on January 29. Abraham Shlonsky, a noted Israeli man of letters, died on May 18, also at 73.

External Relations and the October War. Even before the outbreak of full-scale war in October, Israel was involved in a series of incidents in the field of foreign relations, many of which were violent in nature. Foreign opinion continued to be hostile to Israel, especially in the United Nations, where Israel's enemies commanded a clear majority. Almost the only items of good news were the apparent ending of the USSR's tax on Jewish emigrants in April (though there seemed to be some ambiguity about this) and the visit to Israel by West German Chancellor Willy Brandt (June 7–11). Mrs. Meir made a number of visits abroad, including attendance at a Socialist congress in Paris (January 13–14). On the same trip she visited President Felix

——————— ISRAEL • Information Highlights ———————

Official Name: State of Israel.
Location: Southwest Asia at the eastern end of the Mediterranean Sea.
Area: 7,992 square miles (20,700 sq km).
Population (1973 est.): 3,100,000. *Density,* 378 per square mile (146 per sq km).
Chief Cities (1969 est.): Jerusalem, the capital, 283,100; Tel Aviv-Jaffa, 382,900; Haifa, 214,500.
Government: *Head of state,* Ephraim Katzir, president (took office May 1973). *Head of government,* Golda Meir, prime minister (took office March 1969). *Legislature* (unicameral) —Knesset. *Major political groups*—Labor Alignment; Likud coalition; National Religious party.
Languages: Hebrew, Arabic (both official), English.
Education: *Expenditure* (1967), 7.6% of gross national product. *School enrollment* (1969)—primary, 456,079; secondary, 134,528; technical/vocational, 58,469; university/higher, 49,076.
Monetary Unit: Pound (4.20 pounds equal U. S.$1, Oct. 1973).
Gross National Product (1972 est.): $6,080,000,000.
Economic Indexes: *Industrial production* (1972), 254 (1963= 100); *agricultural production* (1971), 156 (1963=100); *consumer price index* (1972), 174 (1963=100).
Manufacturing (major products): Polished diamonds, processed foods, chemicals, petroleum products, electrical and electronic equipment, textiles, clothing, aircraft.
Major Agricultural Products: Citrus fruits, vegetables, cotton, eggs.
Major Minerals: Potash, phosphate, clay, glass sand, copper.
Foreign Trade (1972): *Exports,* $1,101,000,000. *Imports,* $1,922,000,000. *Chief trading partners* (1971)—United States (took 20% of exports, supplied 24% of imports); United Kingdom (15%—15%); West Germany (13%—13%).
Tourism: Receipts (1971), $178,300,000.
Transportation: *Motor vehicles* (1971), 252,000 (automobiles, ‾174,500); *railroads* (1971), 490 miles (789 km); *merchant fleet* (1972), 698,000 gross registered tons; *major national airline,* El Al Israel Airlines.
Communications: *Telephones* (1972), 563,569; *newspapers* (1971), 24 (daily circulation, 600,000).

Houphouët-Boigny of the Ivory Coast and had an audience with Pope Paul VI. She saw President Richard Nixon in Washington in early March.

Israel incurred widespread criticism for the shooting down (February 21), over the occupied Sinai, of a civilian Libyan airliner; the crash killed 106 persons. A Palestinian commando base near Tripoli, Lebanon, was attacked by Israeli forces on the same day. In another incident involving a civilian airliner, and also exhibiting Israeli bad luck or bad judgment (but not involving loss of life), an Iraqi Airways liner was forced to land in Israel on August 10. Israeli intelligence had believed, erroneously, that several Arab commando leaders were aboard. This action was condemned by the UN Security Council on August 15. In the biggest air battle between Israel and Syria since the 1967 war, 13 Syrian jets were shot down on September 13 over the Mediterranean after Israeli planes had been attacked and one had been lost.

One serious aspect of the deterioration of Israel foreign relations was the virtually complete breach between Israel and the new African states. Over the years good relations had been established with many of them, based on Israel's technical aid and training programs. However, the oil-rich government of Libya has used its funds lavishly to break these contacts, and by the end of 1973, Israeli diplomatic relations with almost all the states of black Africa had virtually ceased.

The war between Israel and the Arab states began on October 6 and gave way to an imperfect and insecure cease-fire by October 24. Its beginning, its course, and its unclear suspension were alike appalling and traumatic events for Israel. It began with an attack by Egypt and Syria launched on Yom Kippur, the holiest of Jewish holy days, and it caught Israel totally off balance. The renowned Israeli air force suffered severe losses because of the unexpected effectiveness of the Soviet-supplied ground-to-air missiles. The initial Egyptian attack

shattered the Bar-Levi line and enabled the Egyptians to occupy some of the Sinai. The Syrian attack won much of the Golan Heights. The counterattacks by Israel in due course carried the war into Syrian territory, and a particularly brilliant surprise move took Israeli forces across the Suez Canal and well on the way to Cairo. At this promising movement, when the lost prestige might have been more than regained, American pressure left a reluctant Israel no alternative but to accede to a cease-fire.

Aftermath of the War. The casualties of the war, as announced on December 9, amounted to 2,355 Israeli soldiers dead, a staggering loss for a nation with so small a population. Nearly 60 more died in the sporadic fighting between October 24 and the end of the year. Another source of anguish was the Syrian refusal to give information about prisoners-of-war, 42 of whose bodies Israel claimed to have discovered in reconquered territory.

Inconclusive negotiations were held along the Suez cease-fire line to effect a disengagement of troops there. These negotiations were then transferred to the Geneva conference, which met for the first time on December 21. The conference was to consider not only military disengagement but also the broader aspects of peace in the Middle East. Little progress could be made, however, until Israel held its parliamentary elections on December 31, since the line to be taken in the Geneva peace talks depended on the election's results.

It was clear that the Labor Alignment, in power since independence, was on the defensive against charges from the opposition Likud of incompetence and unpreparedness in the October war. Unofficial returns on Jan. 1, 1974, showed that the Labor Alignment polled only 39.9% of the vote, compared with 46.2% four years earlier. Its seats in Parliament dropped from 56 to 51, while those held by the Likud rose from 32 to 39. As a result, Prime Minister Meir could only rule by forming a coalition government with other parties, which might be more intransigent in negotiating peace with the Arabs. (See also MIDDLE EAST.)

ARTHUR CAMPBELL TURNER
University of California, Riverside

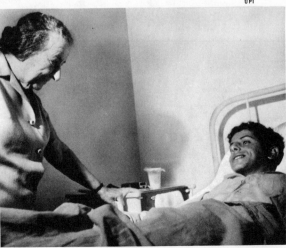

VISITING the wounded in a hospital in Tel Aviv, Israeli Prime Minister Golda Meir talks with a soldier.

UPI

ITALY

Mariano Rumor (left), the new premier of Italy, takes his oath of office before President Giovanni Leone (right) at the Quirinal Palace on July 8, 1973.

A Center-Left government returned to power in Italy in 1973. The economy, which had improved in the spring, suffered badly from the international monetary and energy crises during the summer and fall.

POLITICS

Italy began the year under a Center-Right coalition government, formed in June 1972 by Giulio Andreotti, a Christian Democrat. For the first time in a decade the Communist-leaning Socialist party was excluded from the cabinet, while the conservative Liberal party was included instead. An economic tailspin that began in 1969 was the major cause of dissatisfaction with the Center-Left.

However, Andreotti's inability to make any real improvements in housing, transportation, schools, and hospitals caused voters to swing to the left in municipal elections in November 1972. The Socialists and Social Democrats scored the greatest gains, while the Christian Democrats, neo-Fascists, and Communists all lost ground. In February 1973, Andreotti suffered a serious defeat in the Chamber of Deputies when his own party split, with its left wing calling for a revival of a Center-Left coalition with the Socialists. Thereafter, Andreotti could only mark time until the Christian Democratic congress, held in June.

In the meantime there was violence, sparked by extremists on both the right and left, in such cities as Milan, Rome, and Reggio Calabria. The worst incident occurred in Milan on May 17, when a grenade exploded outside police headquarters during a ceremony honoring a slain officer, resulting in two deaths and 45 injuries. The government feared an international conspiracy might be involved and asked other countries to help investigate the terrorism.

Neo-Fascism. In January, some 1,500 delegates of the neo-Fascist Italian Social Movement (MSI) held their congress in Rome. Italy's fourth-largest party, the MSI received 8.7% of the vote in the 1972 elections. The name of the party was changed to the National Right Wing, and the congress reaffirmed the leadership of Giorgio Almirante, a 58-year-old parliamentary deputy and journalist, who was a minor functionary under Mussolini toward the end of World War II.

ITALY • Information Highlights

Official Name: Italian Republic.
Area: 116,303 square miles (301,225 sq km).
Population (1973 est.): 54,900,000. *Density,* 466 per square mile (180 per sq km).
Chief Cities (1970 est.): Rome, the capital, 2,778,900; Milan, 1,713,500; Naples, 1,278,100; Turin, 1,190,700.
Government: *Head of state,* Giovanni Leone, president (took office Dec. 1971). *Head of government,* Mariano Rumor, premier (took office July 1973). *Legislature—*Parliament: Senate and Chamber of Deputies. *Major political parties—*Christian Democratic; Communist; Socialist; National Right Wing; Liberal; Social Democratic; Republican.
Language: Italian (official).
Education: *Expenditure* (1969), 19.2% of total public expenditure. *School enrollment* (1969)—primary, 4,728,-075; secondary, 3,640,274; technical/vocational, 917,-337; university/higher, 622,416.
Monetary Unit: Lira (584.95 lire equal U.S.$1, July 1973).
Gross National Product (1972 est.): $111,500,000,000.

Economic Indexes: *Industrial production* (1972), 152 (1963=100); *agricultural production* (1971), 119 (1963=100); *consumer price index* (1972), 142 (1963=100).
Manufacturing (major products): Automobiles, petroleum products, machinery, processed foods, chemicals.
Major Agricultural Products: Wheat, grapes (ranks 1st among world producers, 1972), tomatoes, citrus fruits.
Major Minerals: Mercury (ranks 3d among world producers, 1971), antimony, lead, manganese, marble.
Foreign Trade (1972): *Exports,* $18,548,000,000. *Imports,* $19,282,000,000. *Chief trading partners* (1971)—Common Market (took 45% of exports, supplied 42% of imports); United States (10%—9%).
Tourism: Receipts (1972), 2,060,000,000.
Transportation: *Motor vehicles* (1971), 12,285,300 (automobiles, 11,298,600); *railroads* (1971), 10,078 miles (16,218 km); *merchant fleet* (1972), 8,187,000 gross registered tons; *major national airline,* ALITALIA.
Communications: *Telephones* (1972), 10,321,581; *newspapers* (1971), 75 (daily circulation, 7,899,000).

Within the next few months, however, the neo-Fascists received several setbacks. Italy's president, Giovanni Leone, denounced the party, and on May 24 the Chamber of Deputies voted, 485 to 59, to strip Almirante of his parliamentary immunity. This permitted the start of criminal proceedings against him on charges of reorganizing the outlawed Fascist party and advocating the use of violence to gain political ends.

Wiretapping. During the spring, Italians learned that they had a "Watergate affair" of their own. Judicial authorities investigated charges of widespread wiretapping that included among its alleged victims the premier, the president, the pope, the Bank of Italy, foreign embassies, and various politicians. By April, more than 20 persons had been arrested. There was speculation that the bugging was related to rings of rival spies and "superpolice" in the service of political factions, financial tycoons, and foreign espionage agents.

Fall of the Center-Right. Andreotti's Center-Right government lost its narrow majority in parliament on May 28, when the minor Republican party announced during a debate on the banning of private cable television that it could no longer support the government. The crisis reached its height in early June when the Christian Democratic party—which has been aptly described as an "uneasy federation of nine quarreling factions"—held its national congress in Rome. The majority of delegates preferred returning to the Center-Left alliance with the Socialists that had existed before 1972. On June 12, Andreotti and his cabinet submitted their resignations to President Leone, who asked them to stay on as a caretaker government until a new cabinet could be formed. On June 17 the Christian Democratic national council elected former Premier Amintore Fanfani, a longtime advocate of a Center-Left program, to the powerful position of party secretary. Mariano Rumor, minister of the interior, was the party's choice for premier-designate.

The Rumor Center-Left Government. On June 20, as expected, President Leone asked Rumor to form a government. The final hurdle was overcome when the Socialist party announced on July 5 that it was willing to enter a Center-Left government that did not include any Communists. Two days later, Rumor formed a new government, composed of Christian Democrats, Social Democrats, Socialists, and Republicans. His platform called for reforms in education, housing, and health care, as well as vigorous steps to fight inflation and revive the economy. Rumor assigned the important treasury and budget ministries to, respectively, Ugo La Malfa (Republican) and Antonio Giolitti (Socialist). Aldo Moro, a Christian Democrat, succeeded Giuseppe Medici as foreign minister.

Though the new cabinet commanded a stronger majority in parliament than the preceding one, it was weaker than expected because several prominent politicians refused to accept key posts. Also, unlike earlier cabinets, there was no deputy premier because the secretaries of the Socialist and Social Democratic parties could not agree which party should be assigned the position. On July 20, parliament approved the new government, and four days later the cabinet issued decree-laws that sought to deal firmly with Italy's worsening economy.

ECONOMY

Italy's economic stagnation, which began with the wave of strikes in the fall of 1969, seemed to be dissipating at the end of 1972. Official statistics released in the spring of 1973 showed that industrial

Cyclists crowd Rome's Venezia Square after Italian government ban on Sunday automobile driving.

WIDE WORLD

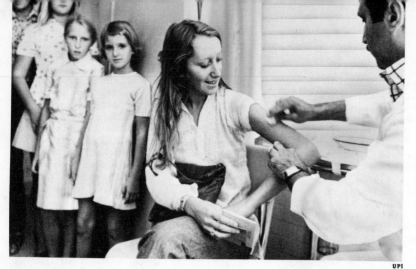

ANTICHOLERA injections are given to children in a Rome hospital in August. Several deaths were reported in Italy in the 1973 outbreak of the disease.

UPI

production in 1972 had risen by 3.9%, as against a drop of 1.3% in 1971. Capital investment rose by 2% in 1972, after dropping 9% in 1971. Such figures were heartening, although they could not compare with those of the halcyon days of the 1960's, when annual increases of more than 5% were registered in the gross national product.

But the 1972 statistics were not without their dark side. Farm output was down by 4.9%. Employment fell by 1.7%, and the number of unemployed rose by 14.4%. Persons leaving school who were unable to find jobs rose by 31.8%. Labor unrest continued to plague the country, though the major unions began in 1973 to accept the need for greater self-discipline. Even so, more man-hours were lost by strikes and absenteeism in Italy than in any other industrial nation. Such essentials as the postal service and airport facilities neared paralysis.

A value-added tax system, which was designed to supersede a confusing variety of sales and excise taxes, went into effect on Jan. 1, 1973. It is similar to systems already adopted by most members of the Common Market. Fearing the effects of the new system, Italians went on a buying spree in late 1972, boosting the year's consumer price index by nearly 8%. Between January and April 1973, inflation was cut to 6.1%.

By the end of May, Guido Carli, governor of the Bank of Italy, discerned reasons for optimism regarding industrial production and private investment. Contributing factors, he said, were increased foreign demand for Italian products and the rapid accumulation of consumer goods prior to the introduction of the value-added tax.

However, the Italian lira remained the weakest currency in the Common Market, although the Bank of Italy held capital reserves of $5.7 billion. The lira was allowed to float in February 1973, and by May it had declined by an average of 10% in relation to other major currencies, thereby increasing the cost of imported food and raw materials. On June 14, two days after the resignation of the Andreotti government, the lira plunged to record lows, precipitating huge outflows of capital, chiefly to Swiss banks. On June 18, to shore up the faltering lira, the government announced it would use short-term credits available from central banks of other Western nations. Such credits, it was estimated, would add another $3 billion to the Bank of Italy's reserves.

On July 25, Rumor's Center-Left government an-

nounced decree-laws freezing prices of such commodities as pasta, olive oil, butter, cheese, and meat, and tightened controls on bread and flour. Rent controls were extended until Jan. 31, 1974. In addition, the price of goods and services of large-scale industries was blocked until July 31, 1974. Since the powerful trade unions supported these measures, the government had no difficulty in obtaining parliamentary approval.

In the fall the government eagerly anticipated receiving substantial aid from the Common Market to improve conditions in the impoverished South. It was expected that over the next three years Italy would receive about $2.5 billion.

Income from tourism declined considerably in 1973, principally as a result of the sharp decrease in the number of Americans traveling abroad. (In 1972, tourists spent $2.06 billion in Italy.) Over the past decade Italy's growth in tourism has averaged only about half that recorded by the international tourism market generally.

Late in the year the government took steps to reform Italy's archaic tax structure. Certain categories of long-term delinquent income taxpayers were offered an amnesty whereby all fiscal penalties would be waived if individual or corporate taxpayers paid at least part of their indebtedness. The formula for such payments will result in the government recovering 40% of unpaid taxes. Starting Jan. 1, 1974, salaried workers will have income taxes deducted from their pay, at rates varying from 10% to 30% on incomes up to $20,000.

Energy Crisis. Italy, already suffering from intermittent gasoline shortages, faced a major crisis in October and November when the oil-producing Arab countries imposed a partial embargo after the Arab-Israeli war. Italy, which is Europe's major oil-refining country, quickly cut off exports to nations outside the Common Market.

Finally, on November 22, the Rumor government announced a series of sweeping measures, including a ban on Sunday and holiday driving beginning December 1, with service stations closing on Saturday afternoons and Sundays. The price of "extra" gasoline was raised by 8%, to $1.32 per gallon, a record level for Europe. Speed limits of 62 miles per hour were set for secondary highways; 75, for superhighways. Delivery of heating oil was reduced by 20%, and the price was increased by 55%. Government offices were instructed to close by dusk and to cut fuel consumption. Stores were

to close no later than 7 P. M., and cinemas, at 11 P. M. Street lighting was to be cut back by 40%.

Environmental Pollution. Italy seems to be overwhelmed by the effects of unchecked industrialization and inadequate governmental measures to protect the environment. Early in 1973, in the port of Marghera, near Venice, 50,000 people were told to wear gas masks after it was learned that almost every day a worker was hospitalized because of air pollution.

On March 10 the Chamber of Deputies passed a bill appropriating $500 million to curb floods and other environmental dangers to Venice. Funds earmarked by the bill included $400 million that an international consortium, under the auspices of UNESCO, had made available to Italy as low-interest loans in 1971.

A serious outbreak of cholera occurred in Naples and Bari in late summer. Authorities blamed it on eating raw shellfish caught in polluted waters. (Twenty open sewers empty into the Bay of Naples.) Ten people died, and hundreds became seriously ill before a mass vaccination program got underway. In Naples, rioters protested alleged governmental inefficiency, while in the North there were questions about what has been accomplished by the billions of dollars already poured into the poorer South.

INTERNATIONAL RELATIONS

Italy's foreign policy shifted somewhat to the left in 1973. The change may be attributed to at least two reasons. First, the Vatican is now more concerned about the welfare of Catholics in Eastern Europe than in increasing its political influence in Italy. Second, since the United States is more interested in détente with the Soviet Union and larger exports to Eastern Europe, it is less preoccupied with Communist strength in Italy.

Evidence of the changing policy was seen in January, when Foreign Minister Giuseppe Medíci traveled to Peking to sign an agreement for civil air transport between Italy and Communist China. Also in January, Rome announced an agreement with East Germany for immediately establishing diplomatic relations. Ties with West Germany remained friendly, however, and in March, West German President Gustav Heinemann went to Rome for a two-day state visit.

Italians welcomed Britain's entry into the Common Market in January, thinking it might bring greater stability to the fragile Italian democracy. However, others feared that as the Common Market's center of gravity moved northward, Italy might drift into a vague role as a kind of Mediterranean Third World country.

As relations between the Arabs and Israelis worsened in 1973, Italy, heavily dependent on the Arab world for its oil, tilted perceptibly toward a pro-Arab position. For years Italy's state-controlled and private oil concerns had lobbied in favor of such a policy. In March, Foreign Minister Medici visited several Arab countries and Israel. He sought to impress on Israel that Italy was vitally interested in an early reopening of the Suez Canal.

When the Arab-Israeli war broke out in October, Italy did not support American military assistance to Israel, arguing that the clash did not lie within the purview of the Atlantic Alliance. During the conflict, an Italian warship was attacked off North Africa by a Libyan air force jet, wounding two sailors. Libya apologized for the incident.

On December 17, Rome's Fiumicino airport was the scene of a violent attack by Arab terrorists who blew up a Pan American World Airways jetliner and then commandeered a Lufthansa plane to fly them and their hostages first to Athens and finally to Kuwait. Thirty-two persons died.

Except for the Middle Eastern problem, Italy's relationship with the United States remained harmonious. In January the two nations signed an anti-hijacking accord. That same month John A. Volpe was named U. S. ambassador to Italy, the first American of Italian descent to hold the post.

On April 16, Premier Andreotti went to the United States for conversations with President Nixon, which were described as taking place in a spirit of "friendship and complete candor." After leaving Washington, Andreotti visited New York City and Hawaii on his way to Japan.

The military coup d'etat that overthrew the Allende government in Chile in September aroused dismay in Italy. Communists, Socialists, and many Christian Democrats deplored Allende's deposition.

Kidnapping of Getty. On June 10, J. Paul Getty III, 17-year-old grandson of the American oil billionaire, was kidnapped in Rome. In October his captors sent Getty's right ear to a Rome newspaper to prove there was no hoax. After $2.8 million was paid in ransom, Getty was released in southern Italy on December 15. A few weeks later police arrested several Calabrian gangsters whom they accused of the crime.

CHARLES F. DELZELL, *Vanderbilt University*

ITALIAN HOUSEWIFE checks the official price list before buying. Disputes were widespread after the government froze the prices of about 500 items.

UPI

A Tokyo shopper (above) seems uncertain about buying fish after a widespread poisoning scare. (Right) A representative of a chemical firm pays a check for about $3.5 million to the attorney for the families of 67 persons the court said had died from eating fish contaminated by pollutants dumped by the company.

JAPAN

WIDE WORLD

In 1973 the Japanese public was constantly reminded of the fact that their nation had arrived as a major economic power. Even with a decline in Japan's trade surplus, resulting from a revaluation of the yen, its gross national product (GNP) passed $320 billion, making it the third largest in the world. It was predicted that, assuming the energy problems are resolved, in the late 1970's the GNP would approach $900 billion—half that of the United States and twice that of West Germany.

But the Japanese people were also discovering that they were paying high costs for the headlong growth of the 1960's. Inflation, environmental disruption, and international trade problems steadily eroded the popularity of the government of Premier Kakuei Tanaka. In response to public pressure, the government adopted a 5-year plan of an unprecedented nature for 1973–77 to preserve Japan's natural environment, to promote social security, to eliminate an imbalance of payments in international trade, and to support international economic cooperation. If fully effected, this plan would slow down the current annual growth to 9%.

At the end of the year Japan, like the other advanced industrial nations, was feeling the effects of the energy squeeze in the form of oil shortages, the result of production cutbacks by Arab states. Japan was particularly vulnerable because it imports virtually all of its oil, and much of it comes from the Middle East. The government called the energy shortage the most serious crisis since World War II. On November 16 the government announced steps to cut consumption of industrial oil and of electricity by 10%. On December 22, Premier Tanaka declared a state of emergency, ordering an immediate 20% cut in oil and electric power to major industries.

Economists gloomily predicted that the rate of growth for the fiscal year ending March 1974 would drop to 5%. If continued, the rationing could lower the rate to zero or even result in a decline for the first time in the postwar era. Meanwhile, if the government were not to take strong countermeasures, the Japanese might face further sharp inflationary rises of 10–15% in prices. Obviously, the Japanese economy was at a turning point, away from the high growth rates of the 1960's.

INTERNATIONAL AFFAIRS

In the joint communiqué covering conversations with President Nixon in Washington on July 31–August 1, Premier Tanaka touched on major points in Japan's foreign policy. Expressing satisfaction with the continuing dialogue between Japan and the United States, the two leaders called attention to a trans-Pacific volume of trade that was the greatest in history. They noted, with satisfaction, progress in the normalization of relations between their two nations and the People's Republic of China. They expressed hope for a lasting peace in Indochina, and they welcomed (prematurely, it seems) signs of accommodation between the two hostile regimes in Korea. In a separate appearance in Washington, Premier Tanaka urged that bilateral issues between Japan and the United States had to be "reviewed in the perspective of a wider global context." Thus he supplemented the American visit with a tour of Western Europe and another experiment in summit diplomacy in Moscow.

Relations with the United States. Trade balances and yen-dollar ratios continued to dominate the "close relationship" between Japan and America. Economic issues occupied the attention of U. S. Ambassador Robert Ingersoll in Tokyo and Takeshi Yasukawa, appointed ambassador to Washington in June. Ambassador Yasukawa warned that congressional deliberations on the 1973 trade bill might result in the levy of an import surcharge on Japanese goods unless Tokyo limited exports, expanded imports, and effected further yen revaluation. In February, the trade imbalance was running to over $4 billion annually in Japan's favor.

Although Japan's gold and foreign exchange reserves declined from the previous month, at the end of January they stood at $17.9 billion and reached an all-time record in February at $19.1 billion. As a result, on February 3 the Bank of Japan was forced to enter the Tokyo Foreign Exchange Market to buy almost $300 million in dollars and to support the dollar (at a level of 301.10 yen = $1). Trading volume, however, continued at the highest level since August 1971, when President Nixon had announced his dollar defense plan. On February 10, Tokyo closed its foreign exchange mart. On February 13, after the United States unilaterally devalued the dollar by 10%, the government decided to float the yen and to reopen the market. By February 19, the dollar price had settled at 264.40 yen per dollar. Thereafter, the value of the dollar continued to rise fractionally (on November 16, the rate was 275.0 yen = $1). Similarly, on October 1, Japan's gold and foreign exchange reserves had fallen to $14.8 billion.

In May, Tokyo informed Washington of the decision to postpone a visit to America by Emperor Hirohito and the empress. Vocal opposition to any political use of the imperial household by the conservative government was cited as a reason, but it was also known that household staff did not want a visit during the Watergate investigations. Nonetheless, Premier Tanaka and President Nixon met in Washington at the end of July: the former reaffirmed an invitation to President and Mrs. Nixon to visit Japan during 1974, presumably after the emperor and empress had gone to America.

Both the Japanese and American press assumed that the Tanaka-Nixon summit talks revolved mainly around trade and economic problems. The two leaders in their joint communiqué endorsed the objective of an open world of trade and investment and promised to support a reformed international monetary system. They subscribed to continuation of the U. S.-Japan Security Treaty; to the maintenance by the United States of an adequate level of deterrent forces in East Asia; and to "due contributions" by Japan to ease the U. S. burden under the treaty. In a separate TV appearance, however, Premier Tanaka explained Japanese reluctance to own or use nuclear weapons. The President promised to support Japan's claim to a permanent seat on the UN Security Council. The premier announced that his government had pledged a grant of $10 million to further Japanese studies in 10 American universities.

On November 16, U. S. Secretary of State Henry Kissinger wound up a whirlwind tour with two days of talks with Japanese leaders in Tokyo, after he had arranged a cease-fire in the Middle East and had visited Peking. His original purpose—to keep the Japanese informed of the progress of normalization of relations with China—was lost sight of in the near-panic shown when he was unable to give any assurances as to when the Arab states would restore oil production.

Relations with Korea. Both the United States and Japan (since 1965) had recognized the Republic of (South) Korea. One of the reasons for the U. S.-Japan security treaty is to maintain the "American presence" so as to guarantee stability in the Korean peninsula. Both had agreed (with Britain and Australia) on a strategy in the UN General Assembly to continue the UN Command in Korea. Meanwhile, Japan had indicated it would favor UN membership for both South Korea and the Democratic People's

---

JAPAN • Information Highlights

Official Name: Japan.
Location: Off the east coast of Asia.
Area (including Okinawa): 143,734 square miles (372,269 sq km).
Population (1973 est., including Okinawa): 108,300,000. *Density,* 733 per square mile (283 per sq km).
Chief Cities (1970 census): Tokyo, the capital, 8,840,942; Osaka, 2,980,487; Yokahama, 2,238,264; Nagoya, 2,036,053; Kyoto, 1,419,165.
Government: *Head of state,* Hirohito, emperor (acceded Dec. 1926). *Head of government,* Kakuei Tanaka, premier (took office July 1972). *Legislature*—Diet: House of Councillors and House of Representatives. *Major political parties*—Liberal Democratic party; Socialist party; Communist party; Komeito; Democratic Socialist party.
Language: Japanese (official).
Education: *Expenditure* (1969), 20.4% of total public expenditure. *School enrollment* (1969)—primary, 9,403,193; secondary, 9,233,147; technical/vocational, 1,833,786; university/higher, 1,631,319.
Monetary Unit: Yen (270 yen equal U. S.$1, Nov. 1973).
Gross National Product (1972 est.): $279,500,000,000.
Economic Indexes: *Industrial production* (1972), 290 (1963=100); *agricultural production* (1971), 116 (1963=100); *consumer price index* (1972), 160 (1963=100).
Manufacturing (major products): Ships, automobiles, electronic components, textiles, iron and steel, petrochemicals, machinery, electrical appliances, processed foods.
Major Agricultural Products: Rice (ranks 5th among world producers, 1972), wheat, barley, potatoes, vegetables, fruits, tobacco, tea, fish (world rank 2d, 1971).
Major Minerals: Coal, iron pyrites, limestone, copper, sulfur, lead, manganese, mercury.
Foreign Trade (1972): *Exports,* $28,655,000,000; *Imports,* $23,481,000,000. *Chief trading partners* (1971)—United States (took 31% of exports, supplied 25% of imports); Canada (3.6%–5%); Australia (3%–9%).
Tourism: Receipts (1971), $172,000,000.
Transportation: *Motor vehicles* (1971), 19,669,000 (automobiles, 10,572,000); *railroads* (1971), 16,954 miles (27,283 km); *merchant fleet* (1972), 34,929,000 gross registered tons; *major national airlines,* Japan Air Lines; All Nippon Airways.
Communications: *Telephones* (1972), 29,827,936; *newspapers* (1971), 170 (daily circulation, 53,402,000).

TRAVELING Premier Tanaka bows to the army band near Bonn, West Germany, in October (above) and is welcomed to Washington by President Nixon in July.

Republic of (North) Korea. Japan had committed massive credits to Seoul in 1972, a total of $170 million; for 1973, it planned to extend $400 million in credits.

Then on August 8, a bizarre political kidnapping in Tokyo threatened to disrupt relations between Tokyo and Seoul. Kim Dae Jung, a minority leader-in-exile who had unsuccessfully run against General Park in the Korean presidential election of 1971, was seized in a Tokyo hotel. He was spirited out of the city and taken by boat beyond Japan's territorial waters. Apparently because of a worldwide outcry protesting the kidnapping, he was released in South Korea but kept practically under house arrest.

Opposition party leaders in Japan who had not supported the normalization of relations with the Seoul regime, together with an enterprising press, put enormous pressure on the government. Tokyo police were forced to reveal details piece by piece, and there was increasing evidence that the South Korean CIA had been involved. In September, Tokyo decided to postpone minister-level negotiations on further aid to Seoul. Although the government publicly announced that the rupture did not constitute a basic change in Japan's policy toward Korea, Premier Tanaka did admit to the Diet that if it were discovered that Korean officials were implicated in the kidnapping, this would constitute a grave infringement of Japan's sovereignty.

Eventually, a face-saving political compromise was reached between Seoul and Tokyo. On October 26, Kim was released from house arrest. Later, he announced plans for a "symbolic" return to Tokyo on his way to a post at Harvard University. On November 2 in Tokyo, Premier Kim Jong Pil expressed President Park's "regret" over the "great trouble" caused by the incident. While admitting the "personal" involvement of a member of the Korean Embassy staff in Tokyo, Premier Kim assured Japan that his government played no part in the abduction. Discussion turned to economic assistance.

Relations with China. Although Tokyo had moved to reestablish relations with Peking in September 1972—simultaneously breaking diplomatic relations with the Republic of China (Taiwan)—the pace of political cooperation remained slow. It was not until February that China opened a temporary embassy in Tokyo. On March 27, Chen Chu arrived to become Peking's first permanent ambassador. He had previously served as representative to the United Nations. Meanwhile, on February 10, Tokyo named Heishiro Ogawa as Japan's first ambassador to the People's Republic. He had previously served as head of Japan's Foreign Service Training Institute.

Ogawa spent most of his first months in Peking preparing for a visit by Foreign Minister Masayoshi Ohira, scheduled for November and designed to conclude an aviation agreement. This, and parallel commerce, navigation, and other bilateral accords, however, were deadlocked because of existing air links between Japan and Taiwan. Trade between Japan and mainland China did, however, turn sharply upward: for the first six months of 1973, the volume exceeded $871 million.

Relations with the USSR. Premier Tanaka's other exercise in summit diplomacy, talks in Moscow, supplemented his Washington and Western European visits and reflected Japan's concerns for energy supplies. Once again Japan encountered Russian intransigence over a territorial issue left over from World War II.

In September, the premier began a 16-day tour of Western Europe involving talks in France, Britain, and West Germany. There he sought to strengthen his hand for his negotiations with the Soviet leaders, by locating potential energy sources. In conversations held October 8–10 in Moscow with Communist party leader Leonid Brezhnev and Premier Aleksei Kosygin, he learned in detail of Soviet interest in Japanese credits and technical assistance in the development of oil, gas, and timber resources of Siberia. In light of Japan's energy needs, these were significant resources.

With a persistence uncharacteristic of Japanese diplomacy, however, Premier Tanaka referred to the outstanding "northern territories" issue, involving the continued occupation by the USSR of the Habomai, Shikotan, Kunashiri, and Etorofu islands in the Kuril chain. Although the Soviet leaders were visibly annoyed by the stubborn Tanaka stand, they did agree to continue diplomatic negotiations on the status of the islands as well as on unmolested Japanese fishing operations in the area. Obviously, however, further movement toward a peace treaty (Japan and the USSR had merely "normalized" relations in 1956) and cooperation in the development of Siberia would have to await the settlement of the "northern territories" issue.

DOMESTIC AFFAIRS

When Premier Tanaka and President Nixon met in Washington, both leaders found themselves under considerable pressure at home because of somewhat similar problems inherent in advanced societies. According to a nationwide opinion poll conducted by Kyodo news service in October, just after Premier Tanaka returned from Europe, support for him remained low at 26.8% of eligible voters asked for an opinion. This marked a drastic decline from the 62% the premier enjoyed a year before. There was no doubt that two of the problems causing disfavor were the galloping inflation and the alarming growth of environmental disruption.

The Problem of Inflation. Three out of four of the Kyodo respondents believed that the government could not master the inflation with current price policy. Fears were translated into action on Sunday, November 11, as more than 2 million Japanese, organized by the General Council of Trade Unions (*Sohyo*) and other labor groups throughout Japan, demonstrated against the failure to check price increases. Moreover, a group of "liberals" within the majority Liberal-Democratic party (LDP) publicly opposed restrictions on private land transactions in the national development bill, the backbone of Premier Tanaka's celebrated plan to remodel the Japanese archipelago. Together with tightening credit, land prices had skyrocketed.

In July, the Bank of Japan released figures showing the wholesale price index 15% higher than that of a year before. Statistics released by the premier's office itself showed the Tokyo (ward areas) consumer price index at 14.5% higher than the year before (September 1972–September 1973). The nationwide price index was 9% over the level of 1972. Costs of land, necessities—particularly housing and clothing—, and leisure activities led the parade. By November, the Economic Planning Agency warned that energy shortages could further drive up wholesale and retail prices. The energy crisis also led industrialists to call on the government to relax controls over air and water pollution, and thus the problem of inflation was linked to the issue of environment.

The Problem of Pollution. In spite of the energy crisis and a decline in the annual growth rate, the

The Ginza, Tokyo's best-known shopping street, has a familiar American sight: a McDonald's Hamburger stand.

PETER GOULD

EMPEROR HIROHITO and the empress enjoy a stroll in the gardens of their villa at Nasu during their summer vacation.

Japanese seemed determined to develop antipollution technology. Takeo Miki, director general of the Environment Agency, said that the government would continue to place priority on the protection of environment. "The lives of human beings are at stake in environmental problems," Miki stated.

Meanwhile, most Japanese applauded the judicial campaign aimed at a legal definition of environmental disruption (*kōgai,* in Japanese). In succession there had been suits involving chemical pollution in Niigata; extreme air pollution in Yokkaichi, an industrial suburb of Nagoya; the infamous *itai-itai* ("hurts, hurts") in Toyama; and finally, there was a climax in the Minamata disease case. This last took its name from waste-contaminated Minamata Bay, in southern Kyushu, where fish had been infected with organic mercury. This sea food then claimed scores of human victims. On March 20, the district court in Kumamoto issued an order to the Chisso firm to pay $3.5 million in damages to families who had suffered illness or death. Thus the last, like the other three, trials ended in favor of the complainants. (It was in Kumamoto that Japan suffered, at the end of November, one of its worst fires in the postwar period. The fire broke out in a department store and took more than 100 lives.)

Environment and Defense. Although there might not seem to be a connection, Japanese had long identified military installations—the "American presence" on naval and air bases and Self Defense Force (SDF) installations—as blights on the natural environment. Perhaps of greater significance was the legal status of the SDF, questioned in light of the famous Article 9 of the American-inspired constitution of 1947. (This article, according to many Japanese, prohibited use of armed forces as "instruments of national policy.")

The SDF had long planned a missile base at Naganuma, Hokkaido. Local groups protested this invasion of national parklands, and on September 10 the district court in Sapporo ruled that the SDF was unconstitutional. The government argued for the inherent right of self-defense, immediately appealed the verdict, and predicted a reversal in the Supreme Court.

Parties, Politics, and Elections. In the general election held in December 1972, the majority LDP had won a plurality, which nonetheless represented a steadily declining proportion (46.8%) of the popular vote. This became translated into an absolute majority (284) of the lower House of Representatives' total of 492 seats. The Japan Socialists (JSP) picked up strength and ranked as the second party. The Communists (JCP) gained sharply to become the third-largest party, trailed by the Komeito and the Democratic Socialists (DSP).

As a result, Tanaka was reelected premier by the Diet. His second cabinet as usual represented a coalition of LDP faction chiefs: his former opponent, Takeo Fukuda (Administration); Takeo Miki (Environment); Kiichi Aichi (Finance); a younger rival, Yasuhiro Nakasone (International Trade and Industry); and the architect of the new China policy, Masayoshi Ohira (Foreign Affairs). Aichi died in November, and Tanaka chose Fukuda to replace him as minister of finance.

Meanwhile, coalitions of opposition parties, rallying around issues of inflation, yen revaluation, and pollution, were successfully challenging LDP dominance at the local levels. "Progressives" had already captured governorships in Tokyo (the popular Socialist Ryokichi Minobe), Kyoto, Osaka, Saitama, and Okayama. In May, JCP-JSP-sponsored Masao Motoyama defeated the LDP-backed incumbent mayor of Nagoya. Although the LDP did make a respectable showing in the election for the Tokyo Metropolitan Assembly held July 8, a three-party coalition linked to Governor Minobe maintained its majority in the 125-seat body.

As a result of rising opposition, the LDP also encountered obstacles to its legislative program in the Diet. In trouble were bills to raise fares on national railways, to establish an innovative national university at Tsukuba, and to expand SDF personnel. On July 27, the LDP unilaterally extended lower house sessions for a second time, while the opposition boycotted the plenary session. On August 27, the Diet finally ended its record 280-day session.

Premier Tanaka's difficulties were compounded by the fact that, in addition to opposition coalitions outside, strong anti-Tanaka factions were forming inside the LDP. On the left were younger, liberal LDP members who opposed continued obsession with growth; and a faction on the right was led by Takeo Fukuda, minister of finance as of November 25. Fukuda advocated strenuous measures to control inflation, such as a reduction in public works expenditures. In effect, he called for the abandonment of Tanaka's plan to remodel Japan.

ARDATH W. BURKS
Rutgers University

JAPANESE LITERATURE. See LITERATURE.
JOHNSON, Lyndon B. See OBITUARIES.

JORDAN

Although Jordan resumed diplomatic relations with Egypt in September 1973 and entered the fourth Arab-Israeli war in October, by year's end it was difficult to say if King Hussein's position in inter-Arab affairs had improved. In the months preceding the outbreak of hostilities, Hussein's diplomatic and political isolation continued to plague his country's fortunes. The king's close relations with the United States, his refusal to allow Palestinian guerrilla forces on Jordanian soil, and his allegedly conciliatory attitude toward Israel isolated the Jordanian monarch even further as the Arab world escalated the confrontation with Israel from economic threats to actual fighting. His initiatives during the war, taken in part to decrease his isolation among Arabs, were critical for his political future.

Arab-Israeli War. Jordan's participation in the fourth round of the intermittent Arab-Israeli war was limited. This fact may have qualified the success of Hussein's efforts to wrench his desert kingdom out of the diplomatic, political, and economic isolation that had plagued him since the Jordanian civil war of 1970. Up to the outbreak of fighting on October 6, diplomatic maneuvering by Jordan, Egypt, and Syria encouraged speculation that Hussein was going to adopt a more militant policy in Arab-Israeli affairs. Contrary to speculation, however, Hussein conducted a cautious military policy during the war, which was consistent with statements he had made the previous May. In a much publicized May 13 order of the day to officers of the Jordanian army, Hussein had stated that a resumption of hostilities with Israel was premature because of Arab divisiveness and lack of preparation. Moreover, Hussein said that unless figures showed the Arabs had a "one in two chance of defeating Israel," Jordan would not act "impulsively and naively in a war which could only end in catastrophe." Apparently for these reasons, Jordan did not enter the war immediately. But Arab political pressure and battlefield successes made his participation unavoidable.

Waiting until October 10 to order mobilization of the Arab Legion and to call up the reserves, Hussein did not risk the full-scale intervention that had led to the debacle of 1967. On October 13, Hussein dispatched what many considered to be only a token force of two mechanized brigades to the Syrian front and, in spite of Iraqi promises to provide the critical air support Jordan lacked, refused to open the third front along the Jordan-Israel border urged by Arab leaders.

Hussein quickly accepted the October 22 UN Security Council cease-fire resolution. There followed statements by Egyptian President Anwar el-Sadat and Syrian President Hafez al-Assad in which the two leaders seemed to anticipate the establishment of an independent Palestinian state on the Israeli-occupied West Bank of the Jordan as part of a comprehensive solution to the Arab-Israeli problem. Such an arrangement would conflict with Jordan's demand that the West Bank remain under Jordanian sovereignty. This issue isolated Jordan at the Arab summit conference held in Algiers in late November. However, Hussein's war policy probably helped to improve his relations with some Arab states.

Diplomacy. September was a watershed in Jordan's diplomatic year. On September 12, Egypt resumed diplomatic relations with Jordan, apparently because Hussein agreed to consider reactivating the

——— JORDAN • Information Highlights ———

Official Name: Hashemite Kingdom of Jordan.
Location: Southwest Asia.
Area: 37,738 square miles (97,740 sq km).
Population (1973 est.): 2,600,000. Density, 62 per square mile (24 per sq km).
Chief Cities (1970 est.): Amman, the capital, 570,000; Zarqa, 200,000.
Government: *Head of state,* Hussein Ibn Talal, king (acceded Aug. 1952). *Head of government,* Zaid al-Rifai, premier (took office May 1973). *Legislature*—National Assembly: Senate and House of Representatives.
Language: Arabic (official).
Education: *Expenditure* (1969), 9.6% of total public expenditure. *School enrollment* (1969)—primary, 259,388; secondary, 88,090; technical/vocational, 2,801; university/higher, 4,463.
Monetary Unit: Dinar (0.3215 dinar equals U.S.$1, Aug. 1973).
Gross National Product (1971 est.): $575,000,000.
Consumer Price Index (1972), 129 (1963=100).
Manufacturing (major products): Cement, petroleum products, cigarettes, vegetable oil.
Major Agricultural Products: Wheat, tomatoes, barley, fruits, corn, sorghum, olives, grapes, tobacco.
Major Minerals: Phosphate rock, salt, potash.
Foreign Trade (1972): Exports, $48,000,000; Imports, $267,000,000. *Chief trading partners* (1970)—Arab countries (took 71% of exports, supplied 21% of imports); Common Market (supplied 18%); United Kingdom (supplied 14%); Communist bloc (supplied 13%).
Tourism: Receipts (1971), $8,694,000.
Transportation: *Motor vehicles* (1971), 20,700 (automobiles, 15,200); *railroads* (1971), 298 miles (480 km); *major national airline,* ALIA-The Royal Jordanian Airlines.
Communications: *Telephones* (1972), 33,020; *newspapers* (1971), 3 (daily circulation, 36,000).

"Eastern Front" with Israel and allowing some Palestinian units to return to Jordan. On September 18, Hussein exhibited a new spirit of reconciliation with the Palestinian Resistance by declaring an amnesty pardoning all Palestinian guerrillas held in Jordan since 1970. The pardon included a group of commandos captured on February 14 while infiltrating Jordan from Syria; their death penalties had contributed to the midyear deterioration of Jordan's relations with the Arab world. On July 6, Tunisia's President Habib Bourguiba had called for the dissolution of the "artificial" Jordanian monarchy, causing the severing of relations between Jordan and Tunisia on July 17. Syria resumed formal relations on October 4.

In the atmosphere of Arab solidarity accompanying the October war, Hussein's limited participation in the fighting was enough to prompt the restoration of relations with Tunisia and Algeria. Of more importance to Jordan was the resumption on October 17 of Kuwait's annual $40 million subsidy, the object of Jordanian diplomatic efforts since it had been cut off in September 1970.

Internal Affairs. Following the resignation of Premier Ahmed Lawzi, Hussein appointed Zaid al-Rifai as premier on May 26. Premier Rifai is reputed to oppose the Palestine guerrilla movement. The new 19-member cabinet is expected to spearhead the implementation of Jordan's massive three-year development plan.

On April 1, Jordan liberalized its electoral law by enfranchising women voters and making them eligible to sit in the House of Representatives.

In economic matters, Jordan's planning was buoyed by the resumption of the Kuwaiti subsidy alleviating an anticipated $33.6 million budget deficit. Late in April, the Jordan Valley Organization, the body administering the three-year development plan, announced that $37.3 million would be allocated for the irrigation of 20,000 acres (8,000 hectares) and the resettlement of approximately 120,000 people. Jordan continued to receive massive economic aid from the United States.

F. NICHOLAS WILLARD, *Georgetown University*

TORNADO touches down just south of Salina, Kans., September 25. It leveled a trailer park, injuring four people.

UPI

KANSAS

In 1973, Kansas had a most useful legislative session, and the state enjoyed record high production for several major farm crops.

Agriculture. The harvesting of crops in Kansas was at its highest levels in 1973. A record 385 million bushels of wheat was harvested, greatly exceeding the previous high of 315 million in 1972. Excellent growing conditions in most of the state, combined with the wide use of fertilizers, brought high yields. This gain was increased when the federal government, because of diminishing grain supplies, allowed farmers who had oversown to harvest those acres rather than to plow them under.

The 1973 soybean crop, estimated at 27 million bushels, and hay, estimated at nearly 6 million tons, were expected to be all-time highs for Kansas. The production of corn, estimated at 151 million bushels, was the highest in 45 years. An estimated 227 million bushels of sorghum grain was the second highest on record for the state. The high yields combined with higher market prices for crops and livestock in 1973 gave Kansas farmers a long-awaited year of prosperity.

Weather. The rains, which brought bountiful harvests, caused substantial losses at times. Downpours measuring up to nine inches in 24 hours at Winfield and Arkansas City brought flooding in many areas of Kansas, especially in late September and early October. Flood control reservoirs constructed during the preceding 15 years prevented major property damage.

Heavy weather during the year also spawned a few tornadoes, which killed several people and brought damage to a dozen Kansas communities. Most heavily hit was Clay Center, where on September 25 a twister plowed through the center of the city.

Legislation. The 1973 legislative session, which approved a record budget of $1.2 billion, was one of the most productive in years. Education received much of the legislators' attention. Major bills included a new state school-aid plan, supported by appropriations of $186.7 million. State aid was increased for community junior colleges, and Washburn Municipal University of Topeka, and the state's tuition-grant program was increased. Construction of a new clinical facility at the University of Kansas Medical Center in Kansas City was approved. Older teacher retirees were granted liberalized benefits.

Some new tax legislation was also passed. Benefits under the homestead property relief act were liberalized, and a permanent property tax lid was established, with modifications eliminating the budget ceiling on counties, cities, and junior colleges, and authorizing a half-cent countywide sales tax. County property taxes for financing welfare programs were eliminated, and the corporation tax disallowance was extended.

The legislators provided for the joint nomination and election of the governor and lieutenant governor, and for four-year terms for the governor, lieu-

---
KANSAS · Information Highlights

Area: 82,264 square miles (213,064 sq km).
Population (1972 est.): 2,258,000. *Density:* 28 per sq mi.
Chief Cities (1970 census): Topeka, the capital, 125,011; Wichita, 276,554; Kansas City, 168,213; Overland Park, 79,034; Lawrence, 45,698; Salina, 37,714; Hutchinson, 36,885.
Government (1973): *Chief Officers*—governor, Robert B. Docking (D); lt. gov., Dave Owen (R); secy. of state, Mrs. Elwill M. Shanahan (R); atty. gen., Vern Miller (D); treas., Tom R. Van Sickle (R); commissioner of education, C. Taylor Whittier; chief justice, Harold R. Fatzer. *Legislature*—Senate, 40 members (27 Republicans, 13 Democrats); House of Representatives, 125 members (80 R, 45 D).
Education (1972–73): *Enrollment*—public elementary schools, 277,675 pupils, 12,970 teachers; public secondary schools, 213,901 pupils, 12,557 teachers; nonpublic schools, 34,700 pupils, 1,490 teachers; colleges and universities, 104,365 students. *Public school expenditures,* $410,625,000 ($919 per pupil). *Average teacher's salary,* $8,839.
State Finances (fiscal year 1971): *Revenues,* $870,216,000 (3% general sales tax and gross receipts taxes, $158,597,000; motor fuel tax, $84,106,000; federal funds, $218,441,000). *Expenditures,* $825,384,000 (education, $333,257,000; health, welfare, and safety, $138,701,000; highways, $171,821,000). *State debt,* $218,841,000 (June 30, 1971).
Personal Income (1972): $10,371,000,000; per capita, $4,593.
Public Assistance (1972): $135,985,000. *Average monthly payments* (Dec. 1972)—old-age assistance, $66.19; aid to families with dependent children, $193.49.
Labor Force: *Nonagricultural wage and salary earners* (July 1973), 741,300. *Average annual employment* (1972)—manufacturing, 143,000; trade, 169,200; government, 162,800; services, 108,300. *Insured unemployed* (Sept. 1973)—6,100 (1.1%).
Manufacturing (1971): *Value added by manufacture,* $2,560,600,000; Transportation equipment, $553,300,000; food and kindred products, $345,500,000; chemicals and allied products, $328,200,000; nonelectrical machinery, $231,900,000; printing and publishing, $181,400,000; petroleum and coal products, $172,800,000.
Agriculture (1972): *Cash farm income,* $3,066,729,000 (livestock, $1,899,276,000; crops, $921,044,000; government payments, $246,409,000). *Chief crops* (in order of value, 1972)—Wheat (ranks 1st among the states), sorghum grain (ranks 2d), corn, hay.
Mining (1972): *Production value,* $587,678,000 (ranks 15th among the states). *Chief minerals*—Petroleum, $262,592,000; natural gas, $133,500,000; natural gas liquids, $52,400,000; cement, $35,850,000.
Transportation: *Roads* (1972), 134,182 miles (215,939 km); *motor vehicles* (1972), 1,599,109; *railroads* (1972), 7,776 miles (12,514 km); *public airports* (1972), 119.
Communications: *Telephones* (1973), 1,411,900; *television stations* (1971), 12; *radio stations* (1971), 83; *newspapers* (1973), 52 (daily circulation, 664,000).

tenant governor, secretary of state, and attorney general. Small-claims courts were established for grievances involving less than $300. A uniform credit code was established, and the Kansas consumer protection act was passed. The state penal system was reorganized, and administration of social welfare was centralized under state control.

Other legislation included the adoption of a no-fault automobile insurance plan and the approval of longer and heavier trucks on Kansas highways. Finally, the legislators provided for the purchase of an 81-acre site just west of Topeka, containing the historic Pottawatomie Baptist Mission building, which was erected in 1850. A state historical museum is to be built on the site.

NYLE H. MILLER
Kansas State Historical Society

KENTUCKY

In 1973, Kentucky suffered from floods, followed by relatively poor crops. There were manifestations of labor unrest. Many government agencies were reorganized, subject to legislative approval.

Government and Politics. Gov. Wendell H. Ford (D) worked throughout the year to reorganize agencies of the state government. Early in the year he established new departments of Natural Resources and Environmental Protection, Finance and Administration, and Transportation. Later he ordered the creation of a new Human Resources Cabinet, a Department of Justice, an Education and Arts Cabinet, and a Development Cabinet. A Consumer Protection and Regulation Cabinet was being planned. An ombudsman in the Human Resources Cabinet would help citizens in their dealings with the state government. The governor estimated that the reorganization would save the state $5 million annually. The restructuring must be approved by the 1974 General Assembly.

In the November elections, Democrats swept local offices in Louisville and its suburbs and increased their majority in both houses of the legislature. Voters rejected a constitutional amendment that would have provided for annual legislative sessions. A close, nonpartisan race preceding the first election of a mayor for the new Lexington-Fayette County Metro Government was marred by disputed returns from one voting machine. The final outcome was to be decided by the courts.

Floods. Western Kentucky was subject to severe storms and flooding beginning in March and lasting throughout the spring, causing widespread damage to property. In mid-May, President Richard Nixon declared the state a major disaster area, providing financial assistance for the removal of debris and the repair or restoration of public facilities.

Agriculture. A cold, wet spring cut the yield of fruits and strawberries throughout the state, while in western Kentucky the floods delayed the planting of field crops. In consequence, cotton and corn acreages were much reduced. However, farmers for the first time in the state's history planted more than 1 million acres of soybeans.

Auction sales of the 1972 burley tobacco crop, which continued into 1973, brought unprecedented returns of nearly $345 million. The 1973 crop was short, preventing growers from profiting from a 5% increase in marketing quotas, but good prices for the reduced quantity of leaf were expected, as was a further quota increase of 3% for 1974 crops.

──────── KENTUCKY • Information Highlights ────────

Area: 40,395 square miles (104,623 sq km).
Population (1972 est.): 3,299,000. *Density:* 82 per sq mi.
Chief Cities (1970 census): Frankfort, the capital, 21,902; Louisville, 361,958; Lexington, 108,137; Covington, 52,535; Owensboro, 50,329; Bowling Green, 36,253; Paducah, 31,-627.
Government (1973): *Chief Officers*—governor, Wendell H. Ford (D); lt. gov., Julian M. Carroll (D); secy. of state, Mrs. Thelma L. Stovall (D); atty. gen., Ed W. Hancock (D); treas., Drexell Davis (D); supt. of public instruction, Lyman V. Ginger (D); chief justice, John S. Palmore. *General Assembly*—Senate, 38 members (25 Democrats, 11 Republicans, 2 vacancies); House of Representatives, 100 members (72 D, 27 R, 1 vacancy).
Education (1972–73): *Enrollment*—public elementary schools, 450,213 pupils, 19,400 teachers; public secondary schools, 264,394 pupils, 11,980 teachers; nonpublic schools, 62,-600 pupils, 2,720 teachers; colleges and universities, 102,-765 students. *Public school expenditures,* $455,000,000 ($693 per pupil). *Average teacher's salary,* $8,150.
State Finances (fiscal year 1971): *Revenues:* $1,529,623,000 (5% general sales tax and gross receipts taxes, $289,850,-000; motor fuel tax, $111,893,000; federal funds, $495,958,-000). *Expenditures,* $1,423,866,000 (education, $579,170,-000; health, welfare, and safety, $235,265,000; highways, $340,215,000). *State debt,* $1,535,965,000 (June 30, 1971).
Personal Income (1972): $11,878,000,000; per capita, $3,601.
Public Assistance (1972): $201,241,000. *Average monthly payments* (Dec. 1972)—old-age assistance, $61.77; aid to families with dependent children, $120.41.
Labor Force: *Nonagricultural wage and salary earners* (July 1973), 1,038,200. *Average annual employment* (1972)—manufacturing, 266,300; trade, 200,100; government, 189,-600; services, 145,400. *Insured unemployed* (Sept. 1973)—11,800 (1.6%).
Manufacturing (1971): *Value added by manufacture,* $5,168,-200,000. Electrical equipment and supplies, $844,300,000; nonelectrical machinery, $724,300,000; food and kindred products, $673,800,000; tobacco manufactures, $438,000,-000; chemicals and allied products, $407,400,000; primary metal industries, $344,100,000.
Agriculture (1972): *Cash farm income,* $1,122,231,000 (livestock, $593,327,000; crops, $492,067,000; government payments, $36,837,000). *Chief crops* (in order of value, 1972)—Tobacco (ranks 2d among the states), corn, hay.
Mining (1972): *Production value,* $1,053,942,000 (ranks 8th among the states). *Chief minerals*—Coal, $908,000,000; stone, $50,595,000; petroleum, $32,710,000; natural gas, $19,275,000.
Transportation: *Roads* (1972), 69,123 miles (111,240 km); *motor vehicles* (1972), 1,859,987; *railroads* (1972), 3,504 miles (5,639 km); *public airports* (1972), 47.
Communications: *Telephones* (1973), 1,610,100; *television stations* (1971), 10; *radio stations* (1971), 164; *newspapers* (1973), 26 (daily circulation, 773,000).

Coal Mining. After making Kentucky the nation's foremost coal-producing state in 1971 and 1972, mine operators found themselves facing increasing difficulties. Harlan county once again became the site of labor strife as employees of the Eastover Mining Co., a subsidiary of Duke Power Co. of North Carolina, began a strike in July to force acceptance of a United Mine Workers (UMW) contract. Defiance of injunctions led to arrests of pickets and of participants in sunrise worship services at the entrance to the mine. Soon afterward the mine was shut down, and a spokesman for the company, which recognizes the Southern Labor Union, firmly denied any intention of accepting a UMW contract. Both sides filed charges with the National Labor Relations Board. In October a short-lived wildcat strike was called in eastern Kentucky during a dispute between the local UMW district and the national office, but the strike ended after intervention by UMW President Arnold Miller.

A campaign by Attorney General Ed W. Hancock against overweight coal trucks on Kentucky roads had results in 1973, when judges in Pulaski and Perry counties issued injunctions against such vehicles. The injunctions were upheld by the court of appeals, which also ruled that the highway department lacked the authority to issue special permits for the use of the trucks.

JAMES F. HOPKINS
University of Kentucky

KENYA

Kenya celebrated the 10th anniversary of its independence on Dec. 12, 1973. During the decade that elapsed since the end of British colonial rule, Kenya maintained one of the most rapid rates of economic growth in Africa, and the country enjoyed stable political leadership under President Jomo Kenyatta.

Economic Development. Kenya's progress in some areas of development has been spectacular. In a speech early in 1973, Minister for Finance and Economic Planning Mwai Kibaki announced that 75% of school-age children were in school. He stated that the number of students had increased from 750,000 in 1963 to 1,600,000 in 1973.

Kibaki also claimed that agricultural production had doubled during the first decade of independence, with the most dramatic development occurring in tea production. A total of 44,000 acres (18,000 hectares) had been under tea cultivation in 1963. By 1973 the total had expanded to 123,500 acres (50,000 hectares).

An economic report for the year 1972 released in mid-1973 indicated that imports had dropped by 3.5% and exports had risen by 22%. The improved balance of trade reflected, to some extent, improved prices for the country's coffee and sisal. Kenya's trade position could improve further, since in 1973 it replaced South Africa as the beef supplier for Zambia, and it also began to take some beef orders from Europe.

Amid reports of economic growth, a report issued early in the year by the International Labor Office cautioned against overoptimism. The report warned that economic growth was benefiting only a small minority in Kenya and proposed that development strategies concentrate on redistribution of the wealth generated by growth and on the improvement of employment conditions.

Government and Politics. President Kenyatta appointed Robert Matano as minister for informa-tion and broadcasting in January. The selection of Matano, the acting secretary general of the ruling Kenya African National Union (KANU), gave the lower coastal region renewed representation in the cabinet. It had been unrepresented since the death in December 1972 of Minister for Power and Communications Ronald Ngala, one of the country's most prominent politicians. There was a second minor reshuffle of the cabinet in April.

President Kenyatta announced in March that a national election, Kenya's second since independence, would be held in 1974. Members of parliament will be elected in a single party primary. The system was used during the last elections in 1969, when most incumbents were defeated.

Party elections, which had been expected to precede parliamentary elections, remained unscheduled. The threat of the eruption of factional disputes has kept KANU from holding a national party conference since 1966. It has been feared that party elections would affect the political positions of the potential successors to 83-year-old President Kenyatta, and could become a contest between prominent officials, such as Vice President Daniel arap Moi and Foreign Minister Njoroge Mungai.

Lt. Col. Dedan Gichuru was appointed in April as the first African commander of the Kenya Air Force and was promoted to colonel.

New Conference Center. The $9.6 million Kenyatta Conference Center in Nairobi opened in 1973. The 32-story center, the tallest building in black-ruled Africa, became the permanent headquarters of the UN Secretariat for the Environment. The center also housed the 28th annual meeting of the World Bank and the International Monetary Fund in September, the first conference of such stature to be held in Africa.

The new building was expected to make Nairobi an attractive site for international conventions and to stimulate the country's already vigorous tourist trade. Tourism, along with coffee and tea, has been one of Kenya's top earners of foreign exchange. The center was originally planned as party headquarters for KANU, whose operations have virtually ceased.

Foreign Relations. A $55 million aid package from Britain, still the largest supplier of foreign aid to Kenya, was announced in March. The money consisted of one-third outright gift and two-thirds interest-free loans, and much of it will be spent to purchase 220 Kenyan farms owned by British citizens.

Since Kenya's neighbor Uganda forced a mass exodus of Asians with British passports in 1972, Britain encouraged Kenya to continue its more gradual policy of phased removal of Asians with British passports. In January, 400 noncitizen Asian traders and their families were told they would have to leave Kenya by June 1.

Although interstate relations in East Africa were calmer in 1973 than they had been for several years, ties within the East African Community continued to loosen somewhat. The member states—Kenya, Uganda, and Tanzania—began steps in 1973 to create separate income tax divisions to replace the Community-wide structures. Relations between Kenya and Uganda became strained for a time after reports began to circulate that several Kenyans, mostly employees of the East African Community, were missing in Uganda.

JAY E. HAKES
Louisiana State University in New Orleans

————— KENYA • Information Highlights —————

Official Name: Republic of Kenya.
Location: East coast of Africa.
Area: 224,959 square miles (582,644 sq km).
Population (1973 est.): 12,000,000. *Density,* 52 per square mile (20 per sq km).
Chief Cities (1970 est.): Nairobi, the capital, 535,200; Mombasa, 255,400.
Government: *Head of state,* Jomo Kenyatta, president (took office Dec. 1964). *Head of government,* Jomo Kenyatta. *Legislature* (unicameral)—National Assembly. *Major political party*—Kenya African National Union (KANU).
Languages: Swahili, English (both official).
Education: *Expenditure* (1968), 4.8% of gross national product. *School enrollment* (1970)—primary, 1,427,589; secondary, 137,008; technical/vocational, 2,136; university/higher (1968), 4,967.
Monetary Unit: Kenya shilling (6.9 shillings equal U.S.$1, Aug. 1973).
Gross National Product (1972 est.): $1,842,000,000.
Economic Indexes: *Industrial production* (manufacturing, 1968), 143 (1963=100); *consumer price index* (1972), 103 (1971=100).
Manufacturing (major products): Construction materials, processed agricultural products, petroleum products.
Major Agricultural Products: Coffee, tea, sugarcane, sisal, corn, cassava, pyrethrum, fruits, livestock.
Major Mineral: Salt.
Foreign Trade (1972): *Exports,* $267,000,000. *Imports,* $497,000,000. *Chief trading partners* (1971)—United Kingdom (took 19% of exports, supplied 31% of imports); West Germany (9%—8%); United States (6%—9%).
Tourism: *Receipts* (1971), $67,450,000.
Transportation: *Motor vehicles* (1971), 123,600 (automobiles, 104,500); *railroads* (regional total with Tanzania and Uganda, 1971), 3,676 miles (5,915 km); *major national airline* (with Tanzania and Uganda), East African Airways.
Communications: *Telephones* (1971), 85,000; *newspapers* (1970), 4 (daily circulation, 155,000).

KOREA

The movement for the unification of South Korea and North Korea appeared to have faded away in 1973. The South-North Coordinating Committee and the Red Cross talks, which were initiated in 1972 and 1971, respectively, to work toward a negotiated peace and unification of the divided country, became seriously deadlocked. The deadlock was intensified after the abduction of the South Korean opposition leader Kim Dae-jung from his Tokyo hotel on August 8. The kidnapping caused serious friction with Japan and prompted North Korea to demand the replacement of South Korea's negotiators on the coordinating committee, charging they had engineered the abduction.

Meetings of the South-North Coordinating Committee and the Red Cross were suspended in July. The irreconcilable issue seemed to be a difference of priorities. North Korea insisted on first resolving the fundamental issue of an overall political settlement, including a peace agreement formally ending the Korean War, and mutual arms reduction, before going on to economic and cultural exchanges and reuniting separated families. South Korea argued for the establishment of mutual trust through social, economic, and cultural exchanges before beginning more serious talks.

SOUTH KOREA

President Park Chung Hee continued to dominate events in South Korea in 1973.

National Assembly. Following several months of rule by decree, elections for a new 219-member National Assembly were held on February 27. The governing Democratic Republican party won 71 of the 146 contested seats. The opposition New Democratic party won 52 seats, 2 were won by the Democratic Unification party, and 21 were won by Independents. The remaining 73 members were appointed by President Park. The elected representa-

UPI

KOREAN OFFICER leaving South Vietnam gives a farewell kiss to a child during ceremonies at the airport.

tives will serve 6-year terms, the appointed members will serve for 3 years. The new assembly convened on March 12, five months after it had been dissolved by presidential decree.

National Reform. A new national reform program was proclaimed by President Park in March in an effort to eliminate waste of both time and money. Under the new reform measure certain family rites, such as weddings and funerals, will be simplified. It placed a strict limitation on wedding ceremonies and banned printed invitations and postnuptial banquets. Traditional mourning dresses were banned.

Political Incidents. A series of unprecedented political incidents erupted within and without South Korea during the year, all attracting international attention. In early June, Lee Jai Hyon, the chief cultural and information attaché of the South Korean embassy in Washington, requested asylum in the United States, stating that he could no longer serve as spokesman for a government disseminating false information and picturing South Korea as a free country. He charged that the South Korean Central Intelligence Agency (CIA) had conducted illegal surveillance and intimidation operations against Korean residents in the United States.

A Presbyterian pastor, Pak Myong Kyu, and 14 "social action" activists were arrested in Seoul on July 5 on a charge of subversion for having distributed leaflets at an Easter sunrise service calling for a "revival of democracy" and an overthrow of "dictatorial government." They were all released in late October after worldwide press attention and public pressure.

SOUTH KOREA • Information Highlights

Official Name: Republic of Korea.
Location: Northeastern Asia.
Area: 38,022 square miles (98,477 sq km).
Population (1973 est.): 32,848,000. Density, 839 per square mile (324 per sq km).
Chief Cities (1970 census): Seoul, the capital, 5,525,000; Pusan, 1,880,710; Taegu, 1,082,750; Inchon, 646,013; Kwangju, 502,753.
Government: *Head of state,* Park Chung Hee, president (took office Dec. 1963). *Head of government,* Kim Jong Pil, premier (tok office June 1971). *Legislature* (unicameral) —National Assembly. *Major political parties*—Democratic Republican party; New Democratic party.
Language: Korean (official).
Education: *Expenditure* (1969), 21% of total public expenditure. *School enrollment* (1969)—primary, 5,622,816; secondary, 1,701,301; technical/vocational, 259,601; university/higher, 186,675.
Monetary Unit: Won (399 won equal U.S.$1, July 1973).
Gross National Product (1972 est.): $9,050,000,000.
Economic Indexes: *Industrial production* (1972), 416 (1963= 100); *agricultural production* (1971), 146 (1963=100); *consumer price index* (1972), 127 (1970=100).
Manufacturing (major products): Textiles, petrochemicals, clothing, hair products, processed foods, plywood, metal products.
Major Agricultural Products: Rice, barley, wheat, soybeans, sweet potatoes and yams, fish.
Major Minerals: Graphite (ranks 3d among world producers, 1971), coal, tungsten, lead, iron ore, kaolin, talc.
Foreign Trade (1972): *Exports,* $1,633,000,000. *Imports,* $2,-522,000,000. *Chief trading partners* (1970)—United States (took 50% of exports, supplied 28% of imports); Japan (25%—40%).
Tourism: *Receipts* (1971), $52,000,000.
Transportation: *Motor vehicles* (1971), 138,400 (automobiles, 67,600); *railroads* (1971), 2,489 miles (4,006 km); *merchant fleet* (1972), 1,057,000 gross registered tons; *major national airline,* Korean Air Lines.
Communications: *Telephones* (1972), 748,474; *newspapers* (1970), 44 (daily circulation, 4,396,000).

325

On August 8, in broad daylight, the most outspoken political opponent of the South Korean government, Kim Dae-jung, was whisked away from the Grand Palace Hotel in Tokyo by five armed men, who the Japanese charged were South Korean CIA agents. Five days after his abduction, Kim was found unharmed outside his home in Seoul, where he was placed under house arrest. President Park's chief opponent in the 1971 presidential election, Kim had left South Korea shortly before the imposition of martial law in October 1972 and campaigned against Park's government in the United States and Japan.

The aftermath of this incident was a rupture with both Japan and North Korea. Despite the South Korean government's denial of any connection with the kidnapping, Japan deferred further economic aid to South Korea until the Kim case was settled satisfactorily.

South Korean Foreign Minister Kim Yong Shik announced on November 1 that his government and Japan had reached a diplomatic settlement over the abduction. Premier Kim Jong Pil visited Japan to "express regrets" to the Japanese government over the kidnapping.

North Korea warned on August 28 that it would break off discussions with South Korea unless Seoul replaced Lee Hu Rak as head of its delegation to the South-North Coordinating Committee, accusing him as the head of the CIA of having engineered Kim's abduction.

The most serious incident for the South Korean regime was the antigovernment rally by some 300 Seoul National University students on October 2. The demonstration, which was the first in two years, demanded an end to "fascist intelligence rule and government infringement of basic human rights." The students issued a resolution demanding the termination of the CIA and revelation of the whole truth about Kim's kidnapping. They also atacked South Korea's growing economic dependence on Japan.

Census Results. An analytical report of the 1970 census released on June 11, 1973, disclosed that the total population of South Korea was 31,435,000. South Korea ranked third in world population density, after Taiwan and the Netherlands. The report also disclosed that the average life span of a South Korean was 65 years, the rate of migration into the capital was the highest in the world, and the ratio of the urban to rural population was 54:46.

A preliminary census taken in March 1973 placed the population at 32,848,000, an increase of 1.67% annually. Combined with an estimated 14,500,000 in North Korea, the total population of the Korean nation was 47,348,000 as of March 1973.

Relations with the United States. According to a joint communiqué issued at the end of a two-day annual security consultation, held in Seoul on September 13–14, the United States reassured South Korea of its continued readiness to provide assistance in the event of an armed attack. The discussions, led by U. S. Deputy Secretary of Defense William P. Clements, Jr., and South Korean Defense Minister Yu Jae Hung, disclosed that the United States would continue to help modernize the South Korean military and that it had no plans to reduce its own forces in Korea. It rejected North Korean demands for the termination of UN and U. S. support of South Korea.

NORTH KOREA • Information Highlights

Official Name: Democratic People's Republic of Korea.
Location: Northeastern Asia.
Area: 46,540 square miles (120,538 sq km).
Population (1973 est.): 14,500,000. *Density,* 306 per square mile (118 per sq km).
Chief City (1967 est.): Pyongyang, the capital, 840,000.
Government: *Head of state,* Kim Il Sung, president and secretary general of the Korean Workers' (Communist) party (took office Dec. 1972). *Head of government,* Kim Il, premier (took office Dec. 1972). *Legislature* (unicameral) —Supreme People's Assembly.
Language: Korean (official).
Monetary Unit: Won (0.961 won equals U. S.$1, July 1973).
Industrial Production Index (1968), 267 (1963=100).
Manufacturing (major products): Cement, metallurgical coke, pig iron and ferroalloys, textiles, cement.
Major Agricultural Products: Rice, sweet potatoes and yams, soybeans, livestock, fish.
Major Minerals: Graphite (ranks 2d among world producers, 1971), coal, lignite, iron ore, salt, lead, manganese, nickel.
Foreign Trade: *Chief exports*—Metals, farm products. *Chief import*—Machinery. *Chief trading partners*—USSR, China.
Transportation: *Merchant fleet* (1972), 51,000 gross registered tons.

NORTH KOREA

North Korea took advantage of the international détente to bring its international standing up to the level of South Korea in 1973. The World Health Organization (WHO) voted on May 17 to admit North Korea, defeating an attempt by the United States, Japan, and South Korea to defer the issue for a year. North Korea was officially accepted for membership in the UN Conference on Trade and Development on May 29. In June, it was granted observer status at the UN's headquarters in Geneva and New York.

The UN Commission on the Unification of Korea recommended its own dissolution on September 6. It had been boycotted by North Korea since its inception in 1950. On October 1, the UN Political Committee unanimously agreed to invite both South Korea and North Korea to the General Assembly session in November for a debate on the Korean question.

Foreign Affairs. The second session of the Fifth Supreme People's Assembly drafted an unusual letter to the U. S. Congress on April 6 appealing to it to consider termination of U. S. interference in Korean internal affairs and calling for the withdrawal of U. S. troops from South Korea. The Assembly asked the U. S. Congress to accelerate the peaceful reunification of Korea and urged it to take "appropriate, positive measures" to change the Nixon administration's policies toward South Korea.

North Korea's most impressive achievement in 1973 was the winning of greater diplomatic recognition and expansion of its trade relations with European countries. It received diplomatic recognition from Togo, Dahomey, Gambia, Somalai, Libya, Malagasy Republic, Sweden, Finland, Denmark, Norway, Iceland, Iran, and Argentina. However, Chile's new military government broke diplomatic relations with North Korea.

By the end of 1973, North Korea had established diplomatic ties with nearly 60 countries and was affiliated with over 100 international organizations. More than 40 nations had established relations with both South Korea and North Korea.

Transportation. An automated and centrally controlled subway, the first in Korea, was opened in Pyongyang on September 6. A new railroad line between Sinch'on and Ullyul in South Hwanghae Province was opened to traffic on September 30.

KEY P. YANG
Korean Area Specialist, The Library of Congress

Members of the St. Louis (Mo.) Teachers Union picket one of the high schools during a strike that lasted from January 22 to February 18.

LABOR

The U. S. labor movement experienced a relatively quiet year in 1973. Elsewhere, high inflation led to many strikes. This review of major 1973 developments is divided into two sections: (1) U. S. Labor and (2) World Labor. A special report on job dissatisfaction appears on page 331.

U. S. Labor

Perhaps the principal characteristic of labor news in 1973 was the relative quiescence with which workers accepted a limit on the economic gains to be made in collective bargaining contracts—5.5% of direct wages as per the federal Cost of Living Council—while at the same time they saw all or most of these gains washed away in the tides of inflation. Toward the end of the year, after the major contracts had been negotiated and signed, an ominous undertow of frustration appeared to be developing— at least in the rhetoric at the national convention of the American Federation of Labor and the Congress of Industrial Organizations (AFL-CIO). Although the unanimous call at the convention for the resignation of President Nixon was attributed to his handling of the Watergate affair, the rationale of the delegates derived in part from their dissatisfaction with a government that had held down wages while allowing profits and dividends and the cost of living to skyrocket.

The number of employed Americans increased, and the ranks of the unemployed decreased and stabilized at between 4.5% and 4.9% of the work force. About 85% of the increase in employed persons came from new entrants in the job market, and

many of these new entrants were still looking for work. The unemployment rate for veterans of the Vietnam War declined by 1.4% to a figure of 5.1%. The long-range effects of increased automation, an imbalance in world trade, and the gradual change from a product economy to a service economy still have not been alleviated. This, combined with a Consumer Price Index that jumped 7.4% in the year ending Oct. 31, 1972, produced pressures to hold down wages, continued the trend to export not just jobs but also technology to other countries and, ironically, encouraged the beginning of a reverse movement by which foreign money was invested in the United States. Corporate profits continued to grow.

Under Phase 4 of the Nixon economic program, the Cost of Living Council provided general guidelines on both wages and retail price costs, with exceptions being made on an industry-by-industry and to some degree on a company-by-company basis. Food prices at the end of the year stabilized on a plateau considerably higher than at the beginning of the year. The Consumer Price Index for the first three quarters of 1973 was 7.4% higher than in the comparable period of 1972. At the same time, the Gross National Product jumped 8.6% to $1,304 billion. Corporate after-tax earnings were up 32.6%. The purchasing price of the dollar as measured by 1967 standards had dropped to $0.738.

The average first-year wage increase provided by major collective bargaining contracts in the first three quarters of 1973 was 6.0%, down from the average gain of 7.3% in the full year 1972. In the first half of 1973, 18.5 million man-days were lost

AUTO workers form a picket line outside a Chrysler plant in Detroit, Mich., during 9-day strike in September.

UPI

through strikes. During similar periods in 1972 and 1971, respectively, 20.8 and 33.9 million man-days were lost. Most of the strikes were in small units, although public-school teacher strikes—particularly in Detroit—were significant. It appeared that final figures might show that 1973 was the most strike-free year since 1963.

Labor, which had generally taken a neutral stand in the presidential campaign of 1972, once again moved into opposition, prodded not only by inflation and Watergate but also by the administration's reluctance to expend money for programs in the health, education, and welfare fields.

Labor union membership continued to grow at a decreasing rate. Biggest gains were among public employees. The number of union workers engaged in manufacturing actually decreased. Heaviest percentage increases were among teachers, federal government employees, and the state and municipal groups. The American Federation of Teachers and the National Education Association discussed a merger.

COLLECTIVE BARGAINING

Electrical Industry. Based on a change of attitude on the part of the management of General Electric Company and a coordinated bargaining approach on the part of the International Union of Electrical Workers and the 13 other major unions that represented workers in various plants of the General Electric chain, a three-year contract was signed in May. It provided for a base of a 72-cent-an-hour increase over the term of the contract, the continuation of the cost-of-living escalator clause, and improvements in pension and other fringe benefits.

A long climate of bitterness was replaced by a frank, aboveboard, give-and-take approach that even permitted the company to restore the seniority credits of the strikers who had participated in the 101-day walkout of 1969–70. Westinghouse followed with a similar contract.

Trucking. A concern that Teamster President Frank Fitzsimmons might not be able to control his union with the release from prison of former President James R. Hoffa proved to be imaginary as the Teamsters signed their major agreement—the National Master Freight Agreement covering 400,000 truck drivers and 1,200 firms. The contract provided for a 95-cent-an-hour increase over the 33 months of the contract, a cost-of-living escalator clause, and significant increases in pension and health and welfare benefits. Dissident elements in the union that had dumped agreements in earlier years were brought in line, and Fitzsimmons, the leading labor supporter of President Nixon, consolidated his hold on both the office and power of the presidency of the union.

Steel. Perhaps the most significant contract signed was the agreement to provide the mechanism for the resolution of potential disagreement when the master steel contract expires in 1974. Both sides were concerned about the inroads made in the U. S. steel market by foreign steel manufacturers. The union was also critical of management's policy of building stockpiles, which led to a "boom-bust" cycle of heavy production followed by layoffs. The parties agreed that anything not agreed on by the parties—the 10 major steel companies and the United Steel Workers—as a result of 1974 contract negotiations would be submitted to final and binding arbitration with no national strike. In return, the union received a guarantee of at least a 3% annual wage increase in each of the three years of the proposed contract, retention of cost-of-living clauses, a $150 bonus on Aug. 1, 1974, and the right to strike on local issues—subject to a secret ballot and the approval of the national president of the union.

Militant rank-and-file steelworkers called the agreement a "sellout," but by the end of the year it appeared that they reflected the views of only a small minority. In addition, the members of the union were now in the camp of the "haves" as distinguished from the "have-nots," signifying that they had something—homes, cars, vacations—to lose during a long strike.

Railroads. The declining rail industry, which has been the scene of some of the most famous and significant disputes over the years, reached agreement with all but a few of its unions—including all the operating unions—three months before the expiration of the previous contract. The new agreement provided wage increases and shifted part of the employee cost of the pension plans to the employer. As a result of the negotiations Congress passed two laws that complemented the contract provision by shifting the employee contribution that exceeded the social security employee contribution to the employer, liberalized eligibility and increased benefits, and created a labor-management committee to complete the restructuring of the retirement system to bring it into line with the social security program that covers a majority of American workers.

Auto Industry. The automobile workers union, long a leader in innovative, effective collective bargaining, hammered out an agreement with Chrysler that became the pattern for the entire industry. Although a nine-day strike was needed to impress on all parties—management, union, employees, government, and the public—the broad parameters of an acceptable agreement, it was a peaceful strike.

The agreement included wage increases but really focused on other issues of importance to the mem-

bers—pension plans that allowed retirement with full benefits after 30 years of service regardless of age, a company-paid dental plan, and the right of skilled employees to strike over subcontracting. The sticky issue of health and safety in the plant, which is surfacing as a significant issue in all labor-management relations as a result of the Occupational Health and Safety Act of 1970, was resolved with a provision for weekly safety inspections by representatives of labor and management.

Responding to the demands of the rank-and-file workers, the union leadership made "compulsory overtime" the key issue in an industry where management has traditionally retained the right to require overtime. The contract provides that no worker will be required to work more than nine hours in any one day or on Sunday. A worker cannot be required to work three consecutive Saturdays if he has worked the five previous scheduled workdays. The new rules will not be in effect during production starts and production completion periods. The Ford and General Motors contracts follow a similar pattern.

Oil Industry. A significant breakthrough came in this industry where, with one exception, the oil and chemical workers' contracts with the major national oil companies contain a provision for a joint safety and health committee, the hiring of jointly appointed health consultants to explore working conditions at company expense, and the use of the grievance procedure including arbitration to resolve health and safety disputes.

Building Trades. While the local contracts continued to provide wage increases, the national building trades unions were showing increasing concern with the overall outlook for the industry. With new building starts down, greater thought was being given to some reorganization of the bargaining pro-

UPI

MARCHERS support Cesar Chavez (center) and farm workers union in boycott of Los Angeles supermarket.

cedures. To get greater control over locals that were running away with the bargaining process, the per capita tax to support the National Building Trades Department of the AFL-CIO was increased from 4 to 8 cents. It will be used to strengthen local building trades councils, to encourage joint bargaining at the local level, to investigate and provide for the acceptance of new methods of construction and new materials, and to expand organization in nonunion geographical and job areas.

Farm Workers. Perhaps the most important— and certainly the most publicized—labor situation involved the United Farm Workers (UFW), the Teamsters, and the fruit and vegetable industry in California. Led by Cesar Chavez and supported by the AFL-CIO, the auto workers, a variety of religious leaders, and a cross section of political and civic organizations throughout the country, the UFW in the 1960's and 1970's had organized much of the grape and lettuce fields in California. Most of the contracts signed then expired in 1973 and should have been renegotiated. However, the Teamsters, already collective bargaining representatives for the food-processing workers, signed contracts purporting to cover the field workers. Union membership in the UFW quickly dropped from 40,000 to 10,000.

The UFW struck back with nationwide boycotts of Teamster and nonunion lettuce and grapes and picketing of farms. After several abortive attempts, an agreement was reached among George Meany, Chavez, and President Fitzsimmons of the Teamsters. Farm workers were to be in the UFW jurisdiction. However, farm owners who had signed contracts with the Teamsters refused to go along with the agreement, which would force them to abrogate their contracts and to renegotiate new ones. Dissident elements in the Teamsters leadership also resisted the agreement. Fitzsimmons was forced to renege on the agreement, for which Meany vehemently denounced him. At the end of the year the situation was still in flux.

NONFARM PAYROLL EMPLOYMENT IN THE UNITED STATES		
Industry	Annual average 1972	Sept.-October 1973
Total	72,764,000	76,124,000
Mining	607,000	636,000
Contract construction	3,521,000	3,929,000
Manufacturing	18,933,000	20,069,000
Durable goods	10,884,000	11,760,000
Ordnance and accessories	188,200	192,200
Lumber and wood products	612,000	644,100
Furniture and fixtures	492,700	528,300
Stone, clay, and glass products	660,000	701,500
Primary metal industries	1,234,800	1,326,500
Fabricated metal products	1,371,100	1,468,600
Machinery, except electrical	1,864,200	2,072,200
Electrical equipment	1,833,000	2,028,900
Transportation equipment	1,746,800	1,846,000
Instruments and related equipment	455,900	503,900
Miscellaneous manufacturing	425,200	448,100
Nondurable goods	8,049,000	8,309,000
Food and kindred products	1,751,100	1,832,000
Tobacco manufactures	72,000	82,500
Textile mill products	991,000	1,025,500
Apparel and other textile products	1,335,000	1,335,300
Paper and allied products	697,000	720,200
Printing and publishing	1,079,600	1,094,500
Chemicals and allied products	1,002,200	1,033,400
Petroleum and coal products	189,800	193,300
Rubber and plastics products	627,000	694,700
Leather and leather products	304,400	297,000
Transportation and public utilities	4,495,000	4,664,000
Wholesale and retail trade	15,683,000	16,345,000
Wholesale trade	3,918,000	4,123,000
Retail trade	11,765,000	12,222,000
Finance, insurance, and real estate	3,927,000	4,071,000
Services	12,309,000	12,968,000
Government	13,290,000	13,442,000
Federal government	2,650,000	2,608,000
State and local government	10,640,000	10,834,000
Source: Bureau of Labor Statistics, U. S. Department of Labor.		

LEGISLATION AND POLITICS

The labor legislative picture was a mixed bag. Congress amended the Taft-Hartley Act to allow insurance funds to be set up to provide legal services to employees covered by collective bargaining agreements and to allow these funds to be run by a joint employer-employee board of trustees.

Congress passed but President Nixon vetoed a minimum wage bill that would have increased the minimum from $1.60 to $2.00 and $2.20 over two years. The bill would have extended coverage to public-sector employees and to domestic employees and would have permitted employment of full-time students in part-time jobs at a minimum wage below the standard for other workers. In vetoing the bill the President contended that the increase was inflationary. Congress sustained the veto.

Pension reform bills were being considered by Congress. There appears to be general agreement in Congress that such a bill should provide for assured vesting rights after a certain period of employment, portability so that prospective beneficiaries can carry their vested rights from one job to another, and a federally administered insurance program to protect against plans that fail.

The AFL-CIO reversed its historical position and endorsed the Equal Rights Amendment to the Constitution, which is supported by feminist groups. The AFL-CIO amended its own constitution, adding to its antidiscrimination clause a prohibition against discriminating on the basis of sex.

Peter Brennan, a leader of New York City's construction workers, became secretary of labor. Within months, he had lost the support of the AFL-CIO for what President George Meany called his "anti-labor positions" and was not even extended the traditional invitation to address the AFL-CIO's annual convention.

COURT ACTION

In a landmark case, the American Telephone and Telegraph Company agreed out of court to pay cash awards to 13,000 women and 2,000 minority men who had been denied pay and promotion opportunities. The Communications Workers of America, representing a majority of the AT&T's workers, attempted to enjoin the settlement, claiming that it countervened its collective bargaining agreement.

About 15,000 workers between the ages of 40 and 65 were found to be victims of age discrimination by the Department of Labor in fiscal 1973. The Equal Employment Opportunity Commission filed an average of 10 court cases a week in 1973.

Lack of effective enforcement of the Occupational Health and Safety Act of 1970 and limited funding of the administrative process caused much concern—particularly as unions were making safety and health an important part of their bargaining demands. In addition, the unions were unhappy with state laws that had been accepted by the Occupational Safety and Health Administration, and they went to court to enjoin the operation of the South Carolina plan, the first to be accepted by the Federal government. In *Gateway Coal Co.* v. *United Mine Workers,* a circuit court held that union members may refuse to work in a situation where working conditions pose a threat to the health and safety of the workers, but the Supreme Court upset the ruling.

The Supreme Court ruled that the machinists union had violated the National Labor Relations Act by imposing fines on strikebreakers who had resigned from the union before crossing the picket line. The court also found that the National Labor Relations Board had an obligation to determine the reasonableness of fines levied against strikebreakers who did not resign from the union before crossing the lines.

EMPLOYMENT

At the end of October 1973, total employment had increased by 3.3 million persons since December 1972 to a national total of 86 million employed. The number of unemployed dropped to 3.8 million. However, the average number of hours worked regular and overtime were essentially the same as the previous year at 37 and 3.7 hours, respectively, per week. Average hourly earnings in October 1973 were $3.99—25 cents above the October 1972 figure—with adjustment for the rise in the cost of living.

HARVEY L. FRIEDMAN
Director, Labor Relations Research Center
University of Massachusetts

World Labor

Labor wrestled with inflation in all parts of the world during 1973, and this struggle contributed to a surge of strikes in many lands. The economic woes were compounded in many countries by the Arab oil squeeze, imposed in October, which led to industry cutbacks, layoffs of workers, and a threat of recession.

Canada. Labor unrest swept many industries and some government services as unions sought to keep wages ahead of prices. A series of regional strikes on the railroads was climaxed by a 10-day national strike that was ended in early September under an emergency law passed by Parliament. The law provided for wage increases averaging 9.6% for 1973, phased raises totaling 8% for 1974, some fringe benefits, and arbitration of remaining differences.

Generally, union-negotiated wage increases in Canada averaged 8% to 9%, slightly less than the rise in the consumer price index. Unemployment declined to 5.2% at midyear, then rose toward 6% in the last half. The labor force grew, and total employment mounted 5% above 1972 levels.

A nationalist trend among organized workers continued. Some additional locals of international unions—those based in the United States—broke away and joined strictly Canadian unions. The Canadian Labour Congress, in which international unions make up the bulk of the membership, launched a drive against the secession trend.

Japan. Industrial turmoil, record wage increases, and escalating prices plagued the Japanese economy. In the annual "shunto," or spring wage offensive, unions won average pay increases of 20% in the private sector, the highest in recent years. In public-sector enterprises, pay raises averaged 17% to 18%. Consumer prices rose nearly 15% above 1972.

Major strikes and other protest actions occurred on the National Railways and other public-sector enterprises. The Railway Workers Union and the Locomotive Engineers staged slowdowns in April, disrupting passenger train schedules. Commuters, angered by delays on April 24, smashed facilities at stations in the Tokyo area, hurled flares, and caused other damage. The unions then shifted to an all-out stoppage, even though strikes are illegal in
(Continued on page 332)

'Lordstown Syndrome'

Dissatisfaction Among Workers Causes Concern

Does assembly-line work, conceded to be the most efficient system of production, result in worker boredom, alienation, or dissatisfaction?

The feelings of American workers about their jobs, as well as the reactions of government, management, unions, and social scientists to this issue, stirred much debate in 1972 and 1973. Strikes at the Lordstown and Norwood, Ohio, plants of the General Motors Corporation were analyzed by sociologists, economists, labor leaders, and managerial personnel. A U. S. Senate subcommittee headed by Sen. Edward M. Kennedy (D-Mass.) conducted hearings. *Work in America,* an important study by the U. S. Department of Health, Education, and Welfare, was published in 1973. The "work ethic" was analyzed, attacked, defended, and explained.

The basic questions were these: Are workers—in both blue- and white-collar jobs—becoming more unhappy with their normal work and, if that is true, what are the causes and results of their boredom, alienation, or dissatisfaction? Job satisfaction was being linked with productivity at a time when the rate of growth of the U. S. standard of living was slowing and when the U. S. economic standing was under pressure throughout the world.

Union leaders, led by William Winpisinger, the general vice president of the International Association of Machinists, contended that what passed for job dissatisfaction—the so-called Lordstown syndrome—was not new, could be resolved by increasing job security and pay through traditional collective bargaining procedures, and was at most limited to special work situations and special circumstances. Other labor leaders felt that the problem could be alleviated by reducing the work week and developing areas of outside activity. Labor leadership appeared to be concerned that a broader approach might be reminiscent of the human relations and automation theories applied by industrial engineers of earlier decades.

In general, management was not much more sympathetic to the job alienation theory. Its contention was that the workers were generally satisfied, that the assembly line and the compartmentalized assignments of white-collar workers constituted the most efficient system of production, and that too much was being made of a minor problem that management itself could handle without help.

Thus, spokesmen for management and labor, as well as some intellectuals, attacked the academic critics of the work system as "soft-headed, impractical idealists" who did not understand how the system functioned. Meanwhile, however, both management and labor were taking the problem seriously enough to explore new approaches.

Labor rather tentatively strove to improve communication with its members, while at the same time developing a philosophy of "democratizing the work place." In addition, certain limited experimental programs were proposed, based either on the collective bargaining agreement or on direct input from labor union staffs.

Management's response was varied. In some situations it sought to head off union pressure and reduce personnel turnover through limited extension of already existing practices, such as profit-sharing or the 4-day, 40-hour work week. In other instances, it investigated European methods of participative management and the so-called flex-i-time approach. It also set up experiments (almost always in nonunion plants) in job redesign and job enrichment that included the combining of jobs, multiple task force assignment, the improvement of physical surroundings, and the introduction of in-service training programs and job rotation.

Such approaches (dubbed "scientific management") fed the fears of trade unions, because much of what management undertook to do in this area was done unilaterally. It hardly escaped labor's attention that such incentives often went hand in hand with management opposition to the effective operation of the Occupational Safety and Health Act of 1970.

What of the future? On the governmental front, the Worker Alienation Research and Technical Assistance Bill, which would authorize the government to study the total extent of job dissatisfaction, has been introduced as a result of the Kennedy committee's hearings. On the industrial front, a step toward nonmandatory overtime was taken in the agreement that ended the United Auto Workers' brief strike against Chrysler in September 1973, and it seems likely that other contract negotiations may produce limited solutions acceptable to management, labor, consumers, and the government.

HARVEY L. FRIEDMAN

331

(Continued from page 330)

government-owned enterprises. The strike ended after 48 hours with a settlement calling for wage increases of about 17% and a government promise to weigh the unions' long demand for reinstatement of the legal right to strike. Another brief rail strike occurred in December.

Meanwhile, the five-day work week made headway. Unions in the textile industry negotiated an agreement calling for two Saturdays off a month in 1974, all Saturdays off in 1975. As prices rose, unions asked for larger than usual year-end bonuses and for "inflation allowances." At the same time, the Japanese economy, heavily dependent on fuel imports, reeled under Arab oil cutbacks, and the country's 10% annual growth rate fell sharply.

Western Europe. Consumer prices rose by 7% to 15%. Unions strove to win more than compensatory wage increases, striking in many industries.

In Britain, the economy boomed early in the year, pushing real growth to 5% and reducing unemployment to 2.2% of the work force, lowest since 1970. The government imposed a freeze and then wage-price controls. Many unions settled within the guidelines (roughly 8%), but others staged strikes or slowdowns as living costs advanced by nearly 9%. Late in the year the economy was jolted by shortened work weeks and other drastic government restrictions imposed as a result of the fuel shortage, plus union slowdowns during wage disputes in coal mines, power plants, and railways.

In West Germany, many wildcat strikes occurred as inflation spiraled, offsetting 8% to 9% wage increases negotiated by unions. Late in 1973 the government instituted restrictive monetary measures to check inflation. The jobless rate fell to 1%, and the economic growth rate was more than 6%, but fuel cutbacks disrupted industry near the end of the year.

In France, "L'Affaire Lip" involved the seizure and operation by employees of the Lip Watch factory at Besançon, after the owners declared bankruptcy and sought to close the plant. The seizure attracted sympathy and led to government intervention to keep the factory going. Meanwhile, France had an economic boom, many strikes, and an 8% inflationary rate.

In Italy, the "L'Affair Lip" example inspired some plant seizures by workers, which were curbed by government intervention. Chronic strikes that had pockmarked Italy's economy in the past few years continued in 1973. Three-year contracts were negotiated by unions for millions of workers in automotive, metal, chemical, printing, and other industries, mostly without strikes.

Latin America. In 1973, as in 1972, inflation engulfed most Latin American lands. Unions, where they functioned freely, fought to keep wages ahead of prices. In nations ruled by military juntas, wages were occasionally increased to appease labor.

In Chile, strife and economic chaos were widespread. Under Marxist President Salvador Allende, prices tripled in the year that preceded the military coup that overthrew his regime in September and cost Allende his life. Allende had retained his support from labor and the poor by subsidies to restrain food prices, by decreeing large wage increases, and other moves toward income redistribution. However, small businessmen, professionals, and others in the middle class hurt by Allende's policies fought back with strikes and demonstrations. A prolonged strike by 40,000 independent truck owners,

called mainly to resist a threatened government takeover of trucking, was a major factor in precipitating the coup.

The junta eliminated most Allende subsidies and devalued the escudo, causing prices to soar still more. Wage increases authorized by the junta failed to match price escalation. The Central Workers' Confederation, an Allende ally, was outlawed.

In Argentina, most of the labor movement supported the return of Juan Perón to power, but splits among labor's left and right wings continued. A series of assassinations occurred, mostly of right-wing union leaders, including the head of the General Confederation of Labor. At midyear, as the inflation rate passed 70%, the Labor Confederation and a pro-industry federation, under government prodding, negotiated a two-year no-strike, no-lockout agreement, with moderate wage increases linked to government assurance of price controls.

In Mexico, inflation was moderate, with the consumer price index rising less than 15%, but this was enough to provoke a wave of strikes. In September, national labor and management federations agreed on basic wage increases of 20%; many plants refused to go along and were struck. The Mexican Labor Confederation pressed for the five-day, 40-hour week, and won it in some major industries.

In Bolivia, labor struck for 48 hours in September in protest against the arrest of 89 union leaders accused of a Marxist plot against the military government.

Brazil was a bright spot, with an inflation rate of 12%, down from 15.7% in 1972 and from 100% in the 1960's, and with an economic growth rate of 9%.

RUBEN LEVIN, *Editor, "Labor" Newspaper*

LAOS

Nearly two decades of almost continuous civil warfare, increasingly internationalized through the years, came to an end for much-bombed Laos in early 1973. Agreement to set up a coalition regime of conservatives and Communists was reached in September, the third attempt at such political cooperation in 20 years. But a new government had yet to be formed by the year's end, even though the anti-Communists' longtime ally, the United States, had militarily disengaged itself from the once "secret war" in Laos.

War's End. A cease-fire ending the war between Premier Souvanna Phouma's government and Communist Pathet Lao forces was reached on February 21, following stepped-up American bombing of Communist positions and supply lines. U. S. B-52 bombers initially ended their air assault against the Communists less than a day after the cease-fire truce but returned to the skies, albeit only temporarily, in April in response to what Washington called a "major violation of the cease-fire." Fighting subsequently fell to a very low level, with only minor incidents reported late in the year.

The cease-fire left the Communists in control of four fifths of the country, excluding the administrative and royal capitals of Vientiane and Luang Prabang. Two thirds of the country's 3 million-plus population live in the cities and adjacent areas controlled by the government.

When the fighting ended in February, a month after the January agreement terminating direct U. S. participation in the war in adjacent Vietnam, there were 40,000–70,000 North Vietnamese troops in the

country (the higher figure being a U. S. intelligence estimate). Joined with these forces, most of whom manned the Ho Chi Minh Trail, were approximately 30,000 Pathet Lao troops. Government forces numbered about 50,000.

Subsequent Settlement. Critics of the February cease-fire agreement described the pact as a victory for the Communists, largely because it left the Pathet Lao in control of 80% of the National territory. The subsequent political settlement, signed in September after months of difficult negotiations, seemed to favor the government, however. Prince Souvanna Phouma would remain as premier, with various ministerial portfolios equally divided between the two sides. The non-Communists were given the ministries of defense, interior, finance, education, and health, while the Pathet Lao portfolios included foreign affairs, information, economics and planning, public works, and religion.

The "national union" government, agreed upon in September, represented the third attempt since 1954 to set up a coalition regime to rule the Laotian kingdom. Similar pacts, which created union administrations in 1957 and 1962, broke down in succeeding years, partly because of American support of conservative efforts to undercut cooperation between non-Communists and Communists.

The September pact provided for all foreign forces to leave the country within 60 days—including 200 U. S. military experts and advisers and 15,000–20,000 American-financed "volunteers" from neighboring Thailand. The Pathet Lao promised that North Vietnamese troops would quit the country altogether, but Laotian critics—and some American officials—expressed their doubts.

Politics. Far-right Laotian opponents of the Pathet Lao, including many military leaders, opposed both the February and September agreements. Exiled generals, living across the Mekong River in Thailand, attempted a coup in August to block establishment of a union government. The action failed because of top army (and strong American) support of Premier Souvanna Phouma. Coup leader Gen. Thao Ma lost his life in the attempt. Several other plotters later were executed by the army.

U. S. Role. The American military role increased dramatically in the first week of the year. (Further details of past secret aspects of this role

PRINCE Souvanna Phouma heads a new coalition government formed in 1973, the third in recent history.

were revealed in testimony before the Senate Armed Services Committee in 1973.) The January agreement on Vietnam was followed by an intensification of the U. S. air war over Laos. It was designed to force the Communists to agree to a cease-fire. U. S. foreign policy adviser Henry Kissinger visited Laos in February for the same purpose.

Having advocated such a settlement, the United States subsequently sought to effect a rapid, and silent, military departure from Laos. B-52 bombing resumed briefly in April, ostensibly to bolster the settlement, but the U. S. withdrawal continued nonetheless. The American military presence was cut back to "fewer than 50" attachés. American military aid was kept to the congressionally mandated ceiling of $375 million.

Economy. The end of the Laotian war had two effects on the country's economy. It punctured the prosperity that had been based on heavy American spending. That spending, of course, declined as the United States cut back its operations in Laos. However, it also fed the hope that the political agreement would be followed by substantial increases in agricultural output.

Coffee and timber did register modest production gains—as did tin, among minerals. Domestic food production continued to fall short of consumption, and many food items (including rice) had to be imported, as well as most manufactures.

Foreign Policy. Renewed "neutralism" was the avowed foreign policy aim of the proclaimed coalition government. There was evidence, however, that both North Vietnam and Thailand might not yet be willing to discontinue all of their interventionist activities. China, meanwhile, continued its road-building in de facto occupied northern Laos, branches of which went to the Thai and North Vietnamese borders.

RICHARD BUTWELL
State University of New York at Brockport

─────── **LAOS • Information Highlights** ───────

Official Name: Kingdom of Laos.
Location: Southeast Asia.
Area: 91,429 square miles (236,800 sq km).
Population (1973 est.): 3,200,000. *Density,* 34 per square mile (13 per sq km).
Chief Cities (1970 est.): Vientiane, the capital, 150,000; Luang Prabang, the royal capital, 25,000.
Government: *Head of state,* Savang Vatthana, king (acceded Nov. 1959). *Head of government,* Prince Souvanna Phouma, premier (took office June 1962). *Legislature* (unicameral)—National Assembly.
Languages: Lao (official), French.
Education: *Expenditure* (1969), 10.7% of total public expenditure. *School enrollment* (1969)—primary, 216,577; secondary, 13,105; technical/vocational, 1,625; university/higher, 559.
Monetary Unit: Kip (600 kips equal U. S.$1, Aug. 1973).
Gross National Product (1971 est.): $198,000,000.
Consumer Price Index (1972), 378 (1963=100).
Manufacturing (major products): Cigarettes, textiles.
Major Agricultural Products: Rice, corn, coffee, cotton, tobacco, cardamon, vegetables, forest products.
Major Minerals: Tin, iron ore.
Foreign Trade (1970): *Exports,* $7,000,000; *Imports,* $114,000,000. *Chief trading partners*—United States, Japan, Thailand.
Transportation: *Motor vehicles* (1971), 14,100 (automobiles, 12,100); *major national airline,* Royal Air Lao.
Communications: *Telephones* (1972), 1,936; *newspapers* (1967), 7 (daily circulation, 8,000).

In Santiago, Chile, army troops surround the Presidential Palace in September coup that overthrew the Marxist government of President Allende.

LATIN AMERICA

Military coups in Chile and Uruguay and the return to power of Juan Perón in Argentina highlighted events in Latin America in 1973. Elected president by a coalition of conservatives and social revolutionaries, Perón, a pro-fascist in the World War II era, swung again to the right upon taking office. In neighboring Chile and Uruguay the reaction against the left was more pronounced, as authoritarian governments ended two of Latin America's longest experiences with democratic rule.

In the long run, however, these political changes may prove less significant than another 1973 event: the adherence of oil-rich Venezuela to the Andean Pact. This cleared the way for the creation of an economic community with a population and income second only to those of Brazil in Latin America, and with unmatched natural resources, including more than half of the region's known oil reserves.

The Common Markets. With the admission of Venezuela in February 1973 the Andean Group (Bolivia, Chile, Peru, Ecuador, Colombia) grew to include six nations encompassing a total of 2 million square miles (over 5 million sq km), inhabited by 70 million people with a total income of $33 billion. Venezuela's large foreign-exchange reserves were seen as a prime source of capital for future subregional development. Outside interest in the Group increased in 1973 as Mexico, admitted to associate membership in January, pledged $6 million to the Andean Development Corporation, the Group's leading institution.

In August 1973, representatives of four of the five original members of the Central American Common Market (CACM) met in Guatemala City and pledged renewed efforts to make CACM an effective mechanism for the social and economic development of the subregion. Honduras remained outside the group, although it began negotiating a treaty with El Salvador to settle the border dispute that had prompted Honduras to withdraw from CACM in 1970.

In the West Indies, CARIFTA, the Caribbean Free Trade Association, was transformed into CARICOM, the Caribbean Common Market.

Development Loans. United States aid for Latin American economic and social development continued to be channeled through such multinational institutions as the World Bank and the Inter-American Development Bank (IADB), over which Washington had a veto power. Early in 1973, John M. Porges replaced Henry J. Constanzo as the U. S. executive director of the IADB, and a change in bank policy was soon evident. Peru, which previously had been denied aid because of its "unfair" seizure of American property, received loans totaling more than $12 million from the IADB in 1973, for health and agricultural purposes. The World Bank also lent Peru money in 1973 for agricultural and educational development.

The volume of IADB lending to Latin America as a whole increased in 1973 as the bank aimed at an annual level of $1 billion over the next five years, compared with the $600–800 million level of 1970–72. The IADB was already the largest lender to Latin America and was given some credit for the region's annual economic growth rate of about 6%.

Panama Canal Controversy. Latin America briefly occupied the center of the world stage in

March 1973 as the UN Security Council met in Panama on the invitation of Panamanian strongman Oscar Torrijos Herrera. The Panamanian setting was ideal for the expression of anti-imperialist and anti-American sentiment. The Security Council obliged Torrijos by voting 13 to 1 for a resolution calling on the United States to relinquish to Panama sovereignty over the Panama Canal. The United States killed the resolution, exercising its veto power for the third time in UN history. U. S. Ambassador to the UN John Scali conceded that some modification was necessary in the treaty that gave the U. S. control "in perpetuity" over the Canal Zone, but insisted that this was a matter to be worked out between the two countries without UN interference.

The United States, Cuba, and the OAS. Although Castro continued to denounce the United States as the principal oppressor of the Third World, his government concluded an agreement with Washington in February to combat airline hijackings.

The question of readmitting Cuba to the Organization of American States (OAS) came up at the OAS general assembly in Washington in April. Proponents of Cuba's readmission, lacking the votes to pass a resolution inviting the Communist island to return to the fold (an invitation which the Castro government indicated it would refuse if offered), worked successfully for adoption of a declaration opening the OAS to "a plurality of ideologies." Acceptance of this principle, it was felt, cleared the way for Cuba's re-entry at a future date. That time seemed much closer in May when a Peronist government came to power in Argentina and promptly established diplomatic relations with Havana.

While the U. S. continued to insist on the exclusion of Cuba and the maintenance of the official OAS embargo on trade with the island, now honored mostly in the breach, there were indications that a reassessment of U. S. policy toward Cuba and toward Latin America in general was under way. Charles A. Meyer, the former Sears, Roebuck executive who had served the Nixon administration since 1969 as assistant secretary of state for Latin American affairs, resigned in January and was replaced by a career diplomat, Jack B. Kubish. At the OAS general assembly the United States supported the creation of a high-level commission to study the organization's operations and structure and make recommendations for charter revision, to be acted upon at the next general assembly in April 1974.

In May 1973, Secretary of State William Rogers made a 17-day swing through eight Latin American nations and the United States ended its aid boycott of Peru. Rogers' successor as secretary of state, Henry Kissinger, indicated at his confirmation hearings in September that he planned consultations with Washington's "friends in Latin America" which might lead to a change in U. S. policy toward Cuba. However, the subsequent elimination of Chile's socialist government, Castro's staunchest supporter in Latin America, eased pressure on the United States for modification of its Cuban policy. At year's end there was no noticeable movement toward a U. S.-Cuban rapprochement.

Military Sales. In June the United States announced that it was willing to sell F-5E jet fighters to Argentina, Brazil, Colombia, Venezuela, and Chile. The U. S. balance of payments problem was cited as a reason for this lifting of the ban on the sale of supersonic warplanes to Latin American countries. It was pointed out that if the United

States continued the ban, the Latin Americans would take their business to European suppliers, as Brazil had done in 1972 when it purchased 16 Mirage fighters from France. Immediately after the U. S. announcement, Brazil placed an order with the Northrop Corporation for 48 F-5E's.

In Chile, where the armed forces traditionally maintained cordial relations with the U. S. military, the USSR was tempting the air force with offers of MIG-21 fighters. By making F-5E's available to Chile, the United States helped prevent Soviet penetration of the Chilean armed forces.

The Coup in Chile. On Sept. 11, 1973, the Chilean military moved to overthrow the three-year-old government of President Salvador Allende Gossens. Political and economic crises preceded the coup. While other Latin American countries were maintaining at least modest growth rates, the Chilean economy was stagnating. Production of copper, the mainstay of Chile's export economy, fell substantially after the 1971 nationalization of the mines, and agricultural production was disrupted by government attempts at agrarian reform and by unauthorized seizures of land by peasant groups. By mid-1973 practically all of Chile's foreign-exchange reserves had been spent on food imports, which were running about 300% above the pre-Allende level. The rate of inflation exceeded 300% a year.

Rationing and a system of government food-distribution centers protected slum dwellers from the worst effects of the inflation, but there was little protection for the middle classes. Their standard of living steadily eroding, threatened with the nationalization of their businesses and professions, the Chilean bourgeoisie went on strike and took to the streets in protest demonstrations. A strike of 40,000 truck owner-drivers, the second in less than a year, was supported by sympathy closings of shops and professional offices. By early September the nation was paralyzed.

The Chilean military coup of September 1973 was one of the bloodiest in recent Latin American history. The rebel command, headed by Gen. Augusto Pinochet Ugarte, was determined not only to break the political and economic deadlock but to extirpate Marxism from Chile. President Allende died, perhaps by his own hand, during an army and air force assault on the presidential palace. Scores of the late president's supporters, especially in the slums around Santiago, were summarily executed by Pinochet's troops.

With the military firmly in control of Chile, Pinochet was sworn in as president, Congress was dissolved, political parties were "suspended," Marxist organizations were outlawed, press censorship was imposed, and homes were ransacked for "subversive" literature, which soldiers burned in the streets. The new regime severed diplomatic relations with Cuba and began talks with U. S. officials about compensation for U. S. property seized under Allende and about ways to attract foreign investment back to Chile. While many Latin American governments expressed shock and dismay at the coup and the death of Allende, the rulers of Brazil were delighted by the turn of events in Chile.

Military Control in Uruguay. Earlier in the year Brazil had assisted in the establishment of what was virtually a military dictatorship in Uruguay. The Uruguayan armed forces, given a free rein by President Juan María Bordaberry to destroy the Tupamaro guerrillas in 1972, completed the task

and found themselves with a new sense of importance and little to do in 1973. By June, military power had so far surpassed that of traditional democratic forces in government that Bordaberry felt compelled to dissolve Congress, impose censorship, and outlaw the country's chief labor organization to prevent his own ouster. These measures provoked a general strike, which government forces broke within a week with the help of 300 truckloads of supplies from Brazil and an emergency loan of $30 million from the Brazilian government.

After mid-1973, Bordaberry was little more than the servant of the Uruguayan military, faithfully approving the decree-laws they handed him. In November the last center of open opposition to the dictatorship was eliminated as troops occupied the hitherto inviolable National University and arrested leftist student leaders and faculty.

The Brazilian Regime. Uruguay's new, army-dominated government seemed hardly more than a reflection of that of its giant neighbor, Brazil. The military coterie that had ruled Brazil since 1964 showed no signs of losing its grip in 1973. Seeing no need for a civilian front man in the presidency, the military selected a four-star general, the fourth in a row since the 1964 coup, for the next presidential term. Gen. Ernesto Geisel was scheduled to succeed incumbent President Emílio Garrastazú Médici in 1974 after an official ballot in the rubber-stamp Electoral College. Geisel promised to continue the economic and social policies of his predecessors, which had produced an economic growth rate of nearly 12% a year and a drastic curtailment of political freedom.

Opponents of the regime charged that it ignored the needs of the poor, put money only in the pockets of the rich, tortured political prisoners, and trampled on basic human rights. These sentiments were forcefully expressed in May 1973 in a 30-page document issued by the Roman Catholic bishops of some of the country's poorest dioceses. With the press rigorously censored, the pulpit served as the principal forum for the expression of dissenting views in Brazil. The government suppressed publication of the bishops' manifesto, but otherwise ignored the protests from the Church.

In the meantime, the boom continued. Strong gains were made in industrial production and in commercial agriculture, with Brazil surpassing Cuba to become Latin America's and the world's leading producer of sugar. At the end of 1973, however, the world energy crunch was giving Brazilian technocrats cause for concern, for their country was relatively poor in both petroleum and coal. (See feature article on Brazil, page 46.)

Problems for Mexico. Mexico, traditionally an exporter of petroleum, found its oil wells running dry in 1973 and hard pressed to produce enough fuel for its own expanding industry. During the year the Mexican economy as a whole sustained its steady growth, at about half Brazil's rate.

Socially and politically, Mexico's authoritarian one-party regime faced problems in 1973 similar to those of Brazil's military dictatorship. An expanding economy was generating visible wealth for a few and raising the expectations of the masses, who remained, for the most part, mired in poverty. Most Mexican families had incomes below $100 a month, and more than a third of Mexico's working-age population was unemployed. The pressure for radical changes was greater in Mexico than in Brazil (where

the condition of the lower class was even worse) because of the close contact between Mexicans , of every class and the super-rich society of the United States, and because of the uncensored Mexican press, which has been relatively free to point out inequities. During 1973 some Mexican newspapers went further and broke an unwritten rule of self-regulation by giving prominence to stories about social and political unrest in the country.

Peronist Argentina. In Argentina, whose citizens enjoy a high per capita income by Latin American standards, President Juan Perón was saying that the country's main problems were political, not economic. Good weather boosted the 1973 grain harvest by about 25% over the previous year, and comparable gains were registered in beef production, at a time when export prices for Argentine foodstuffs were soaring. But the rosy economic picture was clouded by a recurrence of political violence.

Early in 1973 the violence of recent years subsided as Argentines looked forward to the presidential elections of March 11. The armed forces, which had misgoverned the country for 17 years, promised to surrender power to the winner at the polls, although they refused to permit the candidacy of the 77-year-old Perón, then in exile in Spain. Héctor J. Cámpora, a stand-in for Perón, won the election, was inaugurated president in May, welcomed "the Old Man" (*"El Viejo"*) home from Spain in June, and resigned in July. In September new elections were held, which Perón won with 61.5% of the vote.

Perón's return to Argentina, however, was marred by a bloody gun battle between rival groups of his supporters. Two days after Perón's election as president, José Rucci, chief of the powerful Peronist labor movement and a close friend of the former dictator, was assassinated by leftist guerrillas. Perón then virtually declared war on Argentina's leftists, including those who claimed to be Peronists, while insisting that his government was still staunchly anti-imperialist. Backing off from their confrontation with the still-popular Perón, Argentine urban guerrillas concentrated their fire on foreign businesses and businessmen, especially Americans. At year's end the foreign community in Argentina was terrorized by a wave of bombings, kidnappings, and murders, which the government deplored but seemed powerless to stop.

Other Developments. There were significant, if less spectacular, political developments in other Latin American countries. Bolivian strongman Hugo Banzer Suárez, under pressure from both left and right, promised presidential elections in 1974, which the army later forced him to reschedule for 1975. In Ecuador the military government of President Guillermo Rodríguez Lara faced labor unrest and demonstrations by students demanding a return to constitutional rule. Paraguay's dictator since 1954, Alfredo Stroessner, was "reelected."

In December, Venezuela held presidential elections. Two center candidates monopolized more than 85% of the vote, with Carlos Andrés Pérez, of the opposition Democratic Action party, clearly defeating his principal rival, Lorenzo Fernández, the candidate of outgoing President Rafael Caldera's Christian Social party.

NEILL MACAULAY
University of Florida

LATIN AMERICAN LITERATURE. See LITERATURE.

Law

Daniel Ellsberg and his wife, Patricia (right), leave the Los Angeles federal building after the dismissal on May 11 of the Pentagon Papers case.

UPI

Major developments of 1973 in the chief areas of law, in the United States and among nations, are surveyed under the headings (1) U.S. Supreme Court; (2) U.S. Legislation and Case Law; and (3) International Law.

Other legal developments are reviewed in the special feature on Watergate (beginning on page 14); CENSORSHIP; CIVIL LIBERTIES AND CIVIL RIGHTS; CRIME; DISARMAMENT; POLICE; PRISONS; and United Nations.

U. S. Supreme Court

The 1972–73 term of the U.S. Supreme Court, the first in which the four appointees of President Nixon served for the full term, saw the court continue its movement away from the liberal doctrines of the Warren Court. The trend was particularly marked in decisions on obscenity, criminal law, and legislative reapportionment issues. On the other hand, the court outraged conservative views by striking down state laws against abortion; it blocked Nixon administration policy by a strong stand against public aid to parochial schools; and it generally supported efforts to protect the environment.

The four Nixon appointees—Chief Justice Warren E. Burger and Justices Harry A. Blackmun, Lewis F. Powell, Jr., and William H. Rehnquist—generally voted together, as did the liberal trio of William O. Douglas, William J. Brennan, and Thurgood Marshall. Thus White and Stewart were the swing men, the Burger bloc needing the vote of only one of them to control the court. It was White, more often than Stewart, who supplied this vote.

A Gallup poll taken after the term was over gave the Burger Court an overall favorable rating of 37%, compared with a 33% rating for the Warren Court in 1969. This poll showed that 46% of respondents wanted new Supreme Court appointees to be conservatives, 30% would prefer liberals, and 24% had no opinion.

The court handed down 140 signed opinions, of which only 34 (24%) were unanimous. In the preceding term the output was 129 signed opinions, 42 (32%) of which were unanimous. The court also issued 33 per curiam opinions, 16 of them unanimous. Including both signed and per curiam opinions, Douglas was the leading dissenter with 82, followed by Brennan with 56, Marshall 53, Stewart 42, Rehnquist 39, Burger 21, White 20, Blackmun 15, and Powell 14.

There were 31 5-to-4 decisions, in 21 of which all three liberals were in dissent. Stewart was the fourth justice joining them in 16 dissents, while Powell and White each voted with them twice and Blackmun once. The chief justice was on the losing side in six 5-to-4 decisions, but only once were the four Nixon appointees joined in dissent.

A stir occurred during the term when a committee of lawyers and law school professors, appointed by Burger, issued a report declaring the court overworked. It proposed that the justices' function of deciding which cases to accept for review be delegated to a new national court of appeals, composed of federal court of appeals judges on a rotating basis. This controversial suggestion was defended by the chief justice, but attacked by former Chief Justice Earl Warren and Justice Douglas.

ABORTION

In its most surprising action the court held unconstitutional (7–2) the criminal abortion laws of Texas and Georgia, and announced guidelines strictly limiting the power of the states to regulate abortion. Blackmun, relying on the constitutional right to privacy, held that during the first three months of pregnancy, decisions on abortion must be left entirely to the woman and her physician. During the second trimester the state can set standards for the conditions under which abortions are performed in order to preserve the health of the mother or the potential life of the unborn infant. In the third trimester the state, to safeguard the unborn infant, can ban all abortions except those to save the mother's life. The court declined to find that the word "person" in the Constitution includes unborn children. White and Rehnquist dissented in the cases *Roe* v. *Wade* and *Doe* v. *Bolton*.

OBSCENITY

The court, 5-to-4, with White joining the Nixon four, revised the Warren Court's obscenity rulings and opened the way for considerable limitation on distribution of sexually oriented materials (*Miller* v. *California, Paris Adult Theater* v. *Slaton, Kaplan* v. *California*). The previous rule was that matter appealing to prurient interest was obscene only if utterly without redeeming social value. The new rule permits finding of obscenity if the material lacks serious literary, artistic, political, or scientific value. Also, the offensiveness of the matter can be judged

against local, not national, community standards. Whereas the Warren Court had been concerned mainly with protecting juveniles and unwilling adults from forced exposure to obscene materials, Burger ruled that adult book stores and theaters from which juveniles are excluded, and against which adults who would be offended are warned, were not exempt from state regulation.

ELECTIONS

In *Mahan* v. *Howell,* the court challenged the strict "one person, one vote" requirement for election districts, and over the three liberals' protests, accepted population deviations as high as 16% in redistricting the Virginia legislature. The new rule, that integrity of local government boundaries justifies greater flexibility in state legislative apportionments than in congressional districting, was also applied in cases from Connecticut and Texas. But multi-member districts for state legislatures were held racially discriminatory (*Georgia* v. *United States, White* v. *Regester*).

In another assault on "one person, one vote," the court upheld (6–3) a plan for electing a waterstorage district's board of directors that limited the right to vote to landowners in the district and weighted their votes according to the assessed valuation of their land (*Salyer Land Company* v. *Tulare Water District*).

FIRST AMENDMENT

The federal Hatch Act prohibiting partisan political activity by federal employees, and a similar Oklahoma statute, were upheld by votes of 6-to-3 and 5-to-4 against charges that they restrained the free speech rights of public employees (*U. S. Civil Service Commission* v. *National Association of Letter Carriers, Broadrick* v. *Oklahoma*).

In *Columbia Broadcasting System, Inc.* v. *Democratic National Committee,* the court agreed (7–2) with the Federal Communications Commission that broadcasters are not required to sell advertising time to groups wishing to publicize their views on public issues. The FCC fairness doctrine, upheld by the court in 1969, requires broadcasters to provide full and fair coverage of public issues. But licensees are not "common carriers," the court said, and they retain discretion to decide what public-issue advertising they will accept.

RELIGIOUS ESTABLISHMENT

President Nixon in his 1974 budget had provided a tax credit for parents who paid tuition to send their children to parochial or other nonpublic schools. But the court in three decisions involving New York and Pennsylvania laws (*Committee for Public Education and Religious Liberty* v. *Nuquist, Levitt* v. *Committee,* and *Sloan* v. *Lemon*) appeared to hold all such aid plans unconstitutional. Burger, White, and Rehnquist dissented.

EQUAL PROTECTION

Several courts, including the California supreme court, had recently held that financing public schools by local property taxation is unconstitutional because it results in grossly unequal support for education in different areas. The U. S. Supreme Court, in *San Antonio Independent School District* v. *Rodriguez,* refused (5–4) to adopt this position. The majority held that education was not a right guaranteed by the Constitution, and that property tax financing did not disadvantage an identifiable class of poor persons. The minority, with White joining the liberals, saw the decision as "a retreat from our historic commitment to equality of educational opportunity."

There were two important school segregation cases. In 1972 a federal judge had issued an unprecedented order directing the merger of the predominantly black Richmond, Va., schools with the largely white county system. This order was reversed by the federal court of appeals. The Supreme Court (with Powell, a native of Richmond, not participating) divided 4-to-4, leaving the ban on the merger in effect (*School Board of Richmond* v. *State Board of Education of Virginia*).

The court's first Northern school desegregation case, coming from Denver, raised the issue of "de facto" segregation, as opposed to "de jure" (required by law). Holding that deliberate segregation of any school would make the entire system suspect, the court returned the case (7–1) to the district court (*Keyes* v. *Denver School District No. 1*).

Norwood v. *Harrison* held unanimously that Mississippi may not provide textbooks at public expense for "white" academies set up to avoid integration.

The court was unanimous in three other racial discrimination cases. White tenants in an apartment complex that discriminated against nonwhites were held to have standing under the 1968 Civil Rights Act to file suit challenging the discriminatory practices (*Trafficante* v. *Metropolitan Life Insurance Co.*). A swimming pool association with a discriminatory policy was held not to be a private club, and so in violation of federal civil rights acts (*Tillman* v. *Wheaton-Haven Recreation Assn., Inc.*). And *Ham* v. *South Carolina* ruled that black defendants had a constitutional right to query prospective jurors about prejudice against Negroes.

On the women's liberation front, *Frontiero* v. *Richardson* invalidated (8–1) statutes discriminating against female members of the armed forces in standards for determining dependency of spouses, while in a case involving both sex discrimination and freedom of the press the court upheld (5–4) a municipal ordinance forbidding newspapers to carry job ads designated by sex (*Pittsburgh Press Co.* v. *Pittsburgh Commission on Human Relations*).

A state cannot deny admission to the bar solely because the applicant is an alien (*In re Griffiths*), nor can a state exclude all aliens from permanent civil service jobs (*Sugarman* v. *Dougall*).

WELFARE AND POVERTY LAW

In 1971 the court had ruled that persons unable to pay court costs could not be denied access to the divorce courts. But in *United States* v. *Kras,* the court held (5–4) that the filing fee cannot be waived for indigents seeking to file for bankruptcy. Stewart, dissenting, protested the view that "some of the poor are too poor even to go bankrupt."

The court upheld (7–2) a state law requiring able-bodied welfare recipients to seek work or be put on public works projects (*New York State Department of Social Services* v. *Dublino*). But amendments to the federal food stamp plan intended to prevent hippie communes from receiving food stamps were declared unconstitutional (*U. S. Department of Agriculture* v. *Moreno*), and denial of state health and welfare benefits to illegitimate children was held a violation of equal protection (*New Jersey Welfare Rights Organization* v. *Cahill*).

CRIMINAL LAW

The court decided 36 cases involving criminal justice, all but 7 by divided votes, and 23 of the 36 decisions sustained the prosecution. For the most part, however, the court did not reverse controversial rulings of the Warren Court. Rather its tactic was to qualify them, make exceptions, and refuse to extend them to new circumstances.

In several cases the court broadened police power to search or to secure evidence. *Schneckloth* v. *Bustamonte* ruled (6–3) that in obtaining a suspect's consent to search without a warrant, the police need not inform him of his constitutional right to refuse consent. *Cady* v. *Dombrowski* approved (5–4) police search of a car without warrant, after the driver's arrest for drunken driving and the towing of the car to a garage. *Couch* v. *United States* ruled (7–2) that a taxpayer's financial records turned over to an accountant for preparation of his income tax return may be subpoenaed by the government and are not protected by the privilege against self-incrimination.

The action of a government narcotics agent in aiding an illicit drug ring by securing necessary ingredients for them was held (5–4) not to constitute illegal entrapment, because the suspects were predisposed to commit the offense without the agent's help (*United States* v. *Russell*).

Tollett v. *Henderson* ruled (6–3) that a defendant who pleaded guilty could not later attack his conviction on the ground that blacks were excluded from the grand jury that indicted him, despite his attorney's not having told him he could challenge the composition of the grand jury. *Preiser* v. *Rodriguez* ruled (6–3) that state prisoners may not use federal civil rights laws and federal courts to attack their convictions until they exhaust all possible state appeals.

Decisions favorable to the defendant included a widely publicized case from Mississippi. The court ruled (8–1) that state court judges had construed the rules on hearsay evidence so as to deny a fair trial to a black man charged with murdering a policeman (*Chambers* v. *Mississippi*).

Having upheld the use of six-man juries in state criminal trials (1970), the court in *Colgrove* v. *Battin* extended their use to federal civil cases.

PROTECTION OF THE ENVIRONMENT

Members of Congress, invoking the federal Freedom of Information Act, sued to obtain classified documents prepared for the President on an underground nuclear test planned in Alaska. But in *Environmental Protection Agency* v. *Mink* the court held (6–3) that that statute specifically excluded matters required by executive order to be kept secret because of national defense or foreign policy.

The 1899 Rivers and Harbors Act was vigorously interpreted against industrial polluters in *United States* v. *Pennsylvania Industrial Chemical Corp.*, and a Florida oil-spill prevention and pollution-control act was unanimously upheld in *Askew* v. *American Waterway Operators, Inc.* A 4-to-4 vote in *Fri* v. *Sierra Club* upheld lower-court rulings directing the Environmental Protection Agency to disapprove any state air quality control plans that allowed worsening of air quality, even though this might hinder the state's economic development. But municipal regulations banning the nighttime takeoff of jet aircraft from a local airport were invalidated

POLICE in Knoxville, Tenn., impound pornography after the Supreme Court's "local standards" decision.

in *Burbank* v. *Lockheed Air Terminal Inc.* on the ground that federal statutes had preempted state and local control over aircraft noise.

BUSINESS REGULATION

In an important consumer-protection ruling the court held that the 1968 Truth in Lending Act provides redress against deceptive magazine subscription salesmen (*Mourning* v. *Family Publications Service, Inc.*). *Weinberger* v. *Hynson* upheld the right of the Food and Drug Administration to remove ineffective drugs from the market.

After 12 years of litigation the court reversed history's largest antitrust damage judgment, which TWA had secured against the Hughes Tool Company for allegedly delaying TWA acquisition of jet aircraft (*Hughes Tool Co.* v. *Trans World Airlines*).

THE INDOCHINA WAR

As in previous terms, the court refused (7–2) to consider attacks on the constitutionality of U. S. involvement in the Vietnam War (*Sarnoff* v. *Shultz*). In July 1973, after the court had recessed, Judge Orrin G. Judd of the U. S. District Court for the Eastern District of New York, granted an injunction against the bombing in Cambodia, holding it unauthorized and unlawful. The Second Circuit Court of Appeals immediately stayed the injunction, and Marshall, supervising justice for the circuit, refused to intervene. Sponsors of the suit then appealed to Douglas, who did cancel the stay on August 4. But within six hours Marshall, having communicated with the other justices, countermanded Douglas' order. The bombing stopped on August 15 by act of Congress.

C. HERMAN PRITCHETT
University of California, Santa Barbara

U. S. Legislation and Case Law

Civil rights, transportation, and the impact of Watergate on the administration of justice highlighted case law and legislation during 1973.

Legislation. An increasing demand throughout the United States, especially by middle-income families, for prepaid legal services, led to the enactment of an amendment to the 1947 Labor Management Relations Act that authorizes such plans as a fringe benefit in labor contracts. The new legislation permits employers to contribute to jointly administered trust funds established for the purpose of paying for these legal services, just as they already were authorized to do for medical and dental care. Employer contribution can be negotiated as part of the collective bargaining process.

There has been increasing debate, on a national scale, as to the role that public transportation should play in relationship to highway programs. In response, a Federal-Aid Highway Act of 1973, approved on August 13, not only authorizes the expenditure of $17.9 billion over fiscal years 1974–76 for interstate, rural, and urban highways, but also dramatically shifts congressional emphasis from straight highway programs toward helping to solve urban congestion problems. The new law extends and strengthens the provisions of the Federal-Aid Highway Act of 1970 (which authorized a completely new federal aid urban system of streets and highways carrying the major portion of city traffic) by an increase in the act's funding by increments progressing from $100 million to $700 million per year. The law will allow the use of these funds to buy passenger buses for urban systems and to improve rail systems. It also authorizes the expenditure of $3 billion from the general revenues of the federal government for grants and loans to states for capital expenditures for urban mass transit.

In order to improve the ability of the Veterans Administration to deliver quality medical care, Congress removed legislative restrictions on the scope of treatment by enacting the Veterans' Health Care Expansion Act of 1973. This act permits outpatient and ambulatory care to eligible veterans, as well as nursing-home care for veterans with service-connected disabilities. Wives and dependent children of retired veterans and those who died from service-connected disabilities are also granted medical care.

When a state enacts no-fault legislation, it avoids long-delayed court trials to determine liability for a motor vehicle accident. Instead, the insurer of the party, without regard to fault, promptly pays for damages according to prescribed schedules. By 1973 five states, Connecticut, Florida, Massachusetts, Michigan, and New Jersey, had adopted comprehensive no-fault auto insurance plans. Seven other states have enacted some form of modified first-party benefit insurance. Sen. Warren G. Magnuson, chairman of the Committee on Commerce, has introduced a bill entitled a "National No-Fault Vehicle Insurance Act." It establishes minimum standards for a state motor vehicle insurance law.

Case Law. A state that arbitrarily establishes a residency requirement for divorce could violate the due process and equal protection clauses of the 14th Amendment, and unlawfully penalize the constitutionally protected right of interstate travel. The state must show a compelling interest, and it must distinguish between bona fide domiciliaries and non-domiciliaries. Thus, Hawaii could require that a person seeking a divorce in its courts be a domiciliary. But when it provided for a one-year residency requirement, not "tailored" with "precision," the U. S. District Court for Hawaii stated that this was discriminatory against newly arrived, bona fide domiciliaries (*Mon Chi Heung Au* v. *Lum*). On the other hand, Iowa's one-year residency requirement, which was enacted to prevent the state from becoming a "divorce mill" due to its liberal divorce laws, was upheld by the U. S. District Court for the Northern District of Iowa as reflecting a compelling state interest (*Sosna* v. *Iowa*).

Do indigent parents against whom a custody petition is instituted have a right to appointed counsel at the state's expense? The Supreme Judicial Court of Maine, which was deciding this issue for the first time, answered the question in the affirmative. The court held that to do otherwise would deny the parents due process; it rejected the trial court's reliance on the generally accepted distinction between "criminal" and "civil" proceedings (*Danforth* v. *State Department of Health and Welfare*).

Women's rights were upheld in some interesting cases. A New Jersey statute that provides for all sentences of convicted women to be "indeterminate within five years" was held to be unconstitutional by the New Jersey Supreme Court because it denied them equal protection under the 14th Amendment (*State* v. *Chambers*). A female offender cannot receive different sentencing treatment than a male offender would receive for the same offense.

In *Healy* v. *Edwards*, the U. S. District Court for the Eastern District of Louisiana held that Louisiana cannot excuse women from jury service merely by their failing to file a written declaration of their wish to serve, even though the state's constitution and laws provided for such an exemption. To do so, the court said, denied women the equal protection of the law, and denied due process to litigants concerned.

The California Supreme Court ruled that a city ordinance which prohibited commercial establishments from serving food or drink and providing entertainment by "topless" women and "bottomless" persons of either sex was constitutional; it held that the ordinance neither denied freedom of speech and expression nor equal protection of the law (*Crownoner* v. *Musick*).

Administration of Justice. Much more has been involved, legally and morally, in the Watergate affair than the dramatic constitutional confrontation created by President Nixon's claims of absolute immunity from the judicial process and absolute executive privilege. Also to be considered are the effects on the legal profession and the administration of justice. The American Bar Association is particularly concerned about its responsibility to determine the professional standing of those lawyers involved in Watergate who violated the criminal law or the bar's ethical proscriptions. The ABA also intends to investigate the need for "some depoliticization of the federal law enforcement process." With the purpose of restoring public confidence in the fairness and integrity of the system of administering justice in the United States, both the ABA and the Judiciary Committee of the House of Representatives were separately preparing to investigate these sensitive problems.

JULIUS J. MARKE
Law School, New York University

International Law

Major developments in international law during 1973 took place in the areas of war and peace, law of the sea, and the World Court.

War and Peace. During the June visit to Washington of Leonid I. Brezhnev, Soviet party chairman, 11 United States–Soviet agreements were signed. These included "basic principles" that were to govern future negotiations of limits on strategic offensive arms, and an "Agreement on Prevention of Nuclear War." The latter pledges the parties to "avoid military confrontations" and to "enter into urgent consultations" if there appears to be a risk of nuclear conflict.

Another event was the creation of international forces to moderate hostilities in Vietnam and the Middle East. The January 27 Paris "Agreement on Ending the War and Restoring Peace in Vietnam" created an international commission consisting of Canada, Hungary, Indonesia, and Poland. It was to observe and report on implementation of the agreement, but had no enforcement powers. In the Middle East, the cease-fire ordered by the UN Security Council in October was supervised by a 7,000-man UN Emergency Force drawn mainly from Austria, Canada, Finland, Indonesia, Poland, and Sweden.

Law of the Sea. After five years of preparation in a General Assembly committee, the Third UN Conference on the Law of the Sea opened in December with an organizational session at New York. The first substantive session was set for Caracas, Venezuela, in June 1974. Proposals covered all aspects of the law of the sea, including fishing, navigation, mining, pollution, territorial limits, and sea-bed and subsoil rights. Many were of immediate importance for major coastal states such as Canada and the United States. U. S. firms appear ready to harvest manganese nodules at great depths and require a stable legal framework to do so; and in both Canada and the United States, fishing interests threatened by distant-water fleets are pressing for the extension of protective laws.

World Court. The International Court of Justice (ICJ) began 1973 with three cases, decided one, and received three new cases, to end the year with five pending. A disturbing feature of the five cases was the failure of the respondents, Iceland, France, and India, to appear at oral hearings on the grounds that the court lacked jurisdiction. Such refusals have not prevented the court from deciding the jurisdiction issue, and will not prevent it, where it finds jurisdiction, from deciding on the merits.

Fisheries Jurisdiction Cases. Iceland's extension of its exclusive fisheries zone from 12 to 50 nautical miles had been brought to the ICJ in 1972 by Britain and West Germany, whose trawlers continued to fish in the zone and clashed with Icelandic patrol vessels. The court ordered Iceland to permit British and West German vessels to fish in the new zone, subject to catch limits set by the court, pending a final judgment.

On February 2, the World Court held that dispute settlement clauses in 1961 agreements gave it jurisdiction to hear both cases. As Iceland had contested ICJ jurisdiction, but did not appear, the court took pains to consider every conceivable argument. It reviewed the negotiating history, confirming its view that Iceland had agreed to submit fisheries jurisdiction disputes. Relying on legal principles in the 1969 Vienna Convention on the Law of Treaties, the court held the 1961 agreements valid. As to Iceland's claiming "changed circumstances resulting from the ever-increasing exploitation of the fishery resources in the seas surrounding Iceland," the court held that, if proven, such changes would be relevant on the merits, but not on the issue of jurisdiction. The "changed circumstances" doctrine requires a radical transformation of obligations still to be performed, which would not be true of an obligation to submit a dispute to the ICJ. The court ordered written arguments on the merits, with Iceland's brief due by Jan. 15, 1974.

On November 13, Iceland and Britain agreed that, without prejudice to their respective legal positions, a specified number of British trawlers would be permitted to fish within the 50-mile limit for two years. The temporary agreement excludes freezer and factory trawlers altogether, and excludes British vessels from specified conservation areas and areas reserved to small Icelandic boats.

Nuclear Tests Cases. French atmospheric nuclear weapons tests in the South Pacific were challenged on May 9 in cases brought by Australia and New Zealand. The applicants charged that radioactive fallout resulting from French nuclear tests created a serious public health hazard, in violation of international law, and asked the ICJ for a provisional order directing France to halt atmospheric tests. On June 22, the court granted the order. Although the court was not then in a position to reach final conclusions on jurisdiction or on the merits, it appeared that fallout from the French tests might cause irreparable damage to Australia and New Zealand, and the court held that France should avoid nuclear tests causing such radioactive fallout, pending a final judgment.

Disregarding the order, France conducted a nuclear weapons test in the atmosphere over Mururoa in the South Pacific on July 21. The next stage in the cases was to be the exchange of written arguments on jurisdiction in early 1974. If the court found jurisdiction, it would then reach the issue of France's duty to prevent environmental damage.

Trial of Pakistani Prisoners of War. The fate of 195 Pakistanis captured by India during the 1971 civil war in Bangladesh was brought to the World Court by Pakistan in May. Pakistan alleged that India planned to hand the prisoners over to Bangladesh for trial on charges of genocide and crimes against humanity, and asked the court to declare that Pakistan has the exclusive right to try persons accused of genocide committed on Pakistani territory. Pakistan argued that the alleged genocide took place in Bangladesh while it was part of Pakistan, and thus the accused must be tried in Pakistan under Article 6 of the Genocide Convention.

Relying on its reservations as to ICJ jurisdiction under the Genocide Convention and under Article 36 of the ICJ statute, India declined to appear at hearings on provisional measures. Pakistan, anticipating negotiations with India, stated its case at the hearings but then asked the court to postpone consideration of provisional measures. On August 28, the parties agreed to proceed to repatriate Pakistani prisoners, leaving the status of the 195 prisoners to negotiation between Pakistan and Bangladesh. In the light of discussions between the parties, the World Court case was discontinued on December 15 at Pakistan's request.

DANIEL G. PARTAN
Boston University

LEBANON

In 1973, President Suleiman Franjieh's government confronted another year of political and economic problems for Lebanon caused by the presence of Palestinian guerrillas in the country. Israeli raids against Palestinian camps in Lebanon and a mid-year clash between guerrillas and the Lebanese army contributed to a series of governmental crises. There were three prime ministers in less than four months.

Despite losses in revenue resulting from the fighting between the army and guerrillas, Lebanon had a prosperous economic year, highlighted by an agreement with Iraq under which Lebanon increased its annual earnings for oil pumped through its territory to Mediterranean ports.

Israeli Attacks. On February 21, Israeli commandos attacked two Palestinian refugee camps near Tripoli, killing 30 and wounding 60. The army's failure to resist or retaliate opened Premier Saeb Salam's government to charges by the opposition, led by Kemal Jumblat, that there must be a tacit agreement between Lebanese and Israeli authorities allowing such attacks.

Early on April 10, Israeli raiders landed by boat south of Beirut and entered the city, conducting operations that left three Palestinian leaders dead and a guerrilla headquarters destroyed. The raiders escaped unscathed. In the face of demonstrations in the capital that day protesting the army's inactivity, President Franjieh accepted Premier Salam's resignation.

Salam remained in office until April 18 when Amin al-Hafez was designated premier and formed a predominantly right-wing cabinet. The ministry dealing with the Palestinians was awarded to a member of the rightist bloc led by former President Camille Chamoun.

Clash with Guerrillas. Hafez's tenure was not peaceful; hostilities broke out between the army and Palestinian guerrillas after three weeks of tension. Following the arrest of two Palestinians, fighting erupted on May 2 between the Lebanese army and guerrillas near refugee camps outside Beirut. The violence raged until May 11, when Arab mediation brought about a fourth cease-fire. During the hostilities the army used tanks and aircraft. The Syrian-based Palestine Liberation Army intervened, and the Syrian border was closed. Premier Hafez offered his resignation, but it was not accepted. A state of emergency was declared, which lasted from May 7 to May 23.

On May 17, representatives of the army and the major guerrilla organization reached an agreement under which the terms of the guerrilla's continued presence in Lebanon were defined. Although an official version was not published, it was believed to reaffirm agreements reached by the government and the Palestinians in the past year.

Cabinet Crisis. Premier Hafez offered his second resignation in five weeks on June 14 after the two Sunni Muslim members of his government boycotted a cabinet meeting. They had insisted that four ministries should be held by Sunnites under Lebanon's denominational system of representation. It was not until July 8 that the new premier, former Interior Minister Takieddin Solh, was able to form a new 22-member government, the largest in Lebanon's independent history.

Premier Solh, in an extraordinary July 25 session of the legislature, outlined the domestic and foreign policies his government would support. He reaffirmed his support for the Palestinian cause and pledged to strengthen the army, develop the state administrative system, and enact reforms in health, education, and communications while continuing to follow Lebanon's traditionally independent foreign policy.

This independence allowed Lebanon to remain neutral in the October Arab-Israeli war. However, a seat was sought at the peace negotiations that were held in Geneva.

Student Unrest. The year 1973 began with a series of student demonstrations supporting teachers dismissed during a January strike for better pay and conditions in the state school system. The violence culminated in riots on April 3–6 in which over 200 students were arrested and many wounded when police fired on the demonstrators. Tension was eased when the government announced that it would consider reforms.

Economy. Despite inflationary pressures and an estimated $65 million revenue loss during May's hostilities, Lebanon's economy profited from a 20% growth rate in industrial exports and from an agreement with Iraq increasing oil royalties from $8.7 to $12 million annually.

Lebanon forced the hand of American-owned MEDRECO (Mediterranean Refining Co.) by seizing its facilities at Zahrani on July 31, following the company's threat to shut down its operations until the Lebanese government agreed to higher prices. A final agreement was not reached, but the American company agreed to continue refining oil for domestic consumption.

A $432 million budget was announced in September. Earlier, in June, Lebanon received from the United Nations a $10 million development grant and $800,000 to aid in the world campaign against hashish plantings. Lebanon's exports to the east were hampered by Syria's closed border.

F. NICHOLAS WILLARD
Georgetown University

--------- LEBANON • Information Highlights ---------

Official Name: Republic of Lebanon.
Location: Southwest Asia.
Area: 4,015 square miles (10,400 sq km).
Population (1973 est.): 3,100,000. Density, 715 per square mile (276 per sq km).
Chief Cities (1964 est.): Beirut, the capital, 893,000 (metropolitan area); Tripoli, 127,600.
Government: *Head of state,* Suleiman Franjieh, president (took office Sept. 1970). *Head of government,* Takieddin Solh, premier (took office June 1973). *Legislature* (unicameral)—Chamber of Deputies. *Major political groups* —Maronite Christians; Sunnite Muslims; Shiite Muslims; Greek Orthodox.
Languages: Arabic (official), French, English.
Education: *School enrollment* (1969)—primary, 450,499; secondary, 150,875; technical/vocational, 2,198; university/higher, 38,519.
Monetary Unit: Lebanese pound (2.53 pounds equal U.S.$1, Aug. 1973).
Gross National Product (1971 est.): $1,770,000,000.
Consumer Price Index (1972), 115 (1966 = 100).
Manufacturing (major products): Processed foods, textiles, petroleum products, tobacco products, cement.
Major Agricultural Products: Cereals, fruits, vegetables, tobacco, wheat.
Major Mineral: Salt.
Foreign Trade (1971): *Exports,* $256,000,000; *Imports,* $677,000,000. *Chief export customers* (1971)—Saudi Arabia; Kuwait; Jordan; Iraq. *Chief import suppliers* (1971)—United States; West Germany; France.
Tourism: Receipts (1971), $175,200,000.
Transportation: *Motor vehicles* (1971), 163,800 (automobiles, 146,300); *railroads* (1971), 259 miles (417 km); *merchant fleet* (1972), 117,000 gross registered tons; *major national airline,* Middle East Airlines/Airliban.
Communications: *Telephones* (1972), 300,000; *newspapers* (1970), 52.

Plenty of light and an emphasis on openness are features of the reference department of the new, prize-winning Burlington Public Library, Burlington, Ontario.

libraries

Challenges to the well-being of U. S. libraries came from both the executive and the judicial branches of the federal government during 1973. A budgetary proposal of the administration threatened the very existence of direct aid to libraries, and the U. S. Supreme Court ruled that state and local officials can censor material—including that found in libraries—if, "taken as a whole," the material has no "serious literary, artistic, political, or scientific value." Other national events included a slowing of the drive to unionize libraries, publication by the National Commission on Libraries and Information Science of its first annual report, continuation of the commission's regional hearings, and further attempts to obtain revision of the copyright law. International developments were highlighted by Americans' visits to libraries on the Chinese mainland—the first such visits in more than 20 years.

Obscenity Ruling. In a series of five obscenity cases, all involving 5-to-4 decisions handed down on June 21, the U. S. Supreme Court held that the former definition of obscene material as that which is "utterly without redeeming social value" from the standpoint of the "national community" imposes an excessive burden of proof on prosecutors. According to the court's majority, a jury may test whether a work appeals to prurient interest or is patently offensive by determining whether the "average person" applying "contemporary community standards" finds it obscene, not just in some "minor portion" necessary to its scientific, artistic, or literary integrity but in its totality.

Rejecting national standards of what is obscene as "abstract" and unworkable, Chief Justice Warren E. Burger offered this opinion: "It is neither realistic nor constitutionally sound to read the First Amendment as requiring that the people of Maine or Mississippi accept public depiction of conduct found tolerable in Las Vegas or New York City." Librarians therefore face this issue: Will what the "average person" in a community deems obscene limit the materials a library may stock for a constituency of users that includes "not average" as well as "average" individuals? Indeed, librarians are puzzled by the concept of "average person" in a particular locality and wonder whether a work found objectionable in one community can be legally obtained on interlibrary loan from a library in another locality.

Although the implications of the Supreme Court's ruling were not entirely clear as the year ended, librarians were disturbed by a passage in Justice William O. Douglas' dissenting opinion in one of the cases (*Paris Adult Theater I* v. *Slaton*): "What we do today is rather ominous as respects librarians. The net now designed by the Court is so finely

meshed that taken literally it could result in raids on libraries. Libraries, I had always assumed, were sacrosanct, representing every part of the spectrum. If what is offensive to the most influential person or group in a community can be purged from a library, the library system would be destroyed."

Unionization. The drive to unionize library staffs continued during 1973, but union organizers were slowed in their efforts by the tightness of the job market and the consequent fear among librarians that union activity might result in dismissal with little prospect of finding a satisfactory position. Such fear seemed well founded when, on June 15, the University of Chicago terminated four staff members who had sought to organize its library. Although the university dismissed two other librarians who had not been involved in the quest for collective bargaining and insisted that the reduction in staff was the only way to maintain existing acquisition levels, it presented no public evidence that its action was genuinely budgetary and prompted by financial problems.

National Planning and Federal Library Activity. On March 7 and October 3, the National Commission on Libraries and Information Science held public meetings in Atlanta and Boston, respectively. In addition to its regular sessions in Washington, D. C., the commission plans a public hearing in San Antonio on April 24, 1974. In its annual report for 1971–72, published on Jan. 31, 1973, the commission suggested a threefold purpose for these regional hearings: (1) to provide an opportunity for librarians and information scientists, as well as the consumers of their services, to present their views to the commission; (2) to promote an understanding of the commission's mission and ongoing activity; and (3) to expose commission programs and plans to early critique by those who will be most directly affected by them.

Operating on a limited budget of just over $400,-000 during the 1973 fiscal year, the commission set forth its priorities for study and action under the following categories: the patterns of organization of library services, the information needs of various types of users or potential users, the financing of libraries, the adequacy of present library and information systems, the application of new technology, and the needs for staffing. The commission also received the first two of its exploratory contract studies on users' needs and the funding of public libraries. One of these—by Charles P. Bourne of the Institute of Library Research at the University of California, Berkeley—dealt with current groups of users and their needs for information. Another—by Edwin B. Parker of the Institute for Communication Research at Stanford University—offered a view of society in the period 1975–80, with comment on how anticipated changes will affect users of library and information systems.

In other action, the commission supported increased appropriations for the Library of Congress, recommended that Congress enact a revision of the copyright law as soon as possible, and suggested that if the local property tax is an inappropriate base for the finding of public education, it may well be inadequate for the support of public and school libraries. Because of its deep interest in the financing of libraries, the commission has authorized a pilot study by the Public Administration Service of Chicago on the local funding of libraries in 25 states.

In a related development on January 26, U. S. Sen. Claiborne Pell (D-R. I.), proposed a 1976 White House Conference on Library and Information Services. This convocation—at which the library and information science community, leaders in education and in science and technology, and the public would be represented—might consider the recommendations of the National Commission on Libraries and Information Science.

Work continued during 1973 on the James Madison Memorial Building of the Library of Congress. In the fall of 1975, furniture and bookstacks will be installed in the Madison building, and the move of materials into the new structure is expected to begin in early 1976, the country's bicentennial year. The Librarian of Congress agreed, in April, to study the feasibility of cooperative procurement of library materials with the directors of the National Library of Medicine and the National Agricultural Library.

Federal Legislation. The administration's budget request, departing from a 17-year tradition, suggested that no moneys designated for specific types of libraries—public, school, or academic—be appropriated for the 1974 fiscal year. As an alternative to direct support, President Richard M. Nixon proposed that local governments sustain those library activities begun with direct federal aid by means of the more circuitous system called revenue sharing, a plan wherein libraries would vie with other agencies for federal funds made available to localities. The administration's zero funding recommendation came as a rude shock to U. S. librarians, even though federal appropriations to the various types of libraries for construction and services—in addition to training, research, and resources—had been running considerably below the levels authorized by Congress during the last six fiscal years.

On June 26, the House of Representatives passed an appropriations bill that rejected the President's budget recommendation by including $163.7 million for major library programs and $37.5 million for instructional equipment. In the absence of Senate action, President Nixon signed a continuing resolution on July 1, which authorized interim appropriations through September 30 at the level of the appropriations bill passed by the House. Although the funding levels in the House bill for the fiscal year 1974 are below those appropriated for the 1973 fiscal year and although costs rise inexorably, librarians were thankful, as 1973 ended, that at least some funds had been made available. From Boston to Los Angeles, librarians dimmed their lights on May 8 to suggest symbolically what might happen to even basic library services if the administration's budget proposals were approved.

Copyright Revision. The Senate Subcommittee on Patents, Trademarks, and Copyrights again considered legislation to replace the outmoded Copyright Act of 1909. The central tension between authors and publishers, on one hand, and educators and librarians, on the other, developed over what constitutes "fair use" in copying. Librarians would like legal permission to make single copies of a work for teaching, research, or interlibrary loan. Publishers are concerned that what starts with incidental copying often is repeated to the extent that it constitutes republication. The compromise legislation now before the Senate includes a fourfold test of fair use couched in very broad language. The criteria for fair use are the amount of material

Public Library In Boston Gets A New Addition

Designed by Philip Johnson and John Burgee, the addition houses 600,000 volumes and can accommodate 1,200 persons. The wing's central court (*right*) is lit by nine skylights. Located in Copley Square, the original McKim, Mead and White library (*below, left*) was constructed in 1895.

to be photocopied, the purpose for which the work is being copied, the economic effect on the copyright owner, and the character of the material.

Neither librarians and educators nor authors and publishers are satisfied with the rather vague wording of the compromise bill. In the meantime, U. S. Rep. Ogden Reid (D-N. Y.) introduced legislation on February 27 that would provide compensation to authors at the rate their works circulate from libraries, as is now the case in European systems such as those in Sweden and Denmark.

Other Events Around the Nation. On March 7, Mayor John Lindsay of New York approved a community information system, known as the Citizens Urban Information Center program, to be housed in the Brooklyn Public Library and its many branches. Within the system, each center will have a librarian and two well-informed residents of the immediate neighborhood. The program will provide the people who live and work in the communities surrounding each center with information on the workings of local, state, and federal government; urban services and citizen rights; and private and public agencies that stand ready to help them. If the Brooklyn experiment is successful, the system will be enlarged to cover the other boroughs of New York City.

In early 1973, the Office of Library Independent Study and Guidance Projects of the College Entrance Examination Board received $150,000 from the Council on Library Resources, Inc., to be used to stimulate interest in the public library as a logical place of independent study for college credit. With council support, the office "will assist individual libraries with specific problems, stage workshops for librarians, act as a national clearinghouse on projects, publish a manual and other training publications for librarians, and provide evaluative and research services."

National Library Week. The themes of National Library Week, April 8–14, 1973, were "Get Ahead.

Read" and "Widen Your World. Read." In its celebration of reading, this annual event (the 16th), sponsored by the American Library Association and the National Book Committee, again failed to recognize the presence of nonprint media in libraries.

Library Education. The number of graduate library schools accredited by the American Library Association (ALA) increased to 58 in 1973 with the approval of the master's degree program offered by the School of Library Service of Dalhousie University, Halifax, Nova Scotia. At the outset, the ALA Committee on Accreditation had refused to accredit the school. Acting on appeal and on the recommendation of a special subcommittee, the ALA Executive Board reversed the decision and granted the school approval, retroactive to 1970–71.

Under revised appeal procedures, the board will be able to contest accreditation decisions by the committee and to appoint select committees for their review, but the board will not have the authority to grant approval unilaterally, as it did in the Dalhousie case. The new appeals procedure has been subject to considerable dispute, since the ALA constitution permits the Executive Board to overturn an action by any unit of the association and, in turn, provides that the ALA Council (the governing body) may overturn any decision of the board.

Awards. The 1973 Beta Phi Mu Award for distinguished service to education for librarianship went to Lester E. Asheim, former dean of the Graduate Library School at the University of Chicago. The Melvil Dewey Award for recent creative professional achievement, particularly in such fields as management and the tools and techniques of librarianship, was given to Virginia Lacy Jones, dean of the School of Library Service, Atlanta University. The Joseph W. Lippincott Award for distinguished service in the library profession went to Jesse H. Shera, dean emeritus of the School of Library Science, Case Western Reserve University. Doralyn J. Hickey,

First of "instant libraries" planned by West Virginia, this one in the town of Man was built in record 21 days.

associate professor in the School of Library Science, University of North Carolina, was awarded the Margaret Mann Citation for outstanding professional contribution in cataloging and classification.

To Glen A. Zimmerman of the Library of Congress went the Esther J. Piercy Award for contributions in the field of technical services by younger members of the profession. The Isadore Gilbert Mudge Citation for distinguished contribution to reference librarianship was given to William A. Katz, professor in the School of Library Science, State University of New York at Albany. Eleanor Kidder of Seattle, Wash., received the Grolier Award for achievement in guiding and stimulating the reading of children and young people.

International Library Activities. On May 27 the Soviet Union became an adherent of the Universal Copyright Convention (drafted in 1952; effective in 1955). The convention does not apply retroactively, but the Soviet Union will respect the copyrights of the other member countries.

American visitors to the People's Republic of China were especially impressed by the National Library at Peking—an institution of great size and comprehensiveness. The country's bookstores stock traditional Chinese fiction and nonfiction as well as works by and about Chairman Mao Tse-tung.

Other international developments during 1973 included the Special Library Association's withdrawal from the International Federation for Documentation because of the latter's recognition for membership of the Council for Scientific and Industrial Research, an agency of the government of South Africa. The withdrawal was in protest against the federation's involvement with an official organization of a government practicing apartheid. Grenoble, France, was the site of the 39th meeting of the International Federation of Library Associations, Aug. 27–Sept. 1, 1973. The 1974 session of the federation will be held in Washington, D. C.

DAN BERGEN
University of Rhode Island

AMERICAN LIBRARY ASSOCIATION

In its first year under the administration of its new executive director, Robert Wedgeworth, the American Library Association (ALA) launched an extensive review of its programs and operations with a view to the changing needs of the association and its goals. New units were established and other significant projects were undertaken at the annual conference and throughout the year.

Conference and Projects. The 92d annual conference of the ALA was held in Las Vegas, Nev., June 24–30, 1973. Jean E. Lowrie became president and Edward G. Holley became president-elect and first vice president of the ALA. At the conference, the ALA Council established the Intellectual Freedom Round Table and the Office for Research. The Council also provided for merging of the Association of Hospital and Institution Libraries and the Library Service to the Blind Round Table to form the Health and Rehabilitative Services Division, effective after the 1974 annual conference. In a program at the conference sponsored by several ALA divisions, Allie Beth Martin told about developments since the publication of *A Strategy for Public Library Change* (1972). Plans were formulated for making cassette tapes of the program available.

In January an ad hoc committee was formed to study and make recommendations on the ALA's international responsibilities. The committee held hearings in June and was to report its findings in January 1974.

ALA members met with their congressmen in Washington, D. C., and across the country and sent many letters and telegrams urging continued federal support of major library programs, which the White House had recommended for termination. The result was a congressional vote in June to continue the programs. The U. S. Supreme Court denied the ALA's petition for a rehearing on its obscenity decisions of June 21.

The ALA received a grant of $128,000 from the H. W. Wilson Foundation to conduct a study of the education of librarians. The ALA Committee on Accreditation has begun visits to all library schools with previously accredited programs.

Publications. The following are some ALA publications of special interest to libraries, issued in 1973: *Agricultural Education in a Technical Society: An Annotated Bibliography of Resources; Famous American Playhouses:* Vol. 1, 1716–1899; Vol. 2, 1900–1971 (the first two volumes in a projected seven-volume set, Documents of American Theater History); *Guide to the Development of Educational Media Selection Centers; How To Catalog a Rare Book* (2d ed.); *Serial Publications: Their Place and Treatment in Libraries* (2d ed.); *Total Community Library Service; Voices of Brooklyn.*

Awards. Numerous awards were made in 1973, in addition to those cited above under *Awards.*

The J. Morris Jones–World Book Encyclopedia–ALA Goals Award was divided between two ALA units—the ALA Legislation Committee, to form a national legislative network for libraries; and the Association of College and Research Libraries, to prepare a revision of *Standards for College Libraries* (1959). This annual award amounts to $25,000.

The Newbery Medal for the most distinguished children's book was awarded to Jean George for *Julia of the Wolves.* The Caldecott Medal for the most distinguished picture book went to Blair Lent for *The Funny Little Woman.* The Mildred L. Batchelder Award for the most outstanding book originally published in a foreign language and in a foreign country was given to William Morrow & Co., Inc., for its 1971 publication of *Pulga* by Siny van Iterson.

The Eunice Rockwell Oberly Award went to Olga Lendway for *Bibliography of Corn* and *Bibliography of Wheat;* and the Clarence Day Award, to Sol and Mary Ann Malkin, publishers and editors of the *AB Bookman's Weekly.* Betty Ryder of the Pasadena (Calif.) Public Library received the Hammond Incorporated Library Award.

The H. W. Wilson Library Periodical Award was given to *Illinois Libraries,* published by the Illinois State Library and edited by Irma Bostian. Beta Phi Mu memorial awards were given to the Wayne State Fund (Wayne State University) in memory of Patricia B. Knapp and to the Ralph R. Shaw Visiting Scholar Program Fund (Graduate School of Library Service, Rutgers University) in memory of Ralph R. Shaw. The Association of Hospital and Institutional Libraries Exceptional Service Award went to Robert S. Bray, formerly of the Library of Congress; and the Francis Joseph Campbell Citation, to Marjorie S. Hooper of the American Printing House for the Blind, Lexington, Ky.

CURTIS E. SWANSON
American Library Association

LIBYA

Relations between Libya and Egypt deteriorated in 1973, partly because Egypt showed no interest in the immediate unification of the two countries and partly because Egypt agreed to a cease-fire with Israel on terms that were unacceptable to Libya. Col. Muammar el-Qaddafi, Libya's head of state, seized foreign oil companies in Libya, increased the price of oil, and embargoed oil shipments to those supporting Israel in the Arab-Israel war.

Relations with Egypt. The erratic and radical Qaddafi resigned as Libya's head of state and president of the Revolutionary Command Council (RCC) on July 11, when Egyptian President Anwar el-Sadat refused to proceed immediately with the projected union of Libya and Egypt. Then on July 23 he canceled his resignation before a cheering crowd at Benghazi, but warned that he would again leave office if union were not based on those principles he had advocated. He wanted a reluctant Egypt to adopt fundamentalist Islamic reforms amounting to "a cultural revolution."

Qaddafi had resigned two days after returning from his unsuccessful 18-day visit to Egypt in response to a message from Sadat, who demanded that Qaddafi call off a motorized caravan of some 40,000 Libyans headed for Cairo. Sadat warned the Libyan leader that otherwise he would be held responsible for the consequences. Sadat disapproved of efforts to complete unity "under emotional pressure before the political and economic foundations were laid for it." He was determined that unity should take place in stages. It was on July 20 that Qaddafi cabled Sadat that the "unity procession" was a surprise to him, and that he had already left office on July 11. The RCC rejected the resignation (his fourth in three years), threatening in its turn to resign if he persisted. Meanwhile the procession was ordered back.

Yet, on August 29, Qaddafi and Sadat announced the "birth of a new Arab state," but without actual unification. They agreed that on September 1, the original date for full unification, a series of steps

------- LIBYA • Information Highlights -------

Official Name: Libyan Arab Republic.
Location: North Africa.
Area: 679,360 square miles (1,759,540 sq km).
Population (1973 est.): 2,100,000. *Density,* 2.6 per square mile (1 per sq km).
Chief Cities (1970 est.): Tripoli, joint capital, 264,000; Benghazi, joint capital, 170,000.
Government: *Head of state,* Col. Muammar el-Qaddafi, president of the Revolutionary Command Council (took office Sept. 1969). *Head of government,* Maj. Abdul Salam Jallud, premier (took office July 1972). *Chief organ of government*—Revolutionary Command Council. *Major political party*—Libyan Arab Socialist Union.
Language: Arabic (official).
Education: *Expenditure* (1967), 11.6% of total public expenditure. *School enrollment* (1969)—primary, 310,846; secondary, 50,779; technical/vocational, 1,457; university/higher, 3,663.
Monetary Unit: Dinar (0.2961 dinar equals U. S.$1, Oct. 1973).
Gross National Product (1971 est.): $3,946,000,000.
Economic Indexes: *Agricultural production* (1971), 145 (1963 =100); *consumer price index* (1972), 97 (1970=100).
Manufacturing (major products): Petroleum products, processed foods.
Major Agricultural Products: Wheat, barley, tomatoes, dates, olives.
Major Minerals: Petroleum, gypsum, salt, limestone.
Foreign Trade (1972): *Exports,* $2,938,000,000; *Imports,* $1,043,000,000. *Chief trading partners* (1970)—Italy (took 17% of exports, supplied 26.5% of imports); United Kingdom (17%–10.5%); United States (5%—21%).
Tourism: Receipts (1972), $5,000,000.
Transportation: *Motor vehicles* (1970), 145,500 (automobiles, 100,100); *major national airline,* Libyan Arab Airlines.
Communications: *Telephones* (1972), 49,794; *newspapers* (1971), 7.

toward ultimate unification would be initiated. Their two countries would set up a 100-member constituent assembly. A resident minister from each state would serve in the other's capital, and a higher planning council would be established comprising their two premiers and chief ministers. A joint central secretariat would be formed to aid the resident ministers and the constituent assembly. Free trade areas would be designated along their frontiers, and a new common currency unit, the dinar, would be used. As soon as the assembly created a constitution and agreed on a candidate for chief of state, a referendum would be held in each country on some undetermined date.

While averting an immediate rupture with the still aggrieved Qaddafi, Sadat successfully courted the diplomatic and financial support of the Libyan's political foe, King Faisal of Saudi Arabia.

Relations between Libya and Egypt seemed to reach the breaking point on December 1 when Qaddafi ordered the Libyan embassy in Cairo closed. He firmly opposed the cease-fire signed by Egypt and Syria in the October war with Israel. He had not been consulted beforehand by Egypt. Even earlier, as it became evident that most Arab chiefs were agreeable to a peace conference under United Nations auspices, Qaddafi boycotted the meeting of the Arab leaders in Algeria in late November.

Nationalization and Embargo of Oil. On June 11, Qaddafi nationalized Libyan assets of the Bunker Hunt Oil Company of Dallas and its partner, British Petroleum, as a penalty for what he called the pro-Israeli position of the United States. He said, "The time has come for us to deal America a strong slap on its cool, arrogant face." On August 11 he took 51% control of all the oil companies in Libya. This affected such firms as Texaco, Mobil, Shell, Exxon, and Socal. Then on October 19 all exports of crude oil and petroleum items to the United States were stopped. The price of oil was nearly doubled.

Relations with Non-Arab States. On March 21 two Libyan fighters fired on a U. S. transport plane 75 miles (120 km) off the Libyan coast. Libya rejected the U. S. protest and denounced the "spy aircraft." The United States yielded on October 13 to Libya's demand that the passports of foreigners visiting Libya should be written in Arabic. Previously, a U. S. diplomat had been rejected because of noncompliance with this demand in Tripoli.

The indefatigable Qaddafi vistied Yugoslavia on November 18 and France on November 23 in search of weapons for Libya and perhaps for Egypt and Syria, according to reports.

Libya was plagued with airline incidents. On February 21, Israeli fighter planes shot down a civilian Libyan jetliner over the Sinai desert, killing 106 persons. Israel said the pilot ignored warnings to land, while Libya called it a "criminal act." On July 24 four hijackers blew up a Japanese commercial jetliner at Benghazi after the crew and passengers were let out. On August 16 a mentally unbalanced Libyan citizen hijacked a Lebanese airliner to Israel to "show that not all Arabs hate the Jews." On September 29 two Arab terrorists, who exacted a promise from the Austrian government to close a center near Vienna for Jews emigrating from the USSR, landed near Tripoli after threatening to blow up their plane.

JOHN NORMAN
Pace University, Westchester

LITERATURE

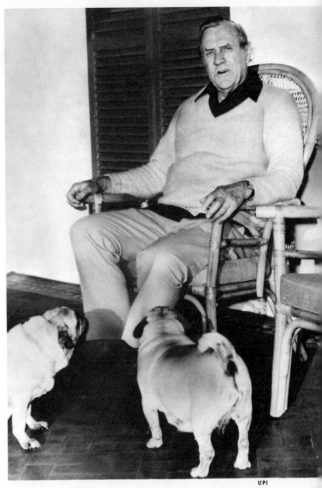

UPI

Australia's Patrick White, winner of the 1973 Nobel Prize in literature, was cited by the Swedish Royal Academy of Science for "epic and psychological art."

In October the Swedish Royal Academy of Science awarded the 1973 Nobel Prize in literature to Australian novelist Patrick White (see BIOGRAPHY). Earlier, the renowned British-American poet W. H. Auden died in Vienna, Austria (see OBITUARIES).

General developments in world literature during 1973 are discussed in this article under the following headings: (1) AMERICAN LITERATURE; (2) CHILDREN'S LITERATURE; (3) ENGLISH LITERATURE; (4) FRENCH LITERATURE; (5) GERMAN LITERATURE; (6) ITALIAN LITERATURE; (7) JAPANESE LITERATURE; (8) LATIN AMERICAN LITERATURE; (9) SOVIET LITERATURE; and (10) SPANISH LITERATURE. A review of 1973 literary news throughout Canada begins on page 160.

American Literature

American literature fared well in 1973. Although no towering masterpiece was published during the year and no intruding literary genius ruffled the ranks of the establishment with his innovations, quite a number of fine books appeared, most of them by the best-known writers. Publishers, hampered by spiraling costs, were obviously nervous about issuing too many books by writers of little or no reputation. However, many of the nation's leading fiction writers published novels or short-story collections, several established poets published collections of verse, and literary critics finally began to turn their attention to the black poets. There were also a number of outstanding works of biography and American history and a large number of books on politics and other topics of current interest.

Novels. Philip Roth, Kurt Vonnegut, Jr., and Gore Vidal, all solidly established novelists, published new novels during 1973, none of which surpassed their former work. Thornton Wilder, who was an established author before these three noted novelists were out of their infancy, also published a new work, which, while it does not surpass his former books, shows no evidence that his talents are diminishing.

Wilder, at the age of 77, wrote *Theophilus North,* an entertaining novel made up of a number of closely related short stories revolving around the central figure of the narrator-protagonist, who bears some resemblance to the author. The stories are set in Newport, R. I., in the summer of 1926. They tell how Theophilus North proves helpful to the townspeople while protesting that he does not wish to become involved in the life of Newport. Wilder writes with the liveliness and wit long associated with his works. He is full of the wisdom that is ordinarily associated with old age, but in Wilder's case it was always there.

Vonnegut's eighth novel, *Breakfast of Champions, or Goodbye Blue Monday!,* hilariously chronicles the disintegration of an automobile dealer, who, after his wife commits suicide by eating Drano, goes mad because of the harmful chemicals in his system. The book contains many entertaining digressions in which its author reduces what is wrong with U. S. culture to gentle satire. Vonnegut seems to be using this novel to say goodbye to old characters and to test and discard old ideas in preparation for a new kind of writing in the future.

Gore Vidal, from his haven in Switzerland, has taken a sidelong glance at American history and produced a fictional biography—*Burr,* a historical novel based on the life of Aaron Burr. Vidal has portrayed this traditional villain (in elementary American history textbooks) as an admirable character, while giving questionable pictures of the stalwart founding fathers. It is a wry comment on American history and politics written with tongue in cheek, and if read in the proper spirit it is a delightfully entertaining book, even if it is not a lasting contribution to American scholarship.

Philip Roth's *Great American Novel* does not live up to its title. It is a comic story about an inept World War II baseball team—belonging to an imagined third major league—that is made up of misfits because all able-bodied men are fighting the war. Although the novel contains a great deal of humor, Roth fails to sustain interest through its 382 pages.

Perhaps the most brilliant novel of the year was Thomas Pynchon's *Gravity's Rainbow,* about the search for a V-2 rocket during World War II. The rocket symbolizes a "sexual love of death" that Pynchon believes is the force behind modern history. The work is complex and well constructed. It con-

tains allusions to literature, the arts, history, and the sciences and covers most of the first half of the 20th century in flashbacks and references. Richard Locke of *The New York Times Book Review* called it "one of the longest, most difficult, and most ambitious American novels in years," and said that the only possible standard by which to judge the work is that of Nabokov.

Other established writers also published new works. Joyce Carol Oates brought out another of her passionate novels exploring the psychology of human relationships. *Do With Me What You Will* tells the story of a woman of extraordinary physical beauty who at first lets men use her but finally undergoes a sexual awakening. In *Ninety-Two in the Shade,* Thomas McGuane continues to write on the theme of men in violent rivalry that had served as the basis of his two previous novels, *The Sporting Club* (1969) and *The Bushwacked Piano* (1971).

The popular writer Jimmy Breslin published a new novel, *World Without End, Amen.* Its protagonist is a New York City policeman, whose alcoholism, bribe-taking, and unhappy marriage are quickening his disintegration. To get away from it all, he takes a trip to Northern Ireland, where he becomes involved with the Catholic revolutionaries, but he ultimately returns to New York and sinks back into his old ways with barely noticeable change. The best parts of the novel are the scenes depicting the life of a New York policeman, which are full of humor and local color.

John Gardner, who so delightfully rewrote *Beowulf* from the monster's point of view in *Grendel,* produced a contemporary pastoral novel in *Nickel Mountain.* Set in a small town in upstate New York, the book emphasizes the goodness of its hero, who faces the challenges and disappointments of rural life to emerge an even better man. While conventional in form and story, *Nickel Mountain* works beautifully and never becomes a cliché.

Other novels include Tom Wicker's *Facing the Lions,* a political novel; Edmond White's *Forgetting Elena,* an excellent first novel; Don Wakefield's *Starting Over,* about divorce; Marge Piercy's *Small Changes,* about women's lib; Beryl Bainbridge's *Harriet Said,* a thriller about two girls who wreak vengeance on the adult world; and Joy Williams' *State of Grace.*

The late poet John Berryman's uncompleted *Recovery,* his only novel, was published posthumously in 1973. It concerns a former physician and alcoholic writer who is overly concerned with his writing and discovering truth—much like Berryman himself.

Short Fiction. Short-story collections were few in number but of generally high quality. Again the established writers led in the publishing of works in this difficult literary genre.

Isaac Bashevis Singer's *A Crown of Feathers* is a collection of 24 remarkably human short stories about Polish Jews. In the title story, a Jewish girl has a vision of her dead grandmother, who says that Christ is the son of God and as a sign she will find in her pillow a crown of feathers surmounted by a cross. After converting to Christianity and marrying a Polish squire, the girl discovers her grandmother was being impersonated by the devil. She divorces her Catholic husband and marries her former Jewish suitor, who forces her to undergo a series of severe penances, which ultimately kill her. On her deathbed she yearns for a vision that will reveal to her the real truth. She dies ransacking her pillow, in search of a crown of feathers with the Hebrew letters representing the name of God, and no one understands what she is looking for. The theme of this story is that "if there is such a thing as truth it is as intricate and hidden as a crown of feathers."

John Cheever's collection of 10 short stories, *The World of Apples,* is one of his best. A majority of the stories deal with the problems at the core of married life, principally the lack of love of either the husband or wife. The title story is about a much-honored expatriate writer, who wonders why he has not received the Nobel Prize, and sets about to purify his thoughts after having descended to the low level of writing dirty limericks. Cheever writes with humor and humanity, exposing the foibles of his characters.

There is a mixture of the serious and the light-hearted in *God Was Here but He Left,* a collection of five short stories by Irwin Shaw. The title story, about a lonely 36-year-old woman who is pregnant with an illegitimate child, is touching. The second story, *Where All Things Fair and Wise Descend,* is about a young man who acquires a tragic sense of life. The final three stories are mixtures of fantasy and satire, treating science, sports, and sex. Bernard Malamud's *Rembrandt's Hat* is a collection of stories, most of which are excellent. *The Congressman Who Loved Flaubert,* a collection of stories by the former Washington journalist Ward Just, is also noteworthy.

Poetry. Little new poetry appeared in 1973, but a few collections of works by some of America's leading contemporary poets were published. In fact, Robert Lowell published three books of verse.

Lowell's *History* contains more than 360 poems, of which 80 are new and the others revised. They treat history through the ages and relate world history to Lowell's own personal history. There are 67 revisions of older poems in *For Lizzie and Harriet* and 103 new poems in *The Dolphin.* Lowell continues to write in his personal, "confessional" style. The revisions in these collections are improvements over the original, and the new poems are on the same high level as his past work.

The Fall of America is a new poetic work by Allan Ginsberg. In it he contemplates the emptiness of middle age. He writes about the state of America and the state of his life and is unhappy about both. Joyce Carol Oates came out with a third volume of verse, entitled *Angel Fire.* The work was accepted with far less enthusiasm than her fiction. Margaret Atwood's *Power Politics* is a sequence of short poems on the battle of the sexes. Robert Bly's *Sleepers Joining Hands* contemplates chaos, violence, and death in America and worries about the impossibility of discerning what is true and how one should act.

Books on Writers and Their Works. A number of works of literary criticism and several biographies of American writers were published during the year. Perhaps the most important of the latter was the completion of a two-part biography of America's first great playwright, Eugene O'Neill, and a group of books on black writers.

O'Neill, Son and Artist is the conclusion of the Louis Sheaffer's biography of Eugene O'Neill, which was begun in *O'Neill, Son and Playwright* (1968). The second volume traces O'Neill's life and career from the production of *Beyond the Horizon* in 1920 to his death in 1953. It is a carefully researched

and detailed account of everything that happened to O'Neill in both the personal and professional worlds. Sheaffer emphasizes the importance of O'Neill's early attachment to his parents and uncovers much new material on O'Neill's three marriages, particularly on his unhappy third marriage with Carlotta. The two volumes together constitute an invaluable study of a great playwright and a tragically beautiful story in their own right. *The Fourteenth Chronicle* contains the collected letters of John Dos Passos, with introductory essays by Townsend Ludington that are biographical in content.

Among the books on black writers that appeared in 1973 were two important studies of one of America's most important black novelists, Richard Wright. Kenneth Kinnamon's critical-biographical *The Emergence of Richard Wright: A Study in Literature and Society* chronicles Wright's life from his birth near Natchez, Miss., in 1908 through the publication of his novel *Native Son* in 1940. Kinnamon emphasizes the social forces that shape Wright's thoughts and play such an important role in his books; evaluates Wright's works; and attempts to assess Wright's contribution to American literature. Another important critical-biographical book on Wright, Michel Fabre's *The Unfinished Quest of Richard Wright*, was translated from the French by Isabel Barzun. Together these books provide invaluable background for any serious study of Wright and his works.

Stephen Henderson, coauthor of *The Militant Black Writer in Africa and the United States,* published *Understanding the New Black Poetry,* an anthology with a long interpretive essay. In the essay he gives his definition of black poetry and suggests ways in which to approach it. *Black Poets of the United States* is a valuable study by the French critic Jean Wagner, translated into English by Kenneth Douglas. Wagner evaluates the major poets from 1890 to 1940 with insight and care. Also noteworthy is *Report from Part One,* an autobiographical work by the black poetess Gwendolyn Brooks.

In *The Anxiety of Influence,* Harold Bloom of Yale University offers his theory of poetry. He holds that when poetic influence involves two strong authentic poets, it always involves a misreading of the poet who is the influence. This misinterpretation is necessary to produce something new and individual rather than an extension or emulation of the work of influence. This theory is in direct contrast to the still-revered theory of T. S. Eliot, as stated in his 1919 essay *Tradition and the Individual Talent,* that the poetry of the past and the literary tradition of a culture, must be reflected in new poetic works.

One of America's most respected critics, Lionel Trilling, published two slim books in 1973. *Sincerity and Authenticity, The Charles Eliot Norton Lectures, 1969–1970* traces authenticity and sincerity in literature from Shakespeare—where he feels sincerity is first found—to the present. *Mind in the Modern World, the 1972 Jefferson Lecture in the Humanities* is an examination of the tradition of anti-intellectualism in America and of the "growing intellectual recessiveness" of U. S. colleges and universities.

The Dream and the New Deal is a carefully researched history of the Federal Writers' Project of the Great Depression, by Jesse Mangione, who was national coordinating editor of the project.

Other Biographies. There were also a number of biographies of people not in the literary field. The

---

CONRAD AIKEN (1889–1973)

WIDE WORLD

Conrad Aiken, one of the most distinguished American men of letters, died in Savannah, Ga., on Aug. 16, 1973. A prolific and versatile writer, Aiken published some 50 books, including 35 volumes of poetry, five novels, several collections of short stories and critical essays, and the third-person autobiography *Ushant* (1952). In 1930 he won the Pulitzer Prize for his *Selected Poems* (1929). Best known for his subtle, often ambiguous, introspective verse, characterized by poignant lyrics, resonant cadences, and brilliant imagery, he has been ranked by some critics with Ezra Pound and T. S. Eliot.

Conrad Potter Aiken was born in Savannah, Ga., on Aug. 5, 1889. When he was 11, his father murdered his mother and killed himself, and this horrible and tragic occurrence had a profound and lasting effect on Aiken. Other less traumatic influences included the works of Edgar Allan Poe and the liberal Unitarianism of his New England relatives, with whom he stayed after the deaths of his parents. At Harvard University, his associations with George Santayana, one of his teachers, and T. S. Eliot, a classmate, contributed to the development of his distinctive literary style. After graduating from Harvard in 1912, Aiken settled in Cambridge, Mass., to devote himself to freelance writing. His experimental efforts to adapt the contrapuntal effects of music to poetry formed the basis for his Pulitzer Prize-winning verse. Aiken also immersed himself in Freudian psychology, which he applied to his verse and prose. His first novel, *Blue Voyage* (1927), is an early example of the stream-of-consciousness technique.

Aiken served as a contributing editor of *Dial* from 1917 to 1919, and he was editor of the *Selected Poems of Emily Dickinson* (1924). From 1950 to 1952 he was consultant in poetry to the Library of Congress. His later poetry includes *A Seizure of Limericks* (1964), and *Thee* (1967). Among the honors he received were the National Book Award (1954), the Bollingen Prize (1956), and the National Medal for Literature (1969).

HENRY S. SLOAN

---

subjects of these biographies ranged from Marilyn Monroe to President Franklin Delano Roosevelt. There was also a magnificent book of memoirs by the playwright Lillian Hellman.

Hellman's *Pentimento: A Book of Portraits* is a series of articles, mainly sketches of the people she has known. The title is a term used in art to describe the transparent state of old paint, which allows parts of a painting below the surface one to show through in bits and pieces. *Pentimento* is written with the intellectual strength and insight that is characteristic of all of Miss Hellman's work.

The fourth volume of Frank Freidel's massive biography of Franklin D. Roosevelt was published in 1973. *Franklin D. Roosevelt: Launching the New Deal* covers the latter part of 1932 and the first six months of 1933—the so-called "interregnum," during which Roosevelt was president-elect and President Herbert Hoover was helpless as the economy of the nation was crumbling, and the Hundred-Day Congress at the beginning of Roosevelt's first term,

which passed an unparalleled amount of legislation. The high level of scholarship and writing that characterized the first three volumes of the work are maintained in this one. The biography, when completed, will surely be a major contribution to the study of 20th century American history.

The third volume of Forrest C. Pogue's projected five-volume biography of General of the Army George C. Marshall was also published in 1973. *George C. Marshall, Organizer of Victory, 1943–45* covers the most important years in Marshall's life. The work is a thorough documentation of an illustrious career.

In *The Devil and John Foster Dulles*, Townsend Hoopes gives an entertaining portrait of the indomitable secretary of state. The book was put together from some 300 tape-recorded interviews with Dulles, resulting in a remarkably lifelike picture of the man who was so influential in U. S. foreign affairs. George Wheeler gives a frank account of the life of the financier Pierpont Morgan, without glossing over the man's faults, in *Pierpont Morgan and Friends: The Anatomy of a Myth*.

Robert W. Johannsen's *Stephen A. Douglas* is a masterful work that will probably be the definitive biography for some time to come of the statesman who opposed Lincoln. It is a detailed, well-organized, and objective book that is also straightforward in its writing.

In *Kissinger*, Stephen R. Graubard advocates that what Henry Kissinger wrote in the 1950's and 1960's is connected with the work he has been doing in foreign policy since 1969.

Bell, Robert V. Bruce's biography of the inventor of the telephone, reveals much about Bell's personal life that had never been published. The book deals with Bell both before and after his great invention and shows him to have been a fine human being.

In commemoration of the 75th anniversary of his birth, a number of books on the composer George Gershwin were published in 1973. They included *The Gershwins* by Robert Kimball and Alfred Simon, *Gershwin: His Life and Music* by Charles Schwartz, and a revised edition of *The Gershwin Years* by Edward Jablonski and Lawrence D. Stewart.

Hour of Gold, Hour of Lead is a compilation of the diaries and letters of Anne Morrow Lindbergh from 1929 to 1932 covering the first happy years of her marriage to Charles Lindbergh and the catastrophic kidnapping and murder of their 20-month-old child in 1932.

In 1973, *The Dictionary of American Biography* published its third supplement, covering Americans who died between 1941 and 1945.

The film idol and sex goddess Marilyn Monroe was the subject of the lavishly illustrated *Marilyn*, written by Norman Mailer. Mailer characterized his book as a "novel biography," implying that it is not to be taken too seriously.

History and Current Events. In addition to the biography of Roosevelt discussed above, there were a number of other books on the U. S. presidency. This was appropriate in view of the furor over the presidency caused by the Watergate case and the wide discussion of presidential impeachment.

In *The Imperial Presidency*, Arthur M. Schlesinger, Jr., gives an overall view of the American presidency. He writes about all U. S. presidents from Washington to Nixon, pointing out patterns in presidential behavior and the acquisition of powers. The chief concern of the book is the power of the president in making war, and careful attention is paid to the Vietnam War. In *The Living Presidency*, Emmet John Hughes is also concerned with the military powers of the president and suggests a number of institutional changes to guard against misuse of presidential power.

The Making of the President 1972 is another of Theodore H. White's excellent journalistic accounts of presidential election campaigns.

John Kenneth Galbraith's *Economics and the Public Purpose* asserts that economics is closely tied to politics and the struggle for power. The book demonstrates how the great corporations are able to impose their own particular ideas on others. Emma Rothschild's *Paradise Lost* is a study of General Motors and the built-in obsolescence of the auto.

The Dance of Legislation by Eric Redman focuses on efforts of various congressmen to pass the bill establishing the National Health Service Corps, which brings doctors to areas that have none. The aim of the book is to show the true worth and power of Congress, in answer to those who believe in a strong presidency and think that the power of Congress is limited to amending and delaying bills.

The American Disease by David F. Musto is a history of narcotics control in the United States from the end of the Civil War to the present. Robert Sherrill's *The Saturday Night Special* is a cynical and despairing study of the gun trade in the United States and a questioning of the type of society that can permit so little control of such lethal weapons. Sherrill's concerns are reflected in the full title of his book: *The Saturday Night Special and Other Guns with which Americans Won the West, Protected Bootleg Franchises, Slew Wildlife, Robbed Countless Banks, Shot Husbands purposely and by Mistake, and Killed Presidents Together with the Debate over Continuing Same.*

The bleak period in which workers in the motion-picture industry were blacklisted because of the investigations of the House Un-American Activities Committee in the 1950's is the subject of Stefan Kanfer's *A Journal of the Plague Years*. The committee, which unsuccessfully sought to prove that the motion-picture industry was Communist controlled, blacklisted many writers, actors, and other film personnel who had at some time been a member of the Communist party. Many who were subpoenaed refused to cooperate and were imprisoned for contempt. Kanfer tells the story of the investigations and what resulted from them as a plea for increased political awareness and the adoption of safeguards against anything of this sort happening again.

ROBERT V. HUBER

Children's Literature

Hardcover children's books published in 1973 remained at the same level as the previous year, approximately 2,000 titles. Paperbacks continued to make gains in retail sales as publishers began placing even greater emphasis on that aspect of production. There were countless hardcover books and paperbacks, fiction as well as fact, on witchcraft, the occult, death and senility, drugs and sex. A number of books for the very young, explaining the facts of life, were more graphic and explicit than heretofore. Minorities, especially Puerto Ricans and Mexican-Americans, continued to receive attention.

1973 CALDECOTT MEDAL for the most distinguished picture book for children was awarded to The Funny Little Woman, as retold by Arlene Mosel and illustrated by Blair Lent.

The Funny Little Woman

RETOLD BY
Arlene Mosel

PICTURES BY
Blair Lent

E. P. DUTTON & COMPANY

"Ungrateful dumpling," scolded the little woman, as she knelt and reached for it.

But just then the earth gave way, and head over heels she tumbled and tumbled

Awards. The major awards presented in 1973 for children's books published in 1972 were as follows: The American Library Association's John Newbery Medal for the most distinguished contribution to literature for children went to Jean Craighead George for her novel *Julie of the Wolves,* a story about a 13-year-old Eskimo girl living with a wolf pack on the Arctic tundra. The ALA's Randolph Caldecott Medal for the most distinguished picture book was given to Blair Lent for his illustrations in *The Funny Little Woman,* a Lafcadio Hearn tale, set in Old Japan and retold by Arlene Mosel, about a cheerful woman falling into a demonic subterranean realm.

Mollie Hunter received the 31st annual award of the Child Study Association of America for reflecting honestly and realistically the world in which young people are growing up, in *A Sound of Chariots*—a skillful interweaving of the sights, sounds, and feelings an impoverished young girl experiences in the death of her father and her vigorous affirmation of her own life and future. The National Book Award for children's books was won by Ursula K. Le Guin for *The Farthest Shore,* the concluding volume in her intricate fantasy trilogy.

Fiction. Among the books published in 1973, perhaps the most outstanding was *The Juniper Tree and Other Tales from Grimm* (2 vols.), selected by Lore Segal and Maurice Sendak. Translated by Lore Segal (four tales were translated by the late Randall Jarrell) and superbly illustrated by Sendak, the stories are seldom found in standard children's collections and "are among the strangest, most grotesque, mysterious and haunting in Grimm." While most of the readers will be adults, children will be attracted by the book's richness and meaning.

The best picture books for the 4–7 age group were as follows: Harve and Margot Zemach's *Duffy and the Devil,* a retelling of a 19th century Cornish play, based on the Rumpelstiltskin story; *How Does a Czar Eat Potatoes?* written by Anne Rose and illustrated by Janosch, contrasting the life of the czar and a peasant family; Uri Shulevitz' *The Magician,* about the prophet Elijah performing a miracle on Passover Eve; Anne Rockwell's *Games,* a playfully illustrated compendium of indoor and outdoor activities; Peter Spier's *The Star-Spangled Banner,* the story of the U. S. national anthem, set to handsome, robust illustrations; and a collection of Danish nursery rhymes in N. M. Bodecker's *It's Raining Said John Twaining.*

For the 6–10 group the most outstanding titles were *A Prairie Boy's Winter,* in which the Canadian primitive painter William Kurelek reminisces in text and 20 full-page paintings about his own childhood; *The Real Thief* by William Steig, about a goose wrongfully accused of robbing the king's treasure; *The Clay Pot Boy,* Cynthia Jameson's adaptation from a Russian tale, with illustrations by Arnold Lobel; Glen Rounds' *The Day the Circus Came to Lone Tree,* an account of the pandemonium that ensues when a circus opens in a frontier town; and Jean Fritz's *And Then What Happened, Paul Revere?* a story of the patriot's ride and of his life.

The most distinguished titles for readers 9 years old and up were Susan Cooper's *The Dark Is Rising,* a powerful fantasy of the conflict between good and evil; Eleanor Cameron's *The Court of the Stone Children,* an elegantly styled story of a modern girl communing with a ghost from the time of Napoleon; *The Winged Colt of Casa Mia* by Betsy Byars, an imaginative story about a boy and his uncle united

1973 NEWBERY MEDAL for the most distinguished children's book went to Jean Craighead George (above) for Julie of the Wolves, which was illustrated by John Schoenherr.

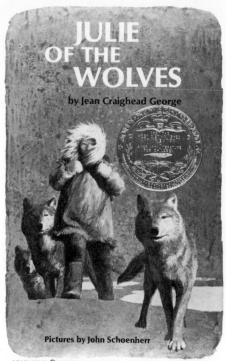

in concern for a flying colt; John Bellairs' *The House With a Clock in Its Walls,* a chilling account of the search for a doomsday clock; Julia Cunningham's *The Treasure Is the Rose,* a finely spun tale of a widow besieged in her crumbling castle by three brigands; Marilyn Sachs' *A Pocket Full of Seeds,* a poignant story of a French-Jewish girl's years of loneliness in occupied France; and two books by Vera and Bill Cleaver—*The Whys and Wherefores of Littabelle Lee,* about a spunky Ozark girl trying to help her indigent grandparents, and *Me Too,* a novel about a girl's frustration in working with her retarded twin sister.

Among novels for teenagers the most notable were Alice Childress' *A Hero Ain't Nothin' But a Sandwich,* a well-wrought story of a 13-year-old heroin user and how his near-addiction affects his family; Bette Greene's *Summer of My German Soldier,* a tragic tale of a young Jewish girl's friendship with a German prisoner of war escapee in Arkansas during World War II; *Nilda* by Nicholasa Mohr, an autobiographical novel of a Puerto Rican girl growing up in New York City; E. L. Konigsburg's *A Proud Taste for Scarlet and Miniver,* a highly creative portrait of Eleanor of Aquitaine; Otfried Preussler's *The Satanic Mill* (translated by Anthea Bell), a macabre tale about a devil's apprentice; and *The Friends* by Rosa Guy, about a friendship between a West Indian girl and a Harlem girl.

Nonfiction. In nonfiction for the age group 9 and up, three titles stood out: *Tomfoolery,* verbal tricks from American folklore, collected by Alvin Schwartz; Paul and Dorothy Goble's *Lone Bull's Horse Raid,* a dramatic distillation from anthropological writings, with illustrations in the style of the Plains Indians; and *Cathedral,* written and illustrated by David Macaulay, which follows the long and complex construction of an imaginary 14th century Gothic cathedral.

GEORGE A. WOODS
Editor, Children's Books, "The New York Times"

English Literature

The dominant literary forms in 1973 continued to be the novel, the memoir, and the biography. Many of England's most prominent novelists published works of fiction during the year, and hardly a week passed without the appearance of a notable book about an important figure from the English literary or political past. In 1973, also, contrary to fashion, one of the most widely read and discussed books was an anthology of modern poetry.

Fiction. Iris Murdoch's *The Black Prince* is a philosophical melodrama about the mysteries of love and art. The artist and lover is Bradley Pearson, a 58-year-old retired tax collector, who is anxious to finish a long-contemplated novel. His literary ideal is Flaubertian. He wants his work to be complex, gem-like, and exquisitely designed. However, life in its "foul contingency" intrudes. Instead of being allowed to get on with his novel, Bradley is besieged by frantic callers at his London flat, and the relation of his life and art becomes hopelessly tangled. Unable to write his masterpiece, he hurts and gets hurt, falls calamitously in love with a young girl, and is inspired to compose a book more honest and commanding than any he could conceive in his dreams. Ingenious in plot, expansive in its sense of personality, provocative in its philosophical speculations, *The Black Prince* should rank as one of Miss Murdoch's best novels.

In *The Summer Before the Dark,* Doris Lessing also studies a crisis in the life of a middle-aged protagonist. No longer needed by her husband and children, Kate Brown is thrown back on her own resources for the first time in several decades and experiences the pleasures and terrors of unexpected freedom. In this work Mrs. Lessing transcends the ordinary through the precision and depth of her psychological observation. We follow Kate Brown into previously unexplored areas of her emotional life and through unsettling encounters with the life

styles of the hedonistic young. The journey is illuminating for her as well as for the reader.

Graham Greene's *The Honorary Consul* may be described as a Latin American melodrama with metaphysical overtones. It entertained and provoked many readers, but struck some as "a trick done once too often." According to this view, the famous Greene conventions—the failed priest, the squalid exoticism, the burned-out diplomat, and the aphoristic reflections on the nature of evil—had hardened into predictable formulae. Greene's admirers, however, argued that great writers often return to obsessive themes and that *The Honorary Consul* represented the perfection rather than the repetition of Greene's fictional conventions.

In Angus Wilson's *As If By Magic*, Hamo Langmuir, a homosexual plant geneticist, and his goddaughter, Alexandra, both try to find solutions to the turmoil of modern life in currently fashionable forms of mysticism and uncommon sexual experience. Wilson criticizes as false the nostrums they pursue and ultimately reject. Admired by some for its exuberance, its daring, and its moral passion, the work was criticized by others for the imbalance between its ideas, which are absorbing and up-to-the-moment, and its fictional art, which is predictable and repetitious.

Anthony Powell came within one volume of finishing his remarkable *roman fleuve, A Dance to the Music of Time*. Set at a cultural conference in Venice in 1958, *Temporary Kings* is a melancholy, autumnal, brilliantly observed work of art.

Richard Hughes also published a novel in a series: *The Wooden Shepherdess*, volume 2 of his trilogy, *The Human Predicament*, a series that began in 1961 with the highly regarded *The Fox in the Attic*. The second installment was generally received with less enthusiasm than the first.

Two novelists of unusual comic gifts provided superior entertainments. Kingsley Amis' *The Riverside Villas Murder*, a detective story set in the 1930's, is a brisk, elegant evocation of a period style. Michael Frayn's *Sweet Dreams* is a fanciful fable about contemporary notions of heaven. Another writer famous for her idiosyncratic comedy did not fare as well. Muriel Spark's sinister allegory *The Hothouse by the East River* was felt by many readers to be by turns too whimsical and too obscure.

Writers of lesser renown were sometimes overshadowed by the attention given to these older established talents. However, the following novels should not be neglected in any survey of the year's fiction: *In the Country of the Skin* by Peter Redgrove; *A Distant Likeness* by Paul Bailey; *Love on the Coast* by William Cooper; *A Lot to Ask* by P. N. Newby; *The Upstart* by Piers Paul Read; *A Temporary Life* by David Storey; and *Elizabeth Alone* by William Trevor. There were also two fine collections of short stories: *Inklings* by Dan Jacobson and *A Bit of Singing and Dancing* by Susan Hill.

Nonfiction. One of the most widely read works of nonfiction published in 1973 was *Portrait of a Marriage* by Nigel Nicolson. Relying in part on his mother's candid, unpublished autobiographical narrative and in part on his own memories and research, Nicolson tells the story of the relationship between his father, Harold Nicolson, and his mother, Vita Sackville-West. "It is the story," he says, "of two people who married for love and whose love deepened with every passing year, although each was constantly and by mutual consent unfaithful to the other. Both loved people of their own sex, but not exclusively. Their marriage not only survived infidelity, sexual incompatability, and long absences, but became stronger and finer as a result. Each came to give the other full liberty without inquiry or reproach. Honor was rooted in dishonor. Their marriage succeeded because each found permanent and undiluted happiness only in the company of the other." Reviewers disagreed about the quality of the Sackville-West autobiographical material but most readers found Nicolson's biographical reconstruction fascinating.

Several other memoirs will also serve as important records of public and private life in our time. *At the End of the Day* was the concluding volume in Harold Macmillan's account of his years as prime minister. *The Infernal Grove*, the second installment of Malcolm Muggeridge's autobiography, covers the years between the author's preoccupation with communism in the mid-1930's and the end of World War II. *Memories II* contains Julian Huxley's reminiscences about being the first director-general of UNESCO. Of considerable literary interest was the first complete publication of *Memoirs*, the autobiography and journal of the poet William Butler Yeats, edited by Denis Donoghue. Although some of the material had been published before, there were new disclosures about London literary life, Irish politics, and Yeats' relationship with women.

Several political and literary figures were subjects of biographies that should be definitive for many years. Antonia Fraser's *Cromwell, Our Chief of Men,* is a long, intricate study of one of England's most enigmatic political leaders. Equally enigmatic, if less significant, was Roger Casement, the late 19th, early 20th century martyr for Irish political independence, who was the subject of a perceptive biography by Brian Inglis. H. G. Wells was well served by Norman and Jeanne MacKenzie in *The Time Traveller.* The first 43 years of Aldous Huxley's life were chronicled by Sybille Bedford in the first of a two-volume biography. Enid Starkie, the eccentric professor of French at Oxford, who helped make Rimbaud and Baudelaire known to English readers, was the subject of a sympathetic yet candid life study by Joanna Richardson.

Less suitably treated were Shakespeare and Ronald Firbank. In his *Shakespeare the Man,* A. L. Rowse proposed a new candidate for the dark lady of the sonnets: Emilia Lanier, daughter of a court musician, Baptist Bassano. Rowse's announcement received wide publicity in the media. However, qualified Shakespearean scholars were convinced that Rowse's energy was more impressive than his evidence and that the case remains open. Firbank, the eccentric author of *The Flower Beneath the Foot* and other exquisite comic novels, was the subject of a hectoring, unselective study by Brigid Brophy, *Prancing Novelist*—exactly the wrong kind of memorial for a writer of Firbank's narrow and peculiar gifts.

Several collections of literary, theater, and film criticism were notable. To celebrate his 70th birthday, Cyril Connolly collected some of his most recent book reviews and miscellaneous essays in *The Evening Colonnade.* Graham Greene's *Pleasure Dome: Film Criticism, 1935–1940,* reminded readers that he was one of the earliest and most observant of movie reviewers. *The Concept of the Avant-Garde* provided evidence that John Weightman is one of the most stimulating commentators on current French

literature and culture. Shortly before his death in 1973, W. H. Auden saw his last book through the press: *Forewords and Afterwords,* a compilation of reviews, brief essays, and prefaces.

Two extended critical studies of general interest were published by Raymond Williams and Donald Davie. In *The Country and the City,* Professor Williams explored the treatment of the rural scene in four centuries of English literature. In *Thomas Hardy and British Poetry,* Professor Davie offered a polemical commentary on Hardy's verse and on the work of several later writers who were perhaps influenced by the poet and novelist.

Finally, H. J. Dyos and Michael Wolff brought together 40 new essays by leading scholars on nearly every aspect of urban life in mid-19th century England. *The Victorian City: Images and Realities* should remain an important source book for students of 19th century history and culture.

Poetry. The most widely read volume of English poetry published in 1973 was not an original book of poems but an anthology: Philip Larkin's *The Oxford Book of Twentieth Century Verse.* Since Larkin, who was born in 1922, is recognized as the leading poet of his generation and since the Oxford anthologies play an important role in shaping contemporary taste, the book stirred enormous controversy. Larkin printed 584 poems by 207 poets, and this allowed everyone to play lynch the anthologist. Most reviewers complained that the choice was too personal, permissive, and undiscriminating. Retitling the volume *The Larkin Book of Modern Verse,* Alfred Alvarez argued that the official Oxford offering should be something "synoptic and dignified, a comprehensive roll-call of the honored and almost dead to go along with the memorial blue covers and gold-lettering." Larkin did provide his roll-call: Eliot, Hardy, Yeats, Kipling, Lawrence, Auden, Betjeman, and Graves are the acknowledged masters. But he also included too much third-rate work by forgotten or forgettable talents. However, the reviews of the Larkin volume and the many letters to the editors of English journals will themselves be seen by future generations as a revealing chapter in contemporary literary history.

The controversy about the Oxford anthology did not obscure the merit of new books by D. J. Enright, Ted Walker, and Anthony Thwaite. Enright's *The Terrible Shears,* spare, ironical, and intelligent, is a sequence of autobiographical poems about childhood and adolescence in Leamington. Walker's *Gloves to the Hangman* reinforced his reputation as one of the best recent nature poets and also revealed a new talent for satire. Thwaite's third book, *Inscriptions: Poems 1967–1972,* was admired for the breadth of its subject matter and the subtlety of its handling of the role of the past in the lives of the living.

There were several other volumes of interest. They included *Shrapnel* by George MacBeth; *Instamatic Poems* by Edwin Morgan; *Funland* by Dannie Abse; *An Exploded View* by Michael Longley; *The Portraits and the Poses* by Edwin Brock; *Sad Grave of an Imperial Mongoose* by Geoffrey Grigson; *The Unreliable Nightingale* by Brian Patten; and *Poems 1970–1972* by Robert Graves.

Obituaries. The world of English letters lost two of its most outstanding figures. The poet W. H. Auden and the novelist and short story writer Elizabeth Bowen both died in 1973. (See OBITUARIES.)

LAWRENCE GRAVER
Williams College

French Literature

The year 1973 was a productive one in French literature. While most of the genres were well represented, the novel reigned supreme.

Novels. Several established authors published novels in 1973. The famous playwright Eugène Ionesco wrote his first novel, *Le Solitaire.* It reflects many of the preoccupations of his dramas—a concern with the absurd, with outlandishness, with anguish, and with the "nausea" of emptiness. Near the end it is lightened somewhat with a small bright vision that may represent a small element of hope.

Romain Gary wrote *Les Enchanteurs,* a curious novel combining realism and fantasy, drama and stylized buffoonery. The story is somewhat confused but merry and untramelled and often fascinating, with some beautiful descriptions of the life and adventures of two generations of Italians in the Russia of Empress Catherine the Great. In *Un Taxi mauve,* Maurice Déon provides some admirable descriptions of the Irish countryside. He is a born narrator able to amuse and enchant his readers without talking down to them. In *Le Jeu du souterrain,* Françoise Mallet-Joris uses an ingenious theme to bring up the problems of literary creation, of writing as a craft, of human values and criteria, and of the illusions of love and life.

Other novels by well-known writers include Maurice Schuman's *Les Flots roulant au loin,* a long tale set in Denmark and treating the nature of myth and of tragedy; Christine de Rivoyre's *Boy,* the nostalgic portrait of a charming young man in pre–World War I society about to plunge into the unknown; and Jean Freustié's *Harmonie ou les horreurs de la guerre,* a World War II story.

Among serious books by lesser-known novelists, the most interesting included Marie Cardinal's *La Clef sur la porte,* an important document on the subject of today's young people; Daniel Depland's *La Mouche verte,* the endless apocalyptic soliloquy of a woman who owns a bistro in the Charente region; Suzanne Prou's *La Terrasse des Bernardini,* a precise and cruel novel about the memories of a rich old lady and her companion, remarkable for its fine writing and psychological perceptiveness; Anne Loesch's *La Grande Fugue,* set in wartime and postwar Algeria; and Henri Bonnier's *Un Prince.*

A very special book, half novel and half poetry, was Jean-Marie Le Clezio's *Les Géants,* a lyrical denunciation of today's world through the unconventional symbolic device of a supermarket, called the Hyperpolis, located by the seashore.

In addition to literary fiction, France also produced its share of so-called popular novels. Such novels of "escape" are generally constructed according to well-proven formulas. They satisfy the average reader's wish to visit places socially defined as "fun places" or places associated with power, to sail on a millionaire's yacht, to occupy a luxurious hotel suite. Among the most successful books of this type in 1973 were Pierre Rey's *Le Grec,* based on the life of a Greek shipbuilder, a combination of Onassis and Niarchos, and the action-adventure stories *Rosebud* by Paul Bonnecarrière and Jean Hemingway and *Fracasso* by Voldemar Lestienne. Another perennially popular type of novel is that dealing with a current problem or trend, treated with an abundance of realistic detail. An example of this type of fiction was Guy des Cars' *Le Donneur,* about artificial insemination.

Nonfiction. With *Tout compte fait,* Simone de Beauvoir completed her four-volume autobiography. In this work she comments on the events of the last 10 years. In *La Soupe chinoise,* Claude Courchay presents the views of a young anarchistic teacher. Pierre Daninos, in *Les Nouveaux carnets du Major Thompson,* casts an ironic but sympathetic glance at the France of the 1970's. Jean Ferniot's *Pierrot et Aline,* the genuine tape-recorded story of an average French family between 1930 and 1970, could almost be described as a "roman-vérité."

Several interesting works in the area of science were published in 1973. They include the penetrating essay *Science et bonheur des hommes,* by Louis Leprince-Ringuet and *Grandeur et tentations de la médecine,* by Jean Bernard.

In the field of literary history and criticism, three works were noteworthy. They were *Jean Lorrain* by Pierre Kyria, *Léon-Paul Fargue* by Louise Schub, and *Céline, le voyeur-voyant* by Erika Ostrowsky.

Poetry. A few major poets published collections in 1973. The most famous is Henri Michaux, whose 11-poem collection *Moments* contains superb passages of heady and powerful verse. Paul Morand published *Poèmes,* early verse written between 1914 and 1924. Another noteworthy volume was André Frénaud's *La Sorcière de Rome,* a compelling meditation on the Rome of marble facades and gas pumps, on the history of the Eternal City, on time and death. The younger generation of poets was represented by Jacques Izoard, who wrote *La Patrie empaillée,* and Dominique Rouche, who published *Hiulques Copules.*

PIERRE BRODIN
Lycée Français de New York

German Literature

The conservative trend in German literature, quite pronounced in 1972, continued in 1973. Although old uncertainties remained, their mere exposure no longer sufficed and many works of a strongly critical nature were published. Generally, an emphasis on craftsmanship was seen to be replacing the older emphasis on political attitudes.

In February 1973, such figures as Hans Habe, Alexander Lernet-Holenia, and Hubertus zu Löwenstein, advocating the independence of literature from narrow party politics, established the writers' organization the *Freier deutscher Autorenverband.* They and others formed it in protest against the unionization and collectivization policies of the older *Verband deutscher Schriftsteller.*

Fiction. In German fiction in 1973 there was critical observation of the past as well as of the present. Literary collages, such as Martin Walser's *Der Sturz,* Wolfgang Hildesheimer's *Masante,* Jakov Lind's *Nahaufnahme,* Uwe Johnson's *Jahrestage,* and Walter Kempowski's *Uns geht's ja noch gold* left most of the critics unsatisfied. Walter Höllerer's novel *Die Elephantenuhr* also proved difficult. However, the craftsmanship of Hans Joachim Sell's stories *Zerstörung eines Parks* and of Hans Erich Nossack's novel *Die gestohlene Melodie* won critical acclaim. Also well received were Ingeborg Bachmann's stories, *Simultan* and Christine Brückner's tales, *Überlebensgeschichten.*

Other books published included the novels *Süsskind von Trimberg* by Friedrich Torberg, *Das Vorbild* by Siegfried Lenz, and Ernst Jünger's *Die Zwille* —a highly controversial work. Readers were unsure whether in it Jünger pleaded for the independence of art from politics or advocated authoritarianism. The world of fantasy was represented in *Deutsche Suite* by Herbert Rosendorfer. Two posthumously published works were *Bekenntnisse eines Pedanten* by Johannes Urzidil and *Engelhart oder Die zwei Welten* by Jakob Wassermann.

Nonfiction. One of the year's big best sellers was the autobiography *Eines Menschen Zeit* by Peter Bamm, who was an opponent of the Hitler regime. The work presents his judgment of the Goebbels propaganda machine and the falsified information fed to the German people during World War II. The book also affords intimate glimpses of Alfred Döblin, Albert Einstein, Fritz Klein, and Bruno Werner. Others who shared Bamm's anti-Nazi attitudes and also published memoirs in 1973 were Fritz Günther von Tschirschky, Reinhold Treviranus, and Hans Habe. Other autobiographical works dealing with the Nazi regime were Hermann Rauschning's *Gespräche mit Hitler* (1939), now issued in its uncensored form, and Hermann Langbein's *Menschen in Auschwitz.* Two nonpolitical memoirs, both about the famous theatrical impresario Max Reinhardt were *Der Liebhaber* by his son Gottfried and *Wie Max Reinhardt wirklich lebte* by his second wife, Helene Thiemig. A humorous memoir was the best seller *Das Scheusal* by Alice Herdan-Zuckmayer.

In other nonfiction, Joachim Fest's new definitive biography of Hitler, titled simply *Hitler,* and Klaus Mehnert's study *Moskau und die Neue Linke* were highly praised. The letters of Carl Gustav Jung, published in 1973, aroused great interest. In a body of significant critical essays, Elias Canetti, winner of the 1972 Büchner Prize, pleaded for a liberal literature free from Marxist party supervision.

Poetry. Among the poets who published in 1973 were Walter Helmut Fritz, Katrine von Hutten, Karl Krolow, Walter Neumann, and Alfred H. Vogt. The unconventional works of Franz Tumler, *Sätze von der Donau,* and Friedreich Hundertwasser, *Regentag,* fall into the realm of prose poetry.

Drama. Among the older moderns, Marieluise Fleisser found a sympathetic public. On the other hand, Friedrich Dürrenmatt's *Die Mitmacher* was noisily rejected. Carl Zuckmayer, honored by the city of Düsseldorf with the Heinrich Heine Prize, was working on a new play, *Der Rattenfänger,* which was produced late in the year. Friendly receptions were accorded the plays of Franz Xaver Kroetz, Heinrich Henkel, Renke Korn, and Thomas Bernhard.

East German Authors. Because of the changed political climate, East German authors attracted more attention in West Germany in 1973. Among the East German authors, all approved by their government, who gained attention in West Germany were Günter Kunert, Volker Braun, and Ulrich Plenzdorf. Braun's play *Die Kipper* and Plenzdorf's drama *Die neuen Leiden des jungen W*(erther), both conveyed the message that the aims of Marxist socialism must be pursued intelligently. Plenzdorf's novel of the same name was a best seller in East Germany. However, the more trenchant criticism of Wolf Biermann in *Deutschland, ein Wintermärchen* was unwelcome to the East German party bosses in spite of his enthusiastic Marxist attitude. The lyrics, *Gezählte Tage,* of Peter Huchel, who left East Germany in 1971, and the poems *Zimmerlautstärke,* by Reiner Kunze, could only be published in the West.

ERNST ROSE
Author of "A History of German Literature"

Italian Literature

In 1973, Italian literature was once again particularly rich in fiction. Among the many fiction awards offered, the prestigious Venetian Campiello Prize was the most prominent.

Fiction Awards. The Venetian Campiello Prize, awarded to five outstanding authors, came to the foreground of the Italian literary scene. The major award of 4 million lire (about $7,000) went to Carlo Sgorlon for his *Il trono di legno,* a novel about a boy from Friuli who has been abandoned by his parents. He leaves his native village as an adolescent and roams around the world in search of excitement. After many adventures, including involved love affairs with two sisters, he returns to his native, rustic old province in northern Italy, which preserves the heritage of its remote past (the name "Friuli" comes from the ancient Roman *Forum Julii*) and offers peace and stability. And here he finally finds his identity, and enchantment as well, in the marvellous stories told him by a peasant patriarch, seated on a great wooden chair, a kind of throne. In this captivating tale, Sgorlon succeeded in blending the realistic and regional with the magical and symbolic. The work brims with strange coincidences, mysteries, and mythological allusions.

The other Campiello finalists were led by Mario Cassola. The latest novel of the well-known author, *Monte Mario,* is a delicately drawn psychological portrait of Elena, a young woman living in Rome who is torn between exercising her freedom to love and accepting her aversion to love. A more sophisticated work is *Amore e Psyche* by Raffaele La Capria. The novel depicts a day in the life of an intellectual who works in a television studio and is beset by the anxieties, doubts, and worries so often endured in today's world. The protagonist's inner torment and complexity are reflected in the taut style and involved verbal structure of the work.

Similarly complex, Giorgio Saviane's *Il mare verticale* is more like a poetic composition than a straight narrative. Its fusion of avant-garde linguistic experiments with traditional stylistic modes caused some Italian critics to view the work as representative of the fiction that has appeared following the decline of neorealism.

The final author in the Campiello group was Luigi Magnani, a musicologist and professor of art history. His *Nipote di Beethoven* is an imaginary diary kept by Karl, the actual nephew of the great composer. Karl Beethoven has traditionally been regarded as a very difficult person and a source of Beethoven's sufferings. Magnani rejects these viewpoints as legend and, claiming documentary evidence, gives a more sympathetic image of the young man and his difficult relationship with his uncle.

Other Fiction. Luigi Malerba's *Il protagonista* is an erotic, symbolic extravaganza told in the first person by a male sex organ. The work is sustained by the author's irony, sense of parody, and verbal virtuosity. *Il protagonista* seems to be representative of a current tendency toward light, entertaining fiction with the emphasis on humor.

It is not a coincidence that readers, obviously tired of the despair and gloom that have prevailed in the literature of recent years, turned to such works as Manlio Cancogni's *Allegri, gioventù,* billed as "the funniest book of the year," or Franco Ferrucci's *Il capello di panama,* a picaresque tale filled with rogues, eccentrics, and various amusing, dreamlike figures. This popular attitude also explains the success of *Il pretore di Cuvio* by Pietro Chiara, a skillful and lively storyteller, and of *La donna di domenica* by Carlo Fruttero and Franco Lucentini. The latter work, ostensibly a detective story, raises the problem of woman's place in bourgeois society. It became a best seller not only in Italy but in France, Germany, and other European countries. In *Oh, Serafina!,* Giuseppe Berto follows an imaginative and satirical vein to create a comedy of folly, love, and ecology, set in an overpopulated, polluted Milan of factories and supermarkets.

Mention should also be made of an entirely different type of work, a social-protest novel, Saverio Strati's *Noi Lazzaroni,* which combines realism with lyricism. The work is a moving and dramatic evocation of emigrants from the south of Italy, who labor and sweat in foreign countries to escape the misery and destitution of such places as Calabria and Sicily.

Among the outstanding short story collections of 1973 were *Il mare color di vino,* 12 ironical and violent tales by Leonardo Sciascia; *Sulla soglia* by Gianna Manzini, whose art of fantasy and poetry reaches its summit in a story about El Greco; and *In visita* by Elena Croce, who portrays Italian post-World War II cultural circles.

Poetry. Major poetic works included *Diario 71 e 72* by Eugenio Montale, who calls himself "a bitter lover of life." Both the poems and prose pieces of this work offer new samples of his exquisite art. *Poesie d'amore* by Alfonso Gatto illustrates his maxim that "to love means to refer to the totality of existence." Vittorio Sereni's *Poesie scelte* includes his best poems from 1935 to 1965.

Obituaries. The death of Carlo Emilio Gadda, whose work has often been compared with that of James Joyce, represented a great loss to Italian literature. Also deeply felt was the death of Dino Buzzati, who was both a talented painter and an author of short stories.

MARC SLONIM
Sarah Lawrence College Foreign Studies

Japanese Literature

In 1973 one of the most striking features of Japanese literature was the increased activity of women writers. Two of the recipients of the important Akutagawa Prize in 1973 were women. Shizuko Gō won for *Rekuiem* (*Requiem*) and Michiko Yamoto won for *Betti-san-no Niwa* (*Betty's Yard*). Both novels deal with Japanese women during World War II and the postwar period.

In general, Japanese publishing thrived in 1973. There was a veritable "flood of publications" with a large rise in the number of new works published. In 1972 the ratio between new books and reprints or revised editions was 78.5% to 21.5%.

Fiction. The Japanese literary world was saddened in 1973 by the deaths of two well-known novelists: Tomoji Abe and Jirō Osaragi. Abe, who was also a fine translator, notably of Herman Melville's *Moby Dick,* died at the age of 69. His posthumously published novel *Hoshū* (*A Prisoner*) is widely regarded as his masterpiece. Osaragi, the prolific Yokohama-born writer, died at the age of 75. He wrote numerous works of fiction, including historical novels, some of which were adapted for television and film. Among Osaragi's best-known works are *Kurama Tengu* (*The Long-nosed Goblin of the Kurama Temple*), *Kikyō* (*Homecoming*), and *Muteki* (*Fog Horn*). The year 1973 also saw the

publication of the complete works of the late novelist Naoya Shiga.

An event that delighted the literary world was the awarding of the Lotus Prize in the field of Asian and African literature to Hiroshi Noma. He became the first Japanese to be so honored.

There were many new notable works of fiction in 1973. One of the most outstanding was Shōhei Ōoka's *Moya*, an "I-novel" related by an old man to his son, who has been living in New York for a long time. This work is, in a sense, a Japanese version of Henry James' *The Ambassadors*. Another important novel was Shūsaku Endō's *Shikai-no Hotori* (*By the Dead Sea*), a work with a Christian theme. In the remarkable novel *Hiwa* (*A Siskin*), a species of bird related to the goldfinch, the poet-novelist Taku Miki recreates the chaos in post-World War II Manchuria through the eyes of an adolescent boy.

One of the most widely read and discussed books of 1973 was Sakyō Komatsu's *Nihon Chinbotsu* (*The Sinking of Japan*) about the escape of the entire Japanese population from its country of islands all sinking as a result of great earthquakes. The work brought to mind the Great Kantō Earthquake of 1923 and also appealed to the current fascination in Japan with *shūmatsukan* or eschatology, a mystical concern with the final occurrences in the history of mankind.

Several fine works for younger readers were published in 1973. Chief among these are Kunio Tsuji's *Haikyōsha Yurianusu* (*Julian the Apostate*) and Shōjo Nosaka's *Ukiyo Ichidai Onna* (*A Woman in the Floating World*).

Nonfiction. Two literary studies were among the outstanding nonfiction works of 1973. Takeo Okuno's *Burai-to Itan* (*Villainy and Heresy*) is a study of the late novelist Ango Sakaguchi. Sakaguchi is widely regarded as a major representative of the postwar *Buraiha* (Villain School). The other work was Keiji Kataoka's *Ōe Kenzaburō-ron* (*A Study of Kenzaburō Ōe*). Ōe, who was born in 1935, first attracted attention with *The Extravagance of the Dead*, which was published in 1957 and won the Akutagawa Prize. Other interesting works were Sei Itō's *Nihon Bundanshi* (*The History of the Japanese Literary World*) and Hiroshi Noma's *Shinran*, about the medieval Japanese priest who founded Shin Buddhism, or Jōdo Shinshū—the "True Pure Land" sect, which has the largest following of all the Japanese Buddhist sects.

Poetry. In Japan the writing of poetry, especially *haiku* and *tanka* verse, is one of the most popular national pastimes. There are some 50 monthly poetry magazines in Japan with a circulation of about one million. It is therefore quite natural that many collections of *haiku*, *tanka*, and *gendaishi* (modern verse) were published in 1973 as in previous years. Among the most significant collections were *Kusano Shinpei-shi Zenshū* (*Complete Works of Shinpei Kusano's Poetry*) and *Gendai Tanka Taikei* (*Modern Tanka Verse*). A major literary event of 1973 was the publication of the complete works of the late poet Kenji Miyazawa.

Drama. Numerous plays were published and staged in 1973. The most noteworthy among these were Nobuo Kojima's *Issunsaki-wa Yami* (*The Future is All Darkness*); Kōbō Abe's *Ai-no Megane-wa Irogarasu* (*Love Wears Rose-Colored Glasses*); and Jūrō Kara's *Bengaruno Tora* (*Bengal Tiger*).

SHINJI TAKUWA
Kyushu University, Fukuoka, Japan

Latin American Literature

The steady flow of high-quality literature that once again came out of Latin America in 1973 continues to prove that the so-called literary "boom" is not an accident but the natural result of the gradual process of development and maturation of Latin American letters. This high quality continues to be recognized internationally. The Colombian novelist Gabriel García Márquez won the Books Abroad–Newstadt International Prize. Severo Sarduy of Cuba received the French Médicis Prize for the best foreign novel with his *Cobra*.

Fiction. In Argentina several established novelists published well-received works. Manuel Mujica Láinez published *Cécil*, a spiritual biography of an author's failures and frustrations, narrated by Cécil, who is a dog. Jorge Luis Borges brought out a new collection of poems and prose, *El oro de los tigres*. With *Guía de pecadores*, Eduardo Gudiño Keiffer revitalized the picaresque novel while dissecting Buenos Aires society.

Beatriz Guido published the novel *Una madre* and a collection of three tales, *Los insomnes*. Julio Cortázar published two new books. In *La casilla de los Morelli*, he dazzles the reader with his customary display of technical virtuosity. His other work, *Libro de Manuel*, is an ideological novel, emphasizing the struggle against oppression and injustice. In spite of its experimental language and shifting points of view, it is far less complex than most of his other novels.

Manuel Puig published his third novel, *The Buenos Aires Affair*, ostensibly a detective work, although he does away with many of the characteristics of the genre, including plot, detective-protagonist, and lineal development.

In Mexico, Luis Spota wrote *Las cajas* and Vicente Leñero published *Redil de ovejas*. Colombia's Jesús Zárate Moreno was awarded posthumously Spain's Premio Planeta for his novel *La Cárcel*. Cuba's Alejo Carpentier published *Los convidados de plata*, a short story taken from his forthcoming book on the Cuban Revolution, *El año 59*. Guatemala's Augusto Monterroso produced a new collection of tales, *Movimiento perpetuo*. The Uruguayan author Mario Benedetti wrote *Tregua*, using the diary form to express frustration and solitude. Brazil's foremost novelist, Jorge Amado, wrote *Tereza Batista cansada de guerra*, a best seller.

Nonfiction. The gifted Venezuelan author of both fiction and nonfiction Arturo Uslar Pietri won two prizes which recognize his multifaceted talent. For his work in journalism he received Argentina's Alberdi-Sarmiento Prize. For his essay in defense of Spanish culture, Spain conferred on him the Miguel de Cervantes Prize.

Mario Benedetti collected a series of his articles from *Marcha*, as well as some poems and three political speeches, for his *Crónicas del 71*. The Peruvian Mario Vargas Llosa wrote the introduction to a collection of *cartas de desafío* by J. Martorell, published under the title *El combate imaginario*. In Venezuela, Miguel Otero Silva gathered a series of his commentaries from newspapers dating back to 1936 in *Un morrocoy en el cielo*.

Several important scholarly works on literary subjects were published in 1973. Two works dealt with Julio Cortázar; Lida Aronne's *Cortázar: la novela mandala*, an analysis of *Rayuela*, and Juan Carlos Curutchet's *Julio Cortázar o la crítica de la*

BIBLIOTECA NACIONAL, RIO DE JANEIRO

BRAZILIAN novelist Jorge Amado published the best-selling Tereza Batista cansada de guerra in 1973.

razón pragmática. Marcos Ricardo Barnatán wrote Borges. Essential to the understanding of today's literature are Historia personal del "boom" by the Chilean writer José Donoso and El buitre y el ave fénix, in which Ricardo Cano Gaviria analyzes the literary ideas of Vargas Llosa.

Poetry. The Cuban Nicolás Guillén won Italy's Viareggio Prize and his countryman José Lezama Lima received Catalonia's Premio Maldoror. The Argentinian poet José Alberto Santiago Claros won Spain's prestigious Leopoldo Panero prize.

Pablo Neruda, Chile's famed and controversial poet, who died in 1973, published Geografía infructuosa and Iniciación al nixonicidio: alabanza a la revolución chilena. The latter work represents a political attack directed against the U. S. President. Of greater value for judging the new trends in Chilean poetry is Martín Michaverga's Poesía joven en Chile. In Mexico, Rosario Castellanos wrote Poesía no eres tú, and Homero Aridjis published an autobiographical account of his childhood and adolescence entitled El encantador solitario.

Theater. There were several festivals of Latin American theater in 1973, some of the most significant held abroad. One took place in San Francisco with the participation of such playwrights as Aron Abend of Brazil and Emilio Carballido of Mexico. The second Pan-American Theater Festival was held in Chicago. Several Latin American groups participated in the ninth World Theater Festival at Nancy, France. In Guatemala, the 10th Festival of Guatemalan Theater offered seven national plays in 1973.

Obituaries. Chile lost three of its foremost writers: Pablo Neruda, Nobel Prize-winner and dean of Spanish American poets, and the novelists Manuel Rojas and Benjamín Subercaseuax. Mexico lost José Gorostiza, one of its best poets.

MARÍA A. SALGADO
University of North Carolina at Chapel Hill

Soviet Literature

In Soviet literature in 1973, two subjects were given particular attention in the press, in public debates, and in literary conferences. One of the topics under discussion was the concept that Soviet literature is a multinational whole, cemented by common ideology and by the techniques of socialist realism. Adherents of this theory were in strong opposition to what they regarded as a symptomatic awakening of Great Russian nationalistic tendencies. They illustrated their viewpoint with numerous examples of translations from the many different tongues spoken in the USSR and by stressing the widespread and favorable publicity given to the Congress of Afro-Asian writers in Tashkent.

The other issue of major interest in Soviet literary circles was the suggested need for a combative literary criticism inspired by party principles. This idea was widely discussed in an extensive campaign throughout the country.

Fiction dominated the Soviet literary scene in 1973. In addition to works on such traditional subjects of Soviet fiction as those of war and of the Russian working man and woman, there were a number of interesting novels on the theme of the personal feelings and emotions of individuals, apart from political, social, or economic contexts.

Fiction on Personal Themes. The most popular and controversial novel of the year was The South American Variant by Sergei Zalyghin. It is a psychological study of a modern woman in her forties, Irina Mansurov, wife of a dull bureaucrat, mother of a grown son, and holder of a responsible position in the Institute of Scientific Information. She is intelligent, well educated, rational, and logical. Underneath the facade of her well-ordered life, however, there is a growing restlessness. She becomes aware of a longing for a true romantic involvement, a kind of love which she had permitted to pass her by. To make up for lost time, Irina attempts to have an affair with one of her colleagues. However, the experience is unsatisfactory to both of them, and the man finally abandons her. Left to herself again, she remembers someone she had met many years before. He had asked her to elope with him to South America, but she had refused, and now she dreams of him and their relationship.

The enormous success of The South American Variant reflects the intense preoccupation of Soviet readers with the existential problems of personal happiness. Zalyghin's theme, that work and political activity are not enough for the fulfillment of the individual, is also explored by such writers as Daniil Granin in Rain in an Unfamiliar Town, Sergei Krutilin in Wasteground, and Irina Welembovskaia in The Sweet Woman.

Fiction on Soviet Industrial and Rural Life. Novels of industrial production still receive official encouragement These types of works, however, generally lack artistic excellence and more often than not are boring. Two such novels in 1973 were Andrei Startzev's The Dry Pine Forest, about the production of cellulose at a northern mill, and Ilya Shtember's The Ordinary Month, about the daily worries and concerns of the chief engineer of a machine-producing plant.

The party critics constantly urge socially conscious authors to write about the working man and to create a true image of the modern proletarian hero. However, a number of writers have turned

instead to the so-called "village literature," much of which contrasts the solid time-honored virtues of the Russian peasant with the negative aspects of the industrial age, or, Scientific-Technological-Revolution (STR) as the Soviet press calls it. This trend can be seen in the novel *Roads and Crossroads* by Fedor Abramov, in such short story collections as *Way of Life* by Andrei Bitov and *Autumn in Taman* by Viktor Lihonossov, and in works by Vladimir Soloukhin, Vassily Belov, and Sergei Antonov.

War Literature. The year 1973 saw the publication of two important reminiscences from World War II—*Shortly Before the Silence*, a diary by Konstantin Simonov, and *The Teacher's House*, on the battle for Moscow, by George Berezko. Two novels dealing with diplomatic events before and after the war were Daniil Kraminov's *Dusk at Noon*, on events in Munich in the 1930's, and Savva Dangulov's *Kuznetzki Bridge*, on the relationships among the Allies before Yalta.

Miscellaneous Fiction. A number of younger writers were attracted to the comic novel. Humorous and eccentric personages were featured in such works as Fazil Iskander's *Sandro from Cheghema*, Vladimir Yevtushenko's *The Apple Tree of Discord*, and Manuil Semenov's *Galakhova*.

Poetry. Several major poetic works were published. They included Andrei Voznesensky's *The Glance;* Yevgeny Yevtushenko's *The Singing Dam* and *Road Number One;* Yaroslav Smeliakov's *Work and Love;* and Viktor Sosnora's *The Stork.*

MARC SLONIM
Sarah Lawrence College Foreign Studies

Spanish Literature

The spectacular proliferation of literary prizes in 1973, as in recent years, has probably been a major contributing factor in the increasingly heightened creative activity of Spanish writers. While literary contests and prizes connected with civic and commercial promotions do not guarantee the emergence of artistic quality, they can and do facilitate its random appearance.

Fiction. Significant prize-winning novels included José María Carrascal's *Groovy* (Nadal Prize), a critical re-creation of the world suggested by the title word; Gonzalo Torrente Ballester's *La saga/fuga de J. B.* (Ciudad de Barcelona and Crítica Prizes), a fictional critique of the *new* novel and widely considered the best fictional narrative of 1973; and Juan Marse's *Si te dicen que caí* (México Prize), a pointed reconstruction of post-Civil War Barcelona. One of the many new prizes that now abound, the Café Colón de Almería Prize, was awarded to Javier del Amo's *El canto de las sirenas de Gaspar Hauser.*

Among the well-established novelists who published in 1973 were Juan Antonio de Zunzunegui (*La hija malograda*), Antonio Prieto (*Secretum*), Elena Quiroga (*Presente profundo*), Juan Benet (*La otra casa de Mazón*), and Jesús Fernández Santos (*Paraíso encerrado*). Significant novels from lesser-known writers appearing in 1973 included José Ramón Arana's *Can Girona*, Isaac Montero's *Los días de amor, guerra y omnipotencia de David el Callado*, José Luis Martín's *El sabor de la carne*, and Gregorio Gallego's *Los caínes.*

The field of short fiction was especially enriched by Ignacio Aldecoa's posthumous *Cuentos completos*. Other outstanding short-story collections were Marta Portal's *La veintena;* José Luis Martín

Abril's *El viento se acuesta al atardecer;* Rodolfo Arévalo's *Descalzo y otros cuentos;* Meliano Peraile's realistic *Insula ibérica;* Luis Mateo Diez' *Memorial de hierbas;* and Andrés Recio's *El aborto de Juana Zacarías.*

Nonfiction. An impressive number of important scholarly works were published in 1973. Juan López-Morillas' *Hacia el 98* brought together several of this major hispanist's best studies. Other outstanding works included Luis López Martínez's *La novelística de Miguel Delibes;* Dinko Cvitanovic's *La novela sentimental española;* José Bergamín's *Beltenebros y otros ensayos sobre literatura española;* Francisco Rico's *Alfonso el sabio y la General Estoria;* José María Aguirre's *Antonio Machado, poeta simbolista;* and Angeles Prado's *La literatura del casticismo.*

In the field of the essay, important publications included Francisco Umbral's *Diario de un snob* and *Carta abierta a una chica progre* and José Luis Aranguren's *Moralidades de hoy y de mañana*, a probe into the socio-ethical nature of modern man. Also noteworthy were Pedro de Lorenzo's *El libro del político;* Angel María Lera's *Mi viaje alrededor de la locura;* and Dionisio Ridruejo's *Entre literatura y política.*

Poetry. Major poetry prizes went to José Alberto Santiago's *Formalidades* (Leopoldo Panero Prize), Concha de Marco's *Tarot* (Juan Ramón Jiménez Prize), and Alfonso Canales' *Requiem andaluz* (Crítica Prize). Among the most important works by major established poets were Gabriel Celaya's *Función de uno, equis, ene;* Carlos Bousoño's *Las monedas contra la losa;* Dionisio Ridruejo's *Casi en prosa;* Luis Felipe Vivanco's heretofore unpublished *Poemas en prosa;* Gloria Fuerte's *Sola en la sala;* Juan Van-Halen's *Cuaderno de Asia;* Concha Lagos' *La aventura;* Julio Alfredo Egea's *Desventurada vida y muerte de María Sánchez;* Alfonso Canales' *Epica menor;* Carlos Murciano's *Poesía, 1950–1972;* and José María Souvirón's *Poesía entera, 1923–1973.*

Significant publications by younger poets included Angel Berenguer's *Poemas para una ciudad hipotética que pudo llamarse Calamarga*, José María Delgado's *Tras el espejo*, and Enrike Gracia's *Encuentros.*

Theater. The Lope de Vega Prize was awarded to José María Camps, long a refugee in Mexico, for his *El edicto de gracia*. The Juan del Encina Prize went to José Fernando Dicenta for *La jaula*. Unquestionably, however, the highlight of the theatrical season was the much-discussed appearance of plays from important writers identified, for the most part before the Civil War, with literary forms other than the theater. They were *La comedia del diantre* by the novelist Ramón Sender and *El labrador de más aire* by the late poet Miguel Hernández.

Promise was shown in the works of such young dramatists as Luis Lucas (*Diabólica noche de lluvia*), Pedro María Herrero (*Balada de los tres inocentes*), and José María Lacoma (*El señor pesa cada día más*).

Translations. Among recent translations from Spanish into English were Ramón Pérez de Ayala's *Honeymoon, Bittermoon*, by Barry Eisenberg; Miguel Delibes' *Smoke on the Ground*, by Alfred Johnson; and Lope de Vega's *The Knight of Olmedo*, by Willard F. King.

ALFRED RODRIGUEZ
University of New Mexico

MAYOR TOM BRADLEY takes the oath of office administered by former U. S. Chief Justice Earl Warren. Bradley is the first black mayor of Los Angeles. Mrs. Bradley witnesses the ceremony.

UPI

LOS ANGELES

The most newsworthy event in Los Angeles in 1973 was the mayoralty election on May 29, when Thomas Bradley (see BIOGRAPHY) defeated three-term incumbent Samuel Yorty. Bradley is the first black to be elected mayor of an American city as large as Los Angeles—third in the nation, after New York and Chicago.

Elections. In the nonpartisan primary on April 3, Bradley, a former police lieutenant and city councilman, and Yorty, both Democrats, easily outran Jesse Unruh, former speaker of the state assembly, and Tom Reddin, former Los Angeles police chief, in a field of 13 candidates. According to city election laws, any candidate receiving more than 50% of the primary vote is elected mayor. However, since neither Bradley not Yorty attained that percentage, the May runoff was necessary.

In the postprimary campaign, Yorty used conservative appeals with certain "scare" tactics that had racial overtones—an approach that worked four years earlier, when he also faced Bradley in the runoff. This time, however, the technique failed. Many former Yorty voters in the largely white middle-class San Fernando Valley did not vote, and he lost much of his support among the city's Jewish and Mexican-American populations. In the May 29 election, in which only 65% of the registered voters turned out, Bradley was an easy winner, with more than 56% of the vote.

In other election results, the eight incumbent councilmen up for reelection were victorious, with only one having a close race. Burt Pines defeated Roger Arnebergh, city attorney for 20 years, in an election in which the voters seem to have confused the largely routine duties of the city attorney with those of the Los Angeles County district attorney, whose office has considerably more power.

The Bradley Administration. Mayor Bradley took office on July 1. He pledged to maintain close ties with his former colleagues on the City Council. His first months in office were relatively uneventful, although there was a stir when he asked for the resignation of all city commissioners—appointed officials on governing and advisory boards—effective inauguration day. More than half of the commissioners resigned, giving Bradley immediate influence over the makeup of various boards, which are highly important in a city with few direct administrative powers in the hands of the mayor.

The new mayor, in the face of financial pressures, soon became involved in a series of minor differences over budget cuts. He also ran into some resistance in asking for five new major staff positions requiring "executive talent." These positions, he said, were intended to help the mayor's office in dealing with "human problems" and economic development.

School Decentralization. In the continuing efforts to decentralize Los Angeles' mammoth school district into units that might be more manageable under local control, state legislation was introduced to subdivide the single city district into three units. The proposal, similar to a bill that narrowly failed passage in 1970, was defeated.

Rapid Transit. Despite the possibility of fuel shortages and the continued efforts to curtail air pollution, moves to establish an effective rapid-transit system in the greater Los Angeles area made little progress during 1973. (Construction of such a system was one of Mayor Bradley's campaign promises, and he gave it high priority in his administration.) Toward the end of the year, the area's rapid transit district was temporarily forced to curtail bus service and to discontinue it on Sundays because of the fuel shortage, but federal government restrictions were later lifted.

Earlier in the year, a 116-mile transit network, utilizing high-speed trains and buses and subways, was proposed for the Los Angeles area. The system, to cost an estimated $7 billion, would be financed by a sales tax and federal aid. Hopes were expressed for completion by the late 1980's, but the technical, administrative, and financial difficulties experienced by the new San Francisco area rapid transit system discouraged popular support for the plan.

Uneven County Justice. In April, the Rand Corporation reported its findings after a year-long study of criminal justice in Los Angeles County. It noted that differences in treatment exist according to the race or ethnic group of the accused, the individual judge, the arresting agency, and the branch of the district attorney's office. It concluded that "no reasonable set of performance standards currently exists for criminal justice agencies." Los Angeles County District Attorney Joseph P. Busch called for investigations into possible reforms in the justice system.

CHARLES R. ADRIAN
University of California, Riverside

LOUISIANA

Louisiana gained almost $300 million in new annual income by changing the tax on petroleum products in 1973. The Legislature passed new abortion laws and reinstated the death penalty. There were several incidents of violence in the state during the year, as well as floods and a disastrous fire.

Government. Observers credited Gov. Edwin W. Edwards with one of the smartest political moves of any governor in recent years when he used the energy crisis as a springboard to state tax reform, adding $169 million a year to the state treasury. At his urging, the Legislature, in a special "energy crisis" session, doubled the severence tax on natural gas and changed the levy on oil from a volume to a value basis. Louisiana is one of the nation's leading producers of petroleum and natural gas.

The revised taxes were expected to increase the state's income from petroleum and natural gas sources by almost $300 million. Some $130 million of the boost was to be rebated to taxpayers through new tax breaks for individuals and corporations. The remaining $169 million was to be divided among a new state energy commission; salary increases for all state workers, including teachers; highway construction; retirement of the state debt; and rebates to local industries for natural gas tax increases.

In its regular session, the Legislature passed five bills that were designed to curb abortion. The bills allow medical personnel, institutions, and

---------------- LOUISIANA • Information Highlights ----------------

Area: 48,523 square miles (125,675 sq km).
Population (1972 est.): 3,720,100. *Density:* 82 per sq mi.
Chief Cities (1970 census): Baton Rouge, the capital, 165,-963; New Orleans, 593,471; Shreveport, 182,064; Lake Charles, 77,998; Lafayette, 68,908; Monroe, 56,374.
Government (1973): *Chief Officers*—governor, Edwin W. Edwards (D); lt. gov., James E. Fitzmorris, Jr. (D); secy. of state, Wade O. Martin, Jr. (D); atty. gen., William J. Guste, Jr. (D); treas., Mrs. Mary Evelyn Parker (D); supt. of public education, Louis J. Michot (D); chief justice, Joe W. Sanders. *Legislature*—Senate, 39 members (38 Democrats, 1 Republican); House of Representatives, 105 members (101 D, 4 R).
Education (1972–73): *Enrollment*—public elementary schools, 511,298 pupils, 22,306 teachers; public secondary schools, 335,221 pupils, 18,187 teachers; nonpublic schools, 140,-600 pupils, 5,490 teachers; colleges and universities, 131,999 students. *Public school expenditures*, $717,261,-000 ($927 per pupil). *Average teacher's salary*, $9,388.
State Finances (fiscal year 1971): *Revenues*, $1,900,682,000 (3% general sales tax and gross receipts taxes, $233,759,-000; motor fuel tax, $124,592,000; federal funds, $453,-232,000). *Expenditures*, $1,770,162,000 (education, $706,-877,000; health, welfare, and safety, $322,927,000; highways, $307,850,000). *State debt*, $945,378,000 (June 1971).
Personal Income (1972): $13,126,000,000; *per capita*, $3,528.
Public Assistance (1972): $271,285,000. *Average monthly payments* (Dec. 1972)—old-age assistance, $73.98; aid to families with dependent children, $90.75.
Labor Force: *Nonagricultural wage and salary earners* (July 1973), 1,144,000. *Average annual employment* (1972)—manufacturing, 178,800; trade, 262,300; government, 226,-500; services, 167,200. *Insured unemployed* (Sept. 1973)—23,800 (2.6%).
Manufacturing (1971): *Value added by manufacture*, $3,504,-500,000. Chemicals and allied products, $1,011,100,000; food and kindred products, $573,400,000; petroleum and coal products, $413,900,000.
Agriculture (1972): *Cash farm income*, $881,536,000 (livestock, $323,639,000; crops, $506,944,000; government payments, $50,953,000). *Chief crops* (in order of value, 1972)—Soybeans; rice (ranks 3d among the states); cotton lint; sugarcane for sugar and seed (ranks 3d).
Mining (1972): *Production value*, $5,606,248,000 (ranks 2d among the states). *Chief minerals*—Petroleum, $3,203,-357,000; natural gas, $1,807,920,000; natural gas liquids, $360,300,000; sulfur, value not available.
Fisheries (1972): *Commercial catch*, 1,070,597,000 pounds ($71,916,000). *Leading species by value*—Shrimp, $47,-023,000; menhaden, $15,480,000; oysters, $4,418,000.
Transportation: *Roads* (1972), 53,340 miles (85,840 km); *motor vehicles* (1972), 1,832,285; *railroads* (1972), 3,753 miles (6,040 km); *public airports* (1972), 70.
Communications: *Telephones* (1973), 1,980,600; *television stations* (1971), 15; *radio stations* (1971), 133; *newspapers* (1973), 26 (daily circulation, 823,000).

pregnant women to refuse to participate in abortions; prohibit state employees from recommending abortions; make survivors of abortion attempts wards of the state; prohibit advertising of abortion services; and require physicians to fill out long forms if they perform abortions. The death penalty was reinstated for first-degree murder.

A 132-member Constitutional Convention worked throughout the year, preparing a document to be voted on in 1974. At the end of the year, many observers saw little chance for voter approval of the new constitution unless major revisions were made affecting taxation, revenue, and education.

Politics. Corinne Morrison Boggs, widow of U. S. House majority leader Hale Boggs, who was lost in a plane over Alaska in 1972, won her late husband's seat in the House by a large margin in 1973. Mrs. Boggs was the first woman ever elected to Congress from Louisiana.

Former Attorney General Jack P. F. Gremillion began serving a federal prison term in 1973 for perjury. Meanwhile, Agriculture Commissioner Dave Pearce awaited trial on almost three dozen indictments for extortion, theft, and perjury.

In New Orleans, District Attorney Jim Garrison —nationally known for his dissenting views on the official explanation of President John F. Kennedy's assassination—was acquitted of charges that he took bribes from illegal pinball machine operators. In December he was narrowly defeated for reelection by Harry Connick, a former assistant U. S. attorney.

The Courts. State and appellate courts ordered equalization of property tax assessments statewide by 1976. The Louisiana supreme court struck down the state's obscenity statutes, removing legal roadblocks to the showing of such films as *Last Tango in Paris*.

Disasters and Violence. The Mississippi River went on a spring rampage, forcing the opening of flood protection gates for the first time in decades. Agricultural crops were hit hard in some areas. At midyear in New Orleans, 33 persons burned to death in a fire believed to have been deliberately set in a walkup bar frequented by homosexuals.

In January, the nation watched on television as New Orleans police flushed out and killed a sniper, who had killed seven persons, on the roof of a multistory downtown motel. In Baton Rouge two FBI agents fatally shot a black man they were trying to apprehend as an Army deserter, only to find that the actual deserter had used the victim's stolen identification to enlist in the service. A local grand jury declined to indict the federal agents.

EDWIN W. PRICE, JR.
"The Morning Advocate," Baton Rouge

LUXEMBOURG

In April 1973, the European Economic Community (EEC) decided to set up the European Monetary Cooperation Fund in Luxembourg. Britain had wanted the offices of the Fund to be located in Brussels, but Luxembourg had been promised priority when future institutions were to be established. Luxembourg insisted that the promise be honored, threatening to use its veto power to block the Fund. The Fund was formally established on April 6. Luxembourg was designated its temporary seat; a final decision on the permanent seat was postponed. Luxembourg has become an important financial center.

——— LUXEMBOURG · Information Highlights ———

Official Name: Grand Duchy of Luxembourg.
Location: Western Europe.
Area: 999 square miles (2,586 sq km).
Population (1973 est.): 400,000. *Density,* 342 per square mile (132 per sq km).
Chief Cities (1970 census): Luxembourg, the capital, 76,143; Esch-sur-Alzette, 27,575; Differdange, 17,963.
Government: *Head of state,* Jean, grand duke (acceded Nov. 1964). *Head of government,* Pierre Werner, premier (took office Feb. 1959). *Legislature* (unicameral)—Chamber of Deputies. *Major political parties*—Christian Social party; Socialist party; Democratic party; Communist party; Social Democratic party.
Languages: French (official), German, Letzeburgesch.
Education: *Expenditure* (1969), 15.2% of total public expenditure. *School enrollment* (1969)—primary, 36,035; secondary, 18,036; technical/vocational, 9,347; university/higher, 422.
Monetary Unit: Franc (35.86 francs equal U. S.$1, Aug. 1973).
Gross National Product (1972): $1,200,000,000.
Economic Indexes: *Industrial production* (1972), 132 (1963 = 100); *agricultural production* (Belgium-Luxembourg, 1971), 130 (1963 = 100); *consumer price index* (1972), 136 (1963 = 100).
Manufacturing (major products): Iron and steel, chemicals, fertilizer, textiles, nonferrous metals.
Major Agricultural Products: Barley, wheat, oats, grapes.
Major Minerals: Iron ore, slate.
Foreign Trade (Luxembourg-Belgium, 1972): Exports, $16,-081,000,000. Imports, $15,605,000,000. *Chief trading partners* (1970)—West Germany (took 25% of exports, supplied 25% of imports); France (20%—18%); Netherlands (19% —16%).
Tourism: Receipts (with Belgium, 1971), $370,000,000.
Transportation: *Motor vehicles* (1971), 111,600 (automobiles, 98,800); *railroads* (1971), 168 miles (271 km); *major national airline,* Luxair (Luxembourg Airlines).
Communications: *Telephones* (1972), 118,664; *newspapers* (1971), 8.

Economy.

Both agricultural and industrial production increased in 1973 over 1972. In 1973 domestic and foreign demand increased by 8%, considerably above expectation. Living costs, however, increased 7% over those in 1972. To combat inflation the government instituted a stabilization program to supplement the EEC anti-inflation plan. The program provided for the encouragement of savings deposits; the issue of government bonds at attractive interest rates and open to subscription only by small savers; the restriction of building credits for social projects; a 5% increase in the corporation tax, refundable at the first economic recession; and the restriction of consumer credit.

Hereditary Grand Duke. On April 16, Prince Henri became 18 years of age and was given the title of Hereditary Grand Duke of Luxembourg.

AMRY VANDENBOSCH, *University of Kentucky*

MAINE

Legislative action to relieve the property tax burden, a management and cost survey, and an ocean boundary dispute with New Hampshire were among developments making news in Maine in 1973.

Government. The 106th session of the Maine Legislature met in 1973. Significant legislation included bills designed to reform the tax structure of Maine. The allocation to the state of over $25 million in revenue sharing monies made possible the enactment of property tax relief measures, arresting, for the time being, the upward drift of local property taxes. Sales tax exemption for new machinery purchase was also adopted, as was property tax exemption on business inventories, measures designed to improve Maine's economic position.

Management and Cost Survey Report. The Maine Management and Cost Survey was authorized by the 105th Legislature. Nearly 100 individuals were loaned by Maine businesses to form the management and cost team. Under the chairmanship of James Longley, a Portland insurance executive, the team conducted an exhaustive 9-month study of the efficiency of operations of the state government and the University of Maine. Its report, released in September 1973, contained over 800 recommendations designed to save the state $23 million.

In September, the University of Maine rejected the major recommendations of the survey in regard to the university system. The report had urged the university to eliminate the Bangor campus, convert four-year campuses at Ft. Kent, Presque Isle, and Machias into community colleges, and extend trustee authority to the state's network of vocational-technical institutes.

Economic Developments. The economy moved at a slow rate of growth in 1973. High interest rates slowed construction and discouraged property transfers, and poor summer weather reduced tourism. Extraordinary increases in many prices wiped out hard-won gains of past years. Maine voters approved a lottery in November.

Maine's Bureau of Environmental Protection held hearings on the application of the Pittston Company to construct an oil refinery at Eastport. A decision was expected in 1974.

"Lobster War." New Hampshire lobster fishermen were arrested by Maine fish wardens and subsequently fined for trapping lobster in offshore waters claimed by both states in a long-standing boundary dispute. This led New Hampshire's governor to revoke a temporary boundary agreement concluded in 1970 and to remark that Maine "has apparently declared war on us." The U. S. Supreme Court agreed to review the issue. (See also NEW HAMPSHIRE.)

RONALD F. BANKS, *University of Maine*

——— MAINE · Information Highlights ———

Area: 33,215 square miles (86,027 sq km).
Population (1972 est.): 1,029,000. *Density:* 32 per sq mi.
Chief Cities (1970 census): Augusta, the capital, 21,945; Portland, 65,116; Lewiston, 41,779; Bangor, 33,168.
Government (1973): *Chief Officers*—governor, Kenneth M. Curtis (D); secy. of state, Joseph D. Edgar (R); atty. gen., Jon A. Lund (R); treas., Norman K. Ferguson; commissioner of education, Carroll R. McGary; chief justice, Armand A. Dufresne, Jr. *Legislature*—Senate, 33 members (22 Republicans, 11 Democrats); House of Representatives, 151 members (79 R, 72 D).
Education (1972–73): *Enrollment*—public elementary schools, 177,393 pupils, 6,721 teachers; public secondary schools, 70,055 pupils, 4,456 teachers; nonpublic schools, 19,600 pupils, 1,060 teachers; colleges and universities, 32,885 students. *Public school expenditures,* $194,800,000 ($840 per pupil). *Average teacher's salary,* $9,277.
State Finances (fiscal year 1971): *Revenues,* $483,316,000 (5% general sales tax and gross receipts taxes, $91,987,000; motor fuel tax, $39,460,000; federal funds, $126,818,000). *Expenditures,* $443,378,000 (education, $159,628,000; health, welfare, and safety, $92,128,000; highways, $91,280,000). *State debt,* $251,421,000 (June 30, 1971).
Personal Income (1972): $3,675,000,000; per capita, $3,571.
Public Assistance (1972): $88,875,000. *Average monthly payments* (Dec. 1972)—old-age assistance, $83.76; aid to families with dependent children, $138.16.
Labor Force: *Nonagricultural wage and salary earners* (July 1973), 345,000. *Average annual employment* (1972)—manufacturing, 102,600; trade, 68,200; government, 69,700; services, 49,500. *Insured unemployed* (Sept. 1973)—7,200 (2.6%).
Manufacturing (1971): Value added by manufacture, $1,208,-300,000. Paper and allied products, $323,200,000; leather and leather products, $180,300,000; food and kindred products, $169,600,000.
Agriculture (1972): *Cash farm income,* $245,968,000 (livestock, $155,248,000; crops, $89,425,000; government payments, $1,295,000). *Chief crops* (in order of value, 1972)—Potatoes (ranks 3d among the states); hay, apples, oats.
Mining (1972): *Production value,* $20,870,000 (ranks 47th among the states). *Chief minerals*—Cement, value not available; sand and gravel, $5,646,000; stone, $3,404,000.
Fisheries (1972): *Commercial catch,* 149,271,000 pounds ($34,-819,000). *Leading species by value*—Lobsters, $18,587,000; clams, $3,716,000; shrimp, $3,232,000.
Transportation: *Roads* (1972), 21,424 miles (34,478 km); *motor vehicles* (1972), 536,815; *railroads* (1972), 1,666 miles (2,-681 km); *public airports* (1972), 42.
Communications: *Telephones* (1973), 553,600; *television stations* (1971), 7; *radio stations* (1971), 50; *newspapers* (1973), 10 (daily circulation, 274,000).

MALAYSIA

The formation of a National Front coalition, considerable improvement in the economy, and foreign policy initiatives marked 1973 in Malaysia.

The National Front. The enlargement of the multiparty governing coalition was completed on January 1 with the admission of the conservative Malay party, Partei Islam. Earlier, the Sarawak United People's party and Gerakan, both predominantly Chinese parties, had joined the three original Alliance party partners—the United Malays National Organization (UMNO), the Malaysian Chinese Association, and Malaysian Indian Congress. The UMNO remained the dominant government party. The Partei Islam's leader, Dato Asri Haji Muda, and its secretary general, Dato Abu Bakar Hamzah, were given cabinet posts.

For the first time since 1957 all 13 state governments were controlled by parties friendly to the central government. According to Prime Minister Tun Abdul Razak, the National Front represented more than 80% of the electorate and was expected to reduce the intensity of active politicking and thereby ease racial tensions. Fresh parliamentary elections to consolidate the new government's position were predicted for the near future.

The weakened opposition parties, holding only 22 out of 144 parliamentary seats, set about to organize their own united front. Leaders of the Democratic Action party (DAP), Sarawak National party, Pekemas (Social Justice party), and Party Mahrein quickly agreed to form an opposition bloc with a rotating parliamentary leader, a post held by the DAP's Lim Kit Siang for the first year. The four parties also made an electoral arrangement for the forthcoming elections.

Other Governmental Developments. The death of Deputy Prime Minister Tun Ismail, a key UMNO leader since independence, in August necessitated a cabinet reshuffle. Datuk Hussein Onn was appointed to succeed Tun Ismail; he had earlier been chosen as the new deputy president of UMNO. The creation of four new ministerial posts enlarged the cabinet to 24 members.

In July, Parliament passed a constitutional amendment that raised the status of the capital, Kuala Lumpur, to that of a federal territory, directly administered by the central government. The government also provided for 10 new parliamentary seats for West Malaysia to be filled after the next elections.

Economy. A welcome increase in the world price of rubber to a new 10-year high was considered the primary reason for the marked economic growth Malaysia experienced in 1973. The government announced a tripling in West Malaysia's trade surplus in the first five months of 1973, and both Sarawak and Sabah also enjoyed substantial increases in their exports.

Significant new offshore oil strikes were made off the east coast of mainland Malaysia as well as in Sabah and Sarawak. The government decided to set up a national oil corporation and to conclude production-sharing agreements with foreign oil companies, both moves modeled on Indonesian practice. Malaysia signed agreements with three oil firms in April, providing for a 65% share in production by the government, with 35% retained by the oil companies. A similar agreement was made in May with a fourth company.

Three important changes in monetary policy were abruptly announced by the government in May. Since the Malaysian government believed that Britain had effectively dismantled the sterling area in 1972, it adopted new exchange controls. It also decided to terminate the joint interchangeability agreement affecting Malaysian and Singaporean currencies, in effect since 1965. Malaysia's third action was stepping out of the joint stock exchange operated with Singapore and opening a separate stock exchange in Kuala Lumpur. These drastic steps were taken without prior consultation with Singapore. Malaysia's finance minister, Tun Tan Siew Sin, argued that the monetary innovations would accelerate Malaysia's industrialization program and the rate of its economic growth. When Singapore unilaterally floated its currency against the U. S. dollar in June, Malaysia quickly floated its own dollar.

Foreign Policy. Malaysia won additional external support for its proposal to bring about the neutralization of Southeast Asia under Great Power guarantees. The Malaysian plan was endorsed by President V. V. Giri of India during his state visit in March and later by the Yugoslav prime minister, Džemal Bijedić.

Several initiatives illustrated Malaysia's determination to pursue a less pro-Western and more neutral foreign policy. In a step partly designed to influence members of the Association of Southeast Asian Nations (ASEAN), the government announced in March that it would establish diplomatic relations with North Vietnam. Indonesia is the only other member of ASEAN that recognizes Hanoi. Kuala Lumpur also announced that it would exchange ambassadors with East Germany and Iraq. The government continued its negotiations with rep-

--------- MALAYSIA • Information Highlights ---------

Official Name: Malaysia.
Location: Southeast Asia.
Area: 127,316 square miles (329,749 sq km).
Population (1973 est.): 11,800,000. *Density,* West Malaysia, 176 per square mile (68 per sq km); East Malaysia, 23 per square mile (9 per sq km).
Chief Cities (1970 census): Kuala Lumpur, the capital, 451,-728; Pinang (Penang), 270,019; Ipoh, 247,689; Kuching, 63,491; Kota Kinabalu, 41,830.
Government: *Head of state,* Sultan Abdul Halim Muadzam, supreme sovereign (took office Sept. 1970). *Head of government,* Tun Abdul Razak, prime minister (took office Sept. 1970). *Legislature*—Parliament: Dewan Negara (Senate) and Dewan Ra'ayat (House of Representatives). *Major political parties*—Alliance party; Pan-Malayan Islamic party; Democratic Action party; Sarawak National party.
Languages: Malay (official), English, Chinese.
Education: *Expenditure* (West Malaysia, 1967), 14.6% of total public expenditure. *School enrollment* (1969)—primary, 1,627,705; secondary, 591,205; technical/vocational, 13,-155; university/higher, 15,447.
Monetary Unit: Malaysian dollar (2.49 M. dollars equal U. S. $1, May 1973).
Gross National Product (1972 est.): $4,540,000,000.
Economic Indexes: *Industrial production* (1972), 131 (1968 = 100); *agricultural production* (West Malaysia, 1971), 162 (1963 = 100); *consumer price index* (West Malaysia, 1972), 105 (1970 = 100).
Manufacturing (major products): Petroleum products, sugar, rubber goods, steel, fertilizer, sawn wood.
Major Agricultural Products: Rubber (ranks 1st among world producers, 1972), palm oil and kernels (world rank 1st, 1972), rice, tea, pepper, coconuts, spices, fruit, forest products.
Major Minerals: Tin (ranks 1st among world producers, 1971), iron ore, petroleum, bauxite.
Foreign Trade (1972): *Exports,* $1,855,000,000. *Imports,* $1,-727,000,000. *Chief trading partners* (1971)—Singapore (took 22% of exports, supplied 8% of imports); Japan (18%—20%); United States (13%—7%); United Kingdom (7%—15%).
Tourism: Receipts (1971), $10,170,000.
Transportation: *Motor vehicles* (1971), 382,200 (automobiles, 308,900); *railroads* (1971), 1,132 miles (1,822 km); *major national airline,* MAS (Malaysian Airline System).
Communications: *Telephones* (West Malaysia, 1972), 163,897; *newspapers* (1969), 37 (daily circulation, 781,000).

resentatives of the People's Republic of China to establish diplomatic relations. During the visit of an economic mission from Poland in March, an agreement was signed to increase trade and technical cooperation between the two countries.

Kuala Lumpur was the site in February of a special meeting of ASEAN foreign ministers that assessed the regional implications of the Vietnam peace agreement. The delegates decided to coordinate their individual efforts for aiding the reconstruction of Vietnam and the rest of Indochina. They also endorsed a proposal to convene a wider Asian forum representing all Southeast Asian states, but deferred its implementation until "an appropriate time in the future."

C. PAUL BRADLEY
University of Michigan-Flint

MANITOBA

The year 1973—a prosperous one for Manitoba —was highlighted by a general election that brought greater political stability to the province.

Election. On May 25, Premier Ed Schreyer unexpectedly announced a general election for June 28. The governing New Democratic party (NDP), the Progressive Conservative party (the official opposition), the Liberal party, and some Social Crediters and independents waged a vigorous campaign throughout the province. So did the newly formed Group for Good Government, a nonpartisan group of businessmen who supported any candidate likely to defeat a government supporter. Principal issues were the government's four-year record, agricultural and social-welfare policies, northern hydroelectric

------- **MANITOBA** · **Information Highlights** -------

Area: 246,512 square miles (638,466 sq km).
Population (1972 est.): 992,000.
Chief Cities (1971 census): Winnipeg, the capital (246,246); St. James-Assiniboia (71,431), St. Boniface (46,714).
Government: *Chief Officers* (1973)—lt. gov., William J. McKeag; premier, Edward R. Schreyer (New Democratic party); atty. gen., Howard R. Pawley (NDP); min. of finance, Saul Cherniak (NDP); min. of educ., Ben Hanuschak (NDP); chief justice, Samuel Freedman. *Legislature*—Legislative Assembly; 57 members (31 New Democratic party, 21 Progressive Conservative, 5 Liberal).
Education: *School enrollment* (1969–70)—public elementary and secondary, 245,363 pupils (11,194 teachers); private schools, 8,178 pupils (532 teachers); Indian (federal) schools, 5,938 pupils (240 teachers); college and university, 16,597 students. *Public school expenditures* (1970) —$194,706,000; average teacher's salary (1970 est.), $7,886.
Public Finance (fiscal year 1973 est.): *Revenues*, $734,200,- 000 (sales tax, $156,400,000; income tax, $182,100,000; federal funds, $235,000,000). *Expenditures*, $724,900,000 (education, $197,000,000; health and social welfare, $295,- 800,000; transport and communications, $53,600,000).
Personal Income (1971 est.): $3,165,000,000; average annual income per person, $3,203.
Social Welfare (fiscal year 1973 est.): $81,600,000 (dependents and unemployed, $54,200,000).
Manufacturing (1969): *Value added by manufacture*, $486,- 057,000 (food and beverages, $120,046,000; fabricated metals, $47,043,000; printing and publishing, $43,713,000; transportation equipment, $37,388,000; clothing, $35,950,- 000; primary metals, $32,520,000).
Agriculture (1972 est.): *Cash farm income* (exclusive of government payments), $475,091,000 (livestock and products, $237,621,000; crops, $230,725,000.) *Chief crops* (cash receipts)—wheat, $99,117,000 (ranks 3d among the provinces); barley, $44,531,000 (ranks 3d); rapeseed, $19,- 322,000; flaxseed, $13,128,000 (ranks 2d); oats, $10,060,- 000 (ranks 1st).
Mining (1972 est.): *Production value*, $311,154,000. *Chief minerals*—nickel, $179,050,000 (ranks 2d among the provinces); copper, $59,187,000; zinc, $17,516,000; cement, $14,838,000; crude petroleum, $14,559,000; tantalum, $2,- 307,000 (ranks 1st).
Transportation: *Roads* (1970), 48,920 miles (78,727 km); *motor vehicles* (1970), 403,187; *railroads* (1971), 4,746 track miles (7,638 km); *licensed airports* (1971 est.), 19.
Communications: *Telephones* (1970), 436,063; *television stations* (1972), 16; *radio stations* (1972), 14; *daily newspapers* (1972), 7.
(All monetary figures given in Canadian dollars.)

developments, and arguments over the amount of socialism in the NDP's platform for another term.

The result was a government victory, the NDP winning an outright majority of 31 of the 57 seats. Since the 1969 election it had depended on capricious independents for survival. Two cabinet ministers were defeated, however. Progressive Conservatives won 21 seats and the Liberals, 5. The exertions of the Group for Good Government seemed to have had little influence on the outcome.

Economic Developments. Record-breaking prices for agricultural products and a good harvest formed a solid foundation for the economy. Prosperity was reflected in all other sectors, with unemployment declining to 3.2%, the second-lowest provincial rate.

On March 27, Premier Schreyer, in his dual capacity as minister of finance, unveiled a budget that opposition members had difficulty criticizing. The current surplus was $43 million, and almost every taxpayer received some measure of relief. Health insurance premiums were completely eliminated, house owners received tax rebates, and cities and municipalities received sufficient funds to enable them to hold the line on tax rates.

On April 13, Health and Social Development Minister René Toupin announced the government's intention to introduce within four years public insurance for hearing aids, eyeglasses, prescription drugs, dental care, and ambulance service.

Hudson's Bay Archives. On July 31, the governor of the 303-year-old Hudson's Bay Company signed an agreement with Premier Schreyer to transfer the company's archives from London, England, to the custody of the Provincial Archives of Manitoba. These records are an inestimably rich source of information on early exploration and the fur trade.

JOHN A. BOVEY
Provincial Archivist of Manitoba

MARINE BIOLOGY

During 1973 an increased emphasis was placed on studies that stress the various relationships that exist between man's activities and the marine environment. Scientists are concerned with pollution, overharvesting of marine resources, the effects of offshore mining and drilling activities, and the development of offshore nuclear power plants and ports. The sudden recognition of an international energy and resource crisis served to stress the urgency of the situation.

Nature of Marine Environments. Marine biologists planned and initiated several comprehensive research programs. One program, called Marine Ecosystems Analysis (MESA), is designed to accumulate information on the nature of marine communities in areas such as the New York Bight, Puget Sound, and the Alaskan coastline. These areas already or soon will receive pollutants and wastes, and it is likely that they will be the scene of extensive industrial activities such as oil transport or drilling.

Numerous physical and geological oceanographic studies are also being conducted in many parts of the world to gain an understanding of how marine life is related to the physical environment. Computer technology now provides the means with which to make the numerous calculations essential to determining the complex interrelationships and to develop "predictive models" that make it possible, at least in theory, to predict changes in marine bio-

logical systems based on known changes in the physical environment or in man's activities.

Increasing Productivity of the Oceans. Although the oceans cover more than 70% of the surface of the earth, marine scientists now think that 90% of the biological productivity of the seas occurs relatively close to shore and especially over the continental shelf. In recent years the standing stocks, or populations, of many important commercial finfish and shellfish have been declining, and marine and fisheries biologists believe that any increase in the yield of the sea must be through animal husbandry.

Biologists have shown that it is possible through genetic study and selective breeding to develop larger populations that grow more rapidly and to a larger size. At a small marine laboratory in Massachusetts it was recently reported that American lobsters can double or triple their growth rate and eventual marketable size if the stock is properly selected on a genetic basis and given favorable feeding schedules and environmental conditions. Simply increasing water temperature (possibly by using warm waters resulting from cooling processes used in the generation of electricity) can often significantly increase the growth rates or growing periods of many species of finfish and shellfish.

Distribution and Migration Studies. Most marine organisms have complex life cycles involving egg and larval stages that often occupy environments quite different from those of the adults. For example, in most species of crabs, lobsters, clams, and flatfish, the adults live on or near the sea floor, but the larva often spend weeks floating as part of the plankton in the upper layers of the water. Scientists in the United States, Scotland, and other places are investigating larval distribution, vertical migration, and rates of growth. They are concerned with factors such as salinity, temperature, and pollution that affect species distribution and with the role of light in the vertical migration of larvae. The U. S. National Marine Fisheries Service is, for example, conducting a research program (MARMAP) designed to reveal the distribution of larvae and breeding areas over the continental shelf of North America.

Scientists at the Woods Hole Oceanographic Institution are conducting research concerned with the use of human sewage as a source of nutrients for marine phytoplankton within closed aquaria. The single-celled plants produced within an enriched media are then harvested and fed to clams and other shellfish. Waste materials produced by the clams are in turn used as foods by shrimp and other animals. The toxic materials inherent in normal sewage are eliminated, and the nutrients are recycled into valuable foodstuffs.

Upwelling. Marine scientists are also studying areas of upwelling. These areas, usually characteristic of the west coasts of continents, result from certain current systems that carry deep nutrient-rich waters to the surface. The nutrients result in increased primary productivity in increased standing stocks of phytoplankton, and in turn in increases in sardinelike fishes. Occasionally, however, patterns of currents fluctuate with a sudden concomitant change in upwelling, and a decrease in productivity results. This phenomena, called *El Nina* off the coast of South America, results in a sudden decline in marine life, which imposes a severe economic hardship on those dependent on the fishery.

JOHN B. PEARCE, *Ecosystems Investigations Sandy Hook Laboratory, N. J.*

WIDE WORLD

BALTIMORE County Executive Dale Anderson at news conference after indictment in political corruption probe.

MARYLAND

Investigation during 1973 of alleged kickbacks and payoffs by contractors and other businessmen to a few public officials, as well as other criminal charges, shook both political parties in Maryland. Spiro T. Agnew resigned as vice president on October 10, just before his plea of no contest in a federal court in Baltimore to a charge of income tax evasion while he was governor. His fine and probation brought to a climax inquiries by U. S. Attorney George Beall. On August 23 and October 4, Dale Anderson, Agnew's Democratic successor as Baltimore County executive, had been indicted on kickback charges that he vigorously denied in announcing that he would run for a third term. A state court fined a Republican "salute to Agnew" committee for misreporting 1972 contributions.

In April a federal grand jury indicted Democratic state delegate James A. Scott of Baltimore (later murdered) for heroin distribution.

School Busing. On January 29 school busing for racial balance became effective without major incident in Prince Georges County, north and east of Washington, D. C., in accordance with federal court decrees. The new busing affected 33,000 students, a quarter of them black. On January 15, 20,000 white parents had joined a protest motorcade to Washington. Gov. Marvin Mandel proposed state aid for new construction to preserve neighborhood school attendance. Elections on November 6 gave the county a school board that continued to oppose racial busing.

Legislation. The regular session of the General Assembly enacted legislation to lower the age of majority to 18 except for purchase of alcoholic beverages. Other laws increased state aid to schools, expanded special education for handicapped children, eliminated grand juries in some criminal cases, and made assessment of property for tax purposes

——————— MARYLAND • Information Highlights ———————

Area: 10,577 square miles (27,394 sq km).
Population (1972 est.): 4,056,000. *Density,* 404 per sq mi.
Chief Cities (1970 census): Annapolis, the capital, 30,095; Baltimore, 905,759; Dundalk, 85,377; Towson, 77,799; Silver Spring, 77,496; Bethesda, 71,621; Wheaton, 66,247.
Government (1973): *Chief Officers*—governor, Marvin Mandel (D); lt. gov., Blair Lee III (D); secy. of state, Fred L. Wineland (D); atty. gen., Francis B. Burch (D); treas., John A. Luetkemeyer (D); supt. of schools, James A. Sensenbaugh; chief justice, Robert C. Murphy. *General Assembly*—Senate, 43 members (33 Democrats, 10 Republicans); House of Delegates, 142 members (121 D, 21 R).
Education (1972–73): *Enrollment*—public elementary schools, 508,312 pupils, 21,562 teachers; public secondary schools, 412,923 pupils, 20,765 teachers; nonpublic schools, 115,700 pupils, 4,910 teachers; colleges and universities, 150,483 students. *Public school expenditures,* $991,484,000 ($1,188 per pupil). *Average teacher's salary,* $11,787.
State Finances (fiscal year 1971): *Revenues,* $1,894,662,000 (4% general sales tax and gross receipts taxes, $262,820,000; motor fuel tax, $119,123,000; federal funds, $376,096,000). *Expenditures,* $1,842,040,000 (education, $652,679,000; health, welfare, and safety, $383,633,000; highways, $334,377,000).
Personal Income (1972): $19,861,000,000; per capita, $4,897.
Public Assistance (1972): $326,889,000. *Average monthly payments* (Dec. 1972)—old-age assistance, $66.12; aid to families with dependent children, $159.70.
Labor Force: *Nonagricultural wage and salary earners* (July 1973), 1,404,700. *Average annual employment* (1972)—manufacturing, 247,800; trade, 329,900; government, 265,100; services, 256,400. *Insured unemployed* (Sept. 1973) —19,000 (1.8%).
Manufacturing (1971): Value added by manufacture, $4,279,400,000. Food and kindred products, $664,800,000; primary metal industries, $586,400,000; transportation equipment, $515,500,000; electrical equipment and supplies, $442,500,000; chemicals and allied products, $425,600,000; printing and publishing, $293,500,000.
Agriculture (1972): *Cash farm income,* $422,491,000 (livestock, $278,085,000; crops, $134,834,000; government payments, $9,572,000). *Chief crops* (in order of value, 1971) —Corn, hay, tobacco, soybeans.
Mining (1972): *Production value,* $104,551,000 (ranks 36th among the states). *Chief minerals*—Stone, $33,140,000; cement, value not available; sand and gravel, $23,740,000; coal, $11,100,000.
Fisheries (1972): *Commercial catch,* 67,636,000 pounds ($18,261,000). *Leading species by value*—Oysters, $9,899,000; crabs, $2,976,000; clams, $2,544,000.
Transportation: *Roads* (1972), 26,522 miles (42,682 km); *motor vehicles* (1972), 2,002,976; *railroads* (1972), 1,110 miles (1,786 km); *public airports* (1972), 20.
Communications: *Telephones* (1973), 2,739,500; *television stations* (1971), 6; *radio stations* (1971), 85; *newspapers* (1973), 12 (daily circulation, 744,000).

entirely a state responsibility The approved annual budget approximated $2.5 billion.

The governor's constitutionally required plan for legislative redistricting became law when the General Assembly deadlocked in attempts to amend it, but the court of appeals agreed to review the plan before the 1974 elections. Special legislative sessions voted a stiff financial disclosure law for state and local officials and passed the nation's first law giving a governor strong powers to regulate the use of energy.

Lottery. Maryland's newly approved state lottery, in full operation before mid-year, fell below the predicted weekly purchase of 2 million 50-cent tickets. The average was 1.6 million, weekly sales dropping from an initial 3.1 million to 1.4 million by the end of November. Revenue to the state still exceeded $300,000 per week.

Political Prospects. Governor Mandel expected to run for reelection in 1974, probably with the Democratic state officers elected in 1970. On July 3 he announced he would dissolve his 32-year marriage to marry Mrs. Jeanne Dorsey, divorced mother of four children. Opposing the plan, Mrs. Mandel stayed in the executive mansion but the governor moved elsewhere. Most Maryland observers appraised the startling development as not politically decisive. By December no strong Republican candidate had appeared, nor had any Democratic candidate to oppose popular Republican U. S. Sen. Charles McC. Mathias, Jr.

Development. A second Chesapeake Bay bridge opened for summer traffic. Pollution dangers led the state to oppose Atlantic off-shore oil drilling.

FRANKLIN L. BURDETTE, *University of Maryland*

MASSACHUSETTS

A disastrous fire, continuing prison unrest, and the removal of a state judge drew major attention in Massachusetts in 1973.

Chelsea Fire. On a windy Sunday afternoon, October 14, a fire broke out in Chelsea, Mass., a city of about 30,000 directly northeast of Boston. By early evening the fire, which had begun in an area occupied by wooden warehouses and tenement dwellings, had spread to an 18-block section of the city. Over 1,000 firemen from Massachusetts, New Hampshire, and Rhode Island labored throughout the night to bring the blaze under control. Winds up to 70 miles an hour generated, in part, by the fire itself helped to spread the destruction. Over 1,100 persons were left homeless, although no one was killed and there were few injuries.

In the aftermath of the fire—one of the worst in recent urban U. S. history—the federal, state, and local governments as well as many private organizations mobilized to aid victims of the disaster. The National Guard was called out to patrol the fire area, and guardsmen, along with state and local

——————— MASSACHUSETTS • Information Highlights ———————

Area: 8,257 square miles (21,386 sq km).
Population (1972 est.): 5,787,000. *Density:* 735 per sq mi.
Chief Cities (1970 census): Boston, the capital, 641,071; Worcester, 176,572; Springfield, 163,905; New Bedford, 101,777; Cambridge, 100,361; Fall River, 96,898; Lowell, 94,239.
Government (1973): *Chief Officers*—governor, Francis W. Sargent (R); lt. gov., Donald Dwight (R); secy. of the commonwealth, John F. X. Davoren (D); atty. gen., Robert H. Quinn (D); treas., Robert Q. Crane (D); commissioner of education, Gregory Anrig; chief justice, G. Joseph Tauro. *General Court*—Senate, 40 members (33 Democrats, 7 Republicans); House of Representatives, 240 members (186 D, 52 R, 2 Independents).
Education (1972–73): *Enrollment*—public elementary schools, 670,000 pupils, 29,036 teachers; public secondary schools, 520,000 pupils, 28,475 teachers; nonpublic schools, 198,300 pupils, 9,000 teachers; colleges and universities, 298,152 students. *Public school expenditures,* $1,240,000,000 ($1,102 per pupil). *Average teacher's salary,* $11,200.
State Finances (fiscal year 1971): *Revenues,* $2,608,835,000 (3% general sales tax and gross receipts taxes, $190,003,000; motor fuel tax, $140,960,000; federal funds, $626,739,000). *Expenditures,* $2,595,392,000 (education, $703,963,000; health, welfare, and safety, $897,260,000; highways, $282,761,000).
Personal Income (1972): $28,181,000,000; per capita, $4,870.
Public Assistance (1972): $813,354,000. *Average monthly payments* (Dec. 1972)—old-age assistance, $105.52; aid to families with dependent children, $335.38 (includes extra grants for special need).
Labor Force: *Nonagricultural wage and salary earners* (July 1973), 2,326,200. *Average annual employment* (1972)—manufacturing, 601,900; trade, 498,600; government, 337,200; services, 478,500. *Insured unemployed* (Sept. 1973)—72,500 (3.8%).
Manufacturing (1971): Value added by manufacture, $9,494,600,000. Electrical equipment and supplies, $1,344,300,000; nonelectrical machinery, $1,297,600,000; instruments and related products, $766,400,000; printing and publishing, $720,700,000; fabricated metal products, $645,600,000; food and kindred products, $636,900,000.
Agriculture (1972): *Cash farm income,* $154,313,000 (livestock, $83,768,000; crops, $70,067,000; government payments, $478,000). *Chief crops* (in order of value, 1972)—Cranberries (ranks 1st among the states), hay, tobacco.
Mining (1972): *Production value,* $50,405,000 (ranks 43d among the states). *Chief minerals*—Stone, $22,306,000; sand and gravel, $24,902,000; lime, value not available; clays, $520,000.
Fisheries (1972): *Commercial catch,* 248,035,000 pounds ($48,052,000). *Leading species by value*—Flounder, $13,955,000; cod, $6,887,000; scallops, $6,884,000.
Transportation: *Roads* (1972), 29,355 miles (47,241 km); *motor vehicles* (1972), 2,699,793; *railroads* (1972), 1,430 miles (2,301 km); *public airports* (1972), 26.
Communications: *Telephones* (1973), 3,745,600; *television stations* (1971), 11; *radio stations* (1971), 103; *newspapers* (1973), 46 (daily circulation, 2,160,000).

ISRAELI Prime Minister Golda Meir receives an honorary LL.D. from Brandeis University, Waltham, Mass., in March.

police, sealed off the city for three days, permitting only residents and emergency workers to enter. The city was declared a disaster area by federal officials, allowing residents and businessmen to receive special assistance.

Prison Unrest. Continuing problems in the state's prison system led in 1973 to a dramatic shake-up in the department of corrections. Corrections Commissioner John O. Boone, who had held the post for 17 months, was dismissed on June 21 by Gov. Francis W. Sargent. Boone's short tenure as the state's highest prison official was marked by continued controversy, much of it sparked by his plans for reform of the state penal system. Among incidents that led to his stepping down were a work stoppage by prison guards in protest of Boone's policies and disturbances at Walpole State Prison, the largest "maximum security" facility in Massachusetts.

Following Boone's resignation the state police took over control of Walpole, which had been without a permanent superintendent since March 2. It was not until September that a new superintendent, Douglas Vinzant, was named, and the control of the prison was returned to regular officials.

Public attention remained focused on the prisons as isolated incidents continued, including the death by stabbing of Albert De Salvo, who at one time had claimed to be the "Boston Strangler" allegedly responsible for the deaths of 13 women from the Boston area between 1962 and 1964. De Salvo, who was serving time at Walpole on criminal charges other than the stranglings, was found dead in his cell on November 26. In recent years De Salvo had recanted his claim to being the Boston Strangler, and his death made the grim puzzle of the multiple murders even more baffling.

State Judge Dismissed. After hearings by the state courts, the legislature, and the executive branch, Judge Jerome P. Troy of the Dorchester district court was formally removed from office on November 7. Troy had voluntarily stepped down as judge in April after charges were filed against him by the state supreme court. The allegations contended that he lied under oath, employed court officers in his personal business affairs, and displayed a conflict of interest in several instances.

Troy, a judge for 11 years, had been disbarred from legal practice by the state supreme court on July 26 and forbidden to sit as judge pending further proceedings against him. His resignation was requested by Governor Sargent, but Troy refused, declaring that he would fight any attempts to remove him in the courts. Shortly thereafter, the legislature passed a rarely used "petition of address" requesting the governor to remove him. Action by the governor, however, required the concurrence of the nine-member executive council, an advisory body to the governor which must approve certain state appointments. After tense hearings held by the council, it voted 7 to 1, with one abstention, to remove Troy. Troy thus became the fourth judge in the state's history to be so removed.

Redistricting Battle. A major battle over redrawing the state Senate district lines lasted until the autumn of 1973. A major conflict involved drawing the lines so as to create a district in the largely black areas of Boston's Roxbury and Mattapan sections. A "Black Caucus" composed of the black members of the legislature and a consortium of civil rights groups pressed hard for the measure. A compromise bill was passed in September that includes the black Boston area as a new Senate district.

HARVEY BOULAY
Boston University

GUARDS at the Walpole (Mass.) State Prison walk off job to protest corrections department's policies.

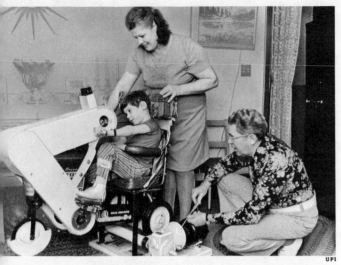

Handicapped children are aided by technology. A child with spastic cerebral palsy (above) uses an exercising tractor, and a blind child (right) plays baseball with ball that has electronic beeper.

medicine

In 1973 the relationship between organized medicine and the federal government came into sharper focus. The structure of the medical care system began to change as a result of legislative and financial policies of the government, reacting in part to increased public demands for high-quality care.

Public interest in vitamins and nutrition also increased. The comparatively strong comeback of some infectious diseases, particularly venereal diseases, clearly demonstrated that even with antibiotics and other modern drugs infectious diseases have not been eradicated. Interest in acupuncture abated slightly, but there were continued attempts to understand the principles involved.

Quality of Medical Care. A revision of the Social Security Act created a system of Professional Standards Review Organizations (PSROs) to review the quality of medical care. By Jan. 1, 1974, the Department of Health, Education, and Welfare (HEW) must designate between 200 and 350 PSRO areas throughout the country. In each area, a review organization will monitor the care given to Medicare and Medicaid patients by the doctors in the area. A National Professional Standards Review Council made up of doctors appointed by the government will supervise the PSROs. Since the role of the PSROs is to review the quality of medical care paid for by federal funds, there is some feeling among physicians that the PSRO system may eventually take complete control of the medical care offered under its direction.

Health Maintenance Organizations (HMOs) are another change in the present system of medical care that is being considered by the government. There are several bills pending in Congress to establish the HMOs called for by President Nixon three years ago. He described an HMO as a new method of delivering health services that "brings together a comprehensive range of medical services into a single organization so that a patient is assured of convenient access to all of them. And it provides needed services for a fixed-contract fee which is paid in advance by all subscribers." The largest and best known medical care organization of this type in the United States is the Kaiser-Permanente program that serves 2.2 million people in California. Pending legislation may provide the impetus for HMOs throughout the country.

Another approach to the standardization of medical care appeared in 1973 as the "problem-oriented" system. This system is basically a record-keeping method in which all the data about a patient are organized into a clearly defined, standardized data base. Next a numbered and titled list of the patient's problems, including medical, social, and demographic status, is prepared. From this, a plan of management for each problem is drawn up. Finally, there are progress notes, each labelled according to the problems.

Supporters of this method of record-keeping suggest that it will assure the quality of diagnosis and treatment given to patients at home and in hospitals. Dr. Lawrence L. Weed, professor of medicine at the University of Vermont, developed the problem-oriented approach. For this, he was the first recipient of the Brookdale Foundation award, which is given to physicians under the age of 50 who make significant contributions to the advancement of medicine.

Financial Problems. Financial pressure applied by the federal government caused some disturbances in the medical field in 1973. The HEW impounded and did not spend $1.1 billion in funds authorized by Congress for health purposes. This led to a cutback in funding and therefore in research at the National Institutes of Health (NIH) as well as in work funded by the NIH at medical schools throughout the country.

The federal government's wage-price freeze fixed

the charges of hospitals and doctors, but not the operating costs of hospitals, and some difficulties for many hospitals became apparent during the year. In November in New York City, workers in voluntary hospitals went on strike to protest failure to receive wage boosts that had been agreed upon by hospital management but rejected by the wage-price regulatory board as inflationary. It was the first large-scale strike against hospitals in the United States. After an eight-day strike that severely curtailed the operation of the hospitals, the workers accepted a 6% wage increase and returned to work.

FDA Rulings on Vitamins. In August the U. S. Food and Drug Administration (FDA) published regulations that concern the use of vitamins. Under the new rules, the FDA established a U. S. Recommended Daily Allowance (RDA) for each of 19 vitamins and minerals recognized as essential. It also decided that a prescription will be required for single doses of Vitamin D larger than 10,000 international units (IU) and for doses of Vitamin A greater than 400 IU. Also included are regulations banning vitamins combined with other substances that have no "scientifically recognized nutritional value," and classifying as a drug any vitamin, food, or food supplement that contains more than three times the RDA of any one vitamin.

Vitamin E. Vitamin E continued to be popular with the public in 1973. First discovered in 1923, vitamin E, or tocopherol, has been tested as treatment for such diverse conditions as acne, allergies, cancer, cystic fibrosis, diabetes, heart disease, and rheumatic fever, but always without success. In recent years there have been reports that vitamin E might be a cure for impotence and sterility, and it has again become a best-seller in over-the-counter usage. Vitamin E is available in the average American diet, and there is still no proof that it has any therapeutic value.

Infectious Diseases. Infectious disease, particularly venereal diseases, continued to make a strong comeback in 1973. There was further extension of the worldwide epidemic of venereal disease. Gonorrhea, estimated at 2½ million cases in 1973, leads all communicable diseases in incidence. Syphilis is in fourth place with about 30,000 new cases in the United States. Yet another venereal disease was reported on the upswing in 1973. This is an infection caused by herpes-simplex virus (HSV-2), which like other venereal diseases is transmitted by sexual contact. Herpes venereal disease may be associated with an increase in cervical cancer, and it is also known to produce fatal infections in newborn infants whose mothers carry the virus.

The incidence of two skin diseases—body lice and scabies—increased. Both are transmitted by close personal contact and are probably associated with the increase in venereal infections. Both diseases are caused by a small parasite living on the skin of the human host. Neither is a serious disease and both are readily treated.

Several other infectious diseases attracted attention. An epidemic of cholera was reported in Italy but eventually was controlled by a vaccine. Only one case of cholera was reported in the United States, and it did not seem to be related to the Italian outbreak. A small outbreak of about 100 cases of typhoid fever occurred in a migrant labor camp near Miami, Fla. Equine encephalitis reappeared in Massachusetts, but it did not lead to any human cases. Two cases of bubonic plague were reported in the United States; neither was fatal.

Meanwhile, there were advances in the development and use of vaccines to prevent infectious diseases. An improved influenza vaccine was announced and produced in advance for the winter of 1973–74. The vaccine provides protection against both the Hong Kong and London types of flu and has fewer side effects than previous vaccines. A new rabies vaccine that uses a killed-virus vaccine grown on human cells was being tested in Switzerland. If successful, it should reduce the number of injections in the treatment program from about 20 to three or four. Progress was also reported in development of vaccines against gonorrhea and meningitis.

Finally, October was designated as Immunization Action Month. Coordinated by the Center for Disease Control and supported by many medical and public health organizations, Immunization Action Month aimed to upgrade the level of immunity against infectious diseases, particularly among children.

Hypertension. An intensified drive against high blood pressure was mounted in 1973. Hypertension, or high blood pressure, is the greatest single cause of death in the United States. At least 10% and perhaps as many as 25% of Americans suffer from this disease, but since in its mild form hypertension does not produce symptoms, many sufferers are unaware of their problem. Hypertension that continues for long periods often leads to heart trouble, kidney disease, and strokes, each of which can be crippling or even fatal. Since determining blood pressure is a simple matter, programs were developed in 1973 to screen larger numbers of patients for hypertension. No new treatment for hypertension was announced recently, but currently available methods are said to be quite effective in controlling the blood pressure of most patients with hypertension.

SIDS. Each year in the United States alone, more than 10,000 infants die suddenly and unexpectedly, victims of what is known as sudden infant death syndrome (SIDS). Victims typically are healthy infants between 1 and 5 months of age. They are put to bed healthy only to be found dead 5 to 6 hours later. The problem is worldwide and has been reported from most parts of the industrialized world. In England it is known as "cot-death." It affects all social and economic groups but seems more common at the lower end of those scales. It is reported in all races, all seasons, climates, hours of the day, and days of the week.

Recent studies at Syracuse University suggest a direction for study of the problem. The data indicate that even normal children have periods during which breathing stops for a few seconds. In children who die of SIDS, the breathing may not resume, especially if the infant is suffering from a cold or other infection. Because of the startling, unexpected pattern of infant death in SIDS, the family and

CONTENTS

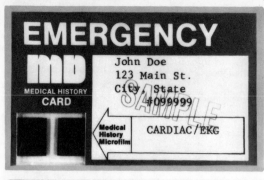

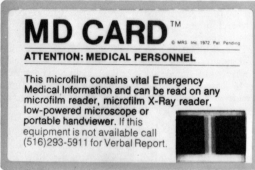

WALLET-SIZED CARD giving vital medical information on microfilm is available to subscribers to the new Medical Identification Systems, Inc., for a $5 fee.

attending doctor may have guilt feelings about the loss of the infant. Specialists who deal with the problem insist that, at the present state of knowledge about SIDS, these deaths are not now preventable. Interest in the problem has led to legislation to provide matching federal funds as an impetus to further investigation of SIDS.

Diagnostic Advances. Several new tests were reported to find disease early in its course. One of the most dramatic tests announced was one to detect a heart attack by checking a urine sample. The test is based on the fact that, during a myocardial infarction, the patient's urine will contain small amounts of myoglobin, a constituent of heart muscle not normally excreted in the urine. The new test provides a ready method for identifying myoglobin that is reported simple enough for household use.

A new technique for differentiating tumors by ultrasound was reported. Using a source of high-frequency sound, this method is reported to deter-

mine the thickness and consistency of the wall of a tumor as well as the internal homogeneity. The method, which does not require entry into the body, is said to differentiate cysts and abscesses from the more serious cancerous masses as well as identifying the type of cancer if one is present.

Using a method of radio-immuno-assay, a test for alpha-1 globulin may be helpful in identifying cancer patients. Alpha-feto-protein is found in fetuses, pregnancy, and patients with cancer of the liver, pancreas, stomach, lungs, or testes. The test is not definite because it is also positive in patients with certain types of liver diseases, but it may be helpful in following the after-treatment course of patients with cancer. Radio-immuno-assay is also being tried for allergy testing.

Acupuncture. Further information about acupuncture comes from China and the United States. Some American physicians now suggest an explanation for the success of acupuncture as an anesthetic for surgery. The theory is that the acupuncture needles stimulate discharge over those fibers in the nervous system that carry messages of pressure and position. These fibers, called proprioceptive fibers, pass their discharges through the spinal column over the same pathways that carry the messages of pain. Stimulation of the proprioceptive fibers is reported to block painful sensations from reaching the brain by competing with the pain-messages for the pathways to the brain. It has been demonstrated that acupuncture needles stimulate proprioceptive impulses by being twirled in the skin. They can also be used to stimulate responses if they are connected to a source of low-voltage electric current. In studies in the United States, skin areas with lowered electrical resistance have been found to correspond roughly to the traditional acupuncture sites.

Acupuncture has been used for more than 2,000 years in China. However, its use for surgical anesthesia dates back just about a decade, and even now, acupuncture is used only for certain operations. Before acupuncture-anesthesia is attempted, four or five days are spent preparing the patient for it, using explanation, reassurance, and trial acupuncture. Preoperatively, small doses of sedatives are usually used to decrease the excitability of the nervous system. Postoperative management of the acupuncture patient is the same in China as it is after conventional Western anesthesia.

IRWIN J. POLK, M.D.
St. Luke's Hospital, New York City

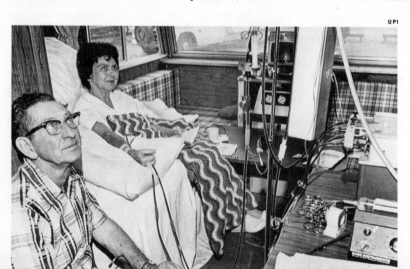

HOME-MADE dialysis machine built into a motor camper allows this California woman to travel and yet receive the treatments she needs to stay alive. Her husband constructed the "artificial kidney," the only one of its type.

Allergies

During 1973 there were significant advances in diagnosing allergies, in recognizing new allergens and allergies, and in understanding the biochemistry of an allergic reaction and how some drugs act to interrupt the reaction.

Diagnostic Advances. Thermography, a method of recording skin temperature, was advanced as a tool for allergists. It can be used to measure the results of standard allergy skin tests that cause an increase in circulation and thus of temperature at the test site. Provocative testing was also increasingly used. In this technique the condition of an air passageway in either the nose or chest is measured, and then the patient is challenged by exposure to a suspected allergen. If a second measurement shows that the passage of air has diminished, the patient is considered to have a positive provocative test for the particular allergen.

Allergens. Buckwheat was found to be a possible cause of allergic reactions. Vitallium, a metal often used in bone surgery, was reported to cause allergy, possibly because of its nickel content. Iron was also reported to cause a contact rash. The most unusual new report concerned human semen, which was found in a closely documented study to cause either immediate or delayed allergic reactions in some women. This reaction has been associated with infertility problems in some patients.

Recognition of New Allergies. A new allergic disease, vibratory angioedema, was described. Its symptoms include swelling of the eyes and lips, hives, flushing, and headaches after exposure to vibrations, massage, and sometimes after exercise. Several scientists investigated exercise-induced asthma, a condition that appears like allergic asthma. It is brought about by exercise, either mild or strenuous, depending on the condition of the patient. It can be prevented by many of the same medicines used to treat allergic asthma. Growth delay in children was recognized as a consequence of chronic infections often associated with allergic rhinitis. Allergies were also documented as the cause of middle-ear fluid and implicated in the hearing and balance disturbances of inner-ear disease.

Biochemistry of an Allergic Reaction. It is known that allergy symptoms are mediated by histamine and other substances and that epinephrine and similar drugs used to treat allergies can interrupt an allergic reaction. It has now been found that these drugs work by activating specific cell sites, known as beta-receptors. These receptors in turn activate the enzyme adenyl-cyclase that causes an increase of the chemical cyclic 3′,5′-adenosine monophosphate, or cAMP, within the cell. This increase of cAMP brings about a decrease in the amount of histamine.

Treatment Advances. A new drug, cromolyn sodium, was released for use in the treatment of asthma. Used by inhalation, cromolyn sodium is effective in preventing both allergic and exercise-induced asthma. Little is known about how it acts on the body.

No other significant treatment techniques were developed, but there was renewed interest in surgical methods for washing the bronchial tubes clear of mucus as a treatment for chronic asthma.

IRWIN J. POLK, M. D.
St. Luke's Hospital, New York City

Cancer

Cancer research in 1973 was characterized by a continuing accumulation of data relating viruses to cancer, by new insight into the role of cyclic nucleotides in the control of cellular proliferation and differentiation, by emphasis on the capacity of the immune system to suppress cancer cells, and by the introduction of two new drugs useful in the management of cancer in man.

Cancer and Viruses. Hopes are increasing for the eventual development of effective vaccines against at least some forms of cancer. Dr. William D. Hardy, Jr., of the Sloan-Kettering Institute for Cancer Research in New York City and co-workers in New York and Boston demonstrated that feline leukemia virus, or FeLV, the virus that causes a lymphosarcoma (a type of cancer) in cats, can be transmitted horizontally—that is, that the virus spreads by contact or contagion. They based their conclusions on immunofluorescent examination of the blood cells of over 2,000 cats, some diseased and some apparently healthy. They found FeLV consistently present in the salivary glands of the virus-positive diseased cats. They proposed that saliva was the most likely vehicle for contagion, with transmission occurring in the course of the cat's grooming themselves and their companions.

The fact of horizontal transmission makes it at least theoretically possible to prevent the spread of the cancer by vaccination with a weakened virus or with a related, but non-tumor-producing virus. Such a vaccine has been successful and in commercial use since 1971 against Marek's disease, a horizontally transmitted, virus-induced lymphoma, or cancer of the lymphatic system, found in chickens.

Cyclic Nucleotides and the Control of Cellular Proliferation. During 1972 and 1973 research in several laboratories has disclosed a relationship between the levels of certain cyclic nucleotides in the cells and the rate of cell proliferation. High intracellular levels of the nucleotide cAMP, or cyclic 3′,5′-adenosine monophosphate, have been found to inhibit cellular proliferation and to promote cell differentiation. Transformed or cancerous cells contain much lower concentrations of cAMP than do normal cells, but exposure of these cells to cAMP or to other chemicals that raise cAMP levels changes the cells toward normality. In contrast, concentrations of cGMP, or cyclic 3′,5′-guanosine monophosphate, have been found to rise rapidly in certain cells—bacteria, human lymphocytes, and mouse fibroblasts—before and during cell proliferation. These findings led Dr. Nelson Goldberg of the University of Minnesota to propose that these two cyclic nucleotides are chemical antagonists and that the balance between the two determines the proliferative state of a tissue.

This theory has been supported in studies on patients with psoriasis, a non-cancerous disorder characterized by patchy areas of markedly accelerated proliferation of skin cells. Dr. John Voorhees of the University of Michigan and Dr. Goldberg compared psoriasis-involved skin and non-involved skin and consistently found decreased cAMP levels and elevated cGMP levels in the diseased skin; in other words, Voorhees and Goldberg found evidence that high cGMP levels are associated with increased cell proliferation.

Cancer and Immunity. The role of the immune system in the control of cancer received increased

PRESIDENT NIXON with his Cancer Advisory Panel (l. to r.): HEW Secretary Weinberger, Dr. Raymond Owen, and chairman Benno Schmidt. Panel proposed 5-year crash program to conquer the disease.

national attention in 1973. Particular emphasis was placed on thymus-derived lymphocytes, or T-cells, as a vital factor in a surveillance mechanism that could detect and kill cancer cells. Individuals having detectable hereditary deficiency in T-cell function have a greatly increased incidence of cancer. Further, T-cell functions are commonly deficient or depressed in patients with some forms of cancer. Although current therapeutic efforts center on non-specific stimulation of the patient's T-cells, transfusions of fully competent T-cells to individuals with cancer is a future possibility. Dr. Soo Duk Lim of Seoul National University, Korea, in collaboration with Dr. Robert A. Good, now at Sloan-Kettering Institute, have had partial success in transfusing competent T-cells in the treatment of leprosy, another disorder where T-cell function is defective.

Cancer Chemotherapy. Bleomycin, an antibiotic that is useful in the management of cancers of the lymphatic system, was licensed for commercial distribution by the U. S. Food and Drug Administration in 1973. In addition, large-scale clinical trials with a second antibiotic, Adriamycin, disclosed that it has therapeutic activity against many human neoplasms. It was uniquely effective against sarcomas, a form of cancer that arises in nonglandular tissues such as bone and muscle and which heretofore has been resistant to anti-cancer drugs.

CHARLES W. YOUNG, M. D.
Sloan-Kettering Institute for Cancer Research

Dentistry

During 1973 there was increased emphasis on dental health education and the prevention of dental diseases, while research on detection and treatment continued. Dental care also came increasingly under prepaid health plans.

Dental Health Education in Schools and the Media. An all-out effort by the dental profession to

educate the public in maintaining oral health is currently being directed to the schools and the communications media. Because school programs are among the most promising means of instructing children and their families in oral health, particular emphasis is placed on school health programs. A newly introduced teaching system for kindergarten through 12th grade includes multimedia curriculum guides, projects, demonstrations, and related activities in art, social studies, and science, as well as plaque control kits to help children establish oral hygiene habits that will last a lifetime. Dental societies are working to introduce this system to schools throughout the United States.

A public information program undertaken by dentistry has resulted in hundreds of magazine and newspaper articles and radio and TV spot announcements. One such story explained the dental hygiene practiced by the Skylab astronauts. An annual science writers' awards program, in its seventh year in 1973, honors writers whose work broadens and deepens the public understanding of dental disease, dental treatment, and dental research. The 1973 competition drew 73% more entries than the previous year—an indication of the greatly heightened interest in dental health.

Prevention. Water fluoridation, topical application of fluorides, use of fluoridated dentifrices, prophylaxis, and good home care are the recognized techniques for prevention and control of dental diseases. Dental health experts and nutritionists alike are increasingly condemning the excessive consumption of sugar. They urge fruit and vegetable snacks and desserts rather than candy, pastry, and sweetened drinks.

Prevention of orofacial injuries is another aspect that is receiving more attention. Such injuries, often very serious, are common in automobile accidents and, more recently, in snowmobile accidents. The incidence of disfiguring orofacial injuries in automobile accidents can be reduced by the use of proper

safety devices such as lap and shoulder belts, and more stringent regulations have been urged for the use of snowmobiles. Mouth injuries also occur in athletics. Dentists have been instrumental in the development of effective protection programs for high school and college football players and are now working toward providing coverage for younger players and for both male and female participants in other sports.

Caries Detection. The dentist's skill, supplemented by X-ray evidence, continues to be the prime method of early caries detection. Other promising detection adjuncts being researched are fiber optic and ultraviolet light illumination.

Other Research. A University of Michigan team reported on skull X-ray studies of ancient and contemporary Nubians and of mummified ancient Egyptian royalty that provide a wealth of new material for orthodontics research. As the National Institute of Dental Research observed its 25th anniversary, attention was focused on the significant advances in caries research achieved through Institute-supported studies. Some National Caries Program developments include an adhesive plastic sealant for pits and fissures of occlusal surfaces, new topical fluoride applications, mouth rinses, and phosphate additives. Research on periodontal disease is now focused on the control of bacterial plaque by chemical agents. In other studies, an ultrasonic toothbrush has been tested for plaque removal, and the transplantation of healthy natural teeth within the dental arch or from one patient to another has been described, with prospects considered good for the use of such vital tooth transplants.

Dental Prepayment. Medicaid has adopted a new program requiring states to provide dental benefits for Medicaid-eligible children up to the age of 21, and suggesting use of the maximum variety of sites for screening and treatment, including day-care centers, health centers, dental schools, and school health facilities. A contract negotiated between the United Auto Workers and the Chrysler Corporation provides a dental care program for 117,000 employees and their dependents. An estimated 18 million Americans now have some kind of prepaid dental care coverage. Dental care for children is an element in various national health insurance plans pending in Congress.

Other Developments. Despite widespread discussion and interest in acupuncture as a means of treating orofacial pain or of achieving anesthesia for dental procedures, acupuncture is still considered experimental. Much additional research is needed in this and in the whole area of pain and associated anxiety and apprehension of dental treatment.

The dental profession has adopted guidelines covering the use of human subjects in clinical research: moral and scientific principles must justify such research; it must be based on findings obtained from laboratory or animal experiments or other scientifically established facts; and informed consent of subjects must be obtained.

Dentists are also becoming increasingly aware that they may be the first to observe signs of oral cancer during routine dental treatment. In a concentrated effort to identify persons with hypertension, a common precursor of cardiovascular disease, dentists are being urged to check their patients' blood pressures.

EILEEN H. FARRELL
Editor, "Dental Abstracts"

Eye Diseases

In 1973 there was emphasis on treating many previously considered incurable congenital and hereditary defects by the use of drugs, enzymes, radioactive isotopes, and other means. There were also advances in knowledge of the fine anatomy of the eye, in vitreous surgery, in diagnostic techniques, and in techniques that will make the treatment of many fairly common eye diseases office procedures in the near future.

Increased Knowledge of the Fine Structure of the Eye. The electron microscope has revealed details of the structure of the iris, ciliary body, choroid, and other structures of the eye that have led to increased understanding of abnormalities and to improve treatment methods.

Surgery on the Vitreous. Only recently have surgeons attempted to deal with the vitreous, a fluid-filled space occupying the central part of the eyeball. The vitreous is subject to many disorders, such as vitreous cysts in association with other ocular abnormalities, including retinitis pigmentosa and uveitis.

Vitreous hemorrhages are also a serious ophthalmologic problem. A study by A-scan ultrasonography has revealed the structure and development of vitreous hemorrhages. The commonest type occur in association with retinal detachment, diabetic and arteriosclerotic retinopathy, and central vein thrombosis. Treatment of vitreous hemorrhages by transcleral cryocoagulation, a method using extreme cold, has been tried in cases of diabetic retinopathy and in Eales disease, and under certain conditions it hastens the absorption of blood. Laser surgery has also been attempted.

Some vitreous surgery approaches involve the use of vitreous implants. The implant materials—air, saline, preserved vitreous, hyaluronic acid, and tropocollagen—are used to reform the globe, restore normal tension, and push the detached retina back against the choroid. Another important advance in vitreous surgery is the anterior approach, the open eye, or "open sky" method, which has proved particularly useful after vitreous loss during cataract surgery.

New Diagnostic Techniques. Among some of the more important diagnostic improvements were a technique that makes it possible to remove for study repeated samples of vitreous humor from the same eye by means of a special needle, and the development of an adjustable mirror contact lens that allows the continuous viewing of the vitreous cavity and ocular fundus, so important for accurately tracing abnormalities. B-scan ultrasonography was also increasingly used to evaluate all eyes with opaque media and all suspected ocular tumors.

Other Advances. Many other treatment advances hold promise for the future. The treatment of chronic simple glaucoma, the extraction of cataracts by phacoemulsification, and the repair of retinal detachments by diathermy, cryotherapy, lasers, and other techniques, will become office procedures. Preserved corneas, scleras, and vitreous and plastic or other artificial lenses will be used to repair injured eyes. Sutures will be largely replaced by tissue binding cement.

ROLAND I. PRITIKIN, M. D.
Author of "Essentials of Ophthalmology"
M. L. DUCHON, M. D.
Consultant in Ophthalmology

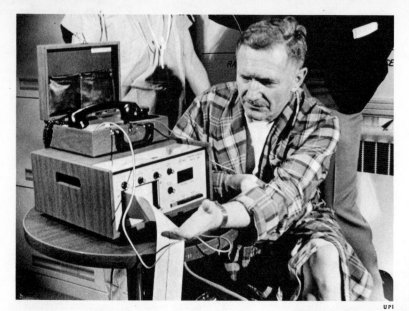

MAX SPIELER (left) *was the first person to receive the new American-made, nuclear-powered pacemaker* (below).

Heart and Vascular Disease

During 1973 advances in the field of cardiovascular diseases included research and observations on venous thrombosis, critical appraisal of coronary artery bypass surgery, continuing interest in hypertension and in the relationship of diet and alcohol to heart disease, and the development and application of new diagnostic techniques.

Venous Thrombosis and Its Complications. Venous thrombosis, or blood clots, in the legs and pelvic veins occurs with alarming frequency in both medical and surgical patients. The intravenous injection of radioactive-labeled fibrinogen and subsequent scanning of the legs is a relatively new method of detecting such clots early. The complication of pulmonary embolism (when these clots travel to the lung) is serious and on occasion fatal. Recent evidence indicates that small doses of the anticoagulant drug heparin administered prior to and for several days following surgery appear to reduce the incidence of thrombosis, without prolonging clotting time.

In some patients in whom blood clots cannot be prevented or controlled with conventional therapy, a new device resembling a small umbrella can be inserted through an incision in a neck vein and advanced to the inferior vena cava, the vein that drains the lower part of the body, where it expands and filters out traveling clots.

Coronary Artery Bypass Surgery. After initial enthusiasm for coronary artery bypass surgery, many cardiologists and cardiac surgeons were requesting a large-scale study of the procedure to compare surgical with medical management. Certain cardiac surgeons suggest that the angiographic demonstration of significant coronary artery narrowing even in the absence of symptoms warrants such surgery, while more conservative cardiac surgeons and many cardiologists believe that cardiac artery bypass surgery should be reserved for those who have severe symptoms not responding to medical therapy.

Sudden Death, CCU's, and Cardiogenic Shock. It is estimated that more than 600,000 people die each year from myocardial infarction and that of these some 400,000 die before reaching the hospital. In the last 10 years or so a significant advance in hospital management of patients with myocardial

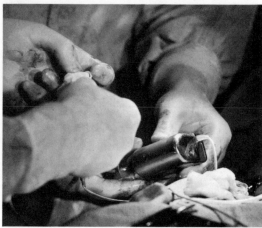

infarction (heart attack) has been coronary care units (CCU). These units have achieved a 50% reduction of in-hospital mortality, largely by the early detection and treatment of disturbances in cardiac rhythm. Today heart muscle or pump failure is the leading cause of death in CCUs. Cardiogenic shock due to pump failure is related to the size of the myocardial infarction, or heart muscle death, and despite heroic measures, the mortality rate remains formidable.

Advances in Diagnosis and Management of Acute Myocardial Infarction. A new technique involving the injection of the radioisotope technetium-99m into a peripheral vein or through a catheter into the pulmonary artery, and its subsequent tracing by a special camera, provides a measurement of cardiac function. A new method of assessing infarct size is based on the blood level of one of the heart muscle enzymes, CPK isoenzyme: the higher the CPK isoenzyme level, the larger the infarct and the worse the prognosis. Another method employing intravenous injection of radioactive potassium, which is rapidly taken up by normal muscle but leaves areas of infarction as "cold" defects, assesses both location and size of an infarct. Experimental studies are being conducted to evaluate measures that will reduce the infarct size.

Hypertension. An estimated 23 million people in the United States have hypertension, but only about one half this number are aware of it and only 10% to 20% are receiving adequate therapy. The National Heart and Lung Institute and various private agencies have launched a nationwide assault on the problem, and large-scale screening procedures have been introduced in some cities. A new drug, diazoxide, most effective in the emergency therapy of severe hypertension, has been released for use.

Diet and Heart Disease. Based on the fact that high blood lipids (cholesterol and triglycerides) may be an important factor in the near-epidemic occurrence of coronary artery disease in the United States, the American Heart Association is urging the American public to reduce calories and cholesterol and saturated fat intake and to increase the proportion of polyunsaturates in the diet. Some investigators, however, caution that excessive ingestion of polyunsaturates may be potentially harmful.

Other Findings. The possible relationship between cardiovascular disease and vitamin E and between cardiovascular disease and alcohol has been investigated. Evidence so far gathered indicates that vitamin E is of no value in preventing or curing cardiovascular disease. Alcohol has been demonstrated as a cause of depressed heart muscle function, but other studies of the role of alcohol in heart disease have been generally inconclusive.

RALPH C. SCOTT, *Cardiac Laboratory*
University of Cincinnati Medical Center

Hospitals

In 1973 money and regulations concerning professional standards and patient's rights were the forces that had the most impact on the 7,200 general-purpose hospitals in the United States.

Financial Problems. Health care was one of three industries left under the confusing controls of the Economic Stabilization Program, although the cost of goods and services that hospitals bought were not. A day of inpatient care rose to an average cost of $105, but the rate of increase was less than that of the overall Consumer Price Index.

At the same time, new technology continues to drive up the cost of hospital care. Among the costly advances are linear accelerators for cancer treatment; an X-ray device meshed with a computer to give a three-dimensional picture of the brain; and a nuclear magnetic resonance device to detect minute levels of elements in the blood. Intensive and coronary care units also continued to grow in number, sophistication, and cost. Most experts agree that the cost of hospital care cannot be lowered, but partly as a cost-conscious move more hospitals are emphasizing outpatient care.

Governments expressed increasing concern about empty beds. As a result the federal government severely cut back its 26-year-old Hill-Burton hospital construction financing program, and 21 state governments passed certificate-of-need laws to regulate new bed construction and the addition of new services. A few states set up commissions to control the cost of hospital care. However, new hospitals continued to be built in the suburbs while the most serious need remained in urban areas.

Health Insurance. Patients who needed kidney dialysis treatments and kidney transplants were covered for the first time under Medicare. Nearly everyone agreed that national health insurance was "an idea whose time has come." However, Congress and special-interest groups were still arguing about which of several national health bills should be adopted. (See SOCIAL WELFARE—*Health Care*.)

Regulations Concerning Care. In most hospitals, doctors have been monitoring the quality of medical care through committees that review tissue after surgery to verify diagnosis and that review use of hospital facilities in individual cases. The federal government passed a tough law mandating a more formal and rigid approach. In 1975, Professional Standards Review Organizations (PSROs) will carry out peer review. Foundations, medical societies, and other organizations will act as PSROs to check on such costly practices as unnecessary surgery, hospitalization, and laboratory tests. In counter reactions, doctors' unions and ultraconservative medical groups grew in power.

Patient's Bill of Rights. The American Hospital Association issued a landmark document, a Patient's Bill of Rights, that said in part that patients have the right to considerate and respectful care; to complete and current information concerning their diagnosis, treatment, and prognosis; to refuse treatment; and to privacy and the protection of information about their care. It remains for physicians to implement the Patient's Bill of Rights, but it was a step toward developing more informed medical-care consumers.

HOWARD L. LEWIS
Managing Editor, "Modern Hospital" Magazine

Mental Health

During 1973 increased attention focused on depression and schizophrenia, on the mental health of children and minority groups, and on crime and antisocial behavior, as well as on drug and alcohol abuse. The establishment of a new federal agency— the Alcohol, Drug Abuse, and Mental Health Administration (ADAMHA) in the Department of Health, Education, and Welfare—to deal with the sociomedical problems of alcohol, drug abuse, and mental health and illness, marked the increasing nationwide recognition of these problems as crucial health issues.

Mental Hospitals. An estimated 275,995 persons were in mental hospitals in 1972, the latest year for which statistics are available; this was less than half of the number in 1955, a peak year. The decrease in hospitalization is linked to new treatment methods, improved psychoactive drugs, and the availability of community care and rehabilitation.

Community Mental Health Services and Centers. In 1973 approximately 700,000 persons received care in federally funded community mental health hospitals. Since passage of the Community Mental Health Centers Act in 1963, the National Institute of Mental Health (NIMH) has provided funds for 540 centers in the United States. As direct federal support was phased out, an increasing number of states enacted community mental health center legislation of their own.

The benefits of the mental health center concept in terms of home-based care and preventive services have been thoroughly demonstrated. Among the services offered by community centers are partial hospitalization, 24-hour-a-day emergency care, inpatient and outpatient services, and consultation and education for community agencies. Many centers provide, or affiliate in developing, drug abuse prevention programs and special services for alcoholics and for children.

Child Mental Health. The extent of mental health problems of children in the United States is shown by 1971 statistics: approximately 140,000 children and youths under 18 years of age received inpatient psychiatric care and an additional 632,000 were treated as psychiatric outpatients, an increase of nearly 20% over 1969 statistics, and an indication of a neglected area in the nation's public health effort. In 1973 federal funds totaling $10 million for the staffing of children's mental health services were provided to the states. NIMH also made available a multi-media package of informational materials designed for the mental health education of teachers.

Mental Health of Minorities. Efforts continued to develop increased knowledge of the stresses of minority life and the impact of the larger community and its activities on minority populations. Research to ascertain issues directly affecting minority groups were supported, and service programs were tailored for these groups.

Depression. Depressive illnesses, which affect millions of Americans, are gaining recognition as a major public health problem. Estimates suggest that as many as 15% of American adults may have significant depressive features at any one time. The drug lithium carbonate was found to be highly effective in preventing relapse among patients formerly hospitalized for severe depression.

Schizophrenia. As part of its International Pilot Study on Schizophrenia, the United Nations World Health Organization (WHO), in cooperation with NIMH and eight other regional research centers, published a major report on schizophrenia in 1973. In the United States, more than 900,000 persons received care for the disorder in 1971.

Crime and Antisocial Behavior. Behavioral scientists sought new ways to prevent crime and antisocial behavior and to rehabilitate young offenders. Attention was paid to resolving conflicts in urban environments, and studies were encouraged to find ways to improve the criminal justice system, the treatment of offenders in institutions, and the training of personnel. Though still in its early stages, a new trend involved the establishment of community-based treatment centers for mentally ill juvenile and adult offenders as an alternative to institutionalization.

Drug Abuse. For the first time in recent decades, nationwide data in 1973 indicated an approaching turnabout in the heroin epidemic that swept the country in the mid-1960's. Reports of the decreasing rates of new addicts were based on a decrease in narcotic-related deaths, official crime statistics, and a major reduction of international drug trafficking. The President's Special Action Office for Drug Abuse Prevention continued its national efforts to attack narcotic and drug abuse problems. By the end of 1973, 300 NIMH-funded community-level drug abuse treatment and rehabilitation service programs were serving approximately 40,000 heroin addicts and other drug abusers.

In a significant research advance, scientists at the Johns Hopkins Medical Institution in Baltimore identified the specific sites in the brain where heroin and other opiates are believed to attach themselves to produce their exhilarating effects on the body. The finding will permit rapid screening of large numbers of potentially non-addicting pain-killing drugs and of narcotic antagonists for the treatment and prevention of addiction.

Alcohol Abuse and Alcoholism. Alcoholism or problem drinking afflicts an estimated 9 million persons in the United States and affects an additional large number of people—the families, friends, employers, and other close associates of the alcoholic. The National Institute on Alcohol Abuse and Alcoholism, in cooperation with state and local agencies, is continuing to make treatment available, develop preventive programs, and give high priority to research, public education, and the training of personnel to cope with the problem.

Citizen Involvement. The National Association for Mental Health, representing approximately 1 million members of voluntary citizen advocacy groups that are a crucial force behind mental health legislation, sponsors an annual Mental Health Research Achievement Award to a scientist who has contributed significantly to research on the causes, treatment, and prevention of mental illness. The recipient in 1973 was Dr. Robert Coles of Harvard.

BERTRAM S. BROWN, M. D.
Director, National Institute of Mental Health

Nursing

The major concerns of nursing in the United States during 1973 included bringing more minority-group students into nursing careers, establishing a certification program to recognize high quality in nursing practice, and assuring continuing education for all nurses to improve professional knowledge and provide better nursing care for the public.

Minority-Group Recruitment. The National Student Nurses' Association (NSNA) launched its Breakthrough to Nursing project, funded for two years by the nursing division of the National Institutes of Health. The project was developed by nursing students in 43 areas of the country, where more than 75 community organizations and health programs worked with the 400 NSNA recruiters to reach prospective candidates in some 200 secondary schools. Nationally, 500 minority-group students were admitted to nursing schools through the project. Some 300 more students, not yet enrolled, were tutored, counseled, and helped to prepare to enter nursing.

Certification and Continuing Education. In May, the American Nurses' Association (ANA) launched a nationwide certification program to provide tangible recognition of a nurse's commitment to high professional standards and to identify for colleagues and clients those nurses who have earned recognition for the quality of their practice. Under the new program, registered nurses—after passing an examination and providing other evidence of excellence in a special area of clinical practice—are certified in that specialty. Certification boards were established for community health, geriatric, maternal and child health, medical-surgical, and psychiatric-mental health nursing. For recertification every five years, certified nurses must submit evidence that they have maintained high standards of practice.

With the advent of certification and with nurses functioning in expanded clinical roles and assuming greater responsibilities in health care, the need for continuing education among nurses was greater than ever before. Mandatory versus voluntary continuing education was a heated topic of discussion at nursing organization meetings and among nurses throughout the country. California became the first state to enact a law requiring evidence of continuing education for relicensure of nurses in the state.

Education. In 1973—the 100th anniversary of the opening of the first U.S. schools of nursing—there were 1,377 nursing education programs in the United States. These were distributed as follows: 541 associate degree two-year programs in community colleges, 293 four-year baccalaureate programs, and 543 hospital-based diploma programs. During the 1972–73 academic year, enrollments in schools of nursing totaled 213,127, an increase of 25,576 over the previous year. Graduates of schools of nursing numbered 51,784—up from 47,001 in 1972.

Nurse Population. The number of practicing registered nurses increased from 748,000 in 1972 to 777,000 in 1973, according to the Interagency Conference on Nursing Statistics. Approximately 551,-000 were employed full-time and 226,000 part-time. The ratio of nurses to population in 1973 increased slightly over that of 1972—from 361 to 370 per 100,000. But the need for nurses continued, especially for nurses with advanced degrees.

ANNE R. WARNER, *National Health Council*

Pediatrics

Although there was little news of a dramatic nature in pediatrics in 1973, there was evidence of continuing improvement in the health of children. Information obtained by the National Center for Health Statistics disclosed that the infant mortality rate for the year ending June 30, 1973, was 18.1 deaths per 1,000 live births—a decrease from an infant death rate of 18.9 per 1,000 in the previous 12 months. This drop of nearly 5% can be attributed to improved care for and survival of premature infants and to the continuing nationwide efforts to identify and treat pregnant women who risk giving birth to premature infants, so that the incidence of prematurity can be reduced. Some states that have well-organized programs for the care of such mothers and of premature infants have succeeded in lowering their infant mortality rate to approximately 12 deaths per 1,000 live births.

Mental Retardation in Infants. Universal screening of newborn infants for phenylketonuria (PKU) was instituted in the United States in the 1960's with the expectation that if these infants can be identified early in life and treated by dietary restriction of the harmful amino acid phenylalanine, the severity of the mental retardation that occurs in untreated infants with PKU could be minimized. A collaborative study from 18 centers treating children who have PKU indicated that the results of dietary treatment were better than anticipated. The mean IQ of 93 children treated for three or four years with a low phenylalanine diet was 100, which is near the mean IQ of normal children, and the spread of the individual tests was the same as that expected in a normal population.

Blood Diseases. Rh-disease, or erythroblastosis foetalis, is an illness characterized by the rapid destruction of red blood cells in some babies with Rh negative mothers. The disease results from the passage of red blood cells, usually at birth, from an Rh+ baby into the mother's circulation, resulting in the formation of maternal antibodies against these foreign cells. During subsequent pregnancies these maternal anti-Rh+ antibodies pass through the placenta into the infant's circulation and destroy the infant's Rh+ cells.

In the 1960's it was learned that if susceptible mothers are given potent anti-Rh antibodies within 72 hours of the delivery of their first Rh+ infant, or abortus, the production of maternal anti-Rh+ antibodies will be minimized. Data available in 1973 indicated that this therapy was highly successful. If all susceptible mothers were treated—and it is estimated that some 80% were being treated in 1973—Rh-disease would be preventable.

An improvement in the management of children with leukemia also became evident in 1973. An increasing number and variety of drugs have gradually been found useful in leukemia therapy. Multi-institutional studies of leukemia therapy, begun in the early 1960's, have shown that certain combinations of these drugs given in regular cycles and sometimes combined with radiotherapy or immunotherapy unquestionably increased the life expectancy of afflicted children. Prior to the advent of drug treatment, less than 1% of children with acute leukemia survived five years. A child who developed acute leukemia in the mid-1960's had less than a 20% chance in living five years. A child who developed leukemia in 1973 was estimated to have better than a 65% chance of surviving five years, and most of them could be expected to be without evidence of disease for prolonged periods. It became appropriate to speak of a "cure" for acute leukemia as a reasonable hope for the future.

Model Act for Treatment of Adolescents. Adolescents under the age of 18 who have venereal disease, who have medical problems related to drug abuse, or who are pregnant often fail to seek medical assistance out of fear that the physician will report their problem to their parents. In 1973 the American Academy of Pediatrics prepared model legislation providing for consent of minors for health services that it hoped would be passed by the legislatures of several states. The proposal provides that minors may be examined and treated without parental knowledge or consent. Where introduced, this bill is expected to be the subject of heated debate.

WILLIAM E. SEGAR, M.D., *University of Wisconsin*

TECHNICIAN takes blood sample from a child in Cleveland's Childhood Lead Poisoning Control Center.

UPI

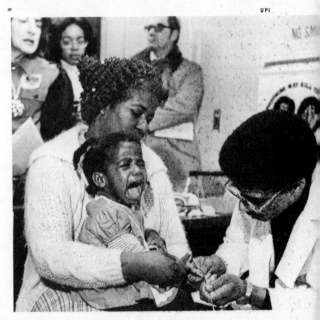

Pharmacology

In 1973 the most important event affecting drug regulation in the United States was a set of decisions by the Supreme Court that gave the Food and Drug Administration (FDA) expanded authority.

Broadened FDA Authority. In summary, the Supreme Court decisions established that: (1) the FDA has the right to classify a product as a new drug, thereby making the use of the product subject to judicial review; (2) the FDA has the authority to group similar drugs in regulatory actions rather than being required to act on a product-by-product basis; and (3) the FDA is not required to grant an administrative hearing to a manufacturer fighting a revocation of a new drug application unless the manufacturer meets FDA requirements for evidence to support claims of effectiveness.

New FDA Commissioner. Alexander M. Schmidt, dean of the Abraham Lincoln School of Medicine at the University of Illinois, was appointed commissioner of the FDA on July 20, succeeding Charles C. Edwards. One of Schmidt's foremost interests is the role that the FDA should play in educating medical students and doctors in the use of drugs.

Advisory Committees. The FDA moved to make broader use of outside advisers and advisory committees in doing the work of the agency. At a time when the secretary of Health, Education, and Welfare. exerted great pressure on agencies to cut the number of advisers sharply to save money, the FDA was allowed to increase the number that it used. The agency hopes to bring in more advisers, and it worked on ways to bring them into the process of approving or disallowing investigational new drug plans and new drug applications. This task is important because FDA approval is required for marketing a drug product.

The plans for advisers were controversial. Proponents said that the agency lacked the scientific competence to accomplish its work satisfactorily and that bringing in outside help was the answer. Opponents pointed to conflict-of-interest problems since most of the outside scientists have participated in drug tests for pharmaceutical companies.

Cold Remedies. The FDA proposed controversial new rules that would cover prescription cough medicines and allergy products. Physicians and the pharmaceutical industry protested that the proposed rules would virtually eliminate all products that have labels making claims for the relief of symptoms of the common cold. The FDA's position was that unless there were adequate and well-controlled studies supporting the claims, the products could not be allowed to remain on the market. At a hearing in the summer, representatives of the pharmaceutical industry and physician witnesses told the agency that cold preparations should be allowed to remain on the market despite the lack of adequate and well-controlled studies. Later, the FDA decided to hold the proposed rules in abeyance pending the report of an advisory committee.

Bioavailability. The FDA published proposed regulations for helping to ensure equivalent bioavailability among products. "Equivalent bioavailability" among products means that one chemical compound in product A will dissolve in the body at the same rate as an identical chemical compound in product B. The question of equivalent bioavailability is of considerable importance because various national health insurance proposals call for payment for drugs at the cost of the lowest-priced member of a class. This mode of payment rests on the theory that equivalent bioavailability can be assumed unless proven otherwise.

Diet Drug Recall. The FDA ordered off the market all but a handful of diet drugs. These drugs usually consisted of dextroamphetamine or amphetamine in combination with other elements such as vitamins or sedatives. These combination products had been used to treat obesity. The FDA concluded that diet drugs containing amphetamines had potential dangers that outweighed their usefulness.

JEANNE F. ANDERSON
Editor, "Washington Drug & Device Letter"

Public Health

The Department of Health, Education, and Welfare (HEW) spearheaded drives in 1973 to improve health care and to combat lead paint poisoning, high blood pressure, venereal diseases, and hepatitis. The department also underwent a reorganization.

HEW Reorganization. The Department of Health, Education, and Welfare made significant changes in the organization of its health programs in 1973. It elevated one Health Services and Mental Health Administration (HSMHA) program, the Center for Disease Control, to agency status. It restructured another, the National Institute of Mental Health, and renamed it the Alcohol, Drug Abuse, and Mental Health Administration. And it divided the remaining HSMHA programs into two new agencies—the Health Services Administration and the Health Resources Administration. As a result, the department's health programs, known collectively as the Public Health Service, were consolidated into six major agencies: the National Institutes of Health, the Food and Drug Administration, the Center for Disease Control, the Health Services Administration, the Health Resources Administration, and the Alcohol, Drug Abuse, and Mental Health Administration.

Concurrently the department worked to improve the availability and quality of health care and to combat a number of specific health problems.

Health Care Review. Acting on authority contained in the 1972 amendments to the Social Security Act, HEW began the process of setting up Professional Standards Review Organizations, or PSROs, across the country. A PSRO is a group of local physicians chartered by HEW to review the quality and appropriateness of medical care provided to Medicare and Medicaid patients by hospitals and other institutions in the group's area. HEW planned to complete the designation of PSRO areas in each state by Jan. 1, 1974, and to have PSROs in operation in most of these areas by 1976.

Lead Paint Poisoning. Special grants were given to 42 cities to establish programs to detect, treat, and prevent the lead poisoning caused by eating the peeling flakes of lead-based paint. These programs sought to screen 200,000 children, especially those under six years of age, in 1973.

High Blood Pressure. The federal government joined with the health professions, pharmaceutical and communications industries, and a range of private and voluntary groups in a nationwide campaign to educate the general public and medical professions on the importance of diagnosing and controlling high blood pressure. This program is a long-range educational effort that may provide a prototype for other health education programs.

VD Plan. The Center for Disease Control augmented its nationwide attack on the venereal diseases by launching a Venereal Disease Communications Plan. The plan is designed to create awareness of the venereal diseases, change attitudes and behavior, increase self-referrals for diagnosis and treatment, and encourage health-care providers to conduct screening and contact-tracing programs. There were approximately 800,000 cases of gonorrhea reported in the United States in fiscal year 1973, an increase of 12% over fiscal 1972.

National Blood Policy. At a meeting with representatives of the nation's blood-banking community, HEW put into effect its plan to upgrade the efficiency and safety of the blood collection and distribution system. Of the 8.8 million units of whole blood collected yearly in the United States, roughly 25% becomes outdated and is never transfused.

Disease is another major problem in the present system. Several studies indicated that there are 17,000 cases of overt post-transfusion hepatitis each year, resulting in about 850 deaths. A major feature of the HEW plan is the elimination of commercial blood banking and the establishment of an all-voluntary donor system. Available data indicate that while commercial blood organizations provide only 15% of the total supply, they account for up to 45% of the post-transfusion hepatitis cases.

Respiratory Diseases

In 1973 there was continued study of influenza and of ways to prevent respiratory diseases.

Influenza. In the United States influenza cases in the winter of 1972–73 reached epidemic proportions, and excess morbidity from influenza was the greatest since the appearance of the Hong Kong virus in 1968–69. There were similar findings in other parts of the world.

As anticipated, the 1972–73 influenza season saw the emergence of a moderately distinctive, but not completely new, variant of the prototype Hong Kong virus causing influenza. The A/England/72 strain became the prevalent type A influenza virus throughout the world during 1973. In the United States the first outbreaks were reported in military installations in the Western states. The first outbreak occurred between Oct. 1 and Nov. 4, 1972, at the U.S. Air Force Academy in Colorado Springs, Colo., and during November and early December influenza spread to military installations in the immediate area.

The first reported outbreak in a civilian area occurred in Baltimore in late November. By Dec. 3, 1972, influenza viruses had been isolated from 14 states, and there were significant ongoing outbreaks in New York City, Baltimore, and the San Francisco Bay area. Soon thereafter outbreaks due to the same strain were being reported throughout the country. By the end of January 1973 morbidity from influenza began decreasing in the northeastern United States, but there were increasing numbers of cases in the Southeastern and Midwestern parts of the country. The epidemic reached a peak during the week ending Feb. 3, 1973. Thereafter it declined, dipping below the epidemic threshold for the first time during the week ending March 17, 1973.

The worldwide influenza picture seemed to mirror that in the United States. In western Europe and the Soviet Union, morbidity and mortality exceeded the previous years' level. Eastern Europe also reported widespread outbreaks.

A strain of influenza B was also responsible for several outbreaks during 1973. The B strains isolated varied: some were known to have been prevalent throughout the world for many years, but others were found to be significantly different, resembling a strain of B influenza isolated in Hong Kong during the epidemic of A influenza in 1972–73. Epidemics of influenza B virus began to be reported in Australia in July 1973, but the specific type of B virus was not indicated. An epidemic associated with the new B virus was reported in Japan in late April 1973.

Another epidemic or pandemic of influenza A due to the 1972 strain was not expected during the 1973–74 winter, but there was a possibility of a widespread pandemic of influenza due to the new B virus. No definite predictions concerning the severity of such an epidemic if it should occur could be made, but past epidemics of influenza B have been milder and asociated with less morbidity and mortality than those due to influenza virus A.

Prevention of Respiratory Diseases. An investigator working in Britain has shown that large quantities of interferon produced by human leukocytes can prevent respiratory diseases due to viruses responsible for influenza and the common cold. Interferon can prevent or modify many virus infections. If quantities large enough could be commercially produced economically, some progress in combatting influenza could be made.

Progress in developing new respiratory disease vaccines continued. Currently there is emphasis on developing mutations of microorganisms known to produce respiratory disease. A report from Washington, D.C., indicated that a temperature-sensitive mutant of respiratory syncytial virus was effective in preventing the major manifestations of disease after it was administered to appropriate volunteer subjects. The investigators' enthusiasm was somewhat dulled, however, because some of the subjects developed what the investigators considered mild but significant disease. The work continues, however, and it is hoped that significant progress may be reported in the next two years.

BERNARD PORTNOY, M.D.
University of Southern California

Surgery

In 1973 there was steady progress in many areas of surgery, with no one achievement overshadowing others. Kidney transplants and heart surgery had increasing success and received considerable attention. New techniques for the surgical treatment of hiatal hernia were explored. Initial efforts at ambulatory surgery were increasingly recognized as successful, and the practice began to spread throughout the country. Psychosurgery, long a controversial issue, was the center of a court case.

Ambulatory Surgery. Along with their medical colleagues, government agencies, and the public, surgeons have appreciated the escalating costs of medical and surgical care. Operations such as kidney transplants and open-heart surgery demand sophisticated equipment and large teams of highly-qualified doctors, nurses, and technicians. This type of surgical care is necessarily expensive. However, other operations, such as hernia repair, tonsillectomy, and appendectomy, can be done efficiently and at reasonable cost. Patients having these operations today are usually discharged from the hospital within three to five days, but even this is not

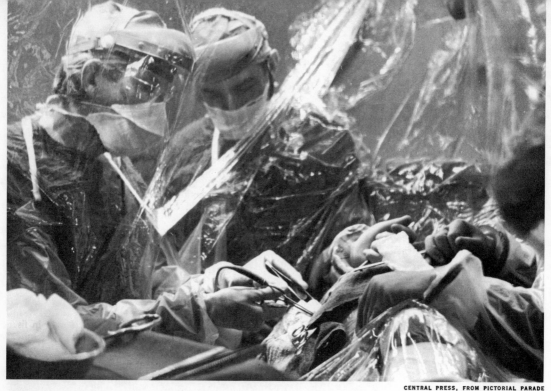

British surgeons operate on a patient from outside a plastic isolation tent, a new technique in air sterilization.

efficient, for the cost of even a four-day hospital stay is many hundreds of dollars. Therefore there has been increasing interest in performing this type of surgery on ambulatory patients.

In 1970 two anesthesiologists in Phoenix, Dr. John Ford and Dr. Wallace Reed, opened a free-standing, ambulatory, surgical facility, which has been called Surgicenter. Its success has been nothing short of phenomenal. The unit may be used by all qualified physicians in the Phoenix area who schedule their cases by telephone. The patient, doctor, and anesthesiologist meet in the facility on the scheduled day of the operation. Either local or general anesthesia is used, and the patient returns to his home a few hours after the operation.

The most commonly performed operations at Surgicenter are dilation and curettage of the uterus, hernia repair, tonsillectomy, and vasectomy. All patients are fully recovered by 4 or 5 P.M., when the unit closes. Because of the efficiency of the unit, costs have been low. Ford and Reed point out some of the reasons for this low cost: no hospital beds, no kitchens, no evening and night shift personnel, minimal laboratory and X-ray facilities, and very efficient management. More than 13,000 operations have been performed in the Phoenix Surgicenter, and 7,000 operations are projected for 1973. Ford and Reed are now building a second Surgicenter in Phoenix.

News of successful ambulatory surgery ventures in Phoenix and elsewhere has spread rapidly, and many units similar to the Phoenix Surgicenter are now under construction across the United States. Some of these are free-standing. Many others are sponsored by and attached to a hospital although they function as quite independent units to handle ambulatory surgical patients only. Because the various units have shown that they can provide first-class care and service at low cost, private insurance

carriers and government agencies have agreed to provide coverage for these services in many states. An expansion of this trend will help to lower medical costs and avoid unnecessary hospitalization.

Pulmonary Embolism. It has been estimated that some 47,000 patients die of pulmonary embolism (blood clots to the lungs) in the United States each year. The blood clots usually arise in inflamed veins in the calves of the legs and may be let free into the venous system and reach the lungs as fatal or non-fatal emboli. When the problem is recognized, the clots can often be prevented or controlled by drugs that tend to keep the blood from clotting (anticoagulants). However, in some cases blood clots have already broken off or break off despite the use of anticoagulants.

Because of the very high risk of fatality from any embolism, an operation to prevent further episodes is justified. The logical procedure is a complete ligation of the inferior vena cava, preventing any large mass from reaching the lungs and forcing blood from the lower parts of the body to find new channels to reach the heart. For several decades Dr. Alton Ochsner of New Orleans has been a leading advocate of this procedure for preventing pulmonary emboli. However, many surgeons feel that. complete occlusion of the inferior vena cava results in impaired venous flow from the legs and uncomfortable late changes such as pain, swelling, and discoloration. To avoid these undesirable effects while still preventing the flow of clots to the lungs, many ingenious devices have been created and used. Dr. William Moretz of Atlanta, Ga., has used a plastic clip that partially occludes the vena cava, yet allows blood to flow freely through it; but this, like complete occlusion, requires a major operation. In an attempt to obviate the operation, surgeons have created many mechanical devices that can be introduced into the vena cava through a

small incision in the groin. These intracaval devices include silastic balloons, Dacron-covered springs, and another wire-springing gadget called an umbrella filter. A recent report by Dr. Kazi Mobin-Uddin and colleagues in Miami noted very gratifying two-year results with the umbrella-type filter.

Hiatal Hernia. Hiatal hernia is fairly common, and its treatment has long been controversial. Hiatal hernia is a protusion of the stomach upward through the opening (hiatus) in the diaphragm through which the esophagus enters the abdomen to join the stomach. Normally, the lowest portion of the esophagus rests within the abdomen and joins the stomach well below the diaphragm. In hiatal hernia, the junction of esophagus and stomach is above the diaphragm and therefore in the chest.

According to many doctors, hiatal hernias are particularly common in middle-aged and elderly people and even more so if they are obese. The cause of hiatal hernia is uncertain, but increased intra-abdominal pressure is felt to be a factor.

The symptom most commonly seen is heartburn, which results when the highly acid juice from the stomach flows over the lining of the esophagus, resulting in irritation. This phenomenon is called "reflux." Other, less frequent symptoms are belching, gasiness, and pain in the upper abdomen. Reflux may also occur in patients without hiatal hernia. The many new technical procedures applied to determine if the patient does or does not have reflux include direct measurement of the acidity in the esophageal wall, direct visualization of the esophageal surface with new, improved fiberopic endoscopes, and careful measurement of intraluminal pressures in the lower esophagus and upper stomach.

Results of the new instrumentation have led to an entirely new concept for the operative treatment of patients with symptomatic reflux, with or without hiatal hernia. In the past, surgeons were content to do an "anatomical repair," bringing the stomach back down to the abdomen and narrowing the size of the esophageal hiatus, but results, particularly long-term results, were poor. Now various techniques aimed solely at preventing reflux are being tested throughout the world, and internists and surgeons are quite optimistic that the new operations will yield better results.

Psychosurgery. Psychosurgery, a procedure in which tiny portions of the brain are destroyed through surgery, radiation, electricity, or ultrasound in an attempt to alter the behavior and emotional makeup of mentally ill patients not responding to conventional treatment was the center of renewed controversy in 1973. Basic issues of law and medical ethics are involved. For example, can an involuntarily hospitalized, mentally ill patient give "informed consent" to an experimental procedure? On July 10 a special three-judge panel in Wayne (Michigan) County Circuit Court ruled that experimental psychosurgery may not be performed on persons confined against their will in state institutions even when such a person's consent is formally obtained. This precedent-setting decision, which some fear will seriously hamper brain research and the development of new psychosurgery techniques, did, however, leave the way open for changes once the psychosurgery procedures are no longer experimental and the benefits clearly outweigh the risks.

IRVING F. ENQUIST
Director of Surgery, Methodist Hospital of Brooklyn

Venereal Disease

Gonorrhea currently ranks first among all reportable communicable diseases in the United States. During the year ending June 30, 1973, there were 809,681 cases reported nationally, an increase of 12% over the number reported the previous year. Increases were reported in all age groups, among both males and females, and in both urban and rural areas. When unreported and undetected cases are considered, the actual incidence in the United States is estimated at about 2.5 million infections per year.

The number of cases of primary and secondary syphilis—the infectious stages of syphilis—has increased steadily since 1969. In fiscal 1973 there were 25,080 cases reported, an increase of 4.5% over the number reported in 1972. It is estimated that there are about 85,000 new cases of syphilis occurring each year. Reported cases of congenital syphilis among infants under one year of age numbered 356 in fiscal 1973, a decrease of 15.6% over the number reported the previous year. Overall, syphilis in all stages numbered 90,609 cases in fiscal 1973. The reservoir of cases needing treatment, most of which are in the latent stages and detectable only by blood tests, is estimated at between 500,000 and 550,000.

Control Programs. Gonorrhea control programs were implemented on a national scale in 1973. Federal assistance to states included the extension of diagnostic and treatment services, culture screening programs to identify and treat those infected (particularly females with asymptomatic disease), and patient interviewing and contact-tracing activities for case detection and prevention purposes. During fiscal 1973 more than 4,939,000 women were culture-tested for gonorrhea, and 4.9% were found positive, with more than 88% being tested in settings other than venereal disease clinics. Over 11,000 female contacts were being examined monthly, and 88% of these received treatment, either therapeutic or preventive. As a result of these efforts, female morbidity rose 36% over that reported in 1972. Male cases increased at the lowest rate in a decade, by only 2%.

Syphilis control activities included the follow-up of positive tests for syphilis to detect untreated cases. During 1973 there were 38 million blood specimens examined, and subsequent follow-up investigations carried out on positive blood tests resulted in approximately 11,000 case reports of infectious syphilis and 54,000 reports of syphilis in other stages. Ninety-six percent of all patients with infectious syphilis were counseled and asked about sexual contacts who might be infected. Contact-tracing activities led to the diagnosis and treatment of an additional 7,200 cases, including 3,500 infectious cases. In addition, some 21,400 contacts were treated prophylactically.

Education and Research. Venereal disease education programs, using all forms of news media to alert the general public, were intensified throughout the United States. Research efforts centered on a continuing search for an effective blood test for gonorrhea, an improved medium for transporting gonorrhea culture specimens, an improved blood test for syphilis, and the development of a vaccine for syphilis and gonorrhea.

JOSEPH H. BLOUNT
Venereal Disease Branch, U. S. Public Health Service

UPI

A tornado whipping through western Massachusetts in August wrapped a tractor-trailer rig around a tree after first removing most of the tree's branches.

meteorology

Weather observations were extended in 1973 by the further use of satellites, buoys, and balloons, and the effects of air-sea interactions were studied. Investigation of and debate over weather modification continued. Other meteorological advances occurred in the areas of climatic change and atmospheric dynamics. The World Meteorological Organization celebrated its centenary in Vienna. Now a UN agency, it comprises 125 nations.

Observations. Weather satellite NOAA-2, launched on Oct. 17, 1972, was replaced by a more sophisticated NOAA-3 on Nov. 7, 1973. NOAA-2 had scanned the atmosphere three-dimensionally from 800 miles (1,290 km) above the earth down to a height of 20 miles (32 km) entirely by sensors rather than TV cameras. It provided information on clouds as small as ½ nautical mile (0.9 km) and also sensed the surface temperature. The key item was the vertical temperature profile from the surface to 100,000 feet (30,480 meters). Every 24 hours, 1.3 million temperature readings were collected.

Stationary weather ships are gradually being displaced by buoys. These buoys have been tested in the Arctic Ocean north of Alaska, surviving 15 months in ice drift with temperatures down to −50°F (−46°C). They relayed data on pressure, temperature, and ice motion to interrogating satellites. Two other 100-ton weather buoys have been anchored in the Gulf of Mexico in water depths of from 8,000 to 10,000 feet (2,400 to 3,000 meters). Their observations of pressure, air and sea temperature, and wind speed are greatly assisting coastal forecasting. Two others are deployed in the Gulf of Alaska and off Norfolk, Va., in the Atlantic.

Observations from floating balloon systems with satellite communications have become available. The French-U. S. Eole program, started in 1971 over the Southern Hemisphere with a release of 480 balloons, was completed in 1973 with 5 balloons still aloft.

Air-Sea Interactions. Sea-surface temperatures are important to large- and small-scale atmospheric conditions. Large oceanic eddies, up to 100 miles (160 km) in diameter, are drifting along the eastern U. S. coast. They are spotted by infrared sensors from satellites. The water of these eddies is up to 8°F (−4.5°C) cooler than the surrounding sea. Clouds moving over these cold-water areas are promptly dissolved by descending air currents induced by the surface cooling.

A joint venture of Soviet and U. S. oceanographers has discovered a similar phenomenon. It is a self-limiting mechanism of rainstorms over tropical waters. Heavy downpours stir up the overheated top layer of 10 meters (33 feet) of the ocean. The cooled surface water stops the updrafts from the warm water that caused the storm, and cloud growth with rain ceases.

A similar process for modifying hurricanes was proposed. This consists of spreading a polymer substance over large water surfaces to suppress the smaller waves, spray, and evaporation. Thus the latent heat of water vapor, which is a major energy source for the hurricane, will be reduced. The search for a long-lived membrane of this type continues.

Weather Modification. Lightning induced forest fires became widespread again in 1973 in the western dry areas of the United States. However, encouraging experiments to decrease electrical conductivity in the atmosphere have been made. Aluminized nylon fibers 4 inches (10 cm) in length, dropped as "chaff" from aircraft, reduce the corona discharges and the cloud-to-ground potential. Storms seeded with the fibers have 66% fewer lightning discharges to the ground than unseeded storms.

British investigations have thrown serious doubts on the accepted cloud-seeding mechanism for rainfall production. They showed that the narrow-size range of small cloud droplets is not altered by seeding but by a dynamic process that creates the large droplets necessary for rain. Nature produces the necessary range of sizes of convective alternation of cloud formation and dissipation, leaving a few large droplets and then reforming the cloud.

Debate over so-called weather warfare continued. The U. S. Department of Defense never admitted use of cloud seeding during hostilities but indicated that it participated in research on weather modification.

Climatic Change. Causes for climatic change remain as obscure as ever. Observations in the Canadian Arctic show that temperatures have lowered. The height above sea level where freezing lasts through the summer has lowered measurably. Glaciers are now static at a level 300 meters (985 feet) lower than a decade ago. Sea ice in Baffin Bay and Davis Strait simultaneously increased.

THE WEATHER IN 1973

A Year of Extremes

The weather in 1973 varied considerably, with extremes of flood and drought prevalent in different parts of the world. A summary of the year's weather highlights is given below.

December 1972–February 1973. Winter brought some weather surprises. U. S. states from the Northeast westward into the Dakotas along the Canadian border were generally more than 2°F (1°C) warmer than average. The South, southern Great Plains, and the Rocky Mountain area were up to 4°F (2°C) colder than average, but an area centered around western Wyoming showed a 10°F (5°C) temperature deficiency.

Precipitation over the conterminous United States was close to average, but some spots in Montana and Arizona had double their usual share. Among the latter was Flagstaff, which had over three times its average snowfall. Salt Lake City, Utah, set an all-time local record with 85 inches (216 cm) of snow. At the same time there was a notable lack of snow in a central stretch from Kansas to New Jersey.

Similar lack of snow was reported from Sweden, where by mid-January no snow cover had been established. In parts of the Soviet Union there was also lack of snow, leading to damage of the winter wheat crop.

In February a severe snow storm hit from Louisiana to North Carolina. Record-breaking amounts, up to 21 inches (53 cm), fell in Georgia and Alabama, causing 17 deaths, leaving 30,000 motorists stranded, and causing $300 million damage.

In January, 46 tornadoes—the highest number ever—occurred in the United States. A twister hit San Justo, Argentina, where 46 were killed and several hundred persons injured. Damaging floods occurred in Oregon, Idaho, and California. In Rio de Janeiro, Brazil, heavy rainstorms ended a heat wave but killed 16 and rendered 5,000 homeless.

Drought plagued Indonesia, Guyana, Cyprus, Morocco, the sub-Saharan Sahel region, South Africa, and Rhodesia, where crop losses were heavy and livestock production was low. In India the cotton crop suffered, and England had the driest winter in a decade.

March–May. Most areas in the United States had a very wet spring. The Mississippi Valley and adjacent areas had record floods. The Mississippi River exceeded flood stage along 1,400 miles (2,255 km) of its course. It reached the highest stage since 1785 at St. Louis, 43.3 feet (13.2 meters), and stayed above flood stage for 76 days, breaking the 1844 record of 58 days. Even though most of the levees held, there were 26 fatalities; 39,000 people were made homeless, and 12.6 million acres (5.1 million hectares) of farmland were flooded. A major flood of the South Platte River in Colorado and Nebraska in early May caused 7,000 persons to flee the rampaging waters that caused $50 million damage.

The season was characterized by an unusually large number of tornadoes, also breaking all previous records. Between January and May, 750 twisters caused 59 deaths and thousands of injuries. Many of these tornadoes occurred in clusters: 21 on March 13 in Texas, Arkansas, and Mississippi, and an astounding 195 between May 26 and 29 mainly in Midwestern and Southern states, the greatest number ever in so short an interval of time.

The Pacific Northwest was very dry, and western Texas and the Dakotas were deficient in precipitation. The Indian pre-monsoon rains were scanty. May showed a nearly worldwide rainfall deficiency, with the Mediterranean area showing the lowest levels in 30 years. The drought in the Sahel area of Africa afflicting six nations (Chad, Niger, Mali, Mauritania, Senegal, and Upper Volta) led to starvation for 10 million people and required international action for relief.

June–August. Summer was cool along the Pacific coast but warm in the North and Northeast. In many Midwestern and Eastern cities warm, stagnant air in July and August led to power shortages and to frequent high levels of air pollution. Precipitation over the United States was very spotty, but the Pacific Northwest suffered from intense drought. The Mississippi River had a second flood crest in early June. Flooding hit New England and Pennsylvania in early July. Vermont was declared a disaster area. A rare tornado struck Massachusetts on August 29, killing 4 and injuring 43 in West Stockbridge.

Although drought prevailed in Finland, Lebanon, and South Africa, floods dominated world weather during the season. The monsoon in South and East Asia caused excessive rain. Early in June the Berisal region of Bangladesh was stricken, and thousands were left homeless. Later that month the swollen Brahmaputra in northeastern India took a large death toll. In Hong Kong, typhoon Dot struck with winds of 100 miles (160 km) per hour and torrential rain. At the end of July it was Japan's turn. In Fukuoka prefecture 9 inches (23 cm) of rain washed 51 houses away and flooded out 20,000 people, causing 18 deaths.

In mid-August northern India and Bangladesh were again hard hit. Rivers from Kashmir to Assam rose above their banks, and severe crop damage ensued. At the end of August the Indus River was on a rampage. In Pakistan's Punjab, 8 million people were affected, 1.5 million were starving, 10,000 villages and 20,000 square miles (51,800 sq km) of cropland were flooded, and damages were estimated at some $250 million.

In the Western Hemisphere, Mexico bore the brunt of floods. In mid-July the rain-swollen Aguanaval River in Coahuila state broke a dam near Encarnación de Díaz, causing 65 deaths. Ten other states were also affected, with a quarter million people made homeless. Toward the end of August a hurricane caused heavy rain in 11 southeastern Mexican states; 70 persons were killed and 400,000 were homeless.

September–November. It was an exceptionally warm autumn over most of the conterminous United States. Many localities in the South and East had record-breaking temperatures for individual days in late November, and along the Gulf Coast it was the warmest November on record. In October, Oklahoma, Kansas, and Nebraska had rainstorms causing damages totaling millions of dollars. Satellite photographs showed that five northern counties in Oklahoma looked like a giant lake. Also unusual was the large number of tornadoes. The worst outbreak, accompanied by torrential rain, swept across northern Mississippi, Alabama, and Tennessee in late November, with 3 deaths and over 100 persons injured.

Early snow hit central Europe in the second week of October, while the French Riviera had the worst rains in 40 years and snow closed the Alpine passes between France and Italy. In the third week of October, 8 inches (20 cm) of rain along the Spanish Mediterranean coast caused floods that killed 93. The Philippines were hit severely in mid-October by three tropical storms, which left over half a million people homeless, killed scores, and severely damaged the rice crop. At the same time a tropical storm killed 19 and destroyed 60,000 homes in the eastern Indian state of Orissa. The southern and central Philippines were devastated again by tropical storms in the third week of November when 33 persons were killed and over 100,000 homes were destroyed in 10 provinces. North Vietnam reported that weather had affected the rice crop so that it reached only 80% of its target. The heaviest rainfall in Mexican history boosted the dry-land harvest of corn, and beneficial rains in Senegal broke the persistent drought south of the Sahara and improved crop prospects for the starving people of the region.

H. E. LANDSBERG

THE FLOODING Mississippi River inundated downtown Hannibal, Mo., in April. The guests of the Mark Twain Hotel, on the site of a swimming hole in Mark Twain's day, were transported by boat service.

New analyses of sediments from cores obtained in the Atlantic and Caribbean have made it possible to reconstruct an approximate temperature curve for the past million years by use of the temperature-sensitive ratio of two oxygen isotopes. Recurrent patterns of from 40,000 to 70,00 years in length are apparent, but eras as warm as the present were relatively rare.

The problem of heat emission by various man-made combustion processes has concerned ecologists. At present this heat amounts to less than one hundredth of one percent of the solar heating. This is dissipated without noticeable global consequences. Projections to the year 2,000 foresee a tenfold increase of thermal pollution. Even that is unlikely to cause global meteorological changes, but it could have profound effects near large settlements.

Atmospheric Dynamics. New insights have been gained into the flow patterns in air. From September through March rather regularly spaced westward-moving pressure waves with associated wind shifts were noted in the tropical Pacific between latitudes 10°N and 10°S. At intervals of 40 to 50 days these pressure waves cause increased cloud and rain formation, moving from the eastern Indian Ocean along the equator to South America.

On a smaller scale in moderate latitudes, it has been discovered that cyclones and anticyclones move faster along their longer axis than in other directions. This tendency had been known for some time to apply to sunspots.

On the local scale, a mathematical model has been developed that successfully permits prediction of sea-breeze circulations. The model has been tested in Florida, where it will predict areas of cloud formation and thunderstorms. In Miami, with south winds the sea breeze will trigger afternoon thunderstorms, but with southeast winds heavy cloud formation and thunderstorms will take place west of the city. The model is now being tried in other topographic settings. In general, automation of thunderstorm forecasts has made much progress.

A relation has been suggested between magnetic storms induced by invasions of particles from the sun and subsequent intensification of pressure troughs in the Gulf of Alaska at 30,000 feet (9,145 meters). Although the mechanism by which the solar events affect weather is unclear, the Aleutian troughs that move into the center of the United States penetrate about 200 miles (320 km) farther south and bring cold weather if they are preceded by northern lights.

H. E. LANDSBERG, *University of Maryland*

GALE FORCE WINDS in Chicago, April 9, sent spray from Lake Michigan smashing into the side of an apartment house. Some of the water reached to above the first-floor lobby.

UPI

MEXICO

Mexican President Luis Echeverría Álvarez, in Britain on a three-day state visit in April, rides with Queen Elizabeth through the streets of Windsor.

Mexico experienced an economic boom in 1973, marked by strong gains in industrial production and export diversification, but it also wrestled with escalating inflation, a worsening trade deficit, and an increase in civil violence. In July elections, President Luís Echeverría's ruling party, the PRI, retained its huge congressional majority, but by December criticism of the president's policies was more widespread than at any time since he took office in 1970. The year was also marred by natural catastrophes of unusual severity.

Natural Disasters. Convulsions of nature inflicted suffering, death, and economic distress in several parts of the country during the summer months. In July and August, hurricane Brenda and heavy rains, producing the worst floods in 40 years, killed hundreds, made thousands homeless, and destroyed valuable crops. Especially hard hit were the states of Nayarit, Guanajuato, Jalisco, Coahuila, Durango, Tamaulipas, and Zacatecas. The government announced the availability of unlimited credit for farmers, but full recovery would take years.

On August 28, an earthquake shook a wide belt in central Mexico extending from the Gulf of Mexico to Mexico City. It caused the death of about 700 persons. Orizaba, Ciudad Serdán, Quecholac, and Puebla were among the cities that suffered extensive damage.

Elections. The government's Institutional Revolutionary party (PRI) once again proved its dominance at the polls. In local and legislative elections on July 1, it swept all seven gubernatorial races, most mayoralty races, and most state legislative races and won 188 seats in the 1973–76 Chamber of Deputies. The National Action Party (PAN) elected 4 deputies, and the Authentic Party of the Mexican Revolution (PARM), 1. Under the country's unique system of proportional representation, PAN was awarded 21 additional seats in the chamber, PARM was given 6, and the People's Socialist Party (PPS), 10. Approximately 15 million of Mexico's 24 mil-

lion registered voters went to the polls, but almost 10% of the votes cast were nullified, sparking charges of electoral anarchy and fraud.

Political Violence. Difficulties with university students continued to plague the Mexican government during 1973. The national university, with an enrollment of over 200,000, was finally able to reopen in the spring after several lengthy and bitter strikes by students and employees, but, by August, the rector had to call police to the campus to put down violence. The causes of the turmoil included overcrowding, inadequate facilities, and underfunding of the institution, which President Echeverría sought to alleviate by increasing the university's budget by about 50%. In addition, the government announced plans to build a second national university in Mexico City, where instruction could begin in 1974.

Student violence and disturbances also occurred in the states of Sinaloa, Sonora, Nuevo León, and Guerrero. At Puebla, in May, a major confrontation between students and state government authorities resulted in gunfire that left four students and five policemen dead and six bystanders injured.

Kidnappings and murders of diplomats and industrialists also presented a major problem. The U. S. consul general in Guadalajara, Terrance G. Leonhardy, was abducted on May 4 by a group calling itself the Armed Revolutionary Forces of the People, which demanded an $80,000 ransom, the release and transportation to Cuba of 30 prisoners, and the publicizing of their statement attacking the Mexican government. Leonhardy was released after all of the conditions had been met by the regime.

Later, however, payment of a $400,000 ransom failed to save the life of the son of the president of the Banco Mexicano, kidnapped on October 5.

On October 10, the British consul in Guadalajara, Anthony Duncan Williams, and Guadalajara industrialist Fernando Aranguren were abducted. The kidnappers demanded $200,000, the dissemina-

EARTHQUAKE on August 28 in Puebla state reduced houses to rubble and killed hundreds of the inhabitants.

tion of an antigovernment "Call to the Nation," and the release of 51 prisoners who were to be flown to North Korea. These demands were not met. Williams was released after five days of confinement, but Aranguren was found dead.

In its political aftereffects, the most serious murder was that of Monterrey industrialist Eugenio Garza Sada, 83, during a kidnapping attempt outside of his brewery on September 17. Also killed in the attempt were two of his aides and two of his attackers. Garza Sada was the leader of the huge Monterrey industrial complex, and his death served to trigger bitter attacks against the regime by business leaders already upset at the government's economic policies and its "left-wing leanings."

Business Expansion and Trade. Stimulated by massive government spending, the gross national product grew at a better than 8% annual rate in the first half of the year. Anti-inflationary measures in the latter part of 1973 were expected to reduce the rate of growth to 7.5% for the year as a whole. Industrial production increased 20%. Tourism grew at a 15% rate. For the first six months of 1973, increases were registered in cement sales (17%), paper production (12%), chemical products (6%), television sets (25%), refrigerators (23%), automobiles (11%), and steel ingots (20%).

Foreign trade increases contributed to economic expansion. For the 12 months ending Sept. 1, 1973, exports rose 18.6%. Of particular significance was the increasing diversification of trade outlets, with exports to China, Canada, Britain, and Japan showing large increases. Despite the rise in export earnings, however, Mexico's balance of trade grew increasingly unfavorable due to an even larger rise in imports.

Inflation. For the average citizen, an abrupt increase in the cost of living was the principal economic problem. After two years during which inflation remained below 5% per year, the projected rate of inflation for 1973 was estimated at between 10% and 20%. Among the factors causing inflationary pressures were worldwide shortages of food and raw materials, rising labor costs, the rising cost of imports, a 19.5% expansion in the money supply in the first quarter of the year, and growing demands for consumer products and capital goods.

The government adopted a 16-point program to combat inflation. It included, among other measures, voluntary price freezes on retail goods, selective government expenditures to increase production, consumer education in better buying practices, and the financing of noninflationary projects. The Minimum Wage Commission raised wages 18% for the period Sept. 17 to Dec. 31, 1973, a measure which benefited 4.5 million workers. In late September, management and labor representatives reached agreement on an emergency wage hike of up to 20% for blue-collar workers, averting a nationwide strike.

Government Planning. Long-range governmental policy goals, such as general economic growth, income redistribution, balanced regional development, rural development, and greater Mexican control of its own economy, were emphasized in 1973 in the proposed national budget. Out of the total budget, 51.5% was programmed for economic development and 24.8% for investment and social protection. A 94% increase in funds allocated for administrative goods and services portended tighter official supervision of the nation's economic affairs.

New laws and governmental actions generally encouraged foreign investment that served national needs, but one new law required that all future foreign direct investments in Mexico be limited to 49% participation and that administrative positions held by non-Mexicans in mixed-capital companies be commensurate with equity holdings. Another law stipulated that foreign technology, patents, and licenses be evaluated by a new National Technology Registry to insure that the country was paying reasonable prices for necessary knowledge.

Several steps were taken during the year to improve living conditions. An urban growth trust fund was created to regulate Mexico City's sprawling

---

MEXICO • Information Highlights

Official Name: United Mexican States.
Location: Southern North America.
Area: 761,602 square miles (1,972,546 sq km).
Population (1973 est.): 56,200,000. *Density,* 70 per square mile (27 per sq km).
Chief Cities (1970 census): Mexico City, the capital, 2,902,969; Guadalajara, 1,194,646; Monterey, 858,107; Ciudad Juárez, 407,000.
Government: *Head of state,* Luís Echeverría Álvarez, president (took office Dec. 1970). *Head of government,* Luís Echeverría Álvarez. *Legislature*—Congress: Senate and Chamber of Deputies. *Major political parties*—Institutional Revolutionary party (PRI); National Action party (PAN).
Language: Spanish (official).
Education: *Expenditure* (1969), 13.5% of total public expenditure. *School enrollment* (1971)—primary, 9,127,226; secondary, 1,008,205; technical/vocational, 257,945; university/higher, 213,199.
Monetary Unit: Peso (12.49 pesos equal U. S.$1, Aug. 1973).
Gross National Product (1972 est.): $38,300,000,000.
Economic Indexes: *Industrial production* (1972), 210 (1963=100); *agricultural production* (1971), 127 (1963=100); *consumer price index* (1972), 138 (1963=100).
Manufacturing (major products): Petroleum products, iron and steel, chemicals, transportation equipment, aluminum, cement, petrochemicals, pharmaceuticals.
Major Agricultural Products: Corn, cotton, sugarcane, wheat, vegetables, fish, livestock.
Major Minerals: Silver (ranks 5th among world producers, 1971), lead, iron ore, zinc, sulfur, petroleum, graphite, gold, manganese, mercury, barite, fluorspar.
Foreign Trade (1972): *Exports,* $1,825,000,000; *Imports,* $2,935,000,000. *Chief trading partner* (1972)—United States (took 70% of exports, supplied 60% of imports).
Tourism: Receipts (1971), $616,300,000.
Transportation: *Motor Vehicles* (1971), 1,926,300 (automobiles, 1,338,400); *railroads* (1971), 15,204 miles (24,468 km); *merchant fleet* (1972), 417,000 gross registered tons; *major national airlines,* Aeronaves de Mexico; Mexicana de Aviación.
Communications: *Telephones* (1972), 1,714,960; *newspapers* (1970), 200.

growth, to acquire land needed for development. Under the new social security law a system of day nurseries was being created for the children of working mothers. Government and petroleum employees were granted a 40-hour work week. The activities of the Basic Commodity Corporation (CONASUPO) were expanded to provide greater savings to consumers and agricultural producers. The government also stepped up its drive to encourage family planning to reduce Mexico's high population growth rate.

International Relations. The Echeverría regime gave strong support to Salvador Allende's Marxist government in Chile. After Allende's ouster and death in September, Mexico gave political asylum to hundreds of Chileans, including Allende's widow, an act that brought some domestic criticism.

In March and April, President Echeverría traveled to Canada, the United Kingdom, France, Belgium, Italy, the Soviet Union, and China seeking wider trade and financial ties and a greater Mexican role in world affairs. As a result of the presidential trips and the commercial missions that preceded them, Mexico received most-favored-nation status from the Soviet Union and China and significantly increased British and French industrial and financial participation in the Mexican economy.

Within Latin America, Mexico expanded its trade with the Central American Common Market and joined the nations of the Andean Group to create a Joint Andean-Mexican Committee to expand trade. It also supported Panamanian demands for full sovereignty over the Canal Zone.

DONALD J. MABRY
Mississippi State University

MICHIGAN

Taxes, controversy over the busing of students to integrate public schools, and a labor dispute dominated the news in Michigan during 1973.

Taxes. A program of tax cuts totaling $380 million, proposed by Gov. William Milliken (R), was completed in May by the Legislature. The program, to take effect in 1974, is worth an estimated $100 a year to the average taxpayer. Major changes in the state income tax law provided large exemptions for dependents and higher credits for property taxes. However, as the year progressed, critics objected that new spending proposals could cause deficits that would force the imposition of new taxes.

An increase in the state gasoline tax from seven to nine cents a gallon took effect on February 1.

Busing. Court battles continued over the busing of school children in numerous state school districts. On June 12, the U. S. Sixth Circuit Court of Appeals affirmed a ruling by District Judge Stephen J. Roth who found *de jure* (by law) segregation in Detroit schools that could be corrected only by integrating Detroit and 52 suburban school districts. However, the Appeals Court returned the case to Roth for further testimony from suburban districts on possible busing plans. In August, 32 additional suburban school districts in the metropolitan area were joined to the suit as defendants.

In Grand Rapids, Federal District Judge Albert Engel dismissed on July 18 a suit started in 1970 by the National Association for the Advancement of Colored People (NAACP) charging racial segregation in Grand Rapids and 11 suburban school districts. The NAACP appealed the decision.

──────── MICHIGAN • Information Highlights ────────

Area: 58,216 square miles (150,779 sq km).
Population (1972 est.): 9,082,000. *Density:* 158 per sq mi.
Chief Cities (1970 census): Lansing, the capital, 131,546; Detroit, 1,513,601; Grand Rapids, 197,649; Flint, 193,317; Warren, 179,260; Dearborn, 104,199; Livonia, 110,109.
Government (1973): *Chief Officers*—governor, William G. Milliken (R); lt. gov., James H. Brickley (R); secy. of state, Richard H. Austin (D); atty. gen., Frank J. Kelley (D); treas., Allison Green; supt. of public instruction, John W. Porter; chief justice, Thomas M. Kavanagh. *Legislature*—Senate, 38 members (19 Democrats, 19 Republicans); House of Representatives, 110 members (60 D, 50 R).
Education (1972–73): *Enrollment*—public elementary schools, 1,160,128 pupils, 37,769 teachers; public secondary schools, 1,032,610 pupils, 51,731 teachers; nonpublic schools, 265,000 pupils, 10,120 teachers; colleges and universities, 344,149 students. *Public school expenditures,* $2,339,000,000 ($1,183 per pupil). *Average teacher's salary,* $12,400.
State Finances (fiscal year 1971): *Revenues,* $4,573,075,000 (4% general sales tax and gross receipts taxes, $878,-097,000; motor fuel tax, $283,843,000; federal funds, $862,-070,000). *Expenditures,* $3,968,650,000 (education, $1,723,-017,000; health, welfare, and safety, $897,318,000; highways, $516,651,000). *State debt,* $1,176,467,000 (June 30, 1971).
Personal Income (1972): $43,746,000,000; per capita, $4,817.
Public Assistance (1972): $1,031,765,000. *Average monthly payments* (Dec. 1972)—old-age assistance, $70.68; aid to families with dependent children, $237.27.
Labor Force: *Nonagricultural wage and salary earners* (July 1973), 3,104,500. *Average annual employment* (1972)—manufacturing, 1,067,300; trade, 609,900; government, 520,-600; services, 441,700. *Insured unemployed* (Sept. 1973)—57,800 (2.3%).
Manufacturing (1971): Value added by manufacture, $20,270,-600,000. Transportation equipment, $7,599,300,000; non-electrical machinery, $2,456,800,000; fabricated metal products, $2,334,100,000; primary metal industries, $1,716,-700,000; food and kindred products, $1,187,300,000; chemicals and allied products, $1,072,100,000.
Agriculture (1972): *Cash farm income,* $1,102,021,000 (livestock, $574,735,000; crops, $466,083,000; government payments, $61,203,000). *Chief crops* (in order of value, 1971) —Corn, hay, dry beans (ranks 1st among the states).
Mining (1972): *Production value,* $670,457,000 (ranks 13th among the states). *Chief minerals*—Iron ore, $159,000,-000; cement, $111,410,000; copper, $69,325,000; sand and gravel, $66,671,000.
Fisheries (1972): *Commercial catch,* 14,213,000 pounds ($2,-985,000). *Leading species by value*—Whitefish, $1,433,000; chubs, $568,000; carp, $95,000; alewives, $42,000.
Transportation: *Roads* (1972), 115,064 miles (185,172 km); *motor vehicles* (1972), 4,739,639; *railroads* (1972), 6,159 miles (9,912 km); *public airports* (1972), 129.
Communications: *Telephones* (1973), 5,586,000; *television stations* (1971), 20; *radio stations* (1971), 203; *newspapers* (1973), 55 (daily circulation, 2,510,000).

On October 5, the schools in Kalamazoo were ordered to discontinue desegregation programs, including busing, started in 1972 under order of a federal district judge. Lansing schools were ordered on August 10 to reinstitute a plan adopted in 1972 to promote integration. The plan had been dropped by a school board that replaced a majority of pro-busing board members ousted in a recall election.

Labor Dispute. A bitter labor dispute resulted in sporadic violence at Kalkaska, the site of a $20 million gas refining plant being built for Shell Oil Co. Trade union members picketed the site to protest the use of out-of-state nonunion workers by the Delta Construction Corp. of Houston, Texas. In June, 500 state police troopers were sent to the scene to maintain order, and more than 65 persons were arrested. The dispute was settled and picketing ended after an agreement overseen by a federal judge. The agreement provided for dismissal of all court actions. Shell and Delta each agreed to donate $250,000 to Kalkaska Township for capital improvements to compensate for the loss of economic benefits to the local community by the use of out-of-state workers.

Lottery. The state lottery, inaugurated in 1972, produced its first "instant" millionaire on February 22 when Hermus Millsaps, 53, a Taylor, Mich., factory worker, won a prize of $50,000 a year for 20 years. Millsaps wore a secondhand pawnshop

suit and rode a bus to Lansing to claim his prize. In a midyear report, the Bureau of State Lottery said it had paid out $33 milion in prize money and had produced $40 million for the state treasury.

Other Developments. Bingo, previously prohibited as a game of chance outlawed by state gambling laws, was legalized by the Legislature. Effective June 30, 1973, the new law permits licensing of bingo games conducted by nonprofit organizations.

Governor Milliken undertook a series of steps, authorized by a 1965 law, to streamline state government. The biggest change was to place all state agencies dealing with environmental problems under the Department of Natural Resources.

Federal courts ruled that Michigan meat laws could not be applied to out-of-state meat processors because federal laws had preempted regulation of interstate commerce. The Legislature then acted to require retailers and restaurants to post notices if they sold meat that did not meet the stricter Michigan standards.

Spring storms and high water combined to cause flooding over wide areas of the Michigan coastline, including parts of east side Detroit. Most damage was afflicted in the heavily populated shoreline areas of Wayne, Macomb, St. Clair, and Monroe counties. Emergency diking of parts of the western shore of Lake St. Clair and Lake Erie was undertaken by the U. S. Army Corps of Engineers.

The state's compulsory no-fault insurance legislation became effective October 1, but is was under court attack by lawyers' groups. The law provides that an accident victim's insurance company pay his claims no matter who may be at fault in the accident.

CHARLES W. THEISEN
The Detroit "News"

MICROBIOLOGY

Several outstanding discoveries were made in various fields of microbiology during 1973.

General Microbiology. New information helps to explain the structure of cell walls and how the cell walls function in allowing certain substances to enter and leave the cell. The cell walls of microbes contain the amino acid D-alanine, which is not present in the cell walls of higher forms of life. Advantage was taken of this difference to prepare a new antibiotic, 3-floro-D-alanine, which appeared to be highly effective against certain bacterial infections.

The nucleic-acid sequence of a single-strand RNA bacteriophage was determined, and it was shown that this phage can be produced in a test tube. These results will lead to a better understanding of the evolutionary pathways available to replicating nucleic acids not only in microbes but possibly in cancer cells and higher forms of life. The polio virus protein also was made in a test tube, using cellular components rather than whole cells in the process.

The discovery that certain heat-sensitive microbial enzymes can be stabilized by attaching them to synthetic polymers has great significance. The enzymes can be used again and again for catalytic studies at high temperatures.

Enzyme inhibitors isolated from microorganisms may play a role in preventing gastric ulcers in animals and man, and possibly even help in controlling alcoholism.

Food Microbiology. Food production and preservation are highly dependent on microbiology. Food-borne diseases continue, especially those caused by microbial toxins, enteric bacteria, and cocci. Studies on fusariotoxin T-2, for example, showed that it is responsible for toxicosis in farm animals, severe mouth lesions in chickens, sloughing of intestinal mucosa in fish, and possibly for alimentary toxic aleukia in humans. *Vibrio parahaemolyticus* in uncooked seafoods has been found to cause gastroenteritis in humans and wound infections in humans and marine invertebrates.

Plant Microbiology. Reports indicated that some viruses may cause diseases in both plants and insects, and that some human viruses may also infect plants. Many new plant diseases were described, including a fungus disease of corn, pollen transmission of ring spot virus in cherry orchards, and bacterial diseases of alfalfa and grapevines.

Soil Microbiology. Advances were made in understanding the process of microbial nitrogen fixation in the soil. These advances may be important if microbes can be induced by genetic means to fix nitrogen in food crops other than legumes.

Microbes that infect other bacteria that cause certain plant diseases, such as blight on soybeans, were isolated from the soil.

Geomicrobiology. Progress was made in determining the role of microorganisms in transforming chemical elements in nature, in using microbes for leaching metals from ores, and in using microbes for oil and gas prospecting. Also, there was some evidence that microbes may be responsible for the formation of seabed nodules, which may become a rich source of manganese, iron, and other metals.

Water and Sewage Microbiology. Isolation of the polio virus and other viruses from natural waters stimulated research on new techniques and standards for water purification. Concurrently, the proper disposal of agricultural, industrial, and municipal wastewaters received increased attention. Indications are that renovation of such wastewaters to potable levels is feasible, and certainly microorganisms can be used to convert some wastes to valuable products such as animal feed.

Microbial Ecology. The importance of microorganisms in various ecosystems is gaining recognition. For example, a bacterial mutant plus nutrients can be put into the ballast water of returning oil tankers. The bacteria multiply rapidly and destroy the remaining oil, sludge, and tar in the tanks, thereby reducing ocean pollution stemming from the dumping of oily ballast water.

Clinical Microbiology and Immunology. New techniques were described for the rapid identification of microorganisms responsible for infectious diseases in animals and human beings.

Advances in immunology included the discovery of the role of certain virus antibodies in serums from patients with multiple sclerosis; the discovery of the antigenic structure of tetanus toxin and the rabies virus; and the successful test vaccination of animals using the syphilis spirochete attenuated by radiation. Advances were also made in tumor immunology, immunogenetics, and the immunology in tissue and organ transplantation.

Industrial Microbiology. New commercial products produced by microorganisms include enzymes, bioinsecticides, single-cell proteins, nucleic acids, and antibiotics.

J. R. PORTER, *University of Iowa*

The cease-fire agreement after the October Israeli-Arab conflict is signed by the delegations from Israel (left) and Egypt (right).

MIDDLE EAST

The year in the Middle East divided into two sharply different phases, the first lasting three quarters of the year, the second the remaining three months. The first nine months of the year were not exceptional. They exhibited the usual unhappy mélange of terrorist activity by Arab organizations, Israeli retaliation, small-scale military clashes, and ineffective UN condemnations. The last quarter of the year was taken up with the violence of the fourth Arab-Israeli war and, after its suspension, subsequent negotiations. Though the war resulted in large losses in men and still more in matériel, the events that followed suggested that future developments in the Middle East might take a happier turn; there was some promise of a stable peace that would be more than a truce between wars.

Terrorist Activities. Arab guerrilla activities resulted in considerable loss of life in 1973. Two American diplomats and one Belgian were shot in cold blood by Black September guerrillas on March 3, in Khartoum, Sudan. President Jaafar al-Numeiry of the Sudan promised to exact retribution from the eight terrorists, who surrendered on March 4. At the end of the year, though still in custody, they had not been brought to trial.

In Nicosia, Cyprus, on April 9, eight Palestinians bombed the residence of the Israeli ambassador and attempted to hijack an El Al airliner at Nicosia airport. One was killed, the other seven captured. Sentenced to long imprisonment, they were in fact set free in December and left for Egypt. In Rome on April 27 an Italian employee of El Al was shot dead by a Black Septembrist. On July 19 a Palestinian gunman, having failed in an attack on the El Al office in Athens, sought refuge in a hotel, took 15 hostages, and in return for their lives obtained safe conduct to Kuwait, where he vanished. The Israeli military attaché in Washington, Col. Yosef Alon, was shot to death on July 1 outside his home in Maryland. On July 20 five Arab guerrillas hijacked a Japanese Boeing 747 on an Amsterdam-Tokyo flight. The plane went first to Dubai and then to Benghazi, Libya, where it was blown up after the passengers and hijackers had disembarked.

Two Arabs who claimed to be Black Septembrists launched at Athens airport on August 5 a grenade and machine-gun attack that killed three persons and wounded 60 others before they were arrested. On August 16, in a more bizarre incident, a "drunken Libyan" hijacked a plane on a Tripoli-Beirut flight and forced it to land at Tel Aviv. Israel authorities committed him to an asylum. The Saudi Arabian embassy in Paris was taken over on September 5 by five Palestinian commandos, who after a siege flew to Kuwait with four hostages and then surrendered. They were let out of jail in October, during the war with Israel, and sent to the front.

It was the turn of surface transportation on September 28, when two Palestinian terrorists took a train into Austria from Czechoslovakia and seized three Jews emigrating from the Soviet Union and an Austrian border guard. They were successful in their objective, which was to extract a promise from the Austrian government to close down the Schönau transit camp used to process immigrants to Israel en route from Russia. The two men were permitted to fly out of Austria unmolested, and the camp was closed. But Jews emigrating from Russia in fact continued to pass through Austria.

On November 25 four Palestinians hijacked a Dutch Boeing 747 over Baghdad and forced it to fly in turn to Damascus, Nicosia, Tripoli, and Malta, where the passengers were released. It then went on to Dubai, where the hijackers surrendered. Nothing more is known of how they fared. The final, and worst, hijacking of the year took place on December 17, when five Arab terrorists at Rome airport bombed one airliner, killing 31 persons, and flew another to Kuwait, where they surrendered, possibly to be handed over by Kuwait to the official Palestinian

Tanks spearhead the Israeli drive toward Damascus, Syria, as night falls on October 12.

organization. This was the first incident of the kind to be clearly denounced by the majority of Arab governments, who had always prior to this shown a good deal of sympathy to Arab terrorists. It was perhaps relevant that the Geneva peace conference was due to open in a few days.

International Incidents. Though the Egyptian-Syrian attacks on Israel did not occur until October, there were a number of hostile incidents in the first nine months of 1973. On January 8, Israeli planes struck Syrian targets in reprisal for Palestinian guerrilla attacks on the Golan Heights staged from Syria. On February 21, Israeli ground forces penetrated 95 miles (155 km) inside Lebanon to damage commando bases inside refugee camps. On the same day, a 113-passenger Libyan jetliner that had strayed over the Israeli side of the canal and had refused orders to land was shot down. Israel admitted an "error of judgment" and decided to compensate the families of the victims.

Not all warlike Mideast incidents involved both Israelis and Arabs. There were prolonged border clashes between Iraq and Kuwait in March 1973; a U.S. Air Force C-130 transport, flying above international waters in the Mediterranean Sea on March 21, was fired on by two Libyan Air Force jets, though not hit; and a week of heavy fighting in the area of Beirut took place early in May between the Lebanese army and Palestinian guerrillas from Syria, before a cease-fire (the third) came into existence.

On April 10, Israel made a raid on Palestinian guerrillas in Beirut; there were some 40 casualties. The raid was explicitly a reprisal for the Arab attacks at Nicosia 24 hours earlier and in general for "the intensification of attacks against Israeli targets abroad." The United Nations reacted predictably, the Security Council on April 22 condemning vaguely "all acts of violence," but specifically the "repeated military attacks conducted by Israel against Lebanon." On May 7, Israel celebrated its 25th anniversary with a military parade in Jerusalem. On August 11, Israeli planes intercepted a Middle East Airlines passenger jet over Lebanon, forced it to land in Israel, and then after an examination of the passengers allowed it to proceed; this action also was condemned by the Security Council. On September 13, in the largest air battle since 1967, Israeli jets that had been attacked by Syrian planes while flying over international waters downed 13 planes for the loss of one.

Probably more important than these military incidents were the political moves among the Arab states which, it can be seen in retrospect, were bringing them together in preparation for launching war on Israel. But the much touted "union" of an eager Libya and a reluctant Egypt was hardly among these moves; it was postponed for a year, and possibly *sine die.* Significant reconciliation talks were held in Cairo in early September among Egypt, Syria, and Jordan. Both Syria and Egypt had broken off relations with Jordan—Syria in the summer of

1971 and Egypt in April 1972. The decision was taken to resume ties. The price Jordan paid was to declare an amnesty for the Palestinian commandos jailed in 1970 after the failure of their attempt to overthrow the Jordanian monarchy. These moves prepared the way for the reopening of an "Eastern front" against Israel. Also significant, financially, for Egypt was the rapprochement with Saudi Arabia that was achieved during the summer.

War. The fourth Arab-Israeli war broke out on Saturday, October 6, when powerful and simultaneous offensives by Egypt and Syria were launched across the Suez Canal and on the Golan Heights. The day—Yom Kippur, the Day of Atonement, which most Israelis spend in the synagogues—was chosen to afford the attackers the maximum advantages of surprise. The Israeli government knew of the military build-up but had concluded, wrongly, that it was not the prelude to a serious attack. (The October mistake is partly to be accounted for by the fact that Israel had made the opposite mistake in May, calling for a costly alert that proved unnecessary.) Israel, a small state than can only field a large army by calling on reservists, cannot remain on alert for long without ruining its economy.

Both Egyptians and Syrians made important initial gains. The Syrians recaptured much of the Golan Heights lost in 1967. The Egyptians smashed through the Bar-Levi defense line (really a connected series of strong-points) and within 24 hours had got some 400 tanks across to the east bank of

the Canal on pontoon bridges. The Israeli air force was less effective than in previous wars, because it lost many planes to the Soviet-supplied ground-to-air missiles, which the Egyptians and Syrians had in plentiful supply.

Other Arab states sent assistance. Jordan did not open a third front, but Jordanian army units took part in the fighting on the Syrian front, as did an Iraqi force of 18,000 men and 200 aircraft, which entered the war on October 10. Morocco and Saudi Arabia also sent units.

The Israeli strategy was to concentrate first on the Syrian front. By October 12 the Syrian army had been driven back beyond the 1967 cease-fire line. The war on the Sinai front began to turn in Israel's favor from October 17, when the Israeli bridgehead established the day before on the west bank of the Canal—a gamble that paid off—was progressively enlarged. By the time of the cease-fire on October 24 a remarkable military situation had developed: the Egyptian army had conquered some 400 square miles (1,035 sq km) of the Sinai desert; on the other hand, the Israelis were in control of some 500 square miles (1,295 sq km) of Egypt proper, were well on the way to Cairo, and had Egyptian forces of some 20,000 men trapped between the main Israeli forces and those west of the Suez Canal.

On October 22, a UN resolution in favor of a cease-fire was adopted. After the truce had been broken, a second cease-fire resolution did produce a cessation of hostilities on October 24.

There was extremely heavy wastage of military equipment during the war. On October 10 the USSR began a substantial airlift of weapons to its Arab clients, and on October 13 in response the United States launched a resupply effort to Israel. The savage intensity of fighting during the 18 days of the war was such that Arab losses were estimated to be 1,500 tanks and 450 aircraft, and Israel's 500 tanks and 120 aircraft. In the 12 days of the Battle of El Alamein in World War II, Rommel and Montgomery together lost only 932 tanks.

The threat of unilateral Soviet intervention to support Egypt led to U. S. forces being placed on worldwide alert on October 25. The United Nations then agreed, with Russian concurrence, to the creation of UN observer corps to police the cease-fire. The war was followed by intense diplomatic efforts by U. S. Secretary of State Henry Kissinger. These led to the transfer of the disengagement talks from the battlefront to the Arab-Israeli peace conference, which opened at Geneva on December 20. Little more than preliminary sparring took place in the initial exchanges, but certainly something new had happened in the chronic and repetitive conflicts of the Middle East situation. There was at least the possibility that the Arabs, fresh from a war in which they had acquitted themselves with more efficiency and élan than on any previous occasion, might be in a psychological mood that would permit the negotiations to get the situation off dead center, and move it in the direction of a "live and let live" peace.

At year's end, it remained to be seen what effect the electoral losses suffered by Premier Golda Meir's party in Israel's parliamentary election of December 31 would have on the negotiations. But it was certain that neither Mrs. Meir's coalition as it stood before the December 31 election, nor the one she put together after it, could agree to give up all the territorial gains made in the Arab-Israeli war of 1967.

The Oil Weapon. A development of an entirely novel kind, and one with immense and unknown ramifications and implications for the future, was the demonstration in the fall of 1973 that the oil-producing Arab states would combine to use oil as a weapon by which to put pressure on states whose policy they disliked. Ministers of the 11 nations of the Organization of Arab Petroleum Exporting Countries agreed in Kuwait, on October 17, on a coordinated program of cuts in petroleum production and exports in an attempt to force a change in the Middle East policy of the United States. They were certainly successful in producing a show of cooperation from most of the European states and from Japan. But the United States, which only gets a fraction of its oil supplies from Arab sources (though the percentage is increasing), was less vulnerable to pressure. (In spite of the embargo, a great deal of Arab oil continued to reach the United States by a variety of circuitous routes.)

On October 20, Saudi Arabia announced it was halting all oil supplies to the United States, and on October 21 all other Arab Persian Gulf producers followed suit. Iran did not restrict supplies, but Iran led the way in the decision, taken December 23, to more than double the price of petroleum as of Jan. 1, 1974—the most shocking of a whole series of price increases announced during the year.

ARTHUR CAMPBELL TURNER
University of California, Riverside

MILWAUKEE

Labor disputes and the completion of two major buildings highlighted events in Milwaukee in 1973.

Labor Problems. A strike by county hospital employees and city school employees and a work stoppage by Milwaukee fireman curtailed essential services for short periods during the year. On January 4, the largest strike in Milwaukee's history began when 11,000 public-employed workers left their jobs, including paraprofessional and other personnel at Milwaukee county hospitals and nonteaching public school employees. In the hospitals, doctors, nurses, and administrators undertook the duties of nurses' aides and other workers.

After moves by city and county officials, including the establishment of a fact-finding board by Mayor Henry W. Maier, the school employees returned to work on January 8; hospital employees returned on January 10. Settlement of the disputes at the end of March included a $10.2 million contract that, among other things, granted a 3% wage increase in 1973 and a similar increase in 1974.

On November 4, when their contract with the city expired, firemen began a work stoppage by reporting themselves ill with what became known as the "red flu." At the request of Mayor Maier, Gov. Patrick J. Lucey sent in 180 National Guardsmen to protect fire stations and assist in fire fighting. The action ended on November 10, when both sides agreed to binding arbitration. The arbitration hearings were scheduled for January 1974.

New Buildings. The 42-story First Wisconsin Center, home of the First Wisconsin Bank, was dedicated on October 6. The tallest building in Wisconsin, it was designed by Skidmore, Owings & Merrill and erected at a cost of $50 million. Meanwhile, the city completed its $14 million Exposition and Convention Center in downtown Milwaukee. The two-story complex, covering a two-block area, was scorned by architectural critics for its boxlike appearance.

Crime. On January 31, two white policemen were shot to death while attempting a routine arrest. As a result of the search of the inner city that followed the crime, the police were charged with brutality by members of the black community. These charges, and related complaints of harassment of blacks by white policemen, were the subject of a year-long probe. A black, Ben Sanders, Jr., was convicted of the slayings in June and sentenced to two consecutive life terms.

Richard C. Nowakowski, chairman of the Milwaukee County Board, was indicted on eight felony counts in March after a grand jury investigation. The charges included violating the state's Corrupt Practices Act, soliciting a person to commit perjury, and accepting a bribe. The case was set for trial in 1974.

Other Developments. Prospects brightened for completing the city's expressway system when Mayor Maier dropped his opposition to completing the downtown freeway loop and the County Board adopted a plan for continued construction of freeways.

Michael Cullen, an antiwar activist and a member of the "Milwaukee 14," a group that burned draft records in 1968, was deported to his native Ireland after being given an "undesirable alien" status by the federal government.

PAUL SALSINI, *The Milwaukee "Journal"*

A surface-mining dragline removes the overburden from a coal seam in Centralia, Wash.

MINING

In 1973 the world's mineral industries were recovering from the worldwide economic recession of 1970–71. The recovery was foreshadowed in 1972—the latest year for which complete mineral production data are available—when there was an average 6.5% increase in the output of 50 minerals compared with an average 5.8% decline in the output of 22 minerals. At the end of 1972, inventories were diminishing and prices began to firm, and in 1973 some inactive marginal mines began to reopen.

Two major areas of interest in 1973 were the impact of the revived world economy upon mineral output and some new developments in economic nationalism, particularly in Australia, Canada, and Ireland.

Economic Nationalism. Over the past decade there has been a growing wave of economic nationalism among the developing nations concerned with furthering their economic development while beset internally with social and economic unrest. These conditions have led to the imposition of very strict controls on mineral development or even to nationalization or expropriation of the mines, often without compensation. As a result, the major U. S., Canadian, and British mining companies have increasingly tended to withdraw from the politically unstable developing nations and to concentrate their efforts in areas that have stable economic and political environments favorable to the very large capital investment and long payback periods characteristic of mineral development. These circumstances, for instance, account for the spectacular rise of Australia as one of the world's largest mineral producers.

Mining in Australia. In Australia, the Labor party took office in December 1972 after 23 years out of power. Surprisingly, in view of the importance of mining to the national economy, the new government has been slow to promulgate a comprehensive minerals policy. At the same time, Prime Minister Edward Gough Whitlam and key officials have expressed strongly nationalistic views with respect to minerals, both in public utterances and in the few actions taken. The latter include mandatory interest-free deposit of 25% of the investment funds borrowed abroad, with the money being held in the Australian Reserve Bank for a minimum of two years; federal government control over all mineral exports from Australia; and withdrawal of tax concessions for natural resource development. Also, no decisions have been made on pending applications for foreign participation in mining. All this has created an atmosphere of uncertainty that has greatly inhibited mineral exploration and has led to the cancellation of several important new projects and the indefinite postponement of others.

Mining in Canada. Canada has long been considered both geologically and politically attractive for mineral development. Although its rise has not been as spectacular as the rise in Australia, the Canadian mining industry has been growing at an accelerating pace. Provincial and federal elections in 1972, which resulted in a strong move to the left, had an adverse impact on Canadian mining in 1973. Both the federal legislative and several provincial legislatures were showing clear intent to capture as much revenue as possible from the minerals sector, for the most part by using means that disregard

(Continued on page 398)

WORLD PRODUCTION OF MAJOR MINERALS[1]

Aluminum (Thousands of metric tons)

	1971	1972
United States	3,559.9	3,738.6
USSR[2]	1,179.1	1,251.6
Japan	893.3	1,014.9
Canada	1,016.7	[2]925.1
Norway	529.6	547.8
West Germany	427.1	444.4
France	383.6	392.7
Australia	223.1	205.8
India	177.7	178.6
United Kingdom	118.8	171.4
Netherlands	116.0	165.9
Ghana	110.6	144.2
Spain	126.0	139.6
China[2]	[11]136.0	136.0
Greece	116.0	129.7
Italy	119.7	121.5
Rumania[16]	111.5	121.5
Poland[15]	99.7	101.5
Brazil	88.9	97.0
New Zealand	21.8	87.1
Austria	90.7	84.3
Switzerland	94.3	83.4
Sweden	75.2	77.0
Total (est.)	10,317.1	10,977.4

Antimony (Metric tons)

	1971	1972
South Africa	14,243	14,568
Bolivia	11,665	13,144
China[2]	11,791	11,791
USSR[2]	6,893	6,984
Thailand	2,294	4,747
Mexico	[11]3,360	[2]4,263
Yugoslavia	[11]2,906	2,876
Turkey	[11]2,209	[2]2,268
Australia	[11]962	1,331
Italy	[11]1,175	[2]1,179
Morocco	1,972	843
Czechoslovakia[2]	599	599
Austria	467	[2]481
Peru	[11]102	80
United States	930	44
Total (est.)	[11]64,298	68,057

Asbestos (Thousands of metric tons)

	1971	1972
Canada	1,482.6	1,447.5
USSR[2]	1,151.8	1,219.9
South Africa	322.2	323.1
China[2]	158.7	199.5
Italy	119.5	132.1
United States	118.7	119.4
Rhodesia[2]	80.0	80.0
Total (est.)	3,583.9	3,703.6

Barite (Thousands of metric tons)

	1971	1972
United States	748.3	821.7
West Germany	408.8	368.6
USSR[2]	300.2	310.2
Mexico	279.7	261.3
Peru	[2]235.8	[2]235.8
Ireland	[11]196.1	199.5
Italy	205.5	181.7
China[2]	139.7	155.1
North Korea[2]	119.7	119.7
Rumania	116.1	116.1
France	109.9	109.7
Thailand	63.5	97.7
Morocco	84.5	93.2
Greece	[11]84.9	[2]85.3
Spain	83.2	[2]84.4
Canada	[11]109.5	66.2
Japan	57.2	60.5
Yugoslavia	[11]64.7	[2]59.9
Iran	59.9	[2]59.9
Poland[2]	55.3	49.9
India	[11]58.7	46.1
Total (est.)	[11]3,837.5	3,863.6

Bauxite (Thousands of metric tons)

	1971	1972
Australia	12,540.5	14,432.3
Jamaica	[11]12,439.9	12,542.5
Surinam	[11]6,717.8	[2]6,908.8
USSR[2]	4,470.4	4,673.6
Guyana	[11]4,233.7	3,726.7
France	3,184.1	3,254.2
Guinea	2,629.4	2,641.6
Greece	[11]2,861.1	2,436.4
Hungary	2,089.9	2,358.1
Yugoslavia	1,958.8	2,196.6
United States	2,019.8	1,840.9
India	[11]1,516.9	1,659.1
Dominican Rep.	1,311.7	[3]1,277.1
Indonesia	1,237.5	1,276.1
Malaysia	977.4	1,075.9
Sierra Leone	590.3	693.9
Haiti	643.1	687.8
Brazil[2]	[11]538.5	605.5
China[2]	548.6	579.1
Ghana	329.2	340.4
Total (est.)	[11]63,506.1	65,881.5

Cement (Millions of metric tons)

	1971	1972
USSR[2]	100.28	104.09
United States	73.67	75.91

Cement (cont'd) (Millions of metric tons)

	1971	1972
Japan	59.45	60.62
West Germany	[11]41.00	43.14
Italy	31.79	33.45
France	28.94	30.28
Spain	16.99	19.44
United Kingdom	17.89	18.04
India	14.89	15.70
Poland	13.08	13.98
China[2]	[11]11.99	13.97
Brazil	9.80	11.37
Rumania	8.52	9.20
Canada	8.22	9.07
Mexico	7.36	8.60
East Germany	8.47	[2]8.49
Turkey	7.55	8.42
Czechoslovakia	7.95	8.04
Belgium	6.93	7.09
South Korea	6.87	6.58
Austria	5.49	6.34
South Africa	5.85	6.11
Total (est.)	[11]605.53	637.32

Chromite (Thousands of metric tons)

	1971	1972
USSR[2]	1,795.9	1,850.3
South Africa	1,643.5	1,482.9
Turkey[2]	603.1	643.9
Albania	[11]534.2	[2]608.6
Rhodesia[2]	362.9	362.9
Philippines	431.7	351.9
India	261.2	281.2
Iran[2]	[11]175.9	179.6
Malagasy Republic	139.7	[2]139.7
Finland	111.6	[2]111.6
Pakistan	24.5	32.7
Cyprus	40.8	29.9
Yugoslavia	34.5	28.1
Japan	31.7	24.5
Total (est.)	[11]6,265.5	6,203.9

Coal (Millions of metric tons)

	1971	1972
USSR	[11]640.7	[2]654.7
United States	508.8	546.5
China[2]	409.9	419.0
East Germany	263.9	249.3
West Germany	221.4	213.1
Poland	179.9	189.9
United Kingdom	147.0	119.7
Czechoslovakia	113.5	113.1
Australia	73.1	83.3
India	75.1	77.8
South Africa	58.7	58.4
North Korea	[11]24.5	34.0
France	35.8	[2]32.7
Yugoslavia	30.9	30.8
Japan	33.6	28.2
Bulgaria	27.0	[2]28.2
Hungary	27.4	25.8
Total (est.)	[11]3,012.9	3,043.7

Copper (mine) (Thousands of metric tons)

	1971	1972
United States	1,380.6	1,510.0
Canada	654.3	726.2
Chile	717.2	724.6
Zambia	651.5	717.0
USSR[2,10]	616.8	664.9
Zaire	405.7	428.9
Peru	212.8	225.0
Philippines	[11]197.5	204.9
Australia	174.2	185.0
South Africa	157.4	161.9
Papua, New Guinea	—	123.9
Poland[2]	90.0	122.4
Japan	121.0	113.6
Yugoslavia	94.4	103.1
China[2]	100.0	100.0
Mexico	63.1	78.7
Bulgaria	45.4	48.1
Rhodesia[2]	29.3	38.3
Rumania	14.2	35.0
Finland	28.4	34.8
S. West Africa	32.0	[2]32.5
Spain	34.0	32.2
Norway	21.7	25.4
Sweden	30.2	24.8
Total (est.)	[11]6,034.3	6,633.4

Diamonds (Thousands of carats)

	1971	1972
Zaire	[11]12,520	13,360
USSR[2]	8,800	9,200
South Africa	7,031	7,395
Ghana	2,562	2,659
Botswana	822	2,403
Sierra Leone	1,935	1,647
S. West Africa	[11]1,648	1,596
Angola	[11]2,413	1,562
Liberia[3]	[11]809	[2]810
Tanzania	837	[3]730
Central African Republic	437	524
Venezuela	499	456
Total (est.)	[11]41,102	43,155

Fluorspar (Thousands of metric tons)

	1971	1972
Mexico	1,180.7	1,042.2
Spain	396.3	487.5
USSR[2]	417.2	426.3
Thailand	427.2	395.0
France	[11]371.9	[2]371.9
Italy	288.2	277.4
China[2]	254.0	254.0
United States	246.8	227.1
United Kingdom	244.8	220.4
South Africa	239.0	210.8
Canada	72.6	163.3
Total (est.)	[11]4,756.0	4,671.3

Gas (natural) (Billions of cubic feet)

	1971	1972
United States	24,088.3	23,997.8
USSR[2]	7,900.0	[2]8,200.0
Canada	2,825.9	3,316.1
Netherlands	1,546.7	2,063.1
Venezuela	1,680.3	1,625.2
Iran	1,305.2	1,469.7
Saudi Arabia	[11]938.3	1,127.0
Rumania	943.6	954.0
United Kingdom	660.6	952.9
Mexico	643.4	660.2
West Germany	562.8	645.1
Total (est.)	[11]54,334.3	51,682.1

Gold (Millions of troy ounces)

	1971	1972
South Africa	31.39	29.25
USSR[2]	6.70	6.90
Canada	2.24	2.08
United States	1.50	1.45
Australia	0.67	0.75
Ghana	0.70	0.72
Philippines	0.64	0.61
Rhodesia[2]	0.50	[2]0.50
Japan	0.26	0.24
Colombia	0.19	0.19
Brazil	0.16	0.17
North Korea	0.16	0.16
Mexico	0.15	0.15
Zaire	0.17	0.08
Total (est.)	46.49	44.71

Graphite (Thousands of metric tons)

	1971	1972
USSR[2]	79.8	79.8
North Korea[2]	75.3	75.3
Mexico	50.9	55.1
South Korea	72.5	40.8
China[2]	30.0	30.9
Austria	21.4	18.8
Malagasy Republic	20.0	18.2
West Germany	[11]12.7	12.7
Norway	8.3	8.2
Total (est.)	390.5	357.8

Gypsum (Thousands of metric tons)

	1971	1972
United States	9,449.1	11,181.5
Canada	[11]6,078.8	7,203.4
France	5,110.5	5,851.4
USSR	[2]4,716.4	[2]4,716.4
United Kingdom	[11]4,274.7	4,162.9
Spain	4,029.7	4,099.6
Italy[2]	3,501.0	3,501.0
Iran	2,249.5	[2]2,267.5
West Germany	1,593.0	1,787.6
Mexico	1,298.0	1,497.4
India	1,087.8	1,077.8
Australia	[11]895.1	[2]1,043.1
Austria	593.6	861.1
Poland	[2]849.9	[2]849 9
China[2]	549.9	599.9
Japan	528.6	464.9
Total (est.)	[11]53,106.7	57,635.7

Iron Ore (Millions of metric tons)

	1971	1972
USSR	203.0	208.0
United States	82.1	76.6
Australia	62.1	63.8
France	55.9	54.3
China[2]	[11]44.7	45.7
Brazil[2]	42.7	42.1
Canada	44.0	40.2
India	34.3	35.0
Sweden	34.4	33.1
Total (est.)	[11]779.3	768.9

Iron (pig) excluding ferroalloys (Millions of metric tons)

	1971	1972
USSR	88.23	[2]91.61
United States	73.81	80.60
Japan	72.73	72.04
West Germany[12]	29.65	31.68
China[13]	27.21	28.11
France	17.90	18.55
United Kingdom	15.26	15.16
Belgium	10.40	11.77
Italy	8.54	9.41
Canada	7.82	[2]8.71
Czechoslovakia[14]	7.96	8.33
Poland	7.04	[2]7.28
India	6.70	6.98
Australia	6.13	6.49

WORLD PRODUCTION OF MAJOR MINERALS[1] (Continued)

	1971	1972
Iron (pig) (cont'd)	(Millions of metric tons)	
Spain	4.83	5.92
Brazil	4.68	5.30
Rumania	4.38	[24].81
Luxembourg	4.59	4.67
South Africa	4.01	4.41
Netherlands	3.76	4.29
Austria	2.85	2.85
Mexico	2.36	2.67
North Korea[2,13]	2.54	2.63
Sweden	2.76	2.53
East Germany	2.03	2.15
Hungary	1.97	2.06
Total (est.)	429.84	452.37
Lead (smelter)	(Thousands of metric tons)	
United States	589.6	631.0
USSR[2]	444.4	462.6
Australia	323.6	348.0
Japan	215.0	223.2
Canada	[11]168.3	189.2
Mexico	136.1	161.7
France	108.2	136.1
West Germany	98.4	101.98
China[2]	99.8	99.8
Bulgaria	[2]99.8	[2]99.8
Spain	[11]75.8	92.1
Belgium	79.3	[2]89.8
Yugoslavia	99.1	87.5
Peru	67.1	85.5
Poland	60.2	65.3
S. West Africa	58.8	63.9
North Korea[2]	63.5	63.5
Italy	48.4	50.6
Sweden	32.2	47.6
Argentina	43.5	39.5
Rumania[2]	36.3	36.3
Zambia	27.7	25.8
United Kingdom	38.6	25.0
Brazil	25.7	25.0
Netherlands	23.7	21.9
Total (est.)	[11]3,175.3	3,379.1
Magnesium	(Thousands of metric tons)	
United States	112.00	109.59
USSR[2]	51.70	54.42
Norway	36.10	36.48
Japan	9.69	10.89
Italy	7.71	[2]7.53
France	[11]7.21	[2]6.98
Canada	6.56	5.30
Total (est.)	232.0	232.9
Manganese Ore		
	(Thousands of metric tons)	
USSR[2]	[11]7,316.8	7,798.4
South Africa	3,235.9	3,270.8
Gabon	1,866.1	1,936.3
Brazil	2,601.3	1,929.2
India	[11]1,840.3	1,623.5
Australia	1,050.0	1,207.0
China[2]	1,000.0	1,000.0
Ghana	598.4	498.2
Zaire	386.9	369.4
Mexico	266.8	295.6
Japan	284.9	260.7
Hungary	167.0	[2]166.9
Morocco	101.4	96.0
Bulgaria	40.8	[2]40.8
Italy	30.6	25.6
Total (est.)	[11]21,014.9	20,708.9
Mercury	(Thousands of flasks)	
Spain	[11]150.83	[2]60.50
USSR[2]	50.00	50.00
Italy	42.61	41.80
China[2]	[1]26.00	26.00
Mexico	35.39	22.51
Yugoslavia	16.59	16.42
Canada	18.50	14.60
Turkey	[11]10.46	[2]11.00
Algeria	7.13	9.20
United States	17.88	7.29
Czechoslovakia	5.63	5.80
Japan	5.56	5.17
Total (est.)	[11]298.55	279.19
Molybdenum	(Thousands of metric tons)	
United States	49.7	50.9
Canada	[11]10.3	11.3
USSR[2]	8.0	8.2
Chile	[11]7.9	5.9
China[2]	1.5	1.5
Total (est.)	77.5	79.5
Nickel (mine)	(Thousands of metric tons)	
Canada	267.0	232.6
USSR[2]	117.9	127.0
New Caledonia	102.3	100.2
Cuba[2]	[11]35.4	36.3

	1971	1972
Nickel (mine) (cont'd)	(Thousands of metric tons)	
Australia	[11]32.5	35.8
Indonesia	[11]19.8	22.4
United States	[11]15.5	15.3
South Africa	12.8	11.7
Total (est.)	[11]634.8	633.1
Petroleum (crude)	(Millions of barrels)	
United States	3,453.9	3,455.4
USSR	2,778.3	2,895.9
Saudi Arabia	1,741.1	2,202.0
Iran	1,661.9	1,843.9
Kuwait	1,167.3	1,201.3
Venezuela	1,295.4	1,178.5
Libya	1,007.7	819.6
Nigeria	558.4	665.3
Canada	491.8	560.7
Iraq	624.3	529.4
Trucial States	[11]350.7	399.2
Indonesia	325.7	395.6
Algeria	279.6	384.9
China[2]	186.2	216.1
Mexico	[11]177.3	185.0
Qatar	156.9	176.5
Argentina	154.5	158.5
Oman	107.4	103.1
Total (est.)	[11]17,662.8	18,597.8
Phosphate	(Thousands of metric tons)	
United States	35,270	37,034
USSR (all forms)	21,623	22,521
Morocco	12,006	14,968
Tunisia	3,161	3,387
China[2]	[11]2,177	2,630
Nauru[3]	[11]1,886	2,000
South Africa	1,729	1,965
Togo	1,715	1,927
Senegal	1,544	1,416
Israel	765	1,106
Christmas Island[3]	[1]990	998
Egypt	[11]713	[2]707
Jordan	650	694
North Vietnam (all forms)[2]	[11]553	599
Total (est.)	[11]87,108	94,206
Potash[5]	(Thousands of metric tons)	
USSR	[11]4,806	[2]5,496
Canada	[11]3,628	3,746
West Germany	2,914	2,844
East Germany	2,425	[2]2,431
United States	2,346	2,412
France	1,999	[2]1,750
Total (est.)	[11]19,788	20,376
Pyrite[9]	(Thousands of metric tons)	
USSR[2]	[11]4,250	4,499
China[2]	1,999	2,017
Spain	[11]2,021	1,925
Japan	2,343	1,580
Italy	1,504	1,382
Finland	866	856
Rumania[2]	840	840
Norway	780	795
United States	821	753
Cyprus	[11]830	638
Sweden	[11]591	[2]600
Portugal	561	553
South Africa	750	439
Total (est.)	[11]21,802	20,342
Salt	(Millions of metric tons)	
United States	40.00	40.86
China[2]	[11]16.51	17.96
USSR[2]	11.97	11.97
West Germany	8.92	9.18
United Kingdom	9.24	8.83
India	[11]5.43	6.50
France	[11]5.49	5.21
Canada	[11]5.03	5.02
Mexico	4.36	[2]4.40
Italy	4.57	4.08
Australia	[11]3.79	4.00
Netherlands	3.17	[2]3.20
Poland	2.96	3.01
Rumania	2.95	[2]2.95
East Germany	2.22	2.25
Total (est.)	[11]144.15	147.44
Silver	(Millions of troy ounces)	
Canada	46.02	47.00
Peru	38.40	40.19
USSR[2]	39.00	40.00
Mexico	36.66	37.48
United States	41.56	37.23
Australia	21.70	22.80
Japan	11.29	10.02
Bolivia	[11]5.37	5.66
East Germany[2]	5.00	5.00

	1971	1972
Silver (cont'd)	(Millions of troy ounces)	
Sweden	[11]3.90	[3]3.90
Honduras	3.64	3.60
Yugoslavia	3.35	3.58
South Africa	3.38	3.29
Chile	[11]2.73	2.86
Argentina	2.05	2.12
Zaire	1.47	2.08
Morocco	1.70	1.87
France	2.11	1.86
Philippines	1.94	1.85
West Germany	1.80	1.74
Spain	1.64	1.64
Ireland	[11]1.43	[2]1.50
Total (est.)	[11]288.88	291.39
Sulfur (elemental)	(Millions of metric tons)	
United States (all forms)	8.76	9.37
Canada (recovered)	4.80	6.95
Poland (Frasch, ore)	2.71	2.94
France (recovered)	1.81	1.73
USSR (all forms)[2]	1.70	1.71
Mexico (all forms)	1.18	.94
Total (all forms) (est.)	23.09	26.21
Tin (mine)	(Thousands of long tons)	
Malaysia	74.2	75.6
Bolivia	[11]29.5	31.1
USSR[2]	28.0	28.0
Thailand	21.3	21.7
Indonesia	19.4	20.9
China[2]	20.0	20.0
Australia	9.6	11.8
Nigeria	7.2	6.6
Zaire	[2]6.4	[2]6.4
Total (est.)	[11]232.2	239.6
Titanium (ilmenite)	(Thousands of metric tons)	
Canada	773.6	834.8
Australia	[11]829.1	708.7
United States	619.5	618.2
Norway	641.4	608.3
Malaysia[3]	156.0	152.1
Finland	139.5	136.1
Total (est.)	[11]3,360.5	3,252.8
(rutile)		
Australia	366.6	317.3
Sierra Leone	[11]11.9	—
Total (est.)	[11]384.4	387.8
Tungsten[6]	(Metric tons)	
USSR[2]	6,984	7,211
China[2]	[16]984	6,894
United States	3,129	3,696
Thailand	2,506	3,342
Bolivia	[11]2,089	2,232
North Korea[2]	2,149	2,149
South Korea	2,058	2,031
Canada	[11]1,663	1,783
Australia	1,547	1,529
Portugal	[11]987	1,383
Brazil	1,398	1,247
Japan	[11]1,058	1,130
Peru	770	856
Total (est.)	36,617	38,454
Uranium Oxide (U_3O_8)	(Metric tons)	
United States	[11]11,150	11,700
South Africa	3,799	5,069
Canada	[11]3,725	4,442
France	[11]1,755	1,742
Niger	[11]430	867
Gabon	545	523
Australia[2]	272	N.A.
Total (est.)[7]	[11]21,696	24,740
Zinc (smelter)	(Thousands of metric tons)	
Japan	[11]716.2	806.1
USSR[2]	650.3	650.3
United States	695.2	574.3
Canada	371.9	476.5
Australia	[11]261.7	296.6
France	218.6	262.8
Belgium	206.8	257.3
Poland	219.9	227.9
West Germany	[11]191.9	213.6
Italy	139.8	155.7
North Korea[2]	99.8	119.7
China[2]	99.8	99.8
Spain	85.6	99.2
Bulgaria	78.3	84.3
Finland	63.7	81.1
Mexico	77.8	79.4
United Kingdom	116.4	73.8
Total (est.)	[11]4,694.1	5,093.2

[1] Output of countries not individually listed and estimates are included in world totals. [2] Est. [3] Exports. [4] Smelter. [5] Marketable in equivalent K_2O. [6] Contained tungsten (W basis). [7] Excludes socialist bloc countries. [8] Excludes ferroalloys. [9] Gross weight. [10] Smelter production. [11] Revised. [12] Includes blast furnace ferroalloys except ferromanganese and spiegeleisen. [13] Includes ferroalloys. [14] Includes blast furnace ferroalloys. [15] Includes secondary. [16] Includes alloys. N.A.=not available.

(*Continued from page 395*)

the technical and economic realities of mining. Proposals ranged from complete takeover of all mineral resources and activities by the provincial government (Manitoba) to some lesser degree of equity participation (British Columbia), marketing control (Quebec), heavy taxes, unrealistic royalties, severance taxes, and the like. The result in British Columbia, for example, has been the postponement of several new mining projects and a steep decline in mineral exploration, which fell more than 30% below 1972 levels.

Mining in Ireland. Some years ago in Ireland, the government decided to encourage mineral development. It took the necessary steps to rationalize and modernize the complex laws and practices governing land tenure and the allocation of mineral rights, and it created a favorable climate for mining investment. The outcome was a repeat of the Australian experience on a much smaller scale and the creation of an important mining industry where virtually none had previously existed. In 1973 new policies were announced and new, less favorable legislation was introduced. The latter has at least temporarily postponed the development of one important new mine and has curtailed exploration.

Japanese and American Policies. The wave of nationalism began to affect the more developed, stable mineral-producing nations in 1973, giving new impetus to the developing concern of the mature industrial countries over how to assure themselves of future supplies of mineral raw materials.

After an exhaustive and careful analysis of its mineral position in 1971, the mineral industries of Japan, in concert with the government, have adopted a policy of geographic diversification of mineral sources. As one result, Japan will not procure more than a specific percentage of its iron-ore requirements from Australia, and this is already leading to large-scale iron mine developments in Brazil, the Republic of South Africa, and West Africa. The United States too has just completed an assessment of its mineral economy, and the final report of the President's Materials Policy Commission arrived at many of the same conclusions and suggestions for new policy reached earlier by the Japanese. Others among the developed industrial nations are following suit.

Precious Metals. Despite the record-high free-market gold price, which reached $127 per ounce in London in June 1973, world gold production fell approximately 3.8% in 1972 and probably will show another decline in 1973. Despite high prices, there has been comparatively little increase in gold mining for several reasons. Greatly increased labor and material costs militate against the reactivation of most old mines. Environmental restrictions, as in the United States, and unfavorable national mineral policies, as in Australia and Canada, also limit activity, especially by small miners.

Silver was relatively quiescent in 1972 and 1973. The price of silver ranged from $1.80 to $2.95 per ounce on the London spot market in 1973, as compared with a range from $1.37 to $2.03 in 1972. Platinum output rose 4.4% in 1972, but larger gains are foreseen for 1973–75 because of the use of platinum in catalytic control of automobile exhaust.

Steelmaking Metals and Ores. Iron ore producers felt the effects of the recession in 1972, and world output fell 1.3%. However, production of pig iron and steel rose 5.2% and 8.8%, respectively,

largely as a result of a second-half increase in orders resulting from stronger economic activity. The activity accelerated in 1973, and fairly severe steel shortages began to appear at year-end. The Japanese twice significantly increased the quantities of iron ore to be delivered under their basic contracts with Australian and Canadian sources during the year. Also, activities leading to the development of new iron mines in South Africa, West African countries, and Brazil were beginning.

The supply of chromite exceeded demand, with consequent weakening of prices from a late 1972 spread of $24–56 per ton, depending on source and grade, to $33–39 per ton toward the end of 1973. Molybdenum output rose slightly in 1972, largely as a result of increasing copper production, of which it is a frequent by-product. However molybdenum prices remained depressed, and several primary producers curtailed or ceased operations. Toward mid-1973, however, improved steel demand resulted in firmer molybdenum prices, declining inventories, and increased mine production.

Mine output of nickel fell 0.3% in 1972 although smelter production rose 2.9%. Mine output was curtailed until about midyear when the market began to strengthen, a trend that continued through 1973. The price of nickel held reasonably steady in 1972, when the low was $1.28 per pound and the high was $1.40. The 1973 low-high range was $1.40–1.50.

Nonferrous Metals. The output of all major nonferrous metals rose in 1972, with copper leading (mine output up 9.9%, smelter output up 8.3%). That trend appears to have held through 1973, but the picture is distorted by an incredible rise in prices outside the United States, where prices were frozen. Copper wirebar on the London Metal Exchange (LME) reached over $1.00 per pound late in 1973 in contrast to the frozen U.S. producer price of 60 cents. Zinc, frozen at 20.31 cents per pound, reached a record 80.56 cents on the LME in November and was expected to go higher. The U.S. producer price for lead was held at 16.5 cents per pound but was upward of 25 cents on the LME. Aluminum ingot cost 25 cents per pound in the United States, while selling at 36–37 cents in Europe.

Canada, in 3d place as a producer of mine copper in 1971, was second only to the United States in 1972, largely as a result of new mines brought into production in British Columbia. Worldwide, a half-dozen major copper mines were in the late planning or early construction stages. Aluminum plants were beginning to expand, and several new zinc projects, especially smelters, were in the works. There appeared to be enough lead available to restrain the development of new facilities.

Outlook. World mineral production appears generally to be growing and expanding geographically. Under normal circumstances, the trend would be expected to hold through 1974. However, the rising tide of economic nationalism may continue to curb some developments, and the growing energy shortage may seriously affect mineral production in many places. There has already been a severe curtailment of aluminum output in the northwestern United States because a drought caused a shortage of hydroelectric power. The shortage of fossil fuels will affect mining operations, the transportation of minerals, and mineral processing.

FRANK H. SKELDING
Director of Corporate Planning
Fluor Utah, Inc.

MINNESOTA

In 1973, Minnesota shared with the rest of the nation an uneasiness about the economy and a concern over the energy crisis—potential shortages of heating fuel being of critical importance to a state where winter temperatures drop well below zero. Politically, the year was marked by the convening of the first Minnesota Legislature ever to be controlled by the Democratic-oriented Liberals.

Legislation. A major reorganization of the executive branch of the state government was authorized by the 1973 Legislature in acts that created new departments of finance and personnel, consolidating functions previously fragmented and giving the governor greater control over them. The reorganization was one of the recommendations made by Gov. Wendell Anderson's Loaned Executives Action Program (LEAP), a six-month study of ways to improve the efficiency and accountability of the state government.

The Legislature abandoned nonpartisan legislative elections—a populist reform in effect since 1913. Beginning in 1974 party designations of the legislative candidates were to appear on the ballots. Fundamental changes in registration procedures allow voters to register by postcard or at the polls.

A bill requiring public decision-making bodies to open all their meetings to the public became law. In the Legislature itself, all sessions, including committee meetings, were similarly opened. The legal

------- **MINNESOTA · Information Highlights** -------

Area: 84,068 square miles (217,736 sq km).
Population (1972 est.): 3,896,000. *Density:* 49 per sq mi.
Chief Cities (1970 census): St. Paul, the capital, 309,828; Minneapolis, 434,400; Duluth, 100,578; Bloomington, 81,970; Rochester, 53,766; St. Louis Park, 48,992; Richfield, 47,231.
Government (1973): *Chief Officers*—governor, Wendell R. Anderson (Democratic-Farmer-Labor); lt. gov., Rudy Perpich (DFL); secy. of state, Arlen I. Erdahl (R); atty. gen., Warren Spannaus (DFL); treas., Van Bjornson (R); commissioner of education, Howard B. Casmey; chief justice, Robert Sheran. *Legislature*—Senate, 67 members (nonpartisan); House of Representatives, 134 members (nonpartisan).
Education (1972–73): *Enrollment*—public elementary schools, 475,839 pupils, 21,455 teachers; public secondary schools, 435,240 pupils, 22,700 teachers; nonpublic schools, 111,800 pupils, 5,270 teachers; colleges and universities, 154,938 students. *Public school expenditures,* $994,000,000 ($1,146 per pupil). *Average teacher's salary,* $11,115.
State Finances (fiscal year 1971): *Revenues,* $1,974,284,000 (3% general sales tax and gross receipts taxes, $212,721,000; motor fuel tax, $130,649,000; federal funds, $439,707,000). *Expenditures,* $1,925,296,000 (education, $799,472,000; health, welfare, and safety, $263,932,000; highways, $296,414,000). *State debt,* $589,147,000 (June 30, 1971).
Personal Income (1972): $16,877,000,000; per capita, $4,332.
Public Assistance (1972): $331,750,000. *Average monthly payments* (Dec. 1972)—old-age assistance $64.98; aid to families with dependent children, $234.29.
Labor Force: *Nonagricultural wage and salary earners* (July 1973), 1,423,200. *Average annual employment* (1972)—manufacturing, 307,500; trade, 332,300; government, 246,000; services, 238,900. *Insured unemployed* (Sept. 1973)—18,600 (1.7%).
Manufacturing (1971): *Value added by manufacture,* $4,827,200,000. Nonelectrical machinery, $1,015,200,000; food and kindred products, $892,500,000; paper and allied products, $448,200,000; printing and publishing, $393,900,000; fabricated metal products, $280,100,000; electrical equipment and supplies, $271,600,000.
Agriculture (1972): *Cash farm income,* $2,543,338,000 (livestock, $1,563,993,000; crops, $799,371,000; government payments, $179,974,000). *Chief crops* (in order of value, 1972)—Corn, soybeans, hay, oats (ranks 1st among the states).
Mining (1972): *Production value,* $626,872,000 (ranks 14th among the states). *Chief minerals*—Iron ore, $564,000,000; sand and gravel, $39,949,000; stone, $15,157,000.
Transportation: *Roads* (1972), 127,744 miles (205,578 km); *motor vehicles* (1972), 2,293,478; *railroads* (1972), 7,700 miles (12,392 km); *public airports* (1972), 139.
Communications: *Telephones* (1973), 2,454,100; *television stations* (1971), 12; *radio stations* (1971), 124; *newspapers* (1973), 32 (daily circulation, 1,128,000).

age of majority in Minnesota was lowered to 18. For the first time, a state minimum wage ($1.80 per hour for adults) was established. The right to strike was granted all but essential public employees. The Equal Rights Amendment to the U. S. Constitution was ratified.

In corrections, a full-time parole board was set up, and the office of ombudsman was established in law to investigate complaints of inmates of correctional institutions. The office had been created by an executive order in 1971 and was the first of its kind in the nation.

The state's continuing concern with the quality of the environment was emphasized by the passage of a state environmental policy act. Funds were provided for a state zoo to be built on a 480-acre site in Dakota county, south of the Twin Cities.

The welfare of the family farmer was the focus of several bills. One prohibits off-farm corporations from engaging in farming. A second gives farmers the right to bargain collectively with agricultural processors. A third increases the farm homestead exemption from 80 acres to 120 acres.

Minneapolis Election. In the November 6 elections in Minneapolis, 33-year-old Democrat Al Hofstede upset incumbent Mayor Charles Stenvig, an independent. The city's voters also elected Democrats to 11 of the 13 City Council seats.

Industrial Pollution. A pioneering lawsuit in the environmental field opened on August 1 in the U. S. District Court in St. Paul–Minneapolis. The plaintiffs—the U. S. government and the states of Minnesota, Michigan, and Wisconsin—contended that the Reserve Mining Company of Silver Bay, Minn., had degraded Lake Superior and was endangering public health. The plant, which opened in 1955, was daily discharging up to 67,000 tons of taconite tailings into the lake. The U. S. Environmental Protection Agency had warned in June that the drinking water of Duluth and nearby communities that comes from Lake Superior contained a high concentration of asbestos fibers, which have been linked to cancer.

Public interest in the trial, which was still in progress at the end of the year, centered on whether the tailings dumped by Reserve were responsible for the potentially dangerous particles. The broader issue under judicial review was whether the waste from the taconite-processing firm had caused serious damage to the lake.

JEANNE SINNEN
University of Minnesota Press

MISSISSIPPI

Floods, municipal elections, and an often-heated legislative session were events of particular interest to Mississippians in 1973.

Floods and Storms. Tornadoes, heavy rains, and devastating floods on the Mississippi, Yazoo, and other rivers plagued the state, particularly the Delta, from mid-March until late May. More than 6,500 families suffered some losses, and total property damage was estimated at well over $100 million. Agriculture was especially hard hit, as more than 3 million acres were overrun by swollen streams and backwaters. Altogether, 52 of Mississippi's 82 counties were declared a major disaster area by President Nixon. By the end of September public and private assistance to disaster victims had surpassed $70 million.

SEN. JOHN STENNIS, on August 3, had almost fully recovered from wounds he received in a January holdup.

Municipal Elections. Elections were held in June in all but 13 of Mississippi's nearly 280 municipalities. Republicans fielded candidates for mayor in 32 municipalities and won 14 victories, an increase of 7 over the 1969 elections. The number of Republicans elected to governing boards also increased from 20 in 1969 to 45 in 1973. While Republicans showed surprising strength in unseating long-term Democratic mayors in Meridian and Tupelo, incumbent Republican mayors suffered defeat in Clarksdale and Hattiesburg.

Blacks, usually running as independents, also registered gains in municipal balloting. Whereas only one biracial town elected a black mayor in 1969, four such towns did so in 1973. In addition, an increased number of racially mixed towns chose one or more black board members.

Legislative Session. The 1973 session of the Mississippi Legislature found lawmakers and Gov. William Waller frequently at odds over major legislation. While the governor did not negate an income-tax cut of $17 million as he had threatened to do if it were passed, he did exercise the item veto to reduce substantially a $106 million capital-improvements appropriation.

Among the Legislature's more important actions was the creation of a continuing Joint Legislative Committee on Performance Evaluation and Expenditures Review. This committee, replacing the long-standing General Legislative Investigating Committee, was given power to audit expenditures made by state and local governments and to bring suit for the recovery of misused funds. Also gaining legislative approval were reapportionment of the state's three most populous counties (Hinds, Harrison, and Jackson); a pay hike for public school teachers; the licensing and regulation of chiropractors; and the establishment of a school of dentistry at the University of Mississippi Medical Center in Jackson.

County Government. County purchasing practices, long a source of speculation and scandal, became the subject of a major controversy in June as the result of allegations of price-fixing and "kickbacks" involving members of county governing boards and companies from which they annually buy large quantities of road culverts. In the wake of the

accusations, the Mississippi Economic Council (the state chamber of commerce) stepped up its perennial campaign for legislation imposing mandatory county-unit road administration and centralized purchasing.

Penitentiary. Both successes and failures marked the state's effort to comply with a 1972 U. S. district court order calling for sweeping reforms at the state penitentiary at Parchman. A major renovation program was begun in 1973, and a prisoner classification system was installed. However, officials had difficulty in eliminating the "trusty system" of guards and also in employing a professional penologist to superintend the prison.

Other Events. President Nixon visited Mississippi in June, honoring the state's senior senator on the occasion of the dedication of the John C. Stennis Center at the Meridian Naval Air Station. Only two months earlier Senator Stennis had sustained near-fatal gunshot wounds when he was the victim of a robbery that took place outside his Washington home.

On June 25 the U. S. Supreme Court ruled that Mississippi's system of providing "free textbooks" must be revamped so as to assure that the state does not aid segregated private schools.

Federal funds for public colleges and universities in Mississippi remained in jeopardy at the end of 1973, pending approval by the U. S. Department of Health, Education, and Welfare of a statewide, higher education desegregation plan.

DANA B. BRAMMER, *University of Mississippi*

MISSISSIPPI • Information Highlights

Area: 47,716 square miles (123,584 sq km).
Population (1972 est.): 2,263,000. *Density:* 47 per sq mi.
Chief Cities (1970 census): Jackson, the capital, 153,968; Biloxi, 48,486; Meridian, 45,083; Gulfport, 40,791.
Government (1973): *Chief Officers*—governor, William Waller (D); lt. gov., William Winter (D); secy. of state, Heber Ladner (D); atty. gen., A. F. Summer (D); treas., Brad Dye (D); supt. of public education, Garvin Johnston (D); chief justice, Robert Gillespie (D). *Legislature*—Senate, 52 members (50 Democrats, 2 Republicans); House of Representatives, 122 members (119 D, 2 R, 1 Independent).
Education (1972–73): *School enrollment*—public elementary, 302,200 pupils, 13,158 teachers; public secondary, 224,118 pupils, 10,226 teachers; nonpublic, 67,500 pupils, 3,000 teachers; colleges and universities, 74,823 students. *Public school expenditures,* $338,875,000 ($689 per pupil). *Average teacher's salary,* $7,145.
State Finances (fiscal year 1971): *Revenues,* $1,045,066,000 (5% general sales tax and gross receipts taxes, $246,322,000; motor fuel tax, $96,081,000; federal funds, $324,892,000). *Expenditures,* $964,613,000 (education, $380,575,000; health, welfare, and safety, $171,818,000; highways, $197,415,000). *State debt,* $495,107,000 (June 30, 1971).
Personal Income (1972): $6,931,000,000; per capita, $3,063.
Public Assistance (1972): $164,198,000. *Average monthly payments* (Dec. 1972)—old-age assistance, $56.95; aid to families with dependent children, $53.07.
Labor Force: *Nonagricultural wage and salary earners* (July 1973), 645,800. *Average annual employment* (1972)—manufacturing, 204,800; trade, 118,900; government, 136,700; services, 72,200. *Insured unemployed* (Sept. 1973)—4,700 (0.9%).
Manufacturing (1971): *Value added by manufacture,* $2,237,200,000. Apparel and other textile products, $254,500,000; lumber and wood products, $211,100,000; chemicals and allied products, $208,000,000; food and kindred products, $207,100,000; electrical equipment and supplies, $190,200,000; transportation equipment, $175,700,000.
Agriculture (1972): *Cash farm income,* $1,210,456,000 (livestock, $549,527,000; crops, $535,054,000; government payments, $125,875,000). *Chief crops* (in order of value, 1972)—Cotton lint (ranks 2d among the states); soybeans.
Mining (1972): *Production value,* $255,716,000 (ranks 28th among the states). *Chief minerals*—Petroleum, $192,938,000; natural gas, $24,242,000; sand and gravel, $14,878,000; clays, $8,650,000.
Fisheries (1972): *Commercial catch,* 260,216,000 pounds ($11,897,000). *Leading species by value*—Shrimp, $4,739,000; menhaden, $2,915,000; red snapper, $944,000.
Transportation: *Roads* (1972), 66,766 miles (107,447 km); *motor vehicles* (1972), 1,175,836; *railroads* (1972), 3,653 miles (5,879 km); *public airports* (1972), 71.
Communications: *Telephones* (1973), 1,032,400; *television stations* (1971), 10; *radio stations* (1971), 138; *newspapers* (1973), 21 (daily circulation, 355,000).

MISSOURI

Large sections of Missouri were ravaged in 1973 by the worst floods in the history of the state. In Missouri politics, a Republican took over as governor and a struggle ensued between the Republican executive branch of the state government and the predominantly Democratic legislature.

Floods. For many Missourians, 1973 was a year of repeated evacuating and subsequent cleaning up and repairing their homes, which time after time were inundated by rampaging flood waters from the Missouri and Mississippi rivers. The worst flooding in the state's history occurred in April, just after March floods had devastated large portions of the state. Most of the areas along the two rivers saw crests reach 12 to 15 feet (3.7–4.6 meters) above the flood stage, surpassing previous records nearly everywhere. When the floods were at their highest, an estimated 1.8 million acres in 82 of the state's 114 counties were under water. Approximately 17,000 persons were forced to evacuate their homes, many of them more than once. In October, new crests flooded parts of 36 counties.

Damage from the spring floods was put at more than $102 million. The communities of West Alton, Smithton, and Old Monroe were among the worst hit. Portage des Sioux, a town of 500 on the Mississippi, was virtually cut off from the rest of the state for three weeks. It could be reached only by helicopter and make-shift ferry service. Floods struck

UPI

MARK TWAIN'S Tom Sawyer and Huck Finn would have been familiar with the spring floods in Hannibal, Mo.

MISSOURI • Information Highlights

Area: 69,686 square miles (180,487 sq km).
Population (1972 est.): 4,753,000. *Density:* 69 per sq mi.
Chief Cities (1970 census): Jefferson City, the capital, 32,-407; St. Louis, 622,236; Kansas City, 507,330; Springfield, 120,096; Independence, 111,630; St. Joseph, 72,691; Florissant, 65,908.
Government (1973): *Chief Officers*—governor, Christopher S. Bond (R); lt. gov., William C. Phelps (R); secy. of state, James C. Kirkpatrick (D); atty. gen., John C. Danforth (R); treas., James I. Spainhower; commissioner of education, Arthur L. Mallory; chief justice, Robert T. Donnelly. *General Assembly*—Senate, 34 members (21 Democrats, 13 Republicans); House of Representatives, 163 members (97 D, 66 R).
Education (1972–73): *Enrollment*—public elementary schools, 737,884 pupils, 24,600 teachers; public secondary schools, 292,124 pupils, 22,075 teachers; nonpublic schools, 104,200 pupils, 4,210 teachers; colleges and universities, 182,738 students. *Public school expenditures,* $806,993,000 ($881 per pupil). *Average teacher's salary,* $9,329.
State Finances (fiscal year 1971): *Revenues,* $1,592,583,000 (3% general sales tax and gross receipts taxes, $325,332,-000; motor fuel tax, $114,960,000; federal funds, $449,-108,000). *Expenditures,* $1,507,610,000 (education, $580,-293,000; health, welfare, and safety, $343,090,000; highways, $327,691,000). *State debt,* $143,981,000 (June 30, 1971).
Personal Income (1972): $19,991,000,000; per capita, $4,206.
Public Assistance (1972): $277,057,000. *Average monthly payments* (Dec. 1972)—old-age assistance, $82.99; aid to families with dependent children, $105.33.
Labor Force: *Nonagricultural wage and salary earners* (July 1973), 1,706,800. *Average annual employment* (1972)—manufacturing, 434,100; trade, 384,500; government, 297,-600; services, 266,100. *Insured unemployed* (Sept. 1973)—26,800 (1.9%).
Manufacturing (1971): *Value added by manufacture,* $7,525,-100,000; Transportation equipment, $1,836,900,000; food and kindred products, $992,400,000; chemicals and allied products, $657,500,000; printing and publishing, $559,300,-000; electrical equipment and supplies, $541,100,000; non-electrical machinery, $508,400,000.
Agriculture (1972): *Cash farm income,* $2,089,847,000 (livestock, $1,237,845,000; crops, $701,799,000; government payments, $150,203,000). *Chief crops* (in order of value, 1972)—Corn; soybeans (ranks 3d among the states); hay; cotton lint.
Mining (1972): *Production value,* $449,717,000 (ranks 17th among the states). *Chief minerals*—Lead, $149,022,000; cement, $80,950,000; stone, $69,342,000; iron ore, value not available.
Transportation: *Roads* (1972), 115,544 miles (185,945 km); *motor vehicles* (1972), 2,497,950; *railroads* (1972), 6,337 miles (10,198 km); *public airports* (1972), 102.
Communications: *Telephones* (1973), 2,979,500; *television stations* (1971), 23; *radio stations* (1971) 49; *newspapers* (1973), 54 (daily circulation, 1,805,000).

---

parts of 36 counties in October, causing damage estimated at $2 million in property and $60 million in crops.

State Government. Christopher S. Bond became Missouri's youngest governor and its first Republican chief executive in 24 years when he was sworn in on Jan. 8, 1973. Bond, who was 33 years old, named 31-year-old John D. Ashcroft (R) of Springfield to replace him as state auditor. This meant that four of the six statewide offices were being held by Republicans. The legislature remained firmly in the control of the Democrats, however, assuring conflict between the two branches of government.

The biggest executive-legislative fight of the year was over the reorganization of the government that had been dictated by the state's voters in 1972. By the end of 1973 the job had not been accomplished, as Bond had vetoed the reorganization plan passed by the legislature and the legislature had refused to accept the governor's plan.

Legislation. Among the most important bills passed by the 1973 session of the legislature was one providing tax relief for the elderly. The program was to become effective when forms for 1973 income taxes are filled out. Persons over 65 years of age who have an annual income of less than $7,500 may use their property tax or a portion of their rent as a tax credit.

The legislature also authorized a 0.5% sales tax to help subsidize bus service in the St. Louis area. The public transit system had been experi-

encing financial difficulties. A new law was passed requiring all governmental meetings, with a few exceptions, to be open to the public.

Investigations. Federal grand juries in Kansas City and St. Louis were investigating possible fraud in collecting sales taxes in the administration of former Gov. Warren E. Hearnes. State Sen. Jasper Brancato and city councilman Sal Capra, both of Kansas City, were indicted for using the mails to defraud in remitting sales tax receipts to the state. Also under investigation were the pardons and paroles granted under Hearnes. Leaders of organized crime in both major cities had been pardoned in the waning days of the Hearnes administration.

RONALD D. WILLNOW
St. Louis "Post-Dispatch"

MONGOLIA

During 1973, Mongolia remained a loyal ally of the USSR, which Mongolian Premier Yumzhagiyn Tsedenbal visited four times for both medical treatment and political consultations. Mongolia also utilized its membership in the Council of Mutual Economic Assistance (CMEA) to receive technical aid from all other council members—Bulgaria, Czechoslovakia, East Germany, Hungary, Poland, Rumania, and the USSR. CMEA countries rendered additional assistance by buying some Mongolian exports at artificially high prices.

Foreign Affairs. A Soviet-Mongolian pact signed in February provided for USSR technical aid in mining copper and molybdenum deposits discovered 150 miles (240 km) northwest of Ulan Bator. Relations between Mongolia and China remained tense because of frequent border incidents, but a treaty between the two countries in March transferred to Mongolian ownership the Chinese hospital and school in Ulan Bator and several construction projects left unfinished by Chinese laborers who were recalled to China in 1964.

A new Czechoslovak-Mongolian treaty of friendship and cooperation was signed on June 18, replacing a similar pact of 1957. Also in June, Mongolia concluded an agreement with North Vietnam pledging free Mongolian economic assistance to the North Vietnamese during 1974–75. New East German–Mongolian cultural exchange, consular, and technical aid treaties were signed in October.

Domestic Affairs. A newly elected Great People's Khural (legislature) met in July without electing a new national president, but authorized Sonomyn Lubsan to continue as acting president with the title of first vice president.

ELLSWORTH RAYMOND, *New York University*

MONTANA

Action to implement the new state constitution; a strengthening of control over natural resources, particularly strip-mined coal; a severe drought; and high agricultural prices highlighted events in Montana in 1973.

Constitutional Changes. The new state constitution became effective July 1, 1973. The legality of the 1972 vote on the constitution was challenged, but it was approved by the state courts and on June 27 by a federal court. In December it was also upheld by the U. S. Supreme Court.

Two provisions of the new constitution attracted widespread interest: one that provided for the legislature to be elected from 100 single-member districts, and another that permits gambling under laws to be enacted by the legislature. The new constitution also directed that property taxes be assessed at the state level; conferred full legal rights on 18-year-olds; made governmental units liable for injury to citizens; guaranteed citizens wider access to information on government activi-

─────── MONGOLIA • Information Highlights ───────

Official Name: Mongolian People's Republic.
Location: East-central Asia.
Area: 604,248 square miles (1,565,000 sq km).
Population (1973 est.): 1,400,000. *Density,* 2.6 per square mile (1 per sq km).
Chief Cities (1969 census): Ulan Bator, the capital, 248,500; Darkhan, 22,800.
Government: *Head of state,* Sonomyn Lubsan, acting president (appointed June 1972). *Head of government,* Yumzhagiyn Tsedenbal, premier and first secretary of the Communist party (took office Jan. 1952). *Legislature* (unicameral)—Great People's Khural.
Language: Khalkha Mongolian (official).
Education: *School enrollment* (1969)—primary, 137,420; secondary, 84,837; technical/vocational, 8,254; university/higher, 7,226.
Monetary Unit: Tugrik (3.32 tugriks equal U. S.$1, June 1973).
Gross National Product (1971 est.): $840,000,000.
Industrial Production Index (1970), 261 (1960 = 100).
Manufacturing (major products): Processed foods, leather goods.
Major Agricultural Products: Wheat, barley, vegetables, livestock (sheep, horses, cattle, goats, yaks), fish.
Major Minerals: Coal, lignite, salt.
Foreign Trade: *Chief exports*—Live animals; hides, skins, and furs; meat; butter; wool and hair. *Chief imports*—Industrial consumer goods; machinery and equipment; fuels; minerals and metals; foodstuffs. *Chief trading partner*—USSR.
Transportation: *Railroads* (1971), 868 miles (1,397 km); *major national airline,* Air Mongol.
Communications: *Telephones* (1972), 25,055; *newspapers* (1970), 2 (daily circulation, 133,000).

─────── MONTANA • Information Highlights ───────

Area: 147,138 square miles (381,087 sq km).
Population (1972 est.): 719,000. *Density:* 5 per sq mi.
Chief Cities (1970 census): Helena, the capital, 22,730; Billings, 61,581; Great Falls, 60,091; Missoula, 29,497; Butte, 23,368; Bozeman, 18,670; Havre, 10,558.
Government (1973): *Chief Officers*—governor, Thomas L. Judge (D); lt. gov., William Christiansen (D); secy. of state, Frank Murray (D); atty. gen., Robert L. Woodahl (R); treas., Hollis G. Connors (R); supt. of public instruction, Dolores Colburg (D); chief justice, James T. Harrison. *Legislative Assembly*—Senate, 50 members (27 Democrats, 23 Republicans); House of Representatives, 100 members (54 D, 46 R).
Education (1972–73): *Enrollment*—public elementary schools, 116,980 pupils, 4,982 teachers; public secondary schools, 55,076 pupils, 3,518 teachers; nonpublic schools, 10,900 pupils, 510 teachers; colleges and universities, 27,197 students. *Public school expenditures,* $150,617,000 ($943 per pupil). *Average teacher's salary,* $8,908.
State Finances (fiscal year 1971): *Revenues,* $391,268,000 (total sales tax and gross receipts taxes, $50,287,000; motor fuel tax, $28,865,000; federal funds, $140,971,000). *Expenditures,* $347,011,000 (education, $127,774,000; health, welfare, and safety, $42,996,000; highways, $109,-594,000). *State debt,* $98,989,000 (June 30, 1971).
Personal Income (1972): $2,802,000,000; per capita, $3,897.
Public Assistance (1972): $36,500,000. *Average monthly payments* (Dec. 1972)—old-age assistance, $61.07; aid to families with dependent children, $151.83.
Labor Force: *Nonagricultural wage and salary earners* (July 1973), 223,400. *Average annual employment* (1972)—manufacturing, 24,900; trade, $51,500; government, 55,500; services, 36,900. *Insured unemployed* (Sept. 1973)—3,500 (2.3%).
Manufacturing (1971): *Value added by manufacture,* $330,400,-000. Lumber and wood products, $95,300,000; food and kindred products $61,400,000; petroleum and coal products, $33,300,000; printing and publishing, $26,700,000; stone, clay, and glass products, $16,400,000; chemicals and allied products, $12,400,000.
Agriculture (1972): *Cash farm income,* $865,222,000 (livestock, $495,517,000; crops, $266,536,000; government payments, $103,169,000). *Chief crops* (in order of value, 1972)—Wheat; hay; barley (ranks 3d among the states); sugar beets.
Mining (1972): *Production value,* $323,823,000 (ranks 22d among the states). *Chief minerals*—Copper, $124,605,-000; petroleum, $102,378,000; sand and gravel, $26,467,-000; cement, value not available.
Transportation: *Roads* (1972), 77,920 miles (125,397 km); *motor vehicles* (1972), 510,696; *railroads* (1972), 4,981 miles (8,016 km); *public airports* (1972), 117.
Communications: *Telephones* (1973), 398,800; *television stations* (1971), 12; *radio stations* (1971), 48; *newspapers* (1973), 13 (daily circulation, 194,000).

ties; and provided for the preliminary appointment of judges by the governor to be followed by election.

Legislative Action. Annual sessions of the legislature provided by the new constitution began in 1973 with both houses and the governorship controlled by Democrats for the first time since 1938. Party unity prevailed as the legislature drafted the strongest laws in the nation regulating strip mining and utility siting in the extensive coal reserves in eastern Montana. An Energy Advisory Council was established to oversee the implementation of these laws, with the lieutenant governor as chairman.

Environmental Issues. Several environmental issues, in addition to coal, were closely watched. Among these were a second open-pit copper mine in Butte, a $22 million expansion of the Anaconda copper smelter, and a $12 million proposed addition to the Hoerner-Waldorf paper pulp mill in Missoula. A Subdivision and Platting Act and a Water Use Act provided for more orderly building expansion in the state, and counties were ordered to provide for disposal of discarded automobiles. An additional tax on mined coal is to be held in a Resources Indemnity Trust Account until this account reaches $200 million.

There were severe drought conditions in wide areas of the state, and extensive range and forest fires raged in August. The reduced production of the leading agricultural products—beef and wheat—was compensated for by the increased market prices of these products.

A strong public reaction to a government proposal to move the U. S. Forest Service offices and laboratories from Missoula to Denver resulted in the government's agreeing to retain the major facilities in Missoula.

MERRILL G. BURLINGAME
Montana State University

MONTREAL

Attracting the attention of Montrealers during 1973 were problems concerning the functioning of the Montreal Urban Community (MUC), the regional government created in 1969 that includes the 29 municipalities on Montreal Island. Other municipal preoccupations in 1973 included the election of school commissioners and preparations for the Summer Olympic Games of 1976.

Community Government. Although numerous strains persisted in the relations between Montreal and the suburban towns, there was a large measure of agreement and cooperation in 1973. The suburban mayors no longer contested the necessity for the larger governmental apparatus, and they were more conciliatory in the matter of integrating police forces. On the other hand, several suburbs still opposed the extension of the Montreal metro (subway). For the first time, the MUC reached accord on a voted budget, which was set at $170.3 million for 1974—a rise of $24 million over 1973. Police services will absorb more than 60% ($104 million) of the total outlay, and the metro extension alone will require an expenditure of $84 million in 1974.

Throughout the year, the question of financing municipal services was heatedly discussed. The MUC, which governs one third of Quebec's population, continues to demand special provincial subsidies.

The publication in June of a report by MUC Chairman Lawrence Hanigan opened debate over reforms to improve the functioning of the MUC. The Hanigan report recommended reducing the number of municipalities from 29 to 19 and grouping the 19 in five geographical sectors. It also proposed that police services be placed under MUC control. At present the budget for the integrated police force is supervised by a "security council" and thus eludes entirely control by popularly elected representatives.

School Commission Elections. In the school elections of June 18, voters elected 100 commissioners within the island's eight school commissions (six Catholic and two Protestant). The commissioners, in turn, elected representatives to the School Council, a new body that began functioning on July 1. The council's mandate is to prepare a plan for restructuring the school system and to determine the bases (language, religion, or area) for reorganizing the commissions.

The election reflected the conflict between partisans of religiously affiliated schools and backers of the "Movement for School Democratization." The latter advocated a restructuring in terms of the needs of the French-speaking majority, elimination of disparities in physical plant, and improvement of free education for adults. In order to stop these "syndicalists," the bloc of English-speaking candidates joined the French-speaking partisans of religious schools. This conservative coalition, which defended the religious educational institutions and the privileges that this kind of scholastic organization has conferred on the English-speaking minority for 137 years, won the election—although only 23% of the electorate participated.

Since July 1, when the law authorizing the reorganization of public instruction in Montreal went into effect, the council and the commissioners have been at their jobs—and in sharp debate. The issues dividing them are the status of the French language and improvement of the less favored educational institutions.

Plans for Olympics. The committee organizing the Olympics initiated important work in 1973. Construction was to begin on a 70,000-seat stadium in early 1974. Mayor Jean Drapeau of Montreal, a principal backer of the Games, has frequently had to reassure an electorate uneasy about financing them. The establishment of a special lottery and the sale of stamps and coins commemorating the Olympics—items already on the market in 1973—ought to cover the entire costs of the sports installations for the Olympic Games, according to Mayor Drapeau.

The choice of Viau Park as the site of the future Olympic Village was loudly contested by champions of the preservation of green spaces. Plans for a temporary village that would permit the recovery of the land after the Games were rejected by the Municipal Council. Even the provincial minister of municipal affairs and the environment failed to win the mayor's approval for a temporary village—although a permanent village will cost more than $100 million.

Mayor Drapeau's ambitious projects (Expo in 1967 and the Olympics in 1976) have been increasingly opposed by citizens' and labor groups. These groups object to the slighting of various social goals.

ROBERT COMEAU
Université du Québec à Montréal

MOROCCO

King Hassan II, Morocco's ruler since 1961, shored up his shaky throne in 1973. His domestic political offensive against radical opponents gained him the support of moderates, and his dispatch in July of Moroccan army contingents to Syria as a sign of solidarity with the Arab cause gained him both support from pro-Arab former opponents and new weight in international diplomacy.

Weakening of the Opposition. Political supporters of the Casablanca-based labor union federation, the UMT, broke with the more radical Rabat branch of the militant National Union of Popular Forces (UNFP) in July, breaking the united front that the UNFP had forged with the moderate Istiqlal party for political negotiations with the king.

Following a series of student strikes in January, the regime outlawed the radical National Union of Moroccan Students (UNEM), while leaving intact the student union (UGEM) dominated by the Istiqlal party. Heading off a strike of college professors in February, government officials embarked on a campaign to discredit university teachers and students, but carefully avoided attacking traditional scholars who normally support the Istiqlal.

In order to undercut the opposition even further by capitalizing on intense domestic feelings of solidarity with the Palestinian exiles, Hassan announced on February 22 his plan to send Moroccan troops to aid the Syrians. Concurrently, he invited leaders of Arabian oil states to Rabat and obtained from them loans of 800 million French francs ($175 million) to cushion Morocco financially against possible French retaliation for the nationalization in July of lands held by French and Spanish colons.

Following the purge of Morocco's armed forces after their involvement in two major coup attempts in 1971 and 1972, the police force has emerged as the most cohesive coercive force backing the throne.

Labor. Increased wildcat strikes, such as that of the rail workers in January, challenged UMT

MOROCCO • Information Highlights

Official Name: Kingdom of Morocco.
Location: Northwest Africa.
Area: 172,413 square miles (446,550 sq km).
Population (1973 est.): 17,400,000. *Density,* 93 per square mile (36 per sq km).
Chief Cities (1970 est.): Rabat, the capital, 374,800; Casablanca, 1,500,100; Marrakesh, 305,000; Fez, 290,000.
Government: *Head of state,* Hassan II, king (acceded Feb. 1961). *Head of government,* Ahmed Osman, premier (took office Nov. 1972). *Legislature* (unicameral)—Chamber of Deputies. *Major political parties*—Movement Populaire; Istiqlal; Union Nationale des Forces Populaires.
Languages: Arabic (official), Berber, French.
Education: *Expenditure* (1969), 16.3% of total public expenditure. *School enrollment* (1969)—primary, 1,142,810; secondary, 295,434; technical/vocational, 8,021; university/higher, 12,770.
Monetary Unit: Dirham (3.90 dirhams equal U. S.$1, July 1973).
Gross National Product (1972 est.): $4,210,000,000.
Economic Indexes: *Industrial production* (mining, 1972), 142 (1963=100); *agricultural production* (1971), 143 (1963=100); *consumer price index* (1972), 120 (1963=100).
Manufacturing (major products): Processed foods, metals, textiles, wine, cement.
Major Agricultural Products: Barley, wheat, citrus fruits, vegetables, sugar beets, tomatoes, grapes, almonds, sheep.
Major Minerals: Phosphate rock (ranks 3d among world producers, 1971), iron ore, coal, manganese, antimony, lead.
Foreign Trade (1972): *Exports,* $639,000,000; *Imports,* $771,000,000. *Chief trading partners* (1971)—France (took 36% of exports, supplied 31% of imports); West Germany (8.5%—7.6%); Italy (5%—6%).
Tourism: Receipts (1971), $152,000,000.
Transportation: *Motor vehicles* (1971), 332,600 (automobiles, 242,100); *railroads* (1971), 1,091 miles (1,756 km); *merchant fleet* (1972), 47,000 gross registered tons; *major national airline,* Royal Air Maroc.
Communications: *Telephones* (1972), 171,544; *newspapers* (1971), 13.

union leadership in 1973. With 57% of Moroccans now under the age of 20, youth is making a mark on the whole society, including the labor unions. Impatient, relatively well educated, and lacking major responsibilities, new union members have taken militant positions that threaten the security of old-time workers and union leaders. Fear of internal agitation and external political challenges by younger workers has induced UMT directors to collaborate with the minister of labor on many levels.

Political Trials. In March the government rounded up two armed bands of Moroccans who, according to the official version, had infiltrated into the country under "a concerted plan" worked out in and funded by Libya. The regime accused Mohammed al-Basri, a UNFP leader living in exile, of masterminding the new plot "to overthrow the regime." A total of 157 arrests followed, including that of younger leaders of the Rabat branch of the UNFP. During the trial most of the defendants publicly complained of police torture and forced confessions.

On April 2, Premier Ahmed Osman suspended the Rabat branch of the UNFP. At the end of August, 72 defendants, including 11 UNFP leaders, were acquitted by the court but remained in jail pending investigation of further charges.

Another 80 young leftist leaders, mostly affiliated with a splinter group of the outlawed Communist party, stood trial in Casablanca for "plotting against the state." In September, 41 of them received sentences ranging from 18 months to 15 years, while 25 tried in absentia face life sentences if apprehended.

Foreign Relations. Morocco became a valuable intermediary for the United States in the Middle East conflict in 1973. Because of its close military ties to the radical Baathist regime in Syria, Morocco may be able to exert a moderate influence on future peace talks between Syria and Israel. Accordingly, the Moroccan foreign minister was included as part of an Arab delegation that visited President Nixon in October, and Henry Kissinger made Morocco his first stop on a "peace tour" in November following the Arab-Israeli war.

Moroccan radio attacks against Libya had intensified after the March events described above, and Morroco's relations with Tunisia also cooled.

Economy. Morocco launched its 1973–77 development plan in July and introduced a new liberal investment law to encourage foreign capital flow into the country. Under the plan a total 26 billion dirhams ($6.7 billion) is to be spent, of which only 11 billion dirhams ($2.8 billion) is to come from internal resources. Planners have stressed the development of light industries, hoping to decrease Moroccan dependence on consumer imports and reduce urban unemployment among the estimated 450,000 presently without jobs.

Morocco's balance of payments improved during 1972. A record amount of money was sent home by approximately 250,000 Moroccan workers in Europe, and 1.1 million tourists visited Morocco in 1972—nearly 24% more than in 1971. An announced rise in the price of phosphate rock, the country's major export earner, from its present level of $15 a ton to $48 in January 1974 should further increase revenues. Morocco is the world's third-largest producer of the mineral and holds one half of known world reserves.

STUART SCHAAR
Brooklyn College, City University of New York

Ryan O'Neal and his daughter, Tatum, played a pair of 1930's confidence tricksters in Paper Moon, *a comedy that was produced and directed by Peter Bogdanovich.*

Motion Pictures

In the film world, 1973 began sensationally with *Last Tango in Paris* and closed sensationally with *The Exorcist.* In between, however, things did not look so good. *Last Tango,* by the Italian filmmaker Bernardo Bertolucci, placed a middle-aged Marlon Brando in a violent, fatal love affair with Maria Schneider, a woman less than half his age. More sexually daring than any other major feature film, it achieved a fashionable notoriety—and wide popular acceptance. *The Exorcist,* based on William Peter Blatty's novel about a teen-age girl who is possessed by the Devil is exceptionally vivid escapist entertainment. It seemed destined to earn a golden reputation in the film industry for its director, William Friedkin (*The French Connection*).

The industry might well be anxious to look for gold. Attendance figures at the box office were down again, slightly. Metro-Goldwyn-Mayer announced that it would end most feature film production. However, Columbia Pictures, also in trouble, especially after such expensive disasters as the musical remake of *Lost Horizon,* announced a determination to stay in the business.

Perhaps the most important and potentially most damaging event of 1973 was the United States Supreme Court's June 21 decision to leave censorship in the arts up to the standards of individual communities. At year's end, however, the first major case involving a film was referred back to the court,

Edward Fox was the "Jackal" in the screen version of Frederick Forsyth's best seller The Day of the Jackal.

405

THE NOSTALGIA boom continued in 1973 with The Way We Were. Here Barbra Streisand (left) and Robert Redford attend a party.

TOGETHER AGAIN: Redford and Paul Newman (right), stars of the 1969 hit Butch Cassidy and the Sundance Kid, team up in 1973's The Sting.

MUSICAL VERSION of Tom Sawyer has Huck Finn (left) and Tom, who are playing hooky from school, celebrate their freedom by bursting into song.

which had to decide whether Mike Nichols' *Carnal Knowledge* was pornographic, and so could be banned by local judges in Georgia.

Audiences. There were continued signs in 1973 that the film audience was fragmenting into several audiences, each with fairly specialized interests and expectations. For example, late in 1973, when 1972's highly successful *Cabaret* had finished its major runs, it was determined that the film had done about half its business in just a few large cities, among them New York, Miami, and San Francisco. In other cities, such as Chicago and Philadelphia, it did poorly—but recouped in the more affluent suburbs. It drew disappointing audiences in small towns, and especially in the rural South. Americans as a whole still seemed to be turning from the habit of movie going. In absolute terms, however, the limited audiences are still huge. Paying higher ticket prices than ever, they still could support some very expensive film production.

In 1973, the market for good imported foreign-language films dwindled to almost nothing except in three or four major cities. However, a steady increase in the nontheatrical market (schools, colleges, film societies) enabled some growing distribution companies to do all their business in this area. This trend is worth noting because the kinds of films that are shown—eventually, the kinds of films that are made—depend ultimately upon producers' and distributors' assumptions about the nature of their audience. In relation to the national population, that audience had become, in significant part, an elite minority.

To cater to such an audience a new organization, the American Film Theater, initiated a subscription series of distinguished plays filmed by well-known casts and directors. Three programs opened in 1973: John Frankenheimer's version of Eugene O'Neill's *The Iceman Cometh;* Edward Albee's *A Delicate Balance,* directed by Tony Richardson; and Peter Hall's filming of Harold Pinter's *The Homecoming.* To many the Pinter seemed good enough to justify the entire enterprise.

Censorship and Public Morality. Despite *Last Tango in Paris,* there were signs (among them, less nudity) that films were drawing back from the relative freedom of recent years. To the outrage of some and the indifference of many, a protracted love scene between Julie Christie and Donald Sutherland in Nicolas Roeg's stylish thriller *Don't Look Now* was remade, softened, to win an R-rating from the Motion Picture Association of America.

However, the vagaries of the rating system were eclipsed by the community-standards ruling of the Supreme Court, which, it was feared, might create chaos in the media. Ironically, hard-core pornography might not be greatly affected, since it could be cheaply produced and then profitably shown in whatever localities accepted it. But films depending on national distribution could be deeply hurt by the pressure to make them universally inoffensive.

Significant Subjects. More pervasive than any subject was a nostalgia for the recent American past. There were depression era comedies, among them Peter Bogdanovich's *Paper Moon* and George Roy Hill's *The Sting.* There was depression era adventure—Robert Aldrich's *The Emperor of the North Pole.* And there was depression era violence—John Milius' *Dillinger.* Sydney Pollack's *The Way We Were* covered the 1930's, the 1940's, and the 1950's. *American Graffiti* was set in the early 1960's.

(Continued on page 410)

American Graffiti, a nostalgic comedy about teenagers in 1962, featured Ronny Howard and Cindy Williams.

UNIVERSAL PICTURES

NOTABLE MOTION PICTURES OF 1973

The following list of films released in the United States in 1973 presents a cross-section of the most popular, most typical, or most widely discussed motion pictures of the year.

Adieu Philippine. Director, Jacques Rozier; screenplay, Rozier and Michel O'Glor. With Yveline Cery, Stefania Sabatini, Jean-Claude Aimimi, Vittorio Caprioli.

The Adversary. Director, Satyajit Ray; screenplay, Ray from story by Sunil Ganuly. With Dhritiman Chatterjee, Krishna Rose.

American Graffiti. Director, George Lucas; screenplay, Lucas, Gloria Katz, and Williard Huyck. With Richard Dreyfuss, Ronny Howard, Paul Le Mat, Charlie Martin Smith, Cindy Williams, Candy Clark.

Ash Wednesday. Director, Larry Peerce; screenplay, Jean-Claude Tramont. With Elizabeth Taylor, Henry Fonda, Helmut Berger.

An Autumn Afternoon. Director, Yasujiro Ozu; screenplay, Ozu and Kogo Noda. With Chishu Ryu, Shima Iwashita, Shin-Ichiro Mikami, Keiji Sada.

Bang the Drum Slowly. Director, John Hancock; screenplay, Mark Harris from his own novel. With Michel Moriarty, Robert de Niro, Vincent Gardenia, Phil Foster, Ann Wedgeworth.

Blume in Love. Director, Paul Mazursky; screenplay, Mazursky. With George Segal, Susan Anspach, Kris Kristofferson, Marsha Mason.

Book of Numbers. Director, Raymond St. Jacques; screenplay, Larry Spiegel, based on novel by Robert Deane Phaar. With Raymond St. Jacques, Freda Payne, Philip Thomas, Hope Clarke.

Brother Sun, Sister Moon. Director, Franco Zeffirelli; screenplay, Suso Cecchi D'Amico, Kenneth Ross, Lina Wertmuller, and Sir Alec Guinness. With Graham Faulkner, Judi Bowker, and Sir Alec Guinness.

Charlie Varrick. Director, Don Siegel; screenplay, Howard Rodman and Dean Riesner from novel by John Reese. With Walter Matthau, Joe Don Baker, Felicia Farr, Andy Robinson, John Vernon.

Charlotte's Web. Directors, Charles A. Nichols and Iwao Takamoto; screenplay, Earl Hamner, Jr. from book by E. B. White. Animated film with the voices of Debbie Reynolds, Paul Lynde, Henry Gibson, Rex Allen.

Cinderella Liberty. Director, Mark Rydell; screenplay, Darryl Ponicsan from his own novel. With James Caan, Marsha Mason, Kirk Calloway, Eli Wallach.

Cops and Robbers. Director, Aram Avakian; screenplay, Donald E. Westlake. With Cliff Gorman, Joseph Bologna.

Day for Night. Director, François Truffaut; screenplay, Truffaut, Jean-Louis Richard, Suzanne Schiffman. With François Truffaut, Jacqueline Bisset, Jean-Pierre Leaud, Valentina Cortese, Jean Pierre Aumont, Dani, Alexandra Stewart, Jean Champion.

The Day of the Dolphin. Director, Mike Nichols; screenplay, Buck Henry from novel by Robert Merle. With George C. Scott, Trish Van Devere, Paul Sorvino, Fritz Weaver.

The Day of the Jackal. Director, Fred Zinnemann; screenplay, Kenneth Ross from the novel by Frederick Forsyth. With Edward Fox, Michel Auclair, Alan Badel, Tony Britton, Michel Lonsdale.

A Delicate Balance. Director, Tony Richardson; screenplay, Edward Albee, from his own play. With Katharine Hepburn, Paul Scofield, Lee Remick, Kate Reid, Joseph Cotten.

Dillinger. Director-scenarist, John Milius. With Warren Oates, Ben Johnson, Michelle Phillips, Cloris Leachman.

A Doll's House. Director, Patrick Garland; screenplay, Christopher Hampton from play by Henrik Ibsen. With Claire Bloom, Anthony Hopkins, Sir Ralph Richardson, Denholm Elliot, Anna Massey.

Don't Look Now. Director, Nicolas Roeg; screenplay, Alan Scott and Christ Bryant from a story by Daphne Du Maurier. With Julie Christie, Donald Sutherland, Hilar Mason, Cielia Matania.

Electra Glide in Blue. Director, James William Guercio; screenplay, Robert Boris. With Robert Blake, Billy (Green) Bush, Mitchell Ryan, Jeanine Riley.

Emperor of the North Pole. Director, Robert Aldrich; screenplay, Christopher Knopf. With Lee Marvin, Ernest Borgnine, Keith Carradine.

Executive Action. Director, David Miller; screenplay, Dalton Trumbo from story by Donald Freed and Mark Lane. With Burt Lancaster, Robert Ryan, Will Geer.

The Exorcist. Director, William Friedkin; screenplay, William Peter Blatty from his own novel. With Ellen Burstyn, Jason Miller, Max von Sydow, Lee J. Cobb, Kitty Winn, Linda Blair.

Fantastic Planet. Director, René Laloux; screenplay, Laloux and Roland Topor from novel by Steven Wul. French-Czech animated feature.

The First Circle. Director, Aleksander Ford; screenplay, Ford from novel by Aleksandr P. Solzhenitsyn. With Gunther Malzacher, Elzvieta Czyzewska, Peter Steen, Vera Chekova.

Five Fingers of Death. Director, Cheng Chang Ho; screenplay, Chiang Yang. With Lo Lieh, Wang Ping, Wang Chin-Feng.

The Flavor of Green Tea Over Rice. Director, Yasujiro Ozu; screenplay, Ozu and Kogo Noda. With Shin Saburi, Michiyo Kogura, Kuniko Miyake, Koji Tsuruta.

The Friends of Eddie Coyle. Director, Peter Yates; screenplay, Paul Monash from novel by George V. Higgins. With Robert Mitchum, Peter Boyle, Richard Jordan, Steven Keats.

Get to Know Your Rabbit. Director, Brian De Palma; screenplay, Jordan Crittenden. With Tom Smothers, Katharine Ross, Orson Welles.

Godspell. Director, David Greene; screenplay, Greene and John-Michael Tebelak from stage musical by Tebelak and Stephen Schwartz. With Victor Garber, David Haskell, Jerry Sroka, Lynne Thigpen.

La Grande Bouffe. Director, Marco Ferreri; screenplay, Ferreri and Rafael Azcona. With Marcello Mastroianni, Ugo Tognazzi, Michel Piccoli, Philippe Noiret, Andrea Ferreol.

The Harder They Come. Director, Perry Henzell; screenplay, Henzell and Trevor D. Rhone. With Jimmy Cliff, Jane Barkley, Carl Bradshaw, Ras Daniel Hartman.

Heavy Traffic. Director-scenarist, Ralph Bakshi. Animated feature with the voices of Joseph Kaufman, Beverly Hope Atkinson, Frank De Kova, Terri Haven.

High Plains Drifter. Director, Clint Eastwood; screenplay, Ernest Tidyman. With Clint Eastwood, Verna Bloom, Mariana Hill, Mitchell Ryan.

The Hireling. Director, Alan Bridges; screenplay, Wolf Mankowitz from novel by L. P. Hartley. With Robert Shaw, Sarah Miles, Peter Egan.

Hitler: The Last Ten Days. Director, Ennio de Concinni; screenplay, De Concinni, Maria Pia Fusco, Wolfgang Reinhardt from book by Gerhard Boldt. With Sir Alec Guinness, Simon Ward, Adolfo Celi, Diane Cilento, Doris Kunstmann.

The Homecoming. Director, Peter Hall; screenplay, Harold Pinter from his own play. With Cyril Cusack, Ian Holm, Michael Jayston, Vivien Merchant, Terence Rigby, Paul Rogers.

I. F. Stone's Weekly. Director-scenarist, Jerry Bruck, Jr. With I. F. Stone.

The Iceman Cometh. Director, John Frankenheimer; play by Eugene O'Neill. With Lee Marvin, Robert Ryan, Fredric March, Jeff Bridges, Martyn Green, George Voskovec, Moses Gunn, Tom Pedi.

Jeremy. Directors, Arthur Barron and Joseph Brooks; screenplay, Barron and Brooks. With Robby Benson, Glynnis O'Connor, Len Bari.

Jesus Christ Superstar. Director, Norman Jewison; screenplay, Jewison and Melvyn Bragg from rock opera by Tim Rice, music by Andrew Lloyd Webber. With Ted Neeley, Carl Anderson, Yvonne Elliman.

A King in New York. Director-scenarist, Charles Chaplin. With Charles Chaplin, Dawn Addams, Oliver Johnston, Maxine Audley, Michael Chaplin.

Lady Caroline Lamb. Director-scenarist, Robert Bolt. With Sarah Miles, Jon Finch, Richard Chamberlain, John Mills, Margaret Leighton, Sir Laurence Olivier.

The Last American Hero. Director, Lamont Johnson; screenplay, William Roberts from articles by Tom Wolfe. With Jeff Bridges, Valerie Perrine, Geraldine Fitzgerald, Art Lund.

The Last of Sheila. Director, Herbert Ross; screenplay, Stephen Sondheim and Anthony Perkins. With Richard Benjamin, Dyan Cannon, James Coburn, Joan Hackett, James Mason, Ian McShane, Raquel Welch.

Last Tango in Paris. Director, Bernardo Bertolucci; screenplay, Bertolucci and Franco Arcalli. With Marlon Brando, Maria Schneider, Jean-Pierre Leaud.

Late Autumn. Director, Yasujiro Ozu; screenplay, Ozu and Kogo Noda. With Sesuko Hara, Yoko Tsukasa, Chishu Ryu, Mariko Okada.

Let the Good Times Roll. Directors, Sid Levin and Robert Abel. With Chuck Berry, Little Richard, Fats Domino, Chubby Checker, Bo Diddley, The Shirelles.

Live and Let Die. Director, Guy Hamilton; screenplay, Tom Mankiewicz from novel by Ian Fleming. With Roger Moore, Yaphet Kotto, Jane Seymour.

The Long Goodbye. Director, Robert Altman; screenplay, Leigh Brackett from novel by Raymond Chandler. With Elliott Gould, Nina van Pallandt, Sterling Hayden, Mark Rydell, Jim Bouton.

Lost Horizon. Director, Charles Jarrott; screenplay, Larry Kramer from novel by James Hilton. With Peter Finch, Liv Ullmann, Sally Kellerman, George Kennedy, Michael York, Olivia Hussey.

Love. Director, Karoly Makk; screenplay, Tibor Dery. With Lily Darvas, Mari Töröcsik, Ivan Darvas.

Love and Pain and the Whole Damned Thing. Director, Alan J. Pakula; screenplay, Alvin Sargent. With Maggie Smith, Timothy Bottoms.

Ludwig. Director, Luchino Visconti; screenplay, Visconti and Enrico Medioli. With Helmut Berger, Romy Schneider, Trevor Howard, Silvana Mangano, Gert Frobe, Helmut Griem.

The Mackintosh Man. Director, John Huston; screenplay, Walter Hill from novel by Desmond Bagley. With Paul Newman, Dominique Sanda, James Mason, Harry Andrews, Ian Bannen, Jenny Runacre.

Magnum Force. Director, Ted Post; screenplay, John Milius and Michael Cimino. With Clint Eastwood, Hal Holbrook, Mitchell Ryan, David Soul.

The Mattei Affair. Director, Francesco Rosi; screenplay, Rosi, Tonino Guerra, Nerio Minuzzo, Tito de Stefano. With Gian Maria Volonte, Luigi Eguarzina, Peter Baldwin.

Mean Streets. Director, Martin Scorsese; screenplay, Scorsese and Mardik Martin. With Robert De Niro, Harvey Keitel, David Proval, Amy Robinson.

Memories of Underdevelopment. Director, Tomás Gutiérrez Alea; screenplay, Alea from novel by Edmundo Desnoes. With Sergio Corrleri, Daisy Granados, Exlinda Nunes, Beatriz Ponchora.

The Merchant of Four Seasons. Director-scenarist, Rainer Werner Fassbinder. With Irm Hermann, Hanna Schygulla, Hans Hirschmuller.

The Nelson Affair. Director, James Gallan Jones; screenplay, Terence Rattigan. With Glenda Jackson, Peter Finch, Michael Jayston, Anthony Quale, Margaret Leighton.

The New Land. Director, Jan Troell; screenplay, Troell and Bengt Forslund from novels by Vilhelm Moberg. With Max von Sydow, Liv Ullman, Eddie Axberg, Monika Zetterlund.

O Lucky Man! Director, Lindsay Anderson; screenplay, David Sherwin from an idea by Malcolm McDowell. With Malcolm McDowell, Sir Ralph Richardson, Rachel Roberts, Arthur Lowe, Helen Mirren, Dandy Nichols.

The Offence. Director, Sidney Lumet; screenplay, John Hopkins. With Sean Connery, Trevor Howard, Vivien Merchant, Ian Bannen.

Oklahoma Crude. Director, Stanley Kramer; screenplay, Marc Norman. With George C. Scott, Faye Dunaway, John Mills, Jack Palance.

The Paper Chase. Director, James Bridges; screenplay, Bridges from novel by John Jay Osborn, Jr. With Timothy Bottoms, Lindsay Wagner, John Houseman.

Paper Moon. Director, Peter Bogdanovich; screenplay, Alvin Sargent from novel by Joe David Brown. With Ryan O'Neal, Tatum O'Neal, Madeline Kahn.

Papillon. Director, Franklin J. Schaffner; screenplay, Dalton Trumbo and Lorenzo Semple, Jr. from book by Henri Charrière. With Steve McQueen, Dustin Hoffman.

Pat Garrett and Billy the Kid. Director, Sam Peckinpah; screenplay, Rudolf Wurlitzer. With James Coburn, Kris Kristofferson, Richard Jaekel, Katy Jurado, Chill Wills, Jason Robards, Bob Dylan.

Payday. Director, Daryl Duke; screenplay, Don Carpenter. With Rip Torn, Ahna Capri, Elayne Heilveil, Michael C. Gwynne.

Playtime. Director-scenarist, Jacques Tati. With Tati, Barbara Dennek, Marc Monjou, George Fave.

Private Parts. Director, Paul Bartel; screenplay, Philip Kearney and Les Rendelstein. With Ann Ruymen, Lucille Benson, John Ventantonio, Laurie Main, Stanley Livingston.

Pulp. Director-scenarist, Michael Hodges. With Michael Caine, Mickey Rooney, Lionel Stander, Lizabeth Scott, Nadia Cassini.

Save the Tiger. Director, John G. Avildsen; screenplay, Steve Shagan. With Jack Lemmon, Jack Gilford, Laurie Heineman, Norman Burton, Patricia Smith.

Scarecrow. Director, Jerry Schatzberg; screenplay, Garry Michael White. With Gene Hackman, Al Pacino, Dorothy Tristan.

Serpico. Director, Sidney Lumet; screenplay, Waldo Salt and Norman Wexler from book by Peter Maas. With Al Pacino, John Randolph, Tony Roberts, Jack Kehoe.

Le Sex Shop. Director-scenarist, Claude Berri. With Berri, Juliet Berto, Jean-Pierre Marielle, Nathalie Delon, Beatrice Romand.

Shaft in Africa. Director, John Guillermin; screenplay, Stirling Silliphant based on characters created by Ernest Tidyman. With Richard Roundtree, Frank Finlay, Vonetta McGee, Neda Arneric.

Siddhartha. Director, Conrad Rooks; screenplay, Rooks from novel by Herman Hesse. With Shashi Kapoor, Simi Garewal, Romesh Sharma.

Sisters. Director, Brian De Palma; screenplay, De Palma and Louisa Rose from a story by De Palma. With Margot Kidder, Jennifer Salt, Charles During.

Sleeper. Director, Woody Allen; screenplay, Allen and Marshall Brickman. With Woody Allen, Diane Keaton, John Beck.

Slither. Director, Howard Zieff; screenplay, W. D. Richter. With James Caan, Peter Boyle, Sally Kellerman, Louise Lasser.

The Spider's Stratagem. Director, Bernardo Bertolucci; screenplay, Bertolucci, Edoardo de Gregorio, and Marilu Parolini from a story by Jorge Luis Borges. With Giulio Brogi, Alida Valli, Tino Scotti.

State of Siege. Director, Costa-Gavras; screenplay, Costa-Gavras and Franco Solinas. With Yves Montand, Renato Salvatore, O. E. Hasse, Jacques Weber, Jean-Luc Bideau.

Steelyard Blues. Director, Alan Myerson; screenplay, David S. Ward. With Jane Fonda, Donald Sutherland, Peter Boyle, Garry Goodrow.

The Sting. Director, George Roy Hill; screenplay, David S. Ward. With Paul Newman, Robert Redford, Robert Shaw.

Such a Gorgeous Kid Like Me. Director, François Truffaut; screenplay, Truffaut and Jean-Loup Dabadie from a novel by Henry Farrell. With Bernadette Lafont, Claude Brasseur, Charles Denner, Guy Marchand, André Bussolier.

Summer Wishes, Winter Dreams. Director, Gilbert Cates; screenplay, Stewart Stern. With Joanne Woodward, Martin Balsam, Sylvia Sidney.

The Tall Blond Man with One Black Shoe. Director, Yves Robert; screenplay, Robert and Francis Veber. With Pierre Richard, Bernard Biler, Jean Rochefort, Mireille Darc.

Ten From Your Show of Shows. Director, Max Liebman; television plays, Liebman, Mel Tolkin, Lucille Kallen, Mel Brooks, Tony Webster, Sid Caesar. With Sid Caesar, Imogene Coca, Carl Reiner, Howard Morris, Louis Nye.

Tom Sawyer. Director, Don Taylor; screenplay, Richard M. Sherman and Robert B. Sherman from *The Adventures of Tom Sawyer* by Mark Twain. With Johnny Whitaker, Celeste Holm, Warren Oates, Jeff East, Jodie Foster, Henry Jones.

A Touch of Class. Director, Melvin Frank; screenplay, Frank and Jack Rose. With George Segal, Glenda Jackson, Paul Sorvino, Hildegard Neil.

Tout Va Bien. Directors, Jean-Luc Godard and Jean-Pierre Gorin; screenplay, Godard and Gorin. With Yves Montand, Jane Fonda, Vittorio Caprioli, Jean Pignol.

The Train Robbers. Director-scenarist, Burt Kennedy. With John Wayne, Ann-Margret, Rod Taylor, Ben Johnson, Christopher George, Bobby Vinton.

Trick Baby. Director, Larry Yust; screenplay, Yust, T. Raewyn, A. Neuberg from novel by Iceberg Slim. With Kiel Martin, Mel Stewart, Dallas Edward Hayes, Beverly Ballard, Vernee Watson.

Under Milk Wood. Director, Andrew Sinclair; screenplay, Sinclair from play by Dylan Thomas. With Richard Burton, Elizabeth Taylor, Peter O'Toole, Glynis Johns, Vivien Merchant, Sian Phillips, Victor Spinetti.

A Warm December. Director, Sidney Poitier; screenplay, Lawrence Roman. With Sidney Poitier, Esther Anderson, Yvette Curtis.

The Way We Were. Director, Sydney Pollack; screenplay, Arthur Laurents from his own novel. With Barbra Streisand, Robert Redford, Bradford Dillman, Louis Chiles, Patrick O'Neal.

Wedding in White. Director, William Freuet; screenplay, Freuet. With Donald Pleasence, Carol Kane, Doris Petrie.

What? Director, Roman Polanski; screenplay, Polanski and Gerard Brach. With Sydne Roman, Marcello Mastroianni, Hugh Griffith, Romolo Valli.

CINEMA 5

YVES MONTAND in State of Siege, his third film with the Russian-Greek director Costa-Gavras.

(Continued from page 407)

Cops-and-robbers films investigated official corruption. Sidney Lumet's *Serpico,* based on the experiences of a real New York City policeman, was the most notable example. But police corruption is also a concern in such films as James William Guercio's motorcycle western *Electra Glide in Blue* and Aram Avakian's happily amoral *Cops and Robbers.*

Assassination was a prominent theme in political films in 1973. There was the attempted assassination of Charles de Gaulle in Fred Zinnemann's *The Day of the Jackal* and a theory about the assassination of President Kennedy in David Miller's *Executive Action.* Costa-Gavras' *State of Siege,* about the kidnapping and killing of a U. S. agent in South America, caused a small political furor of its own. Scheduled to open the American Film Institute's new Kennedy Center theater in Washington, D. C., it was withdrawn at the last minute, presumably because of its antigovernment bias. Later shown commercially in a theater not far from Kennedy Center, it enjoyed initial box office success.

Action Films. *Live and Let Die* was a pleasant continuation of the James Bond adventures. Don Siegel's *Charlie Varrick* celebrated small-time bank robbing as one of the last bastions of individual free enterprise. Robert Altman's *The Long Goodbye* was an ironic and affectionate farewell to Philip Marlowe (beautifully played by Elliott Gould) and the private-eye tradition of Raymond Chandler.

Black films, which recently had filled in the action genres, sometimes with fine results, were in a slight decline. One of the best was Raymond St. Jacques' *Book of Numbers,* a good-humored sidelight on the numbers racket.

An enormous audience existed for the kung fu, or martial-arts melodramas, imported, badly dubbed, from Hong Kong. These films, featuring sensational displays of karate grafted onto rudimentary plots, were long popular in the Chinese community. Their wider success, beginning with Cheng Chang Ho's *Five Fingers of Death,* was new. For a while kung-fu movies seemed almost to dominate the film scene. However, before the end of the year Bruce Lee, the young American-born star of many of these films, had died and audiences began falling off.

Comedies and Musicals. Woody Allen's *Sleeper* hilariously pits a contemporary Woody Allen against a semi-lobotomized society 200 years from now. George Segal became a comic persona in Paul Mazursky's *Blume in Love* and in Melvin Frank's *A Touch of Class.* But the major comedies released in 1973 came out of the past—Jacques Tati's *Playtime* (1967) and Charlie Chaplin's *A King in New York* (1957).

Except for the dismal *Lost Horizon* and Don Taylor's charming setting of Mark Twain material in *Tow Sawyer,* music on film was mostly limited to recordings of rock concerts, documentaries about rock stars, and adaptations of rock stage works. Norman Jewison's *Jesus Christ Superstar* was the most prominent, but David Greene's *Godspell* seemed more successful as a film. *Let the Good Times Roll* is a filmed concert by such pioneer rock stars as Chuck Berry, Bo Diddley, and Little Richard.

Animation. Ralph Bakshi's *Heavy Traffic,* a funny and despairing fantasy about New York City life, was the best animated film of 1973. It easily eclipsed other cartoon projects, such as the adaptation of E. B. White's *Charlotte's Web* or the French-Czechoslovakian science-fiction *Fantastic Planet.*

New Directors. In what was probably the most important manifestation in motion pictures for 1973, a number of younger directors now into their second or third films emerged as major talents. In addition to Bakshi these include Martin Scorsese for *Mean Streets,* an affectionate, agonized study of sub-Mafia crime in New York City's Little Italy; John Hancock for his realization of Mark Harris' fine novel about a dying baseball player, *Bang the Drum Slowly;* and George Lucas for *American Graffiti,* a rich film about the joys and frustrations of wasting time in a California town in the 1960's.

Canada. Among the major offerings of the New York Film Festival, probably the most prestigious of the world's great film festivals, was the French-language *Réjeanne Padovani,* a brilliantly calculated and bitter political melodrama by the Quebeçois Denys Arcand. The English-language *Wedding in White,* directed by William Freuet and shown earlier in 1973, won strong critical praise for its depiction of lower-middle class Canadian life.

Foreign Films. François Truffaut's *Day for Night* was probably the most solid critical success of 1973. A movie about making a movie, it sums up Truffaut's attitude toward his craft. Two major films by Italian directors were Marco Ferreri's *La Grande Bouffe,* a grotesque drama about suicide through overeating, and Francesco Rosi's *The Mattei Affair,* a subdued study of a powerful and mysterious political career. With Tomás Gutiérrez Alea's sophisticated and utterly nonpropagandistic *Memories of Underdevelopment,* Americans had their first look at the post-revolutionary Cuban cinema. From Hungary came Karoly Makk's *Love,* a beautiful film about love and fidelity which offered, in the work of Lily Darvas and Mari Töröcsik, possibly the two best women's performances of the year.

Three films by the Japanese Yasujiro Ozu, one of the supreme masters of world cinema, who died in 1963, opened in 1973. His *Late Autumn, An Autumn Afternoon,* and *The Flavor of Green Tea Over Rice* could be regarded as a small but real symbol of the continuity of experience that makes the movie going and the movie making of this year a part of every year that preceded it.

ROGER GREENSPUN, *Rutgers University*

LOUIS MÉLANÇON

Starring in the Metropolitan Opera's new production of Berlioz' Les Troyens were (l. to r.) Judith Blegen (Ascanius), Shirley Verrett (Dido), and Jon Vickers (Aeneas).

Music

As 1973 began, controversies surrounding the role of music in President Nixon's second inauguration festivities were seen as evidence that art and politics make uneasy bedfellows. This impression was contradicted later in the year when Congress, at Nixon's request, appropriated an unprecedented $106.6 million for the National Foundation for the Arts and Humanities for fiscal 1974, and when the President chose the Philadelphia Orchestra as one of his first "good-will ambassadors" to China.

Everywhere 1973 was a year of contradictions in musical life. A leading manufacturer of high-fidelity components gave New York's Philharmonic Hall (promptly renamed Avery Fisher Hall in his honor) an estimated $8 to $10 million gift in September. However, the Metropolitan Opera, facing its worst financial crisis in 40 years, trimmed back its schedule and cancelled one new production. And though musicians' pay was generally at an all-time high, strikes and threats of strikes by performers marred musical life in several cities.

The Inaugural Controversy. Composer Vincent Persichetti was commissioned to write a work for the official inauguration concert on January 19 to be given by the Philadelphia Orchestra at the Kennedy Center in Washington, D. C. Shortly before the performance, the Presidential Inaugural Committee rejected the work, based on President Lincoln's second inaugural address, claiming that there had been "no firm commitment" to use it. Persichetti and others told the press that the committee feared that references to war and peace in the text might embarrass the President. Some members of

the Philadelphia Orchestra announced that they would not play in the concert, but it took place as scheduled. The program included Tchaikovsky's *Overture 1812* and Copland's *Fanfare for the Common Man.* On the same evening, in Washington Cathedral, a Plea for Peace "Counterconcert" featured former Sen. Eugene McCarthy as speaker and Leonard Bernstein as conductor in Haydn's *Mass in Time of War.* Later in January, the St. Louis Symphony gave the world premiere of Persichetti's *Lincoln Address* with William Warfield as narrator.

Orchestras. The Philadelphia Orchestra and its conductor, Eugene Ormandy, became the first American ensemble to play in China since it came under Communist rule. The orchestra, which arrived in Peking in mid-September, played three programs in the Palace of Nationalities. Among the American works performed were Roy Harris' Third Symphony and Samuel Barber's *Adagio for Strings;* standards included Beethoven and Mozart. The Philadelphians also played the *Yellow River* Concerto for Piano and Orchestra, composed by the Central Orchestral Committee of the People's Republic of China. Yin Cheng-chung was soloist. The orchestra completed its immensely successful tour of China with two performances in Shanghai.

Elsewhere, U. S. orchestras presented a less cheerful picture. The New York Philharmonic was on strike from the end of September to the end of November. In Chicago, four weeks of the fall season were cancelled when the management refused to allow the Chicago Symphony musicians to play after their contract ran out. Agreement on a new contract

came in mid-October. Labor disputes interrupted the seasons of the Denver Symphony and the New York City Opera as well.

Nonetheless, orchestral music around the nation displayed a broad spectrum. In New York, the spring program of the Philharmonic saw the completion of Pierre Boulez's "retrospective" of the music of Haydn and Stravinsky, as well as the world premiere of Luciano Berio's Concerto for Two Pianos and Orchestra, with Boulez conducting and soloists Bruno Canino and Antonio Ballista. In June Boulez introduced a highly successful series of popular-priced "rug concerts," for which the orchestra seats in Philharmonic Hall were removed and replaced by rugs and cushions.

Also in New York, Frederic Waldman's Musica Aeterna Orchestra marked the 75th birthday of Vittorio Rieti in January with the world premiere of his Triple Concerto for Violin, Viola, and Piano. In February, the Symphony of the New World opened a celebration of Black History Week in Philharmonic Hall with a program including the New York premiere of Roger Dickerson's *Requiem for Louis,* in memory of Louis Armstrong, and the world premiere of *Many Thousand Gone* by Kermit Moore. Other spring events included the visits of the London Symphony Orchestra, under André Previn, and of the Chicago Symphony, under Sir Georg Solti, playing a tumultuously greeted concert performance of Act III of Wagner's *Götterdämmerung.*

The Leningrad Philharmonic, under Gennady Rozhdestvensky, sparked the autumn season with a series of four concerts of Soviet and Russian music. In October, the American Symphony Orchestra returned to New York, after a year's hiatus following the retirement of Leopold Stokowski, its founder and former director. The orchestra played in Carnegie Hall under its new music director, Kazuyoshi Akiyama.

Several significant premieres were held outside New York. In January the Pittsburgh Symphony performed Leonardo Balada's *Steel Symphony.* In April the Los Angeles Philharmonic played Arne Nordheim's *Greening for Orchestra,* written for and dedicated to the orchestra's conductor, Zubin Mehta. In May, as part of Tulsa's 75th anniversary and the Tulsa Philharmonic's 25th, music director Skitch Henderson led the orchestra in the world premiere of *Devil's Promenade,* by the Quapaw-Cherokee Indian composer Louis W. Ballard. The world premiere of Marvin David Levy's oratorio *Masada,* commissioned by the National Symphony as a salute to Israel's 25th anniversary, was held at Washington, D. C.'s Kennedy Center in October.

Orchestras other than the Philadelphia took far-flung tours during 1973. The National Arts Centre Orchestra of Canada, under Mario Bernardi, was heard in Moscow, Leningrad, Warsaw, Versailles, Rome, and several British cities. The Cleveland Orchestra, led by Lorin Maazel, toured New Zealand and Australia in the fall, playing at the newly opened Sydney Opera House.

Concert Life. The 85th birthday of the impresario Sol Hurok occasioned a gala at the Metropolitan Opera House in May. Among the artists who feted Hurok were Van Cliburn, Isaac Stern, Margot Fonteyn, and Ned Rorem. Two important birthdays were celebrated in Alice Tully Hall. John Cage's 60th birthday was marked by a retrospective of his music from 1938 to 1972 played by The Ensemble led by Dennis Russell Davies. For cellist

Gregor Piatigorsky's 70th birthday, several artists collaborated with him in a program devoted to the literature of the cello. In a gathering to toast the centenary of Enrico Caruso's birth, five tenors— Vladimir Atlantov of the Soviet Union, Alain Vanzo of France, and the Italians Luciano Pavarotti, Mario del Monaco, and Ferrucio Tagliavini—met in the Teatro San Carlo in Caruso's native city of Naples to sing Italian songs and arias.

Several world premieres of chamber works merited attention. In January, at Alice Tully Hall, the Chamber Music Society of Lincoln Center presented Pierre Boulez' "*. . . explosante/fixe . . .,*" a commissioned work for winds, strings, harp, vibraphone, and halaphone, the last an electronic instrument. Later in the month, the Juilliard Quartet gave the first performance of Elliott Carter's String Quartet No. 3, also in Alice Tully Hall. In September the Contemporary Chamber Ensemble led by Arthur Weisberg, with mezzo-soprano Jan DeGaetani, visited the Scottish National Orchestra's Musica Nova week in Glasgow to premiere Peter Maxwell Davies' *Stone Liturgy* for voice and orchestra, written for Miss DeGaetani.

Two musical comebacks of different kinds stirred worldwide attention in 1973. In Hamburg, Germany, in October, Maria Callas gave her first public performance in eight years. For this concert, the first in a tour of 40 cities, Miss Callas, accompanied by the pianist Ivor Newton, sang duets with Giuseppe di Stefano. Audience response was enthusiastic. Early in the year, England and the continent heard a new two-hour version of *Momente* by Karlheinz Stockhausen. Parts of this work, in progress for more than a decade, had been widely performed before. It now calls for solo soprano, chorus, eight brass instruments, three percussion groups, and two electronic organs.

Opera. In September, after some 14 years in construction, the Sydney (Australia) Opera House opened. The Australian Opera Company christened the house with Sergei Prokofiev's *War and Peace.* The Sydney Symphony Orchestra, with Birgit Nilsson as soloist, played a program conducted by Charles Mackerras.

An important reopening in 1973 was that of the Paris Opera, shut in January 1973 for three months of rehearsals and planning by its new manager, Rolf Liebermann. On March 31 the new regime presented Mozart's *Marriage of Figaro* in the Théâtre Louis XV at Versailles Palace. The work was led by Sir Georg Solti. The performance featured Gundula Janowitz, José Van Dam, and Frederica von Stade. The formal opening of the Opera in its home, the Palais Garnier, took place on April 5 with a new production of the Paris version of Gluck's opera *Orphée et Eurydice.* Nicolai Gedda and Jeannette Pilou sang the title roles. Among the other new productions of Liebermann's debut season were Arnold Schoenberg's *Moses und Aron* and Wagner's *Parsifal.*

In New York the Metropolitan Opera's mounting of *Les Troyens* by Berlioz in October marked Schuyler Chapin's first official season as general manager and Rafael Kubelik's first as the house's music director. It was the first time the epic work had been staged in New York. The production, directed by Nathaniel Merrill and designed by Peter Wexler, was a success. Kubelik conducted in his debut at the Metropolitan, and Jon Vickers portrayed Aeneas. At the first performance Shirley Verrett, substituting for an ailing Christa Ludwig

in the role of Dido, achieved the rare distinction of brilliantly singing both leading female roles in the long work—Cassandra and Dido. In later performances Miss Ludwig was a resplendent Dido. Earlier, the Met's spring season was distinguished chiefly by the debut of Opera at the Forum, an offshoot of the major company for the staging of more intimate and experimental works. At the Forum Theater in Lincoln Center, the "mini-Met" presented a bill of Purcell's *Dido and Aeneas* and Maurice Ohana's *Syllabaire pour Phèdre,* and the Virgil Thomson-Gertrude Stein *Four Saints in Three Acts.*

The New York City Opera offered two new productions in the spring: Alberto Ginastera's *Beatrix Cenci* and Hans Werner Henze's *The Young Lord.* In the fall, after a musicians' strike delayed the opening, the company got its three new productions on the boards in a single week: Gaetano Donizetti's *Anna Bolena* with Beverly Sills, Frederick Delius' *A Village Romeo and Juliet,* and Richard Strauss' *Ariadne auf Naxos.*

Sarah Caldwell's Opera Company of Boston had a fine spring season that included Donizetti's *Daughter of the Regiment,* Bedřich Smetana's *The Bartered Bride,* the Kurt Weill-Bertolt Brecht *Rise and Fall of the City of Mahagonny,* and Verdi's *Don Carlos* with the original French text written for the Paris Opera in 1867.

In Chicago in September, the International Congress of Anthropological and Ethnological Sciences convened at the Studebaker Theater for the world premiere of a commissioned work, Gian Carlo Menotti's *Tamu-Tamu.* The score combines Eastern and Western musical idioms to embody the Congress' theme of "one species, many cultures." At the Chicago Lyric Opera, the first staging of Donizetti's *Maria Stuarda* in that city opened a season that included new productions of Jules Massenet's *Manon* and Wagner's *Siegfried.* The San Francisco

Opera unveiled new stagings of Donizetti's *La Favorita* and Britten's *Peter Grimes,* and revived Strauss' *Die Fledermaus* with Joan Sutherland.

The New Orleans Opera House Association presented Puccini's *Madama Butterfly* in March and Verdi's *Il Trovatore* in May. The association's new home, the $8.5 million New Orleans Theater for the Performing Arts, opened in January with a performance of the Verdi Requiem by the New Orleans Philharmonic Symphony.

For its 25th anniversary, the Canadian Opera Company commissioned an opera from two Canadians, composer Charles Wilson and librettist Eugene Benson. The world premiere of their *Heloise and Abelard* was given in Toronto in September.

Sadler's Wells in London mounted two complete cycles of Wagner's *Ring* tetralogy in August, sung in Andrew Porter's praiseworthy English translations. The Stockholm Royal Opera marked its 200th anniversary with the world premiere of Lars Johan Werle's *Tintomara.* In Turin, 37 years after its destruction by fire, the Teatro Regio reopened in April with Verdi's *I Vespri Siciliani.*

Festivals. The Aldeburgh (England) Festival saw a new opera by Benjamin Britten, an adaptation of Thomas Mann's *Death in Venice,* with Peter Pears as the aging protagonist. At Glyndebourne, Raymond Leppard led highly praised performances of his realization of Monteverdi's *Il ritorno d'Ulisse in patria.* Also in the repertoire was Gottfried von Einem's *Visit of an Old Lady.* The Salzburg Festival was marked by a new production of Mozart's *Idomeneo.* As usual, Herbert von Karajan dominated the festival, this time by making one of his rare forays into Gustav Mahler's orchestral works, a performance of the Fifth Symphony with the Berlin Philharmonic.

At the Athens Festival, Cherubini's *Medea* was sung in the Herod Atticus amphitheater before an

Striking musicians of the New York Philharmonic picket outside Avery Fisher Hall.

THE NEW YORK TIMES

OTTO KLEMPERER (1885–1973)

UPI

Conductor Otto Klemperer, one of the great 20th century interpreters of the German musical repertory, notably of the works of Beethoven, Bruckner, and Mahler, died on July 6, 1973, in Zürich, Switzerland. A major figure on the music scene of pre-Hitler Germany, he was equally renowned later, in exile, as conductor of such ensembles as the Los Angeles Philharmonic Orchestra and the New Philharmonia Orchestra in London. Ranked in stature with Arturo Toscanini and Bruno Walter, Klemperer was noted for his solemn, cerebral approach, sense of orchestral balance, and ability to convey the essence of a composer's music.

The son of a Jewish businessman, Klemperer was born in Breslau, Germany (now Wrocław, Poland) on May 14, 1885. After studying music at the Hoch Conservatory in Frankfurt and the Stern Conservatory in Berlin, he made his debut as a conductor in Berlin at 20. In 1907 he was engaged by the Deutsches Theater in Prague on the recommendation of Gustav Mahler, and in 1910 he joined the Hamburg Opera Company. Between 1913 and 1927 he conducted in the opera houses of Barmen, Strasbourg, Cologne, and Wiesbaden. As director of the Kroll Opera in Berlin from 1927 to 1931, he drew both praise and criticism for his avant-garde productions of works by such modern composers as Stravinsky and Schoenberg.

In 1933, Klemperer, who had been conducting at the Berlin State Opera, fled Germany. He went to the United States where he served as director of the Los Angeles Philharmonic from 1933 to 1939, also sharing the direction of the New York Philharmonic with Toscanini for some years. He also helped reorganize the Pittsburgh Symphony. Although surgery for a brain tumor in 1939 left him partly paralyzed, he continued to win acclaim as a guest conductor in the United States, Europe, and elsewhere. He became music director of the Budapest State Opera in 1947 and remained in that post for three years. From 1959 to 1972 he was conductor of the New Philharmonia Orchestra in London.

HENRY S. SLOAN

audience of 5,000. Leonie Rysanek was superb in the title role. For Israel's 25th anniversary, the Israel Festival featured 21 groups making 100 appearances in 12 locations around the country. Participants included Leonard Bernstein, Zubin Mehta, Isaac Stern, and the late Pablo Casals.

Closer to home, the Cincinnati May Festival marked its centennial with a community-singing spree by 3,000 persons in the Music Hall, an homage to the traditional Cincinnati *Sängerfest,* forerunner of the May Festival. In the professional concerts that were part of the celebration, Cincinnatians hailed fellow native James Levine, the Metropolitan Opera's principal conductor. The Canadian Broadcasting Corporation's Toronto Summer Festival offered 15 free concerts built around 20th century music, with world premieres of works by the Canadian composers Walter Buczynski, Serge Garant, Jean Papineau-Couture, and Murray Schafer.

Awards and Appointments. Guido Ajmone-Marsan, 26, of Chevy Chase, Md., won the first Sir Georg Solti conducting competition in the spring. He led the Chicago Symphony in April just 30 days after his London Symphony debut as winner of the first Ruppert Foundation conducting contest in England. August Everding, the German stage director, was appointed intendant of the Hamburg Opera, replacing Rolf Liebermann. Richard Bonynge was named artistic director of the Vancouver Opera Association, and Pierre Hétu was chosen music director of the Edmonton (Alberta) Symphony Orchestra. Rafael Frühbeck de Burgos will become music director of the Montreal Symphony effective with the 1975–76 season. John Ludwig, manager of the Minnesota Opera Company, was appointed general director of the Wolf Trap Foundation for the Performing Arts. Pierre Boulez announced that he would become director of the Centre des Études de la Musique Contemporaine in Paris in March 1975.

POPULAR MUSIC

With new jazz clubs sprouting up in New York's Greenwich Village and Upper West Side, George Wein, founder and promoter of the Newport Jazz Festival in New York, was encouraged to spread his 10-day fete in July far and wide across the city. Heard in the Wollman Amphitheater in Central Park were Gerry Mulligan's Age of Steam band, the Gato Barbieri octet, Marian McPartland, Max Roach, Charlie Mingus, Stan Getz, and the Modern Jazz Quartet. The Roseland Ballroom was the scene of "A Thirties Ball," featuring the bands of Woody Herman, Duke Ellington, and Count Basie. The Preservation Hall Jazz Band played afloat for Hudson River boatrides.

The Apollo Theater in Harlem heard Howard McGee, Horace Arnold, and Herbie Mann. On July 4, which would have been the late Louis Armstrong's 73d birthday, 100 participating musicians went to the Singer Bowl in Flushing Meadow, Queens, for a concert to rename it the Louis Armstrong Memorial Stadium. The festival ended with a joint concert by Ray Charles, Ellington, and Aretha Franklin at the Nassau Coliseum. Among the Newport artists appearing at Carnegie Hall, Philharmonic Hall, and Radio City Music Hall were Ella Fitzgerald, Mary Lou Williams, Ellington with the Swedish soprano Alice Babs, Sonny Rollins, and the Benny Goodman Quintet.

In May, the resurgence of the solo rock performer was symbolized by Carole King's New York concert, which drew 70,000 to Central Park.

Memories of Woodstock 1969 were stirred by the success in midsummer of the Watkins Glen (N. Y.) Rock Festival, attended by a record 600,000 and musically enlivened by The Grateful Dead, The Band, and the Allman Brothers.

Country music showed the greatest signs of renewed vitality. In sophisticated New York City, radio station WHN went over to an all-county format, and Tammy Wynette and George Jones became the first country act ever to play Philharmonic Hall.

Another trend of the times, the wave of nostalgia currently sweeping the music business, brought Josephine Baker, the U. S.-born black chanteuse whose European career in the 1920's and 1930's is legendary, back to these shores. She appeared at Carnegie Hall and at the Victoria Theater in Harlem.

ROBERT S. CLARK
Contributing Editor, "Stereo Review"

NARCOTICS. See DRUG ADDICTION AND ABUSE.

NEBRASKA

In 1973, local attention in Nebraska centered on a busy legislative session, reduction of income taxes, controversy in education and urban affairs, excellent farm crops and prices, and football.

Legislature and Government. The Nebraska unicameral Legislature continued clashes from the previous session with Gov. J. James Exon (D). Of 15 vetoes, nine were sustained.

The death penalty was reinstated and a strict abortion law was passed. Newsmen received a strong shield law, and Nebraska's ratification of the proposed federal Equal Rights Amendment was rescinded. All cities will have fluoridation of water by January 1975 unless their voters reject it. Repeal of the so-called "Wyoming clause" prepared the way for more vigorous environmental controls.

State school aid of $20 million from federal revenue-sharing funds was provided on a one-time basis. The State Patrol's drug-abuse unit was strengthened. Noteworthy controversies erupted over election of Omaha city councilmen by district, state acquisition of the property of now-defunct Hiram Scott College in western Nebraska, and state school aid. The session reflected remarkable adherence to the governor's budget recommendations.

Taxes. Governor Exon, for the third straight year, prevented the Legislature from increasing state aid to public schools and from shifting school support from real estate to income and sales taxes. The Legislature reduced the 1973 personal income tax from 15% to 13% of federal liability.

NEBRASKA • Information Highlights

Area: 77,227 square miles (200,018 sq km).
Population (1972 est.): 1,525,000. *Density:* 19 per sq mi.
Chief Cities (1970 census): Lincoln, the capital, 149,518; Omaha, 346,929; Grand Island, 31,269; Hastings, 23,580; Fremont, 22,962; Bellevue, 19,449; North Platte, 19,447.
Government (1973): *Chief Officers*—governor, J. James Exon (D); lt. gov., Frank Marsh (R); secy. of state, Allen J. Beerman (R); atty. gen., Clarence A. H. Meyer (R); treas., Wayne R. Swanson (R); commissioner of education, Cecil E. Stanley; chief justice, Paul W. White. *Legislature* (unicameral)—49 members (nonpartisan).
Education (1972–73): *Enrollment*—public elementary schools, 183,000 pupils, 9,300 teachers; public secondary schools, 145,000 pupils, 8,760 teachers; nonpublic schools, 44,500 pupils, 1,960 teachers; colleges and universities, 63,161 students. *Public school expenditures,* $228,000,000 ($735 per pupil). *Average teacher's salary,* $9,080.
State Finances (fiscal year 1971): *Revenues,* $550,416,000 (2.5% general sales tax and gross receipts taxes, $88,953,000; motor fuel tax, $70,293,000; federal funds, $144,330,000). *Expenditures,* $519,028,000 (education, $185,393,000; health, welfare, and safety, $84,233,000; highways, $126,760,000). *State debt,* $70,985,000 (June 30, 1971).
Personal Income (1972): $6,621,000,000; per capita, $4,341.
Public Assistance (1972): $80,237,000. *Average monthly payments* (Dec. 1972)—old-age assistance, $64.11; aid to families with dependent children, $148.89.
Labor Force: *Nonagricultural wage and salary earners* (July 1973), 530,800. *Average annual employment* (1972)—manufacturing, 86,600; trade, 129,600; government, 108,600; services, 90,900. *Insured unemployed* (Sept. 1973)—4,100 (1.0%).
Manufacturing (1971): *Value added by manufacture,* $1,594,100,000. Food and kindred products, $565,300,000; nonelectrical machinery, $189,900,000; electrical equipment and supplies, $139,900,000; fabricated metal products, $99,200,000; chemicals and allied products, $82,900,000; transportation equipment, $79,300,000.
Agriculture (1972): *Cash farm income,* $2,913,467,000 (livestock, $1,915,112,000; crops, $765,031,000; government payments, $233,324,000). *Chief crops* (in order of value, 1972)—Corn (ranks 4th among the states), hay, wheat, grain sorghum (ranks 3d).
Mining (1972): *Production value,* $74,551,000 (ranks 40th among the states). *Chief minerals*—Petroleum, $29,693,000; sand and gravel, $14,165,000; stone, $9,724,000.
Transportation: *Roads* (1972), 98,765 miles (158,943 km); *motor vehicles* (1972), 1,032,693; *railroads* (1972), 5,420 miles (8,722 km); *public airports* (1972), 90.
Communications: *Telephones* (1973), 974,800; *television stations* (1971), 14; *radio stations* (1971), 63; *newspapers* (1973), 19 (daily circulation, 495,000).

Education. The federal Department of Justice ordered the Omaha public schools to desegregate, and litigation began. The boundaries for a state system of community-technical colleges were set. University of Nebraska (Lincoln) tuition was raised, and state college enrollment declined.

Urban Affairs—Omaha. Omaha's voters elected Edward Zorinsky mayor and defeated all but one of the incumbent councilmen. Attempts in the Legislature to dictate election of councilmen by district and to force a metropolitan school merger failed.

Agriculture and Industry. Agricultural production and prices were of major interest to both Nebraska producers and consumers in 1973. Inclement weather delayed completion of the 1972 corn and grain sorghum harvest until April 1973. The 1973 wheat and grain sorghum crops were excellent, although not record-breaking. In spite of a late summer drought and an extremely wet early fall, corn and soybeans set new production records based on both fine yields and increased acreage. Production records were accompanied by record, and rapidly fluctuating, prices for both grain and livestock. By summer, corn, wheat, soybeans, and grain sorghum prices, pushed by worldwide demand, had doubled as compared with a year earlier. Likewise, cattle and hog prices increased by about 50% to all-time high levels. In the fall, prices of both grain and livestock, still fluctuating widely, declined somewhat.

The Fort Calhoun nuclear power plant began operation despite ecologically motivated opposition, and the Cooper Nuclear Station at Brownville neared completion.

Football. Although the University of Nebraska's Cornhusker football team was not as highly rated as it had been in the 1972 season, statewide interest in the team remained high. Led by Heisman Trophy winner Johnny Rodgers, the Cornhuskers had opened the year by defeating Notre Dame in the Orange Bowl. The year ended with the team being invited to play Texas in the Cotton Bowl.

ORVILLE H. ZABEL, *Creighton University*

NETHERLANDS

In 1973, the Netherlands experienced the most protracted ministerial crisis in its history. The economy, though marked by unprecedented prosperity, suffered from a high unemployment rate and severe inflationary pressures. Late in the year there was a major oil crisis as the Arabs cut off oil deliveries to the Netherlands in retaliation for its pro-Israeli stance in the 1973 Arab-Israeli war.

Economy. Domestic and foreign demand for goods remained strong in 1973. In June 1972, imports exceeded exports by 1%; in June 1973, exports exceeded imports by 7%. This enabled the government, in an anti-inflationary measure, to revalue the guilder upward by 5% on September 15. On the negative side, domestic and foreign investment slackened to a low level, and unemployment reached 3.7%. In the first half of 1973, living costs rose 5%.

Politics. The protracted political crisis had begun on July 20, 1972, when the Barend W. Biesheuvel ministry fell. After parliamentary elections in November 1972, the Labor party, the largest in Parliament, emerged with a gain of four seats in the Second Chamber. However, this was still less than a third of the total membership of that body. An attempt was made to form another coalition min-

——— **NETHERLANDS · Information Highlights** ———

Official Name: Kingdom of the Netherlands.
Location: Northwestern Europe.
Area: 15,770 square miles (40,844 sq km).
Population (1973 est.): 13,400,000. *Density,* 837 per square mile (323 per sq km).
Chief Cities (1971 est.): Amsterdam, the capital, 820,406; Rotterdam, 679,000; The Hague, 537,600.
Government: *Head of state,* Juliana, queen (acceded Sept. 1948). *Head of government,* Joop den Uyl, prime minister (took office May 1973). *Legislature*—Staten-Generaal: First Chamber and Second Chamber. *Major political parties*—Catholic People's party; Labor party; People's Party for Freedom and Democracy; Christian Historical Union; Anti-Revolutionary party.
Language: Dutch (official).
Education: *Expenditure* (1968), 25.1% of total public expenditure. *School enrollment* (1969)—primary, 1,450,647; secondary, 1,117,020; technical/vocational, 536,460; university/higher, 211,513.
Monetary Unit: Guilder (2.535 guilders equal U. S.$1, Sept. 1973).
Gross National Product (1972 est.): $40,800,000,000.
Economic Indexes: *Industrial production* (1972), 203 (1963= 100); *agricultural production* (1971), 128 (1963=100); *consumer price index* (1972), 164 (1963=100).
Manufacturing (major products): Metals, processed foods, petroleum products, chemicals, petrochemicals, textiles, machinery and equipment, electrical appliances, clothing.
Major Agricultural Products: Sugar beets, potatoes, wheat, barley, rye, oats, flax, dairy products.
Major Minerals: Natural gas, petroleum, coal, salt.
Foreign Trade (1972): *Exports,* $16,784,000,000; *Imports,* $16,918,000,000. *Chief trading partners* (1971)—West Germany (toook 34% of exports, supplied 32% of imports); Belgium-Luxembourg (14%—15%); France (10%—9%).
Tourism: Receipts (1971), $598,000,000.
Transportation: *Motor vehicles* (1971), 3,140,000 (automobiles, 2,800,000); *railroads* (1971), 1,956 miles (3,148 km); *merchant fleet* (1972), 4,972,000 gross registered tons; *major national airline,* KLM Royal Dutch Airlines.
Communications: *Telephones* (1972), 3,720,817; *newspapers* (1971), 93 (daily circulation, 4,100,000).

istry. After the failure of Jaap Burger, a Socialist Laborite, to form a coalition, Queen Juliana asked the leaders of the Labor and Anti-Revolutionary parties to cooperate in seeking a solution to the deadlock. On May 11, 1973, a new coalition ministry headed by the Laborite Joop den Uyl took office, ending a 163-day crisis.

Joop den Uyl, the first Labor prime minister in 15 years, headed a center-left cabinet—a coalition of Democrats 66, the Political Radicals, and the Labor party as the core plus the Catholic Peoples party and the Anti-Revolutionary, a Protestant center party. The core parties could muster a total of only 56 votes in the 150-member Second Chamber, but with the votes of their allies the coalition commanded 97—a majority of 22. The 16-member cabinet, including the prime minister, was composed of 7 Laborites, 2 Radicals, 1 Democrat, 4 Catholics, and 2 Anti-Revolutionaries. In a speech before Parliament on May 28, den Uyl declared that his government's objective was to "reduce inequality in income, ownership, power and knowledge." The ministry pledged more democracy in industry, government, and education, and promised to reduce military expenditures.

The program was further elaborated at the opening of Parliament on September 18 in the speech from the throne. Reduction in income differentials would be effected by means of the budget; expenditures on social security would be increased; the organization of the judiciary would be completely revised; experiments would be conducted with a view to educational reforms; university education would be restructured; further measures would be taken to control environmental pollution and to combat energy waste; the wealth tax would be raised; and inheritance tax rates would be increased.

On September 5 the Dutch nation celebrated the 25th anniversary of Queen Juliana's accession to the throne.

Foreign Relations. The den Uyl government promised to work for a European community which is more concerned with the well-being of its people, equipped with greater powers and with a truly democratic structure, and pursuing an open policy designed to further the interests of the "third world." It would strive for a détente between East and West. In 1974 a start would be made through the liberation movements to extend humanitarian and development aid to the peoples of colonial territories in Africa.

Oil Crisis. Charging that The Hague supported Israel in the 1973 war, the Arab oil-producing countries imposed an embargo on all oil shipments to the Netherlands in October. (The Netherlands annually imports 139 million barrels of crude oil and exports 116 million barrels of crude and refined products to its neighbors.) To combat the crisis, the government banned nonessential automobile driving and pleasure motorboating on Sundays, and appealed to other Common Market nations to share their oil supplies if necessary. In addition, fear of mounting economic problems brought on by the fuel crisis led to a sharp drop in the value of the guilder in December, and Van Doorn Automobil Fabriek, the principal Dutch auto manufacturer, announced a substantial decrease in sales.

AMRY VANDENBOSCH
University of Kentucky

NEVADA

In 1973 the biggest political news in Nevada was the announcement by Alan Bible, a United States senator since 1955, that he would not be a candidate for reelection in 1974. Gov. Mike O'Callaghan and former governors Paul Laxalt and Grant Sawyer were seriously considering becoming candidates for the position.

Legislation. For the first time in over 35 years, the party of a Nevada governor had a comfortable majority in both houses of the Legislature. Thus, Democratic Governor O'Callaghan's legislative program fared even better than it had in the previous session.

The governor and the 1973 Legislature were aided in meeting the needs of the state by a substantial budget surplus, as the tax revenues for the 1971–1973 biennium greatly exceeded the original estimates. Among the measures enacted by the Legislature were a new death penalty act, a law requiring the registration of lobbyists, and the creation of a Consumers Affairs Division. A liberalized abortion law was also adopted. Nevada became the first state to legalize the practice of acupuncture on a broad scale, although the state board set up to supervise the practice did not issue any licenses until the end of 1973.

The principal change in the election laws was the enactment of a presidential primary system. Nevada's secretary of state will determine which names shall go on the ballot, and each candidate who receives more than 5% of the votes cast in the primary will receive a proportionate number of delegate votes. After emotional hearings, the Legislature decisively refused to ratify the proposed Equal Rights Amendment to the U. S. Constitution.

Economy. The state continued to prosper economically, with gambling and sales tax revenues increasing by almost 12% and 18%, respectively, over the previous fiscal year. Large hotel-casinos

NEVADA • Information Highlights

Area: 110,540 square miles (286,299 sq km).
Population (1972 est.): 527,000. *Density:* 4.6 per sq mi.
Chief Cities (1970 census): Carson City, the capital, 15,468; Las Vegas, 125,787; Reno, 72,863; North Las Vegas, 32,-216; Sparks, 24,187; Henderson, 16,395.
Government (1973): *Chief Officers*—governor, Mike O'Callaghan (D); lt. gov., Harry M. Reid (D); secy. of state, William D. Swackhamer (D); atty. gen., Robert List (R); treas., Michael Mirabelli (D); supt. of public instruction, Kenneth H. Hansen; chief justice, Gordon R. Thompson. *Legislature*—Senate, 20 members (14 Democrats, 6 Republicans); Assembly, 40 members (25 D, 15 R).
Education (1972–73): *Enrollment*—public elementary schools, 72,756 pupils, 2,906 teachers; public secondary schools, 58,917 pupils, 2,505 teachers; nonpublic schools, 2,900 pupils, 90 teachers; colleges and universities, 14,353 students. *Public school expenditures*, $117,500,000 ($971 per pupil). *Average teacher's salary*, $11,472.
State Finances (fiscal year 1971): *Revenues,* $323,588,000 (3% general sales tax and gross receipts taxes, $65,-720,000; motor fuel tax, $26,654,000; federal funds, $69,-906,000). *Expenditures,* $255,971,000 (education, $91,-195,000; health, welfare, and safety, $30,286,000; highways, $63,110,000). *State debt,* $42,561,000 (June 30, 1971).
Personal Income (1972): $2,748,000,000; per capita, $5,215.
Public Assistance (1972): $20,251,000. *Average monthly payments* (Dec. 1972)—old-age assistance, $75.88; aid to families with dependent children, $115.39.
Labor Force: *Nonagricultural wage and salary earners* (July 1973), 241,900. *Average annual employment* (1972)—manufacturing, 9,300; trade, 42,400; government, 39,700; services, 87,700. *Insured unemployed* (Sept. 1973)—6,400 (3.5%).
Manufacturing (1971): Value added by manufacture, $145,-900,000. Chemicals and allied products, $29,700,000; stone, clay, and glass products, $28,100,000; food and kindred products, $19,400,000; printing and publishing, $17,500,000; fabricated metal products, $6,300,000; nonelectrical machinery, $3,500,000.
Agriculture (1972): *Cash farm income,* $113,139,000 (livestock, $94,313,000; crops, $16,207,000; government payments, $2,619,000). *Chief crops* (in order of value, 1971)—Hay, alfalfa seed, barley, wheat.
Mining (1972): Production value, $184,800,000 (ranks 30th among the states). *Chief minerals*—Copper, $108,201,000; gold, $24,013,000; sand and gravel, $13,447,000; diatomite, value not available.
Transportation: *Roads* (1972), 49,702 miles (79,985 km); *motor vehicles* (1972), 372,730; *railroads* (1972), 1,574 miles (2,533 km); *public airports* (1972), 52.
Communications: *Telephones* (1973), 397,400; *television stations* (1971), 7; *radio stations* (1971), 29; *newspapers* (1973), 7 (daily circulation, 153,000).

continued to be built in Las Vegas, and the Reno area enjoyed an unprecedented construction boom with several large hotel-casinos completed and others on the way.

Education. The Legislature passed an act prohibiting the state Board of Education from setting integration rules for local school districts, thus voiding the policy which the board had promulgated a few months before. The Legislature also raised school-support funds again, at the behest of the governor; provided substantial budget increases for the Clark county and Western Nevada community colleges; and passed a resolution calling for the development of a law school in Las Vegas.

DON W. DRIGGS, *University of Nevada*

NEW BRUNSWICK

The year 1973 will be remembered in New Brunswick as the year of the floods, when the St. John River went on a rampage, causing millions of dollars of damage. Important legal agreements were signed with the federal minister of justice in Ottawa, and the province was presented with a new set of electoral boundaries.

Flood Disaster. At the end of April, the St. John River, swollen by rain and melted snow, overflowed its banks and forced the evacuation of 500 persons from homes along a 90-mile stretch of river. The flood waters poured through Fredericton, and the legislature was temporarily closed because of a flooded basement in the parliament building.

The bill for damages due to the flooding of the St. John, and to a lesser extent the Campbellton and St. Croix rivers and Grand Lake, was around $7 million. The federal government compensated New Brunswick for much of the loss, including payments to the victims for damaged homes, property, and small family businesses.

Politics. In the Throne speech opening the spring session of the legislature, Premier Richard Hatfield's Conservative government pledged a "positive, aggressive approach" to development of the province's vital forest-based industries. The government recognized the creation of jobs as its most important task.

In a report on May 9, the New Brunswick electoral boundaries commission proposed important changes in the province's electoral map. The realignment calls for the York-Sunbury constituency to become Carleton York, Carleton-Charlotte to be Charlotte-Saint John, and Saint John-Lancaster to be Saint John.

Federal-Provincial Legal Accords. On January 11, Federal Justice Minister Otto Lang and his New Brunswick counterpart, John Baxter, signed two agreements that cover legal aid for persons accused of wrongdoing and compensation for crime victims. The accords, similar to those previously signed by Ottawa with Quebec and British Columbia, obligate the federal government to meet part of the cost of programs instituted by New Brunswick.

JOHN BEST
Chief, "Canada World News," Ottawa

NEW BRUNSWICK • Information Highlights

Area: 27,985 square miles (72,481 sq km).
Population (1972 est.): 646,000.
Chief Cities (1971 census): Fredericton, the capital (24,254); St. John (89,039); Moncton (47,891).
Government: *Chief Officers* (1973)—lt. gov., Hedard J. Robichaud; premier, Richard B. Hatfield (Progressive Conservative); prov. secy., Omer Leger (P. C.); min. of justice, John B. M. Baxter (P. C.); min. of finance, Jean-Maurice Simard (P. C.); min. of educ., J. Lorne McGuigan (P. C.); chief justice, C. J. A. Hughes. *Legislature*—Legislative Assembly: 58 members (32 Progressive Conservative, 25 Liberal, 1 Independent Conservative).
Education: *School enrollment* (1969–70)—public elementary and secondary, 173,642 pupils (7,822 teachers); private schools, 353 pupils (40 teachers); Indian (federal) schools, 620 pupils (26 teachers); college and university, 9,608 students. *Public school expenditures* (1970)—$108,834,-000; average teacher's salary (1970 est.), $6,404.
Public Finance (fiscal year 1974 est.): *Revenues,* $641,900,-000. *Expenditures* $674,200,000 (education, $140,100,000; health and social welfare, $207,500,000; highways, $69,-900,000.
Personal Income (1971 est.): $1,568,000,000; average annual income per person, $2,469.
Social Welfare (fiscal year 1973 est.): $51,800,000 (dependents and unemployed, $39,000,000).
Manufacturing (1969): Value added by manufacture, $269,-848,000 (food and beverages, $83,072,000; paper and allied industries, $67,200,000; wood industries, $26,049,000; electrical products, $15,023,000; fabricated metals, $12,-824,000; transportation equipment, $15,997,000).
Agriculture (1972 est.): *Cash farm income* (exclusive of government payments), $64,151,000 (livestock and products), $36,807,000; crops, $23,866,000). *Chief crops* (cash receipts)—potatoes, $18,755,000 (ranks 1st among the provinces); vegetables, $1,698,000; fruits, $1,586,000.
Mining (1972 est.): *Production* value, $132,194,000. *Chief minerals*—zinc, $79,056,000 (ranks 1st among the provinces); lead, $16,003,000; copper, $9,583,000; silver, $9,-013,000; cement, $4,232,000; coal, $3,759,000.
Forest Products (1972): Lumber, 313,600,000 board feet.
Fisheries (1972): *Commercial catch,* 325,786,000 pounds ($18,928,000). *Leading species*—lobster, 5,384,000 pounds ($5,122,000); herring, 214,632,000 pounds ($4,732,000); tuna, 8,387,000 pounds ($2,245,000); redfish, 28,616,000 pounds ($1,112,000).
Transportation: *Roads* (1970), 15,260 miles (24,558 km); *motor vehicles* (1970), 201,274; *railroads* (1971), 1,665 track miles (2,697 km); *licensed airports* (1971 est.), 13.
Communications: *Telephones* (1970), 225,852; *television stations* (1972), 11; *radio stations* (1972), 13; *daily newspapers* (1972), 6.

(All monetary figures given in Canadian dollars.)

—— NEW HAMPSHIRE • Information Highlights ——

Area: 9,304 square miles (34,097 sq km).
Population (1972 est.): 771,000. *Density:* 84 per sq mi.
Chief Cities (1970 census): Concord, the capital, 30,022; Manchester, 87,754; Nashua, 55,820; Portsmouth, 25,717.
Government (1973): *Chief Officers*—governor, Meldrim Thomson, Jr. (R); secy. of state, Robert L. Stark (R); atty. gen., Warren B. Rudman (R); treas., Robert W. Flanders; commissioner of education, Newell J. Paire; chief justice, Frank R. Keniston. *General Court*—Senate, 24 members (14 Republicans, 10 Democrats); House of Representatives, 400 members (261 R, 138 D, 1 vacancy).
Education (1972–73): *Enrollment*—public elementary schools, 96,788 pupils, 4,137 teachers; public secondary schools, 71,265 pupils, 3,385 teachers; nonpublic schools, 27,600 pupils, 1,380 teachers; colleges and universities, 27,620 students. *Public school expenditures,* $138,463,000 ($892 per pupil). *Average teacher's salary,* $9,313.
State Finances (fiscal year 1971): *Revenues,* $338,479,000 (total sales tax and gross receipts taxes, $68,857,000; motor fuel tax, $25,177,000; federal funds, $68,705,000). *Expenditures,* $276,519,000 (education, $86,881,000; health, welfare, and safety, $44,224,000; highways, $68,390,000). *State debt,* $179,465,000 (June 30, 1971).
Personal Income (1972): $3,155,000,000; per capita, $4,092.
Public Assistance (1972): $39,920,000. *Average monthly payments* (Dec. 1972)—old-age assistance, $171.82; aid to families with dependent children, $223.15.
Labor Force: *Nonagricultural wage and salary earners* (July 1973), 300,400. *Average annual employment* (1972)—manufacturing, 90,700; trade, 55,100; government, 41,100; services, 48,800. *Insured unemployed* (Sept. 1973)—2,700 (1.1%).
Manufacturing (1971): Value added by manufacture, $1,088,700,000. Electrical equipment and supplies, $198,500,000; nonelectrical machinery, $141,900,000; paper and allied products, $114,000,000; leather and leather products, $110,200,000; food and kindred products, $78,700,000.
Agriculture (1972): *Cash farm income,* $58,493,000 (livestock, $42,829,000; crops, $15,203,000; government payments, $461,000). *Chief crops* (in order of value, 1971)—Hay, apples, sweet corn, potatoes.
Mining (1972): Production value, $10,555,000 (ranks 48th among the states). *Chief minerals*—Sand and gravel, $7,048,000; stone, $3,427,000; gem stones, $42,000.
Transportation: *Roads* (1972), 14,926 miles (24,020 km); *motor vehicles* (1972), 375,436; *railroads* (1972), 817 miles (1,315 km); *public airports* (1972), 16.
Communications: *Telephones* (1973), 486,200; *television stations* (1971), 3; *radio stations* (1971), 39; *newspapers* (1973), 9 (daily circulation, 174,000).

NEW HAMPSHIRE

The year 1973 was marked in New Hampshire by an unproductive session of the legislature, which made a special session early in 1974 inevitable, and by controversies over some of the actions of the new Republican governor, Meldrim Thomson, Jr.

Legislature. Friction arose between the legislature and the governor over the state budgets. An operating budget of $212.8 million for the biennium was approved after the governor had threatened to veto a figure $10 million higher. He killed the $35 million capital budget by a pocket veto. A $4.7 million appropriation provided pay raises for the state's 6,500 employees, but state aid to the university system was cut by $850,000. No effort was made to broaden the state's tax base in the wake of the governor's threat to veto a state sales or income tax.

A bill to form a resources agency to preserve the environment died, but an "Open Space Act" became law, providing that some types of open space land be assessed at the value of their present use rather than as a potential site for development. A "land use change tax" of 10% would be imposed when the use of the land was changed.

To protect consumers, two new laws required public display of prices of more than 200 prescription drugs, and allowed a patient to ask a physician or pharmacist for the generic name of any brand name drug. Other measures gave full legal rights to 18-year-olds, created a state housing authority, revised the structure of the state tax commission, and eliminated superior court trials for offenses not punishable by imprisonment.

After the session's end, Governor Thomson pocket-vetoed a number of bills, including no-fault automobile insurance and partial property tax exemption for the elderly.

Governor. Thomson was frequently accused by critics of overstepping his legal authority to extend his personal power. A search by his agents of confidential business tax records was ruled illegal by the state supreme court. A suit challenging some of his personnel policies was filed by legislators and the state employees' association.

Education. The state board of education applied for a $3 million federal grant to test a controversial voucher method of financing education in selected school districts. If approved by the federal government, the plan would permit parents to send children to any public school in their district or to any private nonsectarian school in the state. Parents would receive vouchers paying the full cost of the public school or applying to the cost of the private school. Foes of the plan hinted at legal action to block it.

Boundary Dispute. A dispute over the offshore boundary between New Hampshire and Maine, affecting lobster-fishing rights, went to the U. S. Supreme Court. A new law of 1973, which Thomson said would aid the state's case, claimed state jurisdiction of a sector of ocean as long as the New Hampshire coastline and extending 200 nautical miles out to sea. (See also MAINE.)

RICHARD G. WEST
Former Senior Editor, "Encyclopedia Americana"

NEW JERSEY

In 1973 attention in New Jersey was focused on gubernatorial politics leading to the November election. Mounting evidence of corruption in the administration of Gov. William Cahill, a Republican, contributed to a landslide victory for the Democrats.

Cahill and Corruption. Suspicions that Governor Cahill's attorney general, George F. Kugler, Jr., had been involved in a cover-up of former Secretary of State Paul Sherwin's acceptance of kickbacks were laid to rest when Kugler was cleared by a state commission. Cahill announced his candidacy for reelection in February, and in the early phases of the campaign it was assumed that he would win. But his campaign was soon damaged by fresh charges of corruption, involving state Treasurer Joseph McCrane, Jr. By the end of May, McCrane had been indicted by state and federal grand juries. The state indictment charged bribery and misconduct designed to use state funds to aid his brother's brokerage business. The federal charges cited a conspiracy to defraud on federal income tax forms by allowing businessmen to write off campaign contributions to Cahill in 1969 as business expenses.

Campaigns and Elections. The mounting evidence of corruption in Cahill's administration brought a strong challenge to his candidacy from within the Republican party and unified the previously divided Democrats. The Republican challenge came from U. S. Rep. Charles W. Sandman, Jr., the chief spokesman for the party's right wing. Sandman attacked corruption and geared his appeal to those he called the "peripheral urban ethnics"—white blue-collar workers living near decaying city centers. His hiring F. Clifton White, Jr., a Goldwater campaign veteran of 1964, as his campaign manager gave his conservative bid national importance.

Area: 7,836 square miles (20,295 sq km).

Population (1972 est.): 7,367,000. *Density:* 969 per sq mi.

Chief Cities (1970 census): Trenton, the capital, 104,638; Newark, 382,288; Jersey City, 260,545; Paterson, 144,824; Elizabeth, 112,654; Camden, 102,551; Clifton, 82,437.

Government (1973): *Chief Officers*—governor, William T. Cahill (R); (acting) secy. of state, Robert M. Falcey (D); atty. gen., George F. Kugler (R); treas., William E. Marfuggi; (acting) commissioner of education, Edward W. Kilpatrick III; chief justice, Richard J. Hughes. *Legislature*—Senate, 40 members (22 Republicans, 16 Democrats, 2 vacancies); General Assembly, 80 members (40 D, 38 R, 1 Independent, 1 vacancy).

Education (1972–73): *Enrollment*—public elementary schools, 991,000 pupils, 41,400 teachers; public secondary schools, 523,000 pupils, 35,600 teachers; nonpublic schools, 260,200 pupils, 10,040 teachers; colleges and universities, 228,313 students. *Public school expenditures,* $1,834,000,000 ($1,352 per pupil). *Average teacher's salary,* $11,750.

State Finances (fiscal year 1971): *Revenues,* $3,104,920,000 (5% general sales tax and gross receipts taxes, $521,686,000); motor fuel tax, $211,721,000; federal funds, $678,053,000). *Expenditures,* $2,639,982,000 (education $812,489,000; health, welfare, and safety, $629,214,000; highways, $469,965,000). *State debt,* $2,038,942,000 (June 30, 1971).

Personal Income (1972): $37,762,000,000; per capita, $5,126.

Public Assistance (1972): $640,594,000. *Average monthly payments* (Dec. 1972)—old-age assistance, $78.46; aid to families with dependent children, $257.09.

Labor Force: *Nonagricultural wage and salary earners* (July 1973), 2,750,300. *Average annual employment* (1972)—manufacturing, 814,800; trade, 578,100; government, 408,200; services, 435,000. *Insured unemployed* (Sept. 1973)—82,300 (3.7%).

Manufacturing (1971): *Value added by manufacture,* $14,393,800,000; chemicals and allied products, $3,487,000,000; electrical equipment and supplies, $1,563,200,000.

Agriculture (1972): *Cash farm income,* $229,710,000 (livestock, $90,194,000; crops, $135,840,000; government payments, $3,676,000). *Chief crops* (in order of value, 1971)—Tomatoes, hay, peaches, potatoes.

Mining (1972): *Production value,* $106,190,000 (ranks 35th among the states). *Chief minerals*—Stone, $41,096,000; sand and gravel, $40,958,000; zinc, $13,884,000.

Fisheries (1972): *Commercial catch,* 190,517,000 pounds ($14,423,000). *Leading species by value,* Clams, $4,409,000; menhaden, $2,262,000; lobsters, $1,828,000.

Transportation: *Roads* (1972), 32,237 miles (51,879 km); *motor vehicles* (1972), 3,737,308; *railroads* (1972), 1,742 miles (2,803 km); *public airports* (1972), 27.

Communications: *Telephones* (1973), 5,208,600; *television stations* (1971), 4; *radio stations* (1971), 61; *newspapers* (1973), 31 (daily circulation, 1,712,000).

GOVERNOR-ELECT Brendan Byrne (left), a Democrat, shakes hands with outgoing Gov. William Cahill, a Republican, who did not survive the primary election in June.

WIDE WORLD

UPI

MASSIVE pileup on the New Jersey Turnpike near Kearny, caused by smog, involved more than 60 vehicles.

The Democrats had become divided in the presidential campaign of 1972 over the candidacy of George S. McGovern, and their chances of winning the governorship seemed slim as long as Cahill remained strong. But Cahill's increasing weakness raised Democratic hopes, and when Superior Court Judge Brendan T. Byrne announced his candidacy on April 24, party leaders welcomed him as a powerful alternative to Cahill. Byrne had a reputation for honesty as an Essex county prosecutor, and was seen as the only person who could unite the McGovern supporters and the traditional party politicians.

The results of the primary on June 5, in which crossover voting was allowed for the first time, showed clear victories for both Sandman and Byrne. Sandman defeated Cahill by almost 60,000 votes. An incumbent governor had never before been beaten in a New Jersey primary, nor had one been challenged for 24 years. Byrne won by comfortable margins over Assemblywoman Ann Klein, who was backed largely by women and the McGovern wing of the party, and over state Sen. Ralph C. De Rose, candidate of the old-line party regulars.

Sandman made no attempt to placate the moderate Republicans and consequently kept the party divided. His chief concern was the income tax, which he said would never come about if he were elected. Byrne, on the other hand, successfully united the Democrats, and that, combined with Sandman's consistently right-wing stands, enabled him to take moderate positions on all the major issues.

In the election, Byrne received 68% of the votes, the greatest landslide in New Jersey's history. The Democratic victory also extended to the legislature. For only the third time in the 20th century the

Democrats controlled the Senate and the Assembly. Even the Republican bastions of Monmouth and Ocan counties were broken.

Other Events. In April the New Jersey supreme court struck down the existing system of financing the state's public schools. Under the disapproved system the schools receive 70% of costs through local property taxes, resulting in a wide disparity between the amounts of money available to suburban and city schools. An appeal to the U.S. Supreme Court was denied in November.

In May, New Jersey voters saw to the final demise of the old Hudson County Democratic organization. Jersey City's Mayor Paul Jordan was reelected over Thomas Gangemi, Jr., of the once powerful Democratic organization, which had been discredited in 1971 when eight of its top members were convicted of shaking down contractors. In November, former Gov. Richard J. Hughes was appointed chief justice of the New Jersey supreme court.

Racial and ethnic tensions in Newark came to a head in the spring with a neighborhood attempt, led by Assemblyman Anthony Imperiale, to block construction of Kawaida Towers, a black apartment complex in a mostly white neighborhood, sponsored by black Assemblyman Imamu Amiri Baraka.

HERMANN K. PLATT
St. Peter's College, Jersey City

NEW MEXICO

Crime and the energy crisis were the major issues causing concern in New Mexico during 1973.

Crime. For the second consecutive year, the FBI's *Uniform Crime Report*, issued in August, showed that Albuquerque, New Mexico's largest city, had the highest crime rate in the nation. Figures revealed that 5,910 serious crimes had been committed for every 100,000 residents in the metropolitan area. Some encouragement was provided by a city police department study that showed a 9.6% drop in crime during the first seven months of 1973.

In March public anger was aroused by the theft of a priceless religious statue, *La Conquistadora*, from the Santa Fe Cathedral. Loss of the treasure, which dates from the 17th century, was one in a series of robberies of Spanish colonial art extending over a period of three years. The state police arrested two Santa Fe youths for the crime in May and recovered *La Conquistadora* and other sacred objects from a cave in the Manzano Mountains.

As a result of the growing problem of lawlessness, the 31st session of the New Mexico legislature had more criminal justice legislation introduced than any previous session. The Organized Crime Act provided for programs to prevent and control organized crime. The Data Processing Act established a uniform system for reporting on criminal justice and highway safety.

Energy Crisis. New Mexico's Bureau of Business Research announced in mid-1973 that the state faced a future shortage of natural gas—the dominant fuel used in homes, commercial establishments, and industrial facilities. Even though New Mexico is a major producer of natural gas, most of its reserves are committed to the interstate market. Propane gas, upon which many of the state's rural residents depend, was also in short supply. The shortages were being studied during the year by the Governor's Task Force on Energy, a body created in

1972 to monitor energy problems and recommend solutions.

Research at the Los Alamos Scientific Laboratory into methods for harnessing geothermal energy was stepped up in 1973. Plans went forward for a series of experiments on underground hot rocks located on the Jemez Plateau. U.S. Sen. Pete V. Domenici (R-N. Mex.) was the cosponsor of a congressional bill that would provide for the development of geothermal energy as a way to alleviate the nation's energy shortage. The State Environmental Improvement Board granted permits for the building of coal gasification plants in northwestern New Mexico.

Indians. In March, two Indian students of the University of New Mexico kidnapped Emmit Garcia, the mayor of Gallup. Garcia was taken from city hall at gunpoint and brought to a nearby store, from which he escaped by plunging through a plate glass window. In an ensuing confrontation with the police, Larry Wayne Casuse, one of the youths, committed suicide. Casuse had been president of the Kiva Club, an Indian organization at the university. The reason for the kidnapping was unknown, but a week earlier Indian students led by Casuse had burned the mayor in effigy in protest against his appointment to the state board of regents.

During the summer the first national Indian Conference on Alcoholism and Drug Abuse was held on the Mescalero Apache Reservation. It was called to establish a board to function as the instrument for all Indian alcoholism programs in the country. San Juan Pueblo opened its own alcohol rehabilitation center, the New Moon Lodge.

MARC SIMMONS, *Author and Historian*

────── **NEW MEXICO • Information Highlights** ──────

Area: 121,666 square miles (315,115 sq km).
Population (1972 est.): 1,065,000. *Density:* 8.5 per sq mi.
Chief Cities (1970 census): Santa Fe, the capital, 41,167; Albuquerque, 243,751; Las Cruces, 37,857; Roswell, 33,908.
Government (1973): *Chief Officers*—governor, Bruce King (D); lt. gov., Robert A. Mondragon (D); secy. of state, Mrs. Betty Fiorina (D); atty. gen., David L. Norvell (D); treas., Jesse D. Kornegay (D); supt. of public instruction, Leonard DeLayo; chief justice, John B. McManus, Jr. *Legislature*—Senate, 42 members (30 Democrats, 12 Republicans); House of Representatives, 70 members (51 D, 19 R).
Education (1972–73): *Enrollment*—public elementary schools, 155,102 pupils, 6,460 teachers; public secondary schools, 133,725 pupils, 5,810 teachers; nonpublic schools, 13,700 pupils, 680 teachers; colleges and universities, 46,721 students. *Public school expenditures,* $227,720,000 ($829 per pupil). *Average teacher's salary,* $8,600.
State Finances (fiscal year 1971): *Revenues,* $668,954,000 (4% general sales tax and gross receipts taxes, $119,076,000; motor fuel tax, $45,278,000; federal funds, $190,695,000). *Expenditures,* $581,229,000 (education, $285,142,000; health, welfare, and safety, $83,960,000; highways, $103,166,000). *State debt,* $135,523,000 (June 30, 1971).
Personal Income (1972): $3,894,000,000; per capita, $3,656.
Public Assistance (1972): $56,871,000. *Average monthly payments* (Dec. 1972)—old-age assistance, $54.70; aid to families with dependent children, $113.10.
Labor Force: *Nonagricultural wage and salary earners* (July 1973), 352,300. *Average annual employment* (1972)—manufacturing, 25,800; trade, 71,200; government, 95,700; services, 60,100. *Insured unemployed* (Sept. 1973)—6,400 (2.8%).
Manufacturing (1971): *Value added by manufacture,* $272,900,000. Food and kindred products, $53,900,000; stone, clay, and glass products, $29,800,000; printing and publishing, $20,900,000; electrical equipment and supplies, $16,900,000; chemicals and allied products, $9,800,000.
Agriculture (1972): *Cash farm income,* $619,944,000 (livestock, $471,737,000; crops, $105,704,000; government payments, $42,503,000). *Chief crops* (in order of value, 1971)—Hay; sorghum grain, cotton lint, lettuce.
Mining (1972): *Production value,* $1,066,139,000 (ranks 7th among the states). *Chief minerals*—Petroleum, $376,976,000; natural gas, $194,080,000; copper, $171,080,000.
Transportation: *Roads* (1972), 68,371 miles (110,029 km); *motor vehicles* (1972), 661,129; *railroads* (1972), 2,120 miles (3,412 km); *public airports* (1972), 65.
Communications: *Telephones* (1973), 568,500; *television stations* (1971), 7; *radio stations* (1971), 73; *newspapers* (1973), 19 (daily circulation, 231,000).

NEW ORLEANS police hunt for a sniper on the roof of a downtown motor lodge. Mark Essex, killed by police the previous night, lies at the lower right of the picture.

GAMMA

NEW ORLEANS

In 1973, New Orleans was shaken by two headline tragedies—a sniper killed 6 persons in an all-day battle atop a downtown hotel and, later in the year, 32 persons were killed in a fire that swept through a French Quarter bar.

The Tragedies. In January, 23-year-old Mark Essex paralyzed the city on a quiet Sunday afternoon when he began shooting at firemen from the roof of the downtown Howard Johnson Motor Lodge. It was believed that Essex had set fires in the hotel and then began shooting guests as they ran from their rooms and later at the firemen who came to put out the fires. A battle with the police ensued. Essex killed six persons, including three policemen, before he himself was gunned down that night by sharpshooters from an armored marine helicopter. At first it was believed that Essex had at least one accomplice, but police later said evidence indicated he was alone.

On a later Sunday, June 24, a flash fire engulfed The Upstairs, a bar in the French Quarter, killing 32 persons. Late in the year, a young man surrendered himself in California and confessed to setting the fire, but police determined his confession to be false and released him. This was the second major fire in New Orleans in seven months. In November 1972, a fire in the top three stories of the 17-story Rault Center in downtown New Orleans had resulted in the deaths of five persons, including four women who leaped to their deaths.

Politics. Lindy Boggs, widow of the U. S. House majority leader, Hale Boggs, who was lost in a plane flight over Alaska in 1972, won a special election to fill her late husband's seat by a landslide margin. Early in 1973 a proposal to expand the City Council from seven to nine members was turned down in a referendum vote. The council later reapportioned its seven seats, but the U. S. Justice Department ordered a delay in the councilmanic elections scheduled for November until there would be no "racially discriminatory effect on voting."

District Attorney Jim Garrison was acquitted of charges that he accepted bribes to aid a pinball machine gambling conspiracy. Shortly after his acquittal, he ran for reelection in a primary election. The contest was extended to a runoff election in December, which Garrison lost. Mayor Moon Landrieu easily won nomination for a second term. The general election was to be held in the spring of 1974.

Construction and Planning. The Superdome, New Orleans' domed stadium, crept toward completion in 1973, although inflation pushed its projected cost to more than $160 million. The stadium was scheduled to open in the middle of the 1974 football season or, at the latest, for the Super Bowl football game of January 1975. But construction problems and labor difficulties made meeting the deadline somewhat doubtful. Some 8,000 new hotel rooms in the city were either in the planning stage or being built. The Superdome was probably responsible for the great increase.

Construction of a new parish (county) prison was begun near the "porous" old one, from which there have been many escapes in recent years. Plans were announced for a new $100 million chemical plant north of the city.

On Jan. 9, 1973, a gala opening was held for the New Orleans Theater of the Performing Arts, a plush new $8.5 million theater-concert hall. A performance of Giuseppe Verdi's *Manzoni Requiem* was given by the New Orleans Philharmonic Symphony Orchestra for the occasion.

In its continuing effort to make the French Quarter a more pleasant place, the City Council ordered all large buses off the Quarter's narrow streets by January 1974. They were replaced with 25-passenger minibuses.

JOSEPH W. DARBY III
"The Times-Picayune," New Orleans

NEW YORK

Gov. Nelson A. Rockefeller resigned in December 1973, climaxing a year marked by passage of no-fault auto insurance and a very strong drug abuse law.

Drug Abuse Law. On January 3 Governor Rockefeller underlined his concern over the need for decisive steps to end drug-related lawlessness in the state. He demanded a "brutal honesty" in dealing with the drug problem and asked the Legislature to impose mandatory life sentences—with no possibility of parole or plea bargaining—for all convicted "pushers" of hard narcotics and for all addicts who commit violent crimes. Criticism from various groups, especially the New York chapter of the American Civil Liberties Union, led to some modification of his request. The final enactment provided for life sentences for drug traffickers, but with the possibility of parole and a limited form of plea bargaining. To enforce the law, 100 new

————— NEW YORK • Information Highlights —————

Area: 49,576 square miles (128,402 sq km).
Population (1972 est.): 18,366,000. *Density:* 384 per sq mi.
Chief Cities (1970 census): Albany, the capital, 115,781; New York, 7,895,563; Buffalo, 462,768; Rochester, 296,233; Yonkers, 204,297; Syracuse, 197,297; Utica, 91,611.
Government (1973): *Chief Officers*—governor, Malcolm Wilson (R); lt. gov., vacancy; acting secy. of state, John Ghezzi (R); atty. gen., Louis J. Lefkowitz (R); treas., Edward F. Moylan; commissioner of education, Ewald B. Nyquist; chief justice, Charles D. Breitel. *Legislature*—Senate, 60 members (37 Republicans, 23 Democrats); Assembly, 150 members (83 R, 67 D).
Education (1972–73): *Enrollment*—public elementary schools, 1,879,000 pupils, 88,300 teachers; public secondary schools, 1,632,000 pupils, 93,300 teachers; nonpublic schools, 742,800 pupils, 29,060 teachers; colleges and universities, 838,278 students. *Public school expenditures,* $5,006,400,000 ($1,584 per pupil). *Average teacher's salary,* $13,450.
State Finances (fiscal year 1971): *Revenues,* $10,869,021,000 (4% general sales tax and gross receipts taxes, $1,175,-898,000; motor fuel tax, $385,314,000; federal funds, $2,-198,057,000). *Expenditures,* $10,492,790,000 (education, $3,-975,860,000; health, welfare, and safety, $2,345,154,000; highways, $933,495,000). *State debt,* $8,639,842,000 (March 31, 1971).
Personal Income (1972): $97,694,000,000; per capita, $5,319.
Public Assistance (1972): $3,868,709,000. *Average monthly payments* (Dec. 1972)—old-age assistance, $97.76; aid to families with dependent children, $272.00.
Labor Force: *Nonagricultural wage and salary earners* (July 1973), 7,076,400. *Average annual employment* (1972)—manufacturing, 1,604,700; trade, 1,440,100; government, 1,240,900; services, 1,392,600. *Insured unemployed* (Sept. 1973)—165,300 (2.8%).
Manufacturing (1971): *Value added by manufacture,* $28,862,-200,000. Printing and publishing, $4,109,900,000; apparel and other textile products, $3,132,500,000; instruments and related products, $3,122,700,000.
Agriculture (1972): *Cash farm income,* $1,121,497,000 (livestock, $830,801,000; crops, $270,757,000; government payments, $19,939,000). *Chief crops* (in order of value, 1972) —Hay, potatoes, grapes, apples (ranks 2d among the states).
Mining (1972): *Production value,* $299,554,000 (ranks 25th among the states). *Chief minerals*—Cement, value not available; stone, $75,862,000; salt, $42,924,000.
Fisheries (1972): *Commercial catch,* 37,377,000 pounds ($22,-123,000). *Leading species by value*—Clams, $13,632,000; oysters, $2,466,000; lobsters, $1,825,000.
Transportation: *Roads* (1972), 106,490 miles (171,374 km); *motor vehicles* (1972), 6,890,844; *railroads* (1972), 5,595 miles (9,004 km); *public airports* (1972), 68.
Communications: *Telephones* (1973), 12,555,500; *television stations* (1971), 29; *radio stations* (1971), 254; *newspapers* (1973), 78 (daily circulation, 7,313,000).

judgeships were created. Perhaps the strongest in the nation, the legislation has been credited with reducing drug abuse in the state.

Budget. On January 16, Governor Rockefeller sent the Legislature an $8.8 billion budget for the fiscal year beginning April 1, an increase of nearly $1 billion over the previous budget. No new taxes were requested, and no new major programs were projected. As finally passed, the budget stood at $8.77 billion, with an $85 million supplement. The budget permitted some increased aid to secondary and higher education and a $544 million increase in state revenue-sharing funds for localities.

No-Fault Auto Insurance. A no-fault automobile insurance bill was signed into law in February. It bars all law suits for bodily injury, excepting persons who suffered certain serious injuries or paid $500 for medical bills in connection with injuries sustained in an automobile accident. The bill was passed after strong opposition by many who argued that such legislation would benefit insurance companies, not the public.

Environment. Environmentalists won a notable victory with the passage of the Adirondack Park bill, which sharply curtailed development on 3.7 million acres of private land in 6-million-acre Adirondack Park.

Other Legislation. Among other legislation passed was a pension revision law that set a minimum retirement age of 62 for most newly hired civil service workers; a welfare measure creating a spe-

cial division in the governor's office to prepare for central welfare computerization as part of a plan for the state's more active role in New York City's welfare program; and a law increasing permissible interest rates on conventional mortgages for one- and two-family homes from 7.5% to 8.5%.

Mass Transit. A major area of concern for Governor Rockefeller was mass transit. In May, he signed into law bills permitting the Port Authority of New York and the state of New Jersey to undertake a $650 million construction program for mass transit, including a rail link between Kennedy International Airport and Manhattan.

A $3.5 billion transportation bond issue subject to voter acceptance was approved by the Legislature in June. This delighted the governor, who instituted a long and arduous campaign of selling the huge mass transit and highway program to the voters in the fall elections. Very strong opposition developed to this measure, and a singular defeat for the governor occurred as voters decisively rejected the transportation bond issue in November.

Elections. Much attention was centered on the race for chief judge of the court of appeals, the state's highest court. In June, Jacob Fuchsberg, a noted trial attorney, defeated Federal Judge Jacob Weinstein by only 755 votes out of more than 760,-000 cast for Democratic candidates. In the November election, Fuchsberg faced the Republican-Liberal candidate Charles Breitel, an associate judge of the court of appeals who had the strong backing of the governor, and the Conservative party candidate, Supreme Court Justice James T. Leff. Judge Breitel carried the state by a margin of more than 300,000 votes over Fuchsberg.

Possibly as a result of the Watergate investigations, Republicans lost their grip on elective offices throughout the state, except for Nassau county. Democrats won many victories. Notable were the election in Westchester of the first Democratic county executive and the Democratic sweep of the Rockland county legislature.

Indictment of Republican State Leaders. Two top leaders of the state Assembly, speaker Perry B. Duryea and majority leader John E. Kingston, were indicted in December on charges of election law violations. The scheme allegedly was to bolster Liberal party candidates at the expense of Democratic candidates and thereby ensure Republican control of the Assembly. Duryea and Kingston pleaded not guilty to the charges on December 13.

Rockefeller Resignation. On December 18, Gov. Rockefeller resigned after having spent 15 years in office. He turned over one of the nation's major political offices to Malcolm Wilson, who had served as lieutenant governor under Rockefeller for 15 years. Wilson, 59, will be governor at least until the next election in November 1974.

Rockefeller said he stepped down to devote himself to the work of two bipartisan national commissions—the Commission on Critical Choices for America and the Commission on Water Quality, both of which are headed by the 65-year-old millionaire. Both commissions were scheduled to complete their work within two years. Although Rockefeller said he did not know whether he would become a presidential candidate in the future, it was widely believed that he would make a fourth try at winning the Republican nomination in 1976.

LEO HERSHKOWITZ
Queens College, City University of New York

NEW YORK CITY

In 1973, New Yorkers faced little racial and social unrest and except for a brief strike by firemen the labor picture was essentially calm. Even the political scene, despite the announced retirement of Mayor John V. Lindsay, was relatively quiet and uneventful.

The firemen's 5½-hour Election Day strike—the first in the city's history—was called for by Richard J. Vissini, president of the Uniformed Firefighters Association. When the strike was later investigated, Vissini admitted that he had lied about the results of the strike vote in order to protect his bargaining position with the city.

Politics and Elections. On March 7, 1973, Mayor Lindsay, citing "personal considerations," announced his decision not to seek a third term for what is frequently called the second hardest job in the country. Numerous candidates soon appeared on the scene. Among the leading candidates for the Democratic nomination were City Controller Abraham Beame, Congressmen Mario Biaggi and Herman Badillo, and Assemblyman Albert H. Blumenthal. Beame took first place in the Democratic mayoral primary held on June 4, but his vote fell far short of the required 40% of the total vote and he thus faced a runoff on June 26 against Badillo, who had finished second.

Beame won easily in the runoff and then faced Republican Congressman John Marchi in the November election, as well as Blumenthal, who ran as the Liberal party candidate, and Biaggi, who held the Conservative party nomination. Biaggi's campaign in the primary and general elections was plagued by his assertion that he had never pleaded the Fifth Amendment in his appearance before a federal grand jury, when in fact it was revealed that he had. Marchi did not receive strong support from Gov. Nelson A. Rockefeller or the Republican party, and Blumenthal had to depend on a weakened Liberal party. It was, therefore, no surprise that Beame won an outstanding victory in November, getting 955,385 votes to 275,362 for Marchi, 263,604 for Blumenthal, and 189,135 for Biaggi.

The Democrats captured all but one of the 38 seats in the City Council and all of the borough presidencies. Democrat Paul O'Dwyer emerged as president of the City Council and Harrison J. Goldin, also a Democrat, overwhelmingly won the election for controller.

An odd aspect of the campaign, although not an unexpected one, was the victory of District Attorney Frank Hogan of New York county, whose 32-year reign in office was continued, despite his nonappearance in the campaign. During the year he had suffered a stroke and had undergone surgery for a lung tumor. In December, Hogan announced his resignation for reasons of health.

Budget and Financing. In May, Mayor Lindsay submitted an expense budget of $10.6 billion for the 1973–74 fiscal year, an increase of 18.8% over the previous budget. After discussion in the Board of Estimate, a slightly reduced budget of $10.16 billion was adopted. It called for a real estate tax increase of 37 cents per $100 of assessed valuation; this was 40 cents less than the increase the mayor had originally proposed. The 37-cent increase brought the basic real estate tax rate in New York City to $6.89 per $100 of assessed valuation. The new budget also restored full transit subsidies for

NEW YORK CITY'S mayor-elect, Abraham Beame, and his wife celebrate victory at campaign headquarters.

the elderly and school children. In addition, it enabled 3,000 new members to be added to the police force, 325 to the transit police, and 175 to the housing police.

The city received $104 million of unexpected funds from the federal government, which was attributed to the loosening of the purse strings as a result of the adverse publicity from the Watergate investigations. An additional $90 million was also allocated by the state Legislature to help close an estimated $211 million budget gap.

Crime. For many citizens crime was the central problem facing New Yorkers in 1973. Concern was expressed by Mayor Lindsay, too, when he announced a record capital budget of $2,448,000,000. He urged that $5 million be allocated to block associations and tenant groups to finance projects on a neighborhood level to help provide citizens safety in the streets and in their homes. Additional money was to be provided for an increase in high-intensity lighting, new security devices in schools, and new voice alarm boxes to reach either police or firehouses. These and other such programs were designed to "insure that the city's extensive public and private programs result in a vital and livable city."

The war on crime was having some effect, according to a report issued by Police Commissioner Patrick V. Murphy. The report showed a decrease of 18% in violent crimes in 1972, although in three serious categories—those of rape, murder, and felonious assault—there was an increase of 12.1%. The overall decrease was due to declines in the incidence of robbery, larceny, burglary, and auto theft. Also, crimes against property were reported to have fallen dramatically.

Shortly after this report and the announced retirement of Lindsay, Commissioner Murphy announced his resignation, stating that he would serve under no other mayor. Donald F. Cawley was appointed commissioner on April 12. He pledged to continue the war on crime, to "elevate the professionalism" of the force, and to root out any "cancers of corruption" that exist. This was an obvious reference to the various disclosures of corruption that have prevailed in law enforcement agencies in past years. In one such scandal, Queens District Attorney

Thomas J. Mackell resigned his office on March 12, only 12 days after he was indicted on charges of covering up a criminal investigation.

Population. The exodus of white middle-class residents from New York City continued in 1973, and the effects could be observed in the changing neighborhoods and public school enrollment. In 1965, whites and Orientals constituted 52% of the school population, but in 1971 only 42% were white or Oriental while blacks represented 35% of the student body and Puerto Ricans, 23%. According to the Health Department, New York City's official 1970 population of 7,895,563 consisted of 5,277,911 whites (66.85%); 1,805,809 nonwhites (22.01%) and 811,843 Puerto Ricans (10.28%). It was estimated that if present trends continued, blacks and Puerto Ricans would constitute a majority of the population in the city in about 12 years.

Construction and Destruction. On April 4, 1973, the $700 million, 1,350 foot twin-towered World Trade Center was dedicated at ceremonies attended by Gov. Nelson Rockefeller and Gov. William Cahill of New Jersey. At about the same time, the famed Lewisohn Stadium, which since 1918 had served as a cultural center where countless New Yorkers heard world-famous musicians for as little as 25 cents, was demolished to make room for an academic center at the City College of the City University of New York.

LEO HERSHKOWITZ
Queens College, City University of New York

NEW ZEALAND

The Labour government elected by a landslide in November 1972 introduced a number of sweeping domestic reforms and showed considerable vigor and independence in foreign policy during 1973.

Foreign Affairs. The New Zealand government strenuously opposed. French nuclear tests in the Pacific. Hugh Watt, New Zealand's deputy prime minister, traveled to Paris in an unsuccessful attempt to persuade President Pompidou to cancel the tests. Then New Zealand's minister of justice, Martyn Finlay, won an interim injunction against France from the International Court of Justice. When France ignored the injunction, the New Zealand government sent a cabinet minister, Fraser Colman, on the frigates *Otago* and *Canterbury* to cruise in protest just outside French territorial waters but within the test danger zone.

In April, after failing to persuade the New Zealand Rugby Union to call off a proposed all-white South African rugby football tour of New Zealand, Prime Minister Norman Kirk postponed the tour until such time as there was clear evidence that South Africa's team had been chosen on merit in truly multiracial trials.

During the year New Zealand recognized the government of the People's Republic of China and also opened new embassies in Moscow and Vienna.

Domestic Affairs. The government established a New Zealand Shipping Corporation to break New Zealand's traditional dependence on privately owned foreign shipping companies.

A dry, cold winter led to the first power restrictions in many years.

In October the government paid NZ$30 million tax free for a half share in the Maui gas field, which has exceedingly rich resources. Supply of fuel from the field is scheduled by 1978.

Also in October the government introduced in Parliament a New Zealand Superannuation Corporation bill providing for the establishment of a compulsory, income-related retirement scheme that, together with a proposed accident compensation scheme, would bring major changes to New Zealand's social welfare system.

In November color television was introduced in New Zealand. Earlier in the year, at the direction of the minister of broadcasting, a four-man committee drafted a detailed plan to give New Zealand two competing state television corporations and one state radio corporation.

The government formulated plans to establish a kibbutz—on the lines of those in Israel—for young people seeking a less materialistic life and also wanting to participate in building the country.

The Economy. New Zealand's economy expanded at a very rapid rate during 1973. But this expansion, combined with record overseas prices for meat exports, made it difficult for the government to control inflation, which continued to rise at an average annual rate of about 10%. In August the government announced a general upward wage adjustment of 8.5%, accompanied by a 30-day price freeze. Thereafter, salaries were frozen until June 30, 1974.

The budget presented to Parliament in May was a popular one. It attacked land and property speculators with a near-confiscatory tax of up to 90% of the capital gain, gave tax relief to those with lower incomes, and increased government spending by 17.4% to a record NZ$2,605,000,000. Much of the increase went to health services, education, and pensions.

Foreign exchange reserves continued at a record level, which not only allowed New Zealand to repay overseas debts as they fell due but also led to a 10% revaluation of the currency in September. Unemployment vanished almost completely during the year.

BARRY GUSTAFSON, *University of Auckland*

--------- NEW ZEALAND • Information Highlights ---------

Official Name: New Zealand.
Location: South Pacific Ocean.
Area: 103,736 square miles (268,675 sq km).
Population (1973 est.): 3,000,000. *Density,* 28 per square mile (11 per sq km).
Chief Cities (1972 est.): Wellington, the capital, 136,400; Christchurch, 166,800; Auckland, 151,900.
Government: *Head of state,* Elizabeth II, queen, represented by Denis Blundell, governor-general (took office Sept. 1972). *Head of government,* Norman Kirk, prime minister (took office Dec. 1972). *Legislature* (unicameral)—House of Representatives. *Major political parties*—Labour party; National party.
Language: English (official).
Education: *Expenditure* (1969), 4.4% of gross national product. *School enrollment* (1969)—primary, 514,774; secondary, 184,301; university/higher, 56,353.
Monetary Unit: New Zealand dollar (0.7476 N. Z. dollar equals U. S.$1, Aug. 1973).
Gross National Product (1971 est.): $7,610,000,000.
Economic Indexes: *Industrial production* (manufacturing, 1970), 156 (1963=100); *agricultural production* (1971), 121 (1963=100); *consumer price index* (1972), 161 (1963=100).
Manufacturing (major products): Processed foods, meat products, wood products, cement, fertilizers.
Major Agricultural Products: Wheat, potatoes, dairy products, sheep, wool, forest products, fish.
Major Minerals: Coal, petroleum, natural gas, mineral sands.
Foreign Trade (1972): *Exports,* $1,766,000,000; *imports,* $1,-531,000,000. *Chief trading partners* (1970)—United Kingdom (took 34% of exports, supplied 28% of imports); United States (16%—10%).
Transportation: *Motor vehicles* (1971), 1,130,500 (automobiles, 938,900); *railroads* (1971), 2,987 miles (4,807 km); *merchant fleet* (1972), 182,000 gross registered tons; *major national airline,* Air New Zealand.
Communications: *Telephones* (1972), 1,281,105; *newspapers* (1970), 40 (daily circulation, 1,058,000).

NEWFOUNDLAND

Following two years of electoral activity and government change, Newfoundland experienced relative quiet in 1973. Industrial development, labor disputes, and municipal elections were prominent in the news, while Premier Frank D. Moores' Progressive Conservative government took no major policy initiatives.

Legislation and Government. Finance Minister John C. Crosbie released in March a 1973 budget which called for record spending of $675 million and borrowing of $218 million, chiefly for minimal expansion of ongoing programs. A restructuring of government departments was carried out in late 1972 to facilitate policy planning and implementation.

Industrial and Labor Developments. Newfoundland witnessed the completion of two large and controversial government-sponsored enterprises in 1973. The $150 million linerboard paper mill in Stephenville began production early in the year but immediately faced the prospect of chronic subcapacity operation because of difficulty in obtaining sufficient pulpwood from distant Labrador forests. In October, New York promoter John Shaheen opened his 100,000-barrel-a-day oil refinery at Come-by-Chance. Of the final $198 million cost, $188 million was loaned or guaranteed by Newfoundland. In February, Premier Moores announced that Shaheen would build at Come-by-Chance a second refinery three times as large as the first but on more favorable terms to his Newfoundland government backers. The Shaheen developments were subjected to public criticism on both economic and environmental grounds.

Labor disputes in various sectors remained in the news throughout the year, reaching a peak in August when the island of Newfoundland was virtually cut off from the mainland by simultaneous strikes by Canadian National Railway employees, who operate ferries carrying both passengers and freight, and St. John's longshoremen, who control incoming seaborne cargo. Many Newfoundlanders felt the shortage of food and other goods, but the disruption most acutely affected several thousand tourists stranded at ferry embarkation points. Other labor disputes included long, bitter strikes by miners at Buchans and fish processors in Bonavista.

Municipal Affairs. William Adams and Noel Murphy—incumbent mayors of St. John's and Corner Brook, respectively—were both defeated in November elections. These upsets climaxed a growing mood of discontent in the province's two largest cities over planning, development, and a lack of public involvement in decisions. Elections in 85 other towns reflected the marked expansion of local government in recent years—from 16 municipalities in 1949 to 273 in 1973. This expansion led to appointment of two royal commissions to review the municipal system.

MARK W. GRAESSER
Memorial University of Newfoundland

NEWSPAPERS. See PUBLISHING.

NIGERIA

Government stability and continued income from petroleum enabled Nigeria to maintain its substantial development programs in 1973 despite the crippling drought that devastated much of West Africa. Nigeria continued to exercise an ever-increasing influence in African affairs.

Domestic Developments. Despite some signs of unrest, there were no serious challenges to the military government during the year. Benin University students demonstrated briefly in January against government interference, and in May there was a brief strike by the 2,000-member Nigerian Association of University Teachers for increased allowances. However, in the face of general prosperity, no group was willing to force an issue with the powerful military government. During the year many high military officials assured the country of a definite return to complete civilian government by 1976.

The Western state, scene of past disturbances, was quiet largely because government policies cushioned sagging cocoa profits. In April a merger of local government councils in the Western state facilitated better relations between towns and the central authorities. Friction developed between the Rivers and East-Central governments concerning the return of property to its Ibo owners.

The Nigerian central government announced a new nationwide census to be taken beginning November 25.

The Federal Budget and the States. Nigeria's prosperity was reflected in the 1.3 billion naira ($5.25 billion) federal budget. The largest segment of the budget (approximately 25%) went to maintain the largest army in sub-Saharan Africa. Much of the remainder went to support the states. The heaviest drain was for the continued reconstruction of the East-Central state, which in 1973–74 budgeted a total expenditure of 139 million naira while its estimated revenue was only 71.8 million naira. Drought conditions in four northern states demand-

ed added expenditure for relief and for funding of long-range projects. The North-East state, even with federal assistance, budgeted a 20% deficit of 15 million naira. Benue Plateau, Kwara, and North-West states were also expected to have deficits.

Economy. The key factor of the Nigerian economy continued to be the expanding petroleum industry, with estimated annual revenues of $750 million —a threefold increase since 1970. The National Oil Corporation, in conjunction with Shell-B.P., was the largest producer, with an output after April of 2 million barrels per day. A promising new discovery of relatively sulfur-free oil was made off-shore of the Western state near Obe.

The vitality of Nigeria's export agriculture continued to decline. The estimated cocoa crop of the Western state was only 245,000 tons, down over 60,000 tons from 1972. Despite aid from the East-Central and Rivers governments, the oil-palm industry has not recovered from the war. Kernel production was only 75% and oil only 21% of the 1963–66 average. Drought conditions in the north seriously limited the peanut harvests, and there were fewer cattle for export than in previous years.

Nigeria continued to develop its industrial and urban sectors with the aid of foreign loans. Cotton-seed crushing mills were opened in the North-Central state, and an aluminum plant was completed near Lagos. In the East-Central state the Niger steel plant at Enugu has been reconstructed, textile mills modernized, breweries expanded, and a new mineral water plant begun. The Western state road system has been improved, and a new $4 million road joined Lagos to Porto Novo in Dahomey. The third wharf extension at Lagos harbor increased the capacity of Nigeria's largest port, and a new World Bank loan of $55 million will enable an even further expansion.

Drought. The drought caused the federal government in January to declare as disaster areas the North-East, North-West, North-Central and Kano states. Transportation on the Niger River south to Lokoja was greatly restricted, the Kano River

stopped flowing in April, and Lake Chad shrunk. By March many towns had acute water shortages, and some urban areas were without water for over a month. Supplies of potable water sold for inflated prices, and industries that required water were shut down or production was cut.

By August an estimated 300,000 cattle had died and many thousands had been prematurely slaughtered. At the same time graineries were emptied months before the regular harvest. In some areas the seed grain and cattle food was eaten. Many crops planted in June and July failed. Even after the onset of rains the millet, maize, and peanut harvests were poor.

Nigerian relief efforts were self-supported and were of two types: one to provide remedies for the current crisis, the other a long-range investment in projects designed to prevent a recurrence of the near-famine conditions. Ten million naira was made available for relief in January, and the funds were increased in July. A crash program to improve the supplies of water to northern cities resulted in greatly improved systems for Kano, Zaria, Ilorin, and Kaduna, and there are four major dams still under construction. Kwara and Benue states plan an expenditure in 1973–74 of more than 8% of their development budgets on dams and water projects.

In the North-Central state the completion of the Bagauda Dam, which delivers 25 million gallons per day, saved the state from greater devastation. In the more desolate North-West and North-East states, the governments invested in bore holes, storage tanks, and small dams.

Foreign Affairs. Nigeria continued to play a dominant role in African affairs, and Gen. Yakubu Gowon, the president, acted as one of the chief spokesmen of African opinion, as his selection as chairman of the Organization of African Unity (OAU) indicated.

Gowon paid state visits to Mali in February and to Britain in June. Important bilateral discussions were held when Britain's Foreign Secretary Douglas-Home visited Lagos in February and when Sudan's President Numeiry made an extensive tour of Nigeria in August.

During the 10th anniversary meetings of the OAU, and later in Ottawa at the Commonwealth heads of government meetings in August, Gowon's moderate position reflected Nigeria's prosperity and the basic pragmatism of its government. However, Nigeria's policy toward white minority rule in Rhodesia and in the Portuguese territories remained inflexibly hostile. Nigeria's closer relations with the Arab world were particularly marked after it was announced in October that Nigeria was severing relations with Israel.

The treaty with Equatorial Guinea covering some 30,000 expatriate workers expired in February, but signing of a new agreement was postponed because of allegations of near slave-like conditions on the plantations in Guinea. In August, following border difficulties, Nigeria began high-level discussions with the Cameroon, but in September Nigeria charged that thousands of farmers and fishermen had been expelled from the creeks of the Rio de Rey.

HARRY A. GAILEY
San Jose State University

NIGERIA • Information Highlights

Official Name: Federal Republic of Nigeria.
Location: West Africa.
Area: 356,668 square miles (923,768 sq km).
Population (1973 est.): 59,600,000. *Density*, 158 per square mile (61 per sq km).
Chief Cities (1971 est.): Lagos, the capital, 900,000; Ibadan, 758,000; Ogbomosho, 387,000; Kano, 357,000.
Government: *Head of state*, Gen. Yakubu Gowon, president (assumed power Aug. 1966). *Head of government*, Gen. Yakubu Gowon.
Languages: English (official), Hausa (official in the north), Ibo, Yoruba, other tribal languages.
Education: *Expenditure* (1965), 2.3% of gross domestic product. *School enrollment* (1969)—primary, 2,345,754; secondary, 222,547; technical/vocational, 16,824; university/higher (1968), 9,775.
Monetary Unit: Naira (0.6579 naira equals U. S.$1, July 1973).
Gross National Product (1971 est.): $6,730,000,000.
Consumer Price Index (1972), 164 (1963 = 100).
Manufacturing (major products): Processed foods, cotton textiles, cement, petroleum products.
Major Agricultural Products: Palm kernels (ranks 1st among world producers, 1972), cacao (world rank 2d, 1972), groundnuts, rubber, cotton, sweet potatoes and yams (world rank 1st, 1972), forest products, fish.
Major Minerals: Petroleum, tin, coal, limestone, natural gas.
Foreign Trade (1972): Exports, $2,180,000,000; Imports, $1,-505,000,000. *Chief trading partners* (1971)—United Kingdom (took 22% of exports, supplied 32% of imports); United States (18%—14%).
Transportation: *Motor Vehicles* (1971), 112,000 (automobiles, 68,000); *railroads* (1971), 2,178 miles (3,305 km); *merchant fleet* (1972), 99,000 gross registered tons; *major national airline*, Nigeria Airways.
Communications: *Telephones* (1972), 86,771; *newspapers* (1970), 21.

NIXON, Richard M. See BIOGRAPHY.
NOBEL PRIZES. See PRIZES AND AWARDS.

NORTH CAROLINA

A new administration, increased public spending, a healthy business scene, and increased black participation in government and business dominated news events in North Carolina in 1973.

New Administration. In January, James E. Holshouser was inaugurated as the first Republican governor to take office in North Carolina in the 20th century. Reorganization of the state government, begun under the previous administration, was continued, but many department heads were removed and generally replaced by Republicans. Dr. Jacqueline Renee Westcott was appointed social services commissioner and is probably the highest-ranking black state official since 1900.

Educational, Cultural, and Recreational Financing. Enrollment in the state's public schools declined for the fifth consecutive year, due to a leveling off of the population climb and to the growth of private schools. Nevertheless the 1973–74 appropriation by the North Carolina General Assembly for public schools was the most generous in its history. Funds were to be used to reduce class size, to provide more public kindergartens, to support construction and expanded programs in community colleges, to support improvements in the University of North Carolina, and to aid private colleges.

───── NORTH CAROLINA • Information Highlights ─────

Area: 52,586 square miles (136,198 sq km).
Population (1972 est.): 5,214,000. *Density:* 105 per sq mi.
Chief Cities (1970 census): Raleigh, the capital, 123,793; Charlotte, 241,178; Greensboro, 144,076; Winston-Salem, 134,676; Durham, 95,438; High Point, 63,259; Asheville, 57,681.
Government (1973): *Chief Officers*—governor, James E. Holshouser, Jr. (R); lt. gov., James B. Hunt, Jr. (D); secy. of state, Thad Eure (D); atty. gen., Robert Morgan (D); treas., Edwin Gill (D); supt. of public instruction, Craig Phillips (D); chief justice, William H. Bobbitt. General Assembly—Senate, 50 members (35 Democrats, 15 Republicans); House of Representatives, 120 members (85 D, 35 R).
Education (1972–73): *Enrollment*—public elementary schools, 799,709 pupils, 32,674 teachers; public secondary schools, 358,840 pupils, 16,707 teachers; nonpublic schools, 28,400 pupils, 1,470 teachers; colleges and universities, 155,109 students. *Public school expenditures,* $858,131,000 ($802 per pupil). *Average teacher's salary,* $9,314.
State Finances (fiscal year 1971): *Revenues,* $2,245,846,000 (3% general sales tax and gross receipts taxes, $286,096,000; motor fuel tax, $226,811,000; federal funds, $511,664,000). *Expenditures,* $2,028,276,000 (education, $1,024,049,000; health, welfare, and safety, $261,876,000; highways, $337,569,000). *State debt,* $576,929,000 (June 30, 1971).
Personal Income (1972): $19,403,000,000; per capita, $3,721.
Public Assistance (1972): $245,406,000. *Average monthly payments* (Dec. 1972)—old-age assistance, $77.73; aid to families with dependent children, $113.95.
Labor Force: *Nonagricultural wage and salary earners* (July 1973), 1,941,400. *Average annual employment* (1972)—manufacturing, 735,500; trade, 335,000; government, 271,100; services, 228,900. *Insured unemployed* (Sept. 1973)—11,600 (0.7%).
Manufacturing (1971): *Value added by manufacture,* $9,824,200,000. Textile mill products, $2,769,500,000; tobacco manufactures, $1,264,700,000; chemicals and allied products, $744,900,000; furniture and fixtures, $686,100,000; food and kindred products, $638,600,000.
Agriculture (1972): *Cash farm income,* $1,716,729,000 (livestock, $642,372,000; crops, $1,016,828,000; government payments, $57,529,000). *Chief crops* (in order of value, 1972)—Tobacco (ranks 1st among the states), corn, soybeans, peanuts (ranks 4th).
Mining (1972): *Production value,* $122,633,000 (ranks 32d among the states). *Chief minerals*—Stone, $66,540,000; sand and gravel, $13,515,000; cement, value not available; phosphate rock, value not available.
Fisheries (1972): *Commercial catch,* 175,410,000 pounds ($11,827,000). *Leading species by value*—Shrimp, $3,549,000; flounder, $1,388,000; crabs, $1,374,000.
Transportation: *Roads* (1972), 86,478 miles (139,169 km); *motor vehicles* (1972), 3,001,520; *railroads* (1972), 4,144 miles (6,669 km); *public airports* (1972), 61.
Communications: *Telephones* (1973), 2,713,600; *television stations* (1971), 19; *radio stations* (1971), 273; *newspapers* (1973), 50 (daily circulation, 1,328,000).

The North Carolina Symphony received a grant-in-aid of $512,000, and a 164-acre site on the western limits of Raleigh was selected for the new $4.5 million North Carolina Museum of Art Building.

As part of a planned expansion of state parks and preserves, the state announced the acquisition of 6,800 acres in Dismal Swamp at a cost of $1.3 million and of 530 acres on the Eno River near Durham for $300,000. The Eno River site is one prime unspoiled region in the highly industrialized Piedmont region. In addition, $14 million was appropriated for the acquisition of new park lands. By executive order the governor established a North Carolina Land Policy Council in anticipation of a land-use act to be presented to the next Assembly.

Health. To ease the shortage of medical services in isolated areas of the state, legislation was passed to set up a series of rural health clinics. A bill of rights for mental patients was also passed, and the law dealing with involuntary commitment to mental institutions was made more restrictive.

Business and Industry. Investments in new and expanded industry during the first half of 1973 exceeded $307 million, an increase of more than $30 million over the same period in 1972. During early 1973 the increased investments created 11,600 new jobs, compared with 7,600 the previous year.

The state legislature raised the minimum hourly wage by 20 cents to $1.80 an hour, thus putting the state minimum above the federal minimum of $1.60. Under black leadership and with a $14 million federal loan guarantee, ground was broken for the first industrial building at Soul City in Warren County, a new town projected to house 44,000 people over the next three decades.

Other Legislative Action. The 1973 Assembly passed a resolution ending the long-standing practice of biennial sessions and provided for annual sessions. It also adopted a one-year budget of $2.9 billion, spending up to the very maximum of projected revenues for the period and thereby abandoning traditional fiscal restraint.

November Election. By a 2-to-1 margin, North Carolina voters defeated a proposal that would have permitted the sale of mixed drinks in certain restaurants. Voters also approved bond issues to provide $300 million for school construction and $30 million for "clean water." In Raleigh, Clarence Lightener was elected mayor; he is the first black mayor in the capital city's history.

WILLIAM S. POWELL
University of North Carolina

NORTH DAKOTA

The year 1973 was a good one for North Dakota farmers. Wheat growers received the highest prices ever for their second-largest crop in history. Prices of other products were up, most at record levels, and farmland values skyrocketed. As for the future, neither the soaring costs of machinery and materials nor the probability of fuel and fertilizer shortages deterred farmers from plowing-up prairies to the fence lines in anticipation of big free-market crops and continued high prices in 1974.

Energy Production. The national energy crisis focused attention on North Dakota's electric generating capability, huge water storage, promising oil fields, and vast reserves of lignite coal for synthetic gas production. As a result, debate raged between those who want to retain the state's rural

——— NORTH DAKOTA • Information Highlights ———

Area: 70,665 square miles (183,022 sq km).
Population (1972 est.): 632,000. *Density:* 8.7 per sq mi.
Chief Cities (1970 census): Bismarck, the capital, 34,703; Fargo, 53,365; Grand Forks, 39,008; Minot, 32,290; Jamestown, 15,385; Dickinson, 12,405; Williston, 11,280.
Government (1973): *Chief Officers*—governor, Arthur A. Link (D); lt. gov., Wayne Sanstead (D); secy. of state, Ben Meier (R); atty. gen., Allen I. Olson (R); treas., Walter Christensen (D); supt. of public instruction, M. F. Peterson; chief justice, Ralph J. Erickstad. *Legislative Assembly*—Senate, 51 members (41 Republicans, 10 Democrats); House of Representatives, 102 members (79 R, 23 D).
Education (1972–73): *Enrollment*—public elementary schools, 94,319 pupils, 4,450 teachers; public secondary schools, 47,216 pupils, 2,685 teachers; nonpublic schools, 12,000 pupils, 530 teachers; colleges and universities, 27,356 students. *Public school expenditures,* $116,760,000 ($855 per pupil). *Average teacher's salary,* $8,362.
State Finances (fiscal year 1971): *Revenues,* $345,575,000 (4% general sales tax and gross receipts taxes, $54,403,-000; motor fuel tax, $22,199,000; federal funds, $108,-306,000). *Expenditures,* $318,744,000 (education, $118,-200,000; health, welfare, and safety, $37,226,000; highways, $82,393,000). *State debt,* $40,582,000 (June 1971).
Personal Income (1972): $2,350,000,000; per capita, $3,718.
Public Assistance (1972): $33,997,000. *Average monthly payments* (Dec. 1972)—old-age assistance, $89.23; aid to families with dependent children, $184.69.
Labor Force: *Nonagricultural wage and salary earners* (July 1973), 184,000. *Average annual employment* (1972)—manufacturing, 10,700; trade, 48,600; government, 50,000; services, 34,300. *Insured unemployed* (Sept. 1973)—1,300 (1.0%).
Manufacturing (1971): Value added by manufacture, $189,-000,000. Food and kindred products, $67,600,000; printing and publishing, $20,500,000; nonelectrical machinery, $19,500,000; fabricated metal products, $15,800,000.
Agriculture (1972): *Cash farm income,* $1,107,838,000 (livestock, $365,261,000; crops, $534,455,000; government payments, $208,122,000). *Chief crops* (in order of value, 1972)—Wheat (ranks 2d among the states), barley (ranks 1st), hay, oats (ranks 2d).
Mining (1972): Production value, $99,546,000 (ranks 37th among the states). *Chief minerals*—Petroleum, value not available; coal, $14,200,000; sand and gravel, $6,831,000; natural gas, $5,472,000.
Transportation: *Roads* (1972), 106,530 miles (171,439 km); *motor vehicles* (1972), 444,066; *railroads* (1972), 5,108 miles (8,220 km); *public airports* (1972), 90.
Communications: *Telephones* (1973), 354,900; *television stations* (1971), 12; *radio stations* (1971), 37; *newspapers* (1973), 11 (daily circulation, 157,000).

environment and preserve its natural resources for future generations and those who want to exploit its mineral wealth to meet present-day needs.

One coal company, which has leased land in six counties having an estimated 3.5 billion tons of lignite ore, combined with a pipeline corporation to build four coal gasification plants and pipe the gas to Midwestern and Eastern cities. In a state whose main occupation is agriculture, the impact of such sudden industrialization is awesome. Each proposed complex, capitalized at $450 million, would employ 1,000 persons with a yearly payroll of $12.5 million and generate $14 million in state and local taxes. Annually, each plant would use 10 million tons of strip-mined coal and divert 17,000 acre-feet of water from Lake Sakakawea.

Furthermore, 12 rural electric cooperatives are building a $200 million generating plant in the Lake Sakakawea area. Three other power utilities sought water permits for additions to existing plants or for new facilities. (State water permits are the key both to expanding electric generation and to establishing gasification projects.)

Government. The Republican-dominated legislature overrode Democratic Gov. Arthur Link's veto of a reapportionment bill that would continue state multi-senator districts. The issue was referred to the voters together with a constitutional amendment that would establish a redistricting commission and prohibit multi-seat districts. On December 4 the voters defeated the amendment and repudiated the legislature. A federal court will redistrict the state.

In other actions, the legislature eliminated the

sales taxes on groceries, adopted a new school financing program that eases the local tax burden, approved income and property tax reforms, and established a new medical school plan. It also rejected the federal Equal Rights Amendment for women.

STAN CANN, *"The Forum," Fargo*

NORTHERN IRELAND. See GREAT BRITAIN.

NORTHWEST TERRITORIES

The Canadian government's northern development policy for the 1970's, which was outlined in 1972, provided the umbrella for national activities in the Northwest Territories during 1973. The legislative framework of the policy embodies the Arctic waters pollution prevention act, the new northern pipeline guidelines, and territorial land-use regulations. The government's priorities place heaviest emphasis on social improvement by methods compatible with northern residents' own aspirations. Other major goals include enhancement of the environment through ecological research and wildlife conservation, stimulation of renewable resource development, and development of light industries and tourism. Progress toward meeting the native peoples' own aspirations was reflected both in legislative action and in a court decision affecting land claims.

Aboriginal Land Claims. In September, the Northwest Territories supreme court granted members of the territories' Indian Brotherhood the right to file a claim of interest in a large area of land, including the Mackenzie River valley, prior to settlement of treaty and aboriginal land claims (see article on Indians in Canada, page 67).

Legislation. During its winter and summer sessions the Territorial Council dealt with a $120 million budget, up $10 million from 1972, and passed a resolution requesting limited control over fiscal affairs. It also passed amendments pertaining to labor standards, child welfare, and control of snowmobiles and enacted an environmental control ordinance and laws to protect job opportunities for native northerners. Six of the elected councillors announced formation of a bloc representing regions of the territories known as bush and barrens.

C. CECIL LINGARD
Former Editor, "The Canada Yearbook"

NORTHWEST TERRITORIES • Information Highlights

Area: 1,304,903 square miles (3,379,699 sq km).
Population (1972 est.): 37,000.
Chief Town (1971 census): Yellowknife, the capital (6,122).
Government: *Chief Officers* (1973)—commissioner, Stuart M. Hodgson; deputy commissioner, John H. Parker; territorial treas., C. McCurdy; director of educ., N. J. Macpherson; judge of the Territorial Court, W. G. Morrow. *Legislature*—Territorial Council, 14 members (10 elected, 4 appointed).
Education: *School enrollment* (September 1972)—elementary and secondary, 11,390 pupils, including 4,111 Eskimos, 1,994 Indians, 5,285 others (611 teachers). *Public school expenditures* (1971–72)—$28,031,700.
Public Finance (fiscal year 1970–71): *Revenues,* $61,848,970 (liquor profits, $2,400,792). *Expenditures,* $72,237,464 (education, $13,363,609; social development, $4,848,947; local government, $4,760,908; industrial development, $3,598,124; health, $3,891,588; capital projects, $13,939,101).
Mining (1972 est.): *Production value,* $126,628,000. *Chief minerals*—zinc, $80,094,000 (ranks 2d among the provinces and territories); lead, $25,606,000 (ranks 3d).
Forest Products (1970): Lumber, 3,873,000 board feet.
Fur Production (1970–71 est.): $1,112,576 value.
Fisheries (1971): *Commercial catch,* $1,003,881 value.
Transportation: *Roads* (1971 est.), 916 miles (1,475 km); *motor vehicles,* 8,474; *railroads,* 129 track miles (208 km); *licensed airports,* 15.
Communications: *Telephones* (1971), 7,200; *television stations* (1972), 4; *radio stations* (1972), 4.
(All figures given in Canadian dollars.)

Huge oil storage tank is towed from Stavanger, Norway, to North Sea's first commercial offshore oil operation.

NORWAY

Political affairs monopolized the attention of most Norwegians in 1973, with elections taking place in September. The Labor party, Norway's most powerful political organization, lost ground in the balloting. Yet, paradoxically, its leader was to head the new coalition government that replaced the minority, non-Labor coalition that had led the nation from late 1972. A trade agreement with the European Economic Community (EEC) was signed in May.

Politics and the EEC. Norway was governed through the first nine months of 1973 by a three-party minority coalition under Prime Minister Lars Korvald, leader of the Christian People's party (CPP). The coalition, including the CPP and the Liberal and Center (farmers) parties, had taken over from a minority Labor government in October 1972, after a popular referendum had rejected Norwegian membership in the European Economic Community. The main goal of the coalition was to negotiate a trade agreement with the EEC, a task which Labor and Conservative party leaders, who favored Norway's full entry into the Common Market, were unwilling to undertake.

Korvald succeeded in concluding the trade pact, which was signed in Brussels, Belgium, in May. In the main, its terms followed the pattern of similar agreements negotiated between the EEC and the other members of the European Free Trade Association (EFTA). It provided for the gradual lowering of tariffs on industrial goods traded between Norway and the EEC over a period of 4½ years, beginning in July 1973. For certain sensitive products, such as paper, aluminum, and ferroalloys, longer transitional periods were to apply.

Pro-Market representatives in the Storting (parliament) criticized the pact, claiming that its terms were unfavorable and would create serious problems for many of Norway's key export industries. Nevertheless, the legislators ratified the agreement unanimously. Even the pro-Marketeers (who outnumbered anti-Market representatives by about 2 to 1) felt that a trade pact with the EEC was better than no arrangement at all.

On a number of other issues, the government had to drop or modify its policies because it lacked the necessary support in Parliament. Due to division among its critics, however, it remained in office until after the September election.

The General Election. The Labor party lost ground steadily in public opinion polls throughout the year. At the general election on Sept. 10, 1973, its share of the vote was only 35.5% compared with its 46.5% share in the previous election, in 1969. It won 62 seats in the enlarged, 155-member Storting (parliament), compared with 74 of 150, in 1969.

Labor's election losses were mainly a result of the EEC dispute. Earlier in the year, many of its anti-EEC members had deserted the party to join a new group, the Socialist Election Alliance (S.V.), which also included the Communists and the Socialist People's party. This group did well at the polls, securing 16 seats and 11.2% of the popular vote.

At the other extreme, a new right-wing, antitax party won 4 seats. The Conservatives continued to hold 29 seats in the Storting. The Center party won

21 seats (a gain of 1); the CPP, 20 (a gain of 6); and the Liberals, 2 (a loss of 11).

New Government. In the new Storting, the Socialist parties had a one-seat majority over the non-Socialists. Because of this, the Labor party's leader, Trygve Bratteli, was asked to form the new government. It took office on October 17.

Bratteli appealed for the "practical cooperation" of representatives of all parties on his domestic program. It was generally believed that he would often have to rely on backing from the 16 S.V. representatives, because of the opposition of non-Socialist parties to a number of Labor's proposals. Many people feared that the S.V. might push Labor to the left, since its policies were more militantly socialist than Labor's on nearly every issue.

Exports and Currency Adjustments. Norway's export industries enjoyed good demand throughout 1973 as a result of the international economic boom. Some exporters suffered, however, from currency devaluations in key markets. The fall in value of the dollar and pound sterling also hit shipowners whose vessels had been chartered on long-term contracts in dollars or pounds.

Offshore Oil Production. Petroleum output continued at a rate of about 40,000 barrels per day from the Ekofisk field of the Phillips Group in Norwegian waters. Under an agreement between Phillips and the Norwegian government, a pipeline was laid during the year which was to begin taking oil from this North Sea field to Britain in 1974. Production from the field was expected to increase considerably at that time, and eventually to reach a peak level of about 800,000 barrels per day.

The Royal Family. A son was born, on July 20, 1973, to Crown Princess Sonja and Crown Prince Harald. He was christened Haakon Magnus.

THOR GJESTER
"Norwegian Journal of Commerce and Shipping,"
Oslo

NOVA SCOTIA

Public interest in Nova Scotia in 1973 focused on labor disputes that plagued the construction industry, oil exploration on Sable Island, and changes in governmental posts. Dr. Clarence L. Gosse, a Halifax surgeon and professor of urology at Dalhousie University, was appointed lieutenant governor of Nova Scotia on September 7, succeeding Victor deB. Oland, whose term expired on October 1. Ian M. McKeigan took office on September 28 as chief justice of Nova Scotia. He succeeded Alexander H. MacKinnon, who died on June 16.

Legislation and Government. The 1973 legislature, which met from January 25 to June 26—one of the longest sessions without a break—enacted 160 of 185 proposed bills. Among the major enactments were bills creating new departments of recreation, tourism, and environment and a bill to control the storage and supply of personal information by consumer-reporting agencies.

Passage of the Maritime Provinces Higher Education Act was a significant move toward developing administrative cooperation among the provinces. Under this act the Maritime Provinces Higher Education Commission was created to plan the future of higher education in the Maritimes. A measure to provide for the licensing of denturists (persons who engage in the practice of denture technology) was the most controversial act of 1973.

─────── NOVA SCOTIA • Information Highlights ───────

Area: 21,068 square miles (54,566 sq km).
Population (1973 est.): 794,500.
Chief Cities (1971 census): Halifax, the capital (122,035); Dartmouth (64,770); Sydney (33,230).
Government: *Chief Officers* (1973)—lt. gov., Dr. Clarence Gosse; premier, Gerald A. Regan (Liberal); atty. gen., Allan E. Sullivan (L); min. of finance, Peter M. Nicholson (L); prov. sec., A. Garnet Brown (L); min. of educ., J. William Gillis; chief justice, Ian M. McKeigan. *Legislature:* Legislative Assembly, 46 members (24 Liberal; 19 Progressive Conservative; 2 New Democratic party); 1 vacancy.
Education: *School enrollment* (1972–73)—public elementary and secondary, 210,574 pupils (10,351 teachers); private schools, 1,405 pupils (141 teachers); college and university, 17,283 students. *Public school expenditures* (1972 est.)—$149,688,755; average teacher's salary (1971–72), $8,309; cost per pupil, $752.
Public Finance (fiscal year 1973 est.): *Revenues,* $503,335,-690 (income tax, $110,958,000; federal funds, $128,749,000; motor vehicles tax, $16,731,480). *Expenditures,* $607,505,-140 (education, $181,149,710; health and social welfare, $223,215,520; highways, $33,140,320; environment, $1,856,-420).
Personal Income (1972): $2,375,000,000; per capita personal income, $2,991.
Social Welfare (fiscal year 1973 est.): $54,893,860 (family and child welfare, $10,340,050; public assistance, $41,-648,990; social aid and rehabilitation, $674,270).
Manufacturing (1970): Value added by manufacture, $308,072,-000 (food and beverages, $78,889,000; paper and allied industries, $44,066,000; transportation equipment, $39,-342,000; wood industries, $14,715,000).
Agriculture (1972): *Cash farm income,* $68,319,000; livestock and products, $53,839,000; crops, $11,399,000. *Chief crops* (cash receipts)—fruits, $4,916,000; vegetables, $1,761,000; potatoes, $1,342,000).
Mining (1972 est.): *Production value,* $55,510,000. *Chief minerals* (tons)—Coal, 1,417,000; gypsum, 5,990,000 (ranks 1st among the provinces); salt, 800,000 (ranks 2d); sand and gravel, 6,000,000.
Fisheries (1972): *Commercial catch,* sea fish, 627,194,000 pounds ($65,539,000). *Leading species by value:* Lobster, $19,341,000; scallops, $16,621,000; cod, $8,476,000; haddock, $4,228,000.
Transportation: *Roads* (1972), 15,414 miles; *motor vehicles* (1972), 360,587; *railroads* (1971), 1,421 track miles; *licensed airports* (1973), 16.
Communications: *Telephones* (1972), 323,762; *television stations* (1973), 21; *radio stations* (1973), 21; *daily newspapers* (1973), 6.
(All monetary figures given in Canadian dollars.)

Alexander M. Cameron, the Liberal candidate, won the June 5 by-election held to fill the legislative seat that had been vacant since Angus MacIsaac, a Progressive Conservative, resigned to run for federal office in 1972. Cameron's victory gave the government of Liberal Premier Gerald A. Regan its largest majority since taking office in 1970.

Economy. The provincial economy remained strong during 1973, with all sectors recording consistent growth. Among the more buoyant sectors of the economy were primary and construction industries, utilities, and manufacturing, followed by trade, finance, and commercial services. The value of shipments for all provincial manufacturing increased, and the flow of farm cash receipts consistently maintained an upward trend. The monthly unemployment rates were lower than in 1972.

But labor unrest remained a troublesome aspect of the economy. Thirty-four collective agreements, involving 19 different unions, were up for renewal during the year. Carpenters, electricians, sheet-metal workers, and nurses struck for higher wages and better fringe benefits. Carpenters remained on strike for nearly seven weeks, and electricians, who held up construction projects worth $200 million took two months to settle their disputes.

Oil Exploration. An oil find on Sable Island—a small island some 100 miles (160 km) off the coast of Nova Scotia—has led to expenditure of $6 million on the drilling of two wells. Reserves are expected to yield 72.8 million cubic feet of natural gas and 1,882 barrels of crude oil a day.

R. P. SETH
Mount Saint Vincent University, Halifax

NUCLEAR ENERGY

An overview of nuclear energy developments relating to the energy crisis appears in a special feature on page 41. Specific developments in the nuclear energy field in 1973 are discussed here.

Federal Reorganization Plans for Energy Research. In legislation submitted to Congress by President Nixon in 1973, an attempt was made to mobilize the nation's research capability to meet growing energy demands. The administration proposed to set up an Energy Research and Development Administration (ERDA) to bring together all of the federal energy research and development activities. Under this plan most of the nonregulatory activities of the Atomic Energy Commission (AEC) —fuel enrichment, reactor development, military applications, physical research, and energy research —would be transferred to ERDA, as would the energy research on fossil fuels supervised by the Interior Department. This transfer would include the AEC's $3.5 billion investment in research facilities and about 24,000 scientists and engineers. The regulatory activity of the AEC, principally the licensing of power reactors, would be transferred to a new Nuclear Energy Commission (NEC), with five commissioners at its head.

Nongovernmental Energy Research. About 80% of the U. S. electrical utility companies banded together in 1973 to form an institute for coordinated research on energy production. Supported by privately and publicly owned utilities, the Electric Power Research Institute (EPRI) does research in nuclear and nonnuclear power generation, power transmission, and energy systems. The institute, headquartered at Palo Alto, Calif., was expected to spend $75 million in its first year of operation, with the total rising to several hundred million yearly in a few years. One of its first expenditures was a $25 million payment toward building a liquid-metal-cooled fast breeder reactor (LMFBR) demonstration plant near Oak Ridge, Tenn., which is financed through governmental and nongovernmental cooperation.

Reactor Sales in the United States. Sales of reactors to U. S. utilities continued at a record pace through 1973. By mid-August, 28 reactors having a total capacity of more than 31,000 megawatts (MW) were sold, whereas 36 reactors having a total capacity of 38,660 MW were sold in all of 1972. As of June 30, 1973, there were 174 reactors in operation, under construction, or ordered in the United States.

Nuclear Power Abroad. Nuclear power production increased significantly in other countries in 1973. Canada's Pickering generating station, operated by Ontario Hydro, has four heavy-water-moderated, natural-uranium-fuel reactors that were expected to turn out 1.6 million MW of electric power per month early in 1974. The Pickering units have been operating at a high capacity, and over one 6-month period Pickering produced more electricity than any other nuclear station in the world.

In breeder reactor developments the French Phenix, a prototype liquid-metal-cooled fast breeder reactor (LMFBR), reached criticality on Aug. 31, 1973. The Soviet BN-350 LMFBR at Schevchenko on the Caspian Sea went critical in November 1972 and started to supply commercial electric power on July 16, 1973. It will also be used to convert 30 million gallons of salt water into fresh water daily.

In the United Kingdom the 250-MW prototype Fast Reactor at Dounray, Scotland, was expected to produce electric power early in 1974.

U. S. Fusion Research. The AEC has decided to accelerate its fusion-reactor development program, with a major goal being the operation of a demonstration reactor by 1995. Many of the feasibility problems appear near solution, and the AEC hopes to achieve fusion "burning" in a deuterium-tritium cycle before 1985.

The success of the ATC (Adiabatic Toroidal Compression) tokamak in achieving high temperatures has encouraged workers in nuclear fusion. Also, neutral-beam heating, in which ion beams are electrically neutralized and allowed to enter the plasma confinement region, has been working well. In an alternative line of fusion research, progress in laser development for laser-induced fusion was reported by the AEC's Lawrence Livermore Laboratory. The laser light initiates an implosion of pellets of deuterium, and this leads to the high pressures and temperatures needed to produce fusion. The Livermore work suggests that mercury-xenon or mercury-argon lasers can supply the needed light.

Radioactive Isotopes in Technology. A 100-watt radioisotope power generator, the most powerful one built so far, was installed by the U. S. Navy at Fort Belvoir, Va., in 1973. This kind of thermoelectric generator uses heat from radioisotopes to heat thermocouples, which in turn produce electricity. Such generators are useful as power sources for beacons, weather stations, oceanographic research, and other applications requiring remote, maintenance-free power sources.

Radioisotopes in Medicine. The use of radioisotope-powered heart pacemakers in humans has produced encouraging results. Well over 100 such devices have been implanted in patients in the United States and Europe without difficulties attributable to the power source.

Scientists at Sandia Laboratories in New Mexico have discovered that sterilizing power is enhanced if both heat and the radiation from radioisotopes are applied simultaneously. Experiments with heat-resistant bacilli have shown that the synergistic effect of heat and radiation can dramatically decrease the radiation dose rates necessary for sterilization. This project was initiated as a possible means of sterilizing spacecraft.

Recovery of Natural Gas. In 1973, the natural gas freed by the Rulison nuclear explosive test in Colorado in the fall of 1969 was ruled safe for use in home heating. The Colorado state board of health noted that most of the original radioactivity in the gas had been dissipated due to normal radioactive decay. In the Rulison test a 43-kiloton nuclear explosive was set off 8,400 feet (2,560 meters) underground. It has raised production from an existing well from 40,000 cubic feet (1,500 cu meters) per day to as much as 16 million cubic feet (450,000 cu meters).

In the AEC's Rio Blanco experiment in Colorado, on May 17, 1973, three 30-kiloton nuclear explosives were detonated at depths of 5,000 to 7,000 feet (1,525 to 2,135 meters). The results of this natural-gas recovery test awaited evaluation at year-end.

ROBERT E. CHRIEN
Brookhaven National Laboratory

NURSING. See MEDICINE.

obituaries • 1973

PICTORIAL PARADE

LYNDON BAINES JOHNSON (1908–1973)
The limits of power and resources.

JOHNSON, Lyndon Baines

Thirty-sixth President of the United States: b. near Johnson City, Texas, Aug. 27, 1908; d. en route to San Antonio from Johnson City, Jan. 22, 1973.

A man who devoted his life to politics, Lyndon Baines Johnson reached the most powerful position in the world only to discover that its power was insufficient to enable him to accomplish his greatest objectives.

Johnson rose from congressional secretary to President, serving in progressively important posts along the way. Moving into the White House in November 1963 after the assassination of John F. Kennedy, Johnson obtained passage of major domestic measures and went on to a landslide victory in the presidential election of 1964. He then expanded his program of domestic reforms, but the country began to respond less rapidly to his innovating tendencies. His popularity and ability to control events declined, chiefly because of his troubled Vietnam policy, and he felt compelled toward the end of his second term in 1968 to forego another presidential race and surrender his office.

EARLY CAREER

Johnson was born in 1908 on a farm in poor southwest Texas farming country, far from the centers of power. He received his early education in public schools and in the Johnson City High School, from which he graduated in 1924. In 1927 he entered the Southwest Texas State Teachers College, earning his degree in a little more than three years.

In 1931, after a brief career as a teacher, Johnson began his rise up the political ladder. His help in the successful congressional campaign of Richard

M. Kleberg in that year led to his appointment as the new congressman's secretary. By 1935, Johnson's energetic service in Washington had earned him the post of state administrator of the National Youth Administration in Texas. Meanwhile, in 1934, he met and married Claudia Alta ("Lady Bird") Taylor. The couple were to have two daughters: Linda Bird, born in 1944, and Lucy (later Luci) Baines, born in 1947.

CONGRESSIONAL YEARS

In 1937, Johnson, an ardent New Dealer, defeated a large field of anti–New Deal candidates to win his own seat in the House of Representatives. There he was to spend 11 years. Capitalizing on his friendship with a powerful Texan, Speaker of the House Sam Rayburn, Johnson made foreign and military affairs his specialty.

As World War II approached, he assisted President Franklin D. Roosevelt in his battles against the isolationists. Early in the war, he served briefly overseas as a naval officer and then returned to Congress, where he worked for the development of the armed forces. He remained a champion of military power after the war and became a firm supporter of the new foreign policy of "containment."

The Senate Years. Johnson was elected to the U. S. Senate on his second attempt, in 1948, his first bid having failed in 1941. He soon attained a position of national leadership. In 1951 he became party whip, and two years later his connections with all factions of the Democratic party and his legislative experience resulted in his selection as his party's leader in the Senate. At first he had only a minority to lead, but the Democrats regained majority status in the congressional elections of 1954 and kept it during the Eisenhower administration.

Johnson's task was difficult. Senators have responsibilities to constituents as well as to party leaders, and power inside the Senate is distributed among committees chaired by men with years of senatorial experience. Furthermore, Johnson's party was divided on many issues, and a Republican was in the White House. Nevertheless, Johnson played his role with unusual success, securing the passage of much major legislation by dint of his talent at finding the common ground that men of power and differing points of view could occupy.

Civil rights provided the most significant illustration of Johnson's techniques and their consequences. In 1957 he faced civil rights proposals by the Eisenhower administration that were supported by Northern Democrats and opposed by the party's Southern members. Seeking a compromise that would hold his party together, Johnson obtained a narrowing of the bill to focus on voting rights. He also obtained agreement to provide for jury trials of those accused of violating the voting rights of others. The result was the first civil rights law since Reconstruction.

The 1960 Campaign. Johnson's support for civil rights, especially the strong support he provided for a second law in 1960 (also concerned chiefly with voting), was part of his move in a liberal direction as the presidential election approached. He had raised his sights to the presidency. To many Northerners, however, he seemed too Southern in viewpoint and style, and for this and other reasons he lost the nomination to Sen. John F. Kennedy. Yet

Kennedy selected Johnson as his vice presidential running mate, partly because he had influence in areas—the South and the Senate—in which Kennedy needed help in order to win the election and gain acceptance for his proposals. Campaigning hard through the fall of 1960, Johnson did help to contain the revolt of Southern Democrats and thereby contributed to the narrow victory margin.

PRESIDENCY

The "1,000 Days" of the Kennedy administration were an active but frustrating period for Vice President Johnson. He performed several important domestic and foreign assignments for the chief executive, but he had private doubts about some of Kennedy's policies, and his relations with certain White House staff members were strained. On Nov. 22, 1963, Johnson suddenly became President when John Kennedy was assassinated in Dallas.

Eager to use the powers that were now his, the new President pressed for enactment of Kennedy's proposals on civil rights and taxes. He employed all of his tested techniques in dealing with Congress and supplemented them with appeals to the people for support. Helped by many others, he obtained passage of Kennedy's proposals and, in the process, broke a major deadlock on domestic issues.

The 1964 Election. Johnson's performance demonstrated that he had become a truly national figure. With his popularity rising, he received the Democratic nomination for a full presidential term in the summer of 1964. The Republicans' nomination of Sen. Barry Goldwater, who disagreed fundamentally with established policies and seemed alarmingly radical to many voters, ensured the President the decisive victory that he felt would endorse his right to leadership and provide a base for further accomplishments. Johnson received more than 61% of the popular vote in November, winning in all states except five in the Deep South and Arizona.

The Great Society Program. Since the spring of 1964, Johnson had talked of and made plans for the building of a "Great Society," and now, with the conservative bloc weakened by the congressional elections, the first session of the 89th Congress converted into law many important proposals, some of which had been bottled up for years. The list included "Medicare" (health insurance for the elderly), another voting rights measure, and new bills supporting the "war on poverty" that Johnson had declared in 1964. This was the most active Congress since 1935 in attacking domestic problems.

Escalation in Vietnam. At the same time, the President enlarged the American role in the war in Vietnam. A Vietcong victory in South Vietnam seemed likely in early 1965, and Johnson feared that such a victory would give the Communists control of a significant area and would suggest that the United States could not protect other countries against revolutionaries that used guerrilla tactics and received outside help. Thus, in February 1965, the President, with confidence in American power and a continuing commitment to containment on a global scale, ordered American planes to bomb North Vietnam and began the rapid expansion of American military ground action and troop levels in South Vietnam. These moves halted the Vietcong drive toward victory but did not check the infiltration of men and supplies from the north or bring the North Vietnamese to the bargaining table on terms acceptable to the President.

IMPORTANT DATES IN JOHNSON'S LIFE

Aug. 27, 1908—Born at Hye, near Johnson City, Texas.

June 1930—Earned B. A. degree at Southwest Texas State Teachers College in San Marcos.

Nov. 17, 1934—Married Claudia Alta Taylor.

August 1935—Became state director of National Youth Administration in Texas.

May 14, 1937—Entered U. S. House of Representatives.

June 1941—Failed in first bid for U. S. Senate seat.

Nov. 2, 1948—Won election to U. S. Senate.

Jan. 2, 1951—Named Senate majority whip.

Jan. 2, 1953—Chosen Democratic floor leader.

Jan. 5, 1955—Became Senate majority leader.

July 1955—Suffered first heart attack.

July 14, 1960—Accepted Sen. John F. Kennedy's offer of the Democratic vice presidential nomination after losing presidential nomination.

Jan. 20, 1961—Sworn in as Vice President.

Nov. 22, 1963—Took oath as President in Dallas on the day of President Kennedy's assassination.

May 22, 1964—Called for "Great Society" program in an address at University of Michigan.

July 2, 1964—Signed sweeping civil rights bill.

Nov. 3, 1964—Elected to full presidential term in landslide victory over Sen. Barry Goldwater.

Feb. 7, 1965—Ordered bombing of targets in North Vietnam and began U. S. troop escalation in Indochina.

Nov. 8, 1965—Signed "Medicare" into law.

June 23 and 25, 1967—Conferred with Soviet Premier Aleksei Kosygin in Glassboro, N. J.

March 31, 1968—Announced reduction of bombing of North Vietnam and decision not to seek reelection.

Jan. 20, 1969—Presidential term ended.

May 22, 1971—The Lyndon Baines Johnson Library dedicated at the University of Texas in Austin.

Jan. 22, 1973—Died en route to San Antonio, Texas, after suffering heart attack in Johnson City.

Love Field, Dallas, Texas, Nov. 22, 1963.

WIDE WORLD

Criticism of Johnson's war policy increased as the fighting dragged on and U. S. casualties mounted. Popular confidence in him declined, and the continuation and enlargement of the war reduced his ability to shape events at home. Rioting erupted in black neighborhoods of many large cities and reached a high level in 1967. Although Johnson admitted the violence revealed that not enough was being done to solve urban problems, he did not call for bold new programs. The war now occupied the top spot on his agenda and consumed billions of dollars that might have been devoted to the treatment of domestic ills.

Announcement of Retirement. Early in 1968, the situation worsened. The Vietcong and the North Vietnamese suddenly mounted a major offensive that contradicted the administration's optimistic pronouncements and enlarged the ranks of Johnson's critics. Two Democrats, Senators Eugene McCarthy and Robert Kennedy, mounted strong challenges to Johnson for the Democratic presidential nomination.

In this situation, Johnson made two decisions. In a dramatic address to the people on March 31, 1968, he announced that he was reducing the bombing in hope of getting negotiations started, indicating that he had lost confidence in escalation. At the same time, he withdrew as a candidate for reelection, stating the hope that this action would serve to unite Americans on the home front. These decisions did not restore his mastery of political developments in the United States during the remaining months of his administration, nor did they result in a negotiated settlement of the war, and he passed on to his Republican successor a set of extremely difficult problems.

Success and Failure. Johnson had used his political skills to acquire enormous power, and had used that power to promote constructive change, but he had tried to do more than the resources of his nation, his office, and his talents would support. He had tried to control events thousands of miles from home at the same time that he attempted to reshape the life of his own nation. But he discovered that his efforts to expand the U. S. role as a global power interfered with his efforts to create a Great Society at home.

Johnson's accomplishments were not insignificant. His civil rights measures considerably increased black participation in political life in the South. Other segments of American society were enormously benefited by the Medicare program, the Higher Education Act of 1965, and other measures. His accomplishments, however, were dwarfed by the more serious problems with which he grappled, such as poverty. Recognizing how limited his power had become, he voluntarily surrendered what remained.

RETIREMENT

Although not an old man, Johnson enjoyed only a brief period of retirement on his Texas ranch. He had driven himself relentlessly throughout a long career and had borne the burden of major responsibilities in difficult times. He suffered a serious heart attack in 1955, went through two abdominal operations while President (1965 and 1966), and had another heart attack in 1972. Arteriosclerosis led to the heart attack that ended his life on Jan. 22, 1973, at the age of 64. He was buried in a small family cemetery close to his birthplace.

RICHARD S. KIRKENDALL, *Indiana University*

AS COMMANDER IN CHIEF, President Johnson visits U. S. troops at Camranh Bay, South Vietnam, in October 1966. The war escalated during his administration.

UPI

AUDEN, W. H.

British-American poet: b. York, England, Feb. 21, 1907; d. Vienna, Austria, Sept. 28, 1973.

One of the dominant voices in 20th century English verse, W. H. Auden exerted a formative influence not only on poetry and verse but also on people and opinions. During the 1930's Auden expressed the views of a romantic radical and after 1940 of a convinced Christian. Auden conveyed his moral acuteness and concern in a graphic, varied, and rich vocabulary. His verse is marked by a fierce and sometimes macabre wit and by a facility that recalls Byron or Browning. His mental landscape, like his geographical, is "Northern," with fells, rocks, scarps, and worn hills, as well as industrial debris, suggesting the polar peril of a new ice age.

Life. Wystan Hugh Auden was born in York, England, on Feb. 21, 1907. His father was a distinguished physician; his mother had been a nurse. Both grandfathers were Anglican clergymen. His home atmosphere, as a result, was both scientific and devout. He intended to become a mining engineer, but in March 1922 a friend asked him, "Do you write poetry?" He never had, but from that instant he knew what he wanted to do, and his first poem was published in 1924. In 1925 he went to Christ Church, Oxford, where he studied English and coedited *Oxford Poetry, 1926* and *Oxford Poetry, 1927*. He dominated his companions in a father-confessorly way. In 1928 the poet Stephen Spender handprinted 26 of Auden's poems in an edition of 45 copies.

After leaving Oxford in 1928, Auden spent a year in Germany, where he "fell in love with the language" and was influenced by the playwright Bertolt Brecht and by German cabaret and theater songs. He also acquired a passion for politics and psychology. On his return from Germany he became the most exciting social poet in England, the leader of the literate left and the poet analyst of a sick society. Auden's *Paid on Both Sides,* a poem published in 1930 in T. S. Eliot's quarterly *Criterion,* was dedicated to the poet C. Day Lewis, whom Auden succeeded that year as an English master at Larchfield Academy, Helensburgh, Scotland.

In 1936, although he had not previously met her, Auden married Erika Mann, the daughter of the German novelist, Thomas Mann, to provide her with a passport so she could leave Nazi Germany. They remained married until Erika died in 1969. In 1937, during the Spanish Civil War, he went to Spain as a stretcher-bearer. That same year he was awarded King George's Gold Medal for poetry. In 1938 he and Christopher Isherwood went to China, then together wrote the play *On the Frontier* (1938) and an essay in prose and verse *Journey to a War* (1939).

In 1939, Auden settled in the United States. He became an American citizen in 1946. He received the 1948 Pulitzer Prize in poetry for *The Age of Anxiety* (1947). From 1956 to 1961 he was professor of poetry at Oxford. Then, in 1972, he again made his home in England as poet in residence at Oxford University. Auden died in a Vienna hotel on Sept. 28, 1973, after spending the summer at his home in the nearby village of Kirchstetten. At his own request, he is buried in the cemetery of the Catholic church in Kirchstetten.

Writings. *Poems* (1930) made Auden's reputation. It included *Paid on Both Sides* and 30 other

W. H. AUDEN (1907–1973)
View from a "Northern" landscape.

poems and was published by Faber and Faber, where T. S. Eliot was an editor. *Poems* castigates and satirizes the bourgeoisie as doomed from without by the inevitable march of Marxism and from within by the interior death-wish that motivates its noisy resistance. However, both writer and reader are part of that bourgeoisie, which Auden loved and later also prayed for. These ideas are expanded in *The Orators* (1932), perhaps the most obscure of Auden's verse.

Auden and Isherwood collaborated on two more plays, *The Dog Beneath the Skin* (1935) and *The Ascent of F6* (1936). Auden and Louis MacNeice, a fellow poet, went to Iceland in 1936, then collaborated on *Letter From Iceland* (1937), a volume of prose and verse.

Among Auden's later volumes of poetry are *For the Time Being: A Christmas Oratorio* (1944), *The Shield of Achilles* (1955), and *Epistle to a Godson* (1972). He translated Dag Hammarskjöld's *Markings* (1964) and, with Chester Kallman, wrote librettos for the operas *The Rake's Progress* (1951), *Elegy for Young Lovers* (1961), and *The Bassarids* (1966).

In addition to the prizes mentioned previously, Auden's awards included the Bollingen Prize, the Gold Medal for Poetry of the National Institute of Arts and Letters, and the National Medal for Literature in 1967. Besides the volumes of poetry, Auden published two collections of essays, *The Dyers Hand* (1962) and *Forwards and Afterwards* (1973).

ANNE FREMANTLE
Author of "This Little Band of Prophets"

UPI

DAVID BEN-GURION (1886–1973)
Idealism and realism.

BEN-GURION, David

Founder of Israel: b. Płonsk, Poland, Oct. 16, 1886; d. Tel Aviv, Israel, Dec. 1, 1973.

David Ben-Gurion belongs in the select company of heroic figures—men such as Washington, Jinnah, Masaryk, or Pilsudski—who have founded or restored nations. More than any other man he was the creator of modern Israel, and he was its first prime minister. He possessed the rare combination of qualities necessary for such a role—the burning idealism that can envision a possible future, and the political realism to bring it to birth. Along with these he had an incredibly stubborn will.

Early Life. The future founder of Israel, whose original name was David Gryn, was born in Płonsk, a small Polish town some 40 miles (65 km) northwest of Warsaw and then part of the Russian Empire. He was the sixth of 11 children. His mother died in childbirth when he was 10. His father practiced law, though apparently lacking formal qualifications. The family was intellectually vigorous, and neither poor nor Orthodox. David received a Jewish education but then ceased observing the rites of his religion. He read very widely, and soon became a remarkable linguist.

"Life in Plonsk was peaceful enough," wrote Ben-Gurion in his memoirs. But the boy was deeply influenced by the writings of the Austrian journalist Theodor Herzl, a pioneer advocate of Zionism, and decided early to emigrate to Palestine and make Zionism his life's work.

In Palestine. David moved to Palestine in 1906, working first as a farm laborer and gaining prominence in the small Socialist-Zionist party, *Poalei Zion.* Soon journalism and politics became his principal activities. Writing his articles under the *nom de plume* Ben-Gurion (the original had been one of the defenders of Jerusalem in 70 A. D. against Titus), he came to adopt this as his own name. In those years and until 1917 he thought it might be possible to obtain a special status for a Jewish Palestine within the Turkish Empire, and so he went to Constantinople to study Turkish law and administration. However, he was expelled by the Turks in 1915 and went to the United States.

In New York, he helped found *Hechalutz* (the Pioneers), which organized Jewish settlements in Palestine between the wars. He also met and married Paula Moonwess, his beloved and formidable wife, who was with him in all his struggles from their marriage in 1917 until her death in 1968.

Encouraged by the issuance of the Balfour Declaration in 1917, Ben-Gurion organized Jewish battalions to fight as part of the British army in the Middle East. He served in 1918 in Egypt as a corporal in the Royal Fusiliers but saw no action.

Emerging Leader. When the labor federation *Histradut* was formed in 1920, Ben-Gurion became its secretary-general, thus acquiring a formidable power base. His position was further enhanced when *Mapai,* the union of Palestinian labor parties, was formed in 1930. In 1935 he became chairman of the Jewish Agency, the executive body of Zionism.

From 1922 until 1948, Palestine was a British mandate. It became the scene of a three-cornered struggle between the Jews, the Arabs, and a British power increasingly restrictive of Jewish immigration. Ben-Gurion was a fighter by instinct and by habit. He had never doubted that the Jewish settlers in Palestine would have to defend their lives and their refound homeland by actual combat. And so, as the mandate neared its end, Ben-Gurion did everything he could to see that the Jewish settlers were militarily ready for the coming struggle.

Israel Restored. The Jewish settlers accepted the 1947 UN decision partitioning Palestine. With Israel's declaration of independence on May 14, 1948, Ben-Gurion became the first prime minister of Israel. In the first war with the Arabs, 1948–49, Ben-Gurion actively led his people to victory. Also, he established firmly the principle that Israel was one state with one army.

Ben-Gurion was prime minister until 1953 and again from 1955 to 1963. He was autocratic and had little patience with dissident colleagues. He frequently used the threat of resignation to get his own way; his withdrawal from government in 1953 and his retirement in 1963 were tactical moves of this kind. During his leadership his personal history was virtually that of his country.

The main features of Ben-Gurion's government were his success in holding together coalitions; the German reparations agreement of 1952; the ambiguous "Lavon affair" (1954–60); the Eichmann trial (1960); and the war of 1956.

In his periods of retreat and after retirement, Ben-Gurion lived a life of scholarly contemplation in the desert *kibbutz* of Sde Boker in the Negev Desert. His death on December 1 followed a cerebral hemorrhage on November 18. After lying in state in Jerusalem, he was laid to rest at Sde Boker on December 3 in a simple ceremony, at his request without eulogy.

ARTHUR CAMPBELL TURNER
University of California, Riverside

BUCK, Pearl S.

American writer and humanitarian: b. Hillsboro, W. Va., June 26, 1892; d. Danby, Vt., March 6, 1973.

Although Pearl Buck, who spent almost half of her life in China, did not achieve serious literary recognition in the United States, she became one of the most widely known of U. S. writers, and she remains the only American woman to have won a Nobel Prize in literature (1938).

She is best known for *The Good Earth* (1931), a novel portraying Chinese peasant life. An instant success, both critically and financially, it won a Pulitzer Prize, was dramatized for both stage and screen, and was translated into more than 30 languages. She produced some 80 other books, including novels, collections of short stories, biographies and other nonfiction, and books for children, as well as many essays, magazine articles, and plays. But her fame is based on her humanitarian activities as well as on her voluminous writing.

Life and Works. Pearl Sydenstricker was born while her Presbyterian missionary parents were on a year's leave from their post in China. She grew up there, speaking both Chinese and English, and at the age of 16 returned to the United States to attend Randolph-Macon Woman's College at Lynchburg, Va., from which she was graduated in 1914. She was married in China in 1917 to John Lossing Buck, an agricultural missionary. Their daughter, Carol, was born in 1921. After her marriage, Pearl Buck taught at Chinese universities, pursued her interest in writing, and with her family made visits to the United States to study or care for personal business. When the marriage failed, she returned permanently to the United States, where in 1935 she was married to Richard J. Walsh, president of the John Day Company, her New York publisher.

Pearl Buck was a child of two civilizations— American and Chinese. This background was the source of her two major themes—the conflict between old and new and between East and West. These themes appear in the two stories contained in her first work, *East Wind: West Wind* (1930). Her masterpiece, *The Good Earth,* combined the regional with the universal in its unromantic portrayal of a peasant's struggle for human fulfillment. It was followed by *Sons* (1932) and *A House Divided* (1935), to form the trilogy *House of Earth* (1935).

In translation, her major effort was a rendering into English of *Shui Hu Chuan,* a classic Chinese novel concerning the right to rebel against bad governments, which she titled *All Man Are Brothers* (1933). In 1936 she published *The Exile,* a biography of her mother, and *Fighting Angel,* a biography of her father. In awarding her the Nobel Prize in 1938, the Nobel committee cited these "masterpieces of biography," as well as her "rich and genuine portrayals of Chinese life." American reaction to the Nobel award was mixed. The editor and author Henry Seidel Canby recognized her achievement in dramatizing Chinese sensibility for a Western audience but noted that she "is clearly not the destined subject of a chapter in literary history."

After 1938, she produced such well-known novels as *Dragon Seed* (1942), *Peony* (1948), *Imperial Woman* (1956), *Command the Morning* (1959), *The Living Reed* (1963), and *Mandala* (1970). Under the pseudonym John Sedges, she wrote several novels, including *The Townsman* (1945). Her autobiographical works are *My Several Worlds* (1954), *A Bridge for Passing* (1962), and *For Spacious Skies* (1966).

Significance. Pearl Buck was sharply critical of the white man in Asia, whether he came to establish trading empires or to preach the gospel. At the same time, she spoke against racism and sexism in the United States.

In 1941 she founded the East-West Association, which for ten years encouraged cultural interchange. In 1949 she founded Welcome House, an organization for unwanted interracial children, and in 1963 she established the Pearl S. Buck Foundation to aid in the adoption and care of Amerasian children. Her own family included nine adopted children, in addition to her daughter, Carol, whose severe mental retardation led her to write *The Child Who Never Grew* (1950) and to work on behalf of the retarded.

Pearl Buck identified her own relation to literary tradition in her Nobel Prize address, published as *The Chinese Novel* (1939). She acknowledged that she shared the Chinese view of the novel as essentially a popular form and stated that she deliberately strove for a mass audience. But she had difficulty in fulfilling her own goals. She placed great emphasis on vividness of character; yet her critics often found her characters flat or improbable. She condemned "explanation" but was criticized for didacticism. And the audience she reached was not so much the common people as what one reviewer called "genteel ladies on wrought-iron garden chairs in Easthamptons all over the world." But Pearl Buck's perceptiveness and candor have great appeal, and her claim to fame seems assured.

JEROME H. STERN, *Florida State University*

PEARL S. BUCK (1892–1973)
Author of "The Good Earth"

WIDE WORLD

UPI

PABLO CASALS (1876–1973)
"I am a man first, an artist second."

CASALS, Pablo

Cellist, conductor, composer, and pianist: b. Vendrell, Catalonia, Spain, Dec. 29, 1876; d. Río Piedras, Puerto Rico, Oct. 22, 1973.

The Spanish-born cellist Pablo Casals is generally regarded as the greatest cello virtuoso of the 20th century and perhaps of all time. His brilliant technique and infinitely expressive style set a standard that, while widely emulated, remained unsurpassed. Although most famous as a cellist, Casals also won great distinction as a conductor, composer, and pianist.

Early Years. Pau Carlos Salvador Defillö de Casals was born at Vendrell, Catalonia, Spain, on Dec. 29, 1876. (Pau is the Catalonian form of Pablo or Paul.) His first teacher was his father, a church organist, under whom he learned to play the organ, piano, violin, flute, and various other instruments. At the age of 12, Casals decided to become a cellist and went to Barcelona, where he studied with José Garcia at the Municipal School of Music. Soon he started to develop a naturalistic approach to technique and his own theories of cello playing, including exact and expressive intonation and rhythmic and melodic accentuation. While a student in Barcelona, he came upon six unaccom-

panied cello suites by Bach, thus initiating a lifelong devotion to that composer, of whose works he became a foremost interpreter.

In 1894, Casals went to Madrid. There he was encouraged and helped financially by Count Morphy, secretary to the queen, and by Queen María Cristina herself. After studying at the Royal Conservatory in Madrid, he went to Paris, where in 1895 he became cellist at the Paris Opéra. His career as a cello virtuoso began in Paris in 1899, when he made his concert debut with the Lamoureux Orchestra. He was an instant success.

Casals began to tour widely in Europe and North and South America, as a soloist and as a coperformer with such distinguished musicians as the violinists Fritz Kreisler and Jacques Thibaud and the pianists Harold Bauer and Alfred Cortot. He made his American debut in 1901 and played at the White House for President Theodore Roosevelt in 1904. In 1905 he formed a chamber music trio with Cortot and Thibaud.

Middle Years. Casals' other great interest, in addition to the cello, was the art of conducting. In 1919 he founded the Pau Casals Orchestra in Barcelona and provided the people of Catalonia, notably the working classes of Barcelona, for whom he set special low admission prices, with splendid performances of classical music. Casals also was a guest conductor of many great orchestras outside Spain.

When the Spanish Civil War broke out in 1936, Casals made no secret of his sympathy for the Republican cause, giving numerous benefit concerts for the wounded and for refugees. He left Spain in 1939, on the eve of Franco's victory and settled in Prades in southern France. During World War II, he courageously refused to have anything to do with the Germans and gave a number of concerts to raise money for victims of the war. In 1950 he founded the Prades Festival, an annual event that attracted many famous musicians and in which he participated both as cello soloist and as conductor.

Later Years. In 1956, Casals visited his mother's birthplace in Puerto Rico and shortly thereafter settled there. In 1957 he married his third wife, Martita Montañes. In that year he also inaugurated the annual Casals Festival in Puerto Rico, which became one of the major international musical events. Even in old age Casals continued to pursue a very active career, not only as a cellist and conductor but also as a recording artist, teacher, and composer. His compositions include the cantata *La visión de Fray Martín* and the oratorio *El pesebre.* Among his most important single appearances were his performance, dedicated by him to the cause of peace, at the United Nations in New York City in 1958 and his recital at the White House in 1961, when he played for President Kennedy. In his final years, Casals' musical activities included an annual visit to the Marlboro Music Festival in Vermont. During UN Day in 1971, Casals conducted the premiere of his *Hymn to the United Nations*, with text by W. H. Auden, in New York. At that time, he was awarded the UN Peace Medal for devoting his life "to truth, to beauty, and to peace."

Throughout his career, Casals, revered equally as a superb musician and as a great human being, tirelessly used his musical genius and his international reputation to further the cause of peace and harmony. His character is best expressed in his own statement, "I am a man first, an artist second."

ROBERT MANN, *Juilliard String Quartet*

COWARD, Sir Noël

British playwright, composer, and actor: b. Teddington, England, Dec. 16, 1899; d. Jamaica, March 26, 1973.

An impressive obituary for Noël Pierce Coward could be written by simply listing his works—more than 50 titles for the theater, more than 250 songs, two volumes of autobiography, a novel, parodies, short stories, poems, and journals, plus work as actor, singer, director, filmmaker, and cabaret entertainer. To the quantity and high quality of these activities must be added the image of the witty sophisticate, who embodied the elegant cynicism and world-weariness of the 1920's. His life ended on an appropriate wave of success—with a revival of *Private Lives* and a revue, *Cowardy Custard,* made up of excerpts from his works, running in London, and another such revue, *Oh, Coward!* in New York.

Life and Works. Noël Coward made his professional debut in London in *The Goldfish* (1911). By the age of 11, he had been prepared for the stage by his mother, who had encouraged his amateur endeavors and arranged for dancing lessons and auditions. After *The Goldfish,* he appeared in a number of plays and became familiar with the wide range of popular theater, and in his teens he began to write poems, stories, songs, and plays. He was in the army briefly in 1918 but was released because of a tubercular condition. His first play to be produced was *I'll Leave It to You* (1920), and he contributed songs to a number of revues.

In 1923, Coward wrote three plays: *Fallen Angels,* a comedy with a daring drunk scene for the two leading ladies; *Hay Fever,* a farce about an eccentric family; and *The Vortex,* a melodrama about an adulteress and her drug-addict son. All three were to be great successes, and it was a coincidence that *The Vortex* was the first produced (1924). It made Coward's reputation as writer, actor, and celebrity. In addition to plays written earlier, the flow of productions for the next few years included two revues—*On with the Dance* (1925) and *This Year of Grace* (1928)—and the operetta *Bitter-Sweet* (1929), which included *I'll See You Again,* the finest of his many songs.

Success proved exhausting and disturbing, and Coward suffered a nervous breakdown. He took a long, recuperative trip to the East and returned with one of his most lasting successes, *Private Lives* (1930), written in only a few days. Its basic pattern —involving the witty couple who cannot live apart but who quarrel most of the time when together— has appeared in a variety of his plays but nowhere else so incisively and elegantly. It confirmed Coward as one of the superior writers of high comedy.

With control and confidence restored, Coward entered upon his finest period. His works included *Cavalcade* (1931), a panoramic view of English society, 1899–1931; *Words and Music* (1932), with what is probably Coward's best-known song, *Mad Dogs and Englishmen; Design for Living* (1932), another skillful high comedy; *Conversation Piece* (1933), a musical comedy; and *Tonight at 8:30* (1935), a group of one-act plays. In 1937 he published the first volume of his autobiography, *Present Indicative.* The second volume, *Future Indefinite,* appeared in 1954.

The outbreak of World War II interrupted the presentation of new Coward plays, but he wrote steadily. In the early 1940's, three of his best plays were produced—*Blithe Spirit* (1941), a farce about ghosts and mediums; *Present Laughter* (1942), a portrait of a self-indulgent but witty actor; and *This Happy Breed* (1942), a chronicle of an unassuming English family from 1919 to 1939.

Blithe Spirit set what was then a London record of 1,997 performances. But Coward's works after the war showed waning energy, although most were moderately successful. The plots and themes that had served him well since the mid-1920's with only slight variations were inadequate in the postwar world. But Coward's reputation was boosted by his success as a nightclub entertainer and author of a novel, *Pomp and Circumstance* (1960). His last theater pieces were a group of plays entitled *Suite in Three Keys* (1966). These were of special interest because in one of them—*A Song at Twilight*— Coward dealt for the first time with the subject of homosexuality.

Assessment. Coward was a distinctive and memorable performer, but critics throughout his career assumed his work would prove ephemeral. Yet his best plays and songs have shown remarkable powers of endurance. They rest on solid craftsmanship, which conceals itself so that the air of spontaneous playfulness persists and the acerbic disdain for the conventional, mixed with a hint of sentiment, is still effective. Coward's best characters are either suave, amoral sophisticates or delightful eccentrics, and his best songs are either patter or sentimental waltzes. He could poke fun at pretension and hypocrisy, but he was no social reformer. He was in the fullest sense what he set out to be in his youth— a man of the theater, an entertainer. For this he was deservedly knighted following his 70th birthday.

MILTON LEVIN, *Author of "Noël Coward"*

SIR NOËL COWARD (1899–1973)
An acerbic disdain for the conventional.

UPI

PABLO PICASSO (1881–1973)
"... the last of the great masters."

PICASSO, Pablo

Painter, sculptor, and printmaker: b. Málaga, Spain, Oct. 25, 1881; d. Mougins, France, April 8, 1973.

Pablo Picasso is considered the greatest artist of his time. His name is inseparable from the art of the 20th century, a period he filled out through a production of more than seven decades in a variety of media. In each of them he probed formal possibilities, invented images, and reflected underlying realities of the age. In so doing, he helped to shape the 20th century world.

Early Years (1881–1904). Picasso was born in Málaga to José Ruiz Blasco, an art teacher, and his wife, María Picasso López. From 1901, he used only the maternal name "Picasso" as his signature.

The family moved, according to the father's teaching posts, first to La Coruña and then to Barcelona, capital of Catalonia. There, at the age of 14, Picasso entered the School of Fine Arts. Two years later he went to Madrid to study, but he soon returned to the lively, intellectually stimulating Catalonian capital. After several restless years spent in Barcelona, Madrid, and Paris, he left Spain in 1904 to settle permanently in Paris.

Imitative Styles. Picasso drew and painted from childhood on. At first, under his father's influence, he worked in the tradition of Spanish realism. Then he began to imitate the dotted style of impressionism and the sinuous line of art nouveau. Probably the first important Parisian painting by Picasso, then 19 years old, is *Le Moulin de la Galette* (1900; Guggenheim Museum, New York).

Blue Period. Mood and pathos expressed through figures of beggars, cripples, harlots, and other outcasts mark Picasso's earliest Parisian style from the end of 1901 through 1904. Blue is the prevalent color of such works as *The Blue Room* (1901; Philips Collection, Washington)—a reflection perhaps of both a personal state of mind and a pessimistic fin-de-siècle sentiment. Despite some early support from such venturesome dealers as Berthe Weill and Ambroise Vollard and the encouraging friendship of the writer Max Jacob, Picasso at that time suffered extreme poverty, making his determination to settle in Paris an act of real courage.

Early Years (1904–1914). The decade before the outbreak of war encompasses the work of the Rose Period and the creation of cubism, Picasso's

most significant contribution to art. In 1904 he took up residence in a rickety building in Montmartre. There he lived for the next five years in material poverty and spiritual elation. His friends included Max Jacob, the Americans Gertrude and Leo Stein, the poet-critic Guillaume Apollinaire, and Fernande Olivier, the first of the many mistresses whose features animated his work. Most important was the friendship of Georges Braque, with whom he later developed the radical cubist style.

Rose Period and Steps to Cubism. Toward the end of 1904, the moody and sometimes sentimental melancholy of the Blue Period gave way to predominantly earthen, brown, and pink hues, as Picasso's subjects moved from the city's cafés and bistros into the roads and the countryside. He came to see his beggars, circus folk, and street singers with a measure of detachment, rendering them less self-consciously and more objectively, as in *The Family of Saltimbanques* (1905; National Gallery).

Picasso's development toward cubism reached its climax with the monumental, justly celebrated *Demoiselles d'Avignon* (1906–07; Museum of Modern Art, New York). After many preparatory works, in which he gradually simplified the design—based on a brothel scene in Barcelona's Avignon Street—and eliminated allegorical subject matter, he arrived at a stylized depiction of angular nude or partially draped women grouped around an arrangement of fruit. This work is a grand recapitulation of Picasso's previous striving and visual inheritance, including El Greco, Cézanne, and Iberian and probably African sculpture. At the same time, the painting's formal innovations contain the basic vocabulary of cubism.

Cubism. By 1909, Picasso had established himself as a painter of exceptional talent. He lived comfortably, vacationed in Spain and Provence, and in his affections replaced Fernande with her friend Marcelle Humbert, whom he called Eva.

In 1910, Picasso's cubist style reached full maturity. In such works as the painting of his dealer Daniel-Henry Kahnweiler, *Portrait of Kahnweiler* (1910; Art Institute of Chicago), Picasso reduces the subject to vestigial remnants that appear in danger of disintegrating into a formal scaffolding. Meaning in such works must be sought in the conjugation of forms—either through analytical dissection (1909–11), in which figurative imagery and color are reduced in favor of structure or, later, through synthetic reconstructions, in which modified formal developments are employed with added color and expanded iconography. Synthetic cubism grows out of collage, in which materials such as wallpaper, cloth, or newspaper simultaneously enrich and adulterate the pure cubist form, as in *Still Life with Chair Caning* (1911–12; Picasso Collection).

Picasso also explored cubism in sculpture, such as the influential and severely beautiful constructions *Guitar* (1912; Museum of Modern Art). Later he developed a playful, colorful, and intimate cubist "rococo" variant.

War Years and Interim (1914–1944). The outbreak of World War I tore the fabric of Picasso's Parisian world. His friends went to the front, and Eva died. Yet the war years were extremely productive for Picasso and brought important stylistic changes.

Realism. The most conspicuous change was an apparent return to realism, as seen in a meticulous pencil drawing, *Portrait of Vollard* (1915; Metro-

politan). For some time Picasso's renewed interest in descriptive rendition, applied to mannerist and neoclassical subjects, kept abreast of a synthetic cubist phase that achieved such masterpieces as the two versions of the *Three Musicians* (1921; Philadelphia Museum of Art and Museum of Modern Art).

Picasso's realist development was reinforced by stage design commissions for the Ballets Russes of Serge Diaghilev. With assistants, he painted a neoclassical fantasy of circus figures on a large curtain for the ballet *Parade* (1917). That and other Diaghilev productions led to new friendships with writers, musicians, and painters linked with Dada, surrealism, and other avant-garde movements. Paul Rosenberg became his dealer, and in 1918, Picasso married the Russian dancer Olga Koklova.

Surrealism. During the 1920's a growing sense of unease is reflected in Picasso's work. There was a change in emphasis from constructed to expressive form and from a style predominantly cubist to one closer to surrealism, although Picasso never formally joined the movement. The clearest revelation of such changes is *Three Dancers* (1925; Tate Gallery, London), depicting three attenuated female figures engaged in a frenetic dance. The underlying cubist structure is used toward expressive ends, foreshadowing the convulsive imagery of *Guernica*.

Other works of the late 1920's and early 1930's include paintings of increasingly distorted, surrealistic figures; metamorphic bronze figures; ingenious assemblages; and many graphics, such as the etchings (1931) for Ovid's *Metamorphoses*. The strained attenuations in many of these works may be, in part, a reflection of personal crisis. This period was marked by separation from the conventional Olga in 1935 and liaisons with the sensual blond model Marie Thérèse Walter and the aloof aristocratic photographer Dora Maar. Both appear in his work.

Expression of Historical Crisis. In the 1930's, Picasso's surrealist images became more overtly symbolic, bespeaking not only his personal emotional turmoil but also the political events of the time. The Spanish Civil War of 1936 generated a patriotism and a humanitarian outrage expressed in the series of etchings *The Dream and the Life of Franco* (1937), and in *Guernica* (1937; Museum of Modern Art), the mural allegory portraying the Spanish town bombed by Franco's forces, which became a byword of victimization through senseless destruction. In both, Picasso falls back on the bullfight imagery that had long captivated him and that he had used with fresh conviction in the etching *Minotauromachy* (1935). The brutally strong bull and the dying horse from the latter reappear transformed in *Guernica*, an unsurpassable expression of violence that may be the most intense creation of its time. Two years after *Guernica* was completed, all Europe was engulfed in war. Picasso hid his work near Bordeaux and enclosed himself in his Paris studio.

Postwar Years (1944–1973). The liberation of Paris in 1944 found Picasso hard at work and enhanced in public stature as a result of his passive resistance against the Germans. In a gesture of naive idealism, he joined the Communist party, providing a lithographed dove for a poster for peace.

Gradually Picasso withdrew from public activity and spent evermore time with the young painter Françoise Gilot in southern France. In 1948 they settled in the pottery town of Vallauris, where Picasso produced pottery and figurines and painted mythological subjects and the murals *War and Peace* (1952) in a deconsecrated 12th century chapel. François left him in 1953, and that year Jacqueline Roque, the cousin of a Vallauris potter, became the last woman to inspire Picasso. After he married her in 1961 (Olga had died in 1955), they settled in Mougins, north of Cannes.

The ever-robust, energetic Picasso continued an undiminished working life. But in these later years the radical innovations of his youth and middle age gave way to detached, self-mocking images, in such recurring themes as the aging artist and young model. Increasingly he turned toward the past, defining Delacroix, Velázquez, and Manet in his own terms. When he died, the world—almost forgetful of his radicalism—mourned him as the last of the great masters.

THOMAS M. MESSER, *Director*
The Solomon R. Guggenheim Museum, New York

Picasso's Guernica *protests the destruction of a Basque town during the Spanish Civil War of 1936–39.*

MUSEUM OF MODERN ART, NEW YORK

obituaries • 1973

The following is a selected list of over 200 prominent persons who died in 1973. Separate articles on major figures appear on the preceding pages. Cross references in this list are to articles in the text where biographical sketches of the subject will be found.

Aichi, Kiichi (66), Japan's minister of finance: b. Tokyo, Oct. 10, 1907; d. there, Nov. 23, 1973. A member of the national legislature since 1950 and holder of finance and other ministry posts since his graduation from the University of Tokyo in 1931, he helped mold the country's financial system and guide its economic development after World War II. As foreign minister (1968–71), he negotiated with the United States for the return (in 1972) of Okinawa to Japan. He was a well-known figure at international economic conferences and at the time of his death a leading adviser in Japan's energy, trade, and financial affairs.

Aiken, Conrad (84), U.S. poet and author: d. Savannah, Ga., Aug. 17. See LITERATURE—*American Literature.*

Allen, George Edward (77), U.S. lawyer and businessman; he was a personal friend of three U.S. presidents—Franklin D. Roosevelt, Harry S. Truman, and Dwight D. Eisenhower: d. Palm Desert, Calif., April 23.

Allen, Ida Bailey (88), U.S. author of cookbooks; wrote more than 50 books, which sold a total of some 20 million copies; specialized in New England recipes: d. Norwalk, Conn., July 16.

Allen, Leo E. (74), U.S. congressman (R-Ill., 1933–61); chairman, House Rules Committee (1947–49 and 1953–55): d. Galena, Ill., Jan. 19.

Allende Gossens, Salvador (65), president of Chile: d. Santiago, Chile, Sept. 11. See CHILE.

Anderson, Margaret C. (82), U.S. magazine editor; founded *The Little Review* in Chicago in 1914; under her editorship for 15 years, it introduced works by Joyce, Eliot, Yeats, Pound, Hemingway, and other prominent writers: d. Le Cannet, France, Oct. 18.

Apostoli, Fred (59), U.S. middleweight boxing champion; he won the title on Nov. 18, 1938, in a bout with Young Corbett and held it until defeated by Ceferino Garcia on Oct. 2, 1939: d. San Francisco, Calif., Nov. 29.

Armstrong, Hamilton Fish (80), U.S. political scientist; editor of the public opinion quarterly *Foreign Affairs* (1928–72): d. New York City, April 24.

Artsimovich, Lev A. (64), Soviet nuclear physicist; a pioneer in the USSR's atomic research program, and a leader in research on peaceful uses of nuclear energy: d. Moscow, March 1.

Auden, W. H. (66), Anglo-American poet: d. Vienna, Austria, Sept. 28. See page 435.

Barker, Lex (53), U.S. film actor, noted for his portrayal of Tarzan; he succeeded Johnny Weissmuller as Tarzan in 1949: d. New York City, May 11.

Batista (y Zaldívar), Fulgencio (72), former Cuban president and military strongman: b. Banes, Oriente province, Cuba, on Jan. 16, 1901; d. Guadalmina, near Marbella, Spain, on Aug. 6, 1973. During most of the period between August 1933, when Batista helped stage a "sergeants' revolution," and New Year's Day, 1959, when he was overthrown by Fidel Castro, he was the dominant force in Cuba. The son of a farm laborer, he began his army career in 1921. As constitutional president from 1940 to 1944 he brought Cuba into World War II on the Allied side and instituted some social reforms. In March 1952 he overthrew the government of Carlos Prío Socarrás. Taking the title of president, he instituted a dictatorship noted for corruption, suppression of constitutional liberties, and hospitality to U.S. business interests. His reform measures failed to stem the growing popularity of Castro, whose revolutionary 26th of July movement in 1953 exerted steady pressure against the Batista regime. After his overthrow nearly five and a half years later, Batista went into exile and during his last years made his home in Portugal and Spain.

Beaumont, Hugh (64), British theatrical producer; one of the most successful producers of his time; produced many British shows in the United States and many U.S. shows in Britain: d. London, March 22.

Beazley, Rev. George G., Jr. (59), U.S. religious leader; leader in ecumenical movement; chairman of the Consultation on Church Union and on central committee of World Council of Churches: d. Moscow, USSR, Oct. 7.

Beebe, Frederick Sessions (59), U.S. publishing executive; was chairman of the board of the Washington Post Company: d. New York City, May 1.

Behrman, S(amuel) N(athaniel), U.S. playwright and screen writer: b. Worcester, Mass., June 9, 1893; d. New York, N.Y., Sept. 9, 1973. A master of sparkling dialogue and ironic wit, he was the author of two dozen urbane, humanistic comedies of manners that often commented on the moral issues of the day, and was long a popular personality of the Broadway theatrical world. He was drawn to literature and the performing arts early in life. After study at Clark University and Harvard and an M.A. at Columbia, he led a precarious existence as a book reviewer, free-lance writer, and press agent, until the 1927 production of his first successful play, *The Second Man.* Among his other plays are *Rain From Heaven* (1934), *End of Summer* (1936), *No Time for Comedy* (1939), and *But for Whom Charlie* (1964). He also wrote the autobiographical *The Worcester Account* (1954), the novel *The Burning Glass* (1968), biographies of Sir Max Beerbohm and Lord Duveen, and many screenplays, including several for Greta Garbo. In 1938 he was a co-founder of the Playwrights' Company.

Bemis, Samuel Flagg (81), U.S. historian: b. Worcester, Mass., Oct. 20, 1891; d. Bridgeport, Conn., Sept. 26, 1973. A "historian's historian" and a leading authority on U.S. diplomatic history, he won two Pulitzer prizes, in history for *Pinckney's Treaty: A Study of America's Advantage from Europe's Distress* (1926), and in biography for *John Quincy Adams and the Foundations of American Foreign Policy* (1949). He was educated at Clark University and at Harvard, where he obtained his doctorate. After teaching at George Washington University and elsewhere, and studying European and Latin American archives, he joined the Yale faculty in 1935. Writing in the "grand style," he published *Jay's Treaty; A Study in Commerce and Diplomacy* (1923), *A Diplomatic History of the United States* (1936), *The Latin American Policy of the United States* (1942), and *John Quincy Adams and the Union* (1956). He edited *The American Secretaries of State and Their Diplomacy* (10 vols., 1927–29). In 1960 he retired from Yale, having been since 1945 Sterling Professor of Diplomatic History and Inter-American Relations.

Ben-Gurion, David (87), founder of Israel: d. Tel Aviv, Dec. 1. See page 436.

Benton, William (72), U.S. businessman, educator, and statesman; pioneered in market research in the 1920's and 1930's and established the realistic radio commercial; vice president of the University of Chicago in 1937–45; became publisher of the *Encyclopaedia Britannica* in 1943; introduced 54-volume *Great Books of the Western World* series; assistant secretary of state for public affairs in 1945–47; as U.S. senator from Connecticut in 1949–53, he opposed Sen. Joseph McCarthy, leading to an investigation and censure of McCarthy: d. New York, N.Y., March 18.

Bertrand, Jean-Jacques (56), Canadian political leader; as premier of Quebec in 1968–70, he tried to hold the French-speaking provinces on a line between federalism and French nationalism: d. Montreal, Feb. 22.

Biddle, George (88), U.S. muralist; best known for fresco panels in Justice Department building, Washington, D.C., depicting everyday people with great dignity: d. Croton-on-Hudson, N.Y., Nov. 6, 1973.

Bikila, Abebe (46), Ethiopian track star; a national hero in Ethiopia, he won the 26-mile marathon at 1960 and 1964 Olympic Games: d. Addis Ababa, Ethiopia, Oct. 25.

Blackmer, Sidney (78), U.S. actor; a founder of Actors Equity Association (1913); appeared in more than 40 Broadway plays, 200 movies, and numerous TV dramas; won a Tony award in 1950 for his performance in *Come Back Little Sheba:* d. New York, N.Y., Oct. 5.

Bonnet, Georges (83), French foreign minister, who signed the 1938 Munich pact with Hitler; was ambassador to the United States (1937) and cabinet member (1925–39, 1956–68): d. Paris, June 18.

Bontemps, Arna (70), U.S. author; was a member of the group of black writers and poets known as the Harlem Renaissance; wrote children's books, histories of the blacks, anthologies, and more than 25 novels, including *God Sends Sunday* (1931), *Black Thunder* (1939), *Drums at Dusk* (1939): d. Nashville, Tenn., June 4.

Bowen, Catherine (Shober) Drinker (76), U.S. author: b. Haverford, Pa., Jan. 1, 1897; d. there, Nov. 1, 1973. She was noted for her best-selling, carefully researched, and partly fictionalized historical biographies, including

Beloved Friend (1937), about Tchaikovsky; *Yankee From Olympus* (1944), about Justice Oliver Wendell Holmes, Jr.; *John Adams and the American Revolution* (1950); and *The Lion and the Throne* (1956), about Sir Edward Coke, which won her a National Book Award in 1957. The daughter of a lawyer who was later president of Lehigh University, she became an accomplished violinist at age 12. She received a teaching certificate from the Institute of Musical Art in New York in 1919 but gave up a musical career to marry Ezra Bowen, a professor. After a divorce, in 1939 she married Dr. Thomas McKean Downs and also began research for her first great nonmusical work, *Yankee From Olympus*, "to bring Justice Holmes out of legal terms into human terms." Among her other books are *Adventures of a Biographer* (1959), *The Craft and the Calling* (1969), and the autobiographical *Family Portrait* (1970).

Bowen, Elizabeth (73), British novelist, noted for her sensitive portrayals of members of upper-middle-class society; books include *Death of the Heart* (1938) and *The Heat of the Day* (1949): d. London, Feb. 22.

Bowen, Ira S. (74), U. S. astronomer; helped build the great Mt. Palomar telescope and was director of combined operations for Palomar and Mt. Wilson observatories (1948–64): d. Los Angeles, Feb. 6.

Brill, Marty (67), U. S. athlete; was All-American halfback for the University of Notre Dame football team; coached teams of La Salle College and Loyola University: d. Los Angeles, April 30.

Brookeborough, Lord (Basil Stanley Brooke) (85), Irish government official; prime minister of Northern Ireland (1943–63); opposed reconciliation with Republic of Ireland: d. Belfast, Northern Ireland, Aug. 18.

Browder, Earl R. (82), American Communist leader: b. Wichita, Kans., May 20, 1891; d. Princeton, N. J., June 27, 1973. As general secretary of the U. S. Communist party from 1930 to 1946 and its presidential candidate in 1936 and 1940, he was the party's standard-bearer during the decade of its greatest influence (1935–45), and he played a major role in its labor union organizing activities. The son of a Populist farmer, he became a Socialist in his teens and served a prison term as a World War I draft resister. A charter member of the U. S. Communist movement, he served it in New York City as an editor, organizer, and delegate to international congresses in the 1920's. Under his leadership, the party adopted a united front policy in the mid-1930's, supporting Franklin D. Roosevelt on a number of issues until the German-Soviet pact of 1939. In 1941–42, Browder was imprisoned on a passport charge, and for the remainder of World War II he firmly supported the Allied war effort. He was expelled from the party as a "right deviationist" in 1946 and later broke with Marxism.

Brown, Joe E(van) (80), U. S. comedian: b. Holgate, Ohio, July 28, 1892; d. Brentwood, Calif., July 6, 1973. One of America's favorite comic artists, he was noted for his huge grin and talent for hilarious pantomime. He began as a circus acrobat in Ohio at the age of nine, performed in vaudeville and burlesque, played professional baseball, and appeared in such Broadway musicals as *Listen, Lester* (1919) and *Greenwich Village Follies* (1921–23). He opened the road tour production of *Harvey* (1945), in which he played the role of Elwood P. Dowd more than 1,000 times. He began his motion picture career in 1928, appearing in some 50 Hollywood films. They include *Hold Everything* (1930), *The Tenderfoot* (1932), *Elmer the Great* (1933), *Show Boat* (1951), and *Some Like It Hot* (1959). He himself thought his best were *Hold Everything* and *Elmer the Great*, reflecting his knowledge of the circus, stage, and sports. He was awarded the Bronze Star for a 200,000-mile tour in World War II, entertaining American servicemen.

Buck, Pearl S. (80), U. S. author: d. Danby, Vt., March 6. See page 437.

Burnett, Whit (72), U. S. editor; as founder-editor of *Story* magazine (1931–71), he published early stories of William Saroyan, Carson McCullers, Truman Capote, and J. D. Salinger: d. Norwalk, Conn., April 22.

Butts, Wally (68), U. S. football coach; served as coach of the University of Georgia football team from 1939 to 1960: d. Athens, Ga., Dec. 17.

Cabral, Amilcar (48), West African political leader; led revolt against the Portuguese rulers of Guinea; founder and president of the nationalist African party for the Independence of Guinea and Cape Verde: d. (assassinated) Conakry, Guinea, Jan. 20.

Calwell, Arthur (76), Australian politician; was a member of the House of Representatives for 32 consecutive years; as minister of immigration (1943–49), he planned and initiated Australia's postwar immigration program; leader of the Labor party (1960–67): d. Melbourne, July 8.

Cannon, Jimmy (63), U. S. sportswriter; sports columnist for the King Features Syndicate and the Hearst newspapers: d. New York City, Dec. 5.

Carey, James B. (62), U. S. labor leader; president of the United Electrical, Radio, and Machine Workers of America (1936–41); founder (1950) and first president of the International Union of Electrical Workers: d. Silver Spring, Md., Sept. 11.

Carrero Blanco, Luis (70), Spanish naval officer and government official: b. Santoña, Spain, March 4, 1903; d. Madrid, Spain, Dec. 20, 1973. Carrero Blanco served Generalissimo Francisco Franco loyally—and largely in the shadows—for decades, and Franco, in effect, designated Carrero as his successor in 1972. Carrero, an honor student at Spain's naval academy, rose through the grades to become an admiral in 1966. In 1937 he had made his way across civil war battle lines to join Franco, who after his victory made Carrero chief of naval operations. In 1941 he was named undersecretary to the presidency of the government, and 10 years later elevated to cabinet rank. Increasingly influential as Franco's hard-line, behind-the-scenes adviser, Carrero was appointed vice-premier in 1967 and premier on June 8, 1973. He was killed by a bomb that exploded under his car. Basque separatists claimed responsibility for the assassination.

Casals, Pablo (96), Spanish-born cellist and conductor: d. Río Piedras, Puerto Rico, Oct. 22. See page 438.

Chandler, Norman (74), U. S. newspaper publisher; built *The Los Angeles Times* into one of the nation's largest and most influential newspapers; led The Times Mirror Company: d. Los Angeles, Calif., Oct. 20.

Chaney, Lon, Jr. (67), U. S. film actor; he was best known for his portrayal of monsters, notably a werewolf in the "Wolf Man" series; won critical acclaim as Lenny in *Of Mice and Men;* was son of the famous silent film star Lon Chaney: d. San Clemente, Calif., July 13.

Chase, Mary Ellen (86), U. S. author, noted for novels depicting life in New England; she was able to derive themes of universal significance from her regional subjects; her novels include *Dawn in Lyonesse* (1938) and *Silas Crockett* (1935); her other writings include the critical study *Thomas Hardy from Serial to Novel* (1927) and the autobiographical *The White Gate* (1954): d. Northampton, Mass., July 28.

Chehab, Gen. Fuad (70), first commander of the Lebanese army, after the nation won its independence in 1946, and president of Lebanon (1958–64): d. near Beirut, April 25.

Cicognani, Amleto Giovanni Cardinal (90), Italian cardinal: b. Brisighella, Italy, Feb. 24, 1883; d. Rome, Italy, Dec. 17, 1973. From 1933 to 1958, he was apostolic delegate in Washington, D. C. He was created cardinal in 1958. After serving as secretary of the Sacred Congregation for the Oriental Church in the Vatican (1960–61), he was appointed papal secretary of state by Pope John XXIII in 1961, retaining that position under Pope Paul VI until 1969.

Condon, Eddie (Albert Edwin) (67), U. S. jazz musician and composer: b. Goodland, Ind., Nov. 16, 1905; d. New York, N. Y., Aug. 4, 1973. A colorful personality in the world of jazz, and one of its great guitarists, he was a leading interpreter of the Dixieland style and helped establish the improvisational "Chicago school" of jazz, which emphasized unscored music played by small bands. Condon began to play with small jazz groups in the Chicago area in his teens and eventually became associated with most of the great figures of the jazz world, including Bix Beiderbecke and Artie Shaw. In the 1930's he played in New York City clubs, and during the World War II years he directed jazz concerts at New York City's Town Hall. In 1946 he opened his own Greenwich Village nightclub, featuring his guitar playing and witty conversation. He made a number of recordings, wrote a jazz column for the New York *Journal-American*, and published the autobiographical *We Called It Music* (1947) and *The Eddie Condon Scrapbook of Jazz* (1973).

Cooper, Merian C. (78), U. S. film producer and director, best known as creator of *King Kong;* other memorable films include *The Lost Patrol, Rio Grande,* and *The Quiet Man:* d. San Diego, Calif., April 21.

Cordiner, Ralph J. (73), U. S. business executive; former chairman of the board and chief executive officer of the General Electric Company; author of *New Frontiers for Professional Managers* (1956): d. Clearwater, Fla., Dec. 5.

Coste, Dieudonné (80), French pioneer long-distance aviator; in 1930 he made the first westward transatlantic flight: d. Paris, May 19.

Costello, Frank (Francesco Castiglia) (82), U. S. underworld figure: b. Cosenza, Italy, Jan. 26, 1891; d. New York, N. Y., Feb. 18, 1973. Known as the "prime minister of the underworld," he amassed a fortune through

such activities as bootlegging, bookmaking, and control of a multi-billion-dollar slot-machine racket, with the help of corrupt law enforcement agents and government officials. In 1951 he was the central figure of Sen. Estes Kefauver's crime investigating committee hearings. The son of a grocer, he came to the United States at the age of four and grew up in New York's Harlem and Greenwich Village, eventually graduating from teen-age street gangs to the big-time rackets of the prohibition era. Convicted of contempt charges growing out of the Kefauver hearings, he also later served a prison term for income tax evasion. In 1957 he survived a gangland assassination attempt. The U. S. government stripped him of his citizenship in 1961.

Coward, Sir Noël (73), English playwright, songwriter, and performer: d. Jamaica, March 26. See page 439.

Cox, Wally (48), U. S. actor; gained popularity in 1953 as a meek, bespectacled teacher in the television series *Mr. Peepers;* appeared on the television game show *Hollywood Squares* from its inception in 1966 until his death: d. Bel Air, Calif., Feb. 14.

Cranko, John (45), South African-born ballet director and choreographer: b. Rustenberg, South Africa, Aug. 15, 1927; d. on flight from Philadelphia, Pa. to Stuttgart, West Germany, June 26, 1973. As director of the Stuttgart Ballet since 1961, he developed it from a unit of the provincial Wurttemberg State Opera into an independent and internationally acclaimed major dance company. After studying at the Festival Ballet Society in Johannesburg and at the University of Cape Town, he went to London in 1946 and became a charter member of the Sadler's Wells Theatre Ballet. His success as a choreographer included such one-act pieces as *Beauty and the Beast* (1949) and *Pineapple Poll* (1951) and the full-length ballet *Prince of the Pagodas* (1956), and staging of the successful musical revue *Cranks* (1955). As director of the revitalized Stuttgart Ballet, he imported talent from all over the world. At the time of his death, the company was returning from its third U. S. tour.

Creasy, John (64), British mystery writer; wrote 650 mystery and detective novels under 28 pen names; among his most popular works are *Inspector Roger West of Scotland Yard, Gideon's Fire,* and the "Toff" series: d. Salisbury, England, June 9.

Darin, Bobby (37), U. S. pop singer: b. Bronx, N. Y., June 14, 1936; d. Los Angeles, Calif., Dec. 20, 1973. A well-known singer of popular songs, he became a star in the 1960's with his interpretations of *Mack the Knife* and such songs of his own composition as *Early in the Morning* and *Dream Lover.* Among his successful motion pictures were *Come September* (1961) and *Captain Newman, M. D.* (1963), for which he received an Oscar nomination.

de Cordova, Arturo (66), Mexican film actor, born Arturo Garcia Rodriguez; played in more than 100 U. S. and foreign films but was best known for his roles in such productions of the 1940's as *For Whom the Bell Tolls* and *Frenchman's Creek:* d. Mexico City, Nov. 3.

De Paris, Wilbur (72), jazz trombonist and bandleader; he led the New Orleans Jazz Band, which held to older forms of jazz; his band toured Africa in 1957 under a State Department program: d. New York, N. Y., Jan. 3.

DeSalvo, Albert H. (40), U. S. criminal, known as the "Boston Strangler"; when on trial for other crimes in 1967, he confessed to the unsolved murders of 13 women in the Boston, Mass., area during 1962–64; he was not tried for the murders and later retracted the confession: d. (of stab wounds) in Walpole, Mass., state prison, Nov. 27.

Drew, George (78), Canadian political leader; was premier of Ontario (1943–48) and national leader of the Conservative party (1948–56): d. Toronto, Jan. 4.

Dunn, Michael (39), U. S. film and stage actor; a 3-foot 10-inch dwarf, he won many favorable notices for his film and stage work, notably for his role as an evil dwarfed hunchback in the movie *Ship of Fools:* d. London, England, Aug. 29.

Edwards, Albert Glenn "Turk" (65), U. S. football player; an All-American tackle at Washington State University in 1929–31; lineman and later coach and vice president of the Washington Redskins; elected to the Pro Football Hall of Fame in 1969: d. Kirkland, Wash., Jan. 10.

Eisendrath, Maurice N(athan) (71), U. S. rabbi: b. Chicago, Ill., July 10, 1902; d. New York, N. Y., Nov. 9, 1973. As head of the 100-year-old Union of American Hebrew Congregations, he served for more than 30 years as spiritual leader of the one million Reform Jews in the United States. A graduate of the University of Cincinnati, he was ordained by the Hebrew Union College in that city in 1926, and then served as a rabbi to congregations in Charleston, W. Va., and Toronto, Canada. In 1943 he was appointed executive director of the Union of American Hebrew Congregations, and in 1946 became its president. Once described as a "Jewish Thomas Paine," Eisendrath championed social justice and civil rights, while condemning racism, McCarthyism, Johnson's and Nixon's Vietnam War policies, and the Watergate scandals. At the time of his death he had been scheduled to deliver a speech sharply criticizing Jews who supported the Nixon administration in order to curry favor for Israel. In 1972, Eisendrath was elected president of the World Union of Progressive Judaism.

Elisofon, Eliot (61), U. S. photographer, cinematographer and painter: b. New York, N. Y., April 17, 1911; d. New York, N. Y., April 7, 1973. A staff member of *Life* magazine (1942–72), he traveled over 2 million miles, covering six continents, to fulfill his mission "to help the world to see." He was especially noted for his work on the art and culture of Africa. A graduate of Fordham University, he began his career as a free-lance photographer. During World War II he photographed military campaigns as well as cultural subjects for *Life,* in Africa, Europe, and the Pacific. Over the years his work included such diverse subjects as the temples of India and Cambodia; Turkish Byzantine architecture; the peoples of the Andes; Africa's Mountains of the Moon; and culinary still lifes. He directed several television programs, including ABC-TV's four-hour *Africa* (1967), and he served as color consultant for Hollywood motion pictures. He was also noted for his delicate watercolor paintings. His *Color Photography* appeared in 1961.

Erskine, Gen. Graves B. (75), U. S. Marine Corps officer, who fought in both world wars; in 1945 he led the Third Marine Division in the landing at Iwo Jima; in 1953 he was promoted to four-star general: d. Bethesda, Md., May 22.

Evergood, Philip (71), U. S. artist, known for social satires; many major U. S. and foreign museums have acquired his paintings: d. Bridgewater, Conn., March 11.

Farber, Sidney (69), U. S. physician; director of research of the Children's Cancer Research Foundation; received (1966) the Lasker Award for Clinical Research for his pioneering work in using drugs to treat malignancies in children: d. Boston, March 30.

Ferretto, Giuseppe Cardinal (81), Italian cardinal; as chief penitentiary of the Roman Catholic Church, he had jurisdiction over all cases of conscience submitted to the Vatican: d. Vatican City, March 17.

Field, Betty (55), U. S. actress; her theater career included roles in *Dream Girl, Three Men on a Horse, Boy Meets Girl,* and *Room Service;* her film credits included *Of Mice and Men, Bus Stop, Picnic,* and *Peyton Place:* d. Hyannis, Mass., Sept. 13.

Firestone, Harvey S., Jr. (75), U. S. businessman; was chief executive officer of the Firestone Tire and Rubber Company (1946–63): d. Akron, Ohio, June 1.

Ford, John (Sean O'Feeney) (78), U. S. motion picture director: b. Cape Elizabeth, Me., Feb. 1, 1895; d. Palm Desert, Calif., Aug. 31, 1973. One of the giants of the U. S. film industry, he directed some 140 motion pictures during a career spanning some 50 years. His epics depicted stark human drama and individual heroism against a background of the great outdoors and characterized by meticulous camera work. A son of Irish immigrants, he served such apprenticeships as stunt man and cameraman in the budding Hollywood film industry before becoming a director in 1917. He received Oscar awards for *The Informer* (1935), *The Grapes of Wrath* (1940), *How Green Was My Valley* (1941), and *The Quiet Man*

Bobby Darin

WIDE WORLD

John Ford

UPI

(1953), and for the documentary short *The Battle of Midway* (1942), which he made while heading the U. S. Navy's film documentary unit in World War II. Among his other memorable films are *The Lost Patrol* (1934), *Stagecoach* (1939), *The Long Voyage Home* (1940), *Fort Apache* (1948), *The Horse Soldiers* (1959), and *The Man Who Shot Liberty Valance* (1962). In April 1973 he received the American Film Industry's first Life Achievement Award and the Presidential Medal of Freedom.

Freed, Arthur (78), U. S. film producer and songwriter; he won Academy Awards for *An American in Paris* (1951) and *Gigi* (1958); his hit songs included *Temptation* and *Pagan Love Song*: d. Hollywood, Calif., April 12.

Frisch, Frankie (74), U. S. baseball player and manager: b. New York, N. Y., Sept. 9, 1898; d. Wilmington, Del., March 12, 1973. He was elected to baseball's Hall of Fame in 1947, having ranked among the greatest second basemen in the history of the game. During 19 seasons with the New York Giants and the St. Louis Cardinals he compiled a batting average of .316. Known as the "Fordham Flash," he grew up in New York's Bronx and became captain of Fordham University's football, baseball, and basketball teams. He began his professional baseball career with the Giants in 1919 and helped them win four consecutive pennants (1921–24). Traded to the Cardinals in 1926, he took part in their successful bids for the pennant in 1928, 1930, and 1931. He managed the Cards' rough-and-tumble "Gas House Gang" from 1933 to 1938, the Pittsburgh Pirates (1940–46), and the Chicago Cubs (1949–51). Frisch also served as a coach and play-by-play radio announcer with the Giants.

Frisch, Ragnar (77), Norwegian economist; shared the first Nobel Prize for economics in 1969 wtih his colleague Jan Tinbergen for their development of econometrics—the application of mathematical models to the analysis of economic processes: d. Oslo, Jan. 31.

Frost, Leslie (77), Canadian politician; premier of Ontario (1949–61): d. Lindsay, Ontario, May 4.

Fuller, Alfred C. (88), Canadian-born U. S. businessman: b. Berwick, Nova Scotia, Canada, Jan. 13, 1885; d. Hartford, Conn., Dec. 4. He was the founder of the Fuller Brush Company and its president until 1943. In that year he became chairman of the board of the multimillion dollar business until his retirement in 1968. At his death there were about 25,000 Fuller Brush salesmen in the United States, Canada, and Mexico.

Gibbon, John H., Jr. (69), U. S. heart surgeon; performed (1953) the world's first successful open-heart surgery using a machine he developed that oxygenated the blood while a hole in the heart was being repaired: d. Philadelphia, Feb. 5.

Gillette, Guy M(ark) (94), U. S. senator: b. Cherokee, Iowa, Feb. 3, 1879; d. there, Mar. 3, 1973. A Democrat from Iowa, noted for his oratorical skill, he served in the House of Representatives from 1933 to 1936 and in the Senate from 1936 to 1945 and 1949 to 1955. The son of a farmer, he entered law practice and Democratic politics after obtaining his law degree from Drake University, Des Moines, in 1900. As a congressman and senator he championed the interests of the farmer and was an independent New Dealer, but he opposed a number of President Franklin D. Roosevelt's policies. An isolationist before World War II, he later turned to internationalism and helped draft the UN charter. He was president of the American League for a Free Palestine from 1944 to 1948, when he was reelected to the Senate. Defeated for a third Senate term in 1954, he served until 1961 as a counsel to Senate committees.

Grable, Betty (Ruth Elizabeth) (56), U. S. actress: b. South St. Louis, Mo., Dec. 18, 1916; d. Santa Monica, Calif., July 2, 1973. The reigning pinup queen of the World War II era and a star of Hollywood musicals during the 1940's and early 1950's, she ranked among the top 10 box-office attractions for 12 consecutive years. Her wholesome charms and "million dollar legs" brought her immense popularity, especially among U. S. servicemen. Encouraged by her mother to pursue a show business career, she began at the age of 13 to appear in chorus spots and bit parts in Hollywood motion pictures. She was launched on the road to stardom when she replaced Alice Faye in the lead of *Down Argentine Way* (1940). Among the more than 40 films in which she appeared were *Tin Pan Alley* (1940), *A Yank in the RAF* (1941), *Coney Island* (1943), *Diamond Horseshoe* (1945), and *My Blue Heaven* (1950). She retired from motion pictures in 1956, but continued to perform occasionally. In 1967 she starred in the Broadway production of *Hello Dolly!*, and in 1972 she was featured in the television special *The Fabulous Forties*. Her marriages to Jackie Coogan and Harry James ended in divorce.

Frankie Frisch

UPI

Betty Grable

WIDE WORLD

Graff, George (86), U. S. lyricist; wrote lyrics for more than 400 songs, including *When Irish Eyes Are Smiling*: d. Stroudsburg, Pa., Jan. 24.

Green, Abel (72), U. S. newspaper editor; was editor of the show business weekly *Variety* since 1933: d. New York City, May 10.

Gustaf VI Adolf (90), king of Sweden since 1960; established a reputation as a beloved and unpretentious monarch: d. Hälsingborg, Sweden, Sept. 15.

Hackworth, Green Haywood (90), U. S. jurist and authority on international law; was legal adviser to the U. S. State Department (1931–46); was a member of the International Court of Justice from its beginnings in 1946 until 1961, serving as president in 1955–57: d. Washington, D. C., June 24.

Hafey, Charles "Chick" (69), U. S. baseball player, who was in the major leagues for 13 seasons; he was the star outfielder for the St. Louis Cardinals and played in four World Series; in 1931 he won the National League batting crown with a .349 average; elected to the Baseball Hall of Fame in 1971: d. Napa, Calif., July 2.

Halliday, Richard (67), U. S. theatrical producer; co-produced many of the stage shows that starred his wife, Mary Martin: d. Brasília, Brazil, March 3.

Hammond, Laurens (78), U. S. inventor and businessman; invented the electric organ in 1935 and established the Hammond Organ Company, which he headed until 1960: d. Cornwall, Conn., July 1.

Hartman, Paul (69), U. S. actor, dancer, and comedian; formed comic ballroom dancing team with his wife, Grace; Broadway stage credits include *Red, Hot, and Blue* and *Angel in the Wings;* film credits include *Inherit the Wind* and *Luv:* d. Los Angeles, Calif., Oct. 2.

Harvey, Laurence (Larusha Mischa Skikne) (44), Anglo-American actor: b. Joniskis, Lithuania, Oct. 1, 1929; d. London, England, Nov. 25, 1973. A veteran of more than 60 British and American films and of the theatre and television, he was best known for his portrayal of the ruthless, self-centered social climber Joe Lampton in the film *Room at the Top* (1958), which earned him an Academy Award nomination. The son of a building contractor, he grew up in South Africa. After World War II military service, he studied at the Royal Academy of Dramatic Art in London, and during the 1950's he appeared with the Royal Shakespeare company and the Old Vic company. In 1947 he made his motion picture debut in *House of Darkness*. He was seen as a debonair playboy type in *Butterfield 8* (1960) and *Darling* (1965), as a conniving theatrical agent in *Expresso Bongo* (1960), and as a brainwashed political assassin in *The Manchurian Candidate* (1962). In 1963 he directed and acted in a film *The Ceremony*, and in 1973 completed directing *Arrow Beach*.

Hawkins, Jack (62), British actor; in a 50-year career he played more than 100 roles on stage and in films, and won acclaim as one of Britain's finest actors; his films include *Ben Hur, The Bridge on the River Kwai, The Prisoner*, and *Lawrence of Arabia*: d. London, July 18.

Hayakawa, Sessue (83), Japanese motion-picture actor; was a Hollywood star of the silent era; later won acclaim for his role in *The Bridge on the River Kwai* (1957): d. Tokyo, Nov. 23.

Heard, William Theodore Cardinal (89), British Roman Catholic prelate; one of the church's foremost experts on canon law: d. Rome, Italy, Sept. 16.

Laurence Harvey   Walt Kelly

Hess, Walter Rudolf (92), Swiss physiologist; co-winner of 1949 Nobel Prize for medicine "for his discovery of the functional organization of the interbrain as a coordinator of the activities of the internal organs"; head of the Physiological Institute of the University of Zürich (1927–51): d. Locarno, Switzerland, Aug. 12.

Higginbotham, Jay C. (67), U.S. jazz trombonist, known for his forceful style; played with Fletcher Henderson and Louis Armstrong: d. New York City, May 26.

Holt, Tim (54), U.S. film actor; starred in 149 films, most of them Westerns: d. Shawnee, Okla., Feb. 15.

Horowitz, Al (65), U.S. chess champion and writer; won U.S. open chess championship three times; founded the *Chess Review* in 1933, and was chess columnist for the New York *Times* (1962–72): d. New York, N.Y., Jan. 18.

Hume, David M. (55), U.S. surgeon, who helped develop the technique of human organ transplants; was chairman of surgery at the Medical College of Virginia (Richmond): d. Van Nuys, Calif., May 19.

Inge, William (Motter) (60), U.S. playwright: b. Independence, Kans., May 3, 1913; d. (apparent suicide) Los Angeles, Calif., June 10, 1973. His penetrating dramas about the dreams and frustrations of ordinary people in small-town America ranked him, along with Arthur Miller and Tennessee Williams, among the most successful dramatists of the Broadway stage in the 1950's. Educated at the University of Kansas and George Peabody Teachers College in Nashville, he was employed for several years as a teacher and journalist. In 1944, while working as a drama critic in St. Louis, he interviewed Tennessee Williams, who inspired him to write plays. His first major drama, *Come Back, Little Sheba* (1950), earned him a New York Drama Critics Circle award as the most promising playwright of the season. It was followed by three more hits: *Picnic* (1953), for which he received a Pulitzer Prize; *Bus Stop* (1955); and *The Dark at the Top of the Stairs* (1957). He also wrote several Hollywood screenplays, including *Splendor in the Grass* (1961), which won him an Academy Award. His subsequent works, among them the novels *Good Luck, Miss Wyckoff* (1970) and *My Son Is a Splendid Driver* (1971), failed to measure up to his earlier successes.

İnönü, Ismet (89), Turkish statesman; he became Turkey's first premier in 1923 and served as the country's second president from 1938 to 1950: d. Ankara, Turkey, Dec. 25.

Ishibashi, Tanzan (88), Japanese statesman, economist, and philosopher; was Japan's minister of finance (1946–47) and premier (1956–57): d. Tokyo, April 24.

Jenks, C. Wilfred (64), British lawyer; spent entire career with International Labor Organization, a UN specialized agency, becoming its director general in 1970: d. Rome, Italy, Oct. 9.

Jensen, J. Hans Daniel (65), German physicist; shared 1963 Nobel Prize in physics for developing the shell model of the arrangement of nuclear particles: d. Heidelberg, Feb. 11.

Johnson, Lyndon B. (64), 36th President of the United States: d. San Antonio, Texas, Jan. 22. See page 432.

Kellaway, Cecil (79), British-American actor, noted for his portrayals of kindly old gentlemen; appeared in more than 75 Hollywood films; nominated for Academy Awards for performances in *The Luck of the Irish* (1949) and *Guess Who's Coming to Dinner* (1967): d. Hollywood, Calif., Feb. 28.

Kelly, Walt(er Crawford) (60), U.S. cartoonist: b. Philadelphia, Pa., Aug. 25, 1913; d. Hollywood, Calif., Oct. 18, 1973. For nearly 25 years Kelly created the nationally syndicated comic strip *Pogo*, featuring a friendly opossum and his animal companions in the Okefenokee swamp and presenting sharp political satire as well as innocent nonsense to 20 million newspaper readers. The son of a theatrical scene painter, Kelly was cartoonist and editor of his high school newspaper. He worked as an animator for Walt Disney studios in Hollywood from 1935 to 1941 and then illustrated children's books. The first *Pogo* strips appeared in the short-lived New York *Star* in 1948, and Kelly began to draw *Pogo* for the New York *Post* in 1949. The strip soon grew immensely popular, and by the early 1950's there were "Pogo for President" clubs on many college campuses. Kelly received the 1952 award of the National Cartoonists Society. In 1954 he was the first comic-strip artist invited to contribute drawings to the Library of Congress collections. Over the years he published 14 Pogo cartoon books.

Kirby, Allan (80), U.S. businessman; former chairman of the Alleghany Corporation, a railroad holding company; inherited a multimillion dollar fortune from his father, a cofounder of the F.W. Woolworth chain stores: d. Harding Township, N.J., May 2.

Klemperer, Otto (88), German conductor and composer: d. Zürich, Switzerland, July 7. See MUSIC.

Koehler, Ted (78), U.S. songwriter; wrote lyrics for many hit songs, including *Stormy Weather* and *Let's Fall in Love*: d. Santa Monica, Calif., Jan. 17.

Konev, Ivan S(tepanovich) (75), Soviet army officer: b. Lodeino, Kirov region, Russia, Dec. 28, 1897; d. Moscow, USSR, May 21, 1973. A top military strategist and expert on mechanized warfare, he led the Soviet Union's first major counterattack against invading Germans in World War II, and in 1944 was promoted to marshal of the Soviet Union. He led his forces in the link-up with U.S. troops on the Elbe in 1945. A Communist party member since 1918, and a civil war veteran of the Red Army, he graduated in 1926 from Frunze Military Academy in Moscow. He survived the Stalinist purges of the 1930's. In 1946 he succeeded Georgi K. Zhukov as commander of Soviet ground forces and deputy defense minister. As an ally of Nikita S. Khrushchev, he headed the 1953 military tribunal that purged the Stalinist secret police chief Lavrenti P. Beria. He became commander of the joint Warsaw Pact forces (1955) and first deputy defense minister (1956). When the Berlin wall went up in 1961, he commanded Soviet forces in East Germany. From 1962 he served as general inspector of the Soviet defense ministry.

Krupa, Gene (64), U.S. jazz drummer and bandleader: b. Chicago, Ill., Jan. 15, 1909; d. Yonkers, N.Y., Oct. 16, 1973. A top personality in the swing era of the 1930's and 1940's, he revolutionized the role of the drummer in a jazz band, changing it from that of timekeeper to soloist. As a member of Benny Goodman's orchestra and as leader of his own bands, he won great popularity. The youngest of nine children of a Chicago alderman, he studied briefly for the Roman Catholic priesthood but dropped out in 1927 and became associated with the "Chicago style" of jazz, which was identified with Benny Goodman, Eddie Condon, and others. In the late 1920's and early 1930's, he played with various ensembles, including those of Red Nichols, Russ Columbo, and Buddy Rogers, before joining Benny Goodman's orchestra in 1935. He left Goodman in 1938 to form his own band, which included vocalist Anita O'Day and trumpeter Roy Eldridge. Krupa also led a new big band from 1944 to 1951, and thereafter played occasionally with smaller ensembles.

Krusen, Frank H. (75), U.S. medical leader; pioneered in the development of physical medicine and rehabilitation; served as head of the physical medicine department at the Mayo Clinic: d. Orleans, Mass., Sept. 16.

Kuiper, Gerard P. (68), Dutch-born U.S. astronomer: b. Harencarspel, Netherlands, Dec. 7, 1905; d. Mexico City, Mexico, Dec. 23, 1973. A major figure in the U.S. space program in the 1960's, he helped pinpoint potential landing sites on the moon through his knowledge of the nature of the lunar surfaces. Among his other outstanding contributions was his discovery of the satellites of the planets Uranus and Neptune in the 1940's.

Lake, Veronica (53), U.S. actress; was a popular film star of the 1940's, identifiable by her long blonde hair, which fell over one eye; her films include *I Married a Witch, Hold That Blonde, Out of This World,* and *Slattery's Hurricane:* d. Burlington, Vt., July 7.

Larraona, Arcadio Maria Cardinal (85), Spanish Roman Catholic churchman, who was one of the Vatican's leading authorities on church law; named a cardinal in 1959; was Prefect of the Sacred Congregation of Rites: d. Rome, May 7.

Lawrence, David (84), U. S. journalist: b. Philadelphia, Pa., Dec. 25, 1888; d. Sarasota, Fla., Feb. 11, 1973. During a career of more than six decades, he reported on national political affairs from Washington. His views, variously described as right-wing Republican and Wilsonian liberal, were reflected in his syndicated newspaper column and his weekly editorials in *U. S. News & World Report*, which he founded in 1947. While attending Princeton University, Lawrence became a reporter for the Associated Press, joining its Washington office in 1910. During service as Washington correspondent for the New York *Evening Post* from 1916 to 1919, he began to write a column that eventually appeared in some 300 newspapers. His *U. S. News & World Report* became one of the most respected American news magazines.

Lazarus, Fred R., Jr. (88), U. S. department store official; a pioneer in retail merchandising, in 1929 he helped form the Federated Department Stores, which he headed until 1966: d. Cincinnati, Ohio, May 27.

Leahy, Frank (64), U. S. football coach: b. O'Neill, Nebr., Aug. 27, 1908; d. Portland, Oreg., June 21, 1973. As head football coach at Boston College for two seasons and at Notre Dame University for 11 seasons, he compiled a lifetime record of 107 games won, 13 lost, and 9 ties. His winning percentage of .892 was exceeded in big-time college football only by the legendary Knute Rockne, under whom he played at Notre Dame in 1930. After serving as assistant coach at Georgetown, Michigan State, and Fordham, he became head coach at Boston College, where, in 1939 and 1940, his teams won 19 of their 20 games. As head coach of Notre Dame's Fighting Irish (1941–43 and 1946–53), Leahy turned out six undefeated teams and four national champions. He won coach-of-the-year honors six times and was elected to the National Football Foundation and Hall of Fame in 1970.

Lee, Bruce (32), Chinese actor; achieved international popularity as star of kung fu karate films: d. Tokyo, July 20.

Lee, Harold B. (74), U. S. religious leader: b. Clifton, Idaho, March 28, 1899; d. Salt Lake City, Utah, Dec. 26, 1973. In July 1972, he was chosen to the post of 11th president of the Mormon Church, the Church of Jesus Christ of Latter-Day Saints.

Lee, Lila (68), U. S. silent film star; won great popularity for roles with Rudolph Valentino and other stars in the 1920's: d. Saranac Lake, N. Y., Nov. 13.

Lefebvre, Joseph Cardinal (80), French Roman Catholic archbishop of Bourges (1943–69) and a cardinal since 1960; was president of the French Episcopal Conference and a member of the Vatican's Congregation for the Doctrine of the Faith: d. Bourges, April 2.

Lefevre, Theo (59), Belgian politician; premier of Belgium (1961–65) and leader of the Christian Social party: d. Brussels, Belgium, Sept. 18.

Leonard, Jack E. (62), U. S. comedian, who specialized in getting laughs with brief, terse insults; starred in vaudeville and nightclubs and on television: d. New York City, May 10.

Levy, Benn W. (73), British playwright; author of *Springtime for Henry* (1931) and *Clutterbuck* (1946); wrote dialogue for first British talking film, Alfred Hitchcock's *Blackmail* (1929): d. Oxford, England, Dec. 7.

Liénart, Achille Cardinal (89), French Roman Catholic ecclesiastic; bishop of Lille (1928–68) and a cardinal from 1930; he advocated Christian trade unionism and workers' rights: d. Lille, Feb. 15.

Lipchitz, Jacques (81), Lithuanian-born U. S. sculptor: b. Druskininkai, Lithuania, Aug. 22, 1891; d. Capri, Italy, May 26, 1973. One of the great masters of 20th century sculpture, he embraced a variety of schools, ranging from cubism, of which he was a pioneer, to monumental structures depicting heroic themes in the manner of Rodin. He moved to Paris in 1909 because opportunities for Jews were limited in czarist Russia, and studied at the École des Beaux-Arts and the Académie Julian. As a member of an avant-garde circle that included Picasso and Braque, he applied their principles to sculpture, and in 1914 he executed his first cubist works. In the 1920's he turned to the more graceful "transparents," using empty space as a component of sculpture. The influence of political events in Europe in the 1930's is reflected in such works as *Prometheus Strangling the Vulture* (1936) and *Rape of Europa* (1938). After he settled in the United States in 1941 his work assumed a more delicate and sensual quality. Lipchitz requested that he be buried in Jerusalem, where many of his works are located.

Loeb, Robert F. (78), U. S. medical scientist and teacher; established the role of the adrenal glands in controlling salt and water metabolism of the body; coeditor (1947–60) of Cecil-Loeb *Textbook of Medicine:* d. New York, N. Y., Oct. 21.

López Contreras, Eleazar (89), president of Venezuela from 1935 to 1941: d. Caracas, Jan. 3.

Lopukhov, Fyodor (86), Soviet ballet master and choreographer, who headed Leningrad's Kirov Ballet in 1922–30, 1944–47, and 1955–58: d. Leningrad, about Feb. 1.

MacEoin, Sean (79), Irish revolutionary; was a leader in Ireland's struggle for independence in the 1920's; served as minister of justice and defense in the 1940's: d. Dublin, July 7.

MacMillan, Sir Ernest (79), Canadian composer-conductor; directed the Toronto Symphony Orchestra (1931–56); his compositions include *Sketches for String Quartet* and *A Song of Deliverance:* d. Toronto, May 6.

Macready, George (63), U. S. actor, noted for his portrayal of villains; he played some 100 major roles on stage and almost as many in motion pictures: his films include *Commandoes Strike at Dawn, Gilda,* and *Johnny Allegro:* d. Los Angeles, July 2.

Magnani, Anna (65), Italian actress: b. Rome, Italy, March 7, 1908; d. there, Sept. 26, 1973. Long considered one of Italy's most skilled dramatic actresses, Miss Magnani won the Academy Award as best actress of 1955 for her tempestuous, down-to-earth portrayal of Serafina Delle Rose in the screen version of Tennessee Williams' *The Rose Tattoo,* her first Hollywood film. After a childhood amid poverty in city slums she studied at the Academy of Dramatic Art in Rome and made her start in show business as a nightclub singer and vaudeville performer. Miss Magnani first appeared in Italian films in the early 1930's but did not attain success until the following decade. Her first major screen role was in *Teresa Venerdi* (1942), and she won international acclaim for her performance in *Open City* (1946). Among her other films are *Angelina* (1947), *Love* (1947), *Volcano* (1953), *The Fugitive Kind* (1960), and *The Secret of Santa Vittoria* (1968).

Malipiero, Gian Francesco (91), Italian composer; an advocate of innovation, he composed operas, musical dramas, symphonies, quartets, and oratorios; compiled the complete works of Monteverdi and Vivaldi: d. Treviso, Italy, Aug. 1.

Mangrum, Lloyd (59), U. S. golfer: b. Dallas, Texas, Aug. 1, 1914; d. Apple Valley, Calif., Nov. 17, 1973. A former U. S. Open champion and leading money winner, Mangrum ranked with Sam Snead and Ben Hogan as one of professional golf's big three during the 1940's and 1950's. He began to play golf as a boy, working as a caddy in Dallas, and he studied the techniques of professional golfers at Los Angeles clubs after moving to the West Coast at age 14. In 1936 he entered tournament competition, and over the next few years he won several minor tournaments. He finished second in the prestigious Masters tourney in 1940. Although Mangrum was seriously wounded in Europe in World War II, he went on to score his greatest victory in 1946 when he won the U. S. Open in a three-way playoff. In 1948 and 1951 he was professional golf's biggest money winner. He won the Vardon Cup twice and the Los Angeles Open four times, and he was on four Ryder Cup teams, once as the captain. He retired from golf in 1960.

Manstein, Fritz Erich von (85), German military officer: b. Berlin, Germany, Nov. 24, 1887; d. Irschenhausen, Federal Republic of Germany, June 10, 1973. An armored warfare expert who was rated by the British historian B. H. Liddell-Hart as "the ablest of all German generals," he engineered the successful blitzkrieg against France in 1940, and led his troops to erstwhile victory in the Crimea and in other campaigns on the Russian front. The son of a Prussian general, he was adopted by a

Gene Krupa   Frank Leahy

German baron who raised him in the Junker tradition. He became a lieutenant in the Potsdam guards at 18, and served as a staff officer in World War I. In 1936 he became deputy chief of staff of the German army. Appointed a field marshal by Hitler in 1942, he was relieved of his command two years later for advocating strategic retreat from Stalingrad. In 1949 he was convicted by a British military court of having committed war crimes during the Russian campaign. After serving four years of an 18-year prison term, he was released, and became a military adviser to the Federal Republic of Germany.

Maritain, Jacques (90), French philosopher: b. Paris, France, Nov. 18, 1882; d. Toulouse, France, April 28, 1973. One of the most influential Roman Catholic thinkers of modern times, he was the leading 20th century exponent of Christian humanism, which applied the doctrines of Thomas Aquinas to problems of the modern industrial age. While adhering to orthodox church dogmas he championed social reform, political democracy, and the ecumenical movement. He strongly influenced leading churchmen, including Pope Paul VI. Reared in an atmosphere of liberal Protestantism, he was educated at the Sorbonne and was converted to Catholicism in 1906. From 1913 on, he taught Thomist philosophy at such institutions as Oxford, Heidelberg, and the Institut Catholique in Paris. After serving as French ambassador to the Vatican from 1945 to 1948, he taught at Princeton University until 1952. He wrote over 50 books, including *Art and Scholasticism* (1930), *True Humanism* (1938), *Man and the State* (1951), and *The Peasant of the Garonne* (1968).

Maynard, Ken (77), U. S. film actor and horseman; appeared in some 300 films, from 1923 to 1969, usually as a bashful cowboy hero: d. Hollywood, Calif., March 23.

Meigs, Cornelia L. (88), U. S. author; wrote more than 40 books for children and several works of history and biography, including *The Violent Men*: d. Harford County, Md., Sept. 10.

Melchior, Lauritz (Lebrecht Hommel) (82), Danish-born U. S. opera singer: b. Copenhagen, Denmark, March 20, 1890; d. Santa Monica, Calif., March 18, 1973. One of the greatest dramatic tenors in the history of opera, he sank over 1,000 performances in Wagnerian roles and was the reigning heldentenor of New York's Metropolitan Opera for nearly 25 years. He began his operatic career as a baritone, making his debut in *Pagliacci* in 1913 at the Royal Opera in Copenhagen. Persuaded to change to the tenor register, he sang with some success in England and Germany in the early 1920's before making his debut at the Metropolitan Opera in *Tannhäuser* in 1926. For 24 seasons he was one of the Met's chief attractions, giving memorable performances in *Siegfried*, *Die Walküre*, *Göttedämmerung*, *Parsifal*, *Tristan und Isolde*, *Lohengrin*, and other Wagnerian operas. He also performed on concert tours, in films, and on radio —activities that he continued after leaving the Met, following a dispute with manager Rudolf Bing in 1950.

Millionshchikov, Mikhail D. (60), Soviet physicist; was president of the Soviet Academy of Scientists and principal spokesman for scientific contacts with the West: d. Moscow, May 27.

Mislimov, Shirali (168), Caucasian peasant, reputedly the oldest person in the world; his age was 168, according to the Soviet news agency Tass: d. Barzavu, USSR, Sept. 2.

Mitford, Nancy (68), expatriate English novelist, essayist, and historian: b. London, England, Nov. 28, 1904; d. Versailles, France, June 30, 1973. A witty observer of upper-class society, she was famous for her controversial essay *The English Aristocracy*, published in *Encounter* magazine in 1955. In it she distinguished between "U" (upper class) and "non-U" way of speaking, claiming that "U" expressions are generally more direct than "non-U" expressions: sick, rich, false teeth ("U") and ill, wealthy, dentures ("non-U"). The essay was reprinted in *Noblesse Oblige* (1956). An aristocrat herself, she was one of six daughters (among them author Jessica Mitford) of the second Baron Redesdale. Her contact with a circle that included Evelyn Waugh and John Betjeman inspired her to pursue a literary career. Her light and humorous novels include *Highland Fling* (1931) and *The Blessing* (1951). Among her historical works are *Madame de Pompadour* (1954), *The Sun King* (1966), and *Frederick the Great* (1970). Miss Mitford lived in France after World War II.

Moberg, Vilhelm (74), Swedish author; considered the greatest contemporary Swedish writer by his countrymen; major works included *The Emigrants* and *The Immigrants*: d. near Stockholm, Sweden, Aug. 8.

Monroe, Vaughn (Wilton) (61), U. S. bandleader and singer: b. Akron, Ohio, Oct. 7, 1912; d. Stuart, Fla., May 21, 1973. One of the most successful singing bandleaders in the big band era of the 1940's and early 1950's, he attained great popularity with his renditions of such hit songs as *Racing With the Moon, Ballerina, Ghost Riders in the Sky*, and *There, I've Said It Again*, sung in his inimitable, slightly off-key nasal baritone. He began to play the trumpet in high school and dropped out of the Carnegie Institute of Technology in 1932 to make his career in popular music. By 1939 he headed his own band, which was heard by millions in nightclubs and theaters and on best-selling recordings. For eight years, beginning in 1945, he headed the popular radio program *Camel Caravan*. He also appeared in motion pictures and on television. After the advent of rock 'n' roll he turned from big bands to smaller ensembles.

Morin, Relman (65), U. S. journalist; was a reporter for the Associated Press news service (1934–72); won Pulitzer prizes for his reporting in 1951 and 1955: d. New York, N. Y., July 16.

Mott, Charles S(tewart) (97), U. S. industrialist and philanthropist: b. Newark, N.J., June 2, 1875; d. Flint, Mich., Feb. 18, 1973. He was a pioneer in the automobile industry and at one time the largest stockholder of the General Motors Corporation. Through his philanthropies, notably the Charles Stewart Mott Foundation, which he founded in Flint in 1926, he financed a variety of educational, medical, and recreational programs. A graduate of Stevens Institute of Technology and a Navy veteran of the Spanish-American War, he became president in 1903 of the family-owned Weston-Mott Company, a manufacturer of axles and wheels. Three years later he moved the company to Flint, Mich., and in 1913 he sold it to General Motors for shares of GM stock. He served as a GM director from 1913 until his death and as a vice president from 1916 to 1937. After three terms as mayor of Flint, he made an unsuccessful bid in 1920 for the Michigan governorship. He established the Flint Junior College, a children's health center, and a summer camp, among other projects, and contributed liberally to universities.

Murphy, Robert (85), U. S. ornithologist; a leading authority on sea birds and a pioneer in conservation; associated with the Museum of Natural History in New York City from 1921 until his death in Stony Brook, N. Y., on March 19.

Naish, J. Carrol (73), U. S. stage, film, radio, and television actor, who played characters of every nationality, relying on his mastery of dialects; he made more than 250 films and starred in the radio series *Life with Luigi* (1948–53): d. La Jolla, Calif., Jan. 24.

Neale, Earle (Greasy) (81), U. S. football coach, noted for innovative offensive and defensive tactics; piloted Philadelphia Eagles to two professional championships; elected to Football Hall of Fame in 1969: d. Lake Worth, Fla., Nov. 2, 1973.

Neill, A(lexander) S(utherland) (89), Scottish educator and psychologist: b. Forfar, Scotland, Oct. 17, 1883; d. Aldeburgh, Suffolk, England, Sept. 24, 1973. A pioneer of the free-school movement, he believed that children must be allowed maximum freedom and spontaneity. The son of a village schoolmaster, he obtained a master's degree from the University of Edinburgh in 1912 and developed his educational theories while working as a teacher and headmaster in Scotland. In 1921 he helped organize an international school near Dresden, Germany, which he brought to England in 1924, establishing it in Leiston, Suffolk, as the Summerhill School. Designed "to make the school fit the child, instead of making the child fit the school," Summerhill discouraged antisocial behavior but it allowed students to make their own rules and to attend classes and examinations at their discretion. Its success inspired the establishment of similar schools elsewhere, including the United States. Among Neill's more than 20 books are *Summerhill: A Radical Approach to Child Rearing* (1960), and the autobiography *Neill! Neill! Orange Peel!* (1972).

Neruda, Pablo (69), the pseudonym of Neftalí Ricardo Reyes Basualto, Chilean poet and diplomat: b. Parral, Chile, July 12, 1904; d. Santiago, Sept. 23, 1973. One of the greatest poets in the Spanish language, he won the 1971 Nobel Prize in literature. Among his major works are *Veinte poemas de amor y una canción desesperada* (1924), the two-volume *Residencia en la tierra* (1933–39), *Tercera residencia* (1947), the epic masterpiece *Canto general* (1950), and the five-volume autobiography in verse *Memorial de Isla Negra* (1964). He grew up in Temuco, Chile, and was educated at a teachers college in Santiago. At 17 he published his first verses, taking the last name of the Czech writer Jan Neruda as his pen name. He soon became highly individualistic style. In the late 1920's and the 1930's he served in diplomatic posts in Asia, Latin America, and Spain.

He was a leading member of the Chilean Communist party for many years, and sat on its central committee. From 1945 to 1948 he was a member of the Chilean Senate. During 1971–72 he served as ambassador to France under the Marxist government of Salvador Allende.

Nichols, Roy F. (76), U. S. historian; won a Pulitzer Prize in 1949 for *The Disruption of American Democracy;* taught at the University of Pennsylvania from 1925 to 1966: d. Philadelphia, Jan. 12.

Notestein, Ada Comstock (97), U. S. educator; president of Radcliffe College from 1923 to 1943; successfully advocated coeducation at Harvard University in 1943: d. New Haven, Conn., Dec. 12.

Nurmi, Paavo (76), Finnish long-distance runner: b. Turku, Finland, June 13, 1897; d. Helsinki, Finland, Oct. 2, 1973. Known as the "Flying Finn," he was one of the great track stars of all time. With his distinctive running style, characterized by long flowing strides, he won nine gold medals and three silver medals in Olympic competition and set 1-mile, 2-mile and numerous other world track records during the 1920's. The son of a carpenter, he went to work in a foundry at 15 and at 17 began to develop the stamina and fleetness that brought him world fame. In the 1920 Olympics at Antwerp he scored his first triumphs, winning gold medals for the 10,000-meter run and the individual and team 10,000-meter cross country events. He reached his peak at Paris in the 1924 Olympics, winning gold medals for the 1,500- and 5,000-meter runs, the 10,000-meter cross country event, and two team events. He won another gold medal at Amsterdam in 1928 for the 10,000-meter event. He also established various world track records during visits to the United States in 1925 and 1929. Disqualified from the 1932 Olympics because of alleged professionalism, Nurmi retired from sports.

Offenhauser, Fred (85), U. S. automobile engineer; builder of four-cylinder engines for racing cars; Offy engines powered the winning car 28 times in Indianapolis 500: d. Los Angeles, Calif., Aug. 17.

Ory, Edward "Kid" (86), U. S. Dixieland jazz musician; organized his first band in 1900, at age 13, and played trombone and led jazz bands almost continuously until he was 80; his most popular composition was *Muskrat Ramble:* d. Honolulu, Jan. 23.

O'Shea, Michael (67), U. S. actor; appeared in over 100 films, including *Captain China, Jack London,* and *Circumstantial Evidence:* d. Dallas, Texas, Dec. 4.

Parkhurst, Helen (86), U. S. educator; devised the Dalton Plan, under which pupils studied in laboratory brigades, with the better students helping the poorer ones and without being subjected to examinations; her book *Education on the Dalton Plan* was published in some 60 languages: d. New Milford, Conn., June 1.

Paxinou, Katina (72), Greek actress; government-sponsored Royal Theater of Athens was created for her and her husband, actor and director Alexis Minotis; won an Academy Award for portrayal of Pilar in U. S. film *For Whom the Bell Tolls* (1943): d. Athens, Feb. 22.

Picasso, Pablo (91), Spanish-born artist: d. Mougins, France, April 8. See page 444.

Pincus, Louis A. (61), world Zionist leader; chairman of the board of the World Zionist Organization and Jewish Agency for Palestine: d. Jerusalem, July 25.

Post, Marjorie M. (86), U. S. businesswoman and philanthropist; inherited Postum Cereal Company on her father's death in 1914 after he had made a fortune on Postum, Post Toasties, and Grape Nuts; by 1929 she and her second husband, Edward F. Hutton, had built the company into the giant General Foods Corporation; gave funds to build and run a Red Cross hospital in France after World War I, financed and supervised Salvation Army feeding station in New York (1929–35), donated cost of Boy Scout headquarters in Washington, D. C., and provided more than $1.5 million for the National Symphony: d. Washington, D. C., Sept. 12.

Radford, Arthur W. (77), U. S. Navy officer: b. Chicago, Ill., Feb. 27, 1896; d. Bethesda, Md., Aug. 17, 1973. A long-time supporter of naval air power, he was chairman of the joint chiefs of staff from 1953 to 1957, the first Navy man ever to serve in the top U. S. military post. He grew up in Iowa and entered the U. S. Naval Academy at 16. After World War I service on a battleship he took flight training and became a squadron commander on an aircraft carrier. During World War II he coordinated the Navy flight-training program and later commanded a task force in major amphibious landings in the Pacific. Promoted to admiral in 1949, he was named commander in chief of the Pacific fleet and high commissioner of the Pacific Islands Trust Territory, serving in those posts until

1953. As head of the joint chiefs he implemented the Eisenhower administration's policies of dependence on airpower and missiles rather than ground troops.

Rahv, Philip (64), U. S. literary critic and educator; his specialty was American literature as well as the works of Kafka and Dostoyevsky; was founding co-editor of *Partisan Review* in 1934; wrote *Images and Ideas* (1949): d. Cambridge, Mass., Dec. 22.

Rankin, Jeannette (92), U. S. congresswoman: b. near Missoula, Mont., June 11, 1880; d. Carmel, Calif., May 18, 1973. The first woman to be elected to the U. S. Congress, she served as a Republican representative from Montana from 1917 to 1919 and from 1941 to 1943. After graduating from the University of Montana in 1902 she devoted herself to social work and the cause of women's suffrage, and over the years she played an active role in peace organizations and women's rights groups. She was among those members of Congress who voted against U. S. entry into World War I and the only one to oppose the declaration of war against Japan in 1941. In 1968 she led a massive women's march in Washington to protest U. S. military involvement in Indochina, and in 1969 she took part in antiwar marches in South Carolina and Georgia.

Razaf, Andy (77), U. S. lyricist; wrote the words to more than 1,000 songs, including *Honeysuckle Rose, Ain't Misbehavin',* and *That's What I Like 'Bout the South:* d. North Hollywood, Calif., Feb. 3.

Richards, Dickinson W. (77), U. S. physician; co-winner of the 1956 Nobel Prize in medicine for "discoveries concerning heart catheterization and pathological changes in the circulatory system": d. Lakeville, Conn., Feb. 23.

Rickenbacker, Edward Vernon (82), U. S. aviator and airline executive: b. Columbus, Ohio, Oct. 8, 1890; d. Zürich, Switzerland, July 23, 1973. The son of a Swiss immigrant construction contractor, he dropped out of school at 13, studied mechanical engineering by correspondence, and became a pioneer racing car driver, winning seven national championships before he was 21. Enlisting in the U. S. Army in 1917 he became Gen. John J. Pershing's driver, and then transferred to the air corps. As commander of the 94th Aero Pursuit Squadron he fought Germany's fabled "flying circus" led by Manfred von Richtofen, the "Red Baron," and was credited with 26 aerial victories. He was America's "ace of aces" in World War I, earning the Congressional Medal of Honor and other decorations. After the war he was unsuccessful in automobile manufacturing. In 1935 he became general manager of Eastern Air Lines and built it into a major and profitable commercial airline, serving as its president and general manager (1938–53) and as board chairman (1954–63). During his career he had many brushes with death, including surviving a plane crash in 1941 and another in 1942.

Rivera, Julio (52), president of El Salvador (1962–67); he ran a constitutional government with independent legislature and judiciary: d. San José Guayabal, El Salvador, July 29.

Robinson, Edward G. (Emmanuel Goldenberg) (79), U. S. actor: b. Bucharest, Rumania, Dec. 12, 1893; d. Los Angeles, Calif., Jan. 26, 1973. Although best remembered as the tough-talking, cigar-chomping, scowling mobster in such gangster films as *Little Caesar* (1930) and *Key Largo* (1948), he skillfully portrayed a wide variety of characters in over 100 movies. Taken to the United States at the age of 10, he decided to become an actor while attending City College in New York. He studied at the American Academy of Dramatic Art and after appearing in stock, vaudeville, and Theatre Guild productions went to Hollywood, where he attained star-

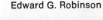

Eddie Rickenbacker   Edward G. Robinson

UPI

dom in *Little Caesar*. Among his other films are *Double Indemnity* (1944), *All My Sons* (1948), and *The Prize* (1963). He acted in some 40 Broadway plays, including *Middle of the Night* (1956), and on radio and television. He was also a noted art collector and philanthropist. Shortly after his death he was awarded a special Oscar for his "outstanding contribution to motion pictures."

Rockefeller, Winthrop (60), U. S. businessman, public official, and philanthropist: b. New York, N. Y., May 1, 1912; d. Palm Springs, Calif., Feb. 22, 1973. A grandson of the oil magnate John D. Rockefeller, he was in his youth the nonconforming member of his illustrious family, but later attained success in ranching and business and as governor of his adopted state of Arkansas (1966–70). A Yale University dropout, he worked for a time as a roustabout in Texas oilfields. In 1953, shortly before his widely publicized divorce from showgirl Barbara "Bobo" Sears, he moved to Arkansas, where he established a prosperous cattle ranch and entered politics. As Arkansas' first Republican governor since Reconstruction, he promoted its agricultural and industrial development. He instituted far-reaching prison reforms, and was moderately successful in furthering school integration and other civil rights goals. In 1940 he helped set up the philanthropic Rockefeller Brothers Fund, and in 1956 he established his own Rockwin Fund to finance health and education projects in Arkansas.

Rodriguez, Tito (50), U. S. bandleader and singer; specialized in Latin American music; noted for smooth, lyrical style: d. New York, N. Y., Feb. 28.

Rollins, Walter E. "Jack" (66), U. S. lyricist; wrote the words for more than 500 songs, including *Frosty the Snowman*: d. Cincinnati, Ohio, Jan. 1.

Romer, Alfred Sherwood (78), U. S. paleontologist; known internationally for his use of comparative anatomy to study the evolution of fossil vertebrates; director (1946–61) of Harvard University's Museum of Comparative Zoology: d. Cambridge, Mass., Nov. 5.

Romnes, Haakon Ingolf (66), U. S. corporation executive, known as H. I. Romnes; during a 44-year career with the American Telephone and Telegraph Company, he rose to become chairman (1967) and chief executive officer 1970–72): d. Sarasota, Fla., Nov. 19.

Rosenman, Samuel I(rving) (77), U. S. judge and presidential adviser: b. San Antonio, Texas, Feb. 13, 1896; d. New York, N. Y., June 24, 1973. A former justice of the New York State Supreme Court, he was one of Franklin D. Roosevelt's closest advisers and drafted many of his major speeches, including the acceptance speech at the 1932 Democratic convention, pledging "a new deal for the American public." Rosenman was said to have assembled FDR's original "brain trust" of scholarly advisers. He graduated from Columbia Law School in 1919 and served as a New York state assemblyman (1922–26). His association with Roosevelt, then candidate for New York governor, began in 1928. Roosevelt appointed him to the state supreme court in 1932. In 1943 he resigned his judgeship to become special counsel to the President. He remained on as adviser to Truman until 1946, and on occasion served the Kennedy administration. In 1970, Rosenman led resistance by 457 lawyers and law professors to the naming of G. Harrold Carswell to the U. S. Supreme Court. Rosenman wrote *Working With Roosevelt* (1952).

Ruiz Cortines, Adolfo (82), Mexican statesman; president of Mexico (1952–58); governor of the state of Veracruz (1944–47): d. Mexico City, Mexico, Dec. 3.

Russell, John (70), U. S. basketball coach, known as Honey Russell; member of Basketball Hall of Fame; coach of noted basketball teams at Seton Hall University (1936–42 and 1950–61) and first coach of Boston Celtics (1946–47): d. Livingston, N. J., Nov. 15.

Ryan, Irene (70), U. S. actress, best known for role of Granny in the popular television series *Beverly Hillbillies*: d. Santa Monica, Calif., April 26.

Ryan, Robert (63), U. S. actor: b. Chicago, Ill., Nov. 11, 1909; d. New York, N. Y., July 11, 1973. An outstanding performer, perhaps best known for his intelligent film portrayals of such villains as the bigoted Marine in *Crossfire* (1947) and the sinister ship's master in *Billy Budd* (1962), he performed with equal skill in more sympathetic roles, such as that of the aging prizefighter in *The Set-Up* (1949). Ryan graduated in 1932 from Dartmouth, where he studied playwriting and was active in sports. After working at such jobs as seaman, miner, and ranch hand, he turned to acting. His performance in the Broadway production of *Clash by Night* (1941) led to his cinematic debut in *Bombardier* (1943). Over the next 30 years he acted in some 90 films. Among his Broadway triumphs were *Mr. President* (1962), *The Front Page* (1969), and *Long Day's Journey into Night* (1971). A champion of liberal causes, he helped organize the

Hollywood chapter of SANE and served on the board of the American Civil Liberties Union. His last films were *Executive Action* and *The Iceman Cometh* (both 1973).

Said, Mohammed Maraghei (92), former premier of Iran and an anti-Communist; as premier in 1944, he rejected Soviet attempts to develop Iranian oil deposits; thereafter, pressure from Moscow forced his resignation, but he was premier again in the late 1940's: d. Teheran, Iran, Nov. 1.

St. Laurent, Louis (91), Canadian statesman: d. Quebec, July 24. See CANADA.

Sanderson, Ivan (62), U. S. naturalist and author; conducted several radio and television nature series; books include *Animal Treasure* (1937) and *Elephants* (1959): d. Columbia, N. J., Feb. 19.

Sands, Diana (39), U. S. actress; rose to stardom in 1959 for her role in the play *A Raisin in the Sun* and re-created that role on the screen in 1960: d. New York, N. Y., Sept. 21.

Santos, Rufino Cardinal (65); Roman Catholic prelate; archbishop of Manila and first Filipino to become a cardinal: d. Manila, the Philippines, Sept. 3.

Saylor, John P. (65), U. S. congressman; senior Republican member of the Pennsylvania congressional delegation, serving in House since 1949: d. Houston, Texas, Oct. 28.

Schiaparelli, Elsa (83), Italian-born French fashion designer: b. Rome, Italy, Sept. 10, 1890; d. Paris, France, Nov. 13, 1973. Advising women to "dare to be different," she revolutionized Paris fashions, beginning in the late 1920's, with her dramatic creations in "shocking pink" and other vivid colors, which considerably brightened the previously drab world of *haute couture*. The daughter of a mathematician, she was privately educated and spent some years in New York's Greenwich Village as an aspiring artist before becoming a French citizen in 1927. She began her fashion career designing sweaters based on an Armenian peasant style. Her Paris salon soon flourished, and her glamorous dresses and cocktail jackets, and such trademarks as padded shoulders and dyed furs, won her international fame. She also marketed successful perfumes, among them *Shocking*. In 1949 she opened a salon in New York City. After retiring from designing in 1954, she continued to work as a consultant.

Senanayake, Dudley (57), former prime minister of Ceylon (now Sri Lanka); served in 1952–53 and again in 1960 and 1965–70; worked to end religious and sectional divisiveness: d. Colombo, Sri Lanka, April 12.

Sherman, Allan (48), U. S. lyricist; became a national celebrity in the 1960's for the album *My Son, the Folksinger* (1962) and other "My Son" parodies: d. Los Angeles, Calif., Nov. 20.

Sisler, George (80), U. S. baseball player: b. Nimisila, Ohio, March 24, 1893; d. St. Louis, Mo., March 26, 1973. A star with the St. Louis Browns in the 1920's, Sisler is ranked as one of baseball's greatest hitters and defensive first baseman. He was the first winner of the American League's most valuable player award (1922) and was among the first players to be voted into baseball's Hall of Fame at its establishment in 1939. His lifetime batting average was .340. He joined the Browns in 1915, after graduating from the University of Michigan. In 1920 and 1922 he held the American League batting title, hitting .407 and .420, respectively. He led the league four times in stolen bases, and his 1920 record of 257 hits remains unbroken. From 1924 to 1927, Sisler was player-manager of the Browns. He ended his active career as a player with the Washington Senators (1928) and the Boston Braves (1928–30).

Skira, Albert (69), Swiss publisher; published limited-edition books illustrated by Picasso and Matisse; published wider-market books on works of art and the history of art: d. Dully, Switzerland, Sept. 14.

Sobeloff, Simon E. (79), U. S. jurist; was solicitor general of the United States (1954–56) and chief judge of the U. S. Court of Appeals (1958–71); advocated civil libertarian principles and the rights of minority groups: d. Baltimore, Md., July 11.

Steichen, Edward (93), U. S. photographer: d. West Redding, Conn., March 25. See PHOTOGRAPHY.

Sutherland, Arthur E. (71), U. S. lawyer and educator; authority and writer on constitutional law; taught at Harvard University (1950–70): d. Cambridge, Mass., March 8.

Szigeti, Joseph (80), Hungarian-American violinist: b. Budapest, Hungary, Sept. 5, 1892; d. Lucerne, Switzerland, Feb. 19, 1973. One of the great violin virtuosos of the 20th century, he was noted for his purity of tone, elegance of style, and flawless musicianship. While excelling in the classical repertoire, he was also an exponent of the works of such modern composers as Béla Bartók, Sergei

Prokofiev, and Darius Milhaud. Szigeti studied at the Budapest Royal Academy and made his debut at 13. After launching his career in Germany and England, he moved to Switzerland, where he taught at the Geneva Conservatory from 1917 to 1924. From the time he made his U. S. debut in 1925 with Leopold Stokowski's Philadelphia Orchestra until his retirement, he was almost continually on tour. He made over 100 recordings, including a Beethoven series with Bartók. In 1951 he became a U. S. citizen. His autobiography, *With Strings Attached*, was published in 1947.

Thompson, Lawrence R. (67), U. S. literary scholar; won a Pulitzer Prize in 1972 for *Robert Frost: The Years of Triumph, 1915–1938*, the last of a 3-volume biography-study of the poet: d. Princeton, N. J., April 15.

Tolkien, J(ohn) R(onald) R(euel) (81), British author: b. Bloemfontein, South Africa, Jan. 3, 1892; d. Bournemouth, England, Sept. 2, 1973. A linguist and scholar, noted for his work in Old English, Middle English, and Chaucer, he won enormous popularity, late in life, with his trilogy *The Lord of the Rings* (1954–55). A vivid and compelling fantasy about the struggle between good and evil, the work is set in "Middle Earth," an imaginary realm, populated by hobbits, elves, and wizards. Moderately successful initially, the trilogy, along with an earlier related work, *The Hobbit* (1937), became the focal point of an international cult among the young, notably U. S. college students, in the 1960's. He was brought to England at an early age and obtained his M. A. at Oxford in 1919. After teaching at the University of Leeds, he joined the Oxford faculty in 1925, remaining there until his retirement in 1959. An outstanding example of his scholarly writing is *Beowulf: The Monsters and the Critics* (1936).

Tourel, Jennie (63), U. S. mezzo-soprano, born of Russian parents; she was best known as an interpreter of French and Russian art songs, but her career in opera spanned 40 years, beginning with her debut as Carmen with the Paris Opéra-Comique in 1933: d. New York, N. Y., Nov. 23.

Truex, Ernest (83), U. S. actor; began his career at the age of 5 in 1895 and subsequently appeared in hundreds of vaudeville acts, plays, films, and television shows: d. Fallbrook, Calif., June 26.

Ulate Blanco, Otilio (82), president of Costa Rica (1949–53): d. San Jose, Costa Rica, Oct. 27.

Ulbricht, Walter (80), East German statesman and political leader: b. Leipzig, Germany, June 30, 1893; d. Dollnsee, north of Berlin, East Germany, Aug. 1, 1973. As leader of the Socialist Unity party and head of the council of state of the German Democratic Republic, he was the dominant figure in East Germany in the 1950's and 1960's. An orthodox Stalinist, he kept East German policies in strict conformity with those of the Soviet Union and developed his country into a leading industrial power. Becoming active in the socialist and trade union movement in his teens, he was a founding member of the German Communist party in 1919 and head of its Berlin organization in the early 1930's. He spent most of the Nazi years in the USSR, and returned to Germany in 1945. A founder of the Socialist Unity party in 1946, he became its first secretary in 1953. In the East German government he served as deputy premier (1949–60), then became chairman of the council of state. The 1953 workers' uprising and refugees' flight from East to West led him to erect the Berlin wall in 1961. He was replaced as party head by Erich Honecker in 1971.

Vandegrift, Alexander A. (86), U. S. Marine Corps commandant; he served in the Marine Corps from 1909 to 1948; led the Marines at Guadalcanal in World War II: d. Bethesda, Md., May 9.

Van Zeeland, Viscount Paul (76), Belgian statesman; premier of Belgium (1936–38) and foreign minister (1948–54): d. Brussels, Belgium, Sept. 22.

Virtanen, Artturi I. (78), Finnish chemist; he won the Nobel Prize in chemistry in 1945 for his work on the preservation of fodder crops; professor of biochemistry at University of Helsinki (1939–48): d. Helsinki, Finland, Nov. 11.

Voisin, Gabriel (93), French aviation pioneer; he was one of the first to fly a heavier-than-air machine (1904); from 1905 to 1918 he designed and manufactured planes: d. Ozenay, France, Dec. 25.

Von Mises, Ludwig (92), Austrian-American economist, author, and teacher; developed theory that business cycle results from expansion and contraction of money supply; regarded as a brilliant teacher; his works include *A Treatise on Economics* (1949): d. New York, N. Y., Oct. 10.

Ward, Clara (48), U. S. gospel singer; led a popular singing group: d. Los Angeles, Calif., Jan. 16.

Watkins, Arthur V. (86), U. S. public official; Republican senator from Utah (1947–59); presided over the Senate select committee that censured Sen. Joseph R. McCarthy in 1954: d. Orem, Utah, Sept. 1.

Watson-Watt, Sir Robert (81), British physicist: b. Brechin, Angusshire, Scotland, April 13, 1892; d. Inverness, Scotland, Dec. 5, 1973. He developed the first practical radar system, providing the British, beginning in 1940, with a powerful defense against German air raids. Watson-Watt was knighted in 1942 and received the United States Medal of Merit in 1946. His autobiography *The Pulse of Radar* appeared in 1959.

Watts, Alan (58), British-born U. S. philosopher; he was a prolific writer on Zen Buddhism and a cult figure for the beat and hippie generations of the 1950's and 1960's: d. Mill Valley, Calif., Nov. 16.

Webster, Ben (64) U. S. musician; jazz tenor saxophonist in bands of Fletcher Henderson, Duke Ellington, and Count Basie: d. Amsterdam, Netherlands, Sept. 20.

Westmore, Bud (55), U. S. makeup artist for films and television; headed the makeup department of Universal Studios for 24 years: d. Sherman Oaks, Calif., June 23.

Westmore, Wally (45), U. S. makeup artist; was a makeup man for Paramount Studios from 1925 to 1968; he and his five brothers dominated the Hollywood makeup business for decades: d. Hollywood, Calif., July 3.

White, Paul Dudley (87), U. S. physician: b. Roxbury, Mass., June 6, 1886; d. Boston, Mass., Oct. 31, 1973. A pioneer in the diagnosis, treatment, and prevention of diseases of the heart and circulatory system, he laid the foundations for modern cardiology through extensive clinical observation and research. He attained international prominence when he became President Eisenhower's chief medical consultant in 1955. The son of a physician, he received his M. D. degree from Harvard Medical School in 1911 and soon thereafter began his lifelong association with Massachusetts General Hospital. From 1914 to 1956 he served on the Harvard faculty. He was among the first to use the electrocardiograph to detect cardiac disorders, and he was a staunch advocate of weight control, prudent diet, and daily exercise. In 1971 he visited the People's Republic of China to study medical advances there. White was a founder of the American Heart Association and the International Society of Cardiology. His book *Heart Disease* (1931) is a standard reference work in its field.

Whittaker, Charles Evans (72), U. S. jurist: b. near Troy, Kans., Feb. 22, 1901; d. Kansas City, Mo., Nov. 26, 1973. A conservative jurist, who regarded the practice of law as a "deliberate science," he served for five years as an associate justice of the U. S. Supreme Court under Chief Justice Earl Warren. A Kansas farm boy and ninth grade "drop-out," he nevertheless studied independently and gained admission to the Kansas City School of Law. Admitted to the Missouri bar in 1923, he practiced trial and corporation law with a prominent firm. President Eisenhower appointed him to the U. S. District Court for western Missouri (1954), to the U. S. Court of Appeals for the eighth circuit (1956), and to the U. S. Supreme Court (1957). He usually supported opinions upholding "law and order," and generally held that claims to individual freedom were outweighed by the demands of government and society. But he occasionally voted to curb government power. He retired from the Supreme Court in 1962.

Wigman, Mary (86), German dancer and choreographer; founder of the modern dance in Europe; emphasized dancing as communication of personal experience to the audience: d. Berlin, Germany, Sept. 18.

Winterhalter, Hugo (64), U. S. popular music arranger; arranged popular tunes that helped to sell millions of records in the 1950's; conducted Hollywood Bowl Orchestra and symphony orchestras in Washington and Milwaukee: d. Greenwich, Conn.. Sept. 17.

Woodward, Maj. Gen. Gilbert H. (56); U. S. military officer; negotiated release of crew of USS *Pueblo* in 1968; chief U. S. delegate in truce talks with North Vietnamese in Saigon in 1973: d. London, England, Oct. 17.

Young, Chic (72), U. S. cartoonist; created (1930) popular comic strip *Blondie*: d. St. Petersburg, Fla., March 14.

Zerba, Cesare Cardinal (81), Italian Roman Catholic clergyman; was secretary of the Sacred Congregation for the Sacraments; author of many books on theology and canon law; made a cardinal in 1965: d. Rome, July 11.

Ziegler, Karl (74), German chemist; co-winner of 1963 Nobel Prize in chemistry for his discovery that polyethylene plastics could be produced by using chemical catalysts: d. Muhlheim, West Germany, Aug. 12.

OCEANIA

In a year of subdued economic and social advance, major developments in Oceania were a sharpened cleavage between English-speaking nations and territories and the French government over the issue of using French Polynesia as a nuclear test site, and Papua New Guinea's attainment of self-government on December 1. In French Polynesia, opposition to the bomb brought demands for independence from France—the first such movement in 16 years.

In most areas inflation accelerated. An overall need for more investment capital was stressed in many quarters. Destruction caused by a hurricane late in 1972 still debilitated some islands.

Political Developments and Regional Cooperation. In April the South Pacific Forum supported Australia's initiative in taking the matter of France's nuclear testing to the World Court. In September the South Pacific Conference, in an unprecedented move into a politically sensitive issue, pressed a motion condemning the tests (which had been held in July). The French representative then withdrew from the Conference.

Among general issues, the area's leaders underscored a need to improve interisland transportation and communications. Some suggested that tariff barriers might usefully be examined, but most were concerned with inflation and economic slackness.

The South Pacific Conference accepted an offer by Australia and New Zealand to contribute U. S.$350,000 each to the South Pacific Commission for special projects, sidetracking France's efforts to hold the commission's budget at earlier levels.

In Papua New Guinea (PNG), Chief Minister Michael Somare carried his country to self-government on December 1, while the 15-man constitution planning committee undertook a "meet the people" tour in an effort to meld ideas on the form of constitution best suited to the country after independence (expected to come in 1974).

Many isolated outbreaks of rioting occurred in PNG. Tensions were related to domestic issues. Strains and conflicts existed between tribes, between the generations, between the urban "elite" and conservative villagers, and between ethnic communities and the central government in its unifying role. In advance of self-government, Somare damped down tensions, saying the move merely recognized existing local control of PNG's internal affairs.

In a move to halt strikes in key industries, Fiji introduced a trade disputes bill in March. A constitutional crisis developed over it when the Opposition secured the speaker's support and the House became deadlocked. The government finally won its point.

In New Caledonia there was a revival of strength for the autonomists, who blamed "Paris bungling" for the nickel industry decline. In New Hebrides, the French influence resisted suggestions of a path to self-determination.

A new political entity, the United Solomon Islands party, was formed by successful candidates to the islands' new Governing Council.

On November 6, voters in American Samoa turned down a new constitution that would have permitted them to elect their governor, now an appointee.

Economic Progress. Oceania's economic gains slowed appreciably under the impact of inflation and the effects of revaluations of the Australian dollar (the basic currency for much of the area). The revaluations resulted in weaker markets for many products and a slackening in tourism.

Some areas reported downturns—notably New Caledonia, where earnings from nickel were depressed, and Papua New Guinea, where an easing in export earnings was aggravated by a decrease in new investment (in anticipation of independence).

Wage inflation and trade slackness affected Fiji. Generally, trade swung away from Australia to New Zealand, but tourists from Australia increased. To improve beef quality, Australia's Murray Grey strain of cattle was introduced. In April, after 90 years of private ownership, sugar processing passed to the government.

Moves began for a regional shipping line for the Pacific islands when Nauru's President Chief Hammer DeRoburt and Tonga's Prime Minister Prince Tuipelehake pledged resources for the purpose.

French Polynesia's inflation continued, and the standard of living marked time. In New Hebrides, low prices for copra, lingering effects of the 1972 hurricane, and a land boom hurt the economy.

Western Samoa hoped to secure a flow of development capital and began preliminary work on a national Development Finance Corporation to provide backing for agriculture and other industries.

R. M. YOUNGER
Author, "Australia and the Australians"

OCEANOGRAPHY

In 1973 oceanography increasingly became the object of international discussions and agreements. A United Nations Conference on the Law of the Sea attempted to reach some international agreements. A long-term threat to open research in the oceans began to materialize as the less-developed nations insisted on the right to regulate scientific exploration within their resource zones offshore. They contend that open research and commercial exploitation of deep-sea resources benefit highly developed countries only, since the other countries lack the technology and economic power to take advantage of the new knowledge—a situation they believe incompatible with the concept of the open ocean and seabed as common heritage for all mankind.

In the United States, ocean research in 1973 remained vigorous but experienced a general budget squeeze in federally funded projects. For example, the highly successful series of Antarctic oceanographic expeditions by the research vessel *Eltanin* were abruptly cancelled, and several other oceanographic ships were laid up.

International Cooperation. There was increasing cooperation between developed maritime nations in such areas as research projects, in pooling of environmental data, in reduction of pollution levels, and in the development of energy, mineral, and fishery resources.

One example of international cooperation in research is the project FAMOUS, or French-American Mid-Ocean Undersea Study. This program includes a detailed investigation of an area in the axial part of the Mid-Atlantic Ridge, where according to a widely accepted theory of sea floor spreading, new oceanic crust is forming. Initial work consisted in surveying a large area south of the Azores by airplane and by research vessels (R/V *Knorr*, USNS *Hayes*, R/V *Charcot*, R/V *Atlantis II*, Navoceano), providing information on bathymetry, magnetics, gravity, sediment distribution, and earthquake activ-

RESEARCH vessel Knorr (above), operated by Woods Hole (Mass.) Oceanographic Institution, lowers water-sampling
tanks (right) at the end of a voyage.

ity. Deep dives by research submarines at selected
sites are planned.

International recognition of the increased seriousness of pollution of the oceans is leading to the
development of international regulations controlling
dumping at sea. A major concern is ship collision,
especially those involving large tankers spilling considerable amounts of oil.

Deep-Sea Environment. Projects within the International Decade of Ocean Exploration (IDOE)
continued. This program is planned, managed, and
largely funded by the National Science Foundation
and is focused on research in environmental quality,
environmental forecasting, seabed assessment, and
living resources. At present, several large-scale
projects are being supported. The Geochemical
Oceans Sections Study (GEOSECS) investigates
processes important in the diffusion, mixing, and dis-
persion of trace compounds and contaminants in the
ocean. The North Pacific Experiment (NORPAX)
is a comprehensive study of large-scale ocean/at-
mosphere interactions. The Mid Ocean Dynamics
Experiment (MODE) is largely concerned with
medium-scale motions in the open ocean and provides information for numerical modeling of ocean
currents and eddies. The project Climate Long-
range Investigation, Mapping, and Prediction
(CLIMAP) investigates sedimentary evidence for
climatic changes over thousands of years. Studies
within the Seabed Assessment Program were conducted on both the African and South American
margins of the Atlantic, on the margins of the
Nazca Plate adjacent to the west coast of South
America, and on the Mid-Atlantic Ridge. The Living Resources Program concentrates on the study of
the physical, chemical, and biological processes in
coastal upwelling ecologic systems.

Coastal Environment. Studies on the physical,
chemical, and biologic processes on the continental
shelves have been intensified. The dynamics of these
offshore regions are especially important in assessing man's impact on the oceanic environment. For

example, according to a recent study, waste disposal
operations are the largest sediment transport and
depositional process now active in the mid-Atlantic
coastal region.

The National Oceanic and Atmospheric Administration (NOAA) continued the Southeastern
Coastal Plains Expedition (SCOPE), a concentrated
two-year environmental study of coastal waters extending from Cape Hatteras, North Carolina, to
near Cape Canaveral, Florida. SCOPE involves
aerial photography and survey of sea-bottom topography, coastal currents, tidal dynamics, and hydro-
graphic properties. The Environmental Protection
Agency (EPA) continued its efforts in monitoring
coastal water quality. Studies showed that of several
thousand coastal and Great Lakes public beaches
surveyed, some 10% were closed at times, mostly
due to sewage system breakdowns.

The National Science Foundation's program Research Applied to National Needs (RANN) emphasized studies in coastal zone regions. Investigations
on effects of waste discharge and dumping on estuaries as well as related projects continued. The
Atomic Energy Commission (AEC) sponsored es-
tuarine and coastal zone research on both coasts of
the United States and in Alaska. This work includes

a systematic study of the fate of Columbia River water and its load as it enters the northeast Pacific Ocean. The central concern is with the pathway of radioactive elements in solution, in sediment, and in the food web. The AEC also accelerated its research into the effects of nuclear power plant operations on marine environments.

Energy Resources. Continental margins are the prime source for oil and gas, and both industry and government are concentrating efforts on offshore research for hydrocarbon reserves. NOAA has focused attention on the northern half of the Atlantic continental shelf and on the shelf off southern Alaska. The U. S. Geologic Survey conducts a systematic investigation of bottom and sub-bottom conditions at Georges Bank off New England and on the shelf off Delaware. Similar studies along the Pacific coast and along Alaska are closely tied to the mapping of earthquake belts and other geologic hazards to forestall environmental damage in the quest for offshore hydrocarbon resources.

Deep-Sea Drilling. In several successful deep-sea drilling expeditions, the research vessel *Glomar Challenger* continued to recover the sedimentary record of the last 120 million years. Drilling in the Antarctic waters has elucidated the timing of the separation of Australia from Antarctica and the subsequent development of the Circum-Antarctic Current. It was discovered that Antarctic glaciation apparently began in the middle Miocene epoch, judging from the occurrence of ice-rafted debris within the cores. Drilling in the western Pacific has revealed much about the formation of island arcs and small ocean basins and the development of the equatorial current system. Many laboratories are

studying the data provided by the deep-sea drilling expeditions. This research emphasized (1) the geochemical evolution of sediments deposited on active ridge crest, where sediments tend to be rich in iron, manganese, copper, zinc, and barium; (2) the determination of plate motions from geophysical data and from sediment rate and facies distribution; and (3) the reconstruction of the ancient ocean environment, including its circulation patterns, calcium-carbonate compensation depth, and bottom-water temperatures.

Remote Sensing. NOAA and NASA (National Aeronautics and Space Administration) are involved in a major cooperative effort to develop satellite systems for use in remote oceanographic sensing programs. Data so collected combined with data from instrumented buoys will be used to relate remote measurements to "sea truth." The goal is to develop the ability to monitor productivity distributions of the oceans by satellite sensing. Aircraft are already used to collect much information, and airborne surveys played an increased role in charting the magnetic field over the ocean and in monitoring sea surface temperature variations by radiation thermometers.

Fisheries and Mariculture. A drastic decline has been observed in the productivity of many important fisheries, especially the great whale fisheries, the renowned Great Banks of the western Atlantic, and the usually highly productive Peruvian anchovy fishery. The Peruvian fishery, an important source for much of the world's supply of fish meal, may be permanently damaged because of overfishing. The high productivity of Peruvian waters (22% of the world's catch) is due to large-scale upwelling within a north-flowing coastal current. As the water on the ocean surface is swept away by the prevailing winds, deeper water rises to replace it. This deeper water is cold and rich in nutrients. At times, however, a warm countercurrent develops and invades the coastal area, preventing upwelling. This phenomenon, called El Niño, greatly reduces productivity. It is believed that the combined effects of El Niño and intensive fishing have reduced the Peruvian coastal fish population sufficiently to jeopardize future harvests. It remains to be seen to what extent the return of normal oceanographic conditions leads to normalization of the fishery.

With the idea of developing technology for artificial upwelling of cold, deep water, experiments were conducted on the north coast of St. Croix in the Virgin Islands. Water is pumped from 2,900 feet (almost 500 fathoms, or 885 meters) depth to the surface where its high nitrate, phosphate, and silicate content stimulates the growth of phytoplankton. Production was increased over tenfold.

WOLFGANG H. BERGER
Scripps Institution of Oceanography

RESEARCH submarine Johnson-Sea-Link (sphere, left), which had been trapped on the bottom of the Atlantic near Key West, Fla. Two of its four crewmen died.

UPI

OHIO

The Ohio legislature used the increased funds provided by the state's new income tax law to raise the biennial budget substantially in 1973. It also enacted an ethics law dealing with the problem of conflict of interest.

The way was cleared for a 1974 gubernatorial bid by former Gov. James A. Rhodes when the Ohio Supreme Court found it legal for him to run for a third but nonconsecutive term. The court later declared his announced competitor, state Sen. Donald E. Lukens, to be ineligible to run until 1978 because

he had been late in filing his personal expense statement from his 1972 campaign for the state senate. Sen. William B. Saxbe was confirmed as the new U.S. attorney general in December, and Governor Gilligan appointed Democrat Howard M. Metzenbaum to serve the remaining year of Saxbe's Senate term.

Budget Increases. Ohio's biennial budget, passed in June, provided for expenditures of $9.96 billion, a 22% increase. Late in 1972, the preceding legislature had voted a 9.8% raise in the pay of state representatives, of the state senators who had been elected that year, and of township and county officials. Seven months later, further increases were provided for legislators, effective in 1975, as well as for the highest elected officials. Education, public welfare, highways, mental health programs, and correctional institutions all received substantial budgetary increases as well.

In the summer the legislature appropriated $81 million to pay for nonreligious auxiliary services in nonpublic schools, a large increase over previous grants. The proposal was at once challenged by the American Civil Liberties Union of Ohio.

Ethics Law. In September an ethics bill was enacted to deal with the problem of conflict of interest. The law provided that virtually all key officials at the state level and many at the local level would be required to file information on their

UPI

POLICE remove student from Antioch College campus. Students struck Yellow Springs, Ohio, school in June.

personal holdings and sources of income, and to make the information available for public scrutiny. Not included were school board members, village officials and employees, township trustees and employees, and county or city board members who are paid less than $1,000 a year. Gov. John J. Gilligan (D) then called for a special legislative session on October 23 to deal with the regulation of campaign contributions and expenditures, a move that raised angry charges of partisanship. The session adjourned after a deadlock on details.

Other Legislation. In addition, the legislature provided equal pay for women doing the same work as men, gave tax exemptions to aid the attack on urban blight, passed an antipollution measure, and repealed "blue laws" prohibiting various business activities on Sunday. It lowered the age of legal adulthood from 21 to 18, although 18-year-olds still would not have the right to purchase alcoholic beverages or serve as policemen or state highway patrolmen. The state's first minimum wage law for persons not covered by federal law affected domestic workers, retail clerks, waitresses, state and local government employees, hotel and motel workers, farm workers, and motion picture employees. Jobless pay and workmen's compensation for those injured on the job were materially increased.

State Lottery. In May, Ohio voters approved a state constitutional amendment calling for a state lottery. The legislature was given power to provide for a lottery with a commission to supervise it. A bill creating such a commission was passed on May 11, three days after the vote.

Other Amendments. The voters in the May primary also approved an amendment giving the legislature the power to call itself into special session and making annual sessions a requirement. In November, four amendments were submitted to the voters, and all passed by decisive margins. One dealt with the taxation of agricultural land, the second removed the $3,000 limitation on the amount of income that can be exempt from the state income tax, the third allowed the establishment of divisions of the Courts of Common Pleas, and the fourth gave Vietnam veterans bonuses of up to $500, with double that amount to be provided if it was used as credit toward college tuition.

FRANCIS P. WEISENBURGER
The Ohio State University

OHIO • Information Highlights

Area: 41,222 square miles (106,765 sq km).

Population (1972 est.): 10,783,000. Density: 263 per sq mi.

Chief Cities (1970 census): Columbus, the capital, 540,025; Cleveland, 750,859; Cincinnati, 452,524; Toledo, 383,818; Akron, 275,425; Dayton, 243,601; Youngstown, 140,909.

Government (1973): *Chief Officers*—governor, John J. Gilligan (D); lt. gov., John W. Brown (R); secy. of state, Ted W. Brown (R); atty. gen., William J. Brown (D); treas., Gertrude W. Donahey (D); auditor, Joseph Ferguson (D); supt. of public instruction, Martin W. Essex; chief justice, C. William O'Neill. *General Assembly*—Senate, 33 members (17 Republicans, 15 Democrats, 1 Vacancy); House of Representatives, 99 members (58 D, 41 R).

Education (1972–73): *Enrollment*—public elementary schools, 1,465,500 pupils, 55,150 teachers; public secondary schools, 950,950 pupils, 50,250 teachers; nonpublic schools, 319,000 pupils, 11,810 teachers; colleges and universities, 351,398 students. *Public school expenditures*, $2,112,000,000 ($945 per pupil). *Average teacher's salary*, $9,800.

State Finances (fiscal year 1971): *Revenues*, $4,136,312,000 (4% general sales tax and gross receipts taxes, $674,557,000; motor fuel tax, $330,139,000; federal funds $730,337,000). *Expenditures*, $3,079,721,000 (education, $1,181,864,000; health, welfare, and safety, $575,298,000; highways, $711,289,000). *State debt*, $1,784,384,000 (June 30, 1971).

Personal Income (1972): $48,656,000,000; per capita, $4,512.

Public Assistance (1972): $612,511,000. *Average monthly payments* (Dec. 1972)—old-age assistance, $62.21; aid to families with dependent children, $158.89.

Labor Force: *Nonagricultural wage and salary earners* (July 1973), 4,064,100. *Average annual employment* (1972)—manufacturing, 1,343,600; trade, 813,800; government, $590,300; services, 615,700. *Insured unemployed* (Sept. 1973)—28,900 (0.9%).

Manufacturing (1971): *Value added by manufacture,* $23,991,700,000. Transportation equipment, $3,479,900,000; nonelectrical machinery, $3,168,100,000; primary metal industries, $2,904,100,000; fabricated metal products, $2,648,200,000; electrical equipment and supplies, $2,207,500,000; chemicals and allied products, $1,843,800,000.

Agriculture (1972): *Cash farm income,* $1,746,310,000 (livestock, $875,527,000; crops, $781,205,000; government payments, $89,578,000). *Chief crops* (in order of value, 1971)—Corn, soybeans, hay, wheat.

Mining (1972): *Production value,* $701,760,000 (ranks 12th among the states). *Chief minerals*—Coal, $293,400,000; stone, $91,634,000; lime, $73,800,000; cement, $65,490,000.

Fisheries (1972): *Commercial catch,* 7,939,000 pounds ($1,026,000). *Leading species by value*—Yellow perch, $679,000; catfish, $270,000; white bass, $214,000.

Transportation: *Roads* (1972), 109,240 miles (175,800 km); *motor vehicles* (1972), 6,043,109; *railroads* (1972), 7,804 miles (12,559 km); *public airports* (1972), 102.

Communications: *Telephones* (1973), 6,667,900; *television stations* (1971), 27; *radio stations* (1971), 226; *newspapers* (1973), 96 (daily circulation, 3,549,000).

OKLAHOMA

One of the nation's costliest prison riots erupted at the Oklahoma State Prison, at McAlester, on July 27, 1973, when 21 guards were taken hostage. The guards were released unharmed the next day, but the rioting, after a brief calm, continued until National Guardsmen drove the prisoners out of cellblocks on July 29.

The prison disaster resulted in the deaths of several prisoners, injuries to both prisoners and prison officials and guards, and property damage, mostly from fire, of $20 million. In the wake of the rioting, Gov. David Hall proposed a comprehensive penal reform program that it was hoped would be approved by the Legislature.

Legislation. The Legislature took steps to exert control over day-to-day governmental operations, particularly in regard to fiscal matters. It also reinstated the death penalty, legalized bingo, and passed an anti-strikebreaking law. However, it rejected the federal Equal Rights Amendment for women and the governor's $43 million proposal for capital improvements.

Government Corruption. The taint of corruption stung the state Democratic administration when the treasurer, Leo Winters, and 13 others were indicted on May 31 for extortion and misuse of funds. Earlier, on May 17, it was revealed that the Internal Revenue Service was auditing income tax returns of Governor Hall and Secretary of State John Rogers. Rogers labeled the move as "political espionage" on the part of the Nixon administration. In Oklahoma

--------- OKLAHOMA • Information Highlights ---------

Area: 69,919 square miles (181,090 sq km).
Population (1972 est.): 2,634,000. *Density:* 36 per sq mi.
Chief Cities (1970 census): Oklahoma City, the capital, 368,-856; Tulsa, 330,350; Lawton, 74,470; Norman, 52,117; Midwest City, 48,114; Enid, 44,986; Muskogee, 37,331.
Government (1973): *Chief Officers*—governor, David Hall (D); lt. gov., George Nigh (D); secy. of state, John Rogers (D); atty. gen., Larry Derryberry (D); treas., Leo Winters (D); supt. of public instruction, Leslie R. Fisher (D); chief justice of the supreme court, Denver N. Davison. *Legislature*—Senate, 48 members (38 Democrats, 10 Republicans); House of Representatives, 101 members (75 D, 26 R).
Education (1972–73): *Enrollment*—public elementary schools, 324,000 pupils, 14,820 teachers; public secondary schools, 290,000 pupils, 13,006 teachers; nonpublic schools, 12,500 pupils, 710 teachers; colleges and universities, 118,746 students. *Public school expenditures,* $385,000,000 ($704 per pupil). *Average teacher's salary,* $8,200.
State Finances (fiscal year 1971): *Revenues,* $1,145,695,000 (2% general sales tax and gross receipts taxes, $101,221,-000; motor fuel tax, $96,631,000; federal funds, $352,827,-000). *Expenditures,* $1,149,352,000 (education, $441,622,-000; health, welfare, and safety, $291,891,000; highways, $204,339,000). *State debt,* $760,141,000 (June 30, 1971).
Personal Income (1972): $10,015,000,000; per capita, $3,802.
Public Assistance (1972): $247,309,000. *Average monthly payments* (Dec. 1972)—old-age assistance, $66.97; aid to families with dependent children, $137.86.
Labor Force: *Nonagricultural wage and salary earners* (July 1973), 832,000. *Average annual employment* (1972)—manufacturing, 138,900; trade, 181,500; government, 191,800; services, 123,300. *Insured unemployed* (Sept. 1973)—12,300 (1.9%).
Manufacturing (1971): Value added by manufacture, $1,834,-400,000. Nonelectrical machinery, $305,700,000; food and kindred products, $243,400,000; fabricated metal products, $187,100,000; electrical equipment and supplies, $172,300,-000; transportation equipment, $150,200,000; stone, clay, and glass products, $141,300,000.
Agriculture (1972): *Cash farm income,* $1,499,074,000 (livestock, $1,081,723,000; crops, $297,951,000; government payments, $119,400,000). *Chief crops* (in order of value, 1971)—Wheat, hay, peanuts, grain sorghum.
Mining (1972): Production value, $1,221,457,000 (ranks 5th among the states). *Chief minerals*—Petroleum, $708,560,-000; natural gas, $299,809,000; natural gas liquids, $102,-760,000; stone, $31,222,000.
Transportation: *Roads* (1972), 107,872 miles (173,598 km); *motor vehicles* (1972), 1,789,483; *railroads* (1972), 5,332 miles (8,581 km); *public airports* (1972), 115.
Communications: *Telephones* (1973), 1,645,100; *television stations* (1971), 9; *radio stations* (1971), 103; *newspapers* (1973), 52 (daily circulation, 869,000).

City, in July, City Manager Nate Ross was dismissed when investigations during the City Council election resulted in charges of corruption in various city agencies.

Indian Affairs. After Arizona, Oklahoma has the largest American Indian population in the United States, and tensions mounted between Indians and whites in several communities. At Indian schools in Hammon, Chilocco, and Canton, as well as at Pawnee Union High School, Indians charged white officials with discrimination against them. At Canton and Pawnee the controversy centered on the long hair worn by many male Indian students.

Education. The Legislature appropriated funds for a medical college and an osteopathic college in Tulsa and for the Health Sciences Center in Oklahoma City. It also passed a precedent-setting public education bill that included teacher salary increases. The governor pledged 50% of all new funds would go to lower schools and 25% to higher education. Tulsa voluntarily desegregated a formerly all-black high school and an all-black junior high school.

Business and Agriculture. Ford Motor Company opened a glass production facility near Tulsa, and General Motors announced that it will build a plant in Oklahoma City. The state had a record-breaking wheat crop in 1973, as rains ended the previous year's drought. However, federal price controls on beef hurt the cattle industry.

Natural Disasters. In May, tornadoes destroyed much of the towns of Union City and Keefeton. In October, rains caused major floods in the communities of Enid and Dover and inundated parts of five counties in north-central Oklahoma, with damage estimated at between $10 and $20 million.

C. B. CLARK
University of Oklahoma

OLDER POPULATION

In 1973 there were events of immediate and long-range significance for older people, most of which promise improvements in their circumstances. There are more than 20.6 million people over 65 years old in the United States, with women making up almost 60% of this population. According to the Census Bureau the percentage of the population over 65 will continue to rise, as will the ratio of older women over older men. Special problems of older women, including emotional problems and economic and social discrimination, are receiving increased attention.

Legislation. In May, President Nixon signed the previously vetoed Older Americans Comprehensive Service Amendments of 1973, which changes and expands federal approaches to dealing with the older population. The amendments created a 15-member federal Council on Aging, appointed by the President with Senate confirmation. The council evaluates federal programs, encourages coordination among them, and recommends improvements in practice and legislation. The Administration on Aging (AoA), focal point for the government's concern for older people, is placed within an Office of Human Development in the Office of the Secretary of Health, Education, and Welfare. The revised act gives new responsibilities to state and community agencies on aging; aims to foster adult education, library services, employment, and activity centers for older adults; seeks expansion of gerontological research and training; and establishes a National Information and Resource Clearinghouse on Aging.

ELDERLY PEOPLE from three New Jersey counties picket the state house in Trenton for reduced utility rates for older persons.

Formulas for apportioning AoA funds among the states and eligibility for some programs are based on the population 60 years and over instead of 65 years and over. This places 30 million people within the scope of AoA and its state and community counterpart agencies.

Community Planning and Services. Under the new amendments the principal thrust will be toward systematic, planned expansion and coordination of services for older persons in states and communities. State agencies on aging designated an aggregate of 600 planning and service areas, 300 to 400 of which will be set up by June 1974, and the remainder during the following year.

Program objectives are: (1) to "maintain maximum independence and dignity in a home environment for older people capable of self-care with supportive services, and (2) remove barriers to economic and personal independence of older persons." Area agencies on aging are charged with identifying persons in need of services, assessing existing community resources, coordinating their efforts, and stimulating expansion of current services and development of new ones as necessary.

Federal funds in the amount of $100 million supplemented by state appropriations were allocated to start the program. It is expected, however, that most support in such areas as housing, transportation, home care, protective services, information and referral, and education will be drawn from other federal-state resources and from communities themselves. Older people will be required to contribute to the extent of their ability.

Meals for the Elderly. A $100 million appropriation for the 1972-enacted program for nutrition for the elderly became available in August 1973, and the first meals were served in September. Rising costs have reduced the projected number of recipients, but by midwinter 200,000 persons were to be receiving meals 5 days a week. Most meals are served to groups for whom social programs are also provided, but some are delivered to homebound elderly.

Income and Housing Problems. Low- and fixed-income older people were hit hard by the 1973 inflation. To offset declining purchasing power, Congress voted an 11% increase in social security benefits, effective in two steps in 1974. (See SOCIAL WELFARE—*Social Security.*) Congress also voted to raise supplemental security income (SSI) payments, to begin January 1974, from $130 to $140 per month

for individuals and from $195 to $210 for couples. The increases are effective July 1, 1974. In November the Administration on Aging and the Social Security Administration launched an SSI-Alert to inform 2.5 million low-income older people who have not received old-age assistance under the new program.

In January 1973 a freeze on housing assistance programs halted construction of housing for the elderly, except for projects in the application stage. In the fall, the administration announced its belief that housing subsidies are not cost-effective and would not be reinstated.

Employment. The Department of Labor investigated 6,067 establishments and found one third guilty of age discrimination; it ordered back payments to 965 workers. A major bus line was found guilty of refusing to hire workers over the age of 40, and an international airline was required to pay $250,000 to 29 airport employees for discrimination in hiring, laying off, and retiring workers aged 40–45 years.

Research and Training. Facilities for research and for training personnel for careers concerned with the problems of aging were enhanced by the opening of the $3.5 million Ethel Percy Andrus Gerontology Center at the University of Southern California and the $6.5 million Weiss Institute of the Philadelphia Geriatric Center. Support for gerontological training was dropped from the federal budget, but most of the 50 to 60 institutions affected were trying to maintain their programs. A survey of the nation's 1,000 community and junior colleges revealed that a third of them were targeting educational opportunities to older adults, training paraprofessional personnel, and providing assistance to groups of older people and to agencies serving them. Multidisciplinary gerontology centers for research, training, and service to action agencies were operating in all 10 federal regions.

The Paris and New York–based International Center for Social Gerontology conducted a 5-day course in Oslo, Norway, for personnel from 25 countries and an International Symposium on Housing and Environmental Design for Older Adults in Washington, D. C. A course on retirement preparation to be held in Madrid (June 17–21, 1974) is expected to attract personnel from management, labor, and adult education.

CLARK TIBBITTS, *Administration on Aging U. S. Department of Health, Education, and Welfare*

ONTARIO

The Progressive Conservative party celebrated its 30th consecutive year in power during 1973. Government policy continued to stress the environment, local problems, and the quality of life rather than any new health and education schemes. Among examples were proposals, introduced at the opening of the legislative session on March 20 and later adopted, for regulating land use to provide parkway belts in urban areas and to preserve the geologically significant Niagara escarpment area. Earlier in the year the province announced that it would pay 75% of the costs of new rapid-transit systems and launched a government program to develop—in conjunction with the West German firm of Krauss-Maffei—a new elevated rapid-transit network. These plans helped Premier William G. Davis win the transit industry's title "Man of the Year" at an October meeting of the American Transit Association in Miami Beach, Fla.

Government and Politics. The policy of decentralization through the transfer of resources to local authorities, begun in 1972, was stepped up in Treasurer John White's first budget, proposed on April 12. Grants to local authorities and school boards were increased to $2.4 billion for the fiscal year 1974. Projected expenditure was $7.67 billion, with estimated revenue of $6.87 billion—a total spending increase of 11.7%. To raise extra revenue, the sales tax was increased from 5% to

--------- ONTARIO • Information Highlights ---------

Area: 412,582 square miles (1,068,589 sq km).
Population (1972 est.): 7,865,000.
Chief Cities (1971 census): Toronto, the provincial capital (712,786); Hamilton (309,173); Ottawa, the federal capital (302,341); London (223,222); Windsor (203,300).
Government: *Chief Officers*—lt. gov., W. Ross MacDonald; premier, William G. Davis (Progressive Conservative); prov. secy., Robert Welch (P. C.); atty. gen., Dalton A. Bales (P. C.); prov. treas., John White (P. C.); min. of educ., Thomas L. Wells (P. C.); chief justice, George A. Gale. *Legislature*—Legislative Assembly: 117 members (76 Progressive Conservative, 22 Liberal, 19 New Democratic party).
Education: *School enrollment* (1969–70)—public elementary and secondary, 1,985,306 pupils (89,929 teachers); private schools, 43,007 pupils (3,316 teachers); Indian (federal) schools, 6,605 pupils (278 teachers); college and university, 108,825 students. *Public school expenditures* (1970)—$1,901,254,000.
Public Finance (fiscal year 1973 est.): *Revenues*, $5,801,400,000 (sales tax, $1,448,000,000; income tax, $1,529,600,000; federal funds, $1,183,000,000). *Expenditures*, $6,363,100,000 (education, $1,890,200,000; health and social welfare, $2,448,200,000; transport and communications, $583,300,000).
Personal Income (1971 est.): $30,560,000,000; average annual income per person, $3,967.
Social Welfare (fiscal year 1973 est.): $2,028,800,000 (dependents and unemployed, $262,800,000).
Manufacturing (1969): *Value added by manufacture*, $10,635,970,000 (transportation equipment, $1,700,090,000; food and beverages, $1,243,342,000; fabricated metals, $985,500,000; primary metals, $938,959,000; electrical products, $831,437,000; chemical and chemical products industries, $816,258,000).
Agriculture (1972 est.): *Cash farm income* (exclusive of government payments), $1,573,869,000 (livestock and products, $1,065,840,000; crops, $464,268,000). *Chief crops* (cash receipts)—tobacco, $141,859,000 (ranks 1st among the provinces); vegetables, $68,543,000 (ranks 1st); corn, $59,443,000 (ranks 1st); fruits, $39,176,000 (ranks 1st); soybeans, $35,784,000 (ranks 1st); wheat, $24,699,000; potatoes, $16,553,000 (ranks 3d).
Mining (1972 est.): *Production value*, $1,521,415,000. *Chief minerals*—nickel, $513,301,000 (ranks 1st among the provinces); copper, $291,563,000 (ranks 1st); zinc, $156,370,000 (ranks 1st); cement, $71,611,000 (ranks 1st); sand and gravel, $60,000,000 (ranks 1st); stone, $39,000,000 (ranks 2d).
Forest Products (1972): Lumber, 1,088,000,000 board feet.
Transportation: *Roads* (1970), 111,979 miles (180,208 km); *motor vehicles* (1970), 3,047,599; *railroads* (1971), 9,935 track miles (15,988 km); *licensed airports* (1971), 93.
Communications: *Telephones* (1970), 3,847,480; *television stations* (1972), 50; *radio stations* (1972), 93; *daily newspapers* (1972), 49.
(All monetary figures given in Canadian dollars.)

7%, with some tax credits allowed to ease the burden on lower-income groups. But the government received a severe shock when public outcry forced it to rescind on April 24 its extension of the 7% sales tax to include energy sources, such as fuel to heat homes.

The major items of expenditure are still health and education—each 30% of the total budget. A new funding system for university financing is being worked out to prevent the severe effects of a drop in enrollment. "Slip year" financing, whereby the new grants are made on the basis of past-year figures, is already operative. Slight increases in student enrollment in the fall of 1973 has quieted the universities' worst fears—that the decline in student enrollment of the past few years would accelerate.

The government had numerous embarrassments in 1973. On March 15 the Liberals won two former Progressive Conservative seats in by-elections, and Premier Davis himself was caught up in controversy. On May 19, after a publicized ski trip to Vermont on a government plane, he indicated that in the future he would reimburse the government for personal trips taken outside the country in provincial aircraft. He was also called upon to testify before a select committee of the legislature investigating the circumstances of the awarding of a $44.4 million contract for a new Ontario Hydro office building to Canada Square Corp. Ltd., owned by Toronto millionaire Gerhard Moog, a friend of Premier Davis. But a subsequent committee report cleared the premier of exercising any undue influence.

There seemed to be a feeling that the government had slipped in public esteem, and Robert Nixon —the Ontario Liberal party leader, who had announced his intention to step down—decided to reconsider and won reelection as party leader in October.

Housing and the Building Industry. Ontario is in "a near-crisis in housing," according to a September 13 report by the Ontario Task Force on Housing, headed by Eli Comay, a former Toronto planning commissioner. Prices of houses in many cities are among the highest on the continent. It is estimated that one family in six needs government assistance to obtain housing it can afford. In response to the report, Premier Davis announced the establishment of a new ministry of housing to help build a million houses in the next decade and a crash program, headed by Comay, to deal with the acute crisis in Toronto, Ottawa, and Hamilton.

After charges of violence, corruption, and union extortion in the lathing, plastering, and dry wall section of the building industry by Morton Shulman, a New Democratic party member of the legislature, the government announced in March the appointment of a royal commission to investigate.

Canadian Nationalism. Expressing alarm that up to 90% of the recreational land in some areas of the province is owned by foreigners, mainly U. S. citizens, the Economic and Cultural Nationalism Committee of the legislature has proposed the prohibition of land sales to anyone except Canadian citizens and landed immigrants. Foreigners currently holding land would retain it but could sell only to Canadian citizens or landed immigrants. Foreign heirs would have to sell within three years. But the government has yet to act on these recommendations.

PETER J. KING
Carleton University

OREGON

Oregon was threatened even more than the rest of the nation by the energy crisis during 1973, but the danger eased by the end of the year. The Democratic-controlled 1973 session of the state legislature was the longest on record—180 days. Its duration resulted in part from the youth and inexperience of many of the legislators and in part from the complexity of its central task—to overhaul the system of tax support for public schools.

Energy Crisis. For a state heavily dependent upon hydroelectric power, the energy crisis was compounded in Oregon by light winter snows and a summer drought, which reduced the flow of the Columbia River to two-thirds its normal level. In September, Gov. Tom McCall declared an emergency. There was a blackout of all commercial lighting, highway lighting was cut back, and state office buildings were darkened at night. Industries in some cases lost up to 25% of their power, and as a result thousands of workers were put out of work.

By the end of the year, heavy rains had restored reservoir levels and eased the prospect of a winter brownout. On December 5, Governor McCall ended most of the emergency restrictions, but urged a continued restraint in the use of power.

Legislature. Majority leaders of both chambers of the Oregon Legislature supported Governor McCall's tax plan, which would have provided for the state's assuming 95% of school costs. The com-

----------- OREGON • Information Highlights -----------

Area: 96,981 square miles (251,181 sq km).
Population (1972 est.): 2,182,000. *Density:* 22 per sq mi.
Chief Cities (1970 census): Salem, the capital, 68,856; Portland, 380,555; Eugene, 78,389; Corvallis, 35,056; Medford, 28,454; Springfield, 27,220; Beaverton, 18,577.
Government (1973): *Chief Officers*—governor, Tom McCall (R); secy. of state, Clay Myers (R); atty. gen., Lee Johnson (R); treas., James A. Redden (D); supt. of public instruction, Dale Parnell; chief justice, Kenneth J. O'Connell. *Legislative Assembly*—Senate, 30 members (18 Democrats, 12 Republicans); House of Representatives, 60 members (33 D, 27 R).
Education (1972–73): *Enrollment*—public elementary schools, 278,863 pupils, 11,740 teachers; public secondary schools, 198,724 pupils, 9,740 teachers; nonpublic schools, 25,700 pupils, 1,170 teachers; colleges and universities, 93,450 students. *Public school expenditures,* $437,208,000 ($1,004 per pupil). *Average teacher's salary,* $9,949.
State Finances (fiscal year 1971): *Revenues,* $1,175,953,000 (total sales tax and gross receipts taxes, $102,518,000; motor fuel tax, $74,498,000; federal funds, $339,741,000). *Expenditures,* $981,815,000 (education, $341,268,000; health, welfare, and safety, $162,834,000; highways, $229,071,000). *State debt,* $832,241,000 (June 30, 1971).
Personal Income (1972): $9,374,000,000; per capita, $4,296.
Public Assistance (1972): $115,304,000. *Average monthly payments* (Dec. 1972)—old-age assistance, $69.42; aid to families with dependent children, $169.64.
Labor Force: *Nonagricultural wage and salary earners* (July 1973), 814,800. *Average annual employment* (1972)—manufacturing, 183,200; trade, 179,200; government, 157,400; services, 125,800. *Insured unemployed* (Sept. 1973)—17,400 (2.8%).
Manufacturing (1971): *Value added by manufacture,* $2,806,600,000. Lumber and wood products, $1,087,500,000; food and kindred products, $379,600,000; paper and allied products, $256,300,000; nonelectrical machinery, $157,200,000; electrical equipment and supplies, $121,200,000.
Agriculture (1972): *Cash farm income,* $668,758,000 (livestock, $288,767,000; crops, $355,433,000; government payments, $24,558,000). *Chief crops* (in order of value, 1971)—Hay, wheat, potatoes, barley.
Mining (1972): *Production value,* $79,805,000 (ranks 39th among the states). *Chief minerals*—Sand and gravel, $30,429,000; stone, $25,669,000; cement, value not available; nickel, value not available.
Fisheries (1972): *Commercial catch,* 92,923,000 pounds ($24,024,000). *Leading species by value*—Tuna, $9,231,000; salmon, $6,987,000; crabs, $2,857,000; shrimp, $2,774,000.
Transportation: *Roads* (1972), 97,453 miles (156,831 km); *motor vehicles* (1972), 1,431,732; *railroads* (1972), 3,068 miles (4,937 km); *public airports* (1972), 98.
Communications: *Telephones* (1973), 1,337,600; *television stations* (1971), 13; *radio stations* (1971), 100; *newspapers* (1973), 22 (daily circulation, 673,000).

plexity of the proposal, however, together with opposition by corporate interests and fears that local control would be lost, led to its defeat by the voters on May 1. The Legislature then devised a compromise package, increasing state support to only 30% and providing property tax refunds for low-income homeowners and tenants. Later phases of the program, if approved by the voters, would establish new local tax bases and increase state support to 50% through higher income taxes.

The Legislature passed a bill requiring meetings of all public bodies—with carefully prescribed exceptions—to be open to the public. Another new law enables a citizen to enlist the aid of the district attorney, if necessary, to obtain access to the records of public agencies. A sweeping shield law for newsmen permits them to refuse to disclose their news sources. A strong conflict of interest bill, requiring officials to disclose their financial interests was vetoed, but the public interest group Common Cause mounted a campaign late in the year to place an even stronger bill before the voters.

A new law bans discrimination against women in the sale or rental of property, granting of credit, purchase of insurance, or use of public accommodations. Workmen's compensation was increased, and a collective bargaining law for public employees was passed. The mutual responsibilities of tenants and landlords were defined in another bill.

The legal age for employment, contract, and marriage without a guardian's consent was lowered to 18, but the drinking age remained at 21. The state's criminal procedures code was revised, replacing the system of commercial bail bonds with less costly public security deposits—a major step toward legal equality for the poor.

Conservation. Conservationists won passage of a bill that places responsibility for the planning of land use on the counties, under state guidelines. They also persuaded the Legislature to mandate purchase of the scenic landmark Cape Kiwanda, despite the insistence of the Highway Commission that it is too hazardous for development as a park.

Conservationists won a more questionable victory over control of the tussock moth, which ravaged forests in a tri-state area centering on Oregon's Blue Mountains. Refusal by the Environmental Protection Agency to allow the use of DDT, despite pressure from the forest industry, was based on the expectation that a virus would, as in past years, check the insect's cycle. But it did not, and more than 600,000 acres were seriously defoliated.

SAMUEL K. ANDERSON
Oregon College of Education

ORGANIZATIONS. See SOCIETIES AND ORGANIZATIONS.

OTTAWA

In 1973, development programs to ease transportation and preserve the environment were the dominant issues in Ottawa, Canada's national capital, with an estimated metropolitan population of 613,000.

Transportation. In January the Ontario provincial government revealed plans for a $195 million elevated rapid-transit system that could be operational by 1978, with the province bearing 75% of the cost. To deal with more immediate problems, a "dial-a-bus" service was introduced into two suburban areas with apparent initial success. The

federal government has completed a new parkway between Ottawa and the city airport, and the federally built Portage Bridge across the Ottawa River was opened in November.

Urban Planning. It is estimated that by the year 2000 the Ottawa-Carleton metropolitan area will have a population of more than 1 million. To meet this growth, the Regional Municipality, comprising 16 municipalities, unveiled a new official urban plan. The plan aimed at preserving natural surroundings while providing adequate transportation and utilities systems. It called for encouraging the growth of new communities, with their own employment base, within the region but outside the Greenbelt around the city proper. Two noteworthy features of the plan are the protection of good agricultural land and the preservation of the natural corridors along the Rideau and Ottawa rivers. Also, to facilitate controlled planning of the downtown area, the city has placed a temporary ban on new development schemes.

Finance. The city of Ottawa estimated a gross operating expenditure of $66,266,800 for 1973, an increase of 8% over 1972. Of this amount, $20 million derived from federal and provincial grants, and $23.8 million from property taxes on a total assessment, residential and commercial, of $791 million. In addition, there was a capital expenditure of $28.5 million. (The city's total capital debt stood at $139.6 million.)

The Regional Municipality budgeted $57.4 million, including $21 million from levies on regional municipalities and $23 million from provincial grants. In addition, the federal government planned expenditures of $32.8 million on new buildings and renovations in the Ottawa area, some of which are administered by the National Capital Commission, of which Edgar Gallant succeeded Douglas Fullerton as chairman in 1973.

Education. The recent trend of declining enrollment in city schools, with a corresponding increase in suburban areas, seemed to have slowed somewhat in 1973. Enrollment in public schools in Ottawa was 49,366 (22,977 elementary; 19,843 secondary English; 6,546 secondary French); in Ottawa Catholic schools, 24,780 (12,463 English; 12,317 French). In suburban areas, public school enrollment was 36,067 (23,435 elementary; 12,632 secondary); Catholic school enrollment, 14,572 (8,585 English; 5,987 French).

In 1973, the Ottawa and Carleton Catholic school boards were threatened with mass resignations of their teachers in a contract dispute. The boards contended that provincially imposed spending limits prevented their meeting teachers' demands.

PETER J. KING, *Carleton University*

PAINTING AND SCULPTURE. See ART.

PAKISTAN

The year 1973 was a crucial one for Pakistan, which was still suffering from the dislocations of the civil war of 1971. A new constitution was adopted, with difficulty; and President Zulfikar Ali Bhutto became the prime minister, with a virtual guarantee of tenure for the next 10 years. The specter of separatism remained, however, with minor guerrilla warfare in Baluchistan province. Prolonged negotiations with India and Bangladesh resulted in agreement on the repatriation of Paki-

stani prisoners of war and the further exchange of populations. A disastrous flood of the Indus River struck the provinces of Punjab and Sind, resulting in many millions of dollars of damage.

Domestic Affairs. The year began with serious and sometimes heated debate over the provisions of a new draft constitution, particularly over the powers of the prime minister. Khan Abdul Wali Khan, leader of the National Awami party, strongly opposed the constitution and threatened to boycott the final stages of the debate and implementation of the document if President Bhutto did not make concessions. In March at least 9 persons were killed in riots over the proposed constitution. In early April, however, Bhutto made enough concessions to obtain the support of all the parties in the National Assembly, and the constitution was adopted.

The third constitution in Pakistan's history, it is federal in nature, providing some autonomy for the four regions of Pakistan (and holding the door open for the eventual return of Bangladesh). But it gives the prime minister strong executive powers and makes it very difficult for him to be removed within the next 10 years. In August, President Bhutto stepped down from the presidency (handing it in turn to Fazal Elahi) and became instead the first prime minister under the new constitution.

The first half of the year was a tumultuous one for Bhutto. He dismissed two provincial ministers, arrested not only a number of military officers for plotting against the government in the spring but also large numbers of political opposition leaders in Baluchistan. Several newspaper editors were also arrested during the year, and rigorous control of the media was instituted. In November the Bhutto-appointed governor of Baluchistan quit because of differences with the central government.

Guerrilla war continued in Baluchistan province, with about 15,000 troops engaged in quelling the disturbances. In February the government seized large quantities of small arms and ammunition in the Iraqi embassy in Islamabad. It was assumed that they were intended for Baluchi tribesmen. The Baluchis live in both Pakistan and Iran, and there has been some cooperation between the two countries on the control of guerrilla activity.

--------- **PAKISTAN · Information Highlights** ---------

Official Name: Islamic Republic of Pakistan.
Location: South Asia.
Area: 310,403 square miles (803,941 sq km).
Population (1973 est.): 68,300,000. *Density,* 220 per square mile (85 per sq km).
Chief Cities (1971 est.): Islamabad, the capital, 50,000 (1967 est.); Karachi, 3,442,000; Lahore, 1,986,000.
Government: *Head of state,* Chaudri Fazal Elahi, president (took office Aug. 1973). *Head of government,* Zulfikar Ali Bhutto, prime minister (took office as president Dec. 1971; as prime minister Aug. 1973). *Legislature*—Parliament: Senate and National Assembly. *Major political parties*—Pakistan People's party; Awami party.
Languages: Urdu (official), English.
Monetary Unit: Rupee (9.931 rupees equal U. S.$1, Aug. 1973).
Gross National Product (1972 est.): $5,085,000,000.
Economic Indexes: *Industrial production* (1971), 160 (1963= 100); *agricultural production* (1971), 121 (1963=100); *consumer price index* (1972), 156 (1963=100).
Manufacturing (major products): Textiles, processed foods, cement, petroleum products, chemicals, metals.
Major Agricultural Products: Rice, wheat, cotton, sugarcane, wool, livestock.
Major Minerals: Natural gas.
Foreign Trade (1972): *Exports,* $697,000,000; *Imports,* $681,-000,000. *Chief trading partners* (1971)—United Kingdom; United States; Hong Kong; Japan.
Transportation: *Motor vehicles* (1971), 215,300 (automobiles, 150,500); *major national airline,* Pakistan International Airlines.
Communications: *Telephones* (1972), 211,088.

In November, Bhutto suggested that the part of Kashmir held by Pakistan could be made a province of Pakistan, at least on an interim basis.

With all his problems, Bhutto remained, at the end of the year, a popular and able leader. He was almost indispensable in the troubled aftermath of the 1971 war with India.

Foreign Affairs. The year 1973 saw President (later Prime Minister) Bhutto play a shrewd and successful role in his complicated dealings with India and Bangladesh. India, in dire economic and political distress itself, held about 90,000 Pakistani prisoners of war and was anxious to disengage from the dispute over them wtih Pakistan. Bangladesh, the former eastern province of Pakistan, was also in a state of economic distress. Among other things it sought Pakistan's recognition of its independence.

The first half of the year was spent in jockeying with India and Bangladesh over (1) the repatriation of prisoners of war from India, (2) the recognition of Bangladesh, (3) the trial in Bangladesh of Pakistani military officers for committing war crimes, (4) the fate of the Bengalis in Pakistan, and (5) the emigration of Biharis from Bangladesh. At the end of August, India and Pakistan agreed, in a pact signed in New Delhi, on the release of Pakistani prisoners of war. The agreement was a major diplomatic victory for Pakistan.

The first group of prisoners was released in September. Those accused of war crimes were to be the last released; by the end of 1973 it seemed unlikely that the accused would be tried. Bengalis in Pakistan were also to be freed, including those who had been arrested for "war crimes" to counter the charges made in Bangladesh against Pakistani prisoners of war. Pakistan agreed to accept from Bangladesh about 50,000 Biharis (East Pakistani, non-Bengali Muslims who had supported Pakistan in the 1971 war).

In November, Bangladesh accused Pakistan of "dragging its feet" in the implementation of the agreement. It was evident that Bhutto was also delaying recognition of Bangladesh until the details of the complex agreement had been implemented to his satisfaction.

In May, Bhutto visited Iran and was given an elaborate and virtually unprecedented reception by the shah. They share many political problems, including those caused by the Baluchi separatist movement. Iran intends to play the role of protector for Pakistan in the months to come.

One of Pakistan's separatist problems arises from the dispute over Pushtunistan with Afghanistan. Pushtunistan is a major part of the Northwest Frontier Province of Pakistan and has been claimed by Afghanistan for years. Dormant for the last several years, the dispute was brought back into prominence by the new ruler in Afghanistan, Gen. Mohammed Daud Khan, who overthrew King Zahir Shah in July. Little is expected to come of Afghanistan's claims, however.

Pakistan strongly supported the Arabs and condemned Israeli aggression in the October Arab-Israeli conflict. The Indians also supported the Arabs. Both nations are oil importers.

The United States relaxed its embargo on the sale of arms to Pakistan in March. In September, Prime Minister Bhutto visited the United States. Although he did not receive any substantial promise of arms, he did get a pledge of "generous and

RELIEF SUPPLIES are dropped by air force helicopter to villagers in a flood-stricken area of Pakistan.

sympathetic" economic assistance. The American ambassadorial post in Islamabad, vacant for some months, was filled during Bhutto's visit to Washington; Ambassador Henry A. Byroade was named to the post.

Economy. Although it is now conceded that Pakistan is in a better position economically because of the breakaway of Bangladesh in 1971, the total economic situation remains fluid and not altogether promising. Inflation, food shortages, and the high rate of population growth have had an adverse effect on the economy. Economic growth levels remain unspectacular. Exports for 1973 will probably total about $650 million.

The worst floods in the history of the nation struck in August. The Indus river system flooded in the Punjab and then dumped its accumulated waters into Sind province. As a result, in Punjab alone over 5 million acres (2,025,000 hectares) of crops were destroyed, a million tons of stored grain were washed away, 70,000 cattle died, a quarter million houses were in ruins, and about 300 people were dead. Approximately 140,000 persons had to be evacuated. In the whole of Pakistan the floods accounted for the deaths of 3,000 persons.

By the middle of September, Bhutto estimated that the flood damage exceeded $300 million. Taxes were imposed for flood relief. The United States pledged assistance, as did the United Nations.

(See also BANGLADESH.)

CARL LEIDEN
University of Texas at Austin

MEETING IN PANAMA in March, the United Nations Security Council discussed Canal Zone problems and other matters. Panama's Aquilino Boyd (left) confers with the Soviet Union's Yakov Malik (right).

PANAMA

During 1973, Panamanians from many sectors of society exhibited growing displeasure over the domestic policies of the authoritarian Omar Torrijos regime. In March, a meeting of the UN Security Council was held in Panama, focusing worldwide attention on the protracted U. S.-Panamanian negotiations over the status of the Panama Canal.

The UN and the Canal Controversy. The Torrijos government won a resolution from the UN Security Council urging an early conclusion of treaty negotiations between Panama and the United States. The Security Council resolution called upon the United States to accept Panama's "effective sovereignty" over the Canal Zone. Although the resolution was vetoed by the United States, the holding of pertinent Security Council sessions on the isthmus and the unprecedented attention given elsewhere in the world to the council's position was seen by Panamanians as a diplomatic triumph.

Following the UN action, both Panama and the United States made unsuccessful efforts to reactivate bilateral negotiations for new treaties regulating the U. S. presence in the zone. The chief U. S. negotiator, Robert Anderson, submitted his resignation in July. Ellsworth Bunker replaced him.

Unpopular Policies. Uncertainties related to the implementation of a new labor code caused complaints and retrenchment among businessmen and industrialists, as well as strikes among laborers demanding management's compliance with the new wage regulations. Business spokesmen, in attacking newly issued housing laws, blasted both the regime's negative attitude toward free enterprise and Communist infiltration at upper administration levels.

Meanwhile, the Catholic hierarchy hit at "certain sectors" of government for promoting economic development of the liberal, capitalist type, "the benefits of which do not reach the underprivileged classes." The bishops also claimed in August that all of the recent attacks on the church by Marxist student leaders enjoyed official support.

Economic Affairs. The country headed into an economic downturn, with inflation and unemployment rising, construction leveling off, and investors

retrenching. The government continued to borrow heavily abroad and pump large amounts of funds into the local economy. A $65 million Eurodollar loan was negotiated in February to pay for the electric and power company, nationalized in 1972.

Even though there appeared to be little likelihood of an early increase in economic benefits from canal operations, a potential bonanza appeared on the horizon in the form of plans for development of abundant and rich copper ore deposits in western Panama. A Canadian firm exploring the deposits, estimated at about 2 billion tons, indicated that mines could be in production 18 months after approval by Panama of an exploitation concession.

International banking continued to grow in Panama. The number of banks reached 50 and deposits topped $2 billion in 1973. While that money has benefited neither local agriculture nor industry, it

――――――― **PANAMA · Information Highlights** ―――――――

Official Name: Republic of Panama.
Location: On the Isthmus of Panama, which links Central America and South America.
Area: 29,209 square miles (75,650 sq km).
Population (1973 est.): 1,600,000. *Density,* 52 per square mile (20 per sq km).
Chief City (1970 census): Panama, the capital, 348,704.
Government: *Military junta,* led by Brig. Gen. Omar Torrijos Herrera (took power Oct. 1968). *Head of state,* Demetrio Lakas Bahas, president. *Legislature* (unicameral)—People's Assembly.
Languages: Spanish (official), English.
Education: *Expenditure* (1969), 34.6% of total public expenditure. *School enrollment* (1969)—primary, 238,593; secondary, 73,371; technical/vocational, 25,449; university/higher, 7,252.
Monetary Unit: Balboa (1 balboa equals U. S.$1, Aug. 1973).
Gross National Product (1972 est.): $1,228,000,000.
Economic Indexes: *Industrial production* (manufacturing, 1971), 178 (1963=100); *agricultural production* (1971), 140 (1963=100); *consumer price index* (1972), 120 (1963=100).
Manufacturing (major products): Processed foods, petroleum products, textiles, wood products, cement, clothing, footwear, pharmaceuticals.
Major Agricultural Products: Bananas, vegetables, rice, forest products, fish.
Major Minerals: Copper, molybdenum.
Foreign Trade (1972): *Exports,* $122,000,000; *Imports,* $438,000,000. *Chief trading partner* (1971)—United States (took 49% of exports, supplied 36% of imports).
Tourism: Receipts (1971), $41,800,000.
Transportation: *Motor vehicles* (1971), 73,300 (automobiles, 55,600); *railroads* (1971), 152 miles (245 km); *merchant fleet* (1972), 7,794,000 gross registered tons; *major national airline,* COPA (Compañia Panamena de Aviación).
Communications: *Telephones* (1972), 107,129; *newspapers* (1971), 11.

did serve to create some 4,000 banking jobs for Panamanians.

Narcotics Crackdown. In an abrupt about-face, Panama's seeming indifference to the international struggle to suppress the traffic in narcotics turned into active cooperation, with the result that smugglers were beginning to avoid the isthmus. Narcotics agents from the United States opened a training course in Panama in September.

LARRY L. PIPPIN
Elbert Covell College
University of the Pacific

PARAGUAY

Presidential and congressional elections, inflation, charges of genocide, and new directions in foreign policy were among the important developments of 1973 in Paraguay.

Elections. President Alfredo Stroessner, who came to power through a violent coup in 1954, was inaugurated for his fifth consecutive term in August 1973, making his the longest-lived regime in contemporary Latin America. He reappointed all but two members of his cabinet. In February elections, the governing Colorado party had received 681,306 of the 904,013 votes cast and thus was constitutionally entitled to two thirds of the seats in both houses of Congress. The remaining seats went to the Liberal and Liberal Radical parties, both of which claimed unfair treatment during the campaign.

Charges of Repression. The regime received criticism in 1973 from several foreign and international bodies. The Inter-American Association for Democracy and Freedom asked the United Nations to hold the Stroessner government responsible for violation of human rights and for arbitrary imprisonment of political opponents. The Inter-American Press Association denounced the absence in Paraguay of freedom of the press.

The administration was also charged with mistreating the Guayaki Indians who live near the site of a proposed hydroelectric project. The UN was asked to investigate, and in the U. S. Congress, Rep.

Charles B. Rangle (D-N. Y.) suggested that the United States might be guilty of complicity in genocide by its aid to Paraguay.

In addition, the U. S. General Accounting Office cited Paraguay as a major transit area for narcotics arriving from Europe. Drug smuggling has long been a profitable business in Paraguay.

Economic Development. Although rising inflation was sending many Paraguayans to Argentina to look for jobs, the gross national product was reportedly on the increase. It had risen by 5% during 1972. The tourist business was a lucrative one, with over 100,000 visitors spending about $15 million a year in Paraguay for mass-produced Paraguayan trinkets alone.

Brazil was being especially helpful to Paraguay's economy in 1973. Brazilian investors were planning to build a sugar mill with a capacity of 300,000 tons a year, a saw mill, and several Brazilian-Paraguayan banks. The Brazilian government also extended a $100 million credit to enable Paraguay to buy the wheat that it needed to offset a severe shortage.

Inter-American Affairs. President Stroessner and Bolivian President Hugo Banzer met in July. The two leaders expressed their continuing concern about the nations' lack of access to the sea. They agreed to improve their transportation links.

Relations with Argentina deteriorated in 1973, due in part to economic disputes and in part to Argentina's displeasure over the signing of a treaty between Paraguay and Brazil calling for joint construction of a huge hydroelectric project on the Paraná River at Itaipu. Paraguay rejected an Argentine protest that the dam would damage the lower Paraná River, which forms part of Argentina's boundary. In a calculated slight, Argentina sent a low-level delegation to Stroessner's inaugural in August. In apparent retaliation, Paraguay closed part of its Argentine border for several days, citing Argentina's inability to suppress terrorists in the border area.

LEO B. LOTT
University of Montana

PAUL VI, Pope. See BIOGRAPHY.
PEDIATRICS. See MEDICINE.

— PARAGUAY • Information Highlights —

Official Name: Republic of Paraguay.
Location: Central South America.
Area: 157,047 square miles (406,752 sq km).
Population (1973 est.): 2,700,000. *Density,* 17 per square mile (7 per sq km).
Chief City (1970 est.): Asunción, the capital, 385,000.
Government: *Head of state,* Gen. Alfredo Stroessner, president (took office Aug. 1954, now serving his 5th term). *Head of government,* Gen. Alfredo Stroessner. *Legislature* —Congress: Senate and Chamber of Deputies. *Major political party* —Colorado party.
Languages: Spanish (official), Guaraní.
Education: *Expenditure* (1969), 2.6% of gross national product. *School enrollment* (1969)—primary, 408,524; general secondary, 44,514; technical/vocational (1968), 2,507; university/higher, 7,454.
Monetary Unit: Guaraní (126 guaraníes equal U. S.$1, Aug. 1973).
Gross National Product (1972 est.): $689,000,000.
Economic Indexes: *Industrial production* (1970), 143 (1963= 100); *agricultural production* (1971), 130 (1963=100); *consumer price index* (1972), 127 (1964=100).
Manufacturing (major products): Meats, leather, wood products, quebracho extract, vegetable oil.
Major Agricultural Products: Cassava, bananas, tobacco, citrus fruits, cattle, forest products.
Major Minerals: Limestone, salt.
Foreign Trade (1972): *Exports,* $86,000,000; *Imports,* $70,- 000,000. *Chief trading partners* (1971)—Argentina (took 27% of exports, supplied 14% of imports); United States (16%—25%); West Germany (5.5%—12%).
Transportation: *Motor vehicles* (1970), 28,300 (automobiles, 15,300); *railroads* (1971), 308 miles (496 km); *major national airline,* LAP (Líneas Aéreas Paraguayas).
Communications: *Telephones* (1972), 26,615; *newspapers* (1971), 11.

PENNSYLVANIA

Pennsylvania was plagued with conflicts among high-ranking state officials in 1973. A prolonged teachers' strike and a proposed reduction in the personal income tax also made news during the year.

Conflicts and Corruption. A long-running dispute between the state police and the Pennsylvania Crime Commission came to a head early in 1973. Attorney General J. Shane Creamer, who headed the crime commission, charged State Police Commissioner Rocco Urella with tapping the telephones of a crime commission unit investigating charges of corruption in the Philadelphia police department. Urella denied the charges and asserted that crime commission investigations duplicated state police efforts. Gov. Milton J. Shapp (D) forced the resignation of Creamer, fired Urella, and chose as his new attorney general Israel Packel, who left his job as superior court judge. The state later sought to prosecute Urella and five former state troopers for wiretapping, but the charges were dismissed by the court on the grounds of insufficient evidence.

Allegations of improper conduct on the part of high-level state officials continued to make news when Alexander Jaffurs was fired from his position as chief counsel for the state's Liquor Control Board (LCB). Jaffurs testified before the House Liquor Control Committee that 13 state legislators and Governor Shapp and his aides had attempted to influence state regulation of the liquor industry through political pressure. He also charged that LCB employees and high state officials had received free liquor from distillers. Governor Shapp denied the charges leveled at him and accused Jaffurs of "incompetence and poor judgment."

State Financing. Threatened with a one-day work stoppage by some 55,000 state workers protesting payless paydays, Shapp yielded to a Republican-controlled House proposal for a $3.5 billion state budget. This was some $50 million less than the governor had asked for. Passage of the budget eased the plight of the state's 750,000 welfare recipients, more than half of whom were without state relief funds for the first two weeks of July. In addition, hardships created by the halting of these funds had been aggravated by a strike of 8,000 social service workers in Pennsylvania, making it difficult to process requests for emergency aid.

At the end of 1973 legislators were still debating the governor's proposed state income tax decrease from 2.3% to 2.1% and the disbursement of some $600 million in nonpreferred funds to state-related universities and various social welfare programs.

───── **PENNSYLVANIA • Information Highlights** ─────

Area: 45,333 square miles (117,412 sq km).
Population (1972 est.): 11,926,000. *Density:* 264 per sq mi.
Chief Cities (1970 census): Harrisburg, the capital, 68,061; Philadelphia, 1,950,098; Pittsburgh, 520,117; Erie, 129,231; Allentown, 109,527; Scranton, 103,564; Reading, 87,643.
Government (1973): *Chief Officers*—governor, Milton J. Shapp (D); lt. gov., Ernest P. Kline (D); secy. of state, Mrs. C. DeLores Tucker (D); atty. gen., Israel Packel (D); treas., Grace M. Sloan (D); secretary of education, John C. Pittenger; chief justice, Benjamin R. Jones. *General Assembly*—Senate, 50 members (25 Democrats, 24 Republicans, 1 vacancy); House of Representatives, 203 members (106 R, 96 D, 1 undecided).
Education (1972–73): *Enrollment*—public elementary schools, 1,229,000 pupils; 52,600 teachers; public secondary schools, 1,139,000 pupils; 57,200 teachers; nonpublic schools, 498,300 pupils; 18,430 teachers; colleges and universities, 401,636 students. *Public school expenditures,* $2,581,434,000 ($1,177 per pupil). *Average teacher's salary,* $11,000.
State Finances (fiscal year 1971): *Revenues,* $5,488,363,000 (6% general sales tax and gross receipts taxes, $1,010,-418,000; motor fuel tax, $377,686,000; federal funds, $1,-004,008,000). *Expenditures,* $5,081,025,000 (education, $1,965,302,000; health, welfare, and safety, $1,138,972; highways, $971,381,000). *State debt,* $3,829,540,000 (June 30, 1971).
Personal Income (1972): $53,029,000,000; per capita, $4,447.
Public Assistance (1972): $1,133,734,000. *Average monthly payments* (Dec. 1972)—old-age assistance, $122.85; aid to families with dependent children, $243.72.
Labor Force: *Nonagricultural wage and salary earners* (July 1973), 4,461,100. *Average annual employment* (1972)—manufacturing, 1,433,800; trade, 862,300; government, 650,-200; services, 715,400. *Insured unemployed* (Sept. 1973)—93,800 (2.5%).
Manufacturing (1971): Value added by manufacture, $21,964,-000,000. Primary metal industries, $3,709,400,000; non-electrical machinery, $2,174,800,000; electrical equipment and supplies, $2,013,900,000; food and kindred products, $1,961,200,000; fabricated metal products, $1,712,200,000; chemicals and allied products, $1,638,400,000.
Agriculture (1972): *Cash farm income,* $1,112,905,000 (livestock, $840,966,000; crops, $249,047,000; government payments, $22,892,000). *Chief crops* (in order of value, 1971)—Hay, corn, potatoes, apples.
Mining (1972): *Production value,* $1,202,631,000 (ranks 6th among the states). *Chief minerals*—Coal, $775,718,000; cement, $165,700,000; stone, $113,360,000; sand and gravel, $33,681,000.
Transportation: *Roads* (1972), 115,658 miles (186,128 km); *motor vehicles* (1972), 6,011,258; *railroads* (1972), 8,273 miles (13,314 km); *public airports* (1972), 68.
Communications: *Telephones* (1973), 7,966,600; *television stations* (1971), 23; *radio stations* (1971), 284; *newspapers* (1973), 106 (daily circulation, 3,990,000).

Education. The 1973–74 school year opened with teachers' strikes in 18 districts throughout Pennsylvania. School doors were closed to some 75,000 pupils and more than 3,800 teachers refused to work without contracts. In nine other school districts, teachers were staffing classrooms on a day-to-day basis while negotiations continued. Disputed items included policy issues as well as wages.

A ruling of the state's Commonwealth Court upheld the right of school boards to determine such things as class size, teacher assignments, preparation time, and school calendars. The Pennsylvania State Education Association, the state's largest teachers' union, appealed the decision to the state supreme court.

State efforts to aid parents of parochial school students were rebuffed when the U. S. Supreme Court ruled a tax credit plan unconstitutional. Some 198,000 families with children in nonpublic schools had been scheduled to receive $35 million in rebates before the court ruling. The plan would have reimbursed parents up to $75 for nonpublic elementary school pupils and $150 for secondary school pupils for payments made for preceding year.

In another school-related matter the state supreme court overturned the traditional doctrine of "sovereign immunity" for local governments. It ruled that Pennsylvania citizens have a right to sue local governments and school boards for negligence.

Financing of public school facilities became more complicated in 1973 with the passage of a so-called "Taj Mahal" law that was intended by the legislators to hold down school construction costs. The new law requires that public hearings be held before the building of any new schools or major additions to certify the need for the new structures. The new law also set cost limits based on intended pupil capacity. The legislators wished to prevent the building of elaborate Taj Mahal-like schools, where smaller simpler, and less expensive buildings would suffice.

Legislature. Most of the bills before the legislature in 1973 were still being debated at the end of the year. One of the most controversial of these was a House bill restoring the death penalty. Despite a recommendation by the Governor's Commission on Capital Punishment that the death penalty not be reinstated in Pennsylvania, the House voted to make capital punishment mandatory for certain types of homicides. After amending the bill to give juries more discretion in deciding whether the death penalty should be imposed, the Senate Judiciary Committee sent the bill to the Senate floor. No decision had been reached on it by the end of the year.

Other major issues awaiting legislative action at the end of 1973 included no-fault auto insurance, state control of hospital rates, the abolition of fixed retail prices on milk, and no-fault divorce.

WILLIAM L. DULANEY
Pennsylvania State University

PERU

The important events of 1973 in Peru were related to the attempt of the military government, headed by President Juan Velasco Alvarado, to blaze an independent trail between a capitalist and a socialist economy. Its task was more difficult due to financial losses caused by the decline of the anchovy catch.

The President's Surgery. On Feb. 23, 1973, General Velasco was operated on for a ruptured ab-

------- **PERU • Information Highlights** -------

Official Name: Republic of Peru.
Location: Western coast of South America.
Area: 496,223 square miles (1,285,216 sq km).
Population (1973 est.): 14,900,000. *Density,* 28 per square
   mile (11 per sq km).
Chief Cities (1970 est.): Lima, the capital, 2,925,000 (metro-
   politan area); Callao, 250,000; Arequipa, 195,000; Trujillo,
   155,000.
Government: *Head of state,* Gen. Juan Velasco Alvarado, presi-
   dent (took office Oct. 1968). *Chief minister,* Edgardo
   Mercado Jarrín, prime minister (took office Feb. 1973).
   Legislature—National Congress (suspended Oct. 1968).
Languages: Spanish (official), Quechua, Aymara.
Education: *Expenditure* (1969), 19.4% of total public expendi-
   ture. *School enrollment* (1968)—primary, 2,334,982; sec-
   ondary, 563,698; technical/vocational, 93,034; university/
   higher, 116,282.
Monetary Unit: Sol (38.70 soles equal U. S.$1, July 1973).
Gross National Product (1972 est.): $7,110,000,000.
Economic Indexes: *Industrial production* (manufacturing,
   1970), 152 (1963=100); *agricultural production* (1971), 124
   (1963=100); *consumer price index* (1972), 167 (1967=100).
Manufacturing (major products): Processed foods, textiles,
   household wares, chemicals, metal products, assembled
   automobiles, fishmeal and fish oil.
Major Agricultural Products: Cotton, sugar, rice, coffee, potatoes, sheep, fish (ranks 1st among world producers,
   1971).
Major Minerals: Copper, silver, lead, zinc, iron ore, petroleum, gold, tungsten, molybdenum, mercury.
Foreign Trade (1972): *Exports,* $943,000,000; *Imports,* $790,-
   000,000. *Chief trading partners* (1971)—United States
   (took 28% of exports, supplied 29% of imports); Japan
   (17%—9.6%); West Germany (15%—12%).
Tourism: Receipts (1971), $44,000,000.
Transportation: *Motor vehicles* (1970), 347,900 (automobiles,
   230,400); *railroads* (1971), 1,299 miles (2,090 km); *merchant
   fleet* (1972), 446,000 gross registered tons; *major national
   airline,* Faucett-Compañia de Aviación.
Communications: *Telephones* (1972), 242,654; *newspapers*
   (1971), 85.

dominal aneurism, and on March 9, after circulatory problems had developed, his right leg was amputated above the knee. While he was ill, the Christian Democratic-sponsored Confederación Nacional de Trabajadores (CNT) and the Communist-dominated Confederación General de Trabajadores (CGTP) joined other groups in a "March of Solidarity" for the ailing president. Notably absent were members of the APRA party and its affiliated labor and peasant groups.

Agrarian Reform. In early March, Gen. Enrique Valdez Angelo, the minister of agriculture, announced that the Peruvian government had expropriated more than 12 million acres (5 million hectares) of farmland and 1.7 million head of livestock under the agrarian reform movement enacted in 1969. Government plans for the 1973–74 period called for expropriation of nearly 10 million more acres (4 million hectares) and 400,000 head of livestock, with compensation awarded to the owners.

On several occasions, General Valdez and Gen. Leonidas Rodríguez Figueroa, the head of SINAMOS (the National Social Mobilization Movement) asserted that small and medium farmers who managed their farms personally and observed the labor laws would be protected. General Rodríguez also promised to investigate reported excesses of SINAMOS promoters who organized occupations of unused land by landless peasants.

Economic Developments. In September, the government announced that foreign trade had reached a record high in 1972 and that a favorable trade balance in the range of $150 million had been recorded in 1972.

On April 26, the Inter-American Development Bank ended a long embargo on Peru by granting a $6 million loan for mining development. The credit was the first authorized by any international bank controlled or influenced by the United States since Peru expropriated the U. S.-owned International

Petroleum Company in 1969. In June the World Bank granted Peru credits of $470 million for 87 developmental projects.

However, on September 24, the U. S.-based Cerro Corporation withdrew its offer to sell the mines and processing plants of its Cerro de Pasco subsidiary to the Peruvian government, charging the Velasco government with "bad faith" in its negotiations. On Dec. 31, 1973, the Velasco government nationalized the Cerro de Pasco holdings and established a new enterprise, Centro-min Peru, to operate the properties.

Petroleum. PETROPERU, the state oil company, signed an agreement with the Japan Petroleum Development Corporation to supply Japan with 375 million barrels of crude oil over a 12-year period, beginning in 1976. In return, the Japanese are to loan Peru up to $350 million for a Trans-Andean pipeline to newly developed oil fields in eastern Peru. PETROPERU also announced that it was going to sell to Brazil 4,000 barrels of oil a day.

Fishing. The favorable balance of trade in 1972 was welcomed given the continuing disappearance of anchovies from coastal fishing waters. In May, the Ministry of Fisheries announced that the 1973 fish catch would be about 4 million tons, compared with an average of about 10 million tons in previous years. The importance of fishing is highlighted by the fact that fishmeal and fish oil exports represented 32% of Peru's foreign exchange earnings in 1972. In April, Peru signed contracts for fishmeal exports at a price of over $440 a ton, compared with a 1972 price of $165.

On May 7, the government announced creation of a new state monopoly, PESCAPERU, which would take control of the ailing fishing industry.

While visiting Peru, Soviet Fisheries Minister Alexander Ishkov announced that the USSR would respect Peru's claim of a 200-mile (320-km) territorial waters limit. The United States continued to defend a 12-mile (19-km) limit, although four California ships were among 22 ships from nine countries applying for Peruvian licenses to fish within the 200-mile oceanic boundary.

NEALE J. PEARSON, *Texas Tech University*

PETROLEUM. See special report beginning on page 34.

PHARMACOLOGY. See MEDICINE.

PHILADELPHIA

Mayor Frank Rizzo's political battles and school and city financial problems dominated the news in Philadelphia during 1973.

Political Disonance. Amid charges and counter-charges of corruption, lying, and "McCarthyism," Mayor Rizzo, a Democrat, feuded with the city's Democratic party leaders. Democratic City Committee Chairman Peter Camiel charged that Rizzo had attempted to bribe him with an offer to let Camiel select architects for city projects in exchange for the Democratic party endorsement of Rizzo's nominee for district attorney. The resulting feud prompted both men to agree to lie detector tests. Rizzo failed and Camiel passed the tests, but the mayor contended: "I have told the truth."

City Council President George X. Schwartz and others accused Rizzo of using a 34-member "special investigation" squad to intimidate his political enemies. In the face of widespread criticism the mayor

SAM PSORAS, PHILADELPHIA DAILY NEWS

PHILADELPHIA'S Mayor Frank Rizzo (right), accused of wrongdoing, submits to a lie detector test.

turned control of the squad back to the city's police commissioner.

Rizzo also fought with the president of the Philadelphia School Board and the school superintendent over financing city schools. He termed Pennsylvania Gov. Milton J. Shapp a "disaster," and attacked former Philadelphia mayors Richardson Dilworth and James Tate. Speculation that Rizzo would run for governor in 1974 was strengthened when a poll, sponsored by Rizzo backers, indicated that the mayor in early summer was running ahead of other gubernatorial prospects.

City Council majority leader Isadore Bellis was indicted on charges of bribery and malfeasance in office for allegedly using his influence to aid companies doing business with the city. The indictment came on the recommendation of a special grand jury convened by District Attorney Arlen Spector to help him root out "systematic police and official corruption."

The Pennsylvania Crime Commission continued its investigation of corruption charges against Philadelphia police and clashed with police officials over access to police personnel files. The commission alleged that acceptance of money for special favors to businessmen is "extremely widespread" among Philadelphia policemen.

City Budget. After three months of debate the City Council unanimously approved a $686 million municipal budget, down some $8 million from that of the previous year and $21 million less than the amount initially proposed by the administration. Resisting pressure from school and civic officials to increase taxes, the Rizzo administration looked to the state legislature for increased financial aid. A proposed real estate assessment would also net an estimated $19 million, to be split between the city and the school district and payable in 1974. The municipal budget earmarked $21 million in assistance to the school district.

Education. The nation's second-longest teacher's strike (72 days) ended in March. The city's 13,000 teachers won substantial salary increases and improved teaching conditions. The strike was

marked by the jailing of two union leaders, the arrest of 790 pickets, and fines of $10,000 a day levied on the Philadelphia Federation of Teachers.

Adding to the problems of the school district was an estimated $71 million budget deficit for the 1973–74 school year. The deficit was reduced to less than $3 million through budget cuts and a combination of state and city council aid.

Crime and Prisons. Serious crimes dropped 5% in Philadelphia during the first six months of 1973. The decrease was attributed to fewer robberies, burglaries, and larcenies. Other categories of major crimes continued to rise.

Security measures were tightened at Holmesburg Prison following the slaying of the warden and deputy warden by two prisoners. New security measures included the installation of metal detectors to detect weapons on prisoners.

WILLIAM L. DULANEY
Pennsylvania State University

PHILATELY. See HOBBIES.

PHILIPPINES

Continuation of martial law, efforts to restore peace and order and promote establishment of the "New Society," and growth of the Philippines' economy were the main developments of 1973.

Referendums. On January 7, President Ferdinand E. Marcos announced in a radio and television address to the nation that he was postponing a plebiscite on the new constitution, which had been scheduled for January 15. The new charter, drafted during the period June 1971–November 1972, included articles providing for an orderly transition from the presidential to the parliamentary form of government. It also allowed President Marcos to hold power during the emergency that led to his proclamation of martial law in September 1972 for the

――――――― PHILIPPINES • Information Highlights ―――――――

Official Name: Republic of the Philippines.
Location: Southeast Asia.
Area: 115,830 square miles (300,000 sq km).
Population (1973 est.): 42,200,000. *Density,* 326 per square mile (126 per sq km).
Chief Cities (1970 census): Quezon City, the capital, 754,452; Manila, 1,330,788; Cebu, 347,116; Iloilo, 209,738.
Government: *Head of state,* Ferdinand E. Marcos, president (took office for 2d term Dec. 1969). *Head of government,* Ferdinand E. Marcos. *Legislature*—National Assembly (unicameral body provided for by new constitution proclaimed by Marcos on Jan. 17, 1973, replacing former bicameral Congress). *Major political parties*—Nationalist party; Liberal party.
Languages: Pilipino (official), English, Spanish.
Education: *Expenditure* (1968), 3.1% of gross national product. *School enrollment* (1968)—primary (1967), 6,406,826; secondary, 1,502,346; university/higher, 627,104.
Monetary Unit: Peso (6.78 pesos equal U. S.$1, Aug. 1973).
Gross National Product (1972 est.): $7,960,000,000.
Economic Indexes: *Industrial production* (1972), 174 (1963= 100); *agricultural production* (1971), 128 (1963=100); *consumer price index* (1972), 187 (1971=100).
Manufacturing (major products): Petroleum products, processed foods, tobacco products, plywood and veneers, paper.
Major Agricultural Products: Rice, corn, coconuts, sugarcane, abaca, sweet potatoes and yams, forest products.
Major Minerals: Copper, gold, nickel, iron ore, chromium ore, mercury.
Foreign Trade (1972): *Exports,* $1,105,000,000; *Imports,* $1,- 397,000,000. *Chief trading partners* (1971)—United States (took 40% of exports, supplied 28% of imports); Japan (35%—30%).
Tourism: Receipts (1971), $32,133,000.
Transportation: *Motor vehicles* (1971), 467,400 (automobiles, 285,100); *railroads* (1971), 654 miles (1,053 km); *merchant fleet* (1972), 925,000 gross registered tons; *major national airline,* Philippine Air Lines.
Communications: *Telephones* (1972), 351,217; *newspapers* (1971), 18 (daily circulation, 785,000).

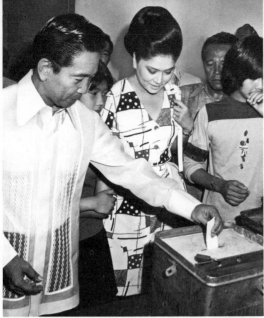

PHILIPPINE President Ferdinand Marcos and his wife vote in the referendum on his continuing in office.

purposes of bringing an end of lawlessness and corruption, rampant inflation, and alleged Communist and Muslim insurgency and creating a "New Society" through sweeping reforms.

The president also announced on January 7 that he was seeking "national consultation" through *barangays* (citizens' assemblies throughout the country, made up of groups ranging in size from a few hundred to several thousand residents 15 years of age and older). A number of issues were proposed for the consideration of these assemblies in a six-day referendum held on January 10–15. On the basis of a national opinion poll of the assemblies, President Marcos announced on January 17 that the assemblies had given approval of themselves as "valid instruments of popular sovereignty"; had ratified the new constitution, except for the article providing for an interim National Assembly, and indicated that they did not wish a plebiscite on the constitution; and had approved the continuation of martial law. Accordingly, the president proclaimed the new constitution on January 17.

In another referendum, held on July 27–28, the people gave assent to the question "Do you want President Marcos to continue in office beyond 1973 and finish the reforms he had initiated under martial law?" Meanwhile, on April 2, the Philippines Supreme Court rejected petitions challenging the validity of the new constitution. The petitions had been filed by groups of opponents representing the abolished Senate, lawyers, citizens, and the press. The court, by a vote of 6 to 4, ruled that the new constitution, as ratified by the Filipino people through the "citizens assemblies," was in force and effect.

Efforts to Restore Peace and Order. President Marcos sought to restore peace and order through the collection of loose firearms (the carrying of firearms by private individuals had been banned in 1972), offers early in the year of amnesty to Communist party members and Muslim rebels, and plans for reconstruction and development of the Muslim southern part of the country. But fighting, heavy at times, continued in the south past midyear.

In pursuance of government plans for the south, the president announced on August 18 that the large province of Cotabato on Mindanao island had been divided into three administrative divisions—Cotabato proper and new provinces named Magindanao and Sultan Kudarat. Likewise, the province of Sulu was divided into Sulu proper and the new province of Tawitawi. In mid-August, President Marcos welcomed a four-nation delegation of the World Islamic Conference, which toured the Muslim areas on a fact-finding mission.

Economy. Efforts continued during the year to rehabilitate and restore the productive capacity of areas of the country damaged by the disastrous floods of July–August 1972. Important public works—including the San Juanico bridge connecting the islands of Samar and Leyte and the Mactan-Mandawe bridge joining Cebu City and the international airport of historic Mactan island—were completed.

An unprecedented collection of taxes gave the government a substantial surplus. The country's international reserves as of August 31 reached a record high of $731 million. There was a favorable balance of trade amounting to $259 million, and various incentives granted to foreign investors attracted foreign capital into the country.

Foreign Affairs. In August, the Philippines' application for membership in the General Agreement on Tariffs and Trade (GATT) was approved by the GATT council. As a member, the Philippines will enjoy most-favored-nation tariff rates among member nations. In September, Foreign Affairs Secretary Carlos Romulo signed letters of agreement on diplomatic relations with Poland, East Germany, Hungary, and Czechoslovakia.

Education. Important reform measures were adopted to enhance the effectiveness of the educational system. One of these requires that high school graduates pass a national entrance examination as a prerequisite for admission to college. Another measure prescribes at least one semester of participation in community development activity as a prerequisite for college graduation.

NICOLAS ZAFRA, *University of the Philippines*

MISS UNIVERSE of 1973, Margarita Moran of the Philippines, paid a visit to New York City in August.

This daguerretype portrait of the poet Edgar Allan Poe brought the highest price ever paid at auction for a single photograph—$9,250—in Chicago in September.

photography

Two important trends in photography became even more prominent during 1973. Electronics continued to play an increasingly important role in professional and amateur equipment, and the changing economic patterns in Western Europe and Japan continued to accelerate the internationalization of the industry.

With regard to the latter, Agfa-Gavaert explored the possibility of establishing production facilities in Portugal to take advantage of relatively low labor costs in that country; Rollei of Germany enlarged its production facilities in Singapore; and an agreement between E. Leitz of Wetzlar, Germany, and Minolta of Japan was substantially expanded when Minolta started to manufacture a new compact model of the Leica in Japan.

Interkamera 73 was held in the spring in Prague, Czechoslovakia. This exhibition was intended mainly for the Eastern Bloc states, but most of the important Western manufacturers were represented. The emphasis was on professional equipment of all types. The eastern European market has been growing in importance, particularly for equipment at the professional level.

Still Cameras. The most advanced new camera to be announced in 1973 was the Rollei SLX66. This 6- by 6-cm single-lens reflex camera goes substantially beyond other professional cameras in its use of electronics to control camera functions. Exposure and film transport are automatic although a manual override is provided. The camera has a fully electronic shutter that is opened and closed by a linear induction motor, which in turn is activated and controlled by the light-measuring system. This is a complete departure from traditional shutter systems. It was expected that this camera would be available in 1974.

When the first Leica camera was introduced in 1924, one of its greatest selling points was its very compact design. Although the basic film format remained unchanged over the years, full-frame 35-mm cameras grew in size and weight as various features were added. This trend was partly arrested in 1973 when two new 35-mm cameras were introduced. The new Leica CL is a very compact 35-mm camera with interchangeable lenses and through-the-lens metering. This camera, made in Japan by Minolta for E. Leitz in Germany, is the lightest Leica ever made. Extensive use of modern lightweight alloys resulted in a substantial overall weight reduction.

The Olympus Optical Company Ltd. of Tokyo, Japan, began nationwide marketing of the Olympus OM-1, a very compact 35-mm single-lens reflex camera. The full-frame 35-mm Olympus retains all of the features normally found on cameras of this type, but it is 35% smaller than any of the others.

Movie Cameras. The Eastman Kodak Company introduced a new synchronized sound movie system for the amateur market. Two new cameras, the Ektasound 130 and Ektasound 140, and two projectors, Models 235 and 245, are available. The cameras use the Super-8 format and have several features that Eastman Kodak first made available on its XL line of Super-8 cameras; specifically, a very wide-opening shutter and a continuous metering system that does not reduce the total amount of light falling on the film. When used with fast color film, this permits filming under most light conditions that the user will encounter.

During filming the synchronized sound is recorded on a magnetic stripe, which is a permanent part of the film. The film is contained in cartridges that are slightly larger than those used with conventional silent Super-8 films, but the new cameras will also accept the smaller silent cartridges. The camera is supplied with an omnidirectional automatic-gain microphone, and a directional unit will be made available.

The Model 235 projector is a replay unit only. The somewhat more expensive Model 245 projector is a record-and-play unit that will allow the user to do a certain amount of editing, or perhaps add a musical background after filming.

Past attempts to add the dimension of sound to amateur film-making fell short because the technology was not available to make the equipment compact and simple to use. The Ektasound system combines compact design and easy operation, and it can be considered the first such system available for the mass market.

The Supermatic 200 sound camera for the professional level is similar in many ways to the Ektasound camera, but it will accept a 200-foot (61-meter) roll of film as well as the standard 50-foot (15-meter) type used in the amateur cameras.

Rapid Motion-Picture Processor. Eastman Kodak planned to market a new high-speed color motion-picture processing system. The Kodak Supermatic-8 processor, which is about the size of an office copying machine, can process 50 feet (15 meters) of Super-8 color film in about eight minutes. The most important initial market for this machine probably will be television studios, where high-speed, on-the-spot processing is particularly desirable. However, it is likely that use of the machine eventually

will spread to small commercial processing establishments. This would mean that amateur film-makers could have their color movies available for viewing minutes after taking them.

Automatic Focusing System. In an automatic focus-control system an electro-optical device measures the distance of a subject from the camera and automatically adjusts the lens accordingly. Such a system is of primary interest in motion-picture photography where it would keep constant track of the distance changes of a moving object.

In the past automatic focusing systems have reached the stage of possible production prototypes, but they were never marketed. Now Bolex has developed a laser ranging system. Basically, the time a light wave takes to reach the moving object and reflect back is measured, thus giving the distance of the object from the camera.

Early versions of the laser measuring device used pulsed light. The ranging accuracy of such a system depends on the time discrimination that can be achieved and the shortness of the pulse. A pulsed laser with a pulse duration and discrimination accuracy of 1 nanosecond (one billionth of a second) can measure distances accurate to about 1 foot (0.3 meter), but this accuracy is not good enough for movie-camera rangefinding at close distances. It is possible to produce laser pulses that last only 0.1 nanosecond and thereby make the system more accurate, but the required equipment is bulky. Bolex worked out a solution to this problem by using a modulated continuous-wave laser system in which the phase of the reflected signal is compared with the phase of the original output signal. The continuous-wave laser equipment needed to achieve the desired accuracy is considerably more compact than the pulsed laser equipment.

The Bolex LR unit, designed in cooperation with the Telecommunications Institute of Vienna's Technical University, was demonstrated in conjunction with a Vario-Switar lens on a slightly modified Bolex H-16 camera. The lens was focused by a servo-motor acting on command from the laser control. Although it is unlikely that automatic focusing will appear as a standard item even on professional equipment in 1974, it is clear that systems of this type will gradually become an accepted feature of cine equipment.

Lenses. Computers and improved production techniques have made it possible to design and mass-produce lenses that just a few years ago existed only in theory or as one-of-a-kind prototypes. Two new zoom lenses with a macro focusing range are in this category.

The Vivitar Series I Macro Zoom Lens is an American-designed, Japanese-manufactured lens that uses the floating-element principle. As a zoom lens, its focal length can vary between 70 mm and 210 mm. When the proper adjustment is made and the lens is switched to the macro range, it can be focused down to 11.5 inches from the focal plane. The maximum magnification in the macro range is 1:2.2. Also, Sun Optical of Japan is marketing an 80- to 240-mm zoom lens with a macro range for close-up photography.

Electronic Flash. The first electronic flash units were massive affairs usable only in professional studios. Shortly after World War II portable electronic flash became available, but the user had to carry a heavy independent power supply. The flash units became smaller and smaller with self-contained power

---

EDWARD STEICHEN (1879–1973)

UPI

One of the world's great artists of the camera, Edward Steichen, who transformed photography into an art form, died at his home in West Redding, Conn., on March 25, 1973, two days before his 94th birthday. A humanist and master craftsman, he believed that "the mission of photography is to explain man to man and each man to himself." Through his pioneering techniques, characterized by meticulous attention to light and shadow, composition, and detail, he tried to capture the essence of flora, fauna, city scenes, and artifacts, as well as the inner personalities of such celebrities as the sculptor Auguste Rodin, the financier J. P. Morgan, the actress Greta Garbo, and the poet Carl Sandburg, his brother-in-law. Steichen's crowning achievement was the *Family of Man* exhibition, which he assembled for New York's Museum of Modern Art in 1955.

Edward Jean Steichen was born in Luxembourg on March 27, 1879. He went to the United States at the age of three and grew up in Michigan and Wisconsin. After leaving school at 15, he devoted his free time to painting, sketching, and experimenting with photography. He first won recognition as a photographer in 1899 at a Philadelphia exhibition. In 1902, after spending some time in Paris, he opened a studio in New York. Three years later, he and Alfred Stieglitz established the Photo-Secession Galleries, a showcase that introduced the works of Rodin, Matisse, Cezanne, and Picasso in the United States. Between 1923 and 1938, Steichen did celebrity portraits for *Vanity Fair*, fashion photographs for *Vogue*, and advertising photographs for the J. Walter Thompson agency.

Steichen served as an aerial photographer with the Army Signal Corps in World War I and was in command of U. S. Navy combat photography in World War II. From 1947 to 1962 he was director of photography for the Museum of Modern Art, which established the Edward Steichen Photography Center in 1964. His documentary exhibit of U. S. poverty during the Depression, *The Bitter Years: 1935–41*, was shown at the museum in 1962. His autobiography is titled *A Life in Photography* (1963).

HENRY S. SLOAN

---

sources, but until the mid-1960's the correct exposure had to be calculated by the user before each picture. The introduction of the Auto-Strobonar by Honeywell in 1965 provided automatic exposure control by using a circuit that monitored the reflected light from the subject and adjusted the output of the flash. However, the monitoring circuit responded to extraneous light sources and sometimes quenched the flash output too quickly, resulting in underexposed negatives. This failing was corrected by improved circuitry in the Auto-Strobonar 770, but one major problem remained to be solved. Regardless of how little energy was required to take a given picture, all of the energy potential in the capacitor was discharged, the unneeded portion being dumped into a quench tube and dissipated as heat. The result was short battery life and frequent replacement or recharge.

At least a dozen manufacturers are now distributing electronic flashguns that tap only the needed amount of power for a given picture. The Braun 2000 is typical of the new energy-saving units, which all have one feature in common. They use a solid-state thyristor circuit designed so that only the power needed for a specific exposure is used and none is wasted. The result is a vast increase in the number of shots between battery change or recharge, particularly when most of the exposures are of nearby subjects.

Miniature TV Camera. The Space & Defense Division of the Fairchild Camera & Instrument Corporation has announced plans to market a palm-sized TV camera weighing only six ounces. The Model MV-100 uses 10,000 silicon photosensors instead of a vidicon tube. At this time the main applications of the MV-100 are expected to be in reconnaissance or surveillance; it is not expected to be used for commercial purposes.

Medical Photography. An ideal photographic system for an operating room would be one that a surgeon or a nurse could pick off an instrument trolley and use on the spot without preparation. This means it must be simple, automatic, easy to handle, and above all sterile. The Meddev Corporation of Los Altos, Calif., has combined these ideas to produce the Surgicam. It consists of a single-lens reflex camera built into a sterilizable case, which looks like an underwater pressure housing. The camera is a modified Alpa reflex camera made by Pignon S. A. of Switzerland.

Photography from Skylab. The Skylab orbiting laboratory, launched early in 1973, has been providing unprecedented opportunities to use photography to increase knowledge of the earth and the universe.

Just a few of the experiments where photography has played a dominant role are described here.

Information acquired by the X-ray and ultraviolet solar photography experiment contributes to the understanding of the characteristics of the solar atmosphere and its distortion by active regions and flares. The objectives of the ultraviolet stellar astronomy experiment are to obtain photographs of ultraviolet line spectra from a large number of stars and to obtain ultraviolet photographs of the clouds of matter and stars in the Milky Way. The ultraviolet airglow horizon photography experiment provides information on ultraviolet absorption by the ozone layer and what effect this has on the lower atmosphere. The data are obtained by making a series of simultaneous photographs with two 35-mm cameras, one of which is equipped with an ultraviolet filter and the other is without the filter. (See also SPACE EXPLORATION.)

Literature. Under the general title of *Literature of Photography*, Arno Press of New York has published a 62-book series consisting of reprints of works originally published between 1840 and 1954. Included are historical accounts, technical manuals, and aesthetic treatises. The series provides more than 3,000 illustrations, of which 1,500 are rare and historically important.

A Century of Cameras from the Collection of the International Museum of Photography at George Eastman House, by Eaton S. Lothrop, Jr., was published in October 1973. Lothrop selected 130 cameras that in his judgment were of particular significance. Each camera is illustrated.

PHILIP L. CONDAX
Curator, Equipment Archives, International Museum of Photography at George Eastman House

PONDER & BEST

COMPACT 35-mm single-lens reflex camera, the Japanese Olympus, is 35% smaller than other models.

FAIRCHILD CAMERA & INSTRUMENT CORP.

MINIATURE television camera weighing only 6 ounces (155 grams) is chiefly for surveillance use.

EASTMAN-KODAK

SOUND MOVIES for the amateur are made easier by the new Kodak Ektasound system, which provides a simple means of recording sound on film...

AERIAL VIEW of the Intersecting Storage Rings (ISR) installation of the European Organization for Nuclear Research in Geneva, Switzerland.

PHYSICS

The year 1973 was an interesting one in physics. Preliminary evidence of the existence of organic-crystal superconductors at relatively high temperatures created controversy; controlled fusion prospects improved slightly; gravity waves were questioned; new elementary particle measurements gave surprising results; and nuclear physics stood at a crossroad. Meanwhile, the manpower surplus in physics continued.

Organic-Crystal Superconductors? Superconductivity is a remarkable physical property that certain materials possess at very low temperatures. A material in a superconducting state has essentially no resistance—no heat is generated when a current is passed through the material. The practical implications are staggering. For instance, an electrical transmission line using superconducting materials is one possible application, and there already are research magnets that use superconducting materials to obtain a very high magnetic field while keeping the magnet and coil size reasonable.

Although superconductivity has been known for many years, its applications thus far are not extensive. The basic problem is that materials do not become superconducting until they reach a very low temperature. So far the highest temperature at which superconductivity has been observed is $22.3°$ K ($-251°$ C), a result obtained with a niobium-germanium compound in 1973. Progress in raising this temperature has been very slow, and many physicists feel that the maximum possible temperature for superconductors is only slightly greater than $22°$ K.

In 1973, preliminary results by a group at the University of Pennsylvania showed that a few crystals of an organic salt became very highly conducting at $58°$ K ($-215°$ C). They experimented with an organic salt called (TTF) (TCNQ), or tetrathiofulvalene-tetracyanoquinodimethan, and found that its conductivity increased to more than 500 times its room-temperature value in a few cases. The discovery of a superconductor at the relatively high temperature of $58°$ K would be a major breakthrough.

However, many (TTF) (TCNQ) crystals were studied, but only three showed this remarkable increase in conductivity; the rest had conductivities that were at most only 10 times their room-temperature value. The three anomalous crystals appeared to be rare, almost perfect crystals.

Although many physicists were openly skeptical of these results, a large number of laboratories were very actively studying organic crystals. Even if these crystals are not true superconductors, they are exceptionally interesting.

Controlled Thermonuclear Fusion. One fundamental problem facing the world is the development of energy sources. Present-day fission reactors provide a first step toward a solution, and prospects are favorable for breeder reactors, which produce more useful fissionable fuel than they consume. Nonnuclear alternatives include solar energy, geothermal energy, coal gasification, and utilization of shale-oil deposits. However, the ultimate alternative to fission processes is controlled thermonuclear fusion.

Uncontrolled fusion of light elements, as in the hydrogen bomb, has been established for 20 years, but the practical problems in controlled fusion are monumental. The basic nuclear reaction is fairly simple; the problem is to heat the materials so that the fusion reaction will occur and to control the process. The temperatures involved are of the order of 100 million degrees Kelvin. At such high temperatures the fusion materials form a plasma (ionized gas). No solid wall material can contain the plasma at the required temperatures, so researchers have tried to use external magnetic fields that serve as a container for the plasma.

The pace of activity in the United States is increasing rapidly. Although no fundamental breakthroughs have been reported, there have been a number of improvements. There is reasonable enthusiasm about the eventual success of a large mag-

CHERENKOV detector (left) is used by ISR physicists for particle identification. The scientists also use the electrostatic separator (below) to filter out unwanted particles.

netic-containment machine, perhaps using the tokamak principle. Tokamak machines became famous in the late 1960's when the excellent results obtained by the Soviet physicist Lev A. Artsimovich were made known. More specialized machines with this design showed promise in the early 1970's. A new approach to the fusion problem is the use of high-powered lasers. In a typical scheme, several laser beams strike a fusion fuel pellet from many sides, resulting in implosion, heating, and nuclear fusion.

The USSR has placed great emphasis on controlled fusion research, and the U. S. Atomic Energy Commission has strongly increased its efforts in this area. The hope is to establish the feasibility of a controlled nuclear-fusion reactor by 1980, and to have fusion reactors available by the year 2000. (See also special report on Energy, page 41.)

Gravity Waves. The discussion over whether gravity waves have been discovered raged on in 1973, with ever-increasing skepticism over the reported identification of this phenomenon. In the past few years, Joseph Weber of the University of Maryland reported observations of gravity waves. According to Einstein's theory of relativity, gravity waves should occur whenever gravitational mass is accelerated. However, these waves have such low energy that detection is exceedingly difficult.

Similar, but not identical, experiments were reported by a number of groups. All results thus far were negative—no gravity waves were observed. J. A. Tyson of Bell Laboratories reported negative results after using equipment with a sensitivity estimated to be 200 times that of Weber's early equipment. Experiments run for a shorter time by V. Braginskii at Moscow State University and R. Garwin and J. Levine of IBM also yielded no positive results.

Assuming that the pulses Weber observed are really gravitational waves, the energy involved in creating them is enormous. Each event would require energy of the order of that obtained by converting the mass of the sun completely into energy. One might expect that other forms of radiation would also be created by such processes. However, no unusual radio-wave or X-ray activity appears to be associated with Weber's events. With all of the activity under way to detect gravity waves, it appeared that the question of their existence would be resolved in the near future.

Elementary Particle Physics. The giant proton accelerator at the National Accelerator Laboratory (NAL) near Batavia, Ill., was in operation in 1973, but only a few results were reported. Meanwhile, construction of a similar machine in Switzerland, the CERN super proton synchrotron, proceeded on schedule. Already particle physicists are concerned about the next step beyond these machines to attain even higher energies. Since the cost of bigger versions of existing machines verges on the astronomical, other more subtle approaches may be the solution.

One basic approach known for many years, but not technically feasible until recently, is the use of magnetic storage rings. Two colliding particles pro-

duce an effective energy many times greater than one particle of the same bombarding energy striking a stationary target, and thus the key point is to use colliding beams. The problem then is one of beam intensity, and that is where the storage rings come into play. By trapping (or storing) beams in magnetic rings, a sufficiently high intensity is reached. Storage rings already are in operation at a variety of large accelerators, and they may well be the way to attain higher energies.

Some of the most interesting results of the year were obtained at CERN, where storage rings were used in studying proton-proton scattering up to an effective energy of 1,500 GeV, far beyond the energy achieved at NAL. The new results have been summarized as: protons are fatter than expected.

Heavy-Ion Physics. Major discussion and interest in nuclear physics in 1973 focused on heavy-ion physics. Many groups devoted a large fraction of their tandem accelerator time to experiments with beams of carbon ions, oxygen ions, sulfur ions, and heavier ions. A wide variety of experiments was performed, emphasizing reaction-mechanism studies and creation of new and unusual isotopes far from the stability line.

Although much exciting heavy-ion physics can be performed with existing accelerators, there was a growing sentiment for building a new heavy-ion accelerator. Such a facility does appear necessary to create the hypothesized superheavy elements.

Although there was appreciable support for such a new facility, there also was major opposition from nuclear physicists who feared the destruction of university nuclear physics laboratories in a growing centralization process. Other urged a waiting period to see what results would be obtained from the German heavy-ion accelerator Unilac, from the renovated Hilac at Berkeley (now super Hilac), and from other small machines.

Superheavy Elements. Another major interest lies in the creation of so-called superheavy elements far beyond those currently known. Scientists have created the elements having atomic numbers from 93 to 105. Since production of these man-made elements has been increasingly difficult, it might appear that the creation of transuranium elements has neared the end of the line. However, calculations based on the shell model of the nucleus indicate there are some mass numbers, called "magic numbers," that correspond to nuclei of great stability. The next magic number beyond element 105 is expected to be near mass number 300. Calculations indicate that a magic-number isotope of element 114 may last for millions of years.

Manpower. Some employment difficulties for physicists continued in 1973 due to effective reductions in federal research spending (essentially fixed spending, with appreciable inflation), lack of growth in the colleges and universities, and changing patterns of industrial research and development. However, the general opinion was that physics was simply the first of the fields in which opportunities for new Ph. D's were contracting. Physics became the test case, carefully studied by academicians of all sorts. They feared a general oversupply of Ph. D's, and wanted to observe carefully how the correction process works.

The number of students majoring in physics continued to decline in 1973, and the fraction of undergraduate physics majors who continued to graduate school in physics dropped even more sharply.

Although there still was an oversupply of physicists, there may be a shortage in the future. As long as science funding is short-range, the funding and the science student population appear locked in boom-or-bust cycles. Scientists have been pleading for long-term budgetary and manpower planning.

GARY MITCHELL
North Carolina State University

PICASSO, Pablo. See OBITUARIES.

POLAND

The year was one of relative stability in Poland's government and politics. There were virtually no changes in the national leadership of the ruling United Polish Workers' Party (PZPR) or of the state apparatus. Edward Gierek, first secretary of the PZPR, and his closest collaborator Piotr Jaroszewicz, the premier, continued policies of economic recovery and modernization inaugurated in 1971.

The Economy. Considerable progress in the economy was evident throughout 1973. According to official midyear estimates, real earnings in Poland increased 11% over 1971, and worker productivity was up by 7.6% over the two-year period. Substantial imports of food and other consumer goods eased chronic shortages in Polish retail stores. Meat and meat products, however, continued in short supply throughout the year. Prices were generally maintained at levels well below those reached in December 1970, when economic discontent brought about widespread rioting and the downfall of the then party leader, Władysław Gomułka.

Government Policies. Among the new measures pursued by the current regime had been a reallocation of priorities, deemphasizing heavy industry in favor of consumer goods. The government had increased efforts to re-equip and computerize manufacturing and distribution facilities and had stressed simplification and increased autonomy in plant management. Efforts were also being made to achieve a massive overhaul of Poland's antiquated road and rail transport system (with the assistance of a United Nations development grant and a U. S. engineering firm). Various tax and regulatory advantages were given to small-scale private enterprises, such as retail, service, and repair shops. The regime was also apparently reassuring apprehensive private farm owners that the party was not about to tamper with their property.

One of the novel features of party policy under Gierek's leadership has been increased two-way communication with various segments of the Polish society, particularly industrial workers. Citizens have been encouraged to bring complaints to the attention of officials and register them in various media, such as billboards, in the major cities.

The Press. Censorship of the press was experimentally lifted in the first half of 1973 in the case of two important party organs, the daily *Trybuna Ludu* and the weekly *Polityka*. Officialy, hopes were expressed that experienced and "responsible" editors would be able to give the press greater spontaneity of expression without indulging in too many "subversive, bourgeois reactionary heresies." This relaxation of controls provoked some controversy within party ranks.

Religion. In church-state relations, a trend toward improvement was upset, at least temporarily, by the publication of a state plan for education in

Official Name: Polish People's Republic.
Location: Eastern Europe.
Area: 120,724 square miles (312,677 sq km).
Population (1973 est.): 34,000,000. *Density,* 272 per square mile (105 per sq km).
Chief Cities (1970 census): Warsaw, the capital, 1,308,100; Łodz, 761,700; Crakow, 583,400; Wrocław, 523,300; Poznan, 469,000.
Government: *President of the Council of State,* Henryk Jabłonski (took office March 1972). *Premier,* Piotr Jaroszewicz (took office Dec. 1970). *First secretary, United Polish Workers' party,* Edward Gierek (took office Dec. 1970). *Legislature* (unicameral)—Sejm. *Major political parties*—United Polish Workers' party; United Peasants' party; Democratic party.
Language: Polish (official).
Education: *Expenditure* (1969), 5.2% of net material product. *School enrollment* (1969)—primary, 5,443,132; secondary, 1,254,757; technical/vocational, 905,781; university/higher, 322,464.
Monetary Unit: Zloty (3.20 zlotys equal U. S.$1, July 1973).
Gross National Product (1971 est.): $48,600,000,000.
Economic Indexes: *Industrial production* (1972), 212 (1963= 100); *agricultural production* (1970), 125 (1957–59=100); *consumer price index* (1972), 109 (1970=100).
Manufacturing (major products): Petroleum products, transportation equipment, chemicals, machinery, metal products, processed foods.
Major Agricultural Products: Rye (ranks 2d among world producers, 1972), oats, potatoes (world rank 2d, 1972), sugar beets, wheat, tobacco, livestock.
Major Minerals: Coal, lignite, salt, zinc, lead, iron ore, sulfur, copper.
Foreign Trade (1972): *Exports,* $4,932,000,000. *Imports,* $5,-335,000,000. *Chief trading partners* (1970)—USSR (took 37% of exports, supplied 30% of imports); East Germany (9%—14%); Czechoslovakia (8%—9%).
Tourism: Receipts (1971), $38,817,000.
Transportation: *Motor vehicles* (1971), 829,600 (automobiles, 555,600); *railroads* (1971), 16,580 miles (26,682 km); *merchant fleet* (1972), 925,000 gross registered tons; *major national airline,* LOT-Polish Airlines.
Communications: *Telephones* (1972), 1,970,856; *newspapers* (1971), 44 (daily circulation, 7,093,000).

mid-May. Stefan Cardinal Wyszynski and other church leaders denounced the plan for its failure to acknowledge any role for the church. Concurrently, demands were made by the episcopate for the establishment of new cultural and religious associations auxiliary to the church itself, and for the right to publish independent Roman Catholic newspapers. With church attendance apparently remaining as high as ever, the prospects seemed good for government concessions to the church and for an attempt to restore the détente undertaken by Gierek and Cardinal Wyszynski in December 1970.

International Affairs. In foreign affairs, Polish relations with West Germany cooled somewhat due to unresolved differences with respect to war reparations payments being demanded by Poland, and to the terms of economic interchange between the two countries. On the other hand, increased efforts were made to strengthen ties between Poland and East Germany, which eagerly sought Polish workers to alleviate its labor shortage. In June, Gierek and Jaroszewicz traveled in East Berlin to secure technical and economic aid from the East Germans.

The Soviet leadership expressed its approval of Gierek's activities by presenting him with the Order of Lenin on his 60th birthday, in January 1973. In May, Chairman Leonid Brezhnev and several other members of the ruling Soviet Politburo paid a well-publicized visit to Poland.

U. S.-Polish relations suffered strain due to the actions of the Polish members of the four-nation International Commission of Control and Supervision in Vietnam. U. S. displeasure over Polish indifference to Vietcong and North Vietnamese violations of the Indochina truce prompted the cancellation of a scheduled visit by Deputy Premier Jan Mitrega to Washington in April.

ALEXANDER J. GROTH
University of California, Davis

POLAR RESEARCH

Scientists from many nations did extensive research in the Arctic and the Antarctic during 1973. Their projects are helping in the assessment of the considerable influence these remote areas have on the rest of the world.

Alaska. The extraction and transportation of crude oil from the North Slope continued to be an issue in 1973. After extensive delay, government approval was given in November for a pipeline from the Prudhoe Bay oil field to Valdez on Alaska's southern coast. The main cause for the delay was concern about environmental effects. (See also ALASKA.)

Since 1970, scientists of the International Biological Program have been working at Barrow and Prudhoe Bay, making field and laboratory experiments and then computerized mathematical models of the tundra ecosystem. The models allow the scientists to predict the effects of nature and man on the tundra and the life it supports. In 1973, most of the field work was finished. Recovery rates were established for oil spills in ponds, the nutrient turnover rate and modeling were used to evaluate damage by off-road vehicles, and methods of stabilizing tundra surfaces after pipeline construction were assessed.

The coming industrialization also will affect man, so University of Alaska scientists have been conducting a long-term economic, demographic, and ethnographic study—called Man in the Arctic—of the rapidly evolving Arctic society. Work in 1973 included analysis of the manpower needs of native communities affected by the Native Claims Settlement Act of 1971 or by development of oil.

Greenland. Danish, Swiss, and American scientists drilled an ice core 400 meters (435 yards) deep on the central Greenland ice dome. Analysis of this and other cores has enabled the reconstruction of world climate cycles over the last 100,000 years and even prediction of future climates. These data, along with radar measurements of ice thickness over large areas and surface measurement of chemical and physical characteristics, are enabling interpretation of past environmental conditions, including global air pollution and the causes of ice ages.

Arctic Ocean. During 1973 environmental data continued to be received via satellite from unmanned stations on the sea ice about 400 kilometers (250 miles) north of Barrow, Alaska. The stations had been placed during the 1972 pilot project of the Arctic Ice Dynamics Joint Experiment (Aidjex), whose ultimate aim is to develop models for predicting the interactions of air, sea, and ice using data from a simple network of observing stations. This information is valuable for navigation and weather prediction in the Arctic and beyond. Work in 1973 involved preparation for the main Aidjex experiment in 1975, which will last a year and involve scientists from Canada, Japan, the Soviet Union, and the United States.

Meanwhile, Soviet scientists established a new station on a drifting ice island 800 kilometers (500 miles) north of the Bering Strait. The station was to play a part in the so-called Polar Experiment, and its scientific results will be of value to the Aidjex project.

Antarctica. At the peak of the 1972–73 summer in the southern hemisphere, about 2,500 researchers and support personnel from 10 nations were in Ant-

arctica, a continent as big as South America. In the winter of 1973, however, less than half that number remained. U. S. research took place at five stations during the year, including one at the South Pole, and at temporary field camps. Much of this research was done in cooperation with the other Antarctic Treaty nations.

Earth Sciences. A drilling project conducted by Japan, New Zealand, and the United States was in its second season in Antarctica, with holes being drilled on Ross Island. Analysis of the cores, which contain layers of basalt, pyroclastics, and, interestingly, ice, has yielded a new volcanic sequence for the island that will help to explain the geology of the McMurdo Sound area. Also, biologists are monitoring the drill sites to determine changes in the ecosystems.

A U. S. Geological Survey party finished a three-summer reconnaissance of the Lassiter and Black Coasts in Antarctica in 1973. Their work so far has shown that the region is a part of the mountain belt that rings the Pacific basin. Copper deposits were found.

A French team supported by U. S. airdrops attempted to traverse 1,700 kilometers (1,060 miles) inland from the Antarctic coast. The party got only 400 kilometers (250 miles) inland before sastrugi—hard, wind-carved hillocks of snow—forced it to turn back. However, scientific observations were made every 10 kilometers (6 miles). A goal of this international project is to learn if (and why) the Antarctic ice cap is getting larger or smaller.

Biology. A U. S. census of seals in the pack ice off Antartica's Oates Coast and George V Coast indicated a density of about four seals per square mile. Scientists estimated that the Antarctic population of crabeater seals, the most common, was 80 million in 1973. A study of ecosystems was begun in 1972–73 in the ice-free Taylor Valley near McMurdo Sound. Data were collected on terrestrial and freshwater systems to determine metabolic pathways. The field party included undergraduate men and women—a first for the U. S. program.

Atmospheric Physics. In Ellsworth Land, Antarctica, the new U. S. station Siple supported studies of the magnetosphere in 1973. Very-low-frequency radio signals from the station's 21-kilometer-long (13-mile-long) antenna were received by the Explorer-45 and IMP-6 satellites and by Siple's geomagnetically conjugate station in Roberval, Quebec, Canada. The goal of this project is to solve some of the outstanding problems of atmospheric physics. Practical benefits may include improved radio communications.

Oceanography. Some of the year's most exciting information came from the deep-sea drilling ship *Glomar Challenger.* The ship took sedimentary cores in the Ross Sea and off Wilkes Land. Core analysis showed that extensive glaciation began in Antarctica at least 20 million years ago (far earlier than previous estimates) and climaxed 4 or 5 million years ago, when the ice cap abruptly shrank to its present size.

In the Weddell Sea, the U. S. icebreaker *Glacier* investigated the formation of Antarctica Bottom Water, the cold, nutrient-rich water that flows as far north as the Caribbean before surfacing to support life.

GUY G. GUTHRIDGE, *Office of Polar Programs National Science Foundation*

Investigator measures ice thickness near the main camp of the Arctic Ice Dynamics Joint Experiment (Aidjex).

WIDE WORLD

NEW ORLEANS plainclothes policeman runs for cover from the bullets of a sniper who shot more than a dozen persons from the rooftop of a motel.

POLICE

The absence of large-scale urban riots and student rebellions during 1973 continued to provide a breathing period for U. S. police forces. Many of them were taking advantage of this respite by attempting to build their relationship within the community, so that the ugly confrontations that had marked the recent period of collective violence—with the police cast in the role of "establishment" villains—would not be repeated in the United States.

Recruitment Changes. Some of the traditional requirements relating to law-enforcement applicants were changing as police sought to develop forces more representative of the communities in which they worked. In New York City, for example, the City Council was considering a measure to raise the maximum age for new policemen from 29 to 35.

The bill expanding age limits for New York recruits was introduced at the request of Police Commissioner Donald E. Cawley. According to its sponsors, the enlistments of older recruits would benefit the working force, since persons in their 30's "frequently have increased maturity, self-control and human understanding not as widely prevalent in younger men and women." It was also hoped that the change would add more Puerto Ricans and blacks to the police force, on the theory that proportionately more men in these disadvantaged groups failed to "lock themselves into careers" in other fields by the age of 35.

"Police Draft" Proposal. A unique suggestion for decreasing police-community alienation was offered during the year by Irving Piliavin of the University of Wisconsin. It called for the use of conscription, much like the military draft, to recruit the bulk of the country's police officers. Piliavin suggested that only minor and inadequate changes in police forces are possible under present approaches. His proposal, he noted, "assumes that there are debilitating effects on patrolmen as a consequence of the tensions, hostilities, and dangers they encounter in patrol duty, and that these de-

bilitating effects cannot be avoided. It therefore seeks to restrict the time which police must spend in this activity."

Piliavin proposed that all males meeting basic eligibility requirements and passing screening procedures (to weed out, for example, those prone to violence) should be drafted at their 21st birthday for police duty. Draftees would serve in police forces for about 30 months, with the first six of these devoted to training, which would be conducted by the federal government. Since most of the draftees would ultimately return to civilian life, Piliavin argues, they would be able to explain to their neighbors the importance of the police role and thus increase community appreciation of policing.

Career police officers could be recruited from draftees who showed particular aptitude and interest in continuing with law enforcement. The argument that the draftees might not perform their duties conscientiously, Piliavin maintains, is contradicted by the record of military police, who are regarded as exemplary enforcement personnel. "Radical remedies for social problems are not easily accepted," Piliavin concluded in his presentation, published at Andover, Mass., in March 1973. "Nevertheless, when the conventional solutions have failed, only the radical remedies remain—unless, of course, we choose to live with our problems."

Federal Bureau of Investigation. The problems of securing citizen confidence in police agencies and maintaining morale within the agencies themselves were highlighted by the difficulties encountered in 1973 by the Federal Bureau of Investigation. Following the death in May 1972 of J. Edgar Hoover, who had guided the bureau since 1924, President Nixon had appointed L. Patrick Gray, 3d, as acting FBI director. Gray, however, became involved in a series of actions in which the best traditions of impartial law enforcement seemed to yield to political expediency. For instance, Gray at one point accepted into his own keeping (and later destroyed) evidence that might have implicated administration figures in criminal acts.

ROCHESTER, N. Y., police use electronic retrieval system in quick search for mug shots or fingerprints.

UPI

free the bureau from the constraints of political control. According to Ruckelshaus, political control was less to be feared than the abuses that might arise from unchecked autonomy.

The Police Establishment. Figures compiled by the FBI on police manpower in the United States indicated that in 1972 there was an average of 2.4 police employees (including civilian employees) per 1,000 inhabitants. Males represented 91.4% of total police employee strength. Cities with populations of 250,000 or more averaged 3.3 police employees per 1,000 inhabitants.

Comparative police manpower figures for nations in the Third World were reported during 1973 by Marshall B. Clinard and Daniel J. Abbott in a study entitled *Crime in Developing Countries.* They point out that in many developing nations, police forces are larger than the military and far more influential. In Ghana, for instance, the police number 21,000 and the military, 8,000, according to the authors. Liberia reported an army of 3,500 and a security force of 20,000, while Nigeria, before its civil war, had 23,000 policemen and only 8,300 troops. These figures indicate the power that can be gained by police forces if they assume military duties and become involved in political matters, courses that have largely been avoided in the United States.

Revelation of this behavior forced Gray's resignation on April 27, 1973, and he was temporarily replaced as acting director by William Ruckelshaus. On July 9, President Nixon announced the appointment of Kansas City police chief Clarence Kelley, a former FBI agent, as permanent FBI director.

Ruckelshaus, after leaving his interim post, announced he was in favor of the appointment of FBI heads for limited terms (7 to 10 years), with any appointment or reappointment subject to confirmation by Congress. However, he opposed removing the FBI from the supervision of the Department of Justice and establishing it as an independent agency —a move sometimes advocated as a step that might

Police Deaths. A total of 112 U. S. law-enforcement officers were killed due to felonious criminal action during 1972, a decrease from the all-time high of 126 in 1971, but still considerably higher than the average of 79 officers slain per year during the period 1963–72. Fourteen officers were slain from ambush in 1972, and 33 were killed while attempting to apprehend robbers or burglars.

Examining these figures, the FBI stressed "a most urgent need for officers to be more alert in connection with all their duties, regardless of how routine these duties may seem or have been in the past. No arrest situation can be considered routine."

GILBERT GEIS, *University of California, Irvine*

NEW YORK CITY police anticrime unit, in attempt to protect city parks, uses "decoy" officers dressed for various recreational activities.

THE NEW YORK TIMES

DEMOCRATIC PARTY unity was emphasized on July 4 in Decatur, Ala., when Gov. George Wallace of Alabama (left) and Sen. Edward Kennedy of Massachusetts (right) shared the platform.

UPI

POLITICAL PARTIES

In a year of political resignations, of investigations, and of charges and countercharges, party activities in the United States in 1973 were unusually muted or decentralized. Spirals of revelations, and in some instances unsupported accusations, stemmed from both official and news media inquiries directly or indirectly related to the burglary in Washington on June 17, 1972, of the Watergate headquarters of the Democratic National Committee. In addition, in October, Spiro T. Agnew resigned as vice president and pleaded no contest to one count of income tax evasion. (See feature article beginning on page 14).

It was unclear, in concrete terms, how these developments would affect forthcoming elections. But leaders of both major political parties were keenly aware that the 1974 elections would involve 34 Senate seats (19 held by Democrats in 1973, 15 by Republicans), all of the seats in the House of Representatives, and 35 governships (23 Democratic, 12 Republican). (See also ELECTIONS.)

DEMOCRATIC PARTY

In the afterglow of substantial congressional victories but a crushing defeat for presidential nominee George S. McGovern in 1972, the Democratic party under the leadership of Robert S. Strauss, chairman of its national committee, strove mightily for unity. On February 6, Strauss moved to mollify officeholders by appointing an advisory council of 40 members, all of them elected officials except the chairman, Arthur B. Krim of New York. At a meeting on March 23 the national committee enlarged its membership to 303 by adding 25 representatives from labor and minority groups. It also enlarged membership in both the charter and delegate-selection commissions.

The charter commission, headed by Terry Sanford, former governor of North Carolina, at a July meeting in Colorado laid plans for the 1974 conference of party delegates mandated by the 1972 national convention. A moderate coalition narrowly prevailed in commission decisions to recommend to the national committee that the conference be restricted to adoption of a charter without considering policy issues. Despite general agreement to hold the conference after the 1974 elections, liberals in the commission predicted renewed battling over proposals for policy making and representation. The commission on delegate selection, with Barbara Mikulski

of Baltimore presiding, held hearings in July, August, and October. Early in October a drafting committee of the commission unanimously abolished the mandatory quota system for selection of women and minority delegates, a step the commission later approved.

Opinion polls as of late June reported Sen. Edward M. Kennedy the choice of 40% of Democrats for the 1976 presidential nomination, with conservative Gov. George C. Wallace of Alabama preferred by 16%. Senators Edmund S. Muskie, Hubert H. Humphrey, George S. McGovern, and Henry M. Jackson trailed. Senator Kennedy encountered liberal criticism for appearing at a July 4 rally in Alabama with Governor Wallace. On September 15 the Democratic party raised $5.4 million through a national telethon appeal, half of the money to go to state Democratic parties and half toward payment of debts of $3.1 million.

REPUBLICAN PARTY

On January 31, President Nixon, constitutionally ineligible for a third consecutive term, declared that he had no favorite 1976 presidential candidate, but expressed high respect for John B. Connally, Jr., former Democratic governor of Texas and later Nixon's secretary of the treasury. Connally announced on May 2 that he had joined the Republican party, the Democrats having "left behind the majority of Americans who occupy the great middle ground."

Polls of voters in June and July showed Republican Senators Charles H. Percy of Illinois and Howard H. Baker, Jr., of Tennessee, the latter vice chairman of the Senate Watergate committee, as running slightly ahead of Democratic Sen. Edward M. Kennedy in separate expressions of preference for the presidency. Other Republican presidential possibilities, often mentioned, ran behind: Gov. Ronald Reagan of California, Gov. Nelson A. Rockefeller of New York, and Connally. After being named to succeed Vice President Agnew, House minority leader Gerald Ford declared that he would not be a 1976 presidential candidate.

In July the Republican National Committee reduced its 1973 budget by $1 million, from $5.5 million, because of slower contributing by large donors. (The committee reported donations of less than $100 were increasing.) A quarter of the staff of 135 was released. Chairman George Bush volunteered to lower by 10% his annual salary of $42,500.

FRANKLIN L. BURDETTE, *University of Maryland*

POPULATION

The population of the world, estimated at almost 3.86 billion in mid-1973, is increasing at the rate of about 2% per year. If this rate of increase continues, the world population will double in 35 years.

The population increase is much more rapid in underdeveloped nations than in developed nations. The populations of Algeria, Iraq, Pakistan, Mexico, and the Philippines, for example, will double in 21 years at current rates, whereas the doubling times for the populations of Canada, the United States, and the United Kingdom are 58 years, 87 years, and 231 years, respectively.

WORLD POPULATION

The world population growth rate is increasing, according to United Nations estimates. The death rate is declining more rapidly than the birthrate, and the age structures of most developing nations favor population growth. Due to recent infant and childhood mortality declines, most developing nations have 40% or more of their populations under 15 years of age, compared with 27% for the United States and only 21% for Sweden. Even if couples in developing nations immediately began to have just enough children to replace themselves, the populations of these nations would continue to grow because of the large proportions of persons entering the reproductive ages.

World Population Policies. More and more governments of underdeveloped countries were recognizing that rapid rates of population growth are detrimental to the achievement of national goals. In a study published in 1973, the American demographer B. Maxwell Stamper concluded that 71% of the combined population of 70 underdeveloped nations lived in a country that had recognized some "population problem" in its national development plans. Eighteen nations, which accounted for 64% of the total population of the 70 nations, also had policies and programs to reduce fertility.

While having no official policy statements about population, several nations do give official support to family-planning activities for other than demographic reasons. The Venezuelan Congress, for example, appropriated funds specifically for family planning for the first time in 1973, giving $363,000 to an affiliate of the International Planned Parenthood Federation.

Only a small proportion, estimated at 13%, of the population of the less-developed world live in a nation with no population policies and no support of family planning.

It has not been possible to measure precisely how much change in a nation's birthrate is due to government efforts to lower fertility. Nations with such programs have been modernizing rapidly, and some reduction in fertility would be expected even if no official program existed. In some countries the official programs are thought to have accelerated a fertility decline that already was in process. According to the Population Council of New York, fertility is "known or surmised to be falling" in 16 developing nations that support family-planning programs, including Egypt, the People's Republic of China, and South Korea.

Population and Food Supplies. While progress was achieved in the population policies of many nations in 1973, the world food-supply situation wors-

BUTTONS urge population control. The letters "ZPG" on the lower button stand for "Zero Population Growth."

ened. As a result of unfavorable weather conditions in 1972, world cereal stocks dropped to the lowest level in 20 years, and food prices accordingly rose rapidly. Given the continuing increase in population, per capita food production in the developing nations as a whole fell back to the levels of the years 1961 through 1965.

The threat of food shortages was most severe in the sub-Saharan zone of West Africa where as many as 6 million persons endured conditions close to famine due to a prolonged drought, according to Addeke H. Boerma, director general of the United Nations Food and Agricultural Organization. The countries of this region that were especially affected were Chad, Mali, Mauritania, Niger, Senegal, and Upper Volta.

The precarious world food situation in 1973 brought about a return to the pessimism of the mid-1960's among some agricultural experts. Good weather and the start of the "green revolution" had created a period of optimism between 1967 and 1970 when it was thought that food production could be increased more rapidly than population growth for at least another decade or two. Now United Nations food experts realize that desired agricultural improvements in many developing nations were not being achieved.

Between 1961 and 1971, food production did not increase as rapidly as the population growth in about half of the world's developing nations, including such large countries as Nigeria, India, Indonesia, the Philippines, Mexico, and Burma. With low world food reserves, the world's population had reached the point where the availability of adequate food supplies, and hence the avoidance of famine, depended on favorable weather for the 1973 harvest. (See also Food.)

VITAL STATISTICS OF SELECTED COUNTRIES

	Estimated population mid-1973[1]	Birthrate per 1,000 population[2]	Death rate per 1,000 population[2]	Current population growth (percent)	Number of years to double population[3]	Population under 15 years (percent)[4]	Population projections to 1985 (millions)[1]	Per capita gross national product (U. S. $)[5]
World	3,860,000,000	33	13	2.0	35	37	4,933	...
North America								
Canada	22,500,000	15.6	7.3	1.2	58	30	27.3	3,700
Cuba	8,900,000	27	8	1.9	37	31	11.0	530
Dominican Republic	4,800,000	49	15	3.4	21	47	7.3	350
El Salvador	3,800,000	42	10	3.2	22	45	5.9	300
Guatemala	5,600,000	43	17	2.6	27	46	7.9	360
Haiti	5,600,000	44	20	2.4	29	43	7.9	110
Honduras	3,000,000	49	17	3.2	22	47	4.6	280
Mexico	56,200,000	43	10	3.3	21	46	84.4	670
Nicaragua	2,200,000	46	17	2.9	24	48	3.3	430
Puerto Rico	2,900,000	25	7	1.4	50	37	3.4	1,650
United States	210,300,000	15.6	9.4	0.8	87	27	235.7	4,740
South America								
Argentina	25,300,000	22	9	1.5	47	30	29.6	1,160
Bolivia	5,000,000	44	19	2.4	29	42	6.8	180
Brazil	101,300,000	38	10	2.8	25	43	142.6	420
Chile	10,400,000	26	9	1.7	41	39	13.6	720
Colombia	23,700,000	45	11	3.4	21	47	35.6	340
Ecuador	6,700,000	45	11	3.4	21	48	10.1	290
Paraguay	2,700,000	45	11	3.4	21	46	4.1	260
Peru	14,900,000	42	11	3.1	23	45	21.6	450
Uruguay	3,000,000	23	9	1.4	50	28	3.4	820
Venezuela	11,900,000	41	8	3.4	21	47	17.4	980
Europe								
Austria	7,500,000	13.8	12.6	0.1	700	24	8.0	2,010
Belgium	9,800,000	13.8	12.0	0.2	347	24	10.4	2,720
Bulgaria	8,700,000	15.3	9.8	0.6	117	23	9.4	760
Czechoslovakia	15,000,000	16.5	11.5	0.5	139	24	16.2	2,230
Denmark	5,100,000	15.8	10.2	0.5	139	24	5.5	3,190
Finland	4,800,000	12.7	9.6	0.3	231	26	5.0	2,390
France	52,300,000	16.9	10.6	0.6	117	25	57.6	3,100
Germany, East[6]	16,300,000	11.7	13.7	−0.2	...	24	16.9	2,490
Germany, West[7]	59,400,000	11.5	11.7	0.0	...	25	62.3	2,930
Greece	9,100,000	15.9	8.3	0.8	87	25	9.7	1,090
Hungary	10,400,000	14.7	11.4	0.3	231	21	11.0	1,600
Ireland	3,000,000	22.4	11.2	0.5	139	31	3.5	1,360
Italy	54,900,000	16.8	9.6	0.7	99	24	60.0	1,760
Netherlands	13,400,000	16.1	8.5	0.8	87	27	15.3	2,430
Norway	4,000,000	16.6	10.0	0.7	99	25	4.5	2,860
Poland	34,000,000	17.4	8.0	0.9	77	28	38.2	1,400
Portugal	9,800,000	21.3	11.1	1.0	70	29	10.7	660
Rumania	21,000,000	19.6	9.5	1.0	70	26	23.3	930
Spain	34,200,000	19.4	8.2	1.1	63	28	38.1	1,020
Sweden	8,200,000	13.8	10.4	0.3	231	21	8.8	4,040
Switzerland	6,500,000	14.4	8.7	1.0	70	23	7.4	3,320
United Kingdom	57,000,000	14.9	11.9	0.3	231	24	61.8	2,270
USSR	250,000,000	17.8	8.2	1.0	70	28	286.9	1,790
Yugoslavia	21,200,000	18.2	9.1	0.9	77	28	23.8	650
Africa								
Algeria	15,500,000	50	17	3.3	21	47	23.9	300
Egypt	36,900,000	37	16	2.1	33	43	52.3	210
Ethiopia	26,800,000	46	25	2.1	33	44	35.7	80
Kenya	12,000,000	48	18	3.0	23	46	17.9	150
Morocco	17,400,000	50	16	3.4	21	46	26.2	230
Nigeria	59,600,000	50	25	2.6	27	43	84.7	120
South Africa	21,700,000	41	17	2.4	29	40	29.7	760
Sudan	17,400,000	49	18	3.1	23	47	26.0	120
Tanzania	14,300,000	47	22	2.6	27	44	20.3	100
Zaïre	18,700,000	44	23	2.1	33	42	25.8	90
Asia								
Afghanistan	18,300,000	51	27	2.4	29	45	25.0	80
Bangladesh	83,400,000	...	...	...	...	...	123.3	...
Burma	29,800,000	40	17	2.3	30	40	39.2	80
China (Mainland)	799,300,000	30	13	1.7	41	...	964.6	160
China (Taiwan)	15,000,000	27	5	2.2	32	43	19.4	390
India	600,400,000	42	17	2.5	28	42	807.6	110
Indonesia	133,500,000	47	19	2.9	24	44	185.1	80
Iran	31,100,000	45	17	2.8	25	46	45.0	380
Japan	108,300,000	19	7	1.2	58	24	122.6	1,920
Korea, North	15,100,000	39	11	2.8	25	...	20.7	330
Korea, South	34,500,000	31	11	2.0	35	40	45.9	250
Malaysia	11,800,000	38	11	2.7	26	44	16.4	380
Nepal	12,000,000	45	23	2.2	32	40	15.8	80
Pakistan	68,300,000	51	18	3.3	21	45	100.9	100
Philippines	42,200,000	45	12	3.3	21	47	64.0	210
Sri Lanka (Ceylon)	13,500,000	30	8	2.2	32	41	17.7	110
Thailand	39,900,000	43	10	3.3	21	43	57.7	200
Turkey	38,600,000	40	15	2.5	28	42	52.8	310
Vietnam, North	22,500,000	...	...	...	...	...	28.2	100
Vietnam, South	19,100,000	...	...	...	...	...	23.9	200
Oceania								
Australia	13,300,000	20.5	8.5	1.9	37	29	17.0	2,820
New Zealand	3,000,000	22.1	8.5	1.7	41	32	3.8	2,700

[1] Estimates from United Nations. [2] Latest available year. North American rates computed by Population Reference Bureau; others from United Nations, adjusted for deficient registration in some countries. [3] Assuming continued growth at current annual rate. [4] Latest available year. Derived from United Nations. [5] 1970 data from International Bank for Reconstruction and Development. [6] Excludes East Berlin. [7] Excludes West Berlin.   Source: Population Reference Bureau, Washington, D. C.

UNITED STATES POPULATION TRENDS

In mid-1973 the total population of the United States was estimated to be 210 million by the U. S. Bureau of the Census. This represented an increase of 30 million persons since the 1960 census, and an increase of 59 million since the 1950 census. The rate of population growth is slowing, however, due to a continuing decline in fertility. The crude birthrate—the total number of births per 1,000 persons—during the 12-month period ending in August 1973 was 15.2—the lowest figure ever recorded in the United States. This figure was about 6% lower than that for the same period in 1972.

About 3.19 million births were registered in the United States during the 12-month period ending in August 1973, 5% less than the number registered during the corresponding period in 1972. In contrast to the national trend, 11 states, including California, Georgia, and South Carolina, registered more births in the first two thirds of 1973 than they did during the same part of 1972.

The declining level of fertility in the United States is due to a reduction in the number of children desired by young women. On the basis of a survey conducted in 1972, the U. S. Bureau of the Census reported that women between 18 and 24 years of age expect to complete childbearing with an average of about 2.1 births. This is a fertility expectation about one-fifth lower than that reported by young women 18 to 24 years old in a similar survey conducted in 1967, when about 2.9 births were expected. Demographers believed the reduction was partly due to the increased availability of abortion, improved contraceptive techniques, and the rapidly rising cost of living.

Long-Range Population Projections. If current levels of fertility persisted for several decades and if immigration into the United States ceased, then in time a stage of zero population growth (ZPG) would be reached. But immigration into the nation is expected to continue. For example, during 1972 the estimated net immigration into the United States was 338,000 persons, or about one fifth of the total population increase in that year. Knowing this, the U. S. Census Bureau assumes a continued net immigration of 400,000 annually in making population projections for the United States. The Census Bureau also broadly assumes that "there will be no disastrous war, widespread epidemic, major economic depression, or similar catastrophe." Given these assumptions, by the year 2000 a fertility level of 2.1 births per woman would result in a U. S. population of about 263 million growing at an annual rate of 0.6%. Zero population growth would not yet have been achieved. Even assuming a lower fertility level of 1.8 births per woman, the population would still be growing in the year 2000 although at a slower rate (0.4%), and the population itself would be smaller in size (250 million persons).

The Energy Crisis of 1973. In the area of population and resources, a major turning point was President Nixon's speech to the nation in November when he asked the public to change certain life styles and the Congress to pass legislation to conserve petroleum products. The crisis was precipitated when several Middle Eastern nations reduced oil exports to the United States.

Among the steps taken or asked by the President were: a public appeal to reduce home and business thermostats to 68 degrees, and to reduce automobile driving speeds to 50 miles per hour; fuel allocations to reduce aircraft flights by 10%; authority to relax environmental protection standards temporarily; and authority to put the nation on year-round daylight saving time.

With a growing population and with widespread desires for ever-increasing per capita consumption levels, the United States has become increasingly dependent on imports of essential industrial commodities such as petroleum. The Middle Eastern oil reductions made many Americans aware of how vulnerable their own personal life styles are to foreign events over which they have no control. Understanding this, the President urged the nation to shift from foreign to domestic sources of energy, particularly coal, even if environmental standards must be modified. The President also called for research and development programs to achieve national energy self-sufficiency by 1980.

CANADIAN POPULATION TRENDS

By mid-1973 the total population of Canada was estimated to have reached 22.5 million persons. The most populous province was Ontario with 7.9 million, followed by Quebec (6.1 million), and British Columbia (2.3 million). The national population grew by 3.8 million, or 21%, since the 1961 census.

The rate of population growth in Canada has been slowing in recent years due to a declining birthrate. In 1971 the Canadian crude birthrate was 16.8, with Quebec's rate of 14.8 per thousand population being the lowest of any province. The declining birthrate has been partially offset by increasing immigration.

Between the 1966 and the 1971 censuses, the average annual net immigration into Canada was 92,800 persons, up considerably from the average of 51,800 per year between the 1961 and the 1966 censuses. During 1972, 20% of all immigrants came from Asia, 19% from the United States, and 15% from the United Kingdom and Ireland.

UNITED NATIONS WORLD POPULATION YEAR

The year 1974, the World Population Year, has been dedicated by the United Nations to evolving a world consensus on population matters. The major event of the year will be a World Population Conference to be held in Bucharest, Rumania, in August. At that time national delegations will formulate the consensus, which hopefully will assist nations in dealing with their population-related problems.

During 1973 and early 1974 four symposia were held to prepare reports that will be used to help governments attending the 1974 conference reach population policy decisions. The topics of the symposia were: population and development; population and family well-being; population, natural resources, and environment; and population and human rights. The main goal of the United States effort is to obtain the maximum involvement of national governments in seeking solutions to world population problems. In March 1973 the executive director of the United Nations Fund for Population Activities, Rafael M. Salas, said: "World Population Year should not be regarded as an end in itself, but as a vital beginning of a sustained effort to achieve worldwide awareness of the need to find a rational balance between people and resources."

ROBERT E. KENNEDY, JR.
University of Minnesota

PORTUGAL

The government of Premier Marcello Caetano was denounced abroad during 1973 for its determination to suppress independence movements in Portuguese Africa. It also seemed to lose support at home, though its existence was not seriously threatened.

Politics. A small expression of dissent from the authoritarian regime was permitted in April, when the first formal meeting of Caetano's opponents in four years took place in the small northern town of Aveiro. Republicans, monarchists, Socialists, Communists, and liberals, whose sole unifying motive was dislike of over 40 years of Salazar-Caetano authoritarianism, assembled but found proceedings heavily censored and the news media prevented from publishing many details. The delegates denounced the long and expensive wars in Angola, Mozambique, and Portuguese Guinea. As elections for a new National Assembly were scheduled for autumn, opponents of the official National Popular Action party formulated a platform for those bold enough to present themselves as Opposition candidates.

Four days before the October 28 elections, 65 Opposition candidates withdrew from the race. They protested official harassment—particularly in their efforts to criticize the fighting in Africa. In the election, the National Popular Action party won all seats (as it likely would have even if the Opposition candidates had not withdrawn).

Economy. The Portuguese economic picture in 1973 was a mixture of prosperity and depression. Prosperity came mainly from the burgeoning tourist industry, which reached a new height during the year. Tourism centered mainly in the Algarve, the southernmost province, a five-hour drive from Lisbon. Here, Lagos has become an air terminal. Luxury hotels have sprung up, along with apartments and casinos, catering principally to foreigners.

An American visitor to the Algarve in the summer of 1973 reported that, because of the newness of tourist facilities, inconveniences existed but were being eliminated. Because of the influx of foreign money brought by tourists, the low prices that have been characteristic of Portugal are disappearing, with an effect on the entire national economy.

The depressed side of the Portuguese economy was apparent in the villages and farm districts, where whole communities are dying, largely because of the departure of young men—partly to escape military service in Africa and partly to gain better wages and employment outside Portugal. In Portugal, a skilled worker earns about $28 for a six-day week, about half of what he can gain in France, where thousands annually migrate, usually clandestinely. By an unofficial estimate, over 700,000 Portuguese, predominantly male, now live and work in France. One result is a severe reduction in the number of men available for the army.

Women's Rights in Portugal. A book published by three Portuguese women in 1972 protesting the status of Portuguese women became internationally known in July 1973. The authors, Maria Isabel Barreno, Maria Velho da Costa, and Maria Teresa Horta, all well-known poets or novelists, had been arrested for collaborating on *New Portuguese Letters,* inspired by the 17th century *Letters of a Portuguese Nun.* Their protest book, including essays, poems, and letters by three fictional Portuguese women—one in a convent, one in a mental hospital, and the third trapped in a hopeless marriage—sold heavily after publication.

Women's liberationists had been rare in Portugal, and the book created a furore. Police confiscated the rest of the edition and brought charges against the authors of outraging public morals and abusing freedom of the press.

Arrested under a new law that makes writers criminally responsible for their work if censors object, the three Marias were released on bail of $700 each and trial was set for July 3. Apparently because Maria Horta is tubercular, the case was postponed until autumn. Then, after an initial session on October 25, the trial was put off until early in 1974. Portuguese intellectuals protested suppression of the book, and there were demonstrations in New York and London.

Foreign Relations. Portugal, which outlaws its small Communist party, declared readiness on February 21 to open trade and diplomatic relations with the Soviet Union and its East European satellites but said the initiative must be theirs.

The U. S. Senate, on June 14, voted to cancel an agreement with Portugal that would have permitted U. S. base rights in the Azores, because the agreement was not presented in treaty form. The arrangement would have given the United States the use of the Azores field and allotted Portugal $30 million in loans and aid.

Premier Caetano visited England in July to commemorate the sixth centennial of the Anglo-Portuguese alliance dating from 1373. Because of a reported massacre by Portuguese troops of the inhabitants of a town near Tete, Mozambique, demonstrations marked his arrival in London. Conversations between the premier and Prime Minister Edward Heath dealt mainly with trade between their two countries, which is heavily unbalanced in British favor.

CHARLES E. NOWELL, *University of Illinois*

PORTUGAL • Information Highlights

Official Name: Portuguese Republic.
Location: Western portion of the Iberian Peninsula in southwestern Europe.
Area: 35,553 square miles (92,082 sq km).
Population (1973 est.): 9,800,000. Density, 275 per square mile (106 per sq km).
Chief Cities (1969 est.): Lisbon, the capital, 830,600; Oporto, 325,400.
Government: *Head of state,* Américo Thomaz, president (took office June 1958). *Head of government,* Marcello Caetano, premier (took office Sept. 1968). *Legislature* (unicameral) —National Assembly. *Official political party*—Acção Nacional Popular.
Language: Portuguese (official).
Education: *Expenditure* (1967), 7.9% of total public expenditure. *School enrollment* (1969)—primary, 989,676; secondary, 405,604; technical/vocational, 135,979; university/higher, 46,725.
Monetary Unit: Escudo (23.67 escudos equal U. S.$1, Aug. 1973).
Gross National Product (1972 est.): $7,800,000,000.
Economic Indexes: *Industrial production* (1972), 203 (1963= 100); *agricultural production* (1971), 103 (1963=100); *consumer price index* (1972), 180 (1963=100).
Manufacturing (major products): Wine, canned fish, processed foods, textiles, ships, electronic equipment, cork.
Major Agricultural Products: Grapes, tomatoes, potatoes, wheat, figs (ranks 1st among world producers, 1971), olives, fish, forest products.
Major Minerals: Wolframite, coal, iron ore, beryl, copper.
Foreign Trade (1972): Exports, $1,287,000,000; Imports, $2,-183,000,000. *Chief trading partners* (1971)—United Kingdom (took 19% of exports, supplied 13% of imports); Portuguese Overseas Provinces (18%—12%); United States (9.7%—6.9%); West Germany (5%—15.7%).
Tourism: Receipts (1971), $308,000,000.
Transportation: *Motor vehicles* (1971), 743,900 (automobiles, 660,400); *railroads* (1971), 2,238 miles (3,602 km); *merchant fleet* (1972), 2,013,000 gross registered tons; *major national airline,* TAP (Transportes Aéreos Portugueses).
Communications: *Telephones* (1972), 809,380; *newspapers* (1971), 31.

POSTAL SERVICE

The mandate received by the U. S. Postal Service as a result of the Postal Reorganization Act of 1970 was to provide optimum service at a reasonable cost but with a phasing out of government subsidies. The service moved toward this goal with moderate success in 1973. The year was marked by three major developments: (1) the gradual realization that the process of mechanization leading to increased productivity would not necessarily balance the budget; (2) the maturation of labor relations, so that the national contract which increased the overall cost of the service by providing for healthy boosts in postal worker wages also created a mechanism to encourage the acceptance of productivity as a valid goal for both labor and management; and (3) the subsequent petition for major rate increases.

Service: Problems and Solutions. The deterioration of service which occurred throughout 1972, peaking at Christmas, continued into 1973. One of the chief problems was the erroneous belief on the part of management officials, mostly from the private sector, that their experience could be precisely transferred to the labor-intensive area of public service. This belief was based on the theory behind the setting up of the Postal Service as a semi-autonomous governmental corporation, namely, that the business-like operation of the post office would provide savings for the taxpayer. These officials, relying on increased automation and mechanization, reduced the number of workers in the Postal Service, at the same time developing capital purchase plans for new and more sophisticated machines.

Disaster struck. Machines did not work, flow patterns were confused, and complaints increased. Questions, many from political figures, were raised as to whether the private approach based on the enhancement of efficiency had already failed. Postmaster General Elmer T. Klassen met with the 86 district managers—mostly long-time postal employees in contrast to the headquarters-regional officials, most of whom had come from private enterprise—and heard frank discussions of field service errors. A series of meetings in the five postal regions provided even more explicit statements from the local postmasters who had direct contact with the public.

As a result, priorities were adjusted so that public *service* was again recognized as being preeminent. The Area Preferential Mail System, which failed to effectively improve service, was downgraded in importance and significantly changed. Additional staff workers were hired. The installation of machinery that had proved itself was expedited. Improved management procedures were introduced. By the end of 1973 the bottleneck had been reduced, although not eliminated.

Labor Relations. Collective bargaining for the second contract under the Postal Reorganization Act of 1970 went well. Union negotiations of four major unions joined in one coordinated bargaining team. Negotiations started in April and concluded in June with the unions ratifying the agreement in July.

Among the features of the agreement were an increase of $1,100, representing an average 14% increase, across the board for all postal personnel over a period of two years; a new cost of living increase clause with no ceiling, which had produced an increase of seven cents per hour by November 1973; an increase in the size of Postal Service contributions to employees' health and life insurance premiums; a limitation on management's right to assign overtime; and an agreement for procedures to negotiate local supplements to the national agreement. Many local agreements were in arbitration at the end of 1973.

Management's demand for unlimited power to lay off the work force was not met, and the original provision for reduction in the work force by attrition and voluntary retirement only was retained. The requests of the unions for a 35-hour work week and for monetary supplements based on geographic differences were turned down.

The final ratification of the national agreement ran into some difficulty. The main reason for dissatisfaction appeared to stem from the feelings of the large-city union locals that they should have received a geographical cost of living differential.

Rates. In the latter part of 1973, the Postal Service asked the Postal Rate Commission for a sizeable increase in postal rates. First-class mail would go from 8 to 10 cents, airmail from 11 to 13 cents, and postcards from 6 to 8 cents. In addition, new increases in second-, third-, and fourth-class mail, parcel post, and book rates were requested. There was also a call for new increases for international mail. The total increase was expected to bring in over $2 billion in new income. An original order of 8 billion new stamps was placed to meet the proposed increase.

These increases were approved first by the Postal Rate Commission and then by the board of governors of the U. S. Postal Service. The Cost of Living Council trimmed the total to be received but did not change the rate structure. Therefore the Postal Service postponed the effective date from January 5 to March 2, 1974.

Progress. A new feature of the postal scene was the promise by the postmaster general that all first-class mail traveling more than 600 miles would go by airmail. This development promises to speed delivery, in spite of the fact that one of the problems of slow delivery has been the lack of available space on many of the airlines. Regular airmail will still have priority at the point of origin and destination.

Mailgram, the postal letter that goes by wire, can now be certified at an extra fee. Increased motorization of delivery was being reexamined in the light of the fuel shortage. The fuel crisis caused the federal government to cut by 11% the amount of diesel fuel requested by the Postal Service for Christmas mail delivery. In response to the criticisms of philatelists and others, a new Stamps Department that is concerned with both the distribution and design of stamps came into existence on July 1, 1973.

Gross income in fiscal 1973 was $9.8 billion, an increase of $400 million over fiscal 1972. The number of pieces of mail delivered increased by 2.5 billion from fiscal 1972 to a total of 89.7 billion. Employed postal personnel decreased slightly from 706,400 to 701,051. The number of post offices remained relatively stable, with 31,385 in operation in 1973.

The Postal Service indisputably made progress in many areas in 1973. The question at the close of the year was whether it had succeeded in gaining the full confidence of the public, the Congress, and its own employees.

HARVEY L. FRIEDMAN
University of Massachusetts

– PRINCE EDWARD ISLAND • Information Highlights –

Area: 2,184 square miles (5,656 sq km).
Population (1972 est.): 114,000.
Chief Cities (1971 census): Charlottetown, the capital, 19,133; Summerside, 9,439.
Government: *Chief Officers* (1973)—lt. gov., J. George McKay; premier, Alexander B. Campbell (Liberal); prov. secy. and atty. gen., Gordon L. Bennett (L); min. of finance, T. Earle Hickey (L); min. of educ., Bennett Campbell (L); chief justice, C. St. Clair Trainor. *Legislature*—Legislative Assembly, 32 members (24 Liberal, 7 Progressive Conservative, 1 Vacant).
Education: *Public school expenditures* (1970)—$16,428,000; average teacher's salary (1970 est.), $5,683.
Public Finance (fiscal year 1973 est.): *Revenues*, $108,000,-000 (sales tax, $21,000,000; income tax, $11,300,000; federal funds, $57,600,000). *Expenditures*, $109,600,000.
Personal Income (1971): $245,000,000; average annual income per person, $2,188.
Manufacturing (1969): Value added by manufacture, $18,471,-000 (food and beverages, $12,789,000; wood industries, $292,000).
Agriculture (1972 est.): *Cash farm income* (exclusive of government payments) (livestock and products, $25,894,000; crops, $15,520,000). *Chief crops* (cash receipts)—potatoes, $12,111,000; vegetables, $901,000.
Mining (1972 est.): *Production value*, $800,000. *Only mineral* —Sand and gravel, $800,000.
Fisheries (1972): *Commercial catch*, 56,588,000 pounds ($9,-509,000). *Leading species*—lobster.
Transportation: *Roads* (1970), 3,487 miles (5,612 km); *motor vehicles* (1970), 40,233; *railroads* (1971), 254 track miles (409 km); *licensed airports* (1970), 2.
Communications: *Telephones* (1970), 34,143; *television stations* (1972), 1; *daily newspapers* (1972), 3.

All figures given in Canadian dollars.

PRINCE EDWARD ISLAND

In 1973, Prince Edward Island celebrated the centennial of its entrance into the Canadian Confederation, but enthusiasm was cooled by a newly formed association, the Brothers and Sisters of Cornelius Howatt (Howatt opposed confederation in 1873).

The provincial economy strengthened during the year, with rising prices for agricultural products and a housing boom initiated by government subsidization in 1972.

Legislation. During the legislative session, from January 23 to March 16, the Liberal government of Premier Alexander B. Campbell presented a budget of $125.2 million, up from $112 million in 1972. The public defender system of legal aid was adopted, and the minimum wage for women was increased to equality with that for men, $1.50 an hour. Legislation to consolidate and rationalize the marketing of agricultural products resulted in an unresolved struggle for control between farmers' organizations and the potato dealers' association.

Industrial Development. Industrial Enterprises Enc., a provincial crown corporation using federal aid, assisted private enterprise in establishing a lumber and chip plant at Souris and in tripling the capacity of a potato-processing plant at McLean. Construction began on a $4 million shopping mall west of Charlottetown. Offshore oil drilling continued with no significant results. Premier Campbell announced that tourist accommodations had been increased by 3,000 units under the island development plan and that tuna sport fishing was expanding.

R. F. NEILL, *Carleton University*

PRISONS

In 1973 the violence that had erupted in the late summer of 1971 in the California and New York prisons of San Quentin and Attica cast further shadows across U.S. prisons. Prison riots, often involving fatalities and extensive damage, continued. Some states initiated programs of reform, amid general public apathy.

Riots and Their Aftermath. Two years after the rebellious uprisings at Attica, and their violent suppression, a New York grand jury was still in session, having already indicted 60 inmates on 1,300 charges. Although most of the 43 deaths, including 11 prison employees and 32 inmates, were apparently caused by state officers retaking the prison, not one state official had yet been indicted. Lawyers for the defense expected the trials to last for more than five years. In California, the year began with a prison strike at San Quentin. Inmates claimed their rebellion was aimed against increased restrictions and security precautions, introduced after the August 1971 prison outburst in which George Jackson was killed.

In Oklahoma, on July 27, four inmates were killed, and the prison, located at McAlester, was almost totally destroyed by fire, with damage estimated at $20 million. The riot began when 21 hostages were seized, and the approximately 800 inmates became for a time uncontrollable. Leaders demanded to meet with Gov. David Hall. The prisoners acceded to the governor's demand to release the hostages, but some 600 inmates, claiming fear of reprisals from other prisoners, refused to reenter their cell blocks and massed in the open yard. It was not until several days later, on August 3, that order was restored by the Oklahoma National Guard. When newsmen and observers were able to enter the prison, the inmates cited lack of rehabilitation programs, poor food, overcrowding, and guards' brutality as the sources of their grievances.

On May 31, at the Homesburg Prison in Philadelphia, Warden Patrick Curran and Deputy Warden Robert F. Fromhold were stabbed to death by two inmates who had come to their offices to discuss questions of religious freedom. The accused convicts were among 1,200 prisoners housed in facilities designed to hold 700.

Race Relations. Racial conflict continued to play an important role in U.S. prisons. On May 13, in the Sumter Correctional Institution in Bushnell, Fla., 45 miles northwest of Orlando, state troopers were eventually able to halt a clash of some 400 prisoners. More than 40 inmates, all white, were hospitalized, some seriously injured by stab wounds. Prison officials speculated that the battle had been sparked by the stabbing of a black inmate by a white the night before.

In California, prison officials attributed more than half of the 34 prison slayings that occurred over the period of a year to the conflict between two gangs of Mexican-American inmates. One, The Imprisoned Mexicans, commonly called the Mexican Mafia, was challenged by a new group calling themselves The New Family. As often occurs in prisons where guards, because of the large numbers of prisoners under their jurisdiction, cannot control the inmates, authority had passed to the prisoners themselves. At stake in the California war, according to officials, was control of narcotics sales, proceeds from the auctioning off of new young arrivals to homosexuals, loan sharking, and smuggling. Chicano inmates find it difficult to remain neutral in the struggle between the rival gangs. A tragic incident was reported by prisoners at the Duel Vocational Facility at Tracy, Calif., in which a young Chicano who refused to align himself with either faction was castrated in the prison workshop.

Juvenile Offenders. The challenges facing the American corrections systems are most apparent in

OKLAHOMA STATE PRISON at McAlester (above) burns as National Guardsmen prepare to act. Inmates (right) later freed their hostages and returned to cells.

the case of young offenders. The following case, although not typical, does represent the kinds of problems facing some authorities. On July 10 two armed youths in Bridgeport, Conn., forced their way into the juvenile detention center and helped a 14-year-old runaway girl escape. After three days of intensive search by both local and state police the youths were captured, hiding alongside a cache of 70 stolen weapons and over 1,000 rounds of ammunition. One of the youths, aged 15, and with a record that included armed assaults, arson, car theft, purse snatches, burglary, and drug abuse, had escaped from the Meriden Reformatory 12 times.

Fruitless Reforms at Walpole. In late June, the Massachusetts correction commissioner, John O. Boone, was dismissed after serving for 17 months, a period marked by considerable reform but also by riots, strikes by guards, and six inmate murders. Walpole, a maximum security prison housing 570 inmates, was the scene of two intense riots, the first causing damage estimated at $1.6 million; the second, $429,000. In March the security guards staged a five-day strike.

When Commissioner Boone first took office, he announced a policy of furlough for prisoners and the use of halfway and community houses to educate prisoners. The reforms, though praised strongly by most penal experts, ran into stiff political opposition when legislators made it plain that they would not tolerate community-based facilities in their own areas. Commissioner Boone's being black also added to the controversy.

National Reform Efforts. In October the National Advisory Commission on Criminal Justice Standards and Goals completed its massive study on the nation's corrections systems. Many of the recommendations were similar to those that had been rejected politically in Massachusetts. The commission suggested a 10-year moratorium on the construction of large prisons and urged instead that corrections become a community-based effort, including small institutions close to the inmates' homes. They recommended an increase in vocational and educational programs as alternatives to prison.

Some states have been taking steps along the reform lines generally recognized as necessary. Connecticut is proceeding with plans to move to community-based institutions, as well as coed prisons. New York officials cite the establishment of a training academy for prison personnel, reduced censorship of mail, some decrease in the amount of time prisoners must remain locked in cells, and an increase in education courses for inmates. Many critics, however, argue that the level and nature of the 1973 reforms are not so much indicators of future improvements, but rather underline the sad state of affairs that have existed so long in the nation's prisons.

DONALD GOODMAN, *John Jay College of Criminal Justice, City University of New York*

STAFF WRITERS Bob Woodward (left) and Carl Bernstein of the Washington Post, who broke the Watergate case, were instrumental in the Post's winning a Pulitzer Prize. They also won prizes of their own for their Watergate reporting.

PRIZES AND AWARDS

In 1973 prestigious awards were given in all fields of endeavor, and the number of prizes continued to increase. Jean Piaget, the Swiss child psychologist, became the first recipient of the $25,000 Kittay International Award of the Kittay Scientific Foundation. One of the first public service awards of the American Institute of Public Service was presented to U. S. Secretary of State Henry Kissinger for his "far-ranging and diligent pursuit of peace."

Carl Bernstein and Robert Woodward of the Washington *Post* received several journalism awards for their investigation of the break-in at Democratic party headquarters in June 1972. The selection of the Washington *Post* as the winner of the Pulitzer Prize for public service in journalism focused attention on the significant role played by the press in disclosing the series of political scandals known as Watergate.

A selected list of the most important and newsworthy prizes and awards announced in 1973 follows.

NOBEL PRIZES

Nobel Prizes were awarded in 1973 in peace, literature, chemistry, physics, physiology or medicine, and economics. The peace prize was presented on Dec. 10, 1973, by King Olav V of Norway. The other awards were presented on the same day by King Carl XVI Gustaf of Sweden. The value of the prize—in 1973 each award was worth about $122,000—has increased steadily due to a successful "long-term policy of investment." The peace prize was awarded jointly to U. S. Secretary of State Henry A. Kissinger and to the North Vietnamese Le Duc Tho (who refused it) for negotiating the Vietnam cease-fire. The literature prize was awarded to the Australian novelist Patrick White for his "epic and psychological narrative art which has introduced a new continent into literature." (For separate articles on these three men, see BIOGRAPHY.)

Chemistry. The 1973 Nobel Prize in chemistry was shared by Ernst Otto Fisher, 55-year-old German chemist at the Technical University of Munich, and Geoffrey Wilkinson, 52-year-old English chemist at the University of London, for their independent studies that could help solve the problem of automobile exhaust pollution.

Physics. The 1973 Nobel Prize in physics was shared by three scientists whose theories have advanced and expanded the study of miniature electronics. Half of the prize was shared by Ivar Giaever, 44-year-old Norwegian-born, naturalized-American physicist at the General Electric Company, and Leo Esaki, 48-year-old Japanese physicist working at International Business Machines, Inc., who were cited for their work with semiconductors and superconductors. The other half of the prize was awarded to Brian D. Josephson, 33-year-old assistant director of research at Cambridge University, who was cited for his theoretical predictions of the properties of electron flow through a tunnel barrier, particularly the phenomena called the "Josephson effect."

Physiology or Medicine. The 1973 Nobel Prize in physiology or medicine was awarded to three pioneers in ethology, the comparative study of behavior, who were cited for their "discoveries concerning organization and elicitation of individual and social behavior patterns." The recipients were Karl von Frisch, 86-year-old Austrian-born bee expert best known for his research on "dance recruitment," the so-called language of bees; 69-year-old Austrian-born Konrad Lorenz of the Max Planck Institute for Behavioral Physiology in West Germany, best known for his work on imprinting; and 66-year-old Nikolaas Tinbergen, professor of animal behavior at Oxford, who was cited for his experimental procedures.

Economics. The 1973 Nobel Prize in economics was awarded to Wassily Leontief, a 67-year-old Russian-born American economist, who was cited as the "sole and unchallenged creator of the input-output technique of economic analysis." The theory developed by Leontif, director of Harvard University's Economics Research Project, is widely used for analyzing sudden economic changes.

PULITZER PRIZES

Winners of the Pulitzer Prizes were announced by the trustees of Columbia University on May 7, 1973. Each prize was worth $1,000 except the public service gold medal. No award was made in the category of editorial cartooning.

Journalism. Local general reporting—the staff of the Chicago *Tribune,* for its exposure of violations of the law in a primary election. Local special reporting—the Sun Newspapers of Omaha, Neb., for a special section on the finances of Boys Town, the home for orphans. Editorial writing—Roger B. Linscott of the Pittsfield, Mass., *Berkshire Eagle,* for his general influence in community affairs. International reporting—Max Frankel of the New York *Times,* for coverage of President Nixon's 1972 trip to China. National reporting—Robert Boyd and Clark Hoyt of the Knight Newspapers, for their disclosure of Sen. Thomas F. Eagleton's history of psychiatric treatment. Spot news photography—Huynh Cong Ut of the Associated Press, for a photograph of a 9-year-old Vietnamese girl fleeing from a napalm bombing. Feature photography—Brian Lanker of the Topeka, Kan., *Capital-Journal,* for a photograph in a sequence on natural childbirth. Commentary—David S. Broder, columnist and political reporter of the Washington *Post.* Criticism—Ronald Powers, television and radio critic of the Chicago *Sun-Times.* Meritorious public service—the Washington *Post,* for its investigation of the Watergate case, a national scandal originating in an attempt to bug Democratic National Headquarters in June 1972.

Letters. History—Michael Kammen, for *People of Paradox: An Inquiry Concerning the Origin of American Civilization.* Biography—William A. Swanberg, for *Luce and His Empire.* Poetry—Maxine Winokur Kumin, for *Up Country.* General nonfiction—Frances Fitzgerald, for *Fire in the Lake: the Vietnamese and the Americans in Vietnam,* and Robert Coles, for *Children of Crisis,* volumes 2 and 3. Fiction—Eudora Welty, for *The Optimist's Daughter.* Drama—Jason Miller, for *That Championship Season.*

Music. Elliott Carter, for *String Quartet No. 3.*

ARTS

American Film Institute, Life Achievement Award—James Cagney.

American Institute of Architects awards: critics' medal—Robin Boyd; collaborative achievement award—Bay Area Rapid Transit District; architectural firm award—Shepley, Bulfinch, Richardson, and Abbott of Boston; fine arts medal—Harry Bertoia; allied professions medal—Hideo Sasaki; industrial arts medal—Elena and Massimo Vignelli; craftsmanship medal—Helena Hernmarch.

Art Dealers Association of America Award for "outstanding achievement in art history" ($3,000)—Meyer Schapiro.

Van Cliburn International Piano Competition awards: first

prize ($10,000)—Vladimir Viardo; second—Christian Zacharias; third—Michael Houstoun.

Dance Magazine Awards—Rudolf Nureyev and William, Harold, and Lew Christensen.

National Academy of Recording Arts and Sciences, Grammy Awards for excellence in phonograph records: record of the year—*The First Time Ever I Saw Your Face,* sung by Roberta Flack; song of the year—*The First Time Ever I Saw Your Face;* album of the year—*The Concert for Bangladesh;* contemporary male vocal performance—Harry Nillson for *Without You;* contemporary female vocal performance—Helen Reddy for *I Am Woman;* contemporary vocal performance by a duo or group—Roberta Flack and Donny Hathaway for *Where Is the Love;* male country vocal performance—Charley Pride for *Charley Pride Sings Heart Songs;* female country vocal performance—Donna Fargo for *Happiest Girl in the Whole U. S. A.;* male rhythm and blues vocal performance—Billy Paul for *Me and Mrs. Jones;* female rhythm and blues vocal performance—Aretha Franklin for *Young, Gifted, and Black;* new artist—*America,* a rock trio; jazz performance by a band—Duke Ellington for *Togo Brava Suite;* solo jazz performance—Gary Burton for *Alone at Last;* classical piano performance—Vladimir Horowitz for *Horowitz Plays Chopin;* classical album of the year—Mahler's *Symphony No. 8,* performed by the Chicago Symphony; original score written for a motion picture—Nino Rota for *The Godfather;* score for an original cast show—Micki Grant for *Don't Bother Me, I Can't Cope.*

National Institute of Arts and Letters awards: art ($3,000)—Rudolf Baranik, Leon Golub, Robert Grosvenor, Raoul Hague, Michio Ihara, Clement Meadmore, and Philip Pearlstein; music ($3,000)—John Heiss, Betsy Jolas, Barbara Kolb, and Curry Tison Street; award of merit medal for sculpture—Reuben Nakian; gold medal for architecture—Louis I. Kahn; Arnold W. Brunner Memorial Prize in Architecture ($1,000)—Robert Venturi; Richard and Hinda Rosenthal Foundation Awards ($2,000)—Thomas Rogers and Jim Sullivan; Charles E. Ives awards ($10,000)—Philip Carlsen, Robert Gerster, and Peter Lieberson; Marjorie Peabody Waite Award ($1,500)—A. Hyatt Mayor.

JOURNALISM

American Newspaper Guild, Heywood Broun Memorial Award ($1,000)—Carl Bernstein and Robert Woodward of the Washington *Post.*

Long Island University, George Polk Memorial Awards: foreign reporting—Jean Thorval and Jean LeClerc du Sablon of Agence France Presse; national reporting—Carl Bernstein and Robert Woodward of the Washington *Post;* metropolitan reporting—Joseph Martin, Martin McLaughlin, and James Ryan of the New York *Daily News;* local reporting—Doris Ellen Olsen of the Santa Maria, Calif., *Times;* community service—Ronald Kessler of the Washington *Post;* investigative reporting—Jean Heller of the Associated Press; magazine reporting—Frances Fitzgerald of the *New Yorker* magazine for *Annals of War: Vietnam;* television reporting—Jim McKay of ABC; television news documentary—CBS News for *60 Minutes* and NBC for *First Tuesday;* news photography—Huynh Cong Ut of the Associated Press; book—Sanford J. Ungar for *The Paper and the Papers;* special award—Lesley Oelsner of the New York *Times* for a series on New York's criminal justice.

Newspaper Guild of New York, Page One Awards: national reporting—Max Frankel of the New York *Times;* foreign reporting—Bernard Weinraub of the New York *Times;* crusading journalism—the New York *Times;* news magazine writing—Frank J. Donner and Eugene Cerruti of the *Nation* magazine.

Overseas Press Club awards: President's Award—the American Committee to Free Journalists Held in Southeast Asia; Robert Capa Gold Medal for still photography—Clive M. Limpkin of the London *Sun; Asia* Magazine Award—Richard Dudman of the St. Louis *Post-Dispatch; Vision* Magazine Ed Stout Award for reporting on Latin America—Lewis H. Oluguld of the Washington *Post;* book on foreign affairs—David Halberstam for *The Best and the Brightest;* magazine reporting from abroad—Joseph Kraft for articles in the *New Yorker* magazine; magazine interpretation of foreign affairs—James A. Michener for an article in the New York *Times Magazine;* television interpretation of foreign affairs—Tom Streithorst of NBC News; television reporting from abroad—CBS News; radio and television documentary—ABC radio and ABC television; radio interpretation of foreign affairs—John Chancellor of NBC News; radio reporting from abroad—CBS radio; cartoon on foreign affairs—Thomas F. Darcy of *Newsday;* photographic reporting-interpretation from abroad—Huynh Cong Ut of the Associated Press; photographic reporting from abroad in a magazine or book—Thomas J. Abercrombie of *National Geographic* magazine; daily newspaper or wire service reporting from abroad—Charlotte Saikowski of the *Christian Science Monitor;* daily newspaper or wire service interpretation of foreign affairs—William L. Ryan of the Associated Press; business reporting from abroad—an eight-man team from the *Stars and Stripes* magazine.

Scripps-Howard Foundation awards: Roy W. Howard Public Service Awards ($2,500)—WABC-TV and the St. Louis *Globe-Democrat;* Ernie Pyle Memorial Award ($1,000)—William Stokes of the Milwaukee *Journal.*

LITERATURE

Academy of American Poets Fellowship Award ($10,000)—W. D. Snodgrass.

American Library Association (ALA) Awards: Newbery Medal—Jean George for *Julie of the Wolves;* Caldecott Medal—Blair Lent, illustrator, for *The Funny Little Woman;* Clarence Day Award—Sol and Mary Ann Malkin, publishers and editors of *AB Bookman's Weekly;* Grolier Award ($1,000)—Eleanor Kidder, retired superintendent of work with young adults, Seattle Public Library; Melvil Dewey Award—Virginia Lacy Jones, dean and professor of the School of Library Service, Atlanta University; Joseph W. Lippincott Award—Jesse H. Shera, professor emeritus of the School of Library Science, Case Western Reserve; Margaret Mann Citation—Doralyn Hickey, associate professor of the School of Library Science, University of North Carolina.

Bancroft Prizes of Columbia University for distinguished writing in U. S. history and international relations ($4,000 each)—John Lewis Gaddis for *The United States and the Origins of the Cold War, 1941–1947;* Frances Fitzgerald for *Fire in the Lake: the Vietnamese and the Americans in Vietnam;* Louis R. Harlan for *Booker T. Washington.*

Bollingen Foundation, Bollingen Prize in Poetry, administered by Yale University ($5,000)—James Merrill.

Governor General's Awards (Canadian): English fiction—Robertson Davies for *The Manticore;* English poetry—Dennis Lee for *Civil Elegies and Other Poems* and John Newlove for *Lies;* French fiction—Antonine Maillet for *Don l'original;* French nonfiction—Jean Hamelin and Yves Roby for *Histoire économique du Québec, 1851–1896;* French poetry—Gilles Henault for *Signaux pour les voyants.*

Mystery Writers of America, Edgar Allan Poe ("Edgar") Awards: mystery novel—Warren Kiefer for *The Lingala Code;* first novel—R. H. Skinner for *Squaw Point;* short story—Joyce Harrington for *The Purple Shroud;* true-crime book—Stephen Fay, Lewis Chester, and Magnus Linklater for *Hoax.*

National Book Awards ($1,000 each): fiction—John Williams for *Augustus* and John Barth for *Chimera;* arts and letters—Arthur M. Wilson for *Diderot;* history—Robert M. Myers for *The Children of Pride* and Isaiah Trunk for *Judenrat;* contemporary affairs—Frances Fitzgerald for *Fire in the Lake: the Vietnamese and the Americans in Vietnam;* biography—James Thomas Flexner for *George Washington: Anguish and Farewell (1793–1799);* poetry—A. R. Ammons for *Collected Poems: 1951–1971;* philosophy and religion—Sydney E. Ahlstrom for *A Religious History of the American People;* science—George B. Schaller for *The Serengeti Lion;* translation—Allen Mandelbaum for his translation of Vergil's *Aeneid;* children's books—Ursula Le Guin for *The Farthest Shore.*

National Book Committee, National Medal for Literature ($10,000)—Vladimir Nabokov.

National Institute of Arts and Letters awards in literature ($3,000): Marius Bewley, Maeve Brennan, Irving Feldman, Frances Fitzgerald, Dorothy Hughes, Philip Levine, Daniel P. Mannix, Cynthia Ozick, Jonathan Schell, and Austin Warren; E. M. Forster Award—Margaret Drabble; gold medal for poetry—John Crowe Ransom; distinguished service to the arts award—Glenway Wescott.

Poetry Society of America Awards: Gold Medal of Achievement—the late Mark Van Doren; Alice Fay di Castagnola Award for a work in progress ($3,500 shared)—Mary Oliver and George Keithley; Shelley Memorial Award ($2,070 shared)—John Ashbery and Richard Wilbur; Melvil Cane Award for a book on poetry ($500)—Jerome J. McGann for *Swinburne: An Experiment in Criticism.*

PUBLIC SERVICE

American Institute of Public Service Awards for distinguished public service ($5,000 each): Henry A. Kissinger, John W. Gardner, Cesar Chavez, and Joseph A. Yablonski.

Anti-Defamation League of B'nai B'rith, National Humanitarian Award—Leonard Woodcock.

Aspen Institute for Humanistic Studies, Statesman-Humanist Award ($10,000)—Willy Brandt.

Albert Einstein Commemorative Awards for outstanding contributions to man's betterment: Arthur Miller, playwright; Willem de Kooning, painter; Joseph Papp, producer; Paul Dudley White, cardiologist; Tom Wicker, columnist.

Four Freedoms Foundation Award—Frank Stanton, retired vice chairman of the Columbia Broadcasting System.

National Association for the Advancement of Colored People (NAACP) Spingarn Medal for the "highest achievement of an American Negro"—Wilson C. Riles.

National Urban Coalition, Lyndon Baines Johnson Award—Rev. Thomas M. Hesburgh, president of the University of Notre Dame.

Presidential Medals for Freedom—John Ford and William P. Rogers.

Rockefeller Public Service Awards for outstanding long-term service to the federal government ($10,000): administration—Phillip S. Hughes; intergovernmental operations—David D. Newsom; human resource development and protection—Martin Marc Cummings; physical resource development and protection—Vincent Ellis McKelvey; professional accomplishment or leadership—Ruth Margaret Davis.

SCIENCE AND TECHNOLOGY

American Academy of Arts and Sciences, Rumford Premium Award ($5,000)—E. Bright Wilson, Jr.

American Chemical Society, Priestley Medal—Paul J. Flory.

American Heart Association, Heart-of-the-Year Award—President Richard M. Nixon.

American Physical Society awards: Tom W. Bonner Prize in nuclear physics ($1,000)—Herman Feshbach; Oliver E. Buckley Solid-State Physics Prize ($1,000)—Gen Shirane; Irving Langmuir Prize in chemical physics ($5,000)—Peter M. Rentzepis; High Polymer Physics Prize ($1,000)—H. Douglas Keith and Frank J. Padden, Jr.

Atomic Energy Commission, Ernest Orlando Laurence Awards ($5,000)—Seymour Sack, Thomas E. Wainwright, Louis Baker, Jr., James R. Weir, Jr., and Sheldon Wolff.

Louisa Gross Horwitz Prize for outstanding research in biology ($25,000 shared)—Harry Eagle of Albert Einstein College of Medicine, Theodore Puck of the University of Colorado, and Renato Dulbecco of Imperial Cancer Research Fund Laboratories, London.

Albert Lasker Clinical Research Awards ($10,000)—William Bennett Kouwenhoven of Johns Hopkins University and Paul M. Zoll of Harvard Medical School.

National Academy of Sciences gold medals for career-long achievement in science ($5,000)—Donald D. Brown, Robert H. Dicke, Donald Wills Douglas, Sr., W. Thomas Edmondson, Hollis D. Hedberg, Samuel Karlin, Kenneth I. Kellermann, Seymour S. Kety, Luna B. Leopold, and Clair C. Patterson.

National Aeronautics and Space Administration (NASA), Exceptional Scientific Achievement Medal—Jacob I. Trombka of NASA's Goddard Space Flight Center.

National Association of Mental Health, McAlpin Research Achievement Award ($10,000)—Robert Coles of Harvard.

National Medals of Science for 1973: Daniel I. Arnon, professor of cell physiology, University of California at Berkeley; Carl Djerassi, professor of chemistry at Stanford University; Harold E. Edgerton, professor emeritus of electrical engineering at the Massachusetts Institute of Technology; William M. Ewing, chief of the Earth and Planetary Sciences Division, Marine Biomedical Institute, University of Texas at Galveston; Arie Jan Haagen-Smit, professor of biochemistry at the California Institute of Technology; Vladimir Haensel, vice president for science and technology at Universal Oil Products Company; Frederick Seitz, president of Rockefeller University; Earl W. Sutherland, Jr., professor of biochemistry at the University of Miami; John Wilder Tukey, associate executive director of the Research Communication Principles Division, Bell Laboratories; Richard T. Whitcomb, aeronautical engineer at NASA's Langley Research Center; Robert Rathbun Wilson, director of the National Accelerator Laboratory.

Vetleson Prize for achievement in the earth sciences, administered by Columbia University ($25,000)—William A. Fowler of the California Institute of Technology.

TELEVISION AND RADIO

Academy of Television Arts and Sciences ("Emmy") Awards: best series—America (NBC); drama series—The Waltons (CBS); single drama—A War of Children (ABC); single variety program—Singer Presents Liza with a "Z" (NBC); single music program—Singer Presents Liza with a "Z"; comedy series—All in the Family (CBS); musical or variety series—The Julie Andrews Hour (ABC); single best performance in a drama—Laurence Olivier in A Long Day's Journey into Night (ABC) and Cloris Leachman in A Brand New Life (ABC); actor in a leading role in a dramatic series—Richard Thomas in The Waltons (CBS); actress in a leading role in a dramatic series—Michael Learned in The Waltons (CBS); actor in a comedy series—Jack Klugman in The Odd Couple (ABC); actress in a comedy series—Mary Tyler Moore in The Mary Tyler Moore Show (CBS); supporting actor in a dramatic series—Scott Jacoby in That Certain Summer (CBS); supporting actress in a dramatic series—Ellen Corby in The Waltons (CBS); supporting actor in a comedy series—Ted Knight in The Mary Tyler Moore Show (CBS); supporting actress in a comedy series—Valerie Harper in The Mary Tyler Moore Show (CBS); writing achievement in drama—John McGreevey for The Waltons (CBS); writing achievement in comedy—Michael Ross, Bernie West, and Lee Kalchein for All in the Family (CBS); original teleplay—Abby Mann for The Marcus-Nelson Murders (ABC); directorial achievement in drama—Joseph Sargent for The Marcus-Nelson Murders (ABC); directorial achievement in comedy, variety, or music

—Bob Fosse for Singer Presents Liza with a "Z" (NBC); sports programing—A. B. C.'s Wide World of Sports (ABC) and The 1972 Summer Olympic Games (ABC); documentaries dealing with historic, artistic, or cultural subjects—America (NBC) and Jane Goodall and the World of Animal Behavior —The Wild Dogs of Africa (ABC); magazine-type program—60 Minutes (CBS); achievement within regularly scheduled news programs—CBS News and CBS correspondents Walter Cronkite, Dan Rather, Daniel Schorr, and Joel Blocker; documentaries dealing with matters of current significance—The Blue Collar Trap (NBC), One Billion Dollar Weapon (NBC), and The Mexican Connection (CBS); children's information programing—The Last of the Curlews (ABC), The A. B. C. Afterschool Special, and N. B. C. Children's Theater.

George Foster Peabody Awards for distinguished achievement in television and radio: television dramatic program—The Waltons (CBS); television documentary—The Search for the Nile (PBS), The Restless Earth (WNET of New York and BBC), China '72: A Hole in the Bamboo Curtain (WWL, New Orleans), Pensions: The Broken Promise (NBC), Willowbrook: the Last Great Disgrace (ABC), and ABC for its coverage of the 1972 summer Olympics; special television award for a "meaningful perspective look at America"—Alistair Cooke for America (NBC); television news reporting—Bill Monroe of the Today show (NBC); television children's programing—The A. B. C. Afterschool Special (ABC), Captain Kangaroo (CBS), and WHRO of Norfolk, Va.; radio programs—the NBC network for Monitor and the NBC-owned and operated stations for two special programs; KOAC of Corvallis, Ore., for Conversations with Will Shakespeare and Certain of his Friends; the Broadcasting Foundation of America; Westinghouse Broadcasting of New York; National Public Radio in Washington, D. C., for All Things Considered, and the Washington school radio project for The Noise Show.

THEATER AND MOTION PICTURES

Academy of Motion Picture Arts and Sciences ("Oscar") Awards for 1973: best film—The Godfather; best foreign-language film—Cries and Whispers; best actor—Marlon Brando in The Godfather; best actress—Liza Minnelli in Cabaret; supporting actor—Joel Grey in Cabaret; supporting actress—Eileen Heckart in Butterflies Are Free; director —Bob Fosse for Cabaret; screenplay based on material from another medium—Mario Puzo and Francis Ford Coppola for The Godfather; original screenplay—Jeremy Larner for The Candidate; nonmusical score—Charles Chaplin, Raymond Rasch, and Larry Russell for Limelight; musical score—Ralph Burns for his adaptation of Cabaret; original song—The Morning After from The Poseidon Adventure; art direction—Rolf Zehetbauer and Jurgen Kiebach for Cabaret; set decoration—Herbert Strabl for Cabaret; editing—David Bretherton for Cabaret; cinematography—Geoffrey Unsworth for Cabaret; costume design—Anthony Powell for Travels with My Aunt; sound—Robert Knudson and David Hildyard for Cabaret; short subject (live action)—Richard Barclay, producer, for Norman Rockwell's World . . . An American Dream; short subject (cartoon)—Richard Williams, producer, for A Christmas Carol; documentary feature film—Howard Smith and Sarah Kernochan, producers, for Marjoe; documentary short subject—Charles and Martina Huguenot van der Linden, producers, for This Tiny World; Jean Hersholt Humanitarian Award—Rosalind Russell; special citations—Charles Boren and the late Edward G. Robinson.

American Theater Wing, Antoinette Perry ("Tony") Awards: best drama—That Championship Season by Jason Miller; best musical—A Little Night Music, produced by Hal Prince; best actor (musical)—Ben Vereen in Pippin; best actress (musical)—Glynis Johns for A Little Night Music; best actor (drama)—Alan Bates in Butley; best actress (drama)—Julie Harris in The Last of Mrs. Lincoln; dramatic supporting actor —John Lithgow in The Changing Room; dramatic supporting actress—Leora Dana in The Last of Mrs. Lincoln; musical supporting actor—George S. Irving in Irene; musical supporting actress—Patricia Elliott in A Little Night Music; director (drama)—A. J. Antoon for That Championship Season; director (musical)—Bob Fosse for Pippin; costume—Florence Klotz for A Little Night Music; lighting—Jules Fisher for Pippin; choreography—Bob Fosse for Pippin; scenic design—Tony Walton for Pippin; score—Stephen Sondheim for A Little Night Music; book—Hugh Wheeler for A Little Night Music; special awards—Mayor John Lindsay, the Actor's Fund of America, and the Shubert Organization.

New York Drama Critics' Circle Theater Awards: best drama—The Changing Room; American drama—The Hot l Baltimore; musical—A Little Night Music.

Village Voice Off Broadway ("Obie") Awards: best plays—Lanford Wilson for The Hot l Baltimore and Joseph A. Walker for The River Niger.

PROTESTANTISM. See RELIGION.
PUBLIC HEALTH. See MEDICINE.

PUBLIC OPINION RESEARCH

In a year dominated by inflation, shortages, and Watergate, public opinion surveys in the United States recorded a steady erosion of public confidence and a marked pessimism about the future.

President Nixon. Satisfaction with the President reached its highest point ever in late January, after the Vietnam peace settlement, when 68% of the public expressed approval of his performance in office. By late April, under the impact of meat shortages, higher food prices, controversy over the bombing in Cambodia and Laos, and emerging Watergate disclosures, this figure has fallen to 48%. By early July, after John Dean III testified before the Senate Watergate hearings, only 40% approved of Nixon's performance, while 49% disapproved and 11% had mixed feelings. In early August the "approve" figure slipped to 31%, the lowest rating given any president in 20 years. The Harris Survey charted a similar trend. In late September, 32% rated Nixon's job performance as excellent or good and 65% called it only fair or poor. By early November, after the President dismissed Archibald Cox, the special Watergate prosecutor, his approval rating, as measured by Gallup, had slipped to 27%. Gallup's final report of the year in December showed a slight recovery to 31%.

The proportion believing that Nixon "should be impeached and compelled to leave office" increased from 19%, when the question was first asked in June, to 37% in early November. At that time, one person in 10 thought Nixon planned the Watergate bugging; 32% said he did not plan it but knew about it in advance, and 34% believed he found out about it after it occurred but tried to cover it up. Only 15% held the opinion that Nixon had no knowledge of the bugging and spoke up as soon as he learned about it. Harris reported more than 60% believed that the President was doing a good job of "working for peace in the world" and "handling relations with Russia," but fewer than 20% approved his handling of Watergate, living costs, corruption in government, and the economy generally.

Economic Issues. Gallup Polls on "the most important problem facing this country today" documented the public's concern with economic matters. The "high cost of living" replaced Vietnam as the No. 1 problem in February, and by September nine Americans in 10 named it as one of the country's two top problems.

The University of Michigan's Survey Research Center reported that consumers' confidence in their personal financial situations and in the economy generally had reached, in August–September, the lowest point ever measured in 25 years of conducting such surveys. Primarily because of rising prices, 36% of the respondents said that they were worse off financially than they were a year earlier, compared with 29% who said this in May and 18% in September 1972. Only 30% expected "good times" during 1974, with 45% expecting "bad times." In 1972, 54% expected good times during 1973 and only 17% expected bad times.

Both Gallup and Harris consistently reported public skepticism about the government's economic policies, and both polls showed that the majority of people favor stricter price and wage controls. Toward the close of the year Harris found 71% of the public in favor of gasoline rationing if the oil shortage continued.

Public Pessimism. More generally, a Gallup Poll in September reported that "the public's outlook is growing more pessimistic." In response to the question, "On the whole, would you say you are satisfied or dissatisfied with the future facing you and your family?", only 53% expressed satisfaction. Ten years ago the figure was 64%; two years ago it was 58%. A Harris Survey sponsored by the Senate Committee on Government Operations, the first poll ever authorized by the Senate, found a majority (53%) agreeing that "there is something deeply wrong in America" and a sharp decline in public confidence in major institutions in society, as compared with a similar survey in 1965. But comparison with figures reported a year earlier indicates that the low point in the public mood may have passed. Thus, while confidence in "the Executive branch of the federal government" continued to decline, confidence in "television news" increased from 17% in 1972 to 41% and is higher than it was eight years ago. Public confidence in the press, the Congress, and higher educational institutions was also up significantly over a year earlier.

Digests of Results. A monthly digest of poll findings, *Current Opinion*, began publication in February. Compiled by the Roper Center for Public Opinion Research at Williams College, each issue reports survey results provided by Gallup, Harris, National Opinion Research Center, the Roper organization, and other polling agencies in the United States and abroad. The only other regularly published source of survey findings is "The Quarter's Polls" in *Public Opinion Quarterly*. This feature summarizes all reported data on one particular topic in each issue and is valuable for showing trends in opinion over long periods of time. Early in the year the Gallup Poll issued a 3-volume index, published by Random House, which contains the findings of all of the surveys it has conducted since its inception in 1935.

Surveying Problems. The American Association for Public Opinion Research (AAPOR) held its 28th annual conference in Asheville, N. C., in May. This organization, consisting of some 900 teachers, practitioners, and users of survey research, discussed the quality standards for surveys, their use in political campaigns, and problems of interviewing arising from increased fear and suspicion by the public. The AAPOR award for distinguished public service to public opinion research was presented to Rensis Likert, founder of the Survey Research Center at the University of Michigan.

Increasing problems of survey research in gaining access to respondents were dramatized in the fall when W. R. Simmons & Associates called off its annual survey of magazine readership because it was not achieving a satisfactory response rate. Among the suspected causes: reluctance of interviewers, who are mostly women, to work in certain urban areas; reluctance of homeowners and apartment dwellers to admit strangers into their homes; cynicism about the purpose and use of many surveys; and a growing concern about privacy. The American Statistical Association, under a grant from the National Science Foundation, has assigned its committee on population sampling to study the matter and make recommendations.

PAUL B. SHEATSLEY
National Opinion Research Center
University of Chicago

PUBLISHING

The publishing world and its 1973 activities are reviewed in this article under three headings— Books, Magazines, and Newspapers.

Books

New obscenity rulings by the U. S. Supreme Court and the Soviet Union's announcement that it was joining the Universal Copyright Convention created drama and turmoil in the book industry in 1973. The industry was also affected by uncertainty over federal book and library appropriations, the continued rise in postal rates, and shortages of paper and other bookmaking materials. Paperback sales continued to zoom while increases in sales of hardcover trade books were only moderate—and inadequate to cover the increase in publishers' overhead. A sea gull, sex, and diet were the subjects of the year's "supersellers."

Major Events and Issues. In a series of obscenity cases, the U. S. Supreme Court rejected national standards of what is obscene and empowered the states and localities to apply "contemporary community standards." Announcement of the decision on June 21 led to formation of a media coalition, composed of library, periodical, film, and civil liberties organizations. The coalition planned to participate in state and federal legislative processes by monitoring bills, proposing model legislation, and supporting positive legislative action. (For details of the decision, see LIBRARIES.)

In a reversal of its traditional position, the Soviet Union accepted the idea of international copyright by joining the Universal Copyright Convention, effective on May 27. The USSR is now required to pay royalties to all authors whose works, copyrighted in a country belonging to the convention, are published in the Soviet Union. Similarly, Soviet authors are entitled to copyright protection in member countries. Soviet publication of foreign copyrighted works without compensation has long been an irritant in U. S.-Soviet relations.

U. S. and other Western observers saw the move as a further attempt to halt the flow of dissident Soviet writings for publication in the West. The likelihood that Soviet authorities would claim copyright control over the works of Soviet citizens seemed to be confirmed when on December 26 the government decreed that Soviet authors could transfer the rights to their works to foreign publishers only through the state-owned All-Union Copyright Agency.

The battle by the book and library communities for federal funds to continue local and national educational programs raged for most of the year. The Nixon administration at first allocated no funds, but in December the President signed a bill that included funds for book and library programs. Some of the funds impounded in fiscal 1973 also were released.

Best Sellers. Richard Bach's *Jonathan Livingston Seagull* topped the fiction best seller list for the second year in a row. Sales of more than 1 million copies in 1973 brought the total number of hardcover sales to well over 3 million. In nonfiction, *The Joy of Sex*, edited by Alex Comfort, was on the national best-seller list every week. Sales of Robert C. Atkins' *Dr. Atkins' Diet Revolution*, the second-leading nonfiction book, continued to climb even after the American Medical Association assailed the diet prescribed by the book as unscientific.

The following, in order of rank, were the best sellers:

FICTION

Jonathan Livingston Seagull, Richard Bach
The Odessa File, Frederick Forsyth
Once Is Not Enough, Jacqueline Susann
Breakfast of Champions, Kurt Vonnegut, Jr.
The Hollow Hills, Mary Stewart
The Billion Dollar Sure Thing, Paul E. Erdman
Harvest Home, Thomas Tryon
Facing the Lions, Tom Wicker
The Honorary Consul, Graham Greene
Burr, Gore Vidal

NONFICTION

The Joy of Sex, Alex Comfort, ed.
Dr. Atkins' Diet Revolution, Robert C. Atkins
The Best and the Brightest, David Halberstam
I'm O.K., You're O.K., Thomas Harris
How To Be Your Own Best Friend, Mildred Newman, et al.
Sybil, Flora R. Schreiber
Harry S. Truman, Margaret Truman
The Implosion Conspiracy, Louis Nizer
Laughing All the Way, Barbara Howar
The Making of the President 1972, Theodore H. White

Paperbacks. The continued strength of the paperback industry enabled paperback houses to pay huge sums for rights to certain books. *The Joy of Cooking* (1st ed., 1931) brought the highest known sum when New American Library purchased rights to it from the hardcover publisher, Bobbs-Merrill, for $1.5 million.

Dell Publishing Co. paid $800,000 for the paperback rights to *Beulah Land*, a new Doubleday novel by Lonnie Coleman, a relatively unknown author. This became the second-highest known sum paid for paperback rights to a fiction book. In 1972, rights to *Jonathan Livingston Seagull* were sold by Macmillan to Avon Books for $1.1 million.

New Companies and Mergers. Several former publishing executives launched their own publishing companies in 1973. The Countryman Press, Taftsville, Vt.—established by Peter S. Jennison, formerly executive director of the National Book Committee —expects to feature books about Vermont and

NORMAN MAILER, at a news conference, defends himself against charges that in Marilyn, his book on Marilyn Monroe, he had plagiarized the work of earlier biographers of the actress, notably Maurice Zolotow.

northern New England. Albert R. Leventhal, formerly with McGraw-Hill, organized Vineyard Books. Thomas H. Lipscomb, formerly with Dodd, Mead, and Orlando Petrocelli, formerly with Auerbach, set up Mason & Lipscomb, Inc., New York, to concentrate on nonfiction titles. Richard Heller, a former Dell and Pyramid editor, formed Richard Heller & Sons, New Rochelle, N. Y., to publish nonfiction.

Random House acquired Ballentine Books, publishers of mass-market paperbacks. Harcourt Brace Jovanovich acquired Pyramid Communications, publishers of mass-market paperbacks and magazines. The first major purchase of a U. S. firm by British interests took place when Morgan Grampain Ltd., publisher of business and consumer magazines, acquired David McKay Co., New York.

DAISY MARYLES
News Editor, "Publishers Weekly"

Magazines

Generally, the magazine industry prospered in 1973. The Magazine Publishers Association reported a record six-month revenue of $636 million for general and farm magazines in the first half of 1973, a rise of 8% over the same period in 1972. American Business Press reported an 8% rise in advertising revenue from 1971 to 1972, from $813.8 million to $882.1 million.

The threat of sharp postal increases continued to hang over the industry. Congress did not act on legislation to defer increases, and the first stage of a new 40% increase was due at the start of 1974.

Mergers and Acquisitions. Another major magazine, *Saturday Review*, collapsed in 1973. *Saturday Review*, which had prospered in the postwar years, had a circulation of more than 500,000 in 1970. After its sale to Nicholas H. Charney and John J. Veronis, in 1971, it was divided into four specialized magazines, with new merchandising subsidiaries. However, high costs and the failure of extensive subscription solicitations led to a crippling deficit. The 49-year-old magazine's bankruptcy was announced in April. In June, Norman Cousins, editor of *Saturday Review* from 1940 to 1971, reacquired the title and merged it into his new biweekly magazine, *World*. *Saturday Review/World* began publication at midyear.

McCall's, the century-old women's magazine with a circulation of 7.5 million, was purchased from Norton Simon, Inc. by a Chicago group headed by the Jay A. Pritzker family, reportedly for $8 million. A Texas combine headed by Arthur Temple acquired 15% of the stock of Time Inc. In return, Time Inc. acquired Temple Industries, specializing in forest products. Temple's group thus became, in the words of the New York *Times,* "a major force in the United States communications industry." In another transaction, the parent corporation of *New York* magazine acquired *Los Angeles* magazine for $500,000.

Editorial. Although broadcasting and newspapers were engaged in conflict with the government over Watergate and other scandals, the involvement of magazines remained marginal. *Time* and *Newsweek* carried their share of the Washington revelations, and political and general magazines published valuable analyses. But there was a gap in the kind of investigative coverage done so well in the past by *Life, Look,* and the *Saturday Evening Post.*

Major editorships shifted during 1973. Lenore Hershey, who succeeded John Mack Carter at the *Ladies' Home Journal,* became that magazine's first

A JOHNSON PUBLICATION

EBONY JR!

MAY 1973
50¢

KWAME AND THE LION
STORIES • GAMES • SURPRISES

JOHNSON PUBLISHING COMPANY

EBONY JR!, *the first national all-black children's magazine in the United States, began publication in March.*

woman editor in this century. Roy Terrell took over for Andre Laguerre at *Sports Illustrated.* Harold T. P. Hayes resigned as a result of a dispute at *Esquire* and was replaced by Don Erickson.

Among the magazines honored by the National Magazine Awards, sponsored by Columbia University, were *Business Week,* which received the general excellence award for coverage of the economy, and *New York* magazine which won the reporting prize for its depiction of life in the New York area. Other prizes went to *The Atlantic Monthly, Horizon,* and *Psychology Today.*

New Ventures. Among magazines that began publication in 1973 were:

New Times, a biweekly national news magazine, published by George A. Hirsch, formerly of *New York* magazine. The editor is Steve Gelman. *New Times* aims at a personal approach to news.

The Chicagoan, a monthly, latest of the city magazines. It was founded by Jon and Abra Anderson, both formerly of the Chicago *Daily News.* The idea behind *The Chicagoan* is to shun "phony boosterism" for "open, frank, and honest" coverage of the city.

Good Food, a monthly, put out by Triangle publications, slated to be sold largely in supermarkets. Its executive editor is Margaret Happel, formerly of the *Ladies' Home Journal.*

Viva, a monthly for women, published by Penthouse International and founded by Bob Guccione.

People, a new weekly issued by Time Inc. on a test basis. Its editor is Richard B. Stolley.

Ebony Jr!, a monthly issued by John H. Johnson, publisher of *Ebony,* who describes it as the first national all-black children's magazine.

JAMES BOYLAN, *Columbia University*

491

Newspapers

Early on the morning of June 17, 1972, due to the alertness of a guard at the Watergate Office Building in Washington, D. C., police arrested five men who had broken into the offices of the Democratic National Committee. It was hardly the biggest news of 1972, but from this event there gradually emerged a series of revelations that exposed a political scandal that reached into the highest office in the land and was to become the nation's chief preoccupation during most of 1973. The development of the Watergate story was, among other things, the century's most stunning journalistic achievement. (See special article beginning on page 14.)

Watergate. The Washington *Post,* which won the 1973 Pulitzer Prize for meritorious public service for its part in exposing the Watergate and related scandals, once again played the classic role of a newspaper in a democracy. Publisher Katherine Graham's investigative reporters Bob Woodward and Carl Bernstein, seizing upon microscopic tips and spending months of time in painstaking research and interviews, laid before the people a weird tale of clandestine government activities, a tale replete with plots and subplots of political espionage and sabotage, "dirty tricks," burglarized files, payoffs, cover-ups, and wiretaps.

As the story developed, other newspapers became equally active in the search for the full truth. In his address of April 30—an address in which he announced resignations of key personnel from his administration—the President himself acknowledged and commended the investigative pursuit of a "determined grand jury, honest prosecutors, a courageous judge, John Sirica, and a vigorous free press."

Threats to the Free Press. Despite this belated commendation from the President, the press did not have an easy year vis-à-vis the government. Several Washington reporters from various media had their telephones tapped when the White House tried to investigate "leaks" in connection with stories about the secret bombing of Cambodia. Throughout the time of its Watergate exposés, the *Post* was scolded, harassed, and accused of political motivation. Renewals of licenses of *Post*-owned broadcasting stations in Florida were challenged.

Subpoenas continued to be issued against newsmen in 1973, and there were some jail terms for refusal to divulge sources. But there was also a movement to shield reporters from the subpoena threat. Early in the year, both houses of Congress were considering such legislation, as were several state legislatures. Three states—North Dakota, Tennessee, and Nebraska—actually passed shield laws. A Gallup poll showed wide public interest and support. As the year wore on, however, the momentum slowed, and the likelihood of a new federal statute affecting reporters' privileges waned.

Toward the end of 1973, interest revived in the wake of Vice President Spiro Agnew's attempt to force newsmen to reveal the sources of leaks relating to his investigation by the federal Department of Justice. By this time, a possible formula for a shield law had emerged. It would guarantee absolute privilege for reporters before grand juries and in legislative investigations, whether state or congressional. It would give qualified privilege when cases reached the courtroom, the qualifiers being these: Does the court believe the reporter has relevant testimony to give? Have all other means to find that evidence been exhausted? Does the court hold that there is compelling, overriding public interest to be served by questioning newsmen?

National News Council. A major development of 1973 in American journalism was the establishment of the National News Council, a body created to investigate complaints against the media, to promote fair and accurate reporting, and to defend freedom of the press against public and governmental pressures. Its 15 members were named in May. At the start, the objects of the council's scrutiny were the national media—networks, wire services, newsmagazines, syndicated services, and newspapers that circulate nationally. Its powers were limited to those of investigation and publicity.

Reaction to the naming of the council was mixed. Some organizations, sensing an intrusion by a quasi-official body, announced that they would not cooperate. These included the New York *Times,* the magazine *Time,* NBC, and others.

Elsewhere, the idea was growing. Britain has had its Royal Commission on the Press for several years. Three Canadian provinces have press councils. Sweden has a press ombudsman. In the United States, Minnesota has a regional council, and, in 1973, a local council was formed in Riverside, Calif.

Newspaper Acquisitions. During the year, Capital Cities Broadcasting Corp. bought the Fort Worth *Star Telegram* for a sum of between $70 million and $80 million. Ridder Publications took over the Wichita (Kans.) *Eagle and Beacon* for $40 million. The Gannett group added dailies in Springfield, Mo., and Muskogee, Okla., while selling its Hartford *Times* to the New Haven *Register.* The Booth Newspapers, a Michigan chain, bought *Parade,* a Sunday supplement. The Montreal *Star* merged into FP Publications, owners of the Ottawa *Journal,* Toronto *Globe and Mail,* and Winnipeg *Free Press.*

Signals of Prosperity. Ad linage in 1973 was running between 8% and 9% higher than the year before, with annual gross advertising revenues at about the $7.2 billion mark. Net earnings showed dramatic increases, partly reflecting inflation, but in some cases marking recoveries from soft spots in previous years. During the first half of 1973, the Times Mirror Company (Los Angeles) reported earnings nearly double those recorded a year earlier. The New York *Times* was not far behind.

Total U. S. newspaper circulation, at 62,510,242 in 1973, had increased by 300,000—the largest one-year gain since 1960. Canadian circulation was 4,780,385, up 340,000 for the year. The number of U. S. dailies increased from 1,749 in 1972 to 1,761 in 1973.

Newsprint Shortage. Difficulties emerged during the year with the supply of newsprint. Even at mill capacity there was a lack as demand was increasing. Many mills, chiefly in Canada, were souring on newsprint, due to low profits and pollution controls. In addition, there were strikes in newsprint mills and on Canadian railroads. Some papers ran out of paper, and a black market appeared.

Deaths in Journalism. John N. Heiskell died in 1973 at the age of 100. He had been editor of the Arkansas *Gazette* of Little Rock since 1902. Death also came to editor and columnist David Lawrence; to Frederick S. Beebe, chairman of the board of the Washington *Post;* to Norman Chandler, retired publisher of the Los Angeles *Times;* and to the famed sports columnist Jimmy Cannon.

RICHARD T. BAKER, *Columbia University*

PUERTO RICO

In 1973, Puerto Rico installed its youngest governor, 36-year-old Rafael Hernandez Colón, and mourned the death of one of its most honored residents, 96-year-old Pablo Casals.

Political Affairs. Governor Hernandez was inaugurated on Jan. 2, 1973. He had been president of the Senate during the preceding administration of Luis Ferré, and, before that, secretary of justice under Gov. Roberto Sanchez Vilella. With Hernandez' accession, the Popular Democratic party, which had gathered 51% of the votes in the 1972 election, returned to power, replacing Ferré's New Progressive party.

Three major projected moves by the government in the area of economic development stirred much political debate. These included a proposal for government purchase of the Puerto Rico Telephone Company, a subsidiary of ITT; the proposed purchase of an unnamed shipping company to give Puerto Rico a merchant marine; and the planned construction of a "superport" for the world's largest tankers, possibly on Mona Island between Puerto Rico and the Dominican Republic, to help Puerto Rico's petrochemical industry.

Economic Growth. The island's net income was $5.3 billion in fiscal 1973, indicating a rise of 6.6% (adjusted for inflation) over that of the preceding year. This rate of growth, down from 7% in 1972, was the lowest in six years.

Death of Casals. Pablo Casals died on Oct. 22, 1973. The world-famous Spanish cellist was the son of a Puerto Rican mother and left a Puerto Rican widow. He had moved to the island from Prades, France, in 1956, at the age of 79. Puerto Ricans came to be grateful not only for his presence among them but also for the annual music festival that bore his name, for his help in establishing a conservatory and a symphony orchestra, and for other contributions to the island's cultural life. (See also OBITUARIES.)

Status of Puerto Rico. In October the United Nations, which had previously been asked by advocates of independence to declare the island a colony of the United States, voted that Puerto Rico, which has long been self-governing in internal affairs, was not a colony and that the United States would not be required to report on it as such to the UN.

The governor appointed an ad hoc advisory committee of seven members, all Popular Democrats, to work with a similar committee to be appointed by the President of the United States on possible modifications of the political relations between the commonwealth and the United States. The executive chairman of the Puerto Rican group was Luis Muñoz Marín, former governor and the founder of the Popular Democratic party.

Student Strike. The University of Puerto Rico was closed from October 15 to November 12, as a result of a strike by its students, who demanded a voice in the management of university affairs. The strike ended when a committee was appointed to work out a compromise. The Inter-American University in San Germín briefly suspended classes for similar reasons, and the students of the Catholic University in Ponce staged a two-day sympathy strike.

EARL PARKER HANSON
*Former Consultant, Department of State
Commonwealth of Puerto Rico*

PULITZER PRIZES. See PRIZES AND AWARDS.

QUEBEC

The principal events of 1973 in Quebec were the reelection of Premier Robert Bourassa's Liberal government by a stunning majority, reverberating revelations concerning the Laporte affair, and the Indian protest over the James Bay project.

Provincial Election. Just when rumors of an upcoming election were circulating in September, the respected minister of social affairs, Claude Castonguay, announced his decision not to run again. A progressive, he was chiefly responsible for the program of social reform pursued in 1973: a new schedule of family allowances, reform of social assistance and the pension system, and citizen participation in hospital administration.

The campaign was short. There was frequent recourse to anti-Communist propaganda against the separatist Parti Québécois (PQ), which for five years has advocated the independence of Quebec in the framework of a social democratic program. The Liberal party declared itself for the preservation of democratic institutions and against the possible installation of a socialist regime. The ardently federalist Liberals won an unexpectedly overwhelming victory on October 29, taking 102 of the 110 Assembly seats (compared with 72 seats in the preceding election). The increase in the Liberal vote, from 45% to 55%, stemmed largely from the collapse of the Union Nationale, the nationalist, conservative party in decline since 1968, and of the right-wing Créditiste party. By violently denouncing the PQ, the leaders of these two parties provoked greater support for the Liberals, who proclaimed themselves more unconditionally federalist than ever.

The Union Nationale failed to retain a single one of the 17 seats they won in 1970. The Créditistes saved only two of the 12 seats they previously held. And so the PQ became the only official opposition party with but six seats. The PQ nonetheless received 30% of the vote, compared with 24% in

─────── PUERTO RICO • Information Highlights ───────

Area: 3,435 square miles (8,897 sq km).
Population (1970 census): 2,712,033. *Density:* 790 per sq mi.
Chief Cities (1970 census): San Juan, the capital, 452,749; Bayamón, 147,552; Ponce, 128,233; Carolina, 94,271; Mayagüez, 68,872; Caguas, 63,215; Guaynabo, 55,310.
Government (1973): *Chief Officers*—governor, Rafael Hernandez Colón (Popular Democratic party); secy. of state, Victor Pons, Jr. (PDP); atty. gen., Pedro Perez Pimentel (PDP); treas., Salvador Casellas (PDP); supt. of public instruction, Ramón A. Cruz; chief justice, Francisco de Jesús Schuck. *Legislature*—Senate, 27 members; House of Representatives, 51 members.
Education (1972): *Enrollment*—public elementary and secondary schools, 697,410 pupils, 23,642 teachers; nonpublic schools (1972), 85,094 pupils; colleges and universities (fall 1972), 64,704 students.
Commonwealth Finances (fiscal year 1972): *Revenues*, $1,143,-200,000. *Expenditures*, $1,607,600,000. *State debt*, $671,-000,000 (June 30, 1972).
Personal Income (1972): $4,824,000,000; per capita, $1,713.
Public Assistance (1972): $103,180,000. *Average monthly payments* (Dec. 1972)—old-age assistance, $18.35; aid to families with dependent children, $46.14.
Labor Force: *Nonagricultural wage and salary earners* (1972), 763,000. *Annual employment* (1972)—manufacturing, 149,-000; trade, 144,000; government, 138,000; services, 133,000. *Insured unemployed* (Sept. 1973)—61,300 (13.1%).
Chief Crops—Sugarcane, coffee.
Mining (1970): *Production value,* $67,040,000. *Chief minerals* —Cement, $27,753,000; sand and gravel, $23,319,000; stone, $13,600,000; lime, $1,505,000.
Transportation: *Roads* (1972), 3,800 miles (6,116 km); *motor vehicles* (1972), 674,051.
Communications: *Telephones* (1972), 369,882; *television stations* (1971), 10; *radio stations* (1971), 70; *newspapers* (1971), 3 (daily circulation, 246,000).

1970. This means that 38% of Quebec's French-speaking citizens voted for the PQ. And although the combined opposition gained 45% of the vote (30% PQ, 10% Créditistes, 5% Union Nationale), it is represented in the Quebec National Assembly by only eight deputies.

The Laporte Affair. An inquiry into organized crime caused anxiety among Liberal deputies when a millionaire who had been under suspicion of illegal activities declared that he had contributed in 1970 to Liberal party coffers. Then, in July, when Deputy Robert Burns of the Parti Québécois established that links existed in 1969 between Pierre Laporte, Liberal minister of labor assassinated in 1970 by the Quebec Liberation Front, and underworld leaders in Montreal, the situation became explosive. The Assembly session was ended abruptly, not to resume until three months later, after the October election. In addition, the police investigation that uncovered links between the underworld and former Montreal police director J. J. Saulnier caused considerable concern at the justice ministry.

James Bay Project. The huge hydroelectric project at James Bay was stopped on November 15 by a court decision obtained by the 6,000 Indians and Eskimos of the region. A subsequent decision of the Quebec court of appeal set this injunction aside, and work was resumed. But the government was obliged to negotiate with the residents of the territory and to offer them significant financial compensation.

The Bourassa Administration. In 1973, the Que-

QUEBEC PREMIER Robert Bourassa votes in the October provincial elections. Bourassa's Liberal party overwhelmed separatist René Lévesque's Parti Québécois.

UPI

QUEBEC • Information Highlights

Area: 594,860 square miles (1,540,669 sq km).
Population (1972 est.): 6,058,000.
Chief Cities (1971 census): Quebec, the capital (186,088); Montreal (1,214,352); Laval (228,010); Verdun (74,718).
Government: *Chief Officers* (1973)—lt. gov., Hugues Lapointe; premier, Robert Bourassa (Liberal); min. of social affairs, Claude Forget (L); min. of justice, Jérôme Choquette (L); min. of finances, Raymond Garneau (L); min. of educ., François Cloutier (L); chief justice, Lucien Tremblay. *Legislature*—National Assembly: 110 members (102 Liberal, 6 Parti Québécois, 2 Créditistes).
Education: *School enrollment* (1969–70)—public elementary and secondary, 1,590,112 pupils (70,700 teachers); private schools, 51,700 pupils (3,500 teachers); Indian (federal) schools, 4,402 pupils (188 teachers); college and university, 66,830 students. *Public school expenditures* (1970 est.)—$1,349,615,000.
Public Finance (fiscal year 1973 est.): *Revenues*, $4,916,500,000 (sales tax, $1,224,600,000; income tax, $1,688,600,000; federal funds, $1,276,500,000). *Expenditures*, $5,228,900,000 (education, $1,451,800,000; health and social welfare, $2,080,700,000; transport and communications, $527,300,000).
Personal Income (1971 est.): $18,244,000,000; average annual income per person, $3,027.
Social Welfare (fiscal year 1973 est.): $720,000,000 (dependents and unemployed, $416,900,000).
Manufacturing (1969): Value added by manufacture, $5,672,740,000 (food and beverages, $773,841,000; paper and allied industries, $574,836,000; transportation equipment, $437,056,000; primary metals, $411,246,000.
Agriculture (1972 est.): *Cash farm income* (exclusive of government payments), $766,633,000 (livestock and products, $632,665,000; crops, $64,099,000). *Chief crops* (cash receipts)—vegetables, $22,604,000 (ranks 2d among the provinces); potatoes, $12,126,000 (ranks 3d); fruits, $9,978,000 (ranks 3d); tobacco, $8,171,000 (ranks 2d).
Mining (1973 est.): *Production value*, $767,303,000. *Chief minerals*—copper, $174,188,000 (ranks 3d among the provinces); asbestos, $165,400,000 (ranks 1st); iron ore, $99,253,000 (ranks 2d); cement, $63,036,000 (ranks 2d).
Forest Products (1972): Lumber, 2,162,600,000 board feet.
Fisheries (1972): Commercial catch, 176,210,000 pounds ($10,436,000). *Leading species*—cod, lobster, redfish.
Transportation: *Roads* (1970), 75,511 miles (121,520 km); *motor vehicles* (1970), 2,115,126; *railroads* (1971), 5,329 track miles (8,576 km); *licensed airports* (1971 est.), 73.
Communications: *Telephones* (1970), 2,616,323; *television stations* (1972), 59; *radio stations* (1972), 64; *daily newspapers* (1972), 15.
(All monetary figures given in Canadian dollars.)

---

bec government undertook few new measures, hesitating to act on several expected reforms. The government remained silent in the face of organized demands for the abolition of Law 63, which facilitates the anglicization of the French-speaking majority. The reform of work laws and rent laws was postponed. Unsatisfied were demands for an environmental protection policy and also for the creation of state-subsidized day-care centers.

As for labor relations, the sentencing to jail for contempt in 1972 of the leaders of the three unions in the Common Front, a confederation of public service employees, did not solve basic problems. After their release in September, they seemed more united and determined to fight the administration's economic and political programs. Their exertions seem to have prevented the premier from imposing Bill 89, which threatened the suppression of the right to strike by public employees.

The Economy. According to Guy St. Pierre, minister of industry and commerce, Quebec had its best year economically in 25 years, with the province's economic growth increasing by about 7.5% over 1972 and personal income rising by 14%. Government sources said that four times more jobs were created in 1973 than in 1972. Private and public investments were up 12.8%. At the same time, however, the cost of living rose at the annual rate of 10%, and the rate of unemployment stood at approximately 8%.

ROBERT COMEAU
Université du Québec à Montréal

RADIO. See TELEVISION AND RADIO.
RAILROADS. See TRANSPORTATION.

CHRISTIAN STEINER, FOR LONDON RECORDS

Zubin Mehta (above) *conducted a new recording of Puccini's* Turandot, *with an all-star cast headed by Dame Joan Sutherland.*

PHOTO COURTESY OF LONDON RECORDS

recordings

The recording industry partially emerged from its fog of confusion in 1973. The number of new classical releases rose, popular records were remarkable for their diversity, and the renewed interest in jazz records continued. In addition, there were important developments in audio equipment.

CLASSICAL RECORDS

Cautious optimism continued to prevail in the classical corner of the record industry in 1973. There seemed to be a tacit realization among the major recording companies that although no great fortunes were to be made with the classics, they were vital for the industry's well-being and deserved a little more encouragement than they had been receiving in the past.

Columbia and RCA. Both Columbia and RCA, the traditional leaders in the U.S. record industry, indicated in the fall of 1973 that they were revitalizing their classical departments. Since the late 1960's both classical departments had been concerned largely with repackaging existing material into extensive series of "Greatest Hits" by various well-known composers. The market for such a spoon-feeding operation appeared to have been saturated after some five years of success.

In addition to expanding their classical roster with a number of new young artists, Columbia embarked on two long-term projects of considerable importance. The company planned to make available on discs a representative survey of music by black composers. It also reactivated its dormant Modern Music Series, concentrating on distinguished American composers, such as Elliott Carter, Aaron Copland, Leon Kirchner, and George Crumb.

After about three years during which the production of new classical records came virtually to a standstill, RCA embarked in 1973 upon a schedule of recording that was to consist of chamber music, featuring the Guarneri and Cleveland quartets; opera, including the first complete recording of

SELECTED CLASSICAL RELEASES IN 1973

BARTÓK, *Concerto for Orchestra:* New York Philharmonic, Pierre Boulez, conductor (Columbia)

BEETHOVEN, *Piano Concertos* (complete): Vladimir Ashkenazy, piano; Chicago Symphony Orchestra, Georg Solti, conductor (London, 4 discs)

BIZET, *Carmen:* Marilyn Horne, James McCracken, and other singers; Metropolitan Opera Orchestra, Leonard Bernstein, conductor (Deutsche Grammophon, 3 discs)

BOULEZ, *Piano Sonatas Nos. 1 & 3:* Charles Rosen, piano (Columbia)

GERSHWIN, *Piano Music:* William Bolcom, piano (Nonesuch)

PFITZNER, *Palestrina:* Nicolai Gedda, Dietrich Fischer-Dieskau, Hermann Prey, Helen Donath, and other singers; Sinfonieorchester des Bayerischen Rundfunks, Rafael Kubelik, conductor (Deutsche Grammophon, 4 discs)

PROKOFIEV, *Symphonies* (complete): Orchestre National de l'O.R.T.F., Jean Martinon, conductor (Vox, 6 discs)

PUCCINI, *La Boheme:* Mirella Freni, Luciano Pavarotti, and other singers, London Philharmonic Orchestra, Herbert von Karajan, conductor (London, 2 discs)

PUCCINI, *Turandot:* Joan Sutherland, Luciano Pavarotti, Montserrat Caballé, and other singers; London Philharmonic Orchestra, Zubin Mehta, conductor (London, 3 discs)

RACHMANINOFF, *Piano Concerto No. 2:* Arthur Rubinstein, piano; Philharmonic Orchestra, Eugene Ormandy, conductor (RCA)

RAMEAU, *Castor et Pollux:* Soloists; Concentus Musicus, Nikolaus Harnoncourt, conductor (Telefunken, 4 discs)

ROCHBERG, *String Quartet No. 3:* Concord String Quartet (Nonesuch)

ROSSINI, *William Tell:* Montserrat Caballé, Nicolai Gedda, Gabriel Bacquier, and other singers; Royal Philharmonic Orchestra, Lamberto Gardelli, conductor (Angel, 5 discs)

SHOSTAKOVICH, *Symphony No. 15:* Philadelphia Orchestra, Eugene Ormandy, conductor (RCA)

VERDI, *Giovanna d'Arco:* Montserrat Caballé, Placido Domingo, and other singers; London Symphony Orchestra, James Levine, conductor (Angel, 3 discs)

WAGNER, *Parsifal:* Christa Ludwig, René Kollo, and other singers; Vienna Philharmonic Orchestra, Georg Solti, conductor (London, 5 discs)

WAGNER, *The Ring of the Nibelungs,* Birgit Nilsson, Wolfgang Windgassen, and other singers; Bayreuth Festival Orchestra, Karl Böhm, conductor (Philips, 16 discs)

Verdi's *I vespri siciliani;* piano music, with soloists Van Cliburn, Artur Rubinstein, and Peter Serkin; and orchestral music, with the Philadelphia Orchestra under Eugene Ormandy. In addition, RCA dipped into its extensive files of historical recordings to release 15 discs documenting the entire recorded work of Sergei Rachmaninoff.

Other Labels. The major European companies —including Angel, Deutsche Grammophon, London, and Philips—continued to supply collectors with a plethora of new performances by such magnetic superstars as Karajan, Previn, Sutherland, Nilsson, Sills, Fischer-Dieskau, Richter, Arrau, and others. Record buyers primarily interested in repertory— either in the current craze for off-beat 19th century works or in works by contemporary composers— turned to the smaller independent companies that specialize in such out-of-the-way fare, such as Vox, Nonesuch, Genesis, Musical Heritage, Vanguard, CRI, Desto, and Orion.

Quadraphonic Recordings. The success of quadraphonics was still a major question in 1973, but the concept seemed to be gathering new converts. Accordingly, Columbia and RCA expanded their activities in the field. Other companies, including Nonesuch, Connoisseur Society, and Vanguard, either initiated or continued programs in quad recording.

Columbia's "Surround Sound" disc of Bartók's Concerto for Orchestra, conducted by Pierre Boulez, proved to be the most radical deployment yet of quad effects. In this recording, the listener is put directly into the center of the orchestra.

PETER G. DAVIS
Recordings Editor, "The New York Times"

POPULAR RECORDS

Popular music recorded in 1973 was remarkable only in its diversity, which most observers thought resulted not from increasingly catholic taste but from the failure of any obvious leader to emerge and fire up the next trend. It was a year as much reflective as disorganized. The audience, although spread thinner, was broader. Country music and even jazz were factors in the "pop" market, and the blues continued to win friends. It was a year in which fad and fashion seemed to be off on vacation, but the betting was that they would be back.

One of the most successful musical revues of 1973, *Lemmings* (a production of the satirical magazine *National Lampoon*), indirectly ridiculed the audience and directly savaged the trend-fomenting recording stars of previous years, including the Rolling Stones, James Taylor, Joe Cocker, and Joan Baez. In fact, the revue, which was recorded, postulated that these stampedes were ultimately anti-life trips. It ended with a sketch featuring a rock group called Megadeath, which plays music advertised as being so loud it kills its listeners.

Scandal. On May 29, Columbia Records fired its president, Clive Davis, and filed a civil suit, charging him with illegally spending some $94,000 in corporate funds. This occurred in the midst of investigations of a new "payola" scandal in the industry, reputedly involving drugs and prostitutes; but Columbia Records denied that this was connected with its dismissal of Davis.

"Visual" Performers. On the creative side of the industry, many performers were emphasizing the visual in their acts, making it hard to capture their essence on sound recordings. "Glitter Rock," featuring the bizarre stage acts of David Bowie, Alice

REPRISE RECORDS

FRANK SINATRA (above) *ended a short-lived retirement with the making of the new album* Ol' Blue Eyes is Back. *English singer-composer Donovan's new release was* Cosmic Wheels.

EPIC RECORDS

Cooper, and others hit a peak in 1973 and then faded without leaving much impression on the record industry. Bette Midler, calling herself "the Divine Miss M," made a noisy recording debut. Although her act relies heavily upon camp-nostalgia trappings, listeners as well as lookers paid attention, but a line of detractors also quickly formed.

New Hits and Old Regulars. Gilbert O'Sullivan started the year with a hit. His catchy *Alone Again, Naturally* is perhaps the prototype of the commercial single of the 1970's thus far. But then, *Also Sprach Zarathustra* and *Dueling Banjos* were equally commercial. *Also Sprach Zarathustra* is Eumir Deodata's electric rock version of Richard Strauss' tone poem. *Dueling Banjos* is a snippet from the sound-track of one of the year's most popular films, *Deliverance,* and featured only two musicians— Eric Weissberg on the banjo and Steve Mandell on the guitar. Bob Dylan, almost silent in 1972, was an accompanying musician on a few albums in 1973, ap-

SELECTED POPULAR RELEASES IN 1973

BEACH BOYS, *Holland* (Brother MS 2118)
BEE GEES, *Life in a Tin Can* (RSO SO 870)
ROY BUCHANAN, *Second Album* (Polydor PD 5046)
PAUL BUTTERFIELD, *Better Days* (Bearsville BR 2119)
JOE COCKER, *Joe Cocker* (A & M SP 4568)
JUDY COLLINS, *True Stories and Other Dreams* (Elektra EKS 75053)
DONOVAN, *Cosmic Wheels* (Epic KE 32156)
J. GIELS BAND, *Bloodshot* (Atlantic SD 7260)
WAYLON JENNINGS, *Honky Tonk Heroes* (RCA APL1-0240)
GORDON LIGHTFOOT, *Old Dan's Records* (Reprise MS 2116)
PAUL McCARTNEY AND WINGS, *Red Rose Speedway* (Apple SMAL-3409)
DON McLEAN, *Don McLean* (United Artists UAS 5651)
JONI MITCHELL, *For the Roses* (Asylum SD 5057)
MOODY BLUES, *Seventh Sojourn* (Threshold THS 7)
NILSSON, *A Little Touch of Schmilsson in the Night* (RCA APL1-0097)
NITTY GRITTY DIRT BAND, *Will the Circle Be Unbroken* (United Artists UAS 9801)
PROCOL HARUM, *Grand Hotel* (Chrysalis CHR 1037)
ROLLING STONES, *Goat's Head Soup* (Rolling Stones COC 5910)
SIEGEL-SCHWALL BAND, *Sleepy Hollow* (Wooden Nickel WNS 1010)
PAUL SIMON, *There Goes Rhymin' Simon* (Columbia KC 32280)
STEELEYE SPAN, *Parcel of Rogues* (Chrysalis CHR 1046)
JOHN STEWART, *Cannons in the Rain* (RCA LSP-4827)
JERRY JEFF WALKER, *Jerry Jeff Walker* (Decca DL 7 5384)

peared in the film *Pat Garrett and Billy the Kid* and dominated its sound-track album, and, in the autumn, recorded the single hit *Knocking on Heaven's Door.*

The Rolling Stones delivered a fine new album, *Goat's Head Soup.* Joni Mitchell's 1973 album, *For the Roses,* was even more fearlessly introspective than her previous efforts. In British folk-rock, the Pentagle disbanded, but the up-and-coming Steeleye Span released *Parcel of Rogues,* which some critics felt was the best album of its kind ever made. The original Byrds regrouped, at least long enough to record one album.

NOEL COPPAGE
Contributing Editor, "Stereo Review"

JAZZ RECORDS

During 1973 there was a proliferation of two-disc reissue jazz albums, mostly in the form of "two-fers"—two discs for the usual price of one—and a continuing renewal of interest in live jazz performances. This posed the old dilemma of the chicken and the egg. Which came first? Did the reissue programs carried out by most of the independent record companies that have extensive jazz catalogues stimulate this new interest? Or did the new public response inspire the record companies to pay more attention to jazz than they had in previous years? Actually, both events seem to have developed simultaneously and independently.

Reissue Program. The reissue program made immediately available an extensive but compact history of jazz since World War II. This provided golden opportunities for jazz enthusiasts to fill in their collections and offered a provocative introduction to younger listeners. But, of necessity, these reissues dealt with well-established musicians. Some of them, such as John Coltrane, are now dead. Others, such as the Modern Jazz Quartet and Stan Getz, had done well even in the lean years that jazz went through in the 1960's.

Live Performances. The response to live jazz performances was reflected in the fact that audiences were drawn to lesser-known musicians whose work was not included in reissues, although they did have an occasional record to support them. These included Don Cherry and the Jazz Composers Orchestra, Gato Barbieri, guitarists Herb Ellis and Joe Pass, the Baron Von Ohlen Quartet, Johnny Guarnieri, Dick Wellstood, and Dave McKenna.

One of the clearest signs that jazz had returned to a situation in which a recording could once again quickly establish a new group was a disc called *Supersax Plays Bird,* on which an ensemble built around five saxophones played harmonized arrangements of some of Charlie Parker's celebrated alto saxophone solos. As a result of this record, Supersax, as the group is called, was suddenly in demand at the Monterey Jazz Festival and took off from California for a coast-to-coast tour.

DUKE ELLINGTON received an honorary doctor of music degree at Columbia University, and led his orchestra at Yale.
FANTASY RECORDS

FANTASY RECORDS

YALE CONCERT
DUKE ELLINGTON AND HIS ORCHESTRA

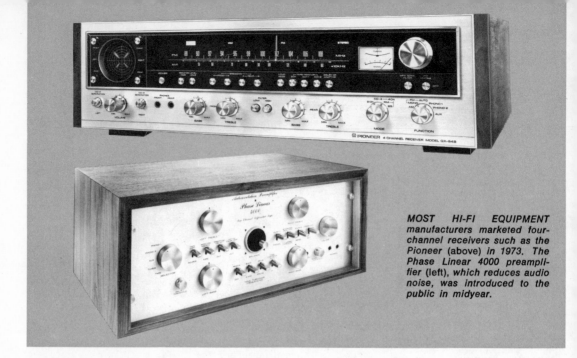

MOST HI-FI EQUIPMENT manufacturers marketed four-channel receivers such as the Pioneer (above) in 1973. The Phase Linear 4000 preamplifier (left), which reduces audio noise, was introduced to the public in midyear.

Release of Held-Up Series. In 1973 a number of Duke Ellington records that had been locked up in various vaults during the 1960's were finally released. They included *The Great Paris Concert* (recorded in 1963), *The Yale Concert* (1968), and *Latin American Suite* (1968). The year's Ellingtonia was also enhanced by an invaluable collection of the recordings made with the band by the greatest of the Ellington singers, Ivie Anderson.

Another locked-up series of recordings began to appear during 1973 when a newly formed company, Onyx, started issuing recordings made privately in Harlem and on 52d Street in New York City during the recording strike of 1942–44. The series, which documents the early years of be-bop, started off with a superb collection of performances by the late Art Tatum, *God Is in the House*. This was followed by an excellent collection of recordings of small groups, *52nd St.*, Vol. 1, and a set featuring Don Byas, *Midnight at Minton's*.

JOHN S. WILSON
"The New York Times" and
"High Fidelity" Magazine

AUDIO EQUIPMENT AND TECHNIQUES

Receivers that can process all available types of four-channel program material were put on the market in 1973. Also, two new types of loudspeaker design and a new noise-reduction system were developed during the year.

Four-Channel Stereo. By the end of 1973 most manufacturers of high-fidelity components were offering four-channel receivers with built-in facilities to process all available types of four-channel program material. These program sources include discrete four-channel recordings from open-reel tape and eight-track tape cartridges, material matrixed via the CBS-SQ and Sansui-QS systems, and the multiplexed phonograph records produced with the RCA-JVC CD-4 system.

Such "do everything" receivers were inevitable outgrowths of four-channel developments. But the SQ and QS sections of the products marketed in 1973 were relatively primitive, incorporating few if any of the separation enhancement techniques developed for the two systems in the recent past. In addition, the CD-4 facilities in these products left the user's choice of suitable associated equipment—phonograph cartridges, turntables, and connecting cables—somewhat up in the air. Still, the consensus of the manufacturers was that equipment that could be advertised as capable of handling any program material—well or indifferently—was a solution to the problem of a confused market.

Sansui and Lafayette did not adopt this strategy. Sansui, developer of the QS-system, quietly introduced a new Vario-Matrix separation-enhancement circuitry in several four-channel receivers, the newest being the QRX-5500. Sansui receivers also

---

SELECTED JAZZ RELEASES IN 1973

GATO BARBIERI, *Bolivia* (Flying Dutchman 10158)
GATO BARBIERI, *Chapter One: Latin America* (Impulse 9248)
COUNT BASIE, *Basic Basie* (BASF 25111)
DON BYAS, *Midnight at Minton's* (Onyx 208)
DON CHERRY AND THE JAZZ COMPOSERS ORCHESTRA, *Relativity Suite* (JCOA 1006)
DUKE ELLINGTON, *Duke Ellington Presents Ivie Anderson* (Columbia KG 32064)
DUKE ELLINGTON, *The Great Paris Concert* (Atlantic 2-304)
DUKE ELLINGTON, *Latin American Suite* (Fantasy 8419)
DUKE ELLINGTON, *Togo Brava Suite* (United Artists UXS 92)
DUKE ELLINGTON, *The Yale Concert* (Fantasy 9433)
HERB ELLIS AND JOE PASS, *Jazz/Concord* (Concord Jazz 1)
JOHNNY GUARNIERI, *Johnny Guarnieri Plays Harry Warren* (Jim Taylor 102)
JIM HALL–RON CARTER, *Alone Together* (Milestone 9045)
DAVE McKENNA, *Cookin' at Michael's Pub* (Halcyon 108)
DAVE McKENNA, *Solo Piano* (Chiaroscuro 119)
BUD POWELL, *Broadcast Performances,* Vol. 1 (ESP BUD 1)
JIMMY RANEY, *Strings and Swings* (Muse 5004)
SUPERSAX, *Supersax Plays Bird* (Capital ST 11177)
ART TATUM, *God Is in the House* (Onyx 205)
BARON VON OHLEN QUARTET, *The Baron* (Creative World 3001)
DICK WELLSTOOD, *Dick Wellstood and His Hot Potatoes* (Seeds 3)
DICK WELLSTOOD, *Alone* (Jazzology 73)
Various small groups, *52nd St.,* Vol. 1 (Onyx 203)

decode SQ material, but lack built-in CD-4 demodulators. Lafayette, long an advocate of the CBS-SQ system, announced late in 1973 the availability of several components with SQ full-logic variable-blend decoding. The new variable-blend technique was said to be an improvement upon the compromised front-to-back separation of the SQ matrix. The Lafayette equipment also offers unenhanced decoding for QS material, but has no CD-4 facilities.

Speaker Systems. Practical new principles for loudspeaker design are rare, but in 1973 the world was presented with two. One was developed by inventor Oskar Heil and manufactured by ESS. The other was proposed by researcher Lincoln Walsh and perfected by the Ohm Corporation.

The Heil principle employs a limp polyethylene diaphragm that is gathered into folds and placed between two massive permanent magnets. When an audio signal is sent to conductive strips on each side of each fold, the diaphragm performs what is called a "meandering" motion—alternate folds expel or inhale air. This produces sound-pressure waves at both sides of the diaphragm. The advantages are said to be low-moving mass for a given acoustical output, high electroacoustical efficiency, a diaphragm relatively free of resonances throughout its operating frequency range, and essentially non-directional acoustic radiation in the horizontal plane. In 1973 this principle was marketed only in a mid-range/tweeter device.

The Walsh principle utilizes a full-range driver that appears conventional in construction. However, the cone does not move as a unitized piston at most frequencies. Instead, it acts as a medium in which flexing motions are propagated, traveling from the apex to the edge in concentric waveforms. The successive waves, passing down the cone's surface, transfer energy to the surrounding air, producing the acoustical output. The advantages of the Walsh principle are said to be essentially non-directional radiation and in-phase propagation of sound in a series of coherent cylindrical wavefronts. Two models were offered in 1973, the Ohm A and the smaller Ohm F. Both systems use drivers that radiate from their rear-cone surfaces and are mounted on large enclosures that assist in developing low-frequency output.

Noise Reduction System. In mid-1973 the Phase Linear Corporation introduced an audio noise reduction system modeled on a signal recovery technique formerly confined to rather specialized scientific applications. According to the manufacturer, the basic operation of this Autocorrelator is controlled by the presence or absence of signals (music) that are above the continuous noise level of the program. In the presence of such signals, the correlator assumes the existence of higher musical harmonics, which may be partly or wholly masked by high-frequency noise. It then passes only the small segments of the audio-frequency band corresponding to the predictable frequencies at which the harmonics would be found. All other frequencies above 2,000 Hz are sharply attenuated, thereby effecting a significant reduction of audible noise.

The Autocorrelator was the first consumer noise-reduction system capable of processing existing recordings without affecting the information content. It was incorporated in the new Phase Linear 4000 stereo preamplifier.

RALPH W. HODGES
Associate Technical Editor, "Stereo Review"

REFUGEES

At the end of October 1973, there were about 10.4 million refugees in Asia, 1.9 million in the Middle East, 1.3 million in Africa, 1.4 million in the Western Hemisphere, and 715,000 in Europe. The grand total of about 16 million refugees showed little change from 1972, although there were shifts in the composition of the world refugee population.

Asia. The 1 million internal refugees in Pakistan created by the fighting between India and Pakistan were resettled in 1973, but there were 1.5 million new refugees in Cambodia as a result of the intense fighting there. Toward the end of the year, the United Nations High Commissioner for Refugees (UNHCR) and the governments of India, Pakistan, and Bangladesh were engaged in the vast and difficult airlift resettlement of Pakistani prisoners of war in India, Bengalis in Pakistan, and non-Bengalis in Bangladesh. This important sequel to the fighting involved more than 200,000 persons.

Middle East. The new outbreak of fighting between Israel and the Arab countries affected the Syrian civilian population in the Golan Heights. However, there was no estimate as to the number of villagers driven from their homes by the fighting.

Africa. There were three major refugee movements in Africa during 1973. Nearly 27,000 Ugandan Asians holding British passports were moved from Uganda to England as a result of Ugandan government expulsion orders. In addition, the government expelled several thousand Asians whose Ugandan citizenship was either canceled or questioned, and they therefore became stateless. The UNHCR found transit hospitality centers and subsequently permanent resettlement for about 3,600 refugees from Uganda.

Repatriation of 325,000 refugees from the southern Sudan was completed in 1973. These refugees returned to their homeland and began to rebuild their homes, farms, and schools. The successful repatriation of this large number of people into their former homeland, which had been destroyed during the fighting, has been described as a miracle. This success was due to the generous and imaginative cooperation of private agencies in many countries, the government of Sudan, and government agencies working through the office of the UNHCR.

Refugees from Burundi totaled approximately 85,000 in 1973. They have settled in Tanzania (4,000), in Zaire (35,000), and in Rwanda (10,000). An additional result of the continuing civil tension in Burundi was the return to Zaire of some 20,000 of its citizens who had been living in Burundi. Moreover, serious tension and strife related to the Burundi uprising resulted in a flight of 5,600 refugees from Rwanda to Burundi, Uganda, and Zaire.

Western Hemisphere. A serious refugee problem developed in Chile as a result of the overthrow of the Allende government in 1973. Significant numbers of refugees from other Latin American countries had fled to Chile and had learned that the new government regarded them as unwanted persons subject to deportation. Many of them were assembled in "peace havens" in Chile for their protection and eventual resettlement.

The movement of refugees into the United States during 1973 involved the resettlement of some 1,500 stateless persons from Uganda.

R. NORRIS WILSON
United States Committee for Refugees

The Very Rev. James P. Morton (left) is installed as the seventh dean of the Episcopal Cathedral of St. John the Divine in New York City by the Right Rev. Paul Moore, Jr.

RELIGION

Developments in the major religions of the world in 1973, including trends, meetings, and principal events, are covered under the following headings: (1) General Survey; (2) Protestantism; (3) Roman Catholicism; (4) Judaism; (5) Eastern Orthodox Church; (6) Islam; and (7) Oriental Religions. A statistical table giving the membership of U. S. denominations is included.

General Survey

In 1973 there was an increasing trend toward conservatism in Christianity. Reappraisals of attempts to relate religion to modern society through liberal thought and aggressive social action led to more emphasis on the search for individual meaning and salvation and a revival of charismatic worship practices. There was also a tendency toward decentralization of religious organizations. The complexities of church-state relations deeply involved Christians, Jews, Muslims, Hindus, and Buddhists.

Conservatism. One example of conservative strength in U. S. Protestantism was the Lutheran Church—Missouri Synod, which reelected a conservative president and sought to require church leaders and members to adhere to conservative interpretations of the Bible and doctrine. Another example was the separation of conservative Presbyterians from the Presbyterian Church in the U. S., on the grounds that it was too liberal, to form the new National Presbyterian Church. Also conservative was the withdrawal by the Consultation on Church Union of a plan of union for 10 major Protestant denominations.

In Roman Catholicism, the Vatican continued to warn against theological and organizational responses to Vatican Council II that it deemed too liberal. It directed the head of the Society of Jesus to remind its members of their vow of loyalty to the pope, and it curtailed experimental forms of religious education, such as postponement of initiation into the sacrament of penance, and other activities throughout the church.

Charismatic and Evangelistic Movements. In both Protestant and Roman Catholic circles, interest in Pentecostal and other charismatic movements featuring spiritual healing and speaking in tongues continued to grow. There were gatherings in North America and Europe, including one of Roman Catholics at the University of Notre Dame, South Bend, Ind., and of Episcopalians in Dallas, Texas. Interdenominational prayer groups were formed, and Protestants participated in Christian communes.

The "Jesus movements" attracted increasing numbers of young people, causing some parents to try to counteract their influence by force. These groups and Key 73, a major interdenominational evangelical drive, made efforts to proselytize, to the dismay of some Jewish leaders. The Unification Church, a Korean-founded group, embarked on a national crusade in the United States as a step toward achieving worldwide significance.

Eastern Interests. The same spiritual and emotional needs that turned some people toward charismatic movements turned others toward various forms of Eastern religions. Many American students were attracted by the emphasis on meditation and prayer

as presented by touring gurus and other spiritual leaders. Many found appeal in Tibetan and other esoteric forms of Buddhism or in witchcraft and other forms of the occult.

Church and State. Many religious bodies were affected by political developments. Religious leaders in the United States were deeply concerned over apparent moral deterioration in the electoral process and in the conduct of some members of the executive branch of the government. Although many denominations reduced their social and political programs, they renewed emphasis on the responsibility of individual members for political participation and reform.

American Jews were disturbed by the Soviet Union's policies to restrict Soviet Jewish emigration to Israel. Congress, supporting their view, was reluctant to grant "most-favored nation" trade status to the USSR. Jews throughout the world, shocked by the Yom Kippur military attack on Israel by Egypt and Syria, gave Israel massive contributions. At the same time, Muslims everywhere expressed solidarity over the Arab-Israeli war.

In southern Asia, Muslim-Hindu differences were intensified by political tensions among India, Pakistan, and Bangladesh. The interests of native Buddhists and Hindu immigrants conflicted in Sri Lanka (Ceylon).

Status of Women. Many groups were rethinking the religious role of women. The Episcopal Church declined to ordain them to the priesthood, but a woman, Claire Randall, was elected executive secretary of the National Council of Churches. Conservative Jews granted women the right to be counted equally with men in a synagogue quorum.

J. A. MARTIN, JR.
Columbia University

Protestantism

Protestant churches in 1973 seemed to be turning away from ecumenism, social action, and other liberal positions toward a more conservative, faith-centered point of view. As many liberal, mainstream churches declined in membership, conservative and charismatic groups increased their appeal.

Conservative Trend. In several denominations, conservative forces won out in controversy with liberals. In the extremely conservative Lutheran Church—Missouri Synod, a bitter theological war between conservatives and moderates reached a climax at its July convention in New Orleans. Delegates reelected conservative president Jacob A. O. Preus and adopted his statement of faith, which required a literal interpretation of the Bible. Preus, planning to oust all professors and clergy who rejected the statement, demanded the dismissal of

U. S. CHURCH MEMBERSHIP

Religious Body	Members	Religious Body	Members
Albanian Orthodox Archdiocese in America	62,000	International Church of the Foursquare Gospel	89,215[6]
American Baptist Association	869,000	International General Assembly of Spiritualists	164,072[2]
American Baptist Churches in the U. S. A.	1,562,636	Jehovah's Witnesses	416,789
American Carpatho-Russian Orthodox Greek Catholic Churches	108,000	Jewish Congregations	5,870,000
American Lutheran Church	2,521,930	Lutheran Church in America	3,069,679
Antiochian Orthodox Christian Archdiocese of New York and all North America	100,000[1]	Lutheran Church—Missouri Synod	2,788,110
Apostolic Overcoming Holy Church of God	75,000[2]	Mennonite Church	88,947
Armenian Apostolic Church of America	125,000	Moravian Church in America, Northern Province	34,555
American Church of America, Diocese of the	300,000	National Baptist Convention, U. S. A., Inc.	5,500,000[7]
Assemblies of God	1,078,332	National Baptist Convention of America	2,668,799[2]
Baptist General Conference	108,474	National Primitive Baptist Convention, Inc.	1,645,000
Baptist Missionary Association of America	193,439	North American Old Roman Catholic Church	60,098
Buddhist Churches of America	100,000[1]	Old Order Amish Church	14,720
Bulgarian Eastern Orthodox Church	86,000	Old Roman Catholic Church (English Rite)	65,128
Christian and Missionary Alliance	127,353	Orthodox Church in America	1,000,000
Christian Church (Disciples of Christ)	1,386,374	Pentecostal Church of God of America, Inc.	115,000[8]
Christian Churches and Churches of Christ	1,036,288	Pentecostal Holiness Church, Inc.	72,696
Christian Methodist Episcopal Church	466,718[3]	Polish National Catholic Church of America	282,411[9]
Christian Reformed Church	286,094	Presbyterian Church in the United States	949,857
Church of Christ, Scientist	[4]	Primitive Baptists	72,000[10]
Church of God	75,890	Progressive National Baptist Convention, Inc.	521,692[8]
Church of God (Anderson, Ind.)	152,787	Reformed Church in America	369,951
Church of God (Cleveland, Tenn.)	287,099	Reorganized Church of Jesus Christ of Latter Day Saints	154,481
Church of God in Christ	425,000[3]	Roman Catholic Church	48,390,990
Church of God in Christ, International	501,000	Romanian Orthodox Episcopate of America	50,000
Church of Jesus Christ of Latter-day Saints	2,133,072	Russian Orthodox Church in the U. S. A., Patriarchal Parishes of the	152,973[3]
Church of the Brethren	181,183	Russian Orthodox Church Outside Russia	55,000[11]
Church of the Nazarene	394,197	Salvation Army	335,684
Churches of Christ	2,400,000[5]	Serbian Orthodox Church for the U. S. A. and Canada	65,000[8]
Congregational Christian Churches, National Association of	85,000	Seventh-day Adventists	433,906
Conservative Baptist Association of America	300,000[1]	Southern Baptist Convention	11,824,676
Cumberland Presbyterian Church	90,368	Triumph the Church and Kingdom of God in Christ	54,307
Episcopal Church	3,217,365	Ukrainian Orthodox Church in America	87,475[12]
Evangelical Covenant Church of America	68,428	Unitarian-Universalist Association	265,408[13]
Evangelical Free Church of America	70,490	United Church of Christ	1,928,674
Free Methodist Church of North America	65,040	United Free Will Baptist Church	100,000[14]
Free Will Baptists	210,000	United Methodist Church	10,509,198
Friends United Meeting	68,773	United Pentecostal Church	250,000
General Association of Regular Baptist Churches	204,357	United Presbyterian Church in the United States of America	3,013,808
General Baptists (General Association of)	65,000	Wesleyan Church	84,499[1]
Greek Orthodox Archdiocese of North and South America	1,950,000	Wisconsin Evangelical Lutheran Synod	383,263
Independent Fundamental Churches of America	139,932		

Figures are mainly for the years 1971 and 1972. [1] 1970. [2] 1956. [3] 1965. [4] Figures not reported. [5] 1968. [6] 1963. [7] 1958. [8] 1967. [9] 1960. [10] 1950. [11] 1955. [12] 1966. [13] 1969. [14] 1952. (Source: National Council of Churches of Christ in the U. S. A., *Yearbook of American and Canadian Churches 1973*.)

THE NEW MODERATOR of the United Presbyterian General Assembly is the Rev. Clinton M. Marsh (left). He is shown with his predecessor, C. Willard Heckel.

Dr. John H. Tietjen, president of Concordia Seminary (St. Louis), on heresy charges.

The Episcopal Church, at its October convention in Louisville, Ky., approved conservative Rt. Rev. John Maury Allin, bishop of Mississippi, as presiding bishop. The House of Deputies, half laymen, confirmed the House of Bishops' choice, however, only after four hours of delaying maneuvers behind closed doors. The reasons for their delay, the first such in Episcopalian history, was the deputies' fear that Allin would repudiate the church's social action programs. The majority of deputies also favored the ordination of women to the priesthood, which Allin opposed, but the ordination proposal was defeated on a technicality.

The battle between conservatives and liberals within the Presbyterian Church in the U. S. (Southern Presbyterian) ended in May in Atlanta with a split that is the first among Presbyterians since they divided into Northern and Southern branches at the time of the Civil War. More than 200 conservative congregations, claiming that other Presbyterians have abandoned a literal interpretation of the Bible, engage in social activism, and approve the ordination of women, decided to form a new denomination, the Continuing Presbyterian Church. According to Southern Presbyterian leaders, 95% of the 1 million membership remain loyal to the old church.

Ecumenism. A few Protestant denominations explored the possibilities of closer relationship. In Britain, Anglicans, Methodists, and the United Reformed Church discussed possibilities of a merger. The Roman Catholic Church and the Baptist Union accepted invitations to discuss unity with each other. The Netherlands Reformed Church and the Reformed Churches of the Netherlands met jointly and established a permanent common synod.

Generally, however, there was decline of interest in ecumenism and the organized church. In the United States one indication was the decision of the Consultation on Church Union (COCU), in Memphis in April, to put aside plans for a proposed merger of 10 major Protestant denominations into a 25-million-member church. Instead it stressed cooperation on a local level. Although the United Presbyterian Church, which had withdrawn from merger talks in 1972, rejoined in 1973, theological

observers said that church unity seemed to be farther away. Many factors contributed to the delay —upsurge of denominational loyalty, concern about denominational property and a new form of church organization, and opposition by local churches to militant social activism by church leaders.

As a parallel development in Canada, the Plan of Union, designed to unite the Anglican Church, the United Church of Canada, and the Disciples of Christ into the "Church of Christ in Canada," met vocal opposition from many Anglicans. In a similar vein, both the U. S. National Council of Churches and the World Council of Churches in Geneva had to cut staff and projects for lack of funds.

Any hopes of closer ties between Protestants and Roman Catholics received a blow when the Vatican Congregation for Doctrine, confirmed by the pope, reaffirmed the dogma of papal infallibility. Protestants universally expressed dismay that this critical doctrine, which seemed to have been softened over the years, should receive renewed emphasis. Although cooperation in many areas will continue, unity remains extremely doubtful.

Evangelism. Evangelism, like ecumenism, suffered a setback. Although many denominations supported Key 73, the evangelistic drive intended to call every person in the United States and Canada to Christ, it failed to win the overall success originally planned. There were many reasons for failure. Jewish leaders accused Key 73 of implied anti-Semitism for trying to convert Jews. Other critics said that Key 73 denied American religious pluralism or that it had overtones of political conservatism. Also, funds were lacking.

Charismatic Movement. The charismatic movement, begun in 1966, continued to grow in mainline denominations. Throughout the United States, Canada, and Europe, Roman Catholics and Protestants attended large convocations at which there were speaking in tongues, faith healing, and appeals to receive the Holy Spirit. Church observers believe that the charismatic movement is growing in appeal because many Christians are tired of the emphasis on church organization.

Gains and Losses. Protestant denominations showed both gains and losses. In the United States the largest Protestant body, the conservative Southern Baptist Convention, reported an increase of 240,000, bringing total membership to more than 12 million. At the same time, membership in more liberal denominations dropped, such as in the Episcopal Church (8% in the last three years), Lutheran Church in America, United Presbyterian Church, United Church of Christ, and American Lutheran Church. Such evidence, however, does not mean that conservative denominations have a higher growth rate than liberal denominations. The most startling drop was in the conservative Lutheran Church—Missouri Synod, which lost 7,000 of its 3 million members.

Outside the United States, Baptists and Anglicans (except in Britain) gained appreciatively. Lutherans decreased, especially in East Germany.

Though membership in many U. S. denominations declined or remained static, contributions increased. According to a survey by the National Council of Churches, the increase was $229 million, or 5.2% over the previous year. Even accounting for its increase in membership, the rate of contribution among Southern Baptists was up, so that total giving was more than $1 billion, the highest of

any Protestant body. A sampling of five conservative small denominations showed an increase of 5.6% in contributions. Highest per capita giving was in the Seventh-day Adventist Church with an average of $417.

The Common Bible. The outstanding religious publication of the year was the Common Bible, which was endorsed by British as well as American Protestant, Roman Catholic, and Orthodox leaders. It is the Revised Standard Version, first published in 1952 by the National Council of Churches.

ALFRED P. KLAUSER
Executive Director, Associated Church Press

Roman Catholicism

During 1973 the life of the Roman Catholic Church was marked by internal theological controversy, renewed emphasis on prayer and interiority, and conflicts with repressive governments. Among important events of 1973 were the 40th International Eucharistic Congress held in February in Melbourne, Australia; the creation of 30 new cardinals in March; the announcement that the 4th World Synod of Bishops on "Evangelization in the Contemporary World" will be held in Rome in October 1974; and the start on Pentecost Sunday, June 10, of preparations for the 1975 Holy Year declared by Pope Paul VI in May.

Theological Controversy. A declaration prepared by the Sacred Congregation for the Doctrine of the Faith and signed June 24 by the pope provoked considerable discussion. The document restated Catholic doctrine, and rejected certain recent errors, on four topics—church unity, papal infallibility, the historical conditioning of dogma, and the priesthood. Although no theologian was mentioned by name, it was understood and confirmed by the Vatican that the section on infallibility was directed against the liberal scholar Hans Küng of Tübingen University, whose *Infallible? An Inquiry* (1970) had touched off vigorous debate. In that work Küng had argued that the permanency of the church in the truth is preserved even if certain historical formulations of its dogmas have been in error. The declaration asserted that such an interpretation could not be reconciled with orthodox Catholic tradition. Küng replied that his work was being condemned without suitable inquiry.

While few Catholic theologians agreed with Küng's views on infallibility, many commented that the declaration had not answered his exegetical and historical arguments. Other theologians found the declaration uneven, more rigid in its understanding of the church's unity than was the view encouraged by Vatican II but recognizing for the first time in official documents the importance of the historical conditioning of dogmatic statements.

Authority. Roman authority asserted itself in other ways, not without causing comment. Many theologians were disturbed that the publishing of the declaration seemed to indicate that the Roman congregations approached theological questions as an exercise in centralized authority rather than in collegial dialogue. Theologians raised a similar objection to the directive issued by two other Roman congregations halting educational experiments that postponed initiation into the sacrament of penance until several years after first communion. The issue was not one of doctrine but of teaching methods. Many American church leaders believed that the directive should and would be reconsidered.

KEYSTONE

CARDINAL MINDSZENTY (left) exiled head of Catholic Church in Hungary, with Cardinal Heenan in London.

Another expression of Roman authority was a new Directory for the Pastoral Ministry of the Bishops, in which they were warned not to voice publicly dissent from the pope. The relation of Roman authority to local churches was also at issue in an October resolution by the Canon Law Society of America "strenuously [to] promote" the continued use of the American Procedural Norms. The use of these norms, which allowed the relatively rapid processing of many marriage cases in American rather than Roman church courts, had been permitted by the Vatican for only one more year.

Interior Renewal. In Catholic life as elsewhere in contemporary culture there was a quickened interest in prayer, meditation, and interiority. One aspect of it was a steadily growing charismatic, or pentecostal renewal. More than 22,000 Catholics attended the annual Charismatic Conference held in June at the University of Notre Dame, South Bend, Ind. Leo Joseph Cardinal Suenens of Belgium told them that the "future of the Church" was coming out of their movement. Serious works were published not only on the charismatic movement but on other forms of prayer as well. Catholics also showed interest in Eastern religions because of their emphasis on contemplation.

Church and State. In many countries there were conflicts between the church and the government. Some of these indicated a shift in traditional alliances and antagonisms. The bishops of Spain urged that the close relation between church and state in their country be ended. The Vatican gave some evidence of a more sympathetic attitude toward Marxism. The first diplomatic contacts with East Germany were established, and a Vatican missionary news agency praised the idealism and moral qualities of the followers of Mao Tse-tung. In Poland, however, bishops urged their people to continue to resist the official atheism of the Marxist government.

In Asia, Africa, and Latin America the church clashed with various governments in protest against the violation of human rights. Catholic bishops in Portugal as well as in Angola denounced Portuguese colonial policies, which sometimes involved brutal torture, as in Mozambique, and the Vatican was urged to do so also. In Rhodesia and South Africa, bishops attacked the institutionalized racism of the governments.

POPE PAUL VI congratulates a member of the Newark Boys Chorus after a Vatican concert on June 23.

In Latin America there was a great deal of ferment within the church itself as the issue of liberation or development was debated. One important question was whether Christians could successfully collaborate with Marxists, as some of the radical clergy had proposed. The tragedy of Chile posed a special challenge. Throughout the unrest of the first eight months of the year, the Cardinal of Santiago tried to reconcile leftist and rightist factions; and, when a military coup overthrew President Allende in September, the church tried, not always with success, to restrain the harsh reprisals inflicted on Allende supporters. The bishops of Brazil and Bolivia protested the imprisonment and torture of political prisoners by rightist regimes.

Ecumenism. The joint working group of the Vatican and the World Council of Churches reported that Catholic membership in the Council remained a possibility, although it was not likely in the immediate future. Collaboration on a number of projects, however, would continue. A commission of Anglicans and Catholics published a common statement on the meaning of the priesthood.

The historic meeting of Israeli Prime Minister Golda Meir with Pope Paul in January provoked controversy over the Vatican's advocacy of the internationalization of Jerusalem. A similar controversy arose over the French bishops' strong condemnation of anti-Semitism.

Other Issues. Vatican representatives participated in the July conference in Helsinki on Security and Cooperation in Europe. Many groups raised the question of the ordination of women to the priesthood, and the Vatican commissioned a study of the role of women in the church and society. U. S. Catholics were disappointed in two major decisions of the Supreme Court, one declaring state laws prohibiting abortion unconstitutional except in rare circumstances, the other declaring almost all forms of public aid to Catholic education unconstitutional.

JOSEPH A. O'HARE, S. J.
Associate Editor, "America"

Judaism

The dominant event of 1973 in world Judaism was the "Yom Kippur War," a tragic culmination to the 25th anniversary year of the State of Israel. Attacks by Arab terrorists and persecution of Soviet and Middle Eastern Jews caused concern. In the United States, a Christian evangelical drive challenged an upsurge in an identity quest by Jewish college youth, and Orthodox spokesmen criticized a Conservative move to extend women's worship rights.

"Yom Kippur War." The surprise attack by Egypt and Syria against Israel on October 6, on Yom Kippur, the sacred, penitential Day of Atonement, struck at the core of world Judaism. Immediately and unanimously, deeply shocked Jews the world over offered their support. Volunteers and donations of money and blood poured into the country. Demonstrations, marches, and prayer and psalm-reading sessions were held in Jewish communities. The response dramatically demonstrated the religious significance of the State of Israel to Jews everywhere.

Israel's 25th Anniversary. The year 1973 was filled with celebrations and other observations commemorating the 25th year of the establishment of the Jewish state. They included assemblies, parades, publications, and television and radio programs reviewing the history of Israel. Some festivities in the United States were highlighted by the attendance of Israeli Prime Minister Golda Meir.

Terrorism and Harassment. In 1973, Arab terrorists aimed at targets outside Israel. Bombs in letters sent to prominent Jewish citizens and organizations, skyjackings, and kidnapping of Jewish diplomats and Israel-bound Soviet Jews elicited a sense of Jewish solidarity.

Soviet harassment—including arrests, torture, and imprisonment—of Jews who sought visas to Israel continued, although the government waived the exorbitant education tax. Undaunted, many Jews persisted in their efforts to leave. In Syria and Iraq, Jews suffered economic oppression, an immigration ban, and physical abuse. Such persecution prompted demonstrations by Jewish youth in many countries, a hunger strike at the Western (Wailing) Wall in Jerusalem, and a Knesset resolution demanding an end to inhumane treatment.

American Judaism. A growing number of Jewish college students were searching for a religious-cultural identity. More of them were observing dietary laws and showing interest in the Hebrew language. There was a proliferation on campus of Jewish publications, petitions for programs of Jewish studies, and prayer groups. Closer ties with Israel and a new image of Jewish militancy projected by such groups as the Jewish Defense League were partly responsible for this trend. As a result, in 1973 more than 350 American colleges offered Jewish studies, several cities established Jewish free universities, and Brandeis University initiated a "Belated Bar Mitzvah Program."

Several Jewish groups set up Jewish cultural programs for youth to counter the effects of Key 73, a missionary drive by more than 130 evangelical Protestant and Catholic denominations. Although some Jewish leaders saw it as a threat to American Judaism, Key 73 had, in fact, little success.

The Committee on Jewish Law and Standards of the Rabbinical Assembly of Conservative Judaism approved a proposal that women now be counted

equally with men as members of a quorum for synagogue prayer. Orthodox leaders objected to this reinterpretation of Jewish law as being without legal sanction, especially since women do not have equal religious responsibilities. The decision is one of 15 modifications of the status of women that Conservative Judaism is considering.

Rabbi Maurice N. Eisendrath, leader of Reform Judaism, died in New York on November 9, just before he was to address the Union of American Hebrew Congregations, which he had led for 30 years. Rabbi Alexander M. Schindler was chosen to succeed him at the helm of Reform Judaism.

LIVIA E. BITTON, *Herbert H. Lehman College*
City University of New York

Eastern Orthodox Church

In 1973, Orthodox churches in Greece and Cyprus were torn by dissension, while the Orthodox Church in the Soviet Union still struggled for its rights. Orthodox churches generally continued to support ecumenism but disapproved of its secular aspects.

Patriarchate of Constantinople. Dimitrios I, Ecumenical Patriarch of the primatial see of Constantinople since 1972, dealt cautiously with other Orthodox churches as he asserted his intentions to continue the ecumenical policies of his famous predecessor, Athenagoras. Dimitrios had difficulties with the Greek Church regarding his traditional jurisdiction over dioceses in northern Greece.

Orthodoxy in Greece. The Church of Greece faced internal crises complicated by the nation's being under military rule. Churchmen continued to criticize Archbishop Ieronymos of Athens, appointed by the state, for dictatorial methods and for reforms that displeased the Patriarch of Constantinople. In April the Council of State confirmed the election of a synod of bishops generally hostile to Ieronymos. Charges of financial mismanagement and dissension in the hierarchy continued to hamper the Church's prestige and influence with the people.

Cyprus. The Cypriot bishops of Paphos, Kitium, and Kyrenia attempted to defrock Archbishop Makarios, president of Cyprus, on the grounds that church law forbids clerics to hold political office. In August, a major synod of senior bishops from Greece and elsewhere upheld Makarios and defrocked his opponents. The attack on the Cypriot ethnarch after 13 years in office is believed to have been inspired by those who favor union with Greece and oppose his conciliatory policy toward Turks and Cypriot Communists. (See also CYPRUS.)

Soviet Union. In the Soviet Union critical voices, such as that of novelist Alexander Solzhenitsyn, continued to be raised against the weakness and passivity of the Orthodox hierarchy. At the same time, state officials regretted the persistence of religious faith and harassed and persecuted religious dissenters. Changes in Soviet foreign policy appeared to explain the presence of fewer Russian churchmen at international gatherings.

Ecumenism. Patriarch Dimitrios of Constantinople made two important statements to the World Council of Churches. Both supported ecumenism, but in March (with Patriarch Nicholas of Alexandria) he criticized the WCC for its secular emphasis and urged it to remember its function as a council of separate and separated Christian bodies. In his August statement he stressed the Orthodox view of ecumenism as the search for church unity

WORLD'S FIRST woman rabbi, Sally J. Priesand, blesses the wine in a cup during a model Seder.

rather than the cooperative effort of divided Christians to interfere in the social and political affairs of the world. The Moscow Patriarchate concurred. Similar views were voiced by the Synod of Bishops of the Orthodox Church in America in a May encyclical denouncing "secular Christianity."

Native Leadership. The Orthodox Church in East Africa, previously under a Greek episcopate, for the first time received three native African bishops from the Patriarchate of Alexandria. The Orthodox diocese of Alaska opened a school to train native Alaskan clergy.

THOMAS HOPKO
St. Vladimir's Orthodox Theological Seminary

Islam

Enmity and conflict characterized much of the Islamic world in 1973. There was strain or violence in the Indian subcontinent, the Philippines, and the Middle East. Such trouble, however, solidified Islamic opinion and produced united action.

Indian Subcontinent. Relations between the countries on the Indian subcontinent were strained over the repatriation of the refugees and prisoners of war resulting from the creation of Bangladesh in 1972. Another grave problem was the plight of the Biharis, non-Bengali Muslims who settled in East Pakistan after the 1947 partition and sided with the Pakistani government in the 1971 fighting. The Bangladesh government does not want them to remain in that country, and both India and Pakistan are reluctant to admit them, thus forcing nearly 1 million Biharis to remain in refugee camps.

Philippines and Africa. Muslim rebels in the southern part of the Philippine Islands took up arms against the Christian government. A conference of Islamic foreign ministers meeting in March in Benghazi, Libya, voiced its support of the rebels' position, established a fund for their benefit, and created a commission to investigate their grievances. Several months later a delegation of the World Islamic League went to Manila to help mediate Muslim-Christian strife but met no real success.

FIFTEEN-YEAR-OLD GURU Maharaj ji, seated on a red-velvet-covered throne, speaks to a crowd of thousands in New York City.

UPI

The continuation of a similar rebellion of Muslims against the non-Muslim government of Chad demonstrated the growing impact of Islam on sub-Saharan Africa. Islam seems more acceptable to native Africans than the Christianity introduced by the colonial powers. In 1973 one third of Africa's population was estimated to be Muslim.

Middle East. For the fourth time in 25 years the Arab-Israeli conflict erupted into full-scale war. After more than two weeks of bitter fighting, a UN-supervised cease-fire went into effect. Although the long-proposed political union of Egypt, Libya, and Syria failed to materialize, Jordanian and Iraqi troops, as well as soldiers from other Islamic countries, served on the front lines. Virtually all Islamic nations condemned Israel.

Inner Tension. Islam, like other great world religions, is undergoing internal dissension as it faces the challenge of adapting age-old traditions to the needs of contemporary society. An example was the referendum on a new Syrian constitution, which omitted the traditional reference to Islam as the state religion. This omission threatened the close relation between church and state that conservative Muslims hold to be an essential part of Islam. There were several clashes between traditionalists and modernists in Homs, Hama, and Aleppo before the constitution was ultimately approved.

KENNETH J. PERKINS, *McGill University*

Oriental Religions

Socioeconomic tensions exacerbated religious feelings in India and Sri Lanka (Ceylon). On the other hand, Pope Paul VI, in the tolerant spirit of Vatican II, joined Protestants in pressing for ecumenical dialogue with Buddhists, Hindus, and Muslims.

Hinduism. Although Hindus still exhibit "deep adoration" for Mahatma Gandhi, there is growing evidence that they give less than total assent to his principle of nonviolence. The landless group of more than 50 million known as "untouchables," whom Gandhi called "harijans," or "Children of God," showed signs of militant protest against the social role traditionally assigned to them, namely that of performing unclean tasks such as sweeping streets, removing human and animal wastes, and tanning hides. They incited hundreds of riots in 1972 and 1973. Publicized cases of untouchables being beaten to death by members of upper castes have further inflamed them.

There were a number of violent demonstrations against the government's closing in April of Aligarh University, the second-largest Muslim school in the world. The government claimed that the university had refused to tailor its courses to the needs of the 40% non-Muslim minority in its student body and that state support for an "island of Muslim education" was unjustified. Demonstrators protested the government's "shattering" of the "minority character" of an institution serving the 55 million Muslims of India.

The continued strength of caste feeling is indicated by the report that 78 persons in a flooded bus died because they refused to use the same rope to haul themselves to safety.

In August, Sheikh Mohammed Abdullah, Kashmiri Muslim leader, announced he would enter Indian national politics. He planned to serve the interests of "the whole country" and thus promote greater amity between Hindus and Muslims.

Buddhism. In March the exiled Dalai Lama of Tibet led 2,500 Hindu untouchables, who have converted to Buddhism, in a mass ceremony in New Delhi. In the last two decades 2 million untouchables are said to have become Buddhists.

In April in Colombo, Sri Lanka, Indian Prime Minister Indira Gandhi and Ceylon's Prime Minister Sirimavo Bandaranaike discussed the tensions that existed between the predominantly Buddhist inhabitants and the Hindu immigrants, who form 25% of the population of Sri Lanka. The Hindus, who are Tamils, ask for their own linguistic and cultural environment, but widespread unemployment prompts the Buddhist majority to seek Tamil repatriation in India.

The strength of Buddhism in South Vietnam was indicated when 200,000 persons, including President Thieu, lined the streets of Hue in February for the funeral of Thich Tinh Kiet, 84, supreme monk of the Vietnam Unified Buddhist Church.

In Japan, there was continued vitality in Buddhist "new religions," such as Soka Gakkai, which combine spiritual discipline with physical and social care of their members.

JOHN B. NOSS
Author of "Man's Religions"

REPUBLICAN PARTY. See ELECTIONS; POLITICAL PARTIES.

RESPIRATORY DISEASES. See MEDICINE.

RHODE ISLAND

The focus of attention in Rhode Island in 1973 was on the economy—a shift from the preceding year's preoccupation with politics.

Economic Developments. The newly elected Democratic governor, Philip W. Noel, had been in office only a short time when it was announced that the U. S. Navy was planning to close down several of its important installations in Rhode Island. For many years Rhode Island's largest employer has been the Navy. In 1971 there were more than 41,000 civilian employees with an annual payroll of $318.7 million.

There were the Naval Air Station at Quonset, the Construction Battalion facility nearby, and the various commands in and around Newport. Among the latter, the key ones were the Atlantic Fleet Cruiser-Destroyer Force comprising 41 ships at Newport, the Underwater Systems Center, and the Naval War College. It was eventually made clear that all the major activities save the War College would be transferred or closed. Most local employees would thus have to find other employment, and the state would have a major economic void to fill.

The Noel administration launched a crash program to measure the potential impact of the closings and to develop solutions to the problems posed. The introduction of new industries that would use the vacated federal land and provide new jobs was among the plans formulated during the year.

Rhode Island, along with the rest of the nation, felt the impact of severe inflation during 1973, and as the year drew to a close, it was girding itself for shortages of gasoline and of the fuel oil that is so vital to New England for both industrial and domestic use.

Governmental Affairs. Two particularly noteworthy governmental developments occurred during the year. The Board of Regents, set up in 1969 as the central governing body for all of the state's educational system, was restructured. Its membership was enlarged from 9 to 15, and three subboards were created within it for the various areas of educational policy.

In another major action, the General Assembly voted to call a special election in August at which the voters would be asked to approve a limited constitutional convention. The electorate agreed, and the convention met on September 4 for 30 days. It agreed to submit constitutional amendments to referendum that would allow a state lottery, revise the grand jury system, bring Rhode Island voter qualifications into line with federal mandates, simplify the process of amending the constitution, raise the pay of legislators, and provide four-year terms for the governor and other state officers. The voters approved all but the last two questions on November 6.

Prison Riot. Difficulties at the state prison, which had begun in late 1972, culminated in a prison riot that caused much damage early in 1973. The reform-minded warden resigned and was replaced amid much criticism and unrest among the prison personnel.

ELMER E. CORNWELL, JR.,
Brown University

——————— RHODE ISLAND • Information Highlights ———————

Area: 1,214 square miles (3,144 sq km).
Population (1972 est.): 968,000. *Density:* 915 per sq mi.
Chief Cities (1970 census): Providence, the capital, 179,116; Warwick, 83,694; Pawtucket, 76,984; Cranston, 74,287; East Providence, 48,207; Woonsocket, 46,820; Newport, 34,562.
Government (1973): *Chief Officers*—governor, Philip W. Noel (D); lt. gov., J. Joseph Garrahy (D); secy. of state, Robert F. Burns (D); atty. gen., Richard J. Israel (R); treas., Raymond H. Hawksley (D); commissioner of education, Fred G. Burke; chief justice, Thomas H. Roberts. *General Assembly*—Senate, 50 members (37 Democrats, 13 Republicans); House of Representatives, 100 members (73 D, 27 R).
Education (1972–73): *Enrollment*—public elementary schools, 116,937 pupils, 5,481 teachers; public secondary schools, 72,756 pupils, 4,003 teachers; nonpublic schools, 36,800 pupils, 1,580 teachers; colleges and universities, 46,891 students. *Public school expenditures*, $200,944,000 ($1,-116 per pupil). *Average teacher's salary*, $10,800.
State Finances (fiscal year 1971): *Revenues*, $497,250,000 (5% general sales tax and gross receipts taxes, $83,287,000; motor fuel tax, $28,550,000; federal funds, $111,005,000). *Expenditures*, $457,316,000 (education, $169,783,000; health, welfare, and safety, $129,233,000; highways, $32,980,000). *State debt*, $386,558,000 (June 30, 1971).
Personal Income (1972): $4,258,000,000; per capita, $4,399.
Public Assistance (1972): $108,075,000. *Average monthly payments* (Dec. 1972)—old-age assistance, $70.19; aid to families with dependent children, $223.04.
Labor Force: *Nonagricultural wage and salary earners* (July 1973), 360,300. *Average annual employment* (1972)—manufacturing, 119,480; trade, 75,500; government, 54,600; services, 59,800. *Insured unemployed* (Sept. 1973)—11,700 (3.8%).
Manufacturing (1971): Value added by manufacture, $1,468,-900,000. Textile mill products, $183,500,000; primary metal industries, $155,200,000; jewelry, silverware, plated ware, $126,600,000; costume jewelry and notions, $123,800,000; nonelectrical machinery, $107,900,000; food and kindred products, $94,800,000.
Agriculture (1972): *Cash farm income*, $17,207,000 (livestock, $8,946,000; crops, $8,204,000; government payments, $57,-000). *Chief crops* (in order of value, 1971)—Potatoes, hay, apples, peaches.
Mining (1972): Production value, $5,552,000 (ranks 49th among the states). *Chief minerals*—Sand and gravel, stone,/ gem stones.
Fisheries (1972): *Commercial catch*, 86,376,000 pounds ($12,-443,000). *Leading species by value*—Flounder, $4,257,-000; lobsters, $4,254,000; clams, $1,157,000; cod, $460,000.
Transportation: *Roads* (1972), 5,461 miles (8,788 km); *motor vehicles* (1972), 509,047; *railroads* (1972), 146 miles (235 km); *public airports* (1972), 7.
Communications: *Telephones* (1973), 573,600; *television stations* (1971), 2; *radio stations* (1971), 22; *newspapers* (1973), 7 (daily circulation, 315,000).

RHODESIA

In early 1973 white-ruled Rhodesia closed its border with black-ruled Zambia because of guerrilla attacks it said were launched from Zambia, and Zambia retaliated by halting the shipment of copper through Rhodesia. A tragic result of the border tension was the shooting deaths of two Canadian women tourists at Victoria Falls.

Border Closing. Mounting attacks from guerrillas allegedly based in Zambia provoked Rhodesian Prime Minister Ian Douglas Smith to close Rhodesia's 400-mile border with Zambia on January 9. Excluded from the closure was Zambia's copper, half of which normally is shipped through Rhodesia and is an important source of revenue for the country. But Zambian Prime Minister Kenneth David Kaunda retaliated by closing Zambia's border with Rhodesia on January 11 and routing all copper exports to the ports of Dar es Salaam in Tanzania and Lobito in Angola.

Hurt economically by the border closing and censured for his action by the Republic of South Africa, Smith reopened Rhodesia's side of the border on February 4. However, Zambia resolutely kept its border closed.

Tourists' Deaths. On May 15 two Canadian women from Ontario were killed and an American from Ohio was wounded when they were fired on from the Zambian side of Victoria Falls while they were hiking on the Rhodesian side. Rhodesia charged that Zambian soldiers—not guerrillas, as first claimed by Zambia—had done the shooting. After an in-

——— RHODESIA • Information Highlights ———

Official Name: Republic of Rhodesia (by unilateral declaration).
Location: Southern Africa.
Area: 150,803 square miles (390,580 sq km).
Population (1973 est.): 5,600,000. *Density,* 36 per square mile (14 per sq km).
Chief Cities (1969 census, metropolitan areas): Salisbury, the capital, 386,040; Bulawayo, 245,040.
Government: *Head of state,* Clifford Dupont, president (took office April 1970). *Head of government,* Ian D. Smith, prime minister (took office April 1964). *Legislature*—Parliament: Senate and House of Assembly. *Major political parties*—Rhodesian Front; Centre party.
Languages: English (official), Bantu languages.
Education: *Expenditure* (1967), 16.9% of total public expenditure. *School enrollment* (1965)—primary, 627,806; secondary, 15,146; technical/vocational, 832; university/higher (1968), 1,064.
Monetary Unit: Rhodesian dollar (0.5921 R. dollar equals U. S. $1, March 1973).
Gross National Product (1971 est.): $1,573,000,000.
Economic Indexes: *Industrial production* (1972), 192 (1963 = 100); *consumer price index* (1972), 125 (1963 = 100).
Manufacturing (major products): Metals and metal products, processed foods, textiles, chemicals, beverages, tobacco products, clothing and footwear.
Major Agricultural Products: Tobacco, sugarcane, tea, groundnuts, cotton, corn, millet and sorghum.
Major Minerals: Asbestos, chromium ore, copper, coal, iron ore, tin, gold.
Foreign Trade (1971): *Exports,* $388,000,000; *imports,* $395,000,000. *Chief trading partner*—South Africa.
Transportation: *Motor vehicles* (1969), 178,600 (automobiles, 126,600); *railroads* (1971), 1,616 miles (2,600 km); *major national airline,* Air Rhodesia.
Communications: *Telephones* (1972), 140,837; *newspapers* (1971), 4 (daily circulation, 85,000).

vestigation, Zambia apologized to the Canadian government for the tragedy.

Newsman Deported. Peter Niesewand, a Rhodesian citizen who is a free-lance reporter for British and French news agencies, was arrested on February 20 for refusing to reveal sources for his reports on Rhodesian army operations against Mozambique-based African guerrillas. In a secret trial on April 6 he was convicted of contravening the Official Secrets Act.

International concern over Niesewand's plight, especially in Britain, probably aided his acquittal by an appeals court on May 1. Deported immediately after his release, Niesewand declared in London on May 5 that his arrest was meant to intimidate the press into silence about government pressure on tribal Africans to accept the 1971 settlement terms with Britain. Africans had rejected these terms because of their strong opposition to continued white rule.

U. S. Chrome Purchases. A bill to halt U. S. purchases of Rhodesian chrome received support from the Nixon administration and from prominent witnesses appearing before the Senate Foreign Relations subcommittee on African affairs on September 6. The bill would repeal an amendment to the Military Procurement Act exempting chrome, a strategic metal, from a U. S. trade embargo against Rhodesia. The embargo was mandated by the United Nations in 1968 to protest Rhodesia's illegal break from Britain in order to retain white control. Witnesses before the subcommittee attacked the argument that by not buying Rhodesian chrome the United States was being forced to buy Soviet chrome at higher cost. They pointed out that by purchasing Rhodesian chrome the United States broke UN sanctions, angered independent Africa, and hurt the U. S. ferrochrome industry.

FRANKLIN PARKER
West Virginia University

ROMAN CATHOLIC CHURCH. See RELIGION.

RUMANIA

In 1973 the chief domestic concerns of Rumania were increasing awareness of the need for further development of heavy industry and the problem of raising the standard of living. Rumanian leader Nicolae Ceauşescu sought also to improve foreign relations with the Communist bloc as well as with many countries of the Western world, including the United States.

Internal Developments. In January, Ceauşescu predicted an industrial growth rate of 12% to 16% and insisted that Rumania would join the ranks of advanced industrial societies by 1990. He stressed the fact that heavy industries, such as steel works and chemical plants, were essential to give Rumania the foundation for the economic independence that it desires. However, about 50% of the population was still in agriculture in 1973.

In September the Rumanian government announced plans to resume construction of the costly Black Sea–Danube River Canal. Work on this waterway was abandoned in 1953.

Ceauşescu Abroad. Ceauşescu visited Pakistan in January. In May he went to Italy, where he signed accords on commercial, technical, and industrial cooperation. At the Vatican he had an audience with Pope Paul VI, who had earlier revealed that the late Rumanian Bishop Iuliu Hossu of Cluj-Gherea had secretly been elevated to the cardinalate in 1969.

In June, Ceauşescu visited West Germany, which is Rumania's most important trading partner after the Soviet Union. There he offered investors a 49% share in enterprises which they wished to finance. During August and September he went to Cuba, Venezuela, Costa Rica, Colombia, and five other Latin American countries, becoming the first Communist bloc leader to personally seek out vast markets on that continent.

——— RUMANIA • Information Highlights ———

Official Name: Socialist Republic of Rumania.
Location: Southeastern Europe.
Area: 91,700 square miles (237,500 sq km).
Population (1973 est.): 21,000,000. *Density,* 223 per square mile (86 per sq km).
Chief Cities (1970 est.): Bucharest, the capital, 1,475,050; Cluj, 202,715; Timisoara, 192,616; Iaşi, 183,776; Braşov, 182,105.
Government: *Head of state,* Nicolae Ceauşescu, president of the State Council and secretary general of the Communist party (took office July 1965). *Chief minister,* Ion Gheorghe Maurer, chairman of the Council of Ministers. *Legislature* (unicameral)—Grand National Assembly. *Political party*—Communist party.
Languages: Rumanian (official), Hungarian.
Education: *School enrollment* (1969)—primary, 2,886,855; secondary, 650,482; technical/vocational, 366,239; university/higher, 151,705.
Monetary Unit: Leu (4.80 lei equal U. S.$1, July 1973).
Gross National Product (1972 est.): $26,500,000,000.
Economic Indexes: *Industrial production* (1970), 229 (1963 = 100); *agricultural production* (1970), 135 (1957–59 = 100); *consumer price index* (1970), 103 (1963 = 100).
Manufacturing (major products): Construction materials, metals, chemicals, machinery, processed foods, textiles, petroleum products.
Major Agricultural Products: Corn, sugar beets, potatoes, wheat, rye, sunflower seeds.
Major Minerals: Petroleum, natural gas, lignite, coal, iron ore, lead, manganese, bauxite.
Foreign Trade (1971): *Exports,* $2,101,000,000; *Imports,* $2,103,000,000. *Chief trading partners* (1970)—USSR (took 26% of exports, supplied 24% of imports); West Germany (8%—17%); Czechoslovakia (8%—6%); Italy (4%—12%); Japan; East Germany.
Tourism: Receipts (1971), $86,100,000.
Transportation: *Motor vehicles* (1970), 45,100; *railroads* (1971), 6,843 miles (11,012 km); *merchant fleet* (1972), 446,000 gross registered tons; *major national airline,* TAROM (Transportarie Aeriene Române).
Communications: *Telephones* (1972), 726,554; *newspapers* (1971), 57 (daily circulation, 3,538,000).

Visitors. In Rumania in January, French Foreign Minister Maurice Schumann promised trade preferences similar to those granted by the European Economic Community (EEC) to developing nations. When this privilege was granted in June, Rumania became the first Warsaw Pact state accorded such preferences. The shah of Iran signed a trade accord in Bucharest in June. Other visitors during the year included Juan Perón of Argentina and Prince Norodom Sihanouk, ousted leader of Cambodia.

Relations with the Bloc. Inflexibly pursuing its decade-old insistence on national equality and sovereignty, Rumania demanded that these principles be universally recognized at preparatory sessions for the Conference on European Security and Cooperation, which opened in July in Helsinki, Finland. Fear of Great Power domination underlay this position, and it placed the Soviet Union in the position of supporting Rumania to suggest that Moscow would not dominate the conference. Associated with Rumania's policy is the demand for the dismantling of all military blocs and withdrawal of foreign troops from all territories. Ceauşescu hoped for a new era in the Balkans marked by peaceful cooperation without nuclear weapons, foreign troops, or military bases in the peninsula.

When Warsaw Pact staff maneuvers were held in Rumania in February, for the first time since 1962, reports of Soviet yielding to Rumania arose. Ceauşescu healed Rumania's breach with the Czech regime, installed by Moscow in 1968, when he visited Prague in March. He discussed common concerns with Marshal Tito in Yugoslavia in August, and he participated in the Crimea summit meeting of Warsaw Pact leaders in July to hear Soviet Communist party chairman Leonid Brezhnev's report of his visits to Germany, France, and the United States. When the bloc states condemned Israel in October, Rumania reiterated its neutral policy and maintained diplomatic relations.

Relations with the United States. Ceauşescu made an important visit to the United States in December. The party leader and President Nixon concluded their talks with a joint statement promising "the continued development of friendly relations" between the two nations. A joint declaration pledging economic, industrial, and technical cooperation was also signed. Ceauşescu also conferred with officials of the International Monetary Fund (IMF) and met with members of the U.S. Chamber of Commerce. During the latter meeting, a U.S.-Rumanian economic council was established.

Earlier in the year, David Rockefeller of the Chase Manhattan Bank had visited Rumania to negotiate improved economic ties. During 1973 also, Rumania purchased three Boeing 707s, signed a $4 million contract with Control Data for joint manufacture of computer equipment, and contracted with General Tire for a $75 million radial tire plant.

SHERMAN D. SPECTOR
Russell Sage College

SAINT LOUIS

The election of a new mayor, the apparent solution of a bus-service crisis, and the resolution of labor disputes that had closed schools and daily newspapers highlighted events in St. Louis in 1973.

Elections. Mayor Alfonso J. Cervantes' desire for a third term died in the March Democratic primary when Comptroller John H. Poelker upset him by 5,600 votes. Poelker then defeated Joseph Badaracco, president of the Board of Aldermen, in the April general election. John F. Bass became the city's second black citywide office-holder when he was elected comptroller. He won over Fred O. Whaley, chairman of the Republican City Central Committee. The Democrats picked up one seat on the Board of Aldermen, giving them a 25 to 4 edge.

Education. St. Louis's 166 public schools were closed from January 22 to February 20 in the city's first teachers' strike. The St. Louis Teachers Association teamed with the Teachers Union to force the board of education to the bargaining table and eventually grant $800 salary increases. Much of the arguing took place in the courtroom, where Circuit Judge Thomas F. McGuire levied fines totaling $680,000 and ordered the jailing of the president of the teachers association when the two groups failed to obey his injunction. Teachers worked off the fines and the jail sentence by doing after-hours work.

In St. Louis County, school districts were under federal court order to reorganize to ensure the desegregation of the all-black Kinloch district.

Bus Service. Bus fares were lowered from 45 cents to 25 cents on Nov. 12, 1973, after a one-half cent sales tax for bus operations was approved by area governments. Until sales-tax revenue began coming in, buses operated mostly on a week-to-week basis as its operators pleaded for governmental subsidies.

Drug Raids. Twelve narcotics agents assigned to the federal Drug Abuse Law Enforcement office in St. Louis were indicted in August for allegedly violating the civil rights of 11 persons in raids on the East Side in April. Victims of the raids, some of whom allegedly had no connection with narcotics, reported they had been terrorized by the agents.

Housing. The crime-infested, financially troubled Pruitt-Igoe public housing development was ordered closed and demolished by the city's Housing Authority. After the federal government approved the action, the remaining 587 families began moving from the project, which once housed 10,000 persons. (See also ARCHITECTURE.)

Labor. The *Post-Dispatch* and the *Globe-Democrat* failed to publish for 46 days in late summer in a dispute with Teamsters Local 610 over automation. During the strike, a new thrice-weekly paper, *St. Louis Today,* was published by staff members of the papers. Other major strikes were against Ozark Air Lines, four wholesale grocery firms, and all new-car dealers.

Local Government. Government and civil leaders proposed a new area-wide government called St. Louis Area Council of Governments to handle planning, transit, airports, and other area-wide services. This proposal set off considerable debate. The hottest controversy was over abortion, as the aldermen attempted to shut down an abortion clinic, and the mayor declared no abortions could be performed in city hospitals. Both matters were being fought in the courts at year-end. A black, Theodore D. McNeal, became head of the St. Louis Police Board.

Commerce. In downtown development, plans were announced to build a 19-story hotel over the vacant Spanish Pavilion and to convert little-used Union Station into a multimillion-dollar commercial development. At its peak Union Station handled as many as 100,000 passengers and 200 trains a day.

RONALD D. WILLNOW
St. Louis "Post-Dispatch"

OIL SPILL in an arm of San Francisco Bay resulted when vandals opened five storage tanks, releasing 200,000 gallons of oil. Clean-up crew herds the slick from the ship channel into a backwater.

SAN FRANCISCO

In 1973 limited service began on the $1.6 billion Bay Area Rapid Transit System (BART). Among other developments, construction of high-rise buildings continued in the downtown and Nob Hill areas, and voters approved a $37.8 million bond issue to protect the city's schools from earthquake damage.

BART System. The BART System was scheduled to begin operation over its entire 75-mile length in 1973. However, one of the most important links in the system, the 3½-mile tunnel under San Francisco Bay, connecting the city with the east bay lines, developed "bugs" in its automated control system that prevented safe operation of trains through the tunnel. It was anticipated that the defects would be eliminated by mid-1974.

Municipal Improvements. The rehabilitation of Market Street, one of the city's major thoroughfares, began in 1973. For months, the street had been torn up as a result of building a two-level underground rail system for streetcars and BART trains. Improvements on Market included construction of 40-foot-wide brick sidewalks and planting twin rows of sycamore trees along much of its length.

In March, Hallidie Plaza, at the junction of Market, Powell, and Fifth streets, was completed and dedicated. The plaza, which provides an attractive open space at one of the city's busiest intersections, is named for Andrew Hallidie, the inventor and first builder of the city's cable cars, which began operating in 1873.

Taxation and Budget. The value of taxable property reached more than $10 billion in 1973—an increase of $340 million over 1972. About 90% of the increase resulted from the construction of new hotels, office buildings, and apartment houses. As a result of this increase and other factors, the property tax rate for the 1974 fiscal year dropped by 34 cents, to $12.25 per $100 assessed valuation.

The 1973–74 city budget was fixed at $634 million. Of this amount, 33% derives from property taxes, 29% from state and federal subsidies, 24% from licenses, fines, and other levies, and 14% from various public service enterprises, such as the city-owned airport and street transportation system.

Population and Crime Statistics. According to the California State Finance Department, San Francisco's population, as of July 1, 1973, was 681,000. This represented a drop of 8,300 from the previous year.

The number of crimes reported declined in most categories during the first nine months of 1973. However, assault and robbery of elderly pedestrians increased sharply despite determined efforts by the police to control the bands of juveniles who are held mainly responsible.

Political Developments. On November 6, voters elected five members of the 11-member Board of Supervisors. Of the 27 candidates, five were incumbents running for reelection, of whom four were successful.

There were 13 propositions on the ballot. The most widely debated was Proposition K, a proposed charter amendment by which members of the Board of Supervisors, now elected by the city at large, would each represent a particular district. The measure was defeated by a margin of almost two to one. Proposition A, authorizing a bond issue of $37.8 million to repair, reconstruct, or replace public schools judged unsafe in the event of a severe earth-

quake, carried handily. On the state level, San Franciscans overwhelmingly rejected Gov. Ronald Reagan's controversial tax limitation plan.

In September, Democratic Mayor Joseph L. Alioto announced that he would not seek a third term. Instead, he will be a candidate in the election for governor in June 1974.

OSCAR LEWIS
Author, "San Francisco: Mission to Metropolis"

SASKATCHEWAN

The Saskatchewan economy appeared buoyant in 1973, sustained by a worldwide demand for agricultural products and consequent high prices. Major events of the year included observance of the centennial of the Royal Canadian Mounted Police (RCMP) and Premier Allan Blakeney's announcement in September of steps to combat inflation.

Legislation. The legislative session, from January 25 to May 4, was the longest in Saskatchewan's history. Premier Blakeney's New Democratic party government used most of the session to further its policy of helping the family farmer remain on the land and to exert further control over future development of the province. Among measures passed was a forest act, which makes all timber-management agreements subject to review.

Economy and Inflation. Cash receipts for farming in the January–July period rose to $761.3 million, from $585.1 million in the same period of the previous year. All other economic indicators—except population, which continued to decline—added statistically to the upswing. How much of the expansion was real and how much a product of general inflationary pressures was a matter of public conjecture.

On September 21, the premier went on a provincewide radio and television hookup to announce

WIDE WORLD

QUEEN ELIZABETH accepts gift of Royal Canadian Mounted Police horse during visit to Saskatchewan.

his government's decision to abolish hospital and medicare premiums, increase social assistance payments, and raise the minimum wage to $2 from $1.75. These steps, the premier said, were the first in a planned series of measures to combat high prices and increasing inflation.

RCMP Centennial. Queen Elizabeth II marked the centennial of the Royal Canadian Mounted Police by presenting a new guidon to the force at ceremonies at Regina Barracks on July 4 (see feature article on page 58). Saskatchewan's association with the Mounties goes back to the beginning in 1873.

Sports. National champions of ten countries entered the Silver Broom World Curling Championship, held at Regina in March. The rink from Sweden won the event, defeating the Canadian champion, Harvey Mazinke and his rink from Regina.

George Reed, fullback of the Saskatchewan Roughriders, set two professional football world records for rushing at Taylor Field, Regina, on August 20, when he scored his 107th touchdown and gained a career total of 12,313 yards.

HELEN A. MCKAY, *Former Head of Adult Services, Regina Public Library*

SAUDI ARABIA

During 1973 the importance of King Faisal as a leading personage in the Arab world greatly increased. He was regarded as a judicious moderate, and his advice was much sought after.

It was estimated that Saudi Arabia, the greatest oil-exporting country in the world, had between $5 to $6 billion on deposit in the Western world. In addition, it was believed that within five or six years the country would have an annual income of $20 billion in oil revenues and an international clout of considerable force.

Oil. In 1972, Saudi Arabia produced slightly under an average of 6 million barrels per day, but by March 1973 production topped 7 million and in July rose to over 8 million. It was expected at that time to reach 9 million barrels per day by the end of the year.

On Feb. 23, 1973, King Faisal issued a royal decree ratifying a general agreement with the Arabian American Oil Co. (Aramco) that had been concluded on Dec. 20, 1972. This agreement called for the

────── SAUDI ARABIA • Information Highlights ──────

Official Name: Kingdom of Saudi Arabia.
Location: Arabian Peninsula in Southwest Asia.
Area: 830,000 square miles (2,149,690 sq km).
Population (1973 est.): 8,400,000. *Density,* 10 per square mile (4 per sq km).
Chief Cities (1965 est.): Riyadh, the capital, 225,000; Jidda, 194,000; Mecca, 185,000.
Government: *Head of state,* Faisal Ibn Abdul-Aziz, king (acceded Nov. 1964). *Head of government,* Faisal Ibn Abdul-Aziz.
Language: Arabic (official).
Education: *Expenditure* (1969), 10% of total public expenditure. *School enrollment* (1969)—primary, 397,153; secondary, 79,469; technical/vocational, 1,777; university/higher, 6,942.
Monetary Unit: Riyal (3.55 riyals equal U. S.$1, Sept. 1973).
Gross National Product (1971 est.): $3,910,000,000.
Manufacturing (major products): Petroleum products, cement, fertilizers, iron and steel.
Major Agricultural Products: Dates, vegetables, wheat.
Major Mineral: Petroleum (ranks 3d among world producers, 1972).
Foreign Trade (1971): *Exports,* $3,844,000,000; *Imports,* $806,-000,000. *Chief trading partners* (1971)—Japan (took 21% of exports, supplied 10% of imports); Italy (11%—4%); Netherlands (9%—4%); United Kingdom (8%—7%).
Transportation: *Motor vehicles* (1970), 115,300 (automobiles, 64,900); *railroads* (1971), 376 miles (605 km); *major national airline,* Saudi Arabian Airlines.
Communications: *Telephones* (1972), 81,600; *newspapers* (1971), 5 (daily circulation, 55,000).

immediate purchase by Saudi Arabia of 25% of Aramco and 51% Saudi ownership by 1982. Later in 1973 the government began to press Aramco to advance the date from 1982, and in November there were reports that the demand was being made for immediate control, involving more than 51% ownership.

With the second devaluation of the U. S. dollar on Feb. 12, 1973, and the floating of European currencies, OPEC (Organization of Petroleum Exporting Countries), of which Saudi Arabia is a member, sought to increase the posted prices of oil. (The posted price is the price that oil companies use in computing the royalties and taxes paid to the producing country.) Because of the devaluation, the posted prices automatically increased 5.8% in accordance with the Teheran Agreement, and OPEC won an additional increase of 6.1% in June. However, by mid-1973 world prices had pushed above posted prices, and Saudi Arabia and other producers complained that the oil companies were thereby getting larger profits than usual. On October 17, OPEC declared a 70% increase in posted prices and a 17% increase in the price of oil sold on their accounts.

With the outbreak of war on October 6 between Israel and Egypt and Syria, Arabs immediately pressed Arab oil-producing countries to halt the shipment of oil to countries giving assistance to Israel. OPEC ministers meeting in Kuwait decreed a monthly 5% cutback in oil production and export to bring world pressure on Israel to withdraw from Arab lands. On November 4, the cutback was raised to 25% with an additional 5% cutback each month until Arab demands were met. A total embargo was placed on all oil shipments directly or indirectly to the United States and the Netherlands, because of their assistance to Israel. However, the monthly 5% cutback was lifted for December and January 1974 for friendly European countries. And on November 27, during the conference of Arab heads of state in Algeria, it was announced that Japan and the Philippines would be exempted from the 5% cut for December.

Defense. During 1973 the U. S. Air Force and Navy became involved in an extensive program to strengthen the Saudi military forces with fighter planes, radar, and advice. Both Northrop F-5E's

and F-5B's were contracted for. A tentative agreement was reached for the purchase of 30 Phantom F-4's, but the final contract was delayed. British firms have contracts for the improvement of airports, depots, runways, and other military facilities. In addition, Britain agreed to supply Westland Sea King attack helicopters and France was to supply 50 Mirage-5 jet and 38 Mirage-3 jets and a number of tanks. King Faisal visited London and Paris to consolidate these military arrangements.

SYDNEY NETTLETON FISHER
The Ohio State University

SEISMOLOGY. See EARTHQUAKES.

SENEGAL

The worst drought conditions of the 20th century struck the countries of Africa's Sahel zone and dwarfed all of Senegal's other problems in 1973. Crop and herd losses and the desiccation of much of northern Senegal had immediate and long-range effects on every facet of the country's political, social, and economic life.

Economic Developments. Senegal's worst drought since 1916 directly affected over 1.5 million people. Loss of livestock in the Sahel zone has been estimated as high as 40%. The millet and sorghum harvests were less than 50% of normal, and Senegal's grain deficit was projected at over 300,000 tons for the year. Groundnut production, the mainstay of Senegal's economy, was expected to be one third of average. Some areas of the country reflected even lower rates of production. In the Saint-Louis region the millet harvest, which was 63,000 tons in 1968, was estimated at only 1,000 tons in 1973. Gum arabic collection, which had reached over 6,000 tons worth $3 million in 1970–71, fell to 118 tons in 1972–73.

The government provided direct aid to some drought victims, made it mandatory for all wage earners to contribute one day's pay to relief funds, and canceled debts incurred by drought area farmers. Senegal also received major shipments of grain from the United States, Europe, and the United Nations Food and Agriculture Organization

────── SENEGAL • Information Highlights ──────

Official Name: Republic of Senegal.
Location: West Africa.
Area: 75,750 square miles (196,192 sq km).
Population (1973 est.): 4,200,000. *Density,* 54 per square mile (21 per sq km).
Chief City (1970 est.): Dakar, the capital, 581,000.
Government: *Head of state,* Léopold Sédar Senghor, president (took office Sept. 1960). *Chief minister,* Abdou Diouf, premier (took office Feb. 1970). *Legislature*—(unicameral) —National Assembly. *Major political party*—Senegalese Progressive Union (UPS).
Languages: French (official), Wolof, Fulani, Mandingo.
Education: *Expenditure* (1965) 14.7% of total public expenditure. *School enrollment* (1968)—primary, 255,493; general secondary, 42,228; technical/vocational (1967), 10,608; university/higher, 2,965.
Monetary Unit: CFA franc (230.21 CFA francs equal U. S.$1, Aug. 1973).
Gross National Product (1971 est.): $800,000,000.
Economic Indexes: *Industrial production* (1972), 157 (1963= 100); *consumer price index* (1972), 123 (1963=100).
Manufacturing (major products): Peanut oil, cement, processed foods, textiles, leather, shoes, chemicals.
Major Agricultural Products: Groundnuts, cotton, millet and sorghum, gum arabic, rice, cassava, fish.
Major Minerals: Phosphate rock, limestone.
Foreign Trade (1972): *Exports,* $213,000,000. *Imports,* $275,-000,000. *Chief trading partners* (1971)—France (took 51% of exports, supplied 47% of imports); Netherlands (7%—3%); West Germany (1.5%—6%).
Transportation: *Motor vehicles* (1971), 63,200 (automobiles, 40,400); *major national airline,* Air Senegal.
Communications: *Telephones* (1971), 28,000; *newspapers* (1971), 1 (daily circulation, 20,000).

(FAO). Long-term aid to build dams across the Senegal and Saloum rivers, improve irrigation and farming, and provide a food reserve for future years has been promised by the World Bank.

Internal Affairs. President Léopold Senghor was reelected to a five-year term on January 28. Running unopposed, he received 99.97% of the vote. The candidates of the ruling Senegalese Progressive Union also won election unopposed to the 100-seat National Assembly. President Senghor reshuffled his cabinet in April, the major change being the appointment of the former minister of national education, Assane Seck, as foreign minister.

Dissatisfaction with Senghor's conservative, pro-French policy continued to be voiced by secondary-school and university students. Sporadic demonstrations occurred in Saint-Louis and Dakar, and a number of schools were set afire. The Senegalese Embassy in Paris was briefly taken over by students in March. The Senegalese Teachers Union was dissolved in March, and three of its leaders were arrested and charged with sedition.

The year's major disturbances erupted in May following the death of Oumar Diop Blondin, a student held prisoner on Gorée. The government claimed he had committed suicide, but radical leaders charged the regime with murder. Army units were called by the government on May 14 to end a 24-hour student strike in Dakar.

Foreign Affairs. The cornerstone of Senegal's policy continued to be close relations with France, in spite of President Senghor's harsh criticism of the French left for its support of the student dissidents. Senegal established a new embassy in Peking and recognized the Vietcong provisional government as well as the Saigon regime.

HARRY A. GAILEY
San Jose State University

SHIPPING. See TRANSPORTATION.

SINGAPORE

The government's initiatives to improve relations with its Southeast Asian neighbors, a setback to monetary cooperation with Malaysia, and continued economic expansion were major developments of 1973 in the Republic of Singapore.

Thai Visit. Prime Minister Lee Kuan Yew made his first official visit to Thailand in January 1973. He and Thai Prime Minister Thanom Kittikachorn agreed on the importance of a continued presence of U. S. troops in Thailand as a major contribution to regional stability. The two governments promised to consult with each other prior to any decision to recognize the People's Republic of China. During Lee's visit the former Thai foreign minister, Thanat Khoman, asserted in a newspaper interview that Singapore wanted to use Thailand as a buffer state to promote its own security.

Visit to Indonesia. In May, Prime Minister Lee visited Indonesia for the first time. The chances of success in Lee's talks with Indonesian President Suharto were enhanced on the first day of the trip, when Lee decorated the graves of two Indonesian marines who had been executed by Singapore for a terrorist bombing there in 1968, during the Sukarno era. Lee's gesture was interpreted as an apology.

In the joint communiqué that followed their talks, the two leaders noted the "increasing cordiality" in their countries' relations. They agreed to

---

SINGAPORE • Information Highlights

Official Name: Republic of Singapore.
Location: Southeast Asia.
Area: 224 square miles (581 sq km).
Population (1973 est.): 2,300,000. *Density,* 9,407 per square mile (3,632 per sq km).
Chief City (1970 census): Singapore, the capital, 2,122,466.
Government: *Head of state,* Benjamin Henry Sheares, president (took office Jan. 1971). *Head of government,* Lee Kuan Yew, prime minister (took office June 1959). *Legislature* (unicameral)—Parliament. Major political party—People's Action party.
Languages: Malay, English, Chinese, Tamil (all official).
Education: *Expenditure* (1969), 15.2% of total public expenditure. *School enrollment* (1969)—primary, 366,881; secondary, 152,110; technical/vocational, 20,635; university/higher, 12,659.
Monetary Unit: Singapore dollar (2.25 S. dollars equal U. S.$1, July 1973).
Gross National Product (1971 est.): $2,482,000,000.
Economic Indexes: *Industrial production* (manufacturing, 1972), 202 (1963=100); *consumer price index* (1972), 113 (1963=100).
Manufacturing (major products): Petroleum products, steel, textiles, tires, wood products, processed foods, electronics, ships, assembled automobiles.
Foreign Trade (1972): Exports, $2,181,000,000; Imports, $3,-383,000,000. *Chief trading partners* (1972)—Malaysia (took 23% of exports, supplied 17% of imports); United States (12%—13%); Japan (7%—20%); United Kingdom (6%—7%).
Transportation: *Motor vehicles* (1971), 204,000 (automobiles, 163,200); *merchant fleet* (1972), 871,000 gross registered tons; *major national airline,* Singapore Airlines.
Communications: *Telephones* (1972), 189,847; *newspapers* (1971), 11 (daily circulation, 367,000).

---

have their senior officials hold "more frequent" consultations and also to expand trade and other economic relations.

Dispute with Malaysia. Relations with Malaysia deteriorated seriously in May when the government in Kuala Lumpur, without prior consultation, abrogated an agreement with the Singapore government that had called for interchangeability of their two currencies and replacement of their joint stock exchange with a separate Malaysian exchange. Acrimonious argument between the two capitals ensued, with each government attempting to undermine the value of the other's currency. In June, Singapore abruptly decided, on a unilateral basis, to float its currency against the U. S. dollar, and Malaysia quickly followed suit.

Economic Developments. In January 1973, the government announced an annual growth rate in its gross domestic product of 15% in 1972, as compared with a 14% gain during the previous year. Manufacturing output showed a 26% increase, as against 24% in 1971.

In a further attempt to make Singapore the leading regional financial center, the government created a new category of foreign banks by granting "offshore" licenses to seven banks of three nations—the United States, Canada, and Britain. Their operations were to be restricted to the Asia dollar market and foreign exchange transactions.

When Prime Minister Lee visited Japan in May 1973 he reportedly won Premier Kakuei Tanaka's acceptance "in principle" of a proposed joint steel enterprise to be operated by Japan, Singapore, Australia, and Indonesia. In August a mission of Japanese steel industrialists, led by officers of the Mitsui firm, visited Singapore.

Defense. Modifications in the Five-Power Defense Agreement appeared imminent when the Australian Labor government decided to withdraw some of its military forces from Singapore.

C. PAUL BRADLEY
University of Michigan-Flint

SOCIAL SECURITY. See SOCIAL WELFARE.

SOCIAL WELFARE

In 1973 many social welfare programs in the United States suffered as a result of pressure from the Nixon administration and resultant confusion and loss of confidence. Significant developments in the field include changes in the Supplementary Security Income (SSI) program and increased interest in some form of national health insurance.

Legislative activity, new or revised programs, and other new developments in the field of social welfare during 1973 are reviewed in this article under the following headings: (1) General Survey; (2) Social Security; (3) Health Care; and (4) Child Welfare.

General Survey

Social welfare programs in the United States were caught in uncertainty and confusion because of conflicts between President Nixon and the Congress during 1973. The conflicts within Congress were not so prominent this year as in some previous years. The administration continued to press for radical changes in the existing system.

To block programs he disliked, President Nixon vetoed appropriation bills, impounded funds for which appropriations were completed, and in other ways attempted to restrict or dismantle programs for which Congress had expressed its support. Some of these presidential actions were successfully challenged in court.

Congress kept some prominent programs in operation by temporary extensions of previous appropriations, while major appropriations bills or court decisions were pending. Meanwhile, many significant programs were quietly eliminated or curtailed, the internal morale of agencies was weakened, and public skepticism mounted as to the willingness or intent of government to carry out its undertakings.

Supplementary Security Income Program. Uncertainty extended even to the new Supplementary Security Income (SSI) program, agreed upon late in 1972 and scheduled to become effective Jan. 1, 1974. Throughout 1973 there were major efforts in both state and federal agencies to prepare for the transfer of persons receiving Old Age Assistance (OAA), Aid to the Permanently and Totally Disabled (APTD), and Aid to the Blind (AB) to the care of the Social Security Administration. The transfer of these 4 million recipients will increase by one tenth the number of persons receiving federal benefits.

It soon became evident that changes would have to be made in the program. The planned-for grants of $130 per month for an individual and $195 for a couple were seen to be too low, even with the permitted additional income of $10 per month for single persons and $15 for couples. Congress agreed to raise the grants, effective July 1, 1974, to $140 per month for an individual and $210 a month for a couple, with the same additional allowances. The provision that states might supplement SSI payments was changed to require all states to supplement SSI payments to the amount of their previous participation in the adult public-assistance programs. Otherwise, large numbers of persons would have received less under the new system than under the old system. A few states, notably Massachusetts, are moving to use the federal program as a base upon which to provide minimum incomes at nearly twice the federal level. Similarly in Canada, where a national program of the same type is in effect, some prov-

inces are supplementing the national program sufficiently to bring minimum incomes for the elderly and handicapped to a level necessary to live decently and in health.

Congress had to deal with other problems regarding SSI. To avoid hardship to 1.5 million persons who would have lost eligibility for food stamps and 150,000 persons who could not have received Medicaid, various provisions were liberalized. However, some observers still consider the complicated food stamp requirements as inequitable for many people. As preparations for implementation of the SSI plan reached a climax, what had been seen as a simplification of federal-state relations began to appear as a nightmare of rules, regulations, and overlapping state and federal responsibilities that threatened a postponement of the effective date. It seems possible, if not probable, that congressional efforts to restrict eligibility and to avoid loopholes have resulted in a costly, unwieldly, bureaucratic structure weighing down a basically sound plan.

Changes in Social Security Benefits and Food Stamp Allotments. To counter inflation, Congress added a 5.6% across-the-board increase in social security benefits, to become effective July 1, 1974. This was in addition to the 20% approved in 1972. In December 1973 this was changed to provide a 7% increase in April 1974 and an additional 4% in July. Inflation also led to semiannual adjustments in food stamp allotments to reflect changes in the cost of living.

Family Assistance Plans. Early in the year the administration announced that it would no longer push for the enactment of the Family Assistance Plan (FAP), first proposed in 1969. This plan would have replaced the state-administered Aid to Families with Dependent Children (AFDC) program with a new federally administered minimum income program for all families with children. After three years of wrangling, Congress had eliminated any version of this from the measure setting up SSI. However, there were indications that both the administration and congressional committees were formulating new welfare reform measures that may be proposed in 1974.

Revenue Sharing. The administration continued to push for the elimination of many specific federal aid programs to states and localities (frequently dating from the Johnson administration) and urged their replacement by a few "special-revenue sharing" funds. These funds would be distributed to states and municipalities on a formula basis, with the local government having much greater leeway in program determination. The burden of protecting the interests of minorities and the disadvantaged would then fall on community action groups. The only revenue-sharing program that made much progress in Congress was the one for education, but no bill was agreed on by the House and Senate.

Administration Attempts to Limit Programs. The administration sought changes in social welfare programs in various ways. Legislation or appropriations that went beyond the scope that President Nixon approved were vetoed. When Congress was unable to override these vetoes, as in the case of the Older Americans Act, the measures were subsequently passed with some or all of the disapproved portions eliminated. In other cases Congress was able to pass measures, such as the increase in social security benefits or the continuation of several Public

Health Services hospitals, contrary to President Nixon's desires, by attaching them to unrelated bills which he would not veto.

Another device used by President Nixon was to withhold, or impound, funds by executive order after he had signed the bills appropriating the funds. Such abrupt actions created great uncertainty among both beneficiaries of the programs and the staffs that administered the programs at the federal, state, and local levels. A series of court decisions denied the President this right, but by that time morale in many agencies had been seriously undermined. In perhaps the most conclusive of its decisions, the court decided that the acting director of the Office of Economic Opportunity (OEO), who had been appointed without Senate confirmation and with the assignment to dismantle the agency, held office illegally and that all steps taken by him to dismantle the agency were also illegal. Several leading members of Congress were plaintiffs in the suit.

A third approach was through administrative regulations changing the rules governing existing programs. The most controversial of the many regulations proposed during 1973 concerned service programs that are associated with public assistance and SSI and that had been rapidly expanding during the past decade. The General Revenue Sharing Act of 1972 set a limit of $2.5 billion on federal matching funds for these services, but the Nixon administration aimed to reduce expenditures to $1.5 billion. Among the changes proposed were the following new regulations: (1) gifts of private funds might not be used to match federal grants; (2) space, equipment, services, or other "in kind" contributions might not be used as matching funds; (3) many services formerly required to be provided by the states would be made optional, and previously optional services would be eliminated for federal funding purposes; (4) national standards for child care services would be eliminated; (5) eligibility of past and potential recipients of public assistance for services would be greatly restricted; and (6) fair hearings and appeals when beneficiaries were aggrieved would be eliminated.

Under such regulations a large portion of the services being provided in many states would have been eliminated or seriously crippled. In the face of thousands of protests, the Department of Health, Education, and Welfare (HEW) first postponed the date for implementation of the new regulations, then issued modified regulations, and later when these changes did not quiet the clamor Congress by law required that the new regulations not be put into effect until new legislation was enacted.

The administration also proposed to enforce, with severe monetary penalties, stringent new regulations regarding state administration of eligibility requirements in public assistance. There was massive resistance, and the states were given up to two years to bring their procedures into line. Such pressures to limit public assistance brought a slight reduction in expenditures in the fiscal year ending June 1973, but later nearly all the states were actively urging potentially eligible elderly and disabled persons to apply for OAA or AB so that they could receive supplements in addition to SSI.

The administration has also reorganized departments in such a way as to reallocate functions and thereby bring them into keeping with administrative purpose. During 1973 the Social and Rehabilitation Service and the National Institutes of Health, both in HEW, were so reorganized. The Office of Economic Opportunity (OEO), especially its legal aid program, has been subject both to executive pressure and to congressional indecisiveness for some years. An independent Legal Services Corporation was proposed, but Congress and the administration have been unable to agree on the amount of control that the President may exercise over it. Congress is fearful that to give the President power to appoint a majority of the members of its board would make the organization a political, rather than a legal, instrument; while the President is fearful that without that type of control the new corporation might irresponsibly disrupt existing political economic and social structures.

Conclusions. The legislative-administrative stalemate over a legal aid program, which is compounded by serious differences within Congress, has generated a large backlog of other legislative proposals having to do with runaway youth, child abuse and neglect, child support, vocational rehabilitation, and many other problems. No serious attention is being devoted to anything resembling the allowances of $20 per month to each child, irrespective of family need, as are given in Canada.

The appropriations bill for the Departments of Labor and HEW for the year beginning in July was held up to reconcile the differences between the House and Senate versions. However, since both houses had approved greater expenditures than the President had indicated he would accept, there was the prospect of another veto. Hence, with the President's popularity in the country sinking and with increasing talk of impeachment in Congress, it appeared that this bill might provide the opportunity for another major confrontation between the President and Congress. Such confrontations have tended to accentuate the negative, rather than establishing positive, investment-type goals for social welfare programs. Whether some states, such as Massachusetts, by asuring their elderly citizens a minimum income high enough to live decently and in health, will demonstrate the utility of a more positive approach to the rest of the nation remains to be seen.

RALPH E. PUMPHREY
Washington University, St. Louis

Social Security

Several significant provisions of the Social Security Act enacted in 1972 went into effect in 1973. Important among these was the extension of Medicare coverage for disabled social security beneficiaries and for certain persons with chronic kidney disease and their dependents for the last half of 1973. Amendments making changes in social security cash benefits, in the Supplemental Security Income (SSI) program, and in the federal-state Medicaid (medical assistance) program were enacted in July and December 1973; most of them were scheduled to become effective in 1974.

Amendments. Legislation enacted in July 1973 included changes relating to the monthly cash benefits: effective January 1974, the annual exempt amounts of beneficiaries' earnings is $2,400 (a beneficiary may earn $200 in a month and still get full benefits for the month); the maximum taxable and creditable amount of earnings was raised, effective for taxable years after Dec. 31, 1973; and monthly cash benefits were to be increased, beginning with the June 1974 benefit. December amendments revised the earlier change in the annual taxable earn-

ings maximum, raising it to $13,200. They also changed the July provision for a benefit increase, providing instead for an 11% increase in two steps —7% payable with the March 1974 benefit and 4% of it payable with the benefit for June. The December legislation also changed the provisions for delayed retirement credits, the special minimum benefit for workers with many years of low earnings in covered employment, and the automatic adjustment provisions for benefit increases and for the retirement-test exempt earnings. The social security contribution rate was not raised, but a shift in the shares for the cash benefits and the hospital insurance benefits reduced the latter by 0.1% and raised the rate for the cash benefits by 0.1% for 1974–77.

Financing. In 1973 employers and employees each paid contributions of 5.85% on the first $10,800 of the worker's earnings. The rate for the self-employed was 8%. For all, 1% of the contribution rate was earmarked for hospital insurance in 1973. The monthly premium for the supplementary medical insurance part of Medicare was $5.80 through Aug. 12, 1973, and $6.30 up to July 1974, when it will be $6.70. The monthly premium for voluntary participation in the hospital insurance program by those aged 65 and over and not otherwise entitled to participate will rise in July 1974 from $30 to $36.

Operations. In the year ending June 30, monthly cash benefits totaled $47,009,807,000. Lump-sum death payments came to $321,125,000. In June the average monthly benefit was $164.80 for retired workers and $181.42 for disabled workers. During one month—June 1973—$617.6 million was withdrawn from the hospital insurance trust fund for payments to hospitals, skilled-nursing facilities, and home health agencies providing services to beneficiaries, and $207.6 million was withdrawn from the medical insurance trust fund for supplementary medical insurance benefits. During the entire fiscal year 1973, a total of $6.6 billion was withdrawn from the hospital insurance trust fund and a total of $2.4 billion from the medical insurance trust fund.

Supplemental Security Income. The new federal Supplemental Security Income (SSI) program, administered by the Social Security Administration, began operations in January 1974. Amendments passed in July and December 1973 revised several provisions in federal legislation. The changes included the setting of new payment levels—at $140 a month for an individual and $210 for a couple, effective January 1974, and the scheduling of further increases for July 1974 to $146 for an individual and $219 for a couple.

ARTHUR E. HESS
Deputy Commissioner of Social Security

Health Care

Rocketing costs of health care, fueled simultaneously by inflation and the increasing sophistication of medical care technology, dominated the health care scene in the United States in 1973 and promised to be a major concern in 1974. Demands for a national health insurance program to help offset the cost of being sick and to help guarantee that health care is available for low-income families grew noticeably during 1973. Congressional leaders predicted that attempts to write a National Health Insurance (NHI) bill would increase during the 1974 session of Congress, although many were reluctant to predict final passage of any bill before the next Congress, the 94th beginning in 1975.

Other significant health care issues during the year included controversy over professional review of the care given by physicians to Medicare and Medicaid patients and growing recognition that alcoholism and the increasing rate of venereal disease are two serious health care problems.

National Health Insurance. Pressures from rising salaries and costs of medical supplies contributed heavily to the increased prices of health care. But another significant factor that bore heavily on the growing interest in National Health Insurance was the technology explosion of recent years. Although such advances in medical practice as organ transplants, kidney dialysis, and radioactive cobalt treatments for cancer victims raised hopes of cures for hitherto incurable diseases, they also presented more families with the possibility of enormous medical bills that have come to be widely known as "catastrophic" health care costs.

A health insurance program to assure that no U. S. family is bankrupted by catastrophic costs has become an increasingly popular trend in Congress. Late in 1973 a National Health Insurance bill was sponsored by Sen. Russell L. Long (D-La.) and Sen. Abraham Ribicoff (D-Conn.). The bill was considered particularly significant because Long is chairman of the Senate Finance Committee that would hold hearings on NHI legislation and Ribicoff is an influential member of the committee. They indicated that they expected to hold hearings on the measure as early as the spring of 1974. The bill combines a "Catastrophic Health Insurance Plan" with a federal program of financing health insurance for low-income individuals and families. The catastrophic plan would cover 80% of a family's medical bills after an initial expense of $2,000 that could be financed by private health insurance. The plan would also pay most hospital expenses after 60 days of inpatient treatment that also could be covered by private health insurance. The plan encourages families to purchase private health insurance for their medical needs up to the "catastrophic" level. Unlike a proposal developed earlier by the Nixon administration, the Long-Ribicoff plan would not flatly require employers to pay 75% of the cost of health insurance for their workers. President Nixon promised a rewritten version of the 1971 administration bill for early 1974.

Although the Long-Ribicoff proposal struck a responsive chord in both the House and the Senate, it was opposed by the AFL-CIO, which is supporting a "womb-to-tomb" National Health Insurance plan, and it was opposed by others who favor more complete coverage.

Wage and Price Controls. Although controls over wages and prices in many sectors of the U. S. economy were relaxed during 1973, the administration announced new Phase 4 strictures on the health care industry. These new measures would take effect Jan. 1, 1974. In revealing details of the new controls, administration officials said they expected that health care would be the last industry to be decontrolled. Some officials openly expressed the view that permanent price controls over health care providers would be necessary as part of a NHI program or until such a program goes into effect.

Phase 4 controls were protested vigorously by virtually every segment of the health care industry, including physician, hospital, dental, nursing home, and other professional organizations. Some filed lawsuits seeking to end the controls, which they

maintained were causing economic hardship on practitioners, particularly hospitals.

Professional Review. An often bitter dispute developed over a section of the 1972 Social Security Amendments that requires Professional Standard Review Organizations (PSROs) to be set up to oversee the care given by physicians to Medicare and Medicaid patients in hospitals. This controversy involved the American Medical Association (AMA), the Senate Finance Committee, and the Department of Health, Education, and Welfare (HEW). Physician organizations opposed the law in general as an invasion of their rights by the government. They fought, in particular, against application of the law by HEW in such a manner that state medical societies, bastions of power within the AMA, were excluded from active participation in all but the smallest states, with the review job going chiefly to county medical societies. In Canada there is already a program of national health insurance, and in 1973 the Canadian Medical Association endorsed the principle that a physician must demonstrate continuing competence to maintain his license to practice and gave high priority to the development of means of implementing this principle.

Major Health Care Issues. There was increased awareness throughout the health care industry of the serious problems of alcoholism and venereal disease. U. S. health care leaders reported progress against alcoholism in 1973. A Conference on Medical Complications of Alcohol Abuse, held by the AMA in October, was marked by widespread confidence among the participants that a "corner had been turned" in efforts against alcoholism. The incidence of venereal disease continued to rise in the United States during 1973, posing one of the country's biggest public health problems (see MEDICINE—*Venereal Disease*).

JEROME F. BRAZDA
Editor, "Washington Report on Medicine and Health"

Child Welfare

In 1973 there was increased trend toward cooperation among federal, state, local, and voluntary agencies in developing and implementing programs within the Office of Child Development (OCD). Illustrative of collaboration were grants to the Children's Division of the American Humane Association and the Mershon Center at The Ohio State University to collect and study information on child abuse and neglect and to survey local programs now operating.

Child and Family Resource Program. An experimental project, named Child and Family Resource Program, was inaugurated. Based on Head Start, the new program is designed to strengthen the role of the family by providing or making available prenatal health and nutrition education, after-school tutoring for primary-grade children, and mental health services and aid to parents in the development of infants and young children. This is achieved through mobilization of existing resources, such as maternal and child health-care clinics, day-care programs, university services, family counseling, and local schools. Exchange of services helps meet the needs of Head Start and other low-income families with young children. Where services are not available, a team of physicians, psychologists, educators, and social workers assists parents in determining the kind of help they need and want. Eleven programs have been funded, one in each of HEW's

10 regions and one under OCD's Indian and Migrant Program.

Action for Foster Children. A joint effort by the Children's Bureau of OCD and the Community Services Administration led to the formation of the National Action for Foster Children Committee. This committee, composed of representatives of national organizations, was created to promote communication and action in behalf of foster children. One of its goals is to stimulate the formation of 100 state, county, and city action committees by April 1974, when an annual National Action for Foster Children Week will be observed.

Education for Parenthood. The demonstration project, Education for Parenthood, begun in 1972 under the joint sponsorship of OCD and the Office of Education, was expanded in 1973 by the involvement of six national voluntary organizations. Grants to Boys Clubs of America, Boy Scouts of America, Girl Scouts of the U. S. A., National Federation of Settlements and Neighborhood Centers, the Salvation Army, and Save the Children Federation will enable each organization to develop programs to help prepare teen-agers for parenthood by working with young children in their own communities. It is estimated that nearly 3 million adult volunteers will play leadership roles and that 300,000 local, state, and national civic, religious, and educational organizations will contribute to the program.

Evaluating Existing Programs. Two programs closely related to Head Start—Parent and Child Centers and Home Start—are being evaluated. Parent and Child Centers provide parent education, counseling, nutrition, and health care coordination to economically deprived families with children under the age of three. The centers are financed by the Office of Economic Opportunity and administered by local Community Action Agencies. An impact study of the 33 centers has been completed, and a final report is expected by early 1974.

Home Start employed paraprofessional women to visit homes to help parents understand and provide for their children. The program, no longer funded by OCD, is being evaluated for its effectiveness.

UNICEF. The United Nations Children's Fund (UNICEF) has 111 member nations and represents almost 850 million children. In its fight against disease, poverty, hunger, and ignorance among children, UNICEF always needs money. For 1973–74, $81 million is available for aid, a substantial increase over that in the previous year, but many unmet needs call for $100 million by 1975.

Child health was the priority in 99 countries, with 41% of UNICEF's aid devoted to building a network of mother-child health centers. Next highest in priority was education, with 27% of assistance going into teacher training, equipment, and textbooks for 83 nations. For 62 countries, malnutrition in children was the major problem, taking 11% of funds. Family-child welfare projects were approved for 54 countries with 6% of aid.

One of the most vital roles for UNICEF is its relief and rehabilitation program. In 1973 emergency programs were funded in Bangladesh, India, the Indochina Peninsula, Pakistan, Sudan, and West Africa. The Bangladesh project, the largest in UNICEF's history, feeds 3 million children a day.

ISABELLA J. JONES, *Executive Vice President*
National Association of Consultants
for Children and Youth

SOCIETIES AND ORGANIZATIONS

This article lists a selection of some of the most noteworthy associations, societies, foundations, and trusts of the United States and Canada. The information for each listing has been furnished by the organization concerned, and includes membership figures, dates of annual meetings, officers, and headquarters location or address.

Alcoholics Anonymous (The General Service Board of A. A., Inc.). Membership: over 650,000 in more than 20,000 affiliated groups. Annual conference: New York, N. Y., April 22–27, 1974. Chairman, John L. Norris, M. D. Headquarters: 468 Park Avenue S., New York, N. Y. Mailing Address: Box 459, Grand Central Station, New York, N. Y. 10017.

American Academy of Arts and Letters. Membership: 50. Annual ceremonial: New York, N. Y., May 1973. President, Aaron Copland; secy., John Hersey. Headquarters: 633 West 155th St., New York, N. Y. 10032.

American Academy of Arts and Sciences. Membership: approx. 2,240. President, Harvey Brooks; secy., A. Hunter Dupree. Headquarters: 165 Allandale St., Jamaica Plain Station, Boston, Mass. 02130.

American Academy of Political and Social Science. Membership: 21,500, including 7,000 libraries. Annual meeting: Philadelphia, Pa., April 5–6, 1974. President, Marvin E. Wolfgang; business mgr., Ingeborg Hessler. Headquarters: 3937 Chestnut St., Philadelphia, Pa. 19104.

American Anthropological Association. Membership: 8,-800. Annual meeting: Mexico City, Mexico, Nov. 1974. President, Joseph B. Casagrande; exec. director, Edward J. Lehman. Headquarters: 1703 New Hampshire Ave. NW, Washington, D. C. 20009.

American Association for the Advancement of Science. Membership: 127,000 and 283 affiliated groups. Meeting: New York City, Jan. 27–31, 1975. President, Roger Revelle; exec. officer, William Bevan. Headquarters: 1515 Massachusetts Ave. NW, Washington, D. C. 20005.

American Association of University Professors. Membership: 85,624. Annual meeting: Washington, D. C., April 26–27, 1974. President, Walter Adams; gen. secy., Bertram H. Davis. Headquarters: One Dupont Circle NW, Washington, D. C. 20036.

American Association of University Women. Membership: 176,000. President, Anne Campbell; gen. dir., Alice L. Beeman. Headquarters: 2401 Virginia Ave. NW, Washington, D. C. 20037.

American Astronomical Society. Membership: 2,800. Meetings: 1974: Lincoln, Neb., March 26–29; Rochester, N. Y., Aug. 19–22; Gainesville, Fla., Dec. 10–13. President, Bart J. Bok; president-elect, Robert P. Kraft; secy., L. W. Fredrick; exec. officer, H. M. Gurin. Address: 211 FitzRandolph Road, Princeton, N. J. 08540.

American Automobile Association. Membership: 16 million in 884 affiliated groups. Annual meeting: Chicago, Ill., Sept. 16–18, 1974. President, Charles J. Gallagher; secy., Knox Farrand. Headquarters: 8111 Gatehouse Rd., Falls Church, Va. 22042.

American Bankers Association. Membership: 18,398 banks and branches. Annual meeting: Honolulu, Hawaii, Oct. 19–23, 1974. President, Rex J. Morthland; secy., George H. Gustafson. Headquarters: 1120 Connecticut Ave. NW, Washington, D. C. 20036.

American Bar Association. Membership: 171,000. Meeting: Honolulu, Hawaii, Aug. 12–16, 1974. President, Chesterfield Smith; secy., Kenneth J. Burns, Jr.; exec. dir., Bert H. Early. Headquarters: 1155 East 60th St., Chicago, Ill. 60637.

American Bible Society. 1972 Scripture distribution: 163,624,325 copies. Annual meeting: New York, N. Y., May 9, 1974. President, Edmund F. Wagner; general secretaries, Laton E. Holmgren and Warner A. Hutchinson; treas., Charles W. Baas. Headquarters: 1865 Broadway, New York, N. Y. 10023.

American Booksellers Association, Inc. Membership: 4,-100. National convention: Washington, D. C., June 2–5, 1974. President, Eliot Leonard; exec. director, G. Roysce Smith. Headquarters: 800 Second Ave., New York, N. Y. 10017.

American Cancer Society, Inc. Membership: 190 voting members; 57 chartered divisions. Annual meeting of members (*no scientific sessions*): New York, N. Y., Oct. 16–18, 1974. President, Justin J. Stein, M. D.; secy., Samuel M. Seegal. Headquarters: 219 East 42d St., New York, N. Y. 10017.

American Chemical Society. Membership: 110,000. National meetings, 1974: Los Angeles, Calif., March 31–April 5; Atlantic City, N. J., September 8–13. President, Bernard S. Friedman; exec. director, R. W. Cairns. Headquarters: 1155 16th St. NW, Washington, D. C. 20036.

American Civil Liberties Union. Membership: 205,000. Exec. director, Aryeh Neier; board chairman, Edward J. Ennis. Headquarters: 22 East 40th St., New York, N. Y. 10016.

American Council of Learned Societies. Membership: 39 professional societies concerned with the humanities and the humanistic aspects of the social sciences. Annual meeting: Washington, D. C., Jan. 17–18, 1974. President, Frederick Burkhardt; vice presidents, Gordon B. Turner and Charlotte Bowman. Headquarters: 345 East 46th St., New York, N. Y. 10017.

American Council on Education. Membership: 1,377 colleges and universities, 120 associated organizations, 56 affiliates, and 69 constituent organizations. Annual meeting: Washington, D. C., Oct. 9–11, 1974. President, Roger W. Heyns; exec. secy., Charles G. Dobbins. Headquarters: One Dupont Circle NW, Washington, D. C. 20036.

American Dental Association. Membership: 118,000. Annual session: Washington, D. C., Nov. 10–14, 1974. President, Carlton H. Williams, D. D. S.; exec. director, C. Gordon Watson, D. D. S. Headquarters: 211 E. Chicago Ave., Chicago, Ill. 60611.

American Economic Association. Membership: 17,500 and 7,650 subscribers. Annual meeting: San Francisco, Calif., Dec. 28–30, 1974. President, Walter W. Heller; secy.-treas., Rendigs Fels. Headquarters: 1313 21st Ave. S., Nashville, Tenn. 37212.

American Farm Bureau Federation. Membership: 2,175,-780 families. Annual meeting: January of each year. President, William J. Kuhfuss; secy.-treas., Roger Fleming. Headquarters: 225 Touhy Ave., Park Ridge, Ill. 60068.

American Geographical Society. Membership: 3,000. Annual dinner: New York, N. Y., Nov. 1974. President, Richard H. Nolte; director, Robert B. McNee. Headquarters: Broadway at 156th St., New York, N. Y. 10032.

American Geophysical Union. Membership: 11.583 individuals and 36 organizations. Meetings, 1974: Washington, D. C., April 8–12 and San Francisco, Calif., Dec. 12–17. President, Philip H. Abelson; gen. secretary, Charles A. Whitten; exec. director, A. F. Spilhaus, Jr. Headquarters: 1707 L St. NW, Washington, D. C. 20036.

American Heart Association. Membership: 91,500 in 55 affiliates, 125 chapters, and about 1,000 local subdivisions. Annual meeting: Chicago, Ill., Nov. 14–19, 1974. President, Richard S. Ross, M. D.; secy., Elwood Ennis. Headquarters: 44 East 23d St., New York, N. Y. 10010.

American Historical Association. Membership: 17,500. Annual meeting: Chicago, Ill., Dec. 28–30, 1974. President, Lynn White; exec. secy., Paul L. Ward. Headquarters: 400 A St. SE, Washington, D. C. 20003

American Horticultural Society. Membership: 24,000 individuals; 380 organizations, institutions, and commercial establishments. National congress: Washington, D. C., Nov. 1974. President, Dr. David G. Leach; exec. director, O. Keister Evans. Headquarters: Mt. Vernon, Virginia 22121.

American Hospital Association. Membership: 19,113 persons; 7,055 institutions. Annual meeting: Washington, D. C., Feb. 3–6, 1974; annual convention (American Health Congress): Chicago, Ill., Aug. 12–15, 1974. Chairman of the board, Horace M. Cardwell; president, John Alexander McMahon; secy., James E. Hague. Headquarters: 840 North Lake Shore Drive, Chicago, Ill. 60611.

American Institute of Aeronautics and Astronautics. Membership: 22,000 plus 4,000 student members. Exec. secy., James J. Harford. Headquarters: 1290 Avenue of the Americas, New York, N. Y. 10019.

American Institute of Architects. Membership: 24,000. National convention: Washington, D. C., May 19–23, 1974. President, Archibald C. Rogers; first vice pres., William Marshall, Jr.; secy., Hilliard T. Smith, Jr. Headquarters: 1735 New York Ave. NW, Washington, D. C. 20006.

American Institute of Biological Sciences. Membership: 11,607, with 43 adherent societies and 8 affiliate organizations. Annual meeting: Arizona State University, Tempe, June 16–21, 1974. President, George Sprugel, Jr.; vice pres. and pres.-elect, David M. Gates; secy.-treas., Richard Greulich; director, John R. Olive. Headquarters: 3900 Wisconsin Avenue NW, Washington, D. C. 20016.

American Institute of Certified Public Accountants. Membership: 96,000. Annual meeting: Seattle, Washington, Oct. 13–16, 1974. President, Samuel A. Dericux; exec. vice pres., Wallace E. Olson; admin. vice pres. and secy., John Lawler. Headquarters: 666 Fifth Ave., New York, N. Y. 10019.

American Institute of Chemical Engineers. Membership: 40,125. Annual meeting: Washington, D. C., Dec. 1–5, 1974. President, Irving Leibson; exec. secy., F. J. Van Antwerpen. Headquarters: 345 East 47th Street, New York, N. Y. 10017.

American Institute of Graphic Arts. Membership: 1,800. President, Robert O. Bach; exec. director, Edward Gottschall. Headquarters: 1059 Third Ave., New York, N. Y. 10021.

American Institute of Mining, Metallurgical and Petroleum Engineers, Inc. Membership: 49,394. Annual meeting: Dallas, Tex., Feb. 24–28, 1974. President, Wayne E. Glenn; exec. director, Joe B. Alford. Headquarters: 345 East 47th St., New York, N. Y. 10017.

American Legion, The. Membership: 2,700,000. National convention: Miami Beach, Fla., Aug. 16–22, 1974. National commander, Robert E. L. Eaton; national adjutant, William F. Hauck. Headquarters: 700 N. Pennsylvania St., Indianapolis, Ind. 46206.

American Lung Association (formerly **National Tuberculosis and Respiratory Disease Association**). Membership: 282 affiliated groups. Annual meeting: Cincinnati, Ohio, May 12–15, 1974. President, Wendell L. Van Loan; managing director, Robert J. Anderson, M.D. Headquarters: 1740 Broadway, New York, N.Y. 10019.

American Management Association. Membership: 50,000. Annual meeting: Sept. 18, 1974. Chairman of the board, Lawrence A. Appley; president and chief exec. officer, James L. Hayes. Headquarters: 135 West 50th St., New York, N.Y. 10020.

American Mathematical Society. Membership: 15,244. Annual meeting: San Francisco, Calif., Jan. 15–18, 1974. President, Saunders MacLane; secy., Everett Pitcher. Headquarters: P. O. Box 6248, Providence, R. I. 02940.

American Medical Association. Membership: 204,000. Annual meeting: Chicago, Ill., June 24–27, 1974. President, Russell B. Roth, M.D.; secy.-treas., Richard E. Palmer, M.D.; exec. vice pres., Ernest B. Howard, M.D. Headquarters: 535 N. Dearborn St., Chicago, Ill. 60610.

American Meteorological Society. Membership: 9,000 including 130 corporate members. President, David S. Johnson; exec. director, Dr. Kenneth C. Spengler; secy.-treas., David F. Landrigan. Headquarters: 45 Beacon St., Boston, Mass. 02108.

American National Red Cross. Adult membership: 36,423,-804 in 3,190 chapters. National convention: Minneapolis, Minn., May 19–22, 1974. Chairman, Frank Stanton; president, George M. Elsey. Headquarters: 17th and D Sts. NW, Washington, D.C. 20006.

American Newspaper Publishers Association. Membership: 1,084. Annual convention: April 22–25, 1974. Chairman, Davis Taylor; president and gen. manager, Stanford Smith. Headquarters: 11600 Sunrise Valley Drive, Reston, Va. 22070. Mail Address: P. O. Box 17407, Dulles International Airport, Washington, D. C. 20041.

American Nurses Association. Membership: 200,000 in 53 states and territorial associations. National convention: San Francisco, Calif., June 10–14, 1974. President, Rosamond C. Gabrielson; exec. director, Eileen M. Jacobi. Headquarters: 2420 Pershing Road, Kansas City, Mo. 64108.

American Philological Association. Membership: 2,800. Annual meeting: Chicago, Ill., Dec. 28–30, 1974. President, Harry L. Levy; secy., Robert W. Carrubba. Headquarters: 431 North Burrowes, The Pennsylvania State University, University Park, Pa. 16802.

American Physical Society. Membership: 29,000 American and foreign. Annual meeting: Chicago, Ill., Feb. 4–7, 1974. President W. K. H. Panofsky; exec.-secy., Dr. W. W. Havens, Jr. Headquarters: 335 East 45th St., New York, N.Y. 10017.

American Psychiatric Association. Membership: 20,158; 67 district branches. Annual meeting: Detroit, Mich., May 6–10, 1974. President, Alfred M. Freedman, M.D.; secretary, Robert W. Gibson, M.D.; medical director, Walter E. Barton, M.D. Headquarters: 1700 18th St. NW, Washington, D.C. 20009.

American Psychological Association. Membership: 35,000. Annual meeting: New Orleans, La., Aug. 30–Sept. 3, 1974. President, Albert Bandura, exec. officer, Kenneth B. Little. Headquarters: 1200 17th St. NW, Washington, D.C. 20036.

American Society of Civil Engineers. Membership: 67,000. Annual meeting: Kansas City, Mo., Oct. 21–25, 1974. President: Charles W. Yoder; exec. director: Eugene Zwoyer. Headquarters: 345 East 47th St., New York, N.Y. 10017.

American Society of Composers, Authors, and Publishers. Membership: 16,100 composers and authors; 5,800 publishers. President, Stanley Adams; secy., Morton Gould. Headquarters: One Lincoln Plaza, New York, N.Y. 10023.

American Society of Mechanical Engineers. Membership: 65,190. President, Daniel C. Drucker; exec. director and secretary, Rogers B. Finch. Headquarters: 345 East 47th St., New York, N.Y. 10017.

American Society of Newspaper Editors. Membership: 800. National convention: Atlanta, Ga., April 16–19, 1974. President: Arthur C. Deck; secy., Warren H. Phillips. Headquarters: Box 551, 1350 Sullivan Trail, Easton, Pa. 18042.

American Sociological Association. Membership: 15,000. Annual meeting: Montreal, Canada, Aug. 26–29, 1974. President, Peter Blau; secy., J. Milton Yinger. Headquarters: 1722 N St. NW, Washington, D.C. 20036

American Statistical Association. Membership: 10,500. Annual meeting: St. Louis, Mo., Aug. 26–29, 1974. President, Jerome Cornfield; secy., Fred C. Leone. Headquarters: 806 15th St. NW, Washington, D.C. 20005.

American Youth Hostels, Inc. Membership: 76,000; 30 councils in the United States. Annual meeting: Boston, Mass., December 1974. President, Lyman Moore; exec. director, Frank D. Cosgrove. Headquarters: National Campus, Delaplane, Va. 22025.

Archaeological Institute of America. Membership: 6500; subscribers, 12,000. President, James B. Pritchard; exec. director, Mary Kathleen Brown; gen. secy., Elizabeth A. Whitehead. Headquarters: 260 West Broadway, New York, N.Y. 10013.

Arthritis Foundation, The. Membership: 76 chapters. Annual meeting: New York City, June 15, 1974. Chairman of the board, Charles B. Harding; president, Daniel E. Button; secy., Richard H. Freyberg, M. D. Headquarters: 1212 Avenue of the Americas, New York, N.Y. 10036.

Association of American Publishers. Membership: approx. 225. Annual meeting: Spring 1974. Chairman of the board, Ross D. Sackett; president, Townsend W. Hoopes; vice pres., Austin J. McCaffrey. Addresses: One Park Ave., New York, N.Y. 10016 and 1826 Jefferson Place NW, Washington, D. C. 20036.

Association of Junior Leagues, Inc. Membership: 223 member Leagues in U.S., Canada, and Mexico. Annual conference: Boca Raton, Fla., May 12–15, 1974. President, Mrs. Rufus C. Barkley, Jr. Headquarters: 825 Third Ave., New York, N.Y. 10022.

Benevolent and Protective Order of Elks. Membership: 1,541,784 in 2,179 Lodges. National convention: Miami Beach, Fla., July 7–11, 1974. Grand exalted ruler, Robert A. Yothers; grand secretary, Homer Huhn, Jr. Headquarters: 2750 Lake View Ave., Chicago, Ill. 60614.

B'nai B'rith. Membership: 510,000 in 4,000 local men's, women's, and youth units. President, David M. Blumberg; exec. vice pres., Rabbi Benjamin M. Kahn. Headquarters: 1640 Rhode Island Ave. NW, Washington, D. C. 20036.

Boys' Clubs of America. Membership: 1,000,000 in 1,014 clubs. National convention: New York, N.Y., May 26–30, 1974. President, John L. Burns; national director, William R. Bricker. Headquarters: 771 First Ave., New York, N.Y. 10017.

Boy Scouts of America. Membership: 6,524,640 boys and leaders in 458 Boy Scout councils. Annual meeting: Honolulu, Hawaii, May 15–17, 1974. President, Robert W. Reneker; chief scout executive, Alden G. Barber. Headquarters: North Brunswick, N. J. 08902.

Camp Fire Girls, Inc. Membership: 600,000 in over 9,000 communities. National council meeting: October 1975. President, Mrs. Albert E. Bollengier; national exec. dir., Dr. Hester Turner. Headquarters: 1740 Broadway, New York, N.Y. 10019.

Canadian Library Association. Membership: 3,100 persons, 900 institutions. Annual conference: Winnipeg, Manitoba, June 22–28, 1974. President: H. C. Campbell. Headquarters: 151 Sparks St., Ottawa, Ont. KIP 5E3.

Canadian Medical Association. Membership: 28,000. Annual meeting: Toronto, Ontario, June 23–28, 1974. President, Dr. P. J. Banks; secy.-gen., J. D. Wallace, M. D. Headquarters: 1867 Alta Vista Drive, Ottawa, Ontario KIG 0G8.

Catholic Library Association. Membership: 3,080. National convention: Pittsburgh, Pa., April 15–18, 1974. President, Dr. Mary-Jo DiMuccio; exec. dir., Matthew R. Wilt. Headquarters: 461 W. Lancaster Ave., Haverford, Pa. 19041.

Chamber of Commerce of the United States of America. Membership about 4,000 trade associations and local chambers, more than 39,000 business members, and nearly 5,000,000 underlying membership. Annual meeting: Washington, D. C., April 28–30, 1974. President, Edward B. Rust; chief exec. officer, Arch N. Booth. Headquarters: 1615 H St. NW, Washington, D. C. 20006.

Council on Foreign Relations, Inc. Membership: 1,600. Annual meeting: New York, N.Y., Oct. 1974. President, Bayless Manning. Headquarters: 58 East 68th St., New York, N.Y. 10021.

Daughters of the American Revolution (National Society). Membership: 196,681 in 2,968 chapters. Continental congress: Washington, D.C., April 15–19, 1974. President general, Mrs. Donald Spicer. Headquarters: 1776 D St. NW, Washington, D.C. 20006.

Freemasonry, Ancient Accepted Scottish Rite of (Northern Masonic Jurisdiction): Supreme Council, 33°. Membership: 511,369 in 380 affiliated groups. Annual meeting: Atlantic City, N. J., Sept. 24–26, 1974. Sovereign grand commander, George A. Newbury; grand secy. gen., Laurence E. Eaton; exec. secy., Stanley F. Maxwell. Headquarters: 33 Marrett Road, Lexington, Mass. 02173.

Freemasonry, Ancient and Accepted Scottish Rite of (Southern Jurisdiction): Supreme Council, 33°. Membership: 610,000 in 216 affiliated groups. National convention: Washington, D. C., Oct. 19–23, 1975. Sovereign grand commander, Henry C. Clausen; grand secy. gen., C. Fred Kleinknecht. Headquarters: 1733 16th St. NW, Washington, D.C. 20009.

Future Farmers of America. Membership: 448,000 in 50 state associations. National convention: Kansas City, Mo., Oct. 15–18, 1974. National advisor, H. N. Hunsicker; exec. secretary, W. P. Gray. Headquarters: Box 15160 Alexandria, Va. 22309.

Garden Club of America, The. Membership: approx. 12,700 in 179 member clubs. Annual meeting: Atlanta, Ga., April 22–24, 1974. President, Mrs. Nicholas R. duPont; corresponding secy., Mrs. Fabian W. Kunzelmann. Headquarters: 598 Madison Avenue, New York, N.Y. 10022.

General Federation of Women's Clubs. Membership: 10,000,000 in 14,000 U. S. organizations and 36 abroad. National convention: Minneapolis, Minn., May 26–June 1, 1974. President, Mrs. Kermit V. Haugan; exec. secretary, Mrs. Wilson Y. Christian. Headquarters: 1734 N St. NW, Washington, D. C. 20036.

Geological Society of America. Membership: 10,205. Annual meeting: Miami Beach, Florida, Nov. 18–20, 1974. President, Clarence Allen; exec. secy., Edwin B. Eckel. Headquarters: 3300 Penrose Place, Boulder, Colorado 80301.

Girl Scouts of the U. S. A. Membership: 3,726,000. National president, Mrs. William McLeod; exec. director, Dr. Cecily C. Selby. Headquarters: 830 Third Ave., New York, N. Y. 10022.

Institute of Electrical and Electronics Engineers, Inc. Membership: 160,000. International convention: New York, N. Y., March 26–29, 1974. President, John J. Guarrera; gen. manager, Donald G. Fink. Headquarters: 345 East 47th St., New York, N. Y. 10017.

Jewish War Veterans of the U. S. A. Membership: 100,- 000 in 750 units. National commander, Ainslee R. Ferdie; national exec. director, Felix M. Putterman. Headquarters: 1712 New Hampshire Ave. NW, Washington, D. C. 20009.

Kiwanis International. Membership: 275,000 in 6,200 clubs in U. S. and abroad. Annual convention: Denver, Colo., June 23–26, 1974. President, William M. Eagles, M. D.; secy., R. P. Merridew. Headquarters: 101 East Erie St., Chicago, Ill. 60611.

Knights of Columbus. Membership: 1,200,000. Annual meeting: Detroit, Mich., Aug. 20–22, 1974. Supreme knight, John W. McDevitt; supreme secretary, Virgil C. Dechant. Headquarters: Columbus Plaza, New Haven, Conn. 06507.

Knights of Pythias, Supreme Lodge. Membership: 175,- 862 in 1,695 subordinate lodges. Biennial meeting: Baltimore, Md., Aug. 11–14, 1974. Supreme chancellor, Andrew A. Oden; supreme secretary, Jule O. Pritchard. Office: 47 N. Grant St., Stockton, Calif. 95202.

League of Women Voters of the United States. Membership: 160,000. National convention: San Francisco, Calif., May 6–10, 1974. President, Lucy Wilson Benson; first vice pres., Gail Bradley. Headquarters: 1730 M St. NW, Washington, D. C. 20036.

Lions International. Membership: 1,020,000 in 26,400 clubs in 149 countries and geographic areas. President, Tris Coffin. Headquarters: York and Cermak Roads, Oak Brook, Ill. 60521.

Modern Language Association of America. Membership: 30,000. Annual convention: New York, N. Y., Dec. 27–30, 1974. President, John H. Fisher; exec. secy., William D. Schaefer. Headquarters: 62 Fifth Ave., New York, N. Y. 10011

National Academy of Sciences. Membership: approx. 1,000. Annual meeting: Washington, D. C., April 22–23, 1974. President, Philip Handler; exec. officer, John S. Coleman. Headquarters: 2101 Constitution Ave. NW, Washington, D. C. 20037.

National Association for Mental Health, Inc. Membership: 1,000 state and local organizations. Annual meeting: Washington, D. C., Nov. 19–22, 1974. President, Linden E. Wheeler; exec. director, Brian O'Connell. Headquarters: 1800 North Kent St., Rosslyn Station, Arlington, Va. 22209.

National Association for the Advancement of Colored People. Membership: 400,000 in 1,500 units. National convention: New Orleans, La., July 1–5, 1974. President, Kivie Kaplan; board chairman, Bishop Stephen G. Spottswood; exec. director, Roy Wilkins. Headquarters: 1790 Broadway, New York, N. Y. 10019.

National Association of Manufacturers. Membership: 12,- 000. Annual meeting: New York, N. Y., Dec. 5–6, 1974. President, E. Douglas Kenna; secy., John McGraw. Headquarters: 1776 F Street N.W., Washington, D. C. 20006.

National Audubon Society. Membership: 300,000. Biennial convention: New Orleans, La., April 17–22, 1975. President, Dr. Elvis J. Stahr; exec. vice pres., Charles H. Callison. Headquarters: 950 Third Ave., New York, N. Y. 10022.

National Conference of Christians and Jews, Inc. Membership: 70 regional offices. Annual meeting: New York, N. Y., Nov. 18–19, 1973. President, Dr. David Hyatt; secy., Oscar M. Lazrus. Headquarters: 43 West 57th St., New York, N. Y. 10019.

National Congress of Parents and Teachers. Membership: 8,236,649 in 37,222 PTA's. National convention: San Antonio, Texas, May 19–22, 1974. President, Mrs. Lillie E. Herndon; secy., Mrs. W. Hamilton Crockford III. Headquarters: 700 North Rush Street, Chicago, Ill. 60611.

National Council of the Churches of Christ in the U. S. A. Membership: 30 Protestant, Anglican, and Orthodox denominations. President, Rev. W. Sterling Carey; gen. secy., Dr. R. H. Edwin Espy. Headquarters: 475 Riverside Dr., New York, N. Y. 10027.

National Council of the Young Men's Christian Associations. Membership: 5,783,817 in 1,855 organizations. National board chairman, E. Stanley Enlund; exec. director, Robert W. Harlan. Headquarters: 291 Broadway, New York, N. Y. 10007.

National Easter Seal Society for Crippled Children and Adults. Membership: 52 state and territorial societies. National convention: San Antonio, Texas, Nov. 12–16, 1974. President, A. Clay Stewart; exec. director, Jayne Shover. Headquarters: 2023 W. Ogden Ave., Chicago, Ill. 60612.

National Education Association of the U. S. Membership: 1,166,203, with units in every state, and 9,369 local affiliates. Annual meeting: Chicago, Ill., June 28–July 3, 1974. President, Dr. Helen D. Wise; exec. secy., Terry E. Herndon. Headquarters: 1201 16th St. NW, Washington, D. C. 20036.

National Federation of Business and Professional Women's Clubs, Inc. Membership: 170,000 in 3,800 clubs. National convention: Chicago, Ill., July 21–25, 1974. President, Miss Jean L. McCarrey; federation director, Mrs. Lucille H. Shriver. Headquarters: 2012 Massachusetts Avenue NW, Washington, D. C. 20036.

National Federation of Music Clubs. Membership: 600,000 in 4,300 clubs and 13 national affiliates. Annual meeting: Fargo, N. D., August 1974; biennial convention, Atlanta, Ga., April 23–May 1, 1975. President, Dr. Merle Montgomery; office manager, Mrs. John McDonald. Headquarters: 600 S. Michigan Ave., Chicago, Ill. 60605.

National Foundation—March of Dimes, The. Membership: 2,500 chapters. President, Joseph F. Nee; exec. vice pres., Charles L. Massey. Headquarters: 1275 Mamaroneck Ave., White Plains, N. Y. 10605.

National Recreation and Park Association. Membership includes professional park and recreation administrators and citizens concerned with conservation of human and natural resources. Annual congress: Denver, Colo., Oct. 20–25, 1974. Executive director, Dwight F. Rettie. Headquarters: 1601 North Kent St., Arlington, Va. 22209.

National Safety Council. Membership: 15,000. National Safety Congress and Exposition: Chicago, Ill., Oct. 29–Nov. 1, 1973. President, Howard Pyle; secy.-treas., H. W. Champlin. Headquarters: 425 N. Michigan Ave., Chicago, Ill. 60611.

National Urban League, Inc. President, Donald H. McGannon; secy., Chester Burger; exec. director, Vernon E. Jordan, Jr. Headquarters: 55 East 52d St., New York, N. Y. 10022.

National Women's Christian Temperance Union. Membership: 250,000 in 6,000 local unions. National centennial convention, Cleveland, Ohio, Aug. 28–Sept. 4, 1974. President, Mrs. Fred J. Tooze; secy., Mrs. Herman Stanley. Headquarters: 1730 Chicago Ave., Evanston, Ill. 60201.

Phi Beta Kappa. Membership: 240,000. Secy., Carl Billman. Headquarters: 1811 Q St. N.W., Washington, D. C. 20009.

Planned Parenthood Federation of America, Inc. (Planned Parenthood–World Population). Membership: 186 affiliates throughout U. S. Annual meeting: St. Louis, Mo., Oct. 17–20, 1974. President, Alan F. Guttmacher, M. D.; chairman of the board, Alan Sweezy, Ph. D.; secy., Mrs. William D. Gregory II. Headquarters: 810 Seventh Ave., New York, N. Y. 10019.

Rotary International. Membership: 743,500 in 15,804 clubs functioning in 150 countries. International convention: Minneapolis-St. Paul, Minn., June 9–13, 1974. President, William C. Carter; gen. secy., Harry A. Stewart. Headquarters: 1600 Ridge Ave., Evanston, Ill. 60201.

Special Libraries Association. Membership: 8,300. Annual conference: Toronto, Ont., June 8–12, 1974. President, Gilles Frappier; exec. director, F. E. McKenna. Headquarters: 235 Park Ave. S., New York, N. Y. 10003.

United States Jaycees, The. Membership: 325,000 in 6,400 affiliated groups. Annual meeting: San Diego, Calif., June 17–20, 1974. President, Rick Clayton, Jr.; exec. vice pres., Ray Roper. Headquarters: Box 7, Tulsa, Okla. 74102.

United Way of America (formerly **United Community Funds and Councils of America, Inc.**). Membership: United Funds, Community Chests, and Community Health and Welfare Councils in 2,240 North American communities. Chairman of the Board of Governors, James R. Kerr; national executive, William Aramony. Headquarters: 801 North Fairfax St., Alexandria, Va. 22314.

Veterans of Foreign Wars of the United States. Membership, V. F. W. and Auxiliary: 2,313,000. National convention: Chicago, Ill., Aug. 16–23, 1974. Commander-in-chief, Ray R. Soden; Adj. general, Julian Dickenson. Headquarters: V. F. W. Building, Broadway at 34th St., Kansas City, Mo. 64111.

World Council of Churches (United States Conference). Membership: 27 churches or denominations in U. S. Chairman, John Coventry Smith. Headquarters: 475 Riverside Dr., New York, N. Y. 10027.

Young Women's Christian Association of the U. S. A. Members and participants: approx. 2,400,000. President, Elizabeth Steel Genné; exec. director, Edith M. Lerrigo. Headquarters: 600 Lexington Ave., New York, N. Y. 10022.

Zionist Organization of America. Membership: 110,000 in 600 districts. 77th National convention: New York, N. Y., June 27–30, 1974. President, Herman L. Weisman; national secy. and exec. director, Leon Ilutovich. Headquarters: 145 East 32d St., New York, N. Y. 10016.

SOUTH AFRICA

Public concerns in South Africa during 1973 remained very much the same as they were the previous year. Prime Minister Balthazar J. Vorster and the ruling National party continued to press forward with the Bantu Homelands, or Bantustans, program, both at home and in South West Africa (Namibia), which despite UN protests is still under South African administration. The program provides the foundations of apartheid policies and has encountered mounting criticism in both areas. Bantustan leaders criticized in particular land questions, finance, and the absence of provision for African cooperation and unity. Labor and student disturbances continued unabated. The government recognized the need for reform in industrial relations and the African wage structure, but it refused to countenance the development of an African trade union movement.

In foreign affairs, the chief issues were the security of the nation's northern borders and disputes at the United Nations over apartheid and the future of Namibia. The government and the country as a whole remained concerned about South Africa's image abroad and its international difficulties, especially its isolation in sports events. One government reaction to its difficulties was a renewal of violent attacks on the opposition press.

Politics. Marais Steyn, head of the United party's division of information and research and a leading veteran of its central executive committee, resigned from his party at the end of August and joined the National party. His resignation followed a clash at the Transvaal United party (UP) congress with the reformist Harry Schwartz and reflected the clash between the liberal reformers and the "Old Guard" conservatives. The UP emerged from its annual congress on November 10 without a confrontation between disputing members and with its balance of power still close to the center. The political activity of the National party, its drive for voter registration, and the release of the provisional delimitation plan for the parliamentary constituencies led the leader of the Opposition to predict an early general election and to alert the UP for April 1974. The Herstigte Nationale party announced that it would contest a substantial number of seats in the next election, and the Progressive party resolved to call a national convention of all races to discuss the future of South Africa.

BLACK ATHLETES participating in the first interracial South African Games enjoy the pool at a hotel in Pretoria declared "multiracial" during the competition.

Domestic Affairs. The year 1973 was marked by an almost continuous series of strikes for wage increases by low-paid African workers. Beginning in Natal and spreading to the Transvaal, the strikes between Jan. 1 and March 31, 1973, alone numbered about 160 and involved more than 61,000 workers. Employers increasingly were forced to consider whether they stood to lose more from these illegal but recurrent strikes or from giving more realistic wage levels to their workers. As one settlement after another was made to deal with one strike after another, attention was increasingly focused on the problems of low-paid workers, and the practices of foreign as well as domestic firms with respect to wages and fringe benefits. The U. S. government published a set of guidelines for U. S. firms suggesting that a reasonable goal for African workers should be a minimum of $140 a month. There was also concern in Britain, and in October the South African government welcomed a five-man delegation from the British Trades Union Congress. The minister of labor reiterated the government's refusal to recognize black trade unions or their

---

SOUTH AFRICA · Information Highlights

Official Name: Republic of South Africa.
Location: Southern tip of Africa.
Area: 471,444 square miles (1,221,037 sq km).
Population (1973 est.): 21,700,000. *Density,* 47 per square mile (18 per sq km).
Chief Cities (1970 census): Pretoria, the administrative capital, 543,950; Cape Town, the legislative capital, 691,296; Johannesburg, 642,967; Durban, 495,458.
Government: *Head of state,* Jacobus Johannes Fouche, president (took office April 1968). *Head of government,* Balthazar J. Vorster, prime minister (took office Sept. 1966). *Legislature*—Parliament: Senate and House of Assembly. *Major political parties*—National party; United party.
Languages: English, Afrikaans (both official); Bantu languages.
Education: *Expenditure* (1961), 4% of national income. *School enrollment* (1963)—primary, 2,546,824; secondary, 532,299; technical/vocational, 76,724; university/higher (1967), 67,363.
Monetary Unit: Rand (0.6729 rand equals U. S.$1, Aug. 1973).
Gross National Product (1972 est.): $18,200,000,000.
Economic Indexes: *Industrial production* (manufacturing, 1972), 167 (1963=100); *agricultural production* (1971), 135 (1963=100); *consumer price index* (1972), 142 (1963=100).
Manufacturing (major products): Textiles, iron and steel, chemicals, fertilizers, assembled automobiles, metals.
Major Agricultural Products: Corn (ranks 4th among world producers, 1972), sugarcane, tobacco, fruit.
Major Minerals: Gold (ranks 1st among world producers, 1971), diamonds (world rank 2d, 1971), chromium ore (world rank 2d, 1971), platinum, coal, iron ore, copper, uranium (world rank 2d, 1971), manganese, asbestos.
Foreign Trade (1972): *Exports,* $2,602,000,000; *Imports,* $3,648,000,000. *Chief trading partners* (1971)—United Kingdom (took 27% of exports, supplied 23% of imports); Japan (12%—10%); United States (8%—16%); West Germany (7%—14%).
Tourism: Receipts (1970), $76,200,000.
Transportation: *Motor vehicles* (1970), 1,961,900 (automobiles, 1,534,700); *railroads* (1971), 13,742 miles (22,115 km); *merchant fleet* (1972), 511,000 gross registered tons; *major national airline,* South African Airways.
Communications: *Telephones* (1972), 1,623,805; *newspapers* (1970), 22.

right to collective bargaining, but in May he introduced legislation that overhauled the traditional machinery and for the first time since 1942 gave African workers limited right to strike.

In one case labor unrest led to tragedy. On September 11, disturbances at the Western Deep Levels Gold Mine at Carltonville led to a riot. After a baton charge failed to quell the riot, the police opened fire, and 12 Africans were killed. The Johannesburg *Star* commented that 1973 was the first year in which public opinion had moved so flexibly on the matters of African pay, education, and communication but that it was also the year of Carltonville. It saw conditions as the by-products of migratory labor and pointed out the need for change.

As a result of reports presented by the Schlebusch Parliamentary Commission of Inquiry into four legal multi-racial organizations opposed to apartheid, the government banned—without trial—eight leaders of the National Union of South African Students and eight African leaders of the South African Student Organization. The government also withdrew the passports of the Rev. C. F. Beyers Naude, director of the Christian Institute, and of other members of the institute's staff who refused to testify before the commission. Subsequently Reverend Naude was tried, fined, and given a three-month suspended sentence for refusing to appear before the commission.

UN Relations. The campaign against South Africa's policy of apartheid continued to mount during 1973. In October the General Assembly refused to accept South Africa's credentials, but the vote did not unseat the delegation, and Prime Minister Vorster announced that South Africa would remain in the United Nations. In November the UN Special Political Committee overwhelmingly adopted a resolution declaring that the South African liberation movements, which are essentially the banned organizations of the African National Congress and the Pan African Congress, were the authentic representatives of the overwhelming majority of the country. That same month the Trusteeship Committee adopted a resolution calling for the imposition of economic sanctions against South Africa and Portugal. On September 13, the UN Special Committee on Apartheid condemned the shooting at Carltonville and called for an impartial inquiry. UN Secretary General Kurt Waldheim asked the government if it would accept a UN representative at the inquiry or agree to an outside investigation, but it refused both requests.

The negotiations between Waldheim and the Nationalist government over the future of Namibia ended in April, and the UN Council on Namibia recommended that the Security Council refuse to sanction further talks since there is no prospect of a satisfactory outcome.

Sports. New Zealand's Prime Minister Norman Kirk has a policy of excluding South African rugby teams and women's tennis teams from competition in New Zealand until racial-discrimination policies are changed. At a special meeting in Paris, South Africa maintained its place in the Davis Cup competition. Arthur Ashe, a U. S. black tennis star, was granted a visa to play in the South African national championships. Similarly, the world champion light-heavyweight boxer Bob Foster, also black, was granted a visa to defend his title against the South African Pierre Fourie in Johannesburg.

RONALD B. BALLINGER
Rhode Island College

—— **SOUTH CAROLINA** • Information Highlights ——

Area: 31,055 square miles (80,432 sq km).
Population (1972 est.): 2,665,000. *Density:* 87 per sq mi.
Chief Cities (1970 census): Columbia, the capital, 113,542; Charleston, 66,945; Greenville, 61,436; Spartanburg, 44,546; Rock Hill, 33,846.
Government (1973): *Chief Officers*—governor, John C. West (D); lt. gov., Earle E. Morris, Jr. (D); secy. of state, O. Frank Thornton (D); atty. gen., Daniel R. McLeod (D); treas., Grady L. Patterson, Jr. (D); supt. of education, Cyril B. Busbee; chief justice, Joseph Rodney Moss. *General Assembly*—Senate, 46 members (43 Democrats, 3 Republicans); House of Representatives, 124 members (103 D, 21 R).
Education (1972–73): *Enrollment*—public elementary schools, 400,000 pupils, 16,080 teachers; public secondary schools, 240,000 pupils, 10,920 teachers; nonpublic schools, 30,600 pupils, 1,590 teachers; colleges and universities, 78,248 students. *Public school expenditures*, $435,000,000 ($751 per pupil). *Average teacher's salary*, $8,310.
State Finances (fiscal year 1971): *Revenues*, $1,072,013,000 (4% general sales tax and gross receipts taxes, $213,-661,000; motor fuel tax, $93,484,000; federal funds $248,-025,000). *Expenditures*, $943,290,000 (education, $444,-598,000; health, welfare, and safety, $113,035,000; highways, $159,097,000). *State debt*, $397,923,000 (June 30, 1971).
Personal Income (1972): $9,188,000,000; per capita, $3,448.
Public Assistance (1972): $87,923,000. *Average monthly payments* (Dec. 1972)—old-age assistance, $51.98; aid to families with dependent children, $81.12.
Labor Force: *Nonagricultural wage and salary earners* (July 1973), 978,600. *Average annual employment* (1972)—manufacturing, 353,600; trade, 160,700; government, 165,200; services, 102,300. *Insured unemployed* (Sept. 1973)—8,400 (1.1%).
Manufacturing (1971): Value added by manufacture, $4,234,-500,000. Textile mill products, $1,440,100,000; chemicals and allied products, $741,700,000.
Agriculture (1972): *Cash farm income*, $608,772,000 (livestock, $214,337,000; crops, $345,150,000; government payments, $49,285,000). *Chief crops* (in order of value, 1971)—Tobacco (ranks 3d among the states); soybeans; cotton lint; corn.
Mining (1972): *Production value*, $71,998,000 (ranks 41st among the states). *Chief minerals*—Cement, value not available; stone, $17,885,000; clays, $11,870,000.
Fisheries (1972): *Commercial catch*, 22,365,000 pounds ($7,-961,000). *Leading species by value:* Shrimp, $5,547,000; crabs, $778,000; oysters, $603,000; spot, $207,000.
Transportation: *Roads* (1972), 59,629 miles (95,961 km); *motor vehicles* (1972), 1,382,965; *railroads* (1972), 3,059 miles (4,923 km); *public airports* (1972), 59.
Communications: *Telephones* (1973), 1,371,800; *television stations* (1971), 11; *radio stations* (1971), 141; *newspapers* (1973), 17 (daily circulation, 579,000).

SOUTH CAROLINA

South Carolina reapportioned its House of Representatives in 1973. The article-by-article revision of the state constitution continued, and the economy was healthy.

Government and Politics. Under the direction of the U. S. Supreme Court, South Carolina reapportioned the state House of Representatives during a special session of the legislature held during the fall. The long-time custom of having at least one representative for each of the state's 46 counties had to be set aside, and counties—some of which had populations of less than 15,000—were combined into single districts. As 1973 ended, supporters of single-member districts were testing the new plan in the federal courts.

The regular session of the General Assembly lasted six months, but little significant legislation was enacted. In the ongoing article-by-article revision of the state constitution begun in 1968, the six amendments approved by the voters in 1972 were considered. Five of these were passed in 1973, providing for reforms in the court system, the executive branch of the government, education, municipal and county government, and procedures governing the removal of officers.

Interim legislative committees were created to study significant problems, including automobile insurance, drug abuse, school bus transportation, legislative pay, income tax laws, and admission laws pertaining to mental patients.

The state department of health and the department of pollution control were merged into a single agency in 1973. The new agency is to be directed by a nonprofessional board rather than being medically oriented. A new law expanded the activities of the department of archives, and financial control of the higher education commission was expanded. Debates occurred in the legislature over the several increases in the price of milk during the year, and there were requests to adjust the rising utility rates.

Black voters outnumbered white voters in three South Carolina counties in 1973, and blacks were elected to three municipal councils for the first time in the state's history. Several counties adopted a manager form of government, and plans were being laid for a vote on the merger of all the governments in Charleston county.

Education. Improvements in education continued under the state's 5-year plan directed toward improved supervision, measurement of student performance, retention of students in school, wide-scale adult education, and expansion of special educational programs. The national teachers examination was discontinued as a basis for teacher pay.

Expansion was authorized for some branches of the state university, and $4 million was appropriated to aid college students attending institutions not supported by the state. Special committees were trying to resolve the problems of medical education in order to overcome the critical shortages in physicians and other medical personnel.

Economy. South Carolina's industries and agriculture prospered in 1973. Industrial expansion reached an all-time high, and all crop yields were good despite a crippling snowstorm and heavy spring rains. Cattle replaced cotton as the third source of farm income, following tobacco and soybeans. Employment was at an all-time high. Major hotels and condominiums were being developed along the state's beaches and on the sea islands and inland lakes.

ROBERT H. STOUDEMIRE
University of South Carolina

SOUTH DAKOTA

There were several significant events in South Dakota in 1973, the most newsworthy of which was the occupation of Wounded Knee by a group of American Indians (see feature article on page 64).

Politics. Gov. Richard Kneip (D) consolidated more than 160 agencies, commissions, and boards into 16 executive departments to "make government more responsive to the people" of South Dakota. On July 1, Kneip personally assumed control of a department of executive management created to deal with budget, personnel, planning, and administrative management. He placed a commission in charge of the state's cement industry, and appointed secretaries to administer the 14 other departments.

Kneip expressed interest in seeking election for a third time in 1974, although South Dakota law prohibits anyone from serving more than two terms. Observers predicted that he might gain court permission to run again, but lose the nomination. He lacks the public support of such fellow Democrats as Lt. Gov. William Dougherty, Attorney General Kermit Sande, and U. S. Sen. James Abourezk.

Legislation. The 1973 legislature passed several significant laws. In addition to ratifying the Equal Rights Amendment to the U. S. Constitution, the

─────── SOUTH DAKOTA • Information Highlights ───────

Area: 77,047 square miles (199,552 sq km).
Population (1972 est.): 679,000. *Density:* 9 per sq mi.
Chief Cities (1970 census): Pierre, the capital, 9,699; Sioux Falls, 72,488; Rapid City, 43,836; Aberdeen, 26,476; Huron, 14,299; Brookings, 13,717; Mitchell, 13,425.
Government (1973): Chief officers—governor, Richard F. Kneip (D); lt. gov., William Dougherty (D); secy. of state, Lorna Herseth (D); atty. gen., Kermit Sande (D); treas., David Volk (R); supt. of public instruction, Donald P. Barnhart; chief justice, Frank Biegelmeier. *Legislature*—Senate, 35 members (18 Democrats, 17 Republicans); House of Representatives, 70 members (35 D, 35 R).
Education (1972–73): *Enrollment*—public elementary schools, 110,222 pupils; 5,212 teachers; public secondary schools, 52,016 pupils; 2,949 teachers; nonpublic schools, 12,100 pupils; 620 teachers; colleges and universities, 28,217 students. *Public school expenditures,* $128,900,000 ($833 per pupil). *Average teacher's salary,* $8,034.
State Finances (fiscal year 1971): *Revenues,* $285,082,000 (4% general sales tax and gross receipts taxes, $53,200,-000; motor fuel tax, $25,326,000; federal funds, $97,282,-000). *Expenditures,* $285,272,000 (education, $110,620,000; health, welfare, and safety, $42,424,000; highways, $78,427,000). *State debt,* $35,615,000 (June 30, 1971).
Personal Income (1972): $2,523,000,000; per capita, $3,716.
Public Assistance (1972): $33,418,000. *Average monthly payments* (Dec. 1972)—old-age assistance, $61.31; aid to families with dependent children, $168.24.
Labor Force: *Nonagricultural wage and salary earners* (July 1973), 204,200. *Average annual employment* (1972)—manufacturing, 18,000; trade, 47,600; government, 57,600; services, 36,700. *Insured unemployed* (Sept. 1973)—1,300 (1.0%).
Manufacturing (1971): *Value added by manufacture,* $226,-200,000. Food and kindred products, $126,800,000; printing and publishing, $20,600,000; stone, clay, and glass products, $15,600,000; nonelectrical machinery, $14,100,-000; fabricated metal products, $12,800,000; lumber and wood products, $9,600,000.
Agriculture (1972): *Cash farm income,* $1,319,258,000 (livestock, $969,470,000; crops, $238,269,000; government payments, $111,519,000). *Chief crops* (in order of value, 1971)—Corn, hay, wheat, oats (ranks 3d among the states, 1972).
Mining (1972): Production value, $69,894,000 (ranks 42d among the states). *Chief minerals*—Gold, $23,869,000; sand and gravel, $19,943,000; stone, $10,517,000.
Transportation: *Roads* (1972), 84,078 miles (135,307 km); *motor vehicles* (1972), 441,689; *railroads* (1972), 3,505 miles (5,641 km); *public airports* (1972), 70.
Communications: *Telephones* (1973), 366,800; *television stations* (1971), 10; *radio stations* (1971), 37; *newspapers* (1973), 13 (daily circulation, 178,000).

legislature passed bills increasing primary and secondary education spending by $6 million, and advancing the minimum wage to $1.60 an hour. Lawmakers refused to approve the governor's third attempt to reform taxation and rejected certain expenditures on education, causing the accumulation of an unprecedented $20 million general-fund surplus.

The Economy. Most South Dakotans prospered as unemployment in the state decreased. Livestock production and farming are the mainstays of the state's economy, and the price of beef, hogs, and crops rose. Those who suffered economic losses included employees of certain meat-processing plants that lost business because of farmers' withholding livestock during the national shoppers' boycott and some gasoline filling-station operators forced by gasoline shortages to close temporarily.

Wildlife. Between January and March at least 40% of the estimated 100,000 ducks wintering at Lake Andes National Wildlife Refuge died of Dutch duck plague, a form of viral enteritis. Wildlife experts sought ways of preventing ducks from assembling at the site in 1974.

Higher Education. Several state-supported institutions of higher learning faced decreased enrollments. Some faculty positions were eliminated. However, the University of South Dakota and South Dakota State University benefited from an increase of $3.7 million in state support, most of which was used to increase faculty salaries.

HERBERT T. HOOVER
University of South Dakota

space exploration

A new chapter in space exploration was begun in 1973 with the success of the U. S. Skylab mission to determine man's ability to live and work in space for extended periods. Unmanned exploration of the planets continued during the year as Pioneer 10 returned data from Jupiter and other spacecraft were sent on missions to Venus, Mercury, and Mars.

MANNED SPACE FLIGHT

The U. S. Skylab program was established to determine man's ability to live and work in space for extended periods of time, to extend the science of solar astronomy beyond the limits of earth-based observations, to develop improved techniques for surveying earth resources from space, and to increase man's knowledge in a variety of other scientific and technological regions.

The initial plans for the Skylab program called for three 3-man crews to travel one after the other to the Skylab space station in earth orbit, live and work there for about one or two months, and then return to earth. The three separate trips were to take place over an eight-month period.

Skylab. The 118-foot (36-meter) long, 85-ton Skylab, the first American space station, was rocketed into space on May 14, 1973. However, barely a minute after the launch atop a Saturn-5 rocket, sensors on the arms of the meteoroid shield alerted flight controllers to serious problems. Unable to withstand the intense vibrations after lift-off, some of the shielding on the outer surface of Skylab ripped free. As it tore away it also wrapped around a winglike solar-cell panel, preventing it from deploying. In addition, Skylab's other solar-cell wing was ripped away. That was bad news indeed because nonoperation of the two solar-cell wings meant that Skylab was deprived of more than half of its electrical power. However, the worst was still to come. Without the shielding, the temperature inside the workshop—the site of the crew quarters—soared dramatically, climbing to 130°F (54°C) and higher, which could have had serious adverse effects on food and film stored on board.

While engineers and flight controllers struggled desperately to save the mission, the launch of the first crew of three astronauts was delayed. First priority was given to cooling off the workshop by maneuvering the spacecraft with its thrusters in order to turn the exposure area away from the sun. After these maneuvers the workshop temperature stabilized close to a tolerable 105°F (40°C). Meanwhile, the engineers worked feverishly to design and build a thermal shield that the astronauts could take to Skylab to lower the temperature to more habitable limits.

While the astronauts awaited a go for their launch from the Cape Kennedy site in Florida, Skylab orbited the earth at an altitude of about 270 miles (435 km) and made one revolution about the earth every 93 minutes.

The space station includes an orbital workshop, an airlock module, a multiple docking adapter, and a telescope mount. The workshop is a cylindrical two-story cabin 48 feet (14.6 meters) long and 22 feet (6.7 meters) in diameter. It has crew quarters, storage areas for food and water, and a large window. The crew quarters include individual sleeping compartments, sit-down and stand-up toilet facilities, a collapsible shower stall, exercise equipment, and a work area for experiments.

The airlock module, 16 feet (4.9 meters) long and having a maximum diameter of 22 feet (6.7 meters), is located between the workshop and the multiple docking adapter. It contains communications, environmental, and electrical equipment and a passage so that astronauts can go outside Skylab for repairs or other tasks.

The multiple docking adapter, 17 feet (5.2 meters) long and 10 feet (3 meters) in diameter, provides the docking port for the ferry craft that brings astronauts to the Skylab and returns them to earth when their mission is completed. A large window in the adapter section enables astronauts to view the earth and perform earth resource studies.

The telescope mount contains eight telescopes, primarily for observing ultraviolet and X-ray emissions from the sun that cannot be studied on earth. An array of solar-cell panels atop the telescope mount is one of the sources for electric power on the space station.

Mission of Skylab 1 Crew. On May 25 astronauts Charles Conrad, Jr., Joseph Kerwin, and Paul Weitz blasted off, riding in a 33-foot (10-meter) long, 15-ton Apollo spacecraft for a rendezvous with the crippled Skylab. After experiencing some difficulties in docking, the astronauts entered the workshop and started the activation of equipment. They succeeded in deploying the sun shield, which lowered the temperature in Skylab to a more tolerable temperature of about 80° F (27° C). The crew was then ready to commence the planned experiments. They made scientific observations of the earth and sun and performed biomedical tests on themselves.

However, before the first week ended, two critical storage batteries had failed, further depleting Skylab's already reduced power supply. In order to provide more electrical power, two of the astronauts took a space walk to free the inoperative solar panel that was jammed in the side of the workshop. After 3½ hours the panel was freed, and sufficient additional power was made available to complete the mission.

The first Skylab mission made significant contributions. Approximately 80% of the sought-for solar data was obtained, 12 of the planned 15 earth resources data runs were accomplished, and all of 16 medical experiments were conducted as required by the operational medical protocols. In addition, the time history of man's adaptation to a zero-gravity environment was obtained for the first time.

After spending a record 28 days in space in a zero-gravity environment, Conrad, Kerwin, and Weitz rode their Apollo ferry craft back to earth and splashed down in the Pacific Ocean on June 22. During their 395 trips around the earth, the Skylab 1 crew slept better, ate more, and were more comfortable than any space voyagers before them. Equally impressive, the astronauts—despite the power shortage in the early part of their mission—completed more than 75% of their scheduled experi-

ments. In doing so, they took about 16,000 photographs of the earth and about 30,000 of the sun.

Before leaving their home in the sky, the astronauts did some space-age housework. They sprayed disinfectant around the Skylab's living quarters, turned off lights and fans, and halted the flow of fresh air into the workshop. That left Skylab shipshape for the next crew of astronauts.

Mission of Skylab 2 Crew. The vacant Skylab remained orbiting under remote control for five weeks while astronauts Alan Bean, Owen Garriott, and Jack Lousma prepared for a second spaceflight mission to continue the research performed by Conrad and his crew. During their mission, Bean, Garriott, and Lousma were to perform observations of the sun and the earth and to observe the behavior of a zoo of spiders, minnows, and other creatures accompanying them into space. But most important for the astronauts were to be the tests on themselves. These tests took on added interest in view of the medical results from the Skylab 1 crew. What most surprised the space doctors was the fact that each member of the Skylab 1 crew had lost about 14% more weight than the experts had anticipated. Furthermore, the three men were slow in making up the few pounds each had lost.

Right on schedule the Skylab 2 crew blasted off from Cape Kennedy on July 28. Catching up with their orbiting space station 8½ hours later, they took a quick close-up look with television cameras, docked their Apollo ferrycraft, and then moved into the 9,550-cubic-foot (270-cubic-meter) laboratory for a 59-day stay.

On the 10th day of the mission, Garriott and Lousma emerged from the Skylab and spent 6½ hours on a space walk—a new record for activity outside an orbiting space vehicle. During that time they deployed a new sun shield to lower the temperatures in the forward and aft compartments, loaded new film cassettes in the solar telescopes, erected panels to detect micrometeoroid impacts, and inspected the Skylab for leaks and damage. Two other space walks were made on the 28th and 57th days of the mission to tend to the experiments and make necessary repairs.

During their stay in the Skylab, the astronauts conducted a highly successful experimental program, exceeding the premission plans by a wide margin. Twenty-six photographic surveys to locate earth resources were included in the mission plans, but the crew completed 39. Subjects of photography coverage included Paraguay, drought areas in West Africa, tropical storm Christine, and the Sargasso Sea. Fifty sites were given to the crew as subjects for Land-Field photography. The Great Salt Lake area was chosen as a site to study the crew's ability to make detailed observations from space on the basis of repetitive passes. The astronauts spent 305 hours making important observations of the sun, including studies of seven flares and a large number of subflare transient events. In the medical tests, the crew augmented the anticipated data by doing hemoglobin tests on all blood samples and adding specific gravity tests to the urine analysis.

Nine investigations suggested by students were assigned to this mission, including a study of how spiders spin webs under zero-gravity conditions. Photographs of the webs spun by the spiders were taken for later analysis.

Bean's crew performed more efficiently than the first crew, but they benefited from the experience of the first crew and had a longer time to work on the tasks. In addition to completing all premission objectives Bean's crew also conducted 12 experiments not previously planned for the mission. The additional experiment activity included 11 metal-composition and metal-processing studies under zero-gravity conditions.

The Skylab 2 crew returned to earth in their Apollo ferry craft, landing in the Pacific Ocean off southern California on September 25 in weakened but otherwise excellent physical condition after a record 59-day 11-hour flight.

Just as impressive as the astronaut's achievements in space was their reaction to earth's gravity on splashdown. Despite feelings of wobbliness, disorientation, and heaviness, the three men started to readapt much faster than space doctors had anticipated—most likely as a consequence of the rigorous exercises they had performed in Skylab.

Mission of Skylab 3 Crew. The third visit to Skylab began on November 16 when astronauts Gerald Carr, Edward Gibson, and William Pogue were launched in their Apollo spacecraft from Cape Canaveral (formerly Cape Kennedy). None of the three had ever flown a space mission before. Their stay in space was to last a maximum of 85 days, as limited by crew health and consumable items on board. The increase in scheduled flight time to a maximum of 85 days was striking evidence of the achievement of the previous Skylab missions in demonstrating that men can indeed remain healthy during long periods of exposure to zero gravity and can recover relatively quickly on returning to earth. All indications from the second mission were that the astronauts' bodies became fully accustomed to space after 40 days.

Carr and his crew carried out much the same tasks as those performed by the first two Skylab crews—a mixture of medical observations, astro-

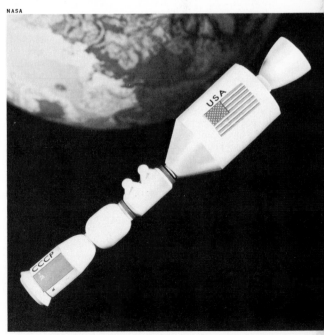

MODELS of the USSR's Soyuz and U. S. Apollo craft docked in earth orbit. Joint mission is set for 1975.

NASA

nomical studies, surveys of earth resources, and zero-gravity technological experiments. However, the most spectacular new experiment was in astronomy. The target was the comet Kohoutek as it flamed across the night sky in mid-December and early January. Because observations from the space station are unobstructed by the earth's atmosphere, Kohoutek provided an unprecedented opportunity to solve long-standing questions on the nature and origin of comets. Carr and his crew also viewed an eclipse of the sun on Christmas Eve and collected data on the planet Mercury.

With the planned return of the Skylab 3 crew in early 1974 the flight portion of the spectacularly successful Skylab program came to at least a temporary end. However, with the wealth of scientific data collected by the three crews, it will be months or years before scientists have fully assessed the true value of the increase in scientific knowledge achieved by the Skylab astronauts.

Salyut 2. On April 3 the USSR launched the 27.5-ton Salyut 2 space station into orbit. Presumably, this launch was to be followed by the launch of a manned Soyuz spacecraft, rendezvous, and transfer of some of the Soyuz crew to the Salyut 2. This sequence of events occurred with Salyut 1 and Soyuz 11 in 1971.

Salyut 2 went through a number of station-keeping maneuvers in a high holding orbit for about 10 days. The apparent purpose of the flight was to test the improved design of on-board systems and instruments. However, on April 14, tracking stations reported that Salyut 2 had broken into at least 15 pieces. On April 28 the Soviet Union announced that the Salyut 2 flight test program had been completed.

Soyuz 12 and Soyuz 13. Soyuz 12 was launched on September 27 by the Soviet Union in its first manned test of a Soyuz spacecraft since the death of three Soyuz 11 cosmonauts in 1971. During their mission on the modified Soyuz 12, Lt. Col. Vasily Lazarev and spacecraft design engineer Oleg Makarov tested an improved system that enables the crew to determine its precise location and orientation independent of ground stations. Soyuz 12 landed on Sept. 29, 1973, completing the first successful manned Soviet mission in more than two years.

Another test of the modified Soyuz-type spacecraft began on December 18 when Soyuz 13 carried Maj. Pyotr Klimuk and flight engineer Valentin Lebedev into earth orbit. They checked the craft's manual and automatic flight control systems and different modes of automatic navigation, apparently in preparation for a rendezvous of manned Soviet and American spacecraft scheduled for 1975. The two cosmonauts returned to earth on December 26, completing an eight-day mission.

UNMANNED SATELLITES AND SPACE PROBES

Jupiter Probes. The American spacecraft Pioneer 10, launched on March 2, 1972, sped past the great planet Jupiter in December 1973. The spacecraft, which had flown safely through the dangerous asteroid belt between Mars and Jupiter, made its closest approach to Jupiter on December 3 when it came within about 80,000 miles (129,000 km) of the largest planet in the solar system. In its 21-month voyage to Jupiter, Pioneer 10 traveled about 620 million miles (998 million km).

During a week when it was close to the planet, the 570-pound (260-kg) spacecraft took about 20 pictures of the orange- and blue-striped Jovian cloud cover, measured the intensities of the planet's magnetic field and radiation belts, and took the planet's temperature. After inspecting Jupiter, Pioneer 10 was on its way toward leaving the solar system entirely—the first man-made object ever to venture forth to the distant stars.

Pioneer 11, a twin of Pioneer 10, was launched on April 5, 1973, for another rendezvous with Jupiter in December 1974. Like its predecessor, Pioneer 11 contains 14 experiments for making measurements of Jupiter's atmosphere, radiation belts, heat balance, magnetic fields, internal structure, and its moons. Shortly after launch a course correction was made. It gave the mission planners the option of directing Pioneer 11 on an equatorial pass with an inspection of one or more of the planet's 12 moons or sending the spacecraft near one of Jupiter's flattened poles. The decision will largely be based on the analyses of the Pioneer 10 experiments.

Mars Probes. Between July 21 and August 9, the Soviet Union launched four spacecraft to explore the planet Mars. Mars 4 and Mars 5, which apparently have the same design, were scheduled to reach the planet in February 1974 after a journey of about 76 million miles (122 million km). Mars 6 and Mars 7, which apparently rely on equipment in Mars 4 and Mars 5 to carry out their missions, were to arrive at the planet in March 1974. The four spacecraft are on an overall mission to explore interplanetary space, to explore Mars during the approach phase, to explore from an orbit around the planet, and to explore from the planet's surface.

During the interplanetary phase the four spacecraft measured the strengths of magnetic fields and cosmic radiation, and they acquired data on solar radio emissions and solar plasma flares. Once at least one of the spacecraft is in orbit and at least one is on the surface, atmospheric measurements and photographs of the surface will be made both from the orbiter and from the landing vehicle. The soft-landing spacecraft will be used to study the physical characteristics of the soil and rocks in addition to attempting to obtain photographs of the immediate landing region. A Mars landing, if successful, will be the first by a Soviet spacecraft. The first penetration to the surface occurred on Dec. 2, 1971, when Mars 3 parachuted a capsule to the Martian surface.

Venus-Mercury Probe. On Nov. 3, 1973, the United States launched Mariner 10 on its journey to the planet Mercury by way of Venus. The spacecraft will sweep by cloud-shrouded Venus at a distance of 3,300 miles (5,300 km) on Feb. 5, 1974. The planet's gravity will bend the trajectory and slow the spacecraft, allowing Mariner 10 to swing within about 620 miles (1,000 km) of Mercury on March 29, 1974. Mariner 10 will be the first spacecraft to use the gravity of one planet to reach another planet. Also, it will be the first to explore Mercury, the smallest planet in the solar system and the nearest one to the sun.

During the close approaches to the planets, Mariner 10 will send back approximately 5,000 pictures of Venus and 3,000 photos of Mercury. The surface of Venus is obscured by a thick cloud cover, so scientists are hoping that the photos will yield more information on the structure of the clouds and their velocities. In addition, an infrared sensor will sweep across Venus to gather cloud-top tem-

(Continued on page 530)

(Right) *Preparing to return to earth, the first Skylab team takes a final look at the workshop.* (Above) *Venturing outside Skylab, Owen Garriott of the second group of men installs a scientific device.*

SKYLAB: Working in Space

In the Skylab program that followed the Apollo missions to the moon, NASA turned from a basic exploration effort to a serious attempt to use manned space flight as an economic, technological, and scientific resource. Placed aboard the orbital workshop were nearly 300 separate experimental systems. With these, the three-man Skylab crews were able to do work in solar science and zero-gravity technology, observe the earth's weather and its natural resources, and study man's ability to function for extended periods in space.

Official emblem of the Skylab program.

Cutaway view of Skylab living and working areas. Above the ring of storage lockers at top is hatch that leads to docking port.

The first Skylab crew, (from left) Joseph Kerwin, Charles Conrad, and Paul Weitz, poses with a model of the space station.

Conrad, outside Skylab, labors to repair damaged solar panel.

As Lousma takes hot shower, water is removed by vacuum system.

As Conrad trims his hair, Weitz holds vacuum tube to remove the clippings.

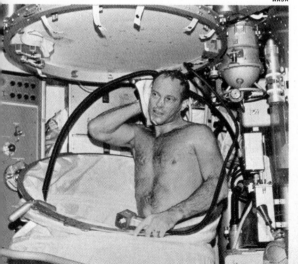

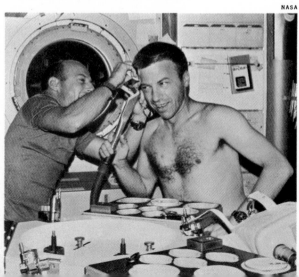

From a height of 270 miles, the orbiting Skylab astronauts look down upon the San Francisco Bay area.

The second Skylab crew flies around the orbiting workshop to inspect it before entering the docking port seen at the front end of the station. The Apollo telescope mount appears on the upper right.

perature measurements. When Mariner 10 flies by Mercury other sensors will determine whether that planet has an atmosphere and, if it does, measure its composition.

Exploration of the Moon. On Jan. 8, 1973, the Soviet Union launched Luna 21, which reached the moon and entered lunar orbit. On January 16, Luna 21 landed on the eastern edge of the Sea of Serenity approximately 112 miles (180 km) north of the Taurus-Littrow valley where the Apollo 17 crew had conducted its surface explorations in 1972.

About 2½ hours after landing, the self-propelled surface vehicle Lunokhod 2 rolled down the gangway from Luna 21 and out onto the lunar surface. The 1,848-pound (838-kg) Lunokhod 2 contained various scientific instruments, including a soil tester, a French-built laser reflector for measuring precise distances from the earth to the moon, and television cameras. During its four-month lifetime, the surface rover transmitted 80,000 pictures of the lunar surface to the earth, including 86 panoramas. When Lunokhod 2 ceased operating in mid-May it had traveled approximately 23 miles (37 km), about 3½ times the distance its predecessor Lunokhod 1 had covered in 1970–71.

The reception of stereoscopic images of the most interesting lunar surface features is making possible a detailed study of their structure. Also, measurements were taken of the physical and mechanical properties of the surface layer of the lunar soils along the route of Lunokhod 2, and analyses were made to determine the chemical composition of the lunar rocks. Prolonged magnetic measurements provided clues to the moon's internal structure.

Meteorological Satellites. On November 6, the United States launched another in its current series of weather satellites, NOAA-3. The 750-pound (340-kg) spacecraft is making meteorological observations of the earth's cloud cover and atmospheric structure. Pictures of the complete global cloud cover are being obtained during both day and night. Another sensor is making continuous radiance measurements, which enable meteorologists to determine the vertical temperature profile of the atmosphere over every part of the earth's surface at least twice daily.

The Soviet Union launched two meteorological satellites in its series in 1973. Meteor 14 and Meteor 15 were placed in earth orbit on March 20 and May 29, respectively.

Communications Satellites. The Intelsat IV F-7 communications satellites was launched on August 23 by the United States for the International Telecommunications Satellite Organization. The satellite was positioned in a geostationary orbit above the equator and over the Atlantic Ocean at 30° west longitude. It has a capacity for 3,000 telephone circuits with its transponders in a spot beam-coverage mode or 12 TV channels or certain combinations of channels and circuits. The satellite has a design life of seven years.

Telesat B (Anik 2), the second of a series of Canadian domestic communications satellites, was launched by the United States for Telesat Canada, a private corporation jointly owned by the Canadian government and telecommunications companies. Telesat B, launched on April 20, will serve primarily as a backup to Telesat A (Anik 1), which was launched in November 1972. Telesat B is stationed above the equator and over the Pacific Ocean at 109° west longitude, five degrees east of Telesat A. Like its predecessor, Telesat B carries 12 transponders and has a capacity for more than 5,000 telephone circuits or 12 TV channels.

In the meantime, the Soviet Union launched five communications satellites for its own needs: two of the Molniya-1 class (Molniyas 1-23 and 1-24) on February 3 and August 30, and three of the Molniya 2 class (Molniyas 2-5, 2-6, and 2-7) on April 5, July 11, and October 19, respectively. The satellites form part of the Orbita network for transmitting telephone, telegraph, radio, and television communications within the Soviet Union. The Molniya satellites also are used as communication relays during manned space-flight operations.

Other Research Satellites. Intercosmos-Copernicus 500, launched by the Soviets on April 19, is a joint endeavor of the Soviet Union, Poland, and

UNMANNED SATELLITES AND PROBES, 1973 HIGHLIGHTS

Name	Launch site and date[1]	Launch vehicle[2]	Spacecraft weight at liftoff (pounds)[3]	Initial apsides of orbit (miles)[4]	Initial period (minutes)	Initial inclination (degrees)	Remarks
Luna 21	B, Jan. 8	N.A.	N.A.	Trajectory to moon			Deployed lunar rover
Molniya 1-23	B, Feb. 3	N.A.	N.A.	292/24,359	703	65.0	Communications satellite
Prognoz 3	B, Feb. 15	N.A.	1,860	366/124,500	5,783	65.0	Solar observatory
Meteor 14	P, March 20	N.A.	N.A.	548/561	102.6	81.2	Meteorological satellite
Salyut 2	B, April 3	N.A.	N.A.	134/162	89.0	51.6	Space station test
Pioneer 11	K, April 5	A-C	572	Trajectory to Jupiter			Fly by Jupiter
Molniya 2-5	B, April 5	N.A.	N.A.	326/24,750	717.7	65.2	Communications satellite
Intercosmos-Copernicus 500	P, April 19	N.A.	N.A.	126/966	102.2	48.5	Solar and ionosphere research
Telesat B (Anik 2)	K, April 20	Delta	1,240	Geostationary orbit at 109° west			Communications satellite
Meteor 15	P, May 29	N.A.	N.A.	529/557	102.4	81.2	Meteorological satellite
Explorer 49	K, June 10	Delta	442	Trajectory to moon			In lunar orbit
Molniya 2-6	P, July 11	N.A.	N.A.	609/24,409	705	65.3	Communications satellite
Mars 4	B, July 21	N.A.	10,200	Trajectory to Mars			Exploration of Mars from orbit and on surface
Mars 5	B, July 25	N.A.	10,200	Trajectory to Mars			
Mars 6	B, Aug. 6	N.A.	10,200	Trajectory to Mars			
Mars 7	B, Aug. 9	N.A.	10,200	Trajectory to Mars			
Intelsat IV F-7	K, Aug. 23	A-C	3,050	Geostationary orbit at 30° west			Communications satellite
Molniya 1-24	P, Aug. 30	N.A.	N.A.	298/23,700	703	65.3	Communications satellite
Molniya 2-7	P, Oct. 19	N.A.	N.A.	391/25,300	736	62.8	Communications satellite
Explorer 50	K, Oct. 25	Delta	877	87,700/180,000	12 days	28.7	Particles and fields
Intercosmos 10	P, Oct. 30	N.A.	N.A.	165/917	102	74.0	Upper atmospheric research
Cosmos 605	B, Oct. 31	N.A.	N.A.	137/263	90.7	62.8	Biological studies
Mariner 10	K, Nov. 3	Delta	1,108	Trajectory to Venus and Mercury			Fly by Venus and Mercury
NOAA 3	V, Nov. 6	Delta	760				Meteorological satellite
AE-C	V, Dec. 13	Delta					Upper atmospheric research

[1] Launch sites: K, Cape Kennedy, Fla.; V, Vandenberg AFB, Calif.; B, Baikonur, USSR; P, Plesetsk, USSR. [2] Launch vehicles: N.A., not available; A-C, Atlas-Centaur. [3] 1 pound equals 0.45 kg. [4] 1 mile equals 1.61 km.

Czechoslovakia in commemoration of the 500th anniversary of the birth of the noted Polish astronomer Nicolaus Copernicus. The satellite carries Polish and Soviet instruments for measuring the radiation of the sun and the ionosphere of the earth.

The United States launched a radio astronomy satellite, Explorer 49, on June 10. It now is listening for sources of low-frequency radio noise in the galaxy and beyond from its position in a lunar orbit. The 442-pound (200-kg) satellite makes use of four radio antennas in an X shape extending 1,500 feet (457 meters) along each diagonal. The spacecraft is making the most extensive study ever undertaken of radio signals that emanate from galactic radio sources, the sun, earth, and Jupiter at frequencies less than 20 megahertz (MHz). Ground-based radio-telescope observations are severely impaired below 20 MHz and are virtually impossible below 10 MHz because of ionospheric effects and terrestrial noise such as thunderstorms and man-made interference.

PITT G. THOME
National Aeronautics and Space Administration

ADVANCES IN SPACE TECHNOLOGY

Space technology underwent consolidation and transition during 1973, but such developments as the manufacture of high-strength or high-purity materials in orbit held great promise for the future.

Skylab Missions. On May 25 the first trio of Skylab astronauts was launched on an orbital mission. This was to be the first of at least three and possibly four orbital endeavors in which three-man crews of astronauts-scientists-engineers would stay in orbit aboard the Skylab space station for as long as three months.

By the end of the second Skylab mission on September 25, enough had been learned of the scientific and engineering physics of operations in orbit to demonstrate that such materials as boron fibers and complicated and expensive crystals could be grown aboard Skylab in a gravity-free environment. Not only were these fibers and crystals grown more expeditiously but also new structures of unexpected strength and purity were achieved. Proposals have been made for manufacturing advanced boron and carbon fibers in orbit to obtain hair-thin fibers with a tensile strength of at least three million pounds per square inch, about 20 times stronger than an equivalent steel fiber.

The Skylab Orbital Workshop program was scheduled to draw to a close with the Skylab 3 crew mission early in 1974, but the likelihood of another long-range orbital mission in 1974 was high. Advanced Skylab workshop missions have been studied by the National Aeronautics and Space Administration, but with limited resources NASA may go on to the shuttle program without another intermediate manned program.

Orbital Shuttle Technology. Despite criticism from some members of Congress and some members of the scientific-technical community, NASA relentlessly pursued its goal of developing the orbital shuttle program by the mid-1970's.

Technical contracts for product improvement or the development of new hardware were awarded to a number of aerospace and electronic companies. The Aerojet Corp. in California, for example, got a contract to develop various elements of attitude-control and propulsion thrustors for the shuttle spacecraft.

NASA studied advanced solid-propellant units for the main shuttle booster and assessed the feasibility of reducing the liftoff thrust of the booster from 2.7 million pounds to about 2.5 million pounds. On the other hand, the redesigned propellant portion of the solid-propellant rockets would weigh about 1 million pounds, versus an earlier design weight of 969,000 pounds.

In design changes the lengths of the rocket motors have been increased to 1,741 inches (44.2 meters), and the overall shuttle liftoff weight, including the booster and the shuttle spacecraft, has been increased from 4,105,000 pounds to 4,165,000 pounds. This would reduce the lift-to-thrust ratio, and the rocket would leave the pad at a slower velocity and acceleration than originally called for.

The Aerojet Corp. has proposed a 120-foot (36.6-meter) long solid-propellant rocket to be cast in a single unit for the shuttle booster. This is an impressive technical undertaking because casting a unit of solid propellant of such large dimensions—about 120 feet long and 30 feet (9 meters) in diameter—has never been attempted before for operational purposes where very high reliability is needed. Competitive solid-propellant companies, including Lockheed, Thiokol, and United Aircraft, have proposed casting the solid propellant in segments like stacked Lifesavers.

NASA had not picked a final solid-propellant system by year-end, and there still was competitive pressure from the liquid-propellant companies to develop a liquid booster for the shuttle.

International Rocket Development. The European space community has decided to join the U.S. orbital shuttle program and has designed various payloads suitable for it. The Europeans hope to make contributions in materials and structures.

Missile Developments. The Aerojet Corp. has developed a variable-thrust space propulsion system for the U.S. Navy AJ-10-53 missile project. These variable-thrust rocket motors are very difficult to design and build because all solid propellants prefer to burn at a constant rate and are difficult to throttle. However, several schemes are possible, including the use of a metal "egg" in the narrow throat of the rocket engine along with the injection of certain liquids into the solid-propellant burning chamber to control combustion.

There was intensive activity during 1973 in the further development of the SRAM (Short-Range Attack Missile) for the U.S. Air Force. Several explosions during the development of the solid-propellant motor AGM-69A, built by Lockheed Corp., created some temporary setbacks for the program.

Advanced Propellant Concepts. The U.S. Air Force showed renewed interest in high-density, high-energy hydrocarbon fuels for use in volume-limited air-breathing propulsion systems. Potential applications for such high-cost fuels include the Subsonic-Cruise Armed-Decoy (SCAD) missile for the Air Force. The bases for these fuels include very volatile liquid hydrocarbons resembling kerosene, or liquid fuels saturated with suspended slurries of metallic substances.

Breakthroughs in such propellant chemistry during 1973 may extend the range of liquid-propellant rockets or air-breathing missiles by 10% to 40% for a given tank volume. Applications are expected to accrue also in the space booster field.

KURT R. STEHLING
U.S. Government Aerospace Consultant

GENERALISSIMO FRANCO (center) at the swearing in of Premier Luis Carrero Blanco (at Franco's right). Carrero Blanco was assassinated in December.

SPAIN

Generalissimo Francisco Franco, aged 80 and apparently in failing health, resigned some of his duties in 1973 but remained titular head of Spain. There was no apparent change in the dictatorial nature of the regime, and a revamped cabinet appeared more conservative than its predecessor. The assassination of Premier Luis Carrero Blanco in December, however, resulted in unexpected uncertainty about the continuity of Spanish leadership. The church hierarchy sought during the year to break its ties with the government.

Politics. Early in 1973, Franco and his designated successor, Adm. Luis Carrero Blanco, seemed to promise Spaniards wider participation in their government. But when, on June 8, Franco turned over to Carrero Blanco most of the day-to-day tasks of running the government, hopes of liberalization were disappointed. Carrero, himself 70 and Franco's confidential aide for 36 years, though vice-premier only since 1967, assumed the title of premier with authority to preside over cabinet meetings and make some decisions hitherto referred to Franco.

The new premier made immediate cabinet changes, which were seen as a victory for the fascistic and conservative Falange faction and an ouster of the "European-oriented technocrats," dominant since 1967. The most significant change was the replacement of Foreign Minister Gregorio López Bravo, who had attempted to obtain the return of Gibraltar by friendly negotiations with Britain, by Laureano López Rodó, an austere nationalist who followed a harder line in his negotiations with the British.

On the morning of December 20, Carrero Blanco was killed when a bomb was detonated under his car outside a Madrid church. The Basque terrorist organization E. T. A. admitted responsibility, and the government later identified six Basque separatists as the assassins. At year's end, Minister of Interior Carlos Arias Navarro was named premier.

Economy. Spain's chief economic interest in 1973 continued to be closer ties with the European Economic Community (Common Market). In 1972, 37% of the country's $3.8 billion in exports went to EEC countries, with an expected 50% in 1973. Spain now bought about 45% of its imports from those countries. The major obstacle to Spain's outright entry into the EEC was the hostility of labor unions and liberal groups in EEC countries to the authoritarian Franco regime.

The cities, though not the rural areas, of Spain showed prosperity. Private car ownership rose from 358,000 in 1961 to 3 million in 1973, and an estimated 10 million Spaniards owned television sets. Unemployment had declined to 1.5% of the 13 million labor force, but this figure did not take account of the many seasonal laborers, especially agricultural, forced to seek employment or better wages outside Spain.

Spanish exports, formerly mainly agricultural, had by 1973 become 79% industrial—most importantly ships, steel, automobiles, chemicals, and electrical equipment. Spanish wages, though rising, remained low; a machine operator in Spain earned about half of what his opposite number earned in Britain and approximately a third of the wages of his West German counterpart. This furnished a powerful incentive for foreign companies to manufacture in Spain, not only for the Spanish market

but for export as well. Also, under the terms of a six-year preferential agreement with Common Market countries, tariffs against Spanish-made goods were lowered by 60% for 1973 and by a projected 75% for 1974.

The negative side was the decay of the countryside and the wholesale migration of rural workers to Spanish cities or other European countries.

As Spanish purchasing power steadily increased in 1973, food-and-beverage frauds reached scandalous proportions. The most common cheating occurred through short-weighting, adulteration, and use of additives. Meat, vegetables, chocolate, fruit, cheese, vinegar, and honey were tampered with to add weight, to dilute, or to liven color. By one report, 62% of what was sold as mineral water (non-carbonated) was really tap water. Wine underwent dilution, and low-grade liquors were sold in bottles bearing elite brand names. A protest meeting in Seville in April proved vehement. But failure by the state's market discipline inspection service to enforce honesty by producers was laid to lack of insistence or discernment by the public.

Tourism. Tourism continued to be a major Spanish industry, with an estimated total of 32 million visitors in 1973, almost equaling Spain's population. A smaller number spent $2.6 billion in 1972. Franco's ministry of information and tourism said in October that the hope was for 38 million tourists spending $6.5 billion by 1975.

This has greatly spurred the nation's industrial expansion and standard of living, yet in 1973 some Spaniards found the huge foreign influx in many ways undesirable. They saw their Mediterranean coast transformed from beautiful seashore to unending stretch of high-rise hotels and apartment buildings for sun-worshiping foreigners. Rising incomes enabled Spaniards to travel more in Spain, but on their vacation trips they found hotel accommodations harder to obtain. One objection was to "package tours," arranged by foreign travel agencies, that engaged blocks of rooms in Spanish hotels at half-price rates, causing Spaniards and foreigners traveling independently to pay more than foreigners in tour groups.

The Church. The Spanish bishops, on January 20, approved by a vote of nearly three to one a document advocating separation of church and state through revision of the concordat of 1953 between the Vatican and Franco's government. The bishops, while not rejecting the idea of Catholicism as the national religion, made plain that they did not wish to be identified with all acts of the state in temporal matters. The government took an unfavorable view of this ecclesiastical action, and vice-premier Carrero Blanco accused the clergy of forgetting all the benefits granted them by the state since Franco's assumption of power.

Despite the bishops' January vote, Archbishop José Méndez Asensio of Pamplona in March invoked the part of the concordat that prohibits the prosecution of priests without their superiors' permission. Several priests of his archdiocese had delivered sermons partially justifying the January kidnapping and holding for ransom of Felipe Huarte, a Pamplona industrialist, by Basque guerrillas, who demanded and obtained pay raises and better working conditions for his employees.

Foreign Affairs. Spain formally recognized East Germany on January 11 and on March 9 announced establishment of commercial and diplomatic rela-

——————— SPAIN • Information Highlights ———————

Official Name: Spanish State.
Location: Iberian Peninsula in southwestern Europe.
Area: 194,897 square miles (504,782 sq km).
Population (1973 est.): 34,200,000. Density, 176 per square mile (68 per sq km).
Chief Cities (1970 census): Madrid, the capital, 3,146,071; Barcelona, 1,745,142; Valencia, 653,690; Seville, 548,072.
Government: Head of state, Francisco Franco, caudillo (leader) (officially assumed power Aug. 1939). Head of government, Carlos Arias Navarro, premier (appointed Dec. 1973). Legislature (unicameral)—Las Cortes Españolas.
Language: Spanish (official).
Education: Expenditure (1969), 2.2% of gross national product. School enrollment (1969)—primary, 3,789,135; secondary, 1,766,488; technical/vocational, 354,227; university/higher, 194,515.
Monetary Unit: Peseta (56.82 pesetas equal U.S.$1, July 1973).
Gross National Product (1972 est.): $42,200,000,000.
Economic Indexes: Industrial production (1972), 250 (1963=100); agricultural production (1971), 117 (1963=100); consumer price index (1972), 182 (1963=100).
Manufacturing (major products): Iron and steel, electrical machinery, automobiles, textiles, chemicals, ships, processed foods, leather, furniture.
Major Agricultural Products: Wheat, rye, barley, corn, citrus fruits, vegetables, olives, potatoes, fish, forest products, sheep.
Major Minerals: Mercury (ranks 1st among world producers, 1971), coal, iron ore, lead, magnesite.
Foreign Trade (1972): Exports, $3,803,000,000. Imports, $6,755,000,000. Chief trading partners (1970)—United States (took 11% of exports, supplied 19% of imports); West Germany (10%—13%); France (8%—10%); United Kingdom (7%—7%).
Tourism: Receipts (1972), $2,600,000,000.
Transportation: Motor vehicles (1971), 3,577,700 (automobiles, 2,784,700); railroads (1971), 8,496 miles (13,672 km); merchant fleet (1972), 4,300,000 gross registered tons; major national airline, IBERIA-Líneas Aéreas de España.
Communications: Telephones (1972), 5,129,501; newspapers (1971), 115 (daily circulation, 3,396,000).

tions with Communist China, following exploratory talks in Hong Kong. Similar negotiations were under way with the Soviet Union, Poland, and other Communist-bloc states. Establishing relations with these Communist countries, unthinkable a few years earlier, caused uneasiness among Spanish conservatives and was bitterly denounced by members of the small Spanish Communist party, most of them in exile, who berated East Germany for recognizing Franco.

The long negotiation between Spain and Britain over the future status of Gibraltar came to at least a temporary halt after the Spanish cabinet changes in June. The new foreign minister, Laureano López Rodó, suspended the protracted discussions his predecessor had held with British Foreign Secretary Sir Alec Douglas-Home and decided to take the dispute to the United Nations. Although the Gibraltarians in 1967 voted overwhelmingly against Spanish sovereignty, Spain called Gibraltar "the last colony left in Europe" and charged that British planes and warships repeatedly violated Spanish air space and waters.

With the outbreak of the Arab-Israeli war in October, Spain clearly took the Arab side. It refused to permit the United States in the course of aid operations to Israel to use U.S.-controlled bases at Torrejón, near Madrid, and Rota, near Cádiz. Spain said the bases could be used only to protect Western European security, not "in a local conflict such as the Arab-Israeli one." U.S. occupation of these bases rested on an executive agreement of 1953, which was to run out in 1975. Spain now sought, evidently because of President Nixon's domestic embarrassments, to tighten controls and to grant renewal only by a firm treaty, hitherto lacking.

CHARLES E. NOWELL
University of Illinois

HORST SCHÄFER

Secretariat

DAN BALIOTTI

Henry Aaron

Sports

BY BILL BRADDOCK
"The New York Times"

After she had humbled Bobby Riggs before the largest audience in the history of the game, Billie Jean King said her victory was "the culmination of 19 years of tennis." Since her match with the 55-year-old self-styled "chauvinist pig" had been billed as the Battle of the Sexes, Mrs. King could rightfully feel that she had achieved something extraordinary for women. Yet she had seen the fulfillment of one of her cherished goals just a few weeks before—the posting of a first prize of $25,000 for women in the United States championships, a purse equal to that for men. This equality was what she had battled for in recent years, and it afforded her greater satisfaction than the squelching of a hustler.

Mrs. King, 29, who won the Wimbledon title for the fifth time in July, had battled the U. S. Lawn Tennis Association and the World Federation in the courts as well as with player associations and had been suspended more than once. She had renewed her efforts in 1972 when she was given $10,000 for winning the U. S. Open while the men's winner received $25,000.

The $100,000 winner-take-all match between Mrs. King and Riggs on September 21 got as much build-up as a heavyweight title fight. There were 30,492 fans in the Houston Astrodome, the largest audience in the history of the game. It was broadcast live on national television and by satellite to 36 other countries for a video audience of 60 million. Riggs, a form U. S. and Wimbledon champion, had soundly defeated Mrs. Margaret Court, the other leading woman player, 6–2, 6–1, on May 13. Thousands who had never seen a tennis match watched as Mrs. King routed Riggs, 6–4, 6–3, 6–3. She had disproved Riggs' theory that women athletes could not perform well under great stress.

"Women can be great athletes, and I think you'll find in the next decade that women athletes will finally get the attention they've deserved through the years, that people will respect us as athletes and not just whether we're good-looking or cute," said Billie Jean.

Mrs. King's premise that the fine athletes would get deserved attention was seen in the sell-out crowds (including 19,694 at Madison Square Garden) to see Olga Korbut and other top Soviet gymnasts and in the willingness of an ice revue to pay $1.5 million to Janet Lynn, a four-time U. S. figure-skating champion, to join it.

The equal-rights struggle was carried on in less highlighted fashion in other sports. In some, the women widened their gains. Robyn Smith, a Stanford graduate, became the first woman jockey to ride a stakes winner in March. Four years before, the male jockeys had tried boycotts to keep females from riding thoroughbred racers.

Women golfers have long had their own tour, but their prize money is much less than the purses distributed to the men. For example, Betty Burfeindt has been on the tour since 1969. She finished fourth in winnings in 1972 with $47,529 and in 1973 with $51,031, or $98,559 in two years and $107,615 in five years. She won three tournaments. In contrast, Jerry Heard in five years on the men's tour also won three tournaments. But he finished fifth in earnings in 1972 with $137,198, 27th in 1973 with $83,285, and made $388,027 in five years.

Much of the struggle for equal rights is being

WIDE WORLD

MARGARET COURT after winning the singles title at the U. S. open tennis championships, at Forest Hills, N. Y.

carried on by girls about the age of Billie Jean Moffitt (now Mrs. King) when she began to play tennis. They have gone to the courts and to municipal officials in their battles for equal privileges. They have challenged the Little League and similar amateur groups for barring them from teams. They are battling schools for team positions and for athletic budgets equal to that given the boys. State after state has upheld their pleas. In Michigan, New Jersey, New York, and Indiana, girls won the right to play on noncontact boys' teams. New York girls have won top roles in cross-country running.

In other breakthroughs, Sue Schneider became a trainer for the Michigan State football team, and Judy Carson is licensed as a football official in Connecticut. In 1972, Mrs. Bernice Gera won a New York court battle that allowed her to become a baseball umpire. After officiating in one minor-league game, she quit. However, she had won her point for womankind.

Women have not penetrated any further into baseball, so it will be many years before a woman can catch up with Babe Ruth's career home run record of 714. By that time the record will probably be held by Atlanta's Henry Aaron. Hammerin' Hank, also known admiringly as "Bad Henry" for being such bad news to pitchers (can a gal be so dubbed?), wound up the season with 713.

Nor was one of the women jockeys up on Secretariat, the 3-year-old Meadow Stable colt that became the ninth winner of thoroughbred racing's Triple Crown by taking the Kentucky Derby, the Preakness, and the Belmont Stakes. The ladies will never get a chance at riding him, either, because the sterling colt was retired to stud after a spectacular 6½-length victory in the Canadian International at Woodbine, near Toronto, on October 28.

Women, however, will be equally involved in the conduct of athletic endeavor in the United States if the bill for federal control of sports, sponsored by Sen. John V. Tunney (D-Calif.), is adopted by Congress. The act is intended to end the struggle between the Amateur Athletic Union and the National Collegiate Athletic Association for control of sports and the sanctioning of international events. Most sports groups object to federal control.

OLGA KORBUT (left) and LUDMILA TURISCHEVA

JANET LYNN

WOMEN IN SPORTS

Women athletes came into their own in 1973, led by Billie Jean King (*opposite*), shown after beating Bobby Riggs. Also pictured here are Janet Lynn, star of *Ice Follies;* Soviet gymnasts Olga Korbut and Ludmila Turischeva; Betty Burfeindt, a leading money winner on the women's golf tour; and jockey Robyn Smith.

BETTY BURFEINDT

BILLIE JEAN KING

ROBYN SMITH

GORDON JOHNCOCK after his victory in the rain-shortened Indianapolis 500. Tragedy again marred race.

AUTO RACING

Two famed drivers, Jackie Stewart and Mark Donohue, retired after a season in which safety, more than ever, was a critical issue. Stewart announced his retirement after regaining the world championship by winning five Grand Prix races and piling up 71 points, 16 more than the runner-up, Emerson Fittipaldi of Brazil, the 1972 champion. Donohue, winner of the Canadian-American Challenge Cup series for sports cars, announced in November that a race in February 1974 would be his last. He will design cars after that. Bobby Isaac, a former stock-car champion, had withdrawn from racing in August.

The energy crisis clouded prospects for the sport in 1974. The problem was not only supplying gasoline for the racers (Indy-type cars use an alcohol-based fuel) but also for the thousands of spectators who drive to the weekend events.

A string of accidents in 1973 had a sobering effect on drivers, influencing several of them to retire. Stewart had seen too many of his friends killed. Roger Williams of Britain died in a fiery crash in the Dutch Grand Prix race, and François Cevert of France, the Scotsman's teammate, was killed in the trials for the U. S. Grand Prix, the season's finale. Conditions at many foreign tracks led the commission that governs racing to ban four of them. The 32-year-old Stewart, who had won the title in 1969 and 1971, raised his Grand Prix victories to a record total of 27 in 99 races.

Disaster at Indianapolis during the trials and the running of the 500-mile race led to revisions in United States Auto Club standards. On May 12, Art Pollard was killed while practicing, and Salt Walther and Swede Savage were injured in efforts to race despite heavy rain on May 28 and 30. Savage died

---

Auto Racing Highlights

World Championship Grand Prix Races

Argentina (Buenos Aires, Jan. 28)—Emerson Fittipaldi, Brazil (driving a Lotus-Ford; distance 199.5 miles; time: 1 hour, 56 minutes, 18.22 seconds; average speed: 102.53 miles per hour)

Brazil (São Paulo, Feb. 11)—Emerson Fittipaldi (200 miles; 1:43:55; 117 mph)

South Africa (Johannesburg, March 3)—Jackie Stewart, Scotland (Tyrrell-Ford; 201.5 miles; 1:43:11:07; 117.5 mph)

Spain (Barcelona, April 29)—Emerson Fittipaldi (176.6 miles; 1:48:18.7; 97.834 mph)

Belgium (Zolder, May 20)—Jackie Stewart (182 miles; 1:42:13.43; 107.73 mph)

Monaco (Monte Carlo, June 3)—Jackie Stewart (158.87 miles; 1:57:44.3; 80.96 mph)

Sweden (Anderstorp, June 17)—Denis Hulme, New Zealand (192.9 miles; McLaren-Ford; 1:56:46; 102.6 mph)

France (Le Castellet, July 1)—Ronnie Peterson, Sweden (Lotus-Ford; 188.5 miles; 1:41:36.52; 115.117 mph)

Britain (Silverstone, July 14)—Peter Revson, Redondo Beach, Calif. (McLaren-Ford; 196.11 miles; 1:29:18.5; 131.75 mph)

Netherlands (Zandvoort, July 29)—Jackie Stewart (187.2 miles; 1:39:12.45; 114.4 mph)

Germany (Neuerburgring, Aug. 5)—Jackie Stewart (198.8 miles; 1:42:03; 116.8 mph)

Australia (Zeltweg, Aug. 19)—Ronnie Peterson (199 miles; 1:28:44; 133 mph)

Italy (Monza, Sept. 9)—Ronnie Peterson (197.4 miles; 1:29:17; 132.338 mph)

Canada (Mosport, Ont., Sept. 23)—Peter Revson (200 miles; 1:59:04.85; 1:16.991 mph)

United States (Watkins Glen, N.Y., Oct. 7)—Ronnie Peterson (199.243 miles; 1:41:15.779; 118.055 mph)

United States Auto Club Championship Trail

Indianapolis 500 (May 30; postponed from May 28–29)—Gordon Johncock, Franklin, Ind. (Eagle-Offenhauser); race ended after 332.5 miles because of rain; winner's time for 133 laps: 2 hours, 5 minutes, 26.59 seconds; average speed 159.036 mph; winner's purse: $236,023)

Schaefer 500 (Pocono International Raceway, Long Pond, Pa., July 1)—A. J. Foyt, Houston, Texas (Gilmore-Foyt; 200 laps; 3:26:58.24; 144.944 mph; $94,808)

California 500 (Ontario, Calif., Sept. 2)—Wally Dallenbach, East Brunswick, N. J. (Eagle-Offy; 200 laps; 3:10:16.97; 157.660 mph; $106,720)

Texas Twin 200's (College Station, Texas, April 7)—Al Unser, Albuquerque, N. Mex. (Parnelli-Offenhauser; 1:18:19; 153.224 mph; $18,651); stock-car race: Gordon Johncock (Chevrolet; 1:30:56.84; 131.952 mph)

Trenton 300 (two 150-mile races, Trenton, N. J., April 15)—first race: A. J. Foyt (1:05:029; 138.355 mph; $8,810); second race: Mario Andretti, Nazareth, Pa. (Parnelli-Offenhauser; 1:00:50; 149.626 mph; $9,435)

Rex Mays 150 (Milwaukee, June 10)—Bobby Unser, Albuquerque, N. Mex. (Eagle-Offenhauser; 1:28:58.278; 108.008 mph; $19,579)

Michigan Twin 200's (Cambridge Junction, July 25)—Roger McCluskey, Tucson, Ariz. (McLaren-Offenhauser; 1:14:28; 161.146 mph; $19,003); stock-car race: A. J. Foyt (Chevrolet; 1:29:16.39; 134.429 mph; $6,596)

Acme Super Saver 500 (stock cars, Pocono Raceway, July 29)—Richard Petty, Randleman, N. C. (Dodge; 3:45:56.07; 132.781 mph; $9,620)

Tony Bettenhausen 200 (Milwaukee, Aug. 12)—Wally Dallenbach, East Brunswick, N. J. (Eagle-Offenhauser; 1:50:47; 108.320 mph; $14,706)

Michigan 250 (two 125-mile races, Cambridge Junction, Mich., Sept. 16)—first race: Billy Vukovich, Fresno, Calif. (Eagle-Offenhauser; awarded victory on appeal, Sept. 24, after Gary Bettenhausen had been named winner; 56:24.41; 134.161 mph; one-lap penalty against Vukovich was erased); second race: Johnny Rutherford, Fort Worth, Texas (McLaren-Offenhauser; 48.04.70; 157.282 mph); overall: Johnny Rutherford

Trenton 200 (Trenton, N. J., Sept. 23)—Gordon Johncock (1:29:47.27; 135.064 mph)

Texas Twin 200's (College Station, Texas, Oct. 7)—Gary Bettenhausen, Tinley Park, Ill. (McLaren-Offenhauser; 1:05.58; 181.918 mph; $15,887); stock-car race: Roger McCluskey (Plymouth; 1:03.22; 143.924 mph; $6,404)

Phoenix 150 (Nov. 3)—Gordon Johncock (1:18:15.03; 115.016 mph)

Nascar Events
Grand National Division

Winston Western (Riverside, Calif., Jan. 21)—Mark Donohue, Reading, Pa. (Javelin; 4 hours, 48 minutes, 33 seconds; average speed 104.055 mph; winner's purse: $15,170)

Daytona 500 (Daytona Beach, Fla., Feb. 18)—Richard Petty, Randleman, N. C. (Dodge; 3:10.50; 157.205 mph; $33,500)

Carolina 500 (Rockingham, N. C., March 18)—David Pearson, Spartanburg, S. C. (Mercury; 4:13:01; 118.649 mph; $14,975)

Atlanta 500 (Atlanta, Ga., April 1)—David Pearson (3:34:52; 139.351 mph; $16,125)

Rebel 500 (Darlington, S. C.)—David Pearson (4:05:14; 122.655 mph; $15,835)

Winston 500 (Talledega, Ala., May 6)—David Pearson (3:47:23; 131.956 mph; $25,845)
World 600 (Charlotte, N.C., May 27)—Buddy Baker (Dodge; 4:26:33; 134.890 mph; $25,200)
Mason-Dixon 500 (Dover, Del., June 3)—David Pearson (4:10:32; 119.745 mph; $13,525)
Alamo 500 (College Station, Texas, June 10)—Richard Petty (3:26:44; 142.114 mph; $15,820)
Tuborg 400 (Riverside, Calif., June 17)—Bobby Allison, Hueytown, Ala. (Chevrolet; 4:00:00; 100 mph; $10,750)
Motor State 400 (Irish Hills, Mich., June 24)—David Pearson (2:36:22; 153.485 mph; $12,210)
Firecracker 400 (Daytona Beach, Fla., July 4)—David Pearson (2:31:27; 158.468; $16,100)
Dixie 500 (Atlanta, Ga., July 22)—David Pearson (3:50:01; 130.211 mph; $15,950)
Talladega 500 (Talladega, Ala., Aug. 12)—Richard Brooks, Porterville, Calif. (Plymouth; 3:26:17; 145.454 mph; $20,815)
Southern 500 (Darlington, S.C., Sept. 3)—Cale Yarborough, Timmonsville, S.C. (Chevrolet; 3:44:25; 134.033 mph; $21,140)
Delaware 500 (Dover, Sept. 16)—David Pearson (4:25:50; 112.852 mph; $15,825)
National 500 (Charlotte, N.C., Oct. 7)—Cale Yarborough (3:26:58; 145.240 mph; $17,725)
American 500 (Rockingham, N.C., Oct. 21)—David Pearson (4:14:57; 117.749 mph; $16,775)

Other Major Sports Car Races

Twenty-Four Hours of Daytona (Daytona Beach, Fla., Feb. 3-4)—Peter Gregg and Hurley Haywood, Jacksonville, Fla. (Porsche-Carrera; 2,552.7 miles; average speed: 106.274 mph)
Monza 1,000 (Monza, Italy, April 25, 621 miles)—Jacky Ickx, Belgium, and Brian Redman, Britain (Ferrari; 4:07; 34.4; 150 mph)
Spa 1,000 (Francorchamps, Belgium, May 6)—Derek Bell, Britain, and Howden Ganley, New Zealand (Gulf-Mirage; 4:05:43.5; 151.92 mph)
Targa Florio (Palermo, Sicily, May 13, 492 miles)—Gijs Van Lennep, Netherlands, and Herbert Muller, West Germany (Porsche-Carrera; 6:54:19.9)
Neuerburgring 1,000 (Adenau, West Germany, May 27)—Jacky Ickx and Brian Redman (5:36:53.4; 111.8 mph)
24 Hours of Le Mans (Le Mans, France, June 9-10)—Henri Pescarolo and Gerard Larrousse, France (Matra-Simco; 3,009 miles; 125.3 mph)
Austrian 1,000 (Zeltweg, June 24)—Henri Pescarolo and Gerard Larrousse (4:48:57.8; 129 mph)
Six-Hours of Endurance (Watkins Glen, N.Y., July 21)—Henri Pescarolo and Gerard Larrousse (672.023 miles; 111.895 mph)

Individual Champions

World Grand Prix—Jackie Stewart, Scotland (71 pts)
United States Auto Club—*Championship Trail:* Roger McCluskey, Tucson, Ariz. (3,705 pts; $170,863); *leading money winner:* Gordon Johncock, Franklin, Ind. ($279,857); *stock car:* Larry (Butch) Hartman, South Zanesville, Ohio ($66,000); *sprint cars:* Rollie Beale, Toledo, Ohio (1,094 pts); *dirt track:* Al Unser, Albuquerque, N. Mex. (460 pts); *Midget division:* Larry Rice, Indianapolis (735 pts)
Nascar—Grand National: Benny Parsons, Ellerbe, N.C. (7,173.80 pts; $114,345); *leading money winner:* David Pearson, Spartanburg, S.C. ($213,966); Grand National East: Tiny Lund, Cross, S.C. (1,294 pts; $18,330); Grand National West: Jack McCoy, Modesto, Calif. (1,673 pts; $15,210)

Sports Car Club of America Champions

Canadian American Challenge Cup (7 races)—Mark Donohue, Reading, Pa. (Sunoco-Porsche; 139 pts; $114,533)
L&M Formula 5,000 (9 races)—Jody Scheckter, South Africa (Lola-Chevrolet; 144 pts; $115,200)
Trans-American Championship Series (6 races)—Peter Gregg, Jacksonville, Fla. (Porsche-Carrera; 71 pts; $17,050); Manufacturers: Chevrolet (42 pts)
VW Gold Cup (8 races)—Bertil Roos, Sweden (Supernova Tui; 86 pts; $13,650)
Solo 2 Championship (Wentzville, Mo., Oct. 20-21)—Overall: John Anderson, Austin, Texas
Press On Regardless Rally (1,700 miles through Michigan, Nov. 1-4)—Walter Boyce and Doug Woods, Ottawa, Ont. (Toyota; 41,847 penalty pts)

Other Sports Car Champions

Tasman Cup (Australia–New Zealand; 8 races)—Graham McRae, New Zealand (McRae-STP)
Monte Carlo Rally (3,000 miles; Jan. 20-26)—Jean Claude Andreaut and Michele Petit, France (Alpine-Renault)
East African Safari (3,000 miles, finish April 23)—Sheh-ker Mehl, Nairobi, Kenya (Datsun)

Sports Car Club of America Road Racing Classic
(Road Atlanta, Flowery Branch, Ga., Nov. 2-4)

A Production—Sam Feinstein, Rydal, Pa. (Cobra; 95.81 mph)
B Production—Bill Jobe, Richardson, Texas (Corvette; 94.71 mph)
C Production—Bob Sharp, Wilton, Conn. (Datsun; 93.64 mph)
D Production—Lee Mueller, Lynwood, Calif. (Healey; 90.47 mph)
E Production—Brian Fuerstenau, Falls Church, Va. (MG; 88.87 mph)
F Production—John Kelly, Rockville, Md. (Spitfire; 88.61 mph)
G Production—Rick Cline, Gainesville, Fla. (Spitfire; 84.18 mph)
H Production—Mike Dale, Kinnelon, N. J. (Sprite; 82.27 mph)
A Sports Racing—Bob Nagel, Bethel Park, Pa. (Lola; 106.73 mph)
B Sports Racing—Jerry Hansen, Wayzata, Minn. (Lola; 105.13 mph)
C Sports Racing—Eric Kerman, Hempstead, N. Y. (Arachnid; 96.11 mph)
D Sports Racing—Ronald Dennis, Madison, Wis. (Ocelot-Suzuki; 87.59 mph)
A Sedan—Carl Shafer, Wyoming, Ill. (Camaro; 94.32 mph)
B Sedan—David Frellsen, Evanston, Ill. (Datsun; 88.44 mph)
C Sedan—Don Devendorf, Los Angeles (Datsun; 84.49 mph)
Formula A—Jerry Hansen, Wayzata, Minn. (Lola; 113.11 mph)
Formula B—Ken Duclos, Boxboro, Mass. (Brabham; 104.64 mph)
Formula C—Michael Gilbert, Redmond, Wash. (Lotus; 92.21 mph)
Formula F—Bob Earl, Sonoma, Calif. (Auto. Development; 95.01 mph)
Formula Vee—Rollin Butler, Greenville, S. C. (Zink; 85.04 mph)
Formula Super Vee—Harry Ingle, Charlotte, N. C. (Zink; 99.48 mph)
President's Cup—Harry Ingle
Outstanding Mechanic—Tom Klausler, Evanston, Ill.

on July 2. The governing body ordered a reduction in fuel capacity and relocation of the tanks to cut the fire hazard, and planned speed-reduction measures.

Roger McCluskey won the USAC big-car championship, but the top money winner was Gordon Johncock, winner of the Indy 500, which was cut by rain to 332.5 miles.

In National Association for Stock Car Auto Racing's top series, the championship went to Benny Parsons. David Pearson was the big winner, though. He finished first in 11 races, mostly on super speedways. His total of $213,966 in purses made him the second Nascar driver to pass the $1 million mark in earnings. Richard Petty, the first to do so, won another $159,665 in 1973.

——— BASEBALL ———

Tug McGraw, a relief pitcher, sparked the late-season revival of the New York Mets with the chant "You Gotta Believe." Before the World Series was over, it seemed that everyone believed the Mets were the best team in the land—everyone except the A's and their fans in Oakland, Calif., a next-door neighbor of McGraw's hometown Vallejo. The A's, trailing 3 games to 2, finally revived themselves and won the next two games for their second straight world championship.

McGraw's chant of faith became the "war song" of Mets fans during the playoffs against the favored Cincinnati Reds for the National League pennant. The Mets had been dismissed as a contender in August when they trailed the leader in their Eastern Division by 12 games. After occupying last place for two months, the New York club began to move up on August 30. With help from their division rivals, the Mets took first place on September 21 by beating the Pirates for their 77th victory. That put them even with their 77 losses, an average of .500. The Mets won five of their last seven games and posted a .509 mark before meeting the Reds (.611) in the pennant series.

The battle among five teams for that division title added excitement to the waning season, in which interest was centered on Henry Aaron's drive

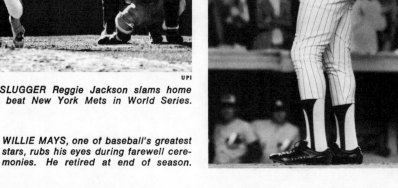

OAKLAND SLUGGER *Reggie Jackson slams home run as A's beat New York Mets in World Series.*

WILLIE MAYS, *one of baseball's greatest stars, rubs his eyes during farewell cere-monies. He retired at end of season.*

to overtake Babe Ruth's record for career home runs. The 39-year-old Atlanta Braves slugger kept whittling away at the mark of 714 and hit his 713th on September 29. In the last game of the season, Aaron lashed out three hits in four times at bat, but he failed to belt the long one that would have tied the record. However, he wound up with a .300 batting average for the season, in addition to 40 home runs.

When the five-way scramble for the Eastern Division title began, Cincinnati was challenged by Los Angeles for Western honors, but a nine-game losing streak stopped the Dodgers. In the American League, the Oakland A's and the Baltimore Orioles were well on the way toward clinching division titles. The only close contest looming was between St. Louis and Pittsburgh for the National East play-off berth. The Cards seemed to be in control with a six-game lead in early August. But Bob Gibson, their ace pitcher, had to have knee surgery, and with their pitching rotation off, the team began to slump. The Pirates, seeking their fourth straight division title, then faltered. Their manager, Bill Virdon, was replaced by Danny Murtaugh, who had retired a third time after the 1971 season. The change was no remedy, mainly because the Mets got well.

A series of injuries had kept the New York club from putting its best team on the field for about half the season. Jerry Grote, the catcher, had missed two months; Bud Harrelson, the shortstop, was gone several weeks; and Cleon Jones, outfielder and a valuable hitter, was ailing. There was clamor about manager Yogi Berra, but the Mets executives rode along with Berra, a believer, who had said all along, "We'd be all right if we could get all of our men on the field."

Then the wounded Mets began to come back. Grote's return to catching duties helped the fine pitching staff live up to its potential. Tom Seaver, Jon Matlack, and Jerry Koosman were reliable starters, and McGraw, who earlier had been ineffec-

tive, was excellent in relief. During the Mets' final surge, McGraw won three games and was credited with nine saves in 13 appearances. In their drive from the cellar to the pennant, the Mets won 24 games and lost 9. Because of postponements due to rain, they actually captured the division title the day after the season ended, winning in Chicago as Pittsburgh lost to San Diego.

In the playoffs, Oakland, which boasted three 20-game winning pitchers (Catfish Hunter, 21–5; Ken Holtzman, 21–16; and Vida Blue, 20–9), sub-dued Baltimore in the fifth and deciding game on the five-hit hurling of Hunter. The Mets had to battle back after the Reds beat Seaver, the National League's Cy Young Award winner, in the opener. An altercation at second base between Pete Rose, the league batting champion, and shortstop Harrel-son in the third game in New York led to a near riot in left field, with the hometown fans throwing a variety of objects at Rose. After the Reds with-drew in protest from the field, Berra and Willie Mays, who had announced he would retire at the end of the season, led a delegation of players who persuaded the fans to calm down.

In the World Series opener at Oakland, Holtz-man beat Matlack, 2–1, on four hits, the A's scoring two unearned runs in the third inning. The second game was a sandlot affair, won by the Mets, 10–7, with four runs in the 12th. Two of the runs came in on errors by Mike Andrews, a substitute second baseman. On the following day, owner Charles O. Finley fired Andrews, sending him home on a medi-cal-disability charge. Commissioner Bowie Kuhn ordered the return of Andrews, who received a standing ovation from the fans. After the series, Kuhn fined Finley $7,000 and put him on probation for his actions.

With the shift of the series to New York, Oak-land took the lead again with a 3–2 victory in 11 innings. But the Mets, behind Matlack, drew even with a 6–1 triumph, and when the Mets won the fifth game, 2–0, on three-hit pitching by Koosman

and McGraw, almost everyone agreed "You Gotta Believe." Almost, except the fans in Oakland where the final two games were played. Reggie Jackson, the league's most valuable player, batted in the runs that led to a 3–1 Oakland victory and tied the series. In the finale, Bert Campaneris and Jackson each hit a homer with a man on in the fourth inning as the A's won, 5–2, retaining the championship and disappointing the believers.

The season had begun on a historical note. The American League made the most drastic change in rules since the game had been standardized a century before. The league set up a procedure for using a· designated hitter to bat for the pitcher. The idea was to produce more runs by taking a weak hitter out of the lineup. This gave a lot of aging good batters, such as Orlando Cepeda, extensions on their careers. After the season, it was shown

UPI

BATTLE IN THE PLAYOFFS: Pete Rose of Cincinnati has upper hand in tussle with New York's Bud Harrelson.

Baseball Highlights

Professional—Major Leagues

AMERICAN LEAGUE
(Final Standings, 1973)

EASTERN DIVISION

	W	L	Pct.
Baltimore	97	65	.599
Boston	89	73	.549
Detroit	85	77	.525
New York	80	82	.494
Milwaukee	74	88	.457
Cleveland	71	91	.438

WESTERN DIVISION

	W	L	Pct.
Oakland	94	68	.580
Kansas City	88	74	.543
Minnesota	81	81	.500
California	79	83	.488
Chicago	77	85	.475
Texas	57	105	.352

NATIONAL LEAGUE
(Final Standings, 1973)

EASTERN DIVISION

	W	L	Pct.
New York	82	79	.509
St. Louis	81	81	.500
Pittsburgh	80	82	.494
Montreal	79	83	.488
Chicago	77	84	.478
Philadelphia	71	91	.438

WESTERN DIVISION

	W	L	Pct.
Cincinnati	99	63	.611
Los Angeles	95	66	.590
San Francisco	88	74	.543
Houston	82	80	.506
Atlanta	76	85	.472
San Diego	60	102	.370

Playoffs—*American League:* Oakland defeated Baltimore, 3 games to 2; *National League:* New York defeated Cincinnati, 3 games to 2

World Series—Oakland defeated New York, 4 games to 3; paid attendance, 7 games, 358,289; total receipts, $3,923,968.37; commissioner's office share, $588,595.26; individual club and league shares, $547,742.91; players' share (series only), $1,144,473.12; players' share of playoffs and series, $1,992,461.17, including full shares of $24,760.87 for each Oakland player and $14,950.17 for each New York player

First Game (Oakland–Alameda County Coliseum, Oct. 13): Oakland 2, New York 1; *second game* (Oakland, Oct. 14): New York 10, Oakland 7 (12 innings); *third game* (Shea Stadium, New York, Oct. 16): Oakland 3, New York 2 (11 innings); *fourth game* (New York, Oct. 17): New York 6, Oakland 1; *fifth game* (New York, Oct. 18): New York 2, Oakland 0; *sixth game* (Oakland, Oct. 20): Oakland 3, New York 1; *seventh game* (Oakland, Oct. 21): Oakland 5, New York 2

All-Star Game (Kansas City, July 24)—National League 7, American League 1

Most Valuable Players—*American League:* Reggie Jackson, Oakland outfielder; *National League:* Pete Rose, Cincinnati outfielder

Cy Young Memorial Awards (outstanding pitcher)—*American League:* Jim Palmer, Baltimore; *National League:* Tom Seaver, New York

Rookies of the Year—*American League:* Al Bumbry, Baltimore outfielder; *National League:* Gary Matthews, San Francisco outfielder

Leading Batters—*Percentage: American:* Rod Carew, Minnesota, .350; *National:* Pete Rose, Cincinnati, .338; *Runs Batted In: American:* Reggie Jackson, Oakland, 117; *National:* Willie Stargell, Pittsburgh, 119; *Home Runs: American:* Jackson, 32; *National:* Stargell, 44

Leading Pitchers—*Earned Run Average: American:* Jim Palmer, Baltimore, 2.40; *National:* Tom Seaver, New York, .207. *Victories: American:* Wilbur Wood, Chicago, 24; *National:* Ron Bryant, San Francisco, 24; *Strikeouts: American:* Nolan Ryan, California, 383; *National:* Tom Seaver, 251

No-Hit Games Pitched—Steve Busby, Kansas City (AL) vs. Detroit, 3–0; Nolan Ryan, California (AL) vs. Kansas City, 3–0; Nolan Ryan vs. Detroit, 6–0; Jim Bibby, Texas (AL) vs. Oakland, 6–0; Phil Niekro, Atlanta (NL) vs. San Diego, 9–0

Hall of Fame Inductees—Roberto Walker Clemente; William G. (Billy) Evans; Monford (Monte) Irvin; George Lange Kelly; Warren Edward Spahn; Michael F. (Mickey) Welch

Professional—Minor Leagues

(When two teams are named, the first team won the regular season championship and the second won the playoff; otherwise, the team named won both.)

American Association (AAA)—Iowa, East Division; Tulsa, West Division and playoff

International League (AAA)—Rochester, American Division; Charlestown, National Division; Pawtucket, playoff

Pacific Coast League (AAA)—Tucson, East Division; Spokane, West Division and playoff

Junior World Series—Pawtucket (International League) defeated Tulsa (American League) 4 games to 1

Mexican League—Southeastern: Jalisco; Southwestern: Tampico; Northeastern: Saltillo; Northwestern: Mexico City Reds and playoff

Eastern League (AA)—Pittsfield, American Division; Reading, National Division and playoff

Southern League (AA)—Montgomery, Western Division and playoff; Jacksonville, Eastern Division

Texas League (AA)—Memphis, Eastern Division and playoff; San Antonio, Western Division

California League (A)—Lodi, first half and playoff; Bakersfield, second half

Carolina League—Lynchburg, first half; Winston-Salem, second half and playoff

Florida State League (A)—Lakeland, Northern Division; West Palm Beach, Southern Division; St. Petersburg, playoff

Midwest League—Wisconsin Rapids, Northern Division first half; Clinton, Northern Division second half; Danville, Southern Division first half; Decatur, Southern Division second half; Wisconsin Rapids, playoff

New York—Pennsylvania League (A)—Auburn; no playoff

Northwest League (A)—Walla-Walla, Eastern Division; Portland, Western Division; Walla-Walla declared champion

Western Carolina League (A)—Gastonia, first half; Spartanburg, second half and playoff

Appalachian (Rookie)—Kingsport

Gulf Coast (Rookie)—Rangers

Pioneer (Rookie)—Billings

Intercollegiate Champions

NCAA—*University Division:* Southern California (defeated Arizona State, 4–3, in final); *College Division:* California at Irvine (defeated Ithaca, 9–6, in final)

NAIA—U. S. International (defeated Eastern Connecticut, 7–2, in final)

Amateur Champions

American Legion—Rio Piedras, Puerto Rico
Babe Ruth World Series—Prince Georges, Md.
Bronco League—Oklahoma City
Colt League—Pasadena, Texas
Connie Mack League—Long Beach, Calif., Great Western Cardinals
Dixie Youth World Series—Fort Oglethorpe, Ga.
Mickey Mantle League—Dallas Hawks
Little League—Taiwan (defeated Tucson, Ariz., 12–0, in final)
Little League Seniors—Taiwan
National Baseball Congress—Fairbanks, Alaska
Pee Wee Reese League—Detroit Southwest PAL Red Sox
Pony League—Santa Clara, Calif.
Sandy Koufax League—Dallas Oak Cliff Lions
Stan Musial League—Dean Realty, Coldwater, Mich.

that the American League had outscored the National, but the figures were inconclusive, although fan interest seemed to be heightened.

Oddly, however, with more batting strength in every team's lineup, 12 American League pitchers won 20 or more games. The National League had only one—Ron Bryant of San Francisco, with 24. Designated hitters failed to bother Nolan Ryan of the California Angels. He broke Sandy Koufax's major league strikeout mark by one, with a total of 383 for the season. He also pitched two no-hit games. However, the Cy Young Award for the American League was voted to Jim Palmer of Baltimore, who had a 22–9 record and a 2.40 earned-run average.

BASKETBALL

Professional

Willis Reed got well just in time to spark the New York Knicks to the National Basketball Association championship in 1973. Reed, voted most valuable player in the playoffs, was aided by some very healthy teammates such as Walt Frazier, Dave DeBusschere, Bill Bradley, Earl Monroe, and Jerry Lucas. In their push to the title the Knicks, who finished second in their division, knocked off three division leaders—Baltimore, Boston, and Los Angeles—each of whom was hampered by injuries to key players.

The Boston Celtics finished the regular season with 68 wins in 82 games and seemed well on their way to reoccupy the top rank they had held during most of the past 10 years. However, John Havlicek, their captain, came up with a shoulder injury late in the third game against the Knicks. He missed one game. The Knicks became the first team to defeat the Celtics in a seven-game series. It took New York only five games to dispose of the Los Angeles Lakers, the defending champions. Superstar Jerry West of the Lakers was hobbled by hamstring muscle pulls, and the Knicks' fine defensive play neutralized Wilt Chamberlain's usually intimidating presence.

During the season, the Philadelphia 76ers set two records for ineptitude. They won only 9 of 82 games and at one stretch dropped 20 in a row.

In the American Basketball Association, Indiana took the title for the second season in a row and the third in four years. The Pacers stopped Louisville in the seventh game, 88–81. Neither club had led its division. The Colonels eliminated Carolina, the Eastern champion, and the Pacers beat Utah, the Western champion, in the semifinals.

Chamberlain, who held dozens of NBA records after 14 years of play in the league, shifted to the ABA as nonplaying coach of the San Diego Conquistadors at the start of the 1973–74 season in October.

College

The University of California at Los Angeles continued to dominate college play in 1973 by winning the National Collegiate Athletic Association championship for the seventh straight year. In so doing, UCLA, coached by John Wooden, swept all 30 of their games, extending their winning streak to 75 over a three-year period and their NCAA tournament victories to 36. The Bruins' performance wiped out the record of 60 held by the University of San Francisco.

Professional Basketball Highlights

National Basketball Association
(Final Standings, 1972–73)

Eastern Conference
Atlantic Division

	W	L	Pct.	Scoring For	Avg. Agst.
Boston Celtics	68	14	.829	112.7	104.5
New York Knickerbockers	57	25	.695	105.0	98.2
Buffalo Braves	21	61	.256	103.3	112.5
Philadelphia 76ers	9	73	.110	104.1	116.2

Central Division

	W	L	Pct.	Scoring For	Avg. Agst.
Baltimore Bullets	52	30	.634	105.0	101.6
Atlanta Hawks	46	36	.561	112.4	112.3
Houston Rockets	33	49	.402	112.8	114.5
Cleveland Cavaliers	32	50	.390	102.7	105.3

Western Conference
Midwest Division

	W	L	Pct.	Scoring For	Avg. Agst.
Milwaukee Bucks	60	22	.732	107.2	99.0
Chicago Bulls	51	31	.622	104.1	100.6
Detroit Pistons	40	42	.488	110.3	110.0
Kansas City-Omaha Royals	36	46	.439	107.6	110.5

Pacific Division

	W	L	Pct.	Scoring For	Avg. Agst.
Los Angeles Lakers	60	22	.732	111.7	103.2
Golden State Warriors	47	35	.573	108.8	105.7
Phoenix Suns	38	44	.463	111.6	112.9
Seattle SuperSonics	26	56	.317	103.7	109.6
Portland Trail Blazers	21	61	.256	106.2	112.4

Eastern Conference playoffs final: New York defeated Boston, 4 games to 3; Western Conference playoffs final: Los Angeles defeated Golden State, 4 games to 1; NBA Championship: New York defeated Los Angeles, 4 games to 1
Most Valuable Player—Dave Cowens, Boston Celtics
Rookie of the Year—Bob McAdoo, Buffalo Braves
Leading Scorer—Nate Archibald, Kansas City-Omaha Royals; 2,719 points; 34 average per game

American Basketball Association
(Final Standings, 1972–73)

Eastern Division

	W	L	Pct.	Scoring For	Avg. Agst.
Carolina Cougars	57	27	.679	115.6	110.7
Kentucky Colonels	56	28	.667	111.9	105.4
Virginia Squires	42	42	.500	115.4	115.8
New York Nets	30	54	.357	103.6	113.2
Memphis Tams	24	60	.286	111.5	118.1

Western Division

	W	L	Pct.	Scoring For	Avg. Agst.
Utah Stars	55	29	.655	115.6	110.1
Indiana Pacers	51	33	.607	114.7	112.5
Denver Rockets	47	37	.560	110.8	107.7
San Diego Conquistadors	30	54	.357	109.0	113.2
Dallas Chaparrals	28	56	.333	110.7	115.1

Eastern Division playoffs final: Kentucky defeated Carolina, 4 games to 3; Western Division playoffs final: Indiana defeated Utah, 4 games to 2; ABA Championship: Indiana defeated Kentucky, 4 games to 3
Most Valuable Player—Billy Cunningham, Carolina Cougars
Rookie of the Year—Brian Taylor, New York Nets
Leading Scorer—Julius Erving, Virginia Squires, 2,268 points; 31.9 average per game

In the final game, played at St. Louis, UCLA defeated Memphis State, 87–66, after the Tennessee quintet had held the champions to a 39–39 tie at halftime. Bill Walton, the lanky center, led the Bruins to their ninth title in 10 years by scoring 44 points, a tourney record. Before the final, UCLA turned back Arizona State, San Francisco, and Indiana. Memphis State, paced by Larry Finch and Larry Kenon, eliminated South Carolina, Kansas State, and Providence.

North Carolina State, ineligible for NCAA play, won all of its 27 games.

Kentucky State failed in its bid for a fourth straight National Association of Intercollegiate Athletics championship, losing in the first round. Guilford took the title by defeating Maryland–Eastern Shore in the final, 99–96. Kentucky Wesleyan won the NCAA College Division championship for the fourth time in eight years, with a 78–76 over-

Amateur Basketball Highlights

Major Tournaments

NCAA (St. Louis, finals, March 26)—University of California at Los Angeles (defeated Memphis State, 87–66); *College Division* (Evansville, Ind., March 14–16): Kentucky Wesleyan (defeated Tennessee State, 78–76, in overtime)

National Intercollegiate (NAIA, at Kansas City, March 12–17)—Guilford (defeated Maryland–Eastern Shore, 99–96, in final)

National Invitation Tournament (New York, March 17–25)—Virginia Tech (defeated Notre Dame, 92–91, in overtime, in final)

Men's AAU (Ashland, Ky., March 29–April 2)—Marathon Oil, Lexington, Ky. (defeated Cincinnati Schlitz, 89–84, in final)

Women's AAU (Gallup, N. Mex., March 27–31)—John F. Kennedy College (defeated Raytown, Mo., Piperettes, 59–52, in final)

National Junior College (Hutchinson, Kans., March 14–17)—Mercer County, N. J., C. C. (defeated Hutchinson J. C., 80–61, in final)

College Conference Champions

(Figures in parentheses represent victories and losses in conference games only.)

Atlantic Coast—North Carolina State (12–0); won championship tournament but was ineligible for NCAA, so Maryland (7–5) gained berth

Big Eight—Kansas State (12–2)

Big Sky—Weber State (13–1)

Big Ten—Indiana (11–3)

Ivy League—Pennsylvania (12–2)

Mid-American—Miami (9–2)

Middle Atlantic—*University Division, East:* St. Joseph's (6–10); *West:* Lafayette (7–3); *College Division, North:* Philadelphia Textile (10–0); *South:* Lebanon Valley (9–2; not eligible for championship) and Widener (9–2)

Missouri Valley—Memphis State (12–2)

Ohio Valley—Austin Peay (11–3)

Pacific 8—UCLA (14–0)

Southeastern—Kentucky (14–4)

Southern—Furman (11–2); won conference tournament

Southwest—Texas Tech (12–2)

Pacific Coast Athletic—Long Beach State (10–2)

West Coast Athletic—San Francisco (12–2)

Western Athletic—Arizona State (10–4)

Yankee—Massachusetts (10–2)

Leading Major Independents

East—Providence (27–4); Syracuse (24–5); St. John's (19–7); Northeastern (19–7)

South—Jacksonville (21–6); South Carolina (22–7); Virginia Tech (22–5); Florida State (18–8)

Midwest—Marquette (25–4); Marshall (20–7)

Southwest—Oral Roberts (21–6); Oklahoma City (21–6); Hardin-Simmons (16–9)

Far West—Denver (17–9); Hawaii (15–11)

UPI

BILL WALTON scores against Memphis State in NCAA title game as UCLA five continued to reign supreme.

time victory over Tennessee State. Immaculata College of Pennsylvania retained the women's intercollegiate crown by beating Queens College of New York, 69–52, in the final.

The United States College All-Stars defeated a touring Soviet team, 4 games to 2.

Boxing

George Foreman, a 24-year-old former Olympic champion, knocked down Joe Frazier six times in 4½ minutes in Kingston, Jamaica, on Jan. 22, 1973, to become the new world's heavyweight champion. Two months later, in San Diego on March 31, Muhammad Ali suffered a broken jaw at the hands of Ken Norton, a former sparring partner, and lost a split decision. It was only the second loss for Ali.

The losses suffered by Frazier and Ali were widely believed at the time to have deflated the price of a return bout between them and to have cost each fighter a rich purse. They had split $5 million in their first fight, won by Frazier, in March 1971. However, boxing fans had not counted on Ali's considerable talent for publicity. The return match, on Jan. 28, 1974, actually brought the principals at least $2.6 million each. Ali won a unanimous decision in the 12-round bout, held in New York.

Several other champions were dethroned and one, Masao Ohba, the World Boxing Association flyweight titleholder, was killed in an auto accident in Tokyo on January 25. He had defended his title successfully against Chartchai Chionoi on January 2. Chartchai, a former champion, won the vacated title by stopping Fritz Chervet of Switzerland in the fifth round on May 17. In defense of his crown, he outpointed Susumu Hanagata of Japan.

Boxing Highlights

World Professional Champions

Flyweight—Chartchai Chionoi, Thailand, World Boxing Association; Venice Borkorsor, Thailand, World Boxing Council

Bantamweight—Arnold Taylor, South Africa, WBA; Rafael Herrera, Mexico, WBC

Featherweight—Ernesto Marcel, Panama, WBA; Eder Jofre, Brazil, WBC

Junior Lightweight—Ben Villaflor, Philippines, WBA; Ricardo Arredondo, Mexico, WBC

Lightweight—Roberto Duran, Panama, WBA; Rodolfo Gonzalez, Long Beach, Calif., WBC

Junior Welterweight—Antonio Cervantes, Colombia, WBA; Bruno Arcari, Italy, WBC

Welterweight—Jose Napoles, Mexico

Junior Middleweight—Koichi Wajima, Japan

Middleweight—Carlos Monzon, Argentina

Light Heavyweight—Bob Foster, Albuquerque, N. Mex.

Heavyweight—George Foreman, Hayward, Calif.

National AAU Championships
(Boston, May 10–12)

106 Pounds—Albert Sandoval, Los Angeles
112 Pounds—Richard Rozelle, Columbus, Ohio
119 Pounds—Mike Hess, Albany, Oreg.
125 Pounds—Howard Davis, New York
132 Pounds—Aaron Pryor, Cincinnati
139 Pounds—Randy Shield, Hollywood, Calif.
147 Pounds—William Tuttle, Bowie, Md.
156 Pounds—Dale Grant, Tacoma, Wash.
165 Pounds—Martin Hagler, Brockton, Mass.
178 Pounds—D. C. Barker, Denver
Heavyweight—James Chapman, Reno, Nev.

Venice Borkorsor of Thailand, the World Boxing Council champion, beat Erbito Salavarria of the Philippines in February.

Romeo Anaya took the WBA bantamweight title from Enrique Pinder of Panama in January but lost it to Arnold Taylor of South Africa on November 3 after beating Pinder again in August. Rafael Herrera of Mexico defeated Rodolfo Martinez for the WBC version of the title and outpointed Borkorsor in defense in October. Eder Jofre of Brazil, a former bantamweight champion, took the WBC featherweight crown away from Jose Legra of Spain and retained it by knocking out Vicente Saldivar on October 20. Ernesto Marcel of Panama twice retained the WBA title.

Jose Napoles, the welterweight champion, and Roberto Duran of Panama, the WBA lightweight king, each won three title bouts. Rodolfo Gonzalez, the WBC lightweight champion, beat two challengers, as did Carlos Monzon of Argentina, the middleweight titleholder. Bob Foster, the light heavyweight champion, defeated Pierre Fourie of South Africa twice. The second bout, staged in Johannesburg, was the first there between a black and a white.

CANADA GAMES

Ontario, the province which had won the three previous biennial meets, was beaten out by British Columbia in the 1973 renewal of the Summer Games. The host province won 6 of the 16 events and 47 gold medals in piling up a total of 176½ points, 6 more than Ontario and 24 more than third-place Quebec. Saskatchewan won the Centennial Trophy for the most improved performance over 1969.

In the 10-day competition in August, which drew 250,690 spectators to Barnaby and Westminster, British Columbia athletes won in baseball, diving, field hockey, rowing, shooting, and soccer. Ontario triumphed in canoeing, lacrosse, swimming, tennis, and track and field.

Younger athletes were the individual stars. In swimming, Becky Smith, 14, of Edmonton, Alberta, and Stephen Pickell, 15, of Vancouver, B.C., won five gold medals each. Ann Dodge, 15, of Fall River, Halifax, took three canoeing, gold medals, and Jan Sparling won three in track.

Canada Games Highlights

Final Point Standings

(Points are awarded on basis of 12 for first, 11 for second, 10 for third, etc., on final standings for each sport.)

British Columbia	176½
Ontario	170½
Quebec	152
Alberta	128
Manitoba	123½
Nova Scotia	118½
Saskatchewan	112
New Brunswick	78
Newfoundland	54
Prince Edward Island	41
Northwest Territories	10
Yukon	7

FOOTBALL
Professional

In regular-season play the Miami Dolphins, undefeated in 1972, lost two games, proving that they were not immortal. But in the Super Bowl on Jan. 13, 1974, at Rice Stadium, Houston, they attained awesome perfection, drubbing the Minnesota Vikings, 24–7. As they had hoped to do, the Dolphins received the opening kickoff and marched to a touchdown. When the Vikings failed to gain, Miami got the ball again and marched to another score and a 14–0 lead. The Dolphins controlled the ball for 11 minutes 13 seconds of the first period, fulfilling another phase of their game plan—to keep the ball out of the hands of Fran Tarkenton, Minnesota's excellent scrambling quarterback.

Most of Miami's marching was done by Larry Csonka, the rugged fullback, who carried for a bowl record of 145 yards. His way was eased by Dolphin interior linemen Wayne Moore, Bob Kuechenberg, Jim Langer, Larry Little, and Norm Evans, who opened gaping holes against the famed defensive bulwark of Carl Eller, Gary Larsen, Alan Page, and Jim Marshall, known as the Purple People Eaters. The Dolphins' less-heralded No-Name Defense was superb in containing the Vikings. Miami's victory, its second in a row, equaled the record of the Green Bay Packers in Super Bowl competition.

The Dolphins, on September 23, had lost a chance to tie the pro record of 17 straight regular-season games, set by the Chicago Bears in 1933–34, when they were beaten by Oakland, 12–7, on

MIAMI fullback Larry Csonka powers his way past Minnesota defenders to score the first touchdown in the 1974 Super Bowl. Csonka picked up 145 yards as Dolphins gained their second straight championship, 24–7.

NATIONAL FOOTBALL LEAGUE
(Final Standings, 1973)

American Conference
Eastern Division

	Won	Lost	Tied	Pct.	Pts.	Opp.
Miami	12	2	0	.857	343	150
Buffalo	9	5	0	.643	259	230
New England	5	9	0	.357	258	300
Baltimore	4	10	0	.286	226	341
N. Y. Jets	4	10	0	.286	240	306

Central Division

	Won	Lost	Tied	Pct.	Pts.	Opp.
Cincinnati	10	4	0	.714	286	231
*Pittsburgh	10	4	0	.714	347	210
Cleveland	7	5	2	.571	234	255
Houston	1	13	0	.071	199	447

Western Division

	Won	Lost	Tied	Pct.	Pts.	Opp.
Oakland	9	4	1	.679	292	175
Denver	7	5	2	.571	354	296
Kansas City	7	5	2	.571	231	192
San Diego	2	11	1	.179	188	386

* Fourth, or wild card, qualifier for playoffs

Playoffs—Oakland defeated Pittsburgh, 33–14, Dec. 22; Miami defeated Cincinnati, 34–16, Dec. 23
Conference Championship—Miami (defeated Oakland, 27–10, at Miami, Dec. 30

National Conference
Eastern Division

	Won	Lost	Tied	Pct.	Pts.	Opp.
Dallas	10	4	0	.714	382	203
*Washington	10	4	0	.714	325	198
Philadelphia	5	8	1	.393	310	393
St. Louis	4	9	1	.321	286	365
N. Y. Giants	2	11	1	.179	226	362

Central Division

	Won	Lost	Tied	Pct.	Pts.	Opp.
Minnesota	12	2	0	.857	296	168
Detroit	6	7	1	.464	271	247
Green Bay	5	7	2	.429	202	259
Chicago	3	11	0	.214	195	334

Western Division

	Won	Lost	Tied	Pct.	Pts.	Opp.
Los Angeles	12	2	0	.857	388	178
Atlanta	9	5	0	.643	318	224
New Orleans	5	9	0	.357	163	312
San Francisco	5	9	0	.357	262	319

* Fourth, or wild card, qualifier for playoffs

Playoffs—Minnesota defeated Washington, 27–20, Dec. 22; Dallas defeated Los Angeles, 27–16, Dec. 23
Conference Championship—Minnesota (defeated Dallas, 27–10, at Dallas, Dec. 30)
League Champion (Super Bowl)—Miami (defeated Minnesota, 24–7, at Houston, Jan. 13, 1974)
Pro Bowl—American Conference 15, National Conference 13, at Kansas City, Mo., Jan. 20, 1974

National Football League Leaders
American Conference

Scoring—Roy Gerela, Pittsburgh (29 field goals, 36 extra points, 123 points)
Scoring (nonkickers)—Floyd Little, Denver (78 pts)
Passing—Ken Stabler, Oakland (163 of 260 for 1,997 yards and 14 touchdowns; 62.7% completions)
Receiving—Fred Willis, Houston (57 for 371 yds)
Interceptions—Dick Anderson, Miami (8)
Rushing—O. J. Simpson, Buffalo (332 for 2,003 yds)
Punting—Jerrell Wilson, Kansas City (45.5 yds average)
Punt Returns—Ron Smith, San Diego (13 yds average)
Kickoff Returns—Wallace Francis, Buffalo (29.9 yds average)

National Conference

Scoring—David Ray, Los Angeles (30 field goals, 40 extra points, 130 points)
Scoring (nonkickers)—Larry Brown, Washington (84 pts)
Passing—Roger Staubach, Dallas (179 for 2,428 yards and 23 touchdowns; 62.6% completions)
Receiving—Harold Carmichael, Philadelphia (67 for 1,116 yds)
Interceptions—Bob Bryant, Minnesota (7)
Rushing—John Brockington, Green Bay (265 for 1,144 yds)
Punting—Tom Wittum, San Francisco (43.7 yds average)
Punt Returns—Bruce Taylor, San Francisco (13.8 yds average)
Kickoff Returns—Carl Garrett, Chicago (30.4 yds average)

Canada

Grey Cup (Toronto, Nov. 25)—Ottawa Rough Riders 22, Edmonton Eskimos 18

UPI

NEITHER SNOW nor the New York Jets can stop O. J. Simpson as he sets a new NFL rushing mark, Dec. 16.

George Blanda's four field goals. They had been undefeated in 18 games, including playoffs. They lost later to Baltimore, 16–3,

Minnesota went into the Super Bowl with the same 12–2 record as Miami in regular-season play. The Vikings won the National Conference championship by downing the Dallas Cowboys, 27–10, the same score by which Miami took the American Conference title against Oakland. The rejuvenated Los Angeles Rams also had a 12–2 record but lost to Dallas in the playoffs.

O. J. Simpson was the season's outstanding player, gaining 250 yards rushing in one game and 2,003 for the season. Both totals bettered league marks. He also led his team, the Buffalo Bills, to a league record in rushing with 3,096 yards.

Just before the start of the season, Congress passed a law forbidding local blackouts of television broadcasts of games sold out three days before the event. After the season the clubs reported that 1,016,565 persons who had tickets did not attend the games. Of the total, 656,290 no-shows were for 113 games that were televised locally under the new rule. The clubs expected a drop in the sale of season tickets.

College

With Notre Dame leading by a point but backed up close to the goal line by a big, belligerent Alabama line and time running out, quarterback Tom Clements coolly faded back to the end zone and drilled a pass upfield to a receiver around the 30-yard line. This imaginative and courageous play, clinched a 24–23 victory and the National Football Foundation's national championship. The game was played in the Sugar Bowl on New Year's Eve before a national TV audience of millions, which was as stunned as Alabama by the thunderbolt that Coach Ara Parseghian ordered Clements to throw.

The play started on the 2-yard line, third down and 8 with about two minutes left. When receiver

QUARTERBACK Tom Clements carries for Notre Dame in 24–23 win over Alabama that clinched No. 1 ranking.

Robin Weber was downed on the 38-yard line, the unbeaten Irish were free to maneuver and run out the clock. It was the first loss in 12 games for Alabama. The deciding points had been scored on a 19-yard field goal by Bob Thomas with 4½ minutes to play, after Alabama had taken the lead on a rare halfback-to-quarterback pass. An earlier Alabama lead of 7–6 was quickly rubbed out by Al Hunter's 93-yard kickoff return for Notre Dame.

The victory was Notre Dame's 11th, but there were other contenders for the mythical national championship. Penn State, like Alabama, had an 11–0 record going into the New Year's finale and outlasted Louisiana State on a slippery field in the Orange Bowl, 16–9. Ohio State had won nine games and been tied by Michigan before routing Southern California, the 1972 champion, 42–21, in the Rose

Bowl in Pasadena, Calif., on New Year's Day.

The writers voting in the Associated Press poll after the bowl games switched their top choice from Alabama to Notre Dame. The Irish had ended Southern California's 23-game nonlosing string, October 27, with a 23–14 triumph, their first in the series since 1966. The UPI poll after the regular season had named Alabama as No. 1.

Then there was Oklahoma, possibly the best but ineligible for postseason games because of recruiting violations. The Sooners won 10 games and tied Southern California, 7–7. They won the Big Eight title, blasting Nebraska, 27–0, and also routed Texas, 52–13. In the Cotton Bowl, Nebraska defeated Texas, 19–3.

Ohio was selected for the Rose Bowl by a Big Ten vote after playing a 10–10 tie with Michigan in a battle for the conference championship. Bo Schembechler, the Michigan coach, accused the conference administrators of being influenced by "petty jealousies."

Penn State's domination of the East, for which it was awarded the Lambert Trophy, was paced by John Cappelletti, a speedy and shifty 210-pound tailback. He was awarded the Heisman Trophy as the nation's outstanding college player.

Two other major unbeaten teams went into postseason play. Miami of Ohio, the Mid-American Conference champion, raised its mark to 11 victories by beating Florida in the Tangerine Bowl, 16–7. Western Kentucky defeated Grambling, 28–20, for its 11th triumph but lost to Louisiana Tech, 34–0, for the Division II small college championship of the NCAA. Wittenberg won Division III NCAA honors by routing Juniata, 41–0. The NAIA Division I title went to Abilene Christian, which trounced Elon, 42–0.

College Football Highlights

Intercollegiate and Conference Champions

National Press Polls—UPI (coaches): Alabama; AP (writers): Notre Dame
National Football Foundation Award (MacArthur Bowl)—Notre Dame
Heisman Trophy—John Cappelletti, Penn State
Eastern (Lambert Trophy)—Penn State
Eastern Small College—Lambert Cup: Lehigh and Delaware; Lambert Bowl: C. W. Post
Atlantic Coast—North Carolina State (6–0)
Big Eight—Oklahoma (7–0)
Big Sky—Boise State (6–0)
Big Ten—Tie between Michigan and Ohio State (7–0–1)
Ivy League—Dartmouth (6–1)
Mid-American—Miami (5–0)
Missouri Valley—Tie between North Texas State and Tulsa (5–1)
Ohio Valley—Western Kentucky (7–0)
Pacific 8—Southern California (7–0)
Pacific Coast A. A.—San Diego State (3–0–1)
Southeastern—Alabama (8–0)
Southern—East Carolina (7–0)
Southwest—Texas (7–0)
Western Athletic—Tie between Arizona and Arizona State (5–1)
Yankee—Connecticut (5–0–1)

Leading Independents

East—Penn State (11–0), Temple (9–1)
South—Tulane (9–2), Memphis State (8–3), Tampa (8–3)
Midwest—Notre Dame (10–0)
Southwest—Houston (10–1)
Far West—Utah State (7–4)

NCAA Small College Bowls
Division II Semifinals

Grantland Rice Bowl (Baton Rouge, La., Dec. 8)—Western Kentucky 28, Grambling 20
Pioneer Bowl (Wichita Falls, Texas, June 8)—Louisiana Tech 38, Boise State 34

Division II Final

Camelia Bowl (Sacramento, Calif., Dec. 15)—Louisiana Tech 34, Western Kentucky 0

Division III

Stagg Bowl (Phenix City, Ala., Dec. 8)—Wittenberg 41, Juniata 0

NAIA Championships

Division I (Shreveport, La., Dec. 8)—Abilene Christian 42, Elon 0
Division II (Huntington, W. Va., Dec. 1)—Northwestern College (Iowa) 10, Glenville State 3; semifinals (Nov. 24)—Northwestern 28, William Jewell 2; Glenville State 14, Carthage College (Wisconsin) 7

Major Bowl and All-Star Games
(Nov.–Dec. 1973; Jan. 1974)

Liberty Bowl (Memphis, Tenn., Dec. 17)—North Carolina State 31, Kansas 18
Blue-Gray All-Stars (Montgomery, Ala., Dec. 18)—Blue 20, Gray 14
Fiesta Bowl (Tempe, Ariz., Dec. 21)—Arizona State 28, Pittsburgh 7
Tangerine Bowl (Gainesville, Fla., Dec. 22)—Miami (Ohio) 16, Florida 7
North-South Shrine Game (Miami, Dec. 25)—South 27, North 6
Peach Bowl (Atlanta, Dec. 28)—Georgia 17, Maryland 16
Astro-Bluebonnet Bowl (Houston, Dec. 29)—Houston 47, Tulane 7
Gator Bowl (Jacksonville, Fla., Dec. 29)—Texas Tech 28, Tennessee 19
Sun Bowl (El Paso, Texas, Dec. 29)—Missouri 34, Auburn 17
East-West Shrine Game (San Francisco, Dec. 29)—East 35, West 7
Sugar Bowl (New Orleans, Dec. 31)—Notre Dame 24, Alabama 23
Cotton Bowl (Dallas, Jan. 1)—Nebraska 19, Texas 3
Orange Bowl (Miami, Jan. 1)—Penn State 16, Louisiana State 9
Rose Bowl (Pasadena, Calif., Jan. 1)—Ohio State 42, Southern California 21
Hula Bowl (Honolulu, Jan. 5)—East 24, West 14
All-American Bowl (Tampa, Fla., Jan. 6)—North 28, South 7
Senior Bowl (Mobile, Ala., Jan. 12)—North 16, South 13

In late November 1973, Jack Nicklaus, who had already been named Golfer of the Year by the Professional Golfers' Association, decided it would be fitting for him to lead the money-winners list too. So he won the Disney World Open, picked up a check for $30,000, and secured the top position for the third straight year with $308,362. This was $34,096 more than second-place Bruce Crampton won. The victory, his seventh of the season, also raised Nicklaus' career total to $2,009,168, the first above the $2 million level. Arnold Palmer, the first golfer to win $1 million, was second with $1,-631,469.

In August, Nicklaus won the PGA title tournament for his 14th major championship, the most by any golfer. He had been tied with Bobby Jones for that honor. With his accomplishments, Nicklaus had one ambition left. "I want to shoot for all four of the major championships [U. S. Amateur and Open, British Open, and PGA] and win them in one year," he said after his triumph in the Disney World Open.

Nicklaus had realized another objective. After winning on the new Nicklaus Golf Center course in Ohio, he turned back the $25,000. He asked that $20,000 be used at Ohio State University (his alma mater) for a scholarship under the name of his father, Charles Nicklaus. The other $5,000 went to the Boy Scouts of America.

Another Ohio State graduate, Tom Weiskopf, won three tourneys and took second once in a five-week span between May 13 and June 10. He finished third in the U. S. Open the following week, two strokes behind the winner, Johnny Miller of San Francisco, and won the British Open in July. Then he took the Canadian Open and won the World Series of Golf, beating Nicklaus, Miller, and Tommy Aaron, the winner of the Masters. The $50,000 he won in that series helped him finish third overall with $245,463.

Miller's only other victory was in the World Cup in Spain. He took individual honors with a 277 as he and Nicklaus won the event for the United States.

Ben Crenshaw, the collegiate champion from Texas, won his first tourney (November 4) after becoming a full-fledged pro and took second in another event. He won $76,749 and plaudits as the "new Palmer."

The women's game was dominated by the established stars. Kathy Whitworth triumphed in seven tourneys, won $82,864, and was named Golfer of the Year for the seventh time in eight years. Mrs. Judy Rankin was second in earnings and captured the Vare Trophy for the best scoring average. Mrs. Susie Berning won the U. S. Open for the third time, and Mary Mills was first in the LPGA tournament.

In amateur competition, Craig Stadler of La Jolla, Calif., won the U. S. championship; Dick Siderowf of Easton, Conn., took the British title; and George Burns 3d of Manhasset, N. Y., captured the Canadian crown. Carol Semple of Sewickley, Pa., won the women's U. S. Amateur, and Mrs. Marlene Stewart Streit took the Canadian title for the 11th time. U. S. amateurs defeated Britain, 14–11, in the Walker Cup competition at Brookline, Mass., and the American pros defeated the British, 19–13, in the Ryder Cup matches.

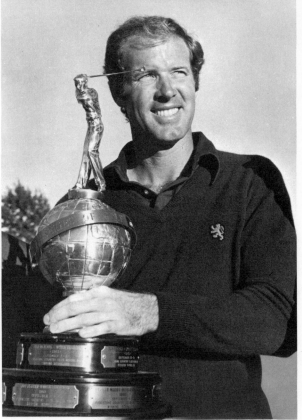

UPI

UPI

GOLFING CHAMPIONS OF 1973: (Above) *Tom Weiskopf holds trophy after winning World Series of Golf. Earlier, he took the British Open.* (Below) *Johnny Miller misses a birdie but fired a 63 in last round to win U. S. Open.*

Golf Highlights

Men's Individual Champions

U. S. Open—Johnny Miller, San Francisco (279)
British Open—Tom Weiskopf, Columbus, Ohio (276)
Masters—Tommy Aaron, Gainesville, Ga. (283)
PGA Tourney—Jack Nicklaus, Lost Tree Village, Fla. (277)
Canadian Open—Tom Weiskopf (278)
Tournament of Champions—Jack Nicklaus (276)
USPGA Match Play—John Schroeder, La Jolla, Calif.
USPGA Senior—Sam Snead, White Sulphur Springs, West Va.
World Senior Pro—Sam Snead (defeated Kel Nagle, Australia, 23 holes)
Vardon Trophy—Bruce Crampton, Australia
Western Open—Billy Casper, Chula Vista, Calif. (272)
World Series of Golf—Tom Weiskopf (137)
Westchester Classic—*Bobby Nichols, Akron, Ohio (272)

Pro Team

Ryder Cup—United States, defeated Britain, 19–13
World Senior Pro—United States

PGA Tournament Winners

American Classic—Bruce Crampton (273)
Atlanta Classic—Jack Nicklaus (272)
B. C. Open—Hubert Green (266)
Byron Nelson Classic—Lanny Wadkins (277)
Campbell-Los Angeles—Rod Funseth (276)
Colonial—Tom Weiskopf (276)
Crosby Pro-Am—*Jack Nicklaus (282)
Disney Open—Jack Nicklaus (275)
Doral-Eastern—Lee Trevino (276)
Florida Citrus—Brian Allin (265)
Hartford Open—Billy Casper (264)
Hawaiian Open—John Schlee (273)
Gleason-Inverrary—Lee Trevino (279)
Heritage—Hale Irwin (272)
Hope Desert Classic—Arnold Palmer (343)
Houston Open—Bruce Crampton (277)
Jacksonville Open—Jim Colbert (279)
Kemper Open—Tom Weiskopf (271)
L & M Open—Bert Greene (278)
Kaiser International—*Ed Sneed (275)
Magnolia—Dwight Nevil (268)
Martin-Tucson—Bruce Crampton (277)
Milwaukee Open—Dave Stockton (276)
Monsanto Open—Homero Blancas (277)
New Orleans—*Jack Nicklaus (280)
Ohio Kings Island—Jack Nicklaus (271)
Philadelphia-IVB—Tom Weiskopf (271)
Phoenix Open—Bruce Crampton (268)
Quad Cities—Sam Adams (268)
Robinson-Shrine—Deane Beman (271)
San Antonio-Texas—Ben Crenshaw (270)
World Open—Miller Barber (570)

Men's Individual Amateur Champions

U. S. Amateur—Craig Stadler, La Jolla, Calif. (defeated David Strawn, Charlotte, N. C., 6 and 5, in 36-hole match)
British Amateur—Dick Siderowf, Easton, Conn.
Canadian Amateur—George Burns 3d, Manhasset, N. Y.
U. S. Public Links—Stan Stopa, New Orleans (294)
U. S. Junior—Jack Renner, San Diego (defeated Michael Brannan, Salinas, Calif., 20 holes, in final)
National Collegiate A. A. (NCAA)—University: Ben Crenshaw, Texas (282); College: Paul Wise, California State, Fullerton
National Intercollegiate (NAIA)—Tie between Jay Overton, Campbell, N. C., and Mike Zack, St. Bernard, Ala. (213)
U. S. Seniors G. A.—Bob Kiersky, Delray Beach, Fla. (147)
USGA Senior—Bill Hyndman 3d, Huntingdon Valley, Pa. (defeated Harry Welch, Salisbury, N. C., 3 and 2, in final)

Other Amateur Tournaments

Amputee—Bick Long, Madison, N. C. (292)
Blind—Joe Lazaro, Waltham, Mass.
Eastern—Vinny Giles, Richmond, Va. (285)
American Senior—Bill Hyndman 3d, Huntingdon Valley, Pa.
Junior College—Frank Zayatz, Chipola (281)
New England—*Bob Caprera, Southbridge, Mass. (292)
North and South—Mike Ford, Yonkers, N. Y.
North and South Senior—Ray Palmer, Grosse Ile, Mich.
Northeast—Ben Crenshaw (275)
Pacific Northwest—Dave Mick, Victoria, B. C.
Porter Cup—Vinny Giles (274)
Southern—Ben Crenshaw (273)
Southeastern—Curtis Strange, Virginia Beach, Va. (288)
Southwestern—Dub Huckabee, Monahans, Texas (285)
Trans-Mississippi—Gary Koch, Temple Terrace, Fla.
Western—Ben Crenshaw
World Junior—Randy Barenaba, Honolulu (290)
World Senior—W. F. Colm, Bakersfield, Calif.

Amateur Team Championships

Walker Cup—United States (defeated Britain, 14–10)
NCAA—University: Florida (1,149); College: California State, Northridge (1,180)
NAIA—Wofford (875)
National Junior College—Miami-Dade North (1,158)
World Senior—United States (453)

Women's Individual Pro Champions

U. S. Open—Mrs. Susie M. Berning, Lake Tahoe, Nev. (290)
LPGA Tourney—Mary Mills Pascagoula, Miss. (288)
Vare Trophy—Judy Rankin
LPGA Player of the Year—Kathy Whitworth

Other LPGA Tour Winners

Alamo Open—Betsy Cullen (218)
American Defender—Judy Rankin (217)
Birmingham Classic—Gloria Ehret (217)
Bluegrass Invitation—Donna C. Young (216)
Burdine's Invitation—JoAnn Prentice (212)
Child Services, Chicago—Betty Burfeindt (212)
Cameron Park—Sandra Palmer (212)
Colgate-Dinah Shore—Mickey Wright (284)
Corpus Christi Civitan—Sharon Miller (210)
GAC Classic—*Judy Rankin (215)
George Washington Classic—Carole Jo Skala (214)
Dallas Civitan—*Kathy Whitworth (213)
Fort Worth Charity Classic—Sandra Haynie (208)
Heritage Village—Susie Berning (207)
La Canadienne—*Jocelyne Bourassa (214)
Lady Carling—Judy Rankin (215)
Lady Errol—Kathy Whitworth (213)
Lady Tara Classic—Mary Mills (217)
Lincoln-Mercury—Sandra Haynie (212)
Marc Equity Classic—Mary Lou Crocker (210)
Naples-Lely Classic—Kathy Whitworth (219)
National Jewish Hospital, Denver—Sandra Palmer (210)
Orange Blossom Classic—Sandra Haynie (216)
Pabst Classic—Judy Rankin (212)
Pompano Beach—*Sandra Palmer (215)
Portland Open—Kathy Whitworth (144)
S & H Green Stamps-Houston—Kathy Whitworth (214)
St. Paul Open—Sandra Palmer (209)
Sealy-Faberge—*Kathy Cornelius (217)
Sears Classic—Carol Mann (68)
Southgate—Kathy Whitworth (142)
Waco—Kathy Whitworth (209)

* Won playoff

Women's Individual Amateur Champions

U. S. Amateur—Carol Semple, Sewickley, Pa. (defeated Ann Quast Sander, Seattle, 1 up, in final)
USGA Senior—Mrs. David Hibbs, Long Beach, Calif.
USGA Girls—Amy Alcott, Pacific Palisades, Calif.
Canadian Amateur—Marlene S. Streit, Fonthill, Ont. (317)
U. S. Intercollegiate—Bonnie Lauer, Michigan State (305)
British Amateur—Ann Irvin, England
Eastern—Lancy Smith, Snyder, N. Y. (219)
North and South—Beth Barry, Mobile, Ala.
Pacific Northwest—Marilyn Palmer, Victoria, B. C.
Trans-National—Liana Zambresky, Pebble Beach, Calif.
Western—Katie Ahern Falk, Milwaukee
World Junior—Suzanne Cadden, Scotland (326)

Team

Intercollegiate—North Carolina at Greensboro (631)

Leading Money Winners in 1973

Men's PGA

Jack Nicklaus	$308,362	Johnny Miller	127,833
Bruce Crampton	274,266	John Schlee	118,017
Tom Weiskopf	245,463	Hubert Green	114,397
Lee Trevino	210,017	John Mahaffey	112,536
Lanny Wadkins	200,455	Forrest Fezler	106,390
Miller Barber	184,014	J. C. Snead	103,601
Hale Irwin	130,388	Homero Blancas	96,964
Billy Casper	129,474	Dave Stockton	96,207

Career Earnings

Jack Nicklaus	$2,009,168	Julius Boros	923,126
Arnold Palmer	1,631,469	Gene Littler	919,895
Billy Casper	1,417,458	Tom Weiskopf	882,332
Lee Trevino	1,064,647	Frank Beard	876,165
Bruce Crampton	1,062,677	Miller Barber	821,462
Gary Player	983,223	George Archer	784,916

Women's PGA

Kathy Whitworth	$82,864	Joyce Kazmierski	38,973
Judy Rankin	72,989	Mickey Wright	36,262
Sandra Palmer	55,440	Sue Berning	31,614
Betty Burfeindt	51,031	Debbie Austin	30,904
Carol Mann	47,735	Gloria Ehret	30,628
Mary Mills	47,639	Donna C. Young	26,242
Sandra Haynie	47,353	Marlene Hagge	24,778
Kathy Cornelius	44,247	JoAnn Prentice	23,632
Jane Blalock	40,711	Beth Stone	22,843

Career Earnings

Kathy Whitworth	$479,666	Marilynn Smith	268,319
Mickey Wright	327,863	Judy Rankin	231,108
Sandra Haynie	312,829	Sandra Palmer	200,145
Carol Mann	300,854	JoAnn Prentice	197,141
Betsy Rawls	293,426	Patty Berg	187,955
Marlene Hagge	273,544		

HARNESS RACING

Sir Dalrae is a 4-year-old horse who got off on the wrong foot, or feet, at the start of his racing career. He began as a 3-year-old trotter, won only once in four races, and developed soreness in his hind legs. His trainer, Jim Dennis, then made him a pacer (a trotter's left foreleg and right hind leg stride together; a pacer's left foreleg and left hind leg move in conjunction), and Sir Dalrae promptly became Harness Horse of the Year. The new pacer, who is owned by the A La Carte Stable of Willard Smith, a Los Angeles restaurateur, won 20 of 27 races and earned $307,354. The son of Porterhouse took 15 straight stakes, in 13 of which he was timed in 2 minutes or less. His total races under 2:00 was 17, one less than the season record set by Albatross in 1972.

In the voting for awards, Sir Dalrae received all but 15 votes for Pacer of the Year, defeating Flirth, the Trotter of the Year, 187–7, for overall honors.

Flirth, the winner of the Hambletonian in two heats, was a 5-vote winner over Starlark Hanover, a 2-year-old, for top trotter honors. In taking the Hambletonian, Flirth, owned by E. Roland Harriman and Elbridge T. Gerry, Sr. and Jr., well-known names in harness racing, bettered the world record for geldings with a time of 1:57⅖.

In other leading trotting events, Arnie Almahurst won the Kentucky Futurity and Tamerlane took the Yonkers Futurity. The top pacing events were split three ways, too. Melvin's Woe won the Little Brown Jug in three heats, Valiant Bret took the Messenger, and Smog won the Cane.

HOCKEY

Boston fans still had a champion, but the title-holders were the New England Whalers of the new World Hockey Association, not the Bruins of the National Hockey League. That championship, along with the Stanley Cup, went back to its usual abode in Montreal. Boston's beloved Bruins, the 1972 champions, were eliminated in the first round.

By midseason, the Montreal Canadiens had pretty well demonstrated that they were best in the East Division of the NHL. The Bruins, who had lost Derek Sanderson (he returned, ailing, near the end of the season) and John Mackenzie to the

Harness Racing Highlights

U. S. Trotting Association Champions

Trotters

2-Year-Old—Starlark Hanover
3-Year-Old—Flirth
4-Year-Old—Spartan Hanover
Aged—Flower Child
Trotter of the Year—Flirth

Pacers

2-Year-Old—Boyden Hanover
3-Year-Old—Melvin's Woe
4-Year-Old—Sir Dalrae
Aged—Mountain Skipper
Pacer of the Year—Sir Dalrae

Harness Horse of the Year

Sir Dalrae (187 votes); Flirth (7); Starlark Hanover (3)

Major Stakes Winners

Trotting

American Championship (Roosevelt)—Spartan Hanover
American Classic (Hollywood)—Elesnar
American National (Sportsman Park, Chicago)—Knightly Way
Colonial (Liberty Bell)—Flirth
Dexter (Roosevelt)—Knightly Way
Hambletonian (DuQuoin, Ill.)—Flirth
Hambletonian Filly Stake (DuQuoin, Ill.)—Colonial Charm
Hoosier Futurity (Indianapolis)—Noble Florie
Kentucky Futurity (Lexington)—Arnie Almahurst
Old Oaken Bucket (Delaware, Ohio)—MacArthur
Prix d'Amerique (Paris)—Dart Hanover
Realization (Roosevelt)—Spartan Hanover
Roosevelt International—Delmonica Hanover
Westbury Futurity (Roosevelt)—Rising Wind
Yonkers Futurity—Tamerlane

Pacing

Adios (Meadows)—Ricci Reenie Time
American Classic (Hollywood)—Invincible Shadow
Cane (Yonkers)—Smog
Canadian Derby (Toronto)—Sir Dalrae
Fox (Indianapolis)—Boyden Hanover
Hoosier Futurity (Indianapolis)—Tippy Time
Little Brown Jug (Delaware, Ohio)—Melvin's Woe
Messenger (Roosevelt)—Valiant Bret
Prix d'Ete (Montreal)—Armbro Nadir
Realization (Roosevelt)—Keystone Pebble
Reynolds (Buffalo, N. Y.)—J. R. Skipper
Roosevelt Futurity—Nevele Bret
Shepard (Yonkers)—Southampton V
U. S. Pacing Series (3 races)—Sir Dalrae, all three

Philadelphia Blazers of the WHA, began to falter. In February, with Boston in third place, the coach, Tom Johnson, was replaced by Bep Guidolin. The Bruins rallied and in March overtook the New York Rangers for second. The New York club, which had retained all of its stars by raising salaries generously to combat the rival league's offers, began to fade. A string of injuries hurt, too.

In the West, the Chicago Black Hawks became the top club early, even though Bobby Hull, their great forward, had jumped to the new league and

UPI

MONTREAL ACE Frank Mahovlich (left) scores against the Chicago Black Hawks in final game of Stanley Cup series. The Canadiens captured the coveted trophy, 4 games to 2.

National Hockey League
(Final Standings, 1972–73)
East Division

	W	L	T	Goals For	Goals Against	Pts.
Montreal	52	10	16	329	184	120
Boston	51	22	5	330	235	107
New York Rangers	47	23	8	297	208	102
Buffalo	37	27	14	257	219	88
Detroit	37	29	12	265	243	86
Toronto	27	41	10	247	279	64
Vancouver	22	47	9	233	339	53
New York Islanders	12	60	6	170	347	30

West Division

	W	L	T	Goals For	Goals Against	Pts.
Chicago	42	27	9	284	225	93
*Philadelphia	37	30	11	296	256	85
Minnesota	37	30	11	254	230	85
St. Louis	32	34	12	233	251	76
Pittsburgh	32	37	9	257	265	73
Los Angeles	31	36	11	232	245	73
Atlanta	25	38	15	191	239	65
California	16	46	16	213	323	48

* Philadelphia awarded second place for better record against Minnesota in games between two clubs.

Stanley Cup Playoffs

Preliminary Series—East Division: Montreal defeated Buffalo, 4 games to 2; New York defeated Boston, 4 games to 1. West Division: Chicago defeated St. Louis, 4 games to 1; Philadelphia defeated Minnesota, 4 games to 2

Semifinals—Montreal defeated Philadelphia, 4 games to 1; Chicago defeated New York, 4 games to 1

Final—Montreal defeated Chicago, 4 games to 2

Individual National Hockey League Awards
(Trophy winners receive $1,500 each from league)

Hart Trophy (most valuable player)—Bobby Clarke, Philadelphia

Ross Trophy (leading scorer)—Phil Esposito, Chicago

Norris Trophy (leading defenseman)—Bobby Orr, Boston

Lady Byng Trophy (sportsmanship)—Gil Perreault, Buffalo

Vezina Trophy (goalie)—Ken Dryden, Montreal

Calder Trophy (rookie)—Steve Vickers, New York Rangers

Conn Smythe Trophy (most valuable in playoffs)—Yvan Cournoyer, Montreal

NHL All-Star Teams

	First Team	Second Team
Goal	Ken Dryden, Montreal	Tony Esposito, Chicago
Defense	Bobby Orr, Boston	Brad Park, N. Y. Rangers
Defense	Guy Lapointe, Montreal	Bill White, Chicago
Center	Phil Esposito, Boston	Bobby Clarke, Philadelphia
Right Wing	Mickey Redmond, Detroit	Yvan Cournoyer, Montreal
Left Wing	Frank Mahovlich, Montreal	Dennis Hull, Chicago

World Hockey Association
(Final Standings, 1972–73)
East Division

	W	L	T	Goals For	Goals Against	Pts.
New England	46	30	2	318	263	94
Cleveland	43	32	3	287	239	89
Philadelphia	38	40	0	288	306	76
Ottawa	35	39	4	279	301	74
Quebec	33	40	5	276	313	71
New York	33	43	2	303	334	68

West Division

	W	L	T	Goals For	Goals Against	Pts.
Winnipeg	43	31	4	285	249	90
Houston	39	35	4	284	269	82
Los Angeles	37	35	6	255	246	80
Alberta	38	37	3	270	256	79
Minnesota	38	37	3	250	269	79
Chicago	26	50	2	245	295	74

Minnesota defeated Alberta, 4–2, in playoff for fourth place

Avco Cup Playoffs

Preliminary Series—East Division: New England defeated Ottawa, 4 games to 1; Cleveland defeated Philadelphia, 4 games to 0. West Division: Winnipeg defeated Minnesota, 4 games to 1; Houston defeated Los Angeles, 4 games to 2

Semifinals—New England defeated Cleveland, 4 games to 1; Winnipeg defeated Houston, 4 games to 0

Final—New England defeated Winnipeg, 4 games to 1

Individual WHA Awards

Most Valuable Player—Bobby Hull, Winnipeg

Best Defenseman—J. C. Tremblay, Quebec

Rookie—Terrence Caffery, New England

Leading Scorer—Andre Lacroix, Philadelphia

WHA All-Star Teams

	First Team	Second Team
Goal	Gerry Cheevers, Cleveland	Bernie Parent, Philadelphia
Defense	J. C. Tremblay, Quebec	Larry Hornung, Winnipeg
Defense	Paul Shmyr, Cleveland	Jim Dorey, New England
Center	Andre Lacroix, Philadelphia	Ron Ward, New York
Right Wing	Danny Lawson, Philadelphia	Tom Webster, New England
Left Wing	Bobby Hull, Winnipeg	Gary Jarrett, Cleveland

Other Professional Champions

American League—Eastern Division: Nova Scotia Voyageurs; Western Division: Cincinnati Swords; Playoffs: Cincinnati defeated Nova Scotia, 4 games to 1

Western League—Regular season and playoffs: Phoenix

Central League—Regular season: Dallas; Playoffs: Omaha

Amateur Champions

Eastern League—Southern Division: Roanoke; Central Division: Cape Cod; Northern Division and playoffs: Syracuse

International League—North Division: Flint; South Division and playoffs: Fort Wayne

United States League—Southern Division: Chicago; Northern Division and playoffs: Thunder Bay, Ont.

Memorial Cup (Canadian junior)—Toronto Marlboros

Allan Cup (Canadian senior)—Orillia (Ont.) Terriers

Amateur Hockey Association of the United States—Pee Wee: Long Island A. C. Flyers; Bantam: Moundview, Minn.; Midget: South Boston, Mass.; Juvenile: Amherst, N. Y.; Intermediate: St. Paul, Minn.; Junior: Ecorse, Mich.

World—USSR; Class B: East Germany

Intercollegiate Champions

NCAA—Wisconsin (defeated Denver, 4–2, in final)

NAIA—Bemidji State (defeated Lakehead, 3–2, in overtime, in final)

ECAC—Division I: Cornell; playoffs: Cornell; Division II: Vermont; playoffs: Vermont

WCHA—Denver; playoffs: Denver and Wisconsin

Central Collegiate—St. Louis; playoffs: Bowling Green

Canadian—Toronto

Canadian Colleges (Canadian Intercollegiate Athletic Union)—Toronto (Ontario universities) defeated St. Mary's (Maritime universities), 3–2

was making the Winnipeg Jets a division champion. The Hawks still had a strong defense in Bill White, Pat Stapleton, and Keith Magnuson in front of the outstanding young goalie, Ken Dryden. The scoring leaders were Dennis Hull, Bobby's younger brother, and Stan Mikita.

Montreal's squad was made up of experienced stars such as Frank Mahovlich, Henri Richard, Yvan Cournoyer, Guy Lapointe, and Jacques Lemaire and a "kid" line of Guy Lafleur, Rejean Houle, and Marc Tardif. In the playoffs the Canadiens eliminated the Buffalo Sabres, 4 games to 2; ousted the Philadelphia Flyers in five games; and then beat Chicago, 4 games to 2, in the final. The victory gave the Canadiens the NHL championship for the 17th time and the Stanley Cup for the 18th season.

The Black Hawks also had little trouble in the playoffs before clashing with Montreal. The Hawks beat St. Louis and New York, each in five games. The Rangers had reached the semifinals by routing the Bruins, 4 games to 1.

The Boston-based Whalers became the powerhouse of the new league. They took control of the East Division in January after the Cleveland Crusaders had held the top spot. In the playoffs Boston lost one game to each club in beating Ottawa, Cleveland, and then Winnipeg in the final. Winnipeg beat the Minnesota Flying Saints in five games and Houston Aeros in four in the early playoffs.

Phil Esposito of the Bruins again led the scorers in the NHL, but the most valuable player award went to Bobby Clark of Philadelphia. Bobby Hull was named MVP in the new league.

HORSE RACING

American sports fans found a new hero in 1973 —a race horse named Secretariat. The 3-year-old chestnut colt received the nickname "Super Red," bundles of mail, and the plaudits of thousands of racing fans for winning the Triple Crown. Secretariat also won $860,404 during the year, ranking fourth in all-time earnings with $1,316,808. He had been syndicated for $6,080,000 and was retired to stud in November.

Secretariat, who had been named Horse of the Year at the end of the 1972 season, quickly began collecting more admirers. On May 5 he won the Kentucky Derby in 1:59⅖, record time for the 1¼-mile event. He took the Preakness, May 19, by 2½ lengths over Sham, who had been second at Louisville, then completed the Triple Crown by winning the Belmont Stakes by 31 lengths on June 9 in the track record time of 2:24 for 1½ miles. Secretariat became the ninth winner of the Triple Crown, and the first since Citation in 1948.

Secretariat's sweep gave the Meadow Stable (headed by Mrs. John B. Tweedy), jockey Ron Turcotte, and trainer Lucien Laurin five victories in the six Triple Crown events in two seasons. The stable's other star performer, Riva Ridge, had won all but the muddy Preakness in 1972. Riva Ridge continued strong in 1973 and was named the best of the older horses. He set a world record of 1:52⅖ for 1³⁄₁₆ miles at Belmont and won $212,452 during the year, raising his earnings to $1,111,497 and

UPI

SECRETARIAT, with jockey Ron Turcotte looking back at the field, breezes to victory by 31 lengths in the Belmont Stakes, June 9, to wrap up racing's Triple Crown.

9th place in the all-time list. He was retired to a stud farm in Kentucky along with Secretariat.

Secretariat, a unanimous choice for Horse of the Year again, did not always win. In 12 races in 1973, he finished first nine times, second twice, and third once. He broke the world record for 1⅛ miles in the Marlboro Cup at Belmont and won $150,000. Secretariat ended his career by winning the Canadian International at Toronto, October 12. Of his 21 races, he won 16, was second three times, third once, and fourth once.

Horse Racing Highlights

Champions of the Year

Eclipse Awards

(Consolidation of polls of the Thoroughbred Racing Associations, the *Daily Racing Form*, and the National Turf Writers Association)
Horse of the Year—Meadow Stable's Secretariat
2-Year-Old Filly—Max H. Gluck's Talking Picture
2-Year-Old Colt—Gluck's Protagonist
3-Year-Old Filly—Harry T. Mangurian's Desert Vixen
3-Year-Old Colt—Secretariat
Older Filly or Mare—Fred W. Hooper's Susan's Girl
Older Colt—Meadow Stable's Riva Ridge
Grass—Secretariat
Steeplechase—William Pape's and Jonathan Sheppard's Athenian Idol
Sprinter—Joe Kellman's Shecky Greene

Major Stakes Winners
(Purses over $100,000)

American Derby (Arlington)—Bemo
Amory L. Haskell Handicap (Monmouth)—West Coast Scout
Arkansas Derby—Impecunious
Arlington Handicap—Dubassoff
Arlington Invitational—Secretariat
Arlington-Washington Park Futurity—Lover John
Beldame (Belmont)—Desert Vixen
Belmont Stakes—Secretariat
Brooklyn Handicap (Aqueduct)—Riva Ridge
California Derby (Golden Gate)—Linda's Chief
California Juvenile—Money Lender
Californian (Hollywood)—Quack
Campbell Handicap (Bowie)—*1st Division:* Vertee; *2d Division:* Delay
Century Handicap (Hollywood)—Cougar II
Champagne Stakes (Belmont)—*1st Division:* Holding Pattern; *2d Division:* Protagonist
Coaching Club American Oaks (Belmont)—Magazine
Delaware Handicap—Susan's Girl
Del Mar Handicap—Red Reality
Flamingo (Hialeah)—Our Native
Florida Derby (Gulfstream)—Royal and Regal
Frizette (Belmont)—Bundler
Futurity (Belmont)—Wedge Shot
Governor (Belmont)—Tentam
Gulfstream Park Handicap—West Coast Scout
Hawthorne Gold Cup—TriJet
Heritage (Liberty Bell)—Better Arbitor
Hialeah Turf Cup—Gleaming
Hobson Handicap (Liberty Bell)—Windtex
Hollywood Derby—Amen II
Hollywood Gold Cup—Kennedy Road
Hollywood Juvenile—Century's Envoy
Hollywood Lassie—Special Goddess

Jersey Derby (Garden State)—Knightly Dawn
Jockey Club Gold Cup (Aqueduct)—Prove Out
Kentucky Derby (Churchill Downs)—Secretariat
Kindergarten Stakes (Liberty Bell)—Determined King
Laurel Futurity—Protagonist
Man o'War Handicap (Belmont)—Secretariat
Marlboro Cup (Belmont)—Secretariat
Metropolitan Handicap (Aqueduct)—Tentam
Michigan 1⅛-Mile (Detroit)—Golden Don
Monmouth Handicap—Our Native
Oak Tree Invitational (Santa Anita)—Portentous
Ohio Derby (Thistledown)—Our Native
Pan American Turf Handicap (Hialeah)—Lord Vancouver
Preakness Stakes (Pimlico)—Secretariat
San Juan Capistrano (Santa Anita)—Queen's Hustler
San Luis Rey (Santa Anita)—Big Spruce
Santa Anita Derby—Sham
Santa Anita Handicap—Cougar II
Santa Margarita (Santa Anita)—Susan's Girl
Sapling (Monmouth)—Tisab
Selima (Laurel)—Dancealot
Sorority (Monmouth)—Irish Sonnet
Strub (Santa Anita)—Royal Owl
Suburban Handicap (Aqueduct)—Key to the Mint
Travers (Saratoga)—Annihilate
United Nations Handicap (Atlantic City)—Tentam
Vanity Handicap (Hollywood)—Convenience
Washington, D. C., International—Dahlia (France)
Widener (Hialeah)—Vertee
Wood Memorial (Aqueduct)—Angle Light
Woodward Stakes (Belmont)—Prove Out

Other Races
(England)

Ascot Gold Cup—Lassalle
Canadian Derby (Northlands)—Wing Span
Canadian International (Woodbine)—Secretariat
Epsom Derby (England)—Morston
Epsom Oaks (England)—Mysterious
Grand National Steeplechase (England)—Red Rum
Grand Prix de Paris—Tennyson
Irish Oaks—Dahlia
Irish Sweeps Derby—Weaver's Hall
King George VI and Queen Elizabeth—Dahlia
Melbourne Derby (Australia)—Gala Supreme
1,000 Guineas (England)—Mysterious
2,000 Guineas (England)—Mon Fils
Prix de l'Arc de Triomphe—Rheingold
Queens Plate (Canada)—Royal Chocolate
St. Leger (England)—Peleid

Quarter Horse
(Ruidoso Downs, N. Mex., Sept. 3)

All-American Futurity (purse $1 million)—Timetothink-rich (John Watson, jockey; winner's purse: $330,000)

Swimming Highlights

World Championships
(Belgrade, Yugoslavia, Sept. 3–9)

Men

100-Meter Freestyle—Jim Montgomery, Madison, Wis. (0:-51.70)
200-Meter Freestyle—Jim Montgomery (1:53.02)
400-Meter Freestyle—Rick DeMont, San Rafael, Calif. (*3:-58.18)
1,500-Meter Freestyle—Steve Holland, Australia (*15:31.85)
100-Meter Backstroke—Roland Matthes, E. Germany (0:-57.47)
200-Meter Backstroke—Roland Matthes (*2:01.87)
100-Meter Breaststroke—John Hencken, Santa Clara, Calif. (*1:04.02)
200-Meter Breaststroke—David Wilkie, Britain (*2:19.28)
100-Meter Butterfly—Bruce Robertson, Canada (0:55.69)
200-Meter Butterfly—Robin Backhaus, Redlands, Calif. (2:-03.32)
200-Meter Individual Medley—Gunnar Larsson, Sweden (2:08.36)
400-Meter Individual Medley—Andras Hargitay, Hungary (4:31.11)
400-Meter Freestyle Relay—United States (Mel Nash, Monroeville, Pa.; Joe Bottom, Santa Clara, Calif.; Jim Montgomery, Madison, Wis., John Murphy, Hinsdale, Ill.; 3:27.18)
400-Meter Medley Relay—United States (Mike Stamm, San Diego, Calif.; John Hencken, Santa Clara, Calif.; Joe Bottom, Santa Clara, Calif.; Jim Montgomery, Madison, Wis.; 3:49.49)
800-Meter Freestyle Relay—United States (Kurt Krumpholz, Irvine, Calif.; Robin Backhaus, Redlands, Calif.; Rick Klatt, Albuquerque, N. Mex.; Jim Montgomery, Madison, Wis.; 7:33.22)
Springboard Diving—Phil Boggs, Akron, Ohio (618.57 pts)
Platform Diving—Klaus DiBiasi, Italy (559.74 pts)

Women

100-Meter Freestyle—Kornelia Ender, E. Germany (*0:-57.54)
200-Meter Freestyle—Keena Rothhammer, Santa Clara, Calif. (2:04.99)
400-Meter Freestyle—Heather Greenwood, Fresno, Calif. (4:20.28)
800-Meter Freestyle—Novella Calligaris, Italy (*8:52.97)
100-Meter Backstroke—Ulrike Richter, E. Germany (1:05.42; her time of 1:04.99 for 100 meters in the medley relay set a new world record)
200-Meter Backstroke—Melissa Belote, Springfield, Va. (2:-20.52)
100-Meter Breaststroke—Renate Vogel, E. Germany (1:13.74)
200-Meter Breaststroke—Renate Vogel (2:40.01)
100-Meter Butterfly—Kornelia Ender (1:02.53)
200-Meter Butterfly—Rosemarie Kother, E. Germany (*2:-13.76)
200-Meter Individual Medley—Andrea Hubner, E. Germany (*2:20.51)
400-Meter Individual Medley—Gudrun Wegner, E. Germany (*4:57.51)
400-Meter Freestyle Relay—E. Germany (Kornelia Ender, Andrea Eife, Andrea Hubner, Sylvia Eichner; *3:52.45)
400-Meter Medley Relay—E. Germany (Ulrike Richter, Renate Vogel, Rosemarie Kother, Kornelia Ender; *4:16.84)
Springboard Diving—Christa Kohler, E. Germany (442.17 pts)
Platform Diving—Ulrike Knape, Sweden (406.77 pts)
Medal Leaders—United States: 15 gold, 16 silver, 7 bronze; East Germany: 13 gold, 6 silver, 9 bronze
*World record

National AAU Outdoor Championships
(Louisville, Ky., Aug. 22–25)

Men

100-Meter Freestyle—Jim Montgomery, Madison, Wis. (0:-52.95)
200-Meter Freestyle—Jim Montgomery (1:53.69)
400-Meter Freestyle—Rick DeMont, Marin, Calif., A. C. (4:00.14)
1,500-Meter Freestyle—Rick DeMont (15:51.02)
100-Meter Backstroke—Mike Stamm, Coronado-Navy B. C. (0:59.35)
200-Meter Backstroke—John Naber, Los Altos, Calif. (2:-05.67)
100-Meter Breaststroke—John Hencken, Santa Clara, Calif. (1:05.17)
200-Meter Breaststroke—John Hencken (2:20.52)
100-Meter Butterfly—Robin Backhaus, Marin, Calif., A. C. (0:56.81)
200-Meter Butterfly—Steve Gregg, Wilmington, Del. (2:-04.11)
200-Meter Individual Medley—Stan Carper, Portland, Oreg. (2:08.80)
400-Meter Individual Medley—Rick Colella, Seattle (4:-36.80)
400-Meter Freestyle Relay—Gatorade S. C., Bloomington, Ind. (Bill Heiss, John Kinsella, Fred Tyler, John Murphy; 3:33.52)
400-Meter Medley Relay—Gatorade S. C. (John Murphy, Peter Dahlberg, Gary Hall, Bill Heiss; 3:56.57)

800-Meter Freestyle Relay—Gatorade S. C. (Bill Heiss, John Kinsella, John Murphy, Fred Tyler; 7:43.33)
1-Meter Dive—Mike Finneran, Columbus, Ohio (498.96 pts)
3-Meter Dive—Phil Boggs, U. S. Air Force (578.73 pts)
Platform Dive—Tim Moore, Columbus, Ohio (519.90 pts)

Women

100-Meter Freestyle—Shirley Babashoff, Huntington Beach, Calif. (0:58.77)
200-Meter Freestyle—Shirley Babashoff (2:04.63)
400-Meter Freestyle—Keena Rothhammer, Santa Clara, Calif. (4:18.07)
1,500-Meter Freestyle—Jo Harshbarger, Bellevue, Wash. (16:54.14)
100-Meter Backstroke—Melissa Belote, Springfield, Va. (1:05.72)
200-Meter Backstroke—Melissa Belote (2:20.75)
100-Meter Breaststroke—Marcia Morey, Decatur, Ill. (1:-16.04)
200-Meter Breaststroke—Lynn Colella, Seattle (2:41.63)
100-Meter Butterfly—Deena Deerdurff, Cincinnati (1:03.85)
200-Meter Butterfly—Lynn Colella (2:18.34)
200-Meter Individual Medley—Kathy Heddy, Summit, N. J. (2:25.41)
400-Meter Individual Medley—Jenny Bartz, Santa Clara, Calif. (5:08.73)
400-Meter Freestyle Relay—Huntington Beach, Calif., A. C. (Terri Clarke, Valerie Lee, Susie Whitaker, Shirley Babashoff; 4:01.37)
400-Meter Medley Relay—Santa Clara S. C. (Nancy Kirkpatrick, Amy Bettencourt, Nina MacInnis, Keena Rothhammer; 4:30.13)
800-Meter Freestyle Relay—Santa Clara S. C. (Diane Gentes, Kelly Rowell, Jenny Bartz, Keena Rothhammer; 2:05.7)
1-Meter Dive—Cynthia Potter, Bloomington, Ind. (431.16 pts)
3-Meter Dive—Carrie Irish, Columbus, Ohio (445.32 pts)
Platform Dive—Deborah Keplar, Columbus, Ohio (370.30 pts)
Team—Santa Clara S. C. (540 pts)

National AAU Indoor Championships
(Cincinnati, April 4–7)

Men

100-Yard Freestyle—Ken Knox, Fort Lauderdale, Fla. (0:-45.269)
200-Yard Freestyle—Tim McDonnell, Los Altos, Calif. (1:-40.04)
500-Yard Freestyle—Jack Tingley, So. California (4:-25.863)
1,650-Yard Freestyle—Jack Tingley (15:19.49)
100-Yard Backstroke—John Naber, Menlo Park, Calif. (0:-51.367)
200-Yard Backstroke—John Naber (1:50.485)
100-Yard Breaststroke—Mark Chatfield, So. California (0:57.36)
200-Yard Breaststroke—Rick Colella, Washington (2:03.186)
100-Yard Butterfly—Bruce Robertson, Vancouver, B. C. (0:-49.598)
200-Yard Butterfly—Robin Backhaus, Redlands, Calif. (1:-49.552)
200-Yard Individual Medley—Steve Furniss, So. California (1:51.599)
400-Yard Individual Medley—Tom Szuba, Michigan (3:-57.78)
400-Yard Freestyle Relay—So. California (Kim Tutt, Steve Tyrell, Edwin McCleskey, Steve Furniss; 3:02.494)
400-Yard Medley Relay—So. California (Steve Cameron, Mark Chatfield, Allen Poucher, Steve Furniss; 3:23.723)
800-Yard Freestyle Relay—So. California (Steve Furniss, Kim Tutt, Jack Tingley, Jim McConica; 6:39.241)
Team—So. California (666 pts)

Men's Diving
(Pittsburgh, March 28–30)

1-Meter—Tim Moore, Columbus, Ohio (501.81 pts)
3-Meter—Lt. Phil Boggs, U. S. Air Force (531.75 pts)
Platform—Steve McFarland, Hurricane S. C. (460.77 pts)

Women

100-Yard Freestyle—Shirley Babashoff, Huntington Beach, Calif. (0:52.55)
200-Yard Freestyle—Keena Rothhammer, Santa Clara, Calif. (1:50.517)
500-Yard Freestyle—Keena Rothhammer (4:52.547)
1,650-Yard Freestyle—Shane Gould, Australia (16:46.659)
100-Yard Backstroke—Linda Stimpson, Los Angeles (0:-58.507)
200-Yard Backstroke—Melissa Belote, Springfield, Va. (2:-05.498)
100-Yard Breaststroke—Cathy Carr, Albuquerque, N. Mex. (1:06.1)
200-Yard Breaststroke—Lynn Colella, Washington (2:20.-594)
100-Yard Butterfly—Deena Deardurff, Cincinnati (0:56.444)
200-Yard Butterfly—Shane Gould (2:02.720)
200-Yard Individual Medley—Leslie Cliff, W. Vancouver, B. C. (2:06.753)
400-Yard Individual Medley—Shane Gould (4:27.115)

Swimming Highlights (continued)

400-Yard Freestyle Relay—Santa Clara S. C. (Diane Gentes, Kelly Rowell, Sharon Berg, Keena Rothhammer; 3:32.801)
400-Yard Medley Relay—Santa Clara S. C. (Nancy Kirkpatrick, Amy Bettencourt, Julie Kriencke, Keena Rothhammer; 3:57.131)
800-Yard Freestyle Relay—Santa Clara S. C. (Kelly Rowell, Sharon Berg, Jenny Bartz, Keena Rothhammer; 7:36.-742)
Team—Santa Clara S. C. (326 pts)

Women's Diving
(Pittsburgh, March 28–30)
1-Meter—Cynthia Potter, Bloomington, Ind. (431.88 pts)
3-Meter—Cynthia Potter (486.75 pts)
Platform—Debby Lipman, Phillips 66, Long Beach, Calif. (354.45 pts)

National Collegiate (NCAA) Championships
(Knoxville, Tenn., March 22–24)
50-Yard Freestyle—John Trembley, Tennessee (0:20.337)
100-Yard Freestyle—John Trembley (0:45.090)
200-Yard Freestyle—Jim McConica, So. California (1:39.62)
500-Yard Freestyle—John Kinsella, Indiana (4:27.593)
1,650-Yard Freestyle—John Kinsella (15:29.209)
100-Yard Breaststroke—John Hencken, Stanford (0.57.11)
200-Yard Breaststroke—David Wilkie, Miami, Fla. (2:03.-407)
100-Yard Backstroke—Mike Stamm, Indiana (0:50.91)
200-Yard Backstroke—Mike Stamm (1:50.561)
100-Yard Butterfly—John Trembley (0:48.68)
200-Yard Butterfly—Gary Hall, Indiana (1:58.486)
200-Yard Individual Medley—Steve Furniss, So. California (1:51.385)
400-Yard Individual Medley—Steve Furniss (3:55.16)
400-Yard Freestyle Relay—Tennessee (Ken Knox, Tom Lutz, Keith Gilliam, John Trembley; 3:00.363)
400-Yard Medley Relay—Tennessee (Kevin Priestley, Rick Stewart, John Trembley, Ken Knox; 3:22.986)
800-Yard Freestyle Relay—Indiana (John Kinsella, Gary Connelly, Fred Tyler, Gary Hall; 6:36.39)
1-Meter Dive—Tim Moore, Ohio State (487.90 pts)
3-Meter Dive—Tim Moore (539.61 pts)
Team—Indiana (358 pts)

SWIMMING

American domination of swimming sank a little more during the world championships in Rumania in September 1973. The United States won 15 events, more than any other single nation but less than half of the championships in the eight-day competition. East Germany, powered by a group of record-breaking women, took 13 gold medals. The other medals were scattered among seven countries.

The East German team broke eight world records, seven of them by the women. The other one was made by Roland Matthes, the backstroke champion who has not been defeated since 1968. The German women were led by Kornelia Ender, freestyle; Ulrike Richter, backstroke; Rosemarie Kother, butterfly; Andrea Huebner and Gudrun Wegner, individual medley (all record-breakers); and Renate Vogel, breaststroke. The squad smashed two relay marks.

Another outstanding non-American swimmer was a 15-year-old Australian, Stephen Holland, who shattered the world mark for the 1,500-meter freestyle by 8 seconds. His time of 15 minutes 31.85 seconds broke the mark he had set in August, which had bettered the listed record by 14.7 seconds. In the earlier performance and again at Belgrade, he broke the record for 800 meters with 8:17.6 and 8:16.27. Other non-American record-breakers were Matthes in the 200-meter backstroke; David Wilkie of Britain in the 200-meter breaststroke; Andras Hargitay of Hungary in the 400-meter medley; and Novella Calligaris of Italy in the women's 800-meter freestyle. Her feat left Shane Gould, the sensational Australian who quit the sport in midyear after two years of record-breaking, with only one of the five records she had held—the 200-meter freestyle.

American swimmers, who also took 16 silver medals at Belgrade, were still No. 1. They held 14 of the major world records, 10 by men and 4 by women. The U. S. record-breakers in the world meet were Rick DeMont in the 400-meter freestyle and John Hencken in the 100-meter breaststroke and the 800-meter freestyle relay.

In the National AAU Outdoor Championships at Louisville in August, Keena Rothhammer of Santa Clara, Calif., set the world mark for the 400-meter freestyle, and Jo Harshbarger of Bellevue, Wash., bettered the mark in the 1,500-meter freestyle.

In the short-course championships at Cincinnati in April, 11 U. S. records were set, after the collegians had bettered six U. S. marks in the NCAA championships at Knoxville, Tenn., in March.

TENNIS

Australia finally regained the Davis Cup in December 1973. The symbol of world supremacy had been held by the United States for five years, during most of which the Australians had failed to gain the final round. However, the Cup rules were altered, giving the Aussies the chance they were hoping for. Noncontract professionals were allowed to play for the prized Cup. Three of Australia's and the world's greatest players—Rod Laver, Roy Emerson, and Ken Rosewall—thus became eligible because their contracts with World Championship Tennis had expired. They defeated the United States for the Cup in Cleveland (Nov. 30–Dec. 2, 1973), winning all five of the matches, which were played indoors for the first time.

The Australian women also regained the Federation Cup in world play and retained the Bonne Bell Cup in competition with the United States.

Individually, the Aussies were very successful. John Newcombe won the U. S. Open as well as his own country's championship, and Margaret Court took three major titles. She defeated her young teammate Evonne Goolagong in the Australian and American finals and stopped Chris Evert, America's sweetheart, in the French title round.

But the Wimbledon crown was won by Billie Jean King for the fifth time. She failed at Forest Hills, partly through heat exhaustion, but triumphed a few weeks later in the much-heralded "Battle of the Sexes" against Bobby Riggs.

The men's title at Wimbledon, which was boycotted by most of the top men players because of a hassle between the pro association and the international federation, was taken by Jan Kodes of Czechoslovakia. He was also the runner-up to Newcombe in the U. S. championship. Ilie Nastase of Rumania, whose talent is often blighted by behavior that antagonizes opponents and officials, won the French Open and the final Masters of the Commercial Union Grand Prix.

Nastase's winnings for the year exceeded $200,-000, as did those of Stan Smith of Pasadena, Calif., the top winner and champion of the World Championship Tennis series. Margaret Court dominated the Virginia Slims competition and became the first woman to exceed $200,000 in earnings. Chris Evert won the Slims final. In her first year as a pro, the young star from Fort Lauderdale, Fla., won over $123,000 and the heart of Jimmy Connors of Belleville, Ill., the 21-year-old who took the U. S. indoor and U. S. pro titles. The young stars were to be married in 1974.

Tennis Highlights

Major Tournaments

Davis Cup—Australia (defeated United States, 5–0, in final round at Cleveland, Nov. 30–Dec. 2)

Wightman Cup (women)—United States (defeated Britain, 5–2, at Brookline, Mass., Aug. 24–25)

Federation Cup (women)—Australia (defeated Japan, 2–1, in final at Bad Hamburg, West Germany, April 30–May 6)

Bon Belle Cup (women)—Australia (defeated United States, 6–3, in Sydney, Dec. 22–24)

Stevens Cup (seniors)—United States (defeated Sweden, 4–1, in final, Aug. 23–25)

U. S. Open (Forest Hills, N. Y., Aug. 29–Sept. 9)—Men's singles: John Newcombe, Australia; women's singles: Margaret Court, Australia; men's doubles: John Newcombe and Owen Davidson, Australia; women's doubles: Margaret Court and Virginia Wade, England; mixed doubles: Billie Jean King, Emeryville, Calif., and Owen Davidson; junior singles: Billy Martin, Palos Verdes, Calif.; senior singles: Bob Howe, Australia; men's 35 singles: Eugene L. Scott, New York; senior doubles: Dick Mateer, Anaheim, Calif., and Homer Richards, Charlotte, N. C.

U. S. National Clay Courts (Indianapolis, Aug. 13–19)—Men's singles: Manuel Orantes, Spain; women's singles: Chris Evert, Fort Lauderdale, Fla.; men's doubles: Frew McMillan, South Africa, and Bob Carmichael, France; women's doubles: Patti Hogan, La Jolla, Calif., and Sharon Walsh, San Rafael, Calif.

U. S. National Amateur Clay Courts (Chattanooga, Tenn., July 2–8)—Men's singles: Pat DuPre, Birmingham, Ala.; women's singles: Janice Metcalf, Claremont, Calif.; men's doubles: Vita Gerulaitis, New York, and Brian Teacher, San Diego; women's doubles: Janice Metcalf and Jane Stratton, Salt Lake City

Men's National Amateur Grass Courts (Southampton, N. Y., Aug. 20–26)—Singles: Jim Delaney, Potomac, Md.; doubles: Vic Amaya, Holland, Mich., and Pat DuPre

Women's National Amateur Grass Courts (Haverford, Pa., Aug. 13–19)—Singles: Candy Reynolds, Knoxville, Tenn.; doubles: Linda Rupert, Bethlehem, Pa., and Sally Greer, Miami, Fla.

Men's National Senior Grass Courts (Philadelphia, Aug. 27–Sept. 2)—Singles: Straight Clark, Haverford, Pa.; doubles: Gardnar Mulloy, Miami, Fla., and Tony Vincent, New York; father and son: Fred McNair 3d and Fred McNair 4th, Bethesda, Md.

U. S. National Senior Clay Courts (Lake Bluff, Ill., July 23–29)—Singles: Frank Sedgman, Australia; doubles: Pancho Gonzales, Malibu, Calif., and Hugh Stewart, Los Angeles

U. S. National Indoor Open—(Salisbury, Md., Feb. 18–25)—Singles: Jimmy Connors, Belleville, Ill.; doubles: Juan Gisbert, Spain, and Jurgen Fassbender, West Germany

U. S. National Women's Indoor (Higham, Mass., March 12–18)—Singles: Evonne Goolagong, Australia; doubles: Olga Morozova and Marina Kroshina, USSR

U. S. Professional (Chestnut Hill, Mass., July 16–23)—Singles: Jimmy Connors, Belleville, Ill.; doubles: Stan Smith, Pasadena, Calif., and Erik van Dillen, San Mateo, Calif.

Other U. S. Champions

National Collegiate (NCAA)—University Division: singles: Sandy Mayer, Stanford; doubles: Sandy Mayer and Jim Delaney, Stanford. College Division: singles: Bob Chappell, Univ. of California at Irvine; doubles: Bob Chappell and Glen Cripe, Univ. of California at Irvine

National Association of Intercollegiate Athletics (NAIA)—Singles: Bob Hochstadter, East Texas State; doubles: Dave Peterson and Tim Butorac, Gustavus Adolphus

Women's National Collegiate—Singles: Janice Metcalf, Redlands; doubles: Linda Rupert and Cathy Beene, Lamar

U. S. Interscholastic—Singles: David Parker, Galesburg, Ill.; doubles: Tim and Chris Delaney, Georgetown Prep

Other Countries

Wimbledon Open (England, June 25–July 8)—Men's singles: Jan Kodes, Czechoslovakia; women's singles: Billie Jean King, Emeryville, Calif.; men's doubles: Jimmy Connors, Belleville, Ill., and Ilie Nastase, Rumania; women's doubles: Billie Jean King and Rosemary Casals, San Francisco; mixed doubles: Billie Jean King and Owen Davidson, Australia; junior singles: Billy Martin, Palos Verdes, Calif.; junior girls: Ann Kiyomura, San Mateo, Calif.; veterans doubles: Don Budge, Los Angeles, and Frank Sedgman, Australia

Australian Open (Melbourne, finals, Jan. 1)—Men's singles: John Newcombe, Australia; women's singles: Margaret Court, Australia; men's doubles: John Newcombe and Malcolm Anderson, Australia; women's doubles: Margaret Court and Virginia Wade, England

French Open (Paris, May 29–June 5)—Men's singles: Ilie Nastase, Rumania; women's singles: Margaret Court, Australia; men's doubles: John Newcombe, Australia, and Tom Okker, Netherlands; women's doubles: Margaret Court and Virginia Wade, England; mixed doubles: Francoise Durr and Jean Claude Barclay, France

Canadian Open (Toronto, Aug. 22–26)—Men's singles: Tom Okker, Netherlands; women's singles: Evonne Goolagong, Australia; men's doubles: Rod Laver and Ken Rosewall, Australia; women's doubles: Evonne Goolagong and Peggy Michael, Pacific Palisades, Calif.

LEADING MONEY WINNERS IN 1973

World Championship Tennis Tour
(Contract Professionals)

Stan Smith	$154,100	Cliff Richey	24,350
Rod Laver	78,200	Brian Gottfried	23,900
Bob Lutz	41,800	Dick Stockton	23,200
Roy Emerson	41,350	Colin Dibley	22,750
John Alexander	31,300	Jaime Fillol	15,600

Virginia Slims Tour
(Contract Professionals)

Margaret Court	$130,725	Betty Stove	33,475
Rosemary Casals	89,625	Francoise Durr	33,275
Kerry Melville	53,650	Chris Evert	32,000
Billie Jean King	50,800	Julie Heldman	29,512
Nancy Gunter	43,112	Janet Newberry	23,725

Commercial Union Grand Prix
Men

Ilie Nastase	$70,000	Jan Kodes	20,500
John Newcombe	43,750	Stan Smith	19,000
Tom Okker	37,500	Tom Gorman	16,250
Jimmy Connors	28,750	Bjorn Borg	12,750
Manuel Orantes	21,250	Arthur Ashe	11,750

Masters Tourney (Boston, Dec. 4–8)—Nastase defeated Okker in final for $15,000 first prize

Women

Chris Evert	$110,949	Kazuko Sawamatsu	20,321
Evonne Goolagong	75,029	Linda Tuero	22,172
Margaret Court	49,333	Pat Pretorius	19,152
Virginia Wade	58,144	Olga Morozova	19,065
Helga Masthoff	38,035	Billie Jean King	18,875

TRACK AND FIELD

In the year following the Olympics, which is supposed to be a "let-down" period, a series of world-record-shattering performances took place in Europe. Two African athletes were foremost, with some spectacular running over a three-week span. The leader was Ben Jipcho of Kenya, who twice broke the world record for the 3,000-meter steeplechase and ran one mile in 3 minutes 52 seconds, the closest anyone had come to Jim Ryun's record of 3:51.1, set in 1967, and his second best of 3:51.3 in the same year.

In Helsinki on June 18, Jipcho's 8:19.8 in the steeplechase lowered the record by a second. Then he cut it to 8:14 on June 27. Five days later, he posted the third-fastest time for the mile.

The other African, Filbert Bayi of Tanzania, with 3:52.6, ran second to Jipcho in the mile at Stockholm, July 2, fourth best in the world. This was four days after his 3:34.6 for the 1,500-meter run at Helsinki had come close to Ryun's mark of 3:33.1. On June 24, Daniel Malan of South Africa had broken the world record for 1,000 meters in a meet in Munich, a site from which he had been barred in the Olympics because of his nationality. His time of 2:16 clipped two-tenths of a second off the previous record.

Meanwhile, in Milan, Marcello Fiasconaro put the Italians back in the record books with a 1:43.7 clocking for 800 meters on June 27. The previous mark of 1:44.3 had been shared by three runners.

Ryun, however, did lose one of his records. Rick Wohlhuter of the University of Chicago Track Club ran 880 yards in 1:44.6 at Los Angeles on May 27, erasing Ryun's 1966 mark of 1:44.9 that did not get into the books for a few years because of an AAU-NCAA sanctioning dispute. Ryun, one of the stars who competed in the first program of professional meets, during the winter, still held the mile and metric mile records, two of the handful that have stood since the mid-1960's. Wohlhuter also anchored his team to a 7:10.4 world record in the two-mile relay on May 12.

Track and Field Highlights

National AAU Indoor Championships
(Madison Square Garden, N.Y., Feb. 23)

Men

60 Yards—Hasely Crawford, Philadelphia Pioneer Club (0:06)
60-Yard Hurdles—Rod Milburn, Southern Univ. (0.07)
600 Yard—Fred Newhouse, Philadelphia Pioneer Club (1:11)
1,000 Yards—Marcel Philippe, Fordham (2:08.8)
Mile—Marty Liquori, New York A. C. (4:03.5)
3 Miles—Tracy Smith, Athletes in Action (13:07.2*)
Mile Walk—Ron Daniel, New York A. C. (6:22)
Mile Relay—Sports International, Washington (Thad Fletcher, Pete Schuder, Bill Barrow, Tommie Turner; 3:17.9)
2-Mile Relay—Univ. of Chicago T. C. (Tom Bach, John Mock, Lowell Paul, Ken Sparks; 7.29)
Sprint Medley Relay—Essex County College (Alfred Daley, Larry Brown, Kevin Joseph, Ainsley Armstrong; 2:04)
Triple Jump—John Craft, Univ. of Chicago T. C. (54 ft 8½ in)
Long Jump—Randy Williams, So. California (26 ft 8¾ in)
High Jump—Dwight Stones, Los Angeles (7 ft)
Pole Vault—Steve Smith, Los Angeles (17 ft 8 in)
Shot Put—George Woods, Los Angeles (69 ft. 9½ in*)
35-Pound Weight Throw—George Frenn, North Hollywood, Calif. (69 ft 7½ in)

*World record

Women

60 Yards—Iris Davis, Tennessee State (0:06.6)
60-Yard Hurdles—Patty Johnson, Club Northwest (0:07.5)
220 Yards—Rosayln Bryant, Murchurettes T. C. (0:24)
440 Yards—Brenda Walsh, Canada (0:55.5)
880 Yards—Cheryl Toussaint, Atoms T. C., Brooklyn, N. Y. (2:08.8)
Mile—Ludmila Bragina, USSR (4:40)
Mile Walk—Lynn Olson, Ferris State (7:37)
640-Yard Relay—New York P. A. L. (Mattline Render, Sharon Osborn, Diedre Wilson, Denise Johnson; 1:11.2)
Mile Relay—Atoms T. C., Brooklyn, N. Y. (Renee DeSandies, Michele McMillan, Gale Fitzgerald, Cheryl Toussaint; 3:50.5)
Sprint Medley Relay—Sports International, Washington (Robin Campbell, . Lacey O'Neal, Jackie Randolph, Esther Stroy; 1:47.9)
Long Jump—Irene Szewinska, Poland (20 ft 6 in)
High Jump—Alice Pfaff, Univ. of Colorado T. C. (5 ft 8 in)
Shot Put—Jan Svendsen, unattached (50 ft ¼ in)

National AAU Outdoor Championships

Men
(Bakersfield, Calif., June 14–16)

100 Yards—Steve Williams, San Diego T. C. (0:09.4)
220 Yards—Steve Williams (0:20.4)
440 Yards—Maurice Peoples, D. C. Striders (0:45.2)
880 Yards—Rick Wohlhuter, Univ. of Chicago T. C. (1:45.6)
Mile—Len Hilton, Pacific Coast Club (3:55.9)
3 Miles—Steve Prefontaine, Oregon T. C. (12:53.4)
6 Miles—Gordon Minty, Golden Triangle T. C. (27:20.8)
3,000-Meter Steeplechase—Doug Brown, Tennessee (8:26.8)
120-Yard Hurdles—Tom Hill, U. S. Army (0:13.2)
440-Yard Hurdles—Jim Bolding, Pacific Coast Club (0:49.2)
3-Mile Walk—John Knifton, New York A. C. (21:36.4)
Long Jump—Randy Williams, Beverly Hills Striders (26 ft 1 in)
Triple Jump—John Craft, Univ. of Chicago T. C. (55 ft 8¾ in)
High Jump—Dwight Stones, Pacific Coast Club (7 ft. 5 in)
Pole Vault—Mike Cotton, Florida T. C. (17 ft 4 in)
Hammer Throw—Ted Bregar, U. S. Naval Academy (215 ft 4 in)
Discus—Mac Wilkins, Oregon T. C. (211 ft 11 in)
Shot Put—Al Feuerbach, Pacific Coast Club (68 ft 1 in)
Javelin—Cary Feldman, Club Northwest (265 ft 3 in)

Women
(Irvine, Calif, June 22–24)

100 Yards—Iris Davis, Tennessee State (0:10.3)
220 Yards—Mabel Fergerson, West Coast Jets (0:23.4)
440 Yards—Mabel Fergerson (0:54.1)
880 Yards—Wendy Koenig, Boulder, Colo. (2:04.7)
Mile—Francie Larrieu, San Jose Cindergals (4:40.4)
2 Miles—Eileen Claugus, Wills Spikettes, Sacramento, Calif. (10:19.4)
100-Meter Hurdles—Patty Johnson, Club Northwest (0:12.9)
400-Meter Hurdles—Gale Fitzgerald, Atoms T. C., Brooklyn, N. Y. (1:00.1)
Mile Walk—Esther Marquez, Sports United (7:54.6)
440-Yard Relay—Tennessee State (Diane Hughes, Teresa Montgomery, Mamie Rawlins, Iris Davis; 0:45.5)
880-Yard Medley Relay—West Coast Jets (Willimae Fergerson, Shirley Lenyoun, Marian Roughley, Mabel Fergerson; 1:43.2)

Mile Relay—Albuquerque Olympettes (Lisa Gibbs, Cindy Ashby, Lisa Chiavaria, Carol Hudson; 3:47)
2-Mile Relay—San Jose Cindergals (Kathy Haughey, Vicki Eberly, Cindy Poor, Francie Larrieu; 9:08)
High Jump—Deanne Wilson, South Coast T. C. (5 ft 9 in)
Long Jump—Martha Watson, Los Angeles T. C. (21 ft 4¾ in)
Discus—Jean Roberts, Delaware Sports (173 ft 3 in)
Javelin—Kathy Schmidt, South Coast T. C. (194 ft 6 in)
Shot Put—Maren Seidler, Mayor Daley Y. F., Chicago (51 ft 8¼ in)
Team—Tie between Los Angeles Track Club and Atoms T. C. (44 pts)

Other AAU Events

56-Pound Weight Throw—Thomas Miller, New York A. C. (40 ft 4½ in)
All-Around—Norm Cyprus, Yonkers, N. Y. (6,756 pts)

Relays

440 Yards—Philadelphia Pioneers (0:41.5)
880 Yards—Philadelphia Pioneers (1:23.7)
1 Mile—United A. A.—BOHAA, Brooklyn, N. Y. (3:13.3)
2 Miles—New York A. C. (7:42.8)
2½-Mile Medley—New York A. C. (10:04.4)
4 Miles—New York A. C. (17:23.1)

Distance Runs

15 Kilometers—Chuck Smead, Santa Barbara (Calif.) A. A. (48:23.6)
15 Kilometers (Masters)—Hal Higdon, Michigan City, Ind. (52:48.8)
15 Kilometers (Junior)—Gary Washington, Indiana (48:10)
20 Kilometers—William Rodgers, Boston A A. (1:03.58)
20 Kilometers (Open)—Phillip H. Davis, Illinois T. C. (1:09:51.6)
20 Kilometers (Masters)—Stephen B. Goldberg, Illinois T. C. (1:12:08.5)
25 Kilometers (Masters)—Hal Higdon (1:22:33)
25 Kilometers (Junior)—Keith Brown, Summit A. C. (1:23:45)
50 Kilometers—Vince Chiapetta, Millrose A. C., New York (3:34:28)
50 Miles—Ed Walkowitz, South Hadley, Mass. (5:31:01.8)
One Hour—Men: Dave White, Orange, Calif. (12 miles, 100 yards; women: Nadia Garcia, California (9 miles, 1,625 yards)

Walks

5 Kilometers (Women)—Susan Brodock, Sports United (27:40)
10 Kilometers—Randy Mimm, Penn A. C. Philadelphia (51:45)
15 Kilometers—Jerry Brown, Boulder, Colo. (1:13:26)
15 Kilometers (Junior)—Jim Bentley, Nevada (1:18:26)
20 Kilometers—John Kelly, California (1:51:07)
25 Kilometers—John Knifton, New York A. C. (2:05:50)
40 Kilometers—John Knifton (3:29:45)
50 Kilometers—Bill Weigle, Boulder, Colo. (4:22:27)
1 Mile (Women)—Esther Marquez, Sports United (7:54)
3 Miles—John Knifton (21:36)
One Hour—Roger Mills, England (8 miles, 252 yards)

Decathlon and Pentathlon Champions

AAU Decathlon—Jeff Bennett, Oklahoma City (8,121 pts)
USTFF Decathlon (Championship)—Ramo Pihl, Brigham Young (7,523)
USTFF Decathlon (Meet)—Jeff Bennett (8,040)
NCAA Decathlon (University Division)—Ramo Pihl (7,782)
NCAA Decathlon (College Division)—Paul Fink, California State at Fullerton (6,960)
NAIA Decathlon—David Bahr, Graceland (7,011)
IC4-A Decathlon—Ron Evans, Connecticut (7,483)
AAU Men's Pentathlon—Rick Wanamaker, Boulder, Colo. (3,499)
AAU Women's Pentathlon—Jane Frederick, Boulder, Colo. (4,281)

Marathons

AAU—Doug Schmenk, Los Angeles (2:15:48)
AAU Masters—Bill Gookin, San Diego (2:32:37)
Boston—Jon Anderson, Eugene, Oreg. (2:16:03)
USTFF (Championship)—Lucien Rosa, Wisconsin-Parkside (2:25:18.4)
USTFF (Meet)—Dennis Delmott, U. S. Marines (2:29:40.8)
NAIA—Lucien Rosa (2:26.01)

Other Team Champions

NCAA College Division—Norfolk State (54 pts)
NAIA—Indoor: Jackson State (43 pts); outdoor: Texas Southern (81 pts)
IC4-A—Indoor: Manhattan (45 pts); outdoor: U. S. Navy (41)

International Competitions

At Munich, West Germany (July 11–12)—United States 122, West Germany 101
At Turin, Italy (July 17–18)—Men: United States 143, Italy 78; women: United States 84, Italy 49
At Minsk, USSR (July 22–23)—Men: USSR 121, United States 112; women: USSR 95, United States 51
At Dakar, Senegal (Aug. 5)—United States 111, Africa 101

Track and Field Highlights (continued)

National Collegiate (NCAA) Indoor Championships
(Detroit, March 9–10)

60 Yards—Gerry Tinker, Kent State (0.06)
60-Yard High Hurdles—Rod Milburn, Southern Univ. (0:06.9)
440 Yards—Terry Erickson, So. Illinois (0:49)
600 Yards—Beaufort Brown, Florida (1:10)
880 Yards—Ken Schappert, Villanova (1:50.4)
1,000 Yards—Tony Waldrop, North Carolina (2:10)
Mile—Dave Wottle, Bowling Green (4:03.4)
2 Miles—Mike Keogh, Manhattan (8:39.7)
Mile Relay—Seton Hall (Mike Tyson, Larry Mustachio, Orlando Greene, Howard Brock; 3:17)
2-Mile Relay—Fordham (Paul Nowicki, Alex Trammell, John Jurgens, Marcel Philippe; 7:31.5)
Distance Medley Relay—Manhattan (John Lovett, Ray Johnson, Joe Savage, Tony Colon; 9:43.8)
Triple Jump—Barry McClure, Middle Tennessee (54 ft 1¾ in)
Long Jump—Randy Williams, So. California (26 ft 4¼ in)
Pole Vault—Terry Porter, Kansas (17 ft)
High Jump—Chris Dunn, Colgate (7 ft 2 in)
Shot Put—Hans Hoglund, Texas–El Paso (64 ft 1¼ in)
35-Pound Weight Throw—Ted Bregar, Navy (68 ft 1½ in)
Team—Manhattan (18 pts)

U. S. Track and Field Federation Outdoor Championships
(Wichita, Kans., June 1–2)

100 Yards—Larry Burton, Purdue (0:09.2)
220 Yards—Mark Lutz, Kansas (0:20.5)
440 Yards—Dennis Schultz, Oklahoma State (0:45.8)
880 Yards—Rudolph Griffith, Texas (1:48.9)
880 Yards (invitation)—Dave Wottle, Bowling Green (1:49.5)
Mile—Rick Wolhuter, Univ. of Chicago T. C. (3:58.8)
3 Miles—Glenn Herold, Wisconsin (13:41.4)
6 Miles—David Koche, Colorado T. C. (28:58.1)
3,000-Meter Steeplechase—Joe Lucas, Georgetown (8:46)
120-Yard Hurdles—Ricky Stubbs, Louisiana Tech (0:13.4)
440-Yard Hurdles—Efron Gipson, Lamar (0:50.2)
440-Yard Relay—Southwest Louisiana (Harold Porter, Pat Gullett, Steve Gullick, Don Credeur; 0:40.1)
Mile Relay—Texas (Ed Wright, Bob Primeaux, John Lee, Don Sturgal; 3:05.7)
High Jump—Dwight Stones, Pacific Coast Club (7 ft 3½ in)
Long Jump—Al Lanier, Cincinnati (26 ft 4¾ in)
Triple Jump—John Craft, Univ. Of Chicago T. C. (55 ft 2 in)
Discus—Gary Ordway, Pacific Coast Club (201 ft 5 in)
Hammer Throw—Peter Galle, Beverly Hills Striders (194 ft 10 in)
Javelin—Sam Colson, Kansas (260 ft 2 in)
Shot Put—Al Feuerbach, Pacific Coast Club (69 ft 9¼ in)
Pole Vault—Jim Speer, Colorado (16 ft 3 in)

U. S. Track and Field Federation Indoor Championships
(Houston Astrodome, Feb. 10)

100 Yards—Don Quarrie, So. California (0.09.4)
400 Yards—John Smith, unattached (0:47.4)
880 Yards—Ken Swenson, Manhattan (Kans.) T. C. (1:52.1)
Mile—Dave Wottle, Bowling Green (4:00.3)
2 Miles—John Hartnett, Villanova (8:36.2)
120-Yard Hurdles—Rod Milburn, Southern Univ. (0:13.3)
Mile Relay—Oklahoma State (Stan Stolpe, Chuck Stilley, James Kurrasch, Dennis Schultz; 3:12.9)
2-Mile Relay—Texas (Ed Wright, Mark Klonower, John Craig, Rudolph Griffith; 7:30)
Long Jump—Randy Williams, So. California (26 ft ¾ in)
High Jump—Chris Dunn, Colgate (7 ft)
Triple Jump—John Craft, Univ. of Chicago T. C. (52 ft 10¼ in)
Pole Vault—Steve Smith, Pacific Coast Club (17 ft)
Shot Put—Al Feuerbach, Pacific Coast Club (68 ft 6½ in)

National Collegiate (NCAA) Outdoor Championships
(Baton Rouge, La., June 7–9)

100 Yards—Ed Hammonds, Memphis State (0:09.4)
220 Yards—Marshall Dill, Michigan State (0:20.9)
440 Yards—Maurice Peoples, Arizona State (0:45)
880 Yards—Earl Kent, Wisconsin (1:47.2)
Mile—Dave Wottle, Bowling Green (3:57.1)
3 Miles—Steve Prefontaine, Oregon (13:05.4)
6 Miles—Charles Maguire, Penn State (28:19.4)
3,000-Meter Steeplechase—Doug Brown, Tennessee (8:28:1)
120-Yard Hurdles—Rod Milburn, Southern Univ. (0:13.1)
440-Yard Hurdles—Robert Primeaux, Texas (0:49.5)
440-Yard Relay—Memphis State (Maurice Wright, Lynn Fox, Ed Taylor, Ed Hammonds; 0:39.6)
Mile Relay—UCLA (Ron Gaddis, Gordon Peppars, Maxie Parks, Benny Brown; 3:04.3)
High Jump—Reynaldo Brown, California Poly (7 ft 4 in)
Triple Jump—Milan Tiff, UCLA (54 ft 2¾ in)
Javelin—Sam Colson, Kansas (279 ft 9 in)
Discus—Mac Wilkins, Oregon (203 ft 11 in)
Long Jump—Finn Bendixen, UCLA (25 ft 10½ in)
Pole Vault—Dave Roberts, Rice (17 ft 4 in)
Hammer Throw—Jacques Accambray, Kent State (221 ft 6 in)
Shot Put—Hans Hoglund, Texas–El Paso (64 ft 6¾ in)
Team—University of California, Los Angeles (52 pts)

Rod Milburn, the world's premier hurdler, added the 110-meter record to his collection with a 13.1 performance at Zurich on July 6. In the dashes, Steve Williams, a New Yorker, running for the San Diego Track Club, became the sixth to share the world record for 100 meters in 9.1 seconds, at Fresno on May 12.

Another athlete who credits his achievement to speed is Dwight Stones of Glendale, Calif. He cleared 7 feet 6 inches in the high jump, on June 24, and expects to hit 7-10 someday. In the weights, Al Feuerbach of Long Beach, Calif., put the shot 71-7, 1½ inches farther than Randy Matson's listed mark. Klaus Wolferman of West Germany threw the javelin 308-8 for a record.

In women's track Paola Cacchi-Pigni of Italy ran the mile in a record 4:29.5, and Renate Stecher of East Germany posted sprinting marks of 10.8 seconds for 100 meters and 22.1 for 200 meters on successive days at Dresden.

——— WORLD UNIVERSITY GAMES ———

In order to better its chances of staging the 1980 Olympics, the Soviet Union put on the World University Games in Moscow, Aug. 15–25, 1973. A U. S. team of about 300 members, all college students, competed in the nine sports—basketball, fencing, gymnastics, swimming, tennis, track and field, volleyball, water polo, and wrestling. Altogether, more than 3,500 athletes from 66 nations competed.

The Soviet Union, whose teams were replete with athletes who represented them in the Olympics, was by far the most successful, taking 68 gold medals for first place, 36 silver for second, and 31 bronze for third. The United States, scoring heavily in swimming only, gained 19 gold medals, 16 silver, and 19 bronze.

The U. S. basketball team, after six easy victories and a 66–60 triumph over Brazil, met the USSR for the title. Paced by David Thompson of North Carolina State, the Americans won, 75–67.

There were unfortunate political outbursts during the activities. Cuban players attacked the Americans during their basketball game, and apologized the next day. Athletes from Israel were hooted by Soviet fans during the ceremonies, and Soviet Jewish fans were mistreated during the competition.

World University Games
(Moscow, August 15–25)
Distribution of Medals

	Gold	Silver	Bronze
Soviet Union	68	36	31
United States	19	15	19
Rumania	4	7	7
Japan	3	8	1
Poland	2	3	5
Britain	2	3	1
Cuba	2	3	1
Czechoslovakia	2	2	1
Italy	2	0	6
Finland	2	0	0
Hungary	1	9	3
Bulgaria	6	7	7
West Germany	1	4	6
East Germany	1	3	7
France	1	2	1
Yugoslavia	1	1	2
Mongolia	1	0	1
Iran	0	4	1
Canada	0	2	5
Australia	0	1	3
Brazil	0	0	5
South Korea	0	0	2
Kenya	0	8	1
Mexico	0	0	1
India	0	0	1

ARCHERY

World Championships
(Grenoble, France, July 25–28)
Men—*Individual:* Viktor Sidoruk, USSR (2,185 pts); *team:* United States (6,400)
Women—*Individual:* Linda Myers, York, Pa. (2,204); *team:* USSR (6,389)

National Field Archery Association Championships
(Aurora, Ill., July 23–27)
Men—*Freestyle: open:* Bobby J. Hunt, Grapevine, Texas (2,794 pts); *amateur:* Terry Ragsdale, White Oak, Texas (2,762); *senior:* Elmer Little, San Diego, Calif. (2,701); *professional:* Dean Pridgen, Kansas City, Mo. (2,792); *youth:* Ricky Sorensen, Orem, Utah (2,582)—*Freestyle Limited: open:* A. L. Lee, Greenwood, S. C. (2,659); *amateur:* Bob Cerney, St. Paul Park, Minn. (2,662); *professional:* Jamie Selkirk, Canton, Ill. (2,673)—*Barebow: open:* Dennis Cline, Sugar Grove, Ill. (2,606); *amateur:* Mike Flier, Pekin, Ill. (2,597); *senior:* Dr. R. E. Szilvassy, Clovis, N. Mex. (2,135); *youth:* Bruce Gates, Jr., Eaton, Ohio (2,122)—*Bowhunter: open:* Cal Vogt, Van Nuys, Calif. (2,586); *amateur:* Alfred Lough, Peoria, Ill. (2,062)
Women—*Freestyle: open:* Barbara Morris, Frankfort, Ky. (2,645); *amateur:* Kathy Cramberg, Dallas City, Ill. (2,683); *senior:* Sandy Elott, Atlanta, Ga. (2,219); *professional:* Eva Troncoso, Monterey Park, Calif. (2,741); *girl:* Linda Loberto, East Meadow, N. Y. (1,651)—*Freestyle Limited: open:* Mary Miller, Garden City, Mo. (2,460); *amateur:* June Mitchell, Chicago (2,474)—*Barebow: open:* Beverly Janis, Americus, Ga. (2,318); *amateur:* Eunice Schewe, Roscoe, Ill. (2,344); *girl:* Sherily Doyle, Taft, Calif. (1,659)—*Bowhunter: open:* Ida B. Lewis, Guthrie, Okla. (1,228); *amateur:* June Jones, Elgin, Ill. (755)

National Archery Association Championships
(Oxford, Ohio, Aug. 6–10)
Men—Darrell Pace, Cincinnati (2,958 pts); *intermediate boys:* Richard Bednar, Suffield, Ohio (2,868); *junior boys:* Don Dabelow, Galveston, Ind. (2,917); *cadet boys:* Tom Stevenson, Jr., Norristown, Pa. (2,974); *team:* Cincinnati Archers (Darrell Pace, John Lamb, Nisel Rippon, Al Kramer; 3,123)
Women—Doreen Wilbur, Jefferson, Iowa (2,833); *junior girls:* Janet McCullough, Sharpsville, Pa. (2,809); *team:* Henderson Archery Club, Phoenix, Ariz. (2,941)

BADMINTON

United States Open Championships (New Britain, Conn., April 12–15)—*Men's singles:* Sture Johnsson, Sweden; *men's doubles:* Don Paup, Long Beach, Calif., and Jim Poole, Northridge, Calif.; *women's singles:* Eva Twedberg, Sweden; *women's doubles:* Diane Hales, Claremont, Calif., and Pam Bristol, Flint, Mich.; *mixed doubles:* Eva Twedberg and Sture Johnsson; *senior men's singles:* Jim Poole; *senior men's doubles:* Jim Poole and Bill Goodman, Wellesley Hills, Mass.; *senior women's doubles:* Ethel Marshall and Bea Massman, Buffalo, N. Y.; *masters men's singles* (50 and over): Ed Phillips, Warwick, R. I.; *masters men's doubles:* Ed Phillips and Harold Seavey, Framingham, Mass.; *masters women's doubles:* Brenda Lumsden and Paula Seavey, Framingham, Mass.; *masters mixed doubles:* Paula Seavey and Robert Bachman, Wellesley Hills, Mass.; *senior mixed doubles:* Jim Poole and Mary Ann Breckell, Los Angeles
United States Junior Championships (Bloomfield Hills, Mich., March 20–23)—*Boys' singles:* Pat Trapnell, Detroit; *girls' singles:* Madalene Steinbroner, Manhattan Beach, Calif.; *boys' doubles:* Bob Gilmour, Garden Grove, Calif., and Mike Kelly, Manhattan Beach, Calif.; *girls' doubles:* Karen Czarnecki, Flint, Mich., and Cindy Young, Altadena, Calif.; *mixed doubles:* Ron Buck, San Francisco, and Madalene Steinbroner
All-England Championships (Wembley, March 21–24)—*Men's singles:* Rudy Hartono, Indonesia; *women's singles:* Margaret Beck, England; *men's doubles:* Ade Chandra and Christian, Indonesia; *women's doubles:* Machiko Aizawa and Etsuko Takenaka, Japan; *mixed doubles:* Derek Ta'bot and Gillian Gilks, England
Canadian Open Championships (Toronto, March 7–10)—*Men's singles:* Jamie Paulson, Toronto; *women's singles:* Nancy McKinley, Toronto; *men's doubles:* Jamie Paulson and Yves Pare, Montreal; *women's doubles:* Margaret Beck, England, and Joke van Beusekom, Netherlands

BILLIARDS

Pocket

World—Lou Butera, Reseda, Calif.
United States Men's Open—Steve Mizerak, Woodbridge, N. J.
United States Women's Open—Jean Balukas, Brooklyn, N. Y.
Men's Intercollegiate—Dan Louie, Washington State
Women's Intercollegiate—Marcia Girolamo, State Univ. of New York at Oswego

BOBSLEDDING

World Championships
(Mt. Van Hoevenberg, Lake Placid, N. Y.)
2-Man (Feb. 11)—West Germany (Wolfgang Zimmerer, driver; Peter Utzschneider, brake; time for four runs: 4:28.77)
4-Man (Feb. 18)—Switzerland (Rene Stadler, driver; Werner Carmichel, Erich Schaerer; Peter Schaerer, brake; time for four runs: 4:22.05)

BOWLING

American Bowling Congress Tournament (Syracuse, N. Y., March 3–May 20)—*Regular Division: singles:* Ed Thompson, Denver, Colo. (762); *doubles:* Jamie Brooks and Jim Paine, Houston, Texas (1,327); *all-events:* Ron Woolet, Louisville, Ky. (2,104); *team:* Skyway Lanes, Chicago (9,316)—*Classic Division: singles:* Nelson Burton, St. Louis (724); *doubles:* Bobby Cooper, Houston, Texas, and George Pappas, Charlotte, N. C. (1,339); *all-events:* Jimmy Mack, Hackettstown, N. J. (1,994); *team:* Stroh's Beer, Detroit (3,050; score posted in 3-game roll-off among six highest teams)—*Booster Division:* Comcrudeslant, Newport, R. I. (2,854)—*Masters:* Dave Soutar, Kansas City (defeated Dick Ritger, Hartford, Wis., by 131 pins, in final)
Women's International Bowling Congress Tournament (Las Vegas, Nev., April 5–July 20)—*Open Division: singles:* Bobby Buffaloe, Costa Mesa, Calif. (706); *doubles:* Dotty Fothergill, North Attleboro, Mass., and Millie Martorella, Rochester, N. Y. (1,238); *all-events:* Toni Calvery, Midwest City, Okla. (1,910); *team:* Fitzpatrick Chevrolet, Concord, Calif. (2,897)—*Division 1:* Barbara Jacques, San Diego, Calif. (680); *doubles:* Carol Sheppard and Laura Blake, Phoenix, Ariz. (1,203); *all-events:* Reta Richardson, Boise City, Okla. (1,769); *team:* Cacco's Hawaii, Honolulu (2,708)—*Division 2: singles:* Marijaye Williams, San Marcos, Texas (620); *doubles:* Jerry Thompson and Judy Hiler, Springfield, Ill. (1,109); *all-events:* Bernadine Sabatta, Lansing, Ill. (1,660); *team:* Killeen Merchants, Killeen, Texas (2,550)—*Queens Tournament:* Dotty Fothergill (defeated Judy Cook, Grandview, Mo., 804–791, in final)
Bowling Proprietors Association of America Open Championships—Men (New York, March 10): Mike McGrath, El Cerrito, Calif. (defeated Earl Anthony, Tacoma, Wash., in final)—Women (with WIBC, at Garden City, N. Y., May 3, final)—Millie Martorella, Rochester, N. Y. (5,533)
Intercollegiate: Association of College Unions–International at ABC Tournament (Syracuse, N. Y., April 12–15)—*Singles:* Jim Fiore, Rensselaer Polytechnic Institute (598); *doubles:* Gary Baker, Northern Colorado, and Rudy Sedillo, Northern Arizona (1,222); *all-events:* Lee Snow, Eastern Michigan (1,946)—National Association of Intercollegiate Athletics (Kansas City, May 4–5): *Singles:* Dave Hudson, Harding (defeated Bob Aleksinski, Great Falls, by 15 pins, in final); *doubles:* Myron Olson and Bob Aleksinski, Great Falls; *all-events:* Bob Aleksinski (3,085); *team:* Great Falls, Mont. (17,273)—Women (Association of College Unions–International, April 7, at WIBC)—*Singles:* Susie Halloway, Indiana (622); *doubles:* Denys Jones, Utah State, and Nancy Young, Lee (1,090); *all-events:* Susie Halloway (1,752)
National Duckpin Bowling Congress (Newington, Conn., March 31–May 13)—*Men: singles:* Fred Belliveau, Norwich, Conn. (466); *doubles:* Larry Shepley and Tom Ramsburg, Frederick, Md. (901); *all-events:* Keith Dashno, Newington, Conn. (1,332); *team:* Dudley Excavating, Washington (2,063)—*Women: singles:* Agnes Claughsey, Hebron, Conn. (435); *doubles:* Rola Ough and Miki Irish, Manchester, Conn. (799); *all-events:* Nancy Brindle, Providence, R. I. (1,214); *team:* Parkville Majors, Baltimore (1,902); *mixed teams:* 4 A's and a B, East Providence, R. I. (1,894); *mixed doubles:* Patsy and Robert Stroessner, Baltimore (866)

BRIDGE, CONTRACT

World Team (Bermuda Bowl, São Paolo, Brazil, May 27, final)—Italy (Giorgio Belladonna, Pietro Forquet, Benito Garozza, Giuseppe Garabello, Vito Pettalao) defeated North America, represented by United States Aces, by 128 international points

American Contract Bridge Association Championships
Spring Nationals
(St. Louis, March 9–20)

Men's Pairs—John E. Kennedy, Jr., and Capt. David Hadden, Shreveport, La.
Women's Pairs—Ann Economidy, Manchester, Mo., and Vivian Williamson, Roswell, N. Mex.
Open Pairs—Jack Rhatigan, Cottage Grove, Minn., and Michael P. Hoffman, Minneapolis
Men's Teams—John Simon, St. Louis; Robert Wolff, Dallas; James Jacoby, Richardson, Texas; Gaylor Kasle and Garey Hayden, Tucson, Ariz.
Women's Teams—Helen Utegaard, Bethesda, Md.; Terry Michaels, Washington; Nancy Gruver, Ellicott City, Md.; and Jo Morse, Silver Spring, Md.

Vanderbilt Knockout Team—Aces (Robert Wolff, Robert Hamman, Robert Goldman, Mark Blumenthal, Dallas; Michael Lawrence, Los Angeles)

Summer Nationals
(Washington, July 20–31)

Mixed Teams—Philip Feldesman, Stanley Tomchin, Edith Sachs, New York, and Ellen Alfandre, Scarsdale, N. Y.
Life Master Pairs—Jack Blair, Tulsa, Okla., and Paul T. Swanson, Morgantown, W. Va.
Senior Master Pairs—Harry Looks, Great Neck, N. Y., and Joel Friedberg, West Hempstead, N. Y.
Grand National Teams—William Seamon, Russell Arnold, Bob Sharp, Miami; Richard Pavlicek and Jim Berry, Fort Lauderdale, Fla.; Jane Jaeger, North Bay Village, Fla.
Spingold Knockout Team—A. E. (Bud) Reinhold, Highland Park, Ill.; Bill Eisenberg, Eddie Kantar, Dr. Richard Katz, Los Angeles; Larry Cohen, Chicago

Fall Nationals
(Las Vegas, Nev., Dec. 7–16)

Life Master Men's Pairs—Edgar Kaplan, New York, and Norman Kay, Philadelphia
Life Master Women's Pairs—June Deutsch and Frieda Arst, Chicago
Mixed Pairs—Marilyn Johnson, Houston, and Bernard Chazen, Fort Lee, N. J.
Blue Ribbon Pairs—Kit Woolsey, Washington, and Steve Robinson, Alexandria, Va.
Reisinger Board-a-Match Team—A. E. (Bud) Reinhold, Highland Park, Ill.; Larry Cohen, Chicago; Dr. Richard Katz, Los Angeles; Peter Weichsel and Alan Sontag, New York

CANOEING

United States Championships
(Seattle, Aug. 10–12)

Men's Kayak

Singles, 500 Meters—Phil Rogosheske, Alexandria, Va. (2:09.85)
Singles, 1,000 Meters—Phil Rogosheske (4:05.08)
Singles, 10,000 Meters—Phil Rogosheske (46:40.7)
Tandem, 500 Meters—Phil Rogosheske and Rob Mitchell, Catherine, Ala. (1:52.25)
Tandem, 1,000 Meters—Jerry Welbourn and John Van Dyke, Potomac R. C., Washington (4:01.22)
Tandem, 10,000 Meters—Jerry Welbourn and Atila Libertini, Conn. (43:21.06)
Fours, 1,000 Meters—Libertini, Van Dyke, Welbourn, and Rogosheske (3:23.84)
Fours, 10,000 Meters—Rusty Pelican O. A., Newport Beach, Calif. (John Glazier, Bob Hahn, Greg Rose, Mike Johnson; 41:31.05)

Women's Kayak

Singles, 500 Meters—Marcia Smoke, Niles (Mich.) C. C. (2:23.48)
Singles, 5,000 Meters—Sperry Rademaker, Floral City, Fla. (25:44.89)
Tandem, 500 Meters—Linda Murray and Nancy Leahy, Washington (2:02.7)
Tandem, 5,000 Meters—Marcia Smoke and Patience Vanderbush, Niles C. C. (24:13.5)
Fours, 500 Meters—Niles C. C. (Marcia Smoke, Loli Flood, Marian Flood, and Patience Vanderbush; 1:53.7)
Fours, 5,000 Meters—Niles C. C. (Marian Flood, Loli Flood, Barbara Hintz, and Ava Tutson; 24:02.4)

Canoe

Singles, 500 Meters—Andy Toro, Rusty Pelican O. A., Newport Beach, Calif. (2:32.09)
Singles, 1,000 Meters—Pete Ross, Yonkers, N. Y. (4:43.6)
Singles, 10,000 Meters—Ray Effinger, Inwood C. C., New York (47:55.04)
Tandem, 500 Meters—Andy Toro and Bob Hahn, Rusty Pelican O. A. (2:13.2)
Tandem, 1,000 Meters—Pete and Gilbert Ross, Yonkers, N. Y. (52:37.5)
Fours, 1,000 Meters—St. Charles C. C. (Ron Diebold, John Diebold, Dan Plankenhorn, Lee Robinson; 4:20.2)

CHESS

World Candidate Pairings

In elimination tournaments, six players won places in the 1974 playoffs for the right to challenge Bobby Fischer of Los Angeles for the world championship. Two other players, former champions Boris Spassky and Tigran Petrosian, both of the USSR, drew byes to the playoffs. The pairings:

Robert Byrne, Ossining, N. Y., vs. Boris Spassky
Tigran Petrosian vs. Lajos Portisch, Hungary
Henrique Mecking, Brazil, vs. Viktor Korchnoi, USSR
Antoly Karpov, USSR, vs. Lev Polugayevsky, USSR

National Championships

United States Open—Norman Weinstein, Allston, Mass. (He was awarded the title on basis of opponents' strength after five players tied for first place. The others in order of their placings were Walter Browne, New York; Duncan Suttles, Vancouver, B. C.; Greg Defotis, Chicago; and Ruben Rodriguez, Quezon City, Philippines.)
United States—Tie between John Grefe, Berkeley, Calif., and Lubomir Kavalek, Washington
United States Junior—Larry Christiansen, Riverside, Calif.
National Open—Walter Brown, New York

CROSS-COUNTRY

AAU (Gainesville, Fla., Nov. 24, 10,000 meters)—Frank Shorter, Florida Track Club, Gainesville (29:52.5); team: Florida T. C. (20 pts)
NCAA—University Division (Spokane, Wash., Nov. 19, 6 miles): Steve Prefontaine, Oregon; team: Oregon. Division II (Wheaton, Ill., Nov. 10, 5 miles): Garry Bentley, South Dakota State (23:49); team: South Dakota State (88). Division III (Wheaton, Nov. 10, 5 miles): Steve Foster, Ashland (24:27); team: Ashland (66)
NAIA (Salina, Kans., Nov. 18, 5 miles)—Tony Brien, Marymount (Kans.) College (23:42.5); team: Eastern New Mexico (33 pts)
IC4-A (New York, Nov. 12, 5 miles)—University: John Hartnett, Villanova (24:00); team: Manhattan (87 pts). College: Charles Duggan, Springfield (24:36.6); team: Bucknell (64 pts)
Masters AAU (Lorain, Ohio, Nov. 17, 10,000 meters)—Hal Higdon, Michigan City, Ind., 40–49 years (33:37.1); Augie Escamilla, San Diego, Calif., 50–59 years (38:02); John Wall, U. S. Naval Reserve, Fort McHenry, Md., 60–69 years (39:01); championship team: Pacific AAU (76 pts)
USTFF (San Diego, Calif., Nov. 24, 6 miles)—Ed Mendoza, Arizona (29:39.6). Hans Menet, Nevada, finished first but was disqualified for fouling Mendoza.
Women's AAU (Albuquerque, N. Mex., Nov. 24, 3 miles)—Francie Larrieu, San Jose (Calif.) Cindergals (17:17); team: San Jose Cindergals (105 pts)
AAU Junior (Buffalo, N. Y., Nov. 11, 6 miles)—Pat Davey, Motor City Striders (30:49.6); team: Motor City Striders (30 pts)
AAU Women's Junior (Albuquerque, N. Mex., Nov. 17, 3 miles)—Kathy Whitcomb, unattached, Colorado (19:12.3); team: Albuquerque Olympette Club (28 pts)

CURLING

World (Regina, Saskatchewan, March 19–24)—Sweden (Bengt Oscarius, skip) defeated Canada, 6–5, in final.
United States (Colorado Springs, March 5–10)—Winchester (Mass.) Curling Club (Charles Reeves, Jr., skip; Barry Blanchard, Henry Shean, Douglas Carlson)
United States Women (Appleton, Wis., Feb. 14–17)—St. Paul Bon Spielers (Marsha Hulstrand, skip; Mrs. Ken Koppy, Linda Barneson, Mrs. Charles Tilden)
Canada (Edmonton, Alberta, March 8–10)—Regina (Harvey Mazinke, skip)
International Juniors (East York, Ontario, April 23)—Sweden (Goran Roxin, skip)

CYCLING

American Amateur Bicycle League of America
National Championships
Road Racing
(Milwaukee, July 28–29)

Senior (120 miles)—John Howard, Houston (4:45:50)
Veteran (40 miles)—Jim Crist, Colorado
Junior (40 miles)—Pat Nielsen, Detroit (1:31:00)
Intermediate (12 miles)—Andrew Peake, Oregon (28:30.8)
Women (32 miles)—Eileen Brennan, Detroit (1:23:06)

Track Racing
(Northbrook, Ill., Aug. 1–4)

Sprints—Roger Young, Detroit (0:12.3)
10 Miles—Mike Neel, Berkeley, Calif. (20:29)
1,000-Meter Time Trial—Steve Woznik, Ridgefield Park, N. J. (1:11.1)
4,000-Meter Pursuit—Mike Neel (5:07)
Team Pursuit—New Jersey (Dave Chauner, John Chapman, Joe Saling, Steve Woznik; 4:48.2)
Women's Sprint—Sheila Young, Detroit (0:13.7)
3,000-Meter Pursuit—Mary Jane Reoch, Washington (4:08.8)
Junior Champion—Gilbert Hatton, So. California (28 pts)

DOG SHOWS

Westminster Kennel Club (New York, Feb. 12–13)—Group winners (3,029 dogs shown)—nonsporting and best in show: Ch. Acadia Command Performance, standard poodle, owned by Edward B. Jenner, of Richmond, Ill., and Mrs. Jo Ann Sering, of Portland, Oreg.; working: Barbara H. Murray's boxer, Ch. Regency's Nite Life, of Corrales, N. Mex.; terrier: Mrs. Jane Esther Henderson's wire fox, Ch. Littleway Haranwal Barrister, of Stockton, N. J.; hound: Dr. and Mrs. Doyle Rogers' Afghan, Ch. Khayam's Apollo, at Pasadena, Texas; toy: Mrs. Mamie R. Gregory's Maltese, Ch. Joanne Chen's Maya Dancer, of La Jolla, Calif.; sporting: Mrs. Peggy Westphal's ascob cocker spaniel, Ch. Sagamore Toccoa, of Bedford, N. Y.
International Kennel Club (Chicago, March 31–April 1)—Group winners (3,095 dogs shown)—terrier and best in show: Mrs. B. G. Frame's West Highland white, Ch. Purston Pinmoney Pedlar, of Indianapolis; toy: Mrs. L. S. Gordon Jr.'s and Mrs. Janet Bennett's Yorkshire terrier, Ch. Continuation of Gleno, of Glenview, Ill.; hound: Sandra and Perry Stone's longhaired dachshund, Ch. Kemper Dachs Waldemar, of Painesville, Ohio; nonsporting: Mrs. Priscilla St. George Ryan's chow chow, Ch. Liontamer Kudos, of Tuxedo Park, N. Y.; working: Timothy Spurlock's standard schnauzer, Ch. Artual Cristofer v. Gurlin, of Bucyrus, Ohio; sporting: Earl Taisey's English springer spaniel, Ch. El Taro's Scotch Flag, of Pasadena, Md.

BEST IN SHOW: Ch. Acadia Command Performance is groomed at the Westminster Kennel Club show. A total of 3,029 dogs was judged.

UPI

FENCING

United States Championships
(Tucson, Ariz., June 23–30)

Individual—Foil: Ed Ballinger, Salle Santelli, New York; *épée:* Scott Bozek, Peabody, Mass.; *saber:* Paul Apostle, Fencers Club, New York; *women's foil:* Tatanya Adamovich, Fencers Club, New York

Team—Foil: Salle Santelli, New York (Ed Ballinger, Marty Lang, Uriah Jones, Vince Surdi); *épée:* New York A. C. (George Masin, Paul Pesthy, Steve Netburn, Robert Braine); *saber:* New York A. C. (Alex Orban, Thomas Losonczy, Csaba Gall, Jack Keane); *women's foil:* Fencers Club, New York (Tatanya Adamovich, Ruth White, Norma Latham, Mary Annavedder); *overall:* Fencers Club, New York

Under 19 Division—*Foil:* Mike McCahey, New Trier, Ill.; *épée:* Tim Glass, Niles, Ill.; *saber:* Miklos Benedek, Newark, N. J.; *women's foil:* Gaye Jacobsen, San Francisco

National Collegiate (NCAA) Championships
(Baltimore, March 15–17)

Individual—Foil: Brooke Makler, Pennsylvania; *épée:* Risto Hurme, New York University; *saber:* Peter Westbrook, New York University
*Team—*New York University (76 pts)

Women's Intercollegiate F. A.
(Trenton, N. J., April 6–7)

Individual: Susan McCourt, California State, Fullerton
Team: Cornell (106 pts)

World Championships
(Göteborg, Sweden, July 6–13)

Foil: Christian Noel, France; *team:* USSR
Épée: Rolf Edling, Sweden; *team:* West Germany
Saber: M. A. Montano, Italy; *team:* Hungary
Women's Foil: Valentina Nikolova, USSR; *team:* Hungary

GYMNASTICS

National AAU Championships
(Buffalo, N. Y., April 26–28)

Men

All-Around—Tie between Yoshi Hayasaki, Illinois, and Yoshiaki Takei, Georgia Southern (108.10 pts)
Floor Exercises—Paul Hunt, University of Illinois (18.400)
Pommel Horse—Yoshi Hayasaki (17.750)
Still Rings—Charles Ropiequet, Carbondale, Ill. (19.175)
Vault—Yoshi Hayasaki (18.250)
Parallel Bars—Yoshiaki Takei (18.725)
Horizontal Bar—Yoshi Hayasaki (18.575)
Team—New York A. C. (300.95)

Women

All-Around—Joan Moore Rice, Mannettes Gym Club, Philadelphia (74.85)
Floor Exercises—Joan Rice (19.300)
Balance Beam—Kim Chace, Riviera Beach Club, North Palm Beach, Fla. (19.100)
Vault—Roxanne Pierce, College Park, Md. (18.775)
Uneven Parallel Bars—Roxanne Pierce (19.100)
Team—Mannettes Gym Club, Philadelphia (218.55)

National Collegiate (NCAA) Championships
(Eugene, Oreg., April 5–7)

All-Around—Tie between Marshall Avener, Penn State, and Steve Hug, Stanford (110.05)
Floor Exercises—Odess Lovin, Oklahoma (18.950)
Vault—John Crosby, Southern Connecticut (18.775)
Rings—Bob Mahorney, Indiana State (19.050)
Pommel Horse—Ed Slezak, Indiana State (18.750)
Parallel Bars—Steve Hug (18.675)
Horizontal Bar—Jon Aitken, Iowa State (18.950)
Team—Iowa State (325.15)

HANDBALL

United States Handball Association Champions
1-Wall—*Singles:* Steve Sandler, New York; *doubles:* Joel Wisotsky and Lou Russo, New York
3-Wall—*Singles:* Paul Haber, San Diego; *doubles:* Joel Wisotsky and Ruby Obert, New York; *masters doubles:* Jim Golden and Dave Rott, Detroit; *golden masters doubles:* Vic Hershkowitz and Harold Hanft, Fort Lauderdale, Fla.

OLGA KORBUT, who thrilled audiences in the 1972 Olympics, takes a break after limbering up for a European gymnastics event in London.

4-Wall—*Singles:* Terry Muck, St. Paul; *doubles:* Ray Neveau, Oshkosh, Wis., and Simie Fein, Milwaukee; *masters singles:* Jim Fitzpatrick, New York; *masters doubles:* Ken Schneider and Phil Elbert, Chicago; *golden masters doubles:* Irv Simon, Los Angeles, and Earl Russell, Long Beach, Calif.
Super Eight Pro Tournament—Fred Lewis, Cleveland

AAU Champions
1-Wall—*Singles:* Joel Davidson, Brooklyn, N. Y.; *doubles—*Wally Ulbrich and Artie Reyer, Brooklyn; *masters doubles:* Bernie Hayden and Herb Isaacson, Brooklyn

YMCA Champions
4-Wall—*Singles:* Terry Muck, St. Paul; *doubles:* Paul Haber, San Diego, and Paul Morlos, San Jose, Calif.; *masters doubles:* Phil Collins and Dick Greco, Chicago

Intercollegiate
4-Wall—*Singles:* Bill Peoples, Montana; *doubles:* Jim Beemon and Scott Hannon, Winona State; *B singles:* Jeff Catron, Youngstown State; *team:* Montana

HORSE SHOWS

American Horse Shows Association Champions
Amateur-Owner Working Hunter—Penny Loeb's No Alibi
Regular Working Hunter—Mr. and Mrs. Kenneth Wheeler's Gozzi
First-Year Green Working Hunter—Debbie Wilson's Market Wise
Second-Year Green Working Hunter—Jane Womble's Third of August

LONDON DAILY EXPRESS

Action in the NCAA lacrosse championship game, won by Maryland (dark uniforms) *over Johns Hopkins, 10–9.*

Junior Working Hunter—Nancy Baroody's War Dress
Green Conformation Hunter—Mr. and Mrs. Wheeler's Vim
Regular Conformation Hunter—Mr. and Mrs. John H. Leib's
  Automation
Small Pony Hunter—Jess Larson's Justa Tinker
Large Pony Hunter—Hollow Hill Farm's Dressing Drink
Amateur-Owner Jumper—Judy Korn's Orange County
Junior Jumper—Keen Tipton's The Intruder
Harness Pony—Mrs. Alan Robson's Debbie's Fashion
Amateur Harness Pony—Debbie Fashion
Hackney Pony—Mrs. Robson's Holiday Debonair
Amateur Hackney Pony—Holiday Debonair
Arabian—Tom F. Ohnemus' Omega Witez
Half-Arabian—Darryl Larson's F. F. Luckett

Equitation Awards
American Horse Show Associations

Dressage—Tracy Lert, Los Altos, Calif.
Hunter Seat—Buddy Brown, South Salem, N. Y.
Saddle Seat—Dana Lyon, Houston, Texas
Stock Seat—Mary Bell, Arcadia, Calif.

National Horse Show

ASPCA Maclay Trophy—Michael Patrick, Canton, Conn.
Good Hands—Dana Lyon, Houston, Texas

ICE SKATING

Speed Skating
World Championships
Men (Deventer, Netherlands, Feb. 17–18)

All-Around—Goran Claeson, Sweden (181.259 pts)
500 Meters—Bill Lanigan, New York (0:42)
1,500 Meters—Sten Stensen, Norway (2:12.70)
5,000 Meters—Goran Claeson (7:47.03)
10,000 Meters—Goran Claeson (15:45.98)

Men, Sprints (Oslo, Norway, Feb. 3–4)

All-Around—Valery Muratov, USSR (161.260 pts)
500 Meters (1st race)—Valery Muratov (0:39.66)
500 Meters (2d race)—Dan Immerfall, West Allis, Wis.
  (0:39.70)
1,000 Meters (1st race)—Jos Valentijn, Netherlands (1:21.80)
1,000 Meters (2d race)—Eppie Bleeker, Netherlands (1:21.11)

Women (Stromsund, Sweden, Feb. 24–25)

All-Around—Atje Keulen-Deelstra, Netherlands (185.949 pts)
500 Meters—Sheila Young, Detroit (0:43.56)
1,000 Meters—Atje Keulen-Deelstra (1:30.41)
1,500 Meters—Galina Stapanskaya, USSR (2:20.88)
3,000 Meters—Sippie Tichelaar, Netherlands (4:50.26)

Women, Sprints (Oslo, Norway, Feb. 3–4)

All-Around—Sheila Young, Detroit (177.515 pts)
500 Meters (1st race)—Sheila Young (0:43.34)
500 Meters (2d race)—Sheila Young (0:43.37)
1,000 Meters (1st race)—Sheila Young (1:30.45)
1,000 Meters (2d race)—Monica Pflug, West Germany (1:29.87)

United States Championships
National Outdoor
(St. Paul, Minn., Jan. 27–28)

Champion—Mike Woods, West Allis, Wis. (22 pts)
⅙-Mile—Bill Heinkel, West Allis, Wis. (0:25.5)
440 Yards—Mike Woods (0:35.2)
880 Yards—Ed Jacquin, St. Louis (1:17.8)
¾-Mile—Mike Woods (2:08.1)
Mile—Mike Woods (3:10.1)

2 Miles—Mike Woods (5:55)
5 Miles—Ed Jacquin (17:18)

Women

All-Around—Nancy Class, St. Paul (16 pts)
⅙-Mile—Nancy Class (0:28.3)
440 Yards—Nancy Class (0:39.7)
880 Yards—Kris Garbe, West Allis, Wis. (1:40.3)
¾-Mile—Kris Garbe (2:43.3)
Mile—Celeste Chlapaty, Skokie, Ill. (3:30.8)

National Indoor
(Hicksville, N. Y., March 10–11)

All-Around—Bill Lanigan, New York (25 pts)
440 Yards—Bill Lanigan (0:38.7)
880 Yards—Bill Lanigan (1:19.4)
¾-Mile—Bill Lanigan (2:02.4)
Mile—Bill Lanigan (2:47)
2 Miles—Bill Lanigan (5:46)

Women

All-Around—Tie between Michele Conroy, St. Paul, and
  Celeste Chlapaty, Skokie, Ill. (13 pts)
440 Yards—Michele Conroy (0:43.3)
880 Yards—Celeste Chlapaty (1:28.9)
¾-Mile—Michele Conroy (no time)
Mile—Celeste Chlapaty (3:06.7)

North American Outdoor
(West Allis, Wis., Feb. 10–11)

Men's All-Around—Jim Chapin, St. Louis
Women's All-Around—Nancy Class, St. Paul

North American Indoor
(Wyandotte, Mich., March 17–18)

Men's All-Around—Benjie Perez, Paramount, Calif.
Women's All-Around—Tie between Celeste Chlapaty, Skokie,
  Ill., and Michele Conroy, St. Paul

JUDO

National AAU Championships
(Atlanta, Ga., April 6–7)

139 Pounds—David Pruzansky, Passaic, N. J.
154 Pounds—Patrick Burris, Anaheim, Calif.
176 Pounds—Bill Sanford, Houston, Texas
205 Pounds—Roy Sukimoto, Los Angeles
Heavyweight—Dean Sedgwick, River Forest, Ill.
Open—Lee Person, Memphis, Tenn.
Grand Champion—Roy Sukimoto

Women's Kata

Nage-No-Kata—Faye Allen, Silver Spring, Md.
Ju-No-Kata—Elizabeth Lee, Los Angeles
Katame-No-Kata—Katen Brockelsby, Deerfield, Ill.
Overall—Frances Glaze and Bonita Hudak, Toledo, Ohio

LACROSSE

National Collegiate A. A. Champion—Maryland (defeated
  Johns Hopkins, 10–9, in overtime final at Franklin Field,
  Philadelphia, June 2); semifinals: Maryland defeated
  Washington and Lee, 18–7; Johns Hopkins defeated Vir-
  ginia, 12–9
National Club—Long Island A. C.
All-Star Collegiate Game—South 14, North 12
Independent College Athletic Conference—Hobart
Junior College—Nassau (N. Y.) Community College
College Division Champions—Central New York; Cortland
  State; *Colonial:* Springfield; *Ivy League:* Brown; *Mid-*

eastern: Maryland; *Midwest:* Denison; *New York Metropolitan:* Hofstra; *Northeastern:* Massachusetts; *Northern New York:* Ithaca; *Rocky Mountain:* Air Force Academy; *South Atlantic:* Washington and Lee; *Wingate Trophy:* Maryland

MOTORBOATING

Unlimited Hydroplane Trophy Winners
Champion Spark Plug Regatta (Miami, May 20)—Pride of Pay 'N Pak; Mickey Remund, driver
President's Cup (Washington, June 3)—Lincoln Thrift, Gene Whipp
Kentucky Governor's Cup (Owensboro, June 17)—Miss Budweiser, Dean Chenoweth
Gar Wood Memorial (Detroit, July 1)—Miss Budweiser
Indiana Governor's Cup (Madison, July 8)—Pride of Pay 'N Pak
Gold Cup (Pasco, Wash., July 22)—Miss Budweiser
Seafair Trophy (Seattle, Aug. 5)—Pride of Pay 'N Pak
Clearwater Cup (Toledo, Ohio, Sept. 2)—Pride of Pay 'N Pak
Spirit of Detroit (Sept. 9)—Miss Budweiser
National Champion—Pride of Pay 'N Pak; Mickey Remund, driver

Distance Races
Griffith Memorial (Miami, May 5, 174 miles)—Art Norris, Miami (Cigarette 36; 3:00:00)
Hennessy Gran Prix (Point Pleasant, N.J., July 18, 181 miles)—Dr. Robert Magoon, Miami (Cigarette 36—Kiekaefer; 2:28:28); *first outboard finisher:* Dick DeWitt, Southgate, Calif. (27 Magnum; 2:11:35); *production class* (113 miles): Thomas Adams, Hallandale, Fla. (27 Magnum); *sports class:* Bob Esposito, Toms River, N.J. (28 Magnum)
Hennessy California Cup (Marina del Rey, Aug. 19, 192 miles)—Art Norris (Cigarette 36; 2:33)
Hennessy Hurricane Classic (St. Petersburg, Fla., Feb. 17, 177.2 miles)—Sandy Satullo, Cleveland (Cigarette 36; 31:35)
Long Beach (Calif.)-Ensenada, Mexico (April 14, 185 miles)—Dr. Robert Magoon, Miami (Cigarette 36-Aeromarine; 3:01)
Miami-Nassau (Oct. 29, 180 miles)—Carlo Bonomi, Italy (Cigarette 38-Aeromarine; 2:39)

Champions
World Offshore—Carlo Bonomi, Italy
National Inboard—Dr. Robert Magoon, Miami
National Outboard—Randy Rabe, St. Petersburg, Fla.
Sam Griffith Memorial Trophy—Carlo Bonomi

PARACHUTING

United States Championships
(Tahlequah, Okla., June 23–July 1)
Men—*Overall:* Chuck Collingwood, U.S. Army (4,035 pts); *accuracy:* John Wolfe, Valdosta, Ga. (0.06); *style:* Chuck Collingwood (7.90)
Women—*Overall:* Gloria Porter, Maple Valley, Wash. (4,868 pts); *accuracy:* Gloria Porter (1.56); *style:* Susan Rademaekers, Oakland, Calif. (9.00)
Team—*10-man:* Jerry Bird's Columbine Turkey Farm, Casa Grande, Ariz. (60); *4-man:* Greene County, Atlanta, Ga. (32.2)

POLO

National Championships
Open (Oak Brook, Ill., Sept. 9)—Oak Brook (Hugo Delmar, Bill Atkinson, Charles Smith, Bobby Beveridge) 9, Willow Bend, Dallas, Texas, 4
20-Goal—Houston 6, Willow Bend 4
16-Goal—Boca Raton 6, Aiken (S.C.) 5
14-Goal—Houston 6, Good Hope, Milwaukee, 5
8-Goal—Maryland 4, Tulsa-Myopia 3
Intercollegiate—Connecticut 19, Virginia 10
Interscholastic—Culver
12-Goal Intercircuit—Chicago-Oak Brook 8, Dallas-Lone Oak 6

International
Coronation Cup (London)—United States 7, England 6

Intracircuit Tourneys
Northwestern 12-Goal—Tulsa Polo and Hunt Club Southern Hills
Central 12-Goal—Wayne
Pacific 8-Goal—Central Valley

RODEO

Rodeo Cowboy Association Champions
All-Around—Larry Mahan, Dallas, Texas (won for sixth time, a record)
Calf Roping—Ernie Taylor, Hugo, Okla.
Bull Riding—Bobby Steiner, Austin, Texas
Saddle Bronco Riding—Bill Smith, Cody, Wyo.
Bareback Bronco Riding—Joe Alexander, Cora, Wyo.

Steer Wrestling—Bob Marshall, San Martin, Calif.
Barrel Racing (women)—Gail Petska, Tecumseh, Okla.
Team Roping—Leo Carrarillo, Donald, Oreg.

ROLLER SKATING

World Championships
(Essen, West Germany, Oct. 16–19)
Men's Singles—Randy Dayney, East Meadow, N.Y.
Women's Singles—Sigrid Mullenbach, West Germany
Pairs—Vicki Handyside and Louis Stoval, Long Beach, Calif.
Dance—Jane Puracchio and James Stephens, Vineland, N.J.

National Championships
Men—*Singles:* Mark Revere, Pontiac, Mich.; *figures:* William Boyd, Seabrook, Md.; *figures international style:* Randy Dayney, East Meadow, N.Y.; *speed:* Danny Butler, Springfield, Mo.
Women—*Singles:* Natalie Dunn, Bakersfield, Calif.; *figures:* Deborah Palm, East Meadow, N.Y.; *figures international style:* Deborah Palm; *speed:* Linda Brooks, Irving, Texas
Pairs—Abe Blass and April Allen Powell, Houston, Texas
Fours—Wayne Melton, Judy Jerue, Richard Toon and Paula Spangle, Garden Grove, Calif.
Dance—*American style:* Joseph and Marie Gaudy, Dover, Del.; *American freestyle:* Kerry Cavazzi and Roseanne Franzone, East Meadow, N.Y.; *international style:* James Stephens and Jane Puracchio, Vineland, N.J.
Men's Relays—*Twos:* Curtis Cook and Steve Torvik, Spokane, Wash.; *fours:* Tom Roycroft, Jim Roycroft, Tom Small, and Tim Small, Hollywood, Fla.
Women's Relays—*Twos:* Marcia Yager and Brenda Haggard, Cincinnati; *fours:* Jan Mitcham, Debbie Davis, Trudy Davis, and Nancy Smith, Dallas, Texas

ROWING

United States Championships
(Camden, N.J., July 14–15)
(Races 2,000 meters unless noted)

Elite Division
Single Sculls—Jim Dietz, New York A.C. (7:08)
Singles, Dash (500 Meters)—Jim Dietz (1:08.2)
Double Sculls—Jim Dietz and Larry Klecatsky, New York A.C. (6:58.9)
Pairs—Jay Forster and Jim Moroney, Vesper B.C., Philadelphia (7:03.6)
Pairs with Coxswain—Walt Updegrove, Mike Staines, and John Gallen, coxswain (7:51.8)
Fours—Vesper B.C. (6:37)
Fours with Coxswain—Vesper B.C. (6:39.3)
Quadruples—New York A.C. (6:47)
Eights—Potomac B.C., Washington (6:24.1)

150-Pound Division
Singles—Larry Klecatsky (7:35.1)
Singles, Dash (500 Meters)—Bill Belden, Undine Barge Club, Philadelphia (1:41.1)
Pairs—John Sonberg and Don Rose, New York A.C. (8:10.5)
Double Sculls—Bill Belden and Fred Duling, Undine B.C. (7:08)
Fours—Mexican National Team (6:44.2)
Fours with Coxswain—Cambridge (Mass.) B.C. (7:14.4)
Quadruples—New York A.C. (6:29.3)
Eights—Cambridge B.C. (6:00.5)

Veteran Division
Double Sculls (1,000 Meters)—Jerry Olrich and Ed Lynch, Cambridge B.C. (3:41.6)

Intermediate Division
Singles—Federico Schleffer, Mexico (7:24.8)
Pairs—Bradford Little and Bob Stevens, Dartmouth R.C. (7:23.7)
Fours with Coxswain—College B.C., Philadelphia (6:47.8)
Eights—Vesper B.C. (6:08.1)

Seniors
Singles—Peter Cortes, Vesper B.C. (7:55)
Pairs—Timothy Wood and Peter Simone, Blood Street Sculls, Olde Lyme, Conn. (7:50)
Fours with Coxswain—Syracuse Chargers (6:43)
Eights—Vesper B.C. (6:38.5)

Intercollegiate Team Champions
IRA Regatta (Lake Onondaga, Syracuse, N.Y., May 31–June 2)—*Varsity:* Wisconsin (6:21); *second varsity:* Wisconsin (6:18.8); *freshmen:* Wisconsin (6:35.1); *varsity pairs:* Dave Brown and Rick Ricci, Trinity (7:55.4); *varsity fours:* UCLA (7:03.6); *freshmen fours:* Brown (7:24.5); *team* (Jim Ten Eyck Trophy): Wisconsin (20 pts)
Dad Vail Trophy (Philadelphia, May 12)—*Varsity:* Massachusetts (6:06.2); *junior varsity:* Marietta (6:09.3); *freshmen:* Marietta (6:00.8)—*Lightweights: varsity:* Marietta (6:11.1); *junior varsity:* Coast Guard Academy (6:27); *freshmen:* Coast Guard Academy (6:13.9); *varsity fours:* Alabama (6:45.2); *varsity pairs:* Jacksonville; *team trophy:* Marietta
Eastern Sprints (Worcester, Mass., May 10–12)—*Heavyweights: varsity:* Northeastern (5:54.6); *second varsity:* Harvard (6:12.6); *freshmen:* Dartmouth (7:22.1); *Rowe Cup:* Harvard (36 pts)—*Lightweights: varsity:* Princeton (6:15.5); *second varsity:* Harvard (7:18.2); *freshmen:* Harvard (7:17.2); *Jope Cup:* Harvard (36 pts)

CAMBRIDGE CREW (foreground) pulls away to a 13-length victory over Oxford in 4¼-mile race on the Thames. Cambridge won event for sixth straight time.

UPI

145-Pound Singles Dash—Bob Kunitz, Wyandotte (Mich.) B. C. (1:34.4)
Junior Doubles—Al Marcoux and André Renart, Quebec (6:54)
155-Pound Eights—Cambridge B. C. (6:17.8)
Team—St. Catharines R. C. (374 pts)

Mid-America Regatta (Marietta, Ohio, May 5)—Varsity: Marietta (5:06.5); junior varsity: Marietta; freshmen: Marietta
Oxford-Cambridge (4¼ miles, April 7)—Cambridge (13 lengths)
Western Sprints (Los Gatos, Calif., May 19)—Varsity: Washington (5:51.4); junior varsity: Washington (5:58); freshmen: Washington (6:05); varsity pairs: Tom Bishop and Jim Coffin, Santa Clara (7:47.6); varsity fours: Washington (6:39.9); freshmen fours: Washington (7:02.5)—Lightweights: eights: UCLA (6:13)
Yale-Harvard (4 miles)—Harvard (19:52.8)
Washington-California—Washington (6:06)
Cups and Trophies—Adams Cup: Harvard beat Navy in postponed race in which Penn could not row because of exams; Bill Cup: Rutgers (5:53); Blackwell Cup: Penn (6:20.3); Callow Cup: Trinity (6:24.6); Carnegie Cup: Cornell (6:18.9); Childs Cup: Penn (6:13.4); Compton Cup: Harvard (6:16); Deering Cup: Columbia (6:27.5); Ewald Cup: Notre Dame (5:50); Goes Trophy (1¾ miles): Navy (8:57); Harborow Cup: Worcester Polytechnic Institute (7:28); Logg Cup: Rutgers (6:31.4); Madeira Cup: Penn (5:50.1); O'Hare Trophy (team): Buffalo State (109 pts); Packard Cup: MIT (6:26); President's (Marist College) Cup: Trinity (5:54.6); Stein Cup: Harvard (6:39.6); Sulger Cup: U. S. Merchant Marine Academy (6:14)

British Henley
(Henley-on-Thames, July 2–7)

Diamond Sculls—Sean Drea, Ireland (7:53)
Silver Goblets (pairs)—Mark Borchelt and Terry Adams, Potomac B. C., Washington (7:42)
Prince Philip Challenge Cup (fours)—Northeastern University (7:13)
Stewards Challenge Cup (fours)—London University (7:03)
Visitors Cup (fours)—First and Third Trinity, Cambridge (7:15)
Wyfold Cup (fours)—Thames Tradesmen, Britain (7:02)
Britannia Challenge Cup (fours)—Isis B. C., Britain (7:19)
Princess Elizabeth Cup (schoolboy eights)—Ridley College School, St. Catharines, Ont. (6:43)
Thames Cup (eights)—Princeton (6:37)
Ladies Plate (eights)—Harvard (6:35)
Grand Challenge Cup (eights)—Trud Kolomna, USSR (6:23)

Canadian Henley
(St. Catharines, Ont., July 26–29)

Single Sculls—Jim Dietz, New York A.C. (7:38.8)
Association Singles—Federico Schleffer, Mexico (7:44.4)
Double Sculls—Jim Dietz and Larry Klecatsky, New York A. C. (7:01)
Pairs with Coxswain—Ken Foote, Walt Jurgins, and John Sullivan, coxswain, Miami R. A. (7:40)
Fours with Coxswain—St. Catharines R. C. (6:46.7)
Eights—Ridley College, St. Catharines, Ont. (5:48.5)
145-Pound Singles—Larry Klecatsky (7:42.2)

SHOOTING

Trapshooting
Grand American Tournament
(Vandalia, Ohio, Aug. 20–25)

Grand American Handicap—Men: Dennis Taylor, Muscoda, Wis. (22½ yds, 99, won shoot-off); women: Jo Ann Nelson, Lone Tree, Iowa (19½ yds, 96); junior: Joseph Loitz, Peotone, Ill. (96, won shoot-off); veterans: C. N. Pierce, Ottumwa, Iowa (22½ yds, won shoot-off); industry: J. H. Muir, White Hall, Pa. (24 yds, 95)
Overall—Men: Larry Gravestock, Amarillo, Texas (958); women: Judy Allison, Elgin, Ill. (903); junior: Leo Harrison 3d, Hannibal, Mo. (932); veterans: Vic Reinders, Waukesha, Wis. (918); industry: Tom Garrigus, Hillsboro, Oreg. (950)
All-Around—Men: Ray Stafford, Denver (390); women: Jane Wall, Orlando, Fla. (371); junior: Joseph Ljutic, Yakima, Wash. (380); veterans: Henry Austin, Champaign, Ill. (375); industry: Tom Garrigus, Hillsboro, Oreg. (386)
Clay Target—Men: John Comly, Lambertville, N. J. (200, won shoot-off); women: Marcella Cook, Winfield, Kans. (195); men's doubles: Veldon Smith, Brownsburg, Ind. (99, won shoot-off); women's doubles: Susan Mattrass, Edmonton, Alberta (91, won shoot-off)

Skeet Shooting
National Skeet Shooting Association Championships
(Savannah, Ga., July 26–Aug. 4)

All-Around—Open: Paul LaPorte, Montreal (547 x 550); women: Karla Roberts, Bridgeton, Mo. (545); junior: Kip Berg, Minneapolis (541); subsenior: John Golla, Fort Lauderdale, Fla. (546); senior: Angel Marchand, San Juan, Puerto Rico (536); veterans: Emery Pappy, Jacksonville, Fla. (539); industry: Jimmy Prall, Little Rock, Ark. (548); military: Cotton Talbot, Virginia Beach, Va. (541); collegiate: Peter Stocks, La Habra, Calif. (545); junior women: Marina Pakis, Hot Springs, Ark. (383 x 400)
Other Individual Champions—.410-gauge: Chris Sumers, El Campo, Texas (100 x 100); women: Karla Roberts (98); junior: John Shima, Oak Park, Ill. (98); senior: J. E. Arnold, Savannah, Ga. (97); veterans: Tom Sanfilipo, Fairfield, Calif. (95); 28-gauge: Wayne Mayes, Attalia, Ala. (100); women: Karla Roberts (99); junior: E. B. Mink 3d, Fort Lauderdale, Fla. (100); veterans: Jack King, Greensboro, N. C. (100); veterans: Emery Pappy (100); 28-gauge: Ron Molenaar, Palos Heights, Ill. (100); women: Joyce Luce, Hebron, Conn. (100); junior: Chip Youngblood, Fort Lauderdale, Fla. (100); senior: Chet Crites, Detroit (100); 12-gauge: Bobbie Lewis, Baxley, Ga. (250 x 250); women: Karla Roberts (249); junior: Bobby Utting, Rush, N. Y. (249); senior: Marchand (247); veterans: Emery Pappy (246)

SKIING

World Cup
Individual—Men: Gustavo Thoeni, Italy (166 pts); leading American: Bob Cochran, Richmond, Vt. (tie for 8th, 93 pts); women: Annemarie Proell, Austria (297 pts); leading American: Marilyn Cochran, Richmond, Vt. (8th, 84 pts)
Team (Nations Cup)—Men: Austria (635 pts); women: Austria (891 pts); combined: Austria (1,526 pts)

United States Championships
Alpine (downhill for women at Boise, Idaho, Feb. 23, and for men at Jackson Hole, Wyo., Feb. 27; slaloms at Mt. Rose, Nev., April 14–15)—Men: Downhill: Bob Cochran, Richmond, Vt. (1:58.68); slalom: Masayoshi Kashiwagi, Japan (1:38.24); giant slalom: Dave Currier, Madison, N. H. (2:05.09)—Women: Downhill: Cindy Nelson, Lutsen, Minn. (1:05.18); slalom: Lindy Cochran, Richmond, Vt. (1:34.60); giant slalom: Debi Handley, Colorado Springs (1:04.08)
Nordic—Jumping (Ishpeming, Mich., Feb. 10): Class A: Jerry Martin, Minneapolis (213 pts); veterans: Don Hurst, Ishpeming, Mich. (143.8 pts); juniors: Scott Clayton, Denver (186.6 pts)—Cross-country (Bloomington, Minn., Jan. 28–Feb. 4)—Men: 15 kilometers: Tim Caldwell, Putney, Vt. (50:21); 30 kilometers: Bob Gray, Putney, Vt. (1:43:58); 50 kilometers: Jod McNulty, Hinsdale, Ill. (2:47:02.1)—Combined: Jumping: Teyck Weed, Etna, N. H.; overall: Teyck Weed (426.9 pts); 40-kilometer relay: East (Tim Caldwell, Mike Gallagher, Jod McNulty, Bob Gray, 2:31:31)—Women: 5 kilometers: Martha Rockwell, Putney, Vt. (18:03); 10 kilometers: Martha Rockwell (37:09); relay: East (Katie Tobey, Mary Heller, Jennifer Caldwell, Martha Rockwell, 1:23:59)

National Collegiate (NCAA) Championships
(Hancock, Vt., March 8–10)

Downhill: Bob Cochran, Vermont (1:46.94); slalom: Peik Christensen, Denver (1:20.30); jumping: Vidar Nilsgard, Colorado (220.7 pts); cross-country: Steiner Hybertsen, Wyoming (53:41); Alpine combined: Peik Christensen; skimeister: Kim Kendall, New Hampshire (336.45 pts); team: Colorado (381.89)

North American Championships
(Thunder Bay, Ontario, Feb. 4–6)

Cross-Country: *15 kilometers:* Tim Caldwell, Putney, Vt. (50:51); *women 5 kilometers:* Shirley Firth, Inuvik, Northwest Territories (18:21); *30-kilometer relay:* United States (Alison Owen, Martha Rockwell, Jana Hlavaty; 55:13)
Jumping (Banff, Alberta, March 24)—Jerry Martin, Minneapolis (213.7 pts)

Canadian-American Trophy Series

Men—*Overall:* Cary Adgate, Bayne City, Mich. (180 pts); *downhill:* Heinz Weizelbaum, West Germany (65); *slalom:* Heinz Weizelbaum (70); *giant slalom:* Cary Adgate (65)
Women—*Overall:* Betsy Clifford, Old Chelsea, Quebec (184 pts); *downhill:* Cindy Nelson, Lutsen, Minn. (60); *slalom:* Betsy Clifford (70); *giant slalom:* Betsy Clifford (70)

SOCCER

United States Championships

Challenge Cup—Maccabi, Los Angeles (defeated Inter Cleveland, 5–3, in final)
Amateur—Inter Philadelphia (defeated San Jose Grenadiers, 3–0, in final)
Junior—St. Elizabeth's, Baltimore (defeated San Diego, 3–2, in final)
North American Soccer League—Philadelphia Atoms (defeated Dallas Tornado, 2–0, in final)

Collegiate Champions

NCAA—*University Division:* St. Louis Univ. (defeated UCLA, 2–1, in sudden-death overtime at Miami, Jan. 4, 1974). In semifinals (Jan. 2) St. Louis defeated Brown, 3–1, and UCLA defeated Clemson, 2–1, in sudden-death overtime. *College Division:* Missouri at St. Louis (defeated California State, Fullerton, 3–1, in final)
NAIA—Quincy (defeated Rockhurst, 3–0, in final)
Junior College—Florissant Valley, St. Louis (defeated Meramac, 2–1, in 7 overtimes in final)

World Cup

(Sixteen survivors of two years of eliminations will begin play in West Germany on June 13, 1974. Games will be played in nine cities with the final in Munich on July 7. The surviving teams and their groups:
Group 1—West Germany, Chile, East Germany, Australia
Group 2—Winner between Spain and Yugoslavia in Feb. 13 match; Brazil, Zaire, Scotland
Group 3—Netherlands, Uruguay, Sweden, Bulgaria
Group 4—Haiti, Italy, Poland, Argentina
Eight top teams will play in second round.)

British Champions

English Association Cup—Sunderland (defeated Leeds, 1–0, in final)
English League Cup—Tottenham (defeated Norwich, 1–0, in final)
Scottish League Cup—Dundee (defeated Glasgow Celtic, 1–0, in final)
Scottish Association Cup—Glasgow Rangers (defeated Glasgow Celtic, 3–2, in final)
English League—*1st Division:* Liverpool; *2d Division:* Burnley; *3d Division:* Bolton; *4th Division:* Southport
Scottish League—*1st Division:* Glasgow Celtic; *2d Division:* Clyde

Other Countries

European Cup—Ajax, Amsterdam (defeated Juventus, Turin, Italy, 1–0, in final)
European Cup Winners Cup—A. C. Milan, Italy (defeated Leeds, England, 1–0, in final)
European Union Cup—Liverpool

SOFTBALL

American Softball Association Champions

Men's Fast Pitch—Clearwater (Fla.) Bombers
Women's Fast Pitch—Stratford (Conn.) Raybestos Brakettes
Men's Open Slow Pitch—Howard Furniture, Denver, N. C.
Women's Slow Pitch—Sweeney Chevrolet, Chattanooga, Tenn.
Industrial Slow Pitch—Pabst International, Springfield, Ohio
16-inch Slow Pitch—Chicago Bobcats
Boys' Slow Pitch—Howard Furniture, Denver, N. C.
Girls' Slow Pitch—Oklahoma City Cobras
Girls' Fast Pitch—Bluff City, Kansas Sunflowers

SQUASH RACQUETS

National Championships

Men

Singles—Vic Niederhoffer, New York
Doubles—Jim Zug, Philadelphia, and Vic Niederhoffer
Veterans Singles—Henri Salaun, Boston
Senior Singles—Floyd Svensson, San Francisco
Senior Doubles—William T. Ketchum and Victor Elmaleh, New York
Team—New York

Women

Singles—Gretchen Spruance, Greenville, Md.
Collegiate Singles—Lee Howard, Radcliffe

Other Championships

Intercollegiate—*Singles:* Peter Briggs, Harvard; *team:* Harvard
North American Open—Sharif Khan, Toronto
International Team—Lapham Cup (singles): Canada 8, United States 7; Grant Cup (doubles): United States 4, Canada 2

SURFING

United States Championships
(Malibu, Calif., Sept. 14–23)

Best Overall—Bob Milfield, Huntington Beach, Calif.
Men—Larry Bertelman, Hawaii
Women—Laura Powers, Western S. A.
Masters—Donald Takayama, Solano Beach, Calif.
Kneeboard—Dale Dobson, San Diego, Calif.
Senior—Rabbit Kekai, Hawaii
Tandem—Steve and Barrie Boehne, Western S. A.
Junior—Jeff Smith, Western S. A.
Boys—Mike Holton, Hawaii
Girls—Linda Davoli, Eastern S. A.

TABLE TENNIS

World Championships
(Sarajevo, Yugoslavia, April 5–15)

Singles—Hsi En-ting, China
Women's Singles—Hu Yu-lan, China
Doubles—Stellan Bengtsson and Kjell Johansson, Sweden
Women's Doubles—Maria Alexandru, Rumania, and Miho Hamada, Japan
Mixed Doubles—Liang Ko-liang and Li Li, China
Jubilee Cup—Bjorne Mellstrom, Sweden
Swathling Cup (men's team)—Sweden
Corbillon Cup (women's team)—South Korea

United States Championships
(Detroit, March 16–18)

Men's Singles—Dal Joon Lee, Parma, Ohio
Women's Singles—Violetta Nesukaitis, Toronto
Men's Doubles—Dell Sweeris, Grand Rapids, Mich., and Alex Tam, Kalamazoo, Mich.
Women's Doubles—Judy Bochenski, Eugene, Oreg., and Patty Cash, San Diego, Calif.
Mixed Doubles—Violetta Nesukaitis and Errol Caetano, Toronto
Men's Senior Singles—Derek Wall, Willowdale, Ontario
Women's Senior Singles—Inez Frazier, Detroit
Senior Doubles—Chuck Burns, Birmingham, Mich., and Sol Schiff, New York
Esquire Singles (over 50)—Max Marinko, Toronto
Junior Singles—Paul Raphel, Los Angeles
Junior Girls' Singles—Judy Bochenski

VOLLEYBALL

United States Volleyball Association Champions

Men's Open—Chuck's Steak House, Santa Monica, Calif.
Women's Open—E Pluribus Unum, Houston, Texas

Other National Champions

YMCA—Columbus, Ohio
YMCA Senior—Balboa Bay, Calif.
NCAA—San Diego State
NAIA—Graceland

WATER SKIING

World Championships
(Bogotá, Colombia, Sept. 13–16)

Men

Overall—George Athans, Kelowna, British Columbia (2,854 pts)
Slalom—George Athans (73 buoys)
Tricks—Wayne Grimditch, Pompano Beach, Fla. (8,980 pts)
Jumping—Ricky McCormick, Independence, Mo. (167 ft)

Women

Overall—Lisa St. John, Fall River Mills, Calif. (2,534 pts)
Slalom—Sylvie Murial, France (60 buoys)
Tricks—Maria Victoria Carrasco, Venezuela (8,140 pts)
Jumping—Liz Allan Shetter, Groveland, Fla. (115 ft)

United States Championships
(Petersburg, Va., Aug. 16–19)

Men's Open

Overall—Wayne Grimditch, Pompano Beach, Fla. (2,935 pts)
Slalom—Kris LaPoint, Castro Valley, Calif. (55 buoys)
Tricks—Tony Krupa, Jackson, Mich. (5,599 pts)
Jumping—Ricky McCormick, Independence, Mo. (161 ft)

Women's Open

Overall—Liz Allan Shetter, Groveland, Fla. (3,701 pts)
Slalom—Liz Shetter (57 buoys)
Tricks—Liz Shetter (4,422 pts)
Jumping—Linda L. Giddens, Eastman, Ga. (118 ft)

Senior Men

Overall—J. D. Morgan, Key West, Fla. (3,598 pts)
Slalom—J. D. Morgan (52 buoys)
Tricks—J. D. Morgan (3,927 buoys)
Jumping—J. D. Morgan (123 ft)

Senior Women

Overall—Thelma Salmas, Novato, Calif. (2,397 pts)
Slalom—Thelma Salmas (38½ buoys)
Tricks—Sandy Monnier, Rock Falls, Ill. (3,267 pts)
Jumping—Thelma Salmas (101 ft)

Masters Tournament
(Callaway Gardens, Ga., July 13–15)

Men
Overall—Mike Suyderhoud, Petaluma, Calif. (2,867 pts)
Slalom—Kris LaPoint, Castro Valley, Calif. (52 buoys)
Tricks—Tony Krupa, Jackson, Mich. (4,920 pts)
Jumping—Ricky McCormick, Independence, Mo. (155 ft)

Women
Overall—Liz Allan Shetter, Groveland, Fla. (3,000 pts)
Slalom—Liz Shetter (55 buoys)
Tricks—Barbara Cleveland, Hawthorne, Fla. (3,590 pts)
Jumping—Liz Shetter (113 ft)

WEIGHT LIFTING

United States Championships
(Williamsburg, Va., June 9–10)

114.5 Pounds—Donald R. Warner, York, Pa. (391¼ pounds, total)
123.5 Pounds—Dwight Tamanaha, Los Angeles (452)
132 Pounds—Roy D. Moore, York, Pa. (518)
148¾ Pounds—Dan Cantore, San Francisco (600¾)
165¼ Pounds—Fred Lowe, York, Pa. (694¼)
181¾ Pounds—Michael Karchut, Chicago (694¼)
198¼ Pounds—Phil Grippaldi, York, Pa. (716¼)
242 Pounds—Bob Bednarski, York, Pa. (749¼)
Super Heavyweight—Jacob Stefan, Los Angeles (776¼)

WRESTLING

National AAU Championships
Freestyle
(Waukegan, Ill., April 26–28)

105.5 Pounds—David Range, Ohio W. C.
114.5 Pounds—Dale Kestel, Michigan W. C.
125.5 Pounds—Don Behm, East Lansing, Mich.
136.5 Pounds—Dave Pruzansky, New York A. C.
149.5 Pounds—Lloyd Keaser, U. S. Marines
163 Pounds—Carl Adams, Ames, Iowa
180.5 Pounds—John Peterson, Wisconsin W. C. (Madison)
198 Pounds—Ben Peterson, Wisconsin W. C. (Madison)
220 Pounds—Russ Hellickson, Wisconsin W. C. (Madison)
Unlimited—Chris Taylor, Ames, Iowa
Team—New York A. C. (79 pts)

Greco-Roman
(Costa Mesa, Calif., June 29–30)

105.5 Pounds—Karoly Kancsar, Nebraska W. C.
114.5 Pounds—Bruce Thompson, Minnesota W. C.
125.5 Pounds—Joe Sade, Oregon W. C.
136.5 Pounds—Gary Alexander, Minnesota W. C.
149.5 Pounds—Phil Frey, Multnomah A. C., Portland, Oreg.
163 Pounds—Mike Jones, Oregon W. C.

JIM CARR of U. S. wrestling team is upended by Arsen Alakhversdiey of USSR in World Cup bouts in Toledo, Ohio. The 114-pound match was won by the Russian.

WIDE WORLD

180.5 Pounds—James Tanniehill, U. S. Army
198 Pounds—Willie Williams, Chicago
220 Pounds—Greg Wojciechowski, Toledo, Ohio
Heavyweight—Mack McCrady, unattached
Outstanding Wrestler—Mike Jones, Albany, Oreg.
Team—Oregon W. C. (53 pts)

National Collegiate (NCAA) Championships
(Seattle, March 8–10)

118 Pounds—Dan Sherman, Iowa
126 Pounds—Mark Massery, Northwestern
134 Pounds—Don Rohn, Clarion State
142 Pounds—Dan Muther, U. S. Navy
150 Pounds—Jarrett Hubbard, Michigan
158 Pounds—Wade Schalles, Clarion State
167 Pounds—Bill Simpson, Clarion State
177 Pounds—Rich Binek, Iowa State
190 Pounds—Greg Strobel, Oregon State
Heavyweight—Chris Taylor, Iowa State
Outstanding Wrestler—Greg Strobel
Team—Iowa State (85 pts)

YACHTING

North American Yacht Racing Union Champions
Men (Mallory Cup)—Dr. John Jennings, St. Petersburg, Fla.
Women (Adams Cup)—Mrs. David Larr, Oyster Bay, N. Y.
O'Day (single-handed)—Jim Hahn, Annapolis, Md.
Junior (Sears Cup)—Glen Brown, Houston, Texas
Interclub (Prince of Wales Trophy)—MIT Nautical Association, Cambridge, Mass.
National Sea Exploring—Mark Rhodes and Warren Hunter, Los Angeles

Ocean and Long-Distance Racing
Annapolis-Newport, R. I. (473 miles, June 16–20)—Equation (Class I), John T. Potter, Oyster Bay, N. Y.; elapsed time: 57.3080 (record); corrected time: 48.2941. Other class winners: Class II: Kate, Robert W. Hubner, Darien, Conn.; Class III: Harpoon, Mark C. Ewing, Trappe, Md.; Class IV: Merrythought, John W. King, Annapolis, Md.; Class V: Lightnin', Ted Turner, Atlanta
Chicago-Mackinac (333 miles)—Bay Bea, Pat Haggerty, Sturgeon Bay, Wis.; 54.7208
Fastnet (England, 605 miles, Aug. 11–16)—Saga, Erling Lorentzen, Brazil; 4:09:11:00 (corrected time)
Marblehead-Halifax (360 miles)—La Forza del Destino, Norman Raben, Mamaroneck, N. Y.; 51:18:24
Miami-Nassau (184 miles)—Cascade, Jerry Milgram, Boston; 16.4932
Newport-Bermuda Multihull (982 miles)—Eclipse, Al Constantino, Greenwich, Conn.; 174.03 hours (elapsed time); 128.78 (corrected time). First to finish: Trumpeter, Philip Weld, Gloucester, Mass.
Newport Harbor (Calif.)-Cebu San Lucas (725 miles)—Moonday, George Wolford (Class B)
Port Huron-Mackinac (260 miles)—Scaramouche, Charles E. Kirsch, Chicago; 38:38:32
San Francisco-San Diego (M. O. R. A., 530 miles)—So Long, Gary Swenson, Anacapa Y. C. (Calif.); 4:23:33:45
St. Petersburg-Isla Mujeres, Mexico (450 miles)—Maraspel IV, Jean Pierre Trouchaud; 53:26:09
St. Petersburg-Fort Lauderdale (404 miles)—Aura, Wally Stenhouse (Class B); 48:3408
Trans-Atlantic (Cape Town–Rio de Janeiro; 3,500 miles)—Stormy (Class I), C. B. Bruynzel, Netherlands; 21 days, 12 hours, 14 minutes, 31 seconds
Trans-Pacific (Los Angeles–Honolulu; 2,225 miles, July 4–15)—Chutzpah (Class D), Stu Cowan, Honolulu; elapsed time: 13 days, 13 hours, 36 minutes, 53 seconds; corrected time: 8:21:21:50. First to finish: Ragtime, Long Beach (Calif.) Y. C. syndicate; time: 10:14:00:40. Other class winners: Class A: Warrior, Al Cassel; Class B: Improbable, D. W. Allen; Class C: Blue Streak, G. L. Myers

Major Trophy Winners
Admiral's Cup (Cowes, England)—West Germany (832 pts)
Miami–Montego Bay, Jamaica (811 miles)—Lightnin' (Class C), Ted Turner, Atlanta; elapsed time: 5:10:47:36; corrected time: 3:14:09:07. Other class winners: Class A: Running Tide, A. G. Van Metre, Annapolis, Md.; Class B: Aura, Wally Stenhouse
American–Australian Cup—St. Francis V, San Francisco (Thomas Blackaller, skipper)
Congressional Cup—Dennis Connor, San Diego (defeated Henry Schofield, Long Beach, Calif., in sail-off)
Everett B. Morris Trophy (outstanding college sailor)—Gary Jobson, State University of New York Maritime College
Kennedy Cup—Bruce Nelson, University of Michigan
Lipton Challenge Cup—America Jane, Newport Harbor (Calif.) Y. C. (Tom Hogan, skipper)
North American Collegiate Championships (Fort Worth, Texas)—Tuthill Trophy (overall team): State of New York Maritime College; Glen Foster Trophy (singlehanded): Gary Jobson, SUNY Maritime College; Morse Trophy (pairs): Tulane; Cornelius Shields Trophy (3-man sloops): SUNY Maritime College
One-Ton Cup—Ydra, owned by Mrs. Marina Spaccarelli, Italy; sailed by Agostino Straulino
U. S. Youth Championships (Wilmette, Ill.)—Singlehanded: Peter Commette, Middletown, N. J.; two-man: Terry Neff and Kevin Gaughan, Oyster Bay, N. Y.
Women's National Collegiate—Massachusetts Institute of Technology (Maria Bozzuto and Shelley Bernstein) Southern Ocean Racing Conference—Munequita, Jack Valley, New Orleans, owner; Click Schreck, skipper (2,233.25 pts)

SRI LANKA (Ceylon)

On May 22, 1973, Sri Lanka observed its first anniversary as a republic. The United Front (UF) government encountered increasing criticism during the year, mainly because of its sponsorship of measures to control the press and its failure to cope with deteriorating economic conditions.

The Economy. The country continued to be plagued by inflation and rising prices, food shortages, low levels of productivity, growing unemployment, heavy burdens for social welfare schemes, a mounting budget deficit, a decline in exports, and an adverse balance of payments. There was also a serious shortage of foreign exchange, about half of which was needed to service the debt, and much of the remainder for food imports. The food shortage was particularly serious. On Oct. 1, 1973, the free rice ration to those below a minimum income level was drastically cut, and later all five university campuses were closed due to food shortages.

In 1973 ceilings were imposed on landholdings, which were limited to no more than 50 acres (about 20 hectares) per person, and on income, limited to about $300 a month. A new compulsory savings scheme was also introduced.

Political Funeral. Nearly a million people turned out for the funeral ceremonies for Dudley Senanayake, a former prime minister and the leader of the opposition United National party, who died on April 12, 1973. This massive outpouring was widely interpreted as a protest against the government. To demonstrate her continued popular support, Mrs. Sirimavo Bandaranaike, the prime minister, organized a huge May Day demonstration.

Press Censorship. A great deal of attention was devoted to two measures which imposed extensive restrictions on freedom of the press. On February 22, the Assembly passed the Press Control Bill, which, on its introduction had been declared unconstitutional by the speaker of the National State As-

SRI LANKA'S Sirimavo Bandaranaike was only woman prime minister at Commonwealth Conference in Ottawa.

sembly and had led to the resignation of a majority of the members of the Constitutional Court. There were no dissenting votes in the Assembly because the opposition members had walked out in protest. The bill provided for a government-appointed council, empowered to punish journalists and publishers for "untrue, distorted, or improper" reports.

On July 19 the Assembly passed a bill authorizing the government to assume majority ownership of the country's largest newspaper group, the Associated Newspapers of Ceylon Ltd. (the so-called "Lake House Group").

Party Shifts. Charging discrimination against the Tamil-speaking minority, the two rival Tamil parties, the Federal Party and the Tamil Congress, banded together in May under the banner of the Tamil United Front. After being expelled from the UF government in September, the Communist party split into pro- and anti-government factions.

International Relations. Following high-level negotiations in February and a state visit to Sri Lanka by India's prime minister, Mrs. Indira Gandhi, on April 27–29, Sri Lanka and India agreed to expand their areas of economic cooperation and to speed the implementation of the Sirimavo-Shastri pact of 1964, which called for repatriation to India of persons of Indian origin in Sri Lanka who had opted for Indian citizenship. The 1973 agreement called for the resolution of the status of 150,000 persons not provided for in the 1964 pact.

Mrs. Bankaranaike participated in the conference of Commonwealth heads of government in Ottawa, Canada (August 2–10) and in the fourth conference of nonaligned nations in Algeria (September 5–9).

NORMAN D. PALMER
University of Pennsylvania

─── **SRI LANKA (Ceylon) • Information Highlights** ───

Official Name: Republic of Sri Lanka.
Location: Island in the Indian Ocean off the southeastern coast of India.
Area: 25,332 square miles (65,610 sq km).
Population (1973 est.): 13,500,000. *Density,* 505 per square mile (195 per sq km).
Chief Cities (1971 census): Colombo, the capital, 563,705.
Government: *Head of state,* William Gopallawa, president (took office May 1972). *Head of government,* Mrs. Sirimavo Bandaranaike, prime minister (took office May 1970); *Legislature* (unicameral)—National Assembly. *Major political parties*—Sri Lanka Freedom party; Lanka Sama Samaja; Tamil United Front; United National party; Communist party.
Languages: Sinhalese (official), Tamil (semiofficial), English.
Education: *Expenditure* (1967), 4.4% of gross national product. *School enrollment* (1969)—primary, 2,298,200; secondary, 355,665; technical/vocational, 7,565; university/higher, 14,400.
Monetary Unit: Rupee (6.218 rupees equal U. S.$1, Aug. 1973).
Gross National Product (1972 est.): $2,200,000,000.
Economic Indexes: *Industrial production* (1966), 115 (1963 = 100); *agricultural production* (1971), 112 (1963 = 100); *consumer price index* (1972), 139 (1963 = 100).
Manufacturing (major products): Milled rice, chemicals, cement, petroleum products, paper and paperboard, tires and tubes.
Major Agricultural Products: Tea (ranks 2d among world producers, 1972), rubber, rice, coconuts.
Major Minerals: Graphite, ilmenite, precious and semiprecious stones, salt.
Foreign Trade (1972): Exports, $315,000,000. Imports, $342,-000,000. *Chief trading partners* (1970)—United Kingdom (took 23% of exports, supplied 14% of imports); China (13%—13%); United States (7%—6%).
Tourism: Receipts (1971), $3,410,000.
Transportation: *Motor vehicles* (1971), 124,400 (automobiles, 88,300); *railroads* (1971), 992 miles (1,596 km); *major national airline,* Air Ceylon.
Communications: *Telephones* (1972), 64,338; *newspapers* (1970), 17 (daily circulation, 612,000).

To help conserve gasoline during the energy crisis, many states reduced highway speed limits. On the Pennsylvania Turnpike a ticket collector waves a homemade sign to remind a motorist of the new maximum speed.

UPI

state government

A healthy fiscal year and increased interest in governmental ethics, taxes, the energy crisis, and environmental problems were major issues for state governments in 1973.

Taxes. A healthy fiscal 1973 enabled many states to lighten the taxpayer's burdens. Most states had surpluses in 1973, the largest being California's $827 million. State tax yields exceeded $66 billion in 1973, and federal revenue sharing provided $1.7 billion. Washington voters chose to remain one of the four states without an income tax by rejecting such a proposal tied to school finance reform.

Income tax breaks were adopted in 11 states, including New York, which suspended its 2.5% surcharge. Only Delaware increased its personal income tax. Corporate income taxes were raised in Delaware, Indiana, Maine, and Montana.

Property tax relief was provided by more than half of the states. By mid-1973 every state had some form of property tax relief for elderly homeowners, with five states initiating such relief in 1973 and 20 others improving their relief programs. Revolutionary property tax relief was enacted in Michigan, Oregon, and Vermont, where all homeowners were given relief geared to their income levels. Homeowner relief was also provided by eight other states. Personal property tax was lowered in four states. State aid to schools was expected to reduce property taxes in Kansas, Maine, and North Dakota. School levies were limited in Idaho and Wyoming and eliminated in Utah. Connecticut cut its sales tax, the highest in the nation, from 7% to 6.5%, but the sales tax was increased in Indiana from 2% to 4% to allow for property tax relief.

Government. While Watergate shook the nation (see feature article beginning on page 14), over 15 state legislatures enacted governmental ethics measures. Disclosure of financial interests that might conflict with governmental duties was required of public officials by 1973 laws in Alabama, California, Maryland, Michigan, Montana, Ohio, and Wisconsin.

Reporting of campaign finances was required in California, Florida, Hawaii, Iowa, Nebraska, New Jersey, and Texas, and campaign spending was limited by Hawaii, Nevada, Utah, and Wyoming. Lobbyists were regulated by Alabama, Maine, Oregon, and Texas.

Ethics codes for employees of state executive branch offices were mandated by the governors of Illinois, Michigan, and Missouri. The right of citizens to have access to governmental meetings was guaranteed by 1973 laws in Missouri, Minnesota, Oregon, and Vermont, leaving only five states without such laws. Legislative committees were opened to public scrutiny in California, Connecticut, North Dakota, Texas, and Vermont.

The right of news reporters to refuse to reveal their sources is assured in 25 states, with action taken in 1973 by California, Indiana, Minnesota, Nebraska, New Mexico, and Oregon.

Reapportionment was conducted by only about 10 state legislatures in 1973, and action was expected by eight others in 1974. Most states had already reapportioned when the U. S. Supreme Court in the Virginia case of *Mahan* v. *Howell* declared that state legislative districts need not meet the strict equality-of-population test required of congressional districts.

Major governmental reorganization was completed in South Dakota, with 160 agencies consolidated into 16 departments. Executive agencies were established or reorganized in at least 18 other states and legislative changes instituted in 16 states.

Top state officials were granted pay raises in 16 states. Legislative compensation was raised in 13 states, and judicial pay raises were provided in 11 states. An initiative measure approved by Washington state voters substituted 5.5% pay raises for top state officials for substantial raises in a 1973 law. In 14 states public employees' salaries were raised, mostly within the 5.5% federal guidelines. The federal Cost of Living Council allowed top Georgia officials to receive only two thirds of their pay raises and reduced raises for 150,000 California state workers from an average 11.3% to 7% maximum.

Education. The threat that states might be required to change their school financing systems was defused when the Supreme Court ruled in *San Antonio* v. *Rodriguez* that Texas' reliance on local property taxes for school finance was constitutional. However, state-by-state court battles on state constitutional grounds seem likely, as New Jersey's system was voided by its supreme court and Idaho's by a district court, but Illinois' was upheld.

State aid to education was increased in most states. North Carolina voters approved $300 million in state school bonds. New or higher funding was provided for kindergartens in nine states and for educating the handicapped in eight states. In New Jersey, for example, voters authorized $25 million for facilities for the handicapped. In at least eight states attempts were made to equalize educational opportunities by providing more aid for poorer districts.

Several states continued to aid private, church-related schools despite a 1973 U. S. Supreme Court decision voiding earlier Pennsylvania and New York laws that aided parents of such pupils. Students attending private colleges were provided state scholarships in six more states.

Consumers. Consumer interest remained high, and by the end of 1973 every state reported having some agency to handle consumer problems. Eight more states enacted no-fault auto insurance, joining 11 others with such laws. Consumers were given the option to buy no-fault auto insurance in two other states. (See also INSURANCE.)

Consumers may cancel door-to-door sales within three days in eight more states, and installment sales were regulated in six more states. Public posting of prescription drug prices was mandated in four states and allowed in three others. "Little FTC" (Federal Trade Commission) laws prohibiting unfair trade practices were passed in eight states. Land sales were regulated in seven states. Tenants were assured rights in seven states and mobile-home owners protected in six states.

Labor. Workmen's compensation laws were improved, with 28 states increasing the maximum disability benefits. At least $3.3 billion in benefits will be paid out in 1973. State minimum wages were increased in seven states.

Abortion Laws. Abortion laws, many more than 100 years old, were voided in many states following the U. S. Supreme Court's decision of January 1973 legalizing abortion. New laws generally in line with the court were enacted in 11 states. However, in defiance of the court, Rhode Island and North Dakota forbade any abortion not necessary to save a woman's life. Three states require that every effort be made to save a viable fetus. Fourteen states called on Congress to propose a constitutional amendment to allow states to regulate abortions. Conscience laws allowing medical personnel to refuse to participate in abortions were passed in 18 states.

Crime. Capital punishment was reinstituted by 19 states in 1973, bringing the total to 21 since the U. S. Supreme Court voided most such laws in 1972. Hard-drug pushers face mandatory life sentences in New York and 30-year terms in Delaware. In Oregon, however, the sentence for marihuana use was reduced, and users may now be punished only by a $100 fine. Gun laws were controversial in many states, and in Illinois cheap handguns, known as "Saturday night specials," were outlawed. Innocent victims of violent crimes may receive state compensation in 11 states with the addition of Illinois and Washington in 1973.

Obscenity cases were newsworthy in several states. Even though the U. S. Supreme Court allowed greater state and local control over obscenity, lower courts voided several state laws because they were not specific enough. New obscenity laws were passed in Florida, Idaho, New Mexico, and Utah.

Environment. In 34 states laws were passed to fight water pollution. Among the large bond issues approved for sewer systems were $210 million in New York, $101 million in New Jersey, and $30 million in Minnesota. Air pollution controls were made more stringent in at least 15 states. Garbage disposal and recycling were the object of new laws in over 16 states, and Connecticut authorized spending $250 million to convert most of the garbage in the state to fuel and reusable material by 1985.

Land policies were also changed. Statewide land-use policies were set by Oregon, Colorado, and Vermont. Coastlines and wetlands were protected by new laws in at least seven states. State take-over or preservation of natural or historic lands was authorized in four more states, and parks and open space areas were financed in five states.

Energy. Many states extended their control over energy-related industries. Power plant locations were regulated by six more states and strip mining by four more states. Those responsible for oil spills were made liable for damages in New York and North Carolina, and a similar 1970 Florida law was upheld by the U. S. Supreme Court. Connecticut regulated petroleum product prices for consumers, and antitrust suits were filed against major oil companies by Connecticut, Florida, and New York. Special energy-crisis powers were granted to governors in Delaware, Maryland, and Washington by their legislatures.

Social Laws. The U. S. constitutional amendment for equal rights for women was ratified by eight more states, bringing to 30 the number of states that have ratified, although Nebraska tried to rescind its approval. Women were guaranteed equal job and credit rights as men by at least 15 states. No-fault divorce laws were enacted by 8 more states.

Legal adulthood was lowered to 18 years by 11 more states, for a total of 41, and lowered to 19 by one other state, making three states that have 19 as the legal age.

State lotteries were approved by voters in Maine, Ohio, and Rhode Island and by law in Illinois, bringing the total of states with lotteries to 11.

ELAINE S. KNAPP, *Editor, "State Government News"*

STEEL

A surging worldwide demand for steel strained available supplies across the globe in 1973 even though many production records were broken.

The International Iron and Steel Institute estimated world raw steel production in 1973 at a record 750 million net tons, an increase of about 9% over the 1972 figure of 691 million net tons. This amounts to a threefold increase since 1953. The American Iron and Steel Institute estimated raw steel production in the United States at 150 million net tons, a 12% increase over 1972.

World Developments. In all countries the growing demand for steel tested the limits of the industry's productive capacity. The United States, because of idle capacity, was able in 1973 to regain its position as world leader in raw steel production, replacing the USSR, leader in 1971 and 1972.

The USSR continued its 5-year plan aiming at a 5% average increase in capacity each year through 1975. Use of continuous-casting machines increased, and the USSR led the world with about 80 machines.

Steel production in the European Coal and Steel Community (ECSC) increased 8% during 1973. Although the mills operated at near capacity rates, steel's poor profit picture held up plans for expansion by the German steel industry and limited that of other European countries.

The Japanese steel industry continued to grow at a record rate, with an increase in raw steel production of 25% in 1973. Nine of the world's ten largest blast furnaces are in Japan.

U. S. Developments. The increase in steel mill shipments in 1973 from 92 to 110 million net tons was nearly 10% more than the increase in production in the United States. Inventories of steel mill products decreased markedly, reflecting both the current demand and confidence that the steel industry would not have a work stoppage. Many products such as galvanized sheets were in short supply, due in part to the diversion of steel capacity to more profitable items.

The tonnage of steel imported into the United States during the first five months of 1973 increased 11.3% over that of the same period in 1972. However, the worldwide demand for steel reversed this trend in later months, resulting in a decrease of 6.7% by the end of September.

New Technology. Recent government regulations to control both air and water quality have encouraged new technology in this field. National Steel Corporation has built new coke plants at Weirton, W. Va., and Granite City, Ill., using new concepts of charging and quenching coke. Inland Steel Company has installed pipeline charging on a new coke battery in East Chicago, Ind., and Bethlehem Steel has developed a new method of removing sulfur from coke oven gases.

The trend from open hearth melting furnaces to basic oxygen and electric furnaces has been accelerated as much by the need for improved control of emissions as by the improved production rates. In 1973 over 55% of the total steel produced was made by the basic oxygen process and 27% by the open hearth process, as compared with 37% and 50%, respectively, five years previous. In the steel finishing area, pickling (descaling) facilities are being converted from sulfuric to hydrochloric acid to facilitate recycling and to reduce the discharge of spent acids.

HOWARD C. LACY
American Iron and Steel Institute

PRODUCTION OF IRON ORE, PIG IRON AND FERROALLOYS, AND RAW STEEL

Country	1972 Iron ore, concentrates and agglomerates (long tons of 2,240 lb)	1972 Pig iron and ferroalloys (short tons of 2,000 lb)	1972 Raw steel[1] (short tons of 2,000 lb)	Country	1972 Iron ore, concentrates and agglomerates (long tons of 2,240 lb)	1972 Pig iron and ferroalloys (short tons of 2,000 lb)	1972 Raw steel[1] (short tons of 2,000 lb)
Algeria	2,707,000	...	...	Luxembourg	4,001,000	5,148,000	...[3]
Angola	5,905,000			Malaysia	522,000	...	
Argentina	246,000	915,000	2,294,000	Mauritania	8,759,000		
Australia	62,497,000	6,669,000	7,496,000	Mexico	5,266,000	2,094,000	4,813,000
Austria	4,084,000	3,138,000	4,485,000	Morocco	394,000		
Belgium	118,000	13,111,000	22,029,000[2]	Netherlands	...	4,661,000	6,139,000
Brazil	32,479,000	5,732,000	7,240,000	New Caledonia	177,000		
Bulgaria	3,189,000	1,675,000	2,425,000	New Zealand	59,000	...	75,000
Burma	2,000			Norway	3,917,000	1,378,000	977,000
Canada	37,400,000	9,615,000	13,073,000	Pakistan	6,000		150,000
Chile	11,318,000	529,000	709,000	Peru	9,842,000	165,000	219,000
China, Mainland	44,289,000	23,148,000	25,353,000	Philippines	2,067,000	...	95,000
China, Nationalist	...	94,000	335,000	Poland	1,968,000	8,190,000	14,771,000
Colombia	591,000	276,000	401,000	Portugal	49,000	386,000	403,000
Cuba		...	60,000	Rhodesia	492,000	276,000	165,000
Czechoslovakia	1,594,000	9,182,000	14,109,000	Rumania	3,543,000	5,071,000	7,937,000
Denmark	15,000	224,000	557,000	Sierra Leone	2,451,000		
Egypt	467,000	551,000	300,000	South Africa	9,941,000	4,883,000	5,842,000
Finland	871,000	1,235,000	1,599,000	Spain	6,791,000	6,493,000	10,472,000
France	54,250,000	20,946,000	26,554,000	Sudan	20,000	...	
Germany, East	295,000	2,370,000	6,283,000	Swaziland	3,149,000		
Germany, West	6,020,000	35,277,000	48,176,000	Sweden	32,601,000	2,596,000	5,769,000
Greece	1,309,000	...	550,000	Switzerland		17,000	600,000
Hong Kong	162,000			Thailand	34,000	11,000	...
Hungary	689,000	2,271,000	3,527,000	Tunisia	886,000	...	
India	33,611,000	7,792,000	7,275,000	Turkey	2,116,000	1,246,000	1,604,000
Iran	2,000			USSR	204,716,000	101,853,000	138,890,000
Ireland			80,000	United Kingdom	8,553,000	16,975,000	27,888,000
Israel		...	100,000	United States	75,284,000	91,338,000	133,241,000[4]
Italy	827,000	10,407,000	21,734,000	Venezuela	16,732,000	573,000	1,230,000
Japan	1,378,000	81,216,000	106,813,000	Vietnam, North	...		5,000
Korea, North	7,874,000	2,646,000	2,205,000	Yugoslavia	3,435,000	1,940,000	2,756,000
Korea, South	413,000	28,000	521,000	Other countries	...	...	737,000
Lebanon		...	20,000				
Liberia	24,408,000	...	...	Total (estimate)[5]	746,781,000	454,541,000	691,081,000

[1] Steel in the first solid state after melting, suitable for further processing or sale. [2] Figures include data from Luxembourg. [3] Included under Belgium. [4] United States data exclude 1,610,000 net tons of steel produced by foundries that reported their output to the Bureau of Census but did not report to American Iron and Steel Institute. [5] Detail does not necessarily add to total because figures were rounded. (Sources: Statistical Quarterly Report for Iron and Steel Industry, West Germany Iron and Steel Federation, Düsseldorf; American Iron and Steel Institute, New York.)

STOCKS AND BONDS

The stock market suffered a sharp setback in 1973 as the list staggered under a large and perplexing array of problems. This was the sixth major decline in the past two decades. The year started with a spurt to a new high for both the Dow Jones industrials and the broader-based Standard & Poor's 500-stock index. But the salutary impact of the Vietnam peace agreement quickly wore off, and stock prices headed downward. Although the decline was punctuated by occasional and sometimes brisk rallies, the bear market atmosphere prevailed to the end of the year, when the list appeared to have found a footing slightly above its early-December low. For the year, Dow Jones industrials suffered a 16.6% loss; Standard & Poor's 500 plunged 17.4%.

The bond market did not escape the downdraft. While bond prices were reasonably good at the start of 1973, they began to erode as the year wore on, reaching a low in early August. A firming tone subsequently appeared, but bonds ended the year at levels only modestly above their earlier lows.

Wall Street was faced with a host of crucial questions—among them, increasing inflation, a devaluation of the dollar, soaring interest rates, the unfolding in the Nixon administration of a string of scandals known as Watergate, the worldwide energy crisis, and finally, mounting pessimism over the Nixon administration's ability to deal with these issues. In times of uncertainty, investors have tended historically either to sell or to stay on the sidelines. They did both in 1973.

Stock Prices. In early January the market moved ahead strongly in an extension of the rally that began in October 1972. Hopes were high. The Vietnam War was ending, and most of the investment community believed that the administration, drawing support from its sweeping victory in the 1972 presidential election, would lead the country into a new era of prosperity. The announcement of Phase 3 of the economic controls program, which dropped mandatory restraints for most industries, sparked a sharp gain for the market to a new high on January 11. Thereafter, stock prices began to give ground as uncertainties over the efficacy of reliance on voluntary compliance came to the fore. Even the signing of the Vietnam peace agreement in late January provided only a brief interruption to the decline.

Concern over inflation, rising interest rates, and the Federal Reserve's tighter monetary stance resulted in a deterioration of confidence in the dollar and brought U. S. securities markets under further pressure. The weakness of the dollar in international currency markets reached crisis proportions and culminated in a 10% devaluation in mid-February—only 14 months after a devaluation under the Smithsonian Agreement of December 1971. Even then, monetary jitters continued. And this uncertainty, together with other economic concerns, kept the stocks list off balance until mid-July.

Despite sporadic rally attempts, there was little news to sustain the bulls. Morale was seriously damaged by such events as the Equity Funding bankruptcy and fraud affair, reports that a large number of brokerage firms were under close surveillance for potential capital problems, the Watergate scandal and the administration's preoccupation with it, and the June 13 price freeze, which was a tacit admission that Phase 3 had not worked.

STOCKS AND BONDS
(Standard & Poor's Indexes)

	Date[1]	425 Industrials	15 Rails	60 Utilities	500 Stocks
1972 high	Dec. 11	132.95	48.31	61.20	119.12
1972 low	Jan. 3	112.19	40.40	52.95	101.67
1973 high	Jan. 11	134.54	45.80	61.57	120.24
1973 low	Dec. 5	103.37	32.50	43.91	92.16
1973 close	Dec. 31	109.14	45.80	46.91	97.55

[1] Dates are for industrials. Rail and utility highs and lows in some instances occurred on other dates.

MOST ACTIVE STOCKS IN 1973—
NEW YORK STOCK EXCHANGE

Stock	Sales	Close	Net Change
American Tel. & Tel.	30,446,100	50⅛	− 2⅝
Gulf Oil	28,980,600	23⅝	− 3⅜
International Tel. & Tel.	27,772,700	26⅜	−33⅞
General Motors	24,577,300	46⅛	−35
Federal National Mortgage Assoc.	24,283,600	16¾	− 3¼
Texaco	23,729,800	29⅜	− 8⅛
Chrysler Corp.	22,175,200	15⅝	−25⅜
American Tel. & Tel. wts.	20,866,100	4¼	− 4⅞
Eastern Airlines	19,670,500	5¼	−17⅜
Exxon Corp.	18,721,000	94⅛	+ 6⅝
American Airlines	18,679,400	8⅝	−16½
Levitz Furniture	18,548,900	3⅝	−23¼
Kresge (S. S.)	18,475,800	32¾	−16⅛
RCA	18,386,200	18½	−20¾
General Electric	18,353,800	63	− 9⅞

MOST ACTIVE STOCKS IN 1973—
AMERICAN STOCK EXCHANGE

Stock	Sales	Close	Net Change
Champion Homes	15,092,600	3¼	−10¾
McCulloch Oil	12,137,600	5⅛	−10⅞
Syntex Corp.	11,756,600	114⅞	+32½
Bowmar Instrument	8,419,700	21⅞	+ ⅜
Imperial Oil	6,875,900	40¼	− 9
Buttes Gas & Oil	6,686,000	30⅝	+ 3⅝
Rapid-American Corp. wts.	5,628,500	3¾	− 1½
Loew's Corp. wts.	5,209,500	5¼	−12⅞
Coit International	5,138,700	2¼	−17⅝
Great Basin Petroleum	5,019,000	3⅛	− ⅛
Texas International	4,615,500	11⅜	+ 5⅛
Banister Continental	4,399,900	17¾	−17⅜
Kaiser Industries	3,994,200	7¼	+ 1¼
Asamera Oil	3,971,400	14¼	+ 1⅛
Warner Communications Pfd. C	3,454,500	2⅝	− 9¾

The list perked up a bit toward fall, reflecting hope that the reimposition of economic restraints under Phase 4 would be the last step before a complete termination of controls. Then came the cyclone. The Middle East war, the Arab oil embargo, and the deepening worldwide energy crisis prompted a devastating six-week drop in stock prices, from near the end of October to early December. In such an atmosphere of doubt and uncertainty, the market became highly sensitive to day-to-day developments in the Middle East. Thus signs of progress toward a possible relaxation of the Arab oil embargo prompted some modest firming at year-end.

Earnings and Dividends. For most companies a substantial earnings improvement occurred in 1973. In terms of Standard & Poor's industrial stock price index, net income (partly estimated) surged 25% to $8.53 a share, from $6.80 in 1972. Dividends, which also moved higher, were equal to $3.48 a share on Standard & Poor's 425-stock index, as against $3.22 in 1972. Standard & Poor's stocks sold at an average price of 12.8 times earnings and had an average return of 3.2%, compared with a 1972 multiple of 19.4 and a yield of 2.4%.

Volume. Total stock trading on the New York Stock Exchange in 1973 slipped a bit from the peak 1972 level. But the total was the second-highest on record, with 4.053 billion shares traded in 1973, compared with 4.138 billion in 1972. American Stock Exchange volume dropped to 759.7 million shares, from 1972's 1.118 billion.

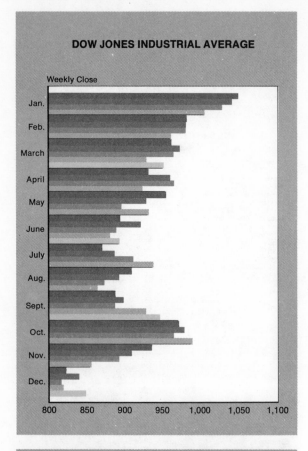

DOW JONES INDUSTRIAL AVERAGE

Weekly Close

Jan. • Feb. • March • April • May • June • July • Aug. • Sept. • Oct. • Nov. • Dec.

800   850   900   950   1,000   1,050   1,100

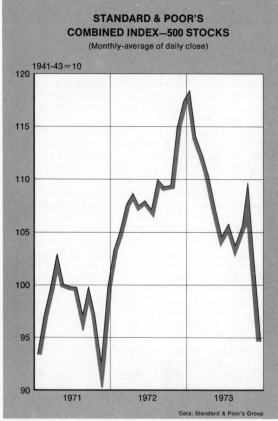

**STANDARD & POOR'S
COMBINED INDEX—500 STOCKS**

(Monthly-average of daily close)

1941-43=10

120 • 115 • 110 • 105 • 100 • 95 • 90

1971   1972   1973

Data: Standard & Poor's Group

Mutual Funds. Mutual fund assets slipped sharply in 1973, according to data released by the Investment Company Institute, the industry's national association. At year-end, fund assets were $46.5 billion, compared with $59.8 billion in December 1972. In every month but July, the funds also continued to experience net redemptions (cashing in by investors of larger dollar amounts of fund shares than they bought). For the second year in a row, the funds closed in a minus stance. For 1973, gross sales totaled $4.36 billion, compared with $4.89 billion in 1972, while gross redemptions were $5.65 billion, compared with $6.56 billion, yielding net cash-ins of $1.29 billion, against 1972's net redemptions of $1.67 billion.

Bond Funds and Bond Prices. The closed-end bond fund became an increasingly popular investment vehicle in 1973. These funds typically have current income as their primary investment goal and are generally sponsored by banks or insurance companies. In the years 1972 and 1973, closed-end bond funds attracted some $3 billion, and the New York Stock Exchange listed 23 such funds at the end of 1973.

The bond market fell prey to many of the pressures that affected stock prices in 1973, with the result that bond prices sagged and yields rose. Yields on highest-grade industrials, which were at a low of 7.01% on January 3, reached a high of 7.83% on August 8 before closing out the year at 7.50%. Coincidentally, the low and the high for short-term taxable government yields were recorded on the same days as the low and the high for industrials. The low for short-term government yields was 6.10%; the high, 8.20%; and the year-end reading, 6.78%.

Both corporate and municipal bond offerings were at a reduced level in 1973, with the corporate sector showing a substantial decline. Public offerings of corporate bonds, including convertible issues, dropped to around $13.5 billion in 1973, from $18.4 billion in 1972. The lower level of corporate financing by bonds was due to a trend toward use of short-term financing, increased liquidity (because of dividend restrictions through part of the year under economic controls), and high interest rates. Municipal offerings dipped slightly to $22.7 billion, from $22.9 billion in 1972. One reason for the lower volume here was the use of federal revenue-sharing funds for capital improvements.

CAROLYN J. COLE, *Standard & Poor's Corporation*

SUDAN

In 1973, President Jaafar al-Numeiry again dominated the Sudanese political scene. Consolidating the peace that he had restored to the Sudan in 1972 after 17 years of civil war between the Muslim North and non-Muslim South, he took a number of steps in 1973 to develop a viable economy for all.

Political Affairs. In January, the president had 12 military men arrested for plotting his assassination. Apart from this, no other attempts against the government were announced during the year. After winning approval of a permanent constitution for the Sudan in May, Numeiry dismissed his cabinet and formed a new one. When he faced strong popular reaction against price increases later in the same month, Numeiry resigned as president but returned when the people demonstrated in his support—just as Egypt's and Libya's leaders had in the past.

The new constitution recognizes only the Sudanese Socialist Union (SSU), which Numeiry has sought to build into a popular force. In the past, Numeiry had been able to rally many Sudanese to his side, including right-wing university students under the influence of the Ikhwan (Muslim Brotherhood) when he led the struggle against communism in the Sudan in 1971. But his popular support did not prevent student riots and a railroad workers' strike that began on September 6. Numeiry declared a state of emergency, and blamed his troubles on the Communists.

North-South Relations. Numeiry has personally played a large role in the cordial relations between the North and South since peace was restored in 1972. But credit for the South's cordiality is also due to the leadership of President Abdel-Alier of South Sudan (the new constitution provides for self-rule by the southern region under a president) and Gen. Joseph Lagu, leader of the Anyana rebels.

Southern President Alier is also vice president of the whole of the Sudan, and 7 of the 21 members of the SSU's Politbureau are Southerners. Incorporation of the Southern guerrillas, including officers, into the Sudanese army has been accomplished with surprising ease. General Lagu enjoys the same rank in the Sudanese Army as General Numeiry.

But regional autonomy is also a reality. Government in the South is controlled essentially by Southerners, and English is gradually replacing Arabic as the principal language in schools and offices in the South. They regard Northern aid and assistance as grudging and always inadequate.

Foreign Affairs. When peace was restored in the Sudan, Numeiry suspended plans to unite with Libya, Egypt, and Syria. Relations with them deteriorated further when the Sudan reestablished relations with the United States, even though Numeiry's policy has been, for the most part, a policy of economic and political nonalignment. He accepts aid from both Communist and capitalist states. During 1973, he sought to improve relations with

the Arab states, agreeing, among other things, to return Sudanese forces to the Suez Canal where they became involved in the fourth Arab-Israeli war in October 1973.

In March, Black September terrorists killed one Belgian and two American diplomats in Khartoum. Numeiry charged the terrorists with murder and suspended all Palestinian liberation activities in the Sudan. But Numeiry later moderated his position, and it is expected that he will eventually commute any sentence that the court might mete out, if it tries the terrorists at all.

WILLARD A. BELING
University of Southern California

SUHARTO. See BIOGRAPHY.
SUPREME COURT. See LAW.
SURGERY. See MEDICINE.

SWEDEN

Major concerns in Sweden in 1973 included elections in September, the death of Gustaf VI Adolf and the succession of Carl XVI Gustaf, and economic problems and efforts to check inflation.

Elections. Results of the September 16 election were somewhat surprising. The Liberals (Folkpartiet) lost 24 seats in the Riksdag (parliament), while the Moderates gained 10 seats and the Center 19 seats, both of the latter parties' votes exceeding expectations. The vote deadlocked the bourgeois and socialist parties at 175 each and caused a parliamentary dilemma. The Social Democrats continued in power, but they could not depend on support from the Communists, who also gained in the election. The Social Democrats will have to frame a broad program to assure bourgeois support. Although the election's shift of five mandates was too few to warrant a judgment, the vote did indicate dissatisfaction with the Liberal party and to some extent displeasure with inflation, the economy, and the Social Democrats.

Death of King and Succession. On September 15, 90-year-old Gustaf VI Adolf died of severe complications following surgery in August. His 27-year-old grandson succeeded as Carl XVI Gustaf in formal ceremonies on September 19. At the funeral of Gustaf VI on September 25, the Swedish people's sincere feeling of loss was displayed by the thousands who watched his cortege wend its way from Hälsingborg to Stockholm and from the castle to the grave at Haga. Constitutional changes approved by the Riksdag in the spring will take the few remnants of power from the new king, and Carl XVI Gustaf will be but a figurehead.

Swedish-American Relations. In January, Prime Minister Olof Palme displayed the Social Democrats' antagonism to U.S. policy in Vietnam and the bombing of Hanoi, referring to villages brutally bombed in World War II as parallels. Even though he understood American reactions, his government appointed a new ambassador to the United States, who was promptly denied acceptance. In addition, the American chargé d'affaires in Stockholm was withdrawn because of Palme's unfriendly actions.

Sweden's Relations with Other Countries. Sweden and Denmark agreed on the construction of a bridge-tunnel connection across the Öresund. Sweden signed treaties for trade and commercial relations with East Germany and with the People's Republic of China, which Foreign Minister Krister

---

SUDAN • Information Highlights

Official Name: Democratic Republic of the Sudan.
Location: Northeast Africa.
Area: 967,497 square miles (2,505,813 sq km).
Population (1973 est.): 17,400,000. *Density,* 16 per square mile (6 per sq km).
Chief Cities (1970 est.): Khartoum, the capital, 261,840; Omdurman, 258,532.
Government: *Head of state,* Gen. Jaafar Mohammed al-Numeiry, president (took office Oct. 1971). *Head of government,* Gen. Jaafar Mohammed al-Numeiry, prime minister. *Legislature* (unicameral)—People's Assembly. *Major political party*—Sudanese Socialist Union.
Languages: Arabic (official), English, French, African languages.
Education: *Expenditure* (1967), 20.3% of total public expenditure. *School enrollment* (1969)—primary, 610,798; secondary, 175,958; technical/vocational, 1,181; university/higher, 11,691.
Monetary Unit: Sudanese pound (0.3482 pound equals U.S. $1, Aug. 1973).
Gross National Product (1971 est.): $1,900,000,000.
Economic Indexes: *Agricultural production* (1971), 145 (1963 =100); *consumer price index* (1972), 113 (1970=100).
Manufacturing (major products): Processed foods, vegetable oil, textiles.
Major Agricultural Products: Sesame seeds (ranks 2d among world producers, 1972), cotton, oilseeds, gum arabic, sorghum, groundnuts, livestock.
Major Minerals: Iron ore, chromium ore, salt, gypsum.
Foreign Trade (1972): *Exports,* $357,000,000. Imports, $353,-000,000. *Chief trading partners* (1971)—USSR (took 15.5% of exports, supplied 4.6% of imports); India (11%—21%); China (9.4%—5.3%).
Transportation: *Motor vehicles* (1970), 43,900 (automobiles, 27,400); *railroads* (1971), 3,383 miles (5,444 km); *merchant fleet* (1972), 36,000 gross registered tons; *major national airline,* Sudan Airways.
Communications: *Telephones* (1971), 46,371; *newspapers* (1970), 22.

SYGMA

Carl XVI Gustaf (standing, right) *accedes to the throne of Sweden in ceremonies at Stockholm Palace.*

Wickman also visited. The government also recognized North Korea and pledged assistance to Iceland for both the damages resulting from the volcanic eruption of Helgafell and the fight against Britain over the 50-mile (80-km) sea boundary.

Economic Problems. In the election campaign the chief issue was inflation and the government's failure to restrain it. According to UN statistics the consumer price index in Sweden rose about 5% in the first six months of 1973. Anti-inflation measures meant lessened industrial growth and a slower rate of advance for the gross national product. It caused a weakening of the krona and forced Swed-

ish currency purchases to maintain the minimum level required by agreement. An adjustment to the devaluation of the U. S. dollar in February, less than anticipated, and the dollar's resurgence against the krona increased monetary headaches. Price freezes and government economic controls could not roll back inflation or even diminish its upward surge. On the other hand, a decline in unemployment and the impressive 5.19 billion kronor surplus in foreign trade at the end of seven months indicated that the Swedish economy might right itself. But September economic reports on costs of living placed Sweden at the top of European countries.

Social Legislation. The Riksdag passed a new marriage law that liberalized civil marriage, dropped the posting of bans, and allowed for divorce by mutual agreement. A six-month waiting period for divorce remained in cases where there were children or only one partner wanted the divorce. Protective provisions for children were stiffened. Proposed legislation would expand health insurance provisions to include dental care and offer more support for pensioners, widows, and children.

Cultural Events. The death of Vilhelm Moberg on August 8 removed one of the most significant figures in Swedish literature. His series on the immigrants, translated, filmed, and now shown in the United States, marked the height of his career that began in 1927 with the novel *Raskens*. The demise of the newspaper *Goteborg Handels- och Sjöfarts-Tidning* also grieved the Swedish public, who lamented the bankruptcy of this 142-year-old newspaper, noted for its long defense of Swedish liberties and for editor Torgny Segerstedt's thunder against the Nazis during World War II.

The 600th anniversary of the death of St. Birgitta was celebrated with joy in the dedication of a new chapel and cloister as parts of·a revived Catholic religious center at Vadstena. The 75th anniversary of the founding of Landsorganisationen (LO), the national labor union, was also observed.

RAYMOND E. LINDGREN
California State University, Long Beach

————— **SWEDEN** • Information Highlights —————

Official Name: Kingdom of Sweden.
Location: Northern Europe.
Area: 173,649 square miles (449,750 sq km).
Population (1973 est.): 8,200,000. *Density,* 47 per square mile (18 per sq km).
Chief Cities (1970 est.): Stockholm, the capital, 740,486; Göteborg, 451,806; Malmö, 265,505.
Government: *Head of state,* Carl XVI Gustaf, king (acceded Sept. 1973). *Head of government,* Olof Palme, prime minister (took office Oct. 1969). *Legislature* (unicameral)—Riksdag. *Major political parties*—Social Democratic party; Center party; Liberal party; Moderate (Conservative) party; Communist party.
Languages: Swedish (official), Lapp.
Education: *Expenditure* (1969), 30.2% of total public expenditure. *School enrollment* (1969)—primary, 606,220; secondary, 655,329; technical/vocational, 227,876; university/higher, 114,875.
Monetary Unit: Krona (4.110 kronor equal U. S.$1, June 1973).
Gross National Product (1972 est.): $38,800,000,000.
Economic Indexes: *Industrial production* (1972), 153 (1963=100); *agricultural production* (1971), 111 (1963=100); *consumer price index* (1972), 154 (1963=100).
Manufacturing (major products): Pulp and paper, iron and steel, machinery and equipment, ships, chemicals, automobiles and transport equipment, lumber, textiles.
Major Agricultural Products: Oats, sugar beets, potatoes, wheat, livestock, forest products.
Major Minerals: Iron ore, lead, sulfur, tungsten, copper.
Foreign Trade (1972): *Exports,* $8,749,000,000. *Imports,* $8,062,000,000. *Chief trading partners* (1971)—United Kingdom (took 13.5% of exports, supplied 16.5% of imports); West Germany (11%—19%); Norway (10.3%—6%); Denmark (10%—8%).
Transportation: *Motor vehicles* (1971), 2,513,000 (automobiles, 2,357,000); *railroads* (1971), 7,563 miles (12,170 km); *merchant fleet* (1972), 5,632,000 gross registered tons; *major national airline* (with Denmark and Norway), Scandinavian Airlines System (SAS).
Communications: *Telephones* (1972), 4,679,691; *newspapers* (1970), 114 (daily circulation, 4,324,000).

—————— SWITZERLAND • Information Highlights ——————

Official Name: Swiss Confederation.
Location: Central Europe.
Area: 15,941 square miles (41,288 sq km).
Population (1973 est.): 6,500,000. *Density,* 396 per square mile (153 per sq km).
Chief Cities (1970 census): Bern, the capital, 162,405; Zürich, 422,640; Basel, 212,857; Geneva, 173,618.
Government: *Head of state,* Ernst Brugger, president of the confederation (took office Jan. 1974). *Head of government,* Ernst Brugger, president of the Federal Council. *Legislature*—Federal Assembly: Council of States and National Council. *Major political parties*—Democratic Radical party; Social Democratic party; Democratic Social Christian party.
Languages: German, French, Italian, Romansch (all official).
Education: *Expenditure* (1969), 19.2% of total public expenditure. *School enrollment* (1969)—primary, 487,583; secondary, 464,023; technical/vocational, 145,937; university/higher, 40,083.
Monetary Unit: Franc (3.029 francs equal U. S.$1, Aug. 1973).
Gross National Product (1972 est.): $27,500,000,000.
Economic Indexes: *Industrial production* (1972), 149 (1963=100); *agricultural production* (1971), 119 (1963=100); *consumer price index* (1972), 144 (1963=100).
Manufacturing (major products): Machinery, chemicals, textiles, watches, clocks, and clock parts, processed foods.
Major Agricultural Products: Potatoes, sugar beets, wheat, barley, forest products, dairy products.
Major Mineral: Salt.
Foreign Trade (1972): *Exports,* $6,828,000,000. *Imports,* $8,470,000,000. *Chief trading partners* (1971)—West Germany (took 15% of exports, supplied 30% of imports); France (9%—13%); Italy (9%—10%); United States (8%—7%).
Tourism: Receipts (1971), $875,000,000.
Transportation: *Motor vehicles* (1971), 1,638,000 (automobiles, 1,482,000); *railroads* (1971), 3,113 miles (5,010 km); *merchant fleet* (1972), 212,000 gross registered tons; *major national airline,* Swissair.
Communications: *Telephones* (1972), 3,213,065; *newspapers* (1971), 99 (daily circulation, 2,360,000).

SWITZERLAND

Swiss political and economic concerns in 1973 were dominated by attempts to control the problems caused by an inflationary spiral that saw a 6.9% increase in the consumer price index in 1972.

Economy. In an effort to bring its economic problems under control, the Swiss government implemented on January 10 a wide-ranging series of anti-inflationary measures aimed at reducing the continued influx of foreign capital by doubling the amount of required bank reserves for foreign as opposed to domestic deposits. Regulations seeking to slow the construction industry were also put into effect, and the government was given the right to supervise developments in the areas of prices, wages, profits, and dividends.

On January 23, as part of the general European reaction to the U. S. dollar crisis, the Swiss government announced that it would no longer hold to a fixed rate of exchange but would allow the Swiss franc to float freely on the European money market.

The value of exports for the first three quarters of 1973 rose 13.9% over the same period in 1972, and imports increased 11.5%. However, the total value of imports over exports continued to increase.

In a related matter, the Swiss government in July reduced slightly the number of foreign nationals allowed to work in Switzerland in seasonal or year-round capacities. Popular pressure, manifested in petitions opposing "overforeignization," ensured that the question of much more severe limitations on the use of foreign labor would be submitted to a national referendum before 1975.

Political Issues. On May 20, a referendum vote resulted in the removal of two articles from the Swiss constitution that had banned the Jesuit order from Switzerland and had prohibited the establishment of religious houses of any order. On September 6, the government announced the formation of a commission to revise the 125-year-old constitution and another to examine possible UN membership.

In June the National Council approved a popular initiative petition for the creation of a national civil service that would be open to conscientious objectors as an alternative way of fulfilling their military service requirement. The Council refused to approve a motion authorizing the federal government to intervene in the controversy between the French-speaking Jurassians and the canton of Bern over the question of separate cantonal status for the Jura region.

On December 5, acting in defiance of the regular leadership of the three major political parties, the Swiss parliament rejected the official city nominees for three cabinet posts and selected other persons from the same parties instead.

PAUL C. HELMREICH, *Wheaton College, Mass.*

SYRIA

The war with Israel in 1973 tended to overshadow the partial democratization of Syria's political system, which had been brought about by the approval of Syria's first permanent constitution in 12 years. Israeli bombing during the war damaged the country's lagging industrial sector, thus offsetting real gains made in the agricultural sector.

The October War. On October 6, three Syrian armored infantry divisions and two armored divisions crossed the Middle East cease-fire lines and engaged Israeli troops in an attempt to regain the Golan Heights, while Egyptian forces simultaneously crossed the Suez Canal and attacked Israeli positions in the Sinai. By nightfall on October 7, the Syrians, with nearly 1,000 tanks and supported by Moroccan and Iraqi troops, reached the pre-1967 boundaries with Israel, captured Mt. Hermon, and encircled the main Golan town of Kuneitra. In the fierce fighting that followed, Israel launched massive counterattacks, bombed key economic and military targets, and checked and then turned the Syrian advance by October 9–10. Israeli forces were

—————— SYRIA • Information Highlights ——————

Official Name: Syrian Arab Republic.
Location: Southwest Asia.
Area: 71,498 square miles (185,180 sq km).
Population (1973 est.): 6,800,000. *Density,* 91 per square mile (35 per sq km).
Chief Cities (1970 census): Damascus, the capital, 836,179; Aleppo, 639,361; Homs, 215,526.
Government: *Head of state,* Lt. Gen. Hafez al-Assad, president (took office March 1971). *Chief minister,* Mahmoud al-Ayubi, premier (took office Nov. 1972). *Legislature* (unicameral)—National Assembly. *Major political parties*—Baath party; Syrian Arab Socialist Union; Arab Socialist Movement; Syrian Communist party.
Language: Arabic (official).
Education: *Expenditure* (1969), 17.1% of total public expenditure. *School enrollment* (1969)—primary, 845,130; secondary, 295,717; technical/vocational, 10,445; university/higher, 37,540.
Monetary Unit: Pound (3.80 pounds equal U. S.$1, Aug. 1973).
Gross National Product (1971 est.): $1,978,000,000.
Economic Indexes: *Industrial production* (1971), 209 (1963=100); *agricultural production* (1971), 96 (1963=100); *consumer price index* (1972), 128 (1963=100).
Manufacturing (major products): Petroleum products, textiles, cement, glass, soap, processed foods.
Major Agricultural Products: Wheat, barley, sugar beets, cotton, grapes, sheep and goats, wool.
Major Mineral: Petroleum.
Foreign Trade (1972): *Exports,* $287,000,000. Imports, $539,000,000. *Chief trading partners* (1970)—Common Market (took 30% of exports, supplied 22% of imports); Communist bloc (26%—24%); Arab countries (25%—18%).
Tourism: Receipts (1970), $12,870,000.
Transportation: *Motor vehicles* (1971), 49,200 (automobiles, 32,800); *railroads* (1971), 336 miles (541 km); *major national airline,* Syrian Arab Airlines.
Communications: *Telephones* (1972), 120,030; *newspapers* (1970), 5.

EUPHRATES DAM at Medinat al Thawra (formerly Tabqa), Syria, which was built with Soviet technical and financial aid, began operations in July.

able to push a vanguard unit to within 25 miles (40 km) of Damascus before being stopped at the strategic town of Saasa. The hostilities came to an end when Syria accepted the UN cease-fire resolution on October 23. At the time of the cease-fire, Israel occupied more Syrian territory than it had before the fighting erupted.

Despite the Israeli success in turning the Syrian offensive, the war was not a repeat of Israel's decisive victory in 1967. Losses to both sides were staggering, and the fighting was marked by the stubborn resistance the Syrians offered to Israeli counterattacks. Equipment losses were offset by massive arms airlifts to Syria from the USSR and to Israel from the United States.

Syria did not attend the opening of the Middle East conference in Geneva on December 21. Citing the refusal of Israel to withdraw from some of the occupied territories before the opening of the talks, Syria claimed that unless the talks took up the question of withdrawal from the occupied territories it would not participate in the discussions of prisoner exchanges and separation of forces.

Internal Politics. Although Syria's first permanent constitution since the 1962 secession from the country's union with Egypt was endorsed by 97.6% of the voters on March 12, it met with opposition from religious groups due to the omission of any clause naming Islam as the state religion. In a demonstration on February 22 in Hama protesting the omission, some 39 persons were killed and 80 wounded. Assad was firm in his view that the constitution should provide for complete religious freedom, although he did admit that the constitution should stipulate that the head of state be Muslim.

The constitution declares that Syria is democratic, socialist, and sovereign, that it is a member of the Federation of Arab Republics, that the Baath party is the leading political organization, that the economy is socialist, and that personal and religious freedoms are sacred. Legislative authority is vested in the National Assembly, although the president, who is elected for seven-year terms, has the power to dissolve the Assembly and assume legislative powers.

In parliamentary elections on May 25–26, the ruling Baath party won 70% of the popular vote and 122 of 186 seats in the Assembly.

The Economy. Syria receives $55 million in military aid from Kuwait and Saudi Arabia. It also used 70% of the revenues received in 1973 to help pay for the import of an estimated $185 million in Soviet arms, despite the need for investment capital. Continued heavy defense spending will be difficult to maintain, however, due to the estimated $500 million in damages inflicted by Israeli bombing on the industrial base. The port facilities at Latakia were severely damaged, as were the oil refineries at Baniyas and Homs. A new $55 million power station was destroyed.

Before the outbreak of the war and the resulting dislocations, the economy had shown signs of a new vigor. In April it was announced that per capita income had risen 11% and that 57% of the 1971–75

SYRIAN TROOPS inspect parts of Israeli aircraft shot down during the October war.

five-year development plan's objectives had been achieved. It was also announced that a 43% increase in exports had shaved the balance-of-payments deficit to $2.5 million. In July, the first stage of the Euphrates Dam was completed, a project expected to double the acreage of irrigated land and triple electrical output. The agricultural sector rebounded in 1973, and the largest cotton crop in seven years was announced in October.

F. NICHOLAS WILLARD
Georgetown University

TANAKA, Kakuei. See BIOGRAPHY.

TANZANIA

Relations with neighboring countries dominated the news in Tanzania, as fighting temporarily broke out along its borders with Uganda, Burundi, and Mozambique in 1973.

Border Incidents. Relations between Tanzania and Uganda have been alternatingly bitter and conciliatory since Tanzania granted asylum to deposed Ugandan President Milton Obote in 1971. The renewal of hostilities in March ended the several-months-long peace with Uganda that followed the October 1972 peace agreement signed in Mogadishu, Somalia. Tanzania expressed fears about its citizens missing in Uganda, charged that Uganda had moved troops to the border in violation of the Mogadishu agreement, and arrested 53 Ugandans for spying. Uganda charged that Tanzania continued to harbor guerrillas sympathetic to Obote.

Most of the accused spies were released after a month and expelled from Tanzania. On May 29, Presidents Idi Amin of Uganda and Julius Nyerere of Tanzania met in Addis Ababa, Ethiopia, to sign a new agreement, which restored the Mogadishu settlement and provided for Ugandan acceptance of

WIDE WORLD

----------- TANZANIA • Information Highlights -----------

Official Name: United Republic of Tanzania.
Location: East Africa.
Area: 364,899 square miles (945,087 sq km).
Population (1973 est.): 14,300,000. *Density,* 36 per square mile (14 per sq km).
Chief City (1970 est.): Dar es Salaam, the capital, 344,900.
Government: *Head of state,* Julius K. Nyerere, president (took office April 1964). *Chief minister,* Rashidi Kawawa, prime minister (took office Feb. 1972). *Legislature* (unicameral)—National Assembly. *Major political party*—Tanganyika African National Union and its affiliate in Zanzibar, Afro-Shirazi party.
Languages: English, Swahili (both official).
Education: *School enrollment* (1968)—primary (1969), 829,-169; secondary, 38,288; technical/vocational, 1,064; university/higher (1969), 1,932.
Monetary Unit: Shilling (6.9 shillings equal U. S.$1, Aug. 1973).
Gross National Product (1972 est.): $1,445,000,000.
Consumer Price Index (1972), 143 (1963=100).
Manufacturing (major products): Textiles, cement, petroleum products, sugar, aluminum.
Major Agricultural Products: Cloves (ranks 1st among world producers, 1972), sisal, cotton, coffee, oilseeds, groundnuts, tea, tobacco, sugarcane.
Major Minerals: Diamonds, gold, gemstones.
Foreign Trade (1972): *Exports,* $284,000,000. *Imports,* $364,-000,000. *Chief trading partners* (1971)—United Kingdom (took 24% of exports, supplied 20% of imports); China (supplied 25%); India (8%).
Tourism: Receipts (1971), $13,520,000.
Transportation: *Motor vehicles* (1971), 73,800 (automobiles, 35,800); *railroads* (regional total with Kenya and Uganda, 1971), 3,676 miles (5,915 km); *major national airline* (with Kenya and Uganda), East African Airways.
Communications: *Telephones* (1972), 40,144; *newspapers* (1969), 4 (daily circulation, 61,000).

responsibility for the missing Tanzanians. After a ministerial conference in July, Uganda agreed to pay compensation for the missing Tanzanians; and in August, Tanzanian Foreign Minister John Malecela said that relations between the two countries were "fully restored."

In March, Burundi attacked the Kigoma district of Tanzania, where many refugees from the civil war in Burundi had fled. Seventy-four people, mostly Burundi refugees and the rest Tanzanian citizens, were killed. Apologies were given by Burundi in April, but fighting recurred in June and July. After talks including representatives of Tanzania, Burundi, and Zaire, an agreement was announced on July 22. Burundi agreed to pay compensation for 10 Tanzanians killed on June 29, and Tanzania agreed to restore commercial relations with Burundi, whose routes to the Indian Ocean it largely controls.

The Tanzanian government reported in January that three Portuguese aircraft from Mozambique had entered Tanzanian airspace and dropped bombs.

Domestic Affairs. Tanzania continued its gradual implementation of its policies of socialism and decentralization. In April the National Assembly passed a bill providing for enforcement of the Arusha Leadership Code, the purpose of which is to prevent political leaders from becoming a wealthy elite. After the 16th biennial conference of the Tanganyika African National Union (TANU) in September, President Nyerere announced that the

capital would be moved from Dar es Salaam to Dodoma, 250 miles (400 km) inland. The move will take place by stages over the next 10 years.

Several important changes occurred in the ministry of home affairs. In April, Saudi Maswanya, the minister for home affairs and a cabinet member for 11 years, resigned because of criticism of the ministry. President Nyerere appointed Al-Haji Omari Muhaji, previously regional commissioner in Tanga, to replace Maswanya. In the same month, Tanzania's police chief, Hamza Haziz, resigned after a coroner ruled that he killed a pedestrian in a hit-and-run automobile accident. Haziz was replaced by S. H. Pundungu.

Relations between Zanzibar and mainland Tanzania became strained when 18 of 81 persons being tried for the assassination of Zanzibar's President Sheikh Abeid Karume in 1972 were held in Dar es Salaam rather than returned to the island for trial. This action displayed a lack of confidence in the Zanzibar People's Court.

Nyerere's Travels. President Nyerere spent an active year traveling outside Tanzania, promoting the cause of liberation movements in southern Africa. He attended the conference of heads of state of Commonwealth countries at Ottawa, Canada, in August; the 7th general conference of the United National Independence Party at Mulungushi, Zambia, also in August; and the 4th conference of nonaligned nations at Algiers, Algeria, in September.

JAY E. HAKES
Louisiana State University in New Orleans

TAXATION

In April 1973 the Nixon administration proposed a number of revisions intended to modify the personal income tax. Some of the proposals were directed toward simplification, including a revised treatment of deductions for medical and drug expenses and casualty losses and a $500 additional miscellaneous deduction to replace itemization for low-income families. Other proposals were directed toward property tax relief for the elderly and a more liberal treatment of income for those over 65. Some proposals were more controversial, such as the proposed elimination of the deduction for gasoline taxes, a partial credit for tuition paid to private elementary and secondary schools, and the elimination of the dividend exclusion. The minimum tax provision, which now applies to those with incomes in excess of $100,000, and which is intended to reduce the use of "tax shelters," would have been extended to those with incomes in excess of $50,000. It was estimated that the proposed revisions would reduce federal revenues by about $600 million annually.

In September, to curb inflation, the administration proposed a surcharge on both corporate and individual incomes, to be refunded at some future time when inflationary dangers had eased. There was also a proposal to vary the rate of investment tax credit between 4% and 15% as an additional fiscal weapon to influence levels of economic activity. The rate is now a flat 7%.

However, the Congress was in no mood for a serious examination of the administration's proposals, and at year-end appeared to be interested primarily in tightening the minimum tax provision, with some attention to federal financing of property tax reform at the state and local level.

Social Security. In recent years both social security taxes and benefits have increased sharply. Additional benefits went into effect on Jan. 1, 1974, and, under new legislation, benefit levels are tied to increases in the consumer price index. If the index rises by 3% over a one-year period, benefits will be automatically increased the following July. There will be further statutory increases in benefits in April and July 1974. Legislation was adopted to raise the taxable earnings base from $12,600 to $13,200. The combined employer-employee rate is now 11.7%.

Revenue Sharing. The State and Local Fiscal Assistance Act, which was adopted in October 1972, provided for a partial doubling-up of payments during 1973. Thus, instead of annual amounts of about $6 billion that states and local governments can expect to receive in the years through 1976, fiscal year 1973 payments amounted to $8.3 billion. These sums were distributed on the basis of one third to the states and two thirds to the some 38,000 local government units excluding school districts. Although a number of the mayors of large cities have objected to the distribution formula, there appears to be no disposition to reexamine the statute until its expiration date approaches in 1976.

State Tax Developments. A number of developments combined to produce an unusual situation in the fiscal affairs of the states. In recent years with the addition and strengthening of a number of state income tax laws, state tax structures have generally become more progressive and revenues have responded more rapidly to increases in economic activity, including the higher incomes produced by inflation. State portions of federal revenue sharing also provided funds. In consequence, for the first time in many years a number of states ended the 1973 fiscal year with a surplus.

In nine states, in spite of the improved revenue picture, taxes were increased with the aim of bringing in $500 million in additional revenue. In 14 states, taxes were reduced by a total of about $1 billion. The favorite type of tax reduction was property tax relief financed by the state. These are known as "circuit-breaker" statutes and are usually directed to relief for elderly homeowners, although some states extend the relief to all low-income families, homeowners and tenants alike. In 1973 eight more states adopted this type of legislation. All states, though not the District of Columbia, now have some form of "circuit-breaker."

U. S. TAX REVENUES
Federal government

Source	Fiscal year 1971	Fiscal year 1972	Fiscal year 1973
		(billions of dollars)	
Individual income.....	$ 86.2	$ 94.7	$103.3
Corporation income....	26.8	32.2	36.1
Social security........	48.6	53.9	64.5
Excises...............	16.6	15.5	16.3
Estate and gift........	3.7	5.4	4.9
Customs..............	2.6	3.3	3.2
Miscellaneous........	3.9	3.6	3.9
Total..............	$188.4	$208.6	$232.2

State and local governments

Source	Fiscal year 1971	Fiscal year 1972	Fiscal year 1973
Property.............	$ 38.3	$ 42.7	$ 45.3
General sales.........	17.7	20.4	22.9
Individual income.....	11.5	15.4	18.0
Corporation income....	3.4	4.2	5.2
Motor fuel...........	6.6	7.2	8.0
Motor vehicle.........	3.3	3.4	3.8
All other.............	13.5	15.2	16.3
Total..............	$ 94.3	$108.5	$119.5

California's fiscal behavior during the year was particularly interesting. With a mounting state surplus the sales tax rate was reduced from 6% to 5%, together with significant reductions in rates of personal income tax. In November, California voters were asked to decide on a constitutional amendment that would have limited the level of state taxes to 8.3% of personal income, with successive reductions to 7% by the year 1990. The amendment was defeated by a margin of 54% to 46%.

U. S. Supreme Court Decisions. In *San Antonio* v. *Rodriguez,* the plaintiff asserted that the school finance pattern in San Antonio, and hence in Texas, was unconstitutional under the equal protection clause of the 14th Amendment because it did not provide equal expenditures per pupil. Although the lower courts ruled in favor of the plaintiff, the Supreme Court held, in effect, that school financing was primarily a state responsibility. Had the ruling gone the other way all states would have faced the need to revamp their school finance systems to assure, at least within narrow limits, equality in educational expenditures.

In spite of the decision a great many states are now moving toward school finance reform to assure greater equality. This may take the form of complete state assumption of the financing of elementary and secondary education.

The court also agreed to hear the case of *Bob Jones University* v. *Schultz,* where the Internal Revenue Service denied a tax exemption on the ground that the university had an admissions policy that was discriminatory on religious grounds. The court's decision was expected in the spring of 1974.

OTHER COUNTRIES

Britain and Ireland entered the European Economic Community, or Common Market, in January 1973. In both countries the value-added tax went into effect in the same month, and Britain introduced further modifications in the tax in April. Belgium, Netherlands, and Luxembourg adopted common legislation to unify their value-added tax and also their excise tax systems. Italy, after long delay, introduced the value-added tax.

A number of developed countries enacted substantial tax increases to curb inflationary pressures. These included West Germany, France, the Netherlands, and Switzerland. These increases were generally in rates of personal income tax, reduced depreciation allowances, and increased levies on gasoline. Japan increased the corporate tax while reducing the personal income tax.

A number of less-developed countries modified their tax systems to encourage additional foreign investment or to strengthen their own export sectors. In Thailand, Brazil, and Turkey, the concessions were combined with a major income tax reform.

The Philippines, by presidential decrees, introduced major changes in the tax structure in 1973. Tax evaders, on liabilities through 1972, were urged to pay a small amnesty tax before April 2. Since that time, under martial law, there has been a strenuous drive on tax evaders and a major increase in the number of those filing income tax returns and in tax collections. Other changes have included increased progressivity in the income tax structure, increased taxes on nonresident aliens, reduced taxes on shipping and airline companies, and a revision of the tariff and customs code.

Federal tax revenues in Canada increased substantially during 1973 as a result of the major reforms introduced in 1972. The resulting pressures for tax reduction took the form of a lower corporation tax rate and more favorable depreciation allowances. In addition, legislation was approved for a major innovation in the personal income tax, whose liabilities, beginning in 1974, will be linked to the consumer price index. As the index increases, personal tax liabilities will be reduced to maintain a roughly equivalent "real" tax burden. In another significant development, as the petroleum crisis deepened after mid-summer, the federal government increased the export tax on crude oil from 40 cents to $1.90 per barrel.

A great many international tax treaties were adopted or under negotiation during 1973. West Germany was most active, negotiating with Singapore, Iceland, Indonesia, South Africa, Zambia, and Liberia. Other major treaties were concluded between Britain and France and between the Netherlands and Indonesia. Norway, Denmark, Finland, Iceland, and Sweden concluded an unusual treaty for the exchange of information from corporate and personal income tax returns. The United States and the USSR concluded their first tax treaty for the avoidance of double taxation, covering copyrights and patents and many other types of income as well.

JESSE BURKHEAD
Syracuse University

TELECOMMUNICATIONS

There were two major events in the field of telecommunications during 1973. One was the approval by the U. S. Federal Communications Commission (FCC) of six corporate applications to build U. S. domestic communications satellite systems. The other was the opening of a trans-Canadian digital data communications network called Dataroute.

Domestic Communications Satellite Systems. In January, the Western Union Corporation won FCC approval of its plan to build the first U. S. domestic communications satellite system. The Western Union system, scheduled to be in operation in 1974, is called Westar. It will make use of two satellites and initially will have earth stations near New York, Chicago, Atlanta, Dallas, and Los Angeles. Westar will provide telegraph, Telex (teletypewriter), and private-line services, and it also may carry network television programs.

The applications of five other companies were approved by the FCC in September. The domestic communications satellite system proposed by the American Telephone and Telegraph Company (AT&T) calls for earth stations at Hawley, Pa., DeLuz, Calif., Hanover, Ill., Woodbury, Ga., and Three Peaks, Calif. The American Satellite Corporation's system was to include earth stations at New York, Dallas, and Los Angeles. The RCA system, with earth stations at New York, Los Angeles, San Francisco, Juneau, and Anchorage, was scheduled to be in operation late in 1975. GTE Satellite Corporation and National Satellite Services, Inc., plan to build domestic satellite facilities having a total value of about $52 million. The Communications Satellite Corporation (Comsat), which must separate its domestic satellite activities from its international satellite activities, was granted an interim authorization for a $180 million four-satellite domestic system. The whole collection of the com-

panies' domestic satellite systems is called Domsat. It will handle telephone, television, telegraph, and data transmission traffic within the United States.

In September, the FCC again demonstrated its policy of opening competition in the telecommunications field. It ruled that the GTE Satellite Corporation could use domestic communications satellites to provide long-distance telephone service in the United States, a service that so far has been provided only by AT&T. FCC members believed that a benchmark for comparison of costs and performance could be established by its ruling. In October, AT&T appealed the FCC's decision.

Canadian Domestic Satellite. Canada's second domestic communications satellite, Anik 2, was launched on April 20. It serves as a backup to Anik 1 for Canadian communications as well as providing some channels for American communications until American domestic communications satellite systems are in operation. Anik 1, the world's first domestic communications satellite, was launched in November 1972.

Trans-Canadian Digital Data Network. Canada's new Dataroute system is designed to provide low rates for a digital data transmission service that is needed because of the increasing flow of business information and the increasing use of computers in Canada. The Dataroute system, designed by Bell Canada and operated by the Trans-Canada Telephone System, links Vancouver, Calgary, Regina, Winnipeg, Toronto, Ottawa, Montreal, Quebec, Moncton, Saint John, and Halifax, with more cities to be added later. The new system utilizes a type of transmission called data under voice. In this technique the digital data signals occupy lower frequency bands than those used for telephone voice signals, and both the data and the voice signals are sent simultaneously. The Dataroute system has an automatic alarm that warns technicians any time

the number of errors on a particular channel exceeds a predetermined level. Dataroute, opened on April 17, is the first transcontinental system of its type to be available commercially from a common carrier.

Telephone Developments. The FCC gave several communications companies permission to lay a $180 million submarine telephone cable from San Luis Obispo, Calif., to Japan via Hawaii and Guam. It is estimated that there will be 1,000,000 calls annually between the People's Republic of China and the United States by 1980.

A new medium-capacity digital transmission system called T2 has been put into commercial service by AT&T. It has a capacity of 96 one-way digital voice circuits per pair of wires and a total capacity of more than 4,400 simultaneous two-way telephone conversations over 52-pair cables. The digital transmission of telephone calls has the great advantage that digital messages are received without significant loss or distortion. In contrast, the conventional analog transmission of telephone calls always is limited by noise and distortion introduced by transmission and amplification.

The Touch-a-Matic phone will be introduced soon. This is a telephone that can automatically dial a call to anywhere in the United States at the touch of a single button. The telephone is capable of dialing 32 prerecorded telephone numbers.

Bell Laboratories is testing a new and compact dialing mechanism for Touch-Tone telephones. It does the same job as the conventional push buttons but takes less than half the space.

The customer service showing the greatest growth in the telephone industry is called "Call Waiting." Call Waiting signals a customer who is talking on the phone that the talker has another caller who is trying to reach him or her.

Pacific Northwest Bell raised the coin telephone rate in Washington from 10 cents to 15 cents in the spring of 1973. The company claimed that a pay telephone station now costs $250, as compared with $90 in the 1950's.

As of the latest FCC report, there were 80 telephone companies fully subject to FCC jurisdiction, including 60 companies with annual revenues of $1 million or more. They reported a total of 109 million phones in service. Since not all companies are within the jurisdiction of the FCC, there are many more telephones in the United States.

Cable Television. Data from the FCC for fiscal year 1972 showed that there were 2,839 cable TV systems serving 5,328 communities in the United States. This represented an annual growth rate of about 5%. Also, the FCC has ruled that pay TV via cable does not need any further authorization.

International Radio Communications. During 1973 the FCC approved recommendations of the International Telecommunications Union, an affiliate of the United Nations, relating to the problem of radio interference due to congested traffic at the lower frequencies. In order to resolve the problem, several higher frequency bands above 10 gigahertz (GHz) were allocated for space communications. However, in solving one problem, another lesser one arose. The use of the higher frequencies presents a difficulty because radio waves with a frequency above 10 GHz have a wavelength that is about the same as the dimension of a raindrop. This leads to transmission losses.

PAUL WEINER, *University of Connecticut*

TELEPHONES IN MAJOR COUNTRIES

Country	Telephones Jan. 1, 1973	% increase over 1972	No. per 100 population
Argentina	1,952,109	6.9	8.10
Australia[1]	4,399,782	6.0	33.95
Austria	1,694,194	9.5	22.72
Belgium	2,305,218	6.6	23.75
Brazil	2,190,000	6.1	2.17
Bulgaria	581,657	8.9	6.77
Canada	10,987,141	7.0	49.98
China, Rep. of	596,663	21.2	3.90
Colombia	1,009,791	0.4	4.49
Czechoslovakia	2,232,481	5.7	15.37
Denmark	1,912,449	6.6	37.93
Finland	1,412,067	9.5	30.47
France	10,338,000	8.3	19.91
Germany, East	2,232,069	3.1	13.10
Germany, West	16,521,149	8.4	26.79
Greece	1,437,578	16.9	16.32
Hong Kong	795,167	15.0	19.38
Hungary	923,966	5.8	8.87
India	1,479,475	9.5	0.27
Israel	619,709	10.0	19.37
Italy	11,345,497	9.9	20.76
Japan[1]	34,021,155	14.1	31.50
Mexico	1,957,972	14.2	3.79
Netherlands, The	4,003,455	7.6	29.91
New Zealand[1]	1,327,134	3.6	44.61
Norway	1,262,254	4.8	32.00
Poland	2,087,032	5.9	6.29
Portugal	873,339	7.9	9.89
South Africa, Republic of[1]	1,706,794	5.1	7.30
Spain	5,712,549	11.4	16.45
Sweden	4,829,047	3.2	59.29
Switzerland	3,404,427	6.0	53.95
Turkey	728,358	11.3	1.94
United Kingdom[1]	17,570,904	8.8	31.39
USSR	13,198,700	10.2	5.31
United States	131,606,000	5.2	62.75
Yugoslavia	910,695	10.9	4.38

[1] 1972 data. Source: AT&T

Britain's National Theatre production of O'Neill's Long Day's Journey Into Night, *starring Laurence Olivier (left, standing), was seen on ABC in March. Others shown are (from left) Constance Cummings, Ronald Pickup, and Denis Quilley.*

television and radio

The long and wide wake of the 1972 Watergate break-in dominated television during 1973, most strikingly in the Senate Watergate hearings. These hearings were part of a long series of news events that were brought vividly to the public by television. Although radio played its part in news coverage, two bizarre phenomena in radio broadcasting seemed to generate the most interest.

TELEVISION

Washington—the Washington of Watergate, the President, the White House, and the Congress—affected public and commercial television during 1973 as it never had before. Events in Washington brought about changes in such diverse areas as program schedules, advertising, public television financing, news coverage, and children's programs. The television broadcasting industry, while adjusting to these changes, marshalled its forces to combat the threat of pay TV via cable.

Watergate. While television could lay little claim to investigative reporting on the Watergate affair, it did broadcast the hearings before the Senate Select Committee on Presidential Campaign Activities, giving the public a show that bettered the Army-McCarthy hearings and the Kefauver crime committee hearings of past years. The Watergate hearings took over the public's attention from May 17 to August 7 and emphasized anew TV's unique strengths: putting the viewer in the middle of the action as it occurs, and transmitting candor or the lack of it as no other medium can. Even as the broadcasts caused injury to many reputations, they made others.

The networks began by vying for the audience, with each providing full coverage of the hearings. But as costs mounted, along with the cries of those addicted to game shows and soap operas, the networks agreed to rotate coverage on a daily basis. Even so, the 319 hours of broadcasting that ended on August 7 cost them somewhere between $7 and $10 million, slightly balanced by an estimated 12% increase in the daytime audience. Public television, turning its night-time hours over to complete tapes of the daily proceedings, picked up an estimated $1 million in new contributions.

The President and Television. President Nixon's feelings toward television were never warm, but they became decidedly frostier during the year. In the early months TV's "instant analysis," immediately following presidential TV addresses, was sharply attacked by the White House. In his TV address on April 30, however, in which he accepted the resignations of his top aides, the President praised "a vigorous free press." After the speech, Nixon told reporters to "give me hell every time you think I'm wrong."

Then there was a turnabout. At the long-delayed press conference televised at San Clemente on August 22, the questions were pointed, and Nixon was

JAMES STEWART, as attorney Billy Jim Hawkins, brandishes a rifle that turned a pageant into a battleground in an episode of the new CBS series Hawkins.

defiant. The presidential press conference on September 5 was more relaxed on both sides, but on October 26, Nixon went on the attack, shocking journalists by his reference to "outrageous, vicious, distorted reporting." From then until the end of the year, the President returned to television for speeches to the public and to specially chosen audiences rather than holding press conferences.

CBS, which in June had given up "instant analysis," announced in November that it was reverting to its earlier practice after a "fair trial" of the no-instant-analysis policy. The CBS decision may have signalled that the Nixon administration's long-term efforts to pressure the three TV networks—ABC, CBS, and NBC—had reached its end. An end to those efforts seemed to be confirmed in late December when Clay T. Whitehead, director of the White House Office of Telecommunications Policy since 1970, announced he would resign in early 1974.

Public Broadcasting. Noncommercial television stations have been a long standing target of White House displeasure. This conflict was underscored early in the year as the relationship between public television and the Nixon administration became highly strained.

The Public Television Act of 1967 had created the Corporation for Public Broadcasting (CPB) to channel federal funds to local public TV stations and their national arm, the Public Broadcasting Service (PBS), and to act as a buffer between the stations and governmental pressure. However, on Jan. 11, 1973, the CPB announced that it was assuming jurisdiction over the creation and scheduling of programs to be carried on the 233-station PBS network in the interest of guaranteeing the "objectivity and balance" required by the original act of Congress. The stations fought back, asserting that control of programming must be exercised by those at the local level—the station licensees and their publics—through PBS.

At immediate issue was CPB's decision not to fund or give network connection to such established programs as William Buckley's *Firing Line, Bill Moyers' Journal, The Advocates,* and *Washington Week In Review* in the 1973–74 season. CPB chairman Thomas B. Curtis worked out a compromise that seemed to favor the position of the licensees, but the CPB voted to defer action on it on April 13. Curtis resigned the following day, later citing as his reasons White House pressure against the compromise and his own lack of faith in the integrity and independence of the CPB board. In May, CPB elected as chairman James R. Killian, vice chairman since CPB's establishment in 1968. Killian worked out an acceptable compromise not markedly different from that of his predecessor.

Public broadcasting continued in its financial plight. Although its hope has long been for five-year funding to provide an effective barrier against political pressure, the President signed a bill authorizing two-year funding of $175 million, a step in the right direction. At year-end, however, CPB found itself with one-year financing of between $47.5 and $50 million, the final amount to be determined by a complex formula, and HEW with $16 million for educational broadcasting grants.

Entertainment Programming. From the 1972–73 season only one new program, *The Waltons,* emerged with distinction and laden with honors to take its place among the top 10. Accordingly, the networks in April announced drastic revisions for the fall—17 programs were to be dropped and 20 new programs of varying lengths, mostly situation comedies and melodrama, were to be added. A 16-week strike by the Writers Guild delayed the premieres and hurried the writing on some programs,

but weak basic concepts may have been the reason for the failure of many of the new shows. Of all the new programs offered in the fall *Kojak,* a police melodrama starring Telly Savalas, emerged as the champ. As always, some fine specials kept the year from being a disaster. Specials with Julie Andrews, documentaries such as the new ABC *Close-up* series, some of the PBS-BBC *Masterpiece Theatre* offerings, and the Joseph Papp *Much Ado About Nothing* on CBS come immediately to mind.

Cable Television. The uncertainty that plagued Americans and their enterprises during 1973 was no stranger to cable television. The Justice Department's antitrust suit against the merger of two giants in the field—Cox Cable Communications, Inc., and American Television and Communications Corp.— and the consequent dropping of the merger put a damper on the industry. There were other unsettled problems, including copyright, jurisdiction over the poles that carry the cable, and inconsistencies in local, state, and federal rules for cable systems.

In contrast, there was joy in the industry over the early success of pay TV via cable, in which motion pictures are transmitted by cable to hotel and motel rooms and sometimes even to private homes for the payment of a specific fee for each showing. Pay TV was seen as a vein of pure gold by cable operators and as an enormous threat by over-the-air broadcasters and theater owners.

In the meantime, cable television continued to grow. There were some 3,000 cable systems in operation in the United States, serving 12% of the homes in the country.

Federal Communications Commission. The Federal Communications Commission (FCC) took steps toward resolving some of the problems that have been its major concerns over the past several years: children's programs, cable TV, domestic satellites, license renewals, cross-ownerships, and so on.

In late November the commission modified its prime-time access rule, adopting a compromise that reduces prime-time access throughout the working week to the half-hour from 7:30 to 8 P. M. in Eastern and Pacific time zones and from 6:30 to 7 P. M. in Mountain and Central time zones, while doing away with the rule entirely on Sundays.

In the domestic communications satellite area, the FCC gave a go-ahead to Western Union in January and to five more companies in September. The Western Union satellite system was expected to be in operation in 1974, and it may carry the TV programs of ABC, CBS, and NBC.

NOTABLE U. S. TELEVISION PROGRAMS OF 1973

AN AMERICAN FAMILY—A 12-part examination of the daily life and problems of the Louds, an affluent, troubled American family, recorded over a seven-month period. PBS, weekly from Jan. 11.

A BOY NAMED TERRY EGAN—Documentary on an autistic child, Terry Egan, and his family, with Daniel Schorr as correspondent. CBS, Oct. 11.

A BRAND NEW LIFE—A drama about the unexpected first pregnancy of a 40-year-old woman, with Cloris Leachman and Martin Balsam. ABC, Feb. 20.

CATHOLICS—A drama examining the many-faceted role of the Catholic Church in contemporary society, starring Trevor Howard, Martin Sheen, and Cyril Cusack. CBS, Nov. 29.

CRIMEWATCH—A program of interviews with law enforcement officials, conducted by Truman Capote. ABC, May 8.

THE DANCE THEATER OF HARLEM—A documentary on the dance group and school established in 1968 and led by Arthur Mitchell, narrated by Brock Peters. PBS, March 26.

A DREAM FOR CHRISTMAS—A drama about the family of Rev. Will Douglas, a black minister who struggles to save his church, which is due to be torn down; with Hari Rhodes and Lynn Hamilton. ABC, Dec. 24.

THE ENERGY CRISIS—An examination of the current energy crisis, narrated by Frank McGee. NBC, Sept. 4.

THE GLASS MENAGERIE—Tennessee Williams' haunting play, starring Katharine Hepburn, Sam Waterston, Joanna Miles, and Michael Moriarty. ABC, Dec. 16.

HOSPITALS, DOCTORS AND PATIENTS—An examination of medical and hospital care in the United States, narrated by Ron Nessen and Ken Alvord. NBC, Aug. 28.

THE INCREDIBLE FLIGHT OF THE SNOW GEESE—A documentary on the annual winter migration of snow geese from Canada to Texas, narrated by Glen Campbell. NBC, Jan. 23.

JULIE ON SESAME STREET—A musical special starring Julie Andrews and featuring Perry Como and Jim Henson's Sesame Street Muppets. ABC, Nov. 23.

LBJ: THE LAST INTERVIEW—An interview with Lyndon Johnson, conducted on January 12, 10 days before his death, with Walter Cronkite. CBS, Feb. 1.

THE LIE—Ingmar Bergman's drama on the disintegration of a modern middle-class marriage, starring Shirley Knight, George Segal, and Robert Culp. CBS, April 24.

THE LILY TOMLIN SHOW—Comedy hour starring Lily Tomlin and featuring Richard Pryor and Richard Crenna. ABC, March 16.

LONG DAY'S JOURNEY INTO NIGHT—Eugene O'Neill's autobiographical drama, starring Laurence Olivier, Constance Cummings, Ronald Pickup, .and Denis Quilley. ABC, March 10.

THE MEN WHO MADE THE MOVIES—A series of eight profiles of great directors, Raoul Walsh, Frank Capra, Howard Hawks, King Vidor, George Cukor, William Wellman, Vincente Minnelli, and Alfred Hitchcock; narrated by Cliff Robertson. PBS, weekly beginning Nov. 4.

MICHELANGELO ANTONIONI'S CHINA—A documentary on China, directed and narrated by the noted Italian director. ABC, Jan. 11.

MUCH ADO ABOUT NOTHING—Shakespeare's play set in the United States in the 1920's and performed with ragtime musical accompaniment, directed by A. J. Antoon and starring Sam Waterston and Kathleen Widdoes. CBS, Feb. 2.

THE MYSTERY OF NEFERTITI—A documentary of the age of the ancient Egyptian ruler Akhenaton and his wife Nefertiti, with commentary by Dr. Ray Winfield Smith. PBS, Oct. 15.

POPULATION: BOOM OR DOOM?—A documentary based on the report of the Population Commission to President Nixon in the spring of 1972, narrated by Herbert Kaplow. ABC, Jan. 6.

RENDEVOUS WITH FREEDOM—A documentary tracing the history of the Jews in the United States, narrated by Sam Jaffe, Zero Mostel, George Segal, Marian Seldes, and Herbert Kaplow. ABC, April 15.

THE ROCKEFELLERS—A documentary on the wealthy and powerful Rockefeller family, with Walter Cronkite as correspondent. CBS, Dec. 28.

SHENYANG ACROBATIC TROUPE OF THE PEOPLE'S REPUBLIC OF CHINA—A performance by one of China's leading acrobatic companies, narrated by Joyce Susskind. ABC, April 18.

TONY AND LENA—A special featuring singers Tony Bennett and Lena Horne. ABC, Sept. 6.

SINS OF THE FATHERS—A documentary on the plight of the thousands of racially mixed children in Vietnam, abandoned by their American soldier fathers; narrated by Robert Northshield. NBC, June 19.

WAR AND PEACE—A 9-part dramatization of Tolstoy's novel, with Anthony Hopkins, Alan Dobie, and Morag Hood. PBS, weekly beginning Nov. 20.

WAR AND PEACE, *the Tolstoy classic, was presented by Public Broadcasting Service in nine episodes. From left are Morag Hood, Rupert Davies, and Joanna David.*

The commission accumulated a mass of material about children's programs in its January hearings and continued to study the data. However, the National Association of Broadcasters' television review board adopted general standards governing commercials aimed at children, standards to become effective not later than Jan. 1, 1974.

For nearly five years the FCC has been considering a rule aimed at breaking up existing cross-ownerships of media in single markets. The antitrust division of the Justice Department, tired of waiting, asked the commission in December to hold hearings on a license renewal application by WTJM-

AM-FM-TV, Milwaukee. It alleged that the owner, the Journal Company, held a monopoly in Milwaukee in view of its ownership of the radio and TV stations and two major newspapers.

In another area the FCC sent waves of shock through network offices by joining forces with a Justice Department suit to break up the networks' hold on programming. The FCC proposed that the networks be barred from producing any entertainment shows, and even perhaps from renting their facilities to producers of programs aired on the networks. The networks answered by pointing out that they produce and own very few of the programs they show, and that they can hardly be expected to maintain expensive production facilities for their news, public affairs, and sports programs if they are unable to gain income by renting their facilities.

June 30 marked the end of Nicholas Johnson's seven-year term on the FCC. The most liberal and consumer-minded member of the commission, Johnson had said he did not seek reappointment, although he did stay on until early December. Another member of the commission, H. Rex Lee, resigned effective December 31. Like Johnson, he was a supporter of public TV.

Federal Trade Commission. A revitalized Federal Trade Commission (FTC) continued to press for truth in advertising. Under Lewis A. Engman, nominated as chairman by the President in January, the FTC successfully pressed Congress to get the advertising of little cigars off the air. It also made moves to rectify, or require proof of, advertising claims for some products in the general areas of proprietary drugs, automobiles, nutrition, beverages, and products aimed at children.

It may have been of concern to American advertisers that Canada took steps toward regaining con-

SUMMARY OF WORLD TELEVISION
(As of March 1973)

Country	Stations	Number of TV sets	Country	Stations	Number of TV sets	Country	Stations	Number of TV sets
Albania	1	2,500	Hong Kong	3	679,000	Paraguay	1	45,000
Algeria	6	260,000	Hungary	11	2,000,000	Peru	18	450,000
Antigua	1	8,500	Iceland	7	43,000	Philippines	17	450,000
Argentina	33	3,800,000	India	1	21,000	Poland	30	5,000,000
Australia	131	2,950,000	Indonesia	11	150,000	Portugal	12	540,000
Austria	170	1,681,000	Iran	12	250,000	Puerto Rico[1]		645,000
Barbados	1	25,000	Iraq	5	500,000	Qatar	1	25,000
Belgium	15	2,383,000	Ireland	23	560,000	Rhodesia	2	58,000
Bermuda	2	20,000	Israel	12	430,000	Rumania	17	1,485,000
Bolivia	1	12,000	Italy	88	11,800,000	Samoa (American)	4	5,000
Brazil	53	7,600,000	Ivory Coast	6	70,000	Saudi Arabia	8	300,000
Bulgaria	8	1,287,250	Jamaica	9	100,000	Singapore	2	169,000
Cambodia	2	30,000	Japan	204	27,327,200	Spain	32	5,200,000
Canada	450	9,060,000	Jordan	1	85,000	Sudan	2	65,000
Chile	31	1,000,000	Kenya	3	35,000	Surinam	1	27,000
China (Mainland)	30	300,000	Korea	11	910,000	Sweden	212	3,700,000
Colombia	18	1,200,000	Kuwait	3	130,000	Switzerland	151	1,729,000
Costa Rica	4	150,400	Lebanon	9	320,000	Syria	5	160,000
Cuba	25	555,000	Liberia	1	8,000	Taiwan	5	2,100,000
Cyprus	2	64,000	Libya	2	1,500	Thailand	5	225,000
Czechoslovakia	28	3,250,000	Luxembourg	2	83,500	Trinidad & Tobago	3	70,000
Denmark	30	1,535,000	Malaysia	21	296,000	Tunisia	9	92,500
Dominican Republic	6	150,000	Malta	1	65,000	Turkey	9	150,000
Ecuador	12	250,000	Martinique	1	9,500	Uganda	6	15,000
Egypt	23	550,000	Mauritius	1	25,000	United Arab Emirates	2	7,500
El Salvador	4	109,300	Mexico	80	4,000,000	United Kingdom	212	16,931,000
Ethiopia	1	7,000	Monaco	1	16,000	United States[2]	927	111,300,000
Finland	67	1,149,300	Morocco	9	300,000	Upper Volta	1	4,000
France	173	13,526,000	Netherlands	18	3,870,000	Uruguay	13	350,000
Germany (East)	28	4,810,000	Netherlands Antilles	2	32,000	USSR	167	40,000,000
Germany (West)	176	21,300,000	New Zealand	24	717,200	Venezuela	31	710,000
Ghana	4	25,000	Nicaragua	2	60,000	Vietnam (South)	1	500,000
Greece	19	450,000	Nigeria	8	75,000	Virgin Islands[1]		23,000
Guam[1]		35,000	Norway	69	900,000	Yemen	4	30,000
Guatemala	3	109,500	Okinawa	2	230,000	Yugoslavia	35	2,320,000
Haiti	3	10,500	Pakistan	4	150,000	Zaire	2	100,000
Honduras	5	45,000	Panama	11	188,000	Zambia	3	18,500

[1] Stations included in U.S. count. [2] Preliminary estimate. (Source: TV Factbook.)

trol of many businesses in which American firms have large interests, and that some of those steps were aimed at TV commercials produced in the United States for use in Canadian markets.

RADIO

Radio's prosperous year in 1973 was marked by two bizarre phenomena. One was the birth and death of a form of talk show that seemingly went rather far beyond accepted community norms. The other was America's first pirate radio station.

Topless Radio. The phrase "topless radio" was promptly pinned on a form of two-way radio program in which a male talk-show host discussed, via telephone, the sexual hangups and problems of his callers-in. Frankness of language and revelation of intimate practices were often the rules of the game. As a result, topless radio shows suddenly popped up in various parts of the country. In April the FFC chose one station as a test case. It fined WGLD in Oak Park, Ill., $2,000 on grounds of obscenity and indecency and invited the licensee to take the matter to the courts as "the final arbiters in this sensitive First Amendment field." The licensee refused to contest the FCC action. Other stations also declined to take on the FCC on this issue, and topless radio died quickly. The FCC said that it was not opposing serious discussion of sex on the air, only salacious discussion.

Pirate Radio. In July the Rev. Carl McIntire, a fundamentalist preacher, finally exhausted all remedies for overturning the FCC's refusal to renew the licenses of his WXUR-AM-FM stations in Media, Pa. The refusal had been based on the stations' persistent violations of the fairness doctrine in presenting only Rev. McIntire's views. Nothing daunted, Rev. McIntire obtained a converted World War II minesweeper, fitted it out with a 10-kilowatt transmitter, and anchored it in international waters outside the 3-mile (4.8-km) limit off Cape May, N. J., from where, he vowed, he would broadcast his message. Calling his operation "Radio Free America," Rev. McIntire began broadcasting in the AM band on September 19. Within a day a federal restraining order shut down the pirate radio ship, and Rev. McIntire prepared for a long court battle. Section 301 of the Communications Act of 1934 bars anyone on a U. S. vessel or aircraft from the use of radio without an FCC license.

JOHN M. GUNN
State University of New York at Albany

TELEVISION AND RADIO ENGINEERING

The growth in the number of commercial and public television broadcasting stations in the United States virtually ended in 1973, but TV broadcasting continued to grow abroad. Sales of television receivers, especially color sets, remained at a high rate. Cable TV continued its steady expansion, both in the United States and abroad. Earth-orbiting satellites were used increasingly for television relaying.

TV Broadcasting. In the United States, 925 television broadcasting stations were on the air at the end of 1973, compared with 922 a year earlier. The 925 stations included 702 commercial and 223 public (noncommercial) TV stations. Of these, 602 operated in the VHF band (channels 2 to 13) and 323 in the UHF band (channels 14 to 69). Outside the United States, television broadcasting continued its steady growth.

Cable TV. Cable TV (CATV) continued to expand in the United States in 1973, and approximately 12% of the nation's 68 million homes were connected to cable systems by year-end. Most of the expansion was accounted for by the growth of existing systems. Many new municipal franchises had been granted for cable construction in larger cities and their suburbs, but actual construction of these systems lagged as prospective cable operators continued to seek fresh sources of programming.

Ways to use satellite relaying to distribute cable programming were under study. The first use of a satellite for this purpose was demonstrated in Anaheim, Calif., in June, using circuits provided by the Canadian Anik 2 satellite.

Cable systems continued to expand abroad, notably in Canada, Japan, Germany, the United Kingdom, Belgium, France, the Netherlands, and Ireland.

TV via Satellite. By 1973 the use of earth-orbiting satellites for TV relaying had become commonplace. Although no domestic television satellites were in use in the United States, several had been authorized and were under construction. Meanwhile, U. S. companies were leasing television relay circuits provided by the two Canadian domestic communications satellites. The launch of an experimental U. S. satellite for direct-to-home television broadcasting, originally scheduled for 1973, was delayed until 1974.

Westinghouse experimented with TV and radio broadcasting from a tethered all-weather balloon floating 10,000 feet (3,000 meters) above the Bahama Islands. This installation provides much wider area coverage than a ground station can.

Television Receivers. Color television receivers continued to account for an increasing percentage of total sales. Total sales in the United States in 1973 were about 17 million sets, of which 9.5

"Now to our White House reporter for his outrageous, vicious, distorted, frantic and hysterical report."

REPRINTED WITH PERMISSION BY NEWSDAY, LONG ISLAND, 1973

million were color sets. New designs emphasized brighter picture tubes and ease of color tuning.

RCA introduced a receiver line intended especially for connection to CATV systems, and industry organizations worked to develop standards for both cable TV receivers and cable distribution systems.

Video Recording and Playback Systems. There was a proliferation of new video recording and playback systems in 1973, featuring new systems using inexpensive plastic disks as well as variations on systems using magnetic-tape cartridges. There was a total lack of standardization, however, as each manufacturer jockeyed for a favorable competitive position. Several systems were offered for sale to the general public, but they had not found widespread public acceptance by year-end.

AM and FM Radio. The Federal Communications Commission (FCC) lifted an eight-year freeze on new AM broadcasting stations and began processing applications for new stations. A treaty between the United States and Mexico for the assignment of FM broadcast channels in the common border area went into effect in 1973.

At the end of 1973, there were 4,500 AM radio stations on the air in the United States, compared with 4,427 in 1972. The FM station total increased from 3,119 at the end of 1972 to 3,500 in 1973, including 700 noncommercial educational stations.

HOWARD T. HEAD, *A. D. Ring & Associates*

TENNESSEE

Legislation providing for a record-high state budget, new educational programs, and a broader state role in social service programs marked the year 1973 in Tennessee.

State Government. The Democrats, controlling the House of Representatives and the Senate, elected Ned McWhirter as House speaker and John Wilder to preside in the Senate and serve as lieutenant governor. They also reelected W. R. Snodgrass, Jr., as comptroller, Joe C. Carr as secretary of state, and Thomas A. Wiseman as treasurer. George King, appointed House bill clerk, became the first black to hold a House position since Reconstruction.

Legislation. Important legislation included provision for a statewide kindergarten program; vocational training in elementary and secondary schools; a rehabilitation center for the handicapped; a contingency fund for higher education; greater state participation in mental health programs and rehabilitation of alcoholics and drug abusers; teacher pay increases averaging $450 a year; bipartisan plans for reapportionment of legislative seats; reinstatement of the death penalty for specific crimes; protection of confidentiality of newsmen's sources; a one-year extension of the half-cent sales tax; and a budget for the operation of the state government of almost $2 billion. More controversial was a requirement that school textbooks include all credible theories, including biblical, on the origin of man.

In January the legislature approved a record-high state budget totaling $1.88 billion for fiscal 1973–74, based on the continuation of the state sales tax of 3.5 cents on the dollar and the expectation of receiving $523 million from the federal government. Also, the state supreme court declared unconstitutional a financial responsibility law for automobile drivers because it did not provide for a hearing prior to license revocation.

Other legislation provided for establishment of alcoholic rehabilitation centers in all three grand divisions of the state and restoration of November 11 as Veterans Day.

Economic Developments. State tax collections in 1973 exceeded the previous year's pace. For example, the amount collected in October was 14% above the previous year, and the total sales tax collections through October—$19.4 million—exceeded the 1972 figure by 15%. Also, the state's 3% unemployment rate was well below the seasonally adjusted national rate.

Industrial expansion included a new Sprague Electric Company plant in Clinton and a new papermaking machine at the Newport mill of the Sonoco Products Company. The TVA installed new devices at two of its steam power plants to monitor air quality and river temperature faster and more accurately than any previous system.

In January government agents in Chattanooga smashed the largest counterfeiting operation in the nation's history, seizing $7 to $10 million in bogus $20 bills.

Education. In March the Sixth Circuit Court of Appeals upheld a ruling of federal court Judge Robert L. Taylor that busing to achieve racial balance in the Knoxville school system was impractical and unnecessary.

The University of Tennessee, recognizing the growing importance of community college programs, began steps to improve relations with the two-year institutions in the state.

STANLEY J. FOLMSBEE, *University of Tennessee*

TENNESSEE • Information Highlights

Area: 422,244 square miles (109,412 sq km).
Population (1972 est.): 4,031,000. *Density:* 97 per sq mi.
Chief Cities (1970 census): Nashville, the capital, 447,877; Memphis, 623,530; Knoxville, 174,587; Chattanooga, 119,082; Jackson, 39,996; Johnson City, 33,770.
Government (1973): *Chief Officers*—governor, Winfield Dunn (R); lt. gov., John S. Wilder (D); secy. of state, Joe C. Carr (D); atty. gen., David M. Pack (D); treas., Thomas A. Wiseman; commissioner of education, Benjamin E. Carmichael; chief justice, Ross W. Dyer. *General Assembly*—Senate, 33 members (19 Democrats, 13 Republicans, 1 American party); House of Representatives, 99 members (51 D, 48 R).
Education (1972–73): *Enrollment*—public elementary schools, 541,221 pupils, 21,300 teachers; public secondary schools, 350,554 pupils, 14,900 teachers; nonpublic schools, 34,800 pupils, 1,920 teachers; colleges and universities, 143,241 students. *Public school expenditures*, $616,850,000 ($730 per pupil). *Average teacher's salary*, $8,450.
State Finances (fiscal year 1971): *Revenues*, $1,422,737,000 (3.5% general sales tax and gross receipts taxes, $264,251,000; motor fuel tax, $140,113,000; federal funds, $434,029,000). *Expenditures*, $1,374,629,000 (education, $561,875,000; health, welfare, and safety, $251,622,000; highways, $291,981,000). *State debt*, $478,299,000 (June 30, 1971).
Personal Income (1972): $14,671,000,000; *per capita*, $3,640.
Public Assistance (1972): $187,474,000. *Average monthly payments* (Dec. 1972)—old-age assistance, $55.48; aid to families with dependent children, $103.50.
Labor Force: *Nonagricultural wage and salary earners* (July 1973), 1,510,400. *Average annual employment* (1972)—manufacturing, 488,300; trade, 296,600; government, 240,200; services, 210,200. *Insured unemployed* (Sept. 1973)—16,500 (1.4%).
Manufacturing (1971): *Value added by manufacture*, $6,728,900,000. Chemicals and allied products, $1,383,100,000; food and kindred products, $641,200,000; electrical equipment and supplies, $620,700,000; apparel and other textile products, $461,900,000.
Agriculture (1972): *Cash farm income*, $907,829,000 (livestock, $514,789,000; crops, $335,287,000; government payments, $57,753,000). *Chief crops* (in order of value, 1971)—Soybeans, tobacco, cotton lint, hay.
Mining (1972): *Production value*, $241,732,000 (ranks 29th among the states). *Chief minerals*—Stone, $53,729,000; coal, $53,400,000; cement, $41,030,000; zinc, $37,841,000.
Transportation: *Roads* (1972), 80,290 miles (129,211 km); *motor vehicles* (1972), 2,135,635; *railroads* (1972), 3,214 miles (5,172 km); *public airports* (1972), 69.
Communications: *Telephones* (1973), 2,225,700; *television stations* (1971), 16; *radio stations* (1971), 213; *newspapers* (1973), 34 (daily circulation, 1,161,000).

TEXAS

A productive legislative session, settlement of two river questions, the beginning of an energy crisis, and investigation into youth-care facilities marked the year 1973 in Texas.

Legislation. The 63d Texas legislature, elected on promises of reform born during the 1971 Sharpstown banking scandal, rewrote much of the state's 19th century legislation. The lawmakers' work included: (1) A new penal code, which replaced one written 117 years before; (2) new drug laws, which included reduced penalties for marihuana possession but tougher penalties for illicit narcotics sales; (3) a revised family code dealing with the rights of juveniles; (4) a law lowering the age of adulthood to 18, allowing 18- through 20-year-olds to enter into contracts, serve on juries, drink alcoholic beverages, and have other rights previously reserved for Texans 21 or over; and (5) stronger ethics laws for public officials.

The same legislators met as a state constitutional convention in January 1974 to write a new Texas constitution. They began their work with a draft prepared in 1973 by a citizens' constitution revision commission.

Airport. In keeping with its reputation for bigness, Texas dedicated the Dallas–Fort Worth Airport, the world's largest, in September. Final construction delayed its opening until early 1974. Sprawled on 17,500 acres between the northern limits of the two cities and costing more than $500 million, the Dallas–Fort Worth Airport, with its individual terminals and electrically powered "people movers," is billed as the prototype of future international airports. Its title of world's largest, however, will soon be lost to Montreal, where an even larger airport is scheduled to open in 1975.

Canal Project. A transportation plan held dear by north Texas businessmen suffered what many consider a fatal blow in 1973. Voters in a 17-county area on March 13 turned down a $150 million bond proposal to finance a Trinity River Canal project, which would have enabled barges to carry goods from the Gulf to Dallas and Fort Worth.

Texas-Louisiana Border. Another Texas river question was settled on March 20 when the U. S. Supreme Court decided by an 8-to-1 vote that the border between Texas and Louisiana is in the middle of the Sabine River and not the western bank, as Louisiana had claimed. The high court's ruling upheld the bulk of the findings of retired Federal Judge Robert Van Pelt of Nebraska, who had acted as special master in the dispute. The decision gave Texas claim to minerals that lie within its half of the river, and these are significant in the case of the oil-rich Sabine.

Energy Shortage. Like the rest of the nation, Texans became aware of a growing national energy shortage in 1973. Although the big state, with its oil and natural gas reserves, was not seriously affected, certain areas of south and central Texas did have a scare in the winter of 1972–73 when gas supplies were curtailed for power plants belonging to Austin, San Antonio, and the Lower Colorado River Authority. The company supplying the gas blamed the curtailment of overestimation of the company's gas reserves in west Texas. The problem was not solved as the year ended, and city officials in that area of the state feared a possible electricity shortage during the winter of 1973–74.

Area: 267,338 square miles (692,405 sq km).
Population (1972 est.): 11,649,000. *Density:* 44 per sq mi.
Chief Cities (1970 census): Austin, the capital, 251,808; Houston, 1,232,802; Dallas, 844,401; San Antonio, 654,153; Fort Worth, 393,476; El Paso, 322,261; Corpus Christi, 204,525.
Government (1973): *Chief Officers*—governor, Dolph Briscoe (D); lt. gov., William P. Hobby (D); secy. of state, Mark W. White, Jr. (D); atty. gen., John Hill (D); treas., Jesse James (D); commissioner of education, J. W. Edgar; chief justice of the supreme court, Joe R. Greenhill. *Legislature*—Senate, 31 members (28 Democrats, 3 Republicans); House of Representatives, 150 members (133 D, 17 R).
Education (1972–73): *Enrollment*—public elementary schools, 1,475,622 pupils, 68,549 teachers; public secondary schools, 1,218,780 pupils, 60,788 teachers; nonpublic schools, 122,100 pupils, 6,000 teachers; colleges and universities, 446,153 students. *Public school expenditures,* $2,598,950,000 ($1,044 per pupil). *Average teacher's salary,* $9,029.
State Finances (fiscal year 1971): *Revenues,* $4,102,131,000 (4% general sales tax and gross receipts taxes, $635,574,-000; motor fuel tax, $333,833,000; federal funds, $1,102,-822,000). *Expenditures,* $3,727,787,000 (education, $1,818,-392,000; health, welfare, and safety, $733,540,000; highways, $672,128,000). State debt, $1,196,337,000 (Aug. 31, 1971).
Personal Income (1972): $47,121,000,000; per capita, $4,045.
Public Assistance (1972): $677,908,000. *Average monthly payments* (Dec. 1972)—old-age assistance, $54.57; aid to families with dependent children, $114,04.
Labor Force: *Nonagricultural wage and salary earners* (July 1973), 4,071,200. *Average annual employment* (1972)—manufacturing, 741,100; trade, 951,200; government, 711,-400; services, 644,200. *Insured unemployed* (Sept. 1973)—27,900 (0.9%).
Manufacturing (1971): *Value added by manufacture,* $13,793,-900,000. Chemicals and allied products, $2,886,200,000; food and kindred products, $1,696,900,000; petroleum and coal products, $1,579,000,000; transportation equipment, $1,262,100,000; nonelectrical machinery, $1,022,100,000; fabricated metal products, $938,000,000.
Agriculture (1972): *Cash farm income,* $4,462,165,000 (livestock, $2,564,846,000; crops, $1,368,752,000; government payments, $528,567,000). *Chief crops* (in order of value, 1972)—Cotton lint (ranks 1st among the states); sorghum grain (ranks 1st); hay; rice (ranks 2d).
Mining (1972): *Production value,* $7,327,231,000 (ranks 1st among the states). *Chief minerals*—Petroleum, $4,548,-517,000; natural gas, $1,520,512,000; natural gas liquids, $536,500,000; cement, $162,400,000.
Fisheries (1972): *Commercial catch,* 117,000,000 pounds ($85,011,000).
Transportation: *Roads* (1972), 248,340 miles (399,654 km); *motor vehicles* (1972), 6,984,269; *railroads* (1972), 13,563 miles (21,827 km); *public airports* (1972), 266.
Communications: *Telephones* (1973), 7,122,400; *television stations* (1971), 56; *radio stations* (1971), 412; *newspapers* (1973), 111 (daily circulation, 3,298,000).

Youth-Care Facilities. A legislative investigation into the state's licensing procedures for youth-care facilities was triggered in June 1973 by the murder indictment of the director of an East Texas school for troubled youths. He was accused of not getting rapid treatment for a 17-year-old female student who took poison.

The investigation soon spilled over from private institutions to state facilities for delinquent and retarded youths. The furor was fueled in August by the findings of U. S. District Judge William Wayne Justice, who ruled that reform schools of the Texas Youth Council (TYC) used methods that constituted cruel and unusual punishment and violated the inmates' rights to treatment. In September a disturbance broke out on the main TYC campuses at Gatesville, precipitating the resignations of key TYC leaders.

Mass Murder. The problem of runaway children also came into the national spotlight as a result of a series of 27 murders of young boys and men in southern Texas. (See also CRIME; HOUSTON.)

Abortion Ruling. Two Texas women helped make legal history in January when they were instrumental in getting the nation's abortion laws overturned by the U. S. Supreme Court. The plaintiff in the case was a Dallas woman, and she was represented by Austin attorney Sarah Weddington.

Weather. Nature was not kind to Texas in 1973. Winter storms caused cattle losses estimated at 150,000, and rains later in the year caused crop damage. The state was spared a hurricane in 1973, but tropical storm Delia made an unusual two landfalls on the upper Texas coast in September.

Names in the News. On Jan. 22, 1973, Lyndon Baines Johnson, Texan and 36th President of the United States, died of a heart attack while at his Texas hill country ranch. He was 64 years old.

Another famous Texas attorney once again came into the national spotlight on November 1, when President Nixon appointed him special U. S. prosecutor to handle the Watergate investigation. He is Houstonian Leon Jaworski, a former president of the American Bar Association, attorney for President Johnson, and Nazi war crime prosecutor.

ADREN ETHERIDGE
Assistant City Editor, The Houston "Post"

THAILAND

The Thai military regime, despite efforts at moderation early in 1973, fell in October in the wake of gigantic student demonstrations, and Premier Thanom Kittikachorn fled to the United States. With the ending of the American role in the Indochina conflict, the presence in Thailand of large numbers of U. S. forces was marked with much uncertainty. Although Thanom had wanted U. S. troops to remain in Thailand, it seemed unlikely that the new regime would continue to share this sentiment.

Domestic Affairs. The year 1973 was tumultuous for the Thais. On Dec. 28, 1972, four Arab terrorists, members of the Black September group, had captured and held the Israeli embassy in Bangkok for 19 hours. After releasing six hostages the terrorists were permitted to leave for Egypt. In March five members of an indigenous terrorist organization called Thai Black September seized a bus and 30 hostages in an abortive bid to get a plane to fly them to Hong Kong. Communist guerrilla activity remained alive in the north.

──────── **THAILAND** • Information Highlights ────────

Official Name: Kingdom of Thailand.
Location: Southeast Asia.
Area: 198,456 square miles (514,000 sq km).
Population (1973 est.): 39,900,000. *Density,* 195 per square mile (76 per sq km).
Chief Cities (1967 est.): Bangkok, the capital, 2,008,000; Thonburi, 606,300.
Government: *Head of state,* Bhumibol Adulyadej, king (acceded June 1946). *Head of government,* Sanya Dharmasakti, premier (took office Oct. 1973). *Legislature* (unicameral)—National Assembly. *Major political parties*—United Thai People's party; Democratic party.
Language: Thai (official).
Education: *Expenditure* (1969), 16.3% of total public expenditure. *School enrollment* (1968)—primary, 5,122,728; secondary, 479,119; technical/vocational, 62,066; university/ higher, 41,848.
Monetary Unit: Baht (20.35 baht equal U. S.$1, Sept. 1973).
Gross National Product (1972 est.): $7,260,000,000.
Economic Indexes: *Agricultural production* (1971), 128 (1963= 100); *consumer price index* (1972), 124 (1963=100).
Manufacturing (major products): Processed foods, textiles.
Major Agricultural Products: Rubber (ranks 3d among world producers, 1972), rice, tapioca, corn, tobacco, fruits, sugarcane, kenaf and jute, forest products, fish.
Major Minerals: Tin, tungsten, lignite, salt, manganese.
Foreign Trade (1972): *Exports,* $1,051,000,000; *Imports,* $1,479,000,000. *Chief trading partners* (1970)—Japan (took 25.5% of exports, supplied 37% of imports); United States (13.4%—15%).
Tourism: Receipts (1972), $130,700,000.
Transportation: *Motor vehicles* (1969), 284,500 (automobiles, 142,000); *railroads* (1971), 2,339 miles (3,764 km); *merchant fleet* (1972), 108,000 gross registered tons; *major national airline,* Thai Airways.
Communications: *Telephones* (1972), 202,023; *newspapers* (1971), 35 (daily circulation, 250,000).

Food shortages, stemming from the serious disintegration of Thai agriculture along with several years of droughts, appeared—although the country has traditionally been able to feed itself and even produce surpluses. Labor unrest mounted steadily, beginning in the spring when illegal strikes in the steel.industry resulted in a victory for the strikers. Field Marshal Thanom Kittikachorn's government was strangely acquiescent in this matter.

In early summer university students began to participate in essentially nonviolent demonstrations over the expulsion of nine students from Ramkanhaeng University for having published a critical satire of the military government. Student strikes succeeded in closing all universities and winning the readmission of those students who had been expelled. The Bangkok Post said in August that "the rise of student power has been one of the most important developments in recent Thai history." The events of October showed that this was no overstatement.

Emboldened by their earlier successes, the students took to the streets of Bangkok in the middle of October and by sheer numbers overwhelmed the police and the army in the capital, burned and sacked several military installations, and demanded the ouster of Premier Thanom, long-time military strongman. This time the uprising was bloody; perhaps as many as 200 students were killed. But the students achieved their objectives.

King Bhumibol accepted the resignations of Kittikachorn, the premier's son (who held a number of offices), and his deputy, Marshal Praphas Charusathien, who then fled the country. An associate of the king, Dr. Sanya Dharmasakti, was named premier, and a new civilian cabinet was formed. The new premier quickly promised a new constitution and new elections.

The leader of the student revolt was Sombat Thamrongthanyawong, secretary general of the National Student Center. He called for the end of foreign aid, particularly that of the United States.

Foreign Affairs. U. S. Vice President Spiro Agnew visited Thailand in February and promised Thanom continued American military and economic aid (military aid has totaled more than $11 billion since 1950). Much of the bombing of Indochina occurred from Thai bases. In the spring about 45,000 American servicemen were stationed at these bases. With the end of the bombing runs a gradual American withdrawal began. In May, Thanom said that an American military presence was still necessary in Thailand. It was disclosed at that time that the United States continued to support about 15,000 "irregular" Thai troops in Laos—at a cost of about $100 million a year.

In October, just before the collapse of his regime, Thanom announced that the United States had agreed to suspend troop withdrawals because of the continued uncertainty of the Indochina situation. With the installation of the new government, the future of the American presence was put in doubt.

The New York *Times* described Thailand in October as a "wobbly Asian domino." It appeared likely that increased anti-American sentiment would characterize the months ahead. By early November the government of Premier Sanya had already moved to improve relations with North Vietnam and Communist China.

CARL LEIDEN
University of Texas at Austin

Peter Cook (wearing glasses) *and Dudley Moore, two of the stars of the 1962 British review* Beyond the Fringe, *returned to Broadway with their two-man show* Good Evening.

theater

A succinct assessment of the New York theater in 1973 would be: new Broadway plays—dismal; Off-Broadway productions—a little better; Broadway musicals—better than average. Every year it seems necessary to search for new ways to describe the shallowness and dullness of the Broadway theater. Two years ago, this survey commented that "legitimate theater in New York reached a new low," but that view could be considered praise in comparison to the 1973 season. Yet investors poured about $23 million into commercial theater last year. They lost over $5 million of it, but the lure of sudden wealth with a hit keeps Broadway alive—however low the quality of that life.

Broadway Plays. The dearth of native American imagination on Broadway is painfully obvious: of 35 nonmusical plays that opened in 1973, 15 were revivals of American and European plays written 20 or more years ago, seven were imports of recent foreign plays, one was an adaptation of Chekhov's fiction, and just 12 (half of them stock situation comedies) were new American works. It is understandable that Broadway "angels" lost millions.

The only impressive new foreign play was David Storey's *The Changing Room,* an understated metaphoric study of the violence and aimless fragmentation of modern life epitomized by the locker-room activities of a British semipro rugby team.

Native revivals were dominated by America's greatest dramatists, Eugene O'Neill and Tennessee Williams. James Earl Jones starred in a bland *The Iceman Cometh;* but another of O'Neill's late plays, *A Moon for the Misbegotten,* was graced by the elegant performances of Jason Robards, Jr., and Colleen Dewhurst. Lincoln Center produced Williams' *A Streetcar Named Desire* in the play's 25th anniversary year. The part of Blanche Du Bois was played brilliantly by Rosemary Harris, who brought out the character's gritty strength and humor, qualities usually overlooked in this great role. *Streetcar* was done again on Broadway later in the year with

Lois Nettleton as a fine Blanche. Williams also had a new play, *Out Cry,* on Broadway. Ironically, this vision of madness, loneliness, and entrapment in family history ran just 12 performances. Broadway also saw a star-studded revival of Clare Boothe Luce's 1937 hit *The Women,* an acid look at New York sophistication and the bitterness resulting from rigid sex-role limitations.

There was no new American play of distinction, or even promise, in 1973. Hopes ran high for the new regime of Joseph Papp, the producer of the New York Shakespeare Festival at Lincoln Center. But these hopes were left unsatisfied (though not utterly extinguished) after Papp's first production, *Boom Boom Room,* the first non-Vietnam play by the young David Rabe. The play is standard American fare: the story of a go-go girl who yearns for self-realization and authenticity. It has moments of insight and sensitivity, but little more.

It is difficult to recall a less rewarding year on Broadway for the home product. Optimistic theatergoers, however, could swallow their disappointment and look forward to 1974 and promised new works by Tennessee Williams and Edward Albee.

Broadway Musicals. During the 1972–73 season the average cost of mounting a Broadway musical was $541,000, and in a few cases costs rose to nearly $1 million. Yet producers were not deterred, and the year saw a better-than-usual crop of musicals. But because big money was involved, the cautious tendency to stick to the tried and true dominated. Revivals or adaptations of successful plays were the rule, original musicals the rare exception. The revival craze went back to 1919 and *Irene,* with Debbie Reynolds in the title role. Other revivals included the Sigmund Romberg favorite *The Desert Song* and a first-rate *The Pajama Game.*

Heading an impressive list of adaptations of previous hits in other forms was *A Little Night Music,* taken from Ingmar Bergman's film *Smiles of* (Continued on page 590)

1973 BROADWAY hits included Raisin *(above),
a musical version of Lorraine Hansberry's*
A Raisin in the Sun; *a revival of the 1919 hit*
Irene *(above, right), starring Debbie Reynolds;*
The Good Doctor *(right), Neil Simon's retelling of several Chekhov stories, with Christopher Plummer (seated); Lerner and Loewe's*
Gigi *(below, right), reversing the usual practice by going from the films to the stage; and*
The Changing Room *(below), a British import.*

BROADWAY OPENINGS IN 1973

PLAYS

The Au Pair Man, by Hugh Leonard; directed by Gerald Freedman; with Julie Harris and Charles Durning; December 27–

Boom Boom Room, by David Rabe; directed by Joseph Papp; with Charlotte Rae, Madeline Kahn, and Robert Loggia; November 8–December 9.

The Changing Room, by David Storey; directed by Michael Rudman; with Rex Robbins, George Hearn, and Tom Atkins; March 6–August 18.

Chemin de Fer, by Georges Feydeau; directed by Stephen Porter; with Rachel Roberts and John McMartin; November 26– (in repertory).

Children of the Wind, by Jerry Devine; staged by Shepard Traube; with James Callahan, Ann Thomas, and Sarah Hardy; October 24–27.

Crown Matrimonial, by Royce Ryton; directed by Peter Dews; with Eileen Herlie and George Grizzard; October 2–December 9.

Don Juan in Hell, by George Bernard Shaw; directed by John Houseman; with Paul Henreid, Ricardo Montalban, Edward Mulhare, and Agnes Moorehead; January 15–February 4.

Emperor Henry IV, by Luigi Pirandello; directed by Clifford Williams; with Eileen Herlie and Rex Harrison; March 28–April 28.

The Enemy Is Dead, by Don Petersen; directed by Arthur Sherman; with Linda Lavin and Arthur Storch; January 14 (one performance).

Finishing Touches, by Jean Kerr; directed by Joseph Anthony; with Barbara Bel Geddes and Robert Lansing; February 8–July 1.

42 Seconds from Broadway, by Louis Del Grande; directed by Arthur Storch; with Henry Winkler and Regina Baff; March 11 (one performance).

Full Circle, by Erich Maria Remarque; adapted by Peter Stone; directed by Otto Preminger; with Bibi Andersson and Leonard Nimoy; November 7–24.

The Good Doctor, by Neil Simon; directed by A. J. Antoon; with Christopher Plummer; November 27–

Holiday, by Philip Barry; directed by Michael Montel; with Rachel Roberts and John McMartin; December 26– (in repertory).

The Iceman Cometh, by Eugene O'Neill, directed by Theodore Mann; with James Earl Jones; December 13–

The Jockey Club Stakes, by William Douglas Home, directed by Cyril Ritchard; with Wilfred Hyde-White, Philip Kerr, Robert Coote, and Geoffrey Sumner; January 24–March 24.

Let Me Hear You Smile, by Leonara Thuna and Harry Cauley; directed by Harry Cauley; with Sandy Dennis and James Broderick; January 16 (one performance).

Look Away, by Jerome Kilty; directed by Rip Torn; with Geraldine Page and Maya Angelou; January 7 (one performance).

Medea, by Euripides; adapted and directed by Minos Volanakis; with Irene Papas; January 17–March 18.

The Merchant of Venice, by William Shakespeare; directed by Ellis Rabb; with Sidney Walker and Rosemary Harris; March 4–April 7.

A Moon for the Misbegotten, by Eugene O'Neill; directed by José Quintero; with Colleen Dewhurst and Jason Robards, Jr.; December 29–

No Hard Feelings, by Sam Bobrick and Ron Clark; directed by Abe Burrows; with Eddie Albert, Nanette Fabray, and Conrad Janis; April 8 (one performance).

No Sex Please, We're British, by Anthony Marriott and Alistair Foot; directed by Christopher Hewett; with Tony Tanner, Stephen Collins, and J. J. Lewis; February 20–March 4.

Out Cry, by Tennessee Williams; directed by Peter Glenville; with Michael York and Cara Duff-MacCormick; March 1–10.

The Plough and the Stars, by Sean O'Casey; directed by Dan Sullivan; with Pauline Flanagan, Roberta Maxwell, Jack MacGowran; January 4–February 10.

The River Niger, by Joseph A. Walker; directed by Douglas Turner Ward; with Mr. Ward, Roxie Roker, and Frances Foster; March 27–November 25.

A Streetcar Named Desire, by Tennessee Williams; directed by Ellis Rabb; with Rosemary Harris and James Farentino; April 26–July 29.

A Streetcar Named Desire, directed by Jules Irving; with Lois Nettleton and Alan Feinstein; October 4–November 18.

Uncle Vanya, by Anton Chekhov; directed by Mike Nichols; with George C. Scott; Nicol Williamson, Julie Christie, and Lillian Gish; June 4–July 22.

Veronica's Room, by Ira Levin; directed by Ellis Rabb; with Arthur Kennedy and Eileen Heckart; October 25–December 29.

The Visit, by Friedrich Dürenmatt; directed by Harold Prince; with Rachel Roberts and John McMartin; November 25– (in repertory).

The Waltz of the Toreadors, by Jean Anouilh; directed by Brian Murray; with Eli Wallach and Anne Jackson; September 13–December 2.

Warp, by Bury St. Edmund and Stuart Gordon; directed by Mr. Gordon; with John Heard and Carolyn Gordon; February 14–18.

The Women, by Clare Boothe Luce; directed by Morton Da Costa; with Alexis Smith, Myrna Loy, Rhonda Fleming, Kim Hunter, and Jan Miner; April 25–June 20.

MUSICALS

Cyrano, book based on Anthony Burgess' adaptation of Edmond Rostand's *Cyrano de Bergerac,* music by Michael J. Lewis, lyrics by Mr. Burgess; directed by Michael Kidd; with Christopher Plummer; May 13–June 23.

The Desert Song, music by Sigmund Romberg; directed by Henry Butler; with David Cryer, Shepperd Strudwick; September 5–16.

Gigi, book and lyrics by Alan J. Lerner, music by Frederick Loewe; directed by Joseph Hardy; with Karen Wolfe, Alfred Drake, Agnes Moorehead, and Maria Karnilova; November 13–

Good Evening, a revue by and starring Peter Cook and Dudley Moore; November 14–

Irene, book by Hugh Wheeler and Joseph Stein, lyrics by Joseph McCarthy, music by Harry Tierney; directed by Gower Champion; with Debbie Reynolds, Patsy Kelly, and George S. Irving; March 13–

A Little Night Music, book by Hugh Wheeler, music and lyrics by Stephen Sondheim; directed by Harold Prince; with Glynis Johns, Hermione Gingold, and Len Cariou; February 25–

Molly, book by Louis Garfinkle and Leonard Adelson, music by Jerry Livingston, lyrics by Mr. Adelson and Mack David; directed by Alan Arkin; with Kay Ballard and Eli Mintz; November 1–December 29.

Nash at Nine, verses and lyrics by Ogden Nash, music by Milton Rosenstock; directed by Martin Charnin; with E. G. Marshall and Virginia Vestoff; May 17–June 2.

The Pajama Game, book by George Abbott and Richard Bissell, music and lyrics by Jerry Ross and Richard Adler; directed by Mr. Abbott; with Barbara McNair, Cab Calloway, and Hal Linden; December 9–

Raisin, book by Robert Nemiroff and Charlotte Zaltzberg, music by Judd Woldin, lyrics by Robert Brittan; directed by Donald McKayle; with Virginia Capers, Joe Morton, Ernestine Jackson; October 18–

Seesaw, book by Michael Bennett, music by Cy Coleman, lyrics by Dorothy Fields; directed by Mr. Bennett; with Michele Lee and Ken Howard; March 18–December 9.

Shelter, book and lyrics by Gretchen Cryer, music by Nancy Ford; directed by Austin Pendleton; with Terry Kiser and Marcia Rodd; February 6–March 3.

Tricks, book by Jon Jory, based on a play by Molière, music by Jerry Blatt, lyrics by Lonnie Burstein; directed by Mr. Jory; with René Auberjonois; January 8–13.

(Continued from page 587)
a Summer Night. It won the Tony award for best musical; its star Glynis Johns was the Tony choice for best musical actress, and the show garnered four other Tonys. Not far behind in excellence was *Raisin,* based on Lorraine Hansberry's celebrated drama of black family life, *A Raisin in the Sun.* William Gibson's *Two for the Seesaw* became *Seesaw* and ran for nine months. The year closed with two other musical adaptations: *Molly,* based on Gertrude Berg's radio and TV series *The Goldbergs,* and a Lerner and Loewe musical version of Colette's romantic novel *Gigi,* which was also one of the all-time most popular films.

It is interesting to note that the only wholly original musical of the year, *Shelter,* lasted less than a month on Broadway. It is small wonder that producers are careful in choosing material on which to spend their average $541,000. And it is small wonder, too, that the Broadway musical, one of the few native American art forms, is now little more than relaxing entertainment with slight relevance to reality, as it sinks further back into the good old days.

Off-Broadway. Lanford Wilson's long-running *The Hot l Baltimore* was the New York Drama Critics choice for best Off-Broadway play. Set in a seedy hotel, the drama compassionately presents a cross section of humanity struggling with the indignities and hassles of a lower-depths world.

The Chelsea Theater Center of Brooklyn, Off-Broadway's most experimental and artistically committed theater, offered two of the season's outstanding ventures: *Kaspar,* the German playwright Peter Handke's extraordinary modernization of the true story of a 16-year-old boy who could not walk or speak. As he learns to master reality in this unsparing criticism of modern life, the boy is bombarded by the media and ends up more alone in his hyperawareness than he was in his early isolation. The Chelsea's production of David Storey's *The Contractor,* another of this British dramatist's slow-rhythm metaphors for reality and nonrelatedness, won deserved plaudits from the critics.

There were new plays by two well-known American dramatists, but neither work lived up to expectations. Mart Crowley (author of *The Boys in the Band*) chronicled 15 years in a conflict-ridden family in his *A Breeze From the Gulf.* Crowley uses the classical situation of American drama, but his play is diffuse and rambling. In *Enclave,* Arthur Laurents takes a rather artificial plot—the "coming out" of a middle-aged homosexual to the chagrin of his circle of smart friends—and satirizes, too cleverly and superficially, the upper-middle-class New York professional world.

In sum, with but few exceptions, Off-Broadway fared as poorly as Broadway did in 1973.

Outside New York. For several years a major part of the truly experimental theatrical activity in the United States was generated by regional theaters, usually foundation-supported and free of the commercial pressures of New York. Many of these theaters are now solidly established. They have lost some of their novelty, but the best of them, such as New Haven's Long Wharf or Washington D. C.'s Arena Stage, continue to mount challenging and serious productions, several of which eventually reach New York. This was the case with the Long Wharf's production of David Storey's *The Changing Room,* which went on to win the New York Drama

Critics' best play of 1973 award. This inspiring company also offered a little-known but very powerful play by D. H. Lawrence, *The Widowing of Mrs. Holroyd.* A starkly realistic drama set in England's mining country, Lawrence's play captures the thwarted, yearning life of the wife of a miner killed in an accident. Reminiscent in atmosphere of his great novel *Sons and Lovers,* the play is very skillful and moving. For work of this high quality, the Long Wharf amply merits recognition and gratitude.

Theatergoers can rely on the Arena Stage for daring and rewarding productions. During recent years the Arena has presented premieres of notable American plays such as *The Great White Hope* and *Moonchildren* (a study of the drifting Vietnam War college generation, which enjoyed a New York revival in 1973). The Arena's most interesting offering of 1973 was the American premiere of the Swiss playwright Max Frisch's 1951 work *A Public Prosecutor Is Sick of It All.* The play typifies the postwar avant-garde as it treats the intermingling of fantasy and reality, and the theme of elusive identity. Here, as in all of Frisch's plays, the psychological exists within a vicious political framework of totalitarianism and violence. The Arena was rewarded for its excellence by being chosen in 1973 by the Nixon administration to be the first U. S. drama company to tour the Soviet Union.

Elsewhere in the United States, some of the best regional theater emanated from colleges. The American College Theater Festival, a selection of the 10 best college productions staged annually at the Kennedy Center in Washington, D. C., burgeoned with 312 entries in the 1973 competition. The University of Illinois entry was a provocative political farce called *Head of State,* comprised largely of quotations from American presidents in the style of "documentary" drama popularized a few years ago by Peter Weiss' *The Investigation.* With regard to U. S. presidents, the Yale Drama School created the ultimate in the demagicalization of "sacred" office with a cabaret-style satiric review on the Watergate affair, with the dean of the school appearing as the beleaguered President. The McCarter Theater, a professional company based at Princeton University, extended its fine work with a production of G. B. Shaw's little-seen farce on family and sex roles *You Never Can Tell,* and also with a stirring revival of John Osborne's *The Entertainer.*

Regional theater provides stars with opportunities to stretch their craft by playing parts usually unavailable to them. The year 1973 saw Faye Dunaway (of *Bonnie and Clyde* fame) trying her hand at *A Streetcar Named Desire* for Los Angeles' Ahmanson Theater and the gifted Al Pacino (of *The Godfather*) as Shakespeare's Richard III for the Theater Company of Boston. The variety and freedom of regional theater impart to it ongoing vitality and importance.

International Theater. Theater in Canada was active and interesting in 1973. The Stratford, Ontario, Shakespeare Festival, which opened 20 years ago with Alec Guinness starring in Tyrone Guthrie's production of *Richard III,* celebrated its two decades with its usual two Shakespeare plays (in 1973, *The Taming of the Shrew* and *Othello*) and one non-Shakespearean play, Oliver Goldsmith's *She Stoops to Conquer.* The Stratford Festival was doubly honored: by an invitation to be the first North American Company to tour the Soviet Union

and by the bestowal of the best actor award of the Outer Critics Circle to Christopher Plummer for his performance in the title role in *Cyrano,* later seen in New York in a musical version.

The Shaw Festival opened its 12th year at Niagara-on-the-Lake, Ontario, with *You Never Can Tell* in a new $3 million theater. Opening night was attended by two prime ministers, Pierre Trudeau of Canada and Indira Gandhi of India. A week later the festival was honored by the attendance of Queen Elizabeth II and Prince Philip. The season's second Shaw production was *Fanny's First Play.* These little-performed Shavian comedies are kept vividly alive by the festival's excellent productions. (See also CANADA: CULTURAL AFFAIRS.)

Theater in England always flourishes. In February 1973, for instance, there were 56 productions running in London, compared with 21 in New York. As usual, several traveled from London to New York, including *Good Evening,* a satirical review by Peter Cook and Dudley Moore (two of the creators of *Beyond the Fringe*). The Royal Court Theatre can invariably be counted on for the best new work in England. During the 1973 season it offered John Osborne's new play *A Sense of Detachment,* Albert Finney in David Storey's antiwar play *Cromwell,* and Paul Scofield in Christopher Hampton's *Savages,* an anticolonial play.

The World Theater Season Festival in London sparkled with international entries. They included the Swedish Royal Dramatic Theater's production of Ibsen's *The Wild Duck,* starring Max von Sydow under Ingmar Bergman's direction; a revival of Lorca's *Yerma* by Spain's Nuria Espert Company (which later went to New York); and two Molière plays by the Comédie Française in honor of the tricentennial of the death of the world's greatest comic dramatist.

Argentinean theater flourishes in Buenos Aires, in part because of a flexible censorship that is unlike Brazil's drastic repression (Brazil has banned 500 plays in the last five years). Most of the serious new plays in Argentina concern national history and current social conflict. Among several noteworthy offerings are: David Viñas' *Túpac-Amaru,* an antiracist, anti-imperialist work, and *El Señor Galindez,* a criticism of the treatment of political prisoners written by the psychoanalyst Edwardo Paulovsky.

East of the Berlin wall, Poland's theatrical scene was especially lively, particularly in the number of Western plays available. During one week, while only two contemporary Soviet plays were on the boards, one could see a dramatization of Kafka's *Amerika,* Ionesco's *Macbeth,* Neil Simon's *The Odd Couple,* Joyce's *Exiles,* O'Neill's *Mourning Becomes Electra, The Man of La Mancha,* and half a dozen other British and American works.

Awards. The major Antoinette Perry (Tony) awards went to: Julie Harris, best actress (*The Last of Mrs. Lincoln*); Alan Bates, best actor (*Butley*); Jason Miller's *That Championship Season,* best play. For musicals: Glynis Johns, best actress (*A Little Night Music*); Ben Vereen, best actor (*Pippin*); best musical, *A Little Night Music.* The Pulitzer Prize for Drama was awarded to *That Championship Season.* (See also PRIZES AND AWARDS.)

Obituary Notes. The theater world mourned the deaths in 1973 of William Inge, Noël Coward, and S. N. Behrman (see also OBITUARIES).

HAROLD FERRAR, *Columbia University*

TORONTO

Toronto, situated on Lake Ontario, is the capital of the province of Ontario and Canada's second-largest city (1973 est. pop. 680,319). Major events in 1973 included a drastic rise in housing prices that totaled 23.6% in the first six months; a visit by Queen Elizabeth in June, during which she opened the $12 million Scarborough Civic Centre; and the January kidnapping and release of Marilyn Lastman, wife of millionaire Mel Lastman, mayor of the Toronto borough of North York.

Government. David Crombie, elected in 1972, is mayor of Toronto. Metro Toronto comprises the city proper and five boroughs, with a population of 2,045,450 (1973 est.). Metro Chairman Albert Campbell, who resigned in July and died in August, was succeeded by Paul Godfrey, aged 34. In 1973 the City Council authorized a major overhaul of the administrative structure, and the federal government announced plans for a $25 million new government office in North York.

Transportation. The federal government ran into criticism over its plans for an 18,000-acre (6,885-hectare) Pickering airport, and over the new Terminal Two at Malton Airport, a half mile long, which was opened in April. The Toronto Transit Commission completed a 2.68-mile (4.3-km) York Mills extension for the Yonge subway; received provincial approval for the controversial route of the $155 million Spadina subway; and planned a 1.6-mile (2.5-km), $40 million Bloor subway extension and a 10-mile (16-km), $400 million Queen subway. The TTC also abolished zones, establishing a single 25-cent citywide fare, and began a dial-a-bus service in the northern suburbs. The proposed Scarborough Expressway met continued opposition, and the Toronto Parking Authority raised its rates.

Development. High-rise development met increasing attacks, and the City Council passed a 45-foot (13.5-meter) height limit for two years in the downtown area to permit further planning. At the request of the Toronto Historical Board, the city designated nearly 400 buildings as historic sites. After several months of investigation, the Ontario Hydro Commission was criticized for its methods in letting the contract for its $44.4 million headquarters to developer Gerhard Moog's Canada Square Corporation. Canadian National Railways began construction of the 1,805-foot (542 meters) CN communications tower, which will be the tallest structure in the world.

Education. The University of Toronto's $42 million Robarts Library was opened, and York University's president David Salter resigned. The Central Mortgage and Housing Corporation began foreclosure proceedings against Rochdale College, which was $5.8 million behind in mortgage payments.

Recreation and Culture. Work proceeded on a 188-acre (75-hectare) aquatic park in the outer harbor, and the province announced that 55,000 acres (22,275 hectares) of parkway corridors would be set aside in the Toronto area. Dr. Walter M. Tovell and Maxwell Henderson were appointed codirectors of the Royal Ontario Museum. Two leading musicians died—Toronto Symphony conductor Karel Ancerl and retired conductor Sir Ernest MacMillan. St. Michael's Catholic Cathedral celebrated its 125th anniversary.

FREDERICK H. ARMSTRONG
University of Western Ontario

SOVIET liner Mikhail Lermontov, *first Russian passenger ship in New York harbor in 25 years, passes World Trade Center towers in June.*

TOURISM

The current craze for nostalgia extended into travel in the United States in 1973. People seemed to be eager to return to the past, with its now distant problems, its quaint tools, and interesting artifacts. Travelers seemed to want to forget the harsh realities of inflation and dollar devaluation. The effect of the fuel shortage was unknown.

Nostalgia. Old towns, ports, mines, trains, and ships drew unusually large crowds in 1973, as did folk and craft festivals. Among the perennially popular sites visited in 1973 were Colonial Williamsburg, Williamsburg, Va., Old Sturbridge, Mass., and Mystic Seaport, Conn. Other heavily visited restored sites included the village of Westville, near Lumpkin, Ga., and Medora, N. Dak. In the old seaport town of New London, Conn., the main street was converted into Captain's Walk, an antique cobbled mall, with trees and shrubs.

Antique ships continued to attract visitors. Maryland started its oystering season in October with Chesapeake Bay Appreciation Day, featuring races of antique shipjack and bugeye sailboats. The old sternwheel steamboat *Delta Queen* has been so popular for its Mississippi River cruises that Congress voted three times over a seven-year period to exempt her from the safety-at-sea laws. In November 1973, the hull of her 379-foot, all-steel, $15.5 million sister ship was dedicated.

World War II battleships, now museum pieces, drew crowds in Massachusetts, North Carolina, Alabama, Texas, Washington, and Hawaii. A U. S. Navy museum opened on a ferryboat in San Diego, Calif., and a naval wax museum opened in Annapolis, Md.

Railroad museums were popular in Chattanooga, Tenn., Atlanta, Ga., Baltimore, Md., and St. Constant, Quebec. Volunteer railroaders and old professionals were operating steam trains in such places as Allaire State Park, N. J., Cass, W. Va., and near Rapid City, S. Dak.

The Tropico Gold Mine, Mill & Goldcamp at Rosamond, Calif., excited '49er fever with its gold mine and refining furnace. Goldpanning championships were held in 1973 as in previous years. Tourists were drawn to Oak Island, near Halifax, Nova Scotia, to watch explorers seeking other gold—perhaps Captain Kidd's.

Fuel Shortage. The impact of faltering fuel supplies on car travel was felt throughout the summer in many parts of the United States. In November 1973, when Middle East oil shipment stopped, President Nixon asked the nation to limit driving speed to 50 mph and requested Sunday closing of gas stations. Gas rationing was also forecast. Airlines reduced flight schedules by 10% to 20%. Bus and rail travel increased. Diminished public mobility was expected to hurt resorts, restaurants, hotels, and the manufacturers of campers, powerboats, private planes, and sports equipment.

Air Travel. In September 1972, the U. S. Civil Aeronautics Board approved the new travel group charters (TGC). Rates were higher than those of affinity-group charters, and registration and payment were required long in advance. One company that specialized in TGC's was successful with them. However, the scheduled airlines and travel agents generally gave up on TGC's.

Late in 1973, Congress was considering authorizing one-stop inclusive-tour domestic charters (ITC)—the sort of plan that makes package tours within Europe inexpensive for Europeans. The scheduled airlines were fighting ITC's, preferring to stick to the old rules requiring three stops on a domestic ITC and a minimum cost of 110% of the scheduled airline fare.

At the end of November, as a result of the fuel shortage, both domestic and international airlines announced fare hikes of from 5% to 6%.

U. S. Rail Travel. The National Railroad Passenger Corporation—Amtrak—continued its efforts "to make the trains worth traveling again" with stewardesses on many trains, weekend city-tour packages, sightseeing and skiing tours, rail/sail tours to Florida and Bermuda, and combination tours with airlines, buses, ships, and rental cars.

The Washington-Montreal *Montrealer* and *Washingtonian* resumed service after a 6-year hiatus, and additional connections to Mexico were introduced. A new computerized reservations and ticketing system was installed. Two fast and elegant French-built turbine trains entered service between Chicago and St. Louis. Amtrak had an option to buy 10 of them. The New York-Boston Turbotrains, however, were frequently out of service. The first of 40 new 3,000-hp locomotives were delivered. Certain trains, such as the *Coast Starlight* between San Francisco and Vancouver, and the *Metroliner* between New York and Washington, were intensively improved. But the majority of trains remained slow, frequently late, and subject to breakdowns. Amtrak's chief need, officials said, was funding to rebuild roadbeds and to straighten and shorten many routes.

Ship Travel. After the Italian government announced in February that it would gradually phase out transatlantic service, it looked as if the *Queen Elizabeth 2* and the *France* would be the sole surviving transatlantic luxury liners. Bucking the trend, the USSR instituted Leningrad-New York service in June with the new *Mikhail Lermontov*.

Twelve shipping lines scheduled over 100 cruises by 29 ships from New York for the winter of 1973–74, as well as numerous fly-cruise packages taking ship in Florida. The first foreign cruise to mainland China was in September when the British *Coral Princess* visited Tientsin. Two Cunarders, *Canberra* and *Adventurer*, were filled to capacity for cruises to see the solar eclipse from the South Atlantic at the end of June. Cunard filled the *Queen Elizabeth 2* for a 3-day cruise from New York City to see the Kohoutek comet in December. Bad weather reduced the success of the latter cruise.

Campers and Motor Homes. General Motors introduced motor homes 23 and 26 feet long, costing $14,000 to $19,000. Ford produced a camper, and Dodge improved the chassis it had been supplying to 85% of the camper manufacturers. There were over 3 million recreation vehicles on the road at the end of 1972, and sales of 250,000 were forecast for 1973. However, the picture turned dark with the onset of the fuel shortage.

Competition for the 250,000 campsites in the 21,000 U. S. public and private campgrounds was acute by 1973. Vehicles often waited in long lines for campsites. Enterprises such as Holiday Inns and Exxon began adding campgrounds to their properties.

Expo '74 Spokane. "Celebrating tomorrow's fresh, new environment" is the theme for Spokane, Washington's world's fair, May 4–Nov. 3, 1974. Besides national and commercial exhibits, amusement rides, and food concessions, there is to be an exhibit by the Smithsonian Institution, tied to the environmental theme. There were plans for symposia to be held on environmental problems, policies, and possible solutions.

National Parks. Protective measures for overused parks continued, with gradual elimination of private cars in favor of buses and promotion of underused parks. A nationwide computerized campsite reservation system was tested at six parks. Former military reservations around New York and San Francisco harbors were being developed into the Gateway National Recreation Area and the Golden Gate National Recreation Area, respectively.

Visit the USA. The National Tourism Review Commission, set up by Congress in 1970, published its report *Destination USA* in June 1973. The report identifies tourism as the largest factor in world trade and states that tourists spent $50 billion in the United States in 1970. It goes on to score the lack of reliable tourism data and the fragmentation of the U. S. effort into about 100 tourism programs by over 50 federal agencies. Proposed remedies include the establishment of a new national tourism administration headed by an undersecretary in the Department of Commerce, the establishment and implementation of a national tourism policy, and strong promotion of tourism by public and private sectors. Meanwhile, it recommends that the United States Travel Service (USTS) be funded at $30 million per year. In Canada, in November 1973, federal tourism promotion was upgraded and placed under an "assistant deputy minister, tourism" in the Ministry of Industry, Trade, and Commerce.

The USTS, hampered by a lack of funds, closed all its foreign offices to the public and promoted 14 U. S. tours to the travel industries of the six countries that provide 87% of the visitor arrivals to the United States: Mexico, Canada, Britain, France, West Germany, and Japan. Cost-effectiveness was being measured by sale of tickets. The Commerce Department reported a 26% gain in travel to the United States from overseas in the first eight months of 1973—a bonus deriving partly from dollar devaluation. Japanese visitors made up the largest group. They totaled 425,076, 61% above 1972.

Bicentennial Progress. The original concept of holding great fairs in 1976 to celebrate the 200th birthday of the United States was rejected in favor of permanent improvements in transportation, housing, and city cores. But progress has been slow.

In Boston a young, vital group, Boston 200, was working closely with Mayor Kevin H. White on bicentennial plans. The celebration began in Boston on Dec. 14–16, 1973, with a reenactment of the Boston Tea Party and other events. Empty tea chests were thrown from the brig *Beaver,* which had been built in Europe. The square-rigged *Beaver* and a pierside museum will remain on permanent display.

New York City's bicentennial plans centered on the South Street Seaport Museum. Also under consideration was a showboat, to carry historic and

ethnic dramas to the waterfront of each of New York's boroughs. Philadelphia and the National Park Service greatly improved the historic area around Independence Hall where, it is hoped, Congress will sit in July 1976. Washington, D. C., will continue its Festival of American Folklife throughout the summer of 1976. The Smithsonian Institution will have its new aviation and space building, and the Kennedy Center for the Performing Arts will be a showcase for the re-creation of many events of the Revolution. Congress authorized a study of proposed transportation improvements, including rapid-transit links for Washington-Annapolis and Yorktown-Williamsburg, as well as fast marine transport (hydrofoil or air-cushion vehicles) connecting Annapolis, Baltimore, and Yorktown, Va.

European Travel. Dollar devaluation and rampant inflation made Europe expensive for North Americans. Many tourists went on charter flights and prepaid package vacations. Travel bargains were still to be had in Greece, Turkey, Israel, Yugoslavia, Iceland, Ireland, Spain, Portugal, and Italy.

ROBERT SCOTT MILNE
Coauthor, "Around the World with the Experts"

Hotels and Motels

In 1973, the U. S. lodging industry registered significant gains in income, occupancy, and number of guest rooms. Hotel/motel income climbed to a record $8.2 billion, a rise of 6% over that of 1972. Average guest-room occupancy rose to 63%, up from 61% a year earlier. New construction boosted the total number of U. S. hotel/motel rooms to 2,715,000, compared with 2,680,000 in 1972.

The number of U. S.-chain hotels and motels rose 9.7% and the number of guest rooms increased 9.4% over 1972 totals, according to the 1973 *Directory of Hotel & Motel Systems.* The number of chains was up to 204 from 193 in 1973. The *Directory* also showed that the 25 largest hotel/motel chains accounted for 63.5% of the total growth in U. S. chain properties, which increased by 483. These larger chains accounted for 67% of the gain in the number of rooms available in U. S. chains.

Holiday Inns, Inc., maintained its position as the world's largest hotel/motel chain by opening 201 inns with a total of 33,413 rooms. The chain

also announced plans for an international system of company-owned and franchised tennis clubs. Other major chains reported the following additions in 1973: Ramada Inns, Inc., 106 inns with 15,236 rooms; ITT Sheraton Corporation of America, 77 hotels and inns with 14,090 rooms; Howard Johnson Company, 32 inns with 4,587 rooms; and Hilton Hotels, 25 hotels and inns with 4,554 rooms.

Two leading economy or budget-priced motel chains, Motel 6 and Days Inns of America, reported the opening, respectively, of 77 inns with 5,000 rooms and 50 inns with 7,000 rooms. Over a dozen new companies entered this field in 1973.

Foreign Investment in U. S. Hotel Market. As devaluation of the dollar and increasing affluence abroad made travel to the United States more attractive, foreign capital started to flow into the American hotel market. Japanese investments in 35 U. S. lodging properties from Guam to New York—including 17 hotels in Hawaii and the first Japanese-style hotel in New York City, the 124-room Kitano—have been estimated at $192 million. Trust Houses Forte, Ltd., a British lodging and food service company, acquired controlling interest in TraveLodge International, Inc., a U. S.-based chain.

New Hotels and Motels. The largest new hotel completed in the United States in 1973 was the $80 million, 2,100-room MGM Grand Hotel in Las Vegas, Nev. Its features include a 2,000-seat jai alai arena and two swimming pools with waterfalls. Other major hotels that opened in 1973 included the 750-room McCormick Inn, Chicago; the 728-room Crown Center Hotel, Kansas City, Mo.; the 460-room Westbury, Chicago; and the 403-room Holiday Inn, Los Angeles Airport.

In London, 50 new hotels, containing nearly 14,000 rooms, were completed in 1973. The largest of these were the 914-room Penta; the 850-room London Tara; the 826-room Tower; and the 640-room Cunard International. Other major new hotels that opened in 1973 outside the United States included the 608-room Munich Penta, Munich, Germany; the 600-room Brussels Sheraton, Brussels, Belgium; and the 500-room Oberoi Sheraton, Bombay, India.

ALBERT E. KUDRLE
American Hotel and Motel Association

UPI

NEW HOTEL in London, the Tower Hotel, rises in "stepped" floors from the side of the River Thames at St. Katherine Docks near the Tower of London.

AMTRAK

New mass transportation equipment under consideration for use in the United States includes Amtrak's French-built turbo train (above) and a battery-powered minibus (right).

ELECTROBUS

transportation

Developments and technological advances in transportation during 1973 are reviewed in this article under the following headings: (1) General Survey; (2) Air Transportation; (3) Highways; (4) Motor Transport; (5) Railroads; and (6) Shipping. A special report on the role of shipping in the Soviet-American grain deal appears on page 602. Additional transportation news appears in separate entries for AUTOMOBILES; ENGINEERING, CIVIL.

General Survey

Transportation activity in the United States increased in virtually all areas during 1973. Major actions included the opening of the Federal Highway Trust Fund to aid urban mass transportation and the approval of the Alaskan pipeline.

Urban Transportation. The most important news of the year was that the $6 billion Highway Trust Fund finally will be tapped to pay for improvements to urban mass transit systems. The Federal-Aid Highway Act of 1973 (Public Law 93-87) was signed into law on August 13.

The act makes two principal changes. It opens the urban highway system authorization to include funds for rail and bus transit, and it opens all highway funds to include expenditures on exclusive lanes, traffic-control devices, bus shelters, parking facilities, and other road-related facilities. The act authorized $780 million in fiscal year 1974, $800 million in fiscal 1975, and $800 million in fiscal 1976 for use in urban areas with a population of more than 200,000.

Starting in fiscal 1974 responsible city officials may propose to substitute a bus or rail transit project for a previously planned highway project within the urban system. However, the $780 million fund for fiscal 1974 is restricted to road use. In fiscal 1975 the trust fund resources may be used to finance up to $200 million in city bus transit projects. In fiscal 1976 the trust fund resources may be used to finance all road, bus, rail, or subway projects without constraint as to mode.

The highway act also authorized $3 billion from general revenue funds for the Urban Mass Transportation Administration's capital grants program, increasing the total to $6.1 billion for capital grants and loans. The federal share for making these grants and loans was set at a mandatory 80% level.

Major grants made by the Urban Mass Transportation Administration in 1973 included $85.3 million to the New York City Metropolitan Transit Authority for construction and rehabilitation of its system; $69.5 million to the Metropolitan Atlanta Rapid Transit Authority for the first phase of its $1.75 billion rail-busway rapid transit system; $56.3 million to the San Francisco Bay Area Rapid Transit for car purchases and automation equipment; and $45.7 million to the Massachusetts Bay Transportation Authority to purchase new lines and new equipment, and make general improvements.

Funds were granted to some communities to help them purchase private transit companies and improve the services. These included $9.5 million to Cincinnati, $6.2 million to the County of Nassau Department of Public Transportation in New York, and $4.5 million to the metropolitan government of Nashville and Davidson county, Tennessee.

Grants for purchase of new equipment are also an important part of the program. Such grants included $23.3 million to the Delaware River Port Authority, $7.9 million to the Southeastern Pennsylvania Transportation Authority, $5.4 million to the Central Ohio Transit Authority, $5 million to the Greater Richmond Transit Company, and $3.4 million to New Orleans.

Small grants are helpful to smaller communities. Grants to study and plan improvements, for example, were made to State College, Pa. ($12,000), Daytona Beach, Fla. ($19,300), Rockford, Ill. ($19,-700), Gainesville, Ga. ($24,900), and Monroe, La. ($29,400). The smaller communities also benefit from grants to help purchase equipment. Examples include $29,000 to Sioux City, Iowa, $32,600 to Frankfort, Ky., and $57,600 to Kenner, La.

Alaskan Pipeline. On November 16, President Nixon signed into law a bill that allows the Interior Department to grant a permit for construction of a 48-inch-diameter (122-cm), 789-mile-long (1,270-km) oil pipeline from Prudhoe Bay south to the year-round port of Valdez. The bill waives the 54-foot (16.5-meter) maximum right-of-way width set in the Minerals Leasing Act of 1920.

The Alyeska Pipeline Service Co., a consortium of Atlantic Richfield, Amerada Hess, Exxon, Mobil, Phillips, Standard Oil of Ohio, and Union Oil companies, will spend an estimated $4.5 billion to finish the pipeline, perhaps by 1977. It may eventually pump about 2 million barrels of oil per day, or about 10% of the nation's daily demand. Because of environmental concerns, about half the line will be above ground and heavily insulated to protect the tundra, and another portion will be built about twice as deep underground as is usual. This accounts for the very high cost.

Crime Losses. The U. S. Department of Transportation (DOT) reported that truck and air carrier losses from lost or stolen cargo amounted to $921 million in 1972, including $900 million in the trucking industry. This is a drain on industry profits as a DOT study showed that for every dollar eliminated in claims, 50¢ can be added to profits.

Fatalities. The National Transportation Safety Board reported that there were 60,288 transportation deaths in 1972, an increase of 2.4% over 1971 and second only to 60,471 in 1969. Highway deaths reached 56,300, including 55,025 from crashes and 1,275 at rail-highway grade crossings. Only rail, marine, and commercial air deaths were down: rail from 607 to 590, commercial shipping from 459 to

352, recreational boating from 1,582 to 1,437, and commercial air from 199 to 190. Deaths in general aviation increased from 1,322 to 1,357.

Railroads. In 1972, Class I line-haul railroads increased their revenue carloadings to 26,061,246, revenue ton-miles to 778,137,000,000, operating revenues to $13,411,116,000, and operating expenses to $10,549,933,000. While their operating income increased 20.1% to $835,149,000 in 1972, the rate of return was only 2.95%.

The average number of railway employees sank 3.4% to 526,091, but the 1972 payroll was $6.4 billion, the highest ever. Average hourly wages rose to $5.03 and yearly wages to $12,213. Because of improved results, in the first 11 months of 1973 the railroads ordered some 95,000 new and rebuilt cars—almost double the 1972 orders—and 1,215 new diesel-electric locomotives.

The Auto-Train Corp., which carries passengers and automobiles between Lorton, Va., and Sanford, Fla., carried 90,000 automobiles and 250,000 passengers in its first 18 months of operation. Because of this success, it will begin service between Louisville, Ky., and Sanford in 1974.

Water Transport. Revenue of the St. Lawrence Seaway Corp. remained level in 1972 at $7.5 million, but total vessel transits continued their annual decline from the peak of 7,341 in 1966, falling to 5,962 in 1972. Total cargo tonnage reached a record of 53.7 million tons, including 45.8 million of bulk cargo and 7.9 million of general cargo. General cargo was down from 8.6 million in 1971, while bulk cargo was up from 44.3 million.

During the first eight months of 1973 the Lake Carriers' Association reported a total bulk commodity tonnage of 93.3 million tons, up from 84.9 million tons in the same period in 1972. Iron ore shipments totaled 54.4 million tons, up from 44.3 million; coal shipments declined from 26 million tons to 23.9 million; and grain shipments rose from 14.6 million tons to 15.1 million.

The Federal Maritime Administration approved a subsidy of $51.6 million for construction of three liquefied natural-gas tankers to be delivered in 1976–77 at a total cost of $309.1 million. The 16.7% subsidy rate is the lowest since the U. S. shipbuilding subsidy program began in 1936.

The American Bureau of Shipping reported that the world's fleets continued to expand. At the start of 1973 there were about 4,600 tankers totaling 193 million deadweight tons, about 11,700 cargo vessels totaling 91 million deadweight tons, about 2,400 bulk carriers totaling 107 million deadweight tons, and about 800 passenger-cargo carriers totaling 2 million deadweight tons.

Canadian Containerports. Seven containerships call at the port of Halifax, and the port handled 1,107,202 tons of cargo in 1972, up from 679,159 in 1971. About 90% of the traffic is brought to or from the port by the Canadian National Railway. At the port of Quebec container traffic increased to 684,560 tons in 1972, up from 601,815 in 1971. The port of Montreal continued to lose container traffic, handling only 1,255,153 tons in 1972, compared with 1,284,088 tons in 1971. The port of Toronto is growing rapidly as it handled 119,728 tons in 1972, up from 56,112 tons of container traffic in 1971. The port of Vancouver reversed its upward trend of recent years when it suffered a severe drop in tonnage, declining from 472,599 tons in 1971 to only 425,348 tons in 1972.

THE CONCORDE, British-French supersonic transport plane, lands on U. S. soil for first time at dedication of new Dallas–Fort Worth Airport in September.

Airports. The Airport Operators Council International reported that O'Hare Airport in Chicago was the nation's busiest, handling 33.5 million passengers annually. Other leading airports included Los Angeles International (22.0 million), Hartsfield in Atlanta (21.2 million), and John F. Kennedy International in New York (20.7 million). In its national airport system plan the Federal Aviation Administration (FAA) announced a need for 697 new airports over the next decade, which would raise the number of national airports to 3,967. The cost of the program was estimated at $6.3 billion. The FAA apportioned $310 million for 1974 under the Airport Development Aid program.

JAMES R. ROMAN, JR.
The George Washington University

Air Transportation

Travel on United States airlines continued to expand in 1973, and a Gallup poll indicated that in the past two years, for the first time, more than half of the U. S. population had flown on a scheduled airliner. However, the rate of growth of the industry entered another downward cycle, causing problems for many airlines that have found it increasingly difficult to tailor their schedules and routes to such cycles.

The airlines were among the first industries to be hit hard by world energy shortages, which, beginning in mid-October, forced them to cancel more than 1,500 of their 13,000 daily flights.

One of the side effects of the fuel crisis was a sharp increase in airline fares. U. S. domestic fares were increased 5% on December 1, and airlines said they would seek further increases in 1974. A series of increases on international routes—attributed to inflation, dollar devaluation, and soaring fuel costs —raised the prices of some of the most popular excursions by 25% during 1973.

After years of escalating problems in their battle against airplane hijackings, Federal Aviation Administration (FAA) and airline security officers were able to curtail the incidence of piracy dramatically with stringent airport search procedures. These included airport security checkpoints, X-ray inspection of luggage carried aboard, and the physical frisking of some passengers.

An increased use of wide-body jumbo jets changed the look of air transportation. Such planes include the Boeing 747, the McDonnell-Douglas DC-10, and the Lockheed L-1011 TriStar.

Traffic. Airline economists began the year with forecasts of a 10% to 15% increase in air traffic, anticipating that the strong growth experienced in 1972 would continue. However, the traffic growth rate began to slump in the spring. By the autumn, domestic travel was running only 2% above 1972, and travel to overseas points was running slightly lower than it had in that year. The slump continued into the fall. By the year's end, airline officials were estimating that the overall domestic traffic gains would average out at 6% to 7%, while international travel gains would be only 4%.

Many industries would consider this a respectable growth rate. But for airlines that had taken delivery of many more large jets on the assumption that 1973 traffic would grow at the 10% to 15% rate of the mid-1960's, the slowdown caused a fiscally disastrous gap between operating expenses and revenue from fares. For example, during the normally lucrative peak summer season, passenger volume increased only 0.5% between the United States and Europe, but the number of seats flown by airlines increased 14.3%. Two airline executives— George A. Spater, chairman of American Airlines, and Sam Higgenbottom, president of Eastern Airlines—were removed as a by-product of the industry's problems. American recalled its 74-year-old founder and long-time chief, C. R. Smith.

Airline economists attributed the sluggish growth to several factors. Among them were consumer caution resulting from inflation, and the decision of the Civil Aeronautics Board (CAB) to phase out discount fares for young and family travelers on domestic routes. With respect to international routes, an additional factor was the sharp drop in the buy-

ing power of the dollar in Europe, Japan, and other countries following two devaluations of the dollar, along with spreading inflation. The economists said that, to a large extent, it appeared that the era when an American could go abroad and buy perhaps 25% or 50% more in tourist accommodations with his money than he could at home was over. However, bargains still existed in Eastern Europe, Spain, Portugal, and a few other regions.

Reverse Tourism. While devaluation of the dollar and widespread inflation meant higher prices for Americans, the same factors touched off a major increase in visits by tourists to the United States. Camera-carrying Japanese tourists became a familiar sight from Manhattan to Hawaii, and middle-income tourists from England, Germany, and other countries appeared in numbers at such places as Las Vegas and Niagara Falls. Tourism to the United States increased by more than 22% in 1973.

Antihijacking Measures. Effective Jan. 5, 1973, under an emergency presidential order issued following an epidemic of hijackings during the preceding year, U. S. airlines were required to inspect all luggage carried aboard their planes by passengers and to check all passengers with electronic metal-sensing instruments in order to determine that they were not carrying weapons. On February 17, a second phase of the emergency order went into effect, which required armed local law enforcement officers to be posted at each boarding area before every commercial flight. Many airports established security checkpoints in their central terminal buildings and prohibited anyone who had not been searched from entering the passenger concourses or boarding areas that extend from the terminals—the so-called "sterile concourse" system. Some passengers, especially businessmen who travel frequently, complained about the checks and particularly about the need to empty their pockets of coins or other metal objects that tripped the weapon detectors. However, improved detection devices reduced such false alarms, and many airlines also purchased X-ray inspection equipment that greatly reduced the number of briefcases and other items that had to be opened.

The security checks had the desired effect; through mid-fall, not a single U. S. airliner had been hijacked since the measures were adopted. Whereas planes had been taken over at a rate of one every two weeks during much of the previous two or three years, the only hijacking to occur in 1973 took place in the first week of January, before the security program was introduced. One measure of the effectiveness of the searches was the number of weapons found through airport checks. In the first six months of the blanket search program, 749 guns, 5,400 knives, and 120 explosive devices were confiscated, according to the FAA.

While airplane hijackings were curtailed in the United States, they continued to plague airlines in other countries. In the most dramatic of such incidents in 1973, a Japan Air Lines Boeing 747 with 143 passengers and crewmen aboard was hijacked in late July by Arab terrorists after it left Amsterdam. The crew and passengers eventually were released, but the plane was blown up in Libya a few days later. Various diplomatic efforts were expended on the hijacking problem. Thus, after five years during which Cuba was by far the chief goal of fugitives commandeering U. S. planes, diplomatic action was taken to close Havana as a place of asylum. The United States and Cuba signed a treaty pledging to extradite or prosecute persons who hijacked planes or boats from the one country to the other. In another effort, delegates from more than 100 nations met for three weeks in Rome to negotiate a treaty by which the nations would take collective action —for example, joint cessation of air service—against a nation that harbored hijackers. The delegates failed to agree on a formula, however, provoking threats of a possible protest strike by international airline pilots in 1974.

A serious air incident occurred in February, when a Libyan Air Lines Boeing 727 strayed into Israeli air space. Israeli fighter pilots intercepted it and, when the pilot did not heed their signals to land, shot the airplane down, killing 108 of the 113 persons aboard. In August, Israeli planes intercepted an Iraqi Airways plane over Lebanon and forced it to land in Israel to be searched for Arab guerrilla leaders. Both of these actions by Israel were condemned by the International Civil Aviation Organization (ICAO), a United Nations agency.

Airplane Manufacture. The slump in U. S. air traffic led to a decrease in orders for new jets, and Boeing, McDonnell-Douglas, and Lockheed all decided to delay development of new models. However, Boeing did decide to build a shortened version of its 747, called the Boeing 747SP. (The initials stand for "special performance.") The new version, 44 feet (13.4 meters) shorter than the regular model, will start service in 1976. Carrying approximately 280 persons instead of 370, it will be used on routes that do not handle enough traffic for the larger plane. Pan American World Airways was the first airline to order the craft.

While manufacturers of jetliners worried about a decline in orders, manufacturers of private planes and executive jets said that they expected 1973 would prove to be one of the best on record. Employment in the commercial transport industry as a whole fell 8.9% during the year, dropping to 70,400 persons. By year-end, the industry was laying off large numbers of personnel because of the fuel crisis. For the entire aerospace industry, including military products and missile and space programs, employment dropped 1%—to 935,000—in 1973.

SST Flights. The British-French Concorde supersonic transport (SST) flew to Texas in September for ceremonies dedicating the new Dallas–Forth Worth Airport, thus becoming the first SST airliner to land in the United States. British Overseas Airways Corporation and Air France announced plans to begin transatlantic service with the Concorde in 1975, although the fuel situation cast doubt on this timetable. U. S. airlines said that they did not plan to buy the $40 million jet because, they concluded, it would have little chance of being profitable.

In June, the Soviet Union's SST prototype, TU-144, crashed during a demonstration at the Paris Air Show. Nevertheless, Soviet officials said that the plane's design was safe and that they would begin commercial operations in 1974 or 1975.

Airport Facilities. The $700 million Dallas–Fort Worth Airport, which covers 17,500 acres (7,088 hectares)—more than twice as much space as any other jetport—was scheduled to open in October, but last-minute problems delayed the opening until early 1974. The airport features its own 13-mile (21-km) automated rapid transit system, extensive land buffers to absorb the kind of jet noise that has bothered airport communities elsewhere, and other innovations that have prompted pilots

and aviation leaders to describe it as the safest airport ever built.

Elsewhere, opposition from community groups and environmentalists delayed construction of new jetports, but there were some major developments. In the New York area, the Newark (N. J.) International Airport reopened after a $400 million facelifting that more than doubled its passenger capacity. In addition, plans were unveiled for a $1 billion jetport for New York on the site of the former Stewart Air Force Base northwest of Manhattan.

CAB Activities. Robert D. Timm succeeded Secor D. Brown, who resigned, as chairman of the CAB. Timm announced that his principal goal would be to raise declining airline earnings. A major part of this program was to encourage airlines to agree to reduce the number of competitive flights on the same routes, which would increase the number of persons per flight as well as reducing the consumption of fuel. The Justice Department criticized this move as a violation of antitrust principles, but the CAB implemented plans to approve such agreements for limited periods on several routes.

The CAB also voted to phase out discount fares for travelers 12 to 22 years old and for families, in three steps to occur on June 1 and Dec. 1, 1973, and June 1, 1974.

ROBERT H. LINDSEY
Transportation Editor, "The New York Times"

Highways

All areas of highway activity in the United States showed gains in 1973. These included more highway construction, increased expenditures, rising costs, more fuel consumption, and increased vehicle registrations.

Interstate Highway System. The Department of Transportation announced that work has been completed or is under way on 41,958 miles of the 42,500-mile Interstate Highway System. As of Sept. 30, 1973, 35,075 miles of the system were in use, and construction was under way on another 3,254 miles. The system consists of 34,185 miles of rural highways and 8,315 miles of urban highways; 82.7% of the rural mileage and 82% of the urban mileage were open to traffic.

About $52.5 billion has been spent on the system since the work started on July 1, 1956, including $39.2 billion for work completed and $13.3 billion for work currently under way. The federal government provides 90% of the funds, and the 50 states provide the balance.

Federal-Aid Highway Program. Under this program the building of primary and secondary state highway systems and their urban extensions is financed by the federal government and the states on an equal-share basis. The program has a cumulative total cost of $35.87 billion for work on 277,583 miles of construction under contracts. This includes 265,351 miles of construction under contracts that were completed since July 1, 1956, at a cost of $27.18 billion, and current contracts involving 12,232 miles of highway at a cost of $5.4 billion. The balance of the funds went for engineering and right-of-way acquisition.

Appalachian Highways. The Appalachian Development Highway System was authorized by Congress in 1965 as part of the area's development act. The act provided for yearly authorizations of funds through fiscal year 1978 to construct up to 2,700 miles of development highways and also up to 1,600 miles of local access roads. The highway provisions of the act are to be carried out by the Appalachian Regional Commission in cooperation with the Federal Highway Administration (FHA). The level of federal aid has been set at $2.09 billion. Through Sept. 30, 1973, a total of $2.205 billion had been obligated, including $1.207 billion in federal funds. Through June 30, a total of 1,757 miles of highways and access roads were completed or under construction. Preliminary work was under way on an additional 795 miles.

Construction Costs. The FHA announced that the costs of highway construction in the United States during the third quarter of 1973 increased to 155.1% of the 1967 average. Over the previous year the increase amounted to 9.9%.

Highway Receipts and Expenditures. The FHA estimated that the states will collect more than $13 billion in revenue from state road-user taxes in 1973, up from $12 billion in 1972. Gasoline taxes accounted for approximately 65% of the total, which does not include tolls. Individual state revenue ranged from a high of $1.357 billion in California to a low of $35.5 million in Wyoming. For 1972 total receipts were $18.5 billion, including $1.7 billion in borrowed funds and $4.8 billion in federal aid. The federal share accounted for 48% of the $9.9 billion in capital expenditures, including $4.3 billion spent on the Interstate Highway System. Other expenditures included $2.3 billion for maintenance, $2.5 billion for administration and other items, $2.7 billion in grants to local governments, and $765 million for bond retirement, for a total expenditure of almost $18.2 billion. The $0.3 billion balance was placed in highway fund reserves. The leading states in highway expenditures include California with expenditures of $1.455 billion, New York with $1.312, and Pennsylvania with $1.149 billion. Rhode Island, on the other hand, spent only $57 million.

The FHA reported that 2,235 federal-aid highway and bridge construction contracts were awarded by state highway departments during the first half of 1973. These contracts had a total value of $2.3 billion. About half of the contracts were for more than $5 million.

For fiscal year 1974 the FHA has apportioned $4.84 billion in federal-aid funds to the states, including $2.6 billion for interstate highways, $1.07 billion for rural highways, $1.07 billion for urban highways, and $100 million for a new priority primary-highway program. California received the highest award, $349 million, while Vermont received the lowest, $19.9 million.

Motor Vehicle Registrations. The FHA estimated that automobile registrations will top the 100 million mark for the first time by the end of 1973, with a total of about 101,327,000 vehicles, resulting in an increase of 4.5% over 1972. Truck and bus registrations increased about 7.4% to about 23,241,000. The total of 124,478,000 vehicles represents a 5.0% increase, or 5,971,952 over the 1972 total of 118,506,048. The motorcycle growth rate slowed in 1973 to 11.0%, resulting in an increase of about 420,000 motorcycles.

California leads the nation with 13.4 million motor vehicle registrations, followed by 7.7 million in Texas, 7.1 million in New York, 6.7 million in Pennsylvania, and 6.4 million in Ohio. The 10 leading states account for 65.0 million vehicles, or 52.2% of the national total.

Fuel Consumption. The FHA predicted that more than 115 billion gallons of fuel would be used by vehicles during 1973, an increase of only 6% as compared with increases of 7% to 8% in recent years. The typical pattern was predicted until fuel shortages began to occur in late spring and summer. Highway use of fuel was estimated at 112 billion gallons, while farming, aviation, boating, and other activities consumed about 3.7 billion gallons.

JAMES R. ROMAN, JR.
The George Washington University

Motor Transport

Truck transportation continued to grow and new records were posted for the number of trucks, ton-miles of freight, and revenues. A 33-month labor contract was negotiated amicably. Several states liberalized size and weight limits for motor trucks, thereby improving the motor transport industry's efficiency and productivity. Rising fuel costs, fuel shortages, and reduced speed limits affected carrier operations in the latter weeks of 1973.

Trucking. The American motor-truck fleet increased by nearly 1.5 million vehicles during 1973. Total registration, excluding government-owned units, reached a record 21.7 million, compared with 20.2 million in 1972. The trucking industry carried about 490 billion ton-miles of intercity freight in 1973, up from 470 billion ton-miles in 1972.

More than 15,000 federally regulated for-hire trucking companies engaged in interstate commerce reported some $21 billion in revenues in 1973, an increase of $2 billion from 1972. Trucking now accounts for more than 54% of the revenues of all forms of regulated transportation—rail, water, air, and pipeline. Many additional billions of dollars in revenues were generated by private and for-hire trucking operations that are not regulated by the government.

The trucking industry provided direct employment for about 9 million persons and had an annual payroll of about $77.5 billion. Continued demand for flexible motor-truck service resulted in record sales of all types and sizes of trucks and trailers in 1973. Trucks consumed over 32 billion gallons of fuel at a cost of more than $7.2 billion, exclusive of state and federal taxes. In 1973, total highway taxes paid by all trucks approached $6.6 billion, including taxes levied for construction of the Interstate and Defense Highway System.

Motor-truck tonnage has grown 1.2 times as fast as industrial production since 1950, but the growth rate slowed somewhat in 1973. The industry faced a continuing fuel shortage throughout 1973, and fuel prices increased 20% to 50%. This increase, plus higher labor costs and other price increases, forced the industry to seek rate increases.

Antipollution and Safety Equipment. Equipment modifications required for safety and environmental reasons were scheduled to be implemented in 1974. These modifications will include more stringent antipollution devices for the larger trucks. The safety and antipollution equipment was expected to increase the cost of a large over-the-road diesel truck tractor by 5% to 10%, and such vehicles already cost anywhere between $25,000 and $28,000. A new antiskid braking system for large truck-trailers, plus proposed noise controls, will further increase equipment costs in 1974.

WILLIAM A. BRESNAHAN
American Trucking Associations, Inc.

Railroads

As freight haulers, U. S. railroads had their busiest year in history in 1973. They produced 840 billion ton-miles of freight service (a ton-mile is one ton moved one mile), more than all trucks, airplanes, and barges combined. As passenger carriers, their performance was less spectacular. All forms of railroad transportation—the National Railroad Passenger Corp. (Amtrak), the privately operated Auto-Train Corp., and commuter lines—produced slightly more than 9 billion passenger-miles of service. This was less than 6% of the national total, excluding automobiles. Buses accounted for 15.5%; airlines, 76.4%; and inland waterways, 2.5%.

Finances. Earnings were another story. As one railroad executive put it: "We're doing more, but enjoying it less." Operating revenues in the first three quarters of 1973 rose to a record of $10.9 billion, an increase of $927 million over the previous year, while operating expenses, taxes, and rents increased by $932 million. This meant that net railway operating income dropped from $582 million in the 1972 period to $577 million in the first nine months of 1973.

For the seventh consecutive year, the rate of return on a net depreciated investment of $28 billion was less than 3%. Also, it was the 18th consecutive year in which the rate of return fell below 4%.

Ordinary (net) income for the first nine months of 1973 was $355 million, up from $303 million in the corresponding 1972 period. Operating income differs from ordinary income in that it is calculated before net income from nonrailroad operations is added and fixed charges, including interest, are deducted.

Despite the financial crunch, railroads were able to invest more than $2 billion in capital improvements in 1973, an increase of about 10% over 1972. This went principally for new freight cars and locomotives, which are relatively easy to finance because they can be repossessed and resold in case of default. Less easy to finance are improvements to roadway and other fixed facilities, and only about $400 million was spent for capital improvements in this area. As a consequence of undermaintenance and deferred maintenance, the railroads' fixed plant continued to deteriorate. The seriousness of this situation was underscored when the bankrupt Penn Central Transportation Co. informed the Federal Railroad Administration (FRA) late in 1973 that it would take $2.9 billion to bring Penn Central's right-of-way up to the minimum standards set earlier in the year by the FRA.

Northeast Crisis. While clouds of varying intensity hovered over the entire railroad industry, a veritable storm raged in the Northeast where six railroads, including the 20,000-mile Penn Central, were in reorganization proceedings under the Federal Bankruptcy Act. After a bankruptcy court threatened to liquidate Penn Central to prevent further erosion of the creditors' estate, a House-Senate conference committee agreed to legislation calling for a massive infusion of federal aid to the six railroads and the bankrupt Ann Arbor railroad. The plan called for the establishment of a United States Railroad Association to trim down and restructure the seven railroads into a single system and the creation of a Consolidated Rail Corp. to operate the new system. Government-guaranteed loans in the amount of $1.5 billion would be issued

to finance the restructuring. Initial estimates were that a system of perhaps 18,000 miles might emerge from the 30,000 miles of main line now in receivership. Creditors of the bankrupt lines would be paid off in stock in the new corporation. While the plan contemplated an eventual return to full private control once the government obligations were paid off, there was considerable feeling in both government and industry circles that the day of viability would never arrive. Instead, the plan would turn out to be the first step toward nationalization of the Northeastern carriers. Present employees of the bankrupt lines would be substantially protected under the plan. The cost of that protection was set at $250 million.

Legislation. While the Northeast plan was the major legislative effort in 1973, the U. S. Department of Transportation (DOT) late in the year prepared another bill to assist all railroads and, it was hoped, to ward off bankruptcies threatening elsewhere in the country. A major provision of the DOT plan would provide up to $2 billion in government-guaranteed loans for all qualifying railroads, both for rolling-stock purchases and roadway improvement.

Meanwhile, Congress did not ignore the passenger side of railroading. The Amtrak Improvement Act of 1973 provided over $150 million in direct grants to Amtrak and increased to $500 million the amount of government-guaranteed loans Amtrak can have outstanding at any given time. This permitted Amtrak to beef up its own program of providing more and better trains despite continuing high operating losses. Two turbine-electric trains were acquired from France in 1973 and put into test service between Chicago and St. Louis. Amtrak had an option for eight additional French turbotrains, and the Rohr Corp., a California-based aerospace firm, negotiated a license to build any future trains of the French design. Amtrak also ordered 57 new Metroliner-type coaches for service in the Washington-New York-Boston corridor, thereby doubling the Metroliner fleet. Additionally, Amtrak was working on designs for 100 new standard passenger coaches. Altogether, Amtrak had 1,900 railroad cars in service in 1973.

A sudden rush back to rails came late in the year as the energy crisis worsened. This caused Amtrak to scour the United States and Canada for about 300 railroad cars not initially purchased when the quasi-public corporation took over intercity passenger service in May 1971. With the reduced capability of U. S. manufacturers to supply new passenger equipment, it appeared likely that Amtrak would go shopping overseas for more rolling stock to meet rising U. S. demands.

Labor. By and large, 1973 was a year of labor peace. In March, the railroads and the brotherhoods reached agreement on new contracts several weeks ahead of the midyear deadline, an unprecedented achievement. These contracts provided for wage increases totaling more than 10%. The settlement also provided for railroad managements to pay that part of an employee's contribution to the Railroad Retirement Fund in excess of what he would be paying under social security. This provision added about $240 million to the railroad industry's annual labor bills. However, the Interstate Commerce Commission permitted the railroads to increase their freight rates by an amount sufficient to pay for this added cost.

Merger. The only merger of consequence was the absorption of the 624-mile Norfolk Southern into the 10,200-mile Southern Railway System.

A report calling for a restructuring of Western railroads into four systems built around the Union Pacific, Southern Pacific, Santa Fe, and the Burlington Northern was rejected by the railroads.

LUTHER S. MILLER
Editor, "Railway Age"

Shipping

Ocean transport boomed in 1973, recovering from a serious slump in 1971 and the first half of 1972. The chief reasons were the large sea movement of wheat to the Soviet Union, China, and the Indian subcontinent, plus increased petroleum imports into the United States until the Arabs embargoed crude-oil exports in mid-October in retaliation for U. S. support of Israel during the Arab-Israeli war. One long-term consequence of that war may be the reopening of the Suez Canal.

(Continued on page 603)

Supertanker Brooklyn, *biggest merchant ship ever built in the United States, is christened at Brooklyn Navy Yard.*

SOVIET freighter Vysotsk loads U. S. wheat at the Port of Longview, Texas, as a grain train replenishes the supply in the elevators.

Big Grain Deal Produced Transportation Headaches

One of the first results of President Nixon's visit to the Soviet Union in May 1972 was a Soviet request to buy U. S. feed grain for consumption by Soviet cattle. This was part of a major Soviet plan to improve the standard of living of its citizens by increasing the ratio of beef to fish protein in their diet. Early in the negotiations, however, the request was changed to wheat for human consumption. Soviet wheat production, due to bad weather and poor management, had dropped from 81.9 million metric tons in 1971 to 62.3 million in 1972.

Agreements. In July 1972, agreement was reached that the United States would sell $750 million dollars worth of grain to the Soviet Union over a three-year period, supplying 19.2 million tons by July 1, 1973. Before this could be done, the U. S. government had to get a commitment from the maritime and longshore unions that they would not block shipments by strikes or picketing. This had happened in 1963 because 50% of the grain shipped was not carried in American flag ships.

In 1963 few Russian vessels were available for that grain transport. In 1972 the Soviet merchant marine was the fifth-largest in the world and so was entitled to its share of this trade. Agreement was reached that one third of the wheat would be transported in U. S. flag vessels, one third in Soviet ships, and one third in ships of other countries. General movement, however, was delayed almost until December because Soviet negotiators refused to assume any of the added cost involved in shipping wheat in U. S. flag vessels rather than in Russian or third-nation vessels. U. S. taxpayers therefore had to make up the difference in shipping costs. This was the first sour note in what generally turned out to be an unhappy affair.

Transportation Problems. Three quarters of the exports have been shipped from the Galveston Bay area of Texas. Ocean transport had hardly begun before a shortage of railway cars and other factors began to affect it unfavorably. Another cause of inefficient delivery was the diversity of government controlling agencies—the Department of Agriculture for the grain elevators, the Interstate Commerce Commission (ICC) for the railroads, and the Maritime Administration of the Commerce Department for ocean shipping.

The consequence was that during the first three months of 1973 as many as 50 ships were anchored off Galveston Bay awaiting berth calls. Some were delayed for as long as 45 days, and charges for demurrage (detention of a vessel) ran as high as about $2,500 for foreign flag ships to about $6,000 for U. S. flag ships.

The first corrective action taken was the diversion of hopper cars from the Northeast to the Midwest–Gulf Coast area. Also, vessel chartering and call-up were done more realistically. As a result, the port situation began to improve by May 1, and by early summer the ship jam off Galveston Bay had been cleared. However, bitter aftereffects remained. A congressional investigating committee summarized the mistakes—too much grain was sold for too quick delivery, four months were lost in negotiations, and too much (75%) of the wheat was funneled through Houston and Galveston.

A countrywide freight-car shortage developed, intensified by shipments of grain to Bangladesh and cotton to China, and it became the worst in history, according to ICC officials. As the U. S. economy began to be unfavorably affected, the Soviet wheat deal became increasingly unpopular as farmers, meat producers, housewives, and businessmen blamed it for their troubles. The grain export impasse was now becoming a national instead of a maritime issue.

Neither the United States nor the Soviet Union has been able to provide the ships to fill their quotas. Third-nation ships, instead of transporting one third of the wheat as planned, were moving more than three quarters of it.

Alternative Inland Transport. The most feasible inland transport for grain is by water in barges. Tulsa, Okla., only a short rail haul from the Kansas wheat fields, has been open to the sea since the Arkansas-Verdigris waterway was opened in 1971, linking Tulsa to the sea via the waterway, the Arkansas River, and the Mississippi River down to New Orleans. Barge companies have been formed in New Orleans for the special transport of grain in unit tows. Thus the delivery of heavy grain exports may take on an entirely new pattern.

JOHN D. HAYES

(Continued from page 601)

World Trade. Merchant fleets are the foundation of world trade and a concrete expression of international relations. The oceans are the last area of free trade. But as movement and competition across them increases and sea law remains largely ineffective, there is little sea order. Collisions, explosions, and sinkings increase; the competence of crews, especially licensed officers, dwindles; traffic conditions in critical seaways, such as the English Channel, are intolerable; and the continental shelves are being polluted. No improvement such as an international sea police is in sight.

Flags of Convenience. The international character of shipping is best exemplified by the first-ranked Liberian fleet. Its registered ships are nearly all owned by citizens or corporations of other countries. U. S. nationals own 32 million tons of shipping under the flags of Liberia and Panama. This American-owned fleet comprises 12% of the world tonnage, whereas merchant ships under the U. S. flag account for only 3.3%. Moreover, many shipowners of maritime nations are shifting to new flags of convenience, either of small countries like Cyprus or former colonies like Bermuda.

National Fleets. Ocean transport was virtually all private enterprise until the creation of the great U. S. merchant fleet of World War II. After that war, the government could sell only a fraction of those ships to its nationals. Soviet merchant vessels have always been nationally owned, but their number in world trade was small until 1956. Now the Soviet fleet is the fifth largest in the world. The growing fleets of developing countries are also national, and they tend to be either state owned or state controlled.

Over 40% of the exported raw materials is from developing countries, but only 7% is carried in ships under flags of these nations. They want to correct this with bilateral agreements. An example is Brazil's agreement with the United States for transport of coffee—40% by vessels of each country and 20% by those under other flags.

The shipping of traditional maritime nations becomes more competitive by resorting to flags of convenience, but some national fleets are growing. The clash between these rival interests creates a continuing problem that international maritime conventions have so far been unable to resolve.

Men in Ships. Over the past decade voyages have become longer and port time shorter, automation has reduced crew size, and ships are larger. The human beings in them, however, remain the same. Boredom and loneliness aboard now are acute problems. These are being attacked in three ways—improved living and recreational facilities, air transport of crew reliefs, and wives on board. The first has brought little improvement; the second affords more family life at home; the third brings family life aboard. Wives of senior officers are often regularly on board, and those of junior officers are allowed for specified periods. Replacement of the seamen is a lesser problem.

Owners resist family inroads on board as they bring problems and added expense. But with ample ship space, the sea village is now a possibility. Family life has long existed on the barges of Europe's inland waterways.

As employment opportunities in Europe and Japan improve, their young men go less to sea and crews are now coming from poorer areas like Spain,

─── **Table 1. MAJOR MERCHANT FLEETS** ───

Gross registered tons[1]

Country	July 1, 1973	1-year gain or loss
Liberia	49,905,000	+5,461,000
Japan	36,785,000	+1,856,000
Britain	30,160,000	+1,535,000
Norway	23,621,000	+ 114,000
Greece	19,295,000	+3,966,000
USSR	17,397,000	+ 663,000
United States	14,912,000	− 112,000
Panama	9,569,000	+1,775,000
World total[2]	289,927,000	+21,587,000

[1] Gross tonnage is volume capacity; deadweight tonnage (dwt) is lifting capacity. [2] Includes other countries in addition to those listed.

─ **Table 2. WORLD MERCHANT SHIPS BY TYPES** ─

Gross registered tons

Type	July 1, 1973	1-year gain or loss	Percent change[1]
Oil tankers	115,365,000	+10,236,000	+ 8.9%
Liquefied gas carriers	2,276,000	+ 389,000	+17.2%
Chemical tankers	652,000	+ 101,000	+15.5%
Bulk/oil carriers[2]	19,539,000	+ 4,666,000	+22.8%
Ore and bulk carriers[2]	53,110,000	+ 4,695,000	+ 8.8%
General cargo	69,506,000	− 1,085,000	− 1.5%
Container ships	5,899,000	+ 1,589,000	+26.9%
Passenger and other	1,688,000	− 32,000	− 0.2%
Nontrading[3]	21,892,000	+ 1,228,000	+ 5.6%
World total	289,927,000	+21,587,000	+ 7.5%

[1] Percent change=col. 2 divided by col. 1. [2] Bulk/oil carrier cargo spaces are fitted to hold either liquid or dry cargo. Ore and bulk carriers transport only dry cargo, either heavy ores or lighter bulk, such as grain and other cereals. [3] Oceanographic and fishing vessels, icebreakers, dredges, etc.
Source: Lloyd's Register of Shipping, 1973

southern Italy, China, and India. The sea offers these people a better livelihood than that provided at home.

U. S. Shipbuilding. The largest ship ever built in the United States, the 225,000-ton *Brooklyn*, was launched June 30 at the former Brooklyn Navy Yard. The new supertanker is 1,094 feet (333 meters) long. Several more are to be constructed in this yard, at San Diego, Calif., and Quincy, Mass., correcting a shipbuilding slump that had largely caused the decline of the U. S. flag fleet.

Shipyards enjoyed a favorable year, and the U. S. fuel shortage gives promise that this will continue. The most encouraging sign is the general drop in construction subsidies from 55% to 34%.

Labor and Management. The retirement of Joseph Curran, founder and former president of the National Maritime Union, gives hope of labor peace as moderate Paul Hall, head of the Seafarers International Union, becomes the leader of sea labor.

Shipping management is embroiled in the courts over the transport of containers by transcontinental railroads instead of through the Panama Canal, which saves up to two weeks time. East coast port authorities, with millions invested in container facilities, have sought injunctions to stop this practice while its legality according to U. S. maritime laws of 1916 and 1920 is determined.

U. S. Coast Guard. The U. S. Coast Guard has taken over port traffic direction in San Francisco and Puget Sound and will do so in Houston in December 1974 and New York in July 1975. Expansion of the role of the Coast Guard has occurred partly as a result of recent laws for ocean pollution control and regulation of growing barge traffic. Among its other duties are search and rescue, merchant marine safety, military readiness, and such worldwide activities as the International Ice Patrol and Amvers, the computerized positioning of merchant ships at sea.

JOHN D. HAYES
Rear Admiral, U. S. Navy (Retired)

— TRINIDAD AND TOBAGO • Information Highlights —

Official Name: Trinidad and Tobago.
Location: Southeastern Caribbean Sea.
Area: 1,980 square miles (5,128 sq km).
Population (1973 est.): 1,100,000. *Density,* 521 per square mile (201 per sq km).
Chief City (1970): Port-of-Spain, the capital, 67,867.
Government: *Head of state,* Elizabeth II, queen, represented by Sir Ellis Clarke, governor-general (took office Jan. 1973). *Head of government,* Eric Williams, prime minister (took office Sept. 1962). *Legislature*—Parliament: Senate and House of Representatives. *Major political parties*—People's National Movement; Democratic Labour party.
Languages: English (official), Hindi, French patois, Spanish.
Education: *Expenditure* (1969), 15.7% of total public expenditure. *School enrollment* (1969)—primary, 227,181; secondary, 32,560; technical/vocational, 3,396; university/higher, 2,218.
Monetary Unit: Trinidad and Tobago dollar (1.95 T. and T. dollars equal U. S.$1, Aug. 1973).
Gross National Product (1971 est.): $961,000,000.
Consumer Price Index (1972), 140 (1963=100).
Manufacturing (major products): Petroleum products, sugar, fertilizers, plastics, textiles, cement.
Major Agricultural Products: Sugarcane, citrus fruits, bananas, coffee, cacao, coconuts.
Major Minerals: Petroleum, natural gas, asphalt, gypsum.
Foreign Trade (1972): *Exports,* $55,000,000. *Imports,* $751,000,000. *Chief trading partners* (1971)—United States (took 40.5% of exports, supplied 17.3% of imports); United Kingdom (9%—13%); Saudi Arabia (supplied 15%).
Tourism: Receipts (1971), $32 900,000.
Transportation: *Motor vehicles* (1971), 94,300 (automobiles, 74,300); *major national airline,* British West Indian Airways.
Communications: *Telephones* (1972), 62,923; *newspapers* (1970), 3 (daily circulation, 140,000).

TRINIDAD AND TOBAGO

The usually green islands of Trinidad and Tobago turned brown in 1973 due to a drought that began in December 1972 and extended into late August. Meanwhile, the nation's long-time leader, Dr. Eric Williams, announced his wish to retire.

Economic Affairs. Agricultural production fell and even industrial activity was threatened as reservoirs, used for generating electricity and for cooling, sank to very low levels. Sugar output (184,900 tons) was the lowest in 10 years, the drought having caused a 20% decline from the previous year in the yield of cane per acre. Also contributing to the poor sugar harvest was the malicious burning of some 700,000 acres of cane. Production of coffee and cacao also declined in 1973, and unemployment and inflation remained serious.

On the other hand, tourism and the petroleum industry registered impressive gains. The number of calls by tourist ships during the winter visiting season rose from 95 in 1971–72 to 138 in 1972–73. Newly operating offshore oil wells were responsible for the increase in petroleum output. A new desulfurization plant entered into full production, and financial means were found to begin processing natural gas for export to the United States.

Williams' Announcement. After 15 years of political leadership, Dr. Eric Williams, the prime minister, announced that while he would prefer to give up the leadership of his party and government he would remain until the general elections early in 1974 would allow the people an opportunity to select a new political leader. In the 1970's the Williams administration had found it hard to deal with persistent guerrilla activity in the isolated hills of northeastern Trinidad and with the general increase in public dissatisfaction with the regime.

Dr. Williams rose to power when Trinidad was still a British colony. He played a key role in the creation of the West Indian Federation. When the federation was dissolved, Dr. Williams led Trinidad and Tobago to full independence.

THOMAS MATHEWS, *University of Puerto Rico*

TUNISIA

President Habib Bourguiba, who celebrated his 70th birthday in August 1973, continued to dominate Tunisian political life and to play the role of peacemaker in the Arab-Israeli conflict.

National Leadership. President Bourguiba appeared to be in better health than in recent years and continued to eliminate political opposition that had risen during his illness. When Bourguiba expelled Ahmed Mestiri from the Destour Socialist party in 1972 for advocating more democracy, he still allowed Mestiri to remain in the National Assembly. But on June 26, the assembly passed a law prohibiting expelled party members from serving in the assembly.

Ahmed Ben Salah, a former minister of national economy, had been sentenced in 1969 to 10 years in prison for high treason. In February, he escaped and fled the country. Bourguiba then staged a trial that on June 14 resulted in the condemnation of Ben Salah's brother and nine others to 3 to 12 years' imprisonment for complicity in the escape. Ben Salah himself was condemned in absentia to an additional 5½ years in prison. He now resides somewhere in Europe where he is seeking to mobilize support, particularly from the left, for his struggle against Bourguiba.

In 1971, Bourguiba had dismissed his lifelong friend and collaborator Bahi Ladgham from the prime ministery because he saw Ladgham as a possible rival. In 1973 Ladgham also resigned under pressure from both the party and the National Assembly.

On April 12, Bourguiba resolved Tunisia's immediate presidential succession problem by announcing that he will run for his fourth 5-year term in elections in November 1974. In the meantime he continued to raise the question of succession after his death—something that obviously weighs on Bourguiba's mind, since, for example, his speeches are loaded with historical reminiscences apparently intended to assure that he will have a large place in Tunisian history after he is gone.

——— TUNISIA • Information Highlights ———

Official Name: Republic of Tunisia.
Location: North Africa.
Area: 63,170 square miles (163,610 sq km).
Population (1973 est.): 5,600,000. *Density,* 89 per square mile (34 per sq km).
Chief City (1966 census): Tunis, the capital, 468,997.
Government: *Head of state,* Habib Bourguiba, president (reelected for 3d 5-year term Nov. 1969). *Chief minister,* Hedi Nouira, premier (took office Nov. 1970). *Legislature* (unicameral)—National Assembly. *Major political party*—Destour Socialist party.
Languages: Arabic (official), French.
Education: *School enrollment* (1968)—primary, 857,514; secondary, 149,414; technical/vocational, 50,587; university/higher, 8,368.
Monetary Unit: Dinar (0.44 dinar equals U. S.$1, Aug. 1973).
Gross National Product (1972 est.): $2,063,000,000.
Economic Indexes: *Industrial production* (1972), 145 (1963=100); *agricultural production* (1971), 120 (1963=100); *consumer price index* (1972), 138 (1963=100).
Manufacturing (major products): Processed foods, wines, petroleum products, olive oil, pulp and wood products.
Major Agricultural Products: Wheat, olives, vegetables, grapes, citrus fruits, forest products.
Major Minerals: Phosphate rock, petroleum, iron ore, zinc, lead.
Foreign Trade (1972): *Exports,* $311,000,000. *Imports,* $460,000,000. *Chief trading partners* (1970)—France (took 24% of exports, supplied 35% of imports); Italy (21%—7.2%); West Germany (10%—8.5%).
Transportation: *Motor vehicles* (1971), 113,600 (automobiles, 72,100); *railroads* (1971), 1,429 miles (2,300 km); *major national airline,* Tunis Air.
Communications: *Telephones* (1972), 88,060; *newspapers* (1969), 4 (daily circulation, 80,000).

Student and Labor Unrest. At the time of Ben Salah's escape in February, university students protested against the Bourguiba regime. Many students identify with Ben Salah simply because he is opposed to the government, without regard to his political ideology. Students also staged solidarity strikes with workers who struck against the failures of the government to settle grievances. The government hopes, apparently, that its appointment of Mohammed Sayah (who at 40 is the youngest member of the cabinet) to head the ministry of youth and sport will help it cope with unrest among the youth.

Foreign Affairs. At the close of 1972, a remarkable debate between Bourguiba and Libyan President Qaddafi on Arab unification was broadcast live over Radio Tunis. Despite Bourguiba's public rebuff of Qaddifi's pan-Arab overtures, however, Libyan relations with Tunisia became relatively cordial during 1973.

There was serious speculation in 1973 that Bourguiba would be acceptable to both Arabs and Israelis to sit down with the Israelis and begin to resolve the Arab-Israeli dispute. After starting out without any preconditions, however, Bourguiba gradually backed off until he declared on July 7 that negotiations would be impossible so long as Israel refused to withdraw from Arab territories. In line with his harder line, Tunisia sent a token Tunisian force into the fourth Arab-Israeli war in October.

WILLARD A. BELING
University of Southern California

TURKEY

On October 29, 1973, the Turkish nation observed the 50th anniversary of the Republic. The Turkish people have more cause for satisfaction with the past than anxiety as to the future. Credit for constructive achievement must rest with ordinary Turkish citizens, who have gained a new self-confidence since the 1960 military coup and show signs of a new dynamism. Despite trials and tribulations, the foundations of the Republic seem sound. Turkey's foreign relations also seem well established, however troubled its alliances appear to be.

Politics. The Turkish armed services continued to play an influential role in Turkish politics during 1973 as they had since 1960, and martial law, especially in Istanbul and Ankara, remained in effect until the fall of 1973. During the early part of 1973, in particular, hundreds of alleged subversives or terrorists were arrested and brought to trial. Politics as usual appeared to be the dominant note. The Supreme Command Council, on February 21, criticized Suleyman Demirel, leader of the Justice party and former prime minister, for not participating in talks to resolve the political stalemate. The Supreme Command Council called for basic reforms, an end to verbal attacks on the armed services, and legal changes to insure honest elections. On February 24 a decree was issued in Ankara requiring all news agencies to submit their news stories to the Supreme Command Council before publication.

The Grand National Assembly began to vote for a new president in March. The early ballots were inconclusive. On March 18 the chief of staff, Gen. Semih Sancar, warned political leaders that the army would step in again if the term of President Cevdet Sunay were not renewed for two more years. The Assembly passed a constitutional amendment creating state security courts to try political crimes, but it rejected an amendment to extend President Sunay's term.

Finally, in its 15th ballot, the Assembly elected Sen. Fahri Korutürk as president. Korutürk, who will serve until 1980, was born in Istanbul in 1903. A retired naval officer, he also was an ambassador to the USSR. On April 10, he accepted the resignation of Prime Minister Ferit Melen and asked Naim Talu to form a government. The Talu program called for strengthening the national, democratic, secular, and social structure of the state, based on law, and the eradication of extremist elements of right and left.

Before the parliamentary elections in October, martial law was lifted after having been in effect for some 29 months. All 450 seats in the National Assembly and one third of the 150 seats in the Senate were filled as some 17 million voters took part. Suleyman Demirel and the Justice party were favored to win, but the Republican People's party, with Bulent Ecevit, the somewhat leftist leader, emerged with 185 National Assembly seats and the Justice party won only 149.

Because no party had a majority, Ecevit was asked to form a government. Like Demirel, Ecevit proposed to repeal the Turkish ban on the cultivation of opium and hashish, arranged in collaboration with the United States. He also proposed political and constitutional reform and amnesty for political prisoners condemned under martial law. On November 7, however, Ecevit abandoned his efforts to form a cabinet. President Korutürk then turned to Suleyman Demirel, who also failed. The crisis was unresolved at year-end, with Naim Talu emerging to lead a kind of caretaker government. The death on December 25 of Ismet Inönü, successor to Ataturk, signaled the end of an era.

TURKEY • Information Highlights

Official Name: Republic of Turkey.
Location: Southeastern Europe and Southwestern Asia.
Area: 301,381 square miles (780,576 sq km).
Population (1973 est.): 38,600,000. *Density,* 119 per square mile (46 per sq km).
Chief Cities (1970 census): Ankara, the capital, 1,208,791; Istanbul, 2,247,630; Izmir, 520,686; Adana, 351,655.
Government: *Head of state,* Fahri Korutürk, president (took office April 1973). *Head of government,* premier. *Legislature*—Grand National Assembly: Senate and National Assembly. *Major political parties*—Justice party; Republican People's party; Democratic party; National Reliance party.
Languages: Turkish (official), Kurdish, Arabic.
Education: *Expenditure* (1968), 20.2% of total public expenditure. *School enrollment* (1972)—primary, 5,100,000; secondary, 1,166,551; technical/vocational, 263,000; university/higher, 170,000.
Monetary Unit: Lira (14 liras equal U. S.$1, Aug. 1973).
Gross National Product (1973 est.): $15,080,000,000.
Economic Indexes: *Industrial production* (1966), 170 (1963=100); *agricultural production* (1971), 134 (1963=100); *consumer price index* (1972), 151 (1968=100).
Manufacturing (major products): Textiles, petroleum products, cement, iron and steel, fertilizers, processed agricultural products.
Major Agricultural Products: Raisins (ranks 1st among world producers, 1972), wheat, cotton, rye, sugar beets, barley, fruits, tobacco, hazelnuts, sheep, cattle.
Major Minerals: Chromium ore (ranks 3d among world producers, 1971), copper, iron ore, coal, lignite, petroleum, mercury, antimony, bauxite.
Foreign Trade (1972): *Exports,* $885,000,000. *Imports,* $1,508,-000,000. *Chief trading partners* (1970)—West Germany (took 20% of exports, supplied 18% of imports); United States (10%—20%); Italy (6.7%—8%); United Kingdom (5.6%—10%).
Tourism: Receipts (1971), $62,900,000.
Transportation: *Motor vehicles* (1970), 311,400 (automobiles, 147,000); *railroads* (1971), 4,976 miles (8,008 km); *merchant fleet* (1972), 743,000 gross registered tons; *major national airline,* Turk Hava Yollari.
Communications: *Telephones* (1972), 654,452; *newspapers* (1971), 432.

Social and Economic Change. Turkey continued to make social and economic progress in 1973. Between 1968 and 1973 the gross national product (GNP) grew from $7.8 billion to $15.08 billion, and per capita GNP from $215 to $420. The annual rate of growth was between 6% and 7%, and in industry 11%. Foreign trade reached $2.4 billion by the end of 1972, when the deficit totaled $623 million, with exports totaling some $885 million and imports $1.5 billion. The number of Turkish workers abroad grew to 654,821, with 544,236 in West Germany (83%). Remittances rose to $740 million in 1972, and estimates for 1973 totaled $900 million.

One symbol of the developing economy was the formal opening of the new Bosporus Bridge in celebration of the 50th anniversary. The six-lane, 3,523-foot (1,074-meter) bridge links Europe and Asia and carries some 22,000 vehicles per day, with toll charges averaging 75 cents per car.

Turkey also gained in education, with more than 5,100,000 students in primary schools and 1,166,551 in secondary education, some 263,000 in vocational schools, and 170,000 in higher learning. By 1973 there were 161 institutions of higher learning, compared with 120 in 1968.

Foreign Relations. Turkey's alliance with the United States and its association with NATO and CENTO remained intact. Although the problem of Cyprus remained unresolved, relations with Greece improved. Relations with the Balkan neighbors developed normally, as did those with the USSR. Turkey refused to permit the United States to fly military equipment to Israel during the Middle East war. Turkey also refused publicly to endorse the Arab position, although it sought improved relations with the Arab world. Turkey's principal trading partners were in Western Europe and the United States, which has extended some $6 billion in assistance since 1948.

HARRY N. HOWARD
The American University

UGANDA

In its third year of military government under Gen. Idi Amin, Uganda continued to play a maverick role in the international community and to be marked by an unsettled political situation at home.

Foreign Relations. Uganda's ties with Arab states, particularly Libya, continued to grow closer in 1973. President Amin, himself a Muslim, issued several statements supporting Arab states during the Middle East conflict. However, relations with several other states were less smooth.

Tensions between Uganda and Tanzania have existed ever since Tanzania provided asylum for former Ugandan President Milton Obote in 1971, although hostilities were reduced temporarily in October 1972, when an agreement between the two states was signed in Mogadishu, Somalia. Serious problems between the two countries began to recur in March 1973, largely as a result of the disappearance of Tanzanian nationals in Uganda. However, on May 29 President Amin met with Tanzanian President Julius Nyerere in Addis Ababa, Ethiopia, where a new accord was reached.

In late July relations improved further when Uganda announced that it had agreed to pay compensation for 24 Tanzanians who disappeared in Uganda in 1972. In late August, Amin issued a strong statement supporting establishment of an East African federation with either Nyerere or Jomo Kenyatta of Kenya as its first president.

Events in 1973 did little to repair the split between Uganda and Britain. The nationalization of British firms begun in 1972 was completed in May. President Amin did not attend the Conference of Heads of Government of Commonwealth Countries, held in Ottawa, Canada, in August, but he issued a statement condemning Britain for its policies in Africa and questioning the continued existence of the Commonwealth.

The United States embassy in Uganda remained vacant for most of the year. U. S. officials were unhappy both about the fact that Uganda detained 112 Zaire-bound Peace Corps volunteers while Amin satisfied himself that they were not Israeli mercenaries, and about a series of notes from Amin to President Nixon on topics ranging from Watergate to Cambodia.

Domestic Affairs. Although Amin's policies of Africanization have undoubtedly won some political support internally, it is clear that much of the country's intellectual and political elite has become disenchanted with his regime. Many in this group initially welcomed Gen. Amin's overthrow of Obote in 1971, but they have become alarmed at the kidnapping and murder of many prominent Ugandan citizens, as well as a number of foreigners, by the army.

During the year Amin frequently juggled personnel in the cabinet, judiciary, and army. The cabinet was in such confusion that permanent secretaries performed the duties of ministers through most of the year. Some departures from the government were voluntary. Early in the year Minister for Education Edward Rugamayo resigned on personal and moral grounds, and Uganda's ambassador to West Germany, John Barigye, quit and condemned Amin for the "reign of terror" in Uganda.

The Ugandan border was reopened to tourist traffic on September 16, ending a ban imposed in 1972. However, restrictions on travel and currency continued to inhibit visits by foreigners.

JAY E. HAKES
Louisiana State University in New Orleans

--------- **UGANDA · Information Highlights** ---------

Official Name: Republic of Uganda.
Location: East Africa.
Area: 91,134 square miles (236,036 sq km).
Population (1973 est.): 9,300,000. *Density,* 111 per square mile (43 per sq km).
Chief City (1969 census): Kampala, the capital, 331,889.
Government: *Head of state,* Gen. Idi Amin, president (took office Feb. 1971). *Head of government,* Gen. Idi Amin. *Legislature* (unicameral)—National Assembly (dissolved Feb. 1971). *Major political parties*—suspended.
Languages: English (official), Swahili, Luganda.
Education: *Expenditure* (1968), 18.1% of total public expenditure. *School enrollment* (1969)—primary, 709,708; secondary, 43,925; technical/vocational, 3,673; university/higher, 2,494.
Monetary Unit: Shilling (6.9 shillings equal U. S.$1, Aug. 1973).
Gross National Product (1971 est.): $1,415,000,000.
Consumer Price Index (1972), 171 (1963=100).
Manufacturing (major products): Processed agricultural products.
Major Agricultural Products: Coffee, millet, cotton, sisal, groundnuts, tobacco, sweet potatoes and yams, cassava.
Major Minerals: Copper, tin, phosphate rock, salt.
Foreign Trade (1972): *Exports,* $260,000,000. *Imports,* $113,-000,000. *Chief trading partners* (1971)—United Kingdom (took 24% of exports, supplied 32% of imports); United States (22%—7%); Japan (supplied 26%); West Germany (supplied 10%).
Transportation: *Motor vehicles* (1970), 43,100 (automobiles, 29,100); *railroads* (regional total with Kenya and Tanzania, 1971), 3,676 miles (5,915 km); *major national airline* (with Kenya and Tanzania), East African Airways.
Communications: *Telephones* (1972), 34,190; *newspapers* (1971), 6 (daily circulation, 78,000).

UPI

USSR

Soviet Jews outside Moscow's ministry of external affairs demonstrate against the denial of exit visas to Israel.

Soviet foreign relations during 1973 were dominated by the uncertain course of U. S.-Soviet relations, which ranged from increasing cooperation early in the year to great tenseness during the autumn Arab-Israel undeclared war. In the first part of the year new Soviet-American agreements were signed to expand trade, increase scientific cooperation, and further limit arms. Soviet leader Leonid Brezhnev's visit to the United States in June resulted in the conclusion of 11 such pacts.

In contrast, the outbreak of the Arab-Israel war in October caused the USSR to airlift arms to Egypt and Syria, while the United States quickly began to airlift arms to Israel. At first the USSR rejected U. S. requests to help mediate the war, and then by a poorly worded diplomatic note prompted the United States to putting all U. S. armed forces on a worldwide military alert, which was obviously aimed against the Soviet Union. Finally the two superpowers did cooperate in bringing about an Arab-Israel truce, but the progress of Soviet-American détente was definitely slowed.

Internally, good weather conditions produced a grain crop of 220 million metric tons, which was the largest in Soviet history and 52 million tons greater than the poor harvest of 1972. Partly because of this agricultural success, annual industrial growth also rose from 6.5% in 1972 to approximately 7.3% in 1973.

Politically, 1973 was noteworthy for the elevation to full Politburo membership of the nation's minister of defense, for the first time since 1957, and of a professional diplomat for the first time in Soviet history. Both were added to this top bureau of the Soviet Communist party apparently because of the increasingly complex nature of Soviet foreign relations.

Throughout 1973, dissident Soviet intellectuals continued to be imprisoned, exiled, demoted, or harassed in an official attempt to weaken the illegal underground press, called *samizdat*.

FOREIGN AFFAIRS

United States. During the first half of 1973, Soviet-American agreements enhanced cooperation between the two countries. These included: an agreement on wildlife conservation (January 31), the grant of U. S. governmental and private long-term credits for the Soviet purchase of American machinery (March), a pact for joint research on air pollution (March), a fisheries agreement embracing the northeast Pacific and western Atlantic oceans, and an agreement on the details of prevention of naval incidents on the high seas (May).

The visit to the United States by Soviet leader Brezhnev from June 16 to 24 resulted in the signing of 11 additional U. S.-Soviet pacts: for five-year cooperation in studies of the world's oceans; for

607

USSR • Information Highlights

Official Name: Union of Soviet Socialist Republics.
Area: 8,649,489 square miles (22,402,200 sq km).
Population (1973 est.): 250,000,000. *Density,* 29 per square mile (11 per sq km).
Chief Cities (1972 est.): Moscow, the capital, 7,300,000; Leningrad, 4,066,000; Kiev, 1,764,000.
Government: *Head of state,* Nikolai V. Podgorny, president (took office 1965). *Head of government,* Aleksei N. Kosygin, premier (took office 1964). *First secretary of the Communist party,* Leonid I. Brezhnev (took office 1964). *Legislature*—Supreme Soviet: Soviet of the Union, Soviet of Nationalities. *Political party*—Communist (sole legal party).
Languages: Russian (official), 80 minority languages.
Education: *Expenditure* (1972), 10% of total public expenditure. *School enrollment* (1973)—primary and secondary, 49,200,000; technical/vocational, 4,500,000; university/higher, 4,600,000.
Monetary Unit: ruble (0.685 ruble equals U. S.$1, Sept. 1973).
Gross National Product (1972 est.): $579,000,000,000.
Economic Indexes: *Industrial production* (1972), 320 (1958 = 100); *agricultural production* (1972), 135 (1958 = 100).
Manufacturing (major products): Steel, cement, chemical fertilizer, electric power.
Major Agricultural Products: Grain (ranks 3d among world producers, 1972), potatoes (world rank 1st, 1972), sugar beets (world rank 1st, 1972).
Major Minerals: Coal (ranks 1st among world producers, 1972), crude petroleum (world rank 2d, 1972), iron ore (world rank 1st, 1972).
Foreign Trade (1972): Exports, $16,891,000,000. Imports, $17,689,000,000. *Chief trading partners* (1972)—East Germany (took 13% of exports, supplied 15% of imports); Poland (10%—11%).
Transportation: *Motor vehicles* (1973), 7,000,000 (automobiles, 2,000,000); *railroads* (1971), 84,000 miles (135,-200 km); *merchant fleet* (1972), 16,734,000 gross registered tons; *major national airline,* Aeroflot.
Communications: *Telephones* (1972), 15,100,000; *newspapers* (1972), 6,878.

five-year joint transportation research; for five-year joint agricultural research; for cultural exchanges between 1974 and 1976 (all the above signed on June 19); for the avoidance of double taxation on the two countries' citizens and business companies (June 20); for the establishment of a Soviet trade mission in Washington and of a U. S. commercial office in Moscow (June 22); for the organization of a U. S.-Soviet Chamber of Commerce (June 22); and for opening new air routes between Moscow and Washington and between New York and Leningrad, to be flown by both Soviet and American airline companies (June 23). More important, however, were the pacts concluded for the acceleration of mutual arms limitation negotiations so that agreement could be achieved in 1974 (June 21); for 10-year joint research on the peaceful uses of atomic energy (June 21); and for the renunciation of nuclear warfare between the two countries and cooperation in preventing it among others (June 22).

On July 6 a U. S. consulate-general was opened in Leningrad, the first there in Soviet history. The U. S.-Soviet Chamber of Commerce was formally organized in both countries, also in July.

Throughout 1973, Soviet-U. S. trade expanded, achieving an annual turnover of approximately $1.5 billion, which was more than double the 1972 level. In 1973 the United States became the largest capitalist trading partner of the USSR. This trade was very one-sided, with U. S. exports (mostly grain) to the USSR greatly exceeding Soviet exports to the United States.

Middle East. Soviet-American governmental relations greatly deteriorated in October, when Syria and Egypt jointly started a brief war by invading Israel on October 6. The Soviet government appeared to have advance notice of the attack, since it evacuated many Soviet civilians from Egypt and Syria a few days before the war began. On October

8 the USSR officially announced its support of the Egyptian, Syrian, and Jordanian demand that those lands that had been taken by Israel in the 1967 Arab-Israel war be returned. On October 9 the USSR was angered when Israeli planes bombed the Soviet cultural center in Damascus, killing or wounding several Soviet citizens. The next day the USSR began airlifting arms to both Syria and Egypt. On October 12, Israeli missile boats sank a Soviet merchant ship in the Syrian port of Tartus. Up to this point the USSR displayed little interest in helping mediate the war.

Then from October 16 to 19, Soviet Premier Aleksei Kosygin visited Egypt and discovered that the Egyptian military situation was starting to deteriorate. Consequently, when U. S. Secretary of State Henry Kissinger visited Moscow to confer with Brezhnev (October 20–21) the Soviet attitude changed, As a result of the Moscow talks, the United States and the USSR submitted a joint resolution to the UN Security Council on October 22, requesting the Arabs and Israel to cease fighting within 12 hours at the existing battle lines. This resolution was adopted by the Council and slowly accepted by both the Arabs and Israel.

On October 24 a poorly worded Soviet note suggested to the United States that the Middle Eastern ceasefire lines be jointly supervised by U. S. and Soviet military observers; it added that otherwise the USSR would do this alone. The U. S. government reacted by putting U. S. forces throughout the world on alert, and by refusing the Soviet offer. By October 28 the USSR officially complained that the United States had misinterpreted the note, that there was no Soviet threat to the Middle East, and that hence the U. S. military alert had been unnecessary. (The alert ended soon after.)

In 1973 the USSR gave technical aid to 12 Mideastern and South Asian countries: Afghanistan, India, Iran, Iraq, Kuwait, Nepal, Pakistan, South Yemen, Sri Lanka, Syria, Turkey, and Yemen. New technical aid pacts were concluded by the USSR during the year with Pakistan (March), Nepal (June), and India (February and November); the one with India was to last 15 years and called for Soviet investment in India's industrial plant. A cultural exchange agreement was signed with Pakistan in February. Two Soviet-Iranian treaties in August defined their common border and provided for cooperation against aerial hijacking. When Afghanistan in July overthrew its king and became a republic, the USSR was the first country to recognize the new government.

Far East. Relations between the USSR and mainland China remained poor in 1973, although the two countries concluded an airways pact in July and a trade agreement in August. Negotiations to delimit the exact Sino-Soviet border continued without result, and China refused a Soviet offer of a nonaggression pact.

Soviet-Japanese agreements were signed in May for the regulation of fishing in the northwest Pacific Ocean and in October for scientific cooperation. Negotiations in October for the long-delayed Soviet-Japanese peace treaty were again fruitless because the USSR refused to return to Japan four small Kuril islands seized by the Soviet Union at the close of World War II.

After the Vietnam peace accord, the USSR in July and August signed technical aid pacts with both North Vietnam and the Vietcong (Communist)

rebels of South Vietnam. Repayment of past Soviet economic loans was waived for the former, while the latter will receive free Soviet aid in the future. In 1973 the USSR also rendered technical aid to Bangladesh, Burma, Malaysia, Mongolia, North Korea, and the Lao Patriotic Front (the legalized political party of the Laotian Communists).

In October most of the Soviet embassy staff was withdrawn from Cambodia, and the USSR pledged its support to Prince Sihanouk's Cambodian government-in-exile, whose forces were waging civil war against the Cambodian government.

Europe. In 1973, Soviet relations with Europe were relatively free from tension and were marked by many new pacts of cooperation. The USSR concluded treaties of shipping and cultural exchange with Sweden; economic cooperation and cultural exchange with West Germany; economic cooperation and cultural exchange with Austria; scientific and economic cooperation with France; and shipping and technical cooperation with Denmark.

In September the Soviet Union established diplomatic relations with Ireland. On October 1, Soviet natural gas began to arrive in West Germany via a pipeline from the USSR.

During the year the Soviet Union rendered technical aid to Finland and Yugoslavia, and received technical assistance from Bulgaria, Czechoslovakia, East Germany, Hungary, Poland, and Rumania. In July the USSR and Yugoslavia signed a trade treaty covering future commerce from 1976 to 1985.

Africa. Soviet technical aid in 1973 was rendered to many African countries: Algeria, Burundi, Central African Republic, Congo, Egypt, Ethiopia, Guinea, Mauritania, Morocco, Nigeria, Senegal, Somalia, Sudan, Tanzania, Uganda, and Zambia. During the year new Soviet technical aid pacts were concluded with Mauritania, Morocco, and the Sudan. The Soviet press also admitted that Soviet arms were being supplied to the rebel nationalists in Portuguese African colonies.

Soviet diplomatic relations were established with Gabon in October and, in the autumn also, with Guinea-Bissau, a new rebel state in Portuguese Africa.

Latin America. The USSR in 1973 attempted to extend its influence in Latin America, with indifferent success. In March the Soviet government supported the resolution of the UN Security Council for termination of U. S. sovereignty over the Panama Canal, a resolution that the United States vetoed. Soviet-Mexican trade and cultural exchange pacts were concluded in April. Soviet technical aid was rendered to Brazil, Cuba, Peru, and, until September, to Chile.

After the anti-Communist coup in Chile, the USSR ceased its aid and on September 21 broke diplomatic relations with the new Chilean government, which was accused of harassing Soviet technicians, seamen, and diplomats.

DEFENSE AND SPACE

Armed Forces. The Soviet armed forces in 1973 totalled about 3,300,000 men. Their impressive equipment included the world's largest totals of tanks (40,000), submarines (400), and intercontinental ballistic missiles (1,618). The Soviet fleet of military transport planes, numbering 1,700, displayed its capability in the autumn by a large-scale airlift of arms to Egypt and Syria during the 1973 Arab-Israel war.

SHARING a joke are Soviet Party Chairman Brezhnev and President Nixon, shown en route to San Clemente.

Showing their ability to operate far from home waters, Soviet naval flotillas during the year paid official visits to France, India, Somalia, and Yugoslavia. During 1973 the USSR maintained a fleet of about 80 naval ships in the Mediterranean Sea and 20 in the Indian Ocean.

Marshal Ivan S. Konev, the great Soviet tank commander of World War II, died on May 21 at the age of 75. Another marshal, 90-year-old Semyon M. Budenny, died on October 28. A hero of the Russian Civil War of 1918–20, he was honored throughout his life.

Space Program. During 1973 the USSR successfully launched 14 unmanned earth satellites and three communications satellites. In contrast an unmanned orbital scientific station, launched during April, went out of control and became useless. This station was part of the preparation for a joint U. S.-Soviet venture in space. A preparatory flight, in September, was successful when a rocket with a two-man crew landed safely after spending two days aloft. Another two-man crew was launched in December in the Soyuz series.

Greater successes were achieved by flights of a lunar and interplanetary nature. In January an unmanned rocket was soft-landed on the moon, releasing an unmanned vehicle that explored the nearby lunar surface until June. In July and August, for the first time in history, four unmanned rockets were launched successively on the same interplanetary route, their common destination being the planet Mars. (See also SPACE EXPLORATION.)

GOVERNMENT AND POLITICS

Personnel Changes. The bad 1972 harvest resulted in several changes in the agricultural hierarchy early in 1973. In February, Politburo member Dmitri S. Polyansky was transferred from the post of first vice-premier to that of minister of agriculture, replacing Vladimir V. Matskevich, who in April became Soviet ambassador to Czechoslovakia. Also in April, Grigori S. Zolotukhin was promoted from the first party secretaryship of Krasnodar Territory to the position of minister of (farm produce) procurement, replacing Ziya N. Nuriyev, who was elevated to the position of vice-premier.

These government personnel shifts were overshadowed on April 27, when a meeting of the Cen-

tral Committee of the USSR Communist party removed both Pyotr Y. Shelest and Gennadi I. Voronov from the all-powerful party Politburo. In May both men were retired, Shelest losing his position as vice-premier and Voronov his position as minister of people's control. Apparently the two were Stalinists who opposed Soviet-U. S. détente.

At the same Central Committee meeting, Defense Minister Andrei A. Grechko and Foreign Minister Andrei A. Gromyko were appointed as full Politburo members, while KGB (police) minister Yuri V. Andropov was promoted from Politburo candidate member to full membership. Grigori V. Romanov was added to the Politburo as a candidate member, also retaining his post as first party secretary of Leningrad. Gromyko is the first professional diplomat ever to hold Politburo membership. His Politburo appointment probably indicates the Politburo's need for experts on foreign affairs.

Ecology. A decree of January 10 ordered numerous measures of environmental improvement to be undertaken during 1973–80, including the construction of incinerators and garbage reclamation plants in all resorts and large cities, the planting of more trees and other greenery in cities, and a cleanup of all mining operations. As a result of previous ecological measures, both the Volga River and Caspian Sea were becoming less impure, though the Soviet press indicated there was still need for further improvement.

The greatest Soviet natural disaster in 1973 was the July envelopment of part of the Central Asian city of Alma Ata by a giant avalanche of mud.

Minority Problems. During 1973 the Soviet press complained about widespread instances of anti-Russian nationalism in the Tadzhik, Turkmen, and Uzbek Soviet republics of Central Asia, and in the Armenian, Azerbaidzhan, and Georgian republics of the Caucasus. In Georgia early in the year the heads of the agricultural, ideological, educational, administrative, and general sections of the republic's central party apparatus were removed, while a vice-premier and the procurement minister lost their positions in the republic government. This Georgian purge was aimed both against local nationalism and the widespread corruption that had become commonplace among Georgian officials.

CULTURE AND SOCIETY

Religion. In response to a request from the U. S. government, the USSR in April suspended the fees previously demanded from emigrating Soviet citizens with college degrees. These high fees, ranging from $4,400 to $30,600 per emigrant, were not specifically directed against Jews, but had hampered Jewish emigration since most Soviet Jews are well educated. Despite the fee suspension, many Soviet Jews still could not obtain permission to leave the USSR, and Jewish emigration in 1973 amounted to little more than the 30,000 persons who departed in 1972.

Though a Soviet law of August 1973 offered benefits to émigrés who wished to return to the USSR, this law was seldom applied to Jewish émigrés to Israel who became dissatisfied with Israeli life and desired to return to the Soviet Union.

Within the USSR during 1973, the authorities harassed several religions besides the Jewish. Twelve leading Buddhist scholars were imprisoned for glorifying the Buddhist religion among Siberian Mongols. Two Orthodox clergy were imprisoned for alleged embezzlement of church funds, and several Baptists were arrested for conducting religious services without official sanction. More than 14,000–16,000 Lithuanian Catholics vainly petitioned the Soviet government to publish enough Bibles for all Catholic families and to cease atheist teaching in Soviet Lithuanian schools.

Meanwhile, the Soviet press complained that many Soviet youths were falling under the influence of religion, and that the Muslim faith was still widespread in Central Asia, the Caucasus, and the Mongol regions of the Volga Valley.

In September, Patriarch Pimen, the official head of the Russian Orthodox Church, attended a meeting of the World Council of Churches at Geneva, Switzerland. At the meeting he publicly stated that both religious freedom and civil liberties existed within the USSR.

Intellectual Unrest. During 1973 the Soviet police made a strong and partially successful effort to suppress the illegal underground literature called *samizdat*, which publishes the reformist views of civil rights advocates, Christian socialists, humanitarian Marxists, and isolationist Slavophiles. Enough *samizdat* writers were arrested, imprisoned, exiled, or incarcerated in mental hospitals to cause the suspension of publication of several illegal journals.

In February the civil rights activist Leonid Plyushch was declared insane by a Ukrainian court. In July the historian Andrei Amalryk, after three years of imprisonment in a corrective labor camp, was sentenced to an additional three years of Siberian exile for his antigovernmental statements. By September the historian Pyotr P. Yakir and the economist Viktor A. Krasin were both sentenced by a Moscow court to three years' imprisonment plus three years of residence outside Moscow for allegedly being paid agents of foreign subversive organizations and for publishing the underground *Chronicle of Current Events*. Since both men publicly confessed their alleged guilt, the prison sentences were reduced to 16 months for Yakir and 13 months for Krasin. Milder punishment was awarded in August to scientist Zhores A. Medvedev, who while performing research in Britain was deprived of Soviet citizenship for allegedly dishonoring it.

Though Soviet dissidents are usually not terrorists, in early September an unknown rebel exploded a bomb in the Lenin Mausoleum, which is adjacent to the Kremlin on Moscow's Red Square.

On September 26 the USSR became the first Great Power to ratify two UN multinational agreements: the International Covenant on Economic, Social, and Cultural Rights, and the International Covenant on Civil and Political Rights. The Soviet press commented that the second covenant permits governments to restrict travel, emigration, and information for reasons of national security.

During the autumn, the Soviet press repeatedly published articles and letters strongly criticizing the atomic scientist Andrei D. Sakharov and Nobel Prize-winning author Aleksandr I. Solzhenitsyn, misquoting them as being opposed to U. S.-Soviet détente. However, both men remained unharmed and continued to issue public statements to the West demanding civil liberties within the USSR.

Culture. On February 21 the Soviet copyright law was amended to give the Soviet government alone the power to permit foreign publication of works written by Soviet citizens. Then on May 27,

UPI

NEW APARTMENT HOUSE in Moscow, built in the form of a ring, offers sports facilities and a children's playground in an enclosed courtyard.

the Soviet Union officially adhered to the International Copyright Convention. In June the Soviet author Vladimir E. Maksimov was expelled from the Moscow Writers Union for publishing a novel abroad without official Soviet permission. To determine which works will be allowed to be published abroad, a USSR copyright agency was established in September, consisting of representatives of the Soviet cultural unions, the ministry of culture, the foreign trade ministry, the USSR Academy of Sciences, and the Novosti press agency.

As part of the Soviet détente with both Western Europe and the United States, the USSR in September stopped jamming the Russian-language radio broadcasts of the Voice of America, the British Broadcasting Corporation, and the Deutsche Welle (the West German official radio). Even earlier, in May, the Soviet government had signed an agreement with the privately owned National Broadcasting Company of the United States for mutual exchange of selected television and radio programs.

During October 25–31, a Soviet-sponsored "World Congress of Peace-Loving Forces" met in Moscow, attended by 3,200 delegates representing 144 countries. Though most of the delegates were Communists, pro-Communists, or extreme leftists, some were liberals simply interested in global peace. The congress met during the 1973 Arab-Israel war, which forced USSR leader Brezhnev to postpone his opening speech of welcome. Some Western liberals also upset the routine of the congress by urging the USSR to grant internal civil liberties. The congress concluded with declarations supporting Soviet foreign policy in détente and denouncing Israel and Western colonialism.

Education. The Soviet press indicated in 1973 that 16% of Soviet pupils graduating from grade school never enter high school, and only 20% of high school graduates continue their education in colleges and universities. Of the entire Soviet population, 61% had completed no more than a grade-school education.

During the year there was much public criticism of grade and high schools in rural areas for shortages of teachers of mathematics, manual trades, drawing, and foreign languages, with many schools having no foreign-language courses. On July 6 a governmental decree ordered the facilities of rural grade and high schools to be drastically improved so that they would equal city schools by 1980. In 1973, 45% of all Soviet schoolchildren were still enrolled in rural schools.

Higher education statistics released during the year revealed that the USSR has 825 colleges and universities staffed by 366,000 college teachers, of whom only 36% hold the Soviet equivalent of Western doctoral degrees. Approximately 36,000 foreign students from 135 countries are studying in Soviet colleges.

During August 15–25, the 1973 World Student Games were held in Moscow, with teams from 72 countries participating. In the total contests the USSR won first place, while the United States was second. The games were marred by anti-Jewish incidents in which Soviet spectators heckled and sometimes harassed Israeli athletes.

ECONOMY

Harvest Success. The greatest Soviet economic successes of 1973 were the grain crop of 220 million metric tons and the cotton crop of 7.5 million tons, both being the largest in Soviet history. These statistics referred to the crops in the fields, not the actual amounts harvested, which were considerably lower. The Soviet press complained that one fourth of the grain crop is normally lost in harvestings. This is so because there is insufficient farm mechanization due to shortages of tractors, tractor spare parts, grain harvesting combines, farm trucks, truck tires, and even farm machine operators. Similarly, 13% of the cotton crop is usually lost because of insect pests and plant disease. Farm shortages were reported in mineral fertilizers and feed for livestock. Probably because of harvesting

losses, the USSR in 1973 continued to import large amounts of grain from the United States and other Western nations.

Industry. Partly because of the good farm crops, Soviet industrial growth in 1973 was about 7.3%. This was well above the 5.8% that had been planned for the year and the 6.5% actually achieved in 1972. Among the major construction projects completed during 1973 were the Kola atomic power station in the Arctic tundra of northwest European USSR near the city of Murmansk, the Shevchenko atomic power plant—which is the first atomic breeder station of commercial size in the world—on the northeastern shore of the Caspian Sea, and the Samotlor-Almetyevsk 1,240-mile (2,000 km) pipeline linking the new West Siberian oil fields to the Volga River, where a connection was made with the Friendship pipeline extending into Eastern Europe. By year-end, the Kama truck plant, the largest in the world and located in east European USSR, was in partial production.

The USSR in 1973 also caught one tenth of the world's fish haul, ranking third after Peru and Japan in the world's fishing catch.

Despite these successes and the fact that the USSR accounted for one fifth of world industrial production, the Soviet government in 1973 placed large orders in the United States, Japan, and Western Europe for industrial machinery. One reason apparently was the inadequate mechanization of Soviet industry, with 40% of coal mining, 44% of lumbering, 45% of consumer-goods manufacture, and 49% of construction admittedly still being performed by hand.

To improve industrial management, the USSR in April decreed that the industrial cabinet ministries abolish their regular branch offices, and in place of them form regional industrial associations with much managerial autonomy; the ministries were to act mainly as planners rather than as direct operators. At the end of the year, the Soviet press accused the ministries of instituting this major change very slowly, for fear of losing ministerial authority.

Transport. In 1973, as before, the railways continued to haul about three fourths of Soviet internal freight. Construction was completed in June of a train ferry linking Sakhalin Island with the East Siberian mainland. Though the Soviet merchant marine consists mainly of freighters, Soviet passenger boat service began in May between Leningrad and New York, with intermediate stops in West Germany, Britain, and France.

Aeroflot, the Soviet airline company, in 1973 conducted regular flights to 65 foreign countries. It added a new Moscow-Aden route via Greece and Egypt. Two Aeroflot regular passenger planes crashed during the year, the first in February in Czechoslovakia and the second during the summer in Jordan. Much worse and more embarrassing was the crash of the Soviet's new supersonic passenger plane, the TU-144, while making a display flight at the annual French air show near Paris. All six Soviet crewmen were killed, along with seven inhabitants of the French village into which the plane fell.

Trade. Though most Soviet foreign trade continued to be conducted with other Communist countries, 1973 was noteworthy for the sharp rise in trade with Western capitalist countries, especially the United States. By mid-1973, six Western banks, including two American, had opened offices in Moscow. Eight American companies were supplying industrial equipment for the Kama truck plant, and many others had signed contracts for industrial aid to other Soviet projects.

By 1973, Soviet foreign aid to non-Communist developing countries totalled more than $8 billion, with approximately 41% going to south Asia, 39% to the Middle East, 16% to Africa, and only 4% to Latin America.

Standard of Living. The Soviet Union's standard of living remained mediocre in 1973, with admitted store shortages of underwear, fur hats and coats, cushions, salt, matches, kerosine, toothpaste, soft drinks, and beer. Before the good crops were harvested, there were also scarcities of bread, potatoes, butter, fruit, and meat. In an effort to increase the supply of consumer goods, a decree of September 9 urged retired people to return to work and lowered income taxes on private artisans. Urban housing, as before, remained overcrowded.

ELLSWORTH RAYMOND
New York University

UPI

BABYSITTERS: Chairman and Mrs. Brezhnev, like proud grandparents anywhere, keep watch over their granddaughter Galina in a Moscow park.

UNITED NATIONS

The UN Security Council, on October 25, voted 14–0 to send peacekeeping forces to the Middle East to police the Israeli-Arab cease-fire. (Below) During the session, Saudi Arabian Ambassador Baroody lashed out at Israeli Ambassador Tekoah.

The explosive Middle East situation, a recurring problem for the United Nations, again dominated the organization's activities in the latter part of 1973. The UN's inherent weakness—the necessity of agreement among the major powers for it to take effective action—was demonstrated by its inability to deal constructively with the Arab-Israeli war until the United States and the USSR jointly sponsored a cease-fire resolution on October 22. As Secretary General Kurt Waldheim said, "We are made up of sovereign nations. We can only accomplish what our members allow us to accomplish."

Since its founding in 1951, UN membership has grown from 51 to 135. The new members are, for the most part, former colonies of the European powers, and they have the voting strength to control the direction that the UN takes, as reflected, for example, by the problems to which the UN devoted most of its time in 1973—Rhodesia, Guinea-Bissau, apartheid, decolonization, and the development of underdeveloped countries. Also, the newer members are responsible for the proliferation of committees, subcommittees, and agencies that deal with subjects the organization did not contemplate considering when it was founded in 1945.

But as its membership grows, the UN increasingly becomes a world organization. The admission of mainland China in 1971 and East and West Germany in 1973 makes it almost universal, leaving only two or three small but controversial areas, such as Korea and Vietnam, outside. The problem that is now facing the UN, as Secretary General Kurt Waldheim expressed it in his annual message on August 26, is that the member nations must decide whether they "really want an organization which is more than a conference machinery and a forum for the pursuit of national policies."

The principal activities of the United Nations in its 28th year are summarized below under the headings: (1) General Assembly; (2) Security Council; (3) Economic and Social Council; (4) Trusteeship and Decolonization; and (5) International Court of Justice.

GENERAL ASSEMBLY

The 28th regular session of the General Assembly opened in New York City on September 18. Leopoldo Benites, the permanent representative of Ecuador since 1960, was elected president. The Federal Republic of Germany, the German Democratic Republic, and the Commonwealth of the Bahamas were admitted to UN membership, bringing the total to 135. During the session, which recessed on December 22, the Assembly considered 110 agenda items, based on recommendations by its General Committee. It acted on 150 resolutions and adopted a treaty aimed at protecting diplomats.

The Assembly opened its overall survey of the world situation on September 24, with the East-West détente as a prominent topic that drew both

favorable and cautionary comments. A number of speakers emphasized the need to find an international solution to the world food crisis, while others commented on the Middle East situation, peace settlement moves in Asia, and the struggle for decolonization in Africa. Among the subjects on which the Assembly acted in 1973 were Guinea-Bissau, the West African drought, Cambodian representation, arms budget cuts, apartheid, self-determination for colonial peoples, disarmament, and the UN university charter.

Guinea-Bissau. Secretary General Waldheim was informed of the proclamation (September 24) establishing the independent state of Guinea-Bissau (Portuguese Guinea) by the first People's National Assembly of the African Party for the Independence of Guinea and Cape Verde. In a resolution on November 2, the Assembly welcomed the independence of Guinea-Bissau by a vote of 93 to 7, with 30 abstentions, and demanded the withdrawal of Portuguese forces, urging the Security Council to take effective steps to "restore the territorial integrity of the Republic." A later resolution, passed by a vote of 94 to 14, wtih 21 abstentions, declared that Portugal represents European Portugal only and not its three African territories.

West African Drought. A resolution calling for a concerted effort to help drought-ridden Chad, Mali, Mauritania, Niger, Senegal, and Upper Volta was approved on October 16 without objection. Member states and UN agencies and programs were urged to provide assistance in various fields.

Cambodian Representation. The Assembly decided on December 5 to postpone until the next session a decision on whether to seat Cambodian representatives of exiled Prince Sihanouk and to expel the present Khmer delegation, representing the government of President Lon Nol. The postponement motion, sponsored by Liberia, was approved by 53 to 50, with 21 abstentions. China, the USSR, East European countries, and a large number of African states were against postponement.

Arms Budget Cuts. After a debate that extended intermittently from mid-November to December 7, the Assembly approved a Soviet-sponsored resolution asking the five permanent members of the Security Council to cut their military budgets by 10% and use a tenth of the funds saved for aid to poorer countries. The vote was 83 to 2 (China and Albania), with 38 abstentions, including the United States, the United Kingdom, and France. The Assembly also invited other states to divert some of their military spending into economic aid. Under the terms of the resolution, a committee composed of the five permanent Security Council members and representatives from the main geographical regions will be set up to distribute such aid funds.

Apartheid. On November 30, the Assembly adopted and opened for signature a new convention designed to outlaw apartheid as a crime against humanity. The convention was adopted by a vote of 91 to 4, with 26 abstentions. In addition to Portugal and South Africa, the opposing votes were cast by the United Kingdom and the United States on the grounds that the convention could adversely affect the structure of existing international law.

Self-Determination. A resolution reaffirming the right of all people under colonial and foreign domination to self-determination and independence was approved on November 30. By a vote of 97 to 5, with 28 abstentions, the Assembly held that sub-jugated peoples had the right to seek liberation by any means available, including armed struggle.

Disarmament. A series of disarmament resolutions, approved on December 6, included those against the use of napalm and other incendiary weapons and chemical and biological weapons. Two resolutions urging a halt to all nuclear weapons tests were approved by votes of 89 to 5, with 33 abstentions, and 65 to 7, with 57 abstentions.

United Nations University. The charter for a UN university, drawn up by the secretary general, with the recommendation that the university's center be located in the Tokyo area, was approved on December 6. The vote was 118 to 0, with 10 abstentions (the USSR, East European countries, Cuba, and Mongolia).

Other Political Questions. Among a number of resolutions passed in December were those relating to guidelines for peacekeeping operations; Palestinian refugees; Israeli practices in occupied territories; human rights in armed conflicts; and host country relations. The last stressed the need for taking effective measures against violence and hostile actions directed at UN missions and personnel in New York City. On November 2, the Assembly designated the 10-year period beginning Dec. 10, 1973, as the Decade for Action to Combat Racism and Racial Discrimination.

Administrative and Budgetary Questions. When Secretary General Waldheim appeared before the Administrative and Budgetary Committee on September 28, he pointed out that nearly 40% of the 1972–73 UN budget required the use of currencies other than U. S. dollars and that the effect of dollar devaluation on UN finances had been serious. The estimated budget for 1974–75 was $513.4 million, up $17.4 million from the previous budget because of currency realignments.

Additional requirements for 1973 were $11 million, but the actual deficit had been kept to $8 million. A saving of $3.9 million resulted from Secretariat austerity measures. Further, the final accounts for 1972 disclosed an under-expenditure of $685,000, and if this amount were applied to the 1973 budget the supplementary requirement for 1973 would be reduced to about $7 million. The secretary general said he was prepared to continue a policy of restraint on personnel recruitment for 1974–75, but he did not feel he could continue the freeze on recruitment because it might adversely affect the performance of the Secretariat.

The Committee on Contributions approved a new scale of assessments for members on October 25. Under it, the U. S. contribution was cut from 31.52% to 25% of the total budget, and the contributions of 116 other members were reduced. The changes were made possible by the accession of the two Germanies and increased contributions on the part of 12 members, including China and Japan.

SECURITY COUNCIL

The Security Council was faced with a variety of problems during the year, including the perennial question of the Middle East, which proved no easier of solution than it had in previous years. Other problems concerned Zambia, Latin America and the Panama Canal, Rhodesia, Namibia, and a Cuban complaint against Chile.

Zambia. Two resolutions were adopted by the Council on February 2, following a five-day debate that originated in a complaint by Zambia against

Rhodesia's economic blockade and military threats in collusion with South Africa. The first, which passed by a vote of 13 to 0, with the United States and the United Kingdom abstaining, called for political action against Rhodesia and South Africa. The second, adopted by 14 to 0, with the USSR abstaining, urged economic assistance for Zambia. The Council authorized sending a mission of four Council members (Austria, Peru, Indonesia, and the Sudan) and six UN experts to Zambia to assess its needs in maintaining systems of communication, unaffected by Rhodesia, to ensure a normal flow of international traffic.

The mission's report to the Security Council was debated in three meetings from March 8 to 10, and two resolutions were passed. One, on which the United States and the United Kingdom abstained, upheld Zambia's complaint. The other, passed unanimously, appealed to all states for immediate technical, financial, and material aid to Zambia.

Latin America. The Council met in Panama City from March 15 to 21. On March 21, a resolution, adopted by a vote of 12 to 0, with the United States, the United Kingdom, and France abstaining, urged states to adopt measures to impede the activities of enterprises that deliberately attempt to coerce Latin American countries. It also requested that states refrain from using or encouraging any type of coercive measures against states of the region.

A second resolution regarding U.S.–Panamanian relations was defeated when the United States cast its third veto in the Security Council. Thirteen members of the Council supported a resolution (the United Kingdom abstained) that noted that the United States and Panama had agreed to reach a fair agreement for the prompt elimination of the causes of conflict between them and called for a "new, just, and fair treaty concerning the Panama Canal, which would fulfil Panama's legitimate aspirations and guarantee full respect for Panama's effective sovereignty over all of its territory." The United States cast its veto on the grounds that the resolution was "unbalanced and incomplete, and therefore subject to serious misinterpretation."

Middle East. In response to a letter from Lebanon referring to an "act of aggression [an assault against Palestinian commando bases] committed by Israel against Lebanon on the morning of 10 April 1973," the Council met seven times to consider the situation in the Middle East. On April 20, the Council requested the secretary general to submit a comprehensive report as soon as possible on UN efforts since 1967 to deal with the Middle East problem. On April 21 a resolution condemning Israel's violation of Lebanon's territorial integrity and sovereignty was passed by a vote of 11 to 0, with China, Guinea, the USSR, and the United States abstaining.

At Egypt's request, the Council met again in June to discuss the secretary general's report, which had been issued on May 21. The Council suspended its session on June 14, resuming it in July, when three meetings were held. On July 26, the U.S. vetoed an eight-power resolution that deplored Israel's continuing occupation of territories occupied since the 1967 war and supported the search for a Middle East solution through the efforts of the secretary general. Five meetings were held in August in response to a letter from Lebanon that said that on August 10 an Israeli air force plane had invaded Lebanese air space and forced an Iraqi

COMMUNIST CHINESE at the United Nations (l. to r.): Chou Nan, a counselor; Deputy Foreign Minister Chiao Kuan-Hua; and UN Ambassador Huang Hua.

civilian plane to fly into Israel and land at an Israeli base. A resolution condemning Israel's action was adopted unanimously on August 15.

After the outbreak of Arab-Israeli hostilities in October, the Council met at the request of the United States. In a stormy session on October 9, Yakov Malik, the Soviet delegate, walked out amid applause as the Israeli representative was speaking.

The Council remained deadlocked and unable to stop the fighting, until, on October 22, it adopted a resolution sponsored by the United States and the USSR, calling for a cease-fire within 12 hours of its passage. A second resolution, on October 23, confirmed the resolution of the previous day and requested the secretary general to dispatch UN observers to supervise the observance of the cease-fire. On October 25, th Council again demanded a cease-fire, and decided to set up immediately a UN Emergency Force, to be composed of personnel from states other than the permanent members of the Security Council. The secretary general was asked to report within 24 hours on the steps taken to that effect. The Council approved the secretary general's report on October 27 and also decided that the Emergency Force should be established for an initial period of six months. The resolutions were adopted 14 to 0, China abstaining on each.

In a further move, on December 15, the Council approved a resolution affirming that the secretary general would "play a full and effective role" at the Geneva conference for a Middle East settlement and requested him to keep the Council informed of developments at Geneva in order to enable it to review the problems on a continuing basis.

Rhodesia. On April 15, the Security Council received a committee report to the effect that Portugal and South Africa persistently refused to implement economic sanctions against Rhodesia. On May 22, the Council adopted a resolution by a vote of 12 to 0, with France, the United States, and the United Kingdom abstaining, that called on states to enact and enforce immediately legislation with severe penalties for persons who evaded or breached sanctions against Rhodesia.

ORGANIZATION OF THE UNITED NATIONS

THE SECRETARIAT
Secretary General: Kurt Waldheim (until Dec. 31, 1976)

THE GENERAL ASSEMBLY (1973)
President: Leopoldo Benites (Ecuador). The 135 member-nations were as follows:

Afghanistan	German Democratic	Niger
Albania	Republic	Nigeria
Algeria	Germany, Federal	Norway
Argentina	Republic of	Oman
Australia	Ghana	Pakistan
Austria	Greece	Panama
Bahamas	Guatemala	Paraguay
Bahrain	Guinea	Peru
Barbados	Guyana	Philippines
Belgium	Haiti	Poland
Belorussian SSR	Honduras	Portugal
Bhutan	Hungary	Qatar
Bolivia	Iceland	Rumania
Botswana	India	Rwanda
Brazil	Indonesia	Saudi Arabia
Bulgaria	Iran	Senegal
Burma	Iraq	Sierra Leone
Burundi	Ireland	Singapore
Cambodia	Israel	Somalia
(Khmer Republic)	Italy	South Africa
Cameroon	Ivory Coast	Spain
Canada	Jamaica	Sri Lanka (Ceylon)
Central African	Japan	Sudan
Republic	Jordan	Swaziland
Chad	Kenya	Sweden
Chile	Kuwait	Syrian Arab Republic
China, People's	Laos	Tanzania, United
Republic of	Lebanon	Republic of
Colombia	Lesotho	Thailand
Congo	Liberia	Togo
Costa Rica	Libyan	Trinidad and
Cuba	Arab Republic	Tobago
Cyprus	Luxembourg	Tunisia
Czechoslovakia	Madagascar	Turkey
Dahomey	(Malagasy	Uganda
Denmark	Republic)	Ukrainian SSR
Dominican	Malawi	USSR
Republic	Malaysia (Malaya)	United Arab
Ecuador	Maldives	Emirates
Egypt	Mali	United Kingdom
El Salvador	Malta	United States
Equatorial Guinea	Mauritania	Upper Volta
Ethiopia	Mauritius	Uruguay
Fiji	Mexico	Venezuela
Finland	Mongolia	Yemen
France	Morocco	Yemen, Democratic
Gabon	Nepal	Yugoslavia
Gambia	Netherlands	Zaire
	New Zealand	Zambia
	Nicaragua	

COMMITTEES
General: Composed of 25 members as follows: The General Assembly president; the 17 General Assembly vice presidents (heads of delegations or their deputies of Cameroon, China, Czechoslovakia, Fiji, France, Ghana, Guyana, Honduras, Netherlands, Spain, Sri Lanka, Tunisia, Uganda, United Arab Emirates, United Kingdom, United States, USSR), and the chairmen of the following 7 main committees, which are composed of all 135 member countries:

First (Political and Security): Otto R. Borch (Denmark).

Special Political: Károly Szarka (Hungary).

Second (Economic and Financial): Zewde Gabre-Sellassie (Ethiopia).

Third (Social, Humanitarian, and Cultural): Yahya Mahmassani (Lebanon).

Fourth (Trust and Non-self-governing territories): Leonardo Díaz González (Venezuela).

Fifth (Administrative and Budgetary): Conrad S. M. Mselle (Tanzania).

Sixth (Legal): Sergio González Gálvez (Mexico).

THE SECURITY COUNCIL (1974)
(Membership ends on December 31 of the year noted; asterisks indicate permanent membership)

Australia (1974)	China*	Mauritania (1975)
Austria (1974)	Costa Rica (1975)	Peru (1974)
Belorussian SSR	France*	USSR*
(1975)	Indonesia (1974)	United Kingdom*
Cameroon (1975)	Iraq (1975)	United States*
	Kenya (1974)	

Military Staff Committee: Representatives of chiefs of staffs of the permanent members.

Disarmament Commission: Representatives of all UN members.

THE ECONOMIC AND SOCIAL COUNCIL (1974)
President: Sergio Armando Frazão (Brazil) 54th and 55th sessions (1973). (Membership ends on December 31 of the year noted. Asterisks indicate the 27 additional members elected for terms beginning Jan. 1, 1974.)

Algeria (1975)	France (1975)	Netherlands (1975)
Argentina (1974)*	German Democratic	Pakistan (1974)*
Australia (1976)	Republic (1976)*	Poland (1974)
Belgium (1976)*	Germany, Federal	Rumania (1976)
Bolivia (1974)	Republic of (1975)*	Senegal (1975)*
Brazil (1975)	Guatemala (1975)*	Spain (1975)
Burundi (1974)	Guinea (1975)*	Sweden (1974)*
Canada (1974)*	India (1974)*	Thailand (1976)
Chile (1974)	Indonesia (1975)*	Trinidad and Tobago
China (1974)	Iran (1976)*	(1975)
Colombia (1976)*	Italy (1976)*	Turkey (1975)*
Congo (1976)	Ivory Coast (1976)*	Uganda (1975)
Czechoslovakia	Jamaica (1976)*	USSR (1974)
(1974)*	Japan (1974)	United Kingdom
Democratic Yemen	Jordan (1976)*	(1974)
(1976)	Kenya (1974)*	United States (1976)
Egypt (1976)*	Liberia (1976)	Venezuela (1975)*
Ethiopia (1974)*	Mali (1975)	Yugoslavia (1975)*
Fiji (1975)*	Mexico (1976)	Zaire (1974)*
Finland (1974)	Mongolia (1975)	Zambia (1976)

THE TRUSTEESHIP COUNCIL (1973–74)
President: Bertrand de Guilhem de Lataillade (France) 40th session (1973).

Australia[1]	France[2]	United Kingdom[2]
China[2]	USSR[2]	United States[1]

[1] Administers trust territory. [2] Permanent member of Security Council not administering trust territory.

THE INTERNATIONAL COURT OF JUSTICE
(Membership ends on February 5 of the year noted.)
President: Manfred Lechs (Poland, 1976)
Vice President: Fouad Ammoun (Lebanon, 1976)

Isaac Forster (Senegal, 1982)	Federico de Castro
André Gros (France, 1982)	(Spain, 1979)
César Bengzon (Philippines, 1976)	Platon Morozov (USSR, 1979)
Sture Petren (Sweden, 1976)	Eduardo Jiménez de Aréchaga (Uruguay, 1979)
Charles D. Onyeama (Nigeria, 1976)	Sir Humphrey Waldock (United Kingdom, 1982)
Hardy C. Dillard (U. S., 1979)	Nagendra Singh (India, 1982)
Louis Ignacio-Pinto (Dahomey, 1979)	José Maria Ruda (Argentina, 1982)

SPECIALIZED AGENCIES
Food and Agriculture Organization (FAO); Intergovernmental Maritime Consultative Organization (IMCO); International Atomic Energy Agency (IAEA); International Bank for Reconstruction and Development (World Bank; IBRD); International Civil Aviation Organization (ICAO); International Development Association (IDA); International Finance Corporation (IFC); International Labor Organization (ILO); International Monetary Fund (IMF); International Telecommunication Union (ITU); United Nations Educational, Scientific and Cultural Organization (UNESCO); Universal Postal Union (UPU); United Nations International Children's Emergency Fund (UNICEF); World Health Organization (WHO); World Meteorological Organization (WMO).

On the same day, another resolution, calling for limitations on purchases of Rhodesia's major exports and a return to 1965 levels of imports from South Africa, Mozambique, and Angola, was vetoed by the United States and the United Kingdom. To reinforce its sanctions machinery, the Council's Sanctions Committee appealed on September 4 for information from private individuals as well as from nongovernmental organizations on possible violations.

Namibia (South West Africa). Guinea, Kenya, and the Sudan requested a meeting of the Security Council on December 10 to consider "the serious situation in Namibia," which is administered by South Africa. Two days later, the Council decided unanimously to discontinue the secretary general's efforts to promote Namibian independence through contacts with the South African government because of lack of progress.

Cuban Complaint Against Chile. The Council met on September 17–18 to consider a Cuban complaint that Chilean armed forces had attacked the Cuban embassy in Santiago and had committed aggression against a Cuban merchant vessel in international waters. However, after discussion, the Council adjourned on September 18 without either tabling a resolution or setting a date for a future meeting.

ECONOMIC AND SOCIAL COUNCIL

On September 24, the United States became the fifth permanent member of the Security Council to ratify requirements that would amend the UN Charter to permit doubling the size of the Economic and Social Council (ECOSOC) from 27 to 54. The 27 new members were chosen by the General Assembly on October 12 to serve on ECOSOC until the end of 1973. On November 23, nine replacement members were elected for three-year terms, beginning on Jan. 1, 1974, and the 27 additional members were elected for terms varying from one to three years, as determined by lot.

The 54th session of ECOSOC was held from April 17 to May 18. It approved resolutions to admit Bangladesh to the Economic Commission for Asia and the Far East; to reaffirm states' sovereignty over their natural resources; to implement special measures in favor of the underdeveloped countries' collective economic security; to examine the impact of multinational corporations on the development process; and to speed economic assistance to specific nations.

ECOSOC's 55th session convened in Geneva from July 4 to August 10. The Council reviewed international development strategy for the UN's Second Development Decade, which has been less effective than planned. Included among its resolutions were those on subjects related to the development of underdeveloped areas, on aid to the drought-stricken Sudano-Sahelian populations, on assistance to southern Sudanese returnees and displaced persons, and on economic assistance to Zambia.

The 55th session was resumed in New York City on October 15, when ECOSOC met for the first time with its new complement of 54 members. It was decided to recommend to the General Assembly that a World Food Conference be convened in 1974 under the auspices of the United Nations.

The Council also decided to transmit to the 28th General Assembly the secretary general's reports on the UN university. The charter for the university, which will be centered in the Tokyo area, with a network of facilities and programs in various parts of the world, was endorsed by the General Assembly on December 6.

TRUSTEESHIP AND DECOLONIZATION

Trusteeship. The 40th session of the Trusteeship Council met in New York City from May 29 to June 22. It reviewed conditions in the only two remaining trust territories—Papua-New Guinea (administered by Australia) and the Pacific Islands (administered by the United States). It was decided that a visiting mission should go to Papua and New Guinea in 1974. A mission, consisting of the representatives of Australia, France, the USSR, and the United Kingdom, visited the Pacific Islands from February 2 to March 7, 1973.

Decolonization. In February 1973, the Special Committee on Decolonization appointed four subcommittees to cover various geographical and subject areas of its responsibilities. As a result of the subcommittees' work, the Special Committee passed two resolutions on Rhodesia in April, both of which reaffirmed the right of the Rhodesian people to self-determination and called for measures to achieve that end.

In July and August the Special Committee adopted six additional resolutions. Among other matters, the resolutions deplored the lack of cooperation by states administering non-self-governing territories and the failure of these states to transmit information about the territories. Other resolutions reaffirmed the right of the peoples of the Comoro Archipelago and Puerto Rico to self-determination and independence.

The Committee completed its work on September 14 and submitted its report to the General Assembly. The report, which was introduced to the Fourth Committee on September 27, concluded that not much progress in decolonization had been made during the year, and that "in particular, the situation in the colonial Territories in southern Africa remained critical and explosive, constituting a growing threat to the peace and security . . . ." of Africa in general.

INTERNATIONAL COURT OF JUSTICE

After public sittings on January 5 and 8, the International Court of Justice decided on February 2 that it had jurisdiction in the territorial-water cases brought by the United Kingdom and the Federal Republic of Germany against Iceland. The cases arose as a result of the Icelandic government's decision to extend, as of Sept. 1, 1972, its exclusive coastline fishing rights from 12 to 50 nautical miles. (The proceedings were instituted by the United Kingdom on April 14, 1972, and by West Germany on June 5, 1972.) In October, Britain and Iceland reached an agreement on the dispute (see also ICELAND).

On May 9, Australia and New Zealand filed applications with the court instituting proceedings against France regarding nuclear tests. Australia and New Zealand sought to establish that proposed French atomic tests in the Pacific were contrary to international law and that an order should be issued to forbid them.

Hearings held later in May resulted in the court's announcement that orders would be made in due course. France sent no representative to the hearings, holding that the court has no jurisdiction in the case. Consideration of an application to intervene in the cases by the government of Fiji was postponed until July 12.

Pakistan, on May 11, filed an application instituting proceedings against India. The application was made in regard to Pakistani prisoners held by India since the Pakistan-India war in 1971 that resulted in Bangladesh independence. India proposed to turn the prisoners over to Bangladesh for trial on charges of genocide and crimes against humanity, while Pakistan contended they should be returned to Pakistan.

A public sitting by the court, scheduled for May 29, was postponed as a result of communications received from both India and Pakistan. Finally, on July 13, the court announced that before it could decide on the question itself, it must first determine if it had jurisdiction in the case. But no decision was necessary, since, on August 28, India and Pakistan reached an agreement relating to the prisoner of war issue. Left unsettled, however, was the question of 195 Pakistani prisoners still being held for possible trial on charges of alleged war crimes. The case was discontinued in December.

(See also LAW—*International Law.*)

RICHARD E. WEBB
Former Director, Reference and Library Division
British Information Services, New York

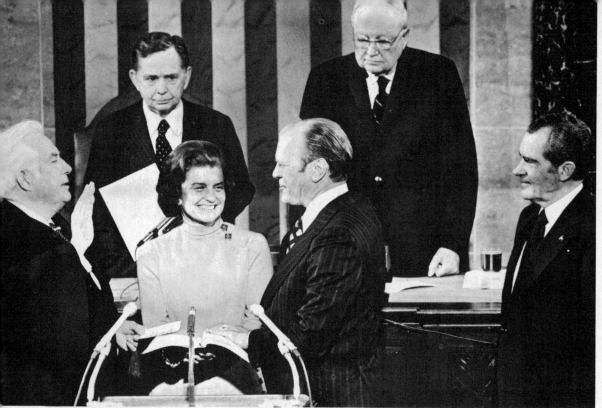

Gerald R. Ford (center) is sworn in as vice president of the United States by Chief Justice Burger. Mrs. Ford holds the Bible, and President Nixon looks on.

UNITED STATES

As 1973 opened, the people of the United States could look to the future with relative confidence and tranquillity. Reflecting the favorable prospects for peace abroad and prosperity at home, President Richard M. Nixon in his second inaugural address, on January 20, called on his fellow citizens "to pledge together to make these next four years the best four years in America's history."

Within the next few months the picture altered dramatically. By year-end, uncertainty and skepticism pervaded the nation's mood, and events that threatened to produce more confusion and divisiveness in the future had been set in motion.

DOMESTIC AFFAIRS

In large measure the drastically altered outlook was due to the Watergate scandal (see feature article beginning on page 14). Apart from its direct impact on the Nixon administration, Watergate undermined the administration's ability to deal with a host of other problems, foreign and domestic, and left the country wondering how much longer Nixon would remain in the White House.

The Administration. Bolstered by his landslide reelection victory, Nixon vigorously set out to reduce the large role in domestic affairs that the federal government had assumed since Franklin D. Roosevelt's New Deal. In his inaugural, Nixon preached self-reliance: "In our own lives, let each of us ask not just what will government do for me, but what can I do for myself?" His $268.7 billion budget for the fiscal year ending June 30, 1974,

called for eliminating or reducing 112 social welfare and education programs. He proposed that 70 other programs be shifted to special revenue-sharing plans in four areas—education, law enforcement, manpower training, and urban community development.

On February 2 the President submitted to Congress an "overview" State of the Union message, which he followed up in subsequent weeks with separate messages containing specific proposals on natural resources and the environment, the economy, human resources, community development, and law enforcement and drug-abuse prevention. The series of State of the Union proposals, the President said in his overview, offered "a fresh approach to government: an approach that addresses the realities of the 1970's." He added, "We must reject the mistaken notion ... that ever-bigger Government is the answer to every problem."

The President's prestige at home was enhanced by success overseas. On January 23 he announced that a cease-fire agreement ending the war in Vietnam would be formally signed in Paris on January 27. His goal of "peace with honor" had been achieved, he said. The nation rejoiced, and the President's approval rating in the Gallup Poll soared in late January to 68%. Soon, 587 freed U.S. prisoners of war made the long journey home from Vietnam.

But as the damaging Watergate disclosures began to unfold, the President's standing in the polls dropped; his approval rating hovered around 30%

at year-end. More than that, the scandal distracted the energies and attention of the President and forced the resignation of his two top White House advisers, H. R. Haldeman and John D. Ehrlichman. To meet the emergency, Nixon in May brought in John B. Connally, Jr., a former secretary of the treasury and a newly converted Republican, as a part-time consultant. In June, former White House aide Bryce N. Harlow and former Secretary of Defense Melvin R. Laird joined Nixon's staff. But Connally left in July, amid reports that he had been unable to gain the President's attention. Laird announced that he would resign early in 1974, and Harlow was expected to follow suit.

In September, the President reprimanded Congress for a "very disappointing" record of carrying out administration initiatives and submitted yet another State of the Union message, which was mainly an attempt to revive his previous legislative proposals. But the Democratic leadership of Congress replied by criticizing Nixon's policies, particularly in the economic field, and little progress was made toward carrying out the President's proposals.

The Vice Presidency. The disclosure in August that Vice President Spiro T. Agnew was under federal investigation for possible violations of criminal law added to the distractions and burdens of the administration. (See special report on page 20.) Following Agnew's October 10 resignation, which climaxed two months of legal and political controversy, Nixon on October 12 nominated Gerald R. Ford (R-Mich.), minority leader since 1965 of the House of Representatives, to succeed Agnew. This was the first application of the 25th Amendment to the U. S. Constitution, ratified in 1967, which provides: "Whenever there is a vacancy in the office of the Vice President, the President shall nominate a Vice President who shall take office upon confirmation by a majority of both houses of Congress."

Ford's confirmation proceedings came as the House Judiciary Committee prepared for a full-scale

<table>
<tr><td colspan="2">UNITED STATES CABINET MEMBERS
(as of Dec. 31, 1973)</td></tr>
<tr><td>Secretary of State—Henry A. Kissinger</td></tr>
<tr><td>Secretary of the Treasury—George P. Shultz</td></tr>
<tr><td>Secretary of Defense—James R. Schlesinger</td></tr>
<tr><td>Attorney General-designate—William B. Saxbe</td></tr>
<tr><td>Secretary of the Interior—Rogers C. B. Morton</td></tr>
<tr><td>Secretary of Agriculture—Earl L. Butz</td></tr>
<tr><td>Secretary of Commerce—Frederick B. Dent</td></tr>
<tr><td>Secretary of Labor—Peter J. Brennan</td></tr>
<tr><td>Secretary of Health, Education, and Welfare—Caspar W. Weinberger</td></tr>
<tr><td>Secretary of Housing and Urban Development—James T. Lynn</td></tr>
<tr><td>Secretary of Transportation—Claude S. Brinegar</td></tr>
</table>

inquiry into possible impeachment charges against Nixon. Many lawmakers asserted that Ford must be considered not only as a candidate for vice president but as a potential chief executive. The 60-year-old congressman's personal background and finances were subjected to intense scrutiny by the Federal Bureau of Investigation on behalf of the Senate Rules Committee and the House Judiciary Committee, which conducted the hearings on the nomination in their respective houses. Howard W. Cannon (D-Nev.), chairman of the Senate committee, called the inquiry "the most exhaustive examination of a nominee ever undertaken by a Senate committee."

Testifying before the Rules Committee, Ford declared he had faith that Nixon was "completely innocent" of wrongdoing in Watergate. But he added that "the public wants the President to prove that, through documents and so forth." Ford also urged increased cooperation between the executive branch and Congress. Before the House Judiciary Commit-

DEMONSTRATORS near the White House urge passing motorists to express their opinions in the controversy over President Nixon's possible impeachment.

UPI

UNITED STATES • Information Highlights

Official Name: United States of America.
Location: North America.
Area: 3,615,123 square miles (9,363,169 sq km).
Population (Dec. 1973 est.): 211,600,000. *Density,* 57.5 per square mile (22 per sq km).
Chief Cities (1970 census): Washington, D. C., the capital, 756,510; New York, 7,895,563; Chicago, 3,369,359; Los Angeles, 2,816,061; Philadelphia, 1,950,098.
Government: *Head of state,* Richard M. Nixon, president (took office for 2d 4-year term Jan. 1973). *Head of government,* Richard M. Nixon. *Legislature*—Congress: Senate and House of Representatives. *Major political parties*—Republican party; Democratic party.
Language: English (official).
Education: *Expenditure* (1972 est.), 8.2% of gross national product. *School enrollment* (1972–73); public elementary, 26,794,070; public secondary, 19,027,673; university/higher, 8,219,691.
Monetary Unit: Dollar.
Gross National Product (3d quarter 1973 est.): $1,304,-500,000,000.
Economic Indexes: *Industrial production* (Nov. 1973), 127.2 (1967=100); *agricultural production* (1973), 115 (1967=100); *consumer price index* (Nov. 1973), 137.6 (1967=100).
Manufacturing (major products): Motor vehicles, aircraft, ships and railroad equipment, industrial machinery, processed foods, chemicals, electrical equipment and supplies, fabricated metals, textiles and clothing, paper and paper products, plastic and rubber products.
Major Agricultural Products: Corn (ranks 1st among world producers, 1972), wheat (world rank 2d, 1972), rye, barley, oats (world rank 2d, 1972), soybeans (world rank 1st, 1972), tobacco (world rank 1st, 1972), cotton (world rank 1st, 1972), sorghum, peanuts, citrus fruits, dairy products, livestock.
Major Minerals: Petroleum (ranks 1st among world producers, 1971), natural gas (world rank 1st, 1971), iron ore (world rank 2d, 1971), silver (world rank 2d, 1971), copper (world rank 1st, 1971), coal (world rank 2d, 1971), zinc, nickel, sulfur, phosphate (world rank 1st, 1971), uranium (world rank 1st, 1971).
Foreign Trade (1972): *Exports,* $49,768,000,000. *Imports,* $55,555,000,000. *Chief trading partners* (1972)—Canada (took 25% of exports, supplied 27% of imports); Japan (10%—16%); West Germany (6%—8%); United Kingdom (5%—5%).
Tourism: Receipts (1972), $2,706,000,000.
Transportation: *Motor vehicles* (1972), 112,999,125 (automobiles, 92,799,052); *railroads* (1972), 205,202 miles (330,225 km); *merchant fleet* (1972), 15,024,000 gross registered tons.
Communications: *Telephones* (1973), 130,968,100; *newspapers* (1973), 1,761 (daily circulation, 62,510,000).

---

tee, Ford said that he himself had no prior knowledge of any of the illegal activities alleged against the 1972 Nixon presidential campaign, and he promised to maintain a measure of independence from the White House.

Appearing in opposition to the nomination, Joseph L. Rauh, Jr., a vice chairman of Americans for Democratic Action, testified that Ford's opposition in Congress to civil rights and social welfare legislation made him unsuited for national leadership. Many Democrats also felt that Ford was too conservative for their tastes. Some believed that he lacked intellectual range, imagination, and administrative experience. But most believed that the President was entitled to select a vice president whose philosophy of government was in accord with his own. Ford's record proved clear of any stain of scandal. And he was popular in Congress, with Democrats as well as Republicans.

Ford's nomination was unanimously approved by the Senate Rules Committee and then on November 27 by a 92–3 vote of the full Senate. After the House Judiciary Committee approved the nomination by a 29–8 vote, the House confirmed him on December 6 by a margin of 387 to 35. Later that day, with Nixon at his side, Ford took the oath as the nation's 40th vice president in brief ceremonies in the House of Representatives. In characteristically modest remarks, Ford reminded the public, "I'm a Ford, not a Lincoln," and promised Nixon

his "support and loyalty." On December 7, Ford was succeeded as House minority leader by Rep. John J. Rhodes of Arizona.

Congress. The 93d Congress' record of significant legislative achievement was not lengthy in 1973. But during the year Congress began to make progress toward reassertng itself as coequal with the executive branch in the workings of the government. These efforts were aided by the President's loss of prestige due to Watergate and were stimulated by Nixon's drive to cut federal spending, which was a major source of friction between the White House and Capitol Hill.

The first battle broke out over impoundment of funds. On February 5, Roy L. Ash, director of the Office of Management and Budget (OMB), reported that the administration had impounded (held in reserve) $8.7 billion in congressionally appropriated funds for such projects as highway construction and rural environmental assistance. The administration's position, as outlined by Ash, was that the President was required to impound funds to avoid violating other statutes, such as the legal limit on the national debt.

Sen. Sam J. Ervin, Jr. (D-N. C.) said that the President must obey appropriation laws—that he had no right to pick and choose which funds to spend or impound. The argument continued through the year, without final resolution. Both the Senate and the House passed measures aimed at restricting the President's power to impound, but they were unable to reconcile their differences. Proposals also were made that Congress develop its own budget to give it a more responsible role in allocating funds.

As the administration continued to impound funds for a variety of programs, the controversy spread into the courts, where the potential beneficiaries sued for the release of the money. They won in most of the more than 30 cases decided by the federal district courts, but the White House usually appealed the rulings.

In a major concession on December 19, the President agreed to release $1.1 billion in impounded funds for health and education programs. But an estimated $13.5 billion for other programs remained impounded, and the administration seemed determined to take the question of the President's constitutional authority to impound to the Supreme Court.

Early in the session, Republicans in Congress rallied behind the President's position on cuts in spending, promising to support his vetoes of funding bills, even if they had voted in favor of the bills in the first place. Five times the President vetoed measures that he regarded as fiscally irresponsible or as contributing to inflationary pressures, and each time Congress was unable to muster the necessary two-thirds majority to override the veto. These were a $2.6 billion bill extending vocational rehabilitation programs to the physically and mentally handicapped, a $120 million bill restoring rural water and sewer system grants, a $185 million proposal providing emergency health service grants, a boost in the minimum wage to $2.20 an hour, and expansion of the disaster aid program of the Small Business Administration.

Nixon's vetoes also prevailed on three bills that he regarded as eroding the authority of the presidency—a measure requiring Senate confirmation of the director and deputy director of the OMB, a bill authorizing $216.7 million for the U. S. Information Agency in 1974 and requiring the agency to

FIRST U. S. PRISONERS OF WAR to return from North Vietnam complete one stage of their journey at Clark Air Base in the Philippines.

turn over any confidential information Congress requested, and a measure cutting off funds for bombing in Cambodia. But the growing strength of Congress was signaled after the bombing cutoff veto, when the White House agreed to a compromise proposal setting August 15 as the terminal date for such bombing. Although he went along with this compromise, Nixon warned that "the abandonment of a friend" by the United States could have "dangerous potential consequences" elsewhere in Asia.

After eight straight failures, Congress succeeded on November 7 in overriding a presidential veto. At issue was a joint congressional measure limiting the President's power to send U. S. troops into combat abroad. As a result of the resolution, the President must notify Congress within 48 hours of dispatching troops and must withdraw them within 60 days unless Congress approves an extension.

Among other major legislation enacted into law were a $20 billion highway bill, authorizing the use of funds from the Highway Trust Fund for mass transit; a farm bill extending government support programs for wheat, feed grains, cotton, and dairy products; limited home rule for the District of Columbia; and an 11% increase in social security benefits. Proposals put off for another year included reform of campaign financing, a trade bill giving the President power to raise or lower tariffs and establish quotas, tax reform, and national health insurance.

The Economy. Regulating the nation's economic affairs proved to be one of the administration's most frustrating problems. On January 11 the President announced the end of the mandatory wage and price controls that had been imposed in 1971, except in the "problem areas" of food, health care, and construction. This marked the official end of the so-called Phase 2 system of federal controls and the beginning of Phase 3, which relied mainly on voluntary compliance with federal standards. The goal of Phase 3, the President said, was to reduce the rate of inflation to 2.5% or less by the end of the year. The Pay Board and the Price Commission, which had regulated wages and prices under Phase 2, were abolished. The Cost of Living Council (CLC) was given added staff and a new director, John Dunlop, a labor relations consultant.

Experience soon demonstrated, though, that the new voluntary approach was inadequate for curbing inflation. The Department of Labor's indices for wholesale and consumer prices rose at an alarming rate. In May the Wholesale Price Index (WPI) jumped 2%, the highest peacetime increase since World War II. During the first quarter of the year the Consumer Price Index (CPI) climbed at an annual adjusted rate of 8.7%. On June 13 the President ordered a freeze for up to 60 days on all prices paid by consumers except those on unprocessed food products at the farm level. He directed Treasury Secretary George P. Shultz and CLC Director Dunlop to prepare more mandatory regulations for a forthcoming Phase 4. "Everyone told reporters, "so let's not argue about that."

On July 18 the President unveiled Phase 4. The freeze on food prices, except for beef, was lifted immediately; industrial and service prices stayed frozen until August 12. Phase 4, like Phase 2, would rely on mandatory compliance with a system of price controls. Price increases would be permitted only to reflect cost increases since the end of 1972. Firms with more than $100 million in annual sales would be required to provide the CLC with advance notice of price rises. The flexible 5.5% guideline for wage increases would continue, with big companies required to give advance notice of salary increases. Nixon reiterated his opposition to accepting wage and price controls as "a perma-
(Continued on page 625)

WIDE WORLD

93d CONGRESS OF THE U.S.

(SECOND SESSION)

SENATE

OFFICERS

President of the Senate: Gerald R. Ford
President Pro Tempore: James O. Eastland (D-Miss.)
Majority Leader: Mike Mansfield (D-Mont.)
Majority Whip: Robert C. Byrd (D-W. Va.)
Minority Leader: Hugh Scott (R-Pa.)
Minority Whip: Robert P. Griffin (R-Mich.)

COMMITTEE CHAIRMEN

Aeronautical and Space Sciences: Frank E. Moss (D-Utah)
Agriculture and Forestry: Herman E. Talmadge (D-Ga.)
Appropriations: John L. McClellan (D-Ark.)
Armed Services: John C. Stennis (D-Miss.)
Banking, Housing, and Urban Affairs: John J. Sparkman (D-Ala.)
Commerce: Warren G. Magnuson (D-Wash.)
District of Columbia: Thomas F. Eagleton (D-Mo.)
Finance: Russell B. Long (D-La.)
Foreign Relations: J. William Fulbright (D-Ark.)
Government Operations: Sam J. Ervin, Jr. (D-N. C.)
Interior and Insular Affairs: Henry M. Jackson (D-Wash.)
Judiciary: James O. Eastland (D-Miss.)
Labor and Public Welfare: Harrison A. Williams, Jr. (D-N. J.)
Post Office and Civil Service: Gale W. McGee (D-Wyo.)
Public Works: Jennings Randolph (D-W. Va.)
Rules and Administration: Howard W. Cannon (D-Nev.)
Veterans' Affairs: Vance Hartke (D-Ind.)

HOUSE

OFFICERS

Speaker of the House: Carl Albert (D-Okla.)
Majority Leader: Thomas P. O'Neill, Jr. (D-Mass.)
Majority Whip: John J. McFall (D-Calif.)
Minority Leader: John J. Rhodes (R-Ariz.)
Minority Whip: Leslie C. Arends (R-Ill.)

COMMITTEE CHAIRMEN

Agriculture: W. R. Poage (D-Texas)
Appropriations: George H. Mahon (D-Texas)
Armed Services: F. Edward Hébert (D-La.)
Banking and Currency: Wright Patman (D-Texas)
District of Columbia: Charles C. Diggs, Jr. (D-Mich.)
Education and Labor: Carl D. Perkins (D-Ky.)
Foreign Affairs: Thomas E. Morgan (D-Pa.)
Government Operations: Chet Holifield (D-Calif.)
House Administration: Wayne L. Hays (D-Ohio)
Interior and Insular Affairs: James A. Haley (D-Fla.)
Internal Security: Richard H. Ichord (D-Mo.)
Interstate and Foreign Commerce: Harley O. Staggers (D-W. Va.)
Judiciary: Peter W. Rodino, Jr. (D-N. J.)
Merchant Marine and Fisheries: Leonor K. Sullivan (D-Mo.)
Post Office and Civil Service: Thaddeus J. Dulski (D-N. Y.)
Public Works: John A. Blatnik (D-Minn.)
Rules: Ray J. Madden (D-Ind.)
Science and Astronautics: Olin E. Teague (D-Texas)
Standards of Official Conduct: Melvin Price (D-Ill.)
Veterans' Affairs: William J. B. Dorn (D-S. C.)
Ways and Means: Wilbur D. Mills (D-Ark.)

SENATE MEMBERSHIP

(As of January 1974: 58 Democrats, 42 Republicans)

Letters after senators' names refer to party affiliation—D for Democrat, R for Republican. Single asterisk (*) denotes term expiring in January 1975; double asterisk (**), term expiring in January 1977; triple asterisk (***), term expiring in January 1979.

ALABAMA
***J. Sparkman, D
*J. B. Allen, D

ALASKA
***T. Stevens, R
*M. Gravel, D

ARIZONA
**P. J. Fannin, R
*B. Goldwater, R

ARKANSAS
***J. L. McClellan, D
*J. W. Fulbright, D

CALIFORNIA
*A. Cranston, D
**J. V. Tunney, D

COLORADO
*P. H. Dominick, R
***F. K. Haskell, D

CONNECTICUT
*A. A. Ribicoff, D
**L. P. Weicker, Jr., R

DELAWARE
**W. V. Roth, Jr., R
***J. R. Biden, Jr., D

FLORIDA
*E. J. Gurney, R
**L. Chiles, D

GEORGIA
*H. E. Talmadge, D
***S. A. Nunn, D

HAWAII
**H. L. Fong, R
*D. K. Inouye, D

IDAHO
*F. Church, D
***J. A. McClure, R

ILLINOIS
***C. H. Percy, R
*A. E. Stevenson III, D

INDIANA
**V. Hartke, D
*B. Bayh, D

IOWA
*H. E. Hughes, D
***R. Clark, D

KANSAS
***J. B. Pearson, R
*R. Dole, R

KENTUCKY
*M. W. Cook, R
***W. Huddleston, D

LOUISIANA
*R. B. Long, D
***J. B. Johnston, Jr., D

MAINE
**E. S. Muskie, D
***W. D. Hathaway, D

MARYLAND
*C. McC. Mathias, Jr., R
**J. G. Beall, Jr., R

MASSACHUSETTS
**E. M. Kennedy, D
***E. W. Brooke, R

MICHIGAN
*P. A. Hart, D
***R. P. Griffin, R

MINNESOTA
***W. F. Mondale, D
**H. H. Humphrey, D

MISSISSIPPI
***J. O. Eastland, D
**J. C. Stennis, D

MISSOURI
**S. Symington, D
*T. F. Eagleton, D

MONTANA
**M. Mansfield, D
***L. Metcalf, D

NEBRASKA
**R. L. Hruska, R
***C. T. Curtis, R

NEVADA
*A. Bible, D
**H. W. Cannon, D

NEW HAMPSHIRE
*N. Cotton, R
***T. J. McIntyre, D

NEW JERSEY
***C. P. Case, R
**H. A. Williams, Jr., D

NEW MEXICO
**J. M. Montoya, D
***P. V. Domenici, R

NEW YORK
*J. K. Javits, R
**J. L. Buckley, R[1]

NORTH CAROLINA
*S. J. Ervin, Jr., D
***J. A. Helms, R

NORTH DAKOTA
*M. R. Young, R
**Q. N. Burdick, D

OHIO
*H. M. Metzenbaum, D[3]
**R. Taft, Jr., R

OKLAHOMA
*H. Bellmon, R
***D. F. Bartlett, R

OREGON
***M. O. Hatfield, R
*B. Packwood, R

PENNSYLVANIA
**H. Scott, R
*R. S. Schweiker, R

RHODE ISLAND
**J. O. Pastore, D
***C. Pell, D

SOUTH CAROLINA
***S. Thurmond, R
*E. F. Hollings, D

SOUTH DAKOTA
*G. S. McGovern, D
***J. G. Abourezk, D

TENNESSEE
***H. H. Baker, Jr., R
**W. E. Brock 3d, R

TEXAS
***J. G. Tower, R
**L. M. Bentsen, D

UTAH
*W. F. Bennett, R
**F. E. Moss, D

VERMONT
*G. D. Aiken, R
**R. T. Stafford, R

VIRGINIA
**H. F. Byrd, Jr., D[2]
***W. L. Scott, R

WASHINGTON
*W. G. Magnuson, D
**H. M. Jackson, D

WEST VIRGINIA
***J. Randolph, D
**R. C. Byrd, D

WISCONSIN
**W. Proxmire, D
*G. Nelson, D

WYOMING
**G. W. McGee, D
***C. P. Hansen, R

[1] Ran as a Conservative. [2] Ran as an independent. [3] Appointed to fill vacancy.

HOUSE MEMBERSHIP

(As of January 1974: 243 Democrats, 189 Republicans, 3 vacancies)

Letters after representatives' names refer to party affiliation—D for Democrat, R for Republican. The abbreviation "At-L." in place of congressional district number means "representative at large." Asterisk (*) before member's name indicates incumbent reelected in 1972 (served in 92d Congress); double asterisk (**) before name indicates nonincumbent elected in 1972; triple asterisk (***) means elected in 1973 to fill vacancy.

ALABAMA
1. *J. Edwards, R
2. *W. L. Dickinson, R
3. *W. Nichols, D
4. *T. Bevill, D
5. *R. E. Jones, D
6. *J. H. Buchanan, Jr., R
7. *W. Flowers, D

ALASKA
At-L. ***D. Young, R

ARIZONA
1. *J. J. Rhodes, R
2. *M. K. Udall, D
3. *S. Steiger, R
4. **J. B. Conlan, R

ARKANSAS
1. *W. V. Alexander, Jr., D
2. *W. D. Mills, D
3. *J. P. Hammerschmidt, R
4. **R. H. Thornton, Jr., D

CALIFORNIA
1. *D. H. Clausen, R
2. *H. T. Johnson, D
3. *J. E. Moss, D
4. *R. L. Leggett, D
5. *P. Burton, D
6. *W. S. Mailliard, R
7. *R. V. Dellums, D
8. **F. H. Stark, Jr., D

9. *D. Edwards, D
10. *C. S. Gubser, R
11. **L. J. Ryan, D
12. *B. L. Talcott, R
13. Vacancy
14. *J. R. Waldie, D
15. *J. J. McFall, D
16. *B. F. Sisk, D
17. *P. N. McCloskey, Jr., R
18. *R. B. Mathias, R
19. *C. Holifield, D
20. **C. J. Moorhead, R
21. *A. F. Hawkins, D
22. *J. C. Corman, D
23. *D. M. Clawson, R
24. *J. H. Rousselot, R
25. *C. E. Wiggins, R
26. *T. M. Rees, D
27. *B. M. Goldwater, Jr., R
28. *A. Bell, R
29. *G. E. Danielson, D
30. *E. R. Roybal, D
31. *C. H. Wilson, D
32. *C. Hosmer, R
33. *J. L. Pettis, R
34. *R. T. Hanna, D
35. *G. M. Anderson, D
36. **W. M. Ketchum, R
37. **Y. B. Burke, D
38. **G. E. Brown, Jr., D
39. **A. J. Hinshaw, R

40. *B. Wilson, R
41. *L. Van Deerlin, D
42. **C. W. Burgener, R
43. *V. V. Veysey, R

COLORADO
1. **P. Schroeder, D
2. *D. G. Brotzman, R
3. *F. E. Evans, D
4. **J. P. Johnson, R
5. **W. L. Armstrong, R

CONNECTICUT
1. *W. R. Cotter, D
2. *R. H. Steele, R
3. *R. N. Giaimo, D
4. *S. B. McKinney, R
5. *R. A. Sarasin, R
6. *E. T. Grasso, D

DELAWARE
At-L. *P. S. du Pont 4th, R

FLORIDA
1. *R. L. F. Sikes, D
2. *D. Fuqua, D
3. *C. E. Bennett, D
4. *W. V. Chappell, Jr., D
5. **W. D. Gunter, Jr., D
6. *C. W. Young, R
7. *S. M. Gibbons, D
8. *J. A. Haley, D

9. *L. Frey, Jr., R
10. **L. A. Bafalis, R
11. *P. G. Rogers, D
12. *J. H. Burke, R
13. **W. Lehman, D
14. *C. D. Pepper, D
15. *D. B. Fascell, D

GEORGIA
1. **R. B. Ginn, D
2. *M. D. Mathis, D
3. *J. T. Brinkley, D
4. *B. B. Blackburn, R
5. **A. Young, D
6. *J. J. Flynt, Jr., D
7. *J. W. Davis, D
8. *W. S. Stuckey, Jr., D
9. *P. M. Landrum, D
10. *R. G. Stephens, Jr., D

HAWAII
1. *S. M. Matsunaga, D
2. *P. T. Mink, D

IDAHO
1. **S. D. Symms, R
2. *O. Hansen, R

ILLINOIS
1. *R. H. Metcalfe, D
2. *M. F. Murphy, D
3. **R. P. Hanrahan, R

4. *E. J. Derwinski, R
5. *J. C. Kluczynski, D
6. *H. R. Collier, R
7. ***C. R. Collins, D
8. *D. Rostenkowski, D
9. *S. R. Yates, D
10. **S. H. Young, R
11. *F. Annunzio, D
12. *P. M. Crane, R
13. *R. McClory, R
14. *J. N. Erlenborn, R
15. *L. C. Arends, R
16. *J. B. Anderson, R
17. **G. M. O'Brien, R
18. *R. H. Michel, R
19. *T. Railsback, R
20. *P. Findley, R
21. **E. R. Madigan, R
22. *G. E. Shipley, D
23. *M. Price, D
24. *K. J. Gray, D

INDIANA
1. *R. J. Madden, D
2. *E. F. Landgrebe, R
3. *J. Brademas, D
4. *J. E. Roush, D
5. *E. H. Hillis, R
6. *W. G. Bray, R
7. *J. T. Myers, R
8. *R. H. Zion, R
9. *L. H. Hamilton, D
10. *D. W. Dennis, R
11. **W. H. Hudnut III, R

IOWA
1. **E. Mezvinsky, D
2. *J. C. Culver, D
3. *H. R. Gross, R
4. *N. Smith, D
5. *W. J. Scherle, R
6. *W. Mayne, R

KANSAS
1. *K. G. Sebelius, R
2. *W. R. Roy, D
3. *L. Winn, Jr., R
4. *G. E. Shriver, R
5. *J. Skubitz, R

KENTUCKY
1. *F. A. Stubblefield, D
2. *W. H. Natcher, D
3. *R. L. Mazzoli, D
4. *M. G. Snyder, R
5. *T. L. Carter, R
6. **J. B. Breckinridge, D
7. *C. D. Perkins, D

LOUISIANA
1. *F. E. Hébert, D
2. ***C. C. Boggs, D
3. *D. C. Treen, R
4. *J. D. Waggonner, Jr., D
5. *O. E. Passman, D
6. *J. R. Rarick, D
7. *J. B. Breaux, D
8. **G. W. Long, D

MAINE
1. *P. N. Kyros, D
2. **W. S. Cohen, R

MARYLAND
1. ***R. E. Bauman, D
2. *C. D. Long, D
3. *P. S. Sarbanes, D
4. **M. S. Holt, R
5. *L. J. Hogan, R
6. *G. E. Byron, D
7. *P. J. Mitchell, D
8. *G. Gude, R

MASSACHUSETTS
1. *S. O. Conte, R
2. *E. P. Boland, D
3. *H. D. Donohue, D
4. *R. F. Drinin, D
5. **P. W. Cronin, R
6. *M. J. Harrington, D
7. *T. H. Macdonald, D
8. *T. P. O'Neill, Jr., D
9. **J. J. Moakley, D[1]
10. *M. M. Heckler, R
11. *J. A. Burke, D
12. **G. E. Studds, D

MICHIGAN
1. *J. Conyers, Jr., D
2. *M. L. Esch, R
3. *G. Brown, R
4. *E. Hutchinson, R
5. Vacancy
6. *C. E. Chamberlain, R
7. *D. W. Riegle, Jr., D

8. *J. Harvey, R
9. *G. A. Vander Jagt, R
10. *E. A. Cederberg, R
11. *P. E. Ruppe, R
12. *J. G. O'Hara, D
13. *C. C. Diggs, Jr., D
14. *L. N. Nedzi, D
15. *W. D. Ford, D
16. *J. D. Dingell, D
17. *M. W. Griffiths, D
18. **R. J. Huber, R
19. *W. S. Broomfield, R

MINNESOTA
1. *A. H. Quie, R
2. *A. Nelsen, R
3. *B. Frenzel, R
4. *J. E. Karth, D
5. *D. M. Fraser, D
6. *J. M. Zwach, R
7. *B. S. Bergland, D
8. *J. A. Blatnik, D

MISSISSIPPI
1. *J. L. Whitten, D
2. **D. R. Bowen, D
3. *G. V. Montgomery, D
4. **W. T. Cochran, R
5. **T. Lott, D

MISSOURI
1. *W. L. Clay, D
2. *J. W. Symington, D
3. *L. K. Sullivan, D
4. *W. J. Randall, D
5. *R. Bolling, D
6. **J. Litton, D
7. *G. Taylor, R
8. *R. H. Ichord, D
9. *W. L. Hungate, D
10. *B. D. Burlison, D

MONTANA
1. *R. G. Shoup, R
2. *J. Melcher, D

NEBRASKA
1. *C. Thone, R
2. *J. Y. McCollister, R
3. *D. T. Martin, R

NEVADA
At-L. **D. G. Towell, R

NEW HAMPSHIRE
1. *L. C. Wyman, R
2. *J. C. Cleveland, R

NEW JERSEY
1. *J. E. Hunt, R
2. *C. W. Sandman, Jr., R
3. *J. J. Howard, D
4. *F. Thompson, Jr., D
5. *P. H. B. Frelinghuysen, R
6. *E. B. Forsythe, R
7. *W. B. Widnall, R
8. *R. A. Roe, D
9. *H. Helstoski, D
10. *P. W. Rodino, Jr., D
11. *J. G. Minish, D
12. **M. J. Rinaldo, R
13. *J. J. Maraziti, R
14. *D. V. Daniels, D
15. *E. J. Patten, D

NEW MEXICO
1. *M. Lujan, Jr., R
2. *H. L. Runnels, D

NEW YORK
1. *O. G. Pike, D
2. *J. R. Grover, Jr., R
3. *A. D. Roncallo, R
4. *N. F. Lent, R
5. *J. W. Wydler, R
6. *L. L. Wolff, D
7. *J. P. Addabbo, D
8. *B. S. Rosenthal, D
9. *J. J. Delaney, D
10. *M. Biaggi, D
11. *F. J. Brasco, D
12. *S. J. Chisholm, D
13. *B. L. Podell, D
14. *J. J. Rooney, D
15. *H. L. Carey, D
16. **E. Holtzman, D
17. *J. M. Murphy, D
18. *E. I. Koch, D
19. *C. B. Rangel, D
20. *B. S. Abzug, D
21. *H. Badillo, D
22. *J. B. Bingham, D
23. *P. A. Peyser, D
24. *O. R. Reid, D

25. *H. Fish, Jr., R
26. **B. A. Gilman, R
27. *H. W. Robison, R
28. *S. S. Stratton, D
29. *C. J. King, R
30. *R. C. McEwen, R
31. **D. J. Mitchell, R
32. *J. M. Hanley, D
33. **W. F. Walsh, R
34. *F. Horton, R
35. *B. B. Conable, Jr., R
36. *H. P. Smith III, R
37. *T. J. Dulski, D
38. *J. F. Kemp, R
39. *J. F. Hastings, R

NORTH CAROLINA
1. *W. B. Jones, D
2. *L. H. Fountain, D
3. *D. N. Henderson, D
4. **I. F. Andrews, D
5. *W. D. Mizell, R
6. *L. R. Preyer, D
7. **C. G. Rose III, D
8. *E. B. Ruth, R
9. **J. G. Martin, R
10. *J. T. Broyhill, R
11. *R. A. Taylor, D

NORTH DAKOTA
At-L. *M. Andrews, R

OHIO
1. *W. J. Keating, R
2. *D. D. Clancy, R
3. *C. W. Whalen, Jr., R
4. **T. Guyer, R
5. *D. L. Latta, R
6. *W. H. Harsha, R
7. *C. J. Brown, R
8. *W. E. Powell, R
9. *T. L. Ashley, D
10. *C. E. Miller, R
11. *J. W. Stanton, R
12. *S. L. Devine, R
13. *C. A. Mosher, R
14. *J. F. Seiberling, D
15. *C. P. Wylie, R
16. **R. S. Regula, R
17. *J. M. Ashbrook, R
18. *W. L. Hays, D
19. *C. J. Carney, D
20. *J. V. Stanton, D
21. *L. Stokes, D
22. *C. A. Vanik, D
23. *W. E. Minshall, R

OKLAHOMA
1. **J. R. Jones, D
2. **C. R. McSpadden, D
3. *C. B. Albert, D
4. *T. Steed, D
5. *J. Jarman, D
6. *J. N. Camp, R

OREGON
1. *W. Wyatt, R
2. *A. Ullman, D
3. *E. Green, D
4. *J. Dellenback, R

PENNSYLVANIA
1. *W. A. Barrett, D
2. *R. N. C. Nix, D
3. *W. J. Green, D
4. *J. Eilberg, D
5. *J. H. Ware III, R
6. *G. Yatron, D
7. *L. G. Williams, R
8. *E. G. Biester, Jr., R
9. **E. G. Shuster, R
10. *J. M. McDade, R
11. *D. J. Flood, D
12. Vacancy
13. *R. L. Coughlin, R
14. *W. S. Moorhead, D
15. *F. B. Rooney, D
16. *E. D. Eshleman, R
17. *H.T. Schneebeli, R
18. *H. J. Heinz III, R
19. *G. A. Goodling, R
20. *J. M. Gaydos, D
21. *J. H. Dent, D
22. *T. E. Morgan, D
23. *A. W. Johnson, R
24. *J. P. Vigorito, D
25. *F. M. Clark, D

RHODE ISLAND
1. *F. J. St. Germain, D
2. *R. O. Tiernan, D

SOUTH CAROLINA
1. *M. J. Davis, D
2. *F. D. Spence, R
3. *W. J. B. Dorn, D
4. *J. R. Mann, D
5. *T. S. Gettys, D
6. **E. L. Young, R

SOUTH DAKOTA
1. *F. E. Denholm, D
2. **J. Abdnor, R

TENNESSEE
1. *J. H. Quillen, R
2. *J. J. Duncan, R
3. *L. Baker, R
4. *J. L. Evins, D
5. *R. H. Fulton, D
6. *R. L. Beard, Jr., R
7. *E. Jones, D
8. *D. H. Kuykendall, R

TEXAS
1. *W. Patman, D
2. **C. Wilson, D
3. *J. M. Collins, R
4. *R. Roberts, D
5. *A. W. Steelman, R
6. *O. E. Teague, D
7. *W. R. Archer, R
8. *R. C. Eckhardt, D
9. *J. Brooks, D
10. *J. J. Pickle, D
11. *W. R. Poage, D
12. *J. C. Wright, Jr., D
13. *R. D. Price, R
14. *J. Young, D
15. *E. de la Garza, D
16. *R. C. White, D
17. *O. Burleson, D
18. **B. C. Jordan, D
19. *G. H. Mahon, D
20. *H. B. Gonzalez, D
21. *O. C. Fisher, D
22. *R. R. Casey, D
23. *A. Kazen, Jr., D
24. **D. Milford, D

UTAH
1. *K. G. McKay, D
2. **W. Owens, D

VERMONT
At-L. *R. W. Mallary, R

VIRGINIA
1. *T. N. Downing, D
2. *G. W. Whitehurst, R
3. *D. E. Satterfield III, D
4. *R. W. Daniel, Jr., R
5. *W. C. Daniel, D
6. *M. C. Butler, R
7. *J. K. Robinson, R
8. **S. E. Parris, R
9. *W. C. Wampler, R
10. *J. T. Broyhill, R

WASHINGTON
1. **J. M. Pritchard, R
2. *L. Meeds, D
3. *J. B. Hansen, D
4. *M. McCormack, D
5. *T. S. Foley, D
6. *F. V. Hicks, D
7. *B. Adams, D

WEST VIRGINIA
1. *R. H. Mollohan, D
2. *H. O. Staggers, D
3. *J. M. Slack, D
4. *K. Hechler, D

WISCONSIN
1. *L. Aspin, D
2. *R. W. Kastenmeier, D
3. *V. W. Thomson, R
4. *C. J. Zablocki, D
5. *H. S. Reuss, D
6. *W. A. Steiger, R
7. *D. R. Obey, D
8. **H. V. Froehlich, R
9. *G. R. Davis, R

WYOMING
At-L. *T. Roncalio, D

PUERTO RICO
Resident Commissioner
**J. Benitez

DISTRICT OF COLUMBIA
Delegate
*W. E. Fauntroy, D

[1] Ran as an independent.

(Continued from page 621)

nent feature of the American economy," and he promised that controls eventually would be dropped. Meanwhile, he said, they were needed to combat "an extraordinary combination of circumstances making for rapid inflation."

But prices continued to climb. The WPI for November was 17.5% above the 1972 level, and the CPI for that month was 8.4% higher than for November 1972. Department of Labor officials calculated that a worker's real earnings were 3.3% lower than the year before, with 1.9% due to rising prices and the rest to higher taxes. Administration officials conceded that controls had become counterproductive. They were having little impact on the general price level. There was some evidence that by discouraging expansion of production capacity, controls were contributing to shortages. In October the administration began decontrolling prices on some products, notably fertilizer and some nonferrous metals, and later, on automobiles. Selective lifting of controls was expected to continue, and some experts believed that the entire system might end in 1974.

If the dollar was losing its purchasing power at home, it was also shrinking in value in overseas currency markets. On February 12, Shultz announced a 10% devaluation of the dollar, the second such action in 14 months. The par value in terms of gold was dropped from $38 an ounce to $42.22. The move was forced by heavy speculation in U.S. currency. The dollar continued to drop in value during the spring, a decline many investors attributed to foreign concern over the impact of Watergate. In August, Nixon urged the nation not to become "mired in Watergate" and warned that "confidence at home and abroad in our economy, our currency and our foreign policy is being sapped by uncertainty." By year-end, largely as a result of the energy crisis, the dollar had strengthened considerably against other currencies. This resulted from the belief that the economies of other leading industrial nations would suffer more from the fuel shortage than would the U.S. economy.

Employment was a relatively bright spot. The jobless rate in January had been 5%, the lowest since July 1970. In November it stood at 4.7%, with 85.7 million persons employed—an increase of more than 3 million from the previous November. The total number of unemployed was 4.3 million. But the administration's satisfaction with these figures was mixed with concern that adjustments to the burgeoning energy crisis would raise the jobless rate.

The Energy Crisis. Late in the year the nation was abruptly alerted to the fact that it was running dangerously low on the sources of power needed to fuel the world's most highly technological society. Although the realization was relatively sudden, there had been plenty of warning that an energy crisis was at hand.

In January the President authorized unlimited purchases of home heating and diesel oil from abroad for the next four months. Secretary of the Interior Rogers C. B. Morton warned, "We're in a bind until we get in hand the economic and technologic techniques to fully exploit our own coal and oil resources." On April 18, Nixon called on Congress to help meet the "possibility of occasional energy shortages and some increase in energy prices." He ended mandatory quotas on oil imports, urged development of domestic sources, and established an

PROTESTING high meat prices, members of the National Consumers Congress picket the White House. Some women hold meat bones, all they can afford, they say.

Office of Energy Conservation in the Department of the Interior to make consumers more conscious of the need to save energy. On June 29, with spot shortages of gasoline being reported across the nation, the President named John A. Love, governor of Colorado, as director of a new White House agency, the Energy Policy Office, with responsibility for developing and directing energy policies. Nixon also announced a 5-year, $10 billion program for energy research and development, to begin in 1975, and ordered federal agencies to set an example by reducing energy consumption by 7%.

The Arab-Israeli conflict in October brought matters to a head. In protest against U.S. support of Israel, the Arab nations announced a total embargo on oil shipments to the United States. Some experts estimated the embargo would cost the United States up to 3 million barrels a day, out of a normal total domestic consumption of 17 million barrels. In a televised address on November 7, Nixon told the nation that "we are heading toward the most acute shortages of energy since World War II." He announced cutbacks in jet fuel allocations, forcing an estimated 10% reduction in air travel. He said allocations of heating oil for homes would be reduced 15% from the 1972 level, and he urged everyone to lower thermostats to achieve a national daytime average of 68° F (20° C).

In another televised energy address on November 25, the President called on gasoline stations to close on Sunday and proposed a 50-mph speed limit on highways. Jet fuel supplies would be subject to further reductions. Nixon set the achievement of energy self-sufficiency by 1980 as a national goal. William E. Simon, deputy secretary of the treasury, was named as head of the newly created Federal Energy Office. The former energy chief, John A. Love, announced his resignation on December 3, complaining that he had found it difficult to get the President's attention.

Truck drivers, indignant at rising fuel costs and lower speed limits, staged dramatic protests against the energy edicts by parking their rigs across major highways to block traffic. Other potential problems loomed. Some economists feared

that the cutbacks in production to conserve energy would raise unemployment, perhaps as high as 8%. And the shortages of oil and gas—commodities that most of the people of the United States had long taken for granted—threatened to have a broad and jarring effect on the life of a nation that prized mobility and creature comforts.

Responding to the crisis, Congress enacted daylight saving time on a year-round basis to conserve electricity. It also approved authorization of a 789-mile (1,270-km) oil pipeline across Alaska. The project, estimated to cost between $3.5 billion and $4.5 billion, is scheduled to be completed by 1977, and by 1980 it is expected to have an output of 2 million barrels a day. But Congress was unable to agree on an omnibus energy bill before it adjourned for the year. The most controversial section of the bill was aimed at preventing "windfall profits" by oil companies. Despite congressional inaction, Simon, the President's chief energy adviser, said that the use of fuel could be curbed by voluntary means. He viewed rationing as a last resort and urged motorists to hold gasoline consumption to 10 gallons a week.

Social Problems. In a radio address on March 4, the President said that "the hour of crisis has passed" for U. S. cities. He cited the decline in mass disorders and the drop in the crime rate. But underlying problems continued to fester. In February the U. S. Civil Rights Commission criticized the federal government for laxness in enforcing civil rights laws. It placed much of the blame on lack of presidential leadership and warned of "a steady erosion of the progress toward equal rights."

Cities remained relatively free of mass violence. But in February, disorder broke out in the rural town of Wounded Knee, on the Pine Ridge Indian Reservation in South Dakota. About 300 armed members and supporters of the American Indian Movement (AIM) seized the community and demanded federal investigations of Indian problems (see feature article beginning on page 62).

ROBERT SHOGAN, *"Los Angeles Times"*

FOREIGN AFFAIRS

The year 1973 constituted a turning point in United States foreign relations. With the agreements of January and March, the war in Southeast Asia was wound down and the United States withdrew militarily. With new ventures in accommodation, détente with the Kremlin and Peking progressed. The proposal for a new Atlantic Charter opened the way for revitalizing the Atlantic alliance. The outbreak of renewed warfare between Israel and the Arab countries tested the new Soviet-American relationship. Negotiations among the Mideast powers and within the United Nations—with the United States playing a leading role—ended the hostilities and led to efforts to resolve long-range issues.

Late in August, President Nixon nominated Dr. Henry A. Kissinger to succeed William P. Rogers as secretary of state, and he took office on September 22. For the first time, one man served both as assistant to the president for national security affairs—which office Kissinger had held since President Nixon's inaugural—and as secretary of state. Despite his many stateside duties, Kissinger continued as one of the president's principal negotiators abroad.

Southeast Asia. Despite the apparent impasse in negotiations to end the Vietnam War late in 1972 and despite the resumption of U. S. bombing and mining of North Vietnam, negotiations—led by Kissinger in Paris and by his deputy, Gen. Alexander M. Haig, in Southeast Asia—produced a series of agreements to end the war. These were formally signed on January 27 by the four principal parties.

An internationally supervised cease-fire took effect at midnight. Four protocols provided for an International Control Commission, comprising Canade, Hungary, Indonesia, and Poland, with headquarters in Saigon; a series of four-party supervisory military commissions in the field; withdrawal of U. S. forces from South Vietnam; release of American prisoners-of-war; and removal of American mines from North Vietnamese waters.

Peace did not come easily to Vietnam, however, and the cease-fire was violated frequently. The Control Commission's rule of unanimity made agreement difficult and sometimes impossible, and the joint military commissions were so obstructed that Canada withdrew in May and was replaced by Iran.

Because the cease-fire appeared to be foundering, a 12-power international conference convened at Paris—consisting of the United States and the other three parties to the original agreements, the four members of the Control Commission, Britain, France, the People's Republic of China, and the Soviet Union. They signed a covering agreement on March 2, reconfirming the January accords, recognizing the sovereignty and territorial integrity of Vietnam and the self-determination of its people, and agreeing to consult if the cease-fire was violated. The American and North Vietnamese diplomats ended their tortuous Paris negotiations on May 1, and after six years Ellsworth Bunker resigned as U. S. ambassador to South Vietnam.

Article 20 of the January agreement required respect for the 1954 and 1962 Geneva accords, which recognized the fundamental rights of Laos and Cambodia and prohibited their use as a base of operations against each other and against other countries. American bombing continued against organized guerrillas within Cambodia during the first half of 1973, although Congress sought to legislate its discontinuance. In May the House of Representatives reversed its previous position and acted to block the transfer of funds for American raids. In July it was revealed that, under presidential order, American bombers had struck secretly in Cambodia as early as 1969, and that reports to Congress and the public had been falsified.

Eventually, by agreement between the President and Congress, American bombing was terminated on August 15, and the longest war in American history came to an end. It had cost more than $150 billion in budgetary expenditures over 15 years and has been unofficially estimated to necessitate continuing costs, including veterans' benefits, amounting to many additional billions.

Presidential War-Making Powers. For several years Congress tried to curtail U. S. military action in Vietnam and restrict presidential authority in declaring war. In November, after several abortive attempts and three years of legislative frustration, Congress passed the war powers act over President Nixon's veto. The act provides that when the President commits U. S. forces to hostilities abroad or substantially enlarges American troops for combat in foreign nations, he must report to Congress within 48 hours the circumstances, authority, and scope of his action. He must stop after 60 days unless

In Washington, Andrei Gromyko and William Rogers sign accords as Chairman Brezhnev and President Nixon chat.

Congress approves his operation, although he may continue another 30 days if necessary to protect American forces. Congress may order the military action halted at any time by passing a concurrent resolution—which is not subject to presidential veto.

Détente. As the United States withdrew from Indochina, President Nixon continued his efforts to broaden diplomatic horizons with the Soviet Union and normalize U. S. relations with the People's Republic of China. Liaison missions were created in both Washington and Peking in May—reviving direct diplomatic exchange that had languished for a quarter of a century—and, during Kissinger's visit to Peking in November, China and the United States agreed to expand their missions and look toward full diplomatic exchanges and a long-range, durable relationship.

In June, Soviet party leader Leonid I. Brezhnev traveled to the United States on an eight-day official visit for summit discussions. He conferred with the President in Washington and at Camp David, Md., met with 25 members of Congress at luncheon, spoke to U. S. businessmen at Blair House, and addressed the American people on television.

During this visit, the U. S. and Soviet governments signed nearly a dozen agreements, including a convention on taxation to relieve the income tax burden of citizens of one country working in the other; four agreements on agriculture, cultural exchange, transportation, and the seas; and three protocols creating a Soviet-American Chamber of Commerce, establishing mutual commercial representative facilities in the two capitals, and expanding commercial air services.

Most important, however, the President and Brezhnev personally signed three major accords—concerned with scientific cooperation in the peaceful uses of atomic energy, with reducing the risk of nuclear confrontation and avoiding nuclear war, and with basic principles of negotiation on strategic arms limitation, seeking a permanent arrangement to replace the interim agreement of 1972.

Kissinger warned the Soviets in early October that there are limits beyond which the United States could not go, that it would oppose Soviet attempts to gain a position of dominance, and that it would resist Soviet ventures to exploit the détente to weaken America's alliances.

Year of Europe. Détente with the Soviet Union also involved the issue of mutual force reductions in Europe, which was intimately related to U. S. relations with its allies. In his annual report on the state of the world, President Nixon called 1973 "the year of Europe," and on April 23, Kissinger proposed a "new Atlantic Charter" to reduce strain within the NATO alliance and convert it into a force that would draw its inspiration from common goals rather than from mutual fears.

Top-level bilateral meetings clarified national positions. President Nixon met with West German Chancellor Willy Brandt in Washington on May 2 and with French President Georges Pompidou in Iceland on June 1, while Kissinger went to London for talks with British Prime Minister Edward Heath. The President expressed hope for the closing of alliance ranks and the charting of concerted strategy for dealing with security and diplomatic issues of common concern.

Major problems troubling the alliance were the relationship of economic and financial considerations with political and military considerations; unilateral as against collective and mutual armed force reduction; East-West coexistence and security; and regional geopolitical stability. Highly intertwined, all of these matters required serious diplomatic bargaining. Facing a series of crucial negotiations in the last half of the year—the United States and

Soviet Union in SALT II, and the Western and Eastern European powers in two conferences on European security and mutual/balanced force reductions—it was essential that the NATO partners first forge a united diplomatic front.

The matter of American military contribution to Europe was affected by the U. S. dollar outflow and the resulting balance of payments problem, the united position taken by Europe against the United States in trade negotiations, the lack of cooperation by the European governments at the time of the Mideast war, and the pressure brought by some members of Congress for unilateral American force reduction. A critical issue was whether trade, international exchange, and defense were to be dealt with separately, as some European countries insisted to their advantage, or whether they were parts of a single package to be treated conjointly, as proposed by the United States.

In both a presidential statement and the NATO Council session in June, the United States reassured its allies that it would not reduce its military forces unilaterally in Europe. The Department of State insisted that the American position remain unchanged because, after years of preparation, negotiations on European security and mutual East-West troop reduction were finally about to begin, and unilateral withdrawal would undermine the bargaining position of the United States and NATO.

Later in the year the conference on security and cooperation convened in Vienna, Austria, and the conference on mutual and balanced force reduction met at Geneva, Switzerland. Meanwhile, the new Atlantic Charter remained in abeyance.

Mideast War. The Middle East erupted into full-scale war when Egyptian and Syrian forces attacked Israel on October 6—the fourth Israeli-Arab war in 25 years, but the first to seriously threaten Soviet-American relations. The United States had two announced basic objectives—the immediate, to end the fighting quickly, and the longer range, to promote a negotiated settlement between Israel and her Arab neighbors.

For several weeks efforts were devoted largely to halting hostilities. At the outset, the United States attempted to moderate the level of outside supply to both sides and worked with the Kremlin on a cease-fire resolution in the United Nations. This initial attempt failed in both respects, and, when the Soviet supply airlift to the Arab countries reached substantial levels by October 12 and the Soviets strengthened their Mediterranean naval forces, President Nixon decided to resupply Israel in order to maintain the military balance between the warring sides.

At Brezhnev's request, Kissinger flew to Moscow where they agreed on a formula embodied in Security Council Resolution 338, approved on October 22, which the three Mideast powers accepted within hours. The formula consisted of three main points: an immediate cease-fire in place, prompt implementation of Security Council Resolution 242 of November 1967 which stipulated general principles for peace, and negotiations between the parties concerned under appropriate auspices to establish peace in the Middle East.

This arrangement did not provide for policing of the cease-fire. The Israelis, pressing for a decisive military conclusion, advanced on the Syrian capital and crossed the Suez Canal, threatening Cairo and cutting off the Egyptian Third Army of approximately 20,000 men in the Sinai desert. The Security Council then reconvened and directed the secretary general to speed UN observers to the scene.

When Egyptian President Anwar Sadat invited the Soviet and American governments to send troops to stabilize the cease-fire, the Kremlin accepted but the United States refused. Because the Kremlin sent a bristling note to Washington threatening to dispatch Soviet troops unilaterally, and American intelligence reports indicated significant Soviet military movements, the President instituted "precautionary measures" on October 25, placing U. S. armed forces on a worldwide alert. What some called a Soviet-American confrontation was averted when the Security Council passed another resolution, authorizing a UN force of 7,000 for constabulary services, not including—on the insistence of the United States—troops of any of the Big Five powers.

With the situation in danger of breaking down as the warring nations maneuvered to augment their negotiating positions, Kissinger went to the Middle East in early November where he was able to induce Egypt and Israel to accept a six-point agreement. Signed formally by their military representatives on November 11 at "Kilometer 101" on the Suez-Cairo road, it provided for: an immediate exchange of prisoners, a corridor through Israeli lines to resupply the Egyptian Third Army with nonmilitary goods, an end of the Arab blockade of the southern end of the Red Sea, negotiations on an agreed cease-fire line, negotiations for a basic, over-all settlement, and UN enforcement of compliance.

The United States continued its complex diplomacy to keep the contending forces in equilibrium until fundamental peace talks began. After another Kissinger trip to the Mideast, and on the joint invitation of the U. S. and Soviet governments, a six-power conference met at Geneva in December, but substantive bargaining was deferred until after the Israeli parliamentary elections on December 31.

Much remained unsettled at the end of 1973—including the critical oil shortage resulting from the embargo instituted by the Arab countries, the festering problems besetting the NATO partnership, and the effects of the war on détente in Europe and on the important East-West negotiations under way. In Israeli-Arab relations, the principal questions were whether the negotiations on the cease-fire would sustain peace and whether the conclusion of a long-range settlement would eventuate.

ELMER PLISCHKE
University of Maryland

UNIVERSITIES AND COLLEGES

A selected list of accredited junior colleges, senior colleges, and universities in the United States and Canada appears on the following pages.

The information given for each school comprises the following data: its degree-granting status (if it is a senior college or university); the composition of its student body (by sex); the legal controlling agency; and the total enrollment of students of college grade as reported by the registrar (U. S. figures are for 1972–73; Canadian figures are for 1971–72).

All the U. S. institutions listed are recognized by *Accredited Institutions of Higher Education*, published by the American Council on Education. The Canadian institutions listed are accredited by the provinces in which they are located.

See also EDUCATION.

MAJOR UNIVERSITIES AND COLLEGES, U.S. AND CANADA

Note: Symbols and abbreviations that follow the name of each school listed are as follows: *Level of Instruction*—(1) 2-year junior college; (2) senior college granting bachelor's and/or first professional degree; (3) senior college granting master's and/or second professional degree; (4) college or university offering a doctoral program *Student Body*—(M) men only; (W) women only; (Coed) coeducational; (Coord) separate colleges for men and women. *Control*—(Public) district, municipal, state, or federal; (Private) proprietary, corporation, or church. *Enrollment*—For the United States, all students of college grade for the academic year 1972–73 excepting correspondence course students. Canadian figures are for 1971–72.

Name and Location	Level of Instruction	Student Body	Control	Enrollment
Abilene Christian College, Abilene, Texas	3	Coed	Pvt-Church of Christ	3,346
Abraham Baldwin Agricultural College, Tifton, Ga.	1	Coed	Public	2,191
Acadia University, Wolfville, Nova Scotia	3	Coed	Pvt-Baptist	2,400
Adams State College, Alamosa, Colo.	3	Coed	Public	2,802
Adelphi University, Garden City, N.Y.	4	Coed	Private	7,712
Adirondack Community College, Glens Falls, N.Y.	1	Coed	Public	1,380
Adrian College, Adrian, Mich.	2	Coed	Pvt-Methodist	1,191
Aeronautics, Academy of, Flushing, N.Y.	1	Coed	Private	1,032
Akron, University of, Akron, Ohio	4	Coed	Public	19,773
Alabama, University of, in Birmingham, Ala.	4	Coed	Public	8,968
Alabama, University of, in Huntsville, Ala.	3	Coed	Public	2,962
Alabama, University of, in Tuscaloosa, Ala.	4	Coed	Public	14,050
Alabama Agricultural and Mechanical College, Normal, Ala.	3	Coed	Public	3,306
Alabama State University, Montgomery, Ala.	3	Coed	Public	3,272
Alameda, College of, Alameda, Calif.	1	Coed	Public	4,986
Alaska, University of, Fairbanks, Alaska (incl. community colleges at Juneau, Kenai, Ketchikan, Kodiak, Palmer, Sitka).	4	Coed	Public	5,469
Alaska Methodist University, Anchorage, Alaska	3	Coed	Pvt-Methodist	1,039
Albany Junior College, Albany, Ga.	1	Coed	Public	1,441
Albany State College, Albany, Ga.	2	Coed	Public	1,803
Albemarle, College of the, Elizabeth City, N.C.	1	Coed	Public	889
Alberta, University of, Edmonton, Alberta	4	Coed	Public	18,243
Albion College, Albion, Mich.	2	Coed	Pvt-Methodist	1,727
Albright College, Reading, Pa.	2	Coed	Pvt-Methodist	1,727
Albuquerque, University of, Albuquerque, N. Mex.	3	Coed	Pvt-Roman Catholic	2,650
Alcorn Agricultural & Mechanical College, Lorman, Miss.	2	Coed	Public	2,535
Alderson-Broaddus College, Philippi, W.Va.	2	Coed	Pvt-Baptist	1,013
Alexander City State Junior College, Alexander City, Ala.	1	Coed	Public	1,142
Alfred University, Alfred, N.Y.	3	Coed	Private	2,441
Allan Hancock College, Santa Maria, Calif.	1	Coed	Public	8,785
Allegany Community College, Cumberland, Md.	1	Coed	Public	1,141
Allegheny College, Meadville, Pa.	3	Coed	Pvt-Methodist	1,782
Alma College, Alma, Mich.	2	Coed	Pvt-Presbyterian	1,229
Alpena Community College, Alpena, Mich.	1	Coed	Public	1,328
Alverno College, Milwaukee, Wis.	2	Coed	Pvt-Roman Catholic	1,145
Alvin Junior College, Alvin, Texas	1	Coed	Public	1,631
Amarillo College, Amarillo, Texas	1	Coed	Public	3,615
American International College, Springfield, Mass.	3	Coed	Private	2,702
American River College, Sacramento, Calif.	1	Coed	Public	14,711
American University, Washington, D.C.	4	Coed	Public	13,778
Amherst College, Amherst, Mass.	3	Coed	Private	1,271
Ana G. Méndez Educational Foundation, Rio Piedras, P.R.	2	Coed	Private	4,178
Anchorage Community College, Anchorage, Alaska	1	Coed	Public	6,988
Anderson College, Anderson, Ind.	3	Coed	Pvt-Church of God	1,754
Anderson College, Anderson, S.C.	1	Coed	Pvt-Baptist	1,044
Andrews University, Berrien Springs, Mich.	4	Coed	Pvt-Seventh-day Adventist	1,476
Angelina College, Lufkin, Texas	1	Coed	Public	1,116
Angelo State College, San Angelo, Texas	2	Coed	Public	4,005
Anne Arundel Community College, Arnold, Md.	1	Coed	Public	4,469
Antelope Valley College, Lancaster, Calif.	1	Coed	Public	4,068
Antioch College, Yellow Springs, Ohio	3	Coed	Private	2,448
Appalachian State University, Boone, N.C.	3	Coed	Public	7,761
Aquinas College, Grand Rapids, Mich.	3	Coed	Pvt-Roman Catholic	1,512
Aquinas Institute of Theology, Dubuque, Iowa	4	Coed	Pvt-Roman Catholic	1,152
Arapahoe Community College, Littleton, Colo.	1	Coed	Public	2,377
Arizona, University of, Tucson, Ariz.	4	Coed	Public	27,552
Arizona State University, Tempe, Ariz.	4	Coed	Public	30,786
Arizona Western College, Yuma, Ariz.	1	Coed	Public	3,014
Arkansas, State College of, Conway, Ark.	3	Coed	Public	4,756
Arkansas, University of, Fayetteville, Ark.	4	Coed	Public	11,804
Arkansas, University of, Pine Bluff, Ark.	2	Coed	Public	2,208
Arkansas Polytechnic College, Russellville, Ark.	2	Coed	Public	2,271
Arkansas State University, State University, Ark.	3	Coed	Public	6,624
Armstrong State College, Savannah, Ga.	2	Coed	Public	2,960
Art Center College of Design, Los Angeles, Calif.	3	Coed	Private	990
Art Institute of Chicago, Schools of the, Chicago, Ill.	3	Coed	Private	1,411
Asbury College, Wilmore, Ky.	3	Coed	Private	1,115
Asheville-Buncombe Technical Institute, Asheville, N.C.	1	Coed	Public	1,320
Ashland College, Ashland, Ohio	2	Coed	Pvt-Brethren	2,437
Assumption College, Worcester, Mass.	3	Coed	Pvt-Roman Catholic	1,632
Athens College, Athens, Ala.	4	Coed	Pvt-Methodist	772
Atlanta University, Atlanta, Ga.	4	Coed	Private	1,156
Atlantic Christian College, Wilson, N.C.	2	Coed	Pvt-Disciples of Christ	1,770
Atlantic Community College, Mays Landing, N.J.	1	Coed	Public	3,213
Auburn Community College, Auburn, N.Y.	1	Coed	Public	2,749
Auburn University, Auburn, Ala.	4	Coed	Public	16,578
Auburn University at Montgomery, Ala.	3	Coed	Public	1,802
Augsburg College, Minneapolis, Minn.	2	Coed	Pvt-Lutheran	3,353
Augusta College, Augusta, Ga.	3	Coed	Public	2,334
Augustana College, Rock Island, Ill.	3	Coed	Pvt-Lutheran	1,991
Augustana College, Sioux Falls, S.Dak.	2	Coed	Pvt-Lutheran	1,112
Aurora College, Aurora, Ill.	2	Coed	Pvt-Advent Christian	1,196
Austin College, Sherman, Texas	3	Coed	Pvt-Presbyterian	3,671
Austin Peay State University, Clarksville, Tenn.	3	Coed	Public	927
Austin State Junior College, Austin, Minn.	1	Coed	Public	994
Averett College, Danville, Va.	2	Coed	Pvt-Baptist	754
Avila College, Kansas City, Mo.	2	Coed	Pvt-Roman Catholic	1,063
Azusa Pacific College, Azusa, Calif.	3	Coed	Private	1,870
Babson College, Babson Park, Mass.	3	Coed	Private	825
Baker University, Baldwin City, Kans.	3	Coed	Pvt-Methodist	10,253
Bakersfield College, Bakersfield, Calif.	1	Coed	Public	2,862
Baldwin-Wallace College, Berea, Ohio	4	Coed	Pvt-Methodist	19,575
Ball State University, Muncie, Ind.	2	Coed	Public	5,026
Baltimore, University of, Baltimore, Md.	3	Coed	Private	1,140
Bank Street College of Education, New York, N.Y.	3	Coed	Private	1,891
Bard College at Charleston, S.C.	2	Coed	Pvt-Baptist	762
Barry College, Miami, Fla.	1	Coed	Pvt-Roman Catholic	1,387
Barstow College, Barstow, Calif.	1	Coed	Public	1,492
Bates College, Lewiston, Me.	2	Coed	Private	1,256
Bayamón Centra lUniversity, Bayamón, P.R.	2	Coed	Private	865

Name and Location	Level of Instruction	Student Body	Control	Enrollment
Baylor University, Waco, Texas	4	Coed	Pvt-Baptist	7,846
Beaver College, Glenside, Pa.	2	Coed	Pvt-Presbyterian	993
Bee County College, Beeville, Texas	1	Coed	Public	1,247
Bellarmine College, Louisville, Ky.	2	Coed	Pvt-Roman Catholic	1,530
Belleville Area College, Belleville, Ill.	1	Coed	Public	6,530
Bellevue Community College, Bellevue, Wash.	1	Coed	Public	5,721
Belmont College, Nashville, Tenn.	2	Coed	Pvt-Baptist	930
Beloit College, Beloit, Wis.	2	Coed	Private	1,788
Bemidji State College, Bemidji, Minn.	3	Coed	Public	4,570
Benedict College, Columbia, S.C.	2	Coed	Pvt-Baptist	1,370
Benedictine College, Atchison, Kans.	2	Coed	Pvt-Roman Catholic	1,170
Bentley College, Waltham, Mass.	2	Coed	Private	3,368
Berea College, Berea, Ky.	2	Coed	Private	1,356
Bergen Community College, Paramus, N.J.	1	Coed	Public	6,163
Berkeley-Charleston-Dorchester Technical Education Center, North Charleston, S.C.	1	Coed	Public	2,403
Berklee College of Music, Boston, Mass.	2	Coed	Private	1,660
Berkshire Community College, Pittsfield, Mass.	1	Coed	Public	2,165
Berry College, Mount Berry, Ga.	2	Coed	Private	1,041
Bethany College, Bethany, W.Va.	2	Coed	Pvt-Disciples of Christ	1,150
Bethany Nazarene College, Bethany, Okla.	3	Coed	Pvt-Nazarene	1,420
Bethel College, St. Paul, Minn.	2	Coed	Pvt-Baptist	1,139
Bethune-Cookman College, Daytona Beach, Fla.	2	Coed	Pvt-Methodist	1,216
Big Bend Community College, Moses Lake, Wash.	1	Coed	Public	850
Biola College, La Mirada, Calif.	3	Coed	Private	1,752
Birmingham-Southern College, Birmingham, Ala.	2	Coed	Pvt-Methodist	1,040
Biscayne College, Miami, Fla.	2	Coed	Pvt-Roman Catholic	958
Bishop College, Dallas, Texas	2	Coed	Pvt-Baptist	1,596
Bismarck Junior College, Bismarck, N.Dak.	1	Coed	Public	1,672
Black Hawk College, Moline, Ill.	1	Coed	Public	4,192
Black Hills State College, Spearfish, S.Dak.	3	Coed	Public	1,838
Blinn College, Brenham, Texas	1	Coed	Public	1,782
Bloomfield College, Bloomfield, N.J.	2	Coed	Pvt-Presbyterian	1,555
Bloomsburg State College, Bloomsburg, Pa.	3	Coed	Public	5,156
Blue Mountain Community College, Pendleton, Oreg.	1	Coed	Public	979
Blue Ridge Community College, Weyers Cave, Va.	1	Coed	Public	1,203
Bluefield State College, Bluefield, W.Va.	2	Coed	Public	1,231
Boise State College, Boise, Idaho	4	Coed	Public	8,808
Boston College, Chestnut Hill, Mass.	4	Coed	Pvt-Roman Catholic	11,787
Boston State College, Boston, Mass.	3	Coed	Public	8,290
Boston University, Boston, Mass.	4	Coed	Private	23,362
Bowdoin College, Brunswick, Me.	3	Coed	Private	1,163
Bowie State College, Bowie, Md.	3	Coed	Public	2,797
Bowling Green State University, Bowling Green, Ohio	4	Coed	Public	16,956
Bradley University, Peoria, Ill.	4	Coed	Private	5,256
Brandeis University, Waltham, Mass.	4	Coed	Private	2,461
Brandon University, Brandon, Manitoba	2	Coed	Public	1,220
Brandywine College, Wilmington, Del.	1	Coed	Private	1,347
Brazosport College, Lake Jackson, Texas	1	Coed	Public	1,654
Brescia College, Owensboro, Ky.	2	Coed	Pvt-Roman Catholic	957
Brevard Community College, Cocoa, Fla.	1	Coed	Public	6,465
Briar Cliff College, Sioux City, Iowa	2	Coed	Pvt-Roman Catholic	901
Bridgeport, University of, Bridgeport, Conn.	3	Coed	Private	7,950
Bridgewater College, Bridgewater, Va.	2	Coed	Pvt-Brethren	852
Bridgewater State College, Bridgewater, Mass.	3	Coed	Public	7,086
Brigham Young University, Provo, Utah	4	Coed	Pvt-Latter-day Saints	24,565
Bristol Community College, Fall River, Mass.	1	Coed	Public	2,981
British Columbia, University of, Vancouver, B.C.	4	Coed	Public	18,993
Brock University, St. Catharines, Ontario	3	Coed	Public	3,622
Brookdale Community College, Lincroft, N.J.	1	Coed	Public	5,622
Broome Community College, Binghamton, N.Y.	1	Coed	Public	4,483
Broward Community College, Fort Lauderdale, Fla.	1	Coed	Public	9,041
Brown University, Providence, R.I.	4	Coed	Private	6,292
Brunswick College, Brunswick, Ga.	1	Coed	Public	1,014
Bryant College, Providence, R.I.	2	Coed	Private	3,461
Bryn Mawr College, Bryn Mawr, Pa.	3	Coed	Private	1,494
Bucknell University, Lewisburg, Pa.	3	Coed	Private	3,100
Bucks County Community College, Newtown, Pa.	1	Coed	Public	5,607
Buena Vista College, Storm Lake, Iowa	2	Coed	Pvt-Presbyterian	816
Burlington County College, Pemberton, N.J.	1	Coed	Public	3,098
Butler County Community College, Butler, Pa.	1	Coed	Public	825
Butler Community College, El Dorado, Kans.	1	Coed	Public	1,586
Butler University, Indianapolis, Ind.	3	Coed	Private	4,239
Butte College, Durham, Calif.	1	Coed	Public	4,170
Cabrillo College, Aptos, Calif.	1	Coed	Public	5,027
Caldwell College, Caldwell, N.J.	2	W	Pvt-Roman Catholic	853
Caldwell Community College & Technical Institute, Lenoir, N.C.	1	Coed	Public	834
Calgary, University of, Calgary, Alberta	4	Coed	Public	9,173
California, University of:			Public	113,420
Berkeley	4	Coed	Public	28,559
Davis	4	Coed	Public	15,294
Irvine (includes California College of Medicine, Los Angeles)	4	Coed	Public	7,384
Los Angeles	4	Coed	Public	29,654
Riverside	4	Coed	Public	5,509
San Diego	4	Coed	Public	7,069
Santa Barbara	4	Coed	Public	12,300
Santa Cruz	4	Coed	Public	4,807
California College of Arts & Crafts, Oakland, Calif.	3	Coed	Private	1,559
California Institute of Technology, Pasadena, Calif.	4	Coed	Private	1,515
California Institute of the Arts, Burbank, Calif.	3	Coed	Private	978
California Lutheran College, Thousand Oaks, Calif.	3	Coed	Pvt-Lutheran	1,363
California Polytechnic State University, San Luis Obispo, Calif.	3	Coed	Public	12,672
California State College, Bakersfield, Calif.	3	Coed	Public	2,770
California State College, Dominguez Hills, Calif.	3	Coed	Public	4,910
California State College, San Bernardino, Calif.	3	Coed	Public	3,217
California State College, Sonoma, Calif.	3	Coed	Public	6,310
California State College, Stanislaus, Calif.	3	Coed	Public	6,433
California State College, California, Pa.	3	Coed	Public	5,439
California State Polytechnic College, Pomona, Calif.	3	Coed	Public	11,016
California State University, Chico, Calif.	3	Coed	Public	13,200
California State University, Fresno, Calif.	3	Coed	Public	16,872
California State University, Fullerton, Calif.	3	Coed	Public	18,844
California State University, Hayward, Calif.	3	Coed	Public	15,520
California State University, Humboldt, Calif.	3	Coed	Public	
California State University, Long Beach, Calif.	3	Coed	Public	30,366
California State University, Los Angeles, Calif.	3	Coed	Public	25,330
California State University, Northridge, Calif.	3	Coed	Public	26,210
California State University, Sacramento, Calif.	3	Coed	Public	20,252
California State University, San Diego, Calif.	3	Coed	Public	31,767
California State University, San Francisco, Calif.	3	Coed	Public	32,665
California State University, San Jose, Calif.	3	Coed	Public	31,951
Calvin College, Grand Rapids, Mich.	3	Coed	Pvt-Christian Reformed	3,185
Camden County College, Blackwood, N.J.	1	Coed	Public	4,303
Cameron College, Lawton, Okla.	2	Coed	Public	3,997
Campbell College, Buies Creek, N.C.	2	Coed	Pvt-Baptist	2,341
Campbellsville College, Campbellsville, Ky.	2	Coed	Pvt-Baptist	743
Cañada College, Redwood City, Calif.	1	Coed	Public	6,346
Canal Zone College, Balboa, C.Z.	1	Coed	Public	1,476
Canisius College, Buffalo, N.Y.	3	Coed	Pvt-Roman Catholic	4,483
Canyons, College of the, Valencia, Calif.	1	Coed	Public	1,885
Cape Cod Community College, West Barnstable, Mass.	1	Coed	Public	2,369
Capital University, Columbus, Ohio	2	Coed	Pvt-Lutheran	2,487
Cardinal Stritch College, Milwaukee, Wis.	2	Coed	Pvt-Roman Catholic	907
Carleton College, Northfield, Minn.	2	Coed	Private	1,552
Carleton University, Ottawa, Ontario	4	Coed	Public	8,454
Carlow College, Pittsburgh, Pa.	2	Coed	Pvt-Roman Catholic	1,065
Carnegie-Mellon University, Pittsburgh, Pa.	4	Coed	Private	4,403

Name and Location	Level of Instruction	Student Body	Control	Enrollment
Carroll College, Helena, Mont.	2	Coed	Public	1,015
Carroll College, Waukesha, Wis.	2	Coed	Pvt-Presbyterian	1,229
Carson-Newman College, Jefferson City, Tenn.	2	Coed	Pvt-Baptist	1,694
Carthage College, Kenosha, Wis.	2	Coed	Pvt-Lutheran	1,648
Case Western Reserve University, Cleveland, Ohio.	4	Coed	Private	9,068
Casper College, Casper, Wyo.	1	Coed	Public	2,740
Castleton State College, Castleton, Vt.	2	Coed	Public	1,534
Catawba College, Salisbury, N.C.	2	Coed	Pvt-United Church of Christ	1,164
Catawba Valley Technical Institute, Hickory, N.C.	1	Coed	Public	1,139
Catholic University of America, Washington, D.C.	4	Coed	Pvt-Roman Catholic	6,654
Catholic University of Puerto Rico, Ponce, P.R.	3	Coed	Pvt-Roman Catholic	6,930
Catonsville Community College, Catonsville, Md.	1	Coed	Public	7,279
Cedar Crest College, Allentown, Pa.	2	W	Pvt-Church of Christ	785
Centenary College, Shreveport, La.	2	Coed	Pvt-Methodist	787
Central Arizona College, Coolidge, Ariz.	1	Coed	Public	3,891
Central College, Pella, Iowa.	2	Coed	Pvt-Episcopal	1,211
Central Connecticut State College, New Britain, Conn.	3	Coed	Public	12,412
Central Florida Community College, Ocala, Fla.	1	Coed	Public	1,432
Central Methodist College, Fayette, Mo.	2	Coed	Pvt-Methodist	744
Central Michigan University, Mt. Pleasant, Mich.	3	Coed	Public	14,317
Central Missouri State University, Warrensburg, Mo.	3	Coed	Public	12,308
Central Oregon Community College, Bend, Oreg.	1	Coed	Public	1,083
Central Piedmont Community College, Charlotte, N.C.	1	Coed	Public	9,301
Central State University, Wilberforce, Ohio.	2	Coed	Public	2,385
Central State University, Edmond, Okla.	3	Coed	Public	10,481
Central Texas College, Killeen, Texas.	1	Coed	Public	4,834
Central Virginia Community College, Lynchburg, Va.	1	Coed	Public	1,892
Central Washington State College, Ellensburg, Wash.	3	Coed	Public	8,355
Central Y.M.C.A. Community College, Chicago, Ill.	1	Coed	Private	4,444
Cerritos College, Norwalk, Calif.	1	Coed	Public	2,680
Chabot College, Hayward, Calif.	1	Coed	Public	18,051
Chadron State College, Chadron, Nebr.	3	Coed	Public	12,741
Chaffey College, Alta Loma, Calif.	1	Coed	Public	2,122
Chaminade College of Honolulu, Hawaii.	3	Coed	Pvt-Roman Catholic	8,345
Champlain College, Burlington, Vt.	1	Coed	Private	1,719
Chapman College, Orange, Calif.	3	Coed	Pvt-Disciples of Christ	1,100
Charles County Community College, La Plata, Md.	1	Coed	Public	4,127
Charles Stewart Mott Community College, Flint, Mich.	1	Coed	Public	13,187
Charleston, College of, Charleston, S.C.	2	Coed	Public	1,300
Chattanooga State Technical College, Chattanooga, Tenn.	1	Coed	Public	3,014
Chemeketa Community College, Salem, Oreg.	1	Coed	Public	1,238
Chesapeake College, Wye Mills, Md.	1	Coed	Public	5,295
Chestnut Hill College, Philadelphia, Pa.	2	W	Pvt-Roman Catholic	862
Cheyney State College, Cheyney, Pa.	2	Coed	Public	2,278
Chicago, City Colleges of, Chicago, Ill.		Coed	Public	46,725
Kennedy-King College, Chicago.	1	Coed	Public	7,868
Loop College, Chicago.	1	Coed	Public	6,931
Malcolm X College, Chicago.	1	Coed	Public	3,779
Mayfair College, Chicago.	1	Coed	Public	4,566
Olive-Harvey College, Chicago.	1	Coed	Public	5,165
Southwest College, Chicago.	1	Coed	Public	8,014
Wilbur Wright College, Chicago.	1	Coed	Public	
Chicago, University of, Chicago, Ill.	4	Coed	Private	8,497
Chicago State University, Chicago, Ill.	3	Coed	Public	5,634
Chipola Junior College, Marianna, Fla.	1	Coed	Public	1,102
Chowan College, Murfreesboro, N.C.	2	Coed	Pvt-Baptist	1,224
Christian Brothers College, Memphis, Tenn.	2	Coed	Pvt-Roman Catholic	862
Christopher Newport College, Newport News, Va.	2	Coed	Public	2,305
Cincinnati, University of, Cincinnati, Ohio.	4	Coed	Public	36,104
Raymond Walters General & Technical College, Cincinnati.				1,890
Cisco Junior College, Cisco, Texas.	1	Coed	Public	930
Citadel, The, Charleston, S.C.	3	Coed	Public	2,884
Citrus College, Azusa, Calif.	1	Coed	Public	8,150
Clackamas Community College, Oregon City, Oreg.	1	Coed	Public	4,117
Claflin College, Orangeburg, S.C.	2	Coed	Pvt-Methodist	713
Claremont Men's College, Claremont, Calif.	2	M	Private	852
Claremore Junior College, Claremore, Okla.	1	Coed	Public	1,049
Clarion State College, Clarion, Pa.	3	Coed	Public	4,717
Clark College, Atlanta, Ga.	2	Coed	Pvt-Methodist	1,236
Clark College, Vancouver, Wash.	1	Coed	Public	4,355
Clark University, Worcester, Mass.	4	Coed	Private	3,194
Clarkson College of Technology, Potsdam, N.Y.	4	Coed	Private	2,434
Clatsop Community College, Astoria, Oreg.	1	Coed	Public	1,937
Clayton Junior College, Morrow, Ga.	1	Coed	Public	2,339
Clemson University, Clemson, S.C.	4	Coed	Public	9,757
Cleveland Institute of Art, Cleveland, Ohio.	2	Coed	Private	822
Cleveland State Community College, Cleveland, Tenn.	1	Coed	Public	2,170
Cleveland State University, Cleveland, Ohio.	4	Coed	Public	14,712
Cochise College, Douglas, Ariz.	1	Coed	Public	2,575
Coe College, Cedar Rapids, Iowa.	2	Coed	Pvt-Presbyterian	1,181
Colby College, Waterville, Me.	3	Coed	Private	1,654
Colby Community College, Colby, Kans.	1	Coed	Public	881
Colgate University, Hamilton, N.Y.	3	Coed	Private	2,519
Colorado, University of, Boulder, Colo.	4	Coed	Public	32,726
Colorado Springs.	3	Coed	Public	2,603
Denver.	3	Coed	Public	6,872
Colorado College, Colorado Springs, Colo.	3	Coed	Private	1,792
Colorado School of Mines, Golden, Colo.	4	Coed	Public	1,688
Colorado State University, Fort Collins, Colo.	4	Coed	Public	17,427
Colorado Women's College, Denver, Colo.	2	W	Private	896
Columbia Basin College, Pasco, Wash.	1	Coed	Public	3,754
Columbia College, Columbia, Mo.	2	Coed	Pvt-Disciples of Christ	784
Columbia College, Columbia, S.C.	2	Coed	Pvt-Methodist	968
Columbia Junior College, Columbia, Calif.	1	Coed	Public	1,677
Columbia State Community College, Columbia, Tenn.	1	Coed	Public	1,504
Columbia Union College, Takoma Park, Md.	4	Coed	Pvt-Seventh-day Adventist	901
Columbia University, New York, N.Y.	4	Coed	Private	15,157
Barnard College, New York.	2	W	Private	1,972
Teachers College, New York.	4	Coed	Private	5,493
Columbus College, Columbus, Ga.	3	Coed	Public	4,097
Columbus Technical Institute, Columbus, Ohio.	2	Coed	Public	2,059
Community College of Allegheny County, Pittsburgh, Pa.:				
Allegheny Campus.	1	Coed	Public	6,692
Boyce Campus.	1	Coed	Public	4,355
Community College of Allegheny County, South Campus, West Mifflin, Pa.	1	Coed	Public	2,624
Community College of Baltimore, Md.	1	Coed	Public	7,135
Community College of Beaver County, Monaca, Pa.	1	Coed	Public	2,743
Community College of Philadelphia, Pa.	1	Coed	Public	6,446
Compton Community College, Compton, Calif.	1	Coed	Public	6,052
Concord College, Athens, W. Va.	2	Coed	Public	1,855
Concordia College, Moorhead, Minn.	2	Coed	Pvt-Lutheran	2,439
Concordia Teachers College, River Forest, Ill.	3	Coed	Pvt-Lutheran	1,593
Concordia Teachers College, Seward, Nebr.	3	Coed	Pvt-Lutheran	1,539
Connecticut, University of, Storrs, Conn.	4	Coed	Public	20,514
Connecticut College, New London, Conn.	3	Coed	Private	2,044
Connors State College, Warner, Okla.	1	Coed	Public	924
Contra Costa College, San Pablo, Calif.	1	Coed	Public	7,622
Converse College, Spartanburg, S.C.	3	W	Private	1,093
Cooke County Junior College, Gainesville, Texas.	1	Coed	Public	2,292
Cooper Union, New York, N.Y.	4	Coed	Private	1,051
Copiah-Lincoln Junior College, Wesson, Miss.	1	Coed	Public	1,543
Coppin State College, Baltimore, Md.	2	Coed	Public	2,585
Cornell College, Mount Vernon, Iowa.	2	Coed	Pvt-Methodist	905
Cornell University, Ithaca, N.Y.	4	Coed	Private	16,546
Corning Community College, Corning, N.Y.	1	Coed	Public	2,428
Costal Carolina Community College, Jacksonville, N.C.	1	Coed	Public	1,080
Cosumnes River College, Sacramento, Calif.	1	Coed	Public	3,021
Creighton University, Omaha, Nebr.	4	Coed	Pvt-Roman Catholic	4,341

Name and Location	Level of Instruction	Student Body	Control	Enrollment
Cuesta College, San Luis Obispo, Calif.	1	Coed	Public	3,665
Cumberland College, Williamsburg, Ky.	1	Coed	Pvt-Baptist	1,751
Cumberland County College, Vineland, N.J.	1	Coed	Public	1,465
Curry College, Milton, Mass.	2	Coed	Private	1,062
Cuyahoga Community College—Metropolitan Campus, Cleveland, Ohio	1	Coed	Public	10,587
Cuyahoga Community College—Western Campus, Parma, Ohio	1	Coed	Public	7,037
Cypress College, Cypress, Calif.	1	Coed	Public	8,303
Dakota State College, Madison, S. Dak.	2	Coed	Public	972
Dalhousie University, Halifax, Nova Scotia	4	Coed	Private	6,103
Dallas, University of, Dallas, Texas	2	Coed	Pvt-Roman Catholic	1,530
Dallas Baptist College, Dallas, Texas	2	Coed	Pvt-Baptist	1,476
Dalton Junior College, Dalton, Ga.	1	Coed	Public	1,262
Dana College, Blair, Nebr.	2	Coed	Pvt-Lutheran	752
Danville Community College, Danville, Va.	1	Coed	Public	1,960
Danville Junior College, Danville, Ill.	1	Coed	Public	3,049
Dartmouth College, Hanover, N.H.	4	Coed	Private	4,139
David Lipscomb College, Nashville, Tenn.	2	Coed	Pvt-Church of Christ	2,061
Davidson College, Davidson, N.C.	2	M	Pvt-Presbyterian	1,118
Davidson County Community College, Lexington, N.C.	1	Coed	Public	5,769
Davis and Elkins College, Elkins, W.Va.	2	Coed	Pvt-Presbyterian	800
Dayton, University of, Dayton, Ohio	4	Coed	Pvt-Roman Catholic	8,272
Daytona Beach Community College, Daytona Beach, Fla.	1	Coed	Public	2,621
Dean Junior College, Franklin, Mass.	1	Coed	Private	1,003
De Anza College, Cupertino, Calif.	1	Coed	Public	6,348
Defiance College, Defiance, Ohio	2	Coed	Pvt-Church of Christ	941
DeKalb College, Clarkston, Ga.	1	Coed	Public	7,197
Del Mar College, Corpus Christi, Texas	1	Coed	Public	1,570
Delaware, University of, Newark, Del.	4	Coed	Public	17,470
Delaware County Community College, Media, Pa.	1	Coed	Public	2,654
Delaware State College, Dover, Del.	2	Coed	Public	1,908
Delaware Technical and Community College, Northern Branch, Wilmington, Del.	1	Coed	Public	2,521
Southern Branch, Georgetown, Del.	1	Coed	Public	2,032
Delaware Valley College of Science & Agriculture, Doylestown, Pa.	2	Coed	Private	1,284
Delgado Vocational-Technical Junior College, New Orleans, La.	1	Coed	Public	5,030
Delta College, University Center, Mich.	1	Coed	Public	6,123
Delta State College, Cleveland, Miss.	3	Coed	Public	3,392
Denison University, Granville, Ohio	2	Coed	Pvt-Baptist	2,155
Denver, University of, Denver, Colo.	4	Coed	Private	8,937
DePaul University, Chicago, Ill.	4	Coed	Pvt-Roman Catholic	9,311
DePauw University, Greencastle, Ind	3	Coed	Pvt-Methodist	2,350
Desert, College of the, Palm Desert, Calif.	1	Coed	Public	5,239
Detroit, University of, Detroit, Mich.	4	Coed	Pvt-Roman Catholic	9,308
Detroit Institute of Technology, Detroit, Mich.	2	Coed	Private	995
Diablo Valley College, Pleasant Hill, Calif.	1	Coed	Public	15,258
Dickinson College, Carlisle, Pa.	2	Coed	Public	1,726
Dickinson State College, Dickinson, N.Dak.	2	Coed	Public	1,280
District of Columbia Teachers College, Washington, D.C.	2	Coed	Public	1,007
District One Technical Institute, Eau Claire, Wis.	1	Coed	Public	2,945
Dixie College, St. George, Utah	1	Coed	Public	2,056
Dodge City Community College, Dodge City, Kans.	1	Coed	Public	1,220
Dominican College of San Rafael, San Rafael, Calif.	3	Coed	Pvt-Roman Catholic	759
Dordt College, Sioux Center, Iowa	2	Coed	Pvt-Christian Reformed	958
Dowling College, Oakdale, N.Y.	2	Coed	Private	955
Drake University, Des Moines, Iowa	4	Coed	Private	7,521
Drew University, Madison, N.J.	4	Coed	Pvt-Methodist	1,798
Drexel University, Philadelphia, Pa.	4	Coed	Private	8,393
Drury College, Springfield, Mo.	3	Coed	Pvt-Church of Christ	2,322
Duke University, Durham, N.C. (incl. Trinity College & Woman's College)	4	Coord	Pvt-Methodist	8,732
DuPage, College of, Glen Ellyn, Ill.	1	Coed	Public	9,091
Duquesne University, Pittsburgh, Pa.	4	Coed	Pvt-Roman Catholic	8,525
Durham Technical Institute, Durham, N.C.	1	Coed	Public	1,189
Dutchess Community College, Poughkeepsie, N.Y.	1	Coed	Public	4,300
Dyersburg State Community College, Dyersburg, Tenn.	1	Coed	Public	753
D'Youville College, Buffalo, N.Y.	2	Coed	Pvt-Roman Catholic	1,239
Earlham College, Richmond, Ind.	2	Coed	Pvt-Friends	1,148
East Carolina University, Greenville, N.C.	3	Coed	Public	11,001
East Central State College, Ada, Okla.	3	Coed	Public	3,082
East Los Angeles College, Los Angeles, Calif.	1	Coed	Public	14,042
East Mississippi Junior College, Scooba, Miss.	1	Coed	Public	1,672
East Stroudsburg State College, East Stroudsburg, Pa.	3	Coed	Public	3,643
East Tennessee State University, Johnson City, Tenn.	4	Coed	Public	9,511
East Texas Baptist College, Marshall, Texas	2	Coed	Pvt-Baptist	740
East Texas State University, Commerce, Texas	4	Coed	Public	8,961
Eastern Arizona College, Thatcher, Ariz.	1	Coed	Public	2,069
Eastern Connecticut State College, Willimantic, Conn.	3	Coed	Public	2,899
Eastern Illinois University, Charleston, Ill.	3	Coed	Public	8,857
Eastern Kentucky University, Richmond, Ky.	3	Coed	Public	10,559
Eastern Mennonite College, Harrisonburg, Va.	3	Coed	Pvt-Mennonite	904
Eastern Michigan University, Ypsilanti, Mich.	3	Coed	Public	20,686
Eastern Montana College, Billings, Mont.	3	Coed	Public	2,786
Eastern Nazarene College, Quincy, Mass.	3	Coed	Pvt-Nazarene	901
Eastern New Mexico University, Portales, N.Mex.	3	Coed	Public	4,298
Eastern New Mexico University-Roswell Campus, N.Mex.	1	Coed	Public	4,342
Eastern Oklahoma State College, Wilburton, Okla.	1	Coed	Public	1,658
Eastern Oregon College, La Grande, Oreg.	3	Coed	Public	1,561
Eastern Washington State College, Cheney, Wash.	3	Coed	Public	7,084
Eastfield College, Mesquite, Texas	1	Coed	Public	6,214
Eckerd College, St. Petersburg, Fla.	2	Coed	Pvt-Presbyterian	996
Edgecliff College, Edgecliff, Ohio	2	Coed	Pvt-Roman Catholic	898
Edinboro State College, Edinboro, Pa.	3	Coed	Public	7,340
Edison Junior College, Fort Myers, Fla.	1	Coed	Public	1,898
El Camino College, Torrance, Calif.	1	Coed	Public	22,483
El Centro College, Dallas, Texas	1	Coed	Public	5,020
Elgin Community College, Elgin, Ill.	1	Coed	Public	3,013
Elizabeth City State University, Elizabeth City, N.C.	2	Coed	Public	1,109
Elizabethtown College, Elizabethtown, Pa.	2	Coed	Pvt-Brethren	1,770
Ellsworth Community College, Iowa Falls, Iowa	1	Coed	Public	915
Elmhurst College, Elmhurst, Ill.	2	Coed	Pvt-Church of Christ	2,701
Elmira College, Elmira, N.Y.	3	Coed	Private	3,025
Elon College, Elon College, N.C.	2	Coed	Pvt-Church of Christ	1,873
Embry-Riddle Aeronautical Institute, Daytona Beach, Fla.	3	Coed	Private	1,604
Emerson College, Boston, Mass.	3	Coed	Private	1,857
Emmanuel College, Boston, Mass.	2	Coed	Pvt-Roman Catholic	1,144
Emory and Henry College, Emory, Va.	2	Coed	Pvt-Methodist	917
Emory University, Atlanta, Ga.	4	Coed	Pvt-Methodist	6,267
Enterprise State Junior College, Enterprise, Ala.	1	Coed	Public	1,952
Erie Community College, Buffalo, N.Y.	1	Coed	Public	5,330
Essex Community College, Baltimore, Md.	1	Coed	Public	1,219
Evangel College, Springfield, Mo.	2	Coed	Pvt-Assemblies of God	5,369
Evansville, University of, Evansville, Ind.	2	Coed	Pvt-Methodist	5,377
Everett Community College, Everett, Wash.	1	Coed	Public	
Fairfield University, Fairfield, Conn.	3	Coed	Pvt-Roman Catholic	3,993
Fairleigh Dickinson University, Teaneck, Madison, Rutherford, N.J.	4	Coed	Private	18,842
Fairmont State College, Fairmont, W.Va.	2	Coed	Public	3,502
Fashion Institute of Technology, New York, N.Y.	2	Coed	Public	5,389
Fayetteville State University, Fayetteville, N.C.	2	Coed	Public	1,643
Fayetteville Technical Institute, Fayetteville, N.C.	1	Coed	Public	2,566
Feather River College, Quincy, Calif.	1	Coed	Public	832

Name and Location	Level of Instruction	Student Body	Control	Enrollment
Ferrum College, Ferrum, Va.	1	Coed	Pvt-Methodist	1,219
Findlay College, Findlay, Ohio	2	Coed	Pvt-Church of God	1,060
Fisk University, Nashville, Tenn.	3	Coed	Private	1,557
Fitchburg State College, Fitchburg, Mass.	3	Coed	Public	3,705
Flathead Valley Community College, Kalispell, Mont.	1	Coed	Public	1,110
Florence State University, Florence, Ala.	3	Coed	Public	3,489
Florence-Darlington Technical Education Center, Florence, S.C.	1	Coed	Public	2,075
Florida, University of, Gainesville, Fla.	4	Coed	Public	23,570
Florida Agricultural & Mechanical University, Tallahassee, Fla.	3	Coed	Public	5,028
Florida Atlantic University, Boca Raton, Fla.	3	Coed	Public	5,681
Florida Institute of Technology, Melbourne, Fla.	3	Coed	Private	2,268
Florida Junior College at Jacksonville, Fla.	1	Coed	Public	9,194
Florida Keys Community College, Key West, Fla.	1	Coed	Public	765
Florida Memorial College, Miami, Fla.	2	Coed	Pvt-Baptist	1,463
Florida Southern College, Lakeland, Fla.	2	Coed	Pvt-Methodist	
Florida State University, Tallahassee, Fla.	4	Coed	Public	19,160
Florida Technological University, Orlando, Fla.	3	Coed	Public	7,405
Floyd Junior College, Rome, Ga.	1	Coed	Public	1,003
Foothill College, Los Altos Hills, Calif.	1	Coed	Public	5,712
Fordham University, Bronx, N.Y.	4	Coed	Pvt-Roman Catholic	13,863
Forsyth Technical Institute, Winston-Salem, N.C.	1	Coed	Public	1,017
Fort Hays Kansas State College, Hays, Kans.	3	Coed	Public	5,058
Fort Lewis College, Durango, Colo.	3	Coed	Public	3,681
Fort Steilacoom Community College, Lakewood Center, Tacoma, Wash.	1	Coed	Public	
Fort Valley State College, Fort Valley, Ga.	3	Coed	Public	2,071
Framingham State College, Framingham, Mass.	3	Coed	Public	4,520
Francis Marion College, Florence, S.C.	3	Coed	Public	1,658
Franklin & Marshall College, Lancaster, Pa.	3	Coed	Private	2,691
Franklin College, Franklin, Ind.	2	Coed	Pvt-Church of Christ	961
Franklin Pierce College, Rindge, N.H.	1	Coed	Private	880
Frederick Community College, Frederick, Md.	1	Coed	Public	1,089
Freed-Hardeman College, Henderson, Tenn.	2	Coed	Pvt-Church of Christ	905
Fresno City College, Fresno, Calif.	1	Coed	Public	13,901
Friends University, Wichita, Kans.	3	Coed	Pvt-Friends	901
Frostburg State College, Frostburg, Md.	3	Coed	Public	2,933
Fullerton College, Fullerton, Calif.	1	Coed	Public	17,060
Fulton-Montgomery Community College, Johnstown, N.Y.	1	Coed	Public	2,279
Furman University, Greenville, S.C.	3	Coed	Pvt-Baptist	
Gadsden State Junior College, Gadsden, Ala.	1	Coed	Public	3,021
Gainesville Junior College, Gainesville, Ga.	1	Coed	Public	1,123
Gallaudet College, Washington, D.C.	3	Coed	Private	1,087
Galveston College, Galveston, Texas.	1	Coed	Public	1,596
Gannon College, Erie, Pa.	3	Coed	Pvt-Roman Catholic	3,491
Gardner-Webb College, Boiling Springs, N.C.	2	Coed	Pvt-Baptist	1,436
Gaston College, Dallas, N.C.	1	Coed	Public	1,923
Gateway Technical Institute, Kenosha, Wis.	1	Coed	Public	3,536
Gavilan College, Gilroy, Calif.	1	Coed	Public	1,867
General Motors Institute, Flint, Mich.	3	Coed	Private	3,018
Genesee Community College, Batavia, N.Y.	1	Coed	Public	1,873
Geneva College, Beaver Falls, Pa.	2	Coed	Pvt-Presbyterian	1,493
George C. Wallace State Technical Junior College, Dothan, Ala.	1	Coed	Public	1,707
George Mason University, Fairfax, Va.	3	Coed	Public	4,223
George Peabody College for Teachers, Nashville, Tenn.	4	Coed	Private	1,959
George Washington University, Washington, D.C.	4	Coed	Private	20,705
George Williams College, Downers Grove, Ill.	3	Coed	Private	1,083
Georgetown College, Georgetown, Ky.	2	Coed	Pvt-Baptist	1,261
Georgetown University, Washington, D.C.	4	Coed	Pvt-Roman Catholic	9,856
Georgia, University of, Athens, Ga.	4	Coed	Public	22,598
Georgia College, Milledgeville, Ga.	3	Coed	Public	2,551
Georgia Institute of Technology, Atlanta, Ga.	3	Coed	Public	8,048
Southern Technical Institute, Marietta, Ga.	2	Coed	Public	1,627
Georgia Southern College, Statesboro, Ga.	3	Coed	Public	6,181
Georgia Southwestern College, Americus, Ga.	2	Coed	Public	2,354
Georgia State University, Atlanta, Ga.	4	Coed	Public	16,955
Germanna Community College, Fredericksburg, Va.	1	Coed	Public	1,006
Gettysburg College, Gettysburg, Pa.	2	Coed	Pvt-Lutheran	1,902
Glassboro State College, Glassboro, N.J.	3	Coed	Public	11,051
Glendale Community College, Glendale, Ariz.	1	Coed	Public	7,090
Glendale Community College, Glendale, Calif.	1	Coed	Public	6,593
Glenville State College, Glenville, W.Va.	2	Coed	Public	1,543
Gloucester County College, Sewell, N.J.	1	Coed	Public	1,924
Goddard College, Plainfield, Vt.	3	Coed	Private	1,922
Golden Gate University, San Francisco, Calif.	3	Coed	Private	5,581
Golden West College, Huntington Beach, Calif.	1	Coed	Public	12,700
Gonzaga University, Spokane, Wash.	3	Coed	Pvt-Roman Catholic	2,932
Gordon College, Wenham, Mass.	2	Coed	Private	1,257
Goshen College, Goshen, Ind.	2	Coed	Pvt-Mennonite	1,257
Goucher College, Baltimore, Md.	2	Coed	Private	1,027
Graceland College, Lamoni, Iowa.	1	Coed	Private[1]	1,271
Grambling College, Grambling, La.	3	Coed	Public	3,888
Grand Canyon College, Phoenix, Ariz.	2	Coed	Pvt-Baptist	772
Grand Rapids Junior College, Grand Rapids, Mich.	1	Coed	Public	5,319
Grand Valley State College, Allendale, Mich.	3	Coed	Public	5,218
Grand View College, Des Moines, Iowa.	1	Coed	Pvt-Lutheran	825
Grays Harbor College, Aberdeen, Wash.	1	Coed	Public	2,837
Grayson County College, Denison, Texas.	1	Coed	Public	2,752
Great Falls, College of, Great Falls, Mont.	2	Coed	Pvt-Roman Catholic	980
Green River Community College, Auburn, Wash.	1	Coed	Public	4,599
Greenfield Community College, Greenfield, Mass.	1	Coed	Public	1,645
Greenville College, Greenville, Ill.	2	Coed	Pvt-Methodist	902
Greenville Technical Education Center, Greenville, S.C.	1	Coed	Public	3,963
Grinnell College, Grinnell, Iowa.	2	Coed	Private	1,314
Grossmont College, El Cajon, Calif.	1	Coed	Public	12,474
Grove City College, Grove City, Pa.	2	Coed	Pvt-Presbyterian	2,130
Guam, University of, Agana, Guam.	3	Coed	Public	2,990
Guelph, University of, Guelph, Ont.	4	Coed	Public	7,310
Guilford College, Greensboro, N.C.	2	Coed	Pvt-Friends	1,411
Guilford Technical Institute, Jamestown, N.C.	1	Coed	Public	1,834
Gulf Coast College, Panama City, Fla.	1	Coed	Public	2,248
Gustavus Adolphus College, St. Peter, Minn.	2	Coed	Pvt-Lutheran	1,941
Gwynedd-Mercy College, Gwynedd Valley, Pa.	2	Coed	Pvt-Roman Catholic	864
Hagerstown Junior College, Hagerstown, Md.	1	Coed	Public	1,422
Hamilton College, Clinton, N.Y.	2	M	Private	932
Hamline University, St. Paul, Minn.	2	Coed	Pvt-Methodist	1,351
Hampden-Sydney College, Hampden-Sydney, Va.	2	M	Pvt-Presbyterian	721
Hampton Institute, Hampton, Va.	3	Coed	Private	2,676
Hanover College, Hanover, Ind.	2	Coed	Pvt-Presbyterian	1,011
Hardin-Simmons University, Abilene, Texas.	3	Coed	Pvt-Baptist	1,624
Harding College, Searcy, Ark.	3	Coed	Pvt-Church of Christ	2,095
Harford Community College, Bel Air, Md.	1	Coed	Public	2,618
Harris Teachers College, St. Louis, Mo.	2	Coed	Public	1,069
Harrisburg Area Community College, Harrisburg, Pa.	1	Coed	Public	4,149
Hartford, University of, West Hartford, Conn.	4	Coed	Private	6,946
Hartford State Technical College, Hartford, Conn.	1	Coed	Public	1,623
Hartnell College, Salinas, Calif.	1	Coed	Public	2,859
Hartwick College, Oneonta, N.Y.	2	Coed	Private	1,725
Harvard University, Cambridge, Mass.	4	Coed	Private	19,322
Hastings College, Hastings, Nebr.	2	Coed	Pvt-Presbyterian	754
Hawaii, Church College of, Oahu, Hawaii.	2	Coed	Pvt-Latter-day Saints	1,078
Hawaii, University of, Honolulu, Hawaii.	4	Coed	Public	22,320
Hawaii Community College, Hilo, Hawaii.	1	Coed	Public	1,148
Heidelberg College, Tiffin, Ohio.	2	Coed	Pvt-Church of Christ	1,210
Henderson County Junior College, Athens, Texas.	1	Coed	Public	1,312
Henderson State College, Arkadelphia, Ark.	3	Coed	Public	3,285
Hendrix College, Conway, Ark.	2	Coed	Pvt-Methodist	1,039

1 Reorganized Church of Jesus Christ of Latter Day Saints.

Name and Location	Level of Instruction	Student Body	Control	Enrollment
Henry Ford Community College, Dearborn, Mich.	1	Coed	Public	11,187
Herkimer County Community College, Herkimer, N.Y.	1	Coed	Public	1,172
High Point College, High Point, N.C.	2	Coed	Pvt-Methodist	1,086
Highland Community College, Freeport, Ill.	1	Coed	Public	1,201
Highland Park Community College, Highland Park, Mich.	1	Coed	Public	3,624
Highline Community College, Midway, Wash.	1	Coed	Public	6,727
Hillsborough Community College, Tampa, Fla.	1	Coed	Public	6,062
Hillsdale College, Hillsdale, Mich.	2	Coed	Private	1,090
Hilo College, University of Hawaii at Hilo, Hawaii	2	Coed	Public	2,044
Hinds Junior College, Raymond, Miss.	1	Coed	Public	3,964
Hiram College, Hiram, Ohio	2	Coed	Pvt-Disciples of Christ	1,335
Hobart & William Smith Colleges, Geneva, N.Y.	2	Coord	Private	1,614
Hofstra University, Hempstead, L.I., N.Y.	4	Coed	Private	12,406
Hollins College, Hollins College, Va.	3	Coed	Private	1,132
Holmes Junior College, Goodman, Miss.	1	Coed	Public	1,055
Holy Cross, College of the, Worcester, Mass.	3	Coed	Pvt-Roman Catholic	2,607
Holy Family College, Philadelphia, Pa.	3	W	Pvt-Roman Catholic	780
Holy Names College, Oakland, Calif.	3	Coed	Pvt-Roman Catholic	735
Holyoke Community College, Holyoke, Mass.	1	Coed	Public	3,177
Honolulu Community College, Honolulu, Hawaii	1	Coed	Public	2,523
Hope College, Holland, Mich.	2	Coed	Pvt-Reformed	2,124
Horry-Georgetown Technical Education Center, Conway, S.C.	1	Coed	Public	1,310
Houghton College, Houghton, N.Y.	2	Coed	Pvt-Methodist	1,215
Housatonic Community College, Bridgeport, Conn	1	Coed	Public	2,413
Houston, University of, Houston, Texas	4	Coed	Public	26,473
Houston Baptist College, Houston, Texas	2	Coed	Pvt-Baptist	1,143
Howard County Junior College, Big Spring, Texas	1	Coed	Public	1,053
Howard Payne College, Brownwood, Texas	3	Coed	Pvt-Baptist	1,525
Howard University, Washington, D.C.	4	Coed	Public-Private	9,850
Hudson Valley Community College, Troy, N.Y.	1	Coed	Public	6,089
Hutchinson Community Junior College, Hutchinson, Kans.	1	Coed	Public	2,231
Idaho, College of, Caldwell, Idaho	3	Coed	Pvt-Presbyterian	962
Idaho, University of, Moscow, Idaho	3	Coed	Public	7,118
Idaho State University, Pocatello, Idaho	4	Coed	Public	6,018
Illinois, University of, Urbana & Chicago, Ill.	4	Coed	Public	59,698
Illinois, University of, at the Medical Center, Chicago, Ill.	4	Coed	Public	3,688
Urbana-Champaign, Urbana, Ill.	4	Coed	Public	35,307
Illinois Benedictine College, Lisle, Ill.	2	Coed	Pvt-Roman Catholic	1,110
Illinois Central College, East Peoria, Ill.	1	Coed	Public	8,834
Illinois, Jacksonville, Ill.	2	Coed	Pvt-Presbyterian and Church of Christ	840
Illinois Institute of Technology, Chicago, Ill.	4	Coed	Private	6,375
Illinois State University, Normal, Ill.	4	Coed	Public	18,819
Illinois Valley Community College, Oglesby, Ill.	1	Coed	Public	2,630
Illinois Wesleyan University, Bloomington, Ill.	2	Coed	Pvt-Methodist	1,717
Immaculata College, Immaculata, Pa.	3	Coed	Pvt-Roman Catholic	1,000
Imperial Valley College, Imperial, Calif.	1	Coed	Public	2,881
Incarnate Word College, San Antonio, Texas	3	Coed	Pvt-Roman Catholic	1,554
Indian River Community College, Fort Pierce, Fla.	1	Coed	Public	2,133
Indiana Central College, Indianapolis, Ind.	3	Coed	Pvt-Methodist	2,289
Indiana State University, Terre Haute, Ind.	4	Coed	Public	13,014
Indiana University, Bloomington, Ind.	4	Coed	Public	31,280
Indiana University Regional Campuses		Coed	Public	
East at Richmond	2	Coed	Public	704
Fort Wayne	3	Coed	Public	4,640
Kokomo	2	Coed	Public	2,088
Northwest at Gary	3	Coed	Public	4,781
Purdue at Indianapolis	4	Coed	Public	16,938
South Bend	3	Coed	Public	5,339
Southeast at Jeffersonville	2	Coed	Public	2,745
Indiana University of Pennsylvania, Indiana, Pa.	3	Coed	Public	10,788
Insurance, College of, New York, N.Y.	2	Coed	Private	1,373
Inter American University of Puerto Rico, San Germán, P.R.	3	Coed	Private-Presbyterian	18,357
Iona College, New Rochelle, N.Y.	3	Coed	Pvt-Roman Catholic	4,371
Iowa, University of, Iowa City, Iowa	4	Coed	Public	20,709
Iowa State University of Science and Technology, Ames, Iowa	4	Coed	Public	19,628
Itawamba Junior College, Fulton, Miss.	1	Coed	Public	930
Ithaca College, Ithaca, N.Y.	3	Coed	Private	4,346
Jackson Community College, Jackson, Mich.	1	Coed	Public	3,609
Jackson State College, Jackson, Miss.	3	Coed	Public	5,100
Jackson State Community College, Jackson, Tenn.	1	Coed	Public	1,476
Jacksonville State University, Jacksonville, Ala.	3	Coed	Public	5,500
Jacksonville University, Jacksonville, Fla.	3	Coed	Private	2,584
James H. Faulkner State Junior College, Bay Minette, Ala.	1	Coed	Public	1,207
Jamestown Community College, Jamestown, N.Y.	1	Coed	Public	2,532
Jefferson College, Hillsboro, Mo.	1	Coed	Public	1,092
Jefferson Community College, Watertown, N.Y.	1	Coed	Public	1,452
Jefferson Davis State Junior College, Brewton, Ala	1	Coed	Public	1,032
Jefferson State Junior College, Birmingham, Ala.	1	Coed	Public	5,830
Jersey City State College, Jersey City, N.J	3	Coed	Public	7,190
John A. Logan College, Carterville, Ill.	1	Coed	Public	1,473
John C. Calhoun State Technical Junior College, Decatur, Ala.	1	Coed	Public	2,860
John Carroll University, Cleveland, Ohio.	3	Coed	Pvt-Roman Catholic	3,785
John Tyler Community College, Chester, Va	1	Coed	Public	1,881
Johns Hopkins University, Baltimore, Md	4	Coed	Private	9,321
Johnson C. Smith University, Charlotte, N.C.	2	Coed	Pvt-Presbyterian	1,043
Johnson State College, Johnson, Vt.	2	Coed	Public	1,142
Joliet Junior College, Joliet, Ill.	1	Coed	Public	4,662
Jones County Junior College, Ellisville, Miss.	1	Coed	Public	2,092
Juilliard School, The, New York, N.Y.	4	Coed	Private	1,165
Juniata College, Huntingdon, Pa.	2	Coed	Private	1,207
Kalamazoo College, Kalamazoo, Mich.	3	Coed	Pvt-Baptist	1,384
Kalamazoo Valley Community College, Kalamazoo, Mich.	1	Coed	Public	4,175
Kansas, University of, Lawrence, Kans.	4	Coed	Public	20,075
Kansas City Kansas Community Junior College, Kansas City, Kans.	1	Coed	Public	2,156
Kansas State College of Pittsburg, Pittsburg, Kans.	3	Coed	Public	4,948
Kansas State Teachers College, Emporia, Kans.	3	Coed	Public	6,506
Kansas State University, Manhattan, Kans.	4	Coed	Public	15,158
Kapiolani Community College, Honolulu, Hawaii	1	Coed	Public	3,001
Kaskaskia College, Centralia, Ill.	1	Coed	Public	1,400
Kauai Community College, Kauai, Hawaii	1	Coed	Public	935
Kearney State College, Kearney, Nebr.	3	Coed	Public	5,210
Keene State College, Keene, N.H.	3	Coed	Public	2,226
Kellogg Community College, Battle Creek, Mich.	1	Coed	Public	3,329
Kennesaw Junior College, Marietta, Ga.	1	Coed	Public	1,784
Kent State University, Kent, Ohio.	4	Coed	Public	19,755
Kentucky, University of, Lexington, Ky.	4	Coed	Public	23,360
Kentucky State University, Frankfort, Ky.	2	Coed	Public	1,961
Kentucky Wesleyan College, Owensboro, Ky.	2	Coed	Pvt-Methodist	772
Kenyon College, Gambier, Ohio.	2	Coed	Pvt-Episcopal	1,441
Keystone Junior College, La Plume, Pa.	1	Coed	Private	1,097
Kilgore College, Kilgore, Texas	1	Coed	Public	2,651
King's College, The, Briarcliff Manor, N.Y.	2	Coed	Private	754
King's College, Wilkes-Barre, Pa.	2	Coed	Pvt-Roman Catholic	2,481
Kirkwood Community College, Cedar Rapids, Iowa	1	Coed	Public	3,074
Knox College, Galesburg, Ill.	2	Coed	Private	1,385
Knoxville College, Knoxville, Tenn.	2	Coed	Pvt-Presbyterian	927
Kutztown State College, Kutztown, Pa.	3	Coed	Public	4,894
Lafayette College, Easton, Pa.	2	Coed	Pvt-Presbyterian	2,213
Lake City Community College, Lake City, Fla.	1	Coed	Public	1,647
Lake Erie College, Painesville, Ohio.	2	Coed	Private	767
Lake Forest College, Lake Forest, Ill.	2	Coed	Pvt-Presbyterian	1,102
Lake Land College, Mattoon, Ill.	1	Coed	Public	2,759
Lake Michigan College, Benton Harbor, Mich.	1	Coed	Public	3,082

Name and Location	Instruction	Body	Control	Enrollment
Lake-Sumter Community College, Leesburg, Fla	1	Coed	Public	1,245
Lake Superior State College, Marie, Mich	1	Coed	Public	1,890
Lakehead University, Port Arthur, Ontario	3	Coed	Private	2,870
Lakeland Community College, Mentor, Ohio	1	Coed	Public	4,144
Lamar University, Beaumont, Texas	3	Coed	Public	10,815
Lambuth College, Jackson, Tenn	2	Coed	Pvt-Methodist	748
Lander College, Greenwood, S.C.	2	Coed	Private	925
Lane College, Jackson, Tenn	2	Coed	Pvt-Methodist Episcopal	821
Lane Community College, Eugene, Oreg	1	Coed	Public	5,287
Laney Community College, Oakland, Calif	1	Coed	Public	11,876
Langston University, Langston, Okla	2	Coed	Public	1,250
Lansing Community College, Lansing, Mich	1	Coed	Public	8,773
Laredo Junior College, Laredo, Texas	1	Coed	Public	2,408
La Salle College, Philadelphia, Pa	3	Coed	Pvt-Roman Catholic	6,362
Lasell Junior College, Auburndale, Mass	1	W	Private	767
Lassen College, Susanville, Calif	1	Coed	Public	1,667
Laurentian University of Sudbury, Sudbury, Ontario	2	Coed	Public	2,062
Laval University, Quebec, Quebec	4	Coed	Pvt-Roman Catholic	9,749
La Verne College, La Verne, Calif	3	Coed	Pvt-Brethren	1,754
Lawrence Institute of Technology, Southfield, Mich	2	Coed	Private	3,362
Lawrence University, Appleton, Wis.	3	Coed	Private	1,294
Lebanon Valley College, Annville, Pa.	2	Coed	Pvt-Methodist	1,329
Lee College, Cleveland, Tenn.	2	Coed	Pvt-Church of God	1,155
Lee College, Baytown, Texas	1	Coed	Public	2,180
Leeward Community College, Oahu, Hawaii	1	Coed	Public	5,236
Lehigh County Community College, Schnecksville, Pa.	1	Coed	Public	2,200
Lehigh University, Bethlehem, Pa.	4	Coed	Private	5,640
Le Moyne College, Syracuse, N.Y.	2	Coed	Pvt-Roman Catholic	1,600
Lenoir Community College, Kingston, N.C.	1	Coed	Public	1,537
Lenoir Rhyne College, Hickory, N.C.	2	Coed	Pvt-Lutheran	1,360
Lesley College, Cambridge, Mass.	3	Coed	Private	1,081
Lethbridge, University of, Lethbridge, Alberta	3	Coed	Public	1,218
Lewis & Clark College, Portland, Oreg.	3	Coed	Pvt-Presbyterian	2,709
Lewis and Clark Community College, Godfrey, Ill	1	Coed	Public	2,286
Lewis-Clark State School, Lewiston, Idaho	2	Coed	Public	1,057
Lewis University, Lockport, Ill.	2	Coed	Pvt-Roman Catholic	1,549
Lincoln Land Community College, Springfield, Ill	1	Coed	Public	2,368
Lincoln University, Jefferson City, Mo.	3	Coed	Public	4,228
Lincoln University, Lincoln University, Pa.	3	Coed	Public	1,060
Linfield College, McMinnville, Oreg.	3	Coed	Pvt-Baptist	1,083
Linn-Benton Community College, Albany, Oreg	1	Coed	Public	2,188
Livingston University, Livingston, Ala	2	Coed	Public	1,423
Livingstone College, Salisbury, N.C.	2	Coed	Pvt-Methodist Episcopal	744
Lock Haven State College, Lock Haven, Pa.	2	Coed	Public	2,397
Loma Linda University, Loma Linda, Calif.	4	Coed	Pvt-Seventh-day Adventist	3,683
Loma Linda University, Riverside, Calif.	2	Coed	Pvt-Seventh-day Adventist	1,930
Lone Mountain College, San Francisco, Calif	3	Coed	Pvt-Roman Catholic	772
Long Beach City College, Long Beach, Calif	1	Coed	Public	24,023
Long Island University, Greenvale, N.Y. (incl. Bklyn. Center; Bklyn. College of Pharmacy; C.W. Post & Southampton campuses, Long Island, N.Y.)	4	Coed	Private	19,215
Longwood College, Farmville, Va.	3	Coed	Public	2,365
Lorain County Community College, Elyria, Ohio	1	Coed	Public	4,024
Loras College, Dubuque, Iowa	3	Coed	Pvt-Roman Catholic	1,488
Lord Fairfax Community College, Middletown, Va.	1	Coed	Public	881
Loretto Heights College, Denver, Colo.	2	Coed	Pvt-Roman Catholic	809
Los Angeles City College, Los Angeles, Calif.	1	Coed	Public	19,622
Los Angeles Harbor College, Wilmington, Calif.	1	Coed	Public	9,213
Los Angeles Pierce College, Woodland Hills, Calif.	1	Coed	Public	16,743
Los Angeles Southwest College, Los Angeles, Calif.	1	Coed	Public	4,087
Los Angeles Trade-Technical College, Los Angeles, Calif.	1	Coed	Public	15,345
Los Angeles Valley College, Van Nuys, Calif.	1	Coed	Public	19,066
Louisburg College, Louisburg, N.C.	1	Coed	Pvt-Methodist	744
Louisiana College, Pineville, La.	2	Coed	Pvt-Baptist	906
Louisiana State University & Agricultural & Mechanical College System, Baton Rouge and New Orleans, La.	4	Coed	Public	39,542
Louisiana Tech University, Ruston, La.	4	Coed	Public	7,758
Louisville, University of, Louisville, Ky.	4	Coed	Public	10,883
Lowell State College, Lowell, Mass.	3	Coed	Public	1,894
Lowell Technological Institute, Lowell, Mass.	4	Coed	Public	6,421
Lower Columbia College, Longview, Wash.	1	Coed	Public	2,062
Loyola College, Baltimore, Md.	3	Coord	Pvt-Roman Catholic	3,540
Loyola Marymount University, Los Angeles, Calif.	3	Coed	Pvt-Roman Catholic	4,050
Loyola University, Chicago, Ill.	4	Coed	Pvt-Roman Catholic	14,178
Loyola University, New Orleans, La.	4	Coed	Pvt-Roman Catholic	4,690
Lubbock Christian College, Lubbock, Texas.	2	Coed	Pvt-Church of Christ	1,060
Lurleen B. Wallace State Junior College, Andalusia, Ala	1	Coed	Public	910
Luther College, Decorah, Iowa.	2	Coed	Pvt-Lutheran	2,040
Lycoming College, Williamsport, Pa	2	Coed	Pvt-Methodist	1,623
Lynchburg College, Lynchburg, Va	3	Coed	Pvt-Disciples of Christ	2,050
Lyndon State College, Lyndonville, Vt.	2	Coed	Public	714
Macalester College, St. Paul, Minn.	3	Coed	Pvt-Presbyterian	2,012
Macomb County Community College, Warren, Mich. South Campus	1	Coed	Public	3,927
Macon County College, Macon, Ga.	1	Coed	Public	13,558
Madonna College, Livonia, Mich.	2	Coed	Pvt-Roman Catholic	1,629
McGill University, Montreal, Quebec.	4	Coed	Private	727
McLennan Community College, Waco, Texas.	1	Coed	Public	14,686
McMaster University, Hamilton, Ontario	4	Coed	Private	2,522
McMurray College, Jacksonville, Ill.	2	Coed	Private	8,428
McMurry College, Abilene, Texas.	2	Coed	Pvt-Methodist	924
McNeese State University, Lake Charles, La.	3	Coed	Pvt-Methodist	1,380
Madison Area Technical College, Madison, Wis.	1	Coed	Public	6,185
Madison College, Harrisonburg, Va.	3	Coed	Public	5,429
Maine, University of at Farmington.	3	Coed	Public	5,550
Maine, University of at Orono.	4	Coed	Public	10,039
Maine, University of at Portland-Gorham.	4	Coed	Public	7,072
Maine, University of at Presque Isle.	2	Coed	Public	1,315
Mainland, College of the, Texas City, Texas.	1	Coed	Public	1,549
Malone College, Canton, Ohio.	2	Coed	Pvt-Friends	851
Manatee Junior College, Bradenton, Fla.	1	Coed	Public	3,125
Manchester College, North Manchester, Ind.	3	Coed	Pvt-Brethren	1,361
Manchester Community College, Manchester, Conn.	1	Coed	Public	3,756
Manhattan College, Bronx, N.Y.	3	Coed	Pvt-Roman Catholic	4,374
Manhattan School of Music, New York, N.Y.	3	Coed	Private	998
Manhattanville College, Purchase, N.Y.	3	Coed	Pvt-Roman Catholic	2,221
Manitoba, University of, Winnipeg, Man.	4	Coed	Public	13,590
Mankato State College, Mankato, Minn.	3	Coed	Public	13,287
Mansfield State College, Mansfield, Pa.	3	Coed	Public	3,182
Marian College, Indianapolis, Ind.	2	Coed	Pvt-Roman Catholic	835
Maricopa Technical College, Phoenix, Ariz.	1	Coed	Public	6,365
Marietta College, Marietta, Ohio.	3	Coed	Private	1,890
Marin, College of, Kenfield, Calif	2	Coed	Private	6,908
Marion College, Marion, Ind.	2	Coed	Pvt-Methodist	738
Marist College, Poughkeepsie, N.Y.	2	Coed	Pvt-Roman Catholic	1,740
Marquette University, Milwaukee, Wis.	4	Coed	Pvt-Roman Catholic	9,907
Mars Hill College, Mars Hill, N.C.	2	Coed	Pvt-Baptist	1,504
Marshall University, Huntington, W.Va.	3	Coed	Public	9,993
Marshalltown Community College, Marshalltown, Iowa.	1	Coed	Public	865
Mary Hardin-Baylor College, Belton, Texas.	2	Coed	Pvt-Baptist	808
Marycrest College, Davenport, Iowa.	2	Coed	Pvt-Roman Catholic	1,009
Marygrove College, Detroit, Mich.	3	Coed	Pvt-Roman Catholic	1,128
Maryland, University of, College Park & Baltimore, Md.	4	Coed	Public	55,204
Maryland Institute, College of Art, Baltimore, Md.	3	Coed	Private	1,542
Marymount Manhattan College, New York, N.Y.	2	Coed	Pvt-Roman Catholic	1,075
Maryville College, Maryville, Tenn.	2	Coed	Pvt-Presbyterian	1,295
Marywood College, Scranton, Pa.	3	Coed	Pvt-Roman Catholic	737
Massachusetts, University of, Amherst, Mass.	4	Coed	Public	23,710
Massachusetts, University of, Boston, Mass.	3	Coed	Public	5,630

Name and Location	Level of Instruction	Student Body	Control	Enrollment
Massachusetts Bay Community College, Watertown, Mass.	1	Coed	Public	3,283
Massachusetts College of Art, Boston, Mass.	2	Coed	Public	1,334
Massachusetts Institute of Technology, Cambridge, Mass.	4	Coed	Private	7,850
Massasoit Community College, Brockton, Mass.	1	Coed	Public	3,225
Mattatuck Community College, Waterbury, Conn.	2	Coed	Public	2,231
Maui Community College, Kahului, Hawaii.	1	Coed	Public	1,311
Memorial University of Newfoundland, St. John's, Nfld.	4	Coed	Public	7,077
Memphis State University, Memphis, Tenn.	4	Coed	Public	21,295
Merced College, Merced, Calif.	1	Coed	Public	5,638
Mercer County Community College, Trenton, N.J.	1	Coed	Public	5,741
Mercer University, Macon, Ga.	4	Coed	Pvt-Baptist	2,304
Mercy College, Dobbs Ferry, N.Y.	3	Coed	Private	1,742
Mercy College of Detroit, Detroit, Mich.	2	Coed	Pvt-Roman Catholic	1,823
Mercyhurst College, Erie, Pa.	2	Coed	Pvt-Roman Catholic	1,251
Meredith College, Raleigh, N.C.	2	W	Pvt-Baptist	1,362
Meridian Junior College, Meridian, Miss.	1	Coed	Public	1,729
Merrimack College, North Andover, Mass.	2	Coed	Pvt-Roman Catholic	2,702
Merritt College, Oakland, Calif.	1	Coed	Public	9,273
Mesa College, Grand Junction, Colo.	1	Coed	Public	2,267
Mesa Community College, Mesa, Ariz.	1	Coed	Public	7,013
Messiah College, Granham, Pa.	2	Coed	Pvt-Brethren	831
Metropolitan Junior College District, Kansas City, Mo.:				
Longview Community College, Lee's Summit	1	Coed	Public	2,949
Maple Woods Community College, Kansas City	1	Coed	Public	1,784
Penn Valley Community College, Kansas City	1	Coed	Public	4,829
Metropolitan State College, Denver, Colo	2	Coed	Public	8,752
Miami, University of, Coral Gables, Fla.	4	Coed	Private	14,465
Miami University, Oxford, Ohio.	4	Coed	Public	16,305
Hamilton Campus.	1	Coed	Public	1,511
Middletown Campus.	1	Coed	Public	1,872
Miami-Dade Junior College, Miami, Fla.	1	Coed	Public	28,025
Michigan, University of, Ann Arbor, Mich.	4	Coed	Public	36,646
Dearborn Campus.	2	Coed	Public	1,978
Flint.	2	Coed	Public	2,555
Michigan State University, East Lansing, Mich.	4	Coed	Public	44,616
Michigan Technological University, Houghton, Mich.	4	Coed	Public	5,018
Middle Georgia College, Cochran, Ga.	1	Coed	Public	1,813
Middle Tennessee State University, Murfreesboro, Tenn.	3	Coed	Public	9,269
Middlebury College, Middlebury, Vt.	4	Coed	Private	1,841
Middlesex County College, Edison, N.J.	1	Coed	Public	6,984
Midland Lutheran College, Fremont, Nebr.	2	Coed	Pvt-Lutheran	819
Midlands Technical Education Center, Columbia, S.C.	1	Coed	Public	1,935
Midwestern University, Wichita Falls, Texas.	3	Coed	Public	4,144
Miles College, Birmingham, Ala.	2	Coed	Pvt-Methodist	1,208
Millersville State College, Millersville, Pa.	2	Coed	Public	6,066
Milligan College, Milligan College, Tenn.	2	Coed	Private	733
Millikin University, Decatur, Ill.	2	Coed	Pvt-Presbyterian	1,579
Mills College, Oakland, Calif.	2	W	Private	1,025
Millsaps College, Jackson, Miss.	2	Coed	Pvt-Methodist	1,087
Milwaukee Area Technical College, Milwaukee, Wis.	1	Coed	Public	16,335
Milwaukee School of Engineering, Milwaukee, Wis.	3	Coed	Private	2,174
Mineral Area College, Flat River, Mo.	1	Coed	Public	985
Minnesota, University of, Minneapolis, Minn.	4	Coed	Public	56,954
Duluth.	3	Coed	Public	5,548
Morris.	2	Coed	Public	1,763
Minot State College, Minot, N.Dak.	3	Coed	Public	2,348
MiraCosta College, Oceanside, Calif.	1	Coed	Public	1,337
Misericordia, College, Dallas, Pa.	2	Coed	Pvt-Roman Catholic	1,030
Mississippi, University of, University, Miss.	4	Coed	Public	8,582
Mississippi College, Clinton, Miss.	3	Coed	Pvt-Baptist	2,430
Mississippi Delta Junior College, Moorhead, Miss.	1	Coed	Public	1,188
Mississippi State College for Women, Columbus, Miss.	3	W	Public	2,655
Mississippi State University, Mississippi State, Miss.	4	Coed	Public	10,924
Missouri, University of:				
Columbia.	4	Coed	Public	50,897
Kansas City.	4	Coed	Public	23,973
Rolla.	4	Coed	Public	10,228
St. Louis.	4	Coed	Public	5,219
Missouri Southern State College, Joplin, Mo.	2	Coed	Public	11,477
Missouri Western State College, St. Joseph, Mo.	2	Coed	Public	3,077
Mitchell College, New London, Conn.	1	Coed	Private	3,276
Modesto Junior College, Modesto, Calif.	1	Coed	Public	961
Mohawk Valley Community College, Utica, N.Y.	1	Coed	Public	915
Molloy College, Rockville Center, N.Y.	2	Coed	Pvt-Roman Catholic	10,006
Moncton, University of, Moncton, New Brunswick.	3	Coed	Pvt-Roman Catholic	4,603
Monmouth College, Monmouth, Ill.	2	Coed	Pvt-Presbyterian	1,161
Monmouth College, West Long Branch, N.J.	3	Coed	Private	3,337
Monroe Community College, Rochester, N.Y.	1	Coed	Public	1,003
Monroe County Community College, Monroe, Mich.	1	Coed	Public	5,049
Montana, University of, Missoula, Mont.	4	Coed	Public	8,943
Montana College of Mineral Science and Technology, Butte, Mont.	3	Coed	Public	1,674
Montana State University, Bozeman, Mont.	3	Coed	Public	8,624
Montclair State College, Upper Montclair, N.J.	3	Coed	Public	13,586
Monterey Peninsula College, Monterey, Calif.	1	Coed	Public	6,395
Montevallo, University of, Montevallo, Ala.	3	Coed	Public	2,850
Montgomery College, Rockville, Md	1	Coed	Public	10,645
Montgomery County Community College, Blue Bell, Pa.	1	Coed	Public	4,294
Montreal, University of, Montreal, Quebec.	4	Coed	Pvt-Roman Catholic	14,681
Loyola College, Montreal, Quebec.	1	Coed	Pvt-Roman Catholic	4,065
Moorhead State College, Moorhead, Minn.	3	Coed	Public	6,460
Moorpark College, Moorpark, Calif.	1	Coed	Public	7,693
Moravian College, Bethlehem, Pa	2	Coed	Pvt-Moravian	1,687
Morehead State University, Morehead, Ky.	3	Coed	Public	6,460
Morehouse College, Atlanta, Ga.	2	M	Private	1,121
Morgan State College, Baltimore, Md.	2	Coed	Public	5,488
Morningside College, Sioux City, Iowa.	2	Coed	Pvt-Methodist	1,527
Morris, County College of, Dover, N.J.	1	Coed	Public	5,375
Morris Brown College, Atlanta, Ga.	2	Coed	Pvt-Methodist Episcopal	1,523
Morris Harvey College, Charleston, W.Va.	2	Coed	Private	2,768
Morton College, Cicero, Ill	1	Coed	Public	2,128
Motlow State Community College, Tullahoma, Tenn.	1	Coed	Public	862
Mount Allison University, Sackville, New Brunswick.	3	Coed	Pvt-United Church	1,338
Mount Holyoke College, South Hadley, Mass.	3	W	Private	1,946
Mount Hood Community College, Gresham, Oreg.	1	Coed	Public	9,045
Mount Mary College, Milwaukee, Wis.	2	W	Pvt-Roman Catholic	830
Mount St. Joseph-on-the-Ohio, College of, Mt. St. Joseph, Ohio.	2	W	Pvt-Roman Catholic	843
Mount St. Mary's College, Los Angeles, Calif.	2	W	Pvt-Roman Catholic	1,227
Mount St. Mary's College, Emmitsburg, Md.	2	Coed	Pvt-Roman Catholic	1,275
Mount St. Vincent, College of, Riverdale, N.Y.	2	Coed	Pvt-Roman Catholic	1,166
Mount St. Vincent University, Halifax, Nova Scotia.	3	Coed	Pvt-Roman Catholic	998
Mount San Antonio College, Walnut, Calif.	1	Coed	Public	15,574
Mount San Jacinto College, Gilman Hot Springs, Calif.	1	Coed	Public	1,739
Mount Union College, Alliance, Ohio.	2	Coed	Pvt-Methodist	1,326
Mount Wachusett Community College, Gardner, Mass.	1	Coed	Public	2,029
Mountain View College, Dallas, Texas.	1	Coed	Public	4,165
Muhlenberg College, Allentown, Pa.	2	Coed	Pvt-Lutheran	1,884
Mundelein College, Chicago, Ill.	2	Coed	Pvt-Roman Catholic	1,224
Murray State University, Murray, Ky.	3	Coed	Public	7,337
Muskegon Community College, Muskegon, Mich.	1	Coed	Public	3,879
Muskingum College, New Concord, Ohio.	2	Coed	Pvt-Presbyterian	1,223
Napa College, Napa, Calif.	1	Coed	Public	4,169
Nassau Community College, Garden City, N.Y.	1	Coed	Public	18,012
Nasson College, Springvale, Me.	2	Coed	Private	860

Name and Location	Level of Instruction	Student Body	Control	Enrollment
National College of Education, Evanston, Ill.	3	Coed	Private	4,088
Naval Postgraduate School, Monterey, Calif.	4	Coed	Public	1,646
Navarro Junior College, Corsicana, Texas	1	Coed	Public	1,081
Nazareth College of Rochester, N.Y.	2	Coed	Pvt-Roman Catholic	1,937
Nebraska, University of, Lincoln, Nebr.	4	Coed	Public	21,581
Nebraska, University of, at Omaha, Nebr.	3	Coed	Public	13,117
Nebraska Wesleyan University, Lincoln, Nebr.	3	Coed	Pvt-Methodist	1,080
Nevada, University of, Reno and Las Vegas, Nev.	4	Coed	Public	11,003
New Brunswick, University of, Fredericton, New Brunswick	4	Coed	Public	5,182
New England College, Henniker, N.H.	2	Coed	Private	1,468
New Hampshire, University of, Durham, N.H.	4	Coed	Public	10,938
New Haven, University of, West Haven, Conn.	3	Coed	Private	5,265
New Mexico, University of, Albuquerque, N.Mex.	4	Coed	Public	19,521
New Mexico Highlands University, Las Vegas, N.Mex.	3	Coed	Public	2,677
New Mexico Institute of Mining & Technology, Socorro, N.Mex.	4	Coed	Public	894
New Mexico Junior College, Hobbs, N.Mex.	1	Coed	Public	1,006
New Mexico State University, Las Cruces, N.Mex.	4	Coed	Public	9,221
New River Community College, Dubin, Va.	1	Coed	Public	1,403
New Rochelle, College of, New Rochelle, N.Y.	3	Coed	Pvt-Roman Catholic	2,520
New School for Social Research, New York, N.Y.	4	Coed	Private	3,985
New York, City University of, New York, N.Y.:				
Bernard M. Baruch College, New York.	3	Coed	Public	14,423
Borough of Manhattan Community College, New York.	1	Coed	Public	10,108
Bronx Community College, Bronx.	1	Coed	Public	12,671
Brooklyn College, Brooklyn.	3	Coed	Public	32,348
City College, New York.	3	Coed	Public	20,654
Graduate School and University Center, New York.	4	Coed	Public	2,668
Herbert H. Lehman College, Bronx.	3	Coed	Public	14,626
Hunter College, New York.	3	Coed	Public	23,251
John Jay College of Criminal Justice, New York.	3	Coed	Public	7,659
Kingsborough Community College, Brooklyn.	1	Coed	Public	7,979
New York City Community College, Brooklyn.	1	Coed	Public	17,106
Queens College, Flushing.	3	Coed	Public	28,688
Queensborough Community College, Bayside.	1	Coed	Public	13,640
Richmond College, Staten Island.	3	Coed	Public	3,478
Staten Island Community College, Staten Island.	1	Coed	Public	9,272
York College, Flushing.	3	Coed	Public	3,267
New York, Polytechnic Institute of, Brooklyn, N.Y.	4	Coed	Private	3,454
New York, State University of, Albany, N.Y.:				
Agricultural & Technical College at Alfred.	1	Coed	Public	3,942
Agricultural & Technical College at Canton.	1	Coed	Public	2,253
Agricultural & Technical College at Cobleskill.	1	Coed	Public	2,454
Agricultural & Technical College at Delhi.	1	Coed	Public	2,336
Agricultural & Technical College at Farmingdale.	1	Coed	Public	12,572
Agricultural & Technical College at Morrisville.	1	Coed	Public	2,766
College of Environmental Science and Forestry, Syracuse.	4	Coed	Public	1,783
Downstate Medical Center, Brooklyn.	4	Coed	Public	1,334
Maritime College, Bronx.	2	Coed	Public	803
State University College at Brockport.	3	Coed	Public	9,762
State University College at Buffalo.	3	Coed	Public	10,660
State University College at Cortland.	3	Coed	Public	5,483
State University College at Fredonia.	3	Coed	Public	5,334
State University College at Geneseo.	3	Coed	Public	5,699
State University College at New Paltz.	3	Coed	Public	8,225
State University College at Oneonta.	3	Coed	Public	5,967
State University College at Oswego.	3	Coed	Public	8,312
State University College at Plattsburgh.	3	Coed	Public	5,885
State University College at Potsdam.	3	Coed	Public	4,936
State University at Albany.	4	Coed	Public	13,571
State University at Binghamton.	4	Coed	Public	7,930
State University at Buffalo.	4	Coed	Public	20,963
State University at Stony Brook.	4	Coed	Public	12,058
Upstate Medical Center, Syracuse.	4	Coed	Public	914
New York Institute of Technology, Old Westbury, L.I., N.Y.	2	Coed	Private	4,678
New York University, New York, N.Y.	4	Coed	Private	30,000
Newark College of Engineering, Newark, N.J.	4	Coed	Public	4,202
Newark State College, Union, N.J.	3	Coed	Public	12,027
Newberry College, Newberry, S.C.	2	Coed	Pvt-Lutheran	764
Newton College, Newton, Mass.	2	Coed	Pvt-Roman Catholic	1,002
Niagara County Community College, Sanborn, N.Y.	1	Coed	Public	3,087
Niagara University, Niagara University, N.Y.	3	Coed	Pvt-Roman Catholic	3,623
Nicholls State University, Thibodaux, La.	3	Coed	Public	5,701
Norfolk State College, Norfolk, Va.	2	Coed	Public	5,858
Normandale State Junior College, Bloomington, Minn.	1	Coed	Public	3,380
North Adams State College, North Adams, Mass.	3	Coed	Public	2,511
North Carolina, University of, Chapel Hill, N.C.:	4	Coed	Public	90,495
Asheville.	4	Coed	Public	1,129
Chapel Hill.	4	Coed	Public	19,320
Charlotte.	4	Coed	Public	5,159
Greensboro.	4	Coed	Public	7,727
Wilmington.	4	Coed	Public	2,417
North Carolina State University at Raleigh.	4	Coed	Public	14,532
North Carolina Agricultural and Technical State University at Greensboro, N.C.	3	Coed	Public	4,510
North Carolina Central University, Durham, N.C.	3	Coed	Public	4,028
North Central College, Naperville, Ill.	2	Coed	Pvt-Methodist	848
North Central Michigan College, Petoskey, Mich.	1	Coed	Public	869
North Central Technical Institute, Wausau, Wis.	4	Coed	Public	1,776
North Dakota, University of, Grand Forks, N.Dak.		Coed	Public	8,282
North Dakota State School of Science, Wahpeton, N.Dak.	1	Coed	Public	3,073
North Dakota State University of Agriculture and Applied Science, Fargo, N.Dak.	4	Coed	Public	7,257
North Florida Junior College, Madison, Fla.	1	Coed	Public	950
North Georgia College, Dahlonega, Ga.	2	Coed	Public	1,423
North Hennepin State Junior College, Minneapolis, Minn.	1	Coed	Public	2,478
North Idaho College, Coeur d'Alene, Idaho.	1	Coed	Public	1,197
North Iowa Area Community College, Mason City, Iowa.	1	Coed	Public	1,681
North Park College, Chicago, Ill.	2	Coed	Pvt-Evangelical Covenant	1,317
North Shore Community College, Beverly, Mass.	1	Coed	Public	6,368
North Texas State University, Denton, Texas.	4	Coed	Public	15,593
Northampton County Area Community College, Bethlehem, Pa.	1	Coed	Public	2,869
Northeast Alabama State Junior College, Rainsville, Ala.	1	Coed	Public	744
Northeast Louisiana University, Monroe, La.	4	Coed	Public	8,861
Northeast Mississippi Junior College, Booneville, Miss.	1	Coed	Public	1,334
Northeast Missouri State University, Kirksville, Mo.	4	Coed	Public	6,236
Northeastern Illinois University, Chicago, Ill.	3	Coed	Public	8,244
Northeastern Junior College, Sterling, Colo.	1	Coed	Public	1,202
Northeastern Oklahoma Agricultural & Mechanical College, Miami, Okla.	1	Coed	Public	2,270
Northeastern State College, Tahlequah, Okla.	3	Coed	Public	5,458
Northeastern University, Boston, Mass.	4	Coed	Private	33,820
Northern Arizona University, Flagstaff, Ariz.	4	Coed	Public	8,915
Northern Colorado, University of, Greeley, Colo.	4	Coed	Public	13,396
Northern Essex Community College, Haverhill, Mass.	1	Coed	Public	3,942
Northern Illinois University, De Kalb, Ill.	4	Coed	Public	23,548
Northern Iowa, University of, Cedar Falls, Iowa.	4	Coed	Public	8,845
Northern Michigan University, Marquette, Mich.	3	Coed	Public	8,053
Northern Montana College, Havre, Mont.	3	Coed	Public	1,065
Northern Oklahoma College, Tonkawa, Okla.	1	Coed	Public	1,325
Northern State College, Aberdeen, S.Dak.	3	Coed	Public	2,350
Northern Virginia Community College, Annandale, Va.	1	Coed	Public	2,550
Northrop Institute of Technology, Inglewood, Calif.	3	Coed	Private	13,974
Northwest Alabama State Junior College, Phil Campbell, Ala.	1	Coed	Public	842
Northwest Community College, Powell, Wyo.	1	Coed	Public	769
Northwest Mississippi Junior College, Senatobia, Miss.	1	Coed	Public	1,009

Name and Location	Level of Instruction	Student Body	Control	Enrollment
Northwest Missouri State College, Maryville, Mo.	3	Coed	Public	5,341
Northwest Nazarene College, Nampa, Idaho.	2	Coed	Pvt-Nazarene	1,007
Northwestern Connecticut Community College, Winsted, Conn.	1	Coed	Public	1,630
Northwestern Michigan College, Traverse City, Mich.	1	Coed	Public	1,936
Northwestern State College, Alva, Okla.	3	Coed	Public	2,208
Northwestern State University of Louisiana, Natchitoches, La.	4	Coed	Public	6,384
Northwestern University, Evanston, Ill.	4	Coed	Private	14,418
Norwalk State Technical College, Norwalk, Conn.	1	Coed	Public	1,650
Norwich University, Northfield, Vt.	4	Coed	Private	1,612
Notre Dame, College of, Belmont, Calif.	4	Coed	Pvt-Roman Catholic	1,518
Notre Dame, University of, Notre Dame, Ind.	4	Coed	Pvt-Roman Catholic	8,575
Nova University, Fort Lauderdale, Fla.	4	Coed	Private	838
Oakland Community College, Bloomfield Hills, Mich.	1	Coed	Public	6,014
Highland Lakes Campus.		Coed	Public	2,345
Orchard Ridge Campus.		Coed	Public	5,675
Oakland University, Rochester, Mich.	4	Coed	Public	8,169
Oberlin College, Oberlin, Ohio.	3	Coed	Private	2,771
Ocean County College, Toms River, N.J.	1	Coed	Public	3,182
Occidental College, Los Angeles, Calif.	3	Coed	Pvt-United Presbyterian	1,826
Odessa College, Odessa, Texas.	1	Coed	Public	3,023
Oglethorpe College, Atlanta, Ga.	3	Coed	Private	929
Ohio Dominican College, Columbus, Ohio.	2	Coed	Pvt-Roman Catholic	949
Ohio Northern University, Ada, Ohio.	4	Coed	Pvt-Methodist	2,583
Ohio State University, Columbus, Ohio.	4	Coed	Public	50,040
Ohio University, Athens, Ohio.	4	Coed	Public	17,677
Ohio Wesleyan University, Delaware, Ohio.	3	Coed	Pvt-Methodist	2,526
Ohlone College, Fremont, Calif.	1	Coed	Public	4,159
Okaloosa-Walton Junior College, Niceville, Fla.	1	Coed	Public	2,291
Oklahoma, University of, Norman, Okla.	4	Coed	Public	23,449
Oklahoma Baptist University, Shawnee, Okla.	2	Coed	Pvt-Baptist	1,701
Oklahoma Christian College, Oklahoma City, Okla.	3	Coed	Pvt-Church of Christ	1,113
Oklahoma City University, Oklahoma City, Okla.	3	Coed	Pvt-Methodist	2,309
Oklahoma College of Liberal Arts, Chickasha, Okla.	2	Coed	Public	1,178
Oklahoma Panhandle State College, Goodwell, Okla.	2	Coed	Public	1,155
Oklahoma State University, Stillwater, Okla.	4	Coed	Public	20,476
Old Dominion College, Norfolk, Va.	3	Coed	Public	11,458
Olivet College, Olivet, Mich.	2	Coed	Pvt-Church of Christ	786
Olivet Nazarene College, Kankakee, Ill.	2	Coed	Pvt-Nazarene	1,781
Olympic College, Bremerton, Wash.	1	Coed	Public	4,658
Onondaga Community College, Syracuse, N.Y.	1	Coed	Public	4,373
Oral Roberts University, Tulsa, Okla.	2	Coed	Private	1,906
Orange Coast College, Costa Mesa, Calif.	1	Coed	Public	20,969
Orange County Community College, Middletown, N.Y.	1	Coed	Public	3,519
Orangeburg-Calhoun Technical Education Center, Orangeburg, S.C.		Coed	Public	1,924
Oregon, University of, Eugene, Oreg.	4	Coed	Public	15,432
Oregon College of Education, Monmouth, Oreg.	3	Coed	Public	3,579
Oregon State University, Corvallis, Oreg.	4	Coed	Public	15,184
Oregon Technical Institute, Klamath Falls, Oreg.	1	Coed	Public	1,781
Otero Junior College, La Junta, Colo.	1	Coed	Public	776
Ottawa, University of, Ottawa, Ontario.	4	Coed	Pvt-Roman Catholic	8,430
Otterbein College, Westerville, Ohio.	2	Coed	Pvt-Methodist	1,301
Ouachita Baptist University, Arkadelphia, Ark.	2	Coed	Pvt-Baptist	1,508
Our Lady of the Lake College, San Antonio, Texas.	3	Coed	Pvt-Roman Catholic	2,031
Ozarks, School of the, Point Lookout, Mo.	2	Coed	Pvt-Presbyterian	1,058
Pace University, New York, N.Y.	3	Coed	Private	10,553
Pacific, University of the, Stockton, Calif.	4	Coed	Private	4,102
Pacific Lutheran University, Tacoma, Wash.	3	Coed	Pvt-Lutheran	3,267
Pacific Union College, Angwin, Calif.	3	Coed	Pvt-Seventh-day Adventist	1,915
Pacific University, Forest Grove, Oreg.	3	Coed	Pvt-Church of Christ	1,186
Palm Beach Junior College, Lake Worth, Fla.	1	Coed	Public	6,740
Palomar College, San Marcos, Calif.	1	Coed	Public	7,074
Pan American University, Edinburg, Texas.	2	Coed	Public	6,896
Paris Junior College, Paris, Texas.	1	Coed	Public	1,101
Parkersburg Community College, Parkersburg, W.Va.	1	Coed	Public	2,512
Parkland College, Champaign, Ill.	1	Coed	Public	4,147
Parks College of Aeronautical Technology, Cahokia, Ill.	2	Coed	Pvt-Roman Catholic	742
Pasadena City College, Pasadena, Calif.	1	Coed	Public	15,746
Pasadena College, Pasadena, Calif.	3	Coed	Pvt-Nazarene	1,673
Pearl River College, Poplarville, Miss.	1	Coed	Public	1,146
Peirce Junior College, Philadelphia, Pa.	1	Coed	Private	1,692
Pembroke State University, Pembroke, N.C.	2	Coed	Public	1,980
Peninsula College, Port Angeles, Wash.	1	Coed	Public	1,192
Pennsylvania, University of, Philadelphia, Pa.	4	Coed	Private	19,614
Pennsylvania State University, University Park, Abington, Allentown, Altoona, Chester, DuBois, Erie, Hazleton, Hershey, McKeesport, Middletown, Monaca, Mont Alto, New Kensington, Schuylkill Haven, Scranton, Sharon, Uniontown, Wilkes-Barre, Wyomissing and York, Pa.		Coed	Public	60,089
Pensacola Junior College, Pensacola, Fla.	1	Coed	Public	5,700
Pepperdine College, Malibu, Calif.	4	Coed	Pvt-Church of Christ	7,699
Peru State College, Peru, Nebr.	2	Coed	Public	940
Pfeiffer College, Misenheimer, N.C.	2	Coed	Pvt-Methodist	1,076
Philadelphia College of Art, Philadelphia, Pa.	3	Coed	Private	1,633
Philadelphia College of Pharmacy & Science, Philadelphia, Pa.	4	Coed	Private	1,070
Philadelphia College of Textiles & Science, Philadelphia, Pa.	2	Coed	Private	2,030
Phillips University, Enid, Okla.	3	Coed	Pvt-Disciples of Christ	1,426
Phoenix College, Phoenix, Ariz.	1	Coed	Public	10,295
Piedmont Technical Education Center, Greenwood, S.C.	1	Coed	Public	1,167
Pikeville College, Pikeville, Ky.	2	Coed	Pvt-Presbyterian	743
Pittsburgh, University of, Pittsburgh, Pa. (Bradford, Greensboro, Johnstown, and Titusville, Pa.)	4	Coed	Private	33,408
Pitzer College, Claremont, Calif.	3	Coed	Private	780
Plymouth State College, Plymouth, N.H.	2	Coed	Public	2,637
Point Loma College, San Diego, Calif.	3	Coed	Pvt-Nazarene	1,273
Point Park College, Pittsburgh, Pa.	2	Coed	Private	2,353
Polk Community College, Winter Haven, Fla.	1	Coed	Public	3,133
Pomona College, Claremont, Calif.	3	Coed	Private	1,293
Porterville College, Porterville, Calif.	1	Coed	Public	1,832
Portland, University of, Portland, Oreg.	4	Coed	Private	1,985
Portland Community College, Portland, Oreg.	1	Coed	Public	12,373
Portland State University, Portland, Oreg.	3	Coed	Public	13,635
Potomac State College of West Virginia University, Keyser, W.Va.	1	Coed	Public	741
Prairie State College, Chicago Heights, Ill.	1	Coed	Public	3,252
Prairie View Agricultural & Mechanical College, Prairie View, Texas.	3	Coed	Public	4,115
Pratt Institute, Brooklyn, N.Y.	3	Coed	Private	4,238
Presbyterian College, Clinton, S.C.	3	Coed	Pvt-Presbyterian	883
Prince Edward Island, University of, Charlottetown, P.E.I.	3	Coed	Public	1,771
Prince George's Community College, Largo, Md.	1	Coed	Public	7,888
Princeton University, Princeton, N.J.	4	Coed	Private	5,503
Principia College, Elsah, Ill.	2	Coed	Pvt-Christian Science	833
Providence College, Providence, R.I.	2	Coed	Pvt-Roman Catholic	3,315
Puerto Rico, University of, Rio Piedras, P.R.	4	Coed	Public	40,697
Puget Sound, University of, Tacoma, Wash.	4	Coed	Pvt-Methodist	4,166
Purdue University, Lafayette, Ind.	4	Coed	Public	26,461
Purdue University Regional Campuses:				
Calumet at Hammond	3	Coed	Public	5,169
Fort Wayne	2	Coed	Public	2,794
North Central Campus	1	Coed	Public	1,354
Quebec, University of, Quebec, Que.	2	Coed	Public	8,080
Queen's University at Kingston, Ontario.	4	Coed	Private	8,861

Name and Location	Level of Instruction	Student Body	Control	Enrollment
Quincy College, Quincy, Ill.	2	Coed	Pvt-Roman Catholic	2,007
Quinnipiac College, Hamden, Conn.	3	Coed	Private	2,927
Quinsigamond Community College, Worcester, Mass.	1	Coed	Public	1,688
Radford College, Radford, Va.	3	Coed	Public	3,670
Randolph-Macon College, Ashland, Va.	2	Coed	Pvt-Methodist	829
Randolph-Macon Woman's College, Lynchburg, Va.	2	W	Pvt-Methodist	742
Redlands, University of, Redlands, Calif.	3	Coed	Pvt-Baptist	2,089
Redwoods, College of the, Eureka, Calif.	1	Coed	Public	4,708
Reed College, Portland, Oreg.	3	Coed	Private	1,198
Reedley College, Reedley, Calif.	1	Coed	Public	2,617
Regis College, Denver, Colo.	2	Coed	Pvt-Roman Catholic	1,330
Regis College, Weston, Mass.	2	W	Pvt-Roman Catholic	844
Rend Lake College, Ina, Ill.	1	Coed	Public	1,105
Rensselaer Polytechnic Institute, Troy, N.Y.	4	Coed	Private	4,660
Rhode Island, University of, Kingston, R.I.	4	Coed	Public	18,961
Rhode Island College, Providence, R.I.	3	Coed	Public	8,204
Rhode Island Junior College, Providence, R.I.	1	Coed	Public	3,850
Rhode Island School of Design, Providence, R.I.	3	Coed	Private	1,270
Rice University, Houston, Texas	4	Coed	Private	3,311
Richard Bland College, Petersburg, Va.	1	Coed	Public	858
Richmond, University of, Richmond, Va.	3	Coord	Pvt-Baptist	4,550
Ricks College, Rexburg, Idaho	1	Coed	Pvt-Latter-day Saints	5,057
Rider College, Trenton, N.J.	3	Coed	Private	5,798
Rio Hondo College, Whittier, Calif.	1	Coed	Public	10,849
Ripon College, Ripon, Wis.	3	Coed	Private	1,052
Riverside City College, Riverside, Calif.	1	Coed	Public	
Rivier College, Nashua, N.H.	3	W	Pvt-Roman Catholic	
Roanoke College, Salem, Va.	3	Coed	Pvt-Lutheran	940
Robert Morris College, Coraopolis, Pa.	1	Coed	Private	1,324
Rochester, University of, Rochester, N.Y.	4	Coed	Private	4,060
Rochester Institute of Technology, Rochester, N.Y.	3	Coed	Private	8,400
Rochester State Junior College, Rochester, Minn.	1	Coed	Public	2,327
Rock Valley College, Rockford, Ill.	1	Coed	Public	6,286
Rockford College, Rockford, Ill.	3	Coed	Private	1,271
Rockhurst College, Kansas City, Mo.	3	Coed	Pvt-Roman Catholic	2,341
Rockingham Community College, Wentworth, N.C.	1	Coed	Public	1,180
Rockland Community College, Suffern, N.Y.	1	Coed	Public	5,897
Roger Williams College, Bristol, R.I.	2	Coed	Private	2,939
Rollins College, Winter Park, Fla.	3	Coed	Private	3,724
Roosevelt University, Chicago, Ill.	3	Coed	Private	6,930
Rosary College, River Forest, Ill.	3	W	Pvt-Roman Catholic	1,352
Rosary Hill College, Buffalo, N.Y.	2	Coed	Pvt-Roman Catholic	1,399
Rose-Hulman Institute of Technology, Terre Haute, Ind.	3	M	Private	1,148
Rowan Technical Institute, Salisbury, N.C.	1	Coed	Public	829
Russell Sage College, Troy, N.Y.	3	W	Private	1,414
Rutgers University, New Brunswick, N.J.	4	Coord	Public	38,358
Ryerson Polytechnical Institute, Toronto, Ontario	2	Coed	Private	7,070
St. Francis College, Brooklyn, N.Y.	2	Coed	Pvt-Roman Catholic	2,736
St. Francis College, Loretto, Pa.	3	Coed	Pvt-Roman Catholic	1,616
St. Francis Xavier University, Antigonish, Nova Scotia	3	Coed	Pvt-Roman Catholic	2,960
St. John College of Cleveland, Ohio	3	W	Pvt-Roman Catholic	754
St. John Fisher College, Rochester, N.Y.	2	Coed	Pvt-Roman Catholic	1,397
St. Johns River Community College, Palatka, Fla.	1	Coed	Public	1,051
St. John's University, Collegeville, Minn.	3	M	Pvt-Roman Catholic	1,724
St. John's University, Jamaica, N.Y.	4	Coed	Pvt-Roman Catholic	13,734
St. Joseph College, West Hartford, Conn.	3	W	Pvt-Roman Catholic	952
St. Joseph's College, Rensselaer, Ind.	3	Coed	Pvt-Roman Catholic	1,161
St. Joseph's College, Calumet Campus, East Chicago, Ind.	2	Coed	Pvt-Roman Catholic	1,688
St. Joseph's College, Philadelphia, Pa.	3	Coed	Pvt-Roman Catholic	6,375
St. Lawrence University, Canton, N.Y.	3	Coed	Private	2,530
St. Leo College, St. Leo, Fla.	2	Coed	Pvt-Roman Catholic	1,141
St. Louis, Junior College District of, St. Louis, Mo.	1	Coed	Public	6,166
Florissant Valley Community College, St. Louis, Mo.	1	Coed	Public	5,758
Forest Park Community College, St. Louis, Mo.	1	Coed	Public	7,310
Meramec Community College, Kirkwood, Mo.	1	Coed	Public	10,307
St. Louis University, St. Louis, Mo.	4	Coed	Pvt-Roman Catholic	1,029
St. Mary's College, Winona, Minn.	3	Coed	Pvt-Roman Catholic	1,481
St. Mary's College, Notre Dame, Ind.	3	W	Pvt-Roman Catholic	1,152
St. Mary's College of Maryland, St. Mary's City, Md.	2	Coed	Public	1,045
St. Mary's Dominican College, New Orleans, La.	3	W	Pvt-Roman Catholic	864
St. Mary's Junior College, Minneapolis, Minn.	1	W	Pvt-Roman Catholic	781
St. Mary's University, Halifax, N.S.	3	Coed	Pvt-Roman Catholic	2,548
St. Mary's University, San Antonio, Texas	3	Coed	Pvt-Roman Catholic	3,964
St. Michael's College, Winooski Park, Vt.	3	Coed	Pvt-Roman Catholic	1,521
St. Norbert College, West De Pere, Wis.	3	Coed	Pvt-Roman Catholic	1,561
St. Olaf College, Northfield, Minn.	3	Coed	Pvt-Lutheran	2,748
St. Peter's College, Jersey City, N.J.	3	Coed	Pvt-Roman Catholic	4,561
St. Petersburg Junior College, St. Petersburg, Fla.	1	Coed	Public	9,204
St. Philip's College, San Antonio, Texas	1	Coed	Public	3,626
St. Rose, College of, Albany, N.Y.	3	Coed	Private	1,563
St. Scholastica, College of, Duluth, Minn.	3	Coed	Pvt-Roman Catholic	959
St. Teresa, College of, Winona, Minn.	3	W	Pvt-Roman Catholic	1,040
St. Thomas, College of, St. Paul, Minn.	3	Coed	Pvt-Roman Catholic	2,456
St. Thomas, University of, Houston, Texas	3	Coed	Pvt-Roman Catholic	1,645
St. Vincent College, Latrobe, Pa.	3	Coed	Pvt-Roman Catholic	1,000
St. Xavier College, Chicago, Ill.	3	Coed	Pvt-Roman Catholic	1,145
Salem College, Salem, W.Va.	2	Coed	Private	1,266
Salem State College, Salem, Mass.	3	Coed	Public	7,119
Salisbury State College, Salisbury, Md.	3	Coed	Public	2,360
Salve Regina College, Newport, R.I.	3	Coed	Pvt-Roman Catholic	724
Sam Houston State University, Huntsville, Texas	3	Coed	Public	10,438
Samford University, Birmingham, Ala.	3	Coed	Pvt-Baptist	2,977
San Antonio College, San Antonio, Texas	1	Coed	Public	16,153
San Bernardino Valley College, San Bernardino, Calif.	1	Coed	Public	13,931
San Diego, University of, San Diego, Calif.	3	Coed	Pvt-Roman Catholic	1,639
San Diego City College, San Diego, Calif.	1	W	Pvt-Roman Catholic	4,404
San Diego Evening College, San Diego, Calif.	1	Coed	Public	13,621
San Diego Mesa College, San Diego, Calif.	1	Coed	Public	7,485
San Francisco, City College of, San Francisco, Calif.	1	Coed	Public	21,484
San Francisco, University of, San Francisco, Calif.	3	Coed	Pvt-Roman Catholic	6,057
San Francisco Art Institute, San Francisco, Calif.	3	Coed	Private	877
San Jacinto College, Pasadena, Texas	1	Coed	Public	7,425
San Joaquin Delta College, Stockton, Calif.	1	Coed	Public	12,500
San Jose City College, San Jose, Calif.	1	Coed	Public	14,897
San Mateo, College of, San Mateo, Calif.	1	Coed	Public	14,158
Sandhills Community College, Southern Pines, N.C.	1	Coed	Public	1,336
Santa Ana College, Santa Ana, Calif.	1	Coed	Public	10,409
Santa Barbara City College, Santa Barbara, Calif.	1	Coed	Public	7,007
Santa Clara, University of, Santa Clara, Calif.	4	Coed	Pvt-Roman Catholic	6,075
Santa Fe, College of, Santa Fe, N.Mex.	2	Coed	Pvt-Roman Catholic	1,177
Santa Fe Community College, Gainesville, Fla.	1	Coed	Public	4,563

Name and Location	Level of Instruction	Student Body	Control	Enrollment
Santa Monica College, Santa Monica, Calif.	1	Coed	Public	12,655
Santa Rosa Junior College, Santa Rosa, Calif.	1	Coed	Public	11,028
Sarah Lawrence College, Bronxville, N.Y.	3	Coed	Private	893
Saskatchewan, University of, Saskatoon and Regina, Sask.	4	Coed	Public	13,748
Sauk Valley College, Dixon, Ill.	1	Coed	Public	1,726
Savannah State College, Savannah, Ga.	2	Coed	Public	2,444
Schoolcraft College, Livonia, Mich.	1	Coed	Public	5,847
Scranton, University of, Scranton, Pa.	3	Coed	Pvt-Roman Catholic	3,692
Seattle Central Community College, Seattle, Wash.	1	Coed	Public	7,197
Seattle Pacific College, Seattle, Wash.	3	Coed	Pvt-Methodist	1,997
Seattle University, Seattle, Wash.	4	Coed	Pvt-Roman Catholic	2,933
Seminole Junior College, Sanford, Fla.	1	Coed	Public	2,097
Sequoias, College of the, Visalia, Calif.	1	Coed	Public	5,650
Seton Hall University, South Orange, N.J.	4	Coed	Pvt-Roman Catholic	9,723
Seton Hill College, Greensburg, Pa.	2	Coed	Pvt-Roman Catholic	774
Shasta College, Redding, Calif.	1	Coed	Public	6,330
Shaw University, Raleigh, N.C.	2	Coed	Pvt-Baptist	1,091
Shepherd College, Shepherdstown, W.Va.	2	Coed	Public	2,004
Sherbrooke, University of, Sherbrooke, Quebec	4	Coed	Pvt-Roman Catholic	4,929
Shippensburg State College, Shippensburg, Pa.	3	Coed	Public	3,924
Shoreline Community College, Seattle, Wash.	1	Coed	Public	7,410
Siena College, Loudonville, N.Y.	2	Coed	Pvt-Roman Catholic	2,046
Sierra Community College, Rocklin, Calif.	1	Coed	Public	4,947
Simmons College, Boston, Mass.	2	Coed	Private	2,754
Simon Fraser University, Burnaby, B.C.	4	Coed	Public	4,123
Simpson College, Indianola, Iowa	2	Coed	Pvt-Methodist	919
Sinclair Community College, Dayton, Ohio	1	Coed	Public	6,350
Sioux Falls College, Sioux Falls, S.Dak.	2	Coed	Pvt-Baptist	844
Sir George Williams University, Montreal, Quebec	4	Coed	Pvt-YMCA	6,094
Siskiyous, College of the, Weed, Calif.	1	Coed	Public	2,196
Skagit Valley College, Mount Vernon, Wash.	1	Coed	Public	3,717
Skidmore College, Saratoga Springs, N.Y.	2	Coed	Private	2,039
Skyline College, San Bruno, Calif.	1	Coed	Public	5,049
Slippery Rock State College, Slippery Rock, Pa.	3	Coed	Public	5,897
Smith College, Northampton, Mass.	4	Coord	Private	2,648
Snead State Junior College, Boaz, Ala.	1	Coed	Public	1,402
Solano Community College, Suisun City, Calif.	1	Coed	Public	6,613
Somerset County College, Somerville, N.J.	1	Coed	Public	1,752
South, University of the, Sewanee, Tenn.	3	Coed	Pvt-Episcopal	991
South Alabama, University of, Mobile, Ala.	4	Coed	Public	5,621
South Carolina, Medical University of, Charleston, S.C.	4	Coed	Public	1,457
South Carolina, University of, Columbia, S.C.	4	Coed	Public	18,667
South Carolina State College, Orangeburg, S.C.	2	Coed	Public	2,640
South Dakota, University of, Vermillion, S.Dak.	4	Coed	Public	6,586
South Dakota School of Mines & Technology, Rapid City, S.Dak.	4	Coed	Public	1,182
South Dakota State University, Brookings, S.Dak.	4	Coed	Public	6,870
South Florida, University of, Tampa, Fla.	4	Coed	Public	18,193
South Georgia College, Douglas, Ga.	1	Coed	Public	1,341
South Plains College, Levelland, Texas.	1	Coed	Public	1,738
South Texas Junior College, Houston, Texas.	1	Coed	Private	4,318
Southeast Missouri State University, Cape Girardeau, Mo.	4	Coed	Public	7,345
Southeastern College, Whiteville, N.C.	1	Coed	Public	1,100
Southeastern Louisiana University, Hammond, La.	3	Coed	Public	5,981
Southeastern Massachusetts University, North Dartmouth, Mass.	4	Coed	Public	5,375
Southeastern State College, Durant, Okla.	2	Coed	Public	3,920
Southern Baptist Theological Seminary, Louisville, Ky.	3	Coed	Pvt-Baptist	1,129
Southern California, University of, Los Angeles, Calif.	4	Coed	Private	19,898
Southern Colorado State College, Pueblo, Colo.	3	Coed	Public	5,773
Southern Connecticut State College, New Haven, Conn.	3	Coed	Public	12,644
Southern Idaho, College of, Twin Falls, Idaho.	1	Coed	Public	1,779
Southern Illinois University, Carbondale, Ill.	4	Coed	Public	32,184
Southern Illinois University, Carbondale.	4	Coed	Public	20,349
Southern Illinois University, Edwardsville.	3	Coed	Public	11,835
Southern Methodist University, Dallas, Texas.	4	Coed	Pvt-Methodist	10,835
Southern Missionary College, Collegedale, Tenn.	2	Coed	Pvt-Seventh-day Adventist	1,421
Southern Mississippi, University of, Hattiesburg, Miss.	4	Coed	Public	8,772
Southern Oregon College, Ashland, Oreg.	2	Coed	Public	4,499
Southern State College, Magnolia, Ark.	2	Coed	Public	1,896
Southern Union State Junior College, Wadley, Ala.	1	Coed	Public	916
Southern University and Agricultural and Mechanical College, Baton Rouge, La.	3	Coed	Public	8,735
Southern Utah State College, Cedar City, Utah.	2	Coed	Public	1,821
Southside Virginia Community College, Alberta, Va.	1	Coed	Public	1,097
Southwest Baptist College, Bolivar, Mo.	2	Coed	Pvt-Baptist	1,171
Southwest Minnesota State College, Marshall, Minn.	2	Coed	Public	2,669
Southwest Mississippi Junior College, Summit, Miss.	1	Coed	Public	894
Southwest Missouri State University, Springfield, Mo.	3	Coed	Public	9,536
Southwest Texas Junior College, Uvalde, Texas.	1	Coed	Public	1,297
Southwest Texas State University, San Marcos, Texas.	3	Coed	Public	11,804
Southwest Virginia Community College, Richlands, Va.	1	Coed	Public	1,351
Southwestern at Memphis, Tenn.	2	Coed	Pvt-Presbyterian	1,110
Southwestern Baptist Theological Seminary, Fort Worth, Texas.	4	Coed	Pvt-Baptist	2,019
Southwestern College, Chula Vista, Calif.	1	Coed	Public	8,188
Southwestern College, Oklahoma City, Okla.	1	Coed	Private	1,393
Southwestern Louisiana, University of, Lafayette, La.	4	Coed	Public	11,436
Southwestern Michigan College, Dowagiac, Mich.	1	Coed	Public	950
Southwestern Oregon Community College, Coos Bay, Oreg.	1	Coed	Public	2,555
Southwestern State College, Weatherford, Okla.	3	Coed	Public	5,563
Southwestern University, Georgetown, Texas.	2	Coed	Pvt-Methodist	819
Spalding College, Louisville, Ky.	3	Coed	Pvt-Roman Catholic	1,048
Spartanburg County Technical Education Center, Spartanburg, S.C.	1	Coed	Public	1,782
Spartanburg Junior College, Spartanburg, S.C.	1	Coed	Pvt-Methodist	2,705
Spelman College, Atlanta, Ga.	2	W	Private	1,069
Spokane Community College, Spokane, Wash.	1	Coed	Public	2,653
Spokane Falls Community College, Spokane, Wash.	1	Coed	Public	3,450
Spring Hill College, Mobile, Ala.	3	Coed	Pvt-Roman Catholic	950
Springfield College, Springfield, Mass.	3	Coed	Private	2,665
Springfield Technical Community College, Springfield, Mass.	1	Coed	Public	4,755
Stanford University, Stanford, Calif.	4	Coed	Private	12,403
State Technical Institute at Memphis, Tenn.	1	Coed	Public	1,925
Stephen F. Austin State University, Nacogdoches, Texas.	3	Coed	Public	10,255
Stephens College, Columbia, Mo.	1	Coed	Private	1,938
Stetson University, De Land, Fla.	4	Coed	Pvt-Baptist	2,924
Steubenville, College of, Steubenville, Ohio.	2	Coed	Pvt-Roman Catholic	1,202
Stevens Institute of Technology, Hoboken, N.J.	4	Coed	Private	2,154
Stonehill College, North Easton, Mass.	2	Coed	Pvt-Roman Catholic	1,987
Suffolk County Community College, Selden, N.Y.	1	Coed	Public	12,387
Suffolk University, Boston, Mass.	3	Coed	Private	3,810
Sul Ross State College, Alpine, Texas.	3	Coed	Public	2,627
Sullivan County Community College, South Fallsburg, N.Y.	1	Coed	Public	1,484
Surry Community College, Dobson, N.C.	1	Coed	Public	1,000
Susquehanna University, Selinsgrove, Pa.	2	Coed	Pvt-Lutheran	1,550
Swarthmore College, Swarthmore, Pa.	2	Coed	Private	1,186
Sweet Briar College, Sweet Briar, Va.	2	W	Private	722
Syracuse University, Syracuse, N.Y.	4	Coed	Private	19,453
Tacoma Community College, Tacoma, Wash.	1	Coed	Public	4,677
Tallahassee Community College, Tallahassee, Fla.	1	Coed	Public	2,483
Tampa, University of, Tampa, Fla.	3	Coed	Private	2,266
Tarleton State College, Stephenville, Texas.	2	Coed	Public	3,027
Tarrant County Junior College, Fort Worth, Texas.	1	Coed	Public	6,752
Taylor University, Upland, Ind.	2	Coed	Private	1,429
Technical Institute of Alamance, Burlington, N.C.	1	Coed	Public	912

Name and Location	Level of Instruction	Student Body	Control	Enrollment
Temple Junior College, Temple, Texas	1	Coed	Public	1,282
Temple University, Philadelphia, Pa	4	Coed	Private	30,065
Tennessee, University of, System:				
Chattanooga	3	Coed	Public	4,920
Knoxville	4	Coed	Public	26,370
Martin	3	Coed	Public	4,990
Medical Units, Memphis	4	Coed	Public	1,736
Nashville	3	Coed	Public	3,726
Tennessee State University, Nashville, Tenn	3	Coed	Public	4,712
Tennessee Technological University, Cookeville, Tenn	3	Coed	Public	6,768
Texarkana College, Texarkana, Texas	1	Coed	Public	2,159
Texas, University of, System, Austin, Texas	4	Coed	Public	72,942
Arlington	4	Coed	Public	14,028
Austin	4	Coed	Public	44,446
El Paso	3	Coed	Public	10,550
Texas Agricultural & Mechanical University, College Station, Texas	4	Coed	Public	16,381
Texas Arts and Industries University, Kingsville, Texas	4	Coed	Public	7,682
Texas Christian University, Fort Worth, Texas	4	Coed	Pvt-Disciples of Christ	6,595
Texas Lutheran College, Seguin, Texas	2	Coed	Pvt-Lutheran	1,095
Texas Southern University, Houston, Texas	3	Coed	Public	6,544
Texas Southmost College, Brownsville, Texas	1	Coed	Public	2,248
Texas Technical Institute, Waco, Texas	1	Coed	Public	1,960
Texas Tech University, Lubbock, Texas	4	Coed	Public	21,494
Texas Wesleyan College, Fort Worth, Texas	2	Coed	Pvt-Methodist	1,766
Texas Woman's University, Denton, Texas	4	Coed	Public	6,259
Thames Valley State Technical College, Norwich, Conn	1	Coed	Public	955
Theodore Alfred Lawson State Junior College, Birmingham, Ala	1	Coed	Public	1,601
Thiel College, Greenville, Pa	2	Coed	Pvt-Lutheran	1,314
Thomas More College, Fort Mitchell, Ky	2	Coed	Pvt-Roman Catholic	1,589
Thomas Nelson Community College, Hampton, Va	1	Coed	Public	2,937
Thornton Community College, South Holland, Ill	1	Coed	Public	4,009
Tidewater Community College, Portsmouth, Va	1	Coed	Public	3,932
Toledo, University of, Toledo, Ohio	4	Coed	Public	14,661
Tompkins-Cortland Community College, Groton, N.Y	1	Coed	Public	1,501
Toronto, University of, Toronto, Ontario	4	Coed	Public	27,161
Tougaloo College, Tougaloo, Miss	2	Coed	Pvt-Disciples of Christ	817
Towson State College, Towson, Md	3	Coed	Public	11,391
Transylvania College, Lexington, Ky	2	Coed	Pvt-Disciples of Christ	726
Treasure Valley Community College, Ontario, Oreg	1	Coed	Public	923
Trent University, Peterborough, Ontario	3	Coed	Private	1,776
Trenton State College, Trenton, N.J	3	Coed	Public	8,891
Trevecca Nazarene College, Nashville, Tenn	2	Coed	Pvt-Church of Nazarene	766
Tri-County Technical Education Center, Pendleton, S.C	1	Coed	Public	1,784
Trinidad State Junior College, Trinidad, Colo	1	Coed	Public	1,407
Trinity College, Hartford, Conn	4	Coed	Private	2,075
Trinity College, Washington, D.C	3	Coed	Pvt-Roman Catholic	754
Trinity College and Divinity School, Deerfield, Ill	2	Coed	Pvt-Evangelical	841
Trinity University, San Antonio, Texas	3	Coed	Pvt-Presbyterian	3,187
Tri-State College, Angola, Ind	1	Coed	Private	1,377
Triton College, River Grove, Ill	1	Coed	Public	8,331
Troy State University, Troy, Ala	3	Coed	Public	3,175
Tufts University, Medford, Mass	4	Coed	Private	5,619
Tulane University, New Orleans, La	4	Coord	Private	8,871
Tulsa, University of, Tulsa, Okla	4	Coed	Pvt-Presbyterian	6,021
Tuskegee Institute, Tuskegee Institute, Ala	3	Coed	Private	3,353
Tyler Junior College, Tyler, Texas	1	Coed	Public	4,029
Ulster County Community College, Stone Ridge, N.Y	1	Coed	Public	2,160
Umpqua Community College, Roseburg, Oreg	1	Coed	Public	969
Union College, Barbourville, Ky	3	Coed	Pvt-Methodist	889
Union College, Lincoln, Nebr	2	Coed	Pvt-Seventh-day Adventist	819
Union College, Cranford, N.J	1	Coed	Private	3,844
Union College and University, Schenectady, N.Y	3	Coed	Private	2,955
Union University, Jackson, Tenn	2	Coed	Pvt-Baptist	946
United States Air Force Academy, Colorado Springs, Colo	2	M	Public	4,201
United States Coast Guard Academy, New London, Conn	2	M	Public	1,080
United States International University (including California Western Campus, Elliott Campus, and School of Performing Arts), San Diego, Calif	4	Coed	Private	4,804
United States Merchant Marine Academy, Kings Point, N.Y	2	M	Public	994
United States Military Academy, West Point, N.Y	2	M	Public	4,417
United States Naval Academy, Annapolis, Md	2	M	Public	4,170
Upper Iowa University, Fayette, Iowa	2	Coed	Private	813
Upsala College, East Orange, N.J	2	Coed	Pvt-Lutheran	1,700
Ursinus College, Collegeville, Pa	2	Coed	Pvt-Church of Christ	1,878
USAF School of Applied Aerospace Sciences, Lowry, Colo	2	M	Public	5,273
Utah, University of, Salt Lake City, Utah	4	Coed	Public	21,221
Utah State University, Logan, Utah	4	Coed	Public	8,746
Utah Technical College at Provo, Utah	1	Coed	Public	3,252
Utah Technical College at Salt Lake, Utah	1	Coed	Public	2,461
Valdosta State College, Valdosta, Ga	3	Coed	Public	4,278
Valencia Junior College, Orlando, Fla	1	Coed	Public	4,312
Valley City State College, Valley City, N.Dak	2	Coed	Public	1,114
Valparaiso University, Valparaiso, Ind	3	Coed	Pvt-Lutheran	4,575
Vanderbilt University, Nashville, Tenn	4	Coed	Private	6,895
Vassar College, Poughkeepsie, N.Y	2	Coed	Private	2,331
Ventura College, Ventura, Calif	1	Coed	Public	9,096
Vermont, University of, Burlington, Vt	4	Coed	Public	9,825
Victor Valley College, Victorville, Calif	1	Coed	Public	2,411
Victoria, University of, Victoria, B.C	4	Coed	Public	4,800
Victoria College, Victoria, Texas	1	Coed	Public	1,621
Villanova University, Villanova, Pa	4	Coed	Pvt-Roman Catholic	10,258
Vincennes University, Vincennes, Ind	1	Coed	Public	2,927
Virgin Islands, College of the, St. Thomas, V.I	2	Coed	Public	1,776
Virginia, University of, Charlottesville, Va	4	Coord	Public	22,030
Mary Washington College, Fredericksburg, Va	2	Coed	Public	2,246
Virginia Commonwealth University, Richmond, Va	4	Coed	Public	16,093
Virginia Military Institute, Lexington, Va	2	M	Public	1,106
Virginia Polytechnic Institute, Blacksburg, Va	4	Coed	Public	16,401
Virginia State College, Petersburg, Va	3	Coed	Public	4,179
Virginia Union University, Richmond, Va	2	Coed	Pvt-Baptist	1,468
Virginia Western Community College, Roanoke, Va	1	Coed	Public	3,337
W. W. Holding Technical Institute, Raleigh, N.C	1	Coed	Public	1,360
Wabash College, Crawfordsville, Ind	2	M	Private	745
Wagner College, Staten Island, N.Y	3	Coed	Pvt-Lutheran	3,298
Wake Forest University, Winston-Salem, N.C	4	Coed	Pvt-Baptist	4,013
Walker College, Jasper, Ala	1	Coed	Private	732
Walla Walla College, College Place, Wash	3	Coed	Pvt-Seventh-day Adventist	1,834
Walla Walla Community College, Walla Walla, Wash	1	Coed	Public	1,643
Walsh College, Canton, Ohio	2	Coed	Pvt-Roman Catholic	894
Walters State Community College, Morristown, Tenn	1	Coed	Public	1,357
Wartburg College, Waverly, Iowa	2	Coed	Pvt-Lutheran	1,312
Washburn University of Topeka, Kans	4	Coed	Public	5,256
Washington, University of, Seattle, Wash	4	Coed	Public	34,125
Washington and Jefferson College, Washington, Pa	2	Coed	Private	1,130
Washington and Lee University, Lexington, Va	3	M	Private	1,667
Washington College, Chesterton, Md	2	Coed	Private	790
Washington State University, Pullman, Wash	4	Coed	Public	14,852
Washington Technical Institute, Washington, D.C	1	Coed	Public	4,664
Washington University, St. Louis, Mo	4	Coed	Private	11,159
Washtenaw Community College, Ann Arbor, Mich	1	Coed	Public	4,217
Waterbury State Technical College, Waterbury, Conn	1	Coed	Public	1,184
Waterloo, University of, Waterloo, Ont	4	Coed	Private	12,284
Waterloo Lutheran University, Waterloo, Ontario	3	Coed	Pvt-Lutheran	2,792
Waubonsee Community College, Sugar Grove, Ill	1	Coed	Public	3,198

Name and Location	Level of Instruction	Student Body	Control	Enrollment
Wayland Baptist College, Plainview, Texas	2	Coed	Pvt-Baptist	927
Wayne Community College, Goldsboro, N.C.	1	Coed	Public	1,617
Wayne State College, Wayne, Nebr.	3	Coed	Public	2,176
Wayne State University, Detroit, Mich.	4	Coed	Public	33,837
Waynesburg College, Waynesburg, Pa.	2	Coed	Pvt-Presbyterian	1,056
Weatherford College, Weatherford, Texas	1	Coed	Public	1,043
Weber State College, Ogden, Utah	2	Coed	Public	9,024
Webster College, St. Louis, Mo.	3	Coed	Private	1,760
Wellesley College, Wellesley, Mass.	3	Coed	Private	1,908
Wenatchee Valley College, Wenatchee, Wash.	1	Coed	Public	1,526
Wentworth Institute, Boston, Mass.	1	M	Private	1,632
Wesley College, Dover, Del.	1	Coed	Pvt-Methodist	1,047
Wesleyan University, Middletown, Conn.	4	Coed	Private	1,834
West Chester State College, West Chester, Pa.	3	Coed	Public	8,186
West Coast University, Los Angeles, Calif.	3	Coed	Private	840
West Florida, University of, Pensacola, Fla.	3	Coed	Public	3,559
West Georgia College, Carrollton, Ga.	3	Coed	Public	5,735
West Liberty State College, West Liberty, W.Va.	2	Coed	Public	2,987
West Los Angeles College, Culver City, Calif.	1	Coed	Public	4,954
West Texas State University, Canyon, Texas	3	Coed	Public	6,574
West Valley College, Campbell, Calif.	1	Coed	Public	13,906
West Virginia College of Graduate Studies, Institute, W.Va.	4	Coed	Public	1,499
West Virginia Inst. of Technology, Montgomery, W.Va.	3	Coed	Public	2,355
West Virginia State College, Institute, W.Va.	2	Coed	Public	3,528
West Virginia University, Morgantown, W.Va.	4	Coed	Public	18,482
West Virginia Wesleyan College, Buckhannon, W.Va.	2	Coed	Pvt-Methodist	1,652
Westark Community College, Fort Smith, Ark.	1	Coed	Public	1,871
Westchester Community College, Valhalla, N.Y.	1	Coed	Public	6,560
Western Carolina College, Cullowhee, N.C.	3	Coed	Public	6,104
Western Connecticut State College, Danbury, Conn.	3	Coed	Public	4,529
Western Illinois University, Macomb, Ill.	3	Coed	Public	14,904
Western Kentucky University, Bowling Green, Ky.	3	Coed	Public	11,481
Western Maryland College, Westminster, Md.	3	Coed	Pvt-Methodist	2,289
Western Michigan University, Kalamazoo, Mich.	4	Coed	Public	22,349
Western Montana College, Dillon, Mont.	3	Coed	Public	897
Western New England College, Springfield, Mass.	3	Coed	Private	3,286
Western New Mexico University, Silver City, N.Mex.	3	Coed	Public	1,448
Western Ontario, University of, London, Ontario	4	Coed	Public	12,788
Western Piedmont Community College, Morganton, N.C.	1	Coed	Public	1,074
Western State College, Gunnison, Colo.	3	Coed	Public	3,555
Western Washington State College, Bellingham, Wash.	3	Coed	Public	10,144
Western Wisconsin Technical Institute, La Crosse, Wis.	1	Coed	Public	2,254
Westfield State College, Westfield, Mass.	3	Coed	Public	3,848
Westmar College, Le Mars, Iowa	2	Coed	Pvt-Methodist	816
Westminster College, New Wilmington, Pa.	2	Coed	Pvt-Presbyterian	2,006
Westminster College, Salt Lake City, Utah	2	Coed	Pvt-Methodist	768
Westmont College, Santa Barbara, Calif.	3	Coed	Private	964
Wharton County Junior College, Wharton, Texas	1	Coed	Public	1,934
Wheaton College, Wheaton, Ill.	3	Coed	Private	2,087
Wheaton College, Norton, Mass.	3	Coed	Private	1,166
Wheelock College, Boston, Mass.	3	Coed	Private	928
Whitman College, Walla Walla, Wash.	3	Coed	Private	1,091
Whittier College, Whittier, Calif.	3	Coed	Private	1,774
Whitworth College, Spokane, Wash.	3	Coed	Pvt-Presbyterian	1,572
Wichita State University, Wichita, Kans.	4	Coed	Public	13,153
Widener College, Chester, Pa.	3	Coed	Private	1,926

Name and Location	Level of Instruction	Student Body	Control	Enrollment
Wilberforce University, Wilberforce, Ohio	2	Coed	Pvt-Methodist Episcopal	1,277
Wilkes College, Wilkes-Barre, Pa.	3	Coed	Private	3,149
Wilkes Community College, Wilkesboro, N.C.	1	Coed	Public	1,115
Willamette University, Salem, Oreg.	3	Coed	Pvt-Methodist	1,595
William and Mary, College of, Williamsburg, Va.	4	Coed	Public	5,588
William Carey College, Hattiesburg, Miss.	2	Coed	Pvt-Baptist	1,002
William Jewell College, Liberty, Mo.	2	Coed	Pvt-Baptist	1,205
William Paterson College of New Jersey, Wayne, N.J.	3	Coed	Public	11,027
William Penn College, Oskaloosa, Iowa	2	Coed	Pvt-Friends	813
William Rainey Harper College, Palatine, Ill.	1	Coed	Public	7,739
William Woods College, Fulton, Mo.	2	W	Private	1,248
Williams College, Williamstown, Mass.	3	Coed	Private	1,719
Williamsport Area Community College, Williamsport, Pa.	1	Coed	Public	2,795
Wilmington College, Wilmington, Ohio	2	Coed	Pvt-Friends	911
Windham College, Putney, Vt.	2	Coed	Private	893
Windsor, University of, Windsor, Ont.	4	Coed	Private	5,838
Wingate College, Wingate, N.C.	1	Coed	Pvt-Baptist	1,550
Winnipeg, University of, Winnipeg, Manitoba	3	Coed	Pvt-United Church	2,378
Winona State College, Winona, Minn.	3	Coed	Public	4,523
Winston-Salem State University, Winston-Salem, N.C.	3	Coed	Public	1,720
Winthrop College, Rock Hill, S.C.	3	Coed	Public	4,068
Wisconsin, University of:				
Eau Claire, Wis.	3	Coed	Public	8,805
Green Bay, Wis.	2	Coed	Public	3,625
La Crosse, Wis.	2	Coed	Public	6,863
Madison, Wis.	4	Coed	Public	34,923
Milwaukee, Wis.	4	Coed	Public	23,293
Oshkosh, Wis.	3	Coed	Public	11,419
Parkside, Wis.	2	Coed	Public	4,366
Platteville, Wis.	3	Coed	Public	4,435
River Falls, Wis.	3	Coed	Public	4,237
Stevens Point, Wis.	3	Coed	Public	9,335
Stout, Wis.	3	Coed	Public	5,641
Superior, Wis.	3	Coed	Public	3,313
Whitewater, Wis.	3	Coed	Public	8,770
Wisconsin, University of, Center System, Madison, Wis.	1	Coed	Public	6,885
Wittenberg University, Springfield, Ohio	3	Coed	Pvt-Lutheran	3,167
Wofford College, Spartanburg, S.C.	3	Coed	Pvt-Methodist	1,034
Woodbury College, Los Angeles, Calif.	2	Coed	Private	1,993
Wooster, College of, Wooster, Ohio	3	Coed	Pvt-Presbyterian	1,836
Worcester Junior College, Worcester, Mass.	1	Coed	Private	1,556
Worcester Polytechnic Institute, Worcester, Mass.	4	Coed	Private	2,537
Worcester State College, Worcester, Mass.	3	Coed	Public	3,874
Wright State University, Dayton, Ohio	4	Coed	Public	12,357
Wyoming, University of, Laramie, Wyo.	4	Coed	Public	9,989
Wytheville Community College, Wytheville, Va.	1	Coed	Public	1,156
Xavier University, Cincinnati, Ohio	3	Coed	Pvt-Roman Catholic	5,991
Xavier University of Louisiana, New Orleans, La.	3	Coed	Pvt-Roman Catholic	1,548
Yakima Valley College, Yakima, Wash.	1	Coed	Public	2,888
Yale University, New Haven, Conn.	4	Coed	Private	9,117
Yeshiva University, New York, N.Y.	4	Coord	Pvt-Jewish	3,440
York College of Pennsylvania, York, Pa.	2	Coed	Private	2,875
York County Technical Education Center, Rock Hill, S.C.	1	Coed	Public	1,007
York University, Toronto, Ont.	4	Coed	Private	11,340
Youngstown State University, Youngstown, Ohio	4	Coed	Public	13,988
Yuba College, Marysville, Calif.	1	Coed	Public	5,253

URUGUAY

Uruguay spent the year 1973 in a state of continued social, political, and economic crisis. The president, Juan María Bordaberry, clung to his post while support from political parties other than his own Colorado party withered away and the military increased its influence despite its disunity.

Political Developments. At his inauguration in March 1972, Bordaberry had outlined a stabilization and recovery program. It sought to promote industrialization, exports, and fiscal stability to achieve a foreign-trade surplus, and it sought fuller employment. The program also aimed to achieve a decrease in political tensions and to eliminate the violence of the urban guerrillas known as the Tupamaros. There was a brief decline in political confrontations, but the Bordaberry program failed to stem a downward economic spiral, and social unrest and criticism soon resumed. By early 1973, public confidence in government mechanisms was at an all-time low.

A partial military coup, on Feb. 12, 1973, left the military even more firmly entrenched in the government. Bordaberry staged a "self coup" of modest dimensions on June 27, and struggled for the rest of the year to retain some semblance of control by ingeniously "improvising" the struggles of the powerful military factions that surrounded him.

During this tug of war, the political freedoms for which Uruguay had long been noted virtually disappeared. The National Convention of Labor (CNT) was suppressed, private property was seized, the press was throttled, free assembly was denied, and torture and arbitrary jailings without due process were practiced.

The armed forces had become active within the political system in the late 1960's under Bordaberry's predecessor, Jorge Pacheco, as the government turned to law-and-order tactics to cope with the terrorism of the Tupamaro guerrillas. Under Pacheco, the military leaders were somewhat rebellious at their assigned role. In 1973, they ceased accepting commands from Bordaberry. After the February coup they produced a 19-point statement which outlined an almost total overhaul of the system. It called for redistribution of land and wealth, elimination of corruption, workers' participation in public and private enterprise management, and explicitly harsh anti-Communist measures. It established a seven-man National Security Council (COSENA), consisting of four cabinet-rank members (not all of whom had to be military officers) and the chiefs of the three military services. This council was to direct government policy without regard to existing law or constitutional guarantees. Bordaberry retained the presidency by approving the plan.

The military expected that all other civilian politicians would also yield, but this did not occur. Military disunity and civilian defiance of both the armed services and the president prevented the organization of COSENA. When the last independent political party withdrew its support from Bordaberry, the president staged his June 27 "minicoup" and dissolved the parliament. He later announced a new Council of State to replace it. Meanwhile, many political leaders were jailed.

Economy. The period 1972–73 was one of raging inflation. Periodic "minidevaluations," of which there were 10 in 1972, continued throughout 1973, with the value of the peso declining from 250 to the U. S. dollar in late 1971 to 911 to the dollar in September 1973. Living costs rose 96% during 1972 and over 100% in 1973. Wages also rose, but under firm control, lagging about 35% behind living costs during the two-year period. Unemployment increased, and tax receipts declined.

Bordaberry sought a favorable trade balance in order to pay foreign debts (estimated at over $550 million) and to revive international confidence in the Uruguayan economy. Export surpluses were achieved in 1973 only by repression of internal consumption, especially that of meat, and by strict import controls. Ranchers were encouraged by these policies to smuggle live cattle to Brazil, while factories that needed imported fuel, raw materials, and subassemblies were operated below capacity. Corruption involving the buying of official favors remained widespread.

Emigration. Continuing domestic tension and unemployment were principally responsible for the emigration of about 240,000 Uruguayans (about 8% of the population) between 1968 and 1973. Young and professionally well-qualified citizens were heavily represented in this group. The countries of preference were Australia, Canada, and the United States.

Inter-American Affairs. U. S. military officers indicated some reluctance in 1973 to give Uruguay technical aid that might contribute to political repression. Meanwhile, Brazilian military influence was on the increase.

On the economic front, Brazil granted $25 million in credits to help Uruguay place its exports in Brazilian markets.

Argentine relations were ruffled briefly by a boundary disagreement affecting the River Plata estuary. Argentina held for the *thalweg* (the channel midline traditionally recognized in international law), while Uruguay insisted on placing the boundary at the geographic midline. The issue was settled by a compromise signed Nov. 19, 1973.

PHILIP B. TAYLOR, JR.
University of Houston

URUGUAY • Information Highlights

Official Name: Eastern Republic of Uruguay.
Location: Southeastern coast of South America.
Area: 68,536 square miles (177,508 sq km).
Population (1973 est.): 3,000,000. *Density,* 41 per square mile (16 per sq km).
Chief City (1963 census): Montevideo, the capital, 1,202,757.
Government: *Head of state,* Juan M. Bordaberry, president (took office March 1972). *Head of government,* Juan M. Bordaberry. *Legislature*—General Assembly (suspended June 1973). *Major political parties*—Colorado party; Blanco (Nacional) party.
Language: Spanish (official).
Education: *Expenditure* (1967), 2% of gross national product. *School enrollment* (1968)—primary, 369,816; general secondary, 123,426; technical/vocational, 35,648; university/higher, 18,650.
Monetary Unit: Peso (911 pesos equal U. S.$1, Sept. 1973).
Gross National Product (1972 est.): $2,025,000,000.
Economic Indexes: *Industrial production* (1970), 121 (1963 = 100); *agricultural production* (1971), 103 (1963 = 100); *consumer price index* (1972), 5,076 (1963 = 100).
Manufacturing (major products): Textiles, construction and building materials, meat products, beverages, chemicals.
Major Agricultural Products: Wheat, corn, rice, livestock, wool.
Major Minerals: Marble, building stone, gravel.
Foreign Trade (1972): *Exports,* $197,000,000; *Imports,* $187,000,000. *Chief trading partners* (1971)—West Germany (took 12% of exports, supplied 10% of imports); Brazil (11.7%—16%); United Kingdom (7.4%—8.3%); United States (4.8%—10.5%).
Transportation: *Motor vehicles* (1970), 209,000 (automobiles, 121,000); *railroads* (1971), 1,848 miles (2,974 km); *merchant fleet* (1972), 143,000 gross registered tons; *major national airline,* PLUNA (Primeras Lineas Uruguayas de Navegación Aérea).
Communications: *Telephones* (1972), 235,226; *newspapers* (1969), 31.

UTAH

Utah enjoyed a unique position in state finances for 1973 because, for the fifth consecutive year, the state would be able to finance all state operations during fiscal 1974–75 with no tax increase. In fact, it was expected that some tax reductions could be made in the coming year. A special session of the Utah Legislature, meeting in October 1973, eliminated the state property tax levy for schools for 1974 and provided a one-time income tax credit of $6 per person. This latter tax reduction was expected to total $6 million and will be financed from sales tax revenue.

Unusual Level of Affluence. The October 1973 position of "affluence in state finances," although it resulted from a combination of circumstances, could not be expected to reoccur in the future. Contributory factors included federal revenue-sharing funds and a court decision that changed the method of computing state corporate income tax liability, with some retroactive effect.

In addition, according to a Utah Foundation Report, revenue collections in recent years had exceeded advance estimates. Inflation, and also an unparalleled boom in construction and the sale of durable goods, had been major factors in a continued high level of tax collections.

Toward the end of the year, however, it became obvious that the worldwide energy crisis would have a major adverse impact on Utah because tourism is a major industry of the entire state.

─────── **UTAH • Information Highlights** ───────

Area: 84,916 square miles (219,932 sq km).
Population (1972 est.): 1,126,000. *Density:* 13 per sq mi.
Chief Cities (1970 census): Salt Lake City, the capital, 175,-885; Ogden, 69,478; Provo, 53,131; Bountiful, 27,956; Orem, 25,729; Logan, 22,333; Murray, 21,206.
Government (1973): *Chief Officers*—governor, Calvin L. Rampton (D); secy. of state, Clyde L. Miller (D); atty. gen., Vernon B. Romney (R); treas., David L. Duncan (D); supt. of public instruction, Walter D. Talbot; chief justice, E. R. Callister, Jr. *Legislature*—Senate, 29 members (16 Republicans, 13 Democrats); House of Representatives, 75 members (44 R, 31 D).
Education (1972–73): *Enrollment*—public elementary schools, 162,775 pupils, 5,950 teachers; public secondary schools, 142,164 pupils, 5,775 teachers; nonpublic schools, 4,700 pupils, 200 teachers; colleges and universities, 73,228 students. *Public school expenditures*, $212,500,000 ($739 per pupil). *Average teacher's salary*, $8,990.
State Finances (fiscal year 1971): *Revenues*, $612,774,000 (4% general sales tax and gross receipts taxes, $101,300,-000; motor fuel tax, $40,816,000; federal funds, $187,076,-000). *Expenditures*, $545,100,000 (education, $285,814,000; health, welfare, and safety, $73,005,000; highways, $100,939,000). *State debt*, $102,603,000 (June 30, 1971).
Personal Income (1972): $4,217,000,000; per capita, $3,745.
Public Assistance (1972): $64,405,000. *Average monthly payments* (Dec. 1972)—old-age assistance, $66.38; aid to families with dependent children, $193.44.
Labor Force: *Nonagricultural wage and salary earners* (July 1973), 417,700. *Average annual employment* (1972)—manufacturing, 59,400; trade, 91,100; government, 104,900; services, 65,400. *Insured unemployed* (Sept. 1973)—5,700 (2.0%).
Manufacturing (1971): *Value added by manufacture*, $864,200,-000. Transportation equipment, $115,700,000; food and kindred products, $103,000,000; nonelectrical machinery, $67,500,000; fabricated metal products, $63,600,000; printing and publishing, $51,600,000; petroleum and coal products, $44,100,000.
Agriculture (1972): *Cash farm income*, $260,042,000 (livestock, $201,636,000; crops, $44,545,000; government payments, $13,861,000). *Chief crops* (in order of value, 1971)—Hay, wheat, barley, sugar beets.
Mining (1972): *Production value*, $536,795,000 (ranks 16th among the states). *Chief minerals*—Copper, $274,299,000; petroleum, $79,648,000; coal, $32,800,000; molybdenum, value not available.
Transportation: *Roads* (1972), 40,981 miles (65,951 km); *motor vehicles* (1972), 711,267; *railroads* (1972), 1,750 miles (2,816 km); *public airports* (1972), 54.
Communications: *Telephones* (1973), 683,500; *television stations* (1971), 3; *radio stations* (1971), 42; *newspapers* (1973), 5 (daily circulation, 265,000).

Local Government. A Salt Lake County Study Commission, consisting of housewives, businessmen, educators, farmers, and lawyers, was formed early in the year to consider possible changes and improvements in Salt Lake county government. The objective of public hearings was to recommend possible consolidation of the governmental units of Salt Lake county, Salt Lake City, and special districts. Alternatives to the present commission form of government included merging of unincorporated areas, a community council plan, and a city-county government structure along the lines of the Urban County Plan. The commission's findings were to be presented to the County Commission in February 1974.

Utah's Judicial System. A major change in Utah's handling of criminal cases, enacted in 1971, took effect on Jan. 1, 1973. The office of district attorney was abolished, and responsibility for prosecution of criminal charges was turned over to the county attorneys. Although fears had been expressed that county attorneys in rural areas might not be qualified to practice before the courts, and might not be capable of handling felony prosecutions, the state's experience during 1973 allayed these anxieties. On the other hand, justices' courts, while still considered necessary in rural areas, continued to be criticized for alleged abuses.

LORENZO K. KIMBALL, *University of Utah*

VANCOUVER

In 1973 a new City Council took office in Vancouver, pledging to make British Columbia's largest city more people-oriented through an emphasis on green and open spaces and a curtailment of the random construction of high-rise buildings. In September, the council approved a $3.4 million plan for turning a six-block section of Granville Street, Vancouver's main thoroughfare, into a pedestrian mall by July 1, 1974.

On October 24, Vancouver voters rejected a proposal to elect aldermen by a ward system and voted to retain the present system of electing members at large. However, the voters were in favor of expanding the council from 10 members to from 12 to 15.

Port of Vancouver. The port of Vancouver, the second largest in North America, was partly idle in the summer of 1973 because of a rail strike that lasted almost seven weeks. The 56,000 strikers were ordered back to work by the federal government.

In October longshoremen demonstrated against Canadian cargo being shipped through U. S. ports because of inadequate container facilities in Vancouver. About 50% of the cargo traveling between the Orient and western Canada was being shipped through Seattle. Meanwhile, construction was underway on the $25 million Vanterm container terminal, due for completion in February 1975. Vanterm was expected to handle 6% of the port's total tonnage, which in 1973 was estimated at 43 million tons.

Hundreds of volunteers joined in clean-up operations along the shores of Burrard Inlet, after some 50,000 gallons of crude oil were spilled at the entrance to Vancouver harbor on September 25. The oil, which caused extensive pollution, escaped from a ruptured fuel tank on the 10,000-ton British freighter *Erawan*, when it collided with the Japanese-owned container vessel *Sun Diamond*.

Sports. At the beginning of August 1973, some 3,000 young athletes from across Canada came to the Vancouver suburbs of Burnaby and New West-

minster for the largest athletic event ever held in the country—the 1973 Canada Summer Games. In September, Mayor Art Philipps' bid for the 1980 Winter Olympics was approved by the Canadian Olympic Committee, but had yet to be considered by the International Olympic Committee, which was to make its final decision in October 1974. The million people of Greater Vancouver were able to watch a second major league hockey club in action when the Philadelphia Blazers of the World Hockey Association became the Vancouver Blazers in 1973.

DEBRA CRAINE, *"The Canadian Press," Vancouver*

VENEZUELA

With the election of a new president and Congress scheduled in December, attention in Venezuela in 1973 was monopolized largely by politicians. Under Venezuelan law, a president is limited to a single five-year term, and President Rafaél Caldera, whose Christian Social party (COPEI) had ended 20 years of rule by the Democratic Action party (AD) in 1968, was scheduled to leave office in March 1974. Contrary to some predictions, the AD swept back into power on Dec. 9, 1973, electing its candidate, Carlos Andrés Pérez, to the presidency. Economically, the year 1973 was improved for Venezuelans by the rise in the value of petroleum on world markets. In February 1973, Venezuela became the sixth member of the very promising common market known as the Andean Group.

December Election. Although 14 presidential hopefuls, supported by 20 parties, vied for the presidency, only Pérez and the candidate of COPEI, Lorenzo Fernández, were considered serious contenders. One Venezuelan with a considerable popular following—the former president Marcos Pérez Jiménez—was barred from running by a constitutional amendment that denied participation to anyone convicted of a felony. (Pérez Jiménez had once been convicted of embezzlement.) In future presidential elections, the large field of candidates was expected to be cut by a requirement that only those parties with a minimum membership of 250,000 registered voters would be allowed to present candidates.

In fact, the pattern of campaign expenditures in 1973 was enough to concentrate popular attention on the two centrist candidates, and, between them, they won over 85% of the votes. The election was a clear-cut victory for Pérez, who received nearly 50% of the presidential ballots as against less than 40% for his chief opponent. His party, the AD, captured a majority of seats in both houses of Congress. Pérez was to be inaugurated in March 1974.

Last Months of the Caldera Administration. Relations between President Caldera and the opposition-controlled Congress were strained during his last year in office. The president several times accused the legislature of obstructive tactics.

A major governmental concern was the politicization of the secondary school students who were angry about limited access to the university and poor educational facilities in general. In February 1973 some 5,000 students took to the streets to protest the alleged death by torture of one of their number. The government denied any responsibility. Students and other factions demonstrated again in May against visiting U. S. Secretary of State William Rogers.

Economic Developments. In his state of the union message early in 1973, President Caldera

──────── VENEZUELA • Information Highlights ────────

Official Name: Republic of Venezuela.
Location: Northeastern South America.
Area: 352,143 square miles (912,050 sq km).
Population (1973 est.): 11,900,000. *Density,* 34 per square mile (13 per sq km).
Chief Cities (1969 est.): Caracas, the capital, 1,600,000; Maracaibo, 625,100; Barquisimeto, 280,100.
Government: *Head of state,* Rafaél Caldera, president (took office March 1969). *Head of government,* Rafaél Caldera. *Legislature*—Congress: Senate and Chamber of Deputies. *Major political parties*—Democratic Action party (AD); Christian Social party (COPEI).
Language: Spanish (official).
Education: *Expenditure* (1969), 20.9% of total public expenditure. *School enrollment* (1969)—primary, 1,681,947; secondary, 448,214; technical/vocational, 146,421; university/higher, 74,666.
Monetary Unit: Bolívar (4.30 bolívares equal U. S.$1, Aug. 1973).
Gross National Product (1972 est.): $11,620,000,000.
Economic Indexes: *Industrial production* (1972), 124 (1963 = 100); *agricultural production* (1971), 156 (1963 = 100); *consumer price index* (1972), 120 (1963 = 100).
Manufacturing (major products): Processed foods, paper and paperboard, beverages, petroleum products, metal products, furniture, clothing.
Major Agricultural Products: Coffee, cacao, bananas, sugarcane, cotton, rice, corn, dairy products.
Major Minerals: Petroleum (ranks 5th among world producers, 1971), natural gas (world rank 4th, 1971), iron ore, gold, nickel, diamonds, coal.
Foreign Trade (1971): *Exports,* $3,155,000,000; *Imports,* $1,931,000,000. *Chief trading partners* (1970)—United States (took 35% of exports, supplied 48.5% of imports); Netherlands Antilles (20% of exports); Canada (11.2% of exports).
Tourism: Receipts (1971), $60,500,000.
Transportation: *Motor vehicles* (1969), 752,000; *railroads* (1971), 109 miles (175 km); *merchant fleet* (1972), 411,000 gross registered tons; *major national airline,* VIASA (Venezolana Internacional de Aviación).
Communications: *Telephones* (1972), 443,668; *newspapers* (1971), 42 (daily circulation, 998,000).

pointed to the following accomplishments during 1972: creation of 116,000 new jobs, construction of 60,000 homes for persons of moderate income, and a growth of 10.5% in the gross national product. During the preceding four years, the Caldera administration claimed, it had completed 12 ports, 12 airports, 25 hospitals (3,177 beds), 1,736 primary school buildings and 36 high school buildings (4,314 rooms), and a variety of irrigation, flood control, sewage disposal, and transportation projects.

Venezuela raised the price of its petroleum several times in 1973, with huge increases occurring toward the end of the year. Rumania agreed to supply equipment for exploring and exploiting Venezuelan oil and to begin importing the product. Petroleum production increased by 5.13% during the first nine months of 1973.

After delaying for some years, Venezuela joined the Andean Group, an economic community that was gradually lowering tariff barriers and rapidly expanding trade between its members. Venezuelan capital was expected to play an important part in the further development of the Andean region.

Foreign Affairs. In February, President Caldera visited seven Latin American countries, his visit to Argentina being the first official one made by a Venezuelan president. President Nicolae Ceauşescu of Rumania paid a state visit to Venezuela in September. Venezuela was also rumored to be on' the brink of reestablishing diplomatic ties with Cuba, which had been broken in 1963.

Venezuela and Colombia resumed their negotiations in Rome over a territorial dispute. Also in 1973, a boundary revision added to Venezuela about 4,000 square miles (10,000 sq km) of land previously disputed with Brazil, most of it in the southwestern part of the state of Bolívar.

LEO B. LOTT
University of Montana

——————— VERMONT • Information Highlights ———————

Area: 9,609 square miles (24,887 sq km).
Population (1972 est.): 462,000. *Density:* 49 per sq mi.
Chief Cities (1970 census): Montpelier, the capital, 8,609; Burlington, 38,633; Rutland, 19,293; Bennington, 14,586; Brattleboro, 12,239.
Government (1973): *Chief Officers*—governor, Thomas P. Salmon (D); lt. gov., John S. Burgess (R); secy. of state, Richard C. Thomas (R); atty. gen., Kimberly B. Cheney (R); treas., Frank H. Davis (R); commissioner of education, Robert A. Withey; chief justice, P. L. Shangraw. *General Assembly*—Senate, 30 members (22 Republicans, 8 Democrats); House of Representatives, 150 members (89 R, 60 D, 1 Independent).
Education (1972–73): *Enrollment*—public elementary schools, 68,514 pupils, 3,165 teachers; public secondary schools, 44,801 pupils, 3,185 teachers; nonpublic schools, 12,300 pupils, 750 teachers; colleges and universities, 24,715 students. *Public school expenditures,* $126,230,000 ($1,211 per pupil). *Average teacher's salary,* $9,110.
State Finances (fiscal year 1971): *Revenues,* $309,020,000 (3% general sales tax and gross receipts taxes, $19,476,000; motor fuel tax, $17,382,000; federal funds, $91,903,000). *Expenditures,* $304,511,000 (education, $107,739,000; health, welfare, and safety, $55,414,000; highways, $73,461,000). *State debt,* $288,795,000 (June 30, 1971).
Personal Income (1972): $1,786,000,000; per capita, $3,865.
Public Assistance (1972): $46,215,000. *Average monthly payments* (Dec. 1972)—old-age assistance, $72.53; aid to families with dependent children, $233.55.
Labor Force: *Nonagricultural wage and salary earners* (July 1973), 163,300. *Average annual employment* (1972)—manufacturing, 38,400; trade, 31,200; government, 28,000; services, 30,300. *Insured unemployed* (Sept. 1973)—3,600 (2.8%).
Manufacturing (1971): *Value added by manufacture,* $562,200,-000. Nonelectrical machinery, $70,200,000; printing and publishing, $55,000,000; food and kindred products, $42,-000,000; lumber and wood products, $37,400,000.
Agriculture (1972): *Cash farm income,* $180,158,000 (livestock, $160,981,000; crops, $18,349,000; government payments, $828,000). *Chief crops* (in order of value, 1971)—Hay, apples, maple syrup, potatoes.
Mining (1972): *Production value,* $35,862,000 (ranks 44th among the states). *Chief minerals*—Stone, $28,044,000; sand and gravel, $3,693,000; asbestos, value not available; talc, value not available.
Transportation: *Roads* (1972), 14,512 miles (23,354 km); *motor vehicles* (1972), 237,153; *railroads* (1972), 766 miles (1,233 km); *public airports* (1972), 13.
Communications: *Telephones* (1973), 265,200; *television stations* (1971), 2; *radio stations* (1971), 22; *newspapers* (1973), 9 (daily circulation, 120,000).

VERMONT

Heavy rains in late June 1973 resulted in flooding of areas east and south of Vermont's Green Mountains. The extent of damage was compared to the disastrous flood of 1927, but there was a minimal loss of life.

Legislative Action. In spite of intense lobbying by the beverage industry and small grocers, public indignation over roadside littering resulted in legislative reaffirmation of a "bottle ban" bill approved in 1972. The bill requires a five-cent deposit on beer and soda bottles and cans, effective September 1. Brewers raised beer prices far above the container charge, and retail grocers' associations circulated petitions, held meetings, and put pressure on Gov. Thomas Salmon to call a special session of the legislature to repeal the law. These efforts failed, however, and the "bottle ban" was viewed as complementing the new state Land Capability and Development Plan to set standards for land development.

The legislature approved two major property tax changes. The first provided for property tax relief, amounting to $10.8 million, based on a sliding scale related to income. The second, resulting from land speculation, heavily taxed capital gains on real estate sales of land held for less than six years.

The legislature also passed a dental health care bill that represents a major breakthrough in public health concepts. Under the bill's provisions, the state will assume part payment of children's dental costs for low- and moderate-income families.

The legislature reluctantly approved a reapportionment plan for the state Senate, after the state supreme court overturned a plan enacted in 1972. The court further ordered that the House of Representatives be reapportioned by March 1, 1974.

Education. Problems on all levels of education resulted in considerable dispute in 1973. Bond issues for public schools were defeated in protest over high tax rates. There also was opposition to a reorganization plan for the University of Vermont, with threats of legislative action when the university's agricultural programs were thought to be endangered. To meet objections, some aspects of the plan were withdrawn and others were modified.

Labor Dispute. The 18-month-old strike against Burlington-area contractors continued in 1973. Governor Salmon was criticized for not helping to end the strike by refusing to circumvent requirements that the lowest bidders be granted state building contracts.

ANDREW E. NUQUIST
University of Vermont

VETERINARY MEDICINE

In 1973 veterinary medicine was concerned with brucellosis in bison in the Yellowstone National Park and with surplus populations of dogs and cats.

Brucellosis in Yellowstone Bison. Brucellosis in the Yellowstone National Park bison herd became a focal point of attention when cattle ranchers and animal disease-control authorities expressed alarm over the possibility that the disease might spread to cattle that sometimes graze on the same open ranges as do the bison. Brucellosis, an infectious disease caused by the bacterium *Brucella abortus*, seriously impairs reproduction in cattle, thereby causing economic difficulties for ranchers and dairymen and ultimately affecting the production of beef and milk. Moreover, brucellosis can be transmitted from cattle to man, producing in man undulant fever.

In addition, there is concern that the brucellosis eradication program, started many years ago and credited with reducing brucellosis in both cattle and man to an extremely low level, could suffer serious setbacks if reservoirs of brucella bacteria are allowed to persist. Disease-control personnel in the U. S. Department of Agriculture claim that rounding up the bison and testing them for brucellosis is possible, though difficult. Some disease authorities think that half of the bison might be infected and that removal of infected bison and vaccination of the calves will remove most of the threat.

Opposing the disease control proposal are ecologists and the U. S. Department of the Interior, which administers the park. They believe that the bison have adjusted to the presence of brucellosis, are in natural balance with their environment, and should not be disturbed. Moreover, they do not regard the threat to cattle as serious, provided that better policing of the park boundaries is practiced. There is also concern that testing and culling of infected bison might disturb the survival capability of the herd.

Surplus Populations of Dogs and Cats. The excess of ownerless and unwanted dogs and cats has reached acute proportions in many major U. S. metropolitan areas. Nationwide, it is estimated that between $350 and $500 million is spent annually to dispose of the millions of excess animals.

The excess stems from uncontrolled and indiscriminate breeding. Too many pet owners fail to restrict dogs and cats or take measures that will render them incapable of reproduction. Veterinary medical groups, humane societies, and other interested organizations generally agree that the surplus cannot be eliminated without a widespread public education campaign and vigorous efforts to sterilize dogs and cats. Ovariohysterectomy, or spaying of the female, and orchiectomy, or castration of the male, are safe surgical operations that effectively sterilize and are widely available from veterinarians. Some interested groups favor the use of existing private veterinary facilities, while others believe that public-supported clinics should be established. Bills were introduced in Congress to provide for public funding of spay clinics and the training of paraprofessional personnel to perform the surgery.

Other measures believed important to reduction of the excess include stricter enforcement of existing animal-control laws, higher licensing fees for dogs and cats capable of reproducing, widespread licensing of cats, and research to develop methods of sterilization or contraception.

ARTHUR FREEMAN, D. V. M., *Editor in Chief, American Veterinary Medical Association*

VIETNAM

One war ended—and another began—in Vietnam in 1973, as the United States disengaged from its combat role in the country. The 12-year "Second Vietnamese War"—which began in 1961 following seven years of uneasy peace after the "First Vietnamese War" (to exterminate French colonial rule)—came to an end on January 28 with a formal cease-fire agreement. By October, however, the chief Vietnamese combatants in that conflict were again engaged in a fierce military struggle.

SOUTH VIETNAM

President Nguyen Van Thieu's government successfully withstood the 1972 Communist offensive, which began on March 31, and emerged as the ruler of most of the people of South Vietnam when the January cease-fire took effect. Thieu put considerable pressure on his powerful U. S. ally in late 1972 and early 1973 in order to influence the peace agree-

——— SOUTH VIETNAM • Information Highlights ———

Official Name: Republic of Vietnam.
Location: Southeast Asia.
Area: 67,108 square miles (173,809 sq km).
Population (1973 est.): 19,100,000. *Density,* 280 per square mile (108 per sq km).
Chief Cities (1968 est.): Saigon, the capital, 1,681,900; Da Nang, 334,200; Hue, 156,500.
Government: *Head of state,* Nguyen Van Thieu, president (reelected Oct. 1971). *Head of government,* Nguyen Van Thieu. *Legislature*—National Assembly: Senate and House of Representatives.
Languages: Vietnamese (official), French, English.
Education: *Expenditure* (1969), 4.2% of total public expenditure.
Monetary Unit: Piastre (525 piastres equal U. S.$1, Oct. 1973).
Gross National Product (1971 est.): $2,350,000,000.
Economic Indexes: *Industrial production* (1971), 216 (1963= 100); *consumer price index* (1972), 875 (1963=100).
Manufacturing (major products): Processed foods, textiles.
Major Agricultural Products: Rice, rubber, corn.
Major Minerals: Zinc, graphite, phosphate.
Foreign Trade (1972): *Exports,* $13,000,000; *Imports,* $707,-000,000. *Chief trading partners* (1970)—France (took 48% of exports, supplied 6% of imports); Japan (12.5%—16%); United States (2.4%—47%).
Tourism: Receipts (1972), $9,230,000.
Transportation: *Motor vehicles* (1970), 89,700; *railroads* (1971), 426 miles (685 km); *major national airline,* Air Vietnam.
Communications: *Telephones* (1972), 38,133; *newspapers* (1970), 56 (daily circulation, 1,221,000).

ment and to acquire additional military equipment and ammunition to fight the enemy without direct American help in the future. The Saigon regime held its own against renewed Communist pressure after the U. S. disengaged its forces and was at least as strong at the end of 1973 as it had been at the time of the cease-fire.

Cease-fire. The January 28 cease-fire agreement —which provided for the withdrawal of all American combat personnel within 60 days but only required North Vietnam not to replace its forces in the south—was essentially a cover for U. S. disengagement. The pact did not bring peace to Vietnam; the 90-day deadline for South Vietnam and the Vietcong to settle their political differences expired in April with no agreement between the two sides. President Thieu's government was left in control of most of South Vietnam's people, but half of the land was in Communist hands.

Thieu remained in office pending an election, a major victory for the non-Communist side. Such voting was to be supervised by a National Council of Reconciliation and Concord that would include Thieu elements, Communists, and "neutralists," but talks between the Vietcong and the government

UPI

SOUTH VIETNAMESE soldiers and villagers in a hamlet just west of Saigon read a newspaper with headlines telling of the cease-fire that was signed in Paris on June 14, 1973.

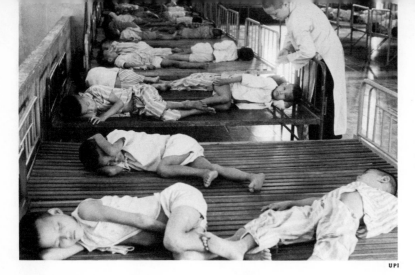

CHILDREN, many of them war orphans, find refuge in this orphanage in the Saigon area.

failed to agree on elections. Similarly, the Joint Military Commission comprising government and Communist representatives had broken down by year's end. The International Control Commission, comprising Indonesia, Poland, Hungary, and Canada (succeeded by Iran when the Canadians quit the commission), was of no help in preventing war from flaring anew.

The war that the cease-fire ended cost the U. S. 45,948 combat dead—and the South and North Vietnamese-Vietcong 184,546 and 927,124 battle fatalities, respectively. Financial cost to the U. S. was officially put at $109.5 billion. In June, the United States and North Vietnam reached a supplementary agreement to strengthen the already much-violated January cease-fire—which it really did not do.

Renewed War. A surge of fighting in the immediate wake of the cease-fire largely involved small infantry clashes and short-lived shelling attacks. This had abated by midyear, following particularly bloody fighting in early June. North Vietnam and the satellite Vietcong took the lead in breaking the cease-fire, but South Vietnam countered with a very vigorous air assault on Communist concentrations. In October the Vietcong issued an order to its personnel that was widely interpreted as signaling the beginning of a new phase in the conflict. Fighting in November was the fiercest since the cease-fire.

The United States cut supplies of artillery, heavy weapons, and ammunition to South Vietnam by one third in an attempt to reduce the level of violence. This action had no effect, however, on what the departing Canadian ICC team called "massive" and "unrelenting" North Vietnamese infiltration. More than 50,000 combatants on both sides lost their lives —a larger number than all the American combat dead between 1961 and 1973.

Politics. President Thieu maneuvered during the year to consolidate his hold on the South Vietnamese political process. In March, he launched a new political party, the Democracy party, on the eve of a trip to the United States to meet with President Nixon. In May-June, the party swept village council elections throughout the non-Communist portion of South Vietnam. In August, Thieu supporters won all 31 races in a Senate election—the first countrywide vote since the cease-fire.

Economy. The economy was troubled as U. S. spending fell back dramatically and prices rose rapidly. The gross national product declined 15%

as a result of reduced American military expenditures. Rice and other commodities were in short supply. Prices in general rose 55% in 1973, but rice, cooking oil, and gas doubled in cost, and sugar tripled. Foreign exchange reserves fell $10 million a month.

Foreign Relations. The United States, the USSR, China, and nine other countries including North and South Vietnam met a month after the January cease-fire pact—as required by that settlement—but they agreed only to "respect" the cease-fire, not to guarantee it. In April, President Thieu visited the United States, where President Nixon promised him more aid, but no intervention. Defense Secretary Schlesinger stated subsequently, however, that the United States would provide air support in the event of "overt" North Vietnamese "aggression."

NORTH VIETNAM

Hanoi's leaders used the end of direct U. S. participation in the Vietnamese fighting—not least of all the termination of American bombing—to rebuild their shattered economy and to seize the military initiative against Saigon.

Communist Strategy. The United States repeatedly charged that North Vietnam was shipping huge quantities of war material and sending a large number of troops into the south in violation of the January agreement. Some 70,000 fighting men, 400 tanks, more than 200 artillery pieces, and 15 anti-aircraft artillery regiments appear to have been moved into Communist-held areas of South Vietnam, where they joined forces and equipment already there at the time of the cease-fire. A road network 250 miles (400 km) in length was constructed south from the border, and 12 airfields were built or rebuilt.

───── **NORTH VIETNAM · Information Highlights** ─────

Official Name: Democratic Republic of Vietnam.
Location: Southeast Asia.
Area: 61,294 square miles (158,750 sq km).
Population (1973 est.): 22,500,000. *Density*, 360 per square mile (140 per sq km).
Chief City (1960 census): Hanoi, the capital, 414,620.
Government: *Head of state*, Ton Duc Thang, president (took office Sept. 1969). *Head of government*, Pham Van Dong, premier (took office July 1954). *First Secretary of Vietnam Workers' (Communist) party*, Le Duan. *Legislature* (unicameral)—National Assembly.
Language: Vietnamese (official).
Monetary Unit: Dong (2.35 dong equal U. S.$1, July 1973).
Manufacturing (major products): Processed foods, cement.
Major Agricultural Products: Rice, sugarcane, tea, sweet potatoes and yams.

HIS FAMILY mourns the death of a South Vietnamese soldier killed after the cease-fire.

WIDE WORLD

In October, the Provisional Revolutionary Government—the Vietcong—called on "all officers and combatants" to "fight back" as long as the Saigon government "has not discontinued its war acts." The "Third Vietnamese War"—to reunify the country on Communist terms—appeared to have begun.

With the fighting escalating late in the year, U. S. Secretary of State Kissinger and North Vietnam negotiator Le Duc Tho met in Paris on December 20. The two 1973 Nobel Prize-winners discussed the ineffective cease-fire.

Politics. Establishment of the cease-fire, and developments thereafter, signaled the return of Lao Dong (Workers') party Secretary Le Duan to de facto leadership of North Vietnam. Le Duan had opposed the extraordinary personnel commitment inherent in the March 31, 1972, offensive, and its failure—and the need for a political settlement—boosted the longtime party secretary's political star.

Economy. Economic factors, particularly the chronic—and worsening—rice shortage, played a part in North Vietnam's agreement to a cease-fire. Despite unfavorable weather, the 1973 winter-spring rice crop, although not meeting government goals, was declared to be satisfactory. Great effort was accorded to rebuilding industrial facilities, roads, and bridges, as well as to increasing agricultural production.

Big Power Relations. The United States appeared to have agreed to a five-year reconstruction aid program for North Vietnam early in the year, but the latter's peace-shattering military acts and U. S. congressional opposition probably sidetracked such assistance forever. In June, Le Duan and Premier Pham Van Dong journeyed to Peking, where China promised "very generous" aid—partly to make up the shortfall occasioned by the failure of Hanoi to obtain expected American aid. The Peking trip was followed in July by a similar mission to Moscow.

RICHARD BUTWELL
State University of New York at Brockport

VIRGIN ISLANDS

In 1973 there was a continuation of the wave of violence that began on St. Croix in 1972 and that has since blighted the peaceful existence of the inhabitants of the Virgin Islands. In August a jury found five Black Muslims guilty of the murders of eight persons at the Fountain Valley Golf Club on St. Croix in September 1972. By mid-October 1973, 13 other persons, mostly whites, had been killed on St. Croix.

Observers attributed the outbreak of violence to the deeply felt frustrations of the native black youth, notably returned veterans, who have found their assimilation into a tourist-industrial society blocked by outside interests. These native people resent the white continentals who monopolize the economically productive activities that have brought affluence to a select group of residents.

Government efforts to deal with the social and economic problems of the native population were frustrated in 1973 by a shortage of federal funds for health, education, public works, and social welfare. News of the violence on St. Croix reduced tourism on the islands. While the call of cruise ships increased 34.6% over 1972, the number of tourists arriving by airplane for longer sojourns declined by about 12% during the tourist season.

The government authorized the establishment of a second oil refinery complex, the Virgin Islands Oil Refinery Corporation. Scheduled to be in operation by the end of 1974, it is expected to produce about 100,000 barrels a day. Of this, 72% will be low-sulfur fuel to be exported to the eastern coast of the United States.

Republican Gov. Melvin H. Evans appointed a Democrat, Athniel C. Ottley, lieutenant governor. Ottley replaced Republican David Mass, who resigned for reasons of health from this normally elective post.

THOMAS G. MATHEWS
University of Puerto Rico

------ **VIRGIN ISLANDS · Information Highlights** ------

Area: 133 square miles (344 sq km).
Population (1970 census): 62,468.
Chief Cities (1970 census): Charlotte Amalie (St. Thomas), the capital, 12,220; Christiansted (St. Croix), 3,020; Frederiksted (St. Croix), 1,531.
Government (1973): *Chief Officers*—governor, Melvin H. Evans (took office Jan. 4, 1971) (R); lt. gov., Athniel C. Ottley (D); atty. gen., Verne Hodge. *Legislature*—Territorial Legislature, 15 members.
Education (1971–72): *Enrollment*—public schools, 19,010 pupils; nonpublic schools, 5,360 pupils; colleges and universities (fall 1971), 473 full-time students, 1,173 part-time students. *Average teacher's salary* (1971), $8,500.
Per Capita Personal Income (1971): $3,000.
Mining: *Chief mineral*—Stone.
Transportation: *Roads* (1972), 420 miles (676 km); *motor vehicles* (1972), 30,254.
Communications: *Telephones* (1972), 26,820; *television stations* (1973), 3; *radio stations* (1973), 6; *newspapers* (1973), 2 daily, 1 weekly.

VIRGINIA

In 1973, Virginia voters returned former Gov. Mills Godwin to the governor's chair. His narrow victory over Lt. Gov. Henry Howell dramatized two trends in recent Virginia politics—the development of a two-party system, and the liberalization of voter attitudes.

Election Campaign. Godwin had first been elected as a Democrat in 1965, defeating Linwood Holton, a Republican. Once a stalwart in the conservative Byrd machine, Godwin established a progressive record as governor, including advocacy of dropping Virginia's pay-as-you-go financial policy. Out of office in 1970, he continued to play an active role in state Democratic politics until 1972, when the McGovern takeover of the state Democratic party prompted him to support President Nixon.

For his part, Henry Howell had established a reputation as Virginia's leading liberal politician. He barely lost the Democratic nomination for governor in 1969. In 1971, he ran for lieutenant governor as an independent and won in a three-way race.

When Godwin formally announced his candidacy, he indicated he would not seek the Republican nomination but would accept it if offered. By this strategy, he hoped to avoid a separate Republican nomination that would divide the moderate or conservative vote and make Howell a winner. No prominent Republican announced in opposition to Godwin, and therefore Godwin was easily nominated at the Republican state convention. To balance the ticket, John Dalton of Radford, a leader of the party's moderate faction, was nominated for lieutenant governor. A relative unknown, Pat Echols, received the nod for attorney general.

When Howell announced his candidacy as an independent, no other Democrat chose to run. For the first time in the 20th century, the Virginia Democratic party had produced no gubernatorial candidate. The party's nominee for lieutenant governor, Harry Michael, and its nominee for attorney general, the incumbent Andrew Miller, declined to endorse either candidate for governor.

The Godwin-Howell clash presented Virginia citizens with a clear conservative-liberal contrast, judging by the rhetoric. Although Howell moderated his liberal stands on busing and the right-to-work law, he retained strong support from Negro and labor groups and refurbished his populist image as spokesman for the consumer and the common man. Howell's strongest issue was his call for repeal of the sales tax on food and drugs.

Godwin campaigned on his record of progress for Virginia while governor, and he condemned Howell as a radical threat to Virginia's stability.

Election Results. Godwin defeated Howell in November, 522,858 to 508,205, thus becoming Virginia's second Republican governor in this century. Dalton and Miller were elected as lieutenant governor and attorney general, respectively. Gov. Linwood Holton did not run because the state constitution forbids two consecutive gubernatorial terms.

In the elections for the House of Delegates, independents gained at the expense of Republicans and Democrats. The old House had 25 Republicans, 71 Democrats, and 4 independents. The new House had 20 Republicans, 65 Democrats, and 15 independents, the last group including mainly Godwin supporters. With an independent in the U. S. Senate and a healthy minority of independents in the legislature, Virginia can probably claim first rank among the states for independents in high office.

Legislation. The Virginia General Assembly met in regular session early in 1973. It authorized an off-year minibudget providing supplemental appropriations, especially for education. Three bond issues were approved for turnpike, hospital, and educational facilities, and the state's five environmental agencies were combined into one department. The Assembly also established a new, simplified system of state courts, and it changed the controversial blue laws again to permit all sales of food on Sunday but no other store openings.

The Assembly declined to ratify the Equal Rights Amendment for women, and it defeated proposals for parimutuel betting and no-fault insurance.

City-Suburb School Consolidation. The U. S. Supreme Court upheld a lower court decision that public schools in the city of Richmond should not be consolidated with public schools in the adjacent suburban counties of Chesterfield and Henrico. (See also EDUCATION).

Car Assembly Plant. Volvo, the Swedish automobile manufacturer, said it would build a car assembly plant in Chesapeake, Va. Production was to start in 1976, providing jobs for about 3,000 workers. The facility will make Volvo the first foreign car manufacturer in the United States.

WILLIAM LARSEN, *Radford College*

--------- **VIRGINIA • Information Highlights** ---------

Area: 40,817 square miles (105,716 sq km).
Population (1972 est.): 4,764,000. *Density:* 118 per sq mi.
Chief Cities (1970 census): Richmond, the capital, 249,430; Norfolk, 307,951; Virginia Beach, 172,106; Newport News, 138,177; Hampton, 120,779; Portsmouth, 110,963; Alexandria, 110,938.
Government (1973): *Chief Officers*—governor, Linwood Holton (R); lt. gov., Henry E. Howell, Jr. (Independent-Democrat); secy. of state, Cynthia Newman (R); atty. gen., Andrew P. Miller (D); acting treas., Frank B. Miller, Jr.; supt. of public instruction, Woodrow W. Wilkerson; chief justice, Harold F. Snead. *General Assembly*—Senate, 40 members (33 Democrats, 7 Republicans); House of Delegates, 100 members (71 D, 25 R, 4 Independents).
Education (1972–73): *Enrollment*—public elementary schools, 665,310 pupils, 30,500 teachers; public secondary schools, 404,035 pupils, 23,000 teachers; nonpublic schools, 65,600 pupils, 3,740 teachers; colleges and universities, 157,158 students. *Public school expenditures*, $918,434,000 ($920 per pupil). *Average teacher's salary*, $9,842.
State Finances (fiscal year 1971): *Revenues*, $1,998,536,000 (3% general sales tax and gross receipts taxes, $229,423,000; motor fuel tax, $161,034,000; federal funds, $431,954,000). *Expenditures*, $1,737,029,000 (education, $758,125,000; health, welfare, and safety, $247,367,000; highways, $383,061,000). *State debt*, $354,945,000 (June 30, 1971).
Personal Income (1972): $20,287,000,000; per capita, $4,258.
Public Assistance (1972): $229,171,000. *Average monthly payments* (Dec. 1972)—old-age assistance, $74.87; aid to families with dependent children, $167.57.
Labor Force: *Nonagricultural wage and salary earners* (July 1973), 1,633,600. *Average annual employment* (1972)—manufacturing, 383,300; trade, 325,200; government, 324,500; services, 238,400. *Insured unemployed* (Sept. 1973)—7,200 (0.6%).
Manufacturing (1971): *Value added by manufacture*, $5,172,800,000. Chemicals and allied products, $777,600,000; tobacco manufactures, $547,100,000; food and kindred products, $511,500,000; electrical equipment and supplies, $473,200,000; transportation equipment, $339,900,000; textile mill products, $344,600,000.
Agriculture (1972): *Cash farm income*, $679,148,000 (livestock, $385,752,000; crops, $273,833,000; government payments, $19,563,000). *Chief crops* (in order of value (1971)—Tobacco; hay; corn; peanuts.
Mining (1972): *Production value*, $440,756,000 (ranks 18th among the states). *Chief minerals*—Coal, $305,000,000; stone, $71,579,000; cement, value not available.
Fisheries (1972): *Commercial catch*, 663,845,000 pounds ($25,992,000). *Leading species by value*, Crabs, $4,302,000; clams, $3,658,000; oysters, $2,821,000; scallops, $1,856,000.
Transportation: *Roads* (1972), 61,508 miles (98,985 km); *motor vehicles* (1972), 2,410,216; *railroads* (1972), 3,895 miles (6,268 km); *public airports* (1972), 52.
Communications: *Telephones* (1973), 2,812,400; *television stations* (1971), 12; *radio stations* (1971), 182; *newspapers* (1973), 32 (daily circulation 1,032,000).

Model of Expo '74 World's Fair, which is scheduled to open in May 1974 in Spokane, Wash.

WASHINGTON

In 1973 the Washington Legislature established fall sessions and sanctioned certain types of gambling. Sharp salary increases for elected state officials were overturned by the voters. In Spokane, preparations were being made for the world's fair to be held there in 1974.

The Legislature. Persistently plagued with overloaded calendars, the Legislature adopted the concept of a continuous legislature by calling for short sessions in the fall, by having standing committees meet for three days each month, and by adopting annual general elections to reduce the long ballots that have plagued the biennial elections.

In response to voters, who in 1972 had amended the state constitution to permit lotteries, the legislators passed a bill that permits limited forms of gambling. It legalized limited-profit bingo for nonprofit organizations, social card games, and certain pinball machines. The bill also gave first-class cities the right to outlaw any of these forms of gambling locally or to tax them.

Three of the other principal bills passed by the Legislature in 1973 were overturned by the state's voters in November. They were a comprehensive tax measure establishing individual and corporate income taxes; a bill lowering the legal drinking age to 19; and an enormous pay raise for the legislators and other elected state officials. This was the sixth time since 1934 and the second time in three years that voters rejected attempts to abolish their constitutional protection against an income tax. The tax measure was crushed by a 3–1 margin, the lower drinking age was defeated by only a little more than 1% of the vote, and the salary raise was overturned by a resounding 80% vote.

The response of the public and the mass media to the pay hike had been immediate and indignant.

Although most felt that the legislators deserved a raise, since they had not received one in several years, they were angered by the size of the raises and by the fact that the measure had been enacted during the late hours of the final day of the session without debate. At a time when the federal Cost of Living Council's wage increase guideline of 5.5% was in effect, legislators had voted to increase their own salaries 193%, the governor's 45.5%, the lieutenant governor's 120%, and other elected officials' from 15.1% to 80%. Voters quickly collected a stunning 799,000 signatures—out of approximately 900,000 voters—to place the action on the November ballot, where all increases were rolled back to 5.5%.

Extortion Trial. The long-running trial in King county charging conspiracy by police and elected officials to operate a payoff and extortion system ended in May. Superior Court Judge James W. Mifflin acquitted eight men, who were or had been law enforcement officers, but convicted a former police chief and a police captain. The judge, in acquitting the eight, observed that there was ample evidence that there had been a payoff system, but the prosecution had failed to link the defendants directly to a conspiracy to participate in the system.

Expo '74. Spokane was busily preparing for the world's fair, Expo '74, to be held in that city. Pavilions were being built in a 100-acre park that occupies two islands and the banks of the Spokane River, surrounding the river's spectacular falls. The theme of the fair was to be "Celebrating Tomorrow's Fresh, New Environment." Some 5 million visitors were expected to visit Expo '74, which was to run from May through October 1974.

WARREN W. ETCHESON, *University of Washington*

WASHINGTON, D. C.

On Dec. 24, 1973, President Nixon signed into law a home rule bill for the District of Columbia. Action on the measure in the House of Representatives had been prompted by the coalescence, for the first time in nearly a century, of a newly constituted District of Columbia Committee, chaired by Rep. Charles C. Diggs, Jr. (D-Mich.), strong lobby groups, and a Washington atmosphere relatively free of local urban dissensions. The bill, which pointed toward a goal that the Senate had approved eight times since 1941, provided for a limited home rule, with an elected mayor and an elected 13-member City Council, but retained control of the District budget by Congress. A charter referendum on the elected city government approved in the bill was scheduled for May 7, 1974.

The House bill proposed a separate national capital enclave inside Washington, including the Capitol, the White House, and other federal government buildings, to be run by an appointed director. The bill was sent to a conference committee in order to resolve differences with the Senate version, and the enclave, to be known as the downtown Monument area, was approved.

Other Federal Legislation. An appropriation of more than $950 million was granted for fiscal 1974, an increase of nearly $52 million over the prior fiscal year. Also appropriated was $8.6 million for the renovation of Union Station as a National Visitor Center. Amendments to the D. C. election law extended the time to file nomination papers, reduced the number of signatures needed to place on the ballot a third-party presidential candidate, and eliminated run-off elections by permitting plurality victories for some offices.

City Government. Mayor-Commissioner Walter E. Washington received a third term by presidential appointment and Senate confirmation. The three-year terms of three councilmen expired on February 1. President Nixon appointed Antoinette Ford, Republican former White House fellow, to replace the Rev. Carlton W. Veazey, who did not wish to serve another term. Dr. Henry S. Robinson, Republican, was reappointed for his second term. Marguerite C. Selden, Democrat, a retired assistant superintendent of the D. C. school system, replaced Democrat Stanley J. Anderson, who had served on the Council since its creation in 1967.

Crime. Nationwide attention focused on the January 18 murder of seven members of the Hanifi sect of orthodox Islam in a home donated by professional basketball player Kareem Abdul-Jabbar, and on the January 30 shooting (non-fatal) of Sen. John C. Stennis (D-Miss.) in a robbery attempt in front of his Washington home. But general crime totals reported in the first nine months of 1973 were 10.3% lower than for the same period in 1972. All categories of crimes against persons and property were lower except for 4.3% more homicide.

Transportation. During the year, three private transit companies serving the District of Columbia and the Maryland-Virginia suburbs joined Metro, Washington's publicly owned rapid transit system. Work on the 98-mile Metro subway system continued, with 27 miles of line and 31 of the proposed 86 stations under construction. Transit authorities expected the first subway trains to operate by 1976 on a line beginning at Union Station, running through tunnels under the Potomac River and ending at the National Airport in Virginia. The completion of the entire project was scheduled for 1980.

Education. Hugh J. Scott, 39, the first black superintendent of Washington's school system, who had lost the support of a majority of the school board, resigned in October at the expiration of his three-year term. Barbara A. Sizemore, a 45-year-old black woman chosen by the school board from 99 applicants, became the new superintendent responsible for 140,000 pupils, 94% of them black. Mrs. Sizemore had gained a national reputation in Chicago as director of the Woodlawn Experimental Schools Project, noted for innovations in community control and instructional methods.

Washington residents elected five aspirants to the 11-member school board. Only one of the three incumbents who ran won in races for two at-large and three district seats. The composition of the board became five men, three blacks and two whites, and five women, four blacks and one white, with one seat to be filled at a run-off election.

Religion. Patrick Cardinal O'Boyle, age 77, retired as Roman Catholic archbishop of Washington, a post he had held for 25 years. On March 9 the Most Rev. William Wakefield Baum, a leading American ecumenist during his service as bishop in Missouri, became archbishop and head of the diocese.

ELEANOR G. FELDBAUM, *University of Maryland*

WATERGATE AFFAIR. See special report beginning on page 14.

WEATHER. See METEOROLOGY.

WELFARE. See SOCIAL WELFARE.

WEST INDIES. See CARIBBEAN.

WEST VIRGINIA

Legislative action—or, more precisely, inaction—occupied West Virginia's attention in 1973. On the brighter side, indicators showed improvements in the state's economic outlook.

Legislative Developments. In February, after three years of deliberation, the state supreme court ruled that the one-man-one-vote principle handed down in earlier rulings by the U. S. Supreme Court need not be strictly observed on the state level. This question, of concern to both Democrats and Republicans, considerably eased legislators' doubts, and leaders of both parties predicted record accomplishments during the regular 60-day session that began later that month.

However, these predictions went unfulfilled. Republican Gov. Arch A. Moore, inaugurated on January 15 as West Virginia's first two-term executive, was faced with a hostile Democratic-controlled Legislature, and even among Democrats there was considerable internecine strife. As a result, neither the regular session nor the special session in May–June produced any significant legislation.

Victims of legislative inaction, partisanship votes, or gubernatorial vetoes included such measures as legalization of branch banking, tax aid to private colleges, a new capital punishment statute, judicial reforms that called for sweeping changes in the justice-of-the-peace system, no-fault automobile insurance, and a state lottery.

Finally, after considerable jockeying between the governor and committees of both the regular and

---
WEST VIRGINIA • Information Highlights

Area: 24,181 square miles (62,629 sq km).
Population (1972 est.): 1,781,000. *Density:* 73 per sq mi.
Chief Cities (1970 census): Charleston, the capital, 71,505; Huntington, 74,315; Wheeling, 48,188; Parkersburg, 44,208; Morgantown, 29,431; Weirton, 27,131.
Government (1973): *Chief Officers*—governor, Arch A. Moore, Jr. (R); secy. of state, Edgar Heiskell III (R); atty. gen., Chauncey H. Browning, Jr. (D); treas., John H. Kelly (D); supt. of free schools, Daniel B. Taylor; chief justice, Thornton G. Berry, Jr. *Legislature*—Senate, 34 members (24 Democrats, 10 Republicans); House of Delegates, 100 members (57 D, 43 R).
Education (1972–73): *Enrollment*—public elementary schools, 236,225 pupils, 8,795 teachers; public secondary schools, 177,882 pupils, 7,917 teachers; nonpublic schools, 11,700 pupils, 530 teachers; colleges and universities, 60,883 students. *Public school expenditures,* $289,545,000 ($749 per pupil). *Average teacher's salary,* $8,505.
State Finances (fiscal year 1971): *Revenues,* $978,861,000 (3% general sales tax and gross receipts taxes, $191,-807,000; motor fuel tax, $55,363,000; federal funds, $321,-526,000). *Expenditures,* $871,391,000 (education, $321,989,-000; health, welfare, and safety, $113,436,000; highways, $304,331,000). *State debt,* $628,039,000 (June 30, 1971).
Personal Income (1972): $6,365,000,000; per capita, $3,574.
Public Assistance (1972): $81,408,000. *Average monthly payments* (Dec. 1972)—old-age assistance, $103.42; aid to families with dependent children, $157.04.
Labor Force: *Nonagricultural wage and salary earners* (July 1973), 543,000. *Average annual employment* (1972)—manufacturing, 122,800; trade, 101,700; government, 98,-300; services, 70,500. *Insured unemployed* (Sept. 1973)—9,100 (2.1%).
Manufacturing (1971): *Value added by manufacture,* $2,387,-700,000. Chemicals and allied products, $840,700,000; primary metal industries, $491,000,000; stone, clay, and glass products, $317,800,000; electrical equipment and supplies, $117,700,000; fabricated metal products, $103,-700,000; food and kindred products, $91,900,000.
Agriculture (1972): *Cash farm income,* $120,461,000 (livestock, $90,209,000; crops, $26,928,000; government payments, $3,324,000). *Chief crops* (in order of value, 1971)—Hay, apples, corn, tobacco.
Mining (1972): *Production value,* $1,389,069,000 (ranks 4th among the states). *Chief minerals*—Coal, $1,235,000,000; natural gas, $64,800,000; stone, $19,169,000.
Transportation: *Roads* (1972), 35,941 miles (57,840 km); *motor vehicles* (1972), 826,154; *railroads* (1972), 3,569 miles (5,744 km); *public airports* (1972), 23.
Communications: *Telephones* (1973), 827,700; *television stations* (1971), 9; *radio stations* (1971), 82; *newspapers* (1973), 29 (daily circulation, 491,000).

special legislative sessions, a record budget of more than $1 billion was enacted. The budget bill prompted the state supreme court to uphold the governor's right to exercise an item veto on the budget bill. Other enacted legislation included a consumer credit and protection bill, a 5% salary increase for teachers, and a $50 million appropriation for school construction.

Constitutional Amendments. In November, voters approved four amendments to the state constitution. The amendments permitted a sheriff to succeed himself; provided property tax relief for elderly and low-income groups; authorized a bonus for Vietnam War veterans; and permitted an additional $200 million bond issue for roads, particularly for upgrading secondary roads.

Economic Improvements. At the end of September, 18 of 23 business indicators registered gains for West Virginia, led by cash farm sales, electric power production, and new building permits. Toward the end of the year, as the nation was gripped by the energy shortage, the importance of West Virginia's coal reserves and electricity generating potential was reflected in additional upturns in economic indicators.

Other Developments. Two matters caused considerable public concern during 1973. The first was the continuing reorganization of higher education facilities, as the Board of Regents, overriding the Legislature, merged state colleges at Bluefield and Concord. The second was the apparent continued delay in plans to modify or eliminate coal-slag dams similar to the one that collapsed in Buffalo Creek Valley in 1972, claiming 118 lives.

W. R. McLEOD
West Virginia University

WISCONSIN

In 1973, Democratic Gov. Patrick J. Lucey used his executive budget for 1973–75 to initiate changes in Wisconsin state policies. The $2.75 billion budget —a record—resulted in major modifications in education, tax, and welfare programs.

Budget Provisions. In education, the budget bill changed the school-aid distribution formula so that local school districts having high property valuations in relation to school enrollment would share some of their state aid with districts that have lower per-pupil valuations. In addition, state aid was increased by $220 million.

In regard to taxation, the budget benefited both industry and low-income groups. In response to complaints that the state was losing industry, the budget eliminated property taxes on manufacturing equipment and machinery. It also extended property tax relief, previously limited to the elderly, to all property owners and tenants over 18, raised financial eligibility from $5,000 to $7,000, and broadened farmer homestead tax-relief provisions.

Governor Lucey proposed that the state assume both financial responsibility and administration of local welfare programs. The Legislature approved state payment but rejected state control.

Other Legislative Action. After Wisconsin voters on April 3 approved, 597,000 to 367,000, a state constitutional amendment permitting licensed bingo games, the Legislature passed a bill to implement the amendment. It also enacted a major probate reform bill, permitting legatees to process estates without legal aid or court approval, and authorized salary

increases for elected state officials. However, the Legislature rejected the governor's proposal to close the state reformatory and some other penal institutions.

Gubernatorial Task Forces. Governor Lucey's task forces, an integral part of his administration, made several important recommendations in 1973. One called for drastic revision of the state's health care system, arousing considerable opposition among doctors. Another recommended an overhaul of state campaign finance laws, urging that the government subsidize state campaigns and that limits be placed on candidate spending and on individual donations.

Economy. High levels of activity in manufacturing and agriculture resulted in 1973 in the highest employment in Wisconsin's history—1,968,000 in September. The number of industrial plants constructed or enlarged also established a record. Farm commodity sales were likewise at record levels, but it is probable that rapidly rising costs cut into farmers' profits.

Events at Madison. In 1973, two developments at Madison, site of the principal campus of the University of Wisconsin, aroused national interest. On Aug. 24, 1970, the university's Army Mathematics Research Center, a target of antiwar protest, was blown up, and a graduate student was killed. In 1973, Karleton Armstrong, a former university student, was extradited from Canada, where he had

sought refuge, and was indicted for murder, bombing, and arson. Armstrong pleaded guilty and, after plea bargaining, was sentenced on November 1 to 23 years in prison. Three other accused persons, including Armstrong's brother, were still at large.

On April 3, Paul R. Soglin, a self-styled radical in his student days, defeated William Dyke as mayor of Madison. In 1968, Soglin was elected alderman and thereafter was twice arrested for participating in antiwar demonstrations. Assuming a more conservative stance, Soglin succeeded in ousting Dyke in a bitter and close election.

PAUL SALSINI
The Milwaukee "Journal"

WOMEN'S LIBERATION MOVEMENT

American women achieved further social gains in 1973 and began to benefit from recent antisex discrimination legislation. By a vote of 7–2 the U. S. Supreme Court on January 22 struck down restrictive Texas and Georgia abortion laws, thereby overturning antiabortion laws in 44 other states and protecting hard-won liberalization in this area.

Equal Rights Amendment. Unexpected opposition slowed ratification of the Equal Rights Amendment (ERA), providing that "equality of rights under the law shall not be denied or abridged by the United States or any state on account of sex." The amendment was ratified during the year by Minnesota, New Mexico, Oregon, South Dakota, Vermont, Wyoming, Connecticut, and Washington, bringing the total of ratifying states to 30. Eight more states must approve the amendment by March 22, 1979, for it to become law.

The National Organization for Women raised a $100,000 ERA Emergency Fund to finance efforts to press for the amendment's approval. The National Federation of Business and Professional Women's Clubs voted $250,000 for the cause. The AFL-CIO, previously a major foe, voted to support the amendment at its national convention in Miami Beach in October.

Economic Gains. As of June 30, 1973, the Department of Labor had ruled that over $65 million was due in back pay to 142,597 women employees because they illegally had been paid less than men for the same work since the Equal Pay Act took effect in 1964. In the biggest sex-discrimination settlement ever awarded, the American Telephone and Telegraph Company in January agreed to pay $15 million in back wages as well as wage increases costing more than $30 million a year.

As a result of suits filed by the Department of Labor, the New England Telephone Company was ordered to pay $436,000 in back wages to 454 women employees, and the Corning Glass Company paid more than $600,000 to 960 men and women employees.

The Equal Employment Opportunity Commission (EEOC) has been investigating similar complaints of discriminatory practices against a dozen other large companies, among them Ford, General Electric, General Motors, and Sears, Roebuck. The four denied the accusations. The EEOC received a record 48,899 complaints during fiscal 1973, a third of them citing sex discrimination. Between March 1972, when the EEOC was empowered to use federal courts to enforce its decisions, and October 1973, the EEOC initiated 144 court actions, 69 of which charged sex discrimination.

WISCONSIN • Information Highlights

Area: 56,154 square miles (145,439 sq km).
Population (1972 est.): 4,520,000. *Density:* 82 per sq mi.
Chief Cities (1970 census): Madison, the capital, 172,007; Milwaukee, 717,372; Racine, 95,162; Green Bay, 87,809; Kenosha, 78,805; West Allis, 71,649; Wauwatosa, 58,676.
Government (1973): *Chief Officers*—governor, Patrick J. Lucey (D); lt. gov., Martin J. Schreiber (D); secy. of state, Robert C. Zimmerman (R); atty. gen., Robert W. Warren (R); treas., Charles P. Smith (D); supt. of public instruction, Barbara Thompson; chief justice, E. Harold Hallows. *Legislature*—Senate, 33 members (18 Republicans, 15 Democrats); Assembly, 99 members (62 D, 37 R).
Education (1972–73): *Enrollment*—public elementary schools, 574,918 pupils, 27,208 teachers; public secondary schools, 420,305 pupils, 23,934 teachers; nonpublic schools, 189,-000 pupils, 7,580 teachers; colleges and universities, 175,066 students. *Public school expenditures,* $1,019,-962,000 ($1,134 per pupil). *Average teacher's salary,* $10,812.
State Finances (fiscal year 1971): *Revenues,* $2,272,057,000 (4% general sales tax and gross receipts taxes, $339,-258,000; motor fuel tax, $137,062,000; federal funds, $372,-906,000). *Expenditures,* $2,128,719,000 (education, $817,-029,000; health, welfare, and safety, $311,081,000; highways, $249,210,000). *State debt,* $679,377,000 (June 30, 1971).
Personal Income (1972): $19,014,000,000; per capita, $4,207.
Public Assistance (1972): $363,929,000. *Average monthly payments* (Dec. 1972)—old-age assistance, $154.28; aid to families with dependent children, $274.36.
Labor Force: *Nonagricultural wage and salary earners* (July 1973), 1,636,900. *Average annual employment* (1972)—manufacturing, 493,600; trade, 346,000; government, 275,-900; services, 249,500. *Insured unemployed* (Sept. 1973)—17,700 (1.3%).
Manufacturing (1971): *Value added by manufacture,* $8,476,-400,000. Nonelectrical machinery, $1,746,600,000; food and kindred products, $1,274,400,000; transportation equipment, $880,900,000; paper and allied products, $775,-600,000; electrical equipment and supplies, $762,700,000; fabricated metal products, $672,200,000.
Agriculture (1972): *Cash farm income,* $1,906,897,000 (livestock, $1,598,147,000; crops, $251,644,000; government payments, $57,106,000). *Chief crops* (in order of value, 1971)—Corn, hay, oats, potatoes.
Mining (1972): *Production value,* $82,660,000 (ranks 38th among the states). *Chief minerals*—Sand and gravel, $34,057,000; stone, $23,297,000; iron ore, value not available; lime, $4,810,000.
Fisheries (1972): *Commercial catch,* 43,661,000 pounds ($2,-521,000). *Leading species by value*—Chubs, $766,000; carp, $300,000; alewives, $262,000; buffalofish, $142,000.
Transportation: *Roads* (1972), 103,352 miles (166,324 km); *motor vehicles* (1972), 2,230,174; *railroads* (1972), 5,926 miles (9,537 km); *public airports* (1972), 100.
Communications: *Telephones* (1973), 2,606,500; *television stations* (1971), 18; *radio stations* (1971), 174; *newspapers* (1973), 37 (daily circulation, 1,222,000).

I'M TIRED OF COOKING AND WASHING AND BEING EXPLOITED!

FROM NOW ON, CALL ME Ms. MULLINS!

SURE--GET BACK TO YOUR WORK, Ms. MULLINS...

I DON'T GET IT-- IT FEELS TH' SAME...

Moon Mullins and other comic strips took an increasing interest in the lighter side of Women's Lib.

Many employers increased women's wages voluntarily or under government pressure. Women also made progress against discrimination in credit, and two women's banks were planned in New York City. Gains were made in the area of maternity leave and benefits. The City University of New York substituted "parental" for "maternity" in its rules, giving equal benefits to men and women.

A parade of witnesses before the Joint Economic Committee chaired by Rep. Martha Griffiths of Michigan revealed continued discrimination against women even in government agencies responsible for enforcing antidiscrimination measures. Rep. Griffiths promised new legislation "to change the laws to allow women to become the economic equals of men."

Education. Law and medical schools admitted more women in 1973. Women's studies programs grew from two in 1970 to 72 in 1973, and 100 courses on 60 campuses grew to 2,000 on some 500 campuses. Some faculty women won equity raises, but many complaints remained.

A 1973 report by the Carnegie Commission on Higher Education termed the outlook for women "dismal." Chairman Dr. Clark Kerr said that "not before the year 2000 and perhaps not even then will the percentage of women and minority members on faculties be in proportion to their representation in the general labor force."

The Movement. The National Organization for Women (NOW) reelected Wilma Scott Heide as president at its national convention in February. Jane Plitt was employed as NOW's first executive director. A national administrative office was opened in Chicago to supplement a legislative office in Washington and a legal defense fund office in New York. NOW had 400 chapters in all 50 states in 1973, and its membership was approaching 35,000, including 2,000 men.

Wilma Scott Heide and eight other NOW leaders demonstrated before the Supreme Court building in Washington to call attention to the lack of women on the high court. New York NOW members protested "male domination of Wall Street" at the American Stock Exchange in August.

Frances (Sissy) Farenthold of Texas was elected as the first national chairperson of the National Women's Political Caucus. Her election was seen as support for the view of some that the women's movement must be dedicated to broad social issues as well as the concerns of women.

The Women's Equity Action League was active in pressing sex-discrimination charges against schools, hospitals, and other institutions. Special-interest feminist groups continued to grow. The National Black Feminist Organization was formed in New York.

Notable Achievements. Billie Jean King won $100,000 by defeating Bobby Riggs in a "battle of the sexes" tennis match in September. Joni Evans Barnett became the first woman director of physical education at Yale. More women ran in marathons, and girls sued to be allowed to play Little League baseball.

Jeanne M. Holm was promoted to major general in the Air Force, the first woman in U. S. history to hold that rank. Bonnie Tiburzi became the first woman pilot for a major airline (American). Yale named Hannah Gray as its first woman provost. Lenore Hershey became editor of the *Ladies' Home Journal,* and Charlotte Curtis was named editor of the "op ed" page of the New York *Times.* Woman became more visible in television, but advanced only from 22% to 23% of the full-time employees.

Claire Randall became the first woman to serve as general secretary of the National Council of Churches, and Florence Pohlman was named the first woman Navy chaplain. In a radical break with tradition, Conservative Judaism began to allow women to be counted in the "minyan," the quorum of 10 or more adults required for communal worship.

CONFRONTATION: Harry Britton, "husband lib" champion, and the opposition meet near the White House.

FIRST WOMAN pilot hired by a major airline, Bonnie Tiburzi was assigned to American Airlines 727 fleet.

A Women's Hall of Fame was started in Seneca Falls, N.Y., the birthplace of the women's rights movement. The first 20 members were inducted on August 26, the 53d anniversary of the enactment of the 19th Amendment, giving women the vote.

International Developments. Implementing a recommendation of the Royal Commission on the Status of Women in Canada, Labor Minister John Munro named a 28-member Status of Women Council to advise the government. Government contractors in Canada were forbidden to discriminate because of sex or marital status, and sex-labeled help wanted ads were banned. Australia and Britain passed legislation requiring that women be paid equally with men for the same work by 1975.

CAROLINE BIRD, *Author of "Everything a Woman Needs to Know to Get Paid What She's Worth"*

WYOMING

Attention in Wyoming in 1973 was on government, the economy, the environment, and education.

Government. In its regular biennial session the Legislature passed almost 200 bills, including appropriations of more than $300 million for the 1973–75 biennium. In other actions it lowered the age of majority to 19; reinstated the death penalty for some crimes; ratified the federal Equal Rights Amendment for women; raised salaries of state officials, including the governor's—from $25,000 to $37,500; authorized construction of a new governor's mansion; and reduced property taxes.

The Legislature also increased the number of state supreme court judges from four to five and district judges from 12 to 13. Surprisingly, Republican Gov. Stanley K. Hathaway appointed a Democrat to the supreme court and another to one of three vacant district judgeships.

Economy. Oil production fell below 130 million barrels in 1973, from a high of 150 million barrels in 1970. However, the loss was offset by increases in the output of coal, trona, and uranium, as well as

by a higher per-unit value of all minerals, and the state had a record mineral-output valuation of $800 million.

Agriculture, Wyoming's most important industry after mineral production, enjoyed record prices, although several counties suffered setbacks as a result of sheep and cattle losses in spring blizzards. Tourism prospered, but it was anticipated that the fuel crisis would curtail tourist travel in 1974.

Environment. A major piece of legislation was the creation of a Department of Environmental Quality, under an appointed board, with authority to regulate air and water quality and mined-land reclamation. Despite this move, conservationists criticized what they called a development-minded state administration and an industry-oriented press. Their complaints included clear-cutting of timber in national forests; coal strip-mining; proposals for new power plants, transmission lines, and coal-hauling railroads; and the lack of land-use zoning. By the end of the year, the fuel crisis had silenced some critics.

Education. The Legislature created a nine-member higher education council with power to study and make recommendations concerning the administration, programs, and budgets of the University of Wyoming and the state's seven junior colleges. Also, a legislative interim committee scrutinized the programs at these institutions. In the fall semester, junior college enrollment increased to nearly 20,000, up by more than 500 over 1972, while enrollment at the university decreased by 400, to just under 8,000.

T. A. LARSON
University of Wyoming

WYOMING • Information Highlights

Area: 97,914 square miles (253,597 sq km).
Population (1972 est.): 345,000. *Density:* 3.5 per sq mi.
Chief Cities (1970 census): Cheyenne, the capital, 40,914; Casper, 39,361; Laramie, 23,143; Rock Springs, 11,657.
Government (1973): *Chief Officers*—governor, Stanley K. Hathaway (R); secy. of state, Mrs. Thyra Thomson (R); atty. gen., Clarence A. Brimmer (R); treas., James Griffith (R); supt. of public instruction, Robert G. Schrader (R); chief justice, Glenn Parker. *Legislature*—Senate, 30 members (17 Republicans, 13 Democrats); House of Representatives, 62 members (44 R, 17 D, 1 Independent).
Education (1972–73): *Enrollment*—public elementary schools, 45,025 pupils, 2,260 teachers; public secondary schools, 40,992 pupils, 2,337 teachers; nonpublic schools, 2,200 pupils, 110 teachers; colleges and universities, 15,011 students. *Public school expenditures,* $77,600,000 ($960 per pupil). *Average teacher's salary,* $9,900.
State Finances (1971): *Revenues,* $245,970,000 (3% general sales tax and gross receipts taxes, $34,075,000; motor fuel tax, $20,426,000; federal funds, $82,886,000). *Expenditures,* $207,361,000 (education, $72,382,000; health, welfare, and safety, $16,280,000; highways, $73,727,000). *State debt,* $46,504,000 (June 30, 1971).
Personal Income (1972): $1,499,000,000; per capita, $4,345.
Public Assistance (1972): $10,410,000. *Average monthly payments* (Dec. 1972)—old-age assistance, $65.89; aid to families with dependent children, $157.18.
Labor Force: *Nonagricultural wage and salary earners* (July 1973), 132,600. *Average annual employment* (1972)—manufacturing, 7,600; trade, 25,000; government, 32,100; services, 17,700. *Insured unemployed* (Sept. 1973)—600 (0.7%).
Manufacturing (1971): Value added by manufacture, $119,400,000. Petroleum and coal products, $43,400,000; food and kindred products, $15,200,000; printing and publishing, $11,300,000.
Agriculture (1972): *Cash farm income,* $365,916,000 (livestock, $293,786,000; crops, $51,535,000; government payments, $20,595,000). *Chief crops* (in order of value, 1971)—Hay, sugar beets, wheat, barley.
Mining (1972): Production value, $731,840,000 (ranks 11th among the states). *Chief minerals*—Petroleum, $440,820,000; natural gas, $54,740,000; sodium salts, value not available; uranium, $52,694,000.
Transportation: *Roads* (1972), 40,540 miles (65,241 km); *motor vehicles* (1972), 257,337; *railroads* (1972), 1,812 miles (2,916 km); *public airports* (1972), 41.
Communications: *Telephones* (1973), 216,000; *television stations* (1971), 3; *radio stations* (1971), 30; *newspapers* (1973), 10 (daily circulation, 80,000).

YUGOSLAVIA

In 1973 the political turmoil that had characterized Yugoslavia for two years subsided. Economic stabilization, the regime's main goal, failed to materialize. The Yugoslavia-Soviet rapprochement begun in 1971 made further progress, although Yugoslav leaders continued to profess nonalignment.

Political Developments. A lengthy draft of the new Yugoslav constitution and preparations for the 10th Congress of the League of Communists of Yugoslavia (LCY), projected for early 1974, were the predominant domestic preoccupations in Yugoslavia during the year, along with the implementation of President Tito's letter of September 1972, calling for greater action and unity in the LCY. The first meeting of the General Assembly of the Federation—a political body comprising representatives of parliamentary, governmental, party, and social mass organizations—was held in Belgrade on April 23. In his address, Tito declared that decisive steps had been taken against "serious deviations" in the LCY and that the campaign against local nationalists, liberals, and Western influences would not affect Yugoslavia's nonalignment.

The annual LCY conference took place in Belgrade on May 10 and 11. In Tito's absence the main report was presented by Stane Dolanc, secretary of the Executive Bureau of the LCY Presidium and one of the most influential of the younger party leaders. He emphasized the need to strengthen the ideological and political unity of the LCY.

The tightening of party control had ample ramifications within both the LCY and the country at large. In February the penal and judicial procedure codes were modified, and stricter penalties and new offenses were introduced. Throughout the year alleged nationalists were tried and convicted; publications were banned; and publishers and film directors were forced to resign, expelled from the LCY, or sentenced and jailed. On November 12 the Assembly of Belgrade University adopted a resolution whereby professors, in addition to being academically qualified, had to accept the Marxist view of the world and the program, line, and leading role of the LCY.

Large numbers of middle-echelon cadres within the LCY were purged or forced to resign. In June, Gen. Ivan Mišković, long the chief of all Yugoslav intelligence branches and Tito's former adviser on state security, was removed from his post as adviser to the state presidency on state security.

The Economy. Despite some bright spots, economic shortcomings persisted in Yugoslavia throughout 1973. A restructuring of bank credits in May diminished the nonliquidity of enterprises and their heavy indebtedness, and invisible earnings (tourism receipts and remittances of workers temporarily employed abroad) were 35% higher in the first half of 1973 than they had been for the first half of 1972. Joint ventures with Western enterprises also assured a new inflow of capital. By mid-July, 15 joint investment agreements, valued at $343 million, had been signed, compared with 23 in 1972.

Inflation rose 21.4% between April 1972 and April 1973, and there were signs of a further increase. The cost of living was up 24% for the first eight months of 1973, while purchasing power dropped 6.6%. Industrial production showed signs of deceleration between January and October, rising only 6.7% over what it had been during the same period in 1972. The agricultural output, especially of wheat, was slightly lower than that of 1972. The trade deficit was substantial for the first nine months, with exports up 24% and imports up 39%.

Foreign Relations. A visit by Soviet Premier Aleksei Kosygin to Yugoslavia on September 24–October 1 was followed by a joint communiqué stressing the expansion of economic cooperation between the two nations. During the Arab-Israeli war in October, Yugoslavia gave permission to the Soviet Union to use Yugoslav air space for overflights and Yugoslav airfields to refuel in order to supply Egypt and Syria with war materials. On November 12–15, Tito paid an unofficial visit to the Soviet Union, meeting with Communist party chairman Leonid Brezhnev in Kiev.

Close ties were maintained or reinforced with Rumania, Poland, and Hungary, whose top party leaders visited Yugoslavia. Complications with Bulgaria over the Macedonian issue were discussed by Miloš Minić, Yugoslav foreign minister, when he visited Sofia in November. Extensive trade agreements were made with Rumania in July. Trade agreements with the USSR in 1973 totaled $660 million.

A Yugoslav delegation headed by Tito participated in the 4th summit conference of nonaligned nations in Algeria on September 2–8. Addressing the conference, Tito stressed the need for all nonaligned countries to retain their full independence. He sided with the Arabs in their conflict with Israel, condemned several aspects of U. S. foreign policy, and refrained from any criticism of the USSR.

In April, West German Chancellor Willy Brandt visited Yugoslavia and signed an agreement on West German war reparations based on long-term economic cooperation. George Shultz, U. S. secretary of the treasury, and Frederick Dent, U. S. secretary of commerce, visited Yugoslavia in October. Trade between the United States and Yugoslavia in 1973 was valued at $420 million, double that of 1969. A new 5-year trade agreement between Yugoslavia and the European Economic Community, aimed at more cooperation, became operative October 1.

MILORAD M. DRACHKOVITCH, *Stanford University*

------ **YUGOSLAVIA • Information Highlights** ------

Official Name: Socialist Federal Republic of Yugoslavia.
Location: Southeast Europe.
Area: 98,766 square miles (255,804 sq km).
Population (1973 est.): 21,200,000. *Density,* 207 per square mile (80 per sq km).
Chief Cities (1971 census): Belgrade, the capital, 800,000; Zagreb, 565,000; Skopje, 250,000.
Government: *Head of state,* Tito (Josip Broz), president (first elected Jan. 1953). *Prime minister,* Džemal Bijedić (took office July 1971). *Legislature*—Federal Assembly (5 chambers). *Major political party*—League of Communists of Yugoslavia (LCY).
Official Languages: Serbo-Croatian, Slovenian, Macedonian.
Education: *Expenditure* (1969), 5.1% of gross material product. *School enrollment* (1969)—primary, 2,857,291; secondary, 705,746; technical//vocational, 500,484; university/higher, 239,701.
Monetary Unit: Dinar (17 dinars equal U. S.$1, Sept. 1973).
Gross National Product (1972 est.): $12,830,000,000.
Economic Indexes: *Industrial production* (1972), 200 (1963 = 100); *agricultural production* (1970), 124 (1957–59 = 100); *consumer price index* (1972), 339 (1963 = 100).
Manufacturing (major products): Steel and iron, processed foods, chemicals, machinery, textiles.
Major Agricultural Products: Corn, wheat, fruits, potatoes, sugar beets, forest products, fish, livestock.
Major Minerals: Coal, iron ore, petroleum, bauxite, copper.
Foreign Trade (1972): *Exports,* $2,237,000,000; *Imports,* $3,233,000,000. *Chief trading partners* (1971)—USSR (took 15% of exports, supplied 9% of imports); Italy (12%—12%); West Germany (12%—19%).
Tourism: Receipts (1971), $359,400,000.
Transportation: *Motor vehicles* (1971), 1,013,500; *railroads* (1971), 6,420 miles (10,332 km); *merchant fleet* (1972), 1,588,000 gross registered tons; *major national airline,* JAT (Jugoslovenski Aerotransport).
Communications: *Telephones* (1972), 820,860; *newspapers* (1970), 24 (daily circulation, 1,738,000).

—— YUKON TERRITORY • Information Highlights ——

Area: 207,076 square miles (536,327 sq km).
Population (1972 est.): 19,000.
Chief City (1972 est.): Whitehorse, the capital (11,600).
Government (1973): *Chief Officers*—Commissioner James Smith; Executive Committee Members: R. A. Hodgkinson (appointed); Keith Fleming (appointed); N. S. Chamberlist (elected); Mrs. H. P. Watson (elected). Territorial Council —Elected Members: speaker Ron Rivett; Mike Stutter, Don Taylor, Mrs. H. P. Watson, N. S. Chamberlist, Ken McKinnon, Clive Tanner.
Education: *School enrollment* (Sept. 1972)—Elementary and secondary, 4,578 pupils; vocational training center, 430 pupils (20 full-time teachers).
Public Finance (fiscal year 1972 est.): *Revenues*, $24,696,729 (liquor profits, $1,500,000; motor vehicle licenses and fuel tax, $2,248,319; property and school tax, $1,000,000; federal funds, $9,312,576). *Expenditures*, $25,683,434 (education, $5,948,800; health and social welfare, $4,024,507; highways and public works, $4,143,474).
Mining (1972 est.): *Production value*, $102,756,000. *Chief minerals*—zinc, $43,861,000; lead, $34,848,000 (ranks 1st); asbestos, $14,200,000 (ranks 3d); silver, $9,330,000 (ranks 3d); gold, $146,000.
Transportation: *Roads* (1972 est.), 2,500 miles (4.060 km); *motor vehicles*, 14,054; *railroads*, 58 track miles (93 km); *licensed airports*, 9.
Communications: *Telephones* (1970), 6,833; *television stations* (1972), 6; *radio stations* (1972), 2.
(All monetary figures given in Canadian dollars.)

YUKON TERRITORY

In 1973, Yukoners, in a potpourri of ceremonies and activities, celebrated the 75th anniversaries of the Klondike Gold Rush, establishment of the Yukon as a separate territory, the start of construction of the historic White Pass & Yukon Route Railway, and the 100th anniversary of the Royal Canadian Mounted Police. The Yukon also experienced a fairly stable pattern of economic growth in 1973.

Government and Politics. Redistribution of electoral boundaries, expansion of membership in the territorial legislature, and regionalization of government were all under consideration. Both the Liberals and Progressive Conservatives endorsed an extension of territorial government control, and the New Democratic party even advocated immediate provincial status.

Negotiations were in progress, between the Canadian federal government and the Yukon Native Brotherhood, toward achievement of a compensatory aboriginal land-claims settlement.

The territorial government became embroiled with the city of Whitehorse over the alleged misappropriation of funds. The mayor and City Council resigned, and a temporary administrator was appointed until representative and responsible government was restored by a municipal election.

Economy. Although the Quill Creek mine ceased operations, production from five other mines was expected to attain an estimated $150 million for 1973, an increase of $48 million over the previous year. Talk of a smelter to serve the Yukon was heard again in 1973, but remained speculative.

Tourism, the second-largest industry, had about 320,000 visitors, compared with 271,000 in 1972.

Transportation and Communications. Work on the 440-mile Dempster Highway from Dawson, Yukon Territory, to Inuvik and Tuktoyaktuk in the Northwest Territories progressed toward completion for 1976. It was also announced that a road connecting Carcross with Skagway, Alaska, would be constructed by 1976. Extension of the railhead from Whitehorse farther inland was under review.

In February 1973, Yukon communities received for the first time live telecasts via the Canadian Broadcasting Corporation satellite Anik I.

W. BRIAN SPEIRS
Territorial Archivist

ZAIRE

Against a backdrop of almost total quiescence on the domestic political scene, the Mobutu regime continued in 1973 to consolidate its centralized hold over this once-turbulent country. The upward swing of world copper prices helped to restore a healthy balance of payments, while Zaire's influence in foreign affairs increased noticeably.

Domestic Politics. Mobutu's campaign of national "authenticity" (now in its third year) has been acquiring important new dimensions. For one thing, it has been serving as the regime's only coherent ideology, one that paradoxically is being echoed by a number of African countries once regarded as far more sophisticated politically than Zaire. More importantly, it has been supplying the ideological ammunition for a continuing drive toward authoritarian centralization and the dismantling of all actual or potential centers of independent power within the state, be they regional, bureaucratic, economic, or spiritual.

The Catholic Church, which had become embroiled in a major confrontation with secular authorities in 1972, was again under fire during the first half of the year. A December 1972 ban against all privately sponsored youth organizations was generally viewed as directed at church-related groups, and in March no fewer than 31 religious publications (most of them Catholic) were suspended. At the same time, Zaire's senior Catholic dignitary, Cardinal Malula, was again accused of "encouraging subversion."

On November 30, President Mobutu announced the nationalization of all foreign-held real estate as well as the take-over of a wide range of business firms owned by expatriates.

Foreign Affairs. Zaire's major foreign policy moves were the opening of diplomatic relations with China and the severing of its ties with Israel following the third Arab-Israeli war. Both moves are in keeping with Mobutu's ostensible policy of nonalignment. In the same perspective, Zaire also moved to recognize both Germanys, North and South Vietnam, and the two Koreas.

The decision to establish relations with China was followed in January by Mobutu's highly publicized trip to Peking (and by a somewhat less touted visit to India). This episode stirred up a certain amount of interest for Chinese methods and reportedly inspired Zaire's single political party, the MPR (Popular Movement of the Revolution), to decide that every citizen should work eight hours a day and donate their Saturdays to collective labor on public-interest projects. A more concrete by-product of the Sino-Zairese cooperation agreements was the dispatching of over 100 Chinese agricultural experts to Zaire, where they took the place of a similar team from Taiwan.

Zaire's break with Israel came after repeated expressions of support for the UN Security Council's resolution of Nov. 22, 1967, on occupied Arab territories, and after several warnings to Tel Aviv (notably after the downing of a Libyan airliner by the Israelis in February) that continued Israeli intransigence might compel Zaire to choose "between its brothers and its friends."

On the African scene, Zaire's relations with Zambia were particularly close following the closure of the Zambia-Rhodesia border, when Mobutu offered active help to its southern neighbor. Along

with Zambia and Tanzania, Zaire also took part in coordinating support for African freedom fighters operating in southern Africa. Zaire promptly recognized the provisional government of Guinea-Bissau (Portuguese Guinea) in September; but its most remarkable contribution in this field was its role as an intercessor between the two major guerrilla organizations in Angola, Holden Roberto's FNLA and Agostinho Neto's MPLA, which agreed to merge into a Supreme Council for the Liberation of Angola (CSLA), with headquarters in Kinshasa. Finally, Zaire intervened with some success during the year to mediate disputes between Rwanda and Burundi, between Uganda and Tanzania, and between Gabon and Equatorial Guinea.

Economic Developments. Thanks in part to the problems faced by the world's two leading copper-producing nations (Chile and Zambia), the continuing upward trend of world copper prices led to a substantial improvement of Zaire's trade balance. To some extent, however, this has been achieved merely by systematically intensifying the exploitation of the country's ample mineral reserves, with the result that Zaire depends more than ever on its copper exports. Production was expected to top 450,000 metric tons in 1973.

The government has been prepared to resort to substantial borrowing ($50 million in 1972 and an equal amount in 1973) in order to maintain a substantial development budget, amounting to $166.8 million, or 22.8% of the total budget for 1973–74. Roughly one third of this expenditure has been going to the huge Inga hydroelectric scheme ($27 million), which went into production in 1972, and to the Maluku smelter ($28 million), which is powered by the Inga dam. Other major projects include a 1,140-mile (1,825-km) power line from Inga to the Shaba (Katanga) mining belt and the improvement of the country's transportation infrastructure.

Zaire remains far from agricultural self-sufficiency. Agricultural production actually declined by some 10% during 1972, and the prospects for subsistence agriculture were seriously impaired in 1973 by the appearance of a blight of cassava plants.

EDOUARD BUSTIN, *Boston University*

ZAIRE • Information Highlights

Official Name: Republic of Zaire.
Location: Central equatorial Africa.
Area: 905,565 square miles (2,345,409 sq km).
Population (1973 est.): 18,700,000. *Density,* 21 per square mile (8 per sq km).
Chief City (1969 census): Kinshasa, the capital, 1,323,039.
Government: *Head of state,* Mobutu Sese Seko, president (took office Nov. 1965). *Head of government,* Mobutu Sese Seko. *Legislature* (unicameral)—National Assembly. *Major political party*—Popular Movement of the Revolution (MPR).
Languages: French (official), Kikongo and other Bantu languages.
Education: *Expenditure* (1969), 18.7% of total public expenditure. *School enrollment* (1969)—primary, 2,822,908; secondary, 243,998; technical/vocational, 33,985; university/higher, 10,165.
Monetary Unit: Zaire (0.50 zaire equals U. S.$1, Aug. 1973).
Gross National Product (1972 est.): $2,176,000,000.
Consumer Price Index (1972), 460 (1963=100).
Manufacturing (major products): Processed foods, clothing, textiles, soap.
Major Agricultural Products: Palm kernels, coffee, rubber, cacao, groundnuts, cotton, bananas, cassava.
Major Minerals: Industrial diamonds (ranks 1st among world producers, 1971), copper, manganese, tin, gold, cobalt.
Foreign Trade (1971): *Exports,* $669,000,000; *Imports,* $693,-000,000. *Chief trading partners* (1971)—Belgium-Luxembourg; other Common Market countries; United Kingdom; United States.
Transportation: *Motor vehicles* (1971), 123,900 (automobiles, 71,700); *railroads* (1971), 3,145 miles (5,061 km); *major national airline,* Air Zaire.
Communications: *Telephones* (1972), 22,901; *newspapers* (1970), 13 (daily circulation, 200,000).

ZOOLOGY

The effects of decreasing federal support for the sciences were felt by U. S. research zoologists in 1973. However, despite dwindling funds, advances were made in cryobiology and other fields; new observations were made of animal behavior, such as the use of "tools" by blue jays; two fossil invertebrates were discovered; and there was continuing concern expressed over man's effects on ecological systems.

Physiological Research. In the field of cryobiology—the study of life at freezing temperatures—most attempts to preserve multicellular mammalian systems such as tissues and organs by freezing them have failed. Certainly no mammal has been restored to life after having been frozen. Therefore the work done in 1973 by Oak Ridge National Laboratory biologists D. G. Whittingham, Stanley Leibo, and Peter Mazur is of special interest. They developed techniques for freezing, storing, thawing, and reimplanting early mouse embryos in foster mothers. Some were frozen at −321° F (−196° C) and some even at −452° F (−269° C), and were stored for up to eight days. The embryonic mice developed normally and grew into normal adults.

Vampire bats cause losses to the cattle industry of Latin America estimated at $250 million annually. R. D. Thompson, G. C. Mitchell, and R. J. Burns of the U. S. Bureau of Sports Fisheries and Wildlife have reported the successful use of a technique for controlling bat populations. A single low dosage of an anticoagulant, Diphenadione, was given to a number of cattle. Bats feeding on the treated cows lost the ability of blood coagulation, a condition that usually results in death in a few days. The technique led to a 93 percent reduction in the bat population concerned without affecting the cattle in any way, and may find wide use.

Behavioral Observations. Psychologists T. B. Jones and Alan Kamil of the University of Massachusetts noted tool manufacture and use in laboratory-raised blue jays, apparently during a period when inadequate food was available in their cage. The jays tore pieces of paper from a large sheet and used the resulting "tool" to secure food pellets otherwise beyond their reach. Tool use has been observed in some other birds, but never before in blue jays.

Zoologist D. R. Robertson of the University of Queensland in Australia reported some fascinating behavior of a species of tropical fish found in the Great Barrier Reef. The species, one of a group known as "cleaner fishes" because of their habit of removing ectoparasites from the skin of other fishes, lives in social units consisting of a large male and three to six mature and several immature females, all dwelling in a "territory" that the male protects. There is a well-defined pecking order, according to size, among females. It was observed that if the male dies, the largest female undergoes sex reversal—behaviorally within hours and physiologically in 18 days—and takes over as protector.

It has long been known that juveniles of sand dollars have sand grains stored in an intestinal diverticulum, whereas the adults do not. Fu-Shiang Chia of the University of Alberta in Canada has concluded that the sand acts as a weight belt, the young sand dollars taking in and storing heavy grains of more or less uniform size in order to remain in place in their shifting sand environment. As they reach a larger size, the grains are lost.

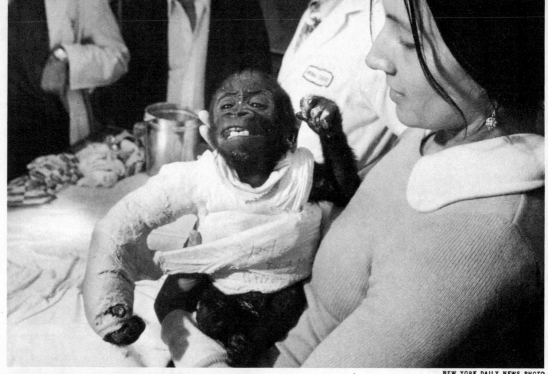

PATTY CAKE, the baby gorilla from New York's Central Park Zoo who had her arm broken in a family scuffle, gets loving attention from a nurse before being reunited with her mother, Lulu.

UPI

Fossil Finds. The oldest known fossil parasitic copepod, a small arthropod, was found in the gill chambers of a fossil fish taken from Lower Cretaceous deposits in Brazil. It was described by Roger Cressey of the Smithsonian Institution and Colin Patterson of the British Museum. Also in 1973, the oldest known fossil pelecypod mollusk, a tiny bivalve, was found in Early Cambrian deposits in New York. It was described by John Pojeta, Jr., and his associates at the U. S. Geological Survey.

Evolutionary Studies. The concept of an evolutionary "clock" holds that the rate of evolution— the rate of development of genetic change—is sim-

ilar in groups having a common ancestor. Anomalies are often interpreted as evidence of incorrect taxonomic placement of the species concerned. However, biochemists Thomas H. Jukes and Richard Holmquist of the University of California's Space Sciences Laboratory have found evidence that the "clock" does not necessarily "run" at the same rate in all animals. Their specific case indicated that the rate of evolution of certain pigments called cytochromes in rattlesnakes is greater than in turtles.

Paleontologist David M. Raup of the University of Rochester has challenged the classical view that the number of different kinds of marine animals rose rapidly during the Cambrian and early Ordovician periods, thereafter declining until the early Triassic and then again increasing on up to present times. His analysis indicates that the diversity of marine animals has instead gradually been reduced from a high that occurred sometime in the Paleozoic Era.

Ecological Concerns. Many words and a few efforts were devoted in 1973 to establishing national parks and natural areas as samples of typical environments little disturbed by man's activities. A report on African national parks expressed doubt that many would survive another 25 years, through a combination of limited financial support, increasing human populations, and the small size of many of the parks. Scientists of the Institute of Biology at the National University of Mexico appealed for natural areas to be set aside in tropical rain forests, which at the present rate of destruction will soon be gone. This loss would result in the extermination of thousands of species of animals before any aspect of their biology could be investigated.

E. Lendell Cockrum
University of Arizona

contributors

Following is a complete list of the distinguished authorities who contributed articles to this edition of the annual. Their professional affiliations are shown, together with the titles of their articles.

ADAMS, GEORGE, Legislative Reference Librarian, Connecticut State Library: CONNECTICUT

ADRIAN, CHARLES R., Professor of Political Science, University of California, Riverside: CALIFORNIA; LOS ANGELES

ALEXANDER, ROBERT J., Professor of Economics and Political Science, Rutgers University: DOMINICAN REPUBLIC; GUYANA

ALLER, LAWRENCE H., Professor of Astronomy, University of California, Los Angeles: ASTRONOMY

ALVEY, EDWARD, JR., Professor Emeritus of Education, Mary Washington College: EDUCATION

AMELIA, WILLIAM F., Public Relations Consultant, The Equitable Trust Co., Baltimore: BALTIMORE

ANDERSON, JEANNE F., Editor, *Washington Drug & Device Letter:* MEDICINE—*Pharmacology*

ANDERSON, SAMUEL K., Professor of History, Oregon College of Education: OREGON

ARMSTRONG, FREDERICK H., Associate Professor of History, Talbot College, University of Western Ontario: TORONTO

BAKER, RICHARD T., Professor of Journalism, Columbia University: PUBLISHING—*Newspapers*

BALLINGER, RONALD B., Professor and Chairman, Department of History, Rhode Island College: SOUTH AFRICA

BANKS, RONALD F., Associate Professor of History, University of Maine: MAINE

BEATTIE, A. J., Senior Lecturer in Political Science, London School of Economics and Political Science: GREAT BRITAIN; HEATH, EDWARD

BELING, WILLARD A., Program Coordinator, Middle East/ North African Program, School of International Relations, University of Southern California: SUDAN; TUNISIA

BERGEN, DANIEL P., Associate Professor, Graduate Library School, University of Rhode Island: LIBRARIES

BERGER, WOLFGANG H., Assistant Professor of Oceanography, Scripps Institution of Oceanography, University of California, San Diego: OCEANOGRAPHY

BEST, JOHN, Chief, *Canada World News,* Ottawa: NEW BRUNSWICK

BIRD, CAROLINE, Author, *The Invisible Scar, Born Female,* and *Everything a Woman Needs to Know to Get Paid What She's Worth;* Consulting Editor, *New Woman:* WOMEN'S LIBERATION MOVEMENT

BITTON, LIVIA E., Assistant Professor of Hebrew and Jewish Studies, Herbert H. Lehman College, City University of New York: RELIGION—*Judaism*

BLACK, KENNETH, JR., Regents Professor of Insurance, Georgia State University; Coauthor, *Life Insurance* and *Cases in Life Insurance:* INSURANCE

BLANKENSHIP, BENJAMIN R., JR., Economic Research Service, U. S. Department of Agriculture: FOOD—*World Food Supply*

BLOUNT, JOSEPH H., Chief, Evaluation and Statistical Services Unit, Venereal Disease Branch, Public Health Service: MEDICINE—*Venereal Disease*

BOULAY, HARVEY, Assistant Professor of Political Science, Boston University: BOSTON; MASSACHUSETTS

BOVEY, JOHN A., Provincial Archivist of Manitoba: MANITOBA

BOWERS, Q. DAVID, Columnist, *Coin World;* Author, *Coins and Collectors:* HOBBIES—*Coin Collecting*

BOYLAN, JAMES R., Graduate School of Journalism, Columbia University: PUBLISHING—*Magazines*

BRADDOCK, BILL, Sports Department, *The New York Times:* AARON, HENRY; KING, BILLIE JEAN; SIMPSON, O. J.; SPORTS

BRADLEY, C. PAUL, Professor of Political Science, University of Michigan—Flint: MALAYSIA; SINGAPORE

BRAMMER, DANA B., Assistant Director, Bureau of Governmental Research, University of Mississippi: MISSISSIPPI

BRAZDA, JEROME F., Editor, *Washington Report on Medicine & Health:* SOCIAL WELFARE—*Health Care*

BRESNAHAN, WILLIAM A., Managing Director, American Trucking Associations, Inc.: TRANSPORTATION—*Motor Transport*

BRODIN, PIERRE, Director of Studies, Lycée Français de New York: FRENCH LITERATURE

BROWN, BERTRAM S., Director, National Institute of Mental Health: MEDICINE—*Mental Health*

BROWN, FREDERICK W., JR., Reporter (Statehouse & Politics), The Denver *Post:* COLORADO

BURDETTE, FRANKLIN L., Professor and Director, Bureau of Governmental Research, University of Maryland: ELECTIONS; MARYLAND; POLITICAL PARTIES

BURKHEAD, JESSE, Professor of Economics, Syracuse University: TAXATION

BURKS, ARDATH W., Professor of Political Science and Associate Vice President for Academic Affairs, Rutgers University: JAPAN; TANAKA, KAKUEI

BURLINGAME, MERRILL G., Professor of History, Montana State University: MONTANA

BUSTIN, EDOUARD, Professor of Political Science, Boston University: ZAIRE

BUTWELL, RICHARD, Chairman, Department of Political Science, State University of New York at Brockport; Author, *Southeast Asia Today—and Tomorrow:* BURMA; CAMBODIA; LAOS; VIETNAM

CAIRNS, JOHN C., Professor of History, University of Toronto: FRANCE; POMPIDOU, GEORGES

CANFIELD, ROBERT L., Associate Professor of Anthropology, Washington University, St. Louis: ETHNIC GROUPS

CANN, STAN, State Editor, *The Forum,* Fargo, N. Dak.: NORTH DAKOTA

CARMONY, DONALD F., Professor of History, Indiana University; Editor, *Indiana Magazine of History:* INDIANA

CARSTENS, HAROLD H., Carstens Publications, Inc.; Past President, Hobby Industry Association of America, Inc.: HOBBIES—*General Survey*

CHALMERS, J. W., Faculty of Education, University of Alberta: ALBERTA

CHILDS, MARQUIS, Contributing Editor, St. Louis *Post-Dispatch:* WATERGATE Feature (in part)

CHINN, RONALD E., Associate Professor and Head, Department of Political Science, University of Alaska: ALASKA

CHRIEN, ROBERT E., Physicist, Brookhaven National Laboratory: ENERGY Feature (in part); NUCLEAR ENERGY

CLARK, C. B., Doctoral Candidate in History, University of Oklahoma: OKLAHOMA

CLARK, ROBERT S., Contributing Editor, *Stereo Review:* MUSIC

COCKRUM, E. LENDELL, Professor of Biological Sciences, University of Arizona: ZOOLOGY

661

COHEN, SIDNEY, Executive Director, Council on Drug and Alcohol Abuse, and Adjunct Professor of Psychiatry, University of California, Los Angeles: DRUG ADDICTION AND ABUSE

COLE, CAROLYN J., Editor, *Facts and Forecasts,* Standard & Poor's Corp.: STOCKS AND BONDS

COMEAU, ROBERT, Professeur d'histoire, Université du Québec à Montréal: MONTREAL; QUEBEC

CONDAX, PHILIP L., Equipment Archives Curator, International Museum of Photography, George Eastman House: PHOTOGRAPHY

COOPER, RICHARD N., Professor of Economics, Yale University; Author, *The Economics of Interdependence—Economic Policy in the Atlantic Community:* BRAZIL Feature (in part)

COPPAGE, NOEL, Contributing Editor, *Stereo Review:* RECORDINGS—*Popular Records*

CORNWELL, ELMER E., JR., Professor of Political Science, Brown University: RHODE ISLAND

CRAINE, DEBRA, News Editor, The Canadian Press, Vancouver: VANCOUVER

CURTIS, L. PERRY, JR., Professor of History, University of California, Berkeley: IRELAND

DARBY, JOSEPH W., III, Assistant City Editor, *The Times-Picayune,* New Orleans: NEW ORLEANS

DAVIS, PETER G., Recordings Editor, *The New York Times:* RECORDINGS—*Classical Records*

DELZELL, CHARLES F., Professor and Chairman, Department of History, Vanderbilt University: ITALY

DOBLER, CLIFFORD, Professor of Business Law, University of Idaho: IDAHO

DOLAN, PAUL, Professor of Political Science, University of Delaware: DELAWARE

DORPALEN, ANDREAS, Professor of History, The Ohio State University: BRANDT, WILLY; GERMANY

DORSEN, NORMAN, Professor of Law, New York University: CIVIL LIBERTIES AND CIVIL RIGHTS

DRACHKOVITCH, MILORAD M., Senior Fellow, The Hoover Institution, Stanford University: YUGOSLAVIA

DRIGGS, DON W., Chairman, Department of Political Science, University of Nevada, Reno: NEVADA

DuBOIS, RUTH MARY (PACKARD), Freelance Fashion Writer, Lecturer, and Columnist: FASHION

DUCHON, M. L., Consultant in Ophthalmology: MEDICINE— *Eye Diseases*

DUFF, ERNEST A., Professor of Political Science, Randolph-Macon Woman's College: COLOMBIA

DULANEY, WILLIAM L., Associate Professor of Journalism, The Pennsylvania State University: PENNSYLVANIA; PHILADELPHIA

DUPREE, LOUIS, American Universities Field Staff: AFGHANISTAN

DUPREE, NANCY HATCH, American Universities Field Staff: AFGHANISTAN

DURRENCE, J. LARRY, Department of History, Florida Southern College: FLORIDA

ENQUIST, IRVING F., M. D., Director of Surgery, Methodist Hospital of Brooklyn: MEDICINE—*Surgery*

ETCHESON, WARREN W., Professor of Business Administration, University of Washington: WASHINGTON

ETHERIDGE, ADREN, Assistant City Editor, The Houston *Post:* HOUSTON; TEXAS

FAIRBROTHERS, DAVID E., Professor and Chairman, Department of Botany, Rutgers University: BOTANY

FARRELL, EILEEN H., Editor, *Dental Abstracts,* American Dental Association: MEDICINE—*Dentistry*

FELDBAUM, ELEANOR G., Research Associate, Bureau of Governmental Research, University of Maryland: WASHINGTON, D. C.

FERRAR, HAROLD, Assistant Professor of English and Comparative Literature, Columbia University: THEATER

FISHER, PAUL, Director, Freedom of Information Center, University of Missouri: CENSORSHIP

FISHER, SIDNEY NETTLETON, Emeritus Professor of History, The Ohio State University: SAUDI ARABIA

FOLMSBEE, STANLEY J., Professor Emeritus of History, University of Tennessee: TENNESSEE

FREEMAN, ARTHUR, Editor in Chief, American Veterinary Medical Association: VETERINARY MEDICINE

FREMANTLE, ANNE, Author, *This Little Band of Prophets;* Book Reviewer, *The New York Times* and *Saturday Review:* AUDEN, W. H.

FRIEDMAN, HARVEY L., Associate Professor of Political Science, and Director, Labor Relations and Research Center, University of Massachusetts: LABOR; POSTAL SERVICE

GAILEY, HARRY A., Professor of History, San Jose State University: GUINEA; NIGERIA; SENEGAL

GEIS, GILBERT, Visiting Professor, Program in Social Ecology, University of California, Irvine; Author, *Man, Crime, and Society:* CRIME; POLICE

GJESTER, THOR, City Editor, *Norwegian Journal of Commerce and Shipping,* Oslo: NORWAY

GLASER, PETER E., Vice President, Arthur D. Little, Inc.: ENERGY Feature (in part)

GOLDEN, FREDERIC, Science Editor, *Time* Magazine: ENERGY Feature (in part)

GOODMAN, DONALD, Associate Professor of Sociology, John Jay College of Criminal Justice, City University of New York: PRISONS

GORDON, MAYNARD M., Editor, *Motor News Analysis* and *The Imported Car Reports:* AUTOMOBILES

GRAESSER, MARK W., Assistant Professor of Political Science, Memorial University of Newfoundland: NEWFOUNDLAND

GRAVER, LAWRENCE, Professor of English, Williams College: ENGLISH LITERATURE

GREENSPUN, ROGER, Associate Professor, Rutgers University; Film Critic, *Penthouse* Magazine: MOTION PICTURES

GROTH, ALEXANDER J., Professor of Political Science, University of California, Davis: POLAND

GULICK, LEWIS, Staff Consultant, House Foreign Affairs Committee: FOREIGN AID

GUNN, JOHN M., Professor of Radio-TV-Film, State University of New York at Albany: TELEVISION AND RADIO— *Television Broadcasting; Radio Broadcasting*

GUSTAFSON, BARRY, Department of Political Studies, University of Auckland: NEW ZEALAND

GUTHERIDGE, GUY G., Director, Polar Information Service, Office of Polar Programs, National Science Foundation: POLAR RESEARCH

HAKES, JAY E., Associate Professor of Political Science, Louisiana State University in New Orleans: KENYA; TANZANIA; UGANDA

HALL, FRANCES L., Director, International Trade Analysis Division, Bureau of International Commerce, U. S. Department of Commerce: INTERNATIONAL TRADE

HALVORSEN, DAVID E., Assistant Managing Editor, *Chicago Tribune:* CHICAGO; ILLINOIS

HANSON, EARL PARKER, Geographer; Former Consultant to the Puerto Rico Department of State: PUERTO RICO

HAYES, JOHN D., Rear Admiral, USN (Ret.); U. S. Naval Academy Alumni Association: TRANSPORTATION—*Shipping*

HAYES, KIRBY M., Professor of Food Science, University of Massachusetts: FOOD—*U. S. Food Industry;* NUTRITION

HEAD, HOWARD T., Partner, A. D. Ring & Associates, Consulting Radio Engineers: TELEVISION AND RADIO—*Television and Radio Engineering*

HELMREICH, E. C., Thomas B. Reed Professor of History and Political Science, Bowdoin College: AUSTRIA

HELMREICH, PAUL C., Associate Professor and Chairman, Department of History, Wheaton College, Norton, Mass.: SWITZERLAND

HERBERT, WALTER B., Consultant on Canadian Cultural Matters; Fellow of the Royal Society of Arts: CANADA: CULTURAL AFFAIRS—*General Survey*

HERRING, RICHARD J., Assistant Professor of Finance, University of Pennsylvania: INTERNATIONAL FINANCE

HERSHKOWITZ, LEO, Professor of History, Queens College, City University of New York: NEW YORK CITY; NEW YORK STATE

HESS, ARTHUR E., Deputy Commissioner, Social Security Administration: SOCIAL WELFARE—*Social Security*

HODGES, RALPH W., Associate Technical Editor, *Stereo Review:* RECORDINGS—*Audio Equipment and Techniques*

HOOVER, HERBERT T., Associate Professor of History, The University of South Dakota: SOUTH DAKOTA

HOPKINS, JAMES F., Professor of History, University of Kentucky: KENTUCKY

HOPKO, THOMAS, St. Vladimir's Orthodox Theological Seminary: RELIGION—*Eastern Orthodox Church*

HOWARD, HARRY N., Adjunct Professor of Middle East Studies, School of International Service, The American University: TURKEY

HUCKSHORN, ROBERT J., Professor and Chairman, Department of Political Science, Florida Atlantic University: NIXON, RICHARD M.

HUTH, JOHN F., JR., Reporter-Columnist, *The Plain Dealer*, Cleveland, Ohio: CLEVELAND

JACOBS, WALTER DARNELL, Professor of Government and Politics, University of Maryland: FORD, GERALD; KISSINGER, HENRY; RICHARDSON, ELLIOT

JAFFE, HERMAN, Department of Anthropology, Brooklyn College, City University of New York: ANTHROPOLOGY

JONES, ISABELLA J., Executive Vice President, National Association of Consultants for Children and Youth: SOCIAL WELFARE—*Child Welfare*

KAMINS, ROBERT M., Professor of Economics, University of Hawaii: HAWAII

KAPLAN, ALAN R., Editor, *Modern Data* Magazine: COMPUTERS

KARSKI, JAN, Department of Government, Georgetown University: BULGARIA; HUNGARY

KEHR, ERNEST A., Director, Stamp News Bureau; Executive Chairman, Philatelic Press Club; Stamp News Editor, The Chicago *Daily News*: HOBBIES—*Stamp Collecting*

KELLER, EUGENIA, Managing Editor, *Chemistry*: CHEMISTRY

KELLY, NORA, Coauthor, *The Royal Canadian Mounted Police: A Century of History*: THE MOUNTIES Feature

KEMPER, ROBERT V., Assistant Professor of Anthropology, Southern Methodist University: DALLAS

KENNEDY, ROBERT E., JR., Associate Professor and Associate Chairman, Department of Sociology, University of Minnesota: POPULATION

KIMBALL, LORENZO K., Associate Professor of Political Science, University of Utah: UTAH

KING, PETER J., Associate Professor of History, Carleton University: ONTARIO; OTTAWA

KIRKENDALL, RICHARD S., Professor of History, Indiana University; Executive Secretary, Organization of American Historians: JOHNSON, LYNDON B.

KLAUSLER, ALFRED P., Executive Director, Associated Church Press; Religion Editor, Westinghouse Broadcasting Co.: RELIGION—*Protestantism*

KNAPP, ELAINE S., Editor, *State Government News*, *State Headlines*, Council of State Governments: STATE GOVERNMENT

KOLEHMAINEN, JOHN I., Chairman, Department of Political Science, Heidelberg College, Tiffin, Ohio: FINLAND

KREITZMAN, STEPHEN N., Professor of Biochemistry, Emory University School of Dentistry: BIOCHEMISTRY

KREPS, CLIFTON H., JR., Wachovia Professor of Banking, University of North Carolina: BANKING

KUDRLE, ALBERT E., Director of Public Relations, American Hotel & Motel Association: TOURISM—*Hotels and Motels*

LACY, HOWARD C., Metallurgical Engineer, American Iron and Steel Institute: STEEL

LAI, DAVID CHUEN-YAN, Associate Professor of Geography, University of Victoria, B. C.: HONG KONG

LANDSBERG, H. E., Research Professor, Institute for Fluid Dynamics and Applied Mathematics, University of Maryland: METEOROLOGY

LARSEN, WILLIAM, Professor of History, Radford College: VIRGINIA

LARSON, T. A., Professor of History, University of Wyoming; Author, *History of Wyoming*: WYOMING

LAWRENCE, ROBERT M., Department of Political Science, Colorado State University: DEFENSE FORCES

LEE, STEWART M., Professor and Chairman, Department of Economics and Business Administration, Geneva College: CONSUMERISM

LEFEVER, ERNEST W., Senior Fellow, Foreign Policy Studies Program, The Brookings Institution: DISARMAMENT AND ARMS CONTROL

LEIDEN, CARL, Professor of Government, University of Texas at Austin: BANGLADESH; EGYPT; PAKISTAN; SADAT, ANWAR EL-; THAILAND

LEVIN, MILTON, Author, *Noël Coward;* Professor of English, Trenton State College: COWARD, NOËL

LEVIN, RUBEN, Editor, *Labor* Newspaper: LABOR—*World Labor*

LEVINE, ROBERT M., Associate Professor of History, State University of New York at Stony Brook: BRAZIL Feature (in part)

LEVY, JAMES R., School of Spanish and Latin American Studies, University of New South Wales: ARGENTINA

LEWIS, HOWARD L., Managing Editor, *Modern Hospital* Magazine: MEDICINE—*Hospitals*

LEWIS, OSCAR, Author, *San Francisco: Mission to Metropolis, The Big Four,* and other books: SAN FRANCISCO

LINDGREN, RAYMOND E., Professor of History, California State University, Long Beach: DENMARK; ICELAND; SWEDEN

LINDSEY, ROBERT H., Transportation Editor, *The New York Times:* TRANSPORTATION—*Air Transportation*

LINGARD, C. CECIL, Former Editor, *The Canada Year Book:* NORTHWEST TERRITORIES

LIVINGSTONE, WILLIAM, Reviewer, *Ballet Review;* Managing Editor, *Stereo Review:* DANCE

LOTT, LEO B., Professor and Chairman, Department of Political Science, University of Montana: PARAGUAY; VENEZUELA

LYNCH, J. JOSEPH, S. J., Director, Fordham Seismic Observatory: EARTHQUAKES

MABRY, DONALD J., Assistant Professor of History, Mississippi State University: MEXICO

MACAULAY, NEILL, Associate Professor of History, University of Florida; Author, *A Rebel in Cuba:* BRAZIL Feature (in part); CUBA; GEISEL, ERNESTO; LATIN AMERICA

McCONNELL, WILLIAM J., Assistant Professor of Political Science, Colorado State University; Colonel, USA (Ret.): DEFENSE FORCES

McCORQUODALE, SUSAN, Assistant Professor of Political Science, Memorial University of Newfoundland: NEWFOUNDLAND

McKAY, HELEN A., Formerly Head of Adult Services, Regina Public Library, Sask.: SASKATCHEWAN

McKAY, W. A., Department of History, Scarborough College, University of Toronto: CANADA; TRUDEAU, PIERRE E.

McLEOD, W. R., Assistant Professor of History, West Virginia University: WEST VIRGINIA

MAJOR ANDRÉ, Literary Critic, Montreal: FRENCH CANADIAN LITERATURE

MALCOLM, ANDREW H., National Correspondent, *The New York Times* (Chicago): AMERICAN INDIAN Feature (in part)

MARCOPOULOS, GEORGE J., Associate Professor of History, Tufts University: CYPRUS; GREECE

MARKE, JULIUS J., Law Librarian and Professor of Law, New York University: LAW—*U. S. Legislation and Case Law*

MARTIN, J. A., JR., Professor of Religion, Columbia University: RELIGION—*General Survey*

MARYLES, DAISY, News Editor, *Publishers Weekly:* PUBLISHING—*Books*

MATHEWS, THOMAS G., Research Professor, Institute of Caribbean Studies, University of Puerto Rico: BAHAMAS; CARIBBEAN; TRINIDAD AND TOBAGO; VIRGIN ISLANDS

MEMOLO, MARCELLA M., Public Information Officer, U. S. Agricultural Research Service: AGRICULTURE—*U. S. Agricultural Research*

MEREDITH, J. R., Director, Bureau of Economics and Statistics, British Columbia: BRITISH COLUMBIA

MESSER, THOMAS M., Director, The Solomon R. Guggenheim Museum, New York: PICASSO, PABLO

MESSNER, STEPHEN D., Head, Department of Finance, School of Business Administration, University of Connecticut: HOUSING

MEYER, EDWARD H., President, Chairman of the Board, and Chief Executive Officer, Grey Advertising Inc.: ADVERTISING

MEYER, RALPH C., Assistant Professor of Political Science, Fordham University at Lincoln Center: ASIA

MIESEL, VICTOR H., Professor of the History of Art, University of Michigan; Author, *Voices of German Expressionism:* ART

MILLER, LUTHER S., Editor, *Railway Age:* TRANSPORTATION—*Railroads*

MILLER, NYLE H., Executive Director, Kansas State Historical Society; Coauthor, *Kansas: A Pictorial History:* KANSAS

MILLINGTON, THOMAS M., Associate Professor of Political Science, Hobart and William Smith Colleges: BOLIVIA

MILNE, ROBERT SCOTT, Society of American Travel Writers; coauthor, *Around the World with the Experts:* TOURISM

MITCHELL, GARY, Associate Professor of Physics, North Carolina State University at Raleigh: PHYSICS

NEILL, R. F., Associate Professor of Economics, St. Patrick's College, Carleton University: PRINCE EDWARD ISLAND

NEWSOM, DONALD W., Professor and Head, Department of Horticulture, Louisiana State University: GARDENING AND HORTICULTURE

NOLAN, WILLIAM C., Associate Professor of Political Science, Southern State College: ARKANSAS

NORMAN, JOHN, Professor of History and Government, Pace University, Westchester: LIBYA

NOSS, JOHN B., Emeritus Professor of Philosophy, Franklin and Marshall College; Author, *Man's Religions:* RELIGION—*Oriental Religions*

NOWELL, CHARLES E., Professor of History, Emeritus, University of Illinois: PORTUGAL; SPAIN

NUQUIST, ANDREW E., Professor Emeritus of Political Science, University of Vermont: VERMONT

NYSTROM, J. WARREN, Executive Director, Association of American Geographers: GEOGRAPHY

O'HARE, JOSEPH A., S. J., Associate Editor, *America:* PAUL VI, POPE; RELIGION—*Roman Catholicism*

PALMER, NORMAN D., Professor of Political Science and South Asian Studies, University of Pennsylvania: GANDHI, INDIRA; INDIA; SRI LANKA

PANO, NICHOLAS C., Assistant Professor of History, Western Illinois University: ALBANIA

PARKER, FRANKLIN, Benedum Professor of Education and Research Associate, Human Resources Institute, West Virginia University: AFRICA; RHODESIA

PARTAN, DANIEL G., Professor of Law, Boston University: LAW—*International Law*

PASTIER, JOHN, Architecture Critic, Los Angeles *Times:* ARCHITECTURE

PEARCE, JOHN B., Acting Laboratory Director, Ecosystems Investigations, Sandy Hook Laboratory, N. J.: MARINE BIOLOGY

PEARSON, NEALE J., Associate Professor of Government, Texas Tech University: CHILE; PERU

PERKINS, KENNETH J., Research Associate, Institute of Islamic Studies, McGill University: RELIGION—*Islam*

PETERSON, ROBERT L., Director, Center for Inter-American Studies, University of Texas at El Paso: CENTRAL AMERICA

PHEBUS, GEORGE E., JR., Supervisor, Processing Laboratory, Department of Anthropology, National Museum of Natural History, Smithsonian Institution; ARCHAEOLOGY—*Western Hemisphere*

PHILLIPS, JACKSON, Vice President, Moody's Investors Service: ECONOMY OF THE U. S.

PIPPIN, LARRY L., Professor of Political Science, Elbert Covell College, University of the Pacific: PANAMA

PLATIEL, RUDY, Reporter, *The Globe and Mail*, Toronto: AMERICAN INDIAN Feature (in part)

PLATT, HERMANN K., Associate Professor of History, St. Peter's College, Jersey City: NEW JERSEY

PLISCHKE, ELMER, Professor of Government and Politics, University of Maryland: UNITED STATES—*Foreign Affairs*

POLK, IRWIN J., Director of Children's Allergy Service, St. Luke's Hospital, New York City: MEDICINE—*General Survey; Allergies*

PORTER, J. R., Professor and Chairman, Department of Microbiology, College of Medicine, University of Iowa: MICROBIOLOGY

PORTNOY, BERNARD, Professor of Community Medicine, Public Health, and Pediatrics, University of Southern California: MEDICINE—*Respiratory Diseases*

POWELL, WILLIAM S., Curator, North Carolina Collection, University of North Carolina: NORTH CAROLINA

PRICE, EDWIN W., JR., Managing Editor, *The Morning Advocate*, Baton Rouge, La.: LOUISIANA

PRITCHETT, C. HERMAN, Professor of Political Science, University of California, Santa Barbara: WATERGATE Feature (in part); LAW—*Supreme Court*

PRITIKIN, ROLAND I., Eye Surgeon and Consulting Ophthalmologist; Author, *Essentials of Ophthalmology:* MEDICINE —*Eye Diseases*

PUMPHREY, RALPH E., Professor of Social Work, Washington University, St. Louis: SOCIAL WELFARE

QUIRK, WILLIAM H., Editorial Director, *Contractors & Engineers* Magazine: ENGINEERING, CIVIL

RANDALL, CHARLES E., Staff, *Journal of Forestry:* FORESTRY AND LUMBERING

RAYMOND, ELLSWORTH, Associate Professor of Politics, New York University; Author, *The Soviet State* and *A Picture History of Eastern Europe:* BREZHNEV, LEONID; KOSYGIN, ALEKSEI; MONGOLIA; UNION OF SOVIET SOCIALIST REPUBLICS

RAYMOND, JACK, Past President and Chief Executive Officer, International Institute for Environmental Affairs; Author, *Power at the Pentagon:* ENVIRONMENT

RODRIGUEZ, ALFRED, Professor of Spanish, University of New Mexico: SPANISH LITERATURE

ROMAN, JAMES R., JR., Associate Professor of Business Administration, The George Washington University: TRANSPORTATION—*General Survey; Highways*

ROSE, ERNST, Author, *A History of German Literature;* Professor Emeritus, New York University: GERMAN LITERATURE

ROSS, RUSSELL M., Professor of Political Science, University of Iowa: IOWA

ROTHMAN, FRANK G., Professor of Biology, Brown University: GENETICS

ROWLETT, RALPH M., Associate Professor of Anthropology, University of Missouri—Columbia: ARCHAEOLOGY—*Eastern Hemisphere*

SALGADO, MARIA A., Associate Professor of Spanish, University of North Carolina at Chapel Hill: LATIN AMERICAN LITERATURE

SALSINI, PAUL, State Editor, The Milwaukee *Journal:* MILWAUKEE; WISCONSIN

SARRATT, WILLIAM A., Editor, *The Fish Boat*, New Orleans: FISHERIES

SAVAGE, DAVID, Instructor, Department of English, Simon Fraser University: CANADIAN LITERATURE

SCHAAR, STUART, Associate Professor of History, Brooklyn College, City University of New York: ALGERIA; MOROCCO

SCHMITT, KARL M., Associate Director, Institute of Latin American Studies; Professor of Government, University of Texas at Austin: HAITI

SCHNEIDERMAN, RONALD A., Senior Editor—Government Electronics and Features, *Electronic News:* ELECTRONICS

SCHWAB, PETER, Associate Professor of Political Science, State University of New York at Purchase: ETHIOPIA

SCOTT, RALPH C., Professor of Medicine, Cardiac Laboratory, University of Cincinnati Medical Center: MEDICINE —*Heart and Vascular Disease*

SEGAR, WILLIAM E., Professor of Pediatrics, University of Wisconsin: MEDICINE—*Pediatrics*

SETH, R. P., Chairman, Department of Economics, Mount Saint Vincent University, Halifax: NOVA SCOTIA

SHEATSLEY, PAUL B., Director, Survey Research Service, National Opinion Research Center, University of Chicago: PUBLIC OPINION RESEARCH

SHOGAN, ROBERT, National Political Correspondent, Washington Bureau, *Los Angeles Times;* Author, *A Question of Judgment: The Fortas Case and the Struggle for the Supreme Court:* WATERGATE Feature (in part); UNITED STATES—*Domestic Affairs*

SIMMONS, MARC, Farrier; Author, *Spanish Government in New Mexico* and *The Little Lion of the Southwest:* NEW MEXICO

SINNEN, JEANNE, Senior Editor, University of Minnesota Press: MINNESOTA

SKELDING, FRANK H., Director of Corporate Planning, Fluor Utah, Inc.: MINING

SLOAN, HENRY S., Associate Editor, *Current Biography:* BIOGRAPHY (in part); OBITUARIES (in part)

SLONIM, MARC, Director, Sarah Lawrence College Foreign Studies: ITALIAN LITERATURE; SOVIET LITERATURE

SPECTOR, SHERMAN D., Professor of History, Russell Sage College; Author, *A History of the Balkan Peoples:* RUMANIA

SPEIRS, W. BRIAN, Territorial Archivist, Yukon Territory: YUKON TERRITORY

STEHLING, KURT R., Aerospace Consultant, U. S. Government: SPACE EXPLORATION—*Advances in Space Technology*

STEPHENS, GENE, Urban Life Center, Georgia State University: ATLANTA; GEORGIA

STERN, JEROME H., Associate Professor, Florida State University: BUCK, PEARL

STOKES, W. LEE, Professor of Geology, University of Utah: GEOLOGY

STOUDEMIRE, ROBERT H., Associate Director, Bureau of Governmental Research and Associate Professor of Political Science, University of South Carolina: SOUTH CAROLINA

SWANSON, CURTIS E., Manager, Public Relations Division, American Library Association: LIBRARIES—*American Library Association*

TABORSKY, EDWARD, Professor of Government, University of Texas at Austin: CZECHOSLOVAKIA

TAKUWA, SHINJI, Professor of English and American Studies, Kyushu University: JAPANESE LITERATURE

TAN, CHESTER C., Professor of History, New York University; Author, *The Boxer Catastrophe* and *Chinese Political Thought in the Twentieth Century*: CHINA; CHOU EN-LAI

TAYLOR, PHILIP B., JR., Professor of Political Science; Director of Latin American Studies, University of Houston: ECUADOR; URUGUAY

TAYLOR, ZACK, Boating Editor, *Sports Afield;* Regional Editor, *Waterway Guide:* BOATING

THEISEN, CHARLES W., Assistant City Editor, The Detroit *News:* DETROIT; MICHIGAN

THOMAS, JAMES D., Professor of Political Science, University of Alabama: ALABAMA

THOME, PITT G., Deputy Director for Earth Observations Flight Program, National Aeronautics and Space Administration: SPACE EXPLORATION—*Manned Space Flight; Unmanned Satellites and Space Probes*

THOMPSON, RICHARD E., President, Revenue Sharing Advisory Service, Inc.: CITIES AND URBAN AFFAIRS

TIBBITTS, CLARK, Director, Division of Manpower Development, Administration on Aging, Department of Health, Education, and Welfare: OLDER POPULATION

TOFANY, VINCENT L., President, National Safety Council: ACCIDENTS AND DISASTERS

TURNER, ARTHUR C., Professor of Political Science, University of California, Riverside: BEN-GURION, DAVID; IRAN; IRAQ; ISRAEL; MIDDLE EAST

VANDENBOSCH, AMRY, Professor Emeritus of Political Science, University of Kentucky: BELGIUM; INDONESIA; LUXEMBOURG; NETHERLANDS; SUHARTO

WALLACE, BEN J., Professor of Anthropology, Southern Methodist University: DALLAS

WARNER, ANNE R., Program and Communications Director, Manpower Distribution Project, National Health Council, Inc.: MEDICINE—*Nursing*

WASHBURN, WILCOMB E., Director, Office of American Studies, Smithsonian Institution; Adjunct Professor, The American University: AMERICAN INDIAN Feature (in part)

WEBB, RICHARD E., Former Director, Reference and Library Division, British Information Services, New York: COMMONWEALTH OF NATIONS; UNITED NATIONS; WALDHEIM, KURT

WEEKS, JEANNE G., Director, Advertising and Public Relations, Harvey Probber Inc.; Associate, Association of Interior Designers: INTERIOR DESIGN

WEINER, PAUL, Professor of Economics, University of Connecticut: TELECOMMUNICATIONS

WEISENBURGER, FRANCIS P., Professor of History, The Ohio State University: OHIO

WELCH, CLAUDE E., JR., Professor of Political Science, State University of New York at Buffalo: GHANA

WEST, RICHARD G., Former Senior Editor, *Encyclopedia Americana:* WATERGATE Feature (in part); NEW HAMPSHIRE

WESTERN, JOE, Kominus Agri-Info Associates: AGRICULTURE—*World Agriculture; U. S. Agriculture*

WHITE, JOHN P., Professor of Political Science, Arizona State University: ARIZONA

WILLARD, F. NICHOLAS, NDEA Title VI Fellow, Department of History, Georgetown University: JORDAN; LEBANON; SYRIA

WILLIS, F. ROY, Professor of History, University of California, Davis: EUROPE

WILLNOW, RONALD D., City Editor, St. Louis *Post-Dispatch:* MISSOURI; SAINT LOUIS

WILSON, JOHN S., Reviewer of Jazz Records, *The New York Times* and *High Fidelity* Magazine; Author, *Jazz: The Transition Years—1940-1960:* RECORDINGS—*Jazz Records*

WILSON, R. NORRIS, Executive Vice President, United States Committee for Refugees: REFUGEES

WOODS, GEORGE A., Children's Books Editor, *The New York Times:* CHILDREN'S LITERATURE

YANG, KEY P., Korean Area Specialist, Orientalia Division, The Library of Congress: KOREA

YOUNG, CHARLES W., Sloan-Kettering Institute for Cancer Research: MEDICINE—*Cancer*

YOUNGER, R. M., Author, *The Changing World of Australia; Australia and the Australians:* AUSTRALIA; OCEANIA

ZABEL, ORVILLE H., Professor of History, Creighton University: NEBRASKA

ZAFRA, NICOLAS, Professor Emeritus of History, University of the Philippines: PHILIPPINES

index

Main article headings appear in this Index as bold-faced capitals; subjects within articles appear as lower-case entries. Main article page numbers and general references are listed first under each entry; the sub-entries which follow them on separate lines direct the reader to related topics appearing elsewhere. Both the general references and the subentries should be consulted for maximum usefulness of this Index. Illustrations are indexed herein. Cross references are to the entries in this Index.